To Robin Corbett MP
with thanks + best wishes

George Barnsby
Feb '98

Socialism in Birmingham and the Black Country
1850-1939

by
George J. Barnsby

INTEGRATED PUBLISHING SERVICES
141 HENWOOD ROAD, WOLVERHAMPTON, WEST MIDLANDS WV6 8PJ

© 1998 George J. Barnsby
All rights reserved.
Reproduction of short extracts for review or teaching purposes is encouraged, but the Copyright owner must be informed through the Publishers.

ISBN 0 905679 10 5

Production by Owain Hammonds Associates,
Ebeneser, Bont-goch, Talybont, Ceredigion, Wales SY24 5DP. Tel: (01970) 832014.

Acknowledgments

For financial assistance, without which this book could not have been published, I wish to thank among others, Democratic Left, the Lipman-Miliband Trust, the Isobel Thornley Bequest Fund, and Bilston Community College. Special mention must be made of the Transport & General Workers Union Midlands and of its branches and sections. But many other trade unions in the West Midlands have also generously contributed and these, together with the valued contribution of individuals are recorded in the List of Sponsors at the back of the book.

For professional competence and friendship I wish to thank all library staff of Birmingham and the four boroughs of the Black Country who also produced many of the illustrations in the book. My thanks also to the staff of national libraries, notably the British Newspaper Library at Colindale.

For technical wizardry in sorting out my Amstrad discs I am indebted to John Hazlehurst and for transcribing these into something acceptable by the printer, Francis King.

For moral assistance and belief in this project over an eight year period I am indebted particularly to my wife, Esme, the Hazlehurst brothers John and Bob together with their wives Elizabeth and Jean, also Nick Matthews now in South Africa, and the London MEP with Black Country connections, Stan Newens.

The Author

Dr George Barnsby was born in 1919 in London. His father, a railway porter, died from the effects of gassing in World War One when the author was three. He attended a Central school and left at fifteen. After six years war service in the ranks (four in Burma) he spent his was gratuity 'seeing if he had any brains' and studied at the London School of Economics. He thus became one of the first generation of working people who were able to go to University and he became a teacher.

He came to the Black Country in 1954 and after several years teaching, mainly at a Secondary Modern School in Bilston, he gave up his job and spent three years at Birmingham University researching what were to become his first two books, *The Working Class Movement in the Black Country 1750 to 1867* and *Social Conditions in the Black Country 1800-1900.*

Prematurely retired from teaching at the age of 63 with a heart condition, he has spent the intervening years producing *Birmingham Working People,* a study of the Birmingham working class movement from 1650 to 1914 and the present book.

He has been a political activist all his adult life. He joined the Communist Party in 1942 and was active in anti-racist politics in the army. He was for twenty years secretary of the Wolverhampton Communist Party, and a member of its Midlands District Committee and Secretariat. He is still active as Honorary Life President of the Wolverhampton Race Equality Council which he helped to found in 1965.

Socialism in Birmingham and the Black Country 1850-1939

Contents

Acknowledgments	i
The Author	ii
List of Illustrations	vii

PART 1
SOCIALISM IN THE BLACK COUNTRY 1850-1914

1   FROM CHARTISM TO SECULARISM 1850-1870 3
Introduction 3; Working Class Politics 1850-69 Chartism and Secularism 4; Bibliography 9

2   REPUBLICANISM AND RETREAT 1870-1884 11
Secularism and Republicanism 1870-74 11; Depression and Restructuring 17; Summary 20; Bibliography 22

3   TRADE UNIONISM IN THE BLACK COUNTRY 1850-75 23
Mining 23; Ironworkers 25; Engineers 26; Tinplate Workers 27; The Builders 31; Lock Makers 34; Nails 35; Chains 38; Glass 40; Nuts and Bolts 42; Other Trade Unions 43; Trades Councils 44; Bibliography 47

4   THE RE-BIRTH OF SOCIALISM 1884-1900 49
The Social Democratic Federation 49; The Socialist League and the Walsall Anarchist 'Bomb Plot' 52; The Fabian Society 55; Clarion and 'Cheerful Socialism' 56; The Independent Labour Party 63; Independent Parliamentary Representation 67; Bibliography 68

5   TRADE UNIONISM 1874-1900 69
The Miners 69; Ironworkers 73; Engineering Unions 79; Tinmen and Ironplate Workers 81; Electricians 82; Builders 83; The Midland Counties Trades Federation 84; The Noble Order of the Knights of Labour 88; Nuts and Bolts 90; Locks 91; Other Crafts 92; Nails 92; Chainmakers 94; Glassmakers 96; Brassworkers 98; Railwaymen 99; Other Manual Unions 99; White Collar Unions 100; Trades Councils 103; Participations at the TUC 105; Bibliography 107

6   FROM LABOUR PARTY TO FIRST WORLD WAR 109
The General Situation 109; SDF/British Socialist Party 110; Clarion 114; Labour Churches 121; Other Socialist Organisations 124; The ILP 125; Parliamentary Representation 1900-14 132; Bibliography 136

7	**DEPRESSION 1903-09 AND THE GREAT UNREST 1910-14**	**137**
	Depression and Distress Committees 137; The Standard of Living 1900-10 139; The Great Unrest 147; Bibliography 159	
8	**CO-OPERATION TO 1914**	**161**
	The Foundations 161; Productive Co-ops 162; Consumer Co-operatives to 1884 168; Other Societies 174; Consumer Co-operatives 1884-1914 174; Administration and Problems to 1914 178; Education Committees 179; The Women's Guild 184; Conclusions 187; Bibliography 194	
9	**WOMEN**	**195**
	Women, Work and Wages 195; Women in Trade Unions 198; Bibliography 200	

PART 2
SOCIALISM IN BIRMINGHAM AND THE BLACK COUNTRY 1914-1939

10	**BIRMINGHAM TRADE UNIONS AND THE WAR**	**203**
	The War and the City 203; The Trades Council and the War 204; 1917 211; 1918 212; The Trade Unions and the War 215; Bibliography 218	
11	**THE CO-OPERATIVE MOVEMENT IN BIRMINGHAM IN WARTIME**	**219**
	Problems and Duties 219; Co-operative Social Organisation 222; The Co-operative Movement and the Food Question 224; The Co-operative Party 226; Bibliography 227	
12	**BIRMINGHAM WOMEN IN WARTIME**	**229**
	Women in Trade Unions 229; Political Women and the War 233; The Women's Social and Political Union 234; The National Union of Women's Suffrage Societies 236; The Women's Co-operative Guild 238; The Women's Labour League 240; The Workers' Suffrage Federation 241; Other Women's Organisations 242; Bibliography 242	
13	**LABOUR MOVEMENT POLITICS IN BIRMINGHAM 1914-1918**	**243**
	BSP and SLP 1914-16 244; The ILP 246; Other Peace Organisations 249; Conscription and Conscientious Objectors 250; 1917 – the year of the Russian Revolutions 255; The Leeds Convention 257; June to December 1917 259; 1918 262; Conclusions 265; Bibliography 267; Appendix – Birmingham Conscientious Objectors 267	
14	**TRADE UNIONS IN THE BLACK COUNTRY 1914-1918**	**271**
	Outbreak of War 271; The Workers' Union 272; The ASE 273; The Trades Councils 276; Bibliography 281	
15	**THE CO-OPERATIVE MOVEMENT IN THE BLACK COUNTRY 1914-1918**	**283**
	Progress and Problems 283; Midland District Reports 285; Walsall and Wolverhampton Societies 287; Conclusions 294; Walsall Locks and Cartgear 294; Bibliography 295	
16	**BLACK COUNTRY LABOUR WOMEN AT WAR 1914-1918**	**297**
	Co-operative Women's Guild Activists 300; Labour Women Political Activists 301; Bibliography 303	
17	**BLACK COUNTRY LABOUR POLITICS 1914-1916**	**305**
	Attitude to the War 305; Conscription and Conscientious Objectors 306; 1918 312; The Khaki Election 314; Bibliography 317; Appendix – Black Country Conscientious Objectors 317	
18	**THE BIRMINGHAM LABOUR MOVEMENT 1919-1926**	**319**
	Ex-Service Politics 319; Hands off Russia 324; The Birmingham Police Strike 1919 326; Unemployment 330; Police Spies and the Campaign for Free Speech 336; The Fight for Peace 340; Adult Working Class Education 343; Women 347; Youth 352; Labour Churches 353; Christian Socialism 356; Leisure and Pleasure 358; The Communist Party 360; Bibliography 365; Appendix – List of Birmingham Police Strikers 366	

19	**THE ILP AND THE LABOUR PARTY**	**369**
	The ILP 369; The Labour Party 374; Bibliography 380	
20	**THE TRADE UNION MOVEMENT IN BIRMINGHAM 1919-1925**	**381**
	Trade Union Advance 1919-20 381; Trades Council 389; Wages and the Standard of Living 390; Bibliography 392	
21	**THE LABOUR MOVEMENT IN THE BLACK COUNTRY 1919-1925**	**393**
	Ex-Service Politics 393; Hands off Russia 395; Unemployment 397; Adult Working Class Education 406; WEA 407; The Communist Party 409; ILP 410; The Labour Party 414; Local Elections to 1925 418; Bibliography 428	
22	**BLACK COUNTRY TRADE UNIONISM 1919-1925**	**429**
	The Trades Councils 429; Black Country Miners 438; Iron Workers 441; Engineers 442; Locks 443; The Workers' Union 447; Unemployment and the Real Standard of Living 447; Bibliography 449	
23	**THE CO-OPERATIVE MOVEMENT IN BIRMINGHAM 1919-1939**	**451**
	Ten Acres & Stirchley 451; TASCOS Social Activity 454; Birmingham Co-operative Society 455; The Slump Years 1921-24 458; Growth Resumed 459; Education Developments 461; The Birmingham Co-operative Party 462; Industrial Co-operation 463; Birmingham Co-operative Personalities 464; Women and the Guilds 466; Conclusions 468; 1930-39 470; Bibliography 471	
24	**THE CO-OPERATIVE MOVEMENT IN THE BLACK COUNTRY 1919-1939**	**473**
	Dudley 473; Halesowen & Hasbury 474; Soho 475; Tipton 476; Wednesbury 476; Walsall 477; Wolverhampton 480; Walsall Locks and Cartgear 486; Summary 488; 1930-39 490; Bibliography 490	
25	**THE GENERAL STRIKE IN THE BLACK COUNTRY**	**491**
	The Miners 491; The General Strike 493; The Miners fight on alone 499; The Return to Work 500; The Settlement 502; Bibliography 503	
26	**THE GENERAL STRIKE IN BIRMINGHAM**	**505**
	Causes 505; Preparations 506; The Nine Days 508; The Long End 527; What could have been 523; Bibliography 529	
27	**THE BLACK COUNTRY LABOUR MOVEMENT 1927-39**	**531**
	Parliamentary and Municipal Representation 531; Against Fascism, Appeasement and War 538; The Peace Ballot 1935 539; Spain and World War 540; Bibliography 545	
28	**BIRMINGHAM FROM GENERAL STRIKE TO WORLD WAR 2**	**547**
	The Trade Unions 1927-39 547; Right v Left 547; The National Minority Movement 551; Elections to 1929 551; The Rise of the Labour Government 552; The Fall of the Labour Government 553; Unemployment 554; Trade Unions 1927-39 556; The Struggle to Prevent War 1932-39 559; Spain, Fascism and War 561; 1938 Czechoslovakia, the Final Betrayal 566; Bibliography 570	
29	**CONCLUSIONS**	**571**
Index		573
Sponsors of this book		577

List of Illustrations

1. Thick Coal Mining in the Black Country.
2. Wolverhampton Society of Tin Plate Workers membership certificate.
3. Birmingham Trades Council Liberal leaders 1880s.
4. (a) Birmingham Labour Church 12th Annual Meeting 1904.
   (b) Labour Church Declaration of Faith.
5. Early twentieth century Birmingham Trades Council leaders.
6. Dr Robert Dunstan, Birmingham Labour and Communist Parliamentary Candidate 1918-1924.
7. The first post-war Hunger March – Birmingham to London 1922.
8. Birmingham Trades Council Executive 1928.
9. Birmingham District Committee Communist Party 1927.
10. May Day procession in Birmingham in 1929.
11. Birmingham – Labour's Victorious Six in the 1929 General Election.
12. Some Black Country Labour MPs from 1906.
13. (a) Walsall Co-operative pamphlet 1829.
    (b) First Walsall Co-operative Society premises 1886.
14. Walsall Co-operative Pioneers.

Cover   William Morris print, Flora.
Front cover   May Day procession in Birmingham in 1929.
Back cover   May Day 1937 cartoon.

Part 1

Socialism in the Black Country 1850-1914

Chapter 1

From Chartism to Secularism 1850-1870

Introduction
The first task is to define the Black Country. Birmingham is, apart from the original tiny village, a political unit, which has grown taking surrounding areas under its jurisdiction. But the Black Country is a physical unit of about 150 square miles and is defined here as that area standing on the unique and magnificent 10-yard seam of coal. Within the many layers compromising this thirty feet wall of coal was ironstone. This led to the development of the great ironworks whose by products of smoke and flame from the open furnaces turned day into night and night into day, according to the awed testimony of those visitors who entered this satanic region. By this definition, Wolverhampton, the largest town of the region, qualifies for inclusion, the coalfield extending to the eastern outskirts of the town. Similarly, in the Walsall area the coalfield dips to reappear further north as the Cannock coalfield. However, both these towns are also central to the industry of the Black Country which must be roughly defined as the area compromising the modern metropolitan boroughs of Wolverhampton, Walsall, Dudley and Sandwell. Birmingham is definitely not in the Black Country.

The economic situation provides the terrain on which the politics of any period are fought out. The period from 1815 to 1850 had been dominated by three Long Depressions of 1815-23, 1826-33 and 1839-43. Each of these Depressions had stimulated particular forms of working class political and trade union organisation which, because Britain was the first nation to have an Industrial Revolution also produced the first working class. The institutions which British working people fashioned were therefore unique and later largely copied by the rest of the world.

The first Long Depression, after the Napoleonic Wars gave rise to working class Political Unions and the 'blasphemous and seditious' newspapers epitomised by William Cobbett's *Political Register*. The second Long Depression brought united action between the middle and working classes with Political Unions in Birmingham and the Black Country leading the struggle for the first Reform Act of 1832. This gave the vote to the middle class, but denied it to working people who had mainly been responsible for agitating for it. So when the third Long Depression occurred there was already in place the first Socialist movement in Britain associated with the name of Robert Owen. This aimed at by-passing capitalism by the creation of co-operative colonies and was also a rationalist, atheist movement attacking religion and the role it played in upholding ruling class hegemony and control.

But the third Depression also gave rise to the most significant working class movement of the century. This was Chartism which aimed, by bombarding Parliament with petitions containing millions of signatures, to peacefully persuade Parliament to grant the vote to all working men. None of these movements was successful in their main aim of universal male suffrage, but all played significant parts in mitigating the elemental upheavals of the capitalist trade cycle which, in its downswings lasting for many years, threatened to starve vast swathes of working people who were not only without political rights, but also without any social services, except the Workhouse.

When we turn to the period after 1850 myths abound. From 1850 to the Great Depression of the 1870s was the period of Britain's industrial supremacy and of vastly expanded industrial output. This, however, does not warrant the assumption that this brought working class prosperity. The 1850s were a 'good' decade with only a small slump in 1855. The 1860s were much worse, however, with full employment only in 1864-65 and trade either moderate or bad in other years. Only from 1870 to 1874 was there a sustained boom and full employment. This was followed by the Great Depression which lasted until almost the end of the century.

Working-class Politics 1850-69 – Chartism and Secularism

Chartism was the main political 'culture' of working people in the Black Country from the end of the 1830s until 1860. Chartism reached its peak here in 1842 when a combination of a campaign for the collection of signatures on the 2nd Petition and a general strike amongst miners and other workers made Black Country Chartism stronger than in almost any other area of Britain. If it had been as strong elsewhere the Charter would almost certainly have had to be granted by the government and democracy would have come to Britain decades earlier. Chartist influence declined thereafter, but until its final demise in 1860 it remained the only organisation and philosophy capable of mobilising working people to political action.

Secularism co-existed with Chartism in the decade 1850-60 and when Chartism disappeared, Secularism inherited its mantle until the early 1870s when a powerful Republican movement arose which was swamped by the Great Depression. It took another ten years before a new Socialist movement arose with the emergence of the Marxist Social Democratic Federation and Socialist League, together with the reformist Fabian Society.

One activity holding Chartists together after 1847 was the Chartist Land Company. This was an immense scheme of Feargus O'Connor involving many thousands of people who made weekly contributions for plots of land on Chartist estates. When they had a fully paid-up £1 share they were entitled to enter a ballot for plots of land on one of five estates. The two-fold aim was to settle workers on the land and also give them a vote as free-holders. O'Connor cut corners to develop the scheme and in 1848 Parliament declared it illegal. By then, however, most of the estates were operating and 15 members in the Black Country and two in Birmingham were allocated land at O'Connorsville in Hertfordshire, Charterville (Minster Lovell in Gloucestershire), Low Bands and Snigs End in Worcestershire, or Great Dodsford near Bromsgrove. This last estate was of particular concern to the West Midlands Chartists who made regular visits and gave assistance when crops failed, new tools were needed etc.

There was also a substantial Chartist revival from 1855 following the disasters of the early part of the Crimean War, during which prices rose sharply. During the period, Bilston was the strongest Chartist centre, but from 1857 to 1860 Dudley took the lead. Here there was an effective nucleus of activists old and new, led by Samuel Cook.

Chartist influence was also strong in the trade unions. But when Ernest Jones gave up the struggle in 1860, Black Country Chartism was left high and dry without national leadership.

During the 1850s Chartists were being reluctantly forced into the realisation that Votes for Working Class Men could only be achieved with broader organisation involving the middle class. This despite the doublecross of 1832 when the middle class had given themselves the vote and denied it to working people.

Dudley was the first town to act. In 1851 a Temple of Investigation is known of through Samuel Cook's famous posters which he displayed in his draper's shop window at the top of the High Street. A resolution to support a modified form of the People's Charter was published 'by order of the Religious and Political Union at the Temple of Investigation'. By 1852 Chartists there were organised into a Dudley Mutual Improvement Society. In January 1853 in successive weeks there were lectures on Land Nationalisation, Paley Refuted, and Secularism, two of which were given by local Chartists.

By the mid-1850s Secularism was well established in Eclectic Institutes across the country and served by John Jacob Holyoake's paper *The Reasoner*. When this paper first appeared in the late 1840s it was said to be 'a weekly paper for Utilitarians, Republicans and Communists'. This shows the Owenite Socialist origins of Secularism. In 1854 and 1855 Dudley secularists met every Sunday at 6pm. at Dudley Hall of Investigation.

In January 1856 a conference in Birmingham, initiated by Christopher Charles Cattell, the leading Birmingham secularist, resolved that 'all friends of free thought should co-operate with the Birmingham and West Midlands Eclectic Society'. Further information could be had from Mr Whittall of York Street, Wolverhampton and Mr Wallwork of Flood Street Dudley. Both of these were Chartist activists. In July there was news of Dudley secularists attending a religious meeting on 'The Absurdities of Atheism'. By October 'a number of friends met each week at Mr Silk's'. These included Silk, Wallwork, Cook, Foster, Smart, Davis, Finney and Weeks. At least the first three were Chartists of long standing.

From 1860 Chartism disappeared and the main Secularist newspaper became Charles Bradlaugh's *National Reformer*. In response to enquiries regarding the policy of the paper, Bradlaugh wrote in 1862:

> Editorially, as to religious questions, the paper is and always has been...the Advocate of Atheism; it teaches that all the religions of the world are based upon error; that humanity is higher than theology; that knowledge is far preferable to faith; that action is more effective than prayer; and that the best worship man can offer is honest work, in order to make one another wiser and happier than heretofore. In politics we are radicals of a very extreme kind; we are advocates of manhood suffrage, we desire shorter Parliaments; laws which are more equal in their application to master and servant; protection from the present state of laws which make pheasants more valuable than peasants; we desire the repeal of all laws against blasphemy... we advocate the separation of Church and State, and join with the financial reformers in their efforts to reduce our enormous and extravagant national expenditure.

Such a policy continued the programme of the Chartists and joined with the Black Country 'infidel' tradition which dated back to Thomas Paine and the French Revolution, later continued by the Owenite Socialists of the 1830s. The hostility to the Church of England is explained by its unfailing support for reactionary national governments and also the role of local clergy as JPs administering the Master and Servants Acts (which made almost every trade union activity illegal) as well as laws depriving working people of all other political rights. The main Methodist body was equally hostile to working class aspirations and it was only among the more submerged sects, notably the Baptists, that there was any sympathy. This atheism of Bradlaugh's was more to the liking of the Black Country militants than the more cautious Secularism (a word he coined) of G.J. Holyoake and his *Reasoner* newspaper which had led the Secularist movement until then.

By 1862 Silk seems to have moved to Birmingham and was active in the movement there. In May there was a notice of Secularism in Oldbury where Mrs Harriet Law (herself a convert to atheism from the Baptists) gave two lectures at the local Temperance Hall. The first was on 'God's Relations with His Chosen People' and the second 'Difficulties with Christianity'. Daniel Wallwork was advertised as lecturing the next week on 'What is Secularism?'. The notice of the meeting was signed by Daniel Wallwork, so it can be assumed that this activity was initiated from Dudley or Birmingham.

There are few reports of Secularism in the Black Country for the next three years and it seems that working class political activity did not develop in these years of unsatisfactory trade, mass unemployment, a considerable growth of trade unions and bitter strikes.

Activity revived in 1866. In July there were meetings in Willenhall and Wolverhampton. In Willenhall Robert Key lectured on 'Infidelity and Christianity' to a 'good audience'. In Wolverhampton Joseph Barker lectured on 'Objections to Christianity' but to a 'poor audience'. In November it was announced that the *National Reformer* could be purchased in Walsall from E. Scholey at the Temperance Coffee House, 68 Dudley St. and C. Whitney, newsagent of Perks Street. Scholey was a Chartist stalwart who had run the Temperance Coffee House in Dudley Street from at least 1855.

In 1867 Secular activity was sufficiently widespread for Birmingham to take another initiative to create district organisation with the Birmingham and Midland Secular Union. J. Morris the Birmingham secretary hoped this would appeal to secularists in West Bromwich, Smethwick, Oldbury, Wednesbury, Walsall, Wolverhampton, Bilston, Brierley Hill, Dudley and Stourbridge. In each of these towns there had been reports of secular meetings in the recent past. A subsequent meeting was called attended by Silk and Bentley of West Bromwich and Gilbert of Willenhall. 'Several friends from Smethwick, Coseley and Brierley Hill gave in names of potential members'.

In November West Bromwich reported two lectures by the national leader, Charles Watts who was touring the area. The first was 'The Orthodox Doctrine of Atonement, is it in Accord with Justice and Right Reason?'. The second was 'The Bible and Science; wherein do they Differ?'. The latter was with special reference to a recent Church Congress held in Wolverhampton. Another report by J.T. Scattergood claimed that West Bromwich was breaking new ground. Christians had been invited, 'but they studiously avoided Watts'. They had assured Scattergood that they had prepared material to come, but had been called away to attend to the sick. Scattergood then invited them to several nights' debate.

Watts had also visited Smethwick that week and had lectured on 'Teaching the New Testament'.

1867 was the year of the second Reform Act which gave the vote to working men in towns. Again, there is little report of Secularist activity, although every Black Country secularist would be active in the wide-spread local agitation promoting the Bill.

1868, in contrast was a year of much secular activity. Regular lectures occurred in Oldbury with the assistance of Birmingham Secular Society and its energetic secretary John Morris. Birmingham also initiated activity in Smethwick where a meeting was held at the Regent Concert Hall, Rolfe Street on the 'Christians' Heaven and Hell'. Morris also reported that Wolverhampton and West Bromwich were 'moving notably in the right direction'.

In February, J. Murray of Bilston contributed 5/-d. to the first of Bradlaugh's many campaigns for election to Parliament as a member for Northampton. In the same month there was a long report of the activities of Dudley Secular Society. A public meeting at the Phoenix Assembly Rooms had drawn an attendance 'much better than expected'. The speaker was Charles Watts who lectured on 'Christianity – the Enemy of Science and Civilisation' with H. Langstone in the chair. Two days later Watts lectured at the same place on 'The Christian Doctrine of Atonement a Fallacy'. The attendance was much larger than before:

> Christians yelled, shouted and hissed, but the speaker and the chairman held their ground and restored moderate order. The speaker severely castigated those of the meek and holy Jesus who so grossly misconducted themselves. A Mr Homer from Sedgley preached and whined for ten minutes, something which, perhaps, would have pleased a Primitive Methodist congregation, but which, was sadly out of place on a Freethought platform. The local preacher said that the mischief of free thought and all other evils were clearly traceable to the Devil. Watts reminded him that he was ignorant of the real origination of evil. His opponent warmly affirmed that nothing in the bible said that the Lord had created evil. Watts cautioned him on his triumphant certainty, but he maintained his proposition. Mr Watts then read the well known passage from Isaiah and handed the book to his crestfallen opponent amid such a burst of applause as seldom has been equalled. The man stared at the book in increasing wonderment and was silent. The incident produced a very marked effect on the Christian part of the audience who were transformed from tigers into lambs and afterwards behaved with extreme circumspection. Our friends were highly gratified at Mr Watts' skill and zeal. There is a large field for the spread of Secular principles here and we hope our friends will lose no time. (J. Truman, Secretary)

This report captures perfectly the views and attitudes of Black Country Owenite Socialism of thirty years earlier.

In March 1868 John Jones, hairdresser, was reported as selling the *National Reformer* at Lea Brook Wednesbury. This is most likely to be John Jones the Bilston barber, who was a leading Chartist from the early 1840s. In West Bromwich the Assembly Rooms were crowded to hear iconoclast Charles Bradlaugh. In May Charles Watts was at the same venue.

In July there was a district complimentary dinner to Bradlaugh. In a series of toasts the health of the Queen was proposed and then Bradlaugh's good health. A toast to a Free Press was followed by Mr Cook of Brierley Hill.

Hill proposed Secular Progress during which he spoke of the great progress that had been made since he was an inmate of Harmony Hall (the famous Owenite Socialist, co-operative colony in Hampshire from 1839 to 1845-GB). John Morris toasted Ladies and Strangers Present and Muir of

Dudley (another Chartist) responded by thanking those who had attended from Wolverhampton, West Bromwich, Walsall, Smethwick, Oldswinsford, Brierley Hill, Oldbury and Bell Broughton.

In August 1868 a notice by Jonathan Lane of Wednesbury announced that 'a few staunch friends had met to see whether we can raise the banner of Secularism here'. It announced a further meeting at Mr Lowe's 34 Cross Street the next Sunday. A society was formed with John Jones as secretary meeting every Sunday at 6pm at 34 Cross street. This was changed in November to 72 Portway Road.

Secularists also flourished at this time in Oldbury. They met every Sunday at what was now called the Freethought Temperance Hall and claimed that for their lectures and readings they had an average weekly attendance of 630. Wolverhampton also had regular meetings every Sunday evening at 6 pm. at 13 St John's Square.

The year ended with the Lecture Room of the column of the *National Reformer* regularly advertising societies in Birmingham, Oldbury, Wolverhampton and Wednesbury.

As Secularism continued to flourish in to 1869 C.C. Cattell from Birmingham was again advocating district organisation, suggesting that it should be centred on Oldbury 'which has a Temperance Room of its own'.

Birmingham Secularism had been for some time moving from the religious to the political field under the impact of such issues as the Reform Act of 1867, the land question, criticism of the monarchy, and education. But Black Country secularists, like their forerunners the Owenite Socialists of the late 1830s, stuck more closely to anti-religious propaganda. For instance, Birmingham Secularists were discussing such topics as the French Revolution, Political Economy, Malthusianism etc and stated that their plan was to vary their programme to discuss scientific, political and social questions instead of allowing theology a monopoly 'and we find it answers very well'. In the Black Country by contrast, meetings in Wolverhampton which were still at 13 St. John's Square, now called the Eclectic Hall, discussed such subjects as Geology and Scripture and at Oldbury, Cattell spoke on the Impossibility of Man's Immortality.

In April in Oldbury a Midlands Secular Union was formed. Cattell, the leading Secularist in the region, was elected secretary and John Silk of West Bromwich, treasurer. Courses of six lectures were arranged for Oldbury and Wolverhampton. Cattell reported that a similar proposal to form a Midland Union eight years before had foundered and showed his hope of basing the Union on the more stable societies of the east Midlands, as well as the west Midlands, when he wrote 'If Leicester and Nottingham, Dudley, Walsall, Wednesbury, Smethwick and many others wish for a union, we will be glad to hear from them'.

Later in the month E. Price, the Wolverhampton secretary reported that David Kirkwood, the Birmingham Secularist, had held meetings in the Eclectic Hall on Geology and Scripture and on the Antiquity of Man. There was no opposition to the meetings and the audience left well satisfied. Charles Watts was booked to lecture on the next Tuesday and Wednesday and Cattell on Sunday.

The Midland Secular Union continued to flourish from the Freethought Temperance Hall in Oldbury. In June, two lectures were reported by Harriet Law, twelve lectures had been arranged for the next three months and hopes were expressed that there would be open-air Sunday meetings at the Wren's Nest and Dudley Castle grounds.

In West Bromwich, at the Assembley Rooms, there had been debates between Harriet Law and Mr T. Jackson. In Wolverhampton at the Eclectic Hall debates were also held and the *National Reformer* could be bought at 65 Snow Hill.

In July, Oldbury departed from religious themes to hear a lecture on the '80th Anniversary of the French Revolution' but returned to more staple fare in August with Cattell lecturing on 'Christianity – The Religion of Persecution' and W. Johnson came from Edinburgh to tell people 'How I became an Infidel'.

Towards the end of July the Midland Secular Union did arrange a summer meeting at the Wren's Nest and Dudley Castle grounds and had a very detailed lecture on the geology of the area, which is outstanding and, of course, germane to the debate on evolution and the bible.

In the autumn of 1869 the Midland Secular Union was strengthened by Birmingham acquiring large premises of its own at St George's Hall, re-named the Birmingham Secular Club and Institute.

Financial help for this project came from as far away as Chipping Norton and Black Country donations can be identified with 10/-d from John Silk of West Bromwich and 5/-d from Smethwick.

Once the hall was opened Birmingham Secularists felt strong enough to assist neighbouring societies. In October a distribution of *National Reformers* in West Bromwich on a Saturday evening was advocated with the suggestion that other Secularists could help either by contributing papers or making a donation to help the upkeep of the hall.

In Oldbury the Midland Secular Union continued to meet with mixed fare. In October '...our friend from Dudley H.V. Mayer lectured on the 'People's Charter – Retrospect and Forecast'. He showed the causes of failure and concluded that all points of the Charter were in fair way of becoming the law of the land. Appreciation was shown by repeated applause. We understand that this is the first lecture given by Mr Mayer. It is sure not to be his last'. The last comment is difficult to understand in view of the fact that Mayer first appeared as H.V. Meira, leading Bilston Chartist in the mid-1850s. In November Cattell lectured on the Wonders of History, but the Union returned to religious themes the next week when J. Johnson of Wolverhampton spoke on the 'Immortality of the Soul' and 'Modern Spiritualism'. At this time we are informed that the work of the Midland Secular Union had been confined to keeping the Oldbury hall supplied with speakers. But the organisation had been fairly supported and they now intended to expand their activities into towns that were doing little or nothing to advance the cause of Secularism.

In December at Oldbury a Mr Price lectured on 'Thomas Paine' and David Kirkwood on 'Dr Livingstone' and 'John Stuart Mill'. G. Lines, the Oldbury secretary reported that a debating society met regularly and elocution classes had begun with recitations of such pieces as The Raven and the speech of Mark Anthony on the death of Caesar. At the Birmingham Secular Club and Institute, Mayer repeated his lecture on Chartism , 'but his strictures of the physical force party brought criticism from the audience'. As well it might, since Chartists in Birmingham and the Black Country had supported Feargus O'Connor, the leader of the so-called physical force Chartists until O'Connor's death in 1855.

1869 closed with much activity in the Black Country, although the Lecture Room column of the *National Reformer* advertised meetings only in Birmingham and Oldbury throughout the year and the Wednesbury and Wolverhampton entries disappeared in mid-November.

In summarising this phase of Black Country secularism the following points can be made. The first is the contrast already drawn with Birmingham, where Secularism was stronger, of the Black Country emphasis on anti-religious propaganda rather than political discussion. This, as I have suggested elsewhere regarding Owenite Socialism, reflects a different religious tradition. In Birmingham, a progressive religious culture dates back at least to the English Revolution of the 1640s and the influx of Dissenters after 1660. This tradition was continued by Joseph Priestley and other Unitarians during the French Revolution and passed on to George Dawson and others into the period under review. In addition, the Church of England clergy were relatively weak in Birmingham. In the Black Country, on the other hand, the clergy of the established church were the 'black slugs' epitomised by Luke Booker, the vicar of Dudley. They were religious terrorists preaching heaven and hell on Sunday and lay terrorists during the week, fining and imprisoning workers under the Master & Servants Acts in their roles as JPs. Progressive christianity was woefully weak in the Black Country compared with Birmingham and the ideological struggle against Christianity and its teachings presented an intellectual stimulus to working people for which there were few other outlets.

The second distinction is the greater continuity between Chartism and Secularism in the Black Country compared with Birmingham. This is a minor surprise as there was virtually no continuity between Owenite Socialism and Chartism in the Black Country thirty years earlier.

Finally there is the question of the influence of Secularism. It is clear that Secularists were mainly working-class people, self-educating themselves through their life time experience. This spanned a most difficult period of the decline of the mass movement of Chartism and the expansion of the national economy as Britain became the Workshop of the World. It is also clear that Secularists were only small groups. But at a time when the mass of working people stubbornly continued hostile or indifferent to religion, when political and trade union rights continued to be withheld, when social conditions were appalling and unemployment widespread (particularly through the 1860s), the influence of Secularism was important as keeping a bridge open over which working class ideology and practice passed from the Utopian socialism of Robert Owen and the mass movement of Chartism to the modern Socialism that emerged in the 1880s.

Bibliography: From Chartism to Secularism 1850-1870

The earlier labour movement has been dealt with by me in: *The Working Class Movement in the Black Country 1750 to 1867* and *Social Conditions in the Black Country 1800-1900.* The Introduction to Chapter 1 of the present book summarises some of this material.

The most important contribution to Black Country labour history for the later period is: Eric Taylor – *The Working Class Movement in the Black Country 1863-1914* (Unpublished Ph.D. thesis Keele University 1974). A copy of this is available at the library of the Wolverhampton University, Dudley campus.

The secular movement has to be researched almost entirely from its newspapers. The two most important of these for Chapter 1 have been: *The Reasoner* (the paper of G.J. Holyoake) and the *National Reformer* (the paper of Charles Bradlaugh).

The remarks concerning the difference between religion in Birmingham and religion in the Black Country were given as a paper to the International Conference of Historians of the Labour Movement and published as *Arbeiterbewegung – Kirche – Religion* by Europaverlang, Vienna 1991.

Chapter 2

Republicanism and Retreat 1870-1884

Secularism and Republicanism 1870-1874
The period examined below started with the Great Boom of the early 1870s. This was the only period of a substantial raising of the standard of living since a similar rise in the years 1845-54. The boom was followed by the Great Depression from 1874 to 1895 which saw the decline of coal mining and the virtual disappearance of iron making as the flooding of the mines, the depletion of ironstone and the failure to change from iron to steel making devastated the Black Country. Such devastation was to be repeated almost exactly one hundred years later.

In 1871 the Midland Secular Union still flourished from the Oldbury Freethought Temperance Hall at Oldbury. The *National Reformer* could still could be obtained at Scholey's in Walsall, from John Jones the Wednesbury hairdresser and at 65 Snow Hill, Wolverhampton. It was still available at Cox's in West Bromwich High Street and from Mayer at 3 Wolverhampton Street, Dudley. In January there was a Thomas Paine Tea Party at Oldbury, reported by J. Lines.

At Wolverhampton, in February, Oliver Trumper was trying to re-establish organisation in the town by calling a meeting at 36 Oxley Street. They had no meeting place, 'but our principles are flourishing', he maintained. Meanwhile Bradlaugh was in the Black Country. He gave three lectures at the Public Hall, Wednesbury 'to crowded audiences', GHR reported. In Walsall, Bradlaugh lectured at the Temperance Hall on the 6th and 7th of February. E.A. Scholey enthused:

> Many came as enemies and went away friends. Others came to grumble and find fault, but are now lavish in their praise. The lecturer made the meeting by his own right of conquest and when a working man gave a vote of thanks he wisely told the audience that the best way of thanking Bradlaugh was to advocate the principles he taught in their factories and workshops.

The opening of a new Republican Club in Birmingham in February heralded the development of a new, powerful movement that was to arise from Secularism and develop parallel with it for some years.

Wednesbury was now becoming a centre of district Secular organisation. The engagement of Harriet Law for two lectures at the Public Hall, Earps Lane, was reported by another new activist T. Battison. In April a Conference occurred presided over by Mayer which formed a South Staffordshire & East Worcestershire Secular Union. Representatives were elected as follows: Dudley – Mayer, Wednesbury – Battison, West Bromwich – John Silk, Walsall – W. Upton, Wolverhampton O. Trumper, Bilston – J. Bailey. Officers elected were president Mayer, treasurer Bray and secretary pro.tem. C. Charles (C.C. Cattell). It is difficult to assess the significance of this new organisation in view of the fact that the Oldbury Union continued to operate. It seems significant that the new organisation should have the weight of the leader of the Birmingham secularists, Cattell, behind it, but no outward sign of tension between the two district organisations can be detected. 1871 was, however, the year that Bradlaugh resigned as the president of the National Secular Society due to overwork and financial problems, although he continued to edit the *National Reformer*. The NSS declined from that time and never again became the powerful, centralised society that it had been.

The new district Union met monthly and in June advertised a public meeting with Charles on 'The Bible – An Immoral Book unfit for Schools'. In August the Union met to re-elect its Committee and decided on delegates for the National Secular Society national conference, which was held that year in Birmingham. The officers elected were: Oliver Trumper – president, George Berry – treasurer, H.V. Mayer – secretary. A committee was also elected of Pattison, Cartwright, Davis, Gilbert, Huins, Holland, Ridgeway and Upton. Mayer was elected as their delegate to the conference. But it was lamented that, 'the only matter for regret is that so many who are known to entertain our views remain aloof and do not share its labours or contribute to its fund'.

When the National Secular Society conference was held in September at St George's Hall, the Black Country delegates were Mayer of Dudley, Radford of Oldbury, Cartwright of Tipton and Trumper of Wolverhampton. During the period of the conference Bradlaugh gave three lectures in Wednesbury and also lectured in Wolverhampton on 'The Impeachment of the House of Brunswick'. Of this meeting Oliver Trumper reported that the audience was largely of working men and this was the first time that Bradlaugh had lectured in Wolverhampton. 'It will help unite working men' he concluded.

In October there was criticism of the vicar of Dudley, the Rev W. Rayner Cosens and the Union was arranging for Charles Watts to visit the area.

The continued existence of the Midland Secular Union centred on the Freethought Temperance Hall at Oldbury indicates a growing strength and influence of Freethought in the Black Country, although the fusion of the two centres would probably have been better. Indeed this was suggested at one of the regular tea parties held at Oldbury.

Towards the end of October 1871 the first Republican Club in the Black Country was inaugurated at Walsall. It met on the same premises as the Secularists in Scholey's Temperance Coffee House in Walsall and Scholey was elected secretary pro.tem.

In November at the monthly meeting of the S. Staffs & E. Worcs Secular Society at Wednesbury the main business was to make arrangements for Watts' coming tour. At the same meeting , 'Miss C. Louisa Trumper, the daughter of our president, admirably recited Shelley's song to the Men of England (page 93 of the Secularists Manual) and received much applause'. In the evening there was a public lecture by Mayer on Prayer and Providence.

Watts lectured in November and rather than tackling the Vicar of Dudley, his programme clearly showed how rapidly Republicanism was developing in the Black Country. In Wednesbury he was due to speak on 'Monarchy', in Walsall on 'Republicanism', in Oldbury on 'Government and the People', in Tipton and in Wolverhampton on 'Two Hundred Years of English Monarchy'. Mayer hoped that 'friends of freethought, republicanism and national thought,' would attend.

Agents for the *National Reformer* in the Black Country at this time were Mayer at Dudley, Scholey Walsall, Jones Wednesbury, Battison at 5 New Street and Cox in High Street West Bromwich and Oliver Trumper at Stafford Street, Wolverhampton.

Republicanism appears to be an exotic bloom to flourish in Britain, especially at a time when the great Victorian expansion was culminating in the frenzied boom of 1870-74. Its flowering was brief – it was destroyed by the Great Depression – but its roots ran deep and it also reflected the widespread poverty and unease that continued to exist at the height of Britain's economic supremacy.

Republicanism was a legacy from the English Revolution of the seventeenth century and looked to the anti-monarchical systems that had emerged from the American and French Revolutions. Central to Republicanism was the land question. The great aristocratic landed estates had vastly prospered during the Victorian expansion and had been added to by the great industrial estates of the Earls of Dudley and others. If the workers in the towns had not participated fully in this vast increase in wealth, the condition of farm labourers was even worse varying from deep poverty to actual starvation. The urban poverty continually stimulated movements for a return to the land as freeholders with a vote. In Chartist times it was Feargus O'Connor's Land Plan; in the 1860s it was a Home Colonisation movement demanding the break-up of the landed estates by Land nationalisation. In the countryside Joseph Arch had at last been able to organise farm workers with his Agricultural Labourers' Union which drew heavily on urban sympathy and solidarity. For a while rural living standards were raised, but the Union collapsed with the agricultural crisis which was part of the Great Depression.

Hostility to the landed interest was extended to the monarchy, seen as the apex and prop of aristocracy. The retirement of Victoria from public life after the death of Albert in 1861 had demonstrated that monarchy was unnecessary and the antics of the heir apparent hardened opinion. Finally, entwined with monarchy and aristocracy was the Church of England the disestablishment of which was the aim of every Dissenter. This also tended to strengthen the forces of Secularism and Atheism.

The begetter of the Republican movement was the Land & Labour League formed in the autumn of 1869. This replaced the Reform League whose work had largely been completed in 1867 although there was considerable dissatisfaction with the results of the Reform Act. For a time the newspaper of the movement was the *Republican*. In November 1870 the paper printed the programme of the Land & Labour League. This included Land Nationalisation, Home Colonisation, national secular gratuitous and compulsory Education, paper money to be issued only by the State, a direct and progressive tax on Property in lieu of all other taxes. reduction of the hours of Labour and Equal Electoral Rights with Payment of Members.

References to the Black Country in the *Republican* in 1871 mainly concern correspondence with the paper. For instance in reply to R. Peters of West Bromwich in March, he is thanked and told that the parcel (of *Republicans* presumably) had been sent. It goes on 'Remember it is the poor themselves who must fight the battle of right against might. Press onwards and upwards. Success is everywhere worshipped. Our time will come.' Peters wrote again in April and was told, 'We endorse the major portion of your letter. We hope to be in a position soon to visit your locality. Nothing would give us greater pleasure than to meet your half-faced Liberal representatives, as you so rightly designate them. We thank you for your earnestness.' In May, Oliver Tromper from Wolverhampton was writing to the paper and was told, 'Soon we hope to be in the position of visiting you for lecturing purposes. Meanwhile, thanks.' In the same month Tromper reported that the nucleus of a Republican Club had been formed in Wolverhampton of about 50 members. Correspondence was to be addressed to Tromper at 88 Stafford Street.

In July J.B. (presumably J. Bailey) of Bilston was told that his letter had been replied to, and R.B. of Horseley Heath, Tipton was chided, 'We sincerely regret the state of your health which aggravates the despondency of the tone of your letter. We do not hide from ourselves that what you say of your own orders is lamentably true.' In August J.P. of Wolverhampton was advised, 'Procure Lewis's Physiology of Common Life.'

The *Republican* newspaper disappeared in 1872 and we return to the *National Reformer* for information on the Secular and Republican movements.

Secular activity continued strongly into 1872. In Oldbury, at the Freethought Temperance Hall, regular meetings included the monthly tea party where fifty people were catered for in February. Reports throughout March from the secretary John Swan reported members meeting to decorate the Hall, a progress report – 'much business has been conducted to raise the Society from the state of embryo in which it has been for so long' – and a meeting which opened with another reading of Marc Anthony's speech over Caesar.

In Wednesbury the S. Staffs and E. Worcs Secular Society continued meeting monthly at Wednesbury. In March they agreed to support George Odger (one of the so-called Junta of trade union leaders centred on London – GB) in support of certain clauses in a Ballot Bill in parliament (another of the Chartist Six points). They also sold a quantity of *Internationals* (presumably the *International Herald* then replacing the *Republican* as the organ of the Republican movement).

Regular meetings of the Walsall Republican Club included one in June when we are told that a 'meeting was taken over', and a resolution passed unanimously that 'Antipas failed to impeach

Republicanism and this proves that B and Sir Charles Dilke are mistaken.' B is presumably Bradlaugh, but the present author cannot match the erudition with which the working men of the 1870s discussed the minutia of Roman republican politics.

In August the S. Staffs & E. Worcs SS held its AGM and elected T. Battison as president, R. Cartwright vice-president, H.V. Mayer secretary and G. Perry treasurer. The new committee was Upton, Holland, T. Davies, Silk, J. Jones, Huins, Ridgway and Wilson.

In October 1872 we have the first notice of the West Bromwich Republican Club when D.A. Beckett of Hallam Place was elected president and the splendidly named Secularist, H. Voltaire Squires of Union Street, Spon Lane as secretary.

In early December there was a slight hiccup at Wednesbury when Battison announce that in view of the small attendance at the usual monthly meeting of the S. Staffs & E. Worcs SS he was calling a special meeting. The matter seems to have been settled by electing A. Holland of 1 Pipes Meadow, Bilston as secretary and F. Wilson and Ridgway as auditors.

By the end of the year Oldbury was still holding its monthly tea parties and weekly meetings. the Guide to the Lecture Rooms column in the *National Reformer* advertised regular activity at Oldbury, Wednesbury, Walsall and West Bromwich Republican Clubs and Walsall announced the opening of a Sunday Reading Room at 68 Dudley Street where E.A. Scholey was the manager.

In January 1873 there were fuller details of the Walsall Sunday Reading Room. It was open from 4pm to 10pm and there were lectures from 7pm to 9pm. The S. Staffs & E. Worcs SS January lecture was by J. Clayton on 'Patriotism'. Bradlaugh was also brought to Wednesbury where he lectured on 'The Bible in India', 'The Bible in China' and 'The Bible in Egypt'.

In February there were tea parties at Oldbury and Wednesbury and Cattell lectured on 'Republicanism' at the Walsall Sunday Reading Room.

In March there was a special meeting of the S. Staffs & E. Worcs SS to consider two important matters. The first was to elect delegates to the first Republican Conference being held in Birmingham on 11 and 12 May. The other matter was to commence taking shares for the building of a Secular Hall in Wednesbury, 'Members are increasingly determined to have our own Hall. Our friend Mr Maybury has promised to take 100 shares'. In further business, W. Pratt was instructed to write to Willenhall Trades Council urging the importance of electoral reform and requesting them to take action in favour of Sir Charles Dilkes' motion for enquiring into the inequalities of the electoral system and Trevelyan's bill to extend household suffrage to the counties. Perry then reviewed recent parliamentary proceedings and a discussion followed in which Blinkhorn, Newman and Pratt participated. It was then arranged for J. Kay to deliver a lecture at the Walsall Temperance Hall and the next lecture at Wednesbury on The Doings of Parliament. After all this business had been transacted A. Holland gave a lecture on 'Secular and Compulsory Education, the only way of Benefitting the Labouring Classes'.

Later in March 1873 Radford reported from Oldbury that Kirkwood of Birmingham had given a lecture on Phrenology and had 'explained the heads of half a dozen people.' This seems a little late to be championing a pseudo-science which had been popular with the Owenite Socialists, but was then losing its appeal, even though one of its strengths was that it postulated equality between male and female brains. Lectures the two following Sundays at Oldbury were Secularism and its General Tendency on Mankind, by Cox of Birmingham and Spenser and his Fairie Queen by J. Parsons.

Among the matters dealt with at the Walsall Penny Sunday Reading Room in April was the receipt of printed copies of the Petition of the borough MP, C. Forster, in support of Trevelyan's reform Bill. Also there were lectures on The Age of Shams, and Co-operatives. At Wednesbury in April at a meeting of the S. Staffs & E. Worcs SS twenty two shares were added to the 100 already subscribed for the proposed Secular Hall and a good attendance was urged for the next meeting which would elect a Committee and a treasurer. R. Cartwright was elected as a delegate to the Birmingham Republican Conference in Birmingham. In Birmingham H.V. Mayer of Dudley was lecturing on Why I became and why I remain a Secularist. Later in April at the monthly Oldbury tea party 'songs from Macauley, Southey and others were rendered by Messrs. Radford Jnr, Cox and other gentlemen'. The Oldbury lecture for the week had been given by Willetts on the Bible and Science, and the same lecturer was due to speak the following week on Prehistoric Man.

In Wolverhampton on 30th April there was a debate at the St. James' School rooms on 'What is God', The Rev J.E. Gladstone, vicar of St. Matthews and the Rev E. Geare, vicar of St. George's, plus other clergymen and scripture readers spoke for the Church. Stanley of Wolverhampton and Reddalls of Birmingham led for the Secularists. Almost 100 were present at a 'very animated discussion' which lasted until 11-30pm. Reddalls then challenged the churches to twelve more nights of debate on 'Is there a God' and 'Is the Character of the Bible God Reliable?'. 'The ministers, thinking discretion the better part of valour refused to meet anyone who thought that matter was eternal and did not think that there was a God', the report from Cookson ended.

In May in Oldbury it was announced that contributions were about to start to a national fund to send Republicans to Parliament. Bradlaugh also spoke in the town on 'Ireland 1793-1873'. Irish politics had a direct bearing on Republicanism in England. The first Irish Land Act of 1870 only highlighted the problems of Irish absentee land owners of vast estates and the eviction of tenants, problems which Gladstone feared would be 'imported over the water' to England. Near the end of this meeting Thomas Davies a veteran Socialist and Chartist 'who had been out of work for some time through trying to befriend someone else', said that he was resolved to go to America. This took members by surprise and not wishing to lose a good friend resolved in starting him in some business. G. Perry has promised him a situation and other members have contributed largely to his support. This. we hope, is one of the things that Secularists are always ready to do.' Holland reported. Bradlaugh also spoke on Ireland to a 'fair audience' at the Public Hall, Wednesbury.

The Republican Conference of May 1873 took place in Birmingham largely because C.C. Cattell had been the driving force behind the initiation of the movement, although by the time of the Conference, Bradlaugh was the leading figure largely seen as 'the coming Cromwell.' and it was the national Secular leaders who dominated the Conference.

Black Country delegates came from Bilston, the S. Staffs & E. Worcs Secular Union, Walsall, West Bromwich and Wolverhampton. The Conference set up a national Republican League and thrashed out a programme of Universal Suffrage, a cautious policy of support for a Republic and Land Reform, abolition of the House of Lords, separate Parliaments for England, Scotland and Ireland if requested, the replacement of the standing army by a citizen force, and the establishment of a national system of compulsory, gratuitous, secular and industrial education.

The main Black Country contribution to the Conference came from H.V. Mayer the Dudley Chartist who put a damper on the proceedings thus:

> ... A Republican myself, I long to see my political aspirations realised. But I am not enthusiastic enough to overlook the obstacles on the way. To deliberately propose to subvert the institutions of a country bespeaks either a considerable amount of confidence, audacity or rashness... I want Republicans to thoroughly comprehend the importance of the change they propose, and to estimate correctly the chances of effecting it... In this England of ours, any political movement must commend itself to the understanding of the nation at large – must be able to challenge the critical consideration of the intelligent and influential, as well as enlist the sympathies of the many... The battle of principles once begun must go on to the end. At every turn new opponents will arise, and fresh objections be urged. The cautious will enquire as to the legality of the thing. The prudent as to its feasibility, the philosopher as to its value, and the statesman as to its expediency... You will have to take into account too, the deplorable apathy of the people themselves... It is no libel upon them to say that six tenths of them –
> Don't care two Injions
> For perlitical opinions.

After much more in like vein Mayer's natural optimism prevailed and he concluded 'Meanwhile, having committed yourself to the cause, let there be no feebleness in you efforts... The task you assay is arduous and great; the difficulties in your way are numerous and formidable, but with courage, energy, patience and perseverance most things are possible.'

Following the Conference, the S. Staffs & E. Worcs Secular Society ordered two hundred copies of the main speeches of the Conference. Ten shillings was also donated to George Reddalls who was publishing a new local paper, the *Secular Chronicle* from Birmingham. Shares for the proposed Secular Hall now stood at 124, the treasurer G. Perry, reported.

After the Conference, Secular and Republican activity continued as before. At West Bromwich

Republican Club a debating class was to meet every Sunday and had been inaugurated by Squires reading a paper on Republicanism.

Scholey reported from the Walsall Sunday Reading Room that attendances had been small in recent weeks, but he expected a very large meeting the next week when friends and advanced Liberals would meet respecting the generous offer of W.H. Duignan, the Walsall solicitor, to donate £100 to a working class candidate for Walsall parliamentary constituency and £25 per annum if he were elected.

Activity continued at the S. Staffs & E. Worcs SS during July and August at Wednesbury. Cattell spoke on the 'Land Question' and promised to return to continue the subject. Officers were elected – Battison (president), Cartwright (vice-president, Moses (secretary) and G. Perry (treasurer). The new committee was Messrs. Jones, Thompson, Ridgway and Holland. At the close of this meeting, 'A Mr Goodhead, a stranger to us, offered us a room at the expense of 3/-d. a week fitted with fireplace and gas. He also promised to sell a piece of land between Darlaston and Wednesbury for £140 and would take twenty shares in the Secular Hall project if his offer were accepted.' This matter was referred to the Committee.

In Walsall Scholey was contemplating new schemes. Truthseekers of all shades of opinion were respectfully invited to a special meeting on a Sunday afternoon in the Billiard Room at 68 Dudley Street to consider forming a society for the investigation of all political, sociological and theological subjects. Republicans, Socialists, Spiritualists and all in favour of unfettered discussion were earnestly invited to attend. This meeting resulted in the formation of a Walsall Free Discussion Society with W. Pratt as secretary pro.tem. At its first discussion at the Temperance Coffee House, S. Parry opened on 'What should be our Future Policy?'. They had done wrong in the past, Parry claimed, by supporting men and not principles. Every man and woman should be allowed a vote. Other speakers were Mr Stringer and J. Pratt. The Walsall Free Discussion continued to meet and seems to have replaced both the Republican Club and the Secular Society in that town.

In the last months of 1873 Burns reported from Bilston that two or three selections by the Secular Glee Club had elicited 'much approbation', at the Oldbury Free Thought Temperance Hall where a meeting had been held on Poetry.

The Guide to the Lecture Halls column in the *National Reformer* in the first week of January 1874 listed the following:

Oldbury Secular Society, Sunday evenings 6-30pm Freethought Temperance Hall, Portway Road.

S. Staffs & E. Worcs. Secular Union, Sunday evenings 7pm at Perry's, Portway.

Walsall Free Discussion Group.

Wolverhampton Republican Club, First Tuesday every month 8pm at the Committee Room, St. George's Hall, Garrick St. Pres: T. Stanley, Sec: H.V. Squires, Wednesfield.

West Bromwich Republican Club, Every Wednesday 8 pm at the People's Hall, Pit Street. Pres: J.L. Reece, Victoria Street. Treasurer: W. Adams.

Spon Lane. Corresponding Sec: T.J. Maxwell, George Street, W. Smethwick.

Financial Sec: D.A. Beckett, Hallam Place.

In February 1874 Walsall Free Discussion Group celebrated the birthday of Thomas Paine. In Wolverhampton a meeting had been held at 35 Culwell St. where songs had been sung selected from the Secularist Manual followed by a lecture on Paine by the secretary J. Cookson. At this meeting Flaganin, a Christian, had been present and the question of forming a Secular Society had been put off until March. 'Flanagin had kindly invited us to meet at his house at 13 Stafford Street.' The March meeting, however, was again at Culwell Street where. John Cookson read an article from the *Republican Herald* on Local Preaching. April's meeting was scheduled for 32 Green Lane, Dudley Road.

Walsall seemed to have been encountering difficulties. In March Professor Allwood spoke on 'Spiritualism' and there was no other report until May when a series of lectures by Wedgwood were adjourned until September.

In July G.W. Foote, the national speaker, lectured in Oldbury and the S. Staffs & E. Worcs Secular

Union started a series of discussion on 'Population' introduced by Cartwright who met with considerable opposition from Holland, Bailey, Jones and Pratt. The series was continued by Holland in August. The Neo-Malthusian view that Malthus had been right and population should be controlled by contraception was highly controversial and an issue on which the Secular movement was to split in 1876. But we are not told here which sides the Wednesbury secularists took.

In September Scholey announced the reopening of the Walsall Free Discussion Group with a library and a wide range of 'advanced' papers. Secularists, Republicans, Internationalists and other 'thorough goers' would find a platform 'where all could fully and fearlessly express their views.' Later in the month there was a meeting to discuss sending delegates to an Electoral Reform Committee.

In Oldbury a meeting was called at the Freethought Temperance Hall to discuss measures to extend Secular organisation in the district. Mayer of Dudley, Cartwright of Tipton, Pratt of Walsall and Reddalls of Birmingham would attend, it was said. When the meeting took place it discussed the desirability of forming a Secular Union or devising other means of utilising the Oldbury hall for Freethought purposes. The meeting decided that nothing could be done at the time and the matter was referred to a conference in Birmingham. But there is no report of the conference and by the end of 1874 only Birmingham Secular Club appeared in the National Reformer's Guide to the Lecture Rooms, such activity as there was in the Black Country going unrecorded.

Depression and Restructuring 1875-1884

By the end of 1874 the Great Boom of 1870-74 was coming to an end and the chill winds of the Great Depression were beginning to blow. The Depression brought working class advance to a halt as masters (as they were still called) strove to transfer the worst effects of falling markets and declining profits on to their employees.

Secularism continued to be the main working class political movement, but Republicanism never got as far as a second annual conference and disappeared as an organised force.

The later 1870s also saw changes in the Secular movement. Bradlaugh's National Secular Society declined as he resigned from the executive and went to America to recoup his debts (1871-74). But after his return to England to unsuccessfully fight the Northampton parliamentary seat, he once again revitalised the NSS. But then he plunged the Society into the difficult neo-Malthusian birth control issue by publishing in 1877 Dr Charles Knowlton's pamphlet Fruits of Knowledge. For this Bradlaugh was immediately prosecuted and found guilty. Although on appeal he found a legal loophole, the question of publicising birth control split the movement and leading Secularists such as Holyoake, Watts and G.W. Foote withdrew from the NSS to form their own British Secular Union with their own publication the *Secular Review*.

In Birmingham the Secularists insulated themselves against these problems with two innovations, which also strengthened, to a lesser extent, the Black Country movement. The first was the publication of a local paper the *Secular Chronicle* from August 1872 to January 1876. The second was the success of an appeal to build their own hall which resulted in th opening of Baskerville Hall (named after the famous Birmingham printer and freethinker) at The Crescent, Cambridge Street in September 1877.

The existence of two national societies and two national newspapers seems to have had little effect in the Black Country, all Societies reporting activities to both papers. The existence of the Birmingham paper the *Secular Chronicle* gave a very important local outlet for advertising Black Country activities and was also used extensively by H.V. Mayer and Francis Neale for scholarly articles on various aspects of Secularism.

In 1875 both the Walsall Free Discussion Group anchored at Scholey's and the S. Staffs & E. Worcs Secular Union met regularly. In July 1875 new ground was broken by George Reddalls, editor of the *Secular Chronicle,* and John Russell with a meeting at Oldswinford and Lye Waste. The report shows the problems of proselytising:

> Secularists are so great a curiosity in this neighbourhood that the people stood at the doors of their houses and congregated in little groups to have a look at us... We heard one old lady explaining that we had come from Birmingham to 'raise the Devil'. Another described us as 'Beelzebub's imps'. Mr

Anthony Watkins, explaining that we had come from Birmingham to 'raise the Devil.' Mr Anthony Watkins – the only Freethinker in Oldswinford – had kindly placed a piece of land at our service, and here, in the morning Mr Reddalls delivered a lecture on 'Why I reject Christianity', to an audience of about 500, including some women. Scarcely had the lecturer started speaking than a number of women assembled behind a hedge and set up a hideous howl, accompanying their voices with the hammering of tea trays with stones, and with the ringing of bells. Nothing daunted, however, Mr Reddalls went on with his discourse, which was attentively listened to despite the frantic efforts of the pious female zealots to prevent him being heard... In the afternoon, the writer delivered a lecture at Lye Waste which was attentively listened to by about 800 or 900 people on 'The Bible – Is it True?' without a single interruption... In the evening about 900 people assembled at the same place to hear Mr Reddalls lecture on 'Popular Misconceptions concerning Secularism'. The greatest order prevailed during the evening... We took with us a large quantity of freethought leaflets and back numbers of the *Secular Chronicle* for distribution, and they were so eagerly sought after that we regretted not having taken more.

John Russell ended his report by suggesting that friends in districts around Birmingham who had no Secular Society should contact the editor of the *Secular Chronicle* with a view to establishing a Midlands Secular Union.

From this activity a Stourbridge branch of the National Secular Society was formed in 1876, with G. Baker as secretary. At the end of the year Scholey published a long list of books donated to the Walsall Sunday Reading Room.

In 1877 Stourbridge & Walsall reported meetings regularly to the *National Reformer,* and the *Secular Review* carried reports of activity in Bilston. Charles Watts lectured at the Town Hall in October on Secularisn the True Gospel for Mankind. and the secretary, A. Holland, hoped that this would be the first of many meetings.

In 1878 the Walsall Sunday Reading Room was advertised as being open on Sunday evenings from 4pm to 8pm for the discussion of social, political and theological topics and 'a variety of interesting works lie on the table for the perusal of visitors.' Stourbridge was still active with a picnic in July and they were probably responsible for a meeting at Kidderminster Town Hall at which a presentation was made to Annie Besant (one of the new leading lights of the Secular world.) In December 1878 there was a large meeting at Birmingham organised by the Malthusian League at which the platform of the Birmingham Secular Society was 'shared with friends from Wolverhampton, Dudley, West Bromwich and several intervening towns and villages.' In Walsall in July 1878 a petition signed by about 50 Secularists was taken to Forster, the town's MP urging him to use his influence on behalf of Edward Truelove, who had been jailed for four months for publishing birth control literature.

In July 1878 John North from Kidderminster reported that together with Stourbridge friends they had taken a river trip from Stourport and had then discussed the question of premises for meetings. In one of the few references to the split in the Secular movement North states, 'After experiencing the spirit animating one section of the Secularist party, we have resolved neither to help nor to hinder until we are convinced that a better and more conciliatory spirit prevails.' It is the National Secular Society here criticised for in the same month it was advertised that both Birmingham and Kidderminster had joined the British Secular Union

For 1879 and 1880 no reports of activity have been found in the *National Reformer* and no Black Country organisations were advertised in the Lecture Room column. But from the *Secular Chronicle* we learn that Holland was still holding the fort in Bilston reporting 'an excellent' tea party commemorating the birthday of Thomas Paine and requesting books and periodicals.

In January 1879 a Midland Social Democratic Association was formed in Birmingham. The leading spirit seems to have been John Sketchley, a veteran Chartist. In April he was appealing to hear from friends in Oldbury, Smethwick, West Bromwich etc. This was the first intimation of the re-birth of Socialism at the depth of the first stage of the Great Depression. The Birmingham *Secular Chronicle* regularly reported its meetings.

Also in April the British Secular Union conference took place in Birmingham at Baskerville Hall. Delegates were present from Birmingham and Kidderminster and Black Country delegates were Mr &

Mrs Adams from for West Bromwich and John Silk from Smethwick. This indicates the split of the movement in the Black Country.

In September Scholey re-opened the Walsall Sunday Reading Room after the summer break with its 'library of 3,000 books on political, social, Freethought and other subjects. The meeting also discussed the possibility of forming a Secular or Freethought Association connected with the building.'

In March 1880 at Kidderminster both the National Secular Society and the British Secular Union had branches as well as there being non-society Secularists. These all worked harmoniously together to successfully promote the candidature of H.V. Squires to the local School Board. In July in Bilston a meeting was held to approve the use of Mr Farley's Cocoa and Coffee House at Horseley Fields, 'the landlord having opened it to us free of charge'. A. Holland was still the secretary. In August at the annual conference of the British Secular Union held at Sheffield only Mr & Mrs Adams of West Bromwich were present from the Black Country.

1881 opened with a Wednesbury and District branch of the National Secular Society meeting at Mrs Griffiths' Oddfellows Arms, James Bridge, with readings from Byron's Vision of Judgement and a Petition in favour of Bradlaugh, who had won the first of three bye elections at Northampton for recognition of the right of an atheist to be a member of Parliament.

In January 1881, among a long list in the Secular Review of 'gentlemen who will be pleased to enrol members' was H.V. Mayer of 3 Wolverhampton Street, Dudley and W. Adams of Spon House, West Bromwich. In March a report of a meeting in West Smethwick to listen to Cattell speaking on 'What the Government ought to do for Ireland', was signed 'JS', who might well have been John Sketchley. In April, John Cartwright for the Wednesbury and District National Secular Society reported to the *Secular Review* that at the last meeting they had read the report in the *National Reformer* of the debate between the Rev Hatchard and Annie Besant and afterwards had 'solos performed on the pianoforte.' Relations between the NSS and the BSU were clearly improving as Bradlaugh's struggle for his Parliamentary seat focused attention on the fight for free speech rather than the right to publish birth control material.

At the fourth annual conference of the British Secular Union in August, Mr & Mrs Adams and John Silk attended from West Bromwich, and there was an unnamed delegate from Dudley. At this time William Adams was advertising in the *Secular Review* as a watchmaker selling the cheapest watches in the world, he claimed. He sold Geneva men's watches at 17/6d and ladies' watches with flowered dials between 17/6d. and 45/-d.

In 1882 while Secular activities flourished in Birmingham.it becomes more difficult to pick up Black Country reports. From the Secular Review we learn only that the Walsall Sunday Reading Room remained open from 3pm to 6pm with discussion from 6pm to 8pm. There are no reports in the *National Reformer* until the autumn when activity of the West Bromwich and District Secular Society at 32 Queen Square is reported by the secretary W. Mole. In September W. Cox lectured on 'Morality with or without the Bible' and in November the society heard 'an able essay on Shelley' and then unanimously voted to join the National Secular Society. Scholey also reported that at the Sunday Reading Room in Walsall in December there had been an 'animated discussion' on Henry George's *Progress and Poverty* which was then beginning to exert an immense influence on radical politics.

In 1883 there were regular reports in the *National Reformer* of activity in West Bromwich. Also in September Wolverhampton Secular Society came to life when a committee met to consider whether to take a regular meeting place. They decided in the affirmative and the first meeting was at the Old Temperance Hall, Bilston Street, when W.W. Collins lectured on 'Does Death end All?'.

1884 is the year of the split in the Secular movement when many turned to Socialism and formed branches of the Social Democratic Federation and Socialist League. The rump soldiered on with their anti-religious propaganda, many of their leading figures, such as Bradlaugh, bitterly anti-Socialist. Thus they removed themselves from the centre of radical politics where they had been since the decline of Chartism, to the periphery where they remain to this day; sympathised with, but not necessarily supported by, all those who live by Humanist principles, but who do not feel the need to indulge in militant, anti-religious propaganda.

In Birmingham secular activity continued strongly from Baskerville Hall reported regularly by the *Secular Review* and less strongly by the Birmingham NSS from the Alexandra Hall, Hope Street, judging by reports in the *National Reformer*. But in the Black Country the former paper tells us of a Wednesbury branch of the NSS meeting at the Coffee House, Upper High Street whose secretary was Mr Smith and the Wolverhampton Secular Society meeting at the Assembly Hall, Charles Street, Stafford Street every Sunday at 7pm and whose annual general meeting took place in August. In addition a Midlands Counties Secular Association was also reported whose secretary was R. Porter of Bilston. Wolverhampton Secular Society continued to meet through 1885 and the last notice for it in the *Secular Review* is March 1886.

The *National Reformer* in 1884 reported both Wolverhampton and Wednesbury activity, but by the end of the year there were no advertisements or notices of any Black Country activity. Even that great Walsall stronghold of E.A. Scholey's Coffee House in its many guises seems to have departed after 30 years of unbroken service to progressive causes. By 1885 neither Birmingham nor Black Country secularism could report regular activity.

Summary

It is clear that there was a direct link between Chartism and Secularism in most Black Country towns. This is in direct contrast with the relationship between Owenite Socialists and Chartists in the 1840s when there was scarcely any overlap between them. Stable Secular organisation was achieved in those towns where there was a committed core of cadres. Elsewhere, there existed isolated militants, and beyond that a core of inactive, but informed sympathisers. On this base there was always the possibility of breaking through to the mass of the population, most of whom were 'infidels' in the sense of their indifference to religion and who had no reason to love the clergy of the established church. This core of rationalist opinion, joined to other radical political opinion exerted a constant pressure on reactionary local political and religious circles for the extension of the franchise and for social amelioration. This became quite threatening in the later 1860s during a decade of surprisingly high unemployment.

The boom of the early 1870s gave a respite to the authorities but it also gave rise to the last great radical attempt to unite middle-class progressives with working class organisation in the Republican movement. Here Joseph Chamberlain was a key local influence almost embracing Socialism at a time when he stood poised to take over the leadership of the Liberal Party.

The Great Depression destroyed Republicanism, and Chamberlain U-turned to become the leader of Imperialism. It took ten years of Depression before the new Socialism was able to break through in 1884. Against this background, the fortunes of Secularists in individual towns can be summarised.

Black Country secularism began in Dudley, the town where Chartism was strongest at the time of the demise of the national movement in 1860. Dudley seems to have been fertile in devising organisations through which the three main strands of religious criticism, extension of the franchise and radical politics could be pursued. But after the death of Samuel Cook in 1861 and the disappearance of Daniel Wallwork it was never again the leading Secular centre, even though it retained the militant and intellectual H.V. Mayers.

Wolverhampton never seems to have assumed a leading role. The town was most active in the period 1866-73 when public premises were established at the Eclectic Hall and a Republican Club set up. This was the period when there was an identifiable leader in Oliver Tromper. Wolverhampton secularism again developed at the very end of the movement in the early 1880s.

West Bromwich adjoins Birmingham and could rely on assistance from that town where Secularism was stronger. The movement does not seem to have developed until the later 1860s when it met regularly at the Assembly Rooms. The town also developed a Republican Club and the Secular movement remained active in the later 1870s. Towards the end of the movement West Bromwich became the centre of district organisation. The leading West Bromwich secularists were Mr & Mrs Adams whose energy and financial assistance helped ensure continuous organisation from at least 1867 to 1884.

Walsall is notable for its anchor man A.E. Scholey who provided from his Temperance Rooms facilities for all progressive causes from Chartism in 1855 up to the disappearance of Secularism in 1884. After a short peak in 1871-73 with Republican politics, both the Secular Society and the Republican Club seem to have been replaced by the Walsall Free Discussion Group. Despite difficulties, it is clear that Secularism had a permanent presence in Walsall during this period.

Stourbridge secularism seems to have developed strongly only from the middle 1870s when the movement as a whole was tending to decline. Its importance was in being able to stimulate activity in surrounding areas such as Oldswinford and the chain and nail districts of Lye Waste, Cradley etc. Activity in Stourbridge coincided with organisation in the adjacent town of Kidderminster (which is not in the Black Country). Stourbridge had been an important centre of Owenite Socialism in the 1830s-40s.

Secular activity was reported from almost every Black Country town and village at some time. But the greatest surprise is the development of consistent district organisation in the two 'minor' towns of Wednesbury and Oldbury.

Oldbury was near to Birmingham and its organisation seems to have been set up by the latter town in 1867, although there had been reports of Secular activity from 1862. The existence of its Freethought Temperance Hall gave it, like Walsall, a public face in the town. Further research on the history of this institution would be useful. The district organisation in Wednesbury was set up a few years later in 1871. It had no regular premises of its own, but it did have an anchor man in John Jones, probably the ex-Bilston, Chartist barber and activity was reported from Wednesbury as early as 1868. Wednesbury had also been an important Chartist centre and in 1843 became the only Chartist organisation in Birmingham or the Black Country to build its own Hall.

It is tempting to see the Midland Secular Union in Oldbury and the S. Staffs. & E. Worcs. Secular Society at Wednesbury as an expression of the national split between the National Secular Society and the British Secular Union, but the national split occurred later, in 1876. By the time of the Stourbridge-Kidderminster development in the later 1870s, the national and local splits do seem to have coincided, and the overtures of Wednesbury to Oldbury in 1881 was probably an attempt to heal this split as well as a commonsense appeal for one district organisation at a time when the movement was rapidly weakening.

Finally an attempt must be made to assess the influence of Secularism during these years when Britain was the Workshop of the World. It is clear that Secularism posed no fundamental threat to the capitalist system in the way that Chartism and some earlier working class movements had. The anti-religious base of Secularism was not broad enough to mobilise support to change society, and the Chartists had been very careful to avoid this narrow base. But, as we have seen. conditions in the Black Country required a robust critique of religion. This had been shown time and time again, notably at the time of the French Revolution with the influence of Thomas Paine and with Owenite Socialism in the 1830s-40s. Secularism was not strong enough to initiate the main reform movements of the time, but its members played important parts in supporting the main campaigns of the times. These issues included church rates, campaigns to abolish income tax, opposition to the Poor Law and support for the Peace Movement; also opposition to colonial wars, support for the defeated revolutionaries of 1848, massive support for Garibaldi and support for the north in the American Civil War. This was climaxed by the struggle for the second Reform Bill of 1867. Black Country support for these movements has been detailed in my *Working Class Movement in the Black Country 1750-1867*. After 1867 the Secularists came into their own with the campaign for the Education Act of 1870 and this was followed by the rapid growth of the Republican movement. This proved to be the peak of the influence of Secularism.

Two points only can be made here. Firstly that even the presence of Secularism in the Black Country has never before been investigated and secondly its influence was clearly not inconsiderable. Its long-term significance is in having provided a bridge from the old Socialism of Owenism and Chartism to the modern Socialism emerging after 1884. In this respect its importance was clearly crucial.

Bibliography: Republicanism and Restructuring 1870-1884

This chapter has been written almost entirely from the Secular newspapers: the *National Reformer;* the *Republican* (1871-72); and the *Secular Chronicle,* the local Birmingham paper 1872-76, and the *Secular Review,* the paper of G.J. Holyoake, Charles Watts and G.W. Foote who withdrew from the National Secular Society in 1877 as a result of the birth control controversy which Bradlaugh embraced, and formed the British Secular Union.

For the history of Secularism in Birmingham, from which town much Black Country Secularism was initiated and where it was stronger than in the Black Country see my *Birmingham Working People – A History of the Labour Movement in Birmingham 1650-1914.*

Chapter 3

Trade Unionism in the Black Country 1850 to the Great Depression 1875

It was noted by Sidney & Beatrice Webb in their classic *History of Trade Unionism* that the density of trade union membership in Staffordshire was less than 5 per cent of the population in 1892 compared with 11 per cent in Northumberland and Durham and more than 6 per cent in Yorkshire and in Wales. Apart from the fact that trade union density in the Black Country is likely to have been very different from that in rural parts of Staffordshire, the only one to contest the Webbs' findings was J.A.C. Baker whose special study was that of the nut and bolt industry. Baker suggested that the Webbs' figures were based on membership of large unions only and that it was smaller unions that were important in the Black Country. Certainly the Black Country was dominated by small firms and domestic production which always made trade union organisation difficult. But where enterprise was on a larger scale, notably the iron industry, organisation was present from the earliest times and the Black Country produced outstanding leaders both local and national. With regard to the myriad smaller crafts such as gun-lock filers, awl makers, fire iron makers etc. many of them acquired a degree of organisation and unity which constitutes a unique contribution to British trade unionism.

The period 1850-67 has been dealt with by me elsewhere, but the premier historian of the period is Eric Taylor whose authoritative PhD thesis *The Working Class Movement in the Black Country 1850-1914* has unfortunately not been published. Black Country trade unionism in these twenty five years of Britain's economic supremacy when wealth was accumulating to industrialists on an unprecedented scale must be related to a closer look at this period from a working class point of view. The decade 1850-60 was a period of fairly full employment during which employers resisted the growth of trade unionism. 1860-70 was a decade of considerable unemployment. This resulted in fierce class battles in the course of which trade unionism was firmly established and the area participated in the national struggle for a legal existence of trade unions which was temporarily won. The decade ended with the establishment over a wide range of industries of conciliation and arbitration machinery and the acceptance by both employers and men of the sliding scale of wages. The years 1870-74 saw a frenetic Great Boom during which trade union membership doubled. Advances in wages and reductions in hours were obtained and trade union leaders emerged as Liberal pillars of society instead of outcast agitators. By 1875 the Great Boom was dead and the Great Depression followed.

Mining

The coal miner dominated the economic scene in the Black Country as the structures of the industry dominated the landscape. By 1865 coal production was at 10 million tons representing about one seventh of all coal mined in Britain.

The problems of the miners were numerous. Their normal wages never made them 'aristocrats of labour' able to support their families comfortably. When in full employment the wage afforded a 'standard of minimum comfort' which was above the poverty line, but only just. In times of slump when the price of coal was reduced, wages fell; more importantly, however, at such times the number of days worked at the pit also fell, so that six days work at 4/6d a day fell to two or three days work at 3/-d. This was starvation level and nothing was to be expected from the Poor Law.

When at work, the mines were operated through the butty system, enabling the coal owners to avoid all responsibility for their workers. In addition the thick coal was worked 'pillar and stall' which meant that the huge 30 feet wall of coal was demolished in a single highly dangerous operation with the result that the death rate in Black Country mines was higher than in any other British and most foreign coalfields. Other problems were tommy (payment of wages in notes exchangeable only at a special shop, usually owned by the butty or owner, at higher prices than those in the local shops), deductions from wages, 'long reckonings' (fortnightly, monthly or longer wage payments), etc. Another problem was 'buildas' (non-payment or under payment for work performed during a day when work was stopped before the end of the normal working day).

These and other grievances had been aired to the Midland Mining Commission of 1843. This had been set up by the government after the Black Country miners had joined the General Strike of 1842 through membership of the Miners Association (the first miners' union to approach national status) and had accepted the leadership and aims of the local Chartists. This had badly frightened the government of the day with the spectre of working-class revolution.

The Miners' Association ceased to exist in 1843, but its name had a resonance for those who appreciated the need for more than local organisation among miners. During the more prosperous early 1850s organisation, if any, was at a local level. From 1858 however, rising prices and unemployment led once again to impossible conditions and a bitter and prolonged strike took place centred around the Earl of Dudley's pits. This was led by the South Staffordshire Miners' Association which amalgamated with the Yorkshire Miners' Association the same year thus giving a lead to national trade union organisation again.

Conditions remained bad and there were strikes in 1861 and 1863. From August to September 1864 there was a general strike of the coalfield arising from a decision to lower wages to 3/-d per day. Violence ensued, blacklegs were blown up and subsequent prosecutions at Stafford made it reminiscent of 1842. The 1864 strike was organised by the Miners' National Association. This had been formed the previous year with representation from South Staffs. greater than that from any other coalfield.

By now the Black Country miners were forcing the local coal owners to recognise their strength and actually sit down and negotiate with them.

After 1851 Mines Inspection began to make inroads into the murder in the pits. From a total of 195 deaths in 1853 the death toll had moved down to 119 by 1866. Support for any prosecutions the Mines Inspectors might bring against coal owners depended crucially on the pressure miners' unions were able to bring to bear against both local magistrates (who were often coalowners) and the government.

This was one of the reasons for the success of the National Association of Miners. Its leader, Alexander McDonald, became an MP in 1874 (the first of two working men MPs) and spearheaded legislation on safety in the pits and decreased working hours. But McDonald was also a leading advocate of the Sliding Scale of wages. This had the advantage of automatically raising wages when coal prices rose, but the two disadvantages of lowering wages in times of slump and never allowing a permanent raising of living standards during booms. More militant miners consistently refused to accept the Sliding Scale. This, together with differences in conditions between miners east of the geological ridge that divides the Black Country, and west of the ridge, created permanent differences which weakened trade union organisation in the area.

To return to the years of the setting up of the National Association of Miners, the Black Country miners formulated their demands at a Conference in February 1864. The Mines Inspection Act was criticised and a resolution passed demanding an 8-hour day. There was a long debate on the 'getting' of the thick coal. A resolution passed unanimously demanded that all coal over 8 feet high should be worked in two divisions (i.e. longwall and not pillar and stall). Another resolution passed demanded that six of any jury of inquest into miners' deaths should consist of practical working men. The Conference also set up a Committee to examine a dispute between Brierley Hill and Dudley districts.

The differences between these districts persisted, however, and were exacerbated by the bitter strike against wage cuts which lasted over the summer and autumn (never the best time for miners to strike and always the best time for coal owners to provoke one) of 1864. By November miners were returning to work. West Bromwich and Oldbury miners were among the last to return on the 13th. of December. In January 1865 Black Country miners broke away from the National Association of Miners and formed the Practical Miners' Association. The president was Thomas Kimberley, a local miner who had clashed with McDonald at national NAM conferences.

The Practical Miners Association did not succeed in becoming a national union and disappeared within a few years. The split was perpetuated when miners east of the Dudley ridge joined the Amalgamated Association of Miners formed in 1869 and those west of Dudley reaffiliated to the Miners' National Association in 1873.

These were the years of the Great Boom which enabled the Black Country miners to make considerable advances in their conditions. By October 1871 wages were at the 'standard of comfort' level of 5/-d. a day. By February wages had risen to the unprecedented height of 5/6d. per day.

An even greater transformation took place in hours of work. In 1871 the nominal working day remained at 12 hours. This gave a six day working week of 72 hours, which would be unsustainable over any lengthy period in such an arduous and dangerous occupation as mining. So miners, if in full work, would take advantage of St. Monday not to work on that day and thus avoid being worked to death. From January 1872 the unions negotiated a drop in hours from 72 to 66. Only two months later the 9-hour day was won bringing hours down to 54. In July 1872 the great aim of an 8-hour day was achieved. Thus in the course of a single year, hours of work were completely transformed. It was too good to last. After 1874 as the Great Boom ended stern struggles lay ahead to try to maintain these gains.

1850-75 can be seen as a period when Black Country miners exerted maximum influence over national mining trade unionism. Beyond this point came the exhaustion of the Black Country coal measures and the flooding of the mines leading to the extinction of the industry in this area.

Iron workers

Ironworks were the nearest the Black Country came to a large-scale industry. In 1860 when there were about 19,000 ironworkers in the Black Country (much the same as the number of coal miners) there were something like 115 ironworks giving an average number employed of 165. Employment ranged from the highly skilled furnacemen through to millmen and forgemen, puddlers, down to large numbers of labourers, including many children. The best estimate for numbers of the latter was 1,200 boys from 10 to 15 given to the Childrens' Employment Commission of 1862. The industry was worked on the sub-contract system, so that craftsmen employed and paid their second hands, labourers etc. and also the children. Output reached its peak in 1856 but permanently declined thereafter as the industry failed to adapt to the Bessemer and later processes of making steel.

Furnacemen and millmen were 'aristocrats of labour' earning wages of £2 to £3 a week when furnaces were in blast, but the wages of puddlers declined through the century and there were large numbers of poorly paid labourers, youths and children. By about 1900 when employment had declined to about 15,000, J.S. Jeans estimated the average wage in Black Country ironworks as only £60 a year. This was the joint lowest (with Derbyshire) of any other British ironmaking area.

Trade union organisation was hampered by the fact that skilled men were also employers of their own labour. Puddling was the most labour intensive process (and also the most arduous) and it was the puddlers who tended to be organised earliest, although all organisation in the first half of the nineteenth was local. In 1830 puddlers were on strike against wage reductions during the Long Depression of 1829-33; during the General Strike of 1842 led by the Miners' Association, at least some forgemen were involved. During the slump of 1848 puddlers were again on strike over wage reductions and the Wolverhampton Chronicle complained that 'they seem intent to remain on strike until their funds are exhausted.' On union organisation in the ironworks we learn from the same source that 'In Stourbridge several works had started at a reduction and pledges required that they would renounce all connection with the union. Those who were members of the union had been receiving support, but the majority who were not in the union were, with their families, in a state of starvation.'

In the second half of the century puddlers were organised at Bradley, and in 1858 a most important strike led to agreement between ironmasters and men to adopt a Sliding Scale of Wages based on the price of iron. In 1863 another puddlers' strike lasting seventeen weeks was opposed by the new, large-scale, joint-stock companies such as the British Iron Company, who were determined to destroy once and for all trade union organisation in the industry. There were large numbers of prosecutions under the Master and Servant Acts and many workers were sent to jail. From February to April 1865 there was a lock-out of ironworkers arising from an insistence of North Staffs ironmasters that S. Staffs ironmasters lock-out their men in sympathy with their lock-out of puddlers who refused to accept wage reductions. Finally, the N. Staffs masters absolved their S. Staffs counterparts from this commitment and the men returned to work, suggesting that they follow the example of the Carpenters and seek peaceful relations with their employers with a system of conciliation and arbitration. Indeed, the Wolverhampton puddlers refused to return to work until the masters accepted such a scheme. This they quickly did and the matter ended with mutual regrets that the recent lock-out had occurred.

By this time, unions of most grades within the ironworks were being formed which linked up with unions in other iron producing parts of the country. 1863-64 were key years in this process. In 1863 both the Associated Ironworkers of Great Britain and the Staffordshire Millmens' Association were formed. In May 1864 the first national conference of the National Association of Puddlers, Rollers and Millmen took place at Brierley Hill. But in 1868 depressed trade and an unsuccessful strike led to the demise of both the Associated Ironworkers of GB and the Staffs. Millmen. The National Association of Ironworkers, a rival of the AIGB set up by northern ironworkers, survived the slump and was reorganised as the National Amalgamated Association of Ironworkers. With the Great Boom of 1870-74 this union took the initiative in resuscitating iron trade unionism in the Black Country, John Kane, the national leader negotiating a wage advance of 10 per cent at Brierley Hill and Wednesbury in 1870. In 1872 Black Country ironworkers joined the union and the next year the union had 10,000 members in S. Staffs & E. Worcs.

In pursuance of the policy of peaceful relations, in 1872 a temporary S. Staffs Iron Trade Board was set up of representatives of masters and men to operate a Sliding Scale of wages and conciliation. This collapsed in 1875 to be replaced by the S. Staffs Mill & Forge Wages Board. With the onset of the Great Depression iron trade unionism in the Black Country again collapsed and it was another decade before ironworkers rejoined a national union.

Engineers

Engineering comprises the five crafts of iron-moulders, machinists, millwrights, smiths and pattern-makers. When the highly significant Amalgamated Society of Engineers was formed in 1851-52 it was the latter four crafts which amalgamated. Ironmoulders continued an independent existence.

One reason for this was that moulding had only recently been liberated from the iron works. It is perhaps significant that Abraham Darby patented his invention of the Iron Bellied Pot which, tapped straight from th furnace, inaugurated the mass market for such iron utensils, but he neglected to patent his vastly more significant subsequent discovery of smelting iron with coke. But iron cast straight from the furnace was of variable quality which could have fatal consequences for the wrong people if the moulding was a cannon. Control of the quality of iron came with its subsequent reheating. But this could not be done until the invention of the reverberatory furnace which separated the heating agent, coal, from the iron. The use of this invention spread from the continent after 1702 but this cupola was very small. The key invention was that of the Black Country ironmaster, John Wilkinson, who in 1794 used a Watt engine to pump the blast. This made it possible to operate on a large scale and thus to separate furnace from foundry. Even then, in the Black Country, furnaces and foundries tended to be operated by ironmasters within the same works and it was in areas outside the coalfields that separate foundries developed. One of the most important of these areas was Lancashire.

It was here that worker organisation first began when the Friendly Ironmoulders' Society was formed in 1809. By 1814 there was a Bilston branch of this society. By 1834 there was a Dudley branch. This we know because two of the early general secretaries of the Friendly Ironmoulders' Society were both Dudley men. The first was William Glasebrook who joined the Dudley Society in 1834 and was national secretary from 1842-53. The other was William Harvey, born in Dudley, who followed as general-secretary from 1853 to 1863. These were important years during which the Society was transformed from the old-fashioned craft union to the highly centralised New Unionism of the 1850s.

Such centralisation, however, led to much bureaucracy which made some other unions reluctant to follow the path of new unionism, and was not without criticism within the Ironmoulders Society. In 1866, for instance, a leading member of the Smethwick branch, Edwin Holmes, attacked the executive for the 'absolute power' that it wielded.

The Friendly Society of Ironfounders, as it became known in 1854, was an exclusive craft union and in the 1860s less skilled workers, such as coremakers, were not eligible for membership. So these formed their own Core Makers' Society which existed independently until it was finally admitted to FSIF membership in 1902.

Other engineering workers who remained outside the Amalgamated Society of Engineers were the Boilermakers and Tinplate Workers. Of the former almost nothing is known as the union was associated with the Iron Shipbuilders and the ports, despite the fact that its products were the most lethal in the Black Country and responsible for numerous deaths when these boilers exploded. The Tinplate Workers are however, of such importance to Black Country trade union history that their development is dealt with separately, below.

The most important development in engineering trade unionism was, however, the formation of the ASE. An earlier attempt to bring engineers together with other unions had been the National Association for the Protection of Labour, which was supported by Bilston blacksmiths in 1830. It was the blacksmiths again who took the initiative in creating the United Trades Association in 1841 which brought together the 'five trades of mechanism'. Despite the failure of these earlier attempts, they were important in laying the basis for the ASE. Both the Blacksmiths and the 'Old Mechanics' (the Journeyman Steam Engine and Machine Builders Friendly Society) were influential in setting up the ASE and the one known contribution of the Black Country was the unanimous decision of the Smethwick 'Old Mechanics' to amalgamate into the ASE. The full name of the ASE was the Amalgamated Society of Engineers, Machinists, Millwrights, Smiths and Patternmakers.

Despite the significance of the ASE to trade union history, its policy of avoiding strikes and seeking conciliation has left little impression locally and neither the local press nor the general histories of the union tell us much of the activities of the ASE in the Black Country in this period 1851-1875. What we can do is to trace the formation of ASE branches. Smethwick was the sole founding branch in the Black Country. Wolverhampton and Wednesbury were next in 1852, Oldbury came in 1857. In 1860 a Dudley branch appeared followed by Walsall in 1866, Bilston the next year and finally West Bromwich in 1880.

Tinplate workers

The activities of the tinplate workers in Wolverhampton are well documented and this activity represents a minor epic in the history of British trade unionism.

The Wolverhampton Tin Plate Workers' Society was formed in 1802. This provides another example of local trade unions being formed in the period of illegality 1799-1825. Its first recorded struggle is a strike in 1819 in the depths of the post-Napoleonic Wars depression and at the height of government repression. The authorities are said to have called in the Bow Street Runners to crush this strike by raiding the rooms occupied by the strikers. They were arrested and charged with the highly dangerous offence of conspiracy. A.T. Kidd tells us that the attack was expected and the 'Red Breasts' were held off until the records of the Society were destroyed. In this way, only the members in the room could be arrested and five of these were transported to Tasmania.

The question of whether trade unions descend directly from medieval gilds has little relevance for the Black Country which, at this time, apart from Walsall, was a collection of small industrial villages. But the crafts within these villages had developed a set of 'industrial relations', elements of which persisted as trades unions developed. Some of the most important of these were the Lists of Prices, the sanctity of announcements of changes in the List price whether made by masters or craftsmen, the maintenance of co-operation with the employer side by side with militant action whenever the craftsman's standard of living was threatened, and attitudes to machinery.

With regard to the last, a letter sent to all Tin Plate Societies throughout the country in August 1820 signed by F. Cook at the Black Horse, Horse Fair, Wolverhampton sets out the opposition of both masters and men to the introduction of new machinery:

> We have been informed by our employers that there is a man in Sheffield now stamping all manner of articles such as Tea Kettle Tops and Coffee Pot Tops etc. and ready for making up in such style that has not been equalled before. We shall not one half of us be in employ long. This man is offering these items at a low rate to induce our employers to buy, but they like us are determined to set their faces against it knowing in the end it will terminate with the ruin of the employer and the employed. It is the wish of our employers that we should as promptly as possible communicate our joint resolution to you which is that we will not buy or make one article up...

The tin plate workers also maintained a price List which, as we shall see was the cause of future disputes with their employers. They also observed the medieval custom of Tramping of which they were take make effective use.

Through the destruction of the records in 1819, the earliest copy of the constitution of the society is from 1834. The full title was The Friendly Society of the United Operative Tin Plate Workers of Wolverhampton. The rule book contained 24 laws. These included the following. The establishment of a Fund for the mutual support of each other and to maintain the rights and interests of the Trade. Every member must have served a legal apprenticeship and attained the age of 21. Officers were to be President and Vice president each with his Right and Left Hand supporters. There were also to be a Warden, two Conductors, a Tyler Doorkeeper and two Stewards. The Committee was to consist of one representative from each shop in the town. Two marshalls or Ale Stewards were also appointed whose duties were to call for liquid refreshment at the order of the President, to serve it out and distribute it impartially. No member was to be allowed to read, sleep, swear, lay wagers or use obscene language during Lodge meetings. Contributions were 5d. a week.

When the next important dispute with tin plate employers occurred in 1822, the various Tin Plate Societies throughout the country were united in a 'Union' of federated societies for mutual protection.

In February 1822 the Wolverhampton society sent a report to all other societies stating that they had been on strike for twelve weeks due to a wage reduction of 10 per cent two years before which had netted the masters £700 and who were now demanding another 10 per cent reduction. For nine weeks the strike had been solid and then five workers had 'ratted'. As a result the union had had a placard posted throughout the town headed 'Notorious Desertion and Robbery'. The placard stated that the undersigned had for nine weeks 'resisted the grevious oppression of avaricious employers' but 'alas the weakness and degeneracy of our nature sold ourselves by yielding to the subtle measure of our adversary, thus branding ourselves with Infamy and Disgrace. By this act we have not only robbed ourselves and our families but also our trade and shop mates whose eternal hatred and contempt we must forever expect as a just punishment for our perfidy.' After much more in like vein the placard ends. 'If pity can be found for such ill-fated beings... such information will be gladly received by the miserable: Joseph Beards Caribee Island, W. Curtis Horseley Field, T. Shale Hallford, W. Hickman and W. Beckett Dudley St.'

The report went on to say that the foreman of the second largest manufactory in the town had resigned as a result of the master bringing an inferior 'rat' into the factory for instruction. The employers had resorted to their old scheme of sending lying messengers in all directions to spread wrong information about the strike and to solicit orders. A financial report showed that £146 had been received from provincial Societies and £150 from the London society towards a strike costing £30 a week. The report was signed by the secretary, F. Stokes.

By the nineteenth week of the strike the Wolverhampton society was supporting its men by sending some of them on 'tramp'. Several were working in London, three others were being sent to London, three to the North Road (where it was hoped they would be employed in Liverpool) and two to the West Road (where there were Societies in Bristol, Cheltenham and Bath). One of the aims was to allow those societies having difficulty raising their levy for Wolverhampton to find work for these members instead. Also, since the Wolverhampton work was going to other districts it was logical to send the Wolverhampton men to where the trade was flowing. This report from Stokes also stated that one employer had had an order served against him for not completing a customer's order and another employer, who had managed to employ a few 'rats' had his goods returned, thus fulfilling the prophecy of the Society that the use of strike-breakers would defeat its own object.

In December 1822 when the strike was almost twelve months old, the union was beginning to consider desperate measures. Of nearly sixty men in the Society twenty were working at the old rates of pay and supporting the strikers, twenty had been sent out on tramp and had found jobs, mostly in London. It was now proposed to send the remaining sixteen men with their families on tramp and support them until they found jobs elsewhere. The potential trampers were in complete agreement with the scheme, it was said. A further financial statement showed that £944 had been contributed to the strike including £67 from Wolverhampton. This report also called for strict enforcement of the 'Unions' rules for tramping to ensure that those with the strikers' Green card received preferential treatment.

This is the last heard of the 1822 strike, but it is likely that improved trade in 1823 made some compromise possible. The Society certainly seems to have survived.

In 1842 at the depth of the third of the Long Depressions of the first half of the nineteenth century and in the year of the Chartist miners' general strike, the Tin Plate workers were again out against another 10 per cent reduction. By this time the general tinplate 'Union' had failed and the Wolverhampton men were relying on voluntary subscriptions from other Societies. However, nothing else has been discovered about this strike either from the *Wolverhampton Chronicle* or from the *Northern Star*.

In 1850 occurred the most important strike of Wolverhampton Tinplate workers. Although a renewed General Union of tinplate workers was not in existence, the Wolverhampton workers had the support of an even wider organisation, the National Association for the Protection of Labour which had been set up in 1830 and to which Wolverhampton Tinplate workers had affiliated in 1845. This bitter and prolonged struggle and the legal conflict which followed attracted considerable national attention. The strike is well documented from the employers side and more than usually so from the workers point of view.

The dispute began over a new printed Book of Prices of 136 pages covering 2,650 separate items. The new Book was accepted by all but two of the employers who asked for time to consider it. During this period they made two-year contracts with as many of their employees as would sign and such other preparations for a strike as they could.

The instigator of the strike was Edward Perry who was determined to crush the union. When Perry rejected the List, the strike began. The strike committee took up quarters at the Swan Tavern in Paul Street close to Perry's works which were picketed. Perry advertised for workers outside Wolverhampton and those who came were jeered at as 'rats' and dead rats thrown at them and hung on the factory gates. The strikers retaliated by calling out the older apprentices, together with those who had originally worked but were now prepared to join the strike, and 'tramping' them. Some were sent to Ireland, some to Scotland and others to villages remote from railway stations.

Perry, unable to recruit sufficient men in Britain, then sent his nephew George Winn, a journalist, to France to bring strike breakers from there. Twenty eight were brought to England and when they landed were given contracts to sign agreeing to work for Perry for twelve months. They were met at Wolverhampton station by Perry and marched in procession to lodgings near the works. The strikers retaliated by engaging a sympathetic Frenchman named Mageurs who had been taken prisoner at the Battle of Waterloo. He soon persuaded the strike breakers to return to France. Again they marched in procession to the station, this time with flags and banners flying accompanied by a brass band.

Refusing to be beaten, Perry repeated the process with Germans. This time they were accommodated inside the factory and no communication with outsiders allowed. A great solidarity meeting with the strikers was held at the Theatre on 30th. October 1850 with delegates from London, Birmingham and elsewhere. The legal right to picket Perry's factory was stressed and Bartlett, the solicitor for the strike committee, spoke about the injustice of men being brought back from their 'tramping' destinations and sent to prison.

At this point, Perry appealed to the Mayor for police protection for him and his strike breakers. The Mayor, together with some of the principal magistrates of the town met at the Town Hall the day after the Theatre meeting to hear both sides and try to arbitrate between them. By this time there was considerable public support in Wolverhampton for the strikers not only among workers, but middle class people too, who saw Perry as deliberately obstructive.

On 23rd November Edward Perry addressed a Letter (really a longish pamphlet) to George Robinson who had been the Mayor when negotiations began clearly revealing Perry's intention not only to destroy trade unionism in his own trade, but also nationally. Perry first objected very strongly to Robinson consulting with any trade unions at all on this matter, quoting the interest taken by Feargus O'Connor's *Northern Star* and the example of a twenty two week strike in Kidderminster which, he alleged, had led to the carpet trade leaving the town. He then claimed that the Tinplate trade was not tied to Wolverhampton and would be driven from the town. If the strike were successful the 'agitators' would move on to the 'ironfounders, brassfounders and other extensive employers of the town and also the proprietors of the colossal iron and coal works of the area', who would have to sustain similar assaults. Already the *Northern Star* was reporting that meetings had been held with the Wrought Iron Coffee Mill Makers and Iron Braziers in Wolverhampton who had both agreed to join the National Association for the Protection of Labour. Perry then went on to claim that in opposing trade unionism he was acting in the best interests of the men themselves, quoting extensively from the London *Times* which was then engaged on one of its anti-union campaigns 'proving' that if trade unionists succeeded in raising wages the working class would be ruined by trade moving elsewhere.

Perry then went on to deal with the workers who had been 'tramped'. According to the statements of five of the wives 'obtained by a respectable neighbour' of Perry's their husbands had been 'made drunk' and 'spirited away.'

Finally, Perry devoted a number of pages to his dissatisfaction with the ex-mayor's attempts to bring the two sides together.

Despite his lack of support in the town, Perry intensified his efforts to find where his contracted workmen were and bring them back to be prosecuted under the Master and Servant Acts for breach of contract. His last desperate throw was to indict the strikers for Conspiracy to molest and intimidate his men to leave their employment. It took three trials to accomplish his purpose.

The first took place at Stafford in August 1851. Perry's witnesses included several men who had been 'tramped' but came back to Wolverhampton to work for Perry. Each claimed that he had been made drunk – an allegation likely to improve the prospect of obtaining a verdict of 'inducement'. The defence urged that the strike was legal and the picketing was within legal limits. The strike had been instigated by Perry who refused to pay the prices fair to all employers and paid considerably less than other employers in the trade. When questioned about the last point Perry produced in court two colanders. One was made of seven pieces of tin, braised, punched and jointed, for which 12/-d. per dozen was paid; the other colander he produced was made by machinery requiring the tinmen only to fix the handles. For these he paid 1/-d. per dozen and the men made more from these than from the hand made ones. This it seems made a considerable impression in the judge and jury who brought in a verdict of guilty. The defence then appealed for an arrest of judgement on technical grounds and the men were bailed. Perry was then summonsed by the men for statements he had made during the trial. These charges were dismissed. The appeal was heard in November 1851 and rejected. W. Peel, T. Winters and F. Green, delegates from the National Association for the Protection of Labour were then sentenced to three months hard labour as were the local men Rowlands, John Gaunt, George Duffield, Thomas Pitt and Thomas Woodnorth. Charles Piatt was given one month's imprisonment. In this way Perry won the strike, but only by a blatant use of the one sided legal situation which pertained at this period when trade unions were no longer illegal, but neither were they legal, because most of the activities which they undertook could be judged illegal.

The final balance sheet of the London Central Defence Committee showed that £2818 had been expended, most of it on the two trials.

It has been held that the Wolverhampton Tinplate strike drained the resources of the National Association for the Protection of Labour and from that time it ceased to play an important part in the trade union movement. The Wolverhampton evidence suggests otherwise. The balance sheet above was signed by William Allen of the Amalgamated Society of Engineers and also by leaders of the Cigar Makers, Book Makers and Cabinet Makers, suggesting that the money came from individual trade unions rather than the NAPL. Moreover, the next mention we have of the Wolverhampton Tinplate Makers is in 1856 when they adopted a new, comprehensive set of rules. At this time they were still affiliated to the NAPL which was then called the National Association of United Trades for the Protection of Industry.

Further details of the Tinplate Workers suggest that they were loathe to develop the friendly side of the union's activity and it was not until 1867 that sickness benefit was embraced and even this amounted to only 2/-d a week and did not become operative until 1870.

Organisation of Tinplate Workers was not confined to this Society. A Co-operative Tinplate Workers of Wolverhampton meeting at the Red Cow, Dudley Street is known for its rules dated 1848. This was also affiliated to the NAPL and relations between the two Societies were cordial. In 1873 a second Society of the Co-operative Workers of Wolverhampton was formed and was 'heartily congratulated' by the original Society. In the bad times of the Great Depression the Co-operative seems to have dissolved and over one hundred members transferred to the original Society.

The 1850 Standard Price List continued to be accepted and by 1870 a situation analogous to that of 1850 occurred; a renewed period of prosperity enabled the Tin Plate workers to claim an advance of 10 per cent This time there was no one mule-headed enough to want to resist it, or to wish to crush the union.

The Society survived the first years of the Great Depression and in 1884 a 10 per cent on the 1850 Price List was again conceded. At this time the Wolverhampton society was extended. Birmingham employers were said to be refusing price increases to their men because Wolverhampton wages were lower. The two Societies therefore merged in 1875 to form the Amalgamated Tinplate Workers of Birmingham, Wolverhampton and District. From this emerged the National Amalgamated Tinplate Workers of Great Britain and subsequently the National Union of Sheet Metal Workers of recent times.

The Builders

The vast increase in the population in the nineteenth century and the enormous building programme of industrial and commercial premises, houses and later, schools meant that building workers were a larger proportion of the work force than they are today. The best estimates that can be made from the existing Census detail is that they represented about 3 per cent of the work force in the Black Country in 1831 and 1901 and this varied up to about 7 per cent in 1861 and 5 per cent in 1881.

Building workers have from very ancient times felt the need to organise. Their problem has always been that it has usually been possible to maintain strong organisation only on large sites. Here the respective strengths of employers and workers are sometimes more equal and improvements in wages and conditions can be won which may or may not prove permanent. The other main problem is that the multiplicity of trades within the industry has led to a plethora of local organisation in each craft reaching for national organisation, and parallel attempts to develop an overall organisation embracing all the trades.

In the first half of the nineteenth century the outstanding feat of organisation was the creation of an all-trades Builders' Union in 1831-34 which helped create the short lived Owenite Grand National Consolidated Trade Union intended to unite all industries into the dream of One Big Union. The centre of the Great Operative Builders' Union was Birmingham where it was led by two Birmingham master builders Walsh and Joseph Hansom. The latter was not only the architect of Birmingham Town Hall but also the originator of the Hansom cab. When the Builders' Union disappeared, the various crafts were left to separate organisation and it was claimed that the Operative Plumbers' Trade & Provident Society had a continuous existence from 1836 based on Birmingham. It is difficult to trace the direct influence of the Builders' Union in the Black Country, but in 1833 delegates were called to Birmingham to form a Society in House Furnishing. Wolverhampton Cabinet Makers with a membership of 19 joined. In the building trades, as in others, trade unionism was sustained by such small Societies as this Wolverhampton one.

After 1850 the New Unionism of amalgamated, centralised Societies spread into the building trades, but the advocates of these new 'monster' unions of the time have overstated their case and both criticism of the bureaucracy they created and the arguments for local autonomy ensured that old type societies existed side by side with the new ones.

Masons continued to be the most ancient and prestigious of the building trade Societies. In May 1853 masons joined together with bricklayers, plasterers and their mates for a strike in Wolverhampton and Bilston. Later, Walsall carpenters and joiners also came out. The military were called to put this strike down.

In 1861 Wolverhampton plumbers, glaziers and painters successfully struck for higher wages and the 10-hour day.

Organisation in the building trades in the Black Country was given its greatest fillip, paradoxically enough, from an attempt to destroy the unions. In 1865 Walsall master builders took up what was a national anti-union campaign by demanding that their men sign the Document. This required the men to state that they were not, and would not become, members of a trade union. A meeting was called in Walsall to consider the matter with R. Westwood of the Stonemasons in the chair. The first resolution, moved by H. Hale, stonemason and E. Millington, carpenter, was passed agreeing to treat the discharge note, or ticket-of-leave, with 'the contempt that it deserved' and that it should be 'resisted to the uttermost' by all grades of operatives. A second resolution moved by a painter W. Palmer resolved to follow the example of the Carpenters in Birmingham and refuse to work until the Document was withdrawn. J. Wright, a carpenter, said that they had the sympathy of the public and disputes could be avoided by a code of rates and regulations before building began. There was some discussion as to whether the bricklayers would follow the example of their Birmingham brethren and remain at work, but ignore the Document; a decision would be taken on Saturday, but bricklayers at the meeting favoured strike action from Saturday. W. Kennedy for the labourers and G. Harding for the plasterers were both in favour of withdrawing from work at once. Other building employers followed the example of their Walsall counterparts and action against the Document quickly spread.

The Wednesbury Operative Carpenters & Joiners meeting at the Fortunes of War public house resolved 'not to accept a discharge note under any consideration'. They further resolved to form themselves into a Society 'to be in a position to protect ourselves against the inroads of unprincipled employers.' A Walsall open air meeting on the Bridge of the Operative Carpenters & Joiners spoke of their determination to resist.

Wolverhampton Carpenters & Joiners meeting at the Noah's Ark Inn, Lichfield St. with Joseph Humphries in the chair, set up an Amalgamated Committee of the building trades of the town which was to meet every night. At the end of the month a meeting was arranged at the Agricultural Hall, Wolverhampton presided over by Councillor Willcock and attended by 500-600 people. But what was to have been a protest meeting turned into a celebration when Barlow of the Stonemasons announced that the employers had withdrawn the Discharge Note and that the operatives had retained 'their birthright as Englishmen.'

All this had occurred in the space of a month between the end of December 1864 and January 1865. Whether the Black Country master builders had been lukewarm in pursuing a course of action which originated at a national level we do not know, but it was a famous trade union victory and had at least two important consequences. It brought about much improved trade union organisation throughout the Black Country and hastened the progress of co-operation between employers and workers. With regard to the latter, the next month employers met in Birmingham to elect delegates to a conference with the trade unions to resolve disputes. This led to the acceptance of conciliation and arbitration procedures advocated by the powerful Amalgamated Society of Carpenters and Joiners, one of the new unions. In April the Wolverhampton ASC&J met to approve proposals to be put to the masters for rules governing the trade for the next year. They also gave a vote of thanks to Rupert Kettle for acting as the arbitrator between masters and men. When the conciliation machinery was put into operation the same month, both masters and men regretted the late lock-out that had occurred.

But the conflicts of 1865 were not at an end. In May Wolverhampton bricklayers and their mates struck. Some small masters conceded the demand for a wage of 29/6d. per week, but others would not. This led to the Operative Plasterers (who had previously worked under the same rules as the bricklayers) meeting with their employers and agreeing separate rules. The bricklayers intensified their strike by calling out the foremen who were then called on by the employers to explain themselves. The union retorted by telling the masters that they would only allow the foremen to be interviewed if each foreman was accompanied by two members of the union. This letter was signed on behalf of both the Manchester and London Orders of the Operative Bricklayers, a division which weakened bricklayers' organisation. The Painters also struck at this time, but only for 12 hours. They had demanded 6d. increase on 24/-d. This was refused on the ground that Birmingham painters worked one hour longer. When the men struck the employers offered 25/-d. to June and 26/-d. thereafter. The men then asked for the 26/-d. straight away and the masters obliged. 'The negotiations were conducted with forbearance on both sides', it was stated.

In August 1865 there was another strike of the building trades in Wolverhampton. In the course of this Benjamin Ward was charged with intimidating a labourer from continuing in the employment of Messrs. Lovatt. Who should be on the bench but Edward Perry of Tinplate fame, and who should be defending Ward but Bartlett the solicitor who had defended the Tinplate Workers. Bartlett began by suggesting that as Perry had been involved in a similar case some years previously it might be better if Perry retired. This caused uproar. Perry's fellow magistrates hoped that he would not retire. Underhill, the prosecutor, said he had never heard such a suggestion as the idea that a man who had been involved in a dispute twelve years before and had since been twice elected Mayor would not act in an impartial way. Perry said that he had no intention of retiring. Barlett's objection was overruled. Underhill then said that Ward had met two labourers and said 'he would make their ears bleed' if they worked for Lovatt. Bartlett then pointed out that these words were not said on the day to which the charge related. He then called witnesses for the defence. These witnesses were asked whether they were among the strikers. Bartlett objected to this question stating that if they said they were, their names would be sent by Lovatt to other builders in the town as he had done with other names. The presiding JP, the Mayor, said that there was sufficient evidence on 14th July, and they had made up their minds. He sentenced Ward to two months hard labour.

Immediately, a similar charge was laid against Michael Murphy of the Builders' Labourers' Society. Again Underhill prosecuted. He stated that Murphy had delivered a note to a building labourer, Rohan, with whom Murphy worked headed 'Four Ashes Inn 21 July'. This read 'You are requested to desist work or you will be heavily dealt with.' Rohan could not read and he took the note to Heveningham, the builder for whom he worked. He said he was working for the same money that the men were claiming. This case was dismissed on the grounds that Rohan was a member of the Labourers' Society and must submit to its rules. Underhill then withdrew a further, similar case.

In November 1865 there was a dinner of the Wolverhampton Operative Carpenters and Joiners at the Noah's Ark Inn to celebrate one year of arbitration in the trade. After the loyal toasts Joseph Humphries spoke about the Society. The branch was formed in 1827, but it was not placed in its present position until 1863. A strike at Bilston had cost the Society £5000 and a delegate conference was held in Manchester to revise the rules. The Wolverhampton Society had doubled its membership in the past year. There were also branches of the Society at Tipton, West Bromwich and Walsall. Wages were now 28/-d. for a 58½ hour week. On conciliation Humphries said that other branches of the building trade had been offended at what the Carpenters did, but they would come round to it themselves.

In August bricklayers and their mates struck again for more money and shorter hours. The most interesting strike at the end of 1865, however, was one at the Walsall Town Hall site which caused employers to complain of the 'tyranny of trade unions.' A. Moult, the Birmingham secretary of the General Builders' Association gave a 'startling account' of this tyranny. Burkitt, a Wolverhampton builder, was building at both Walsall and Congleton Town Halls. He had yielded at Walsall a 25 per cent increase for Stonemasons from February to August. But they then left him to work for a London builder in the vicinity. This caused the Congleton work to cease. To overcome this, Burkitt sub-contracted the work and employed non-union labour. Shortly after, a deputation from the Wolverhampton lodge of the Operative Stonemasons called on Burkitt and threatened to stop the Walsall job if he continued to employ non-union labour. Burkitt then did some of the work himself, only to be met with a threat from the union to 'shelve' the work for one, two, or three years unless he desisted and sacked the bricklayers who had helped him.

From these examples it is clear that building workers had a wide range of actions open to them when trade was good. It is also clear that all crafts within the industry had their national trade societies to which they could turn for assistance in organising, if that were necessary. The most active local societies at this time were the Stonemasons, followed by the Carpenters, then the Bricklayers. Organisation among the Painters was also probably permanent and labourers either acted with the craftsmen for whom they were the mates or organised themselves at times in their own society.

The campaigns of 1864-66 brought hours down from the twelve hour six day week with one hour for dinner giving a 66 hour week to the 58½ hour week spoken of by Humphries. This was an eleven hour day with a 'short' Saturday finishing at 4-30 pm. During the Great Boom of 1870-74 hours were brought down to 54 in summer and 50½ in winter. although in 1900 Walsall summer hours were 55½ and this no doubt applied in some other towns and villages.

Bricklayers' and carpenters' wages were also raised in the boom to 6/-d. a day, but fell back to 5/7½d when the slump hit the building trade rather later in the 1870s than for other industries. Until 1875 the cost of living remained high.

Lock Makers

The Lockmakers' Union had its history written for it by Brian Stenner in 1989 to celebrate its centenary. Records are non-existent until the twentieth century and for the early years Stenner has had to cull the local press. Lock-making is an ancient art known to the Egyptians, but locks are urban appurtenances, so that although locks were made in Willenhall in Tudor times, the Industrial Revolution created the domestic and world market which located the industry in Wolverhampton, Walsall and Willenhall, and eventually in Willenhall almost alone.

Locks, and their necessary keys, were made either in small factories attached to the house of the employer or in domestic workshops attached to the houses of workers. Factory production began in the 1840s and increased with the invention of the Yale lock in the 1860s. But the factories of Josiah Parkes, Chubbs. Yale, Legge etc. co-existed with the small masters, some of whom still survive. The extent of factory organisation can be gauged from an estimate of 1867 that 275 masters employed 3000 people; two employers had over 200 workers, 5 had 100 plus, 10 had 50 plus and 20 had over 25.

Trade union organisation is attested for the 1860s. In 1864 the Wolverhampton and Brewood Industrial and Provident Plate Lock Manufacturing Society was formed. Plate locks were made by only four masters employing 240 men. The men complained that for years they had been 'sorely oppressed' working 14 hours a day for a wage of 15/-d. a week. A strike had taken place and employers had agreed to raise wages, but when the day for this came, the employers reneged on their promise. The men therefore formed a Co-operative. The question of the Lock Co-operative was a key issue in the formation of Wolverhampton Trades Council in 1865. When the Co-op floated loans, the local Amalgamated Society of Engineers and the Tinplate Workers contributed to their funds. A 'gentleman in the town' built a factory for them at North Street, Wolverhampton. By this time the Co-op was employing 80 of the 250 men in the plate lock trade and the four masters fought back by lowering their prices until both masters and Co-op were selling below cost. In these circumstances the trade union movement rallied round. A public meeting was held in the Wolverhampton Agricultural Hall in June, and a Committee was set up to help the Co-op. The Society survived until 1879 when it was wound up, a victim of the Great Depression.

In 1868 file makers at Chubbs struck and the company, like all employers in all ages, countered with a statement on the futility of such a strike which would lead to the introduction of machinery and the loss of jobs.

The Great Boom of the early 1870s led to growing organisation in the trade. A meeting in Willenhall in December 1871 followed one already held in Wolverhampton. The meeting was chaired by the Rev G.H. Fisher who deplored the child labour in the industry. He was followed by another reverend, T.W. Fletcher who thought the men were paid so little because of competition. This had led elsewhere to the setting up of Co-operatives, and the same thing would happen in Willenhall unless wages were increased. A resolution was then put requesting a 10 per cent advance from the masters.

A meeting of employers to consider this request mustered only 30 out of the 170 invited. Vaughan in the chair claimed that his men averaged 25/-d. per week, but even his fellow employers would not swallow this and thought the average was nearer £1. The employers refused to concede the 10 per cent and a strike occurred resulting in the formation of the Willenhall, Walsall & District Lock, Key, Bolt, & General Hardware Burial and Trade Protection Society. The entrance fee was set at 1/-d. and subscriptions were 6d. per fortnight. Those out of work through union activity received 10/-d. a week plus 1/-d. per week for each child under twelve. It was not until the end of 1872 that all employers were persuaded to pay the 10 per cent, despite the unprecedented prosperity of the industry.

A similar struggle took place in Wolverhampton where the Wolverhampton Lock and Keysmith's Death & Trade Association was formed in January 1872. Membership reached a peak of 330 in 1875. The Wolverhampton union survived until 1879.

The Willenhall union had disappeared by 1874 when there were again threats of strikes because wages had fallen behind those in other trades. Dissatisfaction continued and in July 1876 the Willenhall Amalgamated Society of Lock & Keysmiths was formed. Membership reached 300 in 1878. But membership plummeted as the Depression deepened and the union was dissolved in October 1880.

Nails

Nailmaking is an even older craft in the Black Country than locks, nails having been made here since at least the fourteenth century.

With the creation of the world market by the Industrial Revolution, the Black Country is said to have provided 90 per cent of the world's nails. Nail making, like locks, was largely a domestic industry with nail shops attached to the houses of workers who, usually on a Monday, brought their nails to the warehouses of the masters and returned with the iron for the next week's work. Like the iron and coal trades wages were regulated by meetings of masters. This continued until the trade began to disintegrate in the 1860s and competition with the machine made product led to the predominance of the 'fogger' who – at a price – catered for the necessity of nailers to sell their wares more frequently than once a week.

It was in the 1830s that the Industrial Revolution caught up with nail making and machinery introduced which could produce nails five times cheaper than the hand made nails. The workforce thereafter declined from about 50,000 in the 1830s to about 20,000 in the 1860s. Some nails, however, could not be made by machine, notably the horse-shoe nail which had a large overseas market. The hand nail market also continued strong in tea chest nails, certain types for the army and navy and some export markets such as USA and Canada.

The masters' meetings had established a List for nails, and strikes invariably occurred when price reductions were announced. Strikes were frequent and this suggests a considerable degree of informal organisation, for the difficulties of organising domestic workers are always considerable. In the economically catastrophic year of 1842 a great nail strike took place in April as a consequence of successive wage reductions in 1837, 1838 and April 1842. A meeting of 15,000 to 20,000 marched to several nail warehouses and forced some nailmasters to march with them to Dudley. The military were sent for, the Riot Act read and the masters released. The nailmasters then agreed to withdraw the April 1842 List and substitute the 1838 List less 10 per cent. The employers also pledged themselves to abolish tommy and to employ any nailmaker who laid information against masters continuing to pay in truck. According to Emphraim Ball, tommy had only developed in the nail trade after 1830 and by 1865 half the nails made were being taken to the tommy shop. sometimes before every meal, so low had wages fallen. Again, according to Ball, wages at the best of times were only 12/-d. to 16/-d. a week with women's wages 6/-d. to 8/-d. and children's 3/-d. to 5/-d.

Under these circumstances strikes continued. From the 1850s Eric Taylor finds that an acknowledged leader of the nailers was John Price of Halesowen who was usually responsible for initiating strike action, and accompanied by a bellman would then tour the nail towns calling out the men and women. Taylor also traces a number of short lived trade unions. In 1869 a Nail Forgers Friendly Society was formed at Lye. In 1870 an Amalgamated Nailmakers Society enjoyed a brief existence. In 1874 the East Worcestershire and South Staffordshsire Thousand Nailmakers Association was established.

Tommy continued to exist in the Black Country until the twentieth century despite strenuous efforts to eliminate it. Between the nailmaster who operated a tommy shop and the 'fogger' who took nails at less than the list price, the nailer was reduced in the 'prosperous' decade of the 1860s to the condition described by Ball as '20,000 badly fed, badly clothed workers degraded by a system which is a disgrace to England.'

This degradation led to desperate remedies. In 1860 a union was formed which, to Ball's indignation, 'made arbitrary laws and the most extraordinary demands upon their employers'. These demands the nailmasters refused and a strike ensued which was maintained for 20 weeks. During this time there was a recrudescence of the ancient custom of 'dirgying'. This was the Black Country equivalent of machine breaking.

In February 1860 Joseph Brettell and James Weaver were both charged with blowing up the workshop of Thomas Walker, nailmaker of Dudley. Both the accused were represented, presumably paid for by the union. In evidence it was stated that a charred footprint in the snow showed the imprint of a piece of leather or sole of a boot. Both men were remanded in custody, but later discharged for want of evidence. The next month Joseph Worton and Richard Provins were sentenced to eighteen months imprisonment each for cutting the bellows of Thomas Southall of Rowley Regis.

In June during a strike of Spike Nail Forgers at Sedgley, five men were fined for assaulting Harry Morgan who they said worked below the proper prices. A meeting of nailers in Sedgley Bull Ring decided not to accept the masters' reductions.

The strike continued into the autumn. In October Thomas Johnson and Edward Hackett were charged with intimidating workmen of Skidmore & Jones, nailmakers of Netherton. Their men had been on strike for eleven weeks over two men who would not join the union. These two scabs took out iron from the warehouse. The two defendants then called on them and said 'You must not work this iron.'The scabs replied that it was a hard case as the master was willing to pay the proper price. The defendants then said 'You must take it back, we will not allow you to work it until we have received an answer from the Board and if you do you will bring great evil upon other men.' It was contended that these words constituted a threat of intimidation, but the magistrates held that it did not constitute a threat.

1860 had been a year of rapidly rising food prices and public demonstrations in the Black Country about the high price of meat. By 1861 nailers were striking for compensatory wage increases. In January Dudley Horse Shoe Nailmakers struck. A meeting of nailmasters of Staffordshire and Derbyshire resolved that the request was unreasonable, wages having advanced 30 per cent in the previous four years; the strike would be strenuously resisted. The winter of 1861 was particularly severe. Frost had lasted for 24 days with the lowest point 6 degrees fahrenheit. Only on four of these days did the temperature rise above freezing. There were more reports of bellows cutting. At the end of January the *Wolverhampton Chronicle* reported that both masters and men seemed determined to hold out to the last, but the men's funds were exhausted and they were appealing for aid; the stocks of nails were almost gone and the demand for them was great. The strike went on, however. February provided a typical example of the tactics of the masters. A nailmaker named Brownhills was persuaded by the strikers to return his iron to the warehouse of Messrs. Guests. The manager refused to take the iron back and it remained outside the warehouse with other bundles of iron. Although the iron was not taken back by the manager of the warehouse, it was still the responsibility of the nailer, who could be charged under the Master & Servant Acts with neglect of duty; if the iron were stolen the nailer would be charged for it. The iron was eventually taken in by the police. The next day Brownhills, fearing prosecution collected his iron intending to work it. The next morning when he entered his workshop he found his bellows had been cut in such a way 'as to render them entirely useless or repairable.' An open-air meeting at Brierley Hill attended by 600 strikers resolved not to return to work until they were paid another 6d. per thousand nails.

After 32 weeks of the strike it was agreed at Lye in March 1861 that all men could return to work except those at Messrs. Walker. This was because Walker had failed to dismiss men he had taken on as learners during the strike. Of the men who had already returned to Walker's 50 men took their iron back to the warehouse as a result of the above decision. Again it was not accepted and the iron lay outside the warehouse for two days guarded by the police. Despite the ending of the strike, bellows cutting continued at Lye in April by horse shoe nail makers and in May at Netherton.

More long strikes occurred in 1862 and 1863. In June 1863 it was reported at a meeting in Old Hill that horse shoe nail makers had been on strike for 25 weeks and Brazil nailmakers for 17 weeks. A unanimous resolution was passed continuing the strike until proper prices were conceded and agreeing that those not on strike should contribute to those who were. Nailmakers from Birmingham, Belper and Gloucestershire were reported as willing to subscribe for the Black Country nailers. Bellows cutting was reported at Rowley in February, intimidation at Lye in March and assaults on scabs in July.

Also in July 1863 there was a demonstration at Griffin & Walker's warehouse where 70 men brought their nails in on a Monday when a strike had been declared the previous Saturday. In August it was reported that in the course of the strike a 'mob' at Dudley had a barrowful of stones. The horse shoe nail makers strike seems to have ended in September with the masters paying the extra 3d (per thousand nails) demanded at a time when trade was reported 'good'. In November a six weeks strike of Spike Nailers of Sedgley, Coseley and district ended with the 6d. advance demanded.

There seems to have been a lull during the next two years when trade remained good. In August 1865 there was a nailers' strike in Sedgley which quickly won the 6d. advance demanded.

From 1867 the Factory Act Extension Act extended inspection to workshops and thus, for the first time, to the nail trade. But the sub-Inspectors' first job was to find their workshops. This they were advised to do by consulting local trade directories, but this would have revealed only the larger of the nail shops. It was not until 1873 that a sub-Inspector was appointed to reside in the nail and chain districts. Between August 1873 and April 1874 he visited 2,500 workshops. This was the period of the Great Boom. Ephraim Ball in June 1875 told an enquiry into the Working of the Factory and Workshops Act that nailmakers' wages were the highest of the century. They needed to be; the cost of living in the Black Country in the years 1872-74 was 28 per cent higher than in 1850. Any respite from the misery of earlier years was to be welcomed. And such prosperity was to be short-lived.

From the foregoing it is clear that a considerable amount of both formal and informal trade union activity took place among nailers. But no permanent organisation emerged at this time. It is difficult to determine to what extent all nailers were involved. Most of the activity seems to have concerned the heavy nail trade of spikes and Brazils which were made almost exclusively by men. To what extent women and others engaged in the small nail trade were involved it is impossible to determine. This was to change in the subsequent period when 'sweating' became a nationwide scandal.

Chains

Nails and chains are associated together in the public mind and rightly so. Eliza Tinsley & Co. employed between 1000 and 2000 outworkers at this time, but there is no way of knowing how many made chains and how many nails. Both nail and chainmakers shared the same poverty and degradation. Both commodities were made in domestic workshops attached to workers' houses. However there were important differences. Chainmaking employed an expanding workforce into the twentieth century. Census figures show nearly 3000 workers in 1861 and a peak of over 6,000 in 1911. Another difference was that chain making was more concentrated within the nailmaking area and was virtually confined to the small area of Cradley, Cradley Heath, Old Hill, and Lye Waste. The largest chain (e.g. anchor chain) was made in factories, but factories also employed outworkers.

A comprehensive description of conditions in the chain trade was given by Robert Baker, the factory inspector, in 1868, a year after workship inspection began. For a few months in 1847 and again in 1854 men's wages were about 24/-d. a week and women's wages half that. In 1868 and between those years wages averaged no more than half that sum, although 'in-workers' in factories earned more than 'outworkers'. Another major grievance was tommy. Noah Forrest, chain trade union leader, said that 'Up to 1844 groceries and nearly all we consumed was given us instead of money. But after a six month struggle this was put down and not revived.' Other chainmakers who gave evidence to the Commission Investigating the Working of the Factory & Workshops Acts in 1876 were not so sure, and all agreed that those who drank most beer at the public house of the chainmaster were given the most work. Two other grievances were that the essential 'gleeds' (firing material for the hearths) were sold at 20 per cent to 30 per cent higher than their market value; also the charge for carriage of iron from the warehouse and the return journey of completed chains to the warehouse was an unfair imposition.

Such conditions were guaranteed to maintain continual ferment among workers. An important strike of Cradley chainmakers in 1852 claimed that wages had been reduced 50 per cent in the past two years. This was a strike against the principal masters of the trade in large chain – Wood Brothers, Bloomer & Co., Noah Hingley and H.P. Parkes. The men asked for an advance of 30/-d. per ton. The masters conceded two thirds of the claim with a promise of the extra 10/-d. if the spring trade proved good.

It was from 1857, however, that the main protests against these conditions began. In February 1857 a typical case under the Master & Servant Acts was brought when about twenty striking Cradley chainmakers were charged with embezzling iron when in fact the iron in question was lying unworked in their workshops. When this strike ended a prosecution was taken out by the men against Charles Yardley, a chainmaker whose practice was to give out iron at an unspecified price and pay less for the chain if prices had fallen in the interim. This time, during the strike, prices had risen, and the men asked for the higher wage which Yardley refused to pay. The men claimed that the most experienced chainmakers could only earn between 12/-d. and 13/-d. a week and that Hingley's and Wood's were paying 25 per cent more. On this point, the magistrate, Mr Swindell, stated that that had nothing to do with the matter and a man was justified in getting his work done as cheaply as possible. This case was continued but, as with many other cases, no verdict has been found.

In 1858 there was a twelve week strike of 300-400 chainmakers of Cradley and Lye Waste demanding an advance of 3/-d. to 4/-d. per cwt. for half inch chain with proportionate increases for other sizes.

From February 1859 came a year long series of strikes of which a renewal of 'dirgying' was one cause.

By this time the chainmakers had organised a trade union linked with the other heavy chain making area of Newcastle and also had a newspaper. Their demands were for higher wages, gleeds at a fair price and an end to the carriage of iron charges. But the strike might not have taken place except for the issue of 'dirgying'. In February 1859 the premises of three chainmakers were entered at night and their bellows cut. Two of the men had not paid the trade union levy and the third refused to join the union. It was considered, therefore, that these acts had been instigated by the union.

Thomas Homer, the secretary solemnly denied that it had been done by union members or instigated by the union. Despite this, the chainmasters demanded not only that the union pay for the cut bellows (which it was prepared to do) but also that the union support a guarantee fund paid for by a levy on every bundle of iron taken out by a trade unionist to compensate others whose bellows might be destroyed in future. Such a proposal which would have disadvantaged trade unionists and was a barely concealed ploy to destroy the union, could not be accepted. Between 50 and 100 chainmakers were therefore involved in a strike which was supported by fellow trade unionists in the Black Country and those in Newcastle. The strike continued until July 1859 when the employers seem to have capitulated unconditionally and the men returned to work.

But this was only one of a series of strikes. A sympathy strike had taken place in May and June when a proprietor provided chain to the firm whose men were on strike.

The question of the charge for iron was discussed fully by a general meeting in Cradley in June. It resolved that no master should be allowed to charge carriage on either iron or chain and if anyone submitted to the charge they would be fined 10/-d. by the union. The meeting also approved the demand for the '5/-d. list' (i.e. half inch chain at 5/-d.per cwt). But the union revised prices upwards for other sizes of chain, the masters claimed. In July 1859, Homer on behalf of the union requested the 5/-d. list. The masters refused the demand and the strike began on August 6th, a fortnight after Homer had presented the notice. The reply of the masters was to take out summons against many of the men under the Master & Servants Acts for leaving work without notice. They claimed that they were not bound to accept a notice 'from a man not in our employ simply because he styled himself secretary of a union.' The men, on the other hand, argued that the notice was valid citing a tradition that a notice given by a master if read out in the factory and posted on the doors was binding on all, including those who had not heard it or who did not, or could not, read. The Stourbridge magistrates, including a chainmaster, who heard this case rejected the men's claims and ruled that they were not justified in leaving their employment under this notice. In this case, however, it seems that they did not fine or imprison the men.

In the second week of August the men held a mass meeting with Homer in the chair. A letter was read from Gateshead chainmakers promising financial support. A letter was also read from Noah Hingley's accepting the prices asked for by the men and it was agreed that the men employed there should return to work. There were 1,500 chainmakers in Cradley and they were all on strike, it was claimed. At another meeting towards the end of August with 500 to 600 chainmakers present it was agreed to send a deputation to the horse-shoe nailmakers of Quarry Bank who forthwith contributed 'a handsome sum.'

The *Wolverhampton Chronicle* claimed in October that after twelve weeks most strikers had returned, but some were still out. In fact the men had returned to those firms who had agreed to the 5/-d. List. The strike went on until February 1860, when the last employer came in line.

These successful strikes were a landmark for chain makers. Small chain makers benefited by 5/-d. to 8/-d.a week and the masters claimed that higher paid operatives gained 10/- to 12/-d. a week. These were very large increases on the previous starvation wages. The successes would not have been possible without the self-sacrifice and discipline of the chainmakers. For the first five weeks when the strike was general between 1,500 and 3,000 men were paid 7/-d. a week. The strike was then costing £100 a week. This was met in large part by donations from the northern chainmakers totalling £220. After August when the main chainmasters agreed to the increases those who returned to work were levied 2/-d. a week reducing to 6d. a week as other firms came into line. These were very large sums from many whose earnings before the strike had been about 6/-d. a week. Other substantial sums came from other workers in the area. Both the Stourbridge glasscutters and the Spademakers levied their members 3d. a week for the duration of the strike. Finally money came from outside the area. including £30 from the Amalgamated Society of Engineers. The strikes offer a clear example of an industry paying starvation wages whose employers could well afford higher wages. But only trade union organisation and solidarity could wrest improvements from them.

But the successful strikes did not erase hostility to the employers. Bellows cutting occurred during the strikes and continued after. In November 1859 John Garrett was charged at Dudley with destroying three pairs of bellows. He was alleged to have said that he would cut 7 or 8 bellows before the month was out and to have been seen near the house in question with something bright in his hand. Garrett was committed for trial, but the result of the case is not known. In December 1859 another case of bellows cutting went to the Assizes. In February 1860 Benjamin Hancox a chainmaker of Netherton had nine pairs of bellows destroyed, and John Cartwright of Dudley Wood, three. This was the second time that bellows belonging to Cartwright had been cut. Later in the month two men from Lye were sent to Worcester Assizes for the same offence.

Bellows cutting continued after the main strike had ended in a period when nail workshops were being blown up. In June 1860 there was a prosecution for the cutting of eighteen pairs of bellows belonging to Messrs. Steward & Co. who employed 100 chainmakers working in shops surrounded by a high wall. There was also a prosecution of chainmakers for inducing others to leave their work; this was dismissed because of insufficient evidence. Sporadic strikes were still occurring as some chainmasters sought to avoid paying the wage increases. In September the *Wolverhampton Chronicle* reported four pairs of bellows cut belonging to chainmakers of Cradley Heath. The newspaper added the comment, 'The outrages were no doubt committed as a consequence of the trade dispute.' In March 1862 'as a result of recent reductions in the chain trade' 18 pairs of bellows of three employers were destroyed. Bellows cutting continued into 1863 (February) but whether of nail or chainmakers is not clear. Thereafter this type of protest ceased.

The existence of the Operative Chainmakers' Union was central to the successful strikes. The circumstances of its formation were outlined by Noah Forrest for a report of the strike to the National Association for the Promotion of Social Science and printed in their Proceedings. Forrest said that he had been connected with a chainmakers' trade union in the 1840s and 1850s which had co-operated with the masters in virtually eliminating the tommy which was such a considerable cause of the chain makers' poverty. But after several years 'when chainmakers forgot what they had gone through and refused to pay their subscriptions,' Forrest became disgusted, stopped union work and the union failed. When prices dropped to 1844 levels in 1854, Forrest was asked to re-form the union, but he refused. Again he was asked in 1858, but told the men to turn to Thomas Homer. Eventually the Operative Chainmakers' Union was set up in July 1859 with the participation of both Homer and Forrest.

I final word should be said about 'dirgying'. It is strange that the violence of the period was not whipped up into a national anti-trade union campaign; for when the equally impoverished saw grinders of Sheffield resorted to their custom of 'rattening' by blowing up workshops, the 'Sheffield Outrages' of 1865-66 led to the setting up of the Royal Commission on Trade Unions. This, the employers had hoped, would lead to the outlawing of trade unions. In fact it was turned into a trade union triumph ending in the legalising of the trade unions and thus ending that long twilight phase after the repeal of the Combination Acts in 1824-5 when trade unions were no longer illegal, but virtually every activity they undertook could be adjudged illegal. The leaders of the Chainmakers in the Black Country denied that the union or its members were responsible for the violence and there is no evidence to suggest otherwise. It should therefore be argued not that trade unions were responsible for violence, but that only strong trade unionism could render these desperate, primitive methods of violence obsolete. Perhaps the greater violence that occurred in the nail trade where trade union organisation was less advanced than in chains supports this view.

Glass

Although the town of Stourbridge is always associated with glass, most of the glassworks did (and those remaining still do) lie outside the town boundary in Wordsley and Brierley Hill. Nevertheless, it was the Stourbridge fire-clay, and also cheap coal, which brought the Huguenot glass makers to the area in the seventeenth century.

Stourbridge was always one of the less depressed towns of the Black Country. Its dozen or so glasshouses employed about 1300 people in the 1850s which doubled as the industry peaked in the 1870s. Glassmakers operated in 'chairs' of four. The master of the chair, called the Workman, and his Servitor were skilled men; the Footmaker was a labourer, abominably paid, and the fourth was a Boy, who might or might not, be an apprentice. Although the Workmen and the Servitor were skilled men, the high capital cost of a glasshouse precluded them from ever becoming proprietors. The acquisition of the glassmaker's skill entailed a long, on the job, apprenticeship. The skilled men protected their wages and status by controlling the number of apprentices entering the industry and insisted that all hiring of skilled men should come from a pool of unemployed men managed by the union. These arrangements were not without their advantages to the employers since they ensured a steady supply of skilled men. There was therefore a greater than normal incentive to organise, and it is a pity that nothing is known of the several attempts to form trade unions before 1844.

In that year the National Flint Glassmakers' Society of Great Britain and Ireland was formed. It was a powerful, nation wide organisation from the beginning with its two largest branches in Stourbridge and Birmingham. Its insistence on nominating all new men taken on, sometimes led to complaints that these men were not skilled enough or too old. On apprenticeship the union required that there should be only one apprentice to every three 'chairs', or two apprentices to five 'chairs' etc. and that no Footmaker should be discharged to make way for an apprentice.

When the union was formed, the economy was recovering from the Long Depression of 1839-43 and entering the Workshop of the World period. But as has previously been stressed, the period 1850-75 was far from being one of continual full employment. The existence of the *Flint Glassmakers' Magazine* allows us to examine the course of employment in this industry. In the summer of 1852 unemployment was nearly 8 per cent of membership. It fell to less than 1 per cent in 1854. During 1855 it rose to almost 10 per cent and then fell until it was again below 1 per cent in at the end of 1857. Again it rose, but an important strike in 1858-59 distorts the figures. In the 1860s the roller-coaster continued. Unemployment was 8 per cent in 1861, and over 6 per cent in 1862. From 1863 to 1871 it averaged about 4 per cent and then fell to 1 per cent during the Great Boom which, so far as employment in the glass trade was concerned, lasted from 1872 to 1874.

It was on this constantly shifting employment ground that trade unions had to build their policies.

The Flint Glassmakers' Society abhorred strikes and cultivated good relations with their employers. It was a rogue employer, therefore, who embroiled them in the one lengthy strike in this period. The final cause of the Great Strike & Lockout of 1858-59 is disputed, but involved was a case of a proposal to sack a footmaker and take on a yearly-bound apprentice at only 14/-d. a week. In another works there was already 4 apprentices to 9 chairs and the management proposed to take on another apprentice. Another dispute occurred at Grazebrooks' where the management refused to take on a man sent by the union and proposed instead to employ an apprentice. Feeling was already running high at Grazebrooks' who were using the Master & Servant Acts to prosecute men for leaving work without due notice. The strike began in October 1858 in two glasshouses, one of which was Grazebooks'. These employers then sent a black list of all the strikers to every glass employer throughout the country urging them not to employ these men. This was accepted by the employers. The union, still not wishing to extend the strike, then proposed that all glassworks in the Stourbridge district should work only six turns per week, and only if that failed would they call out these works on strike. The response of the masters was to set up the Midland Association of Flint Glass Manufacturers. Its intention from the beginning was to destroy the union. Its rules stipulated that no employee should be taken on without a written character from his last employer; also that all employment of labour should be entirely at the option of the employer.

The union then imposed the six turns per week on Dudley and Birmingham glasshouses as well as Stourbridge, and stated that if this failed, all the Stourbridge men would be called out. The employers reacted immediately by locking out all their men in the midland district from 1 January 1859. The union then called out all its members in Manchester, Warrington, London, Scotland, Belfast and all other glass districts.

The midlands masters then presented the Document requiring anyone they employed to declare that they would not join the union or interfere with the rights of the employers to manage.

The ensuing struggle was very costly. Glass workers' union contributions had been raised from 1/-d. to 5/-d. a week in December before all the men were locked-out. By the end of the strike, in

April 1859 union funds were so low that men were being paid two thirds in cash and one third in promissory notes. £2000 of these notes were issued in all and honoured after the strike.

Throughout the strike, the union was prepared to be conciliatory. Changes to rules on the two questions in dispute were submitted to the masters, but ignored. These changes however, became the basis of the eventual settlement. Both union control of employment and the apprentice provisions were modified without the union conceding the principles on which these rules were based. Thus was the circle squared. The Document was withdrawn and peace, if not harmony, was restored to the industry.

Again we have an example of a national stoppage instigated by employers determined to break union control. The most culpable of these, Grazebrooks', soon after left the glass trade. There was to be no other widespread stoppage until 1902.

After the lockout the union flourished, becoming, in some respects, the strongest in the country with funds per member greatly exceeding those of the formidable Amalgamated Society of Engineers. Membership of the Stourbridge branch rose from about 120 in the early 1850s to about 350 at its peak in the middle 1870s.

There was another important union in the Stourbridge glass trade. This was the United Glass Cutters' Mutual Assistance and Protection Society. It had been reorganised in 1844 and by 1857 the Wordsley (Stourbridge) branch was the largest in the country with a membership about the same as the glass makers. The Glass Cutters also fought a long battle with the employers over apprenticeship; this was in 1865-66. The rules of the society allowed only one apprentice for every five cutters. The employers wanted it changed to one in three. The strike ended, presumably with a compromise. The facts above emerged from witnesses at the Royal Commission on Trade Unions in 1867. Little else is known about the union at this period.

These two trade unions of skilled workers accounted for about one tenth each of the total work force employed in the glassworks. The remaining four fifths would be women or unskilled workers, none of whom were organised and most of whom were poorly paid.

Nuts and bolts

Another small craft to organise was the nut and bolt workers of Darlaston. The significance of the Nut & Bolt Forgers' Protection Society established in 1870 was that it was formed by Richard Juggins, a unique Black Country figure, who used it as the nucleus for the organising of other small crafts in the Black Country.

Nuts and bolts was an expanding trade until the 1880s when foreign competition became acute. Machine methods developed after 1850 and the trade thereafter showed a familiar Black Country pattern of several large factories, numbers of small factories also employing outworkers, and a large number of domestic workers operating from workshops attached to their cottages. In all, a workforce of about 8,000.

The occasion of union organisation was the Factory & Workshops Extension Acts of 1867 which limited the hours of women and young persons to 10 per day and 58 per week. These Acts also prohibited the employment of children under 13 years of age and insisted on medical certificates stating that they were old enough and fit enough to work. These Acts were bitterly opposed by employers, and also by many domestic workers, on the grounds that they raised costs. These difficulties increased when some employers insisted on charging their out-workers 1/-d. instead of the statutory 3d. for these certificates.

A meeting was held in Darlaston in August 1870 of about 200 nut and bolt workers. One of the speakers was the 28 year old Richard Juggins, born in Darlaston with twenty years experience in the trade. The meeting resolved to pay the 3d. for certificates as stipulated in the Factory Acts. When the masters opposed this, the workers brought a test case in Wolverhampton questioning the legality of the 1/-d. fee, As was to be expected, the magistrates found ambiguities in the law and dismissed the mens' case. Two days later the union was formed and Richard Juggins quickly assumed leadership.

In the boom of the early '70s, the larger employers followed the general engineering trade in implementing the 54 hour week which they engineering unions had won. Smaller masters followed suit, but reduced wages pro rata so that the change cost them nothing. Eventually they offered 10 per cent advance on piece rates. This was rejected by Juggins and the union as not fully compensating for the change in hours. The union then presented its own list of prices which the employers claimed involved some increases of up to 25 per cent So this was rejected. The union then brought the Darlaston men out on strike. The masters responded by locking out the Smethwick workers, who were organised as a branch of the Nut & Bolt Forgers' Protection Society. The employers also stated their intention of imposing charges of 3/6d. per week for providing blast and a boy to carry breezes. To add insult to injury they then presented the Document requiring that no workers should be members of the union.

Juggins' employer went even further by declaring that under no circumstances would Juggins ever be employed again in the trade. The dispute lasted several months and ended with a compromise List with charges for blast and carriage of breezes reduced to 1/10d.

Juggins' position was resolved by his becoming paid secretary of the union, a post he held until his death 23 years later. Moreover, from that time he became, 'on the proposal of the largest employer in the trade', the sole Arbitrator for the industry, his decisions being accepted by both employers and operatives. Surely a unique distinction for a trade union leader in Britain.

By 1876 the union had 34 branches throughout the country with nearly 2,000 members and assets approaching £3,000.

Other Trade Unions

Having introduced the most important trade union activity in the Black Country it remains to briefly mention smaller unions. although this cannot include every society.

Of very considerable antiquity is the organisation of print workers, the oldest national 'chapel' known dating from 1685. By 1826 Typographical Societies existed in most large towns. In 1830 the Northern Typographical Union was formed and a Wolverhampton branch was affiliated to it. In 1837 the Wolverhampton chapel proposed a sinking fund to finance weekly payments for strikes, instead of the lump sum of £2, £4 etc. which was paid out in weekly instalments. The union, however, decided that this was too expensive. In 1844 the National Typographical Association was formed and the Midlands district covered most of the old Northern Union branches. The National Typographical Association collapsed in 1848. The next year the Provincial Typographical Association was formed with Birmingham in membership, but not Wolverhampton. A Wolverhampton branch of the PTA was, however, in existence by 1866. The midland branches were the first to call for district trade conferences and in 1884 called a conference of Wolverhampton, Walsall and Dudley societies to form a Black Country Conference.

Besides those already mentioned at least two other productive co-operatives were set up by trade unions in this period. In 1867 a Builders' Co-operative was set up and in 1873 a Walsall Padlock Co-operative was formed.

Finally, something should be said about organisation among white collar workers.

The poor pay and conditions of teachers, together with their professional concern for the pupils they taught led to the development of strong associations in the 1850s, although their general division between Church of England and Non-Conformist schools made unity difficult. These early associations were usually under the patronage of the high and mighty and nothing so 'disgraceful' as trade unionism was ever mentioned. The oldest was the S. Staffs & E. Worcs. Church of England Schoolmasters' Association formed in 1851. A notice of their fourth anniversary dinner announced that Lord Hatherton, the Lord Lieutenant of the County, would be in the chair and the dinner would be donated by the Earl of Dudley. In the 1860s branches of the C of E Schoolmasters' Association such as Wolverhampton and Dudley continued to meet. It is in the later 1870s with the 1870 Education Act promising education for all, and the formation of the National Union of Elementary School Teachers that broader, less sectarian more distinctly trade union organisations developed with the participation of women.

Organisation among shop assistants and clerks was assisted by much public sympathy concerning their impossibly long hours of work.

There had been discussion in 1842 on the hours of shop assistants which were nominally 14 hours a day, but in practice much longer. A success in this campaign came when in 1845 Bilston Market began to close an hour earlier at 11 pm. The movement ebbed and flowed. In 1855 another controversy broke out in Wolverhampton and Bilston. In the latter town shop assistants were said to be still working 14-16 hours a day except for Sundays.

Another aspect of the shorter hours movement was the demand for a five and a half day week instead of six days. In 1860 a Half-Day Holiday Movement was set up in Wolverhampton by a committee of commercial clerks. They 'addressed a circular to the principal merchants, factors and manufacturers' demanding a half day Saturday. This was taken up by the local press and letters of support published. There were also letters against, complaining that where the half-day had been conceded 'it begats unbusinesslike propensities.'

In 1863 a Wolverhampton branch of the Early Closing Movement was formed. The object was to have all shops close at 7 pm except on Saturdays. The existing situation was stated as being that some shops closed at 8 pm on Mondays and at 7 pm the other four days. Other shops did not close until 8 or 9 pm. A particular object was to get the market to close earlier on Saturdays which, it was held, would induce others to do the same.

From such campaigns, with wide local support, trade union organisation of both clerks and shop assistants was to rise later.

The extent of trade union organisation discussed in this chapter suggests that the alleged backwardness of trade unionism in the Black Country was not altogether true. What have not been discussed are the many associations of tiny local trades which came and went, or continued to exist in the form of Friendly Societies. One can instance brushmakers and shoe makers, both with long records of organisation which had branches in Wolverhampton and no doubt other towns. Or organisation among brassworkers, and the leather trades; or glassworkers in Dudley and at Chance's of Oldbury, one of the largest specialist glass producers in the country. Or the regimented railway employees who in 1858 set up in Wolverhampton a Benevolent Society. Trade union branches were to be found not only in the towns, but the neighbouring villages; such was the Tettenhall and surrounding parishes Boot and Shoe Makers. Many more could, no doubt, be found.

Trades Councils

We can round off our study of Black Country trade unionism to 1875 by noting the local umbrella organisations workers found it necessary to create to protect and advance their interests. We have already noted the importance of national organisations such as the U.K.Alliance of Organised Trades in fostering and developing trade unions in the Black Country. But local organisation was essential to co-ordinate actions on national issues and take up local questions common to all trade unionists.

The first of these organisations in the Black Country was the Wolverhampton Trades Council. It was inaugurated in 1865 around both national and local questions. The national issue was the Master & Servant Acts. These were the main instrument of the social control of working people for more than a century and we have already quoted examples of how they were used by employers. It must be emphasised that we are dealing with a period during which working class political parties were illegal; that trade unions were legalised in 1824-25, but not the activities they undertook; working people had no vote for national or local institutions, and the only 'welfare' provision was the Workhouse.

The main provisions of these Master & Servant Acts concerned breaches of contract and default of duty. The former concerned the giving of proper notice before leaving employment for whatever purpose. The latter concerned the spoiling of materials used at work or damage to machinery and plant. If the employer was in default, he was subject to a civil action and damages could be claimed from him. If the employee was at fault, however, this was a criminal matter and the worker was hauled before a magistrate (who might be his own employer) and was liable to three months hard labour. Between 1858 and 1867 there were 10,000 prosecutions in Staffordshire under these Acts. Many of these would be mass prosecutions. Wolverhampton had a higher incidence of these prosecutions than any other borough in the country.

The ways in which these laws were invoked almost defies belief. No strike could take place without fourteen days notice. This made protection against victimisation impossible. Workers had no certainty that the work they did would be paid for. A favourite ploy was to close a workplace before a full days work had been done and not pay for this work. Few workers would have the confidence, or the money, to sue their employer or expect to receive justice if they did. Militant workers were sitting ducks for the Acts. For instance, in 1860 Edward Gough went on a deputation to his butty. He was instantly dismissed with 40/-d. in wages unpaid. He sued the butty, but was told that he had broken his contract by not being in the pit and lost his case. What happened when an employer was on the bench was illustrated in 1853. Twenty six ironworkers were prosecuted for leaving work. They claimed that the management sacked at a moment's notice and they were entitled to do the same. James Bagnall, the magistrate, was also an ironmaster. He sent William Hunt to jail for 21 days saying that he knew from personal experience that Hunt was a ringleader and a dangerous fellow to be connected with any ironworks!

Striking nail makers were, as we have seen, charged with embezzling iron which was lying in their homes unworked. Puddlers, having given the requisite notice of strike were then charged with damage to the puddling furnaces they were not working. In 1858 men refused to enter a pit because it was dangerous. The inspector of Mines sent word that he would not be able to inspect the pit for several days. They were prosecuted for neglect of work and ordered to return to the pit.

The above are only a few of the ways the Acts were used to maintain social control of the workforce and so effective were they that during the period of the Combination Acts (1799-1825) it was never necessary to invoke them in the Black Country; the Master & Servant Acts sufficed.

In 1863 the Glasgow Trades Council initiated a campaign against these Acts and committees were formed throughout the country, including one in Wolverhampton. The Acts were amended in a half-hearted way in 1867 and repealed almost entirely in 1875 when they were replaced by the Employers & Workmen Act.

The local issue that led to the Wolverhampton Trades Council was the setting up of the Plate Lock Co-operative, discussed above.

We have no record of the inaugural meeting, but as the first AGM was in September 1866, it can be assumed that it was September 1865. The Council met every second Tuesday at that bulwark of trade union activity, the Noah's Ark Inn, Lichfield Street. The early officers were well-known trade union leaders in the town. The president was Joseph Humphries, who was also president of the local Amalgamated Society of Operative Carpenters and Joiners, and an ardent advocate of his union's policy of conciliation and arbitration. Humphries was also chairman of the local committee formed to assist the Locksmiths' Co-operative. Vice-president was Edward Davis, delegate from the Tinplate Workers who were active in support of the Locksmiths' Co-op. The secretary of the trades council was Thomas Owen Crumpton, delegate of the Amalgamated Society of Plasterers & Joiners who was also the secretary of the local Master and Workmen's Act Committee set up on the initiative of the trades council. The treasurer was Samuel Godber from the Boilermakers' Union and treasurer also of the Master & Workmen's Committee. The other delegates were:

Thomas Whittall (Secretary Operative Carpenters & Joiners and secretary Locksmiths' Co-operative Committee), Thomas Jones (Secretary of the Locksmiths' Co-operative), H. Law (Painters' Society), Thomas Skett (Carpenters and Joiners), Edward Wooten (Tailors' Society), John Robinson (Tailors' Society), R. Diggory (Tinplate Workers). William Cheers, W. Rowley, David, Harrison, Cull, John Williams, Jackson and Oliver were delegates from unidentified unions. Total delegates were therefore about twenty with an average attendance of about twelve.

The trades council represented mainly the smaller trades. Neither miners nor ironworkers were represented, and the Amalgamated Society of Engineers did not allow affiliation to local trades councils at this time, although the Society nationally was a member of the London Trades Council.

The early years of the Trades Council were crowded with exceptionally fruitful activity. It joined with the Glasgow Trades Council in leading the agitation against the Master & Servant Acts. A bill was promoted in Parliament but did not become law because the government set up a Royal Commission on the matter. John Davis, president of the Locksmiths' Co-op Association, was appointed to give evidence for Staffordshire.

The Trades Council succoured the Lock Co-op through its difficult early years. It also supported affiliation to the First International. The main attraction of the International Working Men's Association to the British trade union movement was that it provided some protection from the import of foreign strike breakers of whom the Tinplate Workers had much experience. Wolverhampton Trades Council also passed the first resolution calling for the Sheffield Conference to consider measures of defence against lock-outs which resulted in the formation of the United Kingdom Alliance of Organised Trades. The agitation for the Reform Act of 1867 which gave the vote to working men in towns was spearheaded locally by the Trades Council together with the local Branch of the Reform League. Finally, the Wolverhampton Trades Council was one of the nine trades councils represented at the inaugural conference in March 1867 of what became the Trades Union Congress.

After this initial burst of activity, the Trades Council subsided into inactivity. So much so that when it revived in the early 1870s even the original year of its foundation was forgotten.

Other trades councils were formed in the boom years of the early 1870s. Walsall & District Trades Council was formed in 1872. Like the Wolverhampton Trades Council, which began to come to life again at this time, the Walsall organisation was also connected with a manufacturing co-operative, in this case the Gun Lock Filers Co-operative. At its first meeting on 9th April 1872, Sam Welsh, editor of the Walsall Free Press and secretary of the Walsall Cottage Hospital where Sister Dora was working, was elected President and Treasurer. In April 1874 a special meeting of the Trades Council at the White Lion Inn, Darlaston, heard of the formation of the Co-op. and pledged its support, At the same meeting the Council had decided to support the locked-out farm labourers and also heard of an impending strike at Wednesbury of Gas Tube Fitters, who were affiliated to the Trades Council. It is likely that Richard Juggins was closely concerned in the formation of Walsall Trades Council. His Nut & Bolt Workers were affiliated to it and he became the Trades Council treasurer.

Juggins' union contributed £50 to the Gun Filers Co-operative, a considerable sum at a time when they were supporting two strikes elsewhere and another two in their own industry.

In June 1874 Walsall Trades Council discussed the formation of a local federation of trades councils. This again is likely to have been a Juggins initiative.

In October 1874, the relations of the Trades Council with the Nut and Bolt Workers became strained. Walsall had proposed a rule that there should be a compulsory levy of trade union affiliates if one fifth of its organisations was on strike. Juggins objected pointing out that Walsall Trades Council had 1200 members of whom two thirds were Nut & Bolt Workers. The next largest society had 250 members and others went down to 25 members; if only half a dozen small societies went on strike there would be a levy on all members, and this was not fair to the Nut & Bolt men. It was further argued that the Smethwick Nut & Bolt branch was affiliated to both Birmingham Trades Council and Wolverhampton Trades Council and neither of these organisations had such a rule.

In 1875 Juggins was treasurer of the Gun Lock Filers' Co-operative which was by then in difficulties, a decision to close it being delayed for a further three months. By June 1875 Walsall Trades was involved in the peace movement with a report from the Midlands Arbitration Society.

In June 1875 we first learn of a Wednesbury Trades Council. It held a meeting with its MP, Alex Brogden. Capper, a trade unionist, said that Wednesbury should have three MPs. one of whom should be a representative of labour. A resolution was also passed condemning the Conspiracy clauses of the recent Labour Laws Amendment Act. Finally a delegate from the Amalgamated Society of Engineers moved a vote of satisfaction on the setting up of the Wednesbury Trades Council and urging all local trade societies to affiliate.

The next month the Wednesbury Trades Council held its 'usual monthly meeting', at the Anchor Hotel, Holyhead Road, with the president in the chair who was Richard Juggins. Juggins had, it seems, initiated the new organisation and transferred his Nut & Bolt Workers to it from Walsall Trades Council as a result of the disagreement discussed above.

Walsall Trades Council continued to meet at Whittimore Street. In August it made donations to various strikes, including that of the Birmingham Tube Workers. It also sent a deputation to try to settle an Awl Blade dispute in Bloxwich.

All trades councils were concerned with the Acts which were replacing the Master & Servant Acts. The Trade Union Act of 1871 had finally legalised trade unions. But the Criminal Law Amendment Act of the same year made picketing during a strike hazardous by declaring 'coercion' an undefined offence; the Act also left trade unionists open to the catch-all and very serious charge of 'conspiracy.' In June Wolverhampton Trades Council contributed 20/-d. to the TUC to further their agitation against the labour laws.

In August 1875 two questions were raised at Wolverhampton Trades Council which were of importance to all Black Country trade unionists. The first was the Temperance question. This was being particularly fiercely pursued at this time by the powerful Liberal and Nonconformist interests and trade unionists wanted to remain neutral. Joseph Humphries the secretary had spoken, it seems, at a Tent Crusade and it was generally agreed that he should have spoken in a private capacity. There was unanimous agreement that the Trades Council should not interfere in the temperance question. This was a decision easier to make than to implement. The other issue was support for Plimsoll legislation which at that time was being withdrawn from Parliament. Some members believed that this was a political question and should not therefore be of concern to the non-political Trades Council. Another delegate argued, however, that this affected engineers on ships and was therefore the concern of the trade union movement.

At the August meeting of the Wednesbury Trades Council it was announced that a district Federation of Engineers with 450 members had affiliated; a delegate jointly with the Nut & Bolt Workers was agreed for the forthcoming TUC; and a resolution in support of Plimsoll was unanimously carried.

In September 1875 Walsall Trades Council held its annual general meeting with Sir Charles Forster MP in the chair. This was respectability indeed. Here it was confirmed that the rule for the levy during strikes had been approved by all affiliated societies except the Nut & Bolt Workers, who had subsequently resigned.

The October meeting of Wednesbury Trades Council strongly criticised local magistrates and called for paid stipendiaries in South Staffs; it condemned the Small Penalties Act; demanded the abolition of truck; supported arbitration in all industrial disputes and again called for direct representation of labour in Parliament.

As the Great Depression descended both trade unions and trades council fell on difficult days and their progress will be followed in a subsequent chapter.

Bibliography: Trade Unionism 1850 to the Great Depression 1875

For the structure of Black Country industry: Timmins S (ed) – *Birmingham and the Midland Hardware Industry* (1866); Allen G.C. – *The Industrial Development of Birmingham and the Black Country 1860-1927*. For trade unionism see: Eric Taylor – *The Working Class Movement in the Black Country 1850-1914*. For the trade cycle and standard of living see my *Social Conditions in the Black Country 1800-1900* chapter 7. For conditions in the mines see: *Midland Mining Commission Report 1843; Mines Inspectors' Annual Reports* from 1851; T.E. Lones – *History of Mining in the Black Country* (1898). For trade unionism in the mining and iron industries Eric Taylor is the best guide. For Tin Plate workers there are two excellent general histories dealing extensively with the Black Country: A.T. Kidd – *History of the Tin Plate Workers and Sheet Metal Workers and Braziers' Societies;* Ted Brake – *Men of Good Character*. For the notorious Perry case see pamphlet and other material in Wolverhampton Central Library archives. For trade unionism in the building trades R.W. Postgate's *The Builders' History* gives the general outline, but local material has to be picked up from the local press. For Locks there is Brian Stenner's *The Lockmakers 1889-1989*. For Nails and Chains, Timmins and Eric Taylor are the best sources. *Factory Inspectors' Reports* are available from 1867. For Glass see the *Flint Glass Makers' Magazine* 1860-1898. For Nuts and Bolts there is J.A.C. Baker – *History of the Nut & Bolt Trade in the West Midlands* (Birmingham M. Comm. 1965). For white collar workers such as Teachers and Shop Assistants there are only the newspaper reports. For Trades Councils see: G. Barnsby – *The History of Wolverhampton, Bilston & District Trades Union Council, 1865-1990* (1994). For Walsall and other Trades Councils see Taylor, and for the origins of Walsall Trades Council the *Walsall Free Press*, March & April 1872. The main capitalist newspapers for the period are the *Dudley Herald, Stourbridge County Express, Walsall Observer* and *Wolverhampton Chronicle*.

Chapter 4

The Re-birth of Socialism 1884-1900

The Social Democratic Federation
Information on the SDF comes from its weekly paper *Justice,* dating from January 1884. The first mention of re-born Socialism in the Black Country was in June 1884 when it was announced that Taylor, Sketchley and other members of the Birmingham Democratic Federation would hold open-air meetings in West Bromwich. Two meetings duly took place in July, one 'under the lamp' in the High Street, and the other 'near the park gates.' There being no discussion at the first meeting, it was announced that another meeting would be held the next week 'dealing with Giffen's statement on the well-being of the working classes'. Giffen and Bowley were both official statisticians pronouncing on the general improvement in working class living standards in the tenth year of the Great Depression which had slashed living standards back to early 1840s levels.

Across the Black Country miners were on strike against wage reductions from 3/8d. per day to 3/4d. Both these rates were starvation level wages. But this was not the end of the matter, for most miners would be working short time. Thus the difference between 5/-d. a day for a full week of six working days which gave miners a reasonable standard of living and three days or less at 3/4d. which would hardly even buy sufficient food for a family of five, meant the return of starvation. West Bromwich socialists reported that SDF manifestoes were being widely distributed and *Justice* sold. 'Our ideas are rapidly spreading and there is every hope of a strong branch being formed shortly.'

The Birmingham socialists were active elsewhere in the Black Country during the strike. Sketchley addressed 5,000 miners at Netherton and Helen Taylor was expected to speak there the following week.

The first advertised agents for *Justice* in the Black Country were G. Tench 186 High St. West Bromwich and Mayer, the veteran Chartist and Secularist at 3 Wolverhampton St. Dudley.

At the end of July, a large meeting at the Theatre Royal, West Bromwich was addressed by Helen Taylor. She said that land and labour were the only sources of wealth and that miners' wives should encourage their striking men.

The strike went on into August. At a meeting in Dudley, the Rev C. Leach from Birmingham compared the £8,000 paid by the Earl of Dudley for a vase with the miserable wages paid to miners.

In October there was a London demonstration of sympathy with the still striking S. Staffs miners with John Burns in the chair. S. Staffs speakers were Benjamin Winwood, Herbert Burrows and a Dudley councillor, Hill. Winwood said he was a working miner who loaded 18-20 tons of coal a day for 3/5d. Hill said that he was a shoemaker, but had been elected by miners because any miner who spoke out would be black-listed by the coal masters.

In the first months of 1885 the formation of Federations of Trades was both a local and a national issue. A regional meeting held at Brierley Hill in February was followed by a national meeting in the same town in March at which both John Burns and H.M. Hyndman attended as delegates from the SDF. Hyndman told the meeting that the Earl of Dudley took £700,000 a year from the blood and sinews of coal and iron workers. A Resolution to form a Federation was moved by a glassworker and a tailor, but it does not seem to have been passed. 'Some trade unionists have still to learn that only by a revolution in the system of production and distribution can the working class be emancipated.' The report, however, took consolation in the progress being made in the Black Country. 'Thanks to Herbert Burrows and other Socialist friends, revolutionary ideas are spreading through the Black Country.'

Towards the end of 1886 Tom Mann made his famous tour of the midlands which led to stable SDF organisation in Birmingham and gave a considerable impetus to Black Country socialism. His successful meetings in Dudley, Wolverhampton and Willenhall, however, were dominated by the economic situation – iron furnaces still in blast operating only three days a week, the chainmakers' strike (which was to last for over one year) in full swing and Willenhall lock makers hard put to make 11/3d a week.

During 1887 meetings initiated from Birmingham took place in Smethwick and West Bromwich. At the August SDF annual conference, a report on branches stated that if Tom Mann could have stayed longer in the Black Country, branches could have been formed, but at that time there were none.

Again in 1888 there was much SDF activity in Birmingham, but little in the Black Country, and that little probably initiated from Birmingham. In West Bromwich a Sunday morning open-air pitch was established opposite the Dartmouth Arms, but a lack of subsequent reports suggests that this was not maintained.

1889 was another good year for the Birmingham SDF and saw considerable activity in Walsall by the Marxist offshoot of the SDF – the Socialist League, but it was another bleak year for the SDF in the Black Country.

Bleak years continued, and it was not until 1893 that news of the inauguration of an SDF branch in the Black Country was recorded. This was at West Bromwich, again on the initiative of Birmingham comrades, where the police were obstructing open-air meetings. 'The police think that the Salvation Army and other religionists are entitled to hold meetings in West Bromwich, but not Socialists.' By May 1893 open-air SDF meetings were being held at the Beeches, West Bromwich and in the Dudley Market place on Sunday evenings. In June the *Justice* SDF Directory confirmed that there were branches in both these Black Country towns. During August Dudley was holding meetings on both Sundays and Wednesdays, and the West Bromwich branch met at the Victoria Coffee House in the High Street.

Open-air activity ceased during the winter, but was resumed in Dudley in May 1894 with Market Place meetings at both 11 am and 6-30 pm on Sundays. Meanwhile West Bromwich was still having problems with its meetings, the Watch Committee having made a decision to ban Socialists. This matter was taken up by the West Bromwich Trades Council and also the Birmingham SDF, with what results we do not know. But by October the SDF branch in West Bromwich was advertising Sunday open-air meetings mornings and evenings at the Fountain. Open-air meetings continued into the winter and at the end of the year West Bromwich branch was holding meetings at the Fountain at 7 pm on Wednesdays and Dudley at 6 pm on Sundays in the Market Place.

In June 1895 open-air meetings were resumed both in West Bromwich and Dudley, but in the former town the police were closing meetings at the Fountain. By this time the Independent Labour Party, which had been formed in 1893 to promote working class candidates for Parliament and local governing bodies, was developing as the strongest Socialist party in the town and this was causing some friction. In West Bromwich it was reported that Tom Mann 'was being brought into the town to work up an ILP branch.' A complainant to *Justice* in July wrote in Provincial Notes, 'It seems to me that the ILP comrades are trying to swamp out of existence the real pioneers of Socialism in West Bromwich. Is it right to come in and take the credit after the ground here has been worked?'

By July 1895 a Smethwick branch had been approved by the general council of the SDF. The branch met at the Six Ways, Grove Lane and the secretary was Cde. Cuin. In August it was reported that Smethwick was flourishing, but West Bromwich was still having problems with the police. Socialists were still forbidden at the Fountain and the comrades had retreated to a patch of waste ground some way from the Fountain. 'Chief-Superintendent Whitehurst was written to, but only told us we would be arrested if we appeared at the fountain.' At this time, Dudley, Smethwick and West Bromwich were all holding regular open-air meetings. Newsagents handling *Justice* at this time included Goddard of Spon Lane, West Bromwich and S. Hodges of 11 Salop St. Wolverhampton.

In October a reporter calling himself Slocum was reporting another busy month in Smethwick, but, 'People in the area are actively afraid of espousing the cause and therefore we are not making new members.' The police were providing a little light relief; at an open-air meeting a police sergeant had ridden up to a meeting on a bicycle and had fallen off it! 'He rose breathing threats and slaughter against us for blocking the road, but there was ample room to pass. It could have been the eloquence of Brown's address. We sold a quire of *Justices* and 15 *Merrie Englands.* The latter is one of the few Black Country references to the remarkable book by Robert Blatchford which sold one million copies in 1895.

Open-air meetings continued at Smethwick until the winter but, like West Bromwich, they were having trouble with the police who were stopping their meetings at the waste ground at Six Ways. They hit back vigorously calling on Birmingham SDFers to help them, and at the end of November, George Lansbury spoke at a meeting there and 'gave us a leap forward.' At a subsequent meeting two comrades, Sale and Skett, had been arrested. The case against them, however, was dismissed by the magistrate after a 'masterly defence by Sale.' They were back at the old spot the next Sunday 'although it was bitterly cold.' At the end of 1895 Dudley, Smethwick and West Bromwich branches were all holding regular open-air meetings.

In the winter of 1895-96 George Lansbury was on an extended SDF tour of the west Midlands and during January 1896 held open-air meetings in Dudley, Smethwick and West Bromwich. Slocum was still reporting for Smethwick. In January he noted that 'the branch was being assailed by the local press' and this was a healthy sign that 'the dovecotes of respectability were being fluttered at seeing the promiscuous doctrine of Socialism gaining ground.' Throughout December, 'our comrades stuck to their posts holding two or three meetings on Sundays, breaking new ground wherever possible and proclaiming the doctrine of discontent with marked success.' Slocum concluded:

> Membership of the branch is steadily increasing, not by droves, but with men who have grasped the broad outlines and appreciating the truths of Socialism are prepared to share in spreading it. *Justice* is becoming as well known as our local points, which must be put down to the energy of Comrade Cole. Our appearances at Six Ways are looked forward to and we can get an audience in spite of the cold.

At the end of February, Slocum reported that because of the spring-like weather they had been able to continue their open-air propaganda throughout the winter to 'large and appreciative audiences.' They had broken new ground by holding indoor meetings at the Boot and Slipper, Rolfe Street on Sunday evenings. The Smethwick agent for *Justice* at this time was J. Mansell of 7 Heath Street.

In July Caroline Martyn, one of the active women leaders of the SDF, died at a tragically early age and a *Justice* obituary noted that she had probably physically overworked herself in the cause of Socialism. Smethwick branch passed a resolution of sympathy with Caroline's relatives whose death had 'robbed the cause of humanity and liberty of one of its most devoted workers.'

But there was little SDF activity reported in the Black Country during the remaining months of 1896. The focus of activity at this time was an Amnesty Committee for the Walsall Anarchists, sentenced for alleged bomb making. This question is fully discussed under the Socialist League section of this chapter.

From this time on the Independent Labour Party seems to have been attracting Labour militants and SDF branches in the Black Country languished. It was not until the jingoism of the early part of the Boer War began to die down that the SDF again began to flourish in the Black Country.

In September 1900 Wolverhampton SDF appeared in the Provincial Lectures column of *Justice,* A. Cain reporting the holding of two public meetings in Wolverhampton on Sundays; one at the Lamp, Cleveland Street at 11am and another at Railway Street at 7pm. These meetings were still continuing in October. In September, Alf Fellows of Wolverhampton SDF spoke at the opening meeting of Birmingham SDF's campaign for the election of working men to the Birmingham School Board. Socialism was stirring again.

The Socialist League and the Walsall Anarchist 'Bomb Plot'

The Socialist League, serviced by its newspaper *Commonweal* was the second of the Marxist socialist organisations to emerge in the 1880s. Its leaders, including William Morris and Marx' youngest daughter Eleanor, split from the SDF at the end of 1884 because of the alleged impossibility of working with the autocrat H.M. Hyndman.

It was not until 1887 that the Socialist League began to make headway in the Black Country. In February John Mahon, a national leader, reported that he had lectured to an advanced Radical club in Walsall, had met a sympathetic audience and 'our literature had been taken up eagerly.' In June A.K. Donald, another national leader, spent a week in the Black Country. This was the period of the epic chainmakers' year long strike to raise wages and fight the truck system. Donald held open-air meetings at Darlaston and at the Sister Dora statue in Walsall. He heard a Roman Catholic priest in Walsall preach on Socialism. On Sunday afternoon, Donald was at Willenhall and in the evening back at Walsall. On Monday he walked from Dudley to Cradley and reported on the general situation in this mining and chainmaking area. Houses, he noted, were undermined by subsidence for which the Earl of Dudley paid no compensation. Some of these houses were built by Building Societies and some working people had lost their life's savings. On Tuesday evening 'several thousands' were present at a meeting addressed by Donald and H. Sanders of the newly formed Walsall branch of the Socialist League. Later in the week Donald spoke at Dudley Market where he stated that chain costing 8¾d to chain masters was selling at between 3/6d and 21/6d. in London.

By the time Donald returned to London, Walsall had a thriving Socialist League branch able to initiate agitation in other parts of the Black Country. In July 1887 Walsall branch reported meetings at Dudley Market on 2nd and 9th each attended by 500 people. During the week, Sanders, Weaver and Deakin, all of the Walsall branch, spoke at Pelsall; on Saturday they were at Walsall Market and on Sunday they went to West Bromwich, Smethwick and Oldbury with good meetings at which 'a fair quantity of literature was sold'. Towards the end of August Mahon was back in the area, holding meetings at Walsall, Wednesbury and Pelsall. The following week Weaver and Deakin spoke at Pelsall, Sanders held 'a large meeting' at Dudley, Sanders and Weaver had 'a most successful meeting' at Wednesbury and Sanders spoke at Walsall.

In the last week of August Sanders and Weaver reported at Wednesbury 'a large and animated meeting with great promise of success.' In Bilston, Sanders 'opened up new ground'. The Walsall branch was also initiating activity in Birmingham with 'a grand meeting' at the Bull Ring. Sanders reported an additional meeting at Darlaston, 'We have been here once or twice before and are always well received.' In Dudley, the concern of the local authorities at Socialist propaganda attracted the attention of the *Express & Star*. It stated that 'Sanders and Webb, agents of the Socialist League from Walsall, held an additional meeting in the Market Place. Police sergeant Sansome told them to move as the meeting was contrary to regulations. Sanders defended the right to sell *Commonweal* and speak. He offered to pay the customary market toll if that was required and said that Socialists had equal rights of meetings with the Salvation Army, jugglers and mountebanks. At Great Bridge, Donald who was back in the area, had held the 'usual meeting' at the Market Place. 'A good crowd listened. There were several disciples of Mr Bradlaugh on the scene, one of whom was firmly convinced that Bradlaugh was a Land Nationaliser. He was invited to write to that celebrated MP and bring back the answer'. Bradlaugh by this time, of course, was very anti-Socialist. At Oldbury, Deakin held an additional meeting, 'People here are exceedingly poor, but were much interested in the address.' At Tipton, Donald held a large meeting at Wednesbury. 'It was the first Socialist meeting ever held there. There was a little interruption from a Tory corn dealer, but he was quickly stopped by the crowd threatening to bonnet the offender.' On Monday in West Bromwich, Donald broke new ground with 'a large meeting listened to attentively'. At Willenhall, Donald did an additional meeting for lock workers on Saturday afternoon. In the evening, Weaver and Donald were at Wolverhampton holding a meeting at the Prince Consort statue, 'It was decidedly the best meeting in the district. The crowd was enormous. A number of objectors and interrupters attempted to break up the meeting, but the crowd soon (taught) these worthies how to behave. Donald was ordered off the chair as he was finishing. He remonstrated with the constable who had drawn his truncheon. He was going to give everyone a lesson, but a little firmness made the bully stay his hand. A serious riot might have occurred in view of the size of the crowd. We were asked to come back.'

In September it was reported from Darlaston and Bilston that although the weather was very stormy, Weaver had got good audiences. In Bloxwich, Weaver also ran into bad weather, but in Dudley on Tuesday 'the usual Market Place meeting was held and although it was very wet Donald got a good audience. The police turned up, but immediately retired.'

Activity continued strongly into the autumn. In Bilston, Sanders had to pay a market toll of 3d. but reported a good crowd. Walsall branch reported meetings at Darlaston, Dudley, Great Bridge, Oldbury, Tipton, West Bromwich, Willenhall and Wolverhampton.

Early in October, A.K. Donald gave a progress report of the Socialist League in the Black Country and the conditions under which the area was suffering:

> The working class are suffering severely from bad trade. The chain strike has now continued for twelve months. Davies of Oldbury became bankrupt putting 1,200 on the poor law, which frightened the Oldbury Guardians. Ultimately, large numbers were put on the highly productive employment of stone breaking!... The S. Staffs coal and iron trades are at a standstill.
>
> There are Socialist League branches at Birmingham and Walsall. Walsall has carried on a big propaganda during the past three months. A drawback in the Black Country is that a surprisingly large number of workers are not able to read. Trade unionism is feebly developed. Some places such as Willenhall had a fairly good society, but this has collapsed. The Tories at Wolverhampton are particularly active trying to disturb our meetings, but they have always been kept in control by the crowds. There was an enormous crowd listening at the Market Place when a crowd of well dressed rowdies came from the Tory club.

Such intensity of Socialist activity and influence occurred during the years 1884-87 which were the worst years of the second phase of the Great Depression of 1874-90. In 1888 trade had picked up and economic conditions became less desperate. As a result, Socialist activity declined and Walsall became the only place in the Black Country where Socialist League activity was strongly organised. The Walsall experience parallels the national one where the Anarchists were ousting William Morris from control of the paper he financed, *Commonweal*. Walsall became, and remained, the sole centre of Anarchism in Birmingham and the Black Country. It maintained its position largely from the activity of three remarkable comrades to whom we have already been introduced – H. Sanders, Deakin and Weaver. The strength of anarchism in Walsall allowed them to make numerous forays into the Black Country and even into Birmingham. But nowhere else in this area was a stable anarchist branch established. In 1892 came the famous Walsall Anarchist Bomb Plot, which the Walsall branch survived into the long period of national campaigns for the release of the prisoners. In the period 1910-14 anarchism was represented by the development of Syndicalism.

An early indication of the anarchist trend in the Walsall branch was when Prince Kropotkin came to Britain in 1887. One of his early visits was to Walsall where in December he lectured to the Literary Institute and then to the Socialist League branch.

Walsall Socialist League maintained an open-air public meeting pitch throughout 1888, including the winter months. But the militant political and trade union struggles had abated and branch discussions were on such academic subjects as 'Workers' Lives in France', 'The Evicted Crofters of the Highlands', and talks on 'Education' and on 'John Ruskin'.

During the summer Sketchley, the veteran Birmingham chartist lectured in Walsall on the 'Currency Question', and local members had a meeting with the Bilston Liberal Club. But from September to December 1888 there were no reports of meetings and only the *Commonweal* notice of a weekly meeting at the Temperance Hall testifies to the existence of the Walsall Socialist League.

Activity seems to have continued at a low level into 1889, but in November a *Commonweal* notice announced that Walsall Socialist League was meeting at a Socialist Club at 18 Goodall Street and meetings were held there nightly.

In February 1890 Peter Kropotkin was once again in the Black Country. Walsall Socialist League reported that he spoke to a large audience at the Institute, Dudley on the 'Colonisation of Siberia'. 'Comrades here took advantage of his being in the district for him to pay us a visit the next day and although there was but little time to organise a meeting a capital audience assembled at the Walsall Unitarian Schoolroom and listened to an eloquent address on the Social Problem. Questions were put at the close and satisfactorily answered.' This report was submitted by JTD and *Commonweal* could be obtained from A. Deakin at 238 Stafford Road. In March Walsall Socialist League observed the ritual that every well-organised socialist body marked – the anniversary of the Paris Commune. This celebration occurred every year until 1917 when it was replaced by the observation of the greater event, the Russian Revolution. In the summer of 1890 the organisation felt strong enough to contemplate the setting up of a Midland Socialist Federation. The inaugural meeting, which took place in July was considered 'an unqualified success.' No executive or other governing body was appointed. Both Parliamentarians (i.e. those within the Socialist League who were now moving to the view that Labour should seek representation at Westminster) and non-Parliamentarians (mainly Anarchists) were represented and Clifton of Nottingham was appointed secretary. This organisation could not be maintained however, in the face of a crisis of the *Commonweal* newspaper. William Morris could no longer sustain the weekly losses of the paper and at the beginning of 1891 it reverted to being a monthly paper and the owners became the London Socialist League. In April it was subtitled A Journal of Revolutionary Socialism and in May, A Revolutionary Journal of Anarchist Communism. By this time only four London branches were advertising in the paper and thirteen provincial societies, one of which was Walsall.

1892 was both the year of the Walsall Anarchist Bomb Plot and also the end of *Commonweal* largely as a result of the Walsall events. The 'Plot' was first revealed with a notice that on Saturday 5th December 1891, 'Comrades had noticed police spies loitering around our Club. On leaving at night the staff increased and comrades were followed home. Some spies were on duty at some of our houses all night.' On 12th January 1892 the front page of *Commonweal* reported, 'Anarchists arrested at Walsall.' Walsall continued to monopolise the front page until April.

The bones of the so-called Plot were that branches of the Socialist League were degenerating into tiny sects advocating everything from robbery to obtain 'revolutionary funds', to the use of bombs. Continental anarchists were also finding their way to Britain, following a spate of bomb attacks in France and elsewhere. The Walsall branch early succumbed to the anarchist trend. In the summer of 1891 Frederick Charles, a well-known anarchist came to Walsall to find work. Later, Auguste Coulon, the suspected agent-provocateur of the plot, sent two anarchist exiles Victor Cailes and George Laplace to Walsall for them to be found work. Cailes stayed, but Laplace returned to London. In August Joseph Deakin, the secretary of the Walsall Socialist Club, met Coulon at an anarchist club in London; enquiries were made of Charles and Deakin said that he was working at an iron foundry. At this, Coulon is stated to have said 'Oh, he will do to make bombs for us.' In October Cailes received a letter in French signed 'Degnai' enclosing a sketch of a bomb which he showed to Charles and Deakin. Cailes applied to Coulon enquiring whether the letter was 'alright' and Coulon replied that it was. They then went ahead to make a casing and involved two other local members, William Ditchfield and John Westley. In December 1891 John Battolla, an Italian anarchist came to Walsall to enquire about the progress of the work. On his arrival he was followed by the Chief Constable of Walsall and Inspector Melville of the CID. From this time both the Socialist Club and its members were under surveillance. On the 6th. January 1892 Deakin went to London with a parcel. He was met by Melville and others who arrested him. The parcel contained not the bomb they expected to find, but a bottle of chloroform.

The next day, Melville came to Walsall and Charles, Cailes and Westley were arrested. The prisoners remained in the Walsall cells for a fortnight, during which time they complained of ill-treatment and Deakin made a confession under rather strange circumstances. This admitted making a bomb but believing that it was for use in Russia. There followed a series of hearings before the Walsall magistrates which lasted another fortnight. The central issue became the relationship of Inspector Melville of the CID with Auguste Coulon. Melville admitted knowing Coulon, but would not say whether he had employed him. The justices supported Melville's refusal to answer questions on this subject on the grounds of 'public duty.' The men were charged under the 1883 Explosives Act of 'feloniously, unlawfully and wickedly conspiring to cause by an explosive substance an explosion in the UK of a nature likely to endanger life.' They were remanded to appear at the next Assizes. At Stafford in March/April 1892 they were tried before a biased judge and a frightened jury. The Attorney-General himself led for the prosecution interlarding his remarks with hair-raising extracts from foreign anarchist literature found on the men. Charles, Cailes and Battolla were sentenced to 10 years penal servitude, Deakin to five years. Westley and Ditchfield were acquitted.

Such is the outline of the 'Plot'. The savagery of the sentences, the use by the police both locally and nationally of informers and the belief that Coulon was an agent-provocateur, led to the case being taken up by the whole Labour movement for the whole period of their imprisonment. These protests were in vain, however, and the men served their sentences.

Modern suspicion was rekindled by the refusal of the Home Office to release papers under the 50 year rule. These were not made available until 1986. They show the Home Office and police continuing to deny that Coulon was involved in the plot or was the instigator of it, although admitting that he was a police spy. But the fact that the 'Plot' would not have gone ahead without Coulon saying that it was 'alright', the fact that Coulon was present when the police first moved on the case with the following of Battolla, and later the arrest of Deakin, indicate that Coulon did more than inform and that he was the prime mover of the project.

The Walsall events played a key part in the disintegration of the Socialist League and its paper *Commonweal* suspended publication from September 1892 to May 1894. It then continued for another year. During this time there were no branch advertisements and no news from Walsall. But the influence of Anarchism established in Walsall was to remain until at least the outbreak of the First World War.

The Fabian Society

The third Socialist organisation emerging in 1884 was the non-Marxist, social-democratic Fabian Society. It was essentially a middle class organisation aspiring to be the think tank of the Labour movement rather than a mass organisation. At first the Society was confined to London. It was not until 1890 with the publication of the first edition of the Fabian Essays that branches were established in the provinces and a monthly journal *Fabian News* established to chronicle the Society's progress. The Birmingham branch, reckoned to be the first provincial society, was set up in 1891. The only place in the Black Country where Fabians seem to have established a branch before 1900 was in Wolverhampton.

The first notice of a Wolverhampton branch was in January 1893 when J.W. Buttery (a Stafford and later Birmingham comrade who was to play an important part in establishing the Independent Labour Party locally) lectured on 'Free Trade and Protection.' Lectures seem to have been fortnightly; on the 17th January Joseph Whittaker (the first leading figure in the social-democratic movement in Wolverhampton) lectured on 'Industrialism' and on the 31st H.G. Robins spoke on 'Old Age Pensions.' Other lectures during the winter and spring of 1893 spanned the spectrum of current political and social issues which the Fabians were busy rationalising into national social-democratic policy. These lectures included W. Bowyer on 'Taxation Direct and Indirect,' J.H. Smith on 'Nationalisation of the Means of Production' and Joseph Whittaker on 'War.'

By August 1893 Wolverhampton Fabians were holding two open-air meetings every week each addressed by three speakers. In December Wolverhampton Fabians were meeting weekly at the Co-operative Store, Stafford Street. Lectures during the month included 'Book Study' by Whittaker, 'Co-operative Production' by James Stephenson, another visit by Enid Stacy and C.W. Wilkes on 'Strikes and their Results.'

Activity continued strongly into 1894, but the Wolverhampton society was encountering the same problems that caused a general decline in the Society elsewhere:

> We have been trying weekly meetings during the past four months, but members do not attend in large numbers because their time and energy is to a great extent absorbed in the Labour Church and

Independent Labour Party work. We propose to abandon small weekly meetings for large monthly meetings.

Some deadheads were struck off this year so our membership remains under 40. The few we have, however, are nearly all prominent trade unionists and some are on the Trades Council.

But in March a full weekly programme included Stevenson on 'Book Study – Progress & Poverty', Higginson on the 'Poor Law', Whittaker on the 'National Debt' and a Fabian Social. In April fortnightly lectures took place – James H. Smith on 'Utility and Value' and Whittaker on the 'Vice of Respectability.' From this time, however, accounts of the Wolverhampton Society disappear from *Fabian News*. The journal continued until 1900, but no Wolverhampton reports have been found after 1894. Nor were there reports of any other Fabian branches in the Black Country.

Clarion and 'Cheerful Socialism'

In the early 1890s some crucial developments were taking place. Most importantly, the Great Depression of 1874-1895 was coming to an end. It had brought two horrifying troughs of mass unemployment 1878-80 and 1884-87 when actual starvation returned to the Black Country. It was the period also of the destruction of the basic Black Country industries of coal and iron and the transition to a heavy engineering economy. From 1888 trade began to improve and some working class families received a regular income sufficient to allow them to accumulate stores of household goods such as furniture, linoleum and even an occasional piano. Innumerable families, however, continued to be serviced by one bread winner bringing home only about £1 a week and here poverty continued to be dire. Before 1914 there was also to be two more periods of mass unemployment, 1892-94 and 1906-09.

The second feature of the early 1890s was that opposition to capitalism and the development of Socialist ideas became permanent and institutionalised.

Two of the institutions responsible for this development were the newspaper *Clarion* and the Independent Labour Party. Each of these will be dealt with separately, although each nourished the other.

Clarion was a remarkable paper started by Robert Blatchford in 1891. Blatchford was the son of strolling players who experienced the depths of poverty. At 20 he became a soldier for seven years and then turned himself into a brilliant journalist eventually earning £1,000 a year with the *Sunday Chronicle*. He was converted to Socialism by a pamphlet of H.M. Hyndman and William Morris which described depths of poverty in Britain which Blatchford denied. He set out to prove Hyndman and Morris wrong. He failed, and when the proprietors of the *Sunday Chronicle* objected to their columns being used to propagate Socialism, Blatchford was forced to resign. He brought out *Clarion* in December 1891.

Blatchford's genius was that he preached Socialism with a human face and made it all fun. Supporters of the paper quickly acknowledged themselves to be Clarionettes. They were much given to the use of pseudonyms; Blatchford himself wrote as Nunquam and some of the brilliant journalists he recruited to the paper were Dangle (Alex Thompson), Mong Blong (his brother Montague), and the Bounder (Edward Fay). *Clarion* really took off in 1893 and became a weekly feast of fun reporting and supporting all Socialist and trade union organisations – SDF, Socialist League, Fabian, ILP, Labour Churches etc. In addition it created a circle of recreational clubs never equalled before or since – Clarion Cycling Clubs, Clarion Choirs and Orchestras, Clarion Field Clubs, Clarion Social Clubs, etc. as well as the incomparable Cinderellas which provided impoverished children with summer, winter and Christmas treats and entertainment.

The first Black Country reference in *Clarion* was in February 1892 when the paper mentioned the twenty five year old Earl of Dudley as best known for having spent £11,000 at one sale for yearling horses. It added that this Staffordshire colliery proprietor had a rent roll considerably in excess of £100,000.

The next month, the Labour candidates standing in the area were publicised and these included for Dudley borough Richard Juggins, the well known trade union leader. The same month, a letter from J.D. Crisp of 66 Raglan Road Smethwick told of the scandal of older boys with boots at the

Birmingham Cinderella treading on shoeless younger boys and taking their Cinderella tickets from them.

There were various Black Country references in 1893 to activists such as J. Baker of Smethwick and W.H. Newman of Dudley, but it was in 1894 that *Clarion* activity began to flourish. In April of that year Birmingham Clarion Cycling Club started their season by coming to Wolverhampton by train, picking up local cyclists and touring Bridgnorth, Bewdley, Stourport, Worcester, Pershore, Evesham and back to Birmingham in an Easter tour.

In September 1894 there was the first detailed report from Wolverhampton. It was signed, in the best *Clarion* tradition, 'Woffler'. He said that never in the history of the metropolis of the Black Country had so much Labour activity been going on. There was discontent at there being only one Labour representative on the local council and only two on the School Board. The ILP was becoming stronger and had established a Labour Club in the area. The Carpenters & Joiners had been on strike for six months and the dispute showed no signs of terminating. Blacklegs were being supplied by the notorious Graeme Hunter. There was likely to be united action by the Trades & Labour Council and the ILP to stand further candidates in the local elections in November. 'If so, things should hum,' Woffler concluded. In the same month the first Midlands conference of the ILP took place; only Wolverhampton, in the Black Country, was represented.

Another report in October stated that the Independent Labour Club 'flourished.' It went on to report that Wolverhampton had been 'honoured' by a recent visit of Princess Louise and her husband:

> The usual tremendous endeavours were made by our resident aristocrats and hangers on to (raise enthusiasm) but the day went off like a damp rocket. The streets were mostly lined with 'respectables', nursemaids and babies, female gossip mongers and idle do-nothing errand boys. Being Monday and little or no work to do in some branches of trade, workmen here and there congregated in groups, but did not cheer, being more concerned to discuss the use or non-use of royalty. Yet the evening paper came out with the heading 'enthusiastic welcome.'

The report also gave further details of the Carpenters' dispute 'which drags on.' Verdicts had been given in the local County court against the agents of Graeme Hunter for detaining the tools of two of the blacklegs who had been sent here. Also, two carpenters who had been sent by the stipendiary to Quarter Sessions for intimidating blacklegs had been discharged there by the Recorder. Finally the report makes mention of the remarkable book Merrie England by Robert Blatchford which, in the course of a year, sold 1million copies. 'No 1d copies of the book are available in Wolverhampton, all of them having been snapped up on their arrival.'

At the end of the year there were reports of Black Country elections. In Wolverhampton William Sharrocks was defeated by a Liberal by only 72 votes in St. Mary's Ward, which 'staggered the Liberals,' but F. Evans 'who was a Clarionette' won St. Mark's. For the Wolverhampton School Board there had been five Labour candidates. Only two were successful, 'but Labour had polled 22,000 votes.' The central Independent Labour Club was also thriving with 500 members. 'Our Saturday evening lectures are popular and our Saturday evening smoking concerts are the talk of the town.' In Smethwick the Rev Travers Sherlock, local Fabian and Socialist, headed the poll for the School Board. There were two other Socialists on the Board. At the local elections Cde Smith, who was a Clarion scout, was to stand for District Council.

In December, Woffler reported the circumstances leading to the election of the first two Labour representatives to the Wolverhampton Board of Guardians. They had been nominated in three wards when the 'wire-pullers' suggested they would be unopposed in one ward if they withdrew from the other two. This was done. The two successful candidates were both Trades Council nominees, Harry Moreton a bootmaker, and William Price of the Typographical Society. These successes occurred at a time when the Trades Council was 'down in the dumps' over the School Board elections when Moreton had lost his place.

In January 1895 the first report of a Bilston Cinderella noted that 300 children had been entertained 'thanks to the Nunquam publican of the Swan, Mr Spittle.' In March it was reported that *Clarion* was now taken by the Wolverhampton Library 'thanks to the efforts of Councillor Stevenson.'

In May Sharrocks was again unsuccessful in taking St. Mary's ward although he polled nearly

5000 votes. Also in May, a Directory of Clarion Scouts showed two troops in the Black Country. At Smethwick D. Austin of 149 Shireland Road was the secretary, and in Wolverhampton L. Pountney who could be contacted at the Labour Club, John Street, was the leader.

Merrie England was beginning to make an impact. In Wolverhampton a clergyman had written to the local paper saying that if Christianity were properly understood there would be no need for books such as Marrie England. 'The book has caused controversy in the press. The latest estimate is of 10,000 sold in the Black Country.'

The effect of working class Guardians of the Poor was soon evident in Wolverhampton when William Price had got the Guardians to 'pass the most far-reaching fair-contract resolution ever passed by a public body.' This included standard wages and hours by all sub-contractors to the Poor Law. Also a no sub-contracting clause and penalties for non-compliance.

In July 1895 a report on the Wolverhampton ILP Club noted that it now had 900 members and 'the best set of rules ever for Labour Clubs.' *Clarion* readers were invited to write for a copy of these model rules. John and Kathleen Bruce-Glasier (two of the most popular ILP and Labour Church figures) had been in Wolverhampton for three days during the election '... and did us a power of good. Many *Merrie Englands* were sold.'

In August a report signed by George Parslow showed some of the tensions of Wolverhampton politics at this time. 'The Liberals who were going to smash the windows of the Labour Club and those of all candidates standing against them in parliamentary, local, school board etc. elections were now talking of not opposing each other. The Trades Council is very dilapidated. Ten years ago it was stigmatised as a Liberal clique. Now it is called an ILP clique and societies are resigning on this account. We will be glad when the Trades Council works with the ILP as it does in other towns.' This report also stated that Clarion Cyclists and Clarion Scouts were doing a good job and that applications to join the ILP were being received from as far afield as Oakengates.

At the end of August Woffler reported a Wolverhampton ILP outing to Tong. In September Caroline Martyn (another very popular national speaker) spent three days in Wolverhampton, during which the Women's Guild of the Co-operative Society had an enjoyable trip to Kingswinford and had prepared a 'first class' programme for the winter. Miss Martyn's lectures were 'an unqualified success.' The last of these had been at the Star Theatre where her subject had been Walt Whitman. She had 'substantially increased the role of the ILP and Socialists.' The Clarion Cyclists were as active as ever at that time. The previous Sunday there had been a ride to Badger Dingle. Later in the month a Cycle Parade was held at Walsall. For the Wolverhampton local elections in November Sharrocks and Evans were adopted by the ILP for St. Matthew's and St. George's wards and the Trades & Labour Council approached for their endorsement in return for support for Trades Council candidates in their various elections. This time unanimous agreement was reached. But the elections were a disappointment, Evans receiving 541 votes, but Sharrocks only 164. In October an ILP Women's Section was formed with more than 60 members. '...some of whom had previously been active in the opposite camp.' This, presumably referred to Liberals. Secretary of the ILP Women's Group was Emma Lloyd. A Clarion band was also formed at this time with Mr Robinson in charge. This report by Woffler also recorded the ten year success of the Wolverhampton & District Co-operative Society which in its first year had 159 members and sales of £1,313. Ten years later its membership was 1104 with sales of £17,574. 'The Society's composition and government are decidedly advanced and local Socialists have a very fair share in its concerns and management.'

In January 1896 came the first indication of Clarion activity in Walsall. Under the *Clarion* column Notes for Clarionettes, Walsall Socialists desirous of forming a Society for the district to distribute literature and hold lectures were invited to contact E. Franklin of 21 Tasker Street, Walsall.

At the end of January Woffler reported the 'brilliant success' of an ILP soiree (usually spelled 'swaree' by Clarionettes) in Wolverhampton. 'To give good entertainment and net a profit of £9 is not bad.' Woffler also reported the annual meeting of Wolverhampton Clarion Cycling Club. 'Numbers for the coming season promise to beat the record by a long way. A fancy dress ball has been arranged at the Exchange Hall for Tuesday February 18th with a good exhibition of cycles. The Clarion band will play for dancing. Dennis Fallow is the hon. sec.' Finally, Woffler reported that Wolverhampton Trades

Council had arranged a meeting of the newly formed Industrial Union of Employers and Employed which Sir Alfred Hickman, a local MP, would address. Other 'big guns' had also agreed to attend and address the trade unionists.

Clarion finances at this time were being considerably boosted by advertisements for cycles and accessories, most of which were made in the west Midlands. Clarion Cycles were manufactured in Birmingham and advertised as 'made by Trade Union labour on an 8-hour day.' JWL of Walsall enquired of the writer of *Clarion* Cycle Notes whether the Clarion cycle could really be recommended. The reply was that he had seen and ridden some which 'excelled anything I have known'. In addition, the secretary of Halifax CCC had written saying that four of their members had bought Clarion cycles and found that they gave 'unbounded satisfaction.' In the same month an advert appeared for Vanguard Cycles made at Bradford Street, Walsall.

At this time Walsall had progressed to a Walsall & District Socialist Society which met every Tuesday evening at the Victoria Coffee House, High Street. Tom Groom (the popular O'Groomie O, and founder of the Clarion Cycling Clubs) from Birmingham, was billed to speak on 'Economic History.' In April 1896 Walsall took the Central Hall in Bradford Street for a meeting by Tom Mann, who spoke on the 'Social Outlook.' Admission was 3d. with front seats 6d.

Wolverhampton ILP celebrated May Day on a most extensive scale. On Friday 1st May there was a Social Night at the Labour Club addressed by James Whittaker. On Sunday came the Third Trades & Labour demonstration on the Wholesale Market beginning at 3pm. Arranged speakers were Carrie Martyn, Emma Lloyd, E.J. Sale, Whittaker, Sharrocks, Councillor Stevens etc. Literature sellers were asked to report to the Central Club at 1-30pm. In the evening, the Star Theatre had been booked for Caroline Martyn 'Queen of the Earth', and the Clarion Orchestra would 'give selections' between 7-30 and 8 pm. Carrie Martyn was also booked to do a series of meetings the following week – at Princes Square on the 4th, Coseley on the 5th, Chester Street, Whitmore Reans on the 6th. Springfields on the 7th, and Bilston Temperance Hall on the 8th. If the rest of the programme was as successful as the Trades & Labour demonstration, it was a productive week.

In June 1896 there was one of the many national demonstrations for the release of the Walsall Anarchists condemned four years previously. This was a mass meeting at Holborn Town Hall 'for the freeing of political prisoners in England.' Speakers were Hyndman, Tom Mann and Hunter Watts from the SDF, Tillett the LCC councillor, Keir Hardie, Pete Curran of the ILP etc.

A report of a summer event organised by the Birmingham CCC and participated in by Wolverhampton cyclists is worth quoting both for its content and also its typical *Clarion* style:

> A Smoking Concert was recently held at Kinver under difficulties. We had just finished a tough struggle with a tough tea and played football after. Our regular pianist failed to turn up. He hasn't done this for years. Birmingham doesn't have one. Wolverhampton had left theirs behind. But we drank each others health. The Perishing Bounder with the indiarubber face sang 'Perhaps', 'The Widow' and other songs till our ribs ached. On Sunday morning we climbed Kinver Edge – well worth doing. Then through Bewdley, Omberley and home. The McSpatkinsons and Edgbastonia Edwards hunted up Dowlo(sic) Bank and have since been over to Horsehay. ... Next Sunday is inter-midlands run to Burton. And Wolverhampton don't leave that Perhaps Not Perisher behind. (O'Groomie O).

In July 1896 West Bromwich Clarionettes invited Socialists to rally round a newly formed ILP branch which met every Tuesday at the top of Paradise Street, or if wet, at the Coffee House near Bull Street. The officers were F. Comyn of 58 George Street and H. Brocklehurst of Hill Top.

During the same month Wolverhampton booked John Bruce-Glasier to speak by the Park at Bath Road at 3pm and 7-30pm. Clarionettes were invited to roll up and bring their friends.

The Cycling Clubs dominated *Clarion* during the summer. In July Wolverhampton CCC entered a Charity Sports Cycle Parade with fourteen other clubs and a silver shield was offered for the best turn-out:

> We adopted a new Pierrot costume designed by Comrade Mrs Atkinson of Birmingham CCC and our members set to work. We put on a fine show with 28 Wolverhampton men and 8 Birmingham men. Thirty three Perishing Bounders lined up, heads erect and under the command of O'Groomie O. It was a brilliant victory. Fourteen Clubs entered having all kinds of fancy dress, but thirteen had no chance. The Silver Shield now adorns the wall of the ILP Club. (Tom Frost).

Socialism was spreading still further in the Black Country in the summer of 1896. In August Socialists in Wednesbury and Darlaston were invited to attend a public meeting at the Market Place, Wednesbury to form a Socialist organisation. Walsall Socialist Society also announced that at their regular Tuesday meetings 'strangers will be welcome' and also disclosed that open-air meetings were being held every Monday evening at 7-30 at the top of Paul Street. Walsall Socialists would also attend the Wednesbury meeting.

'Wulfruna' also reported from Wolverhampton that 'a spirited series of open-air meetings have been held by the Park over the past three months.' Speakers had included Joe Burgess, Enid Stacy, R.J. Sale and Fred Richards, as well as Bruce-Glasier. For the end of August Mrs Bruce-Glasier had been booked to speak at the Park, or if wet, at the Star Theatre. Leading speakers continued to be booked for West Park. In September it was Will Crook and the next month Tom Mann. Both the West Bromwich ILP and the Walsall Socialist Society continued to flourish, the latter having Tom Mann at a meeting at the Temperance Hall in December.

At the end of the year Tom Mann gave a report of the district:

Some weeks ago I reported upon the healthy signs of life among the ILPers of Wolverhampton and district. Having just spent a week there under the auspices of the Midlands Socialist and Independent Labour Party Federation, I am able to report on the position in the Black Country towns of Wolverhampton, Bilston, West Bromwich, Wednesbury, Walsall and Coseley. In all these places there are earnest and vigorous workers for Socialism. The only exception to an ILP is Walsall, which at present is known as a Socialist Society; but it is probable that the name will be changed to fit with the other branches in the district in a few weeks. At Walsall Wood friends are working up the forces, and in a month or so a branch will be formed there. The newly-formed Branch at Dudley is making a healthy advance.

The question up for serious consideration with the Federation is, which of the parliamentary constituencies would be the best to contest; and as it is probable there will be a by-election in the Bilston or South-West Wolverhampton division ere long, the bulk of opinion favours action in this division. Villiers, the Father of the House, is the present Liberal-Unionist MP and since the redistribution of seats there has never been a contest; and for a borough division it will be a difficult one to fight. It is about six miles in length, and covers much of the most unlovely districts to be found even in the Black Country. But there are some fine fellows in Bilston, the chief town of the place, and Wolverhampton will cheerfully throw in their influence... and with Ed.J. Sale as organiser, I see no reason why this division should not be fought and won. Branches or groups should be formed in the seven or eight small townships in the division. Literature must be systematically circulated, and in fine weather regular out-door meetings should be held. The branches must understand that they must raise, in the locality, at least the returning officer's fee, and themselves be prepared to work up the constituency, and not leave it to be worked up by the candidate... however smart a fellow... he may be.

A word of praise to the excellent secretaries in each of the branches of the towns I have referred to. I never met a better set of clear-headed and respectable fellows with a thorough grasp of essential Socialist principles and correct appreciation of the necessity for solid organisation...

In January 1897 details of the Walsall Socialist Society's annual meeting were given. J.E. Hearnes of Selbourne Street was elected corresponding secretary and Mr Hartley finance secretary. Meetings were still being held every Tuesday at the Victoria Temperance Hotel.

In March a notice from Wolverhampton requested that all unattached Clarionettes should 'assist the local comrades to send a good parcel to the ILP national bazaar.' Contributions of either goods or money would be gratefully accepted by Mrs A . Fellows of 56 Victoria Street. The next month her husband, Alf Fellows reported that W. Dilke had been elected unopposed to the Board of Guardians having been nominated in three wards and agreeing to stand down in two of them.

In June there was more national activity on the Walsall anarchists. Large public meetings were held throughout the country organised by the Walsall Amnesty Fund. These culminated in a London meeting at Victoria Park addressed by Herbert Burrows, H.J.H. Wilson MP, Hunter Watts etc. with Pete Curran in the chair. The secretary of the Amnesty Fund was David Nicolls of 6 Windmill Street, London N. Also in June Wolverhampton ILP booked Tom Mann to speak at West Park on 'The Workers' Jubilee; How to Get it and How to Celebrate it.' The next month Wolverhampton Clarion CC repeated their triumph in the fancy costume cycle parade.

A Wolverhampton West ILP branch was set up at Whitmore Reans in September.

> We received samples of tea from Bradford & District ILP Trading Society which, thanks to Joe Burgess, appears perfectly satisfactory. It has been decided that meetings will be held on premises free from all intoxicating drinks. Will all Socialists who have remained outside the movement through the necessity for such a Society send their names to E. Lloyd (secretary) 377 Newhampton Road West. The locality is distinctly working class and is ripe for the propagation of Socialism.

A September report of Wolverhampton CCC confirmed that they had taken the silver shield at the Cycle Parade for the second year and also that the cyclists 'were to the fore in returning Socialists to the town council.' In addition their Cinderella work was attracting the attention of the local papers. *Bicycling News* reported:

> Wolverhampton Clarion Cycling Club do not confine their efforts to cycle runs among themselves, but endeavour to give enjoyment to others. On Saturday last they arranged to take a party of poor children to Ounsdale, one of the pretty spots not many miles away, gave them tea and afterwards amused them with various games. We understand that the object of the Club is purely charitable and is carried out also in other towns by Clubs which we believe are identified with the Independent Labour Party. It is said that financial assistance is needed to carry on this work.

A national list of Cinderellas at this time in *Clarion* totalled nineteen, including, besides the Wolverhampton one, another at Walsall whose secretary was Ellis Franklin at 73 Brace Street.

In November *Clarion* reported the 'resurrection' of the Walsall Socialist Society to 'unbounded enthusiasm'. A class to study Jevons' Political Economy. This class continued the controversy begun in 1884 between Jevons' subjective theory of value (demand determined at the margin) and Marx' labour theory of value which then, and ever since, has split Socialists into Marxists and Social Democrats.

In December the local SDF brought their leader H.M. Hyndman to the Exchange Hall, Wolverhampton to talk on 'The Crisis in India' and to reply to Sir Henry Fowler (the local MP who had been Secretary of State for India in 1894-95 and had been made a Grand Commander of the Star of India.)

1898 began with a balance sheet of the national Walsall Amnesty Fund for the previous year. Income had been £19 and expenditure nearly £27. They proposed producing a leaflet with a brief statement of the case together with the views of public men who supported the case. Agitation was to be resumed in the spring.

During 1898 there were references to Socialist activity west of the Black Country. For instance, an ILP branch was formed at Tong. In April, at Ironbridge Mrs Bonney topped the poll for the Board of Guardians. At Wellington in May a meeting at Pugh's Temperance Hotel, Walker Street, set up a branch of the Workers' Union.

In the summer a five months lock-out of Welsh miners demanding an end to the Sliding Scale was widely supported by the labour movement in the Black Country. In June, Alf Fellows reported that several meetings of ILP branches had been held and good collections for the miners taken. Three open-air meetings had been held the previous Sunday, at 11am on Snow Hill, at 3pm by the West Park and at 6-30pm the Treeharris Male Choir had entertained the audience. 'The principles of Socialism were driven home to large audiences, quite 3,000 people having attended the three meetings. The collection was £14. Coles, Cook and Harris carried a resolution at the last Trades Council to hold a demonstration to support strike funds.' In July, Wolverhampton ILP arranged a meeting at Oldbury. At Langley there was a good meeting for which 'all local works had been well billed.' The speakers (Cook, Parry and Fellows) were escorted from the Five Ways to the place of meeting by the Langley Green band. 500 *Clarions* were distributed and 'eagerly taken up.' The Tredegar Male Choir gave selections. 'The collection of £6 would have been larger if the weather had been fine.' The Welsh miners were eventually driven back to work, defeated by starvation.

During the summer the Dudley ILP secretary, Will Goodman of 20 Martins Hill, appealed for the services of speakers from Birmingham and district.

The September event in Wolverhampton was the visit of the Clarion Van organised by Tom Groom.

The Van was previously advertised by handbills, press notices and the (unsuccessful) prosecution of

Comrade Ben Sewards of Wednesbury which was a victory for the right of free speech and, given a fine day, all records as to propaganda meetings would have been eclipsed. The comrades marshalled at Blakenhall and marched with the Van down Snow Hill to the centre of the town. Quite 1,000 people gathered round Comrade Fellows when he took the chair, and we found it quite a job to keep the road clear. A better disposed or larger crowd never gathered round Villiers' statue. There was a capital sale of literature, but the collection was spoiled by rain. At 2-45pm the Cheslyn Hay band was brought over to mark appreciation for our collections for the Welsh miners. We heard about Socialism from Comrade Enid Widdrington. The Van marched to West Park. Comrade Cook opened in grand style. Comrade Austin of Smethwick gave a stirring address on the 'Necessity for Socialism' and Enid followed with 'Industrial Crises – their Causes and Cure'. But Jupiter Fluvius interfered again while she was speaking. After a good tea at the Club the band started for Queens Square and the crowd was immense at 1,000. Councillor E. Evans opened followed by Ben Seward. Enid was in grand form. There was a retiring collection for the Miners' Lock-out Fund. This was one of the happiest days for yours truly and of the cause in Wolverhampton...

Incidently, Enid Widdrington was the well-known Enid Stacy.

1899 opened with a struggle for free speech in Oldbury which brought both Black Country and Birmingham comrades into the fray. In January G. Clapshaw wrote:

> I'm sorry to report that the fine imposed on Comrade Skett which he refused to pay, preferring to go to jail for 14 days has been paid by distraint on his goods, a £25 pianoforte has been sold for £5. We shall have some hard fighting here in Oldbury before we get peace, but we shall win ultimately for we can see things working for us by alterations in the tone of the local press and instead of 40 people we can command 400 through the police advertising our cause. The case comes on again on January 3rd. We appeal to all readers to help. For this purpose we are banded together with the Dudley branch.

Later in January, J. Austin was asking for greater support for Clapshaw's appeal for help. The place where the ILP hold their meetings did not interfere with pedestrians or vehicular traffic and this was a deliberate attempt on the part of the police to suppress Socialism. By this time another comrade had also been arrested and decided to do 'time' rather than pay a fine. 'Cannot something be done for their families?' Austin concluded.

Clapshaw then added further details. 'I'm sorry to say that the persecution and prosecution of Socialists goes on. On the 3rd of January Skett was fined £3-15-0d. and Stacey (not Enid Stacy, but a local comrade) £6-7-0d. Stacey had two cases against him of obstruction in the Market Place. Both elected to go to jail rather than pay the fines.' Once again Clapshaw appealed for help, 'Comrade Stacey has a wife and two small children. Let us hope that the day is not far distant when such contemptible tyranny will not be tolerated any longer.' Both men went to jail for 21 days.

But a letter from Austin later in the month aired some of the complexities of the situation at Oldbury. After the visit of the Clarion Van it had been decided to set up an Oldbury branch of fifteen members. Seeing that meetings were held in the Market Place by the Salvation Army and, throughout the summer, by the Evangelical Free Church, it was decided to spread ILP propaganda by the same means. But their speaker, Alf Fellows, was harassed by the police and prosecuted. The summons was eventually withdrawn on the payment of costs. It was then decided to work through branch meetings and indoor lectures until the spring and then, if the branch thought it wise, to fight for free speech. At this point, an unattached comrade from Birmingham, W.H. Skett, came forward and, without the consent of the branch, defied the police. The police took up the challenge and had so far had the best of the matter. Prosecutions were based on a pernicious Highways Act which stated that wherever three people were gathered together they created an obstruction. The only way out was to agitate for the amendment of the Act. George Stacey, another unattached Socialist had assisted Skett. Both were imprisoned. The local ILP, not wishing to appear to be cowards, came forward with an appeal for funds. Several other prosecutions took place, and as things were coming to a crisis, it was thought time that the National Administrative Council was informed of the gravity of the situation. So Austin wrote to Bruce-Glasier who was eventually instructed by the NAC to come to Oldbury to investigate. Glasier spoke at a reception after the release of Skett and a local ILP conference was held of representatives from Dudley, Wolverhampton, West Bromwich and Birmingham. At this conference a resolution was passed supporting the original decision of the Oldbury branch. It was further decided that the Oldbury branch would only continue the contest if this was agreed by the local branches in consultation with the NAC. Austin concluded, 'The meeting was decisive and unanimous. At the same time we felt impossibly treated by the authorities... I think we fought pluckily. We engaged the best local counsel. Our men suffered hardships. Others faced the ignominy of police courts and though defeated we are not disgraced. Funds are still required to pay off our debts. Liabilities are at least £5.'

While Oldbury were engaged with the police, in nearby West Bromwich Cinderella work continued. In March, Frank Spires reported that 100 children had been fed and entertained and they hoped to repeat these gatherings every other Saturday. The Birmingham School Board had allowed the free use of a room and a large tin of cocoa from Mr Cadbury had helped considerably. In the same month West Bromwich ILP advertised in *Clarion* for an organiser. A man of energy and some experience was preferred. 'Business ability required more than eloquence.' Applications, with references, were to be made to Henry Brockhouse, hon. sec. Hill Top, West Bromwich.

The same issue of *Clarion* advertised a meeting of Wolverhampton ILP at Hill's Coffee House, North Street, to discuss the best means of increasing the circulation of *Clarion*. In July books and pamphlets were advertised as being sold by J. Start & Son of 1 Salop Street and 86 Worcester Street. A cryptic note in July announced that friendly rivalry between Wolverhampton and Birmingham Clarion Cycling Clubs:

> Poor old Birmingham. Troubles come not in single spies but in thousands. Wolverhampton want to know their grounds for being called 'the Premier Club.' Wolves throw down the scabbard and take up the tuning fork. We want to know what prizes Birmingham have won and how... As for Wolves, the whole world knows what they have done. We wait Brum's answer with baited breath.

In August there was a report from a Walsall Prisoners' Relief Committee based at the Labour Institute, Norwich, stating that it had been formed to obtain relief for those prisoners due to be released on September 18th.

By September West Bromwich's organiser, who had been appointed on Labour Day, was producing results. A Co-operative shop was being successfully manned and the next step was to get a hall and premises for the ILP

In December a Ruskin Hall Correspondence Class was started in Wolverhampton meeting at the Town Hall Restaurant (Mrs Hills), North Street every Wednesday at 8-30pm. Information could be sought from the secretary Arthur Brown of 147 North Street, or the promoters – Alfred Fellows of 56 Victoria Street and Frank J. Tustin of 46 Ewins Street. Prospective customers were advised 'to come early to avoid the rush.'

1899 had seen the beginning of the Boer War and continuing jingoism into 1900 made for a difficult period for Socialists. Activity seems to have picked up in the second half of the year. West Bromwich ILP changed their secretary in July to S. Grimmett of 7 Raglan Road, Handsworth. In October the ILP secretary J. Penny, was advertised as speaking at the Labour Hall, John Street, Wolverhampton. All Socialists were earnestly invited. Throughout the period Start continued to sell *Clarion* from his shops in Wolverhampton.

Another innovation of *Clarion* was Clarion Fellowships which met, usually in the winter, for social, cultural and political discussion, this often being alternative winter activity for the Clarion Cyclists. A Directory in November gave Fellowships at Birmingham, Coventry and the Black Country. The latter were given as Dudley where H. Mayer of 31 Occupation Street was secretary and West Bromwich where the officials were H. Brockhouse of Armdale, Hill Top and F. Qurton 48 Walter Street. But there was also a Fellowship at Wolverhampton where Nunquam spoke on January 11th. on the theme of 'What is Fellowship?' answering the question by saying that Fellowship was to help Socialists in every way since Socialism is Fellowship.

A Clarion Cycling Club Directory in December gave Clubs in Wolverhampton and West Bromwich.

The Independent Labour Party

The creation of the Independent (i.e. independent of the two main capitalist parties of Liberals and Tories) Labour (i.e. working men and women) Party in 1893 was the most important event before the formation of the Labour Representation Committee in 1900 which changed its name to the Labour Party in 1906 after the general election of that year on the return of 29 Labour MPs. The formation of the ILP was preceded by a campaign from 1890 which saw the formation of the first ILP in Bradford and then eleven other towns (including Birmingham and Stafford) before the formation of the Party nationally.

The newspaper of the ILP was the *Labour Leader*. This appeared briefly in 1891 and then regularly from 1894. Joseph Whittaker was a contributor to the newspaper from 1894 with his poetry as well as reports of the first ILP branch formed in the Black Country at Wolverhampton.

This was the 1892-95 period of mass unemployment. 1894 saw the third annual mass May Day demonstration in Wolverhampton when three bands accompanied the procession from St. James Square to the Open Market where four platforms unanimously passed 'similar resolutions to those at Dudley.'

Dudley's demonstration was organised by the Dudley Trades Council. It formed at Queens Cross and headed by a military band marched through the main thoroughfares to the Market Place. Here A.W. Haddleton presided. The speakers included the Reverends A. Gray and A.M. Garner and Messrs. Gibbs, Russell, H. Piercy, J.G. Tomkins and Councillor Lloyd. Here the following resolution was passed with one dissentient.

> This mass rally of working men believes that the time has come to heal all the divisions among labour organisations and to adopt as their end the reorganisation of society on a collective basis. We believe this end will be hastened by the legal enactment of the 8-hour day, a minimum wage for all trades, the nationalisation of the mines and railways and immediate provision of work for the unemployed by municipal and county authorities. We call on workers to elect on local and national governing bodies men of their own class pledged to obtain these objects.

The urgency of the economic clauses was underlined by such reports in the *Labour Leader* as 'Another Victim of Capitalism done to Death.' This told of Thomas Bagley of Cradley Heath who committed suicide with his own chain. Evidence at the inquest showed that he had worked from 6am to 8pm for six days 'for a pittance of 12/-d. from which he had to pay for iron, firing and carriage which left him with 5/-d. The coroner thought it was a pity they could not summon some of the legislators of the country to be present.' A fortnight later there followed:

> Suicide, or rather Murder, of a poor nailmaker of Rowley Regis makes the third within a few days. He found he could make only 7/-d. a week working early to late.

In July, 'the people of Birmingham are astounded at the suicides which are now of daily occurrence... The majority arise from lack of employment.'

An anonymous report of June 1894 from Wolverhampton stated that there was little sign of an ILP candidate to oppose Sir Alfred Hickman the Conservative MP. 'The Liberals there appear to have neither the money nor the organisation. What price an ILPer? There is a fairly strong branch of the ILP in the town but it lacks pugnacity and is too apt to leave everything to a few officials. With the Fabian Society, the ILP is holding four weekly open-air meetings in different parts of the town. An ILP Club is in the process of formation. Better work would be obtained by the division of members into groups or wards for the purpose of propaganda and house to house canvass with ILP literature. This would soon double membership.'

Another report stated that 'Walsall, Dudley, and other black country towns are slowly unfolding their ILP wings and it is quite time for a Midland Federation.' In October 1894 the 1st Conference of Midlands ILPs took place, but Wolverhampton was the only Black Country branch represented.

In February 1895 T.E. of Dudley received a reply from the Answer to Correspondents column of the *Labour Leader* which read:

> No my friend, I did not keep cool. Your warmth and enthusiasm would melt an icicle. I hope one day to have the honour of shaking your hand. I will seriously consider your suggestion about the sheet, but the cost would be much greater than you imagine.

In June there was an excellent summary of the Walsall Anarchists' case by Edward Carpenter. By October Smethwick ILP was functioning under secretary J. Austin and was almost immediately embroiled in a free speech controversy similar to that at Oldbury in 1899, but with happier results.

Both E.J. Sale and W.H. Skett were harassed by the police and summonsed at Smethwick police court. 'Sale made a rattling good speech and the magistrate dismissed the case saying he did not wish to interfere with free speech. A deputation waited on the chief constable, Mr Farndale. It was politely received and every consideration shown. Farndale said we would not be harassed any more, and so far he has kept his word.'

Early in 1896 Birmingham socialists were regretting a suicide from another cause. Herman Severing, an exile from Germany, was persecuted in England for his lack of understanding of English. The Birmingham comrades had 'decided to keep his body from bumbledon' and provide a decent burial. 'About fifty comrades followed him to the grave and there were several wreaths, including one from Smethwick Socialists.'

At the 1896 ILP annual Easter Conference the only local branches qualifying for representation were Birmingham, Bordesley (25 members), Birmingham Central (25 members), Wolverhampton East (26 members) and Wolverhampton West (26 members). Such membership figures may be less than accurate as numbers carried financial obligations and for this reason membership was sometimes understated. But the figures do suggest that Wolverhampton branch of the ILP was not only the strongest in the Black Country but was proportionately considerably stronger than Birmingham, which, of course, was a much larger city. At the 1896 ILP Conference both Birmingham branches were represented and both Wolverhampton branches, the South by J. Whittaker and the West branch by W. Cliffe. The ILP was growing rapidly at this time. At the 1897 Conference Wellington was represented with 29 members, West Bromwich (26 members) by Harry Brockhouse and Wolverhampton South (67 members) by Evan Evans and Alfred Fellows. The official report of the 1897 Conference listed all representatives on local bodies. For the Black Country and Shropshire area these included W. Dilke on the Wolverhampton Board of Guardians, J. Beard and D. Butrey parish councillors at Oakengates and James Stevenson and Evan Evans as Wolverhampton town councillors. At the 1898 Conference where Harry Brockhouse represented 26 members in West Bromwich and Alfred Fellows and Charles Smith represented 82 members in Wolverhampton, the previous list of local ILPers on public bodies was extended to include Harry Brockhouse on the West Bromwich School Board, B. Maddox on the Ironbridge town council and a third town councillor in Wolverhampton, Harry Gibson.

After this, ILP membership tended to decline. At the National Conference of 1899 ninety seven delegates represented 87 branches and 5,277 paid-up members. At this Conference a new Black Country Branch of Dudley, Oldbury & Lye with 43 members was represented by J. Austin. Harry Brockhouse represented West Bromwich with 30 members and William Morris only 33 members in Wolverhampton, although representation on Wolverhampton town council had risen to five with the addition of George Cook and T. Wilson. Wilson stood as an Independent Labour candidate in Dunstall ward because 'although he was an ILPer and an avowed Socialist, he was a government servant and could not stand for a political party.' At the 1900 ILP Conference only 75 delegates representing 74 branches attended, and there was only one delegate from the Black Country, Harry Brockhouse of West Bromwich.

From 1897 when the ILP was growing a journal giving much internal information the *ILP News* was started. Black Country branches at the beginning of 1898 were given as Bilston, Darlaston, Dudley, Smethwick, Stourbridge, West Bromwich and Wolverhampton East & West. Other information during 1898 indicated that West Bromwich branch had made 29/6d. from sales of tea in six months and was, for the first time, solvent. East Wolverhampton, we are told, 'sets an example to other branches by its missionary zeal.' The next month, October, 'propaganda of Wolverhampton comrades in neighbouring towns has resulted in the setting up of a branch at Oldbury.' In November, 'movement in N. Worcestershire is rapidly developing resulting in branches at Stourbridge, Lye and Cradley Heath as well as Oldbury.' This was largely the work of Oliver Jenkins, the Wolverhampton comrade late of Treeharris, who had rendered 'yeoman service.'

In December, local election results at Wolverhampton were highlighted. 'To have placed Comrade Wilson top of the poll against the forces of Toryism, Liberalism and bogus Labour is indeed something to be proud of.'

In January 1899 *ILP News* tells us that West Bromwich ILP had taken a room seating 100 people in a central part of the constituency and Sunday meetings were being arranged on the lines of the Labour Church.

Some idea of the relative strengths of the Black Country branches may be gauged by the following figures of membership and fees paid to the ILP NAC at the beginning of 1899.

Branch	Members	Amount Paid
Cradley Heath	6	Nothing
Dudley	20	Nothing
Oldbury	6	Nothing
Stourbridge	6	Nothing
Wednesbury	15	Nothing
West Bromwich	30	Paid
Wolverhampton East	60	5/-d
Wolverhampton West	12	1/-d

Nationally, 12,322 members had paid up £374.

In March Wolverhampton ILP was reported as having embarked on the milk trade and Councillor George Cook had been appointed manager.

In November 1899 Wolverhampton ILP councillors moved an unsuccessfull motion to change the times of council meetings from 3pm (which suited Liberal and Tory councillors) to 6pm (better suited to Labour councillors who had livings to earn, and also the general public). It was lost by 27 votes to 13.

For 1900 there were the following reports of branch activities. In August Dudley was 'sturdily continuing Sunday meetings on the Market Place. Tom Evans never fails to be at his post either as chairman or lecturer and sometimes both.' In September at West Bromwich they were arranging to give Cinderellas a half day in the country and Harry Brockhouse was to re-run as a candidate for the School Board. The next month a decision was made to build a Socialist Hall. Oliver Jenkins, now of Stourbridge, was as hard at work as ever; the local branch of the Amalgamated Society of Railway Servants, of which Jenkins had become secretary in January, had grown from 80 to 150, 'and still he finds time for ILP work.' In Wolverhampton in October the ILP secretary was changed to H. Tilson at the Central Labour Club, 33 St. John's Street. In December we have the first mention of a Walsall ILP branch when, 'as a result of a visit of the general secretary, a branch of 12 was formed.'

Returning to the *Labour Leader* for 1898, in September, Dilkes, the ILP Poor Law Guardian moved a successful resolution that members of Friendly Societies forced to seek Assistance should not lose the vote. But for this measure to be effective there would be need to change the law, for conditions of relief were written into the national code.

Another example of harassment occurred at Dudley in July 1899:

Comrade Porter of Wolverhampton spoke for the Dudley branch on some waste land where several meetings have been held lately with the permission of the owner, Mrs Matthews. A District Councillor asked the speaker what he would do with £5,000. The crowd, naturally anxious to see the councillor who asked such a silly question surged forward and several stepped on to the footpath with the result that a policeman accused them of wilful obstruction and asked for the speaker's name. But local comrades think the case will go no further.

Dudley branch was very active in this first year of the Boer War. In August Alf Fellows from Wolverhampton 'held forth to a large and appreciative audience on foreign policy and strongly criticised the Transvaal connection.' A fortnight later Comrade Micklewright of Wednesbury had presided over a Dudley meeting where the main speaker was Bruce-Glasier on 'Old Age Pensions.' The meeting passed a resolution against going to war with the Boers. At the end of September Joe Grady stopped over at Dudley on his way to Leicester and lectured on the Transvaal Question. 'He made a good impression by pointing out that war at present was quite unnecessary.'

Such was the state of Socialism in the Black Country in 1900. To be faced was the jingoism and hostility of the Boer War before the next upswing of the movement brought the Labour Party into existence. But before passing to the new century we must look at the early attempts to seek representation in Parliament of working men whose undivided loyalty was to working people freed from all allegiance to either Liberals or Tories.

Independent Parliamentary Representation

From 1884 the new, Socialist political parties came into existence to create a new society organised and controlled by working people. The first step towards this was to elect working men both to local institutions and also to Parliament. In the Black Country they entered a scene where the domination of Gladstonian Liberalism was virtually complete. Gladstone was a hero to working men. The philosophy of trade unions and trades councils was that of Liberal Free Trade. Liberal MPs sat for every Black Country constituency. In 1874 a Tory government had been returned to power. It received much of the opprobrium for the Depression and Disraeli's imperialism saw the horrors of the Bulgarian massacres castigated by Gladstone which brought considerable support to the radical cause nationally including that of William Morris. Gladstone returned in triumph in 1880. In 1884 the Liberals extended the franchise and the next year with Black Country representation raised from five seats to eight the Liberals were returned to power with the Irish nationalists and radical hopes were pinned on Joseph Chamberlain and Sir Charles Dilke.

But the political landscape was changing. The 1885 election broke the Liberal monopoly and three Conservatives were returned to parliament in the Black Country. Alfred Hickman, the Bilston ironmaster had been returned in Wolverhampton, in Wednesbury Wilson Lloyd had defeated the Hon. Philip Stanhope and the new Staffordshire Kingswinford seat had returned a Tory. The loss of a Wolverhampton seat was particularly serious. Hickman was the leading Black Country ironmaster of the day and while Tory ironmasters could be found in the past, this was a portent that the Tory Party was to be the future natural party of the big bourgeoisie and not the Liberal Party. Wolverhampton West was the home of the middle class and also large numbers of more affluent workers ranging from sub-contract master workmen to the rapidly increasing skilled engineer. All of these in the past would have been natural Liberal material. The Great Depression had also begun to undermine the bedrock of Liberalism, Free Trade. On the one hand free trade was just beginning to bring the cheap food which was, for the first time since the end of the Napoleonic Wars, to lower the cost of living. On the other hand Free Trade was allowing entry of the manufactures of Germany, Belgium, the USA etc. whose domestic markets we had lost and who were making inroads into our other foreign markets. Finally there was the question of Imperialism. For all those who deplored Disraeli's swashbuckling foreign ventures which put peace at risk, there were others whose nationalism was stirred. And in 1885 Gordon and his followers were massacred at Khartoum.

But worse was to come. The next year, 1886, Joseph Chamberlain changed the face of British politics for ever by deserting Gladstone over the issue of Irish Home Rule, forming the Liberal Unionists and taking his vast national and local following virtually intact with him into the Tory Party.

The working class was now split five ways – between Gladstonian and Unionist Liberals, a small but ever-present Tory element and the small but rising Socialists.

The 1886 election brought further Liberal set backs. The Tories again took three seats; Hill held Kingswinford, Brooke Robinson ousted Sheridan in Dudley, and J.E. Spencer won West Bromwich. However, Plowden, a Gladstonian Liberal, won back Wolverhampton West and Stanhope won Wednesbury. Sir Charles Forster, another Gladstonian Liberal held Walsall. Fowler, a government minister, but a reluctant Gladstonian Liberal, held Wolverhampton East, but Villiers in Wolverhampton South held his seat as a Liberal Unionist.

With four elections in between, the 1900 position, by which time the Unionists were almost fully integrated into the Conservative Party, was: Liberals in Walsall, W'ton East and W'ton South only. Conservatives in Wednesbury, West Bromwich, Kingswinford, Worcestershire North (Liberal Unionist), Dudley and Wolverhampton West.

Such a loss of Liberal hegemony locally made the question of independent labour representation an urgent matter.

The first attempt to get a working man into Parliament had been in 1872 when John Kane, the ironworkers' union leader, was proposed for Wednesbury, but this was not considered practical at the time. The next attempt was not made until 1891 when the withdrawal of the Liberal candidate left a vacancy in Dudley and Richard Juggins was proposed as a Labour candidate. This was only just agreed by his own Midland Counties Trades Federation and vehemently opposed as 'interference' by the local Liberals, so this project was also dropped.

With the establishment of the Independent Labour Party in 1893 efforts were intensified, but we have seen the resistance at Dudley Trades Council from the Liberal leadership to the proposal of the Wolverhampton ILP of a candidate there. The next opportunity came in 1897 with the death of Villiers. But even the radical Bilston ILP voted for the local Liberal, G.R. Thorne instead of a Labour candidate. Both the organisation and finance for successful Parliamentary candidates had to await the formation of the Labour Representation Committee in 1900.

Bibliography: The Re-birth of Socialism 1884-1900

This chapter has been written almost entirely from the newspapers of the emerging Socialists groups and parties. These are to be found in the British Newspaper Library, Colindale, London: *Justice* for the Social Democratic Federation; *Commonweal* for the Socialist League; *Fabian News* for the Fabian Society; *Clarion* for the various Clarion organisations, Clubs, Scouts, Cyclists, Choirs etc. and also for the Independent Labour Party; *Labour Leader* and ILP News for the Independent Labour Party.

The centenary of the so-called Walsall Anarchist Bomb Plot was celebrated in Walsall in 1992 and included an exhibition at the Art Gallery. For this occasion most of the material relevant to the Plot was collected including a complete copy of the main Home Office file dealing with the Plot and its aftermath File ASS16/27/9. Much of the File ASS16/279 XPO712 was withheld under the Fifty Year Rule and only released in 1986 which kept alive the belief that the Plot was manufactured by the agent-provocateur Auguste Coulon with the connivance of Inspector Melville of the CID and the Home Office. This file has now been examined by myself and others and confirms that this is the most likely explanation. But the contents of the file show nothing that would have justified its retention when the other files were opened. This material is now in the Walsall Local History Centre.

For parliamentary representation the best guide is Eric Taylor's thesis *The Working Class Movement in the Black Country 1863-1914*.

Chapter 5

Trade Unionism 1874-1900

The onset of the Great Depression at the end of 1874 led employers to search for the usual scapegoats for their problems. These crises arise periodically from the internal workings of the capitalist system, and will presumably continue to exist until a satisfactory alternative to the system is found. The scapegoats identified were, of course, high wages, short hours and government interference with such measures as factory acts, limitation on child and juvenile labour, extravagent education, and the actions of trade unions. As in all crises trade union effectiveness sharply declined and with it membership. The effects of the Depression on various sections of workers are detailed below.

The miners

The conditions of the miners at this time have been traced in my book *Social Conditions in the Black Country* and the intricacies of trade union organisation have been skillfully teased out by Eric Taylor, so that only a summary is necessary here.

Coal output reached a maximum of about 11 million tons in 1873 when it was about $8\frac{1}{2}$ per cent of total UK production. It thereafter fell to about 10 million tons a year at the end of the century, but it was by then little more than 4 per cent of UK production. Production figures, however, conceal the changes that were taking place in the coalfield. The old areas of mining which included Bilston, Darlaston and Wednesbury were contracting due to the flooding of the mines whereas the area bounded by Old Hill, Rowley Regis, Cradley and Halesowen was expanding. There was also an independent area of growth around Pelsall, north of the Bentley Fault, which was really an outcrop of the new, thriving Cannock coalfield. Pelsall miners, therefore tended to want to associate themselves with Cannock where wages were higher. These changes can be traced in general population trends. All Black Country towns grew at phenomenal rates up to 1861, But from 1871 growth dropped below the national average and Bilston was the first town to show a loss of 1 per cent population at that time. Thereafter Bilston lost 6 per cent of its population in the following decade and Wednesbury and Dudley 2 per cent each. Strong growth was not again recorded until 1901 by which time the economy of the area had fundamentally changed.

The watering of the mines and the fall in coal production in the declining areas meant that miners in those areas were less able to initiate and sustain militant action to protect their wages, and this affected the miners who were better placed, leading to fundamental differences with regard to strategies and tactics.

Wages had reached the unprecedented height of 5/6d. per day in 1873 and remained at that level until March 1874. By this time coal prices had begun to fall and the coalmasters demanded a wage drop of 1/-d. a day. The miners refused to accept this and a great sixteen week lock-out ensued. The men were at first confident of victory. But the coalmasters refused to negotiate with the trade union leaders objecting to them as 'paid agents' and demanding to deal only with working miners. This despite the fact that the trade unions had to negotiate with the 'paid agent' of the Earl of Dudley, Fisher Smith, who was the leading spirit behind the employers' intransigence. When the employers did meet a deputation of the men at Dudley, 'They were received with ironical cheers, slow stamping of their feet and cries of "No discussion". A resolution was passed to adhere to the 1/-d. reduction. The report in the Labour Press & Miners' Examiner went on:

> They (the employers) imagine they can crush the unions out of existence. Other district employers were more reasonable The settlement in N. Staffs was a 10 per cent reduction (not 20 per cent). South Wales, Wigan etc. will leave the Amalgamated Association of Miners and its elder brother the National Miners' Association free to concentrate on South Staffs and teach Fisher Smith and the smaller fry who swim in the same pool that refusing to negotiate with a sneer on their lips, insulting the deputation of workmen and entering into a contest which threatens to blast industries... will bring no small degree of punishment on themselves.

But the price of coal continued to drop, the strike was bound to fail, and the men went back to work when starvation loomed.

The price of furnace coal fell almost continuously from its peak of 19/d. per ton in 1873 to 5/6d. in March 1889.

The miners' strike had ended with a Sliding Scale agreement signed by E. Fisher Smith for the coalowners and Thomas Halliday, the leader of the Amalgamated Miners' Association. This was the first time that Black Country coalowners had signed a document with a national trade union. The Sliding Scale was a disaster for the men. Wages moved all the way down from 5/6d. in 1874 to 2/4d. in January 1882. The original Sliding Scale had a minimum of 3/6d. a day. The employers took out the minimum in 1877 and wages averaged just over 3/-d. from 1877 to 1881. The miners then negotiated a change from 3d. to 4d. up or down on the price of coal. But wages dropped to 2/4d. from January 1881 and were not raised until 1882 when they were 3/8d. It must be stressed that 2/4d. for a miner with a family was a starvation wage even if a week of six days was worked. But few miners would get this and three and two day weeks were common throughout the Great Depression. It was not until September 1889 that wages touched 4/-d.

In 1883 when a temporary lull in the Depression had raised wages to 3/8d. a joint board of equal numbers of employers and men was formed to regulate wages by Conciliation rather than by Sliding Scale. The board failed to agree a 4d. cut and so an umpire Joseph Rowlands, was chosen. He awarded the 4d. cut. The men refused to accept the award and they were locked-out for another 16 weeks. Again the men had miscalculated. The Depression was entering its second horrendous dip and again they were starved into submission. From 1884 to 1888 the owners refused to meet the men and wages remained at 3/4d. until 1889 when they rose to 3/8d. By April 1890 they were 4/8d. The Great Depression had ended for the miners. From 1900 to 1914 wages averaged about 5/-d. a day.

Black Country miners pondered deeply over these experiences. The Sliding Scale had been a one way ticket to wage reductions. Would they have been any more successful without the Sliding Scale? The main bone of contention was the point from which the scale was calculated. If one took the peak price of furnace coal selling at 19/-d. and wages at 5/6d. the owners' claim for 1/-d. off the pay when the price of coal had fallen to 16/-d. might seem fairly equitable with coal falling 16 per cent and wages falling 18 per cent. But the Great Boom had been entirely exceptional. In that period coal prices had risen 85 per cent but wages had only risen 10 per cent. Much nearer the norm was the 1871 situation of coal at 10/3d and wages at 5/-. Outraged miners were now being expected to accept 4/6d. when coal was 16/-d. whereas when coal had been 10/3d. wages had been 5/-d. It was this built-in injustice in the Scale which cushioned the owners' profits and took wages back to the starvation levels of the 1840s. In the area of flooded mines there was little point in objecting, but other miners had the clout to resist and could have maintained wages, particularly as coal production was actually increasing in some places. In addition, there were always small masters willing to pay higher wages and chafing at the insistence of the large owners led by the Earl of Dudley's representative to enter into prolonged and devastating conflict with the miners. As will be seen, this is the final example of the hegemony of the Earls of Dudley, controlling not only the price of coal and iron but also the level of wages in both these industries. This had always made a mockery of the idea that the Black Country was an area where supply and demand determined prices. It was also part of the larger pattern of social control by employers which I have elsewhere characterised as the Dictatorship of the Bourgeoisie in the Black Country.

The owners attacked miners at every other point. The 8-hour day was their next target after wages. This was the jewel in the crown of the miners who had organised and fought for over one hundred years for safety in the pit, a living wage and reasonable hours of work. They were in no mood to surrender. In 1875 the masters offered either a drop in wages from 4/-d. to 3/6d. or no reduction in return for a 9-hour day. The men preferred to accept the wage drop. The next year the owners again tried to trade wages for hours and failed. The most determined attack came in 1877 when E. Fisher Smith for the owners threatened to end the Sliding Scale and discuss wages on the basis of a 9-hour day. Through all these attempts miners attended crowded meetings and voted overwhelmingly to maintain the 8-hour day. These meetings were highly charged emotionally with miners making such statements as that 'they would rather eat grass' than give up the 8 hours.

The owners next tried to end the beer allowance, and more importantly. concessionary coal. The instrument of the owners for this attack, as for the attack on the 8-hour day, was the Mine Agents' Association. This had been formed in 1867 to combat the Mines Inspector of the time, James Baker, who had tightened up considerably rules under the Mines Inspection Act of 1861 in ways which had not been to the liking of the Agents. It was various associations such as the Mine Agents who took a leading role in the efforts to coerce the miners as the power of the Earls of Dudley declined.

In 1875 Alexander Smith, the mine agents' secretary, read a paper on the subject of concessionary coal. He showed how in 1818 coal owners had attempted to end 'the privilege that allowed wagemen colliers of carrying coal for the supply of their own houses.' on the grounds that it had been 'shamefully abused.' The existing custom was an allowance of one ton of coal for every 24 full turns worked and for single men 48 turns. E. Fisher Smith had a plan to give 10/-d. extra to every man who agreed to accept the money in lieu of coal. Smith claimed that there was no established right for injured miners to receive coal. The present system was also much abused, Smith claimed, with the coal being sold for drink. His parting shot was that concessionary coal was a species of truck and was therefore illegal! The Mine Agents passed a resolution to 'abolish this custom with just and adequate compensation.' This proposition was passed at a time when wage negotiations were in progress. Again crowded meetings of miners defended their coal allowance, knowing only too well that the 10/-d. would soon be absorbed into the normal wage structure.

Beer was always a matter for complaint with regard to quality. But it cost the owners very little and was never strong enough to raise the question of drunkenness. It was attacked in Fisher Smith's 1877 package to end the 8-hour day which also included the ending of all perquisites including coal and beer.

None of these attacks was successful and the owners appear to have desisted collectively only in 1888 when an agreement to set up a Wages Board contained a clause 'that all perquisites to miners be continued as heretofore.'

The other great issue between miners and owners was Employers' Liability. In 1876 mass meetings of miners demanded that 'All persons injured in their employment should be compensated by their employers unless there is negligence on the part of the man.' In 1880 an Employers' Liability bill was passed. This was vehemently opposed by the owners and a deputation led by Fisher Smith went to the House of Commons to protest at the principle of employers' liability and to claim that the existing voluntary arrangements within the coalfield should be extended. When the Act became operative in 1881 the employers found a way of avoiding it by sacking all their employees and re-employing them only on condition that they 'contract out' of the Act by agreeing to pay 3d. a week to a fund which the employer would augment by 25 per cent This 'contracting out' was pronounced legal by a judgement of 1882 Griffiths v the Earl of Dudley. The abuses of the 'voluntary' system had always been matters of grave concern and it was the pressure of the trade union movement, and particularly the miners, which had led to the acceptance of the principle of employer liability. Miners never knew where the money which was 'voluntarily' deducted from their pay went; different pits paid different (but always inadequate) amounts to miners who were injured or the dependents of those who died. Obviously more campaigning would be necessary. It was not until the end of the century that an effective bill conceding the principle of Employers' Liability was passed.

The evolution of miners' attitudes to the Great Depression now claim our attention. Unfortunately, the key working class source, *The Miner,* from which events since 1874 have been traced ceased publication in 1878 and there is a gap of six years before another such source, the *Labour Tribune* appears. For these years we are therefore dependent on the hostile local capitalist press. This source has been skillfully used by Eric Taylor, but conclusions drawn from these sources alone can only be provisional.

The leading union of the 1874 strike had been the Amalgamated Association of Miners. When its leader Thomas Halliday signed the agreement negotiated with Joseph Chamberlain ending the strike and instituting a sliding scale there was not unanimous satisfaction. Opposition seems to have come from associations such as Dudley and Tipton, which happened to be in the National Association of Miners, although the policies of the two unions were not opposed. Acceptance of a sliding scale was not simply an economic matter. It marked a continuation of the political attitudes nurtured during the Workshop of the World period 1850-75, the most important of which was that the interests of masters and men were identical. It is the last purely Liberal phase of trade union development before passing into Lib-Labism and then socialism. Such a philosophy brought social acceptance, support for miners activities by local dignitaries and clergy, prayers at trade union rallies etc. The sliding scale also made trade unions virtually redundant because wages were determined by 'supply and demand.'

Miners's trade unionism held up better in the Black Country than elsewhere, as the struggle to retain the 8-hour day etc. has demonstrated. By 1875, however, the Amalgamated Association of Miners had exhausted its funds in the 1874 strikes and was absorbed into the National Miners' Union. With this a new point of conflict arose. The AAM had required compulsory levies from their members to support other districts on strike; the NMA had a policy of voluntary levies which left a suspicion among Black Country miners that if a local strike occurred they might not be supported by their fellows. As a result, only West Bromwich and Darlaston districts affiliated to the merged union. In 1878 Staffordshire miners challenged the voluntary principle at a miners' conference but were defeated. As a result West Bromwich seceded from the NAM and Darlaston was suspended. Another point of difference with the NAM was that there was a growing trend to adopt a policy of 'play' periods to limit coal output and thus overcome the 'over production' which, by this time was being seen, as a principal cause of the Depression. Such a policy had less application to the east of Dudley where pits were flooding and closing down. Levi Brittain made the clearest statement of union policy at a Sedgley meeting in May 1878. He said that the policy then being adopted in the areas where pits were flooding of emigration of miners was not the answer to the problem. He also admitted that the movement of Black Country miners elsewhere had sometimes been as strike breakers. Better trade union organisation was necessary and also a law prohibiting people who had not been miners before their eighteenth birthday from entering the pits. The main evil was that too much work was done in eight hours.

The removal of the Black Country associations from the NAM had national consequences. The Amalgamated Association of Miners was resurrected at a Darlaston meeting (Rev J. Richardson in the chair). Thomas Halliday (at this time a commercial traveller) said he would accept presidency of the union. Charles Gething of Walsall became the vice-president and the secretary and treasurer were Lancashire men.

In this fragile situation a S. Staffs and E. Worcs Miners' Council was set up in the autumn of 1879 with Charles Gething the first president.

With coal prices temporarily rising again in 1880 the Miners' Council demanded a wage increase. They also debated the continuance of the sliding scale. The vote was 17-17 and only the casting vote of the chairman saved the sliding scale. However, three weeks later there was a 38-10 vote for ending the Birmingham Agreement the most substantial part of which was the sliding scale. Darlaston opposed the decision and Old Hill condemned them for doing so.

National union policy was by this time ambivalent about the sliding scale. Both McDonald and

Halliday had been converted to restriction of output, but in October 1881 the NAM voted unanimously to keep the sliding scale.

In March 1881 a Midland Miners' Federation was formed joining S. Staffs with Shropshire, Cannock and N. Staffs. The first chairman and secretary were Henry Rust and Henry Barnes, both of West Bromwich and both sliding scale supporters.

From the middle of 1881 deep depression descended again and by January 1882 wages were at their lowest point ever of 2/4d. a day. Old Hill miners struck against the 2/4d. and also opposed the sliding scale opting for restriction of output.

By the summer of 1882 coal prices were rising again and Old Hill demanded a 15 per cent increase. The Midland Federation negotiated only 10 per cent and Old Hill left the Fed.

During this period, basic changes were again taking place in the coalfield. The dissolution of the Dudley Association and the retirement of Eli Brittain were the result of a rapid decline of mining in Dudley and Brierley Hill as the flooding spread. There was a further shift in production from the old areas east of Dudley to a rectangle bounded by Old Hill, Rowley Regis, Cradley Heath and Blackheath. The mantle of Dudley Association was taken over by West Bromwich whose influence thus moved across the ridge to as far as Netherton.

Differences concerning the sliding scale increased in December 1882 when the National Association of Miners abandoned this policy and supported restriction of output. The policy was endorsed at a Walsall conference of the Midland Miners' Federation. although West Bromwich and Darlaston were still firmly committed to sliding scale. Their dilemma was resolved in May 1883 however, when the owners gave three months notice to end the sliding scale in pursuance of a drop in wages. It was replaced by a joint board of equal numbers of masters and men. The board met and could not agree, so an umpire, Joseph Rowlands, was appointed who granted the drop the employers were seeking from 3/8d. to 3/4d. The miners refused to accept this and the ensuing strike lasted for sixteen weeks. Again the men were defeated. After that the employers refused to meet the men at all between 1884 and 1888. In October 1888, however, a joint board was again set up and wages continued to be determined by a sliding scale.

The middle '80s saw important changes in coal politics. The 1884 strike undermined still further the dominance of the large coal and iron owners. This had rested on the dominance of the Earl of Dudley, but also on the fact that the large owners mined their coal for their own furnaces. Now, with flooded mines, and steel replacing iron, more coal was mined by small masters or found its way out of the area for house coal or other purposes. Consequently, when the 1884 strike began 4,000 miners out of about 16,000 remained at work but by August 10,000 were working at the old wage. The big owners had their way in the end, but it was a pyrrhic victory; their power was crumbling.

With the West Bromwich association extending its influence to virtually all the declining areas of production, their leaders toyed with the idea of persuading the coal owners to accept the 'alliance philosophy' then being successfully used by W.J. Davis in the Birmingham small trades and Richard Juggins in the Black Country crafts. This involved agreement on prices by both masters and men and the coercion of recalcitrant employers by all men belonging to a trade union and unions refusing to allow men to work at firms not operating the list. This was rejected by the coal owners, and it is indeed difficult to see such a strategy working in what was still the large-scale coal trade. Thus the West Bromwich leaders were left supporting the sliding scale when the Old Hill miners, the Midland Fed and the national union were all opposed to it. The West Bromwich association was further weakened by the development of mining in the Walsall-Pelsall area where miners associated themselves with their fellows in the rapidly growing Cannock coalfield. Benjamin Dean of Walsall, an opponent of the sliding scale, became secretary of a reorganised Midland Federation in 1886 and agent of the Pelsall Miners Federation when it was formed the following year.

The continuation of the Great Depression into the end of its second decade brought a growing realisation of the need for unified trade union action. In 1889 a Birmingham conference of miners drew up a constitution for the Miners' Federation of Great Britain. A key issue for the MFGB was the 8-hour day movement and its split between those miners who wanted it through legal enforcement and those who wanted to gain it by trade union action. The status of the 8-hour day in the Black

Country during these years is not entirely clear. In the 1880s the local papers were reporting 'men taking work at 9 hours'. In 1891 J.B. Cochrane, who was chairman of the Coalmasters' Association, told the Royal Commission on Labour that 'the effects of an 8-hour day would be disastrous', as if the longer day was universal. On the other hand, Thomas Mansell's document *Miners' Wages and Prices of Coal for the Last 45 Years* which shows hours as well as prices from 1864 gives no indication that the owners were able to negotiate a trade off of hours for money between 1872 when the 8-hour day began and 1909. It must be held, therefore, that the 8-hour day continued, at least officially.

Other parts of national policy did affect Black Country miners more directly. Sliding scales were being decisively rejected. At first their continuation was justified on the grounds that the Depression was caused by overproduction and the remedy, therefore, was to limit output by periods of 'play'. This did not necessarily undermine the traditional Liberal philosophy of identity of interests between masters and men. After all, it could be argued that strikes to limit output were in the masters' own interests, if only they would see it! However, the doctrine of the living wage, which was now being preached by union militants was totally subversive of harmony and presumed continuous conflict. At its extreme this trend developed into Syndicalism. But ultimately more important was that the Great Depression had resulted in the re-emergence of Socialism presaging the ultimate solution for the problems of the miners with nationalisation of the industry.

These national trends in the later '80s, with variations for local conditions developed further in the 1890s. The first local reaction to the formation of the Miners' Federation of Great Britain, was for West Bromwich to leave the Midland Fed and thus isolate itself from national organisation. One reason for this was that the national Federation was not only advocating a living wage, but formulating a national wage demand to supersede local bargaining. This further complicated the Black Country situation where the sliding scale continued under the S. Staffs Wages Board. While coal prices held up, local wages kept in step with MFGB demands, but in 1892 when prices were falling the MFGB resolved to 'play the pits' for a week in March. But the local wages board had not demanded wage reductions and the Old Hill miners faced a dilemma. Firstly they hated the sliding scale but were in the humiliating position of having their wages effectively determined by it by virtue of the fact that they worked for the same employers as those operating the sliding scale. Secondly, since they did not face a wage cut, they were placed in a position that national organisation is sometimes likely to bring, of striking for a demand that had little application locally. In this case, the Old Hill men stayed at work. Subsequently efforts were made to involve the S. Staffs Wages Board in 'stop days' to limit output, but the employers refused to co-operate.

The Old Hill dilemma was repeated in 1883 when the MFGB resolved to resist wage cuts and specifically voted that men in areas where wages were not being cut should come out in strike of their fellows. Again, the local wages board did not cut wages and one can hardly resist the thought that this was not entirely without some intention of embarrassing the MFGB. Again, the lock-out was long and bitter. Meanwhile the wages board miners and masters benefitted by the diversion of trade from the locked-out pits. Pelsall also suffered the Old Hill dilemma. At first they came out. Then they returned. Their disloyalty to the union was mitigated by a subsequent MFGB decision that men unaffected by wage cuts could work, but in return would pay a levy to support those still out. In spite of this the masters stubbornly refused to compromise. The dispute was only ended by an intervention by the prime minister and a conference of masters and the MFGB chaired by Lord Rosebery. This decided that wages should be determined periodically by a Board of Conciliation.

Resistance to the drop in wages had increased the prestige of the MFGB and the decisions of the S. Staffs Wages Board were increasingly in line with the national scale negotiated by the MFGB. This was because anything less would lead to defections to the MFGB; on the other hand there was no need to pay more because the wages board men had insufficient industrial strength to enforce it.

The differences between Black Country miners were considerably reduced in 1899 when Thomas Mansell, a new leader, took West Bromwich miners back into the MFGB and the Sliding Scale was finally laid to rest by wages being determined by the National Conciliation Board.

After the great confrontation of 1893 the Great Depression slowly ended. The sharp fluctuations of wages temporarily ceased and wages averaged about 4/8d. per day until the end of the century.

Ironworkers

The Great Depression devastated the iron industry as it did mining. The Black Country's speciality was wrought iron, the art of making which had been brought to near perfection. It came to be widely believed that wrought iron could not be replaced. This was a delusion. The area's output of pig-iron had peaked in 1856 at 777,000 tons representing 22 per cent of production in Great Britain. It progressively declined to 532,000 in 1868. The boom of the early 1870s brought production up to 726,000 tons but by then this represented only 10 per cent of national production. The years of the Depression brought falling, but fluctuating, production with its nadir in the years 1886-87 at under 300,000. By the end of the century it was just below 400,000 tons representing only 4½ per cent of national production.

This failure to maintain pig-iron production when it was rising nationally from 6 million tons in 1874 to 9 million tons in 1900, seems to have been almost entirely the result of entrepreneurial inertia and inefficiency, especially as a vast trade in rolled sheets, particularly corrugated iron, was developing. of which the Black Country became the centre.

Iron prices in the Black Country were always measured against the Earl of Dudley's bar iron. This rose to its peak early in 1873 at £16-12-6d. per ton. For the rest of the year there was much talk of over-pricing and imports of iron. By the beginning of 1874 furnaces were being blown out. Prices fell to £12-12-6d in July and fell steadily thereafter to a low of £8-2-6d. for most of 1879. A slight rise followed, but for much of 1881 the price was the lowest for 25 years at £7-12-6d. It was not until 1890 that the *Engineer* could report prospects as 'better than for a dozen years', but by then the price of iron was still only £8-10-0d.

From 1877 ironmasters began to close their works. Colonel Thomas Thorneycroft was the first culprit, closing his Shrubbery works in Wolverhampton at Christmas claiming that his workers would not accept a wage reduction. 'One thousand new names appeared on the Workhouse and Relieving Officers' books', noted the *Wolverhampton Magazine.* Thorneycroft was the son of G.B. Thorneycroft who had made his fortune n the iron trade and was the first mayor of Wolverhampton. His son was a prodigious inventor. Having liquidated his father's iron and coal empire he was free to devote himself to such fripperies at his mansion of Tettenhall Towers as a theatre with a sprung floor and a cascade of water of water from forty four feet with coloured lights. It is a pity that his talents were not directed to the main economic problem of the Black Country, which at least some other ironmasters were grappling with, namely the development of steel production to replace wrought iron.

Other ironworks also closed and by February 1879 only 24 furnaces out of 147 were in blast. When an ironworks closed either its plant was bought by other ironmasters, or the works were bought at knock-down prices and subsequently restarted. An example of this occurred in January 1878 when Lysaght's of Bristol bought from Thorneycroft Swan Garden Ironworks, which with adjacent Osier Bed had both been threatened with the same fate as Shrubbery. A large number of unemployed gathered and Lysaght made a speech. There were exclamations from women in the crowd such as 'the Lord bless him'. Of the proposed closure of Osier Bed the *Labour Tribune* remarked that it was over fifty years since this ironworks had passed into the possession of William Hanbury Sparrow 'and it is here that he made much of the wealth that has made him probably the richest ironmaster in S. Staffs.'

The effects on ironworkers standards of living can be seen from the record of net wages of a puddler who wrote his reminiscences in the *Labour Tribune.* In 1873 his earnings peaked at £128-17-0d. The following year it fell to £69-18-0d. and averaged £70 for the next three years. On the latter wage a puddler with wife and two children under seven could just maintain a decent life for his family.

But worse was to come. In 1887 a puddler from the advanced Brunswick Works of Patent Shaft & Axletree, whose management were tackling the problems of steelmaking, wrote:

> At the present time the works are giving birth to a new steel trade, whilst its old iron trade seems to be on its deathbed. The forgemen, (puddlers, shinglers etc.) are working at the average rate of two days a week, some are being shifted from one post to another, some shifted off the scene altogether... The average nett earnings of the majority of the puddlers for the year 1886 did not reach £1 a week. For a

man and small family that would barely procure food, fire and clothing, leaving 101 other wants unprovided for. Trades unionism cannot have a worse enemy than a trade of these wretched dimensions… This makes men heartless and low spirited; takes the grit out of men; renders them as flabby as a jelly fish, or rather a mixture of the docile and desperate…

If this was the position at Patent Shaft, the position at more backward ironworks was worse. Under these conditions, and with the sub-contract system still in place, the men inevitably became trapped in sliding scales and conciliation.

Returning to the development of trade unionism, we have seen how by 1873 John Kane's Amalgamated Malleable Ironworkers of G.B. had 10,000 members in S. Staffs. and E. Worcs. Its policy was support for sliding scales for wages and conciliation.

Ironworkers had been locked into an informal sliding scale probably from the beginning of iron production in the Black Country. Certainly the local Ironmasters Association met throughout the period of the Combination Acts (1799-1824) to publicly announce the price of iron, at a time when combinations of both men and masters were illegal. Eventually, from the 1840s this crystallised into the Thorneycroft Scale which fixed the earnings of foremen puddlers at 1/-d. per ton for every £1 per ton of marked iron bars. Millmen's earnings were related to the sliding scale by an 'extra' of 10 per cent.

The pioneers of stable trade unionism in the Black Country iron trade from the 1860s were James Capper, William Aucott and Thomas Piggott. All were in favour of the Sliding Scale and in July 1872 a S. Staffs. Iron Trade Conciliation Board was set up operating a sliding scale ranging from 8/6d. with bar iron at £7-10-0d. per ton to 11/6d. when iron was £11-10-0d. per ton or over. The perceived advantage of the formal sliding scale was that it would avoid the destructive industrial battles of the past when men struck for higher wages as prices rose, and were locked out by the masters resisting wage cuts as iron prices fell. The union leaders can hardly be blamed for not knowing that they were locking themselves into a one way ticket of wage reductions for the next twenty five years.

While trade was good the sliding scale prospered as did the union and there were hopes of a single scale for the whole country which would hopefully have ended the differences and distrust between Black Country ironworkers and 'the men of the North.'

However, the Depression came and trade union membership plummeted. In April 1874 Capper was explaining to his men that a demanded 20 per cent drop had been negotiated down to 7½ per cent with a worsened sliding scale. By 1875 union membership fell to 1,500 and the S. Staffs Conciliation Board also came to an end as Capper and Aucott resigned from the Board no longer able to speak for the majority of ironworkers. For a detailed account of subsequent Wages and Conciliation Boards, Arbitrators, wage reductions and refusal of owners to negotiate with the men one must turn to Eric Taylor's centenary *History of the Midland Iron & Steel Wages Board.* Two main problems dominated these exchanges. One was that the weakness of the men led owners to negotiate with works representatives who were not trade unionists. The second was the weakness of the masters as their trade declined. This led to insufficient ironmasters being represented on the Wages Board to support the prices of iron decided upon.

In 1877 Aucott gave up the ghost and left the industry to become superintendent of Wednesbury Baths, and Capper ceased to be a union member when his lodge disappeared. However neither man completely lost interest in worker representation, although trade unionism was once again reduced to works level where it existed at all.

It was not until 1886 with a temporary lifting of the Depression that north and south could consider forgetting their differences and again begin to work for national organisation. Capper addressed many meetings which passed unanimously in favour of reorganisation, and many new lodges were set up. This impetus continued throughout the year, but by November, Capper was apologising for not attending meetings because of illness. Capper continued with much of his activity despite being reported 'in very weak health' in January 1887.

Trade improvement was indeed brief. In the winter of 1887 soup kitchens appeared in Dudley. The announcement of a cheque for £100 from the Countess of Dudley was cheered, but the *Labour Tribune* tartly remarked that this was bagatelle compared with her total income. A letter from a Lye puddler underlined the conditions to which continued depression and the falling demand for puddled iron had reduced them:

> Let employers who talk of wage cutting look into puddlers' homes and see his half starved and half naked wife and children. Men, who if they have any work to go to must rise at 3 or 4am and slave all day (12 hours) before a blazing furnace for a paltry sum of 4/6d. We need a good, strong union.

The position in the north was that the National Amalgamated Association of Ironworkers had survived under the continued leadership of John Kane. Kane died prematurely in 1876. In his place, Edward Trow who had been born and brought up in the iron trade in the Black Country before moving to the north where he became a leading trade unionist, was elected secretary. In February 1888 a preliminary conference was held in Birmingham to discuss reorganisation. Trow led the northern delegation while the Black Country was represented by James Capper, William Aucott, Thomas Piggott and Benjamin Bradley (who had been the secretary of a short lived local Millmen's Association.) Sufficient progress was made for a delegate conference to be called for April in Manchester.

Sixty seven delegates representing 40,000 iron and steel workers assembled. The Black Country delegation comprised nearly 30 representatives plus Capper and Aucott. Aucott was elected president to loud cheers. This reconciliation of north and south was an emotional burying of the hatchet. Aucott passed lightly over previous difficulties saying, to an appreciative audience that his friend Edward Trow had done splendid work, although they did fall out occasionally (loud cheers and laughter). Thomas Piggott of West Bromwich was elected vice-president.

The Conference set up a new organisation, the National Association of Iron and Steel Workers of G.B. The first contentious issue was that of union funds, which had deeply divided iron workers in the past. A Black Country motion that union funds should be held locally was supported by delegates from Yorkshire, Lancashire and N. Staffs. The objection to local fund holding was that there was no guarantee that such funds would be remitted to assist other areas when they were engaged in strike action; also when lodges closed down the funds were distributed among members instead of being remitted to strengthen the union nationally. Trow moved a northern amendment that funds should be centralised. This rekindled fears that funds would be used to benefit other areas and pass out of control of those who had contributed them. Eventually a compromise was reached whereby funds were held locally by trustees and would be moved when requested by head office only with the consent of all the trustees. On the question of Conciliation and Arbitration there were no differences and a resolution was passed in favour of its retention. After a fiery speech by Trow a resolution supporting labour representation in Parliament was passed 'with acclamation'. This unanimity was based on a belated realisation that the miners had had parliamentary representation for over 20 years and had greatly benefitted from it. At this stage labour representation meant working men Liberals and this philosophy still permeated every aspect of union work. The reasons for this can best be explained by a closer look at the background of the main local leaders at this time.

Edward Trow had been born in Wolverhampton in 1833. He began work with his father at Bagnall's of Wednesbury and became an underhand puddler at thirteen. He was a life long member of the Liberal Party, although a typical Lib-Lab in not believing that the interests of master and men were always the same.

James Capper was born in 1829 and began work at the age of eight. He spent several years in the USA before returning to work with the large Patent Shaft and Axletree Co. as a forehand puddler. With Aucott and Piggott he took part in the 'three stages' of iron trade unionism of 1863, 1872 and 1887. Capper was the men's secretary of the various Conciliation, Arbitration and Wages Boards which dominated the industry. This continued during years when there was no union for him to belong to and periods when the owners refused to negotiate with trade unionists. Capper was a Gladstonian Liberal influential in securing the election of Alexander Brogden to the new Wednesbury constituency in 1868 and in supporting his successor, the Hon. Philip Stanhope.

William Aucott was born a year after Capper in Leicestershire. His father was a Chartist and Methodist. He was barred from the local National school as being of the wrong religion and had no formal education although he could read and write at the age of seven. At fourteen he left the depressed textile industry in Hinkley where his father was a stockinger and was recruited by James Talbot, general manager of John Bagnall's to become an underhand puddler at Wednesbury. He was later to describe bitterly the fate of other young victims of the textile depression saying that they either starved, or migrated to the USA or joined the army and perished in the campaigns of the Crimean War. At the age of twenty, when he was a foreman puddler, he married Talbot's daughter. She shared his religious convictions and they became friends with the Rev Arthur O'Neill, the Birmingham Baptist pastor and former leading Chartist. Such was the influence of Aucott that although he had left the industry in 1877 to become superintendent of Wednesbury Baths, he was elected president of the new union eleven years later. When James Capper's stroke eventually incapacitated him in 1889, Aucott succeeded him as men's secretary to what had then become the Midland Iron & Steel Wages Board. These two posts he continued to hold until 1912 when he retired. Aucott was among the first JPs appointed in Wednesbury in 1893. For sixty two years he was superintendent of the Leabrook Primitive Methodist Sunday School and a leading figure in the Wednesbury Sons of Temperance, which he helped form in 1864. This Lib-Lab trade unionist who inherited the Chartist tradition and who called himself a Socialist died in 1915. All the strengths, weaknesses and contradictions of the mid-nineteenth century working class activist were combined in this remarkable man.

Thomas Piggott was born in 1836 in West Bromwich. He began work at the age of eight at the Bromford Works of Davies & Sons of Oldbury where he eventually became a forehand puddler. Piggott played a leading role in the formation of the Associated Ironworkers of GB in 1863 by bringing the Bromford men out in support of the Brierley Hill strikers. In 1876 he was one of the twelve workmen of the S. Staffs Mill & Forge Wages Board and in 1880 he became vice-president. Piggott was one of the many almost unknown figures connected with individual ironworks who remained rank and file puddlers and struggled over forty years to ensure that, even in the darkest days, trade union organisation continued in the large ironworks. His death was symbolic. He died suddenly in 1887. For almost fourteen weeks before his death he had been out of work as a result of the closure of the Bromford Works, where he had worked all his life. If he was not one of those, described above by the Lye puddler, who died of starvation, the superhuman exertions of the life of a puddler and active trade unionist, together with the cumulative effects of frequent destitution during the Great Depression must share the blame for his untimely demise.

With regard to union policy, one of the main aims of the new Associated Iron & Steel Workers of G.B. was to strengthen Wages Boards and union representation on them. By 1887 there were less than twenty ironworks represented on the Board and the operative representatives were often non-union. One of the first effects of renewed union strength was an agreement with the employers that in all matters affecting the Board, the Board would meet with trade union representatives to decide what action to take. James Capper's enforced resignation in 1888 after his stroke also strengthened trade union influence as his place was taken by William Aucott. Shortly after this the union also gained agreement that all future operative representatives must be members of the union. These important gains were consolidated when ironworks in Derbyshire, Lancashire and South Yorkshire, whose wages had for some time followed the S. Staffs. awards joined the Board as subordinate members, and the old Board was reorganised in 1889 as the Midland Iron & Steel Wages Board. Adherence to the Board of larger numbers of owners inevitably raised the question of the 'alliance philosophy', popular elsewhere in the Black Country of wage and price maintenance by joint employer/worker action. This possibility was reinforced by the rapid, but chaotic growth of the sheet iron and steel trade, notably in corrugated iron, which centred itself in the Black Country.

Encouraged by union membership of 45 lodges with 2,200 members in the Black Country, the union began to tackle the main problems of the sheet trade which concerned both owners and men – the undercutting of prices and low wages. In 1891 a Price List was agreed between producers and union with further agreement that the union should withdraw labour from firms undercutting prices and wages while manufacturers agreed not to provide the defaulting firms with sheets. Here indeed was 'class collaboration' and 'alliance philosophy' in practice. This price and sliding scale arrangement was maintained almost to the end of the century.

The Great Depression ended for most industries in the Black Country in 1895, and from 1890 to 1895 pig-iron output, together with prices and wages, remained low. These years took their toll of union membership as dissatisfaction with the Wages Board grew. But the years 1896-1900 were more prosperous and union membership recovered.

Engineering Unions

Working outwards from the ironworks from which engineers derived their basic material, we come first to the Ironmoulders.

In 1874 at the height of the boom the Friendly Society of Iron Founders had just over 12,000 members. It suffered less than other unions from the subsequent slump and in 1890 still had 11,000 members. The main casting areas and centres of FSIF strength in the Black Country in 1874 were Smethwick where there were 168 members, Toll End 89, Stourbridge 52, Wednesbury 48, Dudley 42, and Bilston 40.

Both Dudley and Bilston branches had, as we know, been in existence before 1838, but Bilston became a victim of the Depression and closed in 1895.

Technical improvements in the industry led to the growth of semi-skilled labour and also the sub-division of labour resulting in new occupations such as core-makers, dressers, pattern makers; also to a division within the industry into light and heavy castings.

In 1890 H. Sanders, a noted militant and socialist from Walsall was called on to organise a strike in Oldham which resulted in the formation of the National Union of Stove Grate Workers. In the same year, again through Sanders' influence, the Amalgamated Society of Casters was formed with its headquarters in Walsall.

Separate organisation in the brass-casting trade was also developing. Until 1872 most casters in Birmingham and the Black Country belonged to the FSIF as iron and brass casting often occurred in the same factories.

It was the genius of W.J. Davis to form the National Society of Amalgamated Brassworkers in Birmingham at the height of the boom in 1872 and successively play off one section of this trade of myriad sub-divisions against all the others. He created one of the most remarkable of all trade unions, which in the subsequent slump developed the Alliance Philosophy of co-operation with the employers. The first annual report showed a total of 5,700 members of whom nearly 400 were in Wolverhampton. Other smaller branches were at Sheffield, Walsall and Rotherham.

Membership at first suffered badly from the Great Depression. It suffered onslaughts on the 9-hour day and accusations that high wages were sending the trade abroad. To where, asked the union? The Depression was world wide. Over-production, originating from the time of the Franco-Prussian war was the main problem. The impact of the Depression can be gauged by the proportion of membership subscriptions spent on unemployment pay. In 1878 this reached nearly 100 per cent and the following year was 146 per cent. In 1880, 1886 and 1888 it was over 80 per cent and even in 1900 was nearly 50 per cent.

In 1883 Davis ceased to be secretary and became one of the first working class factory inspectors. By then membership had declined to 4,149. Davis returned to the union in 1888. Membership then had declined still further to 2,243. In that year Wolverhampton membership had been reduced to 220 members and Walsall from 45 to 21. A year after his return Davis had boosted union membership to 7,625. In 1890 Davis succeeded in creating a Brass Trades Board of Conciliation and in 1897 (at the request of Davis!) the Brass Masters' Association was formed. This represented the climacteric of the Birmingham Alliance Philosophy which aimed at creating closed shops of both workers and employers which would manipulate prices, wages and output on the high moral principle that this best served the interests of both producers and the public. As we shall see, notable as was the achievement, it could not last.

Boiler making was another branch of heavy engineering which was important to the Black Country economy. National trade unionism in the industry began in 1852 with the merging of local societies into the United Society of Boilermakers and Ironship Builders. The first Annual Trade Union Directory of 1861 gives Boilermakers branches at Bilston, Smethwick and Wednesbury, but by how much organisation pre-dates 1861 we do not know. From the annual reports of the union we can give the following membership figures:

	W'ton	Smethwick	Wednesbury	Bilston	Dudley	Great Bridge	Oldbury
1881	52	63	58	9	23	–	–
1890	56	–	68	–	35	35	–
1901	87	61	–	–	50	69	–
1914	90	–	104	18	128	140	40

The emergence of the Great Bridge branch not only reflects the growth of industry in the area after 1840, but probably included also Oldbury and Tipton where there were always boiler making firms and perhaps also Bilston, another important boiler making centre.

Further specialisation in the engineering industry is exemplified by the separate organisation of the Pattern Makers some of whom in 1872, pulled out of the main engineering union and formed the U.K. Pattern Makers Association with just 38 members. By 1883 it had 46 branches of which Smethwick was Branch No.9 with 34 members and Tipton branch 45 with 10 members. By 1900 Smethwick had 49 members, Wolverhampton 21, West Bromwich 26, Darlaston 20 and Dudley 16.

We now turn to the Amalgamated Society of Engineers which was to become the most powerful union in the Black Country. Its influence extended into the Trades Councils and other trade unions, by reason of its financial strength and the aid it was able to offer to other workers in dispute. The union's records are immense with monthly, quarterly and annual reports. Yet it is difficult to write the history of the Black Country branches, and as has been said before, there is little of substance to be found in the local newspapers. What is fully documented is the membership of the branches which overall grew during the Great Depression, but only by about 60 per cent compared with national growth which more than doubled.

	W'ton	Smethwick	Oldbury	Walsall	Wed'bury	Bilston	Dudley	W. Brom	Total
1874	193	212	62	30	100	32	–	–	629
1900	401	297	89	21	87	–	57	73	1025

As with other workers the engineers faced a fierce offensive against the 9-hour day which had been won in the early 1870s. An official return of wages and hours shows that at least in one Wednesbury factory the 51-hour week was operating e.g. nine hours each weekday and the prized Saturday afternoon of a one o'clock finish. But by 1880 hours were back to 54 and this remained general until 1900.

Another problem for the general engineering worker was the increasing specialisation within the industry. This led, as we have seen, to such craftsmen as Pattern Makers hiving off. At the other end, standardisation and mass production led to the growth of semi-skilled machinists. The ASE was a craft union proud of its heritage of having pioneered the new unionism of the 1850s. But its rigid structure made it impossible to admit semi-skilled men until the fundamental reforms of the 1890s initiated by John Burns and Tom Mann. The result was the growth of unions catering for the semi-skilled or their recruitment into the general unions then beginning to appear.

The ASE in the Black Country faced up to this problem by actively encouraging those ineligible to join the ASE to join other unions. In May 1886 the local ASE and the Wolverhampton Trades Council sponsored a meeting to set up the Wolverhampton branch of the National Amalgamated Society of General Toolmakers and Machinists for those working on 'bicycles, tricycles and machining'. A balance sheet a few months later showed that this union had branches in Birmingham, Coventry, Wolverhampton and Smethwick. The ASE was reorganised in 1892 and widened membership to machinists. But by then the damage had been done and the split between skilled and unskilled unions, which weakens trade unionism to this day had begun. The General Toolmakers and Machinists prospered moderately in the ensuing years. In 1896 it had 8 branches with about 750 members. This included 55 in Wolverhampton and 38 in Smethwick

In 1897-8 the ASE was involved in a life and death struggle with a five month Lock-out. This arose over a claim for an 8-hour day. The union suffered one of the heaviest defeats of its history. Not only was the main claim lost, but the employers strengthened their 'right to manage' powers with the right to employ non-union labour and determine workshop practice with regard to piece rates, demarcation etc. Again local material is scarce. There was no overall lock-out in the midlands and most of our information concerns solidarity levies and collections for the engineers by the local trades councils and other unions. No doubt the local ASE branches levied their members as heavily as in the rest of the country, but of this we know nothing.

Tinmen and Ironplate workers

Strictly speaking these workers might be considered under engineering, but the history of the Wolverhampton Tinplate Workers was of such singularity that it demanded special treatment. The militancy of the Tinmen continued into the period 1875-1900, but their history now touched on the rise of a new industry – Ironplate. Gold discoveries in Australia and the USA in the 1850s led to a vast demand for buckets, cooking utensils etc. made both of tin and iron. Tin was soldered; iron was brazed. Thus tin items were both lighter and better finished. Tinmen remained aristocrats concerned to control entry to the trade and also control prices. Iron plate work was rougher and usually badly paid. Demand exploded again with the development of the coating of iron as corrugated iron sheets. This tapped another immense colonial demand. The key development here was the use of soft steel made by the Bessemer and Siemens processes

From 1848 there were two mutually supportive Tin societies. One was the Wolverhampton Society of Operative Tin Plate Workers. The other was the Wolverhampton Co-operative Tin Plate Workers Society. It is likely that the Co-operative organised tinmen working in shops making inferior tin goods. Indeed there was an even lower class of tin goods where the societies refused to recruit at all. Whatever the reason, there was no conflict between the societies. Indeed various unsuccessful attempts were made to unite the two until in 1881 the Co-operative, bankrupted by unsuccessful strikes to maintain prices, was dissolved and its members were admitted to the other society.

With the onset of the boom in the early 1870s changes were made. In March 1873 the Wolverhampton Society requested a 10 per cent advance on the 1850 price list. Before this could be done it was necessary to approach the non-unionised factories where wages were below the List price. Agreement was reached with these shops and they all joined the union. In January 1874 the 10 per cent was conceded.

During this period negotiations were proceeding with the other large Tin Plate organisation in the area, Birmingham. The Birmingham men complained that when ever they applied for an increase they were told that they could not have it because prices were lower in Wolverhampton. So, after rejecting a proposal for national organisation, the two societies merged in 1876 as the Amalgamated Tinplate Workers of Birmingham, Wolverhampton and District with a membership of about 800.

By now the Depression descended and hard times lay ahead. The most important strike was at Jones Brothers of Wolverhampton in 1866 which brought back the bitterness of the 1850s. This was a four year running battle to reduce prices and destroy the union. As with the earlier struggle with Perry, only a small number of workmen were involved. Twenty of the twenty seven workers in the shop were in the Society. The firm imposed reductions and tried to enforce the Document demanding that the men leave the Society. Seven were dismissed for standing by the union. The rest of the men were called out and other members levied to pay to pay married men £1 a week and unmarried men 15/-d. But the Depression defeated the Society and the strike ended in defeat. So parlous was the condition of the union by 1885 that it relaxed its long tradition by allowing members to take work in non-trade jobs, until they could obtain better work.

Such experiences led to a desire of wider unity. In 1889 the Birmingham and Wolverhampton Society merged with several London societies (some engaged in the growing trade of gas meter making) and formed the National Tin Plate Workers of Great Britain with H. Ricket of Wolverhampton secretary, E. Fooks of Birmingham president and F.B. Monk of London vice-president. This brought more than 800 new members, but a truly national organisation failed to develop as such large districts as Lancashire and Scotland declined to join. The problem was that in those districts day work was prevalent whereas in the Midlands the Price List and payment by piece was the life blood of the trade.

The Price List received a new lease of life in the 1890s as the Depression was easing and the question of Fair Wage clauses emerged as an important political issue. A new Price List covering War Office and Admiralty work was quickly produced. These prices were later accepted by municipal and county council authorities. Yet again an element of 'Alliance Philosophy' was emerging.

Meanwhile the Iron Plate trade was developing rapidly and moving from Birmingham to the Black Country. Organisation had begun in 1864 with the Birmingham Iron Plate Workers Trade Protection Society. During the boom years a Wolverhampton Society was formed in 1872. During the Depression organisation in the Black Country almost disappeared, although the Birmingham Society survived. In 1889 with business improving Birmingham put in for a 10 per cent increase. Wolverhampton and Bilston followed suit. The employers refused, but after a few weeks' strike the employers conceded the claim on the condition that the Society produced a new minimum price list and enforce it to the best of its ability within a fourteen mile radius of Birmingham. These terms were agreed at a joint meeting with a newly-formed employers' organisation presided over by an independent chairman, the highly respected secretary of the brassworkers, W.J. Davis. The Birmingham, Wolverhampton and Bilston societies produced a new list of prices, but this was not accepted by the employers. In 1890 the employers distributed a list of their own which was rejected by the men as involving cuts ranging between 10 per cent and 40 per cent Another great strike involving 500 Birmingham, Wolverhampton and Bilston men plus another 130 from Lye then took place. After six or seven weeks the employers withdrew their list and the men returned to work victorious at the old prices. Wider organisation followed when the National Amalgamated Iron Plate Workers Society was set up with headquarters in Birmingham and branches in Wolverhampton, Bilston, Walsall and London. But Lye, where the trade was now concentrating, remained outside the organisation.

As the Depression again descended further desperate strikes took place to maintain prices. With the society almost bankrupt the committee were prepared to let 10 per cent go, but the men would have nothing of it. So another great strike began in 1892. It ended in February 1893 on terms better than might have been expected; the 10 per cent was to be retained for three month to give the union time to enforce Birmingham prices on all outside firms, failing which the 10 per cent would be taken off.

By 1894 Lye had joined the national organisation and was the biggest branch with 350 members. Birmingham had 320, Wolverhampton 300, Bilston 80 and Walsall 20.

Lye iron plate workers were influenced by the Knights of Labour. The role of this American based organisation will be discussed when we examine the smaller crafts and the Midland Counties Trade Federation under the redoubtable Richard Juggins.

Galvanizers were also brought within the orbit of the Iron Plate Workers Society. The Good Intent Society of Galvanizers founded in October 1893 with Issac Grafton as secretary was dissolved in 1899. Iron braziers too joined the national Society and had their own separate list of prices.

By the turn of the century iron plate and tin plate was centred on the Black Country under the designation of hollow ware. Here cast, as well as stamped and pressed goods in tin and iron were often made in the same factory, as exemplified by T & C Clark of Wolverhampton, founded in 1795 and trading until recent years.

Electricians

Trade unionism in the newly developing field of electricity began in the 1890s and in the early days a Wolverhampton branch played an important part. The first union emerged from Manchester in 1889 as the Amalgamated Union of Telegraph and Telephone Construction Men, but changed its title the next year to the Electrical Trades Union of the U.K.

The Wolverhampton branch originated in 1896 from a different part of the industry – the skilled armature winders of the important electrical engineering works of Thomas Parker. It was formed when the union was asked to negotiate a minimum wage of 26/-d. a week for all men over twenty one. In the union's annual report for 1896 F. Sims, the first full time organiser, tells the story in detail. He attended a meeting in Wolverhampton in November 1895 at which a committee of W. Emery, A.B. Blocksedge, Jones, J. Lynch, J. Boucher and Fletcher were elected who agreed to back up Sims at his meeting with the management:

> The secretary duly attended at the time appointed and, after sending in his card and waiting for some time, was allowed to see Mr Parker. After stating his business that gentleman at first refused to discuss the matter with your secretary on the ground that he did not believe that he was representing the men's opinions correctly. Finally he consented to discuss the alleged grievances providing your secretary could get six of his men to attend as a deputation at half past one o'clock... This proposition was accepted and we were pleased to state that we were able to get seven members to attend. The interview duly took place and lasted over one-and-a-half hours. Mr Parker at first refused to allow your secretary to speak on the main question and tried to intimidate the deputation, but finding that they were not frightened and stuck to their demands, he allowed your secretary to state the case on behalf of the union... Finally he decided to give his answer to our requests at the end of the week, but emphatically refused to communicate his reply to your secretary...

Sims had to return to Wolverhampton the following March to finalise the deal. But this was well worth while as it was the first agreement ever signed between an ETU official and an employer in Britain.

This was not the only distinction of the Wolverhampton branch. In 1898 of the 635 members of the union Wolverhampton had 137, a total that was only exceeded by the central London branch with 148. For reasons unknown this situation did not continue. By 1901 Wolverhampton membership had fallen to a more normal level of 34 and, whatever the cause, London suffered the same fate, for the Central branch disappeared altogether.

Builders

It is often claimed that the trade cycle in the building industry differs significantly from that in other industries. The evidence for this in the Black Country is ambiguous. If one takes wages of bricklayers and carpenters in Wolverhampton district these were 8d. an hour from 1877 to 1879 and fell to 7½d. an hour from 1880 to 1890 when they rose again to 8d. This might suggest that the Depression came later in building and perhaps finished earlier, but unemployment during the period might alter the picture. If one takes hours worked as a criterion, the builders faced the same onslaught on hours as workers in other industries. In their case it was a 9 hour day (54 hours a week in summer; 50½ in winter). These attacks were resisted and hours remained unchanged until the end of the century. Just as important as the trade cycle, however, was the overall demand for building during a period when population trends were changing dramatically in the Black Country from a much larger population increase than the national one to a fall in growth and even contraction to below the national level. Here the Censuses suggest that building workers rose to a peak of about 7 per cent of the working male population in 1861 and fell to less than 3 per cent at the end of the century.

With regard to trade union activity, the industry was still plagued with the sectionalism of its many trade unions and the difficulty of organising on small sites; an advantage was that building techniques did not fundamentally change in this period.

In this situation the aristocrats of the trade, the stonemasons, who always earned ½d. an hour over the general craft rate fared surprisingly well, although brickwork continued to oust stone work. In 1870 the Operative Stonemasons' Friendly Society of England and Wales had 304 lodges with 14,000 members. Fifty three of these members were in Wolverhampton and twenty in Walsall. By 1880 fifty lodges had been closed nationally and membership in the Black Country was down to 26 in Wolverhampton and 11 in Walsall. The national union continued to decline until 1886, but growth followed thereafter. By 1901 there were nearly 20,000 members nationally with 81 in Wolverhampton, 19 in Walsall, five at Stourbridge and three in West Bromwich.

Bricklayers seem to have increased throughout the period some of the main towns showing the following trade union membership:

	Dudley	Darlaston	Gornal	Halesown	Walsall	Wednesbury	W. Brom	W'ton
1870	35	34	5	–	64	54	–	35
1878	125	23	67	23	–	62	55	93
1897	133	55	236	74	111	53	–	232

Carpenters were evenly divided between the two main unions of the Amalgamated Society of Carpenters & Joiners and the older General Union of Operative Carpenters & Joiners:

	Dudley	Walsall	Wednesbury	Wolverhampton
AC & J 1874	14	40	14	42
Gen Un 1874	71	52	–	36
AC & J 1881	10	31	8	67
Gen. Un 1881	–	22	–	12
AC & J 1901	55	–	12	–
Gen Un 1901	–	–	–	14

The General Union probably had the larger membership in the Black Country in 1874 at a time when the national membership of the AC & J was nearly 14,000 and the General Union nearly 10,000. This situation was to change radically as the AC & J gained the reputation of ruthlessly poaching members from other unions. By 1881 the national membership of both unions had fallen. But by 1901 AC & J had 30,000 members nationally and it seems that it benefitted at the expense of its rival in the Black Country too.

Other local building unions also existed at times for which less information is available. The plumbers, small in number and usually conservative, were always organised and various builders' labourers unions came and went.

Very little local strike activity is reported in the building trade during the Depression and while this could no doubt be attributed to the builders' belief in Conciliation, no doubt it owed much also to the realism that strikes could not be won in depressed economic conditions.

As the Depression lifted builders' thoughts once again turned to One Big Union and federation of the different building unions was canvassed. National negotiations between the unions achieved nothing, but such a Federation was formed locally.

It arose from one of the few important building strikes of the period. In 1873 the Amalgamated Society of House Decorators and Painters was formed. It made little progress in the Black Country until almost 1890 when its membership in Wolverhampton was 70. In March 1886 its members struck against a ½d. per hour reduction (painters earned ½d. per hour less than the general craft rate) and also against the introduction by the employers of a sliding scale. A Wolverhampton Building Trades Federation was formed and the solidarity of all building workers with the painters was declared. It was suggested that the employers should bring the rate in Walsall. Dudley and adjacent towns up to the Wolverhampton rate (this was ½d. per hour above the other towns) rather than drag the Wolverhampton rate down. W. Sharrocks of the Boilermakers proposed a joint meeting of masters and men with arbitration by members of the Wolverhampton town council who were employers of labour in the building trade. This proposal was accepted.

The result of that strike is not known, but militancy continued to the end of the century when, in 1899 builders' labourers were demanding an increase from 5½d. to 6d. per hour and plumbers demanding an extra ½d. to 9d.

The Midland Counties Trades Federation

Not the least interesting of a number of important contributions made by Black Country trade unionists to the national movement was the Midland Counties Trades Federation.

Federation was an idea whose time had come. In engineering the development of new processes and consequent demarcation disputes led to the Federation of Engineering & Shipbuilding Unions. This was accompanied by federation among employers. The Miners' Federation of Great Britain was formed in 1899 and the General Federation of Trade Unions in 1901. From 1884 there were the new socialist parties and the new unionism dominated by socialists such as John Burns and Tom Mann. They also wanted federation to more effectively pursue socialist policies. But federation also suited the purposes of the collaborationists. Thus federationists were split along the main ideological divide. As far as the Midland Counties Trades Federation was concerned, it was totally Lib-Lab and class collaborationist.

Richard Juggins was the brain behind the formation of the MCTF and it is to the development of his thought as leader of the National Amalgamated Association of Nut & Bolt Workers to which we must turn. Juggins had been responsible for forming the Nut & Bolt Union in Darlaston in 1870 and by 1874 it was a national union, based at the main centre of the trade at Darlaston. The Great

Depression hit the union hard and by 1877 its membership was down to 211 after a five months lockout brought about by a refusal to accept lower prices. The dispute was finally settled with a compromise arbitrated by Joseph Chamberlain. Juggins steered the union through the subsequent years of the Depression to initiate the South Staffordshire Nut & Bolt Wages Board in 1889.

Trades Councils were important to Juggins as a first step towards federation and he utilised both the short-lived S. Staffs & E. Worcs. Trades Council and also the long-lived Walsall Trades Council which eventually broke with Juggins and the MCTF.

The Midland Counties Trades Federation which was formed in 1886 differed from the Trades Councils in a number of ways. Firstly it united as many trades as possible with the aim of mutual support during strikes by financial contributions which each would make. Secondly, the Federation fervently believed that the interests of masters and men were identical and every emphasis was on conciliation and not conflict. Strikes would therefore be matters of last resort and it was assumed that most trades would remain at work when any individual craft was in dispute and the limited funds of the organisation would therefore be sufficient at all times. Thirdly, and most surprisingly, the Federation embraced the pacific principles of the U.S. based organisation, the Knights of Labour, and it was in the Black Country that the Knights made their greatest impact in Britain.

The Federation met the need of the many crafts of the area to have the support of a wider organisation. But the Federation set itself the wider aim of becoming a national organisation federating all trades. Beginning with just three organisations, by 1889 it had forty five affiliates. These included from the Black Country, Anvil Makers, Blastfurnacemen, many chain makers' associations, file cutters, fire brick makers, gas tube men, gun lock filers, ten nailmaking associations, miners from Old Hill, Brierley Hill and Netherton, lock makers, ironplate workers, spade and shovel, and tube workers. From outside the area were chain makers and fibre dressers from Sheffield, who appear to have been connected with the Knights of Labour. Finally in these early years Assemblies of the Knights from Wolverhampton, Lye & Wollescote, and Stamber Mill all in the Black Country and from outside, the Sheffield and North Western Assemblies were all directly affiliated.

The great value of the Federation was not only in its negotiating expertise, but also in its willingness to support strike action where conciliation had failed. Every balance sheet gave details of strike pay. For instance, in the first half of 1890 of an income of about £850 nearly £600 had been spent on strike benefit. Over £200 had gone to Brickmakers, nearly £130 to various Chainmakers and nearly £100 to Willenhall Lockmakers. Perhaps the greatest achievement of the Federation was its sustained support for the nail and chain makers through the whole harrowing decades of the Great Depression and up to 1914 when the sweated labour and starvation wages of these trades stirred the conscience of the whole nation.

By 1891 the Federation had 14,000 members, but for a number of years there was a decline to 4,000. Growth resumed thereafter and membership rose to a maximum of 19,500 in 1900. Thereafter it again declined.

Such growth in the early years was hard earned. Many mass meetings were held to propagate Federation. Typical was one at Wednesbury Town Hall in January 1887. Here the chairman was Eli Bloor, the Birmingham Lib-Lab councillor, whose role was to strengthen the links with the Birmingham crafts. Here he was unsuccessful for there was never the contact one would have expected between the 'alliance philosophy' trades of Birmingham led by W.J. Davis and the equally conciliatory MCTF led by Juggins. The main speaker was the Lib-Lab miners' leader, MP Charles Fenwick, whose job was to attract Black Country miners to the Federation. His speech stressed the unity of interest between capital and labour. Then, as at all these meetings, Juggins moved a resolution, enthusiastically passed, committing all present to join the MCTF. Finally the Bloxwich bit-forgers' secretary together with another national speaker T.R. Threlfall moved a motion supporting working class representation in Parliament. They welcomed the setting up of the Labour Electoral Association and pledged the meeting to returning Labour representatives in the Black Country. Threlfall's importance was that he had moved the resolution at the TUC setting up the Labour Electoral Association, but the LEA was controlled by Lib-Labs who saw the increased number of working class representatives as being Liberals sponsored by the Liberal Party.

The next year a series of mass meetings addressed by such national figures as R.B. Cunninghame-Graham MP, one of the early champions of the chainmakers, and Thomas Burt MP, the president of the Miners' National Union, advocating the extravagent aim of 'bringing about a national federation of all persons engaged in labour' through the development of the MCTF.

In 1889 the occasion of an International Trades Congress in Paris was seized to further cement relations with employers and MPs. A fund to raise £10 to send working men to Paris was contributed to by such notables as the MPs Sir W. Plowden, the Hon. Philip Stanhope, Brooke-Robinson and Staveley Hill; also by Tangye, the progressive Birmingham industrialist, Alfred Hickman and Col. Thorneycroft, the Wolverhampton industrialists etc.

The final delegation consisted of twelve working men chosen by the MCTF as representative of their trades. They were given a warm send-off and went in a special saloon car provided by a local coach proprietor.

The occasion was highly political. July 1889 was the centenary of the fall of the Bastille. It was celebrated with a Paris Universal Exhibition and also two labour gatherings. The first was a meeting of Marxist parties which formed the Second International. The other was a 'Possibilist' i.e. collaborationist conference of reformist trade union leaders which the MCTF delegates attended. Nothing much came from its deliberations, but within a few years both factions were united in the Second International.

The summer of 1890 saw a gala occasion for Darlaston when a presentation was made to Richard Juggins. During the day there was a procession through the crowded, flag bedecked town. In the evening local MPs attended a function in the town hall with trade union slogans such as 'Success to the MCTF', 'Defence not Defiance', 'Come let us Reason Together', etc. Local brass bands played and the chairman then spoke of Juggins' twenty years activity in forming the Nut & Bolt Union and then the MCTF. Listeners were reminded that the MCTF had started with just the three associations of Darlaston Nut & Bolt Workers, Dudley anvil makers and Walsall chain makers and had grown to 12,000 members. Juggins was then presented with an illuminated address and a purse of 100 sovereigns.

Middle class supporters were enrolled as honorary members of the MCTF and the annual report of 1891 when membership peaked at 14,000 showed the Liberal Wednesbury MP Stanhope and the Tory Dudley MP Brooke-Robinson so enrolled as were Wilson Lloyd the important Wednesbury industrialist as well as Richard Tangye. Membership at this time was changing. Female membership had increased. Gas tube makers were more important with branches from Walsall, Wolverhampton, Old Hill, Wednesbury, Birmingham and Middlesbrough. New groups of workers included Darlaston Tramwaymen. From outside the Black Country were London safemakers, brick makers from Shropshire, Saltney chainmakers, fibre dressers not only from Sheffield, but also Manchester and Long Milford. there were also pipe makers from Derby. There had also been progress in the Birmingham area with edge tool makers, spade and shovel and shipping tackle workers affiliated. Altogether the societies outside the Black Country contributed about £300 to the total income of £1,100. There was therefore perhaps some substance to the hope of the auditors that 'instead of a Midland Counties Federation, it will develop into a national one and embrace the whole of the trades of the UK.' The biggest societies were the local ones. Willenhall Lockmakers paid in £163, Cradley Heath chainmakers contributed £156, Wednesbury Tubemakers £72 and Wolverhampton Lockmakers £55. Once again, strike activity had been heavy at over £700 of which £374 went to chainmakers and £216 to tubemakers. During the 1890s the Federation could not escape the political problems which, in a later period, destroyed the whole edifice and made the MCTF an anachronism. The process can be followed through the changing attitudes of honorary members. Before the 1891 Conference, Lloyd made it clear that he did not approve of the agenda and did not intend to attend. He claimed that he had been astonished to find that instead of the conference discussing labour questions these had to a great extent been omitted in favour of 'the so-called Labour programme'. This included such subjects as the disestablishment of the Church and one man one vote. He could only conclude that some members of the Federation desired to turn it into a Radical Association. He had always taken a great interest in trade unions, Lloyd concluded, which in many districts were beneficial both to employers and employees, but the introduction of politics into labour questions was certain to do great harm.

When the AGM opened, the opinions of Wilson Lloyd were discussed and roundly condemned as an attempt to dictate the agenda to working men. Stanhope addressed the conference saying that he saw nothing political in the motions. They affected Conservatives equally with Liberals and he had long been in favour of disestablishment of the Church. Further political matters affected the other Conservative honorary member, Brooke Robinson, for it was proposed that Juggins be nominated a Labour candidate for the Dudley parliamentary seat. This was opposed by important sections of the Federation on financial grounds and also that Juggins' loss to the Federation would outweigh his usefulness as an MP. The eventual resolution to nominate Juggins was passed by 19 votes to 13.

By the tenth anniversary of the MCTF in 1896 the only original honorary member was Tangye. The new ones included both the Tory and the Liberal MPs for Wolverhampton, Sir Alfred Hickman and H.H. Fowler. The tenth anniversary also saw an upturn of membership after a dip from 1891 which had taken membership down to 4,000 by 1894. The rise continued until 1900 when it was at an all time peak of nearly 20,000 members. The 1896 Report also announced an innovation. Boys, previously underpaid had formed their own society and affiliated to the Federation.

In 1895 the Federation suffered a grievous loss with the death of Richard Juggins. Juggins was a figure of national stature and one of the most important and interesting trade unionists that the Black Country has produced. If he had not died at the early age of 53 his impact on the politics of the area would have been even greater. But the two organisations that Juggins had built survived. The MCTF was taken over by Councillor J. Taylor of the Dudley anchor smiths, one of the three original organisations of the Federation. Taylor, however, an archetypal Lib-Lab trade unionist had neither the flair nor the energy of Juggins and it must be speculated whether the Federation might have taken a different direction later had Juggins remained at its head.

For the time being, the Federation grew. In 1898 two important additions were Dudley Corporation Employees and the General Union of Toolmakers, Engineers and Machinists. In 1899 further outsiders affiliated notably Wigan Lockmakers and Coventry Tram men.

At the end of our period in 1900 we can summarise the activities and progress of the MCTF as follows. Parliamentary activity was particularly important. The Fair Wages Clauses and extensions of the Factory and Workshops Acts were particularly relevant. The parliamentary honorary members provided facilities at the House of Commons both for meetings and also for contacting ministers and others. Despite the avowed intention of the Federation to avoid strikes, much of its income was usually devoted to strike pay. There can be no doubt that its ability and willingness to take up the grievances of members with militant action when conciliation had failed was an important reason for its success, particularly as these early years of the MCTF were almost entirely within the period of the Great Depression when successful industrial action was very difficult and many larger unions were disappearing or becoming ineffective.

Another notable feature was that the Assemblies of the Knights of Labour had disappeared by the mid '90s.

Finally, the dream of the Federation becoming a national organisation covering all trades was not to be. Federations based on more militant principles came into existence such as the Miners' Federation of Great Britain. The supreme irony was that when the General Federation of Trade Unions was formed with the blessing of the TUC in 1899, with the same ideas of class collaboration and conciliation as the MCTF, the executive of the latter considered the question carefully, but decided not to affiliate to the National Federation even though they were represented at the inaugural conference. This decision was not maintained and for the whole subsequent period of existence of the MCTF it was affiliated to the GFTU.

The MCTF continued to be an organisation based in the Black Country and supportive of all those small crafts who, left to their own devices, would have been less successful in maintaining their wages and conditions.

Finally, it must again be stressed that the MCTF was the organisational rock around which the chainmakers fought their battles against starvation.

The Noble Order of the Knights of Labour

The meteoric rise and almost equally precipitous decline in the 1880s of the Knights of Labour has few parallels in world labour history. Its influence extended from the USA into Canada and Europe and into Australia. In Britain, its greatest influence was in the Black Country and Birmingham.

The Knights originated in Philadelphia in 1869 as a secret organisation with an elaborate Masonic-type ritual of organisation and high-sounding titles such as Master Workman, Worthy Foreman etc. The value of secrecy was that it protected members from anti-trade union employers in the USA while binding its members together in a universal brotherhood. Born after the Civil War when US employers were prepared to resort to mass murder to prevent trade unions developing, there is a certain parallel between such an organisation and those of British workers during the period of the Combination Acts 1799-1825 when our trade unions were illegal. The Knights was never a Socialist organisation. It believed that the interests of capital and labour were identical, but it recognised that labour was the 'only creator of values' and aimed to create a universal brotherhood through co-operatives and education. Here the parallel is with our Owenite Socialism of the 1830s and '40s.

The Knights made little progress until 1881 when they abandoned secrecy and went public. Growth from that time was astronomic. From 71,000 in 1884 it reached its maximum membership of 700,000 in October 1886. Its fall thereafter was equally swift. By 1890 it was down to 100,000 members and in 1895 20,000. Its role was increasingly taken over by the American Federation of Labour formed in 1886. But the Knights lingered on until the last Assembly joined the AF of L in 1949.

The significance of the Knights for the U.S. labour tradition is that it was the first mass organisation of native-born Americans, earlier movements having been initiated or dominated by immigrant European workers. The Knights initiated the democratic tradition of organising men and women, advocating equal pay for equal work. It organised skilled and unskilled workers. It organised in both north and south of the country. Above all, it organised Negroes and advocated equality of treatment; although its practice fell short of its ideal.

It can be seen that such an organisation would have considerable attractions for the craft workers constituting the Midland Counties Trades Federation, notably peaceful relations with capital, and the avoidance of strikes where possible.

The Knights first appeared in the Black Country through Local Assembly 300 of Pittsburg, which was, in fact, a national union of all the window glass workers of the USA. This 3,000 strong body of skilled craftsmen had gained a monopoly position in the US and were keen to protect this monopoly by contact with glass workers abroad. In November 1884 Local Assembly 3504 was formed of four preceptories of the four large firms making sheet glass in England, namely Pilkingtons and Stock, both of Lancashire. Hartleys of Sunderland and Chance Brothers of Spon Lane, Smethwick. The Spon Lane preceptory was probably the most successful of the four. In 1887 it was reported that 'all or nearly all' of men in the rolled plate department were members.

Assemblies were soon set up in many different trades, but a prime cause of their success in the Black Country was the leadership of Jesse Chapman, the headmaster of a school in Smethwick, and Haydn Sanders, the Walsall socialist. In June 1886 the first mixed assembly of Knights was formed at West Bromwich. Later that year similar local assemblies were formed in Cradley Heath and Handsworth. In 1887 assemblies were formed at Winson Green and Smethwick. In 1888 Wolverhampton, Smethwick, Cradley Heath and Sedgley assemblies were formed, with a further two in Birmingham. In December 1889 an assembly was formed in Bloxwich. The above is taken from a list by Henry Pelling, the historian of the Knights in Britain. To his list we can add the Lye and Wollescote assembly in existence in 1889 and affiliated to the MCTF in 1890 with a separate female section. Also the Stamber Mill assembly, in the town of Stourbridge.

This rapid growth necessitated district organisation and in 1887 the Handsworth District Assembly was created and the next year another one at Cradley Heath.

The Knights were particularly successful in Walsall. Haydn Sanders had been elected a town councillor in 1888 as a Social Democratic Federation candidate. He was also Master Workman of LA

454 and no doubt responsible for the affiliation of such Walsall trade unions as the Bridle Bit Forgers and Saddle Tree Makers. In November 1889 two Knights put up in the Walsall municipal elections and achieved a solid vote, although not elected. In 1890 a Knight was elected to the West Bromwich School Board.

As we have seen the Midland Counties Trades Federation was formed to affiliate to the Knights. We know that local Assemblies and also Sheffield and the North West Assemblies were affiliated to the MCTF, but MCTF never itself affiliated to the Knights. It is also noteworthy that nowhere in its annual reports does the MCTF mention the Knights of Labour but one is left to assume that the Assemblies affiliated to the MCTF could be nothing other than those of the Knights of Labour. On the other hand, the MCTF went to considerable lengths to invite to its public meetings such notables as the trade union MPs Burt and Fenwick, who had personal knowledge of and were sympathetic to the Knights.

In fact the Knights faced many problems in the Black Country. Were they to be trade unions, or federations of trade unions, or to develop as an educational and co-operative non-party political organisation? Were they an eminently respectable organisation seeking reconciliation between capital and labour or were they a subversive, communist organisation advocating anarchy?

The latter became an important issue after the Haymarket bombings in the USA in 1886 and the growth of anarchism in Europe. All these issues were discussed in the West Bromwich paper *Labour Tribune* and it is clear that the issues affected not only a few activists, but the whole body of working people, including the miners and ironworkers.

The religious issue came to centre around the attitude of the Catholic church. The Knights were condemned in 1884 as a socialist and revolutionary organisation. The response of the American leadership under Powderly was to trim their policies to try to demonstrate that they were neither. In 1886 they were rewarded with the withdrawal of this condemnation. An article in *Labour Tribune,* reprinted from the *Catholic Times,* explained that a commission of twelve archbishops in America had decided by 10 votes to 2 that not only were the Knights not hostile to the church, but the reverse; that it was necessary for men to organise to protect themselves from injustice. The Commission strongly condemned the heartless avarice of monopolies which, to increase their revenues, ruthlessly crushed the working men, women and children in their employment.

Typical of the case made for the Knights was a letter in the *Labour Tribune* of Oct 1882. At a time when 'capitalists were resorting to every mean trick to reduce wages and wrench from them the few privileges forced by our ancestors from the employers', how could working men bring about that happy situation when they should enjoy the fruits of their labours? The only answer, he went on, was combination everywhere, and the society giving the greatest facilities for this was the Knights of Labour. The *Labour Tribune* headline was 'A Rosy Picture', making it clear that the paper did not necessarily support the man, although they were not hostile to the Knights.

Influential also were letters from the considerable body of workers who had emigrated to the USA and kept in touch with affairs at home. An ex-West Bromwich miner wrote in November 1888 stating that the *Labour Tribune* circulated there and that trade unionism was growing rapidly. But he warned that the Knights of Labour was a secret organisation condemned by nearly all the churches in America, and they had declared war on the unions. It was nothing more than a political organisation in no way suited to deal with industrial disputes. 'I say men, beware of the designing intrigues of the Knights of Labour', he ended.

In July 1887 a report of an ironworkers meeting at Brierley Hill showed some support for the Knights. Others, however, were opposed to them, one man causing laughter by saying that they were better with the devil they knew and he had more hope of getting money back from the North than from America. Another complained that the Knights were always interfering in politics. Despite these criticisms, support for the Knights continued to be expressed in the *Labour Tribune.* This support continued across the years that the Knights were declining in America.

One disadvantage of being part of an American organisation was that funds were not protected under the Trade Union Acts. The failure of a prosecution in 1890 to recover embezzled funds led to negotiations with the parent organisation to set up an independent body. In August 1891 after two conferences in Smethwick involving at least 30 delegates, mainly from the Black Country and Birmingham, the British Assembly of the Knights of Labour was set up with its headquarters at Cradley Heath. This was registered with the Registrar of Friendly Societies and seems to have included the Cradley Heath district and the Sheffield and Rotherham District, but apparently not the Birmingham District, which remained under its old constitution.

Reports of activities into the 1890s continued. The Knights were influential in the West Bromwich firm of Kenricks where their penchant for negotiation was acknowledged before a strike took place in 1890. In September 1890 at a meeting called by the Wolverhampton Trades Council to further labour representation in the town it was noted that 'Reynolds of the Knights of Labour was present.' Decline of membership was occurring, however and in 1892 national membership was put at only 434.

Influence within the Lib-Lab dominated Local Electoral Associations seems to have been the final sphere of influence of the Knights. After 1891 nothing further is heard of them in the Black Country.

This short-lived success of the Knights in the Black Country is an interesting episode. After its introduction it seems to have put down strong roots as shown by the fact that it was expanding while the parent organisation was declining, and found influence among the big unions of miners and ironworkers as well as the craft unions.

Its history in Britain is positively placid compared with its American experience. US support peaked n 1886 with the great strikes against the railway robber baron Jay Gould, who boasted that he could hire half the working class to kill the other half. Just as important as the strikes were the fantastic boycotts of customers and suppliers such as that against the *New York Tribune* which was sustained for nine years. The boycott has never been an important weapon in England. The decline of the Knights came when the bureaucratic leadership under Terence V. Powderly reacted to red-baiting criticism by forbidding strikes and abandoning the leading trade unionists who were framed for the deaths caused by the Haymarket bomb thrown either by an anarchist or by an agent-provocateur.

But the Knights were eventually eclipsed in America by an organisation more suited to the times – the American Federation of Labour. It is likely that their ultimate failure in the Black Country was due to there being a British organisation able to do everything that the Knights could do – the Midland Counties Trades Federation.

Nuts and bolts

We have seen how the Nut and Bolt Forgers' Protection Society was formed by Juggins in 1871, how it prospered through the boom, and became the National Amalgamated Society of Nut & Bolt Workers in 1874. By 1876 it had 1,900 members in 34 branches as far apart as Accrington, Sunderland, Wales and London, although its main base was always in Darlaston.

By 1877 the boom was over and employers were demanding a revised Price List to replace that of 1872 which the men, in rejecting it, claimed would reduce wages by up to 30 per cent. A protracted five month lock-out followed which ended with Joseph Chamblerlain accepting the role of arbitrator and granting reductions of between 5 per cent and 15 per cent on the 1872 Price List. This was a better settlement than the men might have expected.

This 1877 Price List soon became obsolete and another was negotiated by Richard Chamberlain, who had succeeded Joseph, as arbitrator. This was finalised in 1881.

In the 1880s, however, foreign competition was undermining the nut and bolt trade, and Juggins' thoughts turned to wider organisation to protect the trade. At first he turned to the S. Staffs. & E. Worcs. Trades Council established in 1882. When that failed he turned to the Knights of Labour and the Midland Counties Trades Federation.

As further reductions were demanded by the employers Juggins then turned to the 'alliance philosophy' in the trade. Meetings with employers brought agreement on two points. The first was that the time had come 'for a complete union between employers and workers in the nut and bolt trade.' The second point was that employers should employ only union men and union men would work only for associated employers and withhold labour from non-associated employers. Heroic efforts were made to implement this price fixing cartel. It foundered on the intransigence of one employer, James Wiley owner of the Earle Works in Darlaston, who employed just 25 men.

Juggins, however, persisted with the 'alliance philosophy' and he turned his attention to the formation of a Wages Board. This came into existence in 1889 as the S. Staffs. Nut & Bolt Wages Board. It was formed at a favourable time and brought an immediate 5 per cent wage advance and acceptance of a revised 1887 Price List. But the Great Depression was not yet finished and the next year prices began to fall again. By 1892 operatives were working only two days a week and the employers demanded a 15 per cent reduction. Agreement could not be reached, and the men were reduced to tinkering with the machinery of the Wages Board. It was enlarged to 12 members for each side and the appointment of a secretary for each side imitating the Midlands Iron & Steel Wages Board.

The continued shrinking of the market for hand made nuts and bolts, however, defeated all Juggins' efforts and the increasing number of semi-skilled factory operatives turned not to the MCTF but to the new general unions for organisation.

Locks

The Willenhall Amalgamated Society of Lock and Key Smiths founded in 1876 survived precariously until 1880. Trade unionism was not to revive until the later years of the decade. A Walsall Lockmakers' Society was active in 1887 when the *Ironmonger* reported a settlement at Martin & Taylor's of West Bromwich negotiated by Juggins and William Millerchip (who was to become president of the national union).

The national union was formed on the 9th. March 1889 as the National Amalgamated Lock, Latch and Keysmiths Trade Society. It has survived to the present day. This national union worked closely with the MCTF from its inception. Workers at Chubbs also associated with the National Federation of Labour Unions, a short-lived London based organisation with similar aims to the MCTF set up in the wake of the 1889 Dock Strike, but dominated by the socialists of the Social Democratic Federation. This came about because Chubbs also had a factory in London. The management were determined to end the collaboration of the men. A telegram from Wolverhampton to the London Chubbs' management stated that Williams (an officer of the NFLUs was expected to address a meeting at Horseley Fields, Wolverhampton and 'precautions must be taken to prevent him.' The occasion was a strike at Chubbs' London factory and Williams would be seeking support from Wolverhampton and Willenhall. Whether the firm was successful or not in gagging Williams we do not know.

The national union grew rapidly. By the end of 1889 Mark Stanley was reporting 1,000 members. In this first year the union negotiated a 10 per cent increase in wages to take effect from 1 January 1890. Willenhall employers decided to pay the increase only from 1 February 1890. At a strike meeting of 1,000 people Stanley said that the employers had broken their promise and if the men had done this they would have found themselves in the County Court. Juggins said that when he and Stanley waited on the Wolverhampton employers they were treated with courtesy. At Willenhall this had not been so, although the brass padlock manufacturers had behaved as gentlemen and agreement had been reached with them. The Wolverhampton men supported those from Willenhall, 500 of whom were on strike with 1,200 still at work. Some Wolverhampton employers supported the strike, it was said, and one had contributed £5. By 6 January more employers were paying and the strike ended successfully. This was followed by another successful strike in 1891.

The union ran into unspecified administrative difficulties when Mark Stanley was dismissed as secretary and G. Handley elected in his place with E. Beebee as president.

Membership fluctuated in the 1890s falling to 1,050 in 1894 and rising to 1,670 in 1896.

In 1896 the union decided that trade had improved sufficiently to warrant a demand for another 10 per cent increase in wages. Mass meetings in Wolverhampton, Walsall and Willenhall all agreed on strike action as negotiations had failed. The padlock manufacturers proposed an immediate increase of 5 per cent with a further 5 per cent at the beginning of 1897. This was accepted and talk of a Conciliation Board excited Millerchip and other leaders. However, there was trouble at Legges of Willenhall over union membership at that time and whether the settlement was general is not known.

The settlemen highlights the difficulties of the union at that time. The 'spread' between

Willenhall, Wolverhampton and Walsall was one problem. Another was that of competition among large numbers of small producers making locks so quickly that it was said if a man dropped a lock on the floor he did not bother to pick it up but made a new one. This, with large numbers of outworkers and growing numbers of women made Willenhall, with 60 per cent of its population dependent on the lock trade, a disaster area when trade was bad. In 1896 when the 10 per cent increase was demanded John Taylor (secretary of the MCTF) stated that this would raise average wages to 24/-d. But many were out of work at that time and as the union did not grant unemployment pay, many members were being lost.

However, the remaining years of the century brought better trade and by 1900 the union had nearly 2,000 members and almost £3,000 in the bank. In that year Charles Loat, the secretary of the union, was elected as the first Labour member of the Willenhall Urban District Council. The future looked rosy, but trouble was not far away.

Other crafts

Evidence for the existence of the considerable number of smaller craft trade unions not so far dealt with must be looked for in the records of the umbrella organisations such as the MCTF and the trades councils.

The Dudley based Amalgamated Society of Anvil & Vice Makers, whose secretary was John Taylor, was one of the three founding unions of the MCTF. It remained a pillar of the Federation and when Richard Juggins died in 1895, Taylor became the new secretary. Other small trades affiliated to the MCTF in 1889 included File Cutters of Wolverhampton and also Upper Gornal and the Gunlock Filers of Darlaston whose prices were raised from 3½d. to 7d. in action with the MCTF but which still left them on starvation wages. There were also the Spade and Shovel Workers of Stourbridge & District. The next year these were joined by Lower Gornal brickmakers, Edge Tool Makers at Birmingham, Wolverhampton and Dudley, Dudley Fender Makers and also Fire Iron Makers and the Vermin Trap Makers of Wednesfield. In 1891 Spring Trap Makers joined them and in 1895 the Anchor Smiths of Cradley, the Spring Hook Forgers & Filers of Walsall and also the Walsall Hame Makers affiliated. By 1898 Engine & Cranemen from Wolverhampton, Wednesbury, Tipton and Coseley had also joined the MCTF.

No numbers can be put to the membership of these unions and their size could only be estimated from the financial contributions that they made.

Something of the contribution of these smaller societies to the MCTF can be gauged by their activities on the main committees. In the early days no executive was elected but only a Sub-Committee. In 1890 the officers were Juggins (Nut & Bolt Workers) secretary, John Taylor (Anvil Makers) chairman, John Richards (Nut & Bolt Workers) vice-chair. The three sub-committee members were W. Bardell (Walsall Tube Makers), John Taylor and J. Williams whose union cannot be identified. In 1891 three Trustees were created and these were the heavyweights of the Federation – Thomas Homer (Chains), William Millerchip (Walsall Locks) and H. Homer (Smethwick Chains). Juggins seems to have been his own treasurer and together with the secretary's annual report, a financial statement was given by two auditors.

After the death of Juggins, the annual report came from an executive committee and not the secretary. The EC in 1896 consisted of John Taylor, Thomas Jones (Wednesbury Tubes), William Millerchip, Thomas Sitch, and George Howard (Willenhall Locks). Also Thomas Garvey, William Fell, Joseph Forrest, James P. Price, Elias Eveson, and William Kendall whose societies are not known and none appear on the list of secretaries of affiliated societies.

Nails

From the ending of the Great Boom in 1875 until the early years of the twentieth century the desperate plight of the nail and chain makers created a national scandal, with the Black Country pilloried as the area of White Slavery in England.

The highs and lows of wages must always be related to the trade cycle. In his report for the half year ending April 1875 the factory sub-Inspector for the area said that trade had never been so good.

In his next report he stated that children could earn between 8/-d. and 10/-d. per week and some parents could earn 30/-d. to 60/-d. per week. Not too much credence is to put on some of the pronouncements of the early Factory Inspectors and it would be very exceptional for earnings to reach the higher sum mentioned in each case. By 1879 however, prices had been dropping like a stone and in that year Blenkinsopp, the inspector, reported that trade had never been so bad in his experience and 'nailers have been brought to extreme want by a drop of 30 per cent in prices since August 1878.' By this time, according to evidence at the Royal Commission on Labour showed that male adult wages in nails were 10/-d. to 12/-d. a week.

The Depression was only part of the reason for these low wages. The other was that the domestic nail trade was rapidly disappearing. Tildesley had reported that there were 50,000 nailmakers in the Black Country in 1830. According to the 1871 Census this had fallen to barely 20,000. As the Depression deepened this was to fall still further as the higher paid horse shoe nail succumbed to much cheaper machine production. By 1901 the number of nailers had fallen to just over 4,000 equally divided between men and women. Deteriorating conditions during the Depression strengthened the hand of the Fogger. Loathed by all, he nevertheless was an essential figure accommodating nailers who were forced to sell their nails more than once a week and who provided iron when the 'respectable' nailmasters were not doing so because of a glut of nails. It was always in the hands of the 'respectable' masters to drive out the fogger by providing at list price the services the fogger provided at lower prices, but this they failed to do.

As a consequence of this fall in numbers the nailers were less able to protect themselves. There continued to be a large number of strikes, but by sections only of nailers under almost impossible conditions. This contrasts with the period 1850-75 when the nailers fought bitterly with every weapon, including dirgying, to maintain their conditions.

For trade union activity we turn to the annual reports of the Midland Counties Trades Federation. In 1888 separate organisations of Horse Shoe Nail Makers from Old Hill, Halesowen and Oldswinford were affiliated to the MCTF. There were also Spike Nail Makers from Halesowen and Sedgley, each with a separate female section; also general nailmakers from Oldswinford, again with a female section. Strike activity in that year is attested to by the granting of the considerable amount of £120 to the Horse Shoe Nail Makers of Old Hill and District. The next year Skip Nail Makers of Lye joined them and both Halesowen and Sedgley Spike Nail Makers had received considerable amounts of strike benefit. With the Horse Shoe nail disappearing into factories, the only buoyant part of the trade was the spike nail. This was a heavy nail ranging from 4 inches to 8 or even 9 inches used mainly in ships with a similar nail widely used on the railways known as a 'brog.' The making of these nails gave rise to many of the complaints regarding women making these spikes. The iron came in rods of 56lbs which women were often obliged to carry over long distances. Then the rods had to be cut the right size for the spike. This was done cold with women and men (sometimes as many as five people) holding each other by the waist and jumping up and down on the treadle which operated the oliver (hammer) which struck the cutting instrument. This was considered immodest and totally exhausting. Spike nail makers often worked in pairs, a man 'heading' and a woman 'pointing'. Pointing required the red hot rod to be drawn out over its entire length into a point at the end. This required both the use of the oliver operated by the foot together with blows from a 2lb hammer hitting as hard as a blacksmith shaping horse shoes would strike. This was bad enough, but women sometimes headed as well. This entailed a great deal more exertion with oliver and hammer to fashion the large head of the spike.

Spike nail makers continued to dominate the nailmakers affiliated to the MCTF, but by 1896 there were no nailers at all so associated.

Of the numerous enquiries into the nail and chain trade in this period we can quote the evidence given to the Royal Commission on the Depression of Trade and Industry in 1889 of John Price for fifty years a nailer and for 41 years district chairman of the Nailers' Association. He gave his earnings at that time as 10/6d. a week gross and 8/6d. net after deductions for carriage and gleeds. His wife, who was 68, could earn 3/-d. gross or 2/6d. net. For this he worked 12½ hours each weekday with a two hour break. On Saturdays he worked until 10am when he took his nails to the warehouse. The work was very, very hard he said. No doubt a younger man might have earned somewhat more, but the example illustrates the circumstances of older nailers who had no alternative but to continue working.

Price also discussed general wages. In 1889 prices were between 45 per cent and 55 per cent lower than the peak of 1874. An increase of 10 per cent, which Price thought that masters could well afford would only bring prices back to the 1879 price which was known as the Starvation List.

From their nadir of 1889, the nailers struck back supported by public opinion throughout the country. The most notable of a series of strikes was the 1891 sixteen week strike. This began with a demand for a 10 per cent increase. The *Sunday Chronicle* sent an experienced reporter (almost certainly H.W. Nevinson) into the Black Country. As a result of his reports, the paper offered the nailers £100 a week if they would increase their demand to 50 per cent, a rise which the chainmakers had just achieved. With this and other outside support the 50 per cent was won. This seems to have been followed by a genuine effort by responsible nailmasters to curb the worst excesses of the fogger. In 1892 a Staffs. & Worcs. Wrought Nailmasters Association was formed and in 1893 a short-lived Wages Board for the trade was formed. These promising moves were undermined by the return of the Depression and in 1894 the Factory Inspector was once again reporting trade in the district as depressed as he had ever known it.

Chain makers

Despite the contrast between the declining nail industry and the expanding chain industry there appears to be no discernible difference at all between the inadequacy of the wages and squalor of the conditions of the two sets of workers.

Public concern with 'sweated industries' led to the setting up of the Select Committee of the House of Lords. In its fifth report of 1890 the Committee reported, 'Scarcely any industry came under our notice where there was so much poverty, combined with such severe work and so many hardships.'

The best generalisation with regard to wages remains that for both domestic nail and chain trade male workers would average between 18/6. and 20/-d. per week net in good times and half that in bad times. Women would earn half the wages of men. George Green, the manager for Eliza Tinsley & Co. stated that for heavy chain, after an increase of 15 per cent, men's net pay had averaged 26/11d the previous year. For commoner chain a man making 7 cwt. of chain could earn 24/6. gross less 25 per cent for tools rent and firing leaving 17/6d. net. The average for women on the firm's books was 8/2. per week with deductions of 12½ per cent making 7/2d. net. Young persons and children began with 'blowing' at 2/6d. a week. By the time they were sixteen to eighteen 'if they were sharp and quick' they could be earning 6/-d. to 8/-d. a week. These wages were for a full week's work in a period of temporarily higher wages for one of the largest producers in the Black Country. For those working for a fogger the wage would be much lower. Juggins gave average net earnings for men in domestic chain shops as from 10/d. to 14/-d. at this time.

Non-wage abuses in the trade included 'long reckonings'; Bessano, a JP and by no means a sympathetic observer, stated that sometimes wages were not paid for months and this led to money being borrowed at extortionate rates of interest and payment in truck.

Objections to the employment of women ranged from its immodesty – young girls 'blowing' on a platform at eye level for men – the shedding of clothing in hot weather, and women working on large sizes of iron.

Common abuses were the giving out of the wrong size of iron which meant a visit to an ironchanger and an extra payment, payment for a smaller size of iron than that actually worked, 'errors' in weighing, and complaints regarding the quality of iron.

The first Act of Parliament to protect all working children in the Black Country (the only previous Act had forbidden the working of children in mines) was the Factory Act Extension Act of 1867 which extended the provisions of the Act to Workshops and brought, for the first time, Factory Inspectors into the area. The Act limited the working hours of children under 13 to 30 per week with

15 hours per week schooling for such children until they passed a certain standard. The Factory Acts also limited women's hours to 10½ per day.

Although powerless to raise wages during the Great Depression, the unions pressed strongly through the TUC, through Parliament and by evidence to the many Enquiries of the time, for improved conditions in nails and chains. The most widespread proposal was to limit women to a certain size of iron. Juggins advocated ¼" iron for both nails and chains. An employer, Hingley the MP, advocated ⅜" restriction for chain and ¼" for nails.

The unions believed that the curse of the trade was the married woman whose total wages less the amount she paid for child care while she worked was virtually zero, and that there would be a more civilised family life if women remained at home. Such proposals met with considerable opposition as a general attempt to restrict female work opportunities, and they failed to meet the case of the numerous widows and women caring for disabled husbands, who were obliged to work. Other proposals were to limit women's hours from 6am to 6pm or 7am to 7pm, which would also make workshop inspection easier, but it was claimed that women with household duties would want to work outside those hours. Another proposal was to ban girls under 16 from working, a limit which then applied to brickworks. This raised the vexed issue of birth certificates and the general inadequacy of inspection. A ban on boys and women 'blowing' was yet another proposal.

Another much canvassed proposal was the setting up of Co-operatives. Such solutions dated back to at least the Owenites in Britain and forward to the Knights of Labour. But co-operatives were invariably set up in periods of slump when conditions for their survival were at their worst. Both nail and chain co-operatives had been set up, but all were short lived.

The most radical co-operative plan was put to the Royal Commission on the Depression of Trade & Industry in 1889 by John Lincoln Mahon. a well known socialist from outside the area, endorsed by the Midland Counties Trades Federation. Mahon claimed that co-operatives failed because they were set up by manual workers with no experience of administration. To remedy this Mahon proposed that Parliament should create local boards of management who would be paid partly by salary and partly by commission. The government should then advance money to build factories on the same sort of terms that money was advanced to School Boards. For security the government would have a claim on the buildings and stock, and if the scheme were not successful the government would only have lost a few thousand pounds. The object of the scheme was to supplant all domestic workshops. The chain trade was particularly suited to the scheme because it did not face foreign competition, Mahon claimed. Foggers would disappear as would chainmasters, who were really merchants, very few actually making chain. The question of female labour should be left to the chainmakers themselves most of whom, Mahon claimed, were against wives working. Curtailment of hours would enable more people to be employed, as would the forbidding of children in the trade until they were fourteen years of age. Prices would not necessarily rise, but Mahon advocated deliberately raising prices if an average wage of 30/-d. per week for men was not reached. Any attempt to trade privately in order to lower wages would be stopped by the trade unions and if a conspiracy of capitalists were formed, the state should put it down. Mahon reckoned the scheme would cost about £200,000 and a return of between 3 per cent and 5 per cent could be guaranteed.

Such a utopian scheme had no chance of being accepted, and when that and other options discussed above were rejected the only course left was for the chainmakers to make common cause with the employers and try to implement the 'alliance philosophy'. This transformation was to be accomplished, but not in this period, nor by Richard Juggins, who died in 1895. It was achieved by Thomas Sitch in the years after 1900 with a union which he formed in 1889 and whose early history now claims our attention.

Thomas Sitch was born in Cradley Heath in 1852 and began work at the age of eight as a blower. When he was seventeen and already an experienced chainmaker his family moved to Newcastle-on-Tyne and Thomas went with them. He worked there in the chain trade, interested himself in trade unionism and became the youngest member of the local Trades Council.

He later moved to Saltney, near Chester and worked for Wood & Co. on government contracts. Finding no trade union organisation there he founded in July 1889 the Chainmakers & Strikers

Association of Saltney, Pontypridd & Staffordshire with himself as general secretary and just fifteen members drawn from Wood's factory. This was a union for factory workers only, and being only too well aware of competition from the overcrowded domestic trade, Sitch founded in the same year the National Amalgamation of Chainmakers' & Chainstrikers' Association conceived as an umbrella organisation for all in the trade whether factory or domestic. The Amalgamation supported the great 18 month strike for the 5/-d. list i.e. an increase of 25 per cent in 1892, but funds for this and previous strikes channelled from the factory union through the Amalgamation, exhausted its funds and with the formation of a separate union for domestic workers in 1892, the Cradley Heath & District Chainmakers Association, the factory union was freed from the drain of supporting the outworkers.

In 1894 Sitch returned to Cradley Heath to become full-time secretary of the factory union which, by 1896, had a membership of 850. By 1896 the Chainmakers' & Strikers' Union was well able to look after the factory workers, but the plight of the domestic worker continued dire. An epic year old strike in 1886-87 had been supported by the newly emerged Socialists, and the Liberal press coverage brought nation wide public support. An upturn of trade from 1889 to 1891 brought conditions for further struggles to raise wages and this temporary upturn brought the great Dock Strike of 1889 and organisation of the unskilled and semi-skilled throughout the country. The Midlands Counties Trades Federation was part of this general movement and the support it gave to the domestic chain makers can be followed from its annual reports.

In his 1890 report Juggins stated that the relief the chainmakers had gained in previous years had been under attack by employers intent on reducing them to the state of misery and starvation they had previously experienced. But 'this was not so easily to be done as in days gone by, the operatives being fairly well organised and connected with the Federation... Thus they have been able to hold their own.' The next year the chainmakers of Cradley Heath and District received £374 of the £718 spent by the MCTF on strikes. The auditors reported that the district had not been free of strikes for the whole year. Many victories had been won and although the struggle to prevent reductions was still going on, the number out was considerably reduced.

After 1891 trade again declined and in 1892 the Factory Inspector reported a protracted strike for the 5/-d. List. By 1894 the Inspector was reporting that he had never known the district in such a depressed state. Of the nail and chain trade he reported. 'Price lists are made, but they are not adhered to. Wages are reduced and when they are at starvation level there are strikes or threats of strikes and a new Price List is agreed. Then the same cycle begins all over again.'

From 1895 trade improved and culminated in the boom of 1898-99. The Great Depression had come to an end. During these years of good trade there are few reports of chainworkers' strikes and the factory chainmakers tended to dominate the MCTF, which found better trade more propitious for its policy of conciliation.

Glassmakers

Little is known of trade union organisation in the plate glass industry which consisted in the Black Country of only the semi-monopolistic firm of Chance Brothers of Smethwick, specialising also in optical glass. The little we do know arises from the actions of the American glass makers concerned to protect their monopolistic position by exporting the Knights of Labour to this country. Their activities at Chance's have already been discussed. The Knights do not appear to have infiltrated the flint glass industry of blown table-ware, although the presence of an Assembly of Knights at Stourbridge does not entirely preclude the possibility. But this main branch of the glass trade continued to be dominated by the Flint Glass Makers' Union.

During the Great Depression the industry faced the contradictory situation of a rapidly expanding industry which did not proportionately benefit the Black Country largely because of foreign competition, notably from Germany. The Birmingham and Stourbridge branches continued to dominate the industry nationally and there was a subsidiary Black Country centre at Dudley. In 1874 there were roughly 340 union members in Birmingham and about 320 in Stourbridge. By 1900 the balance was reversed with about 300 members in Birmingham but about 400 in Stourbridge.

The effects of the Depression can be seen from the amounts paid out in unemployment benefit by the Stourbridge branch of the union:

Year	Unemployment Pay (Av. per Week)	Year	Unemployment Pay (Av. per Week)
1874	£2-10-0d.	1881-85	£89
1875	£23	1887-89	£269
1876	£48	1890-97	£71
1879	£211 (Sep-Nov)	1898	£96
1880	£142		

These figures follow the pattern for the rest of the Black Country. Full employment in 1874, a worsening position thereafter culminating with the disaster years of 1879-80. In the 1880s there was some relief, but not much, until two more terrible years in 1888-89. In the 1890s employment was better, but by the end of the century there was another slump.

The existence of the *Glassmakers' Magazine* allows us to follow the reaction of members of this ultra-conservative craft union to the problems of the Depression.

From 1877 the union was saying that the Depression was the worst since 1851 using this as justification for having to raise union contributions. The best means of removing the Depression was to meet with the employers, it was said. But when this was done no agreement could be reached on the way forward. The slump in table-ware was illustrated by Birmingham where in many places 'the trade was all tumblers and chimneys' i.e. all common glasses and globes for oil lamps. A constant concern of both the union and employers was with the retirement age of glass workers. This, the union maintained, was fifty, while the employers claimed that it was fifty five. Apart from the light this throws on working and social conditions, retirement was important to union funds as it was claimed that men 'went through the unemployment scales' before finally retiring; unemployment pay being more generous than superannuation benefit.

In these early years of the Depression, John Ruskin's analysis won much support with the union. It was caused, Ruskin maintained, by:

1. The separation of Masters and Men which was the employers' fault.
2. The loss of custom from bad work.
3. The substitution of machinery for labour had produced a glut.
4. Foreigners had realised that they had hands and brains like us.

By 1879 the drain on union funds for unemployment pay reached crisis point with bankruptcy predicted within twelve months if something was not done. Contributions were raised and rules for benefit tightened up. One issue never addressed was that union payments were paid quarterly. For a man in full benefit, including superannuation, this was more than 1/-d. a week. The result was that large numbers of union members were always in arrears and these had to be paid before any benefits could be claimed.

Disputes in the glass trade in these years were few, a five month strike in 1887 affecting most glassworks being exceptional. Discussion on the reasons for the Depression continued. In 1887 it was noted that the market for glass had quadrupled over the previous twenty years, but union membership remained about the same. This was partly due to the fact that non-trade unionists were increasing and there was much discussion on what to do with these 'nonners'. The main reason for the lack of union recruitment was, however, that the trade was going abroad, particularly to Germany. The Reports of the Royal Commission on the Depression of Trade and Industry in the 1890s brought further discussion on the causes of the Depression. The reason favoured by the employers was Overproduction. To this the unions counterposed Underconsumption. The former represented the laissez-faire view that nothing could be done until the extra production had been worked out of the economic system, while the latter view represented the socialist and interventionist view that the government should take steps to increase consumption.

In the 1890s when trade was improving and the drain on union funds decreased, a branch would move that for the three months of winter unemployment and superannuation pay should be increased by 1/-d. per week. This was usually unanimously approved by the branches.

One problem that better trade led the union to tackle was the disgracefully low wages earned by footmakers which, according to the secretary 'were a lasting disgrace to us as trade unionists'. The masters were approached to raise the wages of footmen and it was resolved that no further footmen be supplied by the union at a wage of less than 18/-d. or 19/-d. per week. It is not clear how successful this campaign was.

The general position facing the trade as the Depression came to an end can be seen from the report of the secretary for 1894:

> It is a sad fact to record that although the demand for glass is far greater than it has ever been in this country it is becoming increasingly more difficult for us to find employment for our members. This fact is proved by the long list of unemployed members that we constantly have before us, many of them good and industrious workers who are spending the best of their days in enforced idleness and consequently have no opportunity to make provision for the time when they will be incapable of working at the trade and have no income except the superannuation funds from the Society which are kept miserably low by the vast amounts that we are compelled to pay in providing for our unemployed.

Brass workers

Brass founding was an ancient craft often carried on in the same premises with iron casting. Such foundries were to be found in every Black Country town, but the national centre of the trade was in Birmingham. Separate trade union organisation for brass workers begins in that city with the setting up by W.J. Davis in 1872 of the Amalgamated Society of Brassworkers. Davis was one of the most remarkable trade union leaders produced in the west Midlands. He did not invent the 'alliance philosophy', nor was he the first to practice it, Juggins and his Nut & Bolt Workers having preceded him, but Davis brought the art of collaboration to its highest form. He organised the brassworkers by playing off one section of employers against another until all were transformed from the level of sweated workers to that of being reasonably paid. Davis was then responsible for bringing the many employers together together into an employers' association the more easily to negotiate with them. Numerous Alliances were then formed, the most famous of which was the Bedstead Alliance (producing most of the beds made in Britain) embracing all employers employing only union labour and all labour working only for Alliance firms. Like similar alliances in the Black Country organised by Juggins and the Midland Counties Trades Federations, these mostly survived the Depression at the cost of accepting ever lower wage levels, and continued into the better years of the later 1890s. Most perished however in the next slump after the Boer War.

The direct influence of Davis and his Alliances is not visible in the Black Country but, from the founding of the union, a Wolverhampton branch was in membership, Wolverhampton being the largest centre of the trade in the Black Country and there was also a Walsall branch.

One of the attractions of the Brassworkers was its generous benefit scales. For a weekly subscription of 9d. (7d. for members under 21) members received £1-2-6d. approved collective dispute pay or 15/-d. approved individual dispute pay. Out of work benefit was 10/-d a week and sick pay 5/-d. Superannuation benefit ranged from 5/-d. to 7/-d. a week and accident benefit was not more than £50. Funeral benefit was £10 for a member, £5 for his wife and £1 for a child. There was an emigration fund paying between £3-10-0d. and £5. Legal expenses were paid in approved cases. If members could not afford to pay for all these benefits there was a 'trade section' giving dispute pay only for a contribution of 6d. per week. For the more affluent, a 1/1d. weekly contribution (11d for those under 21) would buy an improved sick benefit of 11/-d. per week plus a new year dividend of 10/-d.

The fortunes of the union between 1872 and 1900 reflect both the presence of W.J. Davis (he left in 1883 to become one of the first working men Factory Inspectors and returned as secretary of the union in 1889) and the Depression. In 1875 Wolverhampton membership peaked at 401. The next year it declined to 377 when Walsall membership was 45. Walsall membership declined until 1891 when it was 18, but Wolverhampton rose from 1888 when it was down to 221 up to 380 in 1900. Walsall membership was 73 in that year. There had been a Bilston branch in 1878 of 38, but this disappeared. In 1900 there were also branches in Dudley (38 members), Wednesbury (32), Willenhall (16) and West Bromwich (5). National membership had dropped from 5090 in 1875 down to 2243 in

1888. But with the return of Davis he could claim in 1891 that every known brassworker was associated with the union and its total membership was almost 8,000.

In 1899 Davis reported that trade had been improving since 1896 and 'astute observers believed that a great future was opening up for...the whole human race and within a generation or two millions of savages and semi-savages would be exchanging commodities with us'. Davis might have done better to remember his remarks of the previous year when he wrote that 'the present prosperity may not last...' for in 1901 he reported 'a gradual decline in trade'. This presaged the first slump of the new century.

Railwaymen

Early trade unionists on the railways faced special difficulties. Not only were employers bitterly opposed to unions, but they believed that the only way to operate the railways was as quasi-military organisations with military discipline. Security of employment was supposed to compensate for extremely long hours, low wages and the horrific accident rate among operating grades. In addition, those who had the temerity to organise were promptly dismissed.

No doubt early Friendly Societies were a cover for union activity and in April 1858 the local newspaper tells us that railwaymen met in Wolverhampton to discuss setting up a Benevolent Society. National organisation begins, however, with the setting up of the Amalgamated Society of Railway Servants in 1871. Appropriate to its servile name, it was launched by Michael Bass MP a large railway shareholder who sympathised with railwaymen and it was supported by the Archbishop of Canterbury. Until 1900 it may be regarded as much a friendly society as a union and the same applies to the Amalgamated Society of Locomotivemen and Firemen set up in 1880.

Formed during the Great Boom, the Nine Hours Movement sweeping the trade union world particularly attracted railwaymen whose hours could be up to 100 a week. Enthusiastic meetings were held in Wolverhampton and elsewhere and in June 1872 the first delegate meeting of the ASRS was attended by S. Carr of Stourbridge, T. Penzer of Wolverhampton and J. Skinner of Dudley. The Depression scotched the Nine Hours Movement and national membership of the union fell from 17,000 in 1872 to less than 6,000 in 1882. Black Country membership also fell but by less than the national trend. In 1875 in Wolverhampton, an important railway centre, No.1. branch had 150 members and Locomotive branch 110. The next most important branch was Stourbridge with 62 members. Dudley followed with 32 and Bilston had 29. By 1885 membership in the two Wolverhampton branches had fallen to 190. Stourbridge had 55 and Bilston 5.

Growth was resumed after 1889, the year of the Dock Strike and general trade union advance. The All-Grades Movement of 1896-97 resulted in further gains and by 1900 the Black Country position was:

Wolverhampton	5 branches	350 members probably – one branch members not given.
Walsall	3 branches	336 members.
Dudley	2 branches	89 members
Smethwick	1 branch	40 members
Wednesbury	1 branch	13 members
Willenhall	1 branch	Members not given
Old Hill & Dist	1 branch	Members not given

Reports from the Amalgamated Society of Locomotivemen and Firemen show that there was a Wolverhampton branch in 1887. By 1894 Wolverhampton had 28 members and Stourbridge 13. By 1902 the Wolverhampton branch had grown rapidly to 76 members and Stourbridge had 16.

In 1895 there was also a Wolverhampton branch of the much smaller General Railway Workers Union. Membership was not given, but a guesstimate from its financial contribution would suggest about 20.

Other manual unions

From the 1889 London Dock Strike, organisation of the unskilled unexpectedly swelled the ranks of trade unions. As we have seen, some of these unions affiliated to the Midland Counties Trades Federation, but these general unions emerged in the quite different atmosphere of militancy and

Socialism and this was one of the causes of the decline of the MCTF. The two main unions organising unskilled workers in the Black Country were the Workers' Union and the National Union of Gasworkers and General Labourers. The former was effective only after 1900 and eventually merged with the Transport & General Workers' Union; the latter eventually became part of the Municipal and General Workers' Union.

In 1892 branches of the NUG&GL existed in Wolverhampton, West Bromwich (2 branches), Oldbury, Great Bridge, Walsall Wood and Willenhall. By 1894 there were other branches in Oldbury and Stourbridge.

Other trades in membership of the Gasworkers & General Labourers in 1896 were Polishers in both Wolverhampton and West Bromwich; also West Bromwich Spring Makers. In Smethwick, nut and bolt workers were deserting the MCTF and the Machine, Nut, Bolt & Rivet Workers were also members of the NUG&GL.

Tramwaymen were another category of general workers, but these sought separate organisation. Trams were introduced into the Black Country in 1878, but the only union record that we have shows 61 Wolverhampton tram men were members of the Amalgamated Association of Tramwaymen, Hackney Carriage Employees & Horsemen in General in 1900.

Tailors and printers are two categories of craftsmen with long traditions of organisation. The Operative Tailors were in association with Wolverhampton Trades Council from 1865. In 1900 there were branches of the Amalgamated Society of Tailors in Wolverhampton (35 members), Walsall (21), and Stourbridge (6). There is no reason to doubt that organisation was continuous, at least in Wolverhampton.

Printers were less visible after 1875 than before, but again there is little reason to doubt continuity of organisation. The National Typographical Society collapsed in 1848 and a Provincial Typographical Society formed the next year. Birmingham, but not Wolverhampton, was associated with its founding. Musson tells us that in 1884 the midland branches were the first to respond to a call for "missionary work" and that to a meeting to form a Black Country Conference invitations were sent to Wolverhampton, Walsall and Dudley branches. According to the Blocksidge Dudley Annual for 1899, the Dudley & District Typographical Association had been formed in July 1875 and was therefore 'one of the oldest in the surrounding counties'. It collapsed, however, during the Depression and had to be re-formed in 1885.

For the furniture trade we have annual reports from the Friendly Society of Operative Cabinet Makers formed in 1833. Maximum local membership in the first years of the Depression were Wolverhampton 15, Stourbridge 12 and Walsall 8. Despite an amalgamation in 1885 to become the Amalgamated Union of Cabinet Makers only the Wolverhampton branch survived in 1900 with a membership of six.

I conclude this survey of craft unions with mention of those unions only known from their registration, mainly in the 1870s, with the Registry of Friendly Societies. Walsall's leather trade is represented by the Birmingham & Walsall Brown Saddlers Trade & Protection Society and also Walsall Hame Makers' Trade Protection Society; also the horse furniture trade by the Walsall & Bloxwich Bit Forgers & Filers. In building there was the Walsall Builders Labourers' Society and the West Bromwich & District Builders Labourers' Protection, Accident & Burial Society. In chemicals there was the Oldbury & District Chemical & General Workers Society.

White Collar Unions – Shop Workers, Clerks and Allied Trades

We have seen how sympathy for the long hours of shop workers led to the development of the middle-class supported Early Closing Associations. That movement stimulated action by clerks, warehousemen and others. By 1858 this movement had reached Chubbs of Wolverhampton, the only Black Country firm with a considerable London manufacturing base, whose employees befitted from contact with their London colleagues. But the Great Depression retarded both union growth and the shorter hours movement. By 1900 it was said that hours in towns were longer than thirty years previously and even George Snape of the Wolverhampton Grocers' Association was saying that with wages now paid on Friday nights or Saturday mornings there was no need for such long shopping hours.

A limited success was achieved with an amended Act sponsored by Sir John Lubbock stipulating that no young person should be employed for more than 74 hours a week. However, family shops were exempt and the Act was to operate only for two years. The fact that there was no provision for inspection made the Act a dead letter from the start.

By the 1890s the National Union of Shop Assistants had been formed and in 1896 a union sponsored Bill was introduced in parliament by Sir John Dilke. The Bill requested that all shops should close one half day a week on a day to be designated by the local borough authorities, that there should be inspection under the Factory and Workshops Acts, that shops should be provided with seats for women, that there should be continuous employment for not more than five hours, that there should be a sixty minute dinner break and that sanitary conveniences should be provided. The Bill was bitterly opposed and defeated by the trade, and the only success by the end of the century was that one in three of women shop assistants were allowed to sit down when there was no work to be done.

The National Union of Shop Assistants was formed at a Birmingham conference in 1891, but although there were two representatives from Birmingham, no Birmingham or Black Country branches were formed. In 1894 mergers with the NUSA created the National Union of Shop Assistants, Warehousemen & Clerks; still there were no West Midlands branches. In January 1896, however, a Walsall branch was formed whose secretary was S.E. Shaw; but it closed at the end of the year. It was only in 1899 that union organisation took off in the Black Country. In that year 50 men were organised in Wolverhampton; Walsall was back in business with 14 men and six women organised. West Bromwich had 12 men and Dudley had ten men. In 1900 they were joined by Wednesbury with 22 men and five women and Oldbury with 17 men and two women.

Some warehousemen were organised earlier, probably because of their close contact with manual workers; from 1896 Warehousemen & Provers were affiliated to the Midland Counties Trades Federation.

Co-operative employees have always been a bulwark of the shop assistants' union. Their organisation originated in Manchester in 1890 and became the Amalgamated Union of Co-operative Employees in 1895. A midlands council was set up in 1898, further details appear in the chapter on Co-operation.

Organisation among clerks was slower to develop and there were no Black Country branches of the National Union of Clerks until the twentieth century. Various types of clerks did organise, however. The Railway Clerks Association was set up in 1897 and there was a Wolverhampton branch before 1900. Telegraph Clerks also had a union and Telegraph Workers in both Tipton and Dudley were organised and affiliated to the Midland Counties Trades Federation from 1898; whether these workers were linesmen or clerks is not known.

Insurance agents formed the National Union of Life Assurance Agents from 1885 and there was a Wolverhampton branch by 1893. By 1900 there was a branch at Brierley Hill, but the Wolverhampton branch seems to have disappeared.

With regard to municipal employees, the mass unions of today NALGO, NUPE and COHSE are creations of the twentieth century. Organisation was stimulated by the emergence of Labour councillors from the 1880s. Corporation employees in Dudley were affiliated to the Midland Counties Trades Federation by 1898. The rapid development of white collar trade unionism at this period is testified to by the most complete list of affiliates to a local trades council that we have – one for 1904. This shows that to the Wolverhampton Trades Council were affiliated Amalgamated Tailors, Bakers & Confectioners, Musicians Union, Tramway & Vehicle Workers, Shop Assistants, Royal Liver Agents and Co-operative Employees.

Finally a word for the U.K. Commercial Travellers Association. A South Staffs branch was formed in 1895. It had an imposing list of aldermen, ex-mayors, MPs. etc. as its vice-chairmen suggesting that it was half trade association and half trade union. In 1897 it had 'the highly satisfactory' total membership of 125. Its social activity included pic-nics and Smoking Concerts. The latter showed that the members 'appreciated the superior class of Entertainment that your committee try their best to provide.' Besides their reports there is a very good Scrapbook of the association held by Wolverhampton library.

Teachers

We have seen how the early organisation of teachers took the form of associations representing the particular religious denominations responsible for schools, and that these sectarian differences were too great for a united organisation to emerge. This situation changed with the 1870 Education Act which set up local School Boards empowered to create new schools where the existing supply was insufficient to educate all children. The Act became operative in February 1870 and by June the non-sectarian National Union of Elementary Teachers was created.

From 1871 there is a NUET cash book showing contributions received. From that year a South Staffordshire Association was affiliated. More detailed information is not available until NUET Year Books were produced from 1897. From these we learn that Wolverhampton Teachers' Association was formed in 1874, Dudley in 1876, Stourbridge in 1877 and Walsall in 1895. The other Black Country towns were catered for by the South Staffordshire Association, a state of affairs which continued until the enlargement of the four county boroughs in 1966. A wider Midlands District Union was formed in 1894. NUET membership in 1895 was: Wolverhampton 187, Dudley 155, Walsall 92, Stourbridge 90 and S. Staffs 86. Growth continued to the end of the century when Wolverhampton topped the 200 mark.

Problems facing the teachers were many. An official return for 1870 showed the following proportions of children aged between 5 and 13 at school: Smethwick 50 per cent, Wolverhampton 45 per cent, West Bromwich 41 per cent and Dudley 23 per cent. These figures do not mean that no other children went to school nor that all the children stayed at school from age 5 to 13. The normal period of schooling was four years. This gives two four year periods between 5 to 13 and means that in Smethwick, for instance, all children might have gone to school for four years. In reality it is some indeterminate proportion in between since some children stayed at school for more than four years and some children never went to school.

Teachers were wholeheartedly behind the local School Boards in extending educational provision to all children. As always, however, a primary concern was with salaries. Each School Board had its own salary scales, but they could not vary too greatly between adjacent authorities and a rough average based on official returns at various periods shows the following annual salaries for Black Country teachers:

	Masters		*Mistresses*		*Headmasters*	*H'mistresses*
	Cert.	Uncert.	Cert.	Uncert.		
1857	£88	£56	–	£33	£88	£59
1878	£75	£55	£60	£40	£165	–
1882	£80	£55	£67½	£42½	£175	£115
1892	£85	£55	–	£42½	–	–

From the above it can be seen that an experienced, trained male teacher earned in mid-century £1-14-0d a week and uncertificatd teachers, the vast majority, only £1 a week. After 1870 there emerged a class of reasonably well paid Headmasters, but at the expense of the remaining certificated male teachers whose salaries fell sharply during the Great Depression. Beneath the badly paid uncertificated teachers were the Pupil-Teachers learning their craft on the job. In 1878 West Bromwich paid from £15 to £24 per year to their four-year course males and £13 to £22 to their females. Below these again were the Monitors working in the classroom and hoping to become Pupil-Teachers. These were paid 2/-d. a week by West Bromwich in 1886 raised to 2/6d. in 1896. These inadequate salaries were often under attack. As late as 1899 Brierley Hill teachers reported a successful campaign to prevent the School Board lowering headteachers salary and in 1897 the Wolverhampton Teachers' Association supported recurring proposals that salaries should be paid by the government instead of the local religious governors or School Boards.

A further burning issue was Payment by Results imposed on schools by the Revised Code of 1861 which based school grants on examination results. This led to the restriction of the syllabus to the 3Rs and encouraged the exclusion from schools of half-timers, sick or retarded pupils and transformed school inspectors from friends to sworn enemies of teachers.

It is not until the 1890s with the NUET Year Books that reports of Association meetings appear. Most associations must have suffered at some time the malaise of Walsall in 1899 reporting that 'Finances are below nil, the spirit of Unionism as measured by attendances at meetings and the activity of the majority of members stands at 32 degrees F!' In the same year, however, Wolverhampton reported the success of their annual soiree at the Exchange Hall, their pic-nic in Patshull Park and a prominent social side of their affairs.

Another burning issue was the pension which had been taken away from them by the Revised Code. It was not until 1899 that a Superannuation Act restored teachers' pensions. Dudley protested at the age it was to be paid and the amounts payable.

Trades Councils

Wolverhampton Trades Council came into existence in 1865 and Walsall Trades Council in 1872. Their early activities have been covered in Chapter 3. Others, as we have also seen, came into existence as a result of initiatives from Richard Juggins in connection with the Midland Counties Trades Federation. Trades Councils suffered badly from the Great Depression, but the trade union forward movement from 1889 brought renewed strength not only from the new unions of the unskilled, but also by the organisation of municipal employees, and the rapid growth of the railway unions and the lifting of a ban in 1886 on ASE branches affiliating to trades councils. In addition to their roles as supporters and developers of local trades unions and the raising of local issues of common concern to trade unionists, the trades councils found themselves, from 1884, the key players in the efforts to return working men to Parliament and local authority bodies. It is absolutely correct to say that the trade unions brought into existence the Labour Party nationally, and it is equally true to say that the trades councils brought the Labour Parties into existence locally. By the end of the century almost all were Trades and Labour Councils.

Wolverhampton Trades Council experienced all the traumas of this period. Brought back into activity by the Great Boom, it was still a tender plant in 1874 when the Depression struck. By 1877 there were only 1,200 affiliated and funds were so low that it was determined to send £2 to the TUC that year instead of a delegate. After this little is heard until the next great wave of unemployment 1884 to 1887. By this time the new Socialists had appeared and labour representation became a main issue. The Trades Council had always been Liberal in its orientation. The defection of the great bourgeois local hero Joseph Chamberlain in 1886 to the Conservatives as a result of his differences with Gladstone over Irish Home Rule divided the Council still further. Early Labour representation could only be won under the umbrella of the Liberals and the first two labour councillors in Wolverhampton, James Stevenson and F. Evans, were elected on the Liberal ticket and were thus known as Lib-Labs. In 1893 the Independent Labour Party was formed and quickly became the most important Socialist organisation locally. Battle was then joined to convert the Trades Council from Liberal to Socialist policies. ILP candidates were put forward but Trades Council endorsement was essential if the finance to run candidates was to be raised and the support of working men won. In 1895 two ILP candidates were endorsed by the Trades Council, but only by 14 votes to 9. By 1897 there were two Trades Council endorsed ILP councillors in Wolverhampton, R. Evans and H. Gibson, in addition to the two Lib-Labs. In 1895 three Labour candidates were also elected to the Wolverhampton School Board. But Liberal sympathy remained strong, partly because Labour candidates were seen as splitting the progressive vote and partly from respect for C.P. Villiers, the long serving MP. When Villiers actually died in 1897 after representing Wolverhampton for 64 years (although he seldom visited his constituency), the town's leading Liberal G.R. Thorne was supported as Labour was not considered strong enough to put up its own candidate.

Socialism triumphed over Liberalism in 1895 when the Trades Council adopted the policy of independent Labour representation, but the problem of finding the finance to run such candidates was far from solved. An example of growing Socialist influence was the annual May Day processions through the town organised by the Trades Council. The local newspaper, the *Express & Star,* then a Liberal paper, reported the first march in 1892 stating that 7,000 people listened to speakers at two platforms on the Eight Hour Day and other topics. The reporter was much impressed by the growth of Unionism which 'has not a parallel in the history of the town.' It thought that 'the whole of the proceedings had a religious air, so effectively was Christian duty emphasised in relation to the daily task'. Trades Council and Socialist influence continued to increase until 1899 when the jingoism of the Boer War set the movement back temporarily.

Walsall Trades Council, as we have seen. was formed at the top of the boom in 1872 largely, it would seem, as a vehicle for Richard Juggins' Nut & Bolt Workers who became by far its leading affiliate. From 1875 when Juggins left the Walsall Trades Council and transferred to Wednesbury all Trades Council reports disappear from the *Labour Press* which had previously copiously covered them and from which virtually all we know of trades councils' activities is drawn. This paper disappeared in 1878. The next local labour paper was the *Labour Tribune* published from 1886 to 1894. This paper carried no reports of trades councils throughout its existence. It must be assumed, therefore, that Walsall and other Trades Councils lay dormant during this period which coincides with the Great Depression. This could have been an important factor in Juggins' decision to form the Midland Counties Trades Federation in 1886 rather than to continue to work through local trades councils. Trades councils reports again become available in the 1890s through the local Liberal press.

Dean quotes the *Walsall Observer* of 8th March 1897 to suggest that the Trades Council was re-established at that time as the Walsall & District Trades & Labour Representation Committee; but that does not necessarily mean that the 1872 body had been defunct. The *Express & Star* reported an AGM of Walsall Trades Council at the Victoria Temperance Hotel (evidence of the influence of the anti-drink lobby) under the presidency of J. Stokes. The Walsall MP, Sydney Gedge was censured for his activities with regard to the Truck Act and the Workmen's Compensation Act.

Wednesbury was the third of the Black Country trades councils and the second formed under the influence of Juggins. Active only in its early years it also fades from view with the Great Depression. It was re-formed in 1916 and all knowledge of the earlier council has been lost.

In 1882 the South Staffordshire & East Worcestershire Trades Council was formed with its headquarters at Cradley Heath. Taylor tells us that the inaugural meeting brought together chainmakers (both factory and domestic), nailers, rivetmakers, anchorsmiths, sheet iron workers and the usually aloof Flint Glass Makers. Charles Williams of the Horseshoe Nailers' Protection Society was elected secretary. William Husselbee of the glassmakers president, and J. Humphries treasurer. Rules modelled on those of the Birmingham Trades Council were drawn up and a resolution was adopted to restrict the employment of female labour in the nail and chain trades. In March 1883 Henry Broadhurst MP, the stonemasons' secretary introduced a bill into parliament to restrict the employment of women in ironworks and forges. This foundered on the joint resistance of the laissez-faire brigade and feminists who saw this as an attempt to maintain male wage levels by restricting the job opportunities of women. The trades council immediately broke up as a result of this controversy.

Although there is nothing to connect Juggins with the formation of the S. Staffs. & E. Worcs. Trades Council, he was deeply involved in the preparation of the Broadhurst bill. The collapse of the trades council would further predispose Juggins to set up the new umbrella organisation of the MCTF rather than seek to federate the local trades councils.

As the Depression weakened, new trades councils were formed. In 1892 Dudley Trades Council appeared. During that year it met at the Griffin Inn, Stone Street. But from January 1893 it transferred its proceedings to a committee room in Dudley Town Hall, 'kindly granted free by the town council.' Its early secretary was Thomas Mansell of Railway Street, Tipton, who was also the council's representative on the Conciliation Board. In its first decade it was deeply involved in the struggle to change its culture from Liberal to Socialist. Much of it seems to have been provoked from Wolverhampton, aided and abetted by the small Dudley Independent Labour Party. In July 1897 Wolverhampton ILP sought the support of Dudley Trades Council for a Parliamentary candidate, suggesting the names of Tom Mann, Pete Curran, Keir Hardie and Will Thorne. One delegate, Round, said that Keir Hardie was not a fit and proper person, and Tom Mann was not much better. The chairman said that the council should not support a Socialist. Another delegate, Evans, said there was a splendid chance of winning the seat if it were a matter of putting up a Liberal. The discussion was adjourned. When it was resumed the chief Lib-Labs took another line. It was an insult for

Wolverhampton to interfere in the affairs of Dudley. In any case, they didn't want carpet baggers when there were men as good in the district, declared John Taylor. Mansell thought that the attitude of the ILP at Brightside (Sheffield) showed that they were playing into the hands of the capitalists. The chairman, H. Piercey, said he would never give his consent to Dudley interference in the affairs of Wolverhampton. It was unanimously decided to take no action.

But the Socialists persisted. At the same meeting they raised the question of a candidate for the local election in St. Thomas' ward. A letter from Dudley ILP said they had decided to put up Thomas Evans who was both a trade unionist and a delegate to the trades council. The chairman said he would willingly support Evans as a trade unionist, but not as a member of the Independent Labour Party (hear, hear). Smart said that Evans would stand no chance. The chairman said that the ILP had thrown off the mask and declared themselves Socialist to the backbone. This discussion was also deferred. It resumed again in September and again deferred.

Basic information concerning the trades council is taken from Blocksidge's Dudley Almanac where trades council entries appear from 1897 to 1899. After that, no entries appears and yet another trades council disappears from view. It was reformed in 1916 and again, there was no knowledge of the earlier body.

Participation at the TUC

We have seen that some at least of the credit for the formation of the Trades Union Congress goes to Wolverhampton Trades Council for its resolution in 1866 urging that a conference of trades delegates should be held in Sheffield 'to rebut the lock-out system now so prevalent among the capitalists...' This conference took place in July 1866 and Wolverhampton was represented there. The chief outcome was the establishment of the U.K. Alliance of Organised Trades committed to a policy of conciliation and arbitration, amendment of the Master & Servant Acts and advocacy of Co-operation. The occurrence of the Sheffield Outrages about this time, the Hornby v Close decision which left trade unions with their funds unprotected and the government decision to set up a Royal Commission on Trade Unions, all called for a still wider organisation of trade unionists. This occurred in March 1867 when a conference supported by the London Trades Council representing 200,000 trade unionists, including Wolverhampton Trades Council, met in London. This conference is recognised as the forerunner of the permanent, annual TUCs which began in Manchester in 1868. By then, however, Wolverhampton Trades Council had lapsed into inactivity and Birmingham was the nearest Trades Council represented.

The earliest TUC reports give no list of delegates and it is not until the Depression that Black Country representation appears. In 1878 the Amalgamated Society of Tinplate Workers sent T. Phillips of Old Hill, Tettenhall as their delegate in both 1878 and 1879. From 1883 Richard Juggins became a regular attender as a delegate from the Midland Counties Trades Federation and a recognised power at the TUC. In 1883 he stood for the Parliamentary Committee but received only 15 votes. In 1889 he stood again, receiving the more respectable vote of 75, but was not elected. Also in 1889, the year of trade union advance, the Wolverhampton Trades Council had a TUC delegate who took part in the debate on the 8- Hour Question.

In 1888 an International TUC was held. This was not too favourably regarded by the old guard who were beginning to be challenged by the Socialists, Their fears were confirmed when John Burns was elected chairman, but the Lib-Labs were well represented including Juggins representing the MCTF.

From 1890 there were more Black Country delegates. The MCTF was represented by Juggins, T. Jones of Wolverhampton and T. Homer of Cradley Heath. The delegate of the Associated Iron & Steel Workers of GB was William Aucott of Wednesbury, and G. Smith of Old Hill represented the Chain Makers & Strikers. At this Congress Juggins moved the motion on Federation which was to become a reality ten years later, after Juggins' death. In 1891 Juggins represented only the Nut & Bolt Makers; The Chainmakers were represented again by Smith and Homer and Lockworkers by J. Bishop of Willenhall. At the 1892 Congress the MCTF was represented by Juggins and Millerchip and Juggins again stood unsuccessfully for the Parliamentary Committee. These were Congresses at which Lib-Lab principles were being re-asserted against the Socialist challenge.

By 1893 the tide was turning and the TUC voted to support the principle of what is now known as Clause 4, the nationalisation and control of all the means of production and distribution. Black Country representation at this Congress was limited to the MCTF and the Chainmakers. Juggins stood unsuccessfully for the Parliamentary Committee for the last time and polled his highest vote – 185.

In 1894 the MCTF was represented by J. Taylor (who was to be the new secretary on Juggins') death, T. Sitch and E. Day. Locks were represented by Millerchip, and Chains by Noah Forrest. The Ironmoulders delegate was Aucott and the Iron & Steel Workers chose Benyon of Wednesbury

In 1895 the Miners' Federation of Great Britain with its 166,000 workers elected three delegates; one of these was A. Stanley of Hednesford, (a recognition of the growing importance of the Cannock coalfield), and Ben Dean of Walsall. This was the first Congress which excluded trades council delegates under new standing orders.

The 1896 Edinburgh Congress brought a very large Black Country representation. Chain makers of all types including Block, Best, Factory, Hammered and New Block, with memberships ranging from 270 to 50, sent delegates. Locks also sent separate delegates from Willenhall, Walsall and Wolverhampton. For the first time, Charles Gibbs, representing the Birmingham and District Bakers, attended. Another newcomer was Sharrocks of Wolverhampton representing Boilermakers. The MFGB again sent Dean and Stanley and the MCTF Taylor and Jones. These delegates also participated in the proceedings. Sharrocks criticised the inactivity of the Parliamentary Committee regarding the Fair Wages Clauses and Gibbs moved a successful resolution requesting the Parliamentary Committee to initiate a bill limiting hours worked in bakeries. W.J. Davis of the Brassworkers and J. Taylor of the MCTF spoke in support of a resolution to create an Industrial Union of Workers & Employers. This was one of the last of the Lib-Lab initiatives, and it was defeated.

Perhaps it was this motion that brought so many Black Country delegates to far-flung Edinburgh for at the next Congress which was held in Birmingham in 1897 and where one would have expected a large Black Country turn-out, only Gibbs of the Bakers was present.

In 1898 the MCTF, chains, locks, and glass all sent local representatives and T. Jones for the MCTF stood for the Parliamentary Committee receiving 17 votes. In 1899 only Stanley for the Lockmakers attended, but the Black Country delegates participated in both of the last two important initiatives of the trade union movement in the nineteenth century.

The first was the creation of the General Federation of Trade Unions. This presents us with one of the greatest puzzles of Black Country trade union history. From 1886 Juggins had spent all his efforts in creating the Midland Counties Trades Federation and expanding it beyond the midlands. When a national organisation was formed by the TUC one would have expected the MCTF to have welcomed it with open arms and dissolve their Federation within it. This did not happen. Although the MCTF remained affiliated to the GFTU until the demise of the former, there is no mention whatever of the MCTF in the History of the GFTU by Alice Prochaska and it seems to have made no national impact.

There were difficult problems about Federation. We have seen how Juggins brought his Nut & Bolt Workers out of the Walsall Trades Council when it attempted to enlarge its functions to that of a Federation and set up a dispute fund which Juggins thought unfairly committed the funds of his organisation to other unions on strike. Such objections applied nationally. In addition, existing Federations, notably the Miners' Federation of Great Britain, felt they could best protect their members through their own organisation, as did the larger unions such as the ironworkers and engineers. Yet Federation appealed across the board. It appealed to militants who wanted an organisation with the financial resources to support all workers in dispute. Federation also appealed to Lib-Labs who continued to support co-operation with employers, and Conciliation and Arbitration with the ultimate aim of extending the 'alliance philosophy', as practiced by Davis of the Brassworkers and the MCTF, to an ultimate Industrial Union of Workers and Employers.

Federation was discussed at the TUC throughout the 1890s. These schemes were wrecked on the question of the financial provisions, but in 1895 a scheme which diplomatically made no mention of finance, was defeated only by a card vote of 133,000.

The next year a trade union organiser backed by Robert Blatchford and his *Clarion* floated a scheme offering equal payments, equal benefits and equal representation viz. for a fixed payment per member strike benefit could be claimed to the limit of the contribution; and representation on the organisation would be equal to the amounts paid in. The 1897 TUC ordered a report to be presented at the next Congress, but King and Blatchford, believing that nothing would come of the TUC scheme, pre-empted it by calling in July 1898 their own Federal Labour Parliament with an impressive representation of 750,000 and setting up the National & International General Federation of Trades & Labour Unions, with King as secretary. The weakness of the scheme was that it really amounted to a take-over bid for the TUC and had a quasi-syndicalist philosophy hoping to husband sufficient funds to set up Co-operative industries. The alternative responses for the TUC were either to turn itself into a Federation with its Parliamentary Committee replaced by the control of the Federation executive committee with financial teeth, a solution always favoured by militants, or it could create a separate organisation. The TUC chose the latter course.

The 1898 Congress ordered the formation of a Federation and in January 1899 the General Federation of Trades Unions began a separate existence. When formed it represented only a quarter of total TUC membership, but it was quickly recognised as the authorised Federation and King's organisation faded away. The first annual report of 1900 gave both Davis' Brassworkers and the Midland Counties Trades Federation as affiliated bodies. In its 13th.annual report, however, the MCTF states that although it was present at the inaugural conference 'up to the present we have not felt justified in recommending you to join.' It apparently did subsequently recommend affiliation, for it remained connected with the GFTU continuously until at least 1927 and probably until its demise in the 1930s.

What prevented the MCTF from joining the GFTU? It was not likely to have been the presidency which went to Pete Curran an avowed Socialist, because he had been nominated by W.J. Davis when that great Lib-Lab declined the post himself. Nor was it the philosophy of the new organisation which declared its main aim to be the avoidance of strikes and lock-outs and the maintenance of industrial peace.

Nor was it the vexed question of finance. Contributions to the GFTU were 6d per quarter per affiliated member for strike benefit of 5/-d. a week. MCTF was twice as expensive at 1d. per week per affiliated member for the same benefit of 5/-d.

The MCTF might have thought its identity would have been submerged in the larger organisation, but the GFTU at first provided for regional organisation with one centred on Birmingham. Here was the basis for a powerful regional bloc based on the MCTF and W.J. Davis' power based on the Brassworkers which might considerably have influenced the GFTU.

One can only conclude that a great opportunity was missed to strengthen both national and regional organisation, and wonder whether things would have been different if Juggins had still been alive.

The other great initiative of the TUC at the end of the century was the formation of the Labour Party. At a special conference in February 1900, arising from a decision of the 1899 TUC, the Labour Representation Committee was formed which changed its name to the Labour Party in 1906. Present from the Black Country at that historic conference were Councillor J. Taylor JP of Dudley and Councillor W. Millerchip JP of Walsall representing the Midland Counties Trades Federation and Tom Sitch of the Chainmakers and Strikers.

Bibliography: Trade Unionism 1875-1900

Eric Taylor's thesis *The Working Class Movement in the Black Country 1863-1914* is again the best source for trade unionism in the mining, iron, and nail and chain industries. For conditions of workers, the course of the Great Depression, the standard of living and political control by employers see my *Social Conditions in the Black Country 1800-1900* and also *The Dictatorship of the Bourgeosiee in the Black Country* (Communist Party History Group Pamphlet 55 Summer 1972). For miners the working class newspapers are: *Miners' Advocate* 1862-65; *Labour Press & Miners' and Workmen's Advocate* 1874-78; and *Labour Tribune* 1886-94.

For ironmaking the historian of the techniques of the local iron industry is W.K.V. Gale – *The History of the*

Black Country Iron Trade. The economic fortunes of all the basic industries from the employers' point of view have been followed through the pages of the Engineer. For iron trade unionism see Taylor's thesis; his biographies of Aucott, Capper, Groves, Piggott, Harris and Trow in *Dictionary of Labour Biography* Vols 2 & 3. and for an excellent account of the complexities of the sliding scale his centenary *History of the Midland Iron and Steel Wages Board 1876-1976.*

For engineering trade unionism the main source has been the annual reports of the many unions held at the Modern Records Centre of Warwick University and the records of the Amalg. Soc. Engineers at Peckham.

For the remarkable W.J. Davis and his Brassworkers' Union see my *Birmingham Working People, A History of the Labour Movement in Birmingham 1650-1914*. For electricians see G. Schaffer's general history of the ETU – *Light & Liberty* and also annual reports.

For tinplate and iron plate trade unionism see the two national histories of Kidd and Brake quoted in the bibliography of Chapter 3 and for ironplate see Taylor's thesis and his entry for Simeon Webb in the *Dictionary of Labour Biography* vol 1.

Building trade unionism has again had to be picked up from local newspaper reports. Basic statistics for this period are available from the annual reports of the various building trade unions at Warwick.

For the *Midland Counties Trades Federation* and the remarkable Richard Juggins see Taylor's thesis, his entry in the *Dictionary of Labour Biography* vol 1 of Juggins and his piece in *Midland History* vol 1 No.3 Spring 1972. *The Midland Counties Trades Federation 1886-1914.* The annual general meetings were widely reported in the local press and some of the printed annual reports were found by Eric Taylor at the London School of Economics. There is also J.A.C. Baker – *Richard Juggins and Black Country Unionism in the Late Nineteenth Century.*

For the Knights of Labour see Taylor's thesis, and the national history by Henry Pelling 'The Knights of Labour in Britain 1880-1901' in *Economic History Review* No.2. 1956.

For locks, nails, chains and other crafts see MCTF annual reports, Factory Inspectors' Reports, Stenner for Locks, Reports of the S.C. of the House of Lords on the Sweating System 1889-90, and the Royal Commission on Labour 1892-94. Also Taylor's entries for the two Sitches, father and son in the *Dictionary of Labour Biography* vols 1 & 2.

For glass see the *Flint Glassmakers' Magazine* and reports of the union.

For trade unionism on the railways the main source used has been the annual reports at Warwick. Philip Bagwell's standard history of the NUR, *The Railwaymen,* has been disappointing for local material. The newspapers of the rail unions should be more informative, particularly the *Railway Review* now the *Transport Review, Locomotive Review* and *Salaried Staffs' Journal.*

Print workers have always been active in trade union affairs. A.E. Musson's *The Typographical Association* has some local material.

For white collar workers the picture has to be pieced together from local newspapers, from the trade union reports at Warwick University, and the general histories of some of these unions. For these see Clegg H.A. Fox A, & Thompson A.F. in their two volume *History of Trade Unions Since 1889.*

For teachers see my *History of Education in Wolverhampton,* press reports, National Union of Elementary Teachers year books and annual reports at Warwick.

For Trades Council see my *History of Wolverhampton Trades Council 1865-1990.* For Walsall Trades Council see K.J. Dean, *Town & Westminster,* and Minutes of the Trades Council from 1901 at Walsall Local History Centre. For Wednesbury, S. Staffs and E. Worcs. see Taylor's thesis. For Dudley see my 'The Re-formation of Dudley Trades Council in 1916', in *West Midland Studies* Vol 13, 1980.

For Black Country participation at the Trades Union Congress see: R.C. Roberts – *The Trades Union Congress 1868-1921* and TUC Annual Reports. For the GFTU see Alice Prochaska, *History of the General Federation of Trade Unions 1899-1980.*

Chapter 6

From Labour Party to First World War

The General Situation
The twentieth century opened with the jingoism of the Boer War seriously weakening the labour movement. As the war dragged on with Britain inventing concentration camps to contain the Boer guerrillas, nationalism began to subside. With the ending of the war in 1902 the familiar trade cycle exerted its effects. During the war trade had boomed. 1900 had been a year of quite exceptional prosperity to be compared with 1874, but when the war ended unemployment returned. Between 1903 and 1910 there was mass unemployment and mass poverty again. These events had an immediate effect on the political movement. In the 1900 khaki election Labour candidates were swept aside. But in 1905 came the secret pact between Herbert Gladstone and J. Ramsay MacDonald which brought the extraordinary result in the ensuing election of 29 Labour candidates being returned to Parliament. This marks the beginning of the Labour Party. But the mass unemployment brought disenchantment with the actions of the leaders of the Labour Party who after 1910 walked the tightrope of knowing that if they voted against the Liberals, the government would be defeated and worse would happen with the return of the Conservatives. Militants did not see it that way and in July 1907 the movement was electrified by the election of Victor Grayson, a charismatic but unstable Independent Socialist to Parliament for Colne Valley. This strengthened the demand for a Socialist Party instead of a Labour party and resulted in the formation in October 1911 of the British Socialist Party an amalgam of the SDF (by then known as the Social Democratic Party) and many ILP branches and members.

With the end of mass unemployment at the end of the decade another extraordinary movement arose. This was the militancy of the semi-skilled and unskilled determined to obtain a living wage through the strikes of the years 1911 to 1914 which goes under the name of the Great Unrest. But dissatisfaction with Labour politics led trade unionists to the doctrine of Syndicalism, a semi-anarchist doctrine which holds that Syndicates of trade unions can organise not only trade but political matters, thus making governmental bureaucracy unnecessary. Syndicalism was to swiftly destroy the prospects of the British Socialist Party.

To this heady brew must be added the militancy of the Suffragettes and the revolt of Carson and the army against Irish Home Rule. Altogether these events brought fears that Britain was becoming ungovernable and that violent revolution was imminent. The outbreak of war in 1914 brought an end to such fantasies and a sterner discipline than ever before known descended on the nation.

This chapter charts the working out of these events in the Black Country.

SDF/British Socialist Party

We have seen how the Social Democratic Federation was slow to establish itself in the Black Country and only from about 1893 was firm branch organisation established at Dudley, West Bromwich and Smethwick. This was followed by Wolverhampton organisation whose secretary, Alf Fellows was to play a continuing political role in the town.

With the jingoism of the Boer War life became difficult. Wolverhampton branch continued open air meetings twice each Sunday in the summer until at least the autumn of 1900 and Alf Fellows was the member of a committee promoting an SDF candidature for the Birmingham School Board.

In July 1901 Lorenzo Quelch, a national SDF organiser came to Wolverhampton. His first report was cautious. There had been little active propaganda for some time and as a result organisation had suffered. 'A few of us attempted a scratch open-air meeting on Sunday morning which could scarcely be called a success. In the evening we tried a different place. After half an hour there was a very good crowd indeed which listened attentively for an hour.' The next week Quelch reported four public meetings in Wolverhampton. 'On Sunday afternoon the meeting was on the South African War and its Lessons. It was listened to attentively. At the close a man who interrupted was invited to take the platform. He talked of the Boers and their treatment of blacks, but failed to justify the war. A small number of youths encouraged him, but got no support from the main body of the meeting who were evidently with us on this question. A very successful meeting. In the evening we had another good meeting at another place on Social Democracy and Party Politics.' The report went to to cite the 'demoralising' influence of the local ILP Club as one of a number of reasons for recent political inactivity. The majority of members of the Club were 'Radicals, Liberals, Tories or Nothingarians' who not only monopolised the Club, but prevented active ILPers doing anything. He had booked on Thursday to speak after the Sunday concert, but when he approached the chairman he did not know about the arrangement. Quelch concluded that there was a determination to reform the SDF branch and the next week he reported that it had been reformed 'under a capable secretary H. Bailey.'

The criticism of the club was answered the following week by George Tilson secretary of the Club and the local ILP. He said that Quelch had been listening to gossip. The management committee consisted of five ILPers and 4 social members. Club rules required that the president, secretary and treasurer should all be ILP members. The club was open to meetings of the SDF who could have a room free.

Quelch's reorganisation does not seem to have worked and. apart from donations to the paper from Wolverhampton and Walsall comrades in 1902 there is no mention of SDF activity for the following two years.

1905 was the year of the first Russian revolution and a year of advance for the ILP nationally. In July there was an attempt by Birmingham comrades to activate the Black Country. *Justice* readers from Stourbridge, Dudley, Walsall West Bromwich and Smethwick were invited to communicate with W.J. Russell, but little came from this initiative.

Not until July 1906 was there mention of a branch. This was at Smethwick, but was again from a Birmingham initiative for it appeared as a Birmingham branch. In October the secretary appealed in *Clarion* for help from Smethwick and Harborne socialists. There had been over 30 meetings held at the Six Ways, Smethwick and others at Harborne since the branch had been formed three months previously.

In 1907 a Midlands District Council of the SDF was formed and in July another appeal went out for volunteers to form a Wolverhampton branch. This again was not immediately successful, but a call from E.H. Ratcliffe of 8 Westbourne Road, Penn in *Justice* was more successful and in February 1908 a Wolverhampton branch was formed with Ratcliffe as secretary, E. Edwards as president with Comrade Attle. A programme of tri-weekly meetings was immediately arranged with the branch meeting the second Monday of the month at Bradley's Restaurant, Broad Street. By May the chairman was Comrade Whiley; an economics class was being held every Monday, Sherman was the financial secretary, Evans the minute secretary and Meakin the literature secretary. The branch then mustered 24. Activity continued throughout the year and by September the branch was meeting the first Tuesday of the month at the Central Labour Club, St. John's Street.

By 1909 the branch was sharing the general militancy generated by unemployment and the inactivity of the Labour leaders. In April the branch booked Victor Grayson for a meeting at the Wolverhampton Empire with admission by silver collection. In fact Grayson was unable to appear 'because of throat trouble' and the meeting appears to have fallen through. The SDP centre sent in his place Jack Jones who gave 'a fine speech' in the Market Place. Mabbs, the midland organiser had also been in the area and E. Edwards (Reporter) ended his piece, 'The work so admirably commenced by our editor, Harry Quelch a few weeks since is now showing life. We had hoped by Comrade Grayson's visit to clear debts incurred by our open-air propaganda and strike fear into our Liberal and Tory capitalist enemies and inspire hope, energy and manhood in Wolverhampton workers for the cause of Social Democracy.'

Militancy was also spreading into other Black Country towns in 1909. In July an SDF of 40 members was reported in West Bromwich. A local ILPer had recently 'resigned' and together with the SDF were forming the West Bromwich Socialist Society. Their secretary was Annie E. Baker of 16 Lombard St. The formation of a Socsoc followed a national trend in Socialist unity in preparation for the formation of the British Socialist Party.

The *Justice* Directory in January 1910 confirms SDP branches in Wolverhampton (A.P. Mitchell, secretary). Smethwick (Charles Harris) and West Bromwich (Percy Steadman). In April West Bromwich were meeting at their rooms, Ruskin Hall, Lombard Street. In November 'a revolutionary Socialist', Comrade Griffin, contested the local elections for Town Hall Ward, receiving 272 'straight Socialist votes'. This was considered satisfactory in view of the 'strenuous opposition from Liberals, Tories and Protestant Leaguers'. The report also found it 'interesting' that the local ILP branch of 300 members, *all Socialists,* refused to help the Socialist for fear of losing the Liberal vote in wards in where ILP candidates were standing against Tories. The reporter, G. Bridger, ended by announcing a whist drive and dance which would, it was hoped, 'renew the fighting resources of the branch which is in great need of further funds.'

The 1911 *Justice* Directory gave Mitchell and Harris as still secretaries of Wolverhampton and Smethwick SDPs. West Bromwich SDP met at their Rooms 28 New Street and their secretary was W. Cook. 1911 was the year of the formation of the British Socialist Party. Much of the initiative for its creation came from the Birmingham leadership of Leonard Hall; and much of the responsibility for the subsequent rapid decline of the BSP must also be laid at Hall's door. Hall had been one of the ILP leaders responsible for the so-called Green Manifesto discussed and rejected at the 1910 ILP National Conference calling for Labour MPs to vote 'on the merits of each question' and not on the wider tactical issue of the fall of the Liberal government and an incoming Tory Tariff Reform one. Hall then resigned from the ILP and set about creating the Socialist unity which led on to the British Socialist Party. In February a Birmingham & District Socialist Representation Committee was set up. Among the organisations affiliated were the West Bromwich and Smethwick SDPs and the Smethwick Socialist Society. At a March meeting of the Committee Cook of West Bromwich was elected Propaganda Secretary and G. Nicholson of West Bromwich Socsoc and J. Smith of Smethwick Socsoc were elected to the committee. Walsall Socsoc was also represented at this meeting and W.E. Phillips told the meeting that Dudley ILP was considering joining. In May the Committee organised May Day demonstrations in its district including one at Smethwick.

At the April 1911 SDP Conference a motion was passed calling for the establishment of a United British Socialist Party. This was strongly supported by the Birmingham & District Socialist Representation Committee. By this time support for such a Party was being vigorously championed by Victor Grayson, who had lost his seat in a by-election and with the support of Blatchford, was using *Clarion* to push the new party. In some parts of the country branches of a British Socialist Party were being set up in advance of national organisation. One of these was a Committee of the British Socialist Party (Birmingham Section) set up in September. Hall also had a Birmingham Manifesto printed which was to figure at the inaugural conference of the new national party. This took place on September 30th and October 1st 1911. The Birmingham Section seems to have been the largest of the eight already existing branches and had three delegates, Leonard Hall, J. Smith and W.E. Stephens at this Conference. Local Clarion Cyclists were represented through the National Union Clarion Cycling Club and Smethwick ILP was represented by E. Wenlock.

Leonard Hall played a key part at this inaugural conference. He argued strongly for the line of his Birmingham Manifesto. This had two main points. The first was that the impending transition to Socialism was to be achieved by, 'General and combined Strikes developing towards the final Lock-out by the nation of its exploiters.' Some manifestation of the feasibility of this was already being seen in the first stirrings of the Great Unrest which had begun in the Black Country; but it was pure Syndicalist doctrine and was rejected by the majority of the delegates. The second point of the Birmingham Manifesto was that militant socialists should be elected to Parliament and local bodies. This was perfectly acceptable, but their function was 'to cordinate them with the industrial revolution which it is our first and vital business to develop *outside* them.' This would have made the party an appendage to the industrial movement and this again was rejected. Despite these defeats Hall was elected to the executive of the new party. However, he continued to press these views and it was on the question of Syndicalism that the British Socialist Party was to founder.

Nevertheless the new party got off to a bright start. By the 3rd of November a Walsall BSP branch had been formed with 37 members. It met at the Temperance Hall and its secretary was F. Weston. Wolverhampton branch was formed on October 26th. Recruits were sought from Alfred E. Bowen and his report was combined with a plea that the comrade who took the secretary's hat in the excitement of the moment mistaking it for his own should return it! Smethwick BSP was also formed in November and had booked the Town Hall for a Victor Grayson meeting on 10th December. By early December Wolverhampton branch was said to have 37 members and the West Bromwich branch was 'going strong' with nearly 30 members. They met every Wednesday at Wilson's Cafe, Bull Street. Walsall was said to be making 'new members every week' and had a new pro tem secretary E. Bywater.

Progress continued into 1912. In January Walsall had yet another secretary, W. Buck. The next month they had unearthed a Socialist Double Quartet billed to give a selection of folk songs at the Temperance Hall the following Sunday. Here Mr E. Mills of Willenhall would speak on the not very militant subject of 'Some Definitions – Ethical and Economic.' Later in February there were BSP reports from Birmingham (Smethick) where H. Buffey was secretary and Birmingham (West Bromwich) which was still meeting at Wilson's Cafe every Wednesday and 'increasing in numbers.' Walsall intended holding out door meetings at Town's End Bank. West Bromwich BSP booked the Town Hall for a Victor Grayson meeting in April. This meeting attracted support from both Wolverhampton and West Bromwich BSPs. Smethwick BSP arranged May Day celebrations with the national leader Jack Williams. On Saturday May 4th. there was a Fellowship concert and reception to Jack at the Blue Gates Hotel. The next day there were meetings at 11am at the Blue Gates and at 6-30pm at the entrance of West Smethwick Park. Williams was also booked to speak the following Wednesday at Warley Woods. Walsall BSP also arranged a May Day celebration meeting at Town End Bank and followed up with a Ben Tillett meeting at the Town Hall. In the middle of May, West Bromwich BSP members were being urged to attend open-air meetings at St. Michael's Street on Mondays where opposition was said to be 'very strong.' The branch was also committed to supporting a Victor Grayson meeting at the Wolverhampton Empire the next Sunday. The West Bromwich secretary at this time was William Cooke.

But May Day 1912 was the high point of BSP activity in the Black Country. For the reasons for this we must turn to the economic situation and the influence of the Birmingham BSP organisation. As we have seen, the British Socialist Party (Birmingham Section) had played an important part in bringing the national organisation into existence. In June this independent section wound itself up and amalgamated itself with the national body. Its funds were turned over to the Birmingham Federation of the BSP. At this point it was reported that the Birmingham Federation consisted of six active branches with between 350 and 400 members. The next month the Federation peaked with a total of nine branches which included Smethwick and Walsall. From this time the Federation destroyed itself between rival factions of near Syndicalists led by Leonard Hall and a those insisting that the primary task of a political party was politics. This faction was led by Fred Silvester. This very complex struggle need not detain us here; it is dealt with fully in my book *Birmingham Working People*. Only the involvement of the Smethwick branch showing opposition to both Syndicalism and the role that Victor Grayson was playing concerns us. The following is part of a letter as early as November 1911 from T.R. Whittingham to Harry Williams, at that time secretary of the Birmingham Section:

> I adhere to my statement as to Grayson not being asked to speak for the Birmingham Section of the BSP... You say he has been asked three times by 'our' Smethwick organiser. I did not know we had a Smethwick organiser, but if you refer to Comrade Smith, I shrewdly suspect the invitation was extended to Grayson on behalf of the Smethwick Socialist Society and not from the Birmingham Section of the BSP.
>
> Our original obligation, in my opinion, consisted of firmly establishing the BSP on BSP lines and not to establish the BSP on lines advocated by Strike Agitators who may or may not be members of the BSP.

This dispute must be set against the industrial background. Already in August 1911 the Bilston strike of 60 women and girls for the right to join a trade union was eleven weeks old. Strikes throughout the country accompanied it. Already it was being talked about as the Great Unrest. This phase ended, but resumed in June 1912. A Syndicalist outcome to these struggles appeared by no means unlikely.

The Birmingham differences were mirrored in the national BSP. The virtual end came in December 1912 when the Birmingham District Federation of the BSP was disbanded as 'serving no practical purpose.' The weaker branches were to amalgamate, but the balance of the funds were to be donated not to the BSP branches but to the newly established, militant *Daily Herald.*

The BSP continued, but it was little more than the old Social Democratic Federation writ slightly larger. The main reason for the destruction of the hopes for a mass Socialist Party in Britain was that there were not enough Socialists to sustain one. The main body of the ILP, wisely or treacherously, according to one's point of view, refused to join the BSP and got on with the job of strengthening the Labour Party.

Smethwick BSP activity continued at the end of 1912 under an activist W.J. Salmon, and in November a new BSP branch was formed in Wednesbury, secretary F. Whitehouse. Salmon was to be the only Black Country delegate at the second BSF conference in May 1913. In June Tom Quelch was in the Black Country, but it was the class struggle with 35,000 workers on strike that he was reporting and not the strength of BSP branches. In August 1913 another national organiser, Thomas Kennedy, was in Birmingham and the Black Country. In Birmingham he managed to have re-formed the BSP District Council. Moving to the Black Country he held meetings at Oldbury and Handsworth and arranged a complete programme of meetings for these areas. 'Meetings have been good and members made at most', he reported. In November the BSP polled well at the local elections. In Coventry a candidate was returned. In Birmingham Soho, Norman Tiptaft polled 1567 votes against the successful Tory's 1802. In West Bromwich Spon Lane J. Holland polled 855 votes and missed election by 79 votes. W.J. Salmon in Smethwick polled 305 against the winner's 978. In December a 'well attended' meeting of the Birmingham BSP Federation was reported. The *Socialist Record,* a monthly internal organ of the BSP, gave the position of the branches. In February 1913 many were said to be in arrears for cards and stamps, including Wolverhampton. in July a list of branches showed Oldbury (L. Martin secretary), Smethwick (J. Smith), Walsall, Wednesbury, West Bromwich (W. Cooke) and Wolverhampton (still A.P. Mitchell). Of these branches only Walsall appears in the local directories with an entry from 1912 to 1914 in the Walsall Red Book. Its object was given in 1913 as 'the public ownership of land and capital.' In 1914 this was changed to 'the establishment of the Co-operative Commonwealth – that is to say the transformation of capitalist competitive society into a Socialist or Communist Society.' The compromise between syndicalism and political activity had been worked out by the Walsall branch in a section on Methods. First came, 'the education of the people in the principles of Socialism.' Then, 'the closest possible co-operation with trade union organisations and the advocacy of industrial unity of all workers as essential to bring about the socialisation of the means of production'. Finally the place of politics was defined. 'The establishment of a militant Socialist Party in Parliament and on local bodies completely independent of all parties which support the capitalist system.' The officers for 1914 were George Giles (chairman) A. Dixon (vice-chair) J. Johnson (secretary) Miss N. Middleton (literature secretary). The general committee comprised J Deakin, W. Farnol, L. Whitehouse, W. Wallis, J. Lowe and J. Wilson. It is clear that here is a branch, fully staffed, which had worked its way through the ideological controversies of those years by participating in the Great Unrest. The presence of Joe Deakin with his wide experience and influence on the Trades Council suggests that those who would be dismissive of the BSP because of its small numbers need to be cautious. These remarks may also apply to other Black Country branches. However, for 1914 there are no reports of activity in the first part of the year. in August the war broke out. It was supported by the whole national executive of the British Socialist Party. The attitude of the Black Country branches and the opinions of individual members is not known. An entirely new world was about to be born.

Clarion

Up to 1914 *Clarion* continued its key role as purveyor of 'cheerful Socialism' reporting all shades of labour movement opinion and activity whilst promoting its own network of social cum political organisations.

Highly popular were the Clarion Cycling Clubs, but these seem to have gone through two distinct phases during this period. Up to 1906 Wolverhampton CCC flourished. Then it disappears from both the columns of the *Clarion* and the local Directory. It would seem that it was not only Clarion which suffered. In 1905 the Wolverhampton Red Book listed seven cycling clubs and it was likely that Clarion was the largest as clubs such as Wolverhampton Wheelers limited their membership to thirty. From this point the number of cycling clubs listed in the Red Book declines until by 1913 it is only three. But Clarion cycling in the Black Country experienced a revival from 1911 which was still strong in 1914.

In 1900 the only Clarion cycling clubs were the very active Wolverhampton one and another at West Bromwich. In the winter of 1901 Wolverhampton was, as usual, raising funds by a Fancy Dress Ball at the Co-op Hall. The 1902 annual general meeting showed a substantial financial balance. The highlight of the previous year had been a Stafford Meet attended by about 120 cyclists from all parts of the midlands. They had also participated in the Cinderella work taking poor children for outings. The annual ball had been arranged for the Drill Hall.

Reports become fewer from 1903, only a note from Birmingham CCC stating that 'Wolves were coming over', revealing their existence. But Wolverhampton CCC continued until at least 1905 when its headquarters was at the Central Labour Club, John Street. Its president was L. Sproson and secretary W.H. Fisher. Its subscription was 1/-d. per season.

The next appearance of Wolverhampton CCC in the columns of the *Clarion* was not until May 1911 when it was announced that it would meet on Sunday at the ILP Rooms, Bilston Street to 'start a new section.' All those wishing to join were requested to attend. The next week the secretary, V. Leary, announced its opening run to Tong. In June Walsall CCC announced its presence with a 'captains run', starting from the Bridge. By now there were Midland and Birmingham Unions of Clarion Cycling Clubs and a delegation from these had seen Tom Groom about getting the Clarion Van back on the road. Later in June Wolverhampton CCC had a run to Codsall. In July Walsall had a run to Brewood and reported 'fraternising' with West Bromwich CCC. In Wolverhampton there was a 'Saturday impromptu' at the ILP rooms. At the end of July Walsall, whose secretary was J. Johnson, were holding a united picnic in Sutton Park and the next day going to Birmingham where Leonard Hall was to launch the Van. The cycling clubs played an important part in supporting the Midland Van.

Both the reappearance of the cycling clubs and also the Van was at least partly inspired by *Clarion* support for the formation of the British Socialist Party. In September 1911 Walsall CCC announced 'Keep an eye open for a town meeting on October 2nd re. BSP'.

Cycling activity continued into 1912. Wolverhampton began in April with an 'impromptu' on Saturday and a run to Kinver the next day. Walsall CCC were active in May. There are no other reports for 1912, but this was no doubt partly because the servicing of the Van, the excitement of the new BSP and the importance of the Labour Unrest was absorbing most of the cyclists' attention.

Reports resumed in 1913. Walsall were off the mark early with their first run of the season, to Brewood, in early March. In July a cryptic Walsall notice said that 'four members were enraptured with the glories of Hill Hook last week.' Wolverhampton were going to Chaddesley Corbett on the same day, meeting at 10am at the Market Square. New members were heartily welcome. In Wolverhampton the cyclists were also involved in the setting up of a Socialist Society advertising what was probably its inaugural meeting. By the end of the month Wolverhampton CCC was advertising that the Socialist Society was meeting every Monday at 3 Compton Road. Regular rides continued. Wolverhampton and Walsall both went to Brewood in August and Walsall was taking a leaf out of Wolverhampton's book by having an 'Impromptu' on the Saturday. The next week Walsall were off to Coventry 'for a confab on a Club House,' and the following week Walsall and Wolverhampton joined forces for another run to Chaddesley Corbett. In September Walsall was having another 'Impromptu' and asking for prizes for their 1d. draw. Wolverhampton had another run to Brewood and advised those who wanted to take shares in the Club House to contact the secretary. The interest in Club Houses was being stimulated by the suggestion of Tom Groom, the charismatic, ex-Birmingham founder of the cycling clubs, that all Clarion organisations should be amalgamated into local Fellowships. In October Walsall said, 'The season is coming to an end, so lets finish in style with an 'Impromptu'.'

In 1914 Walsall led the way by organising in February a 'fraternal evening' in conjunction with Aston CCC at the Stork Hotel. Hednesford, Wolverhampton and West Bromwich were invited. The next week it announced that the concert had been 'a great success' with thanks to Birmingham, Hednesford and Wolverhampton. 12/6d. had been collected for the Van and the report ended 'Fellowship is a real live thing in Walsall.' In April Walsall were at the North Midland Union's first meet at Uttoxeter. 'We must keep up our old practice of attending this meet to keep them in order. Will Miss Middleton please bring the kettle.' In April Walsall were off on 'an easy run to West Bromwich to hunt up new members and make over a respectable section. Subs. were urgently required. Wolverhampton were off to Birmingham for the Van opener. There had been a good turn out the previous week to Brewood. Fifty members were wanted for this year. In May Walsall and Wolverhampton went to Milford and Walsall were organising social activity each Saturday with a run the next day. The same month they were upset with Stafford. 'Ye Gods, Stafford wants to know if we're extinct!' Late in May the Van was in the Black Country and both Walsall and Wolverhampton were there with support when it came to those towns. Walsall runs continued to the outbreak of war and beyond. But the war brought a smaller paper and reports of activities ended in September.

Clarion Fellowships were no new idea when Tom Groom gave a new impetus to them in 1914. As we have seen there were Fellowships in Dudley, West Bromwich and Wolverhampton in 1899. These continued in the early years of the new century. In January 1901 Wolverhampton Fellowship held a dinner and social at the Co-operative Hall, Stafford Street. Tickets (1/6d. for the dinner and social, 6d. for the social only) could be obtained either at the Co-op Store or from the ILP Club in John Street. The next month the Clarion Fellowship Directory gave a Birmingham one with a secretary who lived in Smethwick and others at Walsall (C. Brown and E. Clarke), Wolverhampton (F.J. Kenney and R. Taylor) and West Bromwich (Fred Hughes.) In June 1901 Wolverhampton Fellowship jointly with Wolverhampton CCC Cinderella organised an outdoor social at Harrows on the Stafford Road. Brakes started at 2-30 pm from Skinner Street. The charge for brake and tea was 2/6d. Subsequently a successful day was reported. Some went by brake, others by bicycle or train. Professor Somers delighted the children with a Punch and Judy show and the Quaver band had added to the enjoyment.

Wolverhampton Fellowship continued to develop. In January 1902 there was a social evening at Hill's Restaurant in North Street where the main item was the popular 'Impromptu'. Later in the month a concert was held at the Co-op Hall, admission free. In February the Fellowship organised a lecture at the YMCA Hall, Darlington Street on the 'Taxation of Land Values.' This was one of a series and in March at the Co-op Hall Harvey Theobald lectured on 'The Nation's Need'. At this time a national Fellowship Tribute 1/-d. Fund was attracting donations from the Black Country and Walter Jones of Stourbridge was on the national committee. Also from Stourbridge, in the days of Oliver Jenkins' activity, a Winter Scheme involving indoor meetings in chain and nail country resulted in the formation of a Fellowship 'group' at Lye. In May 1902 a report from Wolverhampton Fellowship Club announced the end of the winter series of lectures. Summer activity would begin by taking 120 children to the Harrows. A subsequent CCC notice asked for the assistance of as many Fellowshippers and Clarionettes as possible. In August there was another Fellowship outing to the Harrows. However, all was not well. In December 1902 at the AGM at Hill's Restaurant after dealing with the annual report and balance sheet a 'meagre attendance' passed on to discuss the question of disbanding. Of 70 or 80 members only seven attended and the secretary, R. Taylor, felt that members did not want a Fellowship. It was then decided to abandon it. Several reasons might be suggested for this action. It was at a low point of political activity at the time of the Boer War; national Fellowship trends were going the same way. It also came at a time when the Cyclists were soon to disappear and this probably points the main cause. The CCC was a main supporter of the Fellowship and also the Cinderella. Fellowships grew out of the need for a winter activity to supplement summer runs and political work. With a low level of political activity and the existence of the Labour Church, and also the ILP Club and Co-operative guilds there was no doubt an overlapping with an ill-defined role for the Fellowship.

Tom Groom's appeal in 1913 for the amalgamation of all Clarion activities into Fellowships came too late to revive them in the Black Country, although a Fellowship was formed in Birmingham. However, the renaissance of the Cyclists, the close connection of Tom Groom with the CCCs and the Walsall cyclist's comment that 'Fellowship was a reality' in that town, suggests that had not the war intervened more would have been heard of Fellowship.

Other Clarion activity continued, however. in West Bromwich a Clarion Handicraft Guild was formed in 1902. The secretary was Fred Hughes. Handicraft Guilds were growing quickly at this time and a November Directory in the *Clarion* gave 25 nationally including Birmingham, Coventry and West Bromwich. In October 1903 the Directory had twenty two Handicraft Guilds including West Bromwich – secretary H. Thompson. But nothing further is heard of it nor do we know what its activities were. From 1905 there was also a Field Club in West Bromwich. These were more popular and tended to be longer lived. A notice in July stated: 'West Bromwich nature lovers are envious of the gigantic North Staffs Field Club so have formed their own in connection with the Labour Church. Our rambles take place on Saturday afternoons.' Any West Bromwich nature lover was urged to contact secretary Wotton. The next outing was to meet at Dartmouth Park entrance. 'Mr Hales is the leader and he will give a paper on Darwinism. We hope in time to be the South Staffs Field Club.' A fortnight later the following account of the activities of the club appeared:

> Our appeal has not yet proved fruitful. There are some interesting spots nearby. Frinstance Dudley Castle and Wrens Nest and Old Oak House West Bromwich for wet days. There are some delightful country lanes within fifteen minutes walk. (Essentials are): Item – an enquiring mind -do- A good appetite -do- A Pocketful of pill boxes -do- an easy conscience and an oldish pair of boots. We adopt the usual way of rambling. Meet at the appointed trysting place. Fifteen will promise and only five turn up. Wait for stragglers and proceed. Around the lanes examining hedges, banks and fields for flowers, insects, ferns, mosses etc. asking and evading questions until tea time. Then billeting ourselves on some unsuspecting cottages for tea. some of us taking our food and buying tea, others being 'wholehoggers' (with apologies to Suthers). After tea (a by no means unimportant item) someone inflicts a short paper on some more or less uninteresting subject in the more or less humorous ILP way.
>
> After which, sadder and wiser men, we wend our way homeward through fields and lanes, usually dispersing about nine o'clock.

In November a winter programme of lectures included 'Fall of the Leaf', 'Beauty in Minute Life', 'Terrestial Magnetism' and 'Religion of Nature.' The secretary then was H. Lewis. No reports of activity in 1906 and beyond have however, been found and it must be assumed that the Field Club went the same way as the Handicraft Guild.

These Clarion social activities were reinforced every year by the political message of the Clarion Van. The Vans were the brain child of Julia Dawson whose fertile mind and vast energy was also responsible for the Handicraft Guilds and much else nurtured by her woman's columns in the Clarion. Eventually there was a number of these Vans including a motor one. Either the national or a midland van toured the Black Country every year from 1902 to 1914 except 1904-06. The Vans posed large problems of finance, organisation and political support. First, sufficient funds had to be raised or promised to put and keep horse and van its driver and the Vanner on the road. The annual tour meant continuous travel, rough living and abominable conditions when it rained (which it seemed to for whole seasons on end). The Van and its occupants faced possible violence when holding meetings and sabotage when it was parked unless a sufficient political presence was mustered. The Vanner, who had to be an outstanding political propagandist was often obliged to arrange his own schedule and support. He also had to be prepared not infrequently to forego his meagre wages. All these, and other problems faced the Van in the Black Country.

The first mention of the Van was in November 1902 when it was at Stourbridge. This was a natural place to start where Oliver Jenkins was renewing socialist politics and trade unionism and Julia Dawson was interested in the struggles of the chainmakers. It was called a Clarion Van Winter Scheme. Great difficulties were experienced in securing halls in the Stourbridge district, it was reported. The Vale of Hope Institute, available the year before, had been closed to them, although the managers were working men and mostly trade unionists. 'They are afraid of Socialism, Such narrow mindedness indicates the need for Socialist propaganda. In fine contrast was the generosity of Mr Perks of Lye who allowed the Gospel Hall for six meetings without charge. Attendances were comparatively small, as were the collections'. On Monday there was a meeting at Cradley. On Tuesday at Brierley Hill. 'A blighted hole with no saving grace except the presence of one or two Socialists. For two hours we stood in the main street distributing leaflets. It was intensely cold. Pioneer Tom Evans of Dudley was in the chair.' On Wednesday they were at the Cradley Board School again. Not a very big attendance 'although Musto, Jenkins and myself distributed bills during the afternoon.' The next meeting was a failure because the Earl of Beauchamp and Cecil Harmsworth were billed to speak at the Town Hall on Education, 'so all the Stourbridge world and his wife went to see the real live earl.' On the Friday they were at the Primitive Methodist Schoolroom at Brierley Hill. The Van was billed to spend three days in Dudley and then go to Kidderminster and Worcester, returning to Wolverhampton for a week in December. The above report was from the Vanner, Henry L. Barrett who also contributed the next report on Dudley. A meeting at the Temperance Hall which held 1,000 '...got a small audience because of the wretched weather, cold, fog, drizzle and rain throughout the evening. It is scarcely surprising that the audience looked like a few scattered crumbs on a meat dish. Alexander Young of the School Board presided. Tom Evans worked like the brick he is. Our expenses were very heavy and our local sympathisers, however rich in ideas and enthusiasm, are poor in pocket. If *Clarion* readers would decide to come together and take a small room and meet regularly I am convinced that before long a good solid organisation would be created.' The next night there was a meeting at King Street Congregational schools and the following night one at the Dock Lane Mission Rooms with Tom Evans in the chair. But no remarks were made concerning either attendance or weather. The meetings scheduled for Wolverhampton seem to have fallen through 'due to misunderstandings.'

The Van continued touring through the winter. By February 1903 it was at West Bromwich where hardships could be temporarily forgotten. 'To arrive at a town where there is not only a good and active organisation of Socialists but also a comfortable central meeting place is, indeed, a pleasant experience'. On Sunday there was a fairly well attended meeting at the West Bromwich Labour Church. The next day the Van was at Wednesbury, 'One of the most capitalist ridden towns I have ever visited. Work is so slack and organisation so weak that workers hardly dare attend a meeting on Labour Representation. The good old Socialist Comrade Micklewright presided over a gathering of about 50. Tried to form a Socialist group, but men dare not turn up in public.' These were dark days for Socialist pioneers at the end of the Boer War. On Tuesday they were at the Central Labour Hall, West Bromwich under the auspices of the Labour League. Here they held discussions on the formation of a Labour group in the House of Commons. 'Harry Brockhouse is doing excellent work here'. On Thursday they were at Spon Lane Board School, 'Comrade Thompson who fought the election was in the chair.' On Sunday Barrett was 'Honoured by an interview with Chief Baker who came with orders for me to speak at the Birmingham Fellowship'. W.E. Baker was then organising *Clarion* activity in Birmingham including Fellowship and Handicraft Guild work.

In 1904 and 1905 there was no mention of the van, and in 1906 the only notice was that Birmingham (where also there had been no Van activity) was to have its own Van. By April 1907 it

117

was being called the Midland Van and the Vanner appointed was C.D. Drysdale. The Van first appeared in the Black Country in August. At Brierley Hill 'the comrades had difficulty finding a pitch and meetings were somewhat poorly attended'. But at Dudley it was 'Success from every point of view. Audiences were large and enthusiastic, collections and sales were above average and new members joined.'

In September the Van moved to Wolverhampton. Drysdale reported:

> Wolverhampton has been a record in more respects than one. We opened before a very large crowd to the accompaniment of church bells. A deputation went to the church to ask for the bells to be discontinued during the meeting. This was refused. A strongly worded resolution was then put to the meeting and passed. Subsequently a clergyman said that if we had seen the proper authorities we could have endeavoured to come to some amicable arrangement. This little incident together with my answers to questions regarding Grayson... duly reported in the local press was a good advert and all following three meetings were very large. With Mrs Sproson of the Suffragettes Union in the chair we had an additional meeting on Socialism and Women. On Friday we found the pitch occupied by the redoubtable Hunnable of Jarrow and we succeeded in drawing a large proportion of the crowd from that hero. On Sunday night it was a pleasure to address a magnificent crowd of 2,000 to 3,000 people. The subject was Socialism and Christianity. At the end the Rev Bros, Vicar of St. Peters mounted the platform and said he agreed cordially with our ideas and was prepared to admit the truth of my statement that much Christianity was organised hypocrisy.

The next week Drysdale was at Walsall where the visit was adjudged 'fairly successful'. Three meetings had had to be abandoned because of rain. 'The Sunday meeting and others were well attended. Collections and sales were good, but not up to the Wolverhampton standard'.

The Van moved on to Wednesbury. On arrival it found the local Wakes in progress and in consequence the crowd 'somewhat rowdy'. On Tuesday and Wednesday the crowds were good and 'we had the satisfaction of knowing that the visit will have good effects.' On Thursday they were at Great Bridge, 'possibly the most dismal spot in the Black Country which is saying a lot.' Meetings there were 'well attended' however and the Sunday was spent in 'practical pioneering work'.

Then on to West Bromwich where the pitch had the disadvantage of being 'a little out of the way'. But the meetings were an unqualified success 'Owing to the splendid energies of Comrades Brockhouse, Micklewright and others. Audiences were large and enthusiastic and collections (whisper it not in Gath) topped Wolverhampton'.

The Van returned to Wolverhampton in October where an additional attraction had been a debate with a Unionist Tariff Reformer. The Van continued on the road during the winter, but predictably, with less success. There was an appeal for dates in November indicating that the Van was being under-utilised. In December Drysdale 'took Jowett's place in Wolverhampton, but the meeting was not a success.'

An incentive to keep the Van on the road despite the winter difficulties is suggested by the fact that *Clarion*'s was not the only Van around. In January 1908 Birmingham Clarion Scouts were vexed by the fact that Tory Van No.9. had visited Gosta Green and they had not been there to heckle it. In February the Clarion Van was at Smethwick where mass unemployment was the main issue.

In the spring of 1908 Drysdale was protesting about an imposter who first visited the Van at Wolverhampton and said he was Stoker Moody just released from 9 months in jail for his part in naval riots at Portsmouth and calling himself Drysdale's cousin . In April Drysdale went to West Bromwich to take the place of Victor Grayson who should have addressed a meeting there. He left the Van in Wolverhampton with Comrade Attle in charge. In May a successful meeting at the West Bromwich Labour Church was held from the Van which then went to Dudley. Here Drysdale reported, 'Dudley has a reputation of being rather rowdy for Socialist speakers, but for four nights our audiences were large and attentive'.

In June 1908 the accounts of the Midland van were published for the period October 1907 to April 1908. There was a total deficiency of £8-16-8d. Total expenditure had been £119-10-0d. of which the Vanners salary amounted to £65. The income had come from Collections £58, Guarantors £50 and Subscriptions and Branch payments £14-10-0d.

The Van did not return to the Black Country until the autumn. At the end of September on the way to Walsall the Van broke down. However, the following Sunday 'We had two of the largest audiences that have as yet attended Socialist meetings in Walsall'. The Van moved on to Willenhall, 'one of the most poverty stricken places in the Black Country.' Here Drysdale reported that the continuous strain of the summer work had brought him perilously near to break down. His tour of Staffordshire, Warwickshire, Derbyshire and Leicestershire 'had brought some of the largest Socialist meetings ever seen.' The deficit on the Van at that time was £12 and an appeal went out from West Bromwich for those towns through which the Van had passed to meet this. We hear no more of his break down, but Drysdale's trials continued:

> On Monday I had an alarming encounter with a mob of roughs called 'peaky binders.' On arrival the horse was surrounded and 'baksheesh' demanded. When this was refused they tried to enter the Van and drove the horse off. I was surrounded by a howling mob of men, women and children on my own. Failing to gain entry they drove the Van several times against a wall in an attempt to smash it. I was rescued by police and sympathisers.

The location of this encounter was not given, but the Van was around the Black Country at the time. The next week the Van was in Walsall where Drysdale reported that he had lost his voice and his place was taken by Comrade Wilkinson of Walsall.

At the beginning of 1909 a Midland Area meeting was held about the Van. Attle (Wolverhampton), Griffiths (Dudley) and E. Mills (Willenhall) represented the Black Country. One of the items on the agenda was probably the state of the Van for in March we are told that the Van was being 'altered and repaired by a Smethwick comrade.' Within a couple of weeks the Van was back on the road 'greatly improved.' In June the Van was at West Bromwich where:

> On arrival we found that an anti-Socialist Van had been before us and had received a great deal of heckling. The Tories had threatened reprisals. At our first meeting the audience was large and enthusiastic, but the others were spoiled by rain.

The next week Drysdale reported, 'So many of our meetings have been spoiled by rain that we wonder whether we shall have any summer.' Rain continued into August, but by the second week Drysdale was reporting excellent meetings due to a change in the weather. In September Drysdale was enthusiastic about the Van, saying that for effective propaganda it was by far and away the best. 'Our opponents are of the same opinion judging by the number of Protectionist Vans on the road.' But the rains returned in September and Drysdale had to say, 'Although I am reluctant to admit defeat, the bad weather has brought things to an impasse.' This affected the finances of the Van. A Midland Van Committee meeting in November heard that the deficit was then £33 and they could not consider another year's campaign until this had been cleared.

In April 1910 it was announced that the Van would tour again even though the Guarantee Fund was insufficient. The Van mostly toured the north Midlands that season but by September Drysdale's wages were £20 in arrears even though from a propaganda point of view this had been his most successful season. It was not until September that the Van came to the Black Country where it stayed a week at West Bromwich. Here, 'The ILP, SDF and Socialist Society worked loyally in support and the result was a splendid series of meetings.' The Van was now involved in the campaign to create the united British Socialist Party.

It was the summer of 1911 before the Van again came to the Black Country. In July it was announced that the Midland Vanner was to be George Whitehead. In August he was reporting good support from the Clarion Cycling Clubs, and seven meetings held in the Black Country:

> All were successful except in West Bromwich where another speaker put his box three inches from ours. Although I understand there are hundreds of ILPers in West Bromwich none came out to help. A pleasing feature of the other meetings has been a plentiful supply of questions. I thank Comrades Murray and Poultney very heartily for their hospitality.

There is no further mention of the Van until the spring of 1912 when early in May all Clarionettes were requested to make their way to Burton-on-Trent to see the new Midland Motor Van 'opened' by Leonard Hall. It was not until September that the Van reached the Black Country. Whitehead reported two successful meetings in Walsall despite very cold weather. The next week he was to be in Wolverhampton, but there were problems with West Bromwich where the police were only allowing one meeting per week and that only for one hour. He thanked Comrades Bradfield and Bleby for hospitality in Walsall and Wolverhampton. In October there was a Midland Van delegate meeting at Derby. No representatives from Birmingham or the Black Country attended. Here it was decided to store the Van for the winter.

In 1913 there was another new Vanner, Tom Jones. He was in the Black Country in June 'doing splendidly among midland strikers.' In Walsall he had 'the best turn-out of the year', and in Smethwick held a very good meeting among the strikers. He moved on to Stourbridge, but could not find a pitch so went on to Lye where brickmakers were on strike. Here he had 'a good crowd interested for 1½ hours.' On to Dudley where 'a splendid meeting if followed up would result in a good branch'. By the end of the week he was in Wolverhampton. A meeting on the Market Place on the Friday attracted a crowd which 'could have been bigger.' But on Saturday night he had 'a good and interested crowd.' He finished his Wolverhampton mission on the Sunday with a 'rousing' meeting and secured 14 names of those wishing to form a Wolverhampton Fellowship. In September Walsall CCC announced that the Van would be back at Walsall in early September at Town's End Bank in support of the campaign for a Midland Club House and asking supporters to forward their half crowns for shares.

In 1914 the Walsall cyclists were again making the running with 'a record turnout' for a Van meeting in May. At the end of the month the Van was at the Blue Gates, Smethwick. 'Wintry weather, rained off altogether, but a good meeting in the evening. A good crowd listened attentively although the night was cold and cheerless.' Then on to Stourbridge:

> Where we were booked for one day, but owing to no pitches at Lye and Brierley Hill we were forced to stay three days. All three meetings were dismal failures due to (a) the Pitch was unsuitable and (b) although there is a fair sprinkling of local Socialists we were not blessed with their presence. We tried at Wollescote, but it was another small audience. It was interrupted by a thunder storm. On Saturday we were pleased to leave Stourbridge for Dudley where we hoped for better times, but on Saturday night a meeting was impossible because of rain.

Despite the support of both Walsall and Wolverhampton CCCs the going remained tough. Here is the report at the end of May:

> We have done another week's work in the Black Country, and very heavy work it is too. To stand up and speak of Socialism to a crowd who need feeding more than they need education is not an easy or a pleasant task. Our collections were poor although our audiences were good... On Sunday we opened on Dudley Market Place. The morning meeting was poor, but the evening audience was a splendid one. If we had more assistance, collections and literature sales would be better. As it was, the Vanner and another comrade had to make the best of things. On Monday the Market Place was occupied with stalls and we had to go down a side street to hold an unsuccessful meeting. On Tuesday we transferred to Wednesbury where we held three good meetings. Here the people are very poor but they purchased literature in fair quantities. This is a promising place for Socialism if followed up. On Friday we moved to Walsall. The Friday meeting was good, but on Saturday we had the stormiest meeting I have ever experienced. We seemed to have all the drunks that Walsall possessed. Undoubtedly it was organised opposition and reflects discredit on those responsible. Our platform was nearly smashed and fisticuffs engaged in. However, the fort was held and we brought the meeting to a peaceful conclusion. This week we give thanks for hospitality to Mr & Mrs Bleby of Wolverhampton and Miss Middleton of Walsall.

The Black Country tour continued into June. There was a good meeting at Willenhall and then a five day Mission in Wolverhampton. 'What with holidays and rain we have not had very good meetings' On Monday there was opposition from the local 'Tory Labour Party' and, 'our comrades generously forsook the Vanner and helped our opponents to an audience.' The Van then left for Cannock and the Potteries. The next month war broke out. In September the Van Committee decided it was futile to continue propaganda work. It was agreed that the Vanner's services could best be utilised by him visiting the larger towns and helping with the circulation of *Clarion*. The Vanner refused to do this, however. The report ended, 'Clarionettes must therefore do this themselves. It was tried in Birmingham and the results were worth while.' By then *Clarion* was supporting the war, and the Vanner's reluctance may have been because he had reservations about this policy.

Labour churches

Labour Churches began in Manchester in 1891 when a Socialist minister, John Trevor, dissatisfied with the way other organised religionists catered for the needs of working people, set up his own church. The movement spread, particularly in the north. The principles of the new church were:

1. That the Labour Movement is a Religious Movement.
2. That the Religion of the Labour Movement is not a Class Religion, but unites members of all classes working for the abolition of Commercial Slavery.
3. That the Religion of the Labour Movement is not Sectarian or Dogmatic, but Free Religion, leaving each man free to develop his relations with the Power that brought him into being.

It can be seen that such principles covered both believers and agnostics and could even be stretched to include atheists. Services consisted of prayers and readings from radical writers, and hymns from their own Labour Hymn Book, including those of such atheists as Shelley and William Morris. The main item was a 'sermon' from a leading Labour movement figure. Such churches grew rapidly in the 1890s particularly in Yorkshire and Lancashire. In 1893 a Labour Church Union was established and a monthly paper the *Labour Prophet* was established a year earlier. At the end of the century the Union, which never had more that twenty five churches, began to weaken and the paper disappeared in 1897.

It is from the *Labour Prophet* that we learn of the first Black Country Labour Church, in Wolverhampton. The first report came from Joseph Whittaker of 10 Townwell Fold who wrote in July 1893:

> It is going slowly here. We are scarcely more than a dozen. We are heavily hampered by hours of work and bread and butter questions. We have held a sort of Labour Church service in the open air in the East End for the last four or five Sunday nights. We have two or three hymns from the Labour Church Hymn Book, a reading – usually from the *Labour Prophet* and about two addresses. No prayers. This is not exactly a praying region. The first Sunday we sang two hymns, but no adults came by us. About 40 children clustered about us, but of course, we cultured Fabians could not stoop to speak to mere children. The next Sunday was the same – plenty of children but no adults. We were disgusted; but one of us Tom Frost by name was not so superior as his comrades and, to the children's delight began to read to them the Cinderella story from the May *Prophet*. (This was a story by Robert Blatchford – GB). By and bye a few grown-ups came around and we had an adult meeting after all, though only about a dozen. The next Sunday was a shade better and last Sunday we had about forty. So we are going slowly. But why give up the children? Here you are throwing away a fine chance for a real live piece of work. If you must have the adults, let Tom Frost go off somewhere else and draw the children...

This experience led to to the setting up of a Pioneer Group and in October 1893 W.J. Carthy wrote from Wolverhampton saying that the Pioneers had decided to organise themselves for the Labour Church during the winter months, and the Wolverhampton Fabian Society committee had passed a resolution congratulating the Labour Church Pioneers. In January 1894 another report from McCarthy said there had been successful meetings on the first two Sundays of the month and on the third Mrs Bruce Glasier had spoken on War and Peace. 'The Labour Church choir was ably accompanied by stringed instruments and piano, rendering Labour Church hymns very creditably.' F.W. Mee, the Labour JP, had taken the chair. 'Wolverhampton will survive', McCarthy ended. In February, 'Pleasant evenings but not large attendances', were reported, with speakers Enid Stacy on 'Modern Shams' and Mr Carlile from Birmingham on the 'Religion of the Labour Church.' For March and April they had decided on one big meeting a month. The March speaker was Fred Brocklehurst who 'addressed us on Socialism and Character in grand style'. Before the meeting there had been a 'social tea and chat.' The string band had played two selections of music and the choir 'which was a strong one sang Labour hymns splendidly'. In June Joseph Whittaker was 'starting a small class more elementary than Pioneers'. In September William McCarthy was still the Hon. Sec.

But it appears that the Wolverhampton Church did not survive as this was the last report in the *Labour Prophet*. However In October 1897 the *Prophet* had a front page wholly devoted to a biography of Joseph Whittaker, 'story writer and poet'. Whittaker was born in 1871 in some of the worst slums of Wolverhampton to parents of a large family of which only five survived. He left school at twelve and worked for six years in a pawnshop in east Wolverhampton. When he was fourteen his father died and the family home, which by then was in Townwell Fold, another unsalubrious area, was kept together by the brothers and sisters. In 1887 he joined the Wolverhampton Library classes. In 1890 he was out of work for eighteen months and very pessimistic. Then he got a job as a warehouse clerk under a 'Christian philanthropist' and was sacked after four and a half years. During this 'golden age' Whittaker read 'Looking Backward' (an American utopian account of a Socialist USA – GB) with a notion of refuting it, but finding he could not, joined the Wolverhampton Fabian Society of which he was secretary until its decease. He next assisted the formation of the Wolverhampton ILP and ILP Club for which he acted as secretary. He was also secretary of the South Staffordshire Socialist Federation.

Joseph Whittaker began writing at the age of thirteen, contributing to a *Young Folks' Paper* under the pen-name of Ishmael. He contributed to the *Labour Prophet* almost from its commencement. He was also the author of Hymn No.14 in the Labour Church Hymn Book, 'Lift up the People's Banner'. In 1892 he received sufficient orders to print his first book of poems in an edition of 140. This was both a literary and a commercial success and had become a rarity. In 1895 *Divers Tomes* was published which included The Storming of Heaven. In 1896 he was out of work for eight months and in September he went to Blackpool to work on a Labour cum Co-operative cum Trade Union paper which folded and in October 1897 he was again out of work.

Joseph Whittaker does not appear to have returned to Wolverhampton and his subsequent whereabouts and activities are unknown to the present writer. By an irony of fate and a cause of no little confusion he was succeeded in his work by another J. Whittaker (James) who, from 1891 to 1940 was the outstanding Labour and trade union figure in Wolverhampton.

At the end of 1897 the *Labour Prophet* ceased publication and the Labour Church Union was in decline. At its 6th. Annual Conference only seven of twenty seven churches sent delegates. But the Birmingham Labour Church continued to exist and the twentieth century was to see the real development of Labour Churches in Birmingham and the Black Country.

From 1900 *Clarion* and the *Labour Leader,* the paper of the ILP, are our main sources of information, as befits the fact that it is almost impossible to separate the Labour Churches from Clarion and its organisations – Cinderellas, Cyclists, Scouts, Fellowships etc, and also the ILP and the Fabians.

The next and most celebrated of the Black Country Labour Churches was West Bromwich, the *Victoria County History* quoting D.F. Summers' unpublished Edinburgh Ph.D.thesis of 1958 states that there was a meeting (the inaugural one?) in 1899 of the Church at Groves Assembly Rooms with Henry Brockhouse in the chair. By 1901 it was established in its own premises, the People's Hall, which had been built by the local ILP. From this time the Church existed continuously, not only to 1914 but up to 1940.

The People's Hall was a corrugated iron building on a site between Shaftesbury Street and Temple Street between the old Hippodrome and a row of shops. It held nearly 200 people and club and committee rooms were attached. It was lighted by electricity installed by members. Its most important feature was the decoration which was supervised by Walter Crane the celebrated artist of the Labour movement. The cost was £700 of which £400 had been raised. The opening ceremony was on Sunday 10th. November 1901. The building was still the property of the ILP in 1970. In July 1903 the Labour Church Union national conference was held at West Bromwich. In the same month Clarion reported that the West Bromwich Socialist Party had 'one of the prettiest Halls in the country', but it was £600 in debt. A Fancy Fair was to be held in November opened by the Countess of Warwick:

> Only those who live in the Black Country can appreciate the sacrifice involved in active Socialist work and we ask friends outside West Bromwich to help. There will be a Handicraft Guild stall and a fancy stall for ladies. Don't be afraid to embarrass us with an abundance of things. (Henry Thompson 11 Temple Street. Henry Brockhouse, joint secs.).

In September 1904 it was announced that the new season would be opened with a lecture on the Ethical Movement. This was to be followed by a Shakespeare recital. 'It looks like being a good season', said the hon.sec. James Gripton.

By the end of 1905 the Socialist revival was under way. In December Philip Snowden had spoken at the West Bromwich People's Hall and also at the Town Hall. Both meetings had been 'a huge success'. The same month there was a Labour Church associated with the North Worcestershire ILP.

In April 1906 Gavan Duffy was touring the Black Country for the ILP. He announced a packed meeting at West Bromwich Labour Church on 'Today's Life's Problems' and the first mention of Walsall where he 'attended the usual Labour Church meeting held at the Temperance Hall.' The next month Walsall were assisting in setting up a Church in Wednesbury where, 'The YMCA is now becoming a Labour Church'. The contact person was E. Dillon Clarke of Walsall. Fred Hick was touring the Black Country in May and reported a 'splendid' Labour Church meeting at Walsall on 'Is Society an Organism?' Later in the month he attended an executive committee meeting 'In the new Wednesbury Labour Church'. A report on the preparation of the Church said:

> The interior has been transformed from a dull and dreary blank... to a perfect paradise of lime-wash, colouring and paint. With only a few coppers in the war chest we undertook the lease of the building and are looking forward to a brisk propaganda. Comrades at a distance who are puzzling their wits how to dispose of their surplus cash may find a ready demand from: J. Jackson c/o Mr Whitehead at 22 Spring Head, Wednesbury.

Still in May 1906 Hick was again at the West Bromwich Labour Church: 'The place was full and a double the normal collection went to the local hospital.' Hick was again at Wednesbury Labour Church in September talking on 'Socialism and Christianity.'

Some time in 1906 Wolverhampton Labour Church reappeared, for in November the *Wolverhampton Journal* reported that Mrs Pankhurst had delivered two addresses there on 'Votes for Women'. This paper continued to report Labour Church meetings in Wolverhampton. Also in November a debating class was formed at the Church 'to develop ILP speakers', and in December there was a 'large audience' to hear Fred Bramley of the *Clarion* van.

In January 1907 Wolverhampton Labour Church was meeting at the Co-op Hall, Stafford Street where they heard the Black Country's first Labour MP elected the previous year, T.F. Richards. The other new Labour MPs were much in demand at the Wolverhampton Church and in April G.H. Roberts, the Norwich MP gave 'one of the finest expositions of Socialism ever heard in Wolverhampton'. and also in April Charles Duncan MP spoke on 'In Front of the Speaker's Chair'. In May Roberts was back to speak on 'Labour's Aims and Ideals'. Wolverhampton brought their winter season to an end with two lectures by Mrs Bruce Glasier on the 'Meaning of Labour's Victories' and 'Socialism and the Home'. In October Wolverhampton started the new season with a 'magnificent meeting' at the Empire with T.F. Richards and in November opened in their new premises, the Central Hall, School Street, with an address by Councillor R.R. Millard on the text 'He beheld the City and Wept for It.'

There were no other mentions of Black Country Labour Churches in 1907 in either *Clarion* or the *Labour Leader* apart from a report of the first appearance of a choir at the West Bromwich Church in March.

In February 1908 two Wolverhampton Labour Church meetings were reported at the Empire Palace. One was by James Parker MP for Halifax on 'Socialism and Life'. The other was by Charles Duncan MP for Barrow who 'advocated Socialism and censured Sir Henry Fowler (the local MP – GB) for his determined attacks on Socialism' which he had made at a recent public meeting/

In October 1908 Dudley Labour Church was inaugurated. The *Labour Leader* carried a very informative feature article which highlighted the problems of both the area and Labour politics. It is summarised below:

> Like a carbuncle on the backbone of England stands the ancient borough of Dudley. Open to the four winds of heaven, the smoke of the Black Country has little chance to stagnate over its streets. On its highest eminence, above flowing folds of rich foliage rises the castle keep. For miles around the land with its vast mineral resources is the castle desmesne. Tens of thousands of toilers are vassals of the baron and his head men. Uncongenial ground for (even) a virile organisation like the ILP. Yet even this feudal stronghold is being sapped and mined. A small band of comrades has long been at work to break up the old and bring in the new order.

> Week by week the comrades meet to discuss this bit of business or that and the feeling grows – this won't do we are wanderers. We must have a home of our own. But how to find it!

Landlords scenting Socialism were not to be tempted even by the bait of an immediate tenant. But at last an opportunity to acquire premises arrived. It was a derelict building enough, part of an old social club in surroundings neither ornamental nor fragrant. Our scribe, who had been sent to inspect and report returned holding his nose and gasped Ne-var. Weeks passed. We looked further but in vain. The olfactory nerves got blunted. The whisper went round: Better independence on a dunghill than servitude in a wide house. We took the derelict club. The veteran (probably A.V. Mayer – GB) the chairman and the scribe went guarantors. Then began the great concerted action. The scouts, the main body, blocked the traffic of the cul-de-sac. The password was Coats and the response – Off. Instantly the Labour Church began to be. Its consecration had commenced.

It was a long and lofty room; rows of windows on the long sides – one row so high, heavily barred and grated as to suggest durance vile for a suffragette. At a squeeze the room would take 100, but an anteroom would take a dozen more. A cellar with a bombshell capacity of twenty tons, completed the suite.

There then followed a long account of the restoration work by the voluntary labour including its wiring for electricity, the making of collection plates with a monogram 'DLC' and two cartoon engravings of Walter Crane's.

At the opening service the church was well filled. The West Bromwich Labour Church sent along a 'splendid contingent'. There were others from a distance. The president (chosen for the year) was in the chair. The comedy man, dropping for the nonce his role read gravely and well a passage from Carlyle's *Past and Present*. Comrade Henry Brockhouse gave a lucid but brief account of what Labour Churches stand for. The local Socialist parson spoke on the gospel of the Labour Church which he described first as a gospel of revolt – against a crude theology, against conventional religion and against a cruel social order; and second as a message of hope and a call to constructive work. Instead of wasting time sifting theological dogma such as the Resurrection, the Labour Church concerned itself with the resurrection of society. A religion which did not express itself in humane laws stood self-condemned. The religion of the Labour church represented the high aspects of Socialism, the care of the body in order to develop the mind, the emancipation of the wage-slave in order to free his soul, to give him scope for developing the highest and divinest within him.

What is the Labour Church on Sundays is the Labour Hall every week night. it is fast developing into a club, a centre for fellowship and for service – in a word, a citadel of Socialism.

From 1909 Labour Church reports become very scarce. A meeting of the Wolverhampton Church in January 1911 to hear W.C. Anderson reported that the 'Room was easily packed out'. The only report of 1912 was one showing a new Church – the Stourbridge Labour Church which in October heard Norman Tiptaft (a future Birmingham mayor who moved very far from socialism) speaking on 'What Socialism Is'.

These years, and up to 1914, were action packed with the creation of the new British Socialist Party, the Women's Suffrage movement and the Great Unrest. Whether this made the Labour Churches less relevant to the times or whether they were one organisation too many, is difficult to decide. But lack of reports does not necessarily signify extinction. Some, such as Wednesbury and Stourbridge and perhaps even Walsall may not have survived. But West Bromwich Labour Church existed into the 1930s, as did Wolverhampton, while the Dudley Church remained until at least the first World War as insertions in the Dudley Herald Year Books for 1912 to 1914 testify. These show that its location was in King Street. Services were held every Sunday at 6-30pm 'to give expression to the religion of the labour movement' which was 'not theological but respects every individual's personal conviction upon this question.'

Other Socialist organisations

There were two breakaway groups from the Social Democratic Federation in these years. In 1903 the Socialist Labour Party was formed by a group of ultra-pure Marxists who believed that the SDF had departed from the strict revolutionary path. This group was based mainly in Scotland and Socialist growth in the Black Country was too slight to accommodate the revolutionary dogmatism and discipline of this organisation. However, the main influence of the SLP was in the dissemination of Marxist texts, many from translations made in America by Daniel de Leon's Socialist Labour Party there. These and the SLP paper the *Socialist* did circulate in the Black Country and it is likely that their greatest impact was in Walsall where the semi-anarchism from the Walsall Bomb Plot lingered on.

The other breakaway group from the SDF was the Socialist Party of Great Britain. This was a predominantly London group which broke away in 1905. As is the way with the ultra-pure neither of these breakaways would have relations with the other and the SPGB had even less effect in the Black Country than the SLP.

Fabian Society activity was also sparse. We have seen how the Society took hold in Wolverhampton under the secretaryship of Joseph Whittaker, but after that year nothing more is heard. From 1905 with the resurgence of Socialism, the Fabian Society again began to expand outside London. In March 1909 there is one of only two references to Fabian activity in the Black Country that I have found. The first stated, that a branch had been formed in Walsall and a series of lectures arranged at the Co-op Hall, Bridge Street. These were to be taken by Holbrook Jackson on successive Fridays and would be on 'Socialism and the Labour Party', 'Socialism and the Ratepayer' and the 'Coming of Socialism'. Jackson had recently been joint editor with A.R. Orage on the latter's paper the *New Age* which was trying to re-vivify what is called ethical socialism. It is perhaps singular that Fabianism developed in Walsall with its semi-anarchic tradition rather than in Wolverhampton or Dudley with their more orthodox political development. But develop it did and the Society has an entry in the Walsall Red Book for each year from 1909 to 1912.

Another development of ethical socialism with the Socialist revival of 1905 was an enormous growth of Christian Socialism. Two organisations grew from this. One was the Christian Socialist League, an organisation limited to members of the Church of England. Two of its leaders were based in Birmingham, the Hon. Rev James Adderley and the Rev Arnold Pinchard, who was the national president for some time. The League was formed in 1906 and within two years it had 25 branches and 1,000 members. There is no record of a Black Country branch, but as we have seen by their willingness to associate with the Labour Churches, there were a number of Church of England ministers who were Christian Socialists even if they did not belong to the League. The League was no supine organisation and identified with the militant rather than the reformist sections of the movement, tending to support the Syndicalists during the Great Unrest. After this, it associated itself with Guild Socialism.

The Nonconformists, particularly the Congregationalists, were also concerning themselves with the condition of the people question and Socialism. From 1905 the Rev J.A. Shaw in Wolverhampton associated himself strongly with the Labour movement, particularly the ILP. In 1909 the nonconformists formed a Progressive League. In Wolverhampton it first appeared in November 1909 as the League for Progressive Thought, with Shaw as the local president. This League also developed rapidly nationally to 175 branches with between four and five thousand members. Again we know nothing of organisation in the Black Country. But Shaw became a leading figure in the Wolverhampton labour movement, addressing unemployed demonstrations in 1908 and contributing to the local labour movement paper *Wolverhampton Worker* in 1913 and 1914. More will be heard of the Rev Shaw. It seems clear, however, that further research is needed on Christianity and Socialism in the Black Country.

The Independent Labour Party

The ILP became the largest Labour political organisation in the Black Country almost from its inception in 1893. After 1900, together with what became Trades & Labour Councils within local Labour Representation Committees, its activities were dominated by the quest for local representation in Parliament and on local bodies; the ILP providing the organisation and the trade unions the money. In this section it is proposed to deal with the development of the ILP in the various towns, and then deal with national representation separately.

In 1900 the position was that Wolverhampton was the strongest organised town with two branches and something over 70 members. West Bromwich was also well organised with a membership of about 30 and a leader nationally known, Harry Brockhouse. Dudley ILP with 20 members was the next strongest branch. There were also organised branches in Stourbridge, Wednesbury, Oldbury and Cradley Heath, but these were less well equipped to survive the storms of the Boer War.

The Stourbridge branch was the result of the work of Oliver Jenkins. He was a railwayman, well known in Welsh labour circles, who left Merthyr Tydfil in 1897 and settled in the Black Country. In an extraordinary burst of political initiative he organised in rapid succession the local railwaymen and then the Stourbridge Trades Council. With C. Crossland he formed the Stourbridge & District ILP and also a Socialist Society. By 1903 Jenkins had been elected to Lye Urban District Council. He was then sacked by the Great Western Railway for not being at his work on the night of the election. So he became an insurance agent and also opened refreshment rooms at 75 Lower High Street, Stourbridge. Whether these sources of income proved insufficient or whether it was for other reasons, Oliver Jenkins then seems to have left the Black Country and nothing further is known of him.

With Jenkins' departure the ILP branch disappeared and it was not until 1908 that it was re-formed. However. elections are recorded in 1905 for Lye and Wollescote UDC in which trades council and miners' candidates participated which suggest that some of Jenkins' efforts were bearing fruit.

Stourbridge shared in the socialist advance after 1905 and in May 1908 it was announced that a Stourbridge ILP branch had been formed. Its secretary was A. Pearson and it met at the Central Coffee Tavern. In July it was said to be 'strongly advancing' and had received a visit from Crossland who by then appears to have moved to Wolverhampton. The following week the main speaker failed to appear and 'local members Bewcher, Sciven, Music and Harwood went into the breach and conducted themselves like veterans'. The names suggest a hand written report which the editor found difficult to decipher. There is then another gap until February 1911 when it was announced that Stourbridge ILP Labour Rooms had been crowded in the morning and the Picture Palace at night to hear E. Hallas from Birmingham give two 'inspiring' lectures on 'Faust and Socialism' and 'Joseph Chamberlain from a Socialist Standpoint'. The report ended, 'Stourbridge could be a stronghold if the comrades rally round.' There are no other reports, but the emergence of a Labour Church in 1912 suggests that there would be an ILP branch at that time.

Smethwick is just off the coalfield and with only one iron furnace might claim not to be in the Black Country, but with the Soho Foundry within its borders and as perhaps the most important centre of the foundry industry it is linked with both the Black Country and Birmingham. For much of its political development, however, the largest centre was Birmingham and it tended to be connected with that town. ILP records show a branch at Smethwick at the beginning of 1898, but no branch a year later. But in the dark days of 1902 Birmingham ILP set up a preliminary meeting at No.1. Coffee House to which 'all Fellowshippers, Clarionettes and Socialists generally', were invited. This resulted in the setting up of a branch and the election of a secretary. However, branches could be set up with a minimum of only six members and this branch probably disappeared. It was re-formed in July 1906 with reports of the ILP and SDF working harmoniously organising socials and open-air meetings.which were 'going splendidly'. By October the ILP was co-operating with the Trades Council to sponsor technical education in the town at a meeting addressed by Sir Oliver Lodge who 'strongly advocated municipal socialism.' The next month Fred Bramley held two meetings where 'attendances were the biggest ever and the local press most favourable.' At the end of 1907 the branch was 'still growing.' In April 1908 a lecture by the Rev Lewis Donaldson of Leicester on 'Socialism and Christianity' was presided over by a local ILPer the Rev W.J. Archer. Large meetings were also reported with Drysdale and the Clarion Van. By November mass unemployment had driven the branch leftwards and Grayson was speaking in the town in December. Activity continued through 1909. The branch took a room at the town hall and met every Monday. Large town hall meetings were organised in September with Margaret Bondfield and George Lansbury and in October with Margaret McMillan when there was also a social and dance. In December the branch held its fourth AGM with a Bruce Glasier meeting.

Growth continued into 1910 when local electoral activity commenced initiated by a local Labour Representation Committee. The question of a new Socialist Party was agitating Black Country militants at that time and a Smethwick Socialist Society was in place by January. The same month the formation of a choir with 92 members was announced and in February the choir made its debut at a town hall meeting. The next month there was another 'grand social and dance.' In March a Birmingham and District Socialist Representation Committee was set up and Smethwick was being drawn into activity led by Leonard Hall in Birmingham to set up and shape the British Socialist Party. Smethwick belonged to the Birmingham ILP Federation at this time and the founding of the BSP must have weakened the local ILP. It continued to operate with the Federation however which in January 1912 was instructed to try to organise outdoor summer meetings in a number of places, including Smethwick. But the socialist advance was at an end. The Birmingham ILP Federation in 1913 dropped from 25 to 15 branches and Smethwick reports ceased.

However, in Black Country terms, Smethwick was very successful with its electoral activity. The first Labour member of the town council was George Ryder who won a seat in 1906, although he seems to have stood as an Independent rather than Labour. Ryder retained his seat in two elections and was still a councillor in 1914. Ryder was joined by Albert Collins in 1909. This was a last minute nomination and the local newspaper thought he stood as a Ratepayer rather than a Socialist. The fact that neither of these elections were reported in the *Labour Leader* as Labour successes suggests that they were both at first Lib-Labs. In 1910 Wilkinson stood as a Labour Representation Committee candidate in Victoria ward and failed to gain election by only five votes. In 1912 both Ryder in Soho and Collins in Victoria successfully defended their seats and they were joined by George Betts in Spon Lane. In Uplands George Wilkinson failed to be elected by 102 votes. The fact that this was reported in the *Labour Leader* as one gain and three Socialist seats suggests that by this time any question about the status of Ryder and Collins had been resolved. 1913 brought even greater sensations. In Uplands George Wilkinson was rewarded for his perseverance by being elected. A. Morris was elected in Victoria ward and J. Kesterton in Soho, bringing the total of Socialists on the council to six. A fourth LRC candidate, B.G. Lloyd polled 1136 in Bearwood (by far the biggest ward) and lost by 533 votes. This was not the end of the surprises, however. The Workers' Union which was currently bearing the brunt of the Great Unrest stood two candidates. In Spon Lane their candidate polled 305 votes against the Municipal League candidate's 978 and in Sandwell an Independent candidate, M. Chatwin polled 800 against the Workers' Union candidate, J.W. Hinton. In this latter ward Hinton congratulated Chatwin 'who was also a Labour man on his victory for Labour'. The six Socialist councillors represents a quarter of the total Council and Smethwick must be seen as the only Black Country town where the industrial advances of the period 1910-14 were matched with equivalent political gains.

A Wednesbury ILP branch existed at the end of the century and also in 1903, so it is likely that it survived the intervening reactionary period. In November 1905 Whitehead of Wednesbury ILP polled 241 votes but lost to the Liberal by 424 votes because 'Liberals and Conservatives combined to beat Labour.' This was a year when no other Black Country town seems to have contested elections. In the summer of 1907 it was organising open-air meetings in the Market Place. In April 1909 it organised a Victor Grayson meeting at the Town Hall. After surviving for so long it is surprising to read the following in October 1912: 'Wednesbury – Unattached Socialists wishing for a branch of the Labour movement here apply F. Whitehouse 20 Spring Rd.'

Oldbury brings no reports between 1899 and 1906. In May of that year Fred Hicks was campaigning in the Black Country and reported crowds 'compact' which 'showed solid attention.' The branch was continuing Friday night meetings in June when *Labour Leader* sales were three dozen. In August the fragility of the branch was exposed: 'Oldbury requests secretaries not to send draw tickets as they cannot undertake the expense of returning same.' In October the branch had 20 members. In May 1907 the branch was continuing summer outdoor meetings with C.D. Drysdale who had spoken for forty minutes on the 'Politics of a Socialist' to 'a fair crowd.' This was the last report of activity.

Willenhall branch was formed in in May 1908. A Walsall Wood branch was formed in 1909 where Freddie Richards the Wolverhampton Labour MP was said to have spoken to a crowd of 1,000 people. In September 1909 a Netherton ILP branch was reported and the next month a 'Good winter programme had been arranged.' In May 1910 Bilston was reported as a new branch whose secretary was A. Gordon of 34 Wellington Road.

Having dealt with ILP in the smaller towns, we turn to the branches in Wolverhampton, West Bromwich, Dudley and Walsall.

Wolverhampton remained the largest branch in the Black Country. It contested elections in the bad years of 1900 and 1901 and a revival began in May 1902 when the National Administrative Council of the ILP met in Wolverhampton and there were important demonstrations in the Market Square with two platforms and crowds of about 2,500. Speakers had included the two local councillors, Frost and Evans, as well as Philip Snowden and Ramsay MacDonald. 'Resolutions condemning the bread tax and Education Bill and affirming the principles of Socialism and Labour Representation were carried unanimously.' In a crowded meeting at the Co-op Hall with speeches by Bruce Glasier, Snowden and Keir Hardie, the decision to stand a candidate for the Parliamentary division was enthusiastically endorsed. In August the branch was announcing successful open air meetings at the Five Ways but asking for an interchange of speakers with other branches. In November 1903 Ramsay MacDonald was at a large meeting in the town campaigning for Richards. 1904 and 1905 were also campaigning years for Richards who was elected in January 1906.

The socialist revival after 1902 confirmed the position of the ILP as the driving force behind the demand for national and local working class representation influencing not only the Labour movement but also the Liberals.

The first working man to be elected to Wolverhampton council was Abiathar Weaver in 1891. Weaver was a Conservative who refused to join his trade union and so was not a Labour representative. The next came one month later when George Stevenson was elected unopposed. But he had Liberal support and was thus a Lib-Lab. In 1896 Evan Evans became the first 'true' Labour councillor as a nominee of the ILP for Graiseley ward. In 1897 F. Evans, another Lib-Lab was elected for Dunstall and also H. Gibson for Blakenhall. In 1898 J. Steward won the Dunstall ward and in 1899 T. Wilson won Dunstall, which thus became the first ward with three Labour councillors. By 1900 there were five Labour councillors, plus two Lib-Labs and one Con-Lab. In the bad years for Labour of the Boer War they maintained their position on the Council. Cooke lost his St. John's seat in 1901, but was replaced by William Sharrocks at St. Matthew's. Sharrock's victory was particularly noteworthy because he stood both for the ILP and also for the red-bloodied Socialism of the Social Democratic Federation. He lays claim therefore to being the first 'true' Socialist on the Council. although he subsequently stood as the LRC candidate and there is little in his later career to suggest a Marxist background. In 1902 Wilson lost his Dunstall seat, but Thomas Frost gained St. John's. Labour membership of the Council fluctuated between four and five in the years 1902 to 1907 but then came a disaster year in 1908 when the Tories mounted an offensive throughout the town. In that year Evan Evans lost Graiseley and Thomas Frost lost St. John's for Labour representation to fall to two. The years of trade union success 1910-13 brought little electoral reward and by 1914 Labour representation stood at three, the two stalwarts Tom Frost and William Sharrocks and a newcomer, Albert Bent.

West Bromwich ILP benefitted immeasurably from the presence of Harry Brockhouse whose financial resources and personal status solved many problems. Brockhouse attended the annual ILP Conferences from 1897 to 1917 almost without a break and was sometimes the only Black Country delegate. He does not seem to have made any significant contribution to these Conferences, but he was a nationally admired and influential member. For a time after 1907 he was a divisional representative on the National Administrative Council, although generally the midlands representative was J.W. Kneeshaw from Birmingham. His opinions were sought by the national leadership on the question of Parliamentary elections, particularly, as we shall see, on the vexed question of Wednesbury representation. But the only office Brockhouse seems to have sought was the local School Board on which he was serving in 1897 and to which he was re-elected unopposed in 1901.

In the years before the Boer War the the number of members Harry Brockhouse represented was between 20 and 30. The branch appears to have drawn out of the doldrums of the war earlier than some. A report in ILP News in June 1902 (the month the war ended) stated that the branch 'had many irons in the fire and is keeping them all hot.' It instanced the success of the Labour Church and the local Co-operative which was also 'under the wing' of the ILP and increasing both in members and sales. It had 'the usual accessories of Glee Club, Handicraft Guild and Cycle Club.' The most important step had been the setting up of a joint electoral committee of trade unions, ILP, Co-operators and Teachers which promised good results at the November elections. The report went on to state that 'apart from the ILP there is an absolute dearth of public spirit in the town'. However, 'through the Hall, first class lecturers and regular organisation a large body of opinion favourable to Socialism has been created.' One secret of their success was that they had 'avoided the mistake of talking unity and falling out among ourselves over the ideal of one Socialist party.' The report ended 'let our big brothers in Birmingham and Wolverhampton beware lest we pass them in the race.'

West Bromwich ILP was therefore well placed to take advantage of the post-Boer War Socialist upsurge and their activitists in the following years were fully occupied in the broad activities of the Labour Church, Clarion groups etc. which have been detailed elsewhere as well as the Co-operative movement and electoral activity to be detailed below. By 1906 there was a South Staffs ILP Federation with branches in West Bromwich, Wolverhampton, Walsall and Wednesbury. The president was the NAC member, Harry Brockhouse, and the secretary E. Dillon Clarke of Walsall. They were advertising for a full-time organiser for six months at a salary of £2 a week. The man appointed was J.W. Kneeshaw of Hull, who thus came to the West Midlands and subsequently played a leading role in the ILP in this area, particularly in Birmingham.

In 1910 the branch organised the first May Day demonstration with 'an imposing procession reinforced by outlying branches.' Will Crooks was the man speaker. Crooks also spoke at an evening meeting at the Town Hall which was 'packed to overflowing.' This was followed up in September when W.C. Anderson spoke at another Town Hall meeting where 'ten recruits were made and more expected.' In 1911 just as the Great Unrest was beginning, the ILP decline seems to have struck West Bromwich. A report in February of a meeting on 'Socialism and Character' (in itself not a matter likely to be dealt with in a period of advance) reported that 'everyone was delighted, but the audience was not up to the usual standard.' From this time also sectarian innocence was blighted by the emergence of the British Socialist Party and the development of Syndicalism. This decline was confirmed at the end of 1912 when the annual ILP Midlands Federation, of which Harry Brockhouse was chair and Kneeshaw secretary, reported a drop of ILP branches from 88 to 85.

The electoral activity over the period shows much promise but little real achievement. We have seen that Harry Brockhouse was a member of the West Bromwich School Board from 1897. In 1901, when the jingoistic phase of the war was waning, both Harry Brockhouse and Charles Gibbs stood for the School Board. Originally there were fifteen candidates for the eleven seats, but four of the retiring members did not seek re-election so that Brockhouse and Gibbs were returned unopposed. 'Two Labour members will be able to do a vast amount of good in the next three years,' commented *Clarion*. The next target was the Workhouse. In March 1901 the West Bromwich ILP nominated Fred Hughes and the Rev A.E.W. Salt BA, as candidates for the Board of Guardians. 'Money and workers urgently needed' added an appeal. Fred Hughes was not elected but polled 351, a result that was considered 'encouraging.' It was at this point that the Labour Hall project in West Bromwich began to take shape.

In July 1902 a United Labour Electoral Committee in the town sponsored by the ILP and the local Trades Council of which Charles Gibbs, the formidable leader of the Bakers' Union was the most important figure. was formed. Affiliated also to the ULEC at this time was the Labour Church, the Co-operative Society, Typographical Association, Gasworkers, Ironfounders, Postmen, Carpenters etc. The Engineers and Plasterers were expected to join shortly and it was hoped that they would be followed by the Miners and the Teachers. The secretary of the ULEC was the indefatigable Harry Brockhouse. The chairman was Charles Gibbs and the treasurer was Fred Hughes. This was probably the most efficient and energetic trio of Labour leaders to be found in the Black Country at this time. The ULEC lost no time in contesting the local council elections. In October Henry Thompson was nominated by the ULEC to stand in Spon Lane Ward. Thompson was secretary of the Labour Church, a trade union pioneer of the Postmen's Federation, an active ILPer and Co-operator. Joseph Thursfield, secretary of the Carpenters' Society, was nominated to stand in Sandwell ward against the Tory mayor-elect. A weekly broadsheet was being issued. At the election neither was successful, Thompson standing as an ILPer polled 371 against the Liberal's 1157 and Thursfield as a Trade Unionist polled 328 against the Tory's 1043. The first Labour councillor in West Bromwich was elected in 1904. He was Joe Holland who stood in Spon Lane for Labour. He polled 963 against the Tory's 631. In 1906 Dr Scott was nominated as an ILP candidate but does not appear to have stood.

In 1907 Joe Holland lost his seat at Spon Lane to a well known Tory C.S. Bache who polled 895 against Holland's 672. This was a savage contest. 'Bache was supported by the Tories, influential Liberals and the Ratepayers Association. Cries of "Atheist", "Free Love" etc. were widely used. We fought for the first time solely on our own against all parties,' it was reported. This defeat seems to have set the movement back and it was not until 1910 that Labour candidates were again put forward. In that year Smith (ILP) stood in Sandwell and polled 480 votes; Holland stood again at Spon Lane and polled 634; at Town Hall Griffin stood as an SDP candidate and polled 220. None was elected. This defeat again seems to have dampened enthusiasm and elections were not contested again until 1913 when Joe Holland again tried to win Spon Lane and Greets Green was also contested. Neither candidate was successful. These were the last elections before the Great War, so despite the strength and depth of the Labour movement in West Bromwich at that time, there were no Labour members of the Council in 1914.

In Dudley, the public face of the ILP branch seems to have been greatest in its early days. It was one of the first ILP branches in the area to contest the local elections. In 1897 T. Evans polled 65 and was defeated in what was described as the 'first attempt of a young branch.' As we have seen, however, the fiercely Lib-Lab Trades Council made it difficult to formulate a popular Labour strategy in the town. The only time the branch was represented at the ILP national conference seems to have been in 1899 when J. Austin represented a combined branch of 43 members from Dudley, Oldbury and Lye. This was the period when Oliver Jenkins' influence from Stourbridge was at its peak. In May 1900 the *Labour Leader* reported that 'Dudley had opened hostilities on Sunday last at Dudley Market Place where Alf Fellows of Wolverhampton spoke on 'Socialist Ideals' to 'quite a large crowd.' Tom Evans, the secretary of the branch, said meetings would be held there every Sunday. Later in the year the branch was trying to influence the trade union movement by bringing in Bruce Glasier to talk at a joint meeting of the ILP and Bakers and Shop Assistants (Alf Fellows was an important pioneer of the National Union of Shopworkers – GB) and it was hoped that a branch of the Bakers Union would be formed. In May 1902 the ILP at its AGM passed a motion protesting to the town council at the housing and sanitation conditions in the town and 'Tom Evans with the aid of a few other comrades continues to spread light in and around Dudley.' In September open air meetings were being held in the Market Place, Jack Beard of Wellington speaking on 'Commercialism the Cause of Poverty and Socialism the Remedy.' Tom Evans also talked on the sanitary and housing question which the branch were determined to 'keep before the minds of the electorate.' In 1904 the branch was joining the national campaign to protest against the importation of Chinese slave labour into South Africa. But reports were becoming few and the branch was obviously in difficulties. The directory of branches given in the national ILP annual report for 1905 shows a branch in existence in Dudley, but no branch was shown for 1906. There was still no Dudley branch in the 1911 directory and it is interesting that a branch emerges in Netherton in 1909, possibly recognising the difficulty of developing a branch for the rest of the town. The persistence of Lib-Labism in Dudley and indeed Tory influence is attested to by the fact that by 1914 the only working men town councillors were John Taylor, the Midland Counties Trades Federation secretary, who was a Lib-Lab and William Bradford who was a member of the Conservative Party.

Walsall ILP has been left to last because of the singularity of Walsall labour politics. We have seen that it was only in Walsall that the Socialist League with its tendencies towards anarchism established itself and how under the leadership of Sanders, Deakin and Weaver the rest of the Black Country and even Birmingham was influenced. Haydn Sanders owned a small lock works in Walsall. He was also Master Workman of Local Assembly 454 probably formed in 1888 of the Knights of Labour. Most astonishing of all, he was elected to Walsall borough council on the Social Democratic Federation ticket in 1888 and became not only the first Socialist to serve on a local authority in the Black Country, but one of the first in Britain. The next year the Knights put forward two candidates at the local election, neither of whom was successful. Sanders' work on the council merits further investigation. It was sufficient for him to have a square in the town named after him, although he is best known for insulting his fellow councillors by calling them 'bald-headed and pot-bellied.' He was not re-elected and he left Walsall in 1890 at the invitation of the Rotherham pioneers of a new trade union, the National Union of Stove Grate Workers. Here his propensity for militant and spectacular activity is attested to by such examples as the organisation of a 'funeral' of strike breakers with the epitaph:

> Masters they served, men they betrayed,
> If they go to heaven, who will be saved?

Sanders left Walsall just in time not to be associated with the so-called Walsall Anarchist Bomb Plot. Joseph Deakin was not so fortunate and was sentenced to five years imprisonment. He survived to become the dominant figure in Walsall working class politics. From his release Deakin was the leading figure in the local Social Democratic Party which became the British Socialist Party in 1911 and inherited the anarchist tradition through the Syndicalism of that party and also of the Great Labour Unrest of 1910-14 with which we still have to deal. It would seem therefore that there was less space for a pivotal role for the ILP in Walsall than in some other Black Country towns. We have seen a flurry of ILP activity in the Black Country including Walsall in the early days after the party was founded in 1893, but if this resulted in a Walsall branch there was none by 1898. Walsall favoured the politics of unity and it was a Walsall and District Socialist Society operating from at least 1896 and led by the SDF which steered Walsall towards Socialism at the end of the century.

Firm ILP organisation begins with the new socialist advance from 1905. By April 1906 there are reports of both Walsall ILP branch and Walsall Labour Church as established institutions. The ILP was said at this time to have been in existence for only three months and its membership had risen from 11 to 60. There are regular reports of ILP activity from 1907 to 1909. This included both large public meetings and also open-air speaking at Town's End Bank. But by 1910 it is again Socialist Society activity which takes the headlines with a Victor Grayson meeting in November. The turn to the left is further emphasised by Walsall ILP activity being recorded in *Clarion* rather than the *Labour Leader*.

The fragility of the ILP is indicated by considering local electoral activity. The formation of the national Labour Representation Committee in 1900 led to an enquiry from Walsall Trades Council in November 1902 to Ramsay MacDonald as to the implications of forming a local LRC. By 1905 there was a local LRC, although when Alderman Dean moved a resolution calling for local Parliamentary representation, the Trades Council sponsored meeting listed the trade union branches in support but made no mention of the LRC. However, after the 1906 general election successes it was moved by Joseph Deakin at a trades council meeting in February 1906 that the LRC and the trades council merge. The negotiations took a year and it was in February 1907 that the Walsall and District Trades and Labour Council came into existence. It also, at this time affiliated to the LRC nationally, which then became the Labour Party.

Deakin, who was then president of the trades council, voluntarily abdicated his position by proposing the merger, as the socialist parties were not allowed to be affiliated at first and this included not only the SDP to which Deakin belonged, but also the ILP and the Fabians. This matter was put right in August when the local LRC constitution was amended and Socialists were added to the list of Trade, Labour, and Co-operative Societies entitled to affiliate to the LRC. The ILP and Fabians then joined, but the SDP does not seem to have done and so Deakin remained excluded from the Labour Party. Perhaps this was a legacy from the old LRC which had been very much in the hands of the Lib-Lab councillors, Dean and Millerchip. In fact the extended Trades and Labour Council does not seem to have given complete satisfaction for in 1912 a Walsall Labour Association was formed to clarify the difference between the Trades Council and Labour.

This apparent confusion is reflected in the elections results of the period up to 1914. Up to 1910 the only working class councillors were the two Lib-Lab trade union leaders Ben Dean and William Millerchip. Dean had been elected in the Birchills ward in 1890, became an alderman in 1901 and mayor in 1906. Millerchip was elected to the town council in 1898. He was the leading figure in the Walsall Lock Co-operative. In 1910 Dean died and Millerchip left to become manager of the new Labour Exchange. In 1908 William Guest an ILP and Trades Council representative stood in Paddock ward and polled 405 votes against the 923 of Dr Stead the Liberal candidate. In 1912 both Joseph Thickett and Henry Hucker, the leading railway and Trades Council trades unionists, tried to win

131

seats but failed. It was not until June 1913 at a Pleck by-election that Joseph Thickett became the second socialist to follow Haydn Sanders on to the council. In April 1914 Thickett's fellow trade unionist and friend Henry Hucker was returned unopposed to a seat at Caldmore, so that at the outbreak of war in 1914 there were two Socialists on the council.

Parliamentary Representation 1900-1914

Approaching the time when a separate party of working people was to emerge, a short sketch of general development to that point is necessary.

The Industrial Revolution made the Black Country and its commercial and marketing centre in Birmingham a key and perhaps the most important economic area in Britain. But before 1832 neither industrialists nor workers were directly represented in Parliament. A tradition had grown up that one of the two county seats should be held by someone representing industrial interests. This was obviously unsatisfactory particularly as the new towns themselves were not represented. Hence the famous Reform Act of 1832. The key event leading to that Act is said to be the great Reform meeting of 200,000 people in Birmingham. Most of them came from the Black Country incidentally.

One result of that Act was that Birmingham and Wolverhampton were given two seats apiece, Walsall one and Dudley one. This set the pattern of Liberal representation in both seats in Birmingham and Wolverhampton, usually Liberal representation in Walsall and sometimes Tory representation in the Dudley seat controlled by the Earl at 'the Castle.' The Liberals thus became the Party representing the industrial interests. Since they had originated as the champions of Parliament against King in the civil war, the Liberals also represented Nonconformism. They were also the party of Free Trade and, against the evil of drink, assumed the moral mantle of Temperance reformers. With these qualifications they represented themselves as the champions of the unenfranchised working class. Unfortunately, as industrialists they were, violently opposed to factory reform, shorter hours and higher pay. The Tories, on the other hand were the party of aristocracy and landed gentry, the Party of the established Church and they became the party of the Publicans. They could also present themselves as the party interested in factory reform. These divisions are, of course, a generalisation; industrialists could be found who were Tory and landed gentry (important in the Black Country) who were part of the Whig wing of the Liberal Party. As the organised working class movement grew in the Black Country it was, as we have seen, almost invariably Liberal in ideology, although Tory MPs in the area wooed trade unionists with some success.

The problem of the Reform Act of 1832 for the Liberals was that it gave them barely enough votes to be sure of being the natural ruling party. Some working class votes were needed; not all of them, of course, for this led to the nightmare that the vote in the hands of the majority of people with no property would lead them to vote for the appropriation of the property of those who did have property. So the Liberals dallied with 'fancy franchises' descending from the existing £10 property qualification. While they were so doing, a mischievous Tory, Disraeli 'stole their clothes' and passed the 1867 Reform Act. The effect of this act was to give the vote to male heads of households in towns – still very far short of the Chartist demand for male suffrage. The Act also increased the number of seats. At the 1868 election the Liberals swept the board. In Wolverhampton the veteran C.P. Villiers and his partner T.M. Weguelin were returned. Charles Forster retained Walsall and H.B. Sheridan retained Dudley. To the new Wednesbury seat Alexander Brogden was returned.

At this high tide of Liberal fortunes the fulcrum of Liberalism had shifted from Manchester to Birmingham. Here, Joseph Chamberlain, an almost self-made industrialist, retired from business with a fortune in 1874 and was to devote the following years to the twin aims making Birmingham 'the best governed city in the world' with a series of spectacular measures of 'municipal socialism' and also perfecting a new organisation of the Liberal party which was then extended throughout the country. At this time also, the poverty question arose sharply and Chamberlain enunciated the 'doctrine of ransom' threatening the rich that if they were not prepared to tax themselves to provide measures to alleviate the poverty of the mass of the population, their riches would be taken away from them by revolution.

From 1876 Chamberlain moved to the higher stage of Parliament where his radicalism and his huge support were expected to result in proposals for 'national socialism', which would tie working people permanently to the Liberal Party, particularly when Gladstone resigned (an imminent event) and his natural heir, Chamberlain, took over.

Such dreams were to be shattered by the cataclysm of the Great Depression. This changed Joseph Chamberlain from a radical republican to the leading imperialist, holding that problems of poverty at home could only be solved by expansion abroad. The first step in this extraordinary transformation was his break with Gladstone in 1886 over the question of Home Rule for Ireland. Chamberlain broke the Liberal Party by taking his Liberal Unionists over to the Conservative Party with which they soon merged completely. Such was Chamberlain's influence that he took his Birmingham support intact and all Liberal MPs there became in effect Tories, as Liberal Unionists. His influence in the Black Country was almost as great and the position at the 1886 election (when the electorate had again been widened and the number of seats increased) was as follows: Kingswinford – A.S. Hill (Conservative), Worcestershire North – B. Hingley (Liberal-Unionist), Dudley – Brooke Robinson (Con), Walsall – Forster (Gladstonian-Liberal), Wednesbury – P.J. Stanhope (Glad-Lib), West Bromwich – J.E. Spencer (Con), Wolverhampton East – H.H. Fowler (Glad-Lib), W'ton S – C.P. Villers (Lib-Un), W'ton W – W.C. Plowden (Glad-Lib). So now, out of nine seats five were Tory or Liberal Unionist.

It was under these drastically changed circumstances that working people either faced the three alternatives of clinging to the Gladstonian Liberals and developing Lib-Labism, or advocating a separate working class party, or supporting the Liberal-Unionists who were now Tories.

The first firm proposal for a working class candidate arose in Dudley in the early 1890s when Richard Juggins was proposed as a Liberal candidate This foundered both from the hostility of the Dudley Liberal Association and also the luke-warmnesss of his own organisation, the Midland Counties Trades Federation. In the 1890s the Liberal position further deteriorated and it was becoming clearer that any working class MP would only emerge from a separate Labour Party. The instrument for this arose with the creation of the national Labour Representation Committee in 1900 and the development of local LRCs with finance provided by the trade unions and organisation from the political movement.

In the same year that the national LRC was formed, the Tories, who had been in power since the defection of Chamberlain's Liberal Unionists in 1886, called a 'khaki election' to celebrate what was thought to be the near end of the Boer War. Of course, they won it. But there were straws in the wind. No Labour candidates were put forward in the Black Country, but at least there were two Liberal gains to end the seemingly endless swing to the Tories. As the jingoism of the war cooled it was increasingly seen to be an imperialist war fought for the diamond and banking interests of South Africa, supported at home by similar interests led by Joseph Chamberlain.

By the 1906 election the situation was completely changed. The guerrilla war in South Africa had lasted another two years ending with the erection of concentration camps to confine the Boer population, unemployment and depression had again appeared, and the Liberals were framing a policy of sweeping social reforms aimed at keeping working people within the orbit of the Liberals and countering the threat of the Labour Representation Committee.

There were negotiations for Labour candidates in three Black Country constituencies leading up to the 1906 election. By this time the possibility of the LRC ending up the same way as previous such organisations – in the hands of the Liberals – was blocked by two decisions taken at the 1902 annual conference of the LRC. One was that every Labour candidate must sever all connections with the Liberal or Conservative parties. The second was the decision to set up a fund to finance elections from affiliated organisations. The first decision torpedoed negotiations in North Worcestershire and Wednesbury and almost led to failure in the only constituency that was contested and won – Wolverhampton.

With regard to the North Worcestershire seat, this was largely within the influence of the Birmingham and District Labour Representation Committee and a North Worcestershire LRC was therefore set up in 1902 as this was seen as a possible seat to win. Unfortunately, Frank Spires from Birmingham who headed these negotiations was either deceived, or deceived himself, for the two

133

favoured candidates were Albert Stanley, a miners' representative or John Taylor, secretary of the Midland Counties Trades Federation. Either might have accepted nomination as Labour candidates but neither would have renounced their Liberal connections, the miners still retaining their Lib-Lab orientation, and Taylor having been a Liberal councillor for nearly ten years. So plans for a Labour candidate had to be dropped.

In Wednesbury, negotiations were even more complicated. The seat was held by a Conservative with a small majority and the Liberals were having difficulty finding a candidate, which raised hopes that the Liberals would acquiesce in a Labour candidate. The basic dilemma of both parties to these negotiations was, of course, that a Labour candidate was likely to be successful only under two circumstances. One was that he was endorsed by the Liberals and became a Lib-Lab MP tied to the Liberal Party. The other was that the Liberals abstained from opposing Labour candidates and thus allowed a rival Labour Party to emerge. The first proposed Labour candidate was James Conley, a Glasgow city councillor and JP sponsored by the Boilermakers' Union. This matter was aired at a conference in 1902 chaired by William Sharrocks the Wolverhampton councillor, ILP member and boilermaker. Tom Mansell, the miners' leader who had been a Tipton Liberal councillor for the past two years, underlined the dilemma by maintaining that the best chance of Labour representation was by the local Liberals adopting a working man. Sharrocks put the opposite view by saying that they needed a man who would be Labour first, last and always. The meeting finally decided to invite Conley to visit the constituency. When Conley arrived he made clear that he had been a Liberal all his life and if Stanhope (the most popular Liberal and previous MP) stood he would withdraw. Additional urgency was given to the matter by the disclosure that in the confidential negotiations between Ramsay MacDonald and Herbert Gladstone for some sort of limited electoral agreement between the Liberal Party and the LRC that Wednesbury was one of five seats targetted as liable to require the intervention of the Liberal National Committee to decide the candidate. This spurred the Wednesbury Liberals to produce a list of nine possible candidates which included the names of Stanhope, Conley, and Councillor William Millerchip the local Lib-Lab man. In March 1903 the Hon. Philip Stanhope at last made his decision not to stand and the Boilermakers' secretary D.C. Cummings made formal application to the LRC requesting that Conley be adopted as their candidate for Wednesbury. MacDonald wrote back reminding the Boilermakers of the Newcastle Resolutions and asking for their comments. This infuriated the Boilermakers and negotiations were set afoot to form a local Labour Representation Council dominated by Lib-Labs to further the candidacy of Conley.

These developments were watched with concern by Harry Brockhouse in neighbouring West Bromwich who was in touch with Ramsay MacDonald and to whom he wrote disclosing these intrigues. Brockhouse then set in motion intrigues of his own by forming a Wednesbury Labour League committed to finding 500 voters who would support an independent Labour candidate but would vote Tory if a Lib-Lab candidate stood. This effectually scotched Conley's chances and in June 1903 the Wednesbury Liberal Association chose an orthodox employer candidate in Clarendon Hyde, a building contractor, and the Boilermakers withdrew Conley's candidature. Brockhouse then tried to find a Socialist candidate from the Bricklayers' Union. These negotiations did not come to fruition, however, and when the election took place in January 1906 there was a straight fight in Wednesbury between Clarendon Hyde the Liberal, and the custard king A.F. Bird, the Tory.

Only in Wolverhampton were negotiations successful and an LRC candidate not only ran but he won. A broad based Wolverhampton Labour Representation Committee including both the ILP and the Trades Council was made possible as early as 1902 because of the latter's early shedding of its Lib-Lab skin and conversion to Socialism. By December of that year on the recommendation of the local Boot and Shoe Workers. T.F. Richards an executive committee member of that union was enthusiastically adopted as a prospective candidate for one of the Wolverhampton constituencies.

The most promising seat was Wolverhampton West which had been held by the local iron and steel baron, Sir Alfred Hickman, since 1892, but with a smallish majority, despite his local influence, when he had been opposed by a Liberal.

When an election appeared imminent in 1903 the executive of the Boot & Shoe Union, in ignorance of the secret negotiations between MacDonald and Gladstone, passed a resolution recognising that Richards could only be successful with the votes of other political parties and that the Wolverhampton LRC should recognise this and act upon it. Such co-operation seemed to have been achieved when at an Agricultural Hall rally in November 1903 G.R. Thorne the leading Liberal in the town appeared at the hall, apparently uninvited, and was asked to sit on the platform where Ramsay MacDonald was the main speaker, to enthusiastic outbursts of cheering.

The expected dissolution of Parliament did not occur however at that time and Richards continued to campaign vigorously. It seemed that the Liberals would not stand a candidate against him and Richards refrained from advocating any policies likely to upset the Liberals and he invited the support of all parties. By 1905 it was clear that the election could no longer be delayed and Richards set up his organisation recruiting many Liberals, and leading Liberals who spoke at his meetings. The formal alliance was finalised in December 1905 when the local Liberals confirmed that they would stand no candidate and urged support for the Labour man.

But these developments breached the Newcastle Rules and MacDonald asked Richards and the Boot & Shoe Union to explain themselves. Both justified their actions, Richards quoting the example of MacDonald sitting on the same platform as the Liberal, Thorne. Richard's parting shot was that no Labour candidate, including MacDonald himself in Leicester, could succeed without Liberal support. It was perhaps too late to change things at the eleventh hour and Richards goes down in history as the Black Country's first Labour MP and one of the 29 Labour MPs sponsored by the LRC who were victorious at the sensational election of January 1906 which gave a landslide victory to the Liberals and 29 Labour MPs, almost all of whom owed their seats to the absence of a Liberal candidate. Richards' majority over Hickman was only 171 and it is quite clear that he owed his victory to the Liberals. But the ILP paper *Labour Leader* never accepted that Richards was a Labour MP. During the campaign it publicised all the Labour campaigns and after the election analysed the reasons for every success; but never a word was printed about the Wolverhampton campaign. Richards was reduced to blowing his own trumpet in the quarterly report of the General Federation of Trades Unions, but admitted that he had no support from either the local ILP or the SDF.

The only other general elections before 1914 were two in the same year of 1910. In the years since 1906 the political scene had again changed drastically. Voters, not least in the Black Country where the basic industries had been destroyed, were still being seduced by the Protectionism of the Tories led as it was until 1906 by Joseph Chamberlain. When a stroke ended the career of the great radical renegade Lloyd George (the de facto leader of the Liberals) was laying the first foundations of the Welfare State with his reforms at this time and in 1910 was concerned to raise the money for both Old Age Pensions and more battleships by taxing the rich.

On the Labour side there was considerable disenchantment with the performance of the Labour MPs, particularly the refusal to harry the Liberal government over the mass unemployment of the years 1903 to 1908. The result had been the sensational election in 1907 of Victor Grayson who was excluded from the House for his insistence on raising the unemployment question to the point where it endangered the life of the government. This would have led, in the opinion of MacDonald and the other Labour leaders, to the worse evil of a Tory protectionist government, and scupper any chance of a new pact with the Liberals to retain the Labour seats.

In 1909 the House of Lords rejected Lloyd George's budget and the Liberals called an election for January 1910. Both the forward surge of the protectionist Tories and the disenchantment of Labour made it impossible to stand Labour candidates in any other Black Country constituency and in Wolverhampton, where Freddy Richards had long since been dubbed a 'time-serving flunkey' by the militants, he lost his seat to the Tory A.F. Bird by 592 votes. Nationally the result of this election was that the huge Liberal majority was wiped out and they became dependent on the votes of the Irish and Labour.

The second election in December 1910 was necessitated by the Parliament Act which curbed the powers of the Lords. Wolverhampton attempted to find another Labour candidate from James Sexton of the Dock Labourers, T. Warner of the Bleachers and Dyers, W. Walker of the Carpenters and Joiners and G.H. Stuart of the Postmen, without success. Nowhere else in the Black Country was it possible to find a Labour candidate. The election produced virtually the same result as the January one. The Tory surge continued and the only Liberal MPs in the Black Country by this time were J.W. Wilson in Worcestershire North with a wafer thin majority and G.R. Thorne in Wolverhampton East. Elsewhere, all were Unionists, who by this time were completely fused with the Conservatives.

Bibliography: From Labour Party to First World War
Again, the development of the Labour movement must be followed from the working class newspapers; very little is to be found in the local press. For the SDP and the British Socialist Party *Justice* is the paper together with *Socialist Record, Clarion* and the *Labour Leader*. For Leonard Hall and the influence of Birmingham on the British Socialist Party see my *Birmingham Working People*. The main papers on the Birmingham BSP are at the London School of Economics. *Clarion* deals with the Clarion Clubs and Fellowships. For Labour Churches see *Labour Prophet, Clarion* and *Labour Leader*. Also *Wolverhampton Journal* for Wolverhampton Labour Church and *Victoria County History of Staffordshire* Vol XVII off-print pub. by Sandwell Borough Council as *A History of West Bromwich*, p.63 and D.F. Summers' Edinburgh 1939 thesis *The Labour Church and Allied Movements* for West Bromwich Labour Church. For the Socialist Labour Party see the *Socialist*. For the Independent Labour Party see *Labour Leader*. Also Taylor's thesis for local electoral activity and his entries for Joseph Thickett and Henry Hucker in the *Dictionary of Labour Biography* vol 2. Also for Walsall political development see K.J. Dean, *Town and Westminster, A Political History of Walsall from 1906-1945*. For Parliamentary representation in the Black Country to 1914 the material has been taken almost exclusively from Taylor's thesis.

Chapter 7

Depression 1903-09 and the Great Unrest 1910-14

Depression and Distress Committees

There is something to be said for the tradition that sees the Great War of 1914-18 as the real end of the nineteenth century; certainly this cataclysmic event changed the world for ever. But the first fourteen years of the twentieth century saw highly significant changes which altered institutions and ideologies; these must be dealt with.

Taking economic developments first. Technological changes brought the emergence of the modern 'metal-bashing' factories familiar until recent years. These required large numbers of semi-skilled and unskilled labour, much of it female, and this entailed a de-skilling of many existing artisans and craftsmen. With large scale factories came increasing centralisation and monopolisation of capital. Britain's economic position, while still immensely strong, was weakening internationally as competition from the great German cartels and U.S. monopolies continued to bite deeper into our markets. The capitalist trade cycle continued to operate and as the Boer War deteriorated into prolonged guerrilla action mass unemployment returned to the Black Country. This was exacerbated by the fact that prices had been rising ever since 1896 and continued to do so until 1914 while wages remained stationary. Finally, when better times returned after 1909, working people took their revenge in that extraordinary episode known as the Great Unrest. This was a nationwide outburst of industrial militancy which, as we shall see, had a distinctive Black Country twist which raised wages, particularly of the unskilled and semi-skilled by about 20 per cent.

These economic changes brought political developments. Most striking was the conversion of employers from their traditional free trade stance to protectionism. The campaign was led by the local hero Joseph Chamberlain and the pill was sweetened by calling it Tariff Reform.

For working people the reaction to mass unemployment was to develop a theory of the Right to Work claiming that if private capital could not ensure work then it must be provided by the local or national authorities. After 1905 disillusion with the Labour Party led to the emergence of Syndicalism which held that capitalism could only be brought down by a general strike. After this each industry would be controlled by its Syndicate of workers within the industry. Syndicalism was strongly influenced from abroad, notably from France where an assault on democracy in that country from 1909-13 claimed that democracy was a sink of corruption led by Freemasons, Jews, Protestants and aliens conspiring to ruin France and sell her to Germany. This unhealthy brew was stirred in Britain by the two Catholics, Hilaire Beloc and G.K. Chesterton. Their theory was that the intervention of any state led inevitably to loss of freedom and the Servile State. This tended to discredit Socialism and strengthened the case for Syndicalism which was an important element of the Great Unrest.

1900-14 divides therefore into two periods – one of depression and mass unemployment from 1903-09 and another of full employment and the Great Unrest from 1910-14. Both of these periods give ample evidence of the 'Condition of England' – a question greatly exercising minds at the beginning of the century – as it pertained to the Black Country.

Unemployment began to rise in 1903. By 1905 fears of violence, particularly in London, led the government to pass the 1905 Unemployed Workmen's Act which authorised the setting up of local Distress Committees responsible for creating labour registers and bureaux. The act was optional outside London.

A number of Distress Committees were set up in the Black Country. The Walsall Distress Committee began operating in November 1905. It consisted of twelve local councillors, eight members appointed by the Walsall Board of Guardians and five people 'experienced in the relief of distress.' Its first acts were to appoint an Investigating Officer at 25/-d. per week and open a Labour Registry in Goodall Street. For this it requested £100 from the rates. By January 1906 it was reported that 150 had applied to register at the Bureaux. 68 of these were labourers and the others craftsmen, including 25 leather workers. Enquiries were made from Lords Bradford, Lichfield and Hatherton whether they had any land that needed levelling. Work had been found by various corporation committees for twenty men. By the autumn the Distress Committee was requesting that the government grant compulsory purchasing powers for land that could be used to set men to work. Emigration was a much favoured remedy for unemployment at this time and the Committee ruled that anyone agreeing to emigrate should first attend a Salvation Army or Church Army Land Colony for instruction. Six people were approved for assisted emigration and given £10 each, which had to be repaid.

In 1907 when unemployment was rising rapidly in the Black Country, the Committee considered in the autumn that it would not be necessary for a Mayor's Relief Fund to be raised.

But unemployment deepened and the annual report in November 1908 showed that 703 applications had been received of which 522 were found 'deserving' after investigation and placed on the Register. The number for whom the Corporation had found work during the year was 141. During the year all single men had been informed that there was very little possibility of their being given work because priority was being given to married men with families. These single men were therefore advised to join the newly organised Army Reserve for the winter months!

In the winter of 1908-09 unemployment was at its peak. £350 was sought for the opening of Soup Kitchens in all wards and a request that the Mayor's Fund be opened. Only in 1909 is there a record of any government assistance for public works, when the Local Government Board contributed £160 (one third of the cost) to the levelling of a hospital site in Sneyd Lane and various other small schemes. The Committee complained of the smallness of the grant. John Burns (who had been in charge of the Local Government Board from 1906 when the Liberals had won their famous electoral victory) later increased the grant to £1000.

After the winter of 1908-09 unemployment declined and although the Distress Committee remained in existence it had only flurries of activity – in 1912 when there was distress from the Miners' Strike, in 1914 after the outbreak of war when there was considerable unemployment, and finally after the war in 1920-21. The Committee was disbanded in 1924.

Smethwick's Distress Committee can be dealt with more summarily. The only contribution it made to the alleviation of distress in the town was to allocate 'deserving' cases to the Stoneyard associated with the Workhouse. Its first annual report of October 1906 showed that it had received 215 applicants for aid of whom 104 had been admitted to the Stoneyard. The Yard had been open for 37 weeks, 3932 tons of stone had been broken and wages of £397 paid. This amounts to an average of 2/-d. a week paid to each of the 104 'lucky' men. Subsequent annual reports show relative changes in the severity of unemployment, but these figures greatly under estimate actual unemployment:

	1907	1908	1909	1910
Applicants	112	145	276	304
Admitted to Stoneyard	106	110	217	192

As elsewhere, unemployment declined from 1910 and the activities of Smethwick Distress Committee virtually ceased, although it remained in existence until 1930.

Dudley did not at first have a Distress Committee, but the Board of Guardians set up a Special Committee on Unemployment in November 1904. It set up a separate Stoneyard and laid down regulations with regard to work and relief scales. 15cwt of stone would have to be broken to the satisfaction of the Labour Superintendent of the Labour Test Yard. Hours of work were from 9am to 4pm. Relief would be paid daily from the office of the Relieving Officer of the District at the following scales with a maximum of three days work each week: Man and Wife 1/6d. An additional 2d. per day would be paid for every child up to seven. This would give a man with seven children (or more) 2/8d. per day with a maximum of 8/-d. per week. Half of this relief would be paid in food and the other half in money. Single men and those living in Common Lodging Houses were not eligible for Labour Relief, except in special cases. A few months later it was discovered that some men were breaking the required quantity of stone by midday and were then leaving. To prevent this it was laid down that stone would be broken to a size that would pass through a $2^{1}/_{4}$ inch ring. If this were still accomplished before 4 pm then other tasks within the Stoneyard must be performed or more than 15 cwts of stone broken. The minutes of this Special Committee on Unemployment have survived only for 1904-05 and in the absence of evidence for the Distress Committee that was later formed it is not known how Dudley coped with its unemployment problem between 1905 and 1910.

Wolverhampton Distress Committee provides the fullest picture of conditions at this time and it is proposed to use this evidence together with Poor Law material and other sources to investigate the extent of unemployment and the standard of living of both employed and unemployed people at the turn of the century.

The standard of living 1900-10

No one has ever solved the problem of measuring unemployment in the nineteenth century. The best known indicator is the return of trade unions of the percentage of their members unemployed. This features mainly skilled trade unions and measures usually only their numbers receiving unemployed pay. Because this trade union return does not cover unskilled or casual trades nor important ones where falling production was met with short-time working rather than dismissal of workers, I have suggested elsewhere that the trade union indicator should be doubled to measure the true amount of unemployment. Below, as well as the national trade union figures, I have used two new indicators. One is a monthly return in the Employment Gazette published by the Board of Trade of engineering trade unions in an entity entitled 'Wolverhampton, Birmingham and Coventry'. The other is an estimate of short time working in the coal mines in Staffordshire. Both probably underestimate unemployment in the Black Country, the former by including Coventry, the latter by including the developing and thriving Cannock coal field as well as including North Staffs. It was also possible to use another indicator for the iron industry in the nineteenth century; this was the number of furnaces in blast. But by the twentieth century the Black Country iron industry was much reduced, many of the out of blast furnaces would never again be lit and it would be misleading to use this indicator. Staffordshire miners recorded the highest average of 5.76 working days per week in December 1902 and the lowest of 3.68 in the summer of 1905. December and June shifts worked have been averaged to give the figure for each year and unemployment calculated from a base of the highest number of days worked rather than from the 6 working day week. So 1904 gives an average of 5.08 days worked per week which shows the work force employed for 88 per cent of each week and thus an unemployment rate of 12 per cent.

Indexes of Unemployment (%)	1900	1902	1904	1906	1908	1910	1912	1914
National Trade Union	2.5	4.0	6.0	3.6	7.8	4.7	3.2	3.3
B'ham Cov. & W'ton Engs.	–	3.1	5.2	2.0	6.0	3.8	1.8	2.6
Staffordshire Miners.	–	5.0	12.0	23.0	13.0	16.0	8.0	10.0

Clearly, when short time working is converted into unemployment percentages it makes a considerable difference to the figures. Masses of casual workers were subjected to comparable underemployment as well in other trades such as brass and iron and steel.

These percentages can be related to absolute numbers. If one takes a typical town such as Tipton, according to the 1901 Census it had 10,000 employed males. Of these 820 were miners, 1221 ironworkers and 2700 were in engineering. It is likely that unemployment in the town would be over 1000 in bad years such as 1908. This is a rate of 10 per cent and seems too low.

However, it is from the Wolverhampton Distress Committee that the most detailed information is available regarding the unemployed and who they were. The information required from each applicant aped the procedures of the Charity Organisation Society (COS) whose concern was to weed out the 'undeserving poor'which they obstinately continued to believe existed in large numbers despite all the evidence to the contrary. So most of their funds were frittered away on bureaucratic administrative structures and very little went to the poor. This was also true of the Distress Committees to a considerable extent, and the Poor Law. Fortunately, COS which was powerful in Birmingham had only a toe hold in the Black Country, at Walsall.

The Wolverhampton Distress Committee was set up in October 1905. It had Labour councillors and trade unionists on it from the beginning (Messrs Frost, Evans, Sharrocks and Whittaker). The report of July 1907 covers the first full year of its activities. 522 applicants had applied for relief. This amounts to about 2 per cent of Wolverhampton's male work force of about 30,000. Of the applicants 366 were married men with a total of 1209 dependents. 252 were in the prime working ages of up to 40. The largest number (136) was in the age range 40 to 49 when ill-health and waning powers would make re-employment difficult. 84 men were between 50 ad 59 and fifty were over 60. The vast majority (458) were in distress from slackness of trade, works closing or the failure of employers. Another 45 had left because of ill-health or injury.

With regard to the occupations of the claimants 193 were labourers, 79 were from the building trade, 102 from the engineering trade, 45 from the iron trade and 34 were clerks, shop assistants or other white collar occupations. The 522 applicants were investigated and 94 were rejected (37 of 'indifferent character' and 24 as in receipt of Poor Relief). Another 37 found work before the investigation was completed, so 391 applicants were eventually 'entertained'. Of these 279 were eventually found work provided by the local council levelling the East Park, or sewerage schemes or road widening. Total wages paid were £324. The scale of relief represented by these wages should be noted. 164 men received less than £1, 109 received between £2 and £4 and only six received from £4 to £7. Many of these men were unemployed throughout the year. But the 'lucky' man who earned £7 received less than 2/6d. a week and the vast majority earning under £2 had 9d. per week. Clearly this scale of relief could make little difference to the distress of the applicants.

The balance sheet up to March 1907 showed receipts of £478. Of this £115 came from the rates, £250 from the local Voluntary fund, £60 from the national Queen's fund and £50 from the Local Government Board. £106 of this money was unspent, £255 went on relief wages and £112 on administrative expenses.

Subsequent Distress Committee activities followed the same pattern, but the scale of unemployment greatly increased from 1907 to 1910 after which the activities of the Committee virtually ceased.

	1906-07	*1907-08*	*1908-09*	*1909-10*	*1910-11*
Applicants for Relief	552	914	1600	995	317

A feature of the later years was the number of applicants who applied for relief year after year (the original orders from the local Government Board limited relief to two years only, but this was later extended). These were invariably of the higher age groups. So in 1911 of 317 applicants 245 were renewals and 105 of these were over 50 years of age.

Efforts were made to further classify applicants by occupation. In the 1909 report 772 were classified as Labourers (177 general, 174 casual, 118 in the building trade) and 764 as Artisans (418 from engineering, 153 from the iron trade, 105 from the bicycle trade and 85 building craftsmen). In his report Benjamin Lambe, the Investigating Officer, highlighted the length of unemployment by stating that half the relief had been paid to 'renewals' and admitting that a very large percentage of these renewals were virtually permanently unemployed. After the start of levelling work in the mining area of Rough Hills, Lambe stated that it would have been possible to give every married man on the books 'a few days work a week', but this was prevented by the 'clamour' of the single men who 'remained month after month on the register but who never obtained work except through the Committee.' Final figures showed that about 900 married men compared with 223 single men had been relieved. Average earnings for married men had been £2-16-3 (1/-d a week) and for single men £1-3-5d.(6d. a week). Again, the relief is derisory. Even the favoured 15 men who earned the top wage of £7 to £8 in the year averaged only 3/-d. a week.

By June 1910 the tide of unemployment was ebbing. but a new Wolverhampton Investigating Officer, Charles F. Robb, claimed that when he started work in January he had faced a rush of previously rejected applicants who thought that with a change of officer they might be re-registered. He soon scotched this idea, 'I am glad to report that none had succeeded even though some gave false names'. Robb estimated that 19 per cent of those on the register were permanently unemployed mainly because of age or physical disability. He also congratulated the men working at Rough Hills, 'especially in view of the large number unaccustomed to such labouring work and also on account of their advanced age.

Robb's report of September 1911 spoke of the great improvement from the lifting of the Depression, the mildness of the weather and the establishment of the local Labour Exchange. All of these greatly decreased the work of the Committee and the number remaining on the register in June was only 72. From this time the Committee ceased to provide any work even though a hard core of unemployed continued to exist.

If the unemployed could expect little or nothing from Distress Committees were there other sources of relief? Almost everyone would contribute to a Friendly Society or Sick Club while they were in work, but these societies paid no unemployment benefit. They had developed over centuries to provide sickness and death benefit and higher paid workers would contribute to their endowment, annuity or pension benefits. But they never developed unemployment benefit, and when most of them became the source for the distribution of government paid benefits after 1911 they had to set up special Approved Sections.

Only trade unions paid unemployment benefit. The Amalgamated Society of Brassworkers (which had 500 members in the Black Country) in 1905 had a general section whose members over 21 paid 9d. a week. For this they received between £1-2-6d and 15/-d. a week dispute pay, 10/-d. a week out of work benefit, 5/-d. a week sick benefit after 12 months membership, 5/-d to 7/-d. superannuation and up to £50 in trade accident benefit. Funeral benefits of £10 for a member, £5 for his wife and £1 for a child were also paid as were legal fees, where approved. Unemployment benefit was invariably the greatest item of expenditure. At the height of the Great Depression for instance in 1879 unemployment pay with the Brassworkers amounted to 146 per cent of membership contributions. The lowest it fell was 30 per cent in 1902, but by 1904 it was 57 per cent and rising rapidly. The long established Tin Plate Workers Union paid £1 a week dispute benefit, 12/-d. unemployment benefit, 8/-d. sickness pay and an £8 death benefit for a contribution of 1/3d. a week. Most other unions for skilled workers had similar schemes. But when under great strain, unemployment benefit tended to be reduced either in amount or in weeks paid, or weekly contributions were increased or levies made on members.

The Toolmakers Union catering for the new, semi-skilled operator also sought to match the skilled unions in the range of benefits offered for a lower contribution than the 1/-d to 1/6d weekly paid by skilled workers, but they had to restrict total benefits to £10 per member with only £6 in any one year. Even some of the new unions for unskilled workers attempted to pay benefits. The Amalgamated Gasworkers offered 6/-d. a week unemployment pay and 12/-d. dispute pay for a contribution of only 3d. per week. The rival Gasworkers and General Labourers' Union paid sickness but not unemployment pay for a contribution of 4d. a week. A Contingency Fund was available to relieve distress caused by unemployment.

Thus trade unions were the only source to which workers could turn for anything like adequate unemployment relief and this only for the minority who were in trades unions and of these mainly skilled men.

One other possible source of relief not so far investigated is the Poor Law. This offered two equally unattractive alternatives, Indoor and Outdoor Relief. The former was the Workhouse. It can be taken as axiomatic that the Workhouse was always full. For if customers became scarce some on Outdoor relief would be hauled in, because it was always the impossible aim to abolish Out Relief altogether. In times of unemployment it was the old who suffered first, for families who would make every effort to keep their parents out of the hated Workhouse could no longer support them. Figures for two of the four main Poor Law Unions in the Black Country moved as follows:

Numbers receiving Relief in Wolverhampton (December each year)

	1900	1904	1908	1909	1910	1912	1913
Indoor	3904	3899	4179	4369	4256	3721	3719
Outdoor	11981	14528	12095	12824	12098	8425	7351

The following shows the expenditure of the Dudley Poor Law Union on Out Relief for the following years (ending Ladyday):

1900	1904	1906	1908	1909	1910	1912	1914
£18686	£19798	£17553	£16614	£16609	£17417	£12333	£11208

The figures indicate that in Wolverhampton numbers in the Workhouse rose 12 per cent between 1900 and 1909 and Out Relief increased 7 per cent in the same period. In Dudley, Out Relief paid in the worst years of unemployment 1905-09 never even reached the amount paid out in the year of of full employment, 1900. With regard to Relief, we can follow exactly what amounts were paid and to whom by taking the figures from the entirely typical town of Tipton for 1908. In that year a booklet listing every inmate of the Workhouse and all persons in receipt of Out Relief was published. This did not happen often because such information was expensive to produce. Its purpose was punitive; by publicising every name it was hoped that sufficient 'scroungers' would be identified by the general public for the Guardians to save an equal or greater amount than the cost of the collection and printing of the data. It now serves the purpose of allowing future generations to know the names and misfortunes of the very poorest of our antecedents.

About 300 unfortunate citizens of Tipton passed through the Workhouse in that year. Of those about 140 were old people with ages ranging from 60 to 88 years. Six of them died there. Another 32 were children under 10. Of the remainder, only 45 were men of working age. We are told nothing about them, but again it may be taken as axiomatic that although they would be classified as 'Able Bodied' none in fact would be; all would be suffering some mental or physical disability either permanent or temporary, for it was invariably impossible to find men fit enough to do the ordinary heavy work of keeping the Workhouse clean and operating.

Turning to Outdoor Relief in Tipton in 1908, of the approximate number of 400 who were relieved during the year about 250 were over 60 years of age. This represented about 13 per cent of all those over 60 in Tipton. These received weekly amounts of between 2/-d. and 3/-d. a week for single people and 4/-d. to 5/-. for married couples. This left about 150 men and women of working age receiving relief. Of these 49 were widows with children. Another three had husbands in jail, two were deserted wives, three had husbands in asylums and four receiving temporary relief had husbands in hospitals; all of these women had children to support. They were far from generously treated. The modal number of children was three. To keep these and herself the sum granted was usually 4/-d. or 4/6d. a week. Of the remaining women, all had specific mental or physical defects.

The number of Tipton men of working age receiving Out Relief was about 50. Almost all of these were disabled – blind and deaf, crippled, paralysed or with advanced rheumatic, bronchitic or asthmatic conditions etc. Most had a wife and children to support. Only two men of working age, both with children, could possibly pass as suffering from unemployment alone. It is clear therefore that no relief for the unemployed could be expected from the Poor Law.

To summarise. Once unemployed, only a minority of mainly skilled trade unionists would receive limited unemployment benefit. Other skilled and some semi-skilled workers would have savings to subsist on for a limited period, but these would be small. Soup kitchens might be available when unemployment was at its worst providing one meal for the family, or there might be breakfasts at school for the poorest children. When desperation point was reached the Distress Committee could be applied to with limited hopes of assistance and an even more limited amount of relief, if granted. The conclusion can only be that numbers would face actual starvation. For very large numbers it was the source of the malnutrition that afflicted adults and children alike. For almost all, it produced the desperation and heart ache resulting in suicide and the enormous, but as yet unmeasured amount of ill-health of the community. The local newspapers of the day bear testimony to all these things – starvation, suicides and malnutrition.

This leads on to the question of how much was required to keep a family above the level of under-nourishment and the wider question of the standard of living.

For the nineteenth century it has been found possible to roughly measure the standard of living in the Black Country estimating prices from Workhouse contract prices, local wage material, and the state of trade from various local indices. Most of these sources fail us for the twentieth century. They are replaced however by a great deal of national price material and considerable local wage material. Moreover, because of the general alarm at the physical condition of recruits during the Boer War and concern for the effects of the unemployment in subsequent years, wage, price and nutritional data has been from that time regularly and extensively collected. Central to this was the Report of an Enquiry by the Board of Trade into Working Class Rents, Housing, Retail Prices and Standard Rates of Wages in the United Kingdom, 1908. This focused on Wolverhampton and Walsall in the Black Country and from this Report the following material is culled.

The Enquiry collected nearly 2000 food budgets of working people and analysed them in five groups according to the average income of the average family which was found to have 3.1 children. The food budget for the families with income below 25/-d. a week came to 14/5d or 67 per cent of family income. The amounts of food consumed by Black Country families has been taken to correspond almost exactly with the national trends and has been re-costed with Black Country prices (which were lower than the national average):

Bread, 7 x 4lb loaves at 4½d.	2 – 7½d
Flour, 3½ lbs	4½d
Potatoes, 14 lbs	4½d
Meat, 5 lbs	2 – 1d
Bacon, 1 lb	6d
Eggs, 6	6d
Fresh milk, 6 pints	10½d
Cheese ½lb	3½d
Butter ½lb	6d
Vegetables and Fruit	4½d
Tea ½lb	7d
Sugar 2lbs	4d
Fish 1 lb	3d
Other Items (rice, dried fruit, coffee, jams, pickles etc)	1 – 9d
Total	11 – 5d

This food budget accounts for 63 per cent of an 18/-d. wage which is lower than the national average. It provides approximately 10,000 calories a day giving the man 3,000, the wife 2500 with 1500 each for the three children. This would just about be adequate.

Rents in Wolverhampton were given in the Report as being in 1905:

No. of Rooms per Tenement	*Predominant Weekly Rents incl Rates*
2 rooms	2/-d to 3/-d
3 rooms	2/6d to 3/6d
4 rooms in Courts	2/9d to 3/9d
4 rooms not in Courts	3/6d to 5/-d
5 rooms	5/-d to 6/9d
6 rooms	7/-d to 8/6d

The typical dwelling for working men was said to be a two storey house with four rooms. An 1894 return from AEU members showed that the average rent of these skilled trade unionists was 4/6d. a week. This would suggest that they lived in the better 4-roomed of 5-roomed houses. Few workers lived in 6-roomed houses, it was stated. Rents in Walsall were given as slightly higher. In the smaller Black Country towns rents were likely to be lower. All these rents were said to be only 53 per cent of rents in London. An unskilled man with three children on 18/-d. a week would need a 4-roomed house and an inferior such house rented at 2/9d. He would, however, be more likely to live in a three or even two roomed house where his rent would still be about 2/6d.

For the other main items of expenditure we must go further afield. Budgets from Maud Pember Reeves' book, *Round About a Pound a Week,* suggests that expenditure on fuel and light in London varied between 1/4d. and 2/7d. depending on whether ½ or 2 cwts of coal was used. Coal was cheaper in the Black Country and it is unlikely that less than 2 cwts would be adequate for heating, cooking, washing and drying purposes. Expenditure on oil and candles was invariably 5d. Allowing 2cwts of coal for 1/5d. and 5d. for oil, candles, and wood our Black Country family would spend 10 per cent of its income on fuel in the winter, less in summer, say an average of 1/-d. a week.

With regard to clothing, much of this would be acquired second hand. But expenditure on boots and their repair, and socks and stockings could not be avoided. Clothing and boot clubs were common to which a weekly contribution of 1/-d. or 1/6d would keep the family adequately clothed. But a budget of 18/-d. would not stretch to this and we have estimated this expenditure at 6d. per week or 3 per cent of income.

The above accounts for 15/8d. from an income of 18/-d. leaving 2/4d. a week to cover all the expenditure for materials for the washing of humans and clothes, fares, doctor and medicines, household goods such as furniture, floor coverings and bed clothes, crockery and glass, entertainment, postage stamps, pocket money, insurance and tobacco and alcohol. Clearly the budget could not cover the most essential of these items even if the wage earner turned over all of his 18/-d. to his wife. It is clear that such a family lived in dire poverty even when the husband was in work. When catastrophe struck in the shape of the normal exigencies of life of unemployment, sickness, injury and old age, destitution and starvation loomed.

From the Board of Trade Report we can follow what happens to the food budget of the semi-skilled group of workers earning between 20/-d. and 25/-d. per week. Such a worker spent almost 25 per cent more on food. At Black Country prices this would be 14/3d, an increase of 2/10d. per week. Obviously no family earning up to 21/-d. could afford such an increase in expenditure for food as there were, as we have seen, other pressing needs to meet.

Even the worker earning 24/-d. to 25/-d. a week will not be able to increase his food expenditure by that amount and cover all the other expenses referred to above. He remains, even in full employment, in poverty.

So we come to the skilled worker and will take engineering workers, fitters and turners, earning between 30/-d. and 35/-d. a week with a family of 3 children. Their food expenditure would have increased by 45 per cent compared with the 18/-d. a week man making 16/6d. a week. He will, we know, rent a house averaging 4/6d. a week. He will spend on clothing and boots not less than 1/6d. Living in a house with gas laid on he will pay about 8d a week for gas, 1/5d. for 2 cwts of coal and 2d for wood, oil etc. making his heat and fuel bill 2-3d. Soap, soda, starch etc. would take another 6d. His insurance will be his trade union subscription of 1/3d. a week which will give him 10/-d a week unemployment and sickness benefit and also a small pension. Doctors' fees would also have to be paid and prescribed medicines. Large sums were also spent on patent medicines for coughs, constipation, piles, women's ailments, rupture appliances etc. The chemist would also be visited for baby requisites and the modest cosmetic requirements of the wife. To this must be added the cost of any stay in hospital or minor surgery such as adenoids with children or longer stay for diphtheria, scarlet fever etc. All of this would not be likely to average less than 6d. a week.

There remains two categories of essential goods. One is Household Goods and the other is Services comprising fares, postage, entertainment, hairdressing etc. These are difficult to calculate locally and were never measured nationally until a Ministry of Labour enquiry into family budgets of 1938-39. This Enquiry used the weight of 7 per cent of the budget or just over 2/-d. on an income of 30/-d. for Durable Household goods. This looks too generous for Black Country standards, so we allot

1/6d. for all household goods. For Services, the rate was almost 8 per cent and again we make an allotment of 1/6d.

Our calculations so far show that 28/3d. of our skilled man's wage must be spent on essentials. We can now therefore raise the vexed question of tobacco and alcohol both of which were part of both working and social life. By 1914 alcohol consumption in England was down to about 4 pints per head per week, but since about half of the Black Country population was under 10 years this makes a total of 8 pints per adult divided perhaps into 12 pints for a man and 4 for his wife. Workers such as miners and ironworkers would drink more, but this was normally 'small' beer with a low alcoholic content. A skilled engineer would no doubt feel himself entitled to at least 6 pints a week plus beer or even some spirits for his wife. Beer cost between 1d. and 3d. a pint. If 1½d. is taken as average, a justifiable 1/6d. could be spent on drink. If he smoked a pipe or cigarettes he might consume ½oz per day. Stourbridge Workhouse was purchasing tobacco for about 2½d. an oz. in 1900. Retail it would cost more, say 3d. His tobacco bill would then be about 9d.

The final budget amounts to 30/6d. This must be taken as the minimum wage necessary to purchase all the necessities of life. Anything above this wage would provide a margin for savings, or luxury expenditure such as gambling.

We can now take two points. An income of 30/6d. per week provided a 'minimum standard of comfort' for a man. wife and three children. If we halve that amount, we can take 15/3d as the 'subsistence level' below which it was not possible to provide the three basic elements of food, shelter and fuel. Between the subsistence level and minimum comfort level lay poverty. The degrees of poverty varied. Between 15/3d. and 18/-d. the family faced physical deterioration. Above 18/-d. poverty was dire until the point was reached when minimum weekly needs could be met at 24/-d. to 25/-d, but any interruption of income would plunge the family below subsistence level. Minimum weekly needs were met only when income was 24/-d. to 25/-d. a week.

Before trying to assess how many Black Country people lived at these varying levels one must ask what supplementary sources of income were available to augment the family wage. Firstly, the man might work overtime, or moonlight by taking a second job. Much of this no doubt occurred. However, there is a strange lack of evidence for overtime in the literature of the time and it is clear that overtime earnings did not play the important part that they do in modern earnings. With regard to moonlighting a main factor depressing wages in the Black Country was the excess of labour and thus a 'reserve army of labour' in all but the most prosperous years.

Nor is there much evidence that the wife would work. In 1901 in Dudley about 5000 women were in employment according to the Census. Of these only 1132 were married or widowed. We know from the same source there were 712 widows in Dudley between the ages of 20 and 65, the majority of whom would have to find employment to keep themselves and their families. This would mean about 450 married women at work. This is about 5 per cent of married women in Dudley. Other Black Country towns give comparable figures. Married women were more likely to take in washing, or perform some domestic service for more affluent families. Where there was a garden, chickens, or exceptionally pigs, might be kept and fruit and vegetables grown. There is perhaps more evidence of gardens in nail and chain country such as Lye or Cradley, but in the larger towns where gardens existed they were small. Some working class homes also took in a lodger, but this depended on occupying at least three rooms in order let one. At this level there would be little surplus over the lodger's board with all the problems of he or she being able to pay, together with the social problems arising. For a married couple taking a lodger was a measure of last resort; for widows it was likely to be a necessity. Similar difficulties arose if a working class family risked taking a house large enough to permit of sub-letting to another family.

The scope for children to supplement the family income had been drastically limited by the Education Act of 1870. Children's contributions were limited to the usual part-time activities of selling newspapers, errand boys etc. between school or at week-ends, some of the proceeds of which they would want to keep for themselves. A more important contribution would be that made by children between the time of leaving school and getting married. This would be a period when poorest families rose to a lesser degree of poverty, or if several children were at work the standard of minimum comfort or beyond might be achieved. This period was not usually very prolonged, however, and ahead for the couple loomed old age.

But it is clear that some augmentation of the man's wages must be allowed for if poverty is to be measured. Again we turn to Dudley and look at the Census. There were 10,479 married women in Dudley in 1901 and so presumably the same number of married households. There were also 11,848 single or widowed/widowered people above the age of of 15. Many of these would live in the family home, but an unknown proportion of them would constitute separate one person households. If we assume that 15 per cent of such persons lived in households of their own we can add these to the married households and estimate that there was a total of 12251 'households' in Dudley. We know that there was a total of 18941 males and females working in 1901. If one is divided by the other we find that there was an average of 1.5 incomes per household. We must then estimate what percentage of male earnings this 0.5 extra income represents. So we take the percentage of females working compared with men and find this is 32 per cent. We know that women earned half the wages of men. We then want to know the percentages of young girls and young men working, because they would be paid even less than male adults. We then find that 25 per cent of all wage earners were aged from 10 years to 20 years; young girls would earn one quarter of the male adult wage and the young males would average rather more than half assuming that they reached adult wage at either 18 or 21, Deducting these percentages of 32 per cent and 25 per cent from the 0.5 extra wage earner we find that in terms of male wage the extra income was worth 0.38 or 6/10½d making a total weekly wage of 24/10½d. Further additions could be made for part-time children's work and home-grown food, but while this might amount to a useful sum for a small number of families, averaged over all families it would be negligible.

From average family income thus assembled, important deductions must be made. This average income assumes 1.38 male equivalent incomes coming into the house for 52 weeks a year. This would not be the case. Holidays were not universally welcomed – they were usually unpaid. The local wakes week, Christmas, Easter and other public holidays would mean that there would be no income for at least two weeks a year. Sickness might take another two weeks income; the poorer the family the more likely it was to suffer sickness and the least likely it was that the man could afford to stay away from work. But the greatest thief of income was unemployment. Adhering to my previously expressed view that for a realistic figure of both unemployment and short time working, the national trade union figures should be doubled we have the following percentages of unemployment: 1900: 5%; 1901: 6.6%; 1902: 8%; 1903: 9.4%; 1904: 12%; 1905: 10%; 1906: 7.2%; 1907: 7.4%; 1908: 15.6%; 1909: 15.4%; 1910: 9.4%; 1911: 6%; 1912: 6.4%; 1913: 4.2%; 1914: 6.6%. Average income figures would have to be deflated by these amounts to show actual income. Thus in the worst year of 1908 the 24/10½d. wage would be reduced to an average of 19/4½d.

It must be emphasised that averages have been used to measure standards of living over a period: a snapshot at a given moment would give a very different picture. The average encompasses those whose incomes remain the same down to those whose income entirely disappears. More than half of families always lie below the average. Our final step therefore must be to estimate the numbers of families and try to measure not average poverty but absolute poverty.

To do this a number of sources must be used. We can begin with a housing survey in Wolverhampton in 1901 which showed 384 courts in the town with an average of 4.5 houses in each court. Of these 1683 houses 153 were too derelict to occupy and another 87 had been condemned. 58 per cent of them were damp or dilapidated or both. Only the most desperately poor occupied these courts, we are told. They contained, however 8135 people and together with the 166 back-to back houses 'housed' 9 per cent of the population. Smaller towns had larger court populations and more back-to- backs than the larger ones. An analysis of Dudley housing in 1901 shows 4 per cent of the population living four or more persons in two rooms. This might be taken as a measure of the greatest poverty, and the further 7 per cent living six or more in three rooms as the next level of poverty.

If we could identify the numbers of skilled, semi-skilled and unskilled workers we would have another useful index of poverty. The Census is not very helpful in this regard. Occupations are given by trades but with no indication of the grade of labour. I have taken a typical town in 1901, West

Bromwich, and tried to break down the composition of the work force. The figures I came up with were 38 per cent unskilled, 39 per cent semi-skilled and 22 per cent skilled. Although this is nothing more than an educated guess, if we take rough percentages of 40:40:20 it may not be too far from the mark.

I would then summarise the question of poverty as follows: under conditions of full employment not less than 5 per cent of the population lived permanently on or below the line of subsistence of 15/3d. per week for a family of man, wife and three children. This meant that they could not afford to buy sufficient to eat or enough housing space or heat to continue in a state of physical well-being. These consisted of unskilled workers either with large families, or where the only wage earner was sick or injured, or old persons unable to work and without support from their families, or where the main wage earner through drunkenness or gambling failed to provide his family with the subsistence amount. The remaining unskilled workers earning between 18/-d and 20/-d a week (family incomes averaging 24/10½d. to 27/6d) lived in varying degrees of poverty, never reaching the minimum standard of comfort level of 30/6d. These represented perhaps another 35 per cent of the population.

Most semi-skilled men earning between 21/-d. and 29/-d. (family income 29/-to 40/-d.) would reach the minimum standard of comfort. They represented perhaps another 40 per cent of the population.

Skilled workers (perhaps 15 per cent) and professional people (4 per cent of the employed population in West Bromwich in 1901) earning 30/-d. and above family income (41/-d and above) lived above the minimum comfort level.

This equilibrium of 5 per cent destitute and another 25 per cent in poverty was violently disturbed by unemployment. Incomes disappeared. Unskilled and semi-skilled workers dropped below subsistence level immediately, as did skilled workers if unemployment were of long duration. With unemployment never below 7 per cent and ranging up to nearly 16 per cent between 1902 and 1910 destitution vastly increased and one need look no further for explanations of the extraordinary outbreak of militancy among unskilled and semi-skilled workers after 1910 which goes under the name of the Great Unrest.

The Great Unrest 1910-1914

One of the keys to this unprecedented period of militancy in Britain was the rise in the cost of living. Taking the Board of Trade Retail Price Index as 100 in 1900, it rose slowly until 1906 and then jumped to 105; thereafter it rose rapidly to 109 in 1910 and 115 in 1913. The price of clothing rose in the same period from 100 to 116. Rents also were rising. Of essential goods, only the price of coal fell, by 10 per cent. The characteristic of wages, on the other hand, was their 'stationaryness'. Many rates had not varied since the 1880s when they had been slashed by the Great Depression, but benefitted from the substantial fall in the cost of living at that time.

It is difficult to know how national events affected Black Country thinking, but there were portents enough. From the threat of the hitherto complaisant railway workers to strike in 1906 (averted only by adroit footwork on the part of Lloyd George), miners, cotton workers engineers and countless others broke out in general mutiny against agreements signed by trade union leaders on their behalf, and contempt for long established conciliation procedures. Above all, the unskilled were determined to end the perpetual penury in which they lived. By 1911 with the Port of London closed, troops firing on workers on Merseyside, to the 1913 great battles in Dublin where the Irish Transport & General Workers Union led by James Larkin and James Connolly fought the Dublin Tramways Company's lock-out, the country seemed to many to be on the verge of revolution.

To this ferment, the Black Country added an important and unique contribution. We can begin with the great Chainmakers' struggle of 1910.

The trade at this time comprised a prosperous factory section employing about 1,500 men and some women making the larger and sometimes immense chain such as that for the anchor of the Titanic. Alongside this was the sweated domestic trade. This divided into the Hammered Chain trade employing about 2000 women and a heavier Dollied or Tommied trade employing between 800 to 1000 men. The out-workers, both men and women either worked at a stall provided at the workshop of a shop owner, or in their own workshop at their own house. These shop owners, numbering between 400 and 500 were, however, really middlemen, since they sold their chain to the factory owners. The wages of the women continued deplorable. In 1889 at the depth of the Great Depression the Midland Counties Trades Federation estimated average earnings at between 10/-d. and 14/-d. for men and 4/-d. to 4/6d. for women; in 1910 coming out of another slump R.H. Tawney in a careful analysis of 426 women showed that 103 women earned between 4/-d. and 5/-d. and another 170 earned less than that; another 91 earned between 5/d. and 7/-d. and only 61 earned more than 7/-d. Nothing much had changed, despite the fact that these women were working not in a dying trade but in an expanding one. For these earnings a study of hours worked in 1913 divided almost equally into four quartiles of women working less than 30 hours, 30 to 40 hours, 40 to 50 hours, and 50 to 60 hours and above.

The response to the continued sweating conditions was the formation by the women in 1905 of the Cradley Heath and District Hammered and Country Chainmakers' Association. This in 1907 became the Hammered Chain branch of the National Federation of Women Workers whose secretary was the redoubtable Mary Macarthur. Together with Tom Sitch, who was secretary of the men's factory union and his son Charles Sitch who became secretary of the women's union, a formidable leadership of the women was created.

The break through came in 1910 with the setting up of a Trade Board for the chain trade. The basis of the Trade Board was to be the fixing of a minimum hourly rate. Only in this way could the previous vicious circle of agreements made in good times and rates cut in bad times, be broken.

The Trade Boards were, of course, violently opposed by employers, with arguments not unfamiliar to this day: Employers could not afford higher wages; our export trade would be lost; the trade would move abroad; women would not be employed thus creating unemployment; untold suffering would be caused by depriving women who were prepared to work for less than the Trade Board rate of employment.

The Chain Board, comprising six employer representatives, six workers' representatives and three independent members appointed by the Board of Trade, first met in May 1910 and decided 'to fix a rate' for the women's hand hammered trade. At a subsequent meeting a similar decision was taken with regard to the the men's dollied trade. After a lapse of three months to hear objections, the hand hammered rate was to come into existence in August 1910 and the dollied rate in February 1911. After this the Board of Trade fixed the hourly rates at 2½d. for the hammered trade and between 5d. and 7d. for the men's dollied trade. These rates were to apply from the dates stated and after six months would become compulsory.

To this agreement there were two serious problems. The first was that the employers' panel contained both the big factory owners and the middle men, many of whom were part employer and part workman. The other problem was the six months time lag. It was the latter that brought the last great confrontation in the chain trade. In August 1910 both employers and middlemen began requiring that their workers agree in writing to accept less than the Trade Board rate. The intention of the employers was to ignore, and if possible destroy, the minimum rate by building up a large stock of surplus chain. The women refused to sign the agreements, and on the 27th August the employers declared a general lock-out of all workers.

The progress of the dispute can be followed through the pages of the *Stourbridge County Express*. During the first week Mary Macarthur held a large meeting which ended with a procession along the High Street with the women singing Onward Christian Soldiers. An office was opened in the High Street with Charles Sitch and Charles Homer in charge. In an interview Mary Macarthur said the women wanted the legal rate at once and that 900 women were already receiving it. In a letter from George Williams, secretary of the Chain Manufacturers' Society, he claimed that the greater proportion of trade was done by shop men outside his association who were free to pay a lower rate. He put the proposal that all members of his association would pay the Trade Board rate if the chainworkers' union would undertake to see that no woman made chain at under that price. This was a proposition that the union was in no position to enforce and was only one of several attempts the employers made to cloud the issue. Further mass meetings took place. At Grainger's Lane School one thousand women were present. Tom Sitch opened the proceedings by saying that it was the largest meeting ever held in Cradley Heath and he asked who had signed the agreement. Not a hand was raised. When he asked who had not signed the agreement every hand went up. Mary Macarthur then spoke and said that Cradley Heath was renowned around the world as a place of hard, dirty work for low wages. They wanted to alter this so that women had some chance of leading a happy life and not be treated as slaves. A motion was passed pledging refusal to sign contracting-out agreements and support for the Women's Federation in its efforts to secure the full rate. After the meeting there was another impromptu march round the town.

A few days later an official demonstration was arranged. 5000 people gathered outside Grainger's Lane School, it was claimed. Led by the Quarry Bank silver band the procession proceeded to Cradley and Colley Gate and then back to Cradley Heath 'with songs and hymns all the way and great enthusiasm.' Some carried babies. The marchers were then addressed by Julia Varley and Mary Stocks from London.

Such efforts to encourage, enthuse and seek sacrifices for a cause from women who were among the poorest in the land were both necessary and continuous. At the end of the week a further demonstration took place in the Empire Theatre, Cradley Heath. Mary Stocks taught the women two songs to the tune of 'All the Nice Girls love a Sailor' and 'Daisy, Daisy'. Tom Sitch told the 500 women that it was the employers who had sought the dispute and were responsible for it, whatever they said. There had been no organisation previously and the employers thought that they only need to make the workers walk the streets for a week or so for starvation to loom and bring them to heel. All in dispute would receive 5/-d. a week strike pay and other funds were being raised. Sitch concluded by stating that 350 women were receiving Trade Board rates and 200 on 'country chain' were unaffected by the dispute.

The following week hopes of a short struggle were waning. The union declared that it could not undertake unlimited responsibility, although it would do all that was legitimately within its power to see that no one worked under price. But the employers could end the dispute immediately by only accepting chain with a certificate to say that the minimum rate had been paid. On Saturday collectors for the women had been as far afield as Birmingham. Strike pay had been dispensed at Grainger's Lane School – £70 to some 280 women. 'It was significant and pitiable that many women were actually better off' with this 5/-d. An outside reporter (who was probably Henry Nevinson – GB) stated that the position of women who did not receive this benefit was desperate. If they took work they were blacklegs; if they didn't they starved. 'In all England one can find nothing to beat the sheer sordid squalor of Cradley Heath,' he concluded.

On Monday Mary Macarthur paid a flying visit. She was met at the station by women who formed a procession and escorted her to Quarry Bank. One reporter commented: 'Surely one of the most pathetic manifestations to our sense of liberty ever seen. For so long have these women gone on slaving for a pittance that some find it almost impossible to believe that they are actually being enabled to stand up for themselves.' From Quarry Bank there was a procession to Lomey Town Mound in Cradley Heath. Here Mary Macarthur said that £200 had been collected and the Countess of Beauchamp had donated £100. They could now pay 6/-d. a week to trade unionists and 4/-d. to others. 'The eyes of the world are on Cradley Heath,' she concluded.

George Williams made another attempt to explain the employers' position. He said that the Employers' Association consisted of the principal employers. They were all paying the full rate, but they purchased their hammered chain from middlemen over whom they had no control.

That week also brought a statement from Joseph Woodhouse on behalf of the middlemen. He placed the blame squarely on the shoulders of the employers by stating that few middlemen had known that it was possible to contract-out until they were informed of this by the large employers who also provided them with the necessary forms.

A conference of Manufacturers and Chain Makers took place at the Cradley Heath council offices. The employers undertook to 'do all in their power' to ensure that the minimum was paid if the Union would undertake to pay 4/-d. a week to all women who refused to work under the rate. The union representatives replied that they were unable to give such an undertaking.

Contributions to the strike were now being received both from home and abroad. Edward

Cadbury had promised £5 a week and George Cadbury later guaranteed £10 a week. The fund then stood at £700. The existing position was given as 638 women locked out, 320 of whom were unionists and 318 non-unionists.

During this week there was a 'memorable' demonstration at Old Hill. The next day was said to be 'remarkable' for the number of women on the 'country list' coming to the office and announcing that they were not working.

The civic pride of Cradley Heath was being ruffled by 'hordes' of reporters descending on the town and seeking out its worst aspects. Pathe reported that it was sending a team to take 'living pictures.'

The third week of the strike saw another demonstration at the Empire with Edward Cadbury as the main speaker. Charles Sitch reported no change since the conference with the employers. George Williams asked querulously why the women were collecting all this money. The dispute was likely to be over within two weeks, he maintained, and in future employers were likely to employ more themselves and middlemen and women would disappear.

Justice, the paper of the Social Democratic Federation believed that the large employers supported minimum rates because the middlemen would then disappear. 'It is dog eat dog under this system. Big capitalist eat little capitalist.'

The dispute continued and settled into a routine. In the fourth week the usual demonstration was held on the Monday at the Empire Theatre with the Dean of Worcester. Mary Macarthur came and was greeted by 'a goodly number of women.' 500 women were out, it was reported. 200 of them union members and 300 of them not. The fund was now £1500 and the target had been raised to £2000. Williams announced for the employers that 35 manufacturers had signed a White list of both associated and unassociated employers who agreed to pay the full rate. A conference would take place the following Tuesday. The *County Express* rated it 'a most uneventful week.'

The paper's 24 September issue covering the fifth week of the dispute reported 'steady progress.' The White list was published, but it consisted mainly of the larger employers such as Tinsleys. Joseph Whitehouse, spokesman for the middle men stated that they were prepared to pay the trade board rate, but not until the employers agreed to place orders only with middle men who sign the White list. Those willing to sign accounted for 90 per cent of the work and the ending of the dispute rested with the employers, he claimed. The weekly position was given as 600 unionists working under the proper rates with 140 unionists and 280 non-unionists still in dispute.

In the sixth week of the dispute the paper reported no progress until Thursday. On the Sunday there had been yet another large meeting at the theatre this time with Arthur Henderson and John Galsworthy as the main speakers. Here it was reported that the national fund had reached £1700. Then, on the Thursday, the shop men met the middlemen with Mary MacArthur and J.J. Mallon present. At this meeting the proposals put the previous week were agreed. Afterwards, Mary MacArthur thought it was a great step forward and if the big employers would accept the proposals the strike could end the next week with only guerrilla warfare against those who then refused to pay the trade board rates. Later the same day there was a meeting at Grainger's Lane School where Mary MacArthur seems to have been quizzed on her views on the controversy as to whether Cradley Heath was being defamed by over-zealous newspaper reporters. She supposed that critics wanted to hear that Cradley Heath was a beauty spot! To those who were annoyed at the things that had been said they should recognise that these things were true. Cradley Heath was a drab place with no colour or joy in the lives of overworked and underpaid women chain makers. This state of affairs should be altered and she proposed that after the dispute an Institute for trade unionists should be built in Cradley Heath.

The employers rejected the proposals of the middlemen and the dispute went into October with bitterness increasing. The middlemen took Grainger's Lane School to hold a meeting after the breakdown of negotiations with the employers and announced that they were creating a more powerful association. The workers held a 'densely packed' meeting at the school the next evening. The privations of the women were increasing and the dispute seemed to be no nearer solution. Mary MacArthur said that if it was necessary to adopt extreme measures they would. One measure would be to have pickets outside all factories. Some women were asking if it were not better to finish the dispute off with a general strike. She asked the women to trust their leaders and promised that if there were not a final settlement by October 19th. when a further meeting with employers had been arranged she would call the women together to discuss drastic action. A letter from George Williams disclaimed employer responsibility for the continuation of the dispute. He said that all associated employers had signed the White list agreeing to pay trade board rates and they had gone out of their way to get non-associated employers to sign. They considered that they had fully carried out their responsibilities and it was now up to the women's trade union to deal with those who paid under the rate.

The seventh week brought no progress and the *County Express* proclaimed it the quietest week of the dispute. The most exciting news it could report was that the parish council has discussed 'Is Cradley Heath a Hell?'. The general opinion seemed to be that there were thousands of places worse than Cradley Heath. But some councillors raised the question of reforms.

The next week however, a settlement was agreed. At a meeting of the employers in Grainger's Lane School with Mary MacArthur all employers present agreed to deal only with those shopmen or middlemen who signed the White list. They also agreed to use all their influence to induce other employers to do the same. All this on the understanding that it was not to be used as a precedent when dealing with other branches of the trade or with regard to any alterations proposed in reference to the Trade Board. 150 middlemen had signed the White list it was stated.

A packed meeting of women at Grainger's Lane School the same day heard Mary MacArthur announce a 'complete and decisive victory'. It was ten weeks since they had started 'this most wonderful' trade dispute. She thanked Joseph Woodhouse for getting 153 shop owners to sign the list. She thought that the employers had been fair and 'reasonable'. They had fought a system and defeated it. She was sorry about the controversy of the slums of the district, but it had been necessary to tell the truth. The resumption of work would be gradual and the Fund would be kept open until January or February 'to help the wounded'. Some dozen employers had still not signed. She proposed that monthly meetings should continue to be held with good speakers brought down. A scheme under discussion was for girls to learn another craft so that they would not be entirely dependent on chain making. She wanted the women themselves to bring about a better future. 'The meeting was most enthusiastic throughout.' Songs were sung and there were cheers for Mary Macarthur and other workers.

The fears of the employers did not materialise. No one went out of business as a result of the higher wages, no women lost their jobs, nor did the trade move abroad.

The effects of the strike are not easy to assess. There were complaints that women were still earning less than 2½d. an hour. This could have been due to middlemen not paying the rate, or it might have been that when the hourly rate was transcribed into prices for the myriad types of chain, some of them did not yield the 2½d. hourly rate.

Tawney analysed the earnings of 588 women in in 1913 and found that the main groups of women earned between 5/-d. and 8/-d. a week compared with pre-trade board wages of 4/-d. to 7/-d. His comments were: 'If the low earnings still obtaining create amazement...the improvement from a state of things in which under 15 per cent of workers earned over 7/-d. a week to one in which just upon 60 per cent will do so certainly offers some cause for satisfaction.'

Even this limited advance, however, seems to have had a considerable effect on the area. Tawney quotes observers as claiming that 'an enormous difference' could be seen in the women's clothes, appearance and cleanliness; equally important was its effect on the school children who were 'much better fed, better clothed and better shod.'

The chain makers were not the only low paid workers to revolt in 1910. A particularly vicious and long drawn out struggle occurred at Doulton's Sanitary Pipemakers, Rowley Regis in August over a 10 per cent reduction in wages. The strikers accused the local Labour Exchange of supplying blacklegs to the firm. This the manager strenuously denied saying that they would never knowingly send men to a firm where there was a strike. The Doulton's manager, however, took steps to replace the 70 men on strike and took on 33 blacklegs. At the end of that day large numbers of the workers on strike 'wanted to have a word with them.' But the strike breakers thought they would be molested and 'charged the strikers with their bottles.' The strikers retaliated and in a struggle on the tow path six of the blacklegs were pushed into the canal. The ringleaders were ducked twice and others rolled in the dust. 'Some ran to a train, although it was going in the wrong direction.' The next morning the strike breakers were protected by the police. Most of them left, and five were escorted to their homes by the police. The dispute continued until at least November, when there was again violence, but I have not been able to trace the end of the dispute.

The struggle of the chainmakers was also rousing other workers in the area, notably the hollow ware trade. This trade had been significantly transformed by new processes of pressing and stamping and the tin plate trade became dominated by semi-skilled labour and women workers. In addition the cheapness and availability of steel led to the development of iron plate hollow ware. Both sections of the trade faced fierce foreign competition, notably from Germany. As a result the iron plate trade migrated from Birmingham to the Black Country and became centred on Lye where it became a sweated industry. Organisation in the iron plate trade was largely the result of the efforts of Simeon Webb, a Dudley born ex-miner, who was general secretary of the Galvanised Hollow-ware, Sheetmetal and Braziers Association. In 1909 so bad was the state of the industry that the *County Express* had raised the question of a living wage for for hollow-ware workers in Halesowen. The next year the question was again raised, this time by the *Birmingham Post*. Webb welcomed their support and said that he was seeking a minimum wage in the trade, but if he couldn't get that, he wanted a Trade Board. Developments came in the next year.

1911

In 1911 the revolt of the underpaid reached an unprecedented height. To catch both its extent and its effect on the thinking of contemporaries it is necessary to quote verbatim from the annual report of the Workers' Union which spearheaded this advance:

> It is with the greatest possible pleasure that I present the annual report indicating as it does a complete obliteration of all past records, and marking such a gigantic step forward... as could scarcely have been foreseen by the most sanguine member. The year 1911 is simply unprecedented in the history of the workers. Trade is undoubtedly booming as it never boomed before, despite the Tariffist croakers, and the workers have spontaneously taken advantage of that fact to insist on some tangible improvement in their too miserable conditions of life and labour...
>
> The outstanding feature of the tremendous movement called 'Industrial unrest'... was the unanimity with which all sections of the workers, skilled, semi-skilled, labourers of both sexes obeyed the call when it was justified, and stood loyally and steadfastly together until the grievances of all had been recognised, and definite guarantees given of a real desire to improve them.
>
> Nothing of the kind has ever happened before, on such a gigantic scale since the world began...
>
> From the very inception the efforts (of the Union) proved magnificently successful. The strike of Seamen and Firemen, then the Dockworkers absolutely paralysed the great captains of industry, and proved upon what a flimsy basis their autocratic rule had been based...
>
> The seed sown by the Trades Unions in years of depression ripened quickly... and immediately, as if by magic thousands... instantly became members of Trades Unions and before the end of the year membership of the Workers' Union had risen from 5000 to over 20,000...

The local achievements of the Workers' Union in that year rested on two main disputes. The first was centred on the BSA works in Birmingham, but involved also the ASE, Steam Engine Makers, Toolmakers and Brassworkers. The dispute was conducted through a newly created Engineers and Allied Trades Federation to which all unions involved in the dispute belonged. The strike was successful, semi-skilled and unskilled workers receiving advances of 1/-d. a week and advances in other factories being achieved without resort to strike action. The other main dispute was an unsuccessful strike in Bilston, but this had a huge significance in mobilising Black Country workers.

Early in 1911 a branch of the Workers' Union was opened in Bilston. It was joined by workers at John Fellows. Two months later the shop steward was sacked and other members ordered to leave the union. They refused to abandon the union and were then locked out. The numbers involved seemed small – 15 men and 50 women, but the dispute was long and bitter. The police were called in to intimidate the trade unionists and they were arrested en masse as 'disorderly persons'. Fifty summonses were issued and fines were imposed. Fifteen, who refused to pay the fines, went to jail. The collaboration of the police with intransigent employers was deplored. Local campaigns were organised to support the workers and pay their fines. What was remarkable to contemporaries was the solidarity of the women. The management brought strike breakers into the factory and the dispute continued for six months. After this period, it was necessary for the Union to admit defeat. But the nightly propaganda in Bilston had served the wider purpose of publicising the union's policy of a minimum wage. Organisation was set up in other factories in the town and a 22/-d. minimum conceded in some of them.

In August 1911 another great national strike occurred. This time it was the railwaymen again. By this time there was virtual civil war in some parts of the country. The *Express & Star* in August reported paralysis of the Port of London, troops on Merseyside and riots in Glasgow. Liverpool shipowners had declared a lockout and there had been 100 baton charges by the police. Two men had been killed when the troops fired with revolvers. Locally in the Bilston strike, windows had been broken at Fellows's and a policeman injured.

On the railways, since Lloyd George's patched up settlement of the 1907 dispute, a Conciliation Scheme for a minimum period of six years had been in operation. During this time the railway employers refused to recognise and negotiate with the union. By 1911 militants were no longer prepared to wait and unofficial strikes in Liverpool, Manchester and Birmingham made it clear that unless the leaders acted they would lose control of the movement. So a national strike was called for August. 145,000 unionists stopped work. In the Black Country the response was very good. In the Stourbridge district, which included Cradley, Lye, Brettell Lane, Brierley Hill and Round Oak, the *County Express* was talking of a food famine even before the rail strike began and reported that prices were already rising. During the strike they reported that the railways were paralysed, Dudley was isolated and the strike was a success throughout the district. There had been scenes of violence in Birmingham, but locally all was peaceful. The Amalgamated Society of Railway Servants had sent telegrams to all branches stating that 'Your liberty is as stake.' The men immediately struck. At Stourbridge goods depot no trains were leaving. It had been thought that some men would have come to work as the majority were non-union but this did not occur. Only one train had left Dudley station. The Stourbridge strike committee was operating from the Labour Hall in Enville Street. The next week when the three day dispute had ended the paper stated that 190 locomen, 131 traffic, 91 platelayers and 48 goods workers had stopped, making a total of 460 on strike.

In West Bromwich early workmen's trains did not run. On the following day men employed at the GWR station went to work as usual, but after a meeting with an ASRS official they left work and the station was at a complete standstill. In neighbouring Langley, however, violence occurred. Here two trains were held up and signal boxes manned by strike-breakers were attacked. Troops were sent in to restore 'order'.

The soldiers were centred on Wolverhampton. West Riding Regiment detachments had been sent there on the 18th. the first day of the strike. They brought with them two machine guns. The next day the *Express & Star* reported the streets 'presented an animated appearance', the main attraction being the soldiers 'whose fixed bayonets were the cynosure for all eyes.' On the 19th. some of them, with fixed bayonets,took up their positions on the bridge at Bushbury, but there was no disturbance, it was reported. Why should there have been? The only railwayman on duty at Bushbury was the station master. The reasons given for stationing the troops in Wolverhampton was that it was a central position from which to deploy them and also that there were good drill halls at Wolverhampton and Bilston.

The same day there was a large meeting of support and protest on the Market Place. The Catholic priest of St. Joseph's, the Rev J.J. Darmody, opened th meeting by saying 'I bless your sacred cause, on one condition. That you do nothing illegal.' The Rev J.A. Shaw chaired the meeting and Alderman Price Lewis the Liberal leader, and Labour Councillors Walsh, Sharrocks and Whittaker all spoke. A Trades Council representative, A. Bent moved the motion: That this meeting of railwaymen and friends protests at the presence of the military and asks the Mayor, who was responsible for them, to request their removal.

The strike began at midnight. Within an hour the *Express & Star* had reporters at the main railway centres. From the two main stations of Wolverhampton they reported that most men had left work, the signal boxes were deserted, and pickets were very active. By 9am 'nearly everyone was out' at the GWR goods station amounting to 100 men. At the Midland goods depot all had been quiet during the night and 'the pickets had little trouble dealing with would-be infringers of the unwritten law of the union'. This despite the fact that the Midland Railway directors had a few days before the strike announced that they would reward 'loyal servants' with a 50 per cent bonus.

At Bilston 'the men had responded well to the strike call.' The situation at Walsall the *Express & Star* reported was, 'Very satisfactory. The men are holding firm and adopting a peaceful attitude.'

The strikers remained firm throughout the three day strike. When it ended there was general relief, it was said; holiday makers were happy because the trains were running again and Dudley ironworks which had been told that they must close by the following Tuesday and all other firms facing shut-down no doubt shared the 'thankfulness' of the Rev J.J. Darmody.

Of the numerous other strikes in 1911 only a few can be mentioned. In August while the two main disputes were still in progress Nut & Bolt Workers and Rivet Makers from Halesowen, Dudley, Blackheath Old Hill and elsewhere were all in dispute. Earlier, in June, a strike at Izon's of West Bromwich was a reminder that the dispute of hollow-ware workers was still simmering. These strikers were supported by the Birmingham Gasworkers and General Labourers Union, demonstrating that the other unions of the unskilled were active as well as the Workers' Union. And Council and tramway men were active throughout the year in negotiating better wages and conditions.

1912

The year was dominated by the miners' strike. Wages had come under attack during the years of depression of the first decade of the new century and particularly after the Eight Hours Act of 1909 made it impossible to lengthen hours. One area where employers could and did attack was that of 'abnormal places' e.g. difficult places where it was impossible to earn the agreed minimum, This became an important issue both nationally and in the Black Country. It became an integral part, however, of the minimum wage question which the miners, in common with so many other workers, were pressing. On this matter the majority of employers, including those of the Midlands were not opposed, on condition that each district negotiated its own minimum. A minority of employers disagreed, however, and negotiations broke down. A ballot to strike was supported by a large majority and a national strike was declared for the end of February.

District minimum rates requested ranged from 7/6d. per day in the more prosperous coalfields of Yorkshire and Nottingham down to 6-/d. The Midland minimum was set at 7/-d. and 6/-d. with Old Hill miners 'firm for 7/-d.' and 6/-d. being demanded in the less prosperous pits where the minimum in operation was 5/-d. The strike began on Friday 1st. March and all pits were soon closed. By the 2nd. of March there were a million miners idle. This was by far the largest industrial dispute ever known in Britain and the first in which Black Country miners had the support of a truly national organisation. Despite reservations i.e. the differences between miners east and west of Dudley, and the fact that the coal trade was booming and employers therefore inclined to be conciliatory, Black Country miners were solid. In the Gornals, 'success lies with the men,' it was reported. 'There are an estimated 2000 miners in Lower Gornal, Upper Gornal and Gornal Wood. They are all on strike and feel that they are fighting for their rights.' In Dudley, 'The men are as firm as a rock. Never in the history of Dudley has there been such a firm and determined strike.' Nearly 2,000 'determined Pelsall miners' attended a meeting on Pelsall Common. The miners were defended by the Rev J.A. Shaw in a sermon at All Souls church, Wolverhampton where he spoke of the social revolution in progress. The acceptance of differing minimums within the Black Country was bringing problems. At a meeting it was stated that Old Hill men were asking for 7/-d but Dudley men only for 6/3d. Was not a Dudley man worth as much as an Old Hill man, it was asked.

The strike produced the extraordinary position of Asquith, the Liberal prime minister, preparing an Act of Parliament to force the minority of recalcitrant coalowners to accept the minimum rate.

Within a few days, iron masters were threatening to close works because of coal shortages. The Royal Hospital stated that it had sufficient coal stocks to remain open for a month. Particularly important was the question of mine drainage. At first it was announced that pumping would continue, but an incident when miners stopped a boat load of slack from Bloomfield Colliery led the Mines Drainage Commission to stop the Stow Heath engine which had been pumping 20,000 gallons a day.

After the first week of the strike problems multiplied. Many trains ceased to run and travellers turned to the trams. In Wolverhampton, railway employees were 'temporarily dispensed with' and in Walsall they were put on short time. In Wolverhampton the Mayor's Fund was opened to feed poor children and the question of implementing the clauses of the Education Act permitting authorities to provide school meals was raised throughout the Black Country.

Another problem was the search for coal from the pit mounds and the resultant danger. At Parkfields in Wolverhampton a large surface deposit of slack had been discovered and people from as far as Dudley with wheel barrows and baskets were busy taking it away. As the mounds were worked, seams from the pit were disclosed and 'prospectors' toiled twenty four hours a day in candlelight to get the coal and protect their 'claim'. In some cases roofs were propped and sides strengthened, but the dangers were obvious as people began to tunnel into the seam. Two brothers had dug a deep hole when a fall of earth completely buried one of them. 'Prospectors' rushed from other 'claims' and he was rescued alive, but suffering severely from shock. In Dudley some miners were collecting coal from a mound where five men were digging into a seam. The miners warned them that the seam was a death trap. The side collapsed and one of the men was killed. Where pits were active and stopped only by the strike, some coal-pickers were prosecuted by the owners.

As the strike became long drawn out, violence erupted. Riots broke out at Littleton Pit, Cannock Chase, when crowds of several thousands converged to stop strike breakers working. Ponies were brought out of the pit and a large number of tubs thrown down the pit. The unrest spread to Walsall Wood and Bloxwich. On 25th March violence was threatened as owners tried to open pits. A very large crowd of Pelsall miners threatened violence until it was stated that the men at work were repairers and not drawing coal.

The negotiations to end the strike proved protracted. The miners were adamant that a minimum wage of 5/-d. a day for men and 2/-d. for boys should be written into the Bill. This the owners rejected. The union also wanted the district minimums being claimed to be written into the Bill; these minima and often more were already being paid in these prosperous times as coal prices rose fast. Thus the strike was always for the benefit of the minority who were not being paid the minimum. Before resorting to an Act of Parliament, Asquith and Lloyd George tried negotiations, but by 15th March there was complete deadlock and settlement of the strike seemed further off than ever. Asquith then introduced his Bill on March 19th. To try to meet the demands of both sides Asquith's Bill put no figures at all to the minima. Balfour, the Conservative leader, complained that the Liberals were trying to 'force through a colossal revolution in a week.' The Labour MPs consistently moved amendments to include the 5/-d. and 2/-d. minima, but were defeated. The Bill passed its third reading on March 26th. Labour MPs voted against it. It went through the Lords in a couple of days and received the royal assent on March 29th. Who said Parliament cannot act in a hurry when it wants to?

The MFGB then put to the vote whether to accept or reject the new situation arising from the Coal Mines Minimum Wage Act. This conceded the principle of the minimum wage, but left the actual amount to be negotiated through the Conciliation Boards etc. which normally negotiated wages for different areas and regions. Thus the national minimum, which was the policy of the union, was avoided by the employers.

The miners felt they had been tricked. The new law gave them nothing that they did not already have and the minima that they were demanding had not been conceded. The votes were cast in bitter mood. When they were counted 244,000 were against the settlement and 201,000 for it. The Midlands Federation, however, had voted 18,000 to 11,000 to resume work. With only a small national majority to continue the strike, the national leaders recommended a return to work.

The Black Country settlement which was reached on 22 May 1912 was extremely complex and is dealt with fully by Taylor. In brief, for pikemen in the thick coal three grades were established ranging from 6/6d to 5/8d per day. Minimum rates for roadmen and repairers and loaders and fillers were set at 5/4d and 5/-d per day respectively. Differential and lower rates were set for thin coal miners. The award was hedged around with conditions e.g. miners had to work 80 per cent of the time their pit was open to qualify for minimum wage. The response of the two main local associations predictably varied. In the S. Staffs & E. Worcs Association, representing mainly the less productive pits in the coal field, the award was declared by Tom Mansell to be 'highly satisfactory.' To the Old Hill and Pelsall miners the settlement was a betrayal and the Old Hill men came out on strike against it. Not until mid-June were all the pits at work again. The settlement did nothing to improve relations between Black Country miners working in such different circumstances.

1913 – the Labour War

In 1913 the Black Country made its own unique contribution to labour history. Not only did tens of thousands unskilled workers struggle and sacrifice to raise wages from 18/-d a week to 23/-d, but the whole of Black Country society backed their efforts with the feeling that 'it was only right' that they should have the 23/-d. Moreover this struggle, like that of the Chainmakers, was one in which women, previously thought to be unorganisable, played a leading role to emancipate themselves from almost perpetual destitution.

The struggle was led by the Workers' Union, but during its course, many other workers in other unions, notably Council workers, also made important advances.

The beginning is generally thought to be 18th February 1913 when 500 workers at Tangyes struck for a 23/-d minimum wage for men and additional money for men up graded to semi-skilled machinists. (Askwith, however, the government conciliator claimed it started with some women in Dudley.) By the end of the month 1,600 of the 2,400 work force was on strike. Tangyes were known as good employers, but it was not until 3rd March that they offered a 23/-d. minimum which was accepted.

During February, tramwaymen had received a rise and bakers in Wolverhampton, Willenhall and Bilston had won a 2/-d increase to 28/-d a week.

As soon as the 23/-d minimum had been conceded at Tangyes, similar demands were made at Chance Brothers and Griggs Ltd. both of which were granted. Jack Beard, the Workers' Union organiser repeatedly stressed that these were the first wage increases for 18 years.

The next to take action were women at United Hinges (a subsidiary of Kenricks'). They complained that they were only paid when their work left the firm's premises, which might be weeks, and if they left in the meantime they might not be paid at all. When the men came out in sympathy they put in a claim for a 23/-d minimum for unskilled men and 12/-d for women with payment for work on completion.

These events stimulated the interest and enthusiasm which was a feature of the campaign to its end. The Workers' Union began distributing leaflets and holding meetings outside factory gates and large numbers of workers joined the union.

The United Hinge women had now been joined by workers at the main factory, Kenricks, and almost simultaneously the strike spread to Guest, Keen & Nettlefolds in the Stour Valley. Kenrick's conceded the claim on 19th April and GKN and other firms in the West Bromwich area also granted the claim. By now the minimum of 23/-d had been conceded by some of the largest firms in Birmingham including B.S.A. and Metropolitan Carriage & Wagon Co.

But the strikes took a new and bitter turn after Birmingham Carriage workers at Smethwick walked out on the 19th of April and the employers resisted the claim. The Smethwick workers then organised marches to the other carriage works in the area at Oldbury, Wednesbury and Saltley and brought these to a stand still.

By this time the condition of many of the strikers was desperate. Most of those who joined the strikes had not been in the union and even those who were received very little strike benefit. Local tradesmen helped by giving credit. The Soho Co-operative Society in addition gave away 100 loaves a week. The Handsworth Co-operative Women's Guild and the Women's Labour League jointly paid for one shilling parcels of food which were distributed to needy families. Every means was used to raise funds; barrel organs at first used in Smethwick and West Bromwich were soon going as far afield as Manchester and marchers went with them, collecting on the way.

At the end of April the strikes spread to Wolverhampton. Women at Bayliss, Jones & Bayliss recruited to the Workers' Union came out and the union demand for 23/-d and 12/-d was put. Nearly 500 men, women and children walked out. The firm closed the bolt department until the settlement. This put another 600 or 800 out of work. Seven or eight police were at the gate of the works. A representative for the firm said that the strike was the work of agitators and most people were satisfied with their wages. Arthur Ellery, the Workers' Union organiser, met the management and higher prices were fixed for women and girls for a two months trial. In the screw department an extra 2/-d a week was to be paid and also time and a quarter for overtime. The women were said to be satisfied with this offer, but they stayed out with the men until their claim was settled. By then 40 toolmakers at the firm had walked out. Their claim was for a 'florin' a week i.e. 2/-d. By this time many more industrial workers in Wolverhampton were involved.

Wolverhampton gas workers demanded a 24/-d. minimum. It was conceded but not paid; when the men enquired why, the Council stated that this was because already another claim for 25/-d had been put in. The British Electric Traction Co. managed to spread a dispute right across the Black Country by offering different rates in different towns. At Dudley and Stourbridge drivers were offered $5\frac{1}{4}$ d to $6\frac{1}{4}$ d (after three years) and conductors $4\frac{1}{2}$d to $5\frac{1}{2}$d an hour. Cleaners, labourers and permanent way men were offered 5d an hour. There was indignation at Dudley at the 'divide and rule tactics' by BET, better terms were being offered in Wednesbury and better still in West Bromwich and Smethwick, it was claimed. The Amalgamated Society of Tramway & Vehicle Workers held a meeting of employees in all Black Country towns and there was unanimous agreement to reject the terms. By now Wolverhampton Trades Council had adopted the Workers' Union claim of 23/-d and 12/-d and put its main officials, James Whittaker and Harry Bagley at the service of the strikers.

Also at the end of April the strike spread to Wednesbury. Tube workers at John Russell's demanded a 10 per cent increase in piece work prices and 10 per cent for day workers earning up to 25/-d. The management offered to raise wages from 18/-d to 20/-d and 'absolutely' refused any other concession. The offer was refused. At that time all the men were non-unionists, according to the *Wolverhampton Chronicle,* but the Workers' Union offered its help and the men 'were expected to join.' The Russell strikers spread the dispute to other tube works, notably the Alma Works at Walsall and this precipitated further developments in Walsall. By the third week in May 10,000 men were idle according to the press.

To co-ordinate the activity with other unions, notably the two Gasworkers Unions, John Beard of the Workers' Union initiated a Minimum Wage Council. In addition to its basic demand for the 23/-d and 12/-d minimum a claim for 10 per cent increase in piecework prices, 2/-d a week advance for all those earning over 23/-d and scales of earnings for youths and girls was formulated and widely circulated as a leaflet.

New efforts were now directed at Birmingham Carriage where no progress had been made in a month. Marches to Wednesbury and Oldbury brought out the workers at these branches of the firm and two days later John Beard called out workers from the main factory at Saltley. Birmingham Carriage then retaliated by locking out all its 7500 workers. Within a week the number made idle by the strike almost doubled.

In the last week in May the strike spread into Bilston. Thompson's at Ettingshall offered 21/-d to unskilled workers and 23/-d to blacksmiths' strikers, new scales for youths and time and a quarter for overtime. This was not satisfactory to the strikers and with the Workers' Union banner at their head they marched to John Thompson of Bilston. Here the men had already been out once and refused to strike again until proper notice had been given to the management.

Threats were beginning to be made by managements as bitterness increased. Russell's threatened to close their Alma works for ever and Talbot Stead to close theirs for six months. Walsall Trades Council had a large scheme of assistance to strikers. Tube works at Great Bridge, Hill Top and elsewhere were out and Danks' of Netherton had been out nearly a month. In Willenhall 1000 were out. Brickworkers of Lower Gornal & District gave notice to withdraw from agreements. When the Stewart & Lloyd tubeworks at Coombes Wood came to a halt there were 30,000 workers in dispute at the end of May.

The Malleable Iron Founders Association met and decided to oppose the union's claim. When Brotherton's of Wolverhampton became idle the manager, asked to comment on future developments said, 'Ask me in two month's time.' As the weeks went by hardships increased and violence appeared. At Talbot Stead's where the management tried to reopen the works with strike breakers, 3,000 men stormed the factory gate and were repulsed by mounted police. Violence also occurred elsewhere, not always from the strikers' side. A march from Smethwick Carriage Works to the Old Park Works at Wednesbury to persuade these men to join the strike led to a striker being hit with a lump of coal, and but for the efforts of the leaders of the march, an ugly situation would have developed. Efforts were made to spread the strike beyond the Black Country and 25 men from Wednesbury and 25 from Walsall were chosen for a march to Glasgow to close down tube works there.

By June actual starvation was beginning to appear among the strikers. Their sufferings were to some extent increased by the very hot weather. In the second week of June a march of 2,000 strikers took place from Wednesbury to Coombes Wood where it was said that work was being resumed. 'Many were nearly exhausted from the march and from the heat. When this became known many women rushed from their houses bringing loaves for men who had brought with them their own cheese.' The journey had not been necessary, according to the management, the men at work were from Manchester and they were only doing repairs. Julia Varley advised strikers to apply to the Poor Law Guardians for relief; if they were unsuccessful she would lead a march to the Workhouse. Typical was the plight of 1,500 strikers at Monmore Green who had been out for three weeks. Most of them had not been members of the union. The previous week union members had been paid 3/-d. a week if they were married and 1/6d a week if single. This had been raised by 6d and 3d. for the present week. Non-union married strikers received 2/6d. a week and the *Wolverhampton Chronicle* ran a story on 'Life at Monmore on 2/6d a week.' At Ettingshall the Children's Breakfast Fund had benefitted by £3-11-11d. from a sacred concert at Ettingshall Church Institute. An average of 100 children a day were fed with milk, tea, bread and jam. In Wolverhampton the Mayor opened a Relief Fund in June. Funds came from sympathisers far from the Black Country and a national appeal towards the end of June raised £1,000. But even this made little impact on the 37,000 who were said to be on strike by the end of June.

The employers, most of whom were not eligible for membership of the Engineering Employers' Federation formed the Midland Employers' Association and at first refused to meet the unions while the strikes were proceeding. On the 14th June, however, they made the first official contact with the union. A subsequent conference a week later led to an offer of a 21/-d minimum. This the union rejected and put to a ballot of its members. It was rejected by almost a 50 to 1 vote. Bitterness was still increasing and on the 31st June there was a riot at John Fellows of Bilston as 150 police battled to prevent workers charging the works gates and uprooting the pillars holding them. By this time however, some employers were conceding the minimum, most importantly GKN and Garringtons.

George Askwith, the Government's chief conciliator, had been brought in to help with the negotiations and by the 2nd of July when it was announced that only one firm in the whole of Birmingham had not conceded the 23/-d there was a feeling of victory in the air. On the 5th July a resounding welcome was given to two barrel organ teams from Smethwick who had marched to Liverpool and Manchester and back collecting funds. They were met at the Smethwick boundary by a band which accompanied them to Six Ways where a crowd of 5,000 people gave them a tremendous ovation.

A final settlement was agreed on July 7th. This conceded the 23/-d and 12/-d minima for the Birmingham district which included Smethwick and Oldbury. Elsewhere in the Black Country the minimum was 22/-d. to be raised to 23/-d. within six months. These terms were agreed and accepted by Julia Varley and Jack Beard for the Workers' Union, and also by the two Gasworkers Unions. This was approved in a subsequent ballot by 4 to 1.

Thus ended arguably the most important episode in Black Country labour history. The effect of raising wages from 18/-d to 23/-d is difficult to overestimate. Not only did it lift perhaps one third of all Black Country families from a life of perpetual penury to one in which they at least could purchase the main necessities of life, but the social effects of having some control over their lives and the lives of their families brought new attitudes of confidence and self respect. Nor was it only the unskilled who benefitted. During this period numerous other settlements, some recorded and some not, were made. For the semi-skilled worker, an average wage of about 28/-d. emerged, partly as a result of the raising of the unskilled minimum and partly from their own efforts. And settlements for skilled workers were also made in this period which might not have been so easy except for the efforts of the women and the unskilled men. The sacrifices and privations of the strikers had been justified. But what sort of industrial society was it that would not pay a living wage until trade union energy and human sacrifices forced it?

The Great Unrest had still not run its course, however. During 1913 the struggle of women for the vote was reaching a climax. In addition, the national unrest spread to Ireland where from August 1913 to the beginning of 1914 the great struggle of the Irish Transport Workers Union against the lock out of the tramway workers held the attention of all trade unionists, generating support and sympathy, not least in the Black Country.

By 1914 it was widely held that Britain was becoming ungovernable and further manifestations of this spirit of revolt were expected. Instead the Great War broke out and everything changed.

Bibliography: Depression 1903-09 and the Great Unrest 1910-14

There was much discussion and analysis of continuing poverty and unemployment into the twentieth century. Some of the most useful to me have been: A.W. Humphrey – *The Workers' Share, A Study in Wages and Poverty* (1930); L.G. Chiozza Money – *The Nation's Wealth, Will it Endure?* (1914); H.A. Silverman – *The Economics of Social Problems* (1928); A.M. Carr-Saunders & D. Caradog Jones – *A Survey of the Social Structure of England & Wales* (1937); Maud Pember Reeves – *Round About a Pound a Week* (1913).

For unemployment the essential source is the *Department of Employment Gazette* from 1888, also W.R. Garside – *The Measurement of Unemployment in Great Britain 1850-1979*.

For the standard of living see my *Social Conditions in the Black Country,* Chapter 7.

For Distress Committee reports see Wolverhampton library and Walsall Local History Centre; For Dudley Poor Law material see Dudley Local History Centre.

For details of budgets, rents, etc. see *Report of an Enquiry by the Board of Trade into Working Class Rents, Housing, Retail Prices & Standard Rates of Wages in the UK* (1908).

For the Great Unrest see: Eric Taylor's thesis, for the Chain Makers' Strike and for Minimum Rates and the Chain Trade Board see R.H. Tawney – *Studies in the Minimum Wage;* also the *Stourbridge County Express* for the chain strike. For the other strikes see the local press.

For the 'Labour War' of 1913 see the Bellars & Leask pamphlet *Nor Shall the Sword Sleep,* the Workers' Union annual reports at Warwick University and Richard Hyman – *The Workers' Union*.

Chapter 8

Co-operation to 1914

The Foundations of Co-operation

Co-operation is the third element of the Labour movement together with trade unions and working class political parties. Again, because the Industrial Revolution produced in Britain the first working class in the world, Co-operation began in Britain and, as with trade unions and working class political parties, spread to the rest of the world.

All three developments are imperishably connected with Robert Owen, who is one of the great figures of British history and the most important pioneer of the Labour movement.

Owen, born in Wales, was a self-made man who quickly made a fortune in the developing cotton trade. This enabled him to acquire the major share in the New Lanark Mills where, in a remote Scottish location with a tough and illiterate population he put into operation his famous principle that people's characters are formed through their environment. Kind treatment, lower hours than elsewhere, good housing and working conditions, education for children and with all this, high profits, made New Lanark a show piece for the world and Owen a famous man.

The slump after the Napoleonic Wars brought home to Owen the irrationality of capitalism and he advocated the setting up of Co-operative communities to plan production. In doing so, he quickly lost the support of the wealthy and influential who were further alienated by his ideas on natural religion, which led him to be regarded as an atheist.

Undeterred, Owen left Britain in 1824 for America where he founded Co-operative colonies.

When he returned to England in 1829 Owen found that his ideas had been taken up by working people. In conformity with the principle that all value is created by labour, National Equitable Labour Exchanges were set up in 1832 to which craftsmen brought the commodities they had produced to exchange them for other goods or to take away Labour Notes of equal value. This was followed in 1834 by the setting up of the Grand National Consolidated Trades Union with the aim of peacefully transforming society to Socialism by the creation of co-operative enterprises and communities. Such vast millennial schemes were doomed to failure at the time, but became the heritage of working people from that time.

Owen's ideas were particularly important in Birmingham, where the only National Equitable Labour Exchange in the country to liquidate itself voluntarily and show a profit, was situated. Owen subsequently founded what was to become the Universal Community of Rational Religionists with the aim of 'an entire change of the character and condition of man by meetings etc. and by founding Communities of United Interest.' These Owenite Socialists as they came to be called were important in both the Black Country and Birmingham. But the basic aim of supporting the one socialist colony that was established in Britain, Queenwood in Hampshire, was overshadowed by the excitement of propaganda against religion with the great interest and vast prejudice which this generated.

It was not until the 1860s that Co-operation once again attracted the attention of large numbers of working people in the Black Country. Before examining the better known Consumer Co-operatives the origins of which are usually traced to the Rochdale Pioneers of 1844, the progress of the surprisingly important industrial co-ops will be looked at.

Productive Co-operatives

In 1852 the Industrial & Provident Societies Act gave limited, legal protection to persons wishing to form a Society under terms applicable to Friendly Societies for members to engage in Labour, Trade or Handicraft. Between 1850 and 1912 thirty nine Co-operative Societies in the Black Country were registered with the Registry of Friendly Societies, a number of which can be identified as industrial societies.

One was the Lock Co-operative set up as a result of a dispute and which, as we have seen, was a factor in the setting up of the local Trades Council. This was registered under the title of the Wolverhampton & Brewood Industrial & Provident Plate Lock Manufacturing Society Ltd. It operated at North Road in a 'large manufactory' built for it by 'a gentleman in the town.' The men claimed that for many years they had been 'sore oppreseed' with wages of 15/-d. a week for a 14 hour day. A strike had taken place and as a result the employers had agreed to raise wages, but when the time came to do this the employers refused. The men then formed the Co-operative with loans and contributions from the Labour movement. Only four employers made plate locks, employing 240 men. The Co-operative, when set up, employed 80 of these men, it was said. The employers however were hostile, 'prevented them from getting orders, tried to prevent the Co-operative buying materials, spread flase reports about its management, discharged large numbers of workers hoping thereby to embarrass the Co-operative, which would feel morally bound to try to employ them and finally reducing their selling price so that both private employers and the Co-operative were selling below cost.' It was at this point that the Trades Council was formed to support the Co-operative. In October 1865 the Trades Council was told that the Lock Co-operative was 'still suffering from the competition of the masters, but their work was superior, and they had hopes of getting all the trade into their hands.' In August 1866 the situation was reported as much better. 'After facing gigantic obstacles for two years the men would soon be receiving a full wage. Their motto must be Malice towards None, Charity to All.'

The Co-operative flourished during the prosperity of the early 1870s. But in October 1873 the *Engineer* reported that the Co-operative, which had had a hard struggle to establish a position even after receiving important aid from such people as Tom Hughes and Canon Kingsley (both Christian Socialists – GB) had sustained a severe injury when its factory was almost completely gutted by fire. The damage was estimated at £300, but it was insured for only £75. This disaster was overcome and in April 1874 the Co-operative was said to be paying higher wages than other employers in the trade. In April 1875 the Co-operative celebrated its tenth anniversary with a dinner at the Fox Inn, North Road. It was stated that it started with five members and a capital of £13. It now had 75 working members with a capital of £850 and had just declared its first dividend. A letter of congratulation was read from Rupert Kettle (the celebrated, local conciliator – GB) which said 'Your perseverance under difficulties which would have overwhelmed most men has entitled you to your success.' They remembered above all the kind friend who had built them their factory. They now earned between 20/-d. and 23/-d. a week. The advantage of co-operation to the workman was stressed by Mr Jones, the secretary, who said that he now owned £30 of capital and this would have been impossible if he had remained an ordinary worker. Stenner states that entry to the Co-operative cost 1/3d and one or more shares could be bought with a deposit of 6d. and a weekly payment of 3d. until each share was paid up. The profits were divided between management expenses, 5 per cent interest on money borrowed and the remainder to dividends and profit sharing for the workmen.

The Co-operative also claimed to have affected industrial relations. If the Co-operative lowered its prices this would be the certain sign that other employers were justified in doing the same and strikes on that account would be avoided. Conversely employers would not be so likely to reduce their prices when Co-operative prices remained steady. The Co-operative was also supporting conciliation and regretted that the Chamber of Commerce would not join with the Trades Council to form a general conciliation board for the town.

The Co-operative, however, was a victim of the Great Depression. In May 1879 the *Engineer* reported that the Co-operative had circularised all members to consider winding up the concern. In August 1879 it was wound up. The only explanation known comes from a letter to *The Times* stating that this was due to too few orders and too much stock. The Co-operative was in good company. In that year, of 147 iron furnaces in the Black Country 123 were idle and mass bankruptcies of firms large and small were the order of the day. The demise of the Co-operative should be seen against the background of a depression of almost unprecedented depth and after almost 15 years successful operation at a time when most middle class people despised the working class and derided the possibility of them successfully organising a business venture. Nor was this quite the end. In the 1890 Co-operative Union Congress Report, Wolverhampton General Lockmakers' Co-operative appears with 41 members and £41 in capital. It received for goods sold in that year £30, but incurred charges of £49. Whether this was an attempt to form a new Co-operative or whether it arose from the liquidation of the former enterprise is now known. It disappeared in 1895, 'cancelled after notification from the Registrar.'

In the depressed but expanding chain trade the Cradley Heath and District Chain Manufacturing Co-operative was set up in 1887. Reports from the *Co-operative News* for February 1889 indicate that this was an ambitious attempt to do no less than end the sweated domestic chain trade for ever by bringing the women into a Co-operative factory. Appeals were made from London for capital and an impressive list of notables were prepared to contribute. The Duke of Westminster promised £50, as did the Earl of Derby, Lord Rothschild offered £20. The Earl of Dudley, however, was significantly absent. Tangyes offered £100 as did J.T. Brunner MP. Other MPs also offered large sums. Total contributions at that time amounted to £849 and the original appeal for £1,000 of capital was raised to £2,000. However, this co-operative never got off the ground. It appears in the list of producer co-operatives in the annual Co-operative statistics for the years 1887 to 1890, but at no time is any information given regarding members, capital, sales etc. It must therefore be assumed that it never functioned.

In the terminally declining hand nail trade, several attempts were made to start productive co-ops. The Lye Distributive Co-operative Society, first registered in 1861 began to employ some of its members at making nails in 1867. By this time it had a surplus of a few hundred pounds and proceeded very cautiously, selecting only its most sober and trustworthy members to make nails. As a result it acquired a reputation for good workmanship and survived the Great Depression until 1892. The Dudley Industrial Nail Manufacturing Society was established in the first trough of the Great Depression in 1879 and for the first three years enjoyed some success, but membership was never more than 12. From 1883 it lost money and its trade and capital quickly dwindled. But it continued to exist in 1890 when its turnover was £190, charges £20 and net profit £5.

A Midland Nailmakers' Association was formed in 1884, but within three years its members had abandoned nail making in favour of the production of spades and shovels. In 1890 the Society had 8 members with a capital of £288. Its turnover for the year was £916 with trade charges of £137, and a net profit of £34. It disappeared in 1894.

Another domestic trade equally depressed as nails even in the good times of 1870-74 was that of gunfilers. In January 1874 the *Engineer* reported that a Co-operative Gunlock Factory had opened in Darlaston. At the end of the same month it reported 'the success of the gun lock factory in Darlaston is now most doubtful.' In April 1875 further light on the Co-operative was shed by the *Labour Press*. A meeting of the shareholders of the Darlaston Lock Filers' Co-operative Association had been held. These shareholders were mainly the various societies of the Walsall Trades Council and the treasurer was Richard Juggins, at that time also secretary of the Amalgamated Nut & Bolt Workers' Union, so the finances at least were in capable hands. Juggins told the meeting that the Co-operative had a share capital of £225, but a deficit of £82. It had almost been decided to close the Co-operative, he said, but finally agreed to carry on for a further quarter. The position did not improve, however, and in July 1875 it was wound up. The *Labour Press* report stated that the present quarter had not been satisfactory and 'The men were not sufficiently educated to appreciate the benefits of Co-operation. They had orders in hand, but could not get the men to work for them.'

Brick making was another low-paid industry notorious for the heavy loads carried by women. A South Staffordshire Co-operative Brickworks Industrial Society was set up probably in the decade 1863-73. Nothing is known of it, however, apart from its registration.

Also interested in Co-operation were the glass makers whose prosperity largely depended on their being able to limit the amount of labour in the trade. To erect and maintain a full scale glass works, in contrast to the smaller glasshouses known as 'cribs', would have required much greater capital than lock or nail co-operatives. This the union and its members were in a position to provide. A Stourbridge and Wordsley Industrial and Provident Glass Manufacturing Society Ltd. was registered with the number 1125 which suggests a date between 1863 and 1873. Nothing is known of its activities. It was in the depths of the Depression in the mid-1880s that much discussion regarding the desirability of Co-operation was carried on in the pages of the *Flint Glassmakers' Magazine* and the Socialist implications of such activity aired. A limiting factor counselling caution was an existing Co-operative Bottle Works at Castleford in Yorkshire. At the end of the 1880s this Co-operative collapsed. 'We cannot compete with the masters. If we did it would mean lower wages.' It seems clear that it was difficult to find dedicated Co-operators who were prepared to make sacrifices while the business was being developed. The final deficit of the Bottle Works was £584 and nothing more was done about Co-operation.

Requiring even greater capital was entry into ironmaking. Yet a Wolverhampton Co-operative Iron Manufacturing Industrial Society Ltd. number 703 was registered, again suggesting a date during the Great Expansion. Nothing more is known of this Co-operative, however. Another Co-operative was the Cradley Sheet Iron Workers first noticed in the Congress Report of 1892 as Lye and changed in 1894 to Cradley Sheet Iron Workers. It existed until 1902 when it had fourteen members, a capital of £1,000 and a turnover of £11,000.

Industrial co-operation impinged upon ordinary business life in other ways. For instance, in November 1873 the *Engineer* reported a statement made in London that the Earl of Dudley was selling some coal to Co-operatives at 18/-d. per ton when the current price was 23/-d. The paper doubted the accuracy of the report 'since there was no need to reduce the price as all staple trades were well employed.' Another example was a 'stormy' meeting in November 1876 of members of the Leeds Co-operative Society which had invested the enormous sum of £18,000 in the Tipton Green Colliery. It was said to have been solid coal and in such a case would have proved a very profitable investment. But alas, they were not the first investors to be sold a pup, for the colliery had already been worked at least three times!

To end this section on industrial co-operation, however, we will take two cases which proved to be among the most successful, not only in the Black Country, but throughout Britain.

The first is the Dudley Bucket and Fender Co-operative Society Ltd. The salvation of this Co-operative was that, from the beginning, it sold most of its goods to the Co-operative Wholesale Society and not to the general trade and it was eventually absorbed into the other manufacturing interests of the CWS. It began its operations in April 1888 at the end of the second trough of the Great Depression. Its timing was dictated by the fact that it followed a previous industrial co-operative in Dudley called the Dudley Productive Company also producing galvanised goods, which failed in November 1887. The hostility of the general trade to co-operatives can be judged from the statement that the new Co-operative 'experienced great difficulty in removing the prejudice found in the co-operative movement against us, which was chiefly caused by the failure of the former society, as managers of furnishing departments were afraid we should follow suit, and then they would be compelled to obtain their goods from the old firms they had traded with before...'

The first eight months trading resulted in a loss of £853, but in 1889 turnover increased to £4,036; the loss was wiped out, arrears of interest paid and a bonus given to the workers. By 1890 the Co-operative had 16 members with a capital of £758 and a turnover of £5499.

In 1893 this Co-operative adopted the system which best suited the general movement of dividing profits between their customers, their workers and investment in the business. They also installed gas and electrical plant in place of steam. By 1905 turnover was nearly £23,000 and net profit £2,189 divided in the proportions of 32½ per cent to customers, a 25 per cent bonus to workers and the remainder ploughed back into the business. 'Demand for our products compelled us to purchase adjoining property to enlarge our works which are second to none in the town and district. At this time 95 per cent of trade was done with the co-operative movement ... as there exists bitter opposition to us by private traders; but whenever we can (with safety) supply the outside market, we do so.' In 1905 the Co-operative had 167 members including 89 co-operative societies, 'some of which are among the largest distributive societies in England.' Share capital had increased ten-fold from 1893 and was then £7766. Commencing with five workers the Co-operative then had 136, 'Preference is given to trade unionists and trade union rates of pay are paid to all our employees.' This represents a quite extraordinary rate of growth over fifteen years in the face of local business hostility even granted that these were on the whole years of expansion for the economy as a whole.

The Society was fully integrated into the general co-operative movement, sponsoring educational conferences and assisting local consumer co-operatives. It sent delegates to the annual Co-operative Union Congress and always had a display at the exhibition at each Congress where productive co-operatives displayed their wares and invited further business from consumer societies.

The Society continued to prosper and its success attracted the attention of the CWS. The Midland section of the 1909 annual Congress reported that 'The Dudley Bucket and Fender Co-operative Society, one of the most successful productive societies in the movement has now become part of the Co-operative Wholesale Society'.

The second, and even more successful productive co-operative in the Black Country was the Walsall Locks and Cartgear Society which existed for 113 years and eventually fell victim to Thatcher's de-industrialisation of the 1980s.

As with Wolverhampton Lock Co-operative, Walsall Locks originated with a strike and the assistance of the local Trades Council. The Walsall strike, however, occurred in 1872 at the height of the great boom. Towards the end of the year an increase in wages was requested from the masters. This was refused and the men were locked out. By December, £150 had been collected and distributed to those locked out. At the Trades Council meeting that month George Harrison pointed out that such a sum would have sufficed to set up their own workshops in which workers could have well paid and secure employment. The suggestion was acted upon and at the February 1873 meeting Sam Welsh, chairman of the Trades Council, announced that the locksmiths of Walsall had purchased tools and were ready to start work. The society commenced operations the next month.

The original capital was £83 and there were less than ten workers. George Harrison was appointed manager. By 1874 capital had risen to £119 and profits amounted to £75. An appeal for more capital was made to the Labour movement and so busy was the society at that time there was no time even for a proper stocktaking and an estimate had to suffice. Trade continued good and a new workshop was taken in 1876. Turnover in that year was £3457, profits £168, share and loan capital £185 and wages £1847. Net profit was therefore more than 90 per cent of capital, reflecting only palely, no doubt, the profit margins in general businesses during the great boom.

The society at this time seems to have had no connection with the general movement, but was gradually drawn into it. In 1876 it was invited to display its goods at an exhibition of the annual Co-operative Congress. From this time it sent delegates to the Congress and the annual exhibition became one of its most important contacts with the general movement.

The first year of depression for the co-partnership was 1878. It seems to have been met by both economies and greater efficiency. 1879 and 1880 were also bad years, but business improved somewhat thereafter. By 1884 new and larger premises were taken and negotiations for an agent in Holland commenced. This was also the year in which the co-partnership took an active part in initiating the Walsall Distributive Co-operative Society.

Bad trade then returned and provoked a crisis which could have changed the character of the Co-operative. This was the refusal to elect William Millerchip to membership of the society, despite the fact that he had been influential in its inauguration. The refusal arose from the desire of existing members to protect their own interests, particularly when profits were falling; for the more members there were, the less there was to distribute in bonus. In such cases, Co-operatives tended to degenerate into ordinary joint stock companies; according to Beatrice Webb, this was a general weakness of productive co-operatives.

However, the Walsall society took urgent steps to overcome this situation. Millerchip became a member in 1887 and from 1889, 'employees have been systematically made members on application, and every encouragement has been given for them to make such applications'. With the ending of the depression larger premises again became necessary and a loan was sought from the CWS.

The Society does not seem to have suffered from the same hostility as the Dudley Bucket and Fender. It was now sufficiently important to be consulted by the various Masters' Associations in the town and was regularly represented on the town's Employers' Association.

By 1890 share capital had risen to £776, more than four times that of 1876. Net profit was £712. In 1900 share capital was £2872 and by 1913 it was £7290.

In 1892 a new and large factory was opened in Neale Street owned by the Co-operative. Land on the site surplus to requirements was leased for house building with the significant condition that no licenced house be erected on the Society's land.

There now began a period of amalgamations with both other industrial co-operatives in the town and also non-co-operative firms. One result of this was the finalising of the name. In the early years it was at first known as The Walsall Lock and Keysmith Society Ltd; then the Co-operative Walsall Padlock Company and in 1887 it was named the Walsall Industrial Co-operative Lock and Hardware Manufacturing Society Ltd. This was mercifully shortened in 1888 to the Co-operative Padlock Society Ltd.

In 1894 the Society absorbed the Walsall Cart Gear, Chain and Hame Manufacturing Society. Nothing of the origins of this society is known, but in 1890 it had 24 members with a capital of £58 and a turnover of £346. In the same year the Midland Co-operative Locksmiths of Willenhall were absorbed; of this society nothing whatever is known. Further acquisitions followed and by 1914 the co-partnership had absorbed the two firms with which it had been in dispute in 1872 and which had given rise to the Co-operative.

Walsall Locks and Cartgear thus became the sole survivor of a group of firms which produced the cheapest sort of padlocks for export. In 1894 it made 2,500,000 padlocks. But the variety of productions quickly increased until it was making almost every kind of lock, probably the widest in the trade, as well as carrying on the distinct industry of hame, chain and cartgear. A most notable advance had been in the quality of the work undertaken and the firm boasted that no type of lock was considered too difficult for it to undertake.

Halstead, in accounting for the success of the co-operative, states that the industry had for one hundred years afforded scope for numerous and varied inventions. A good number of the patents protecting such inventions stood to the credit of the Walsall Society. The co-partnership had kept abreast of the improvements in design and in mechanical construction necessary to win and to hold the markets of the world. The strength of the firm was the ingenuity of operatives, staff and managerial workers, sometimes under the stimulus of special means adopted to encourage resourcefulness and inventiveness, Halstead concluded.

Certainly the co-operative had negotiated the double crisis of the Great Depression and the transition from an almost wholly domestic industry to one where home industry continued but was subordinate to large scale factory production. What is striking is the combination of entrepreneurial flair and a deep attachment to the co-operative principle. This is epitomised by the career of two of the pioneers; George Harrison who was an originator of the society, the first manager, and who served the enterprise for fifty years. The other was William Millerchip who became chairman of the directors in 1887, served until 1902 when he became secretary of the Lock and Keysmiths' Union, was one of the first Labour councillors in Walsall and a key figure in the distributive Co-operative society in Walsall.

The attachment to Co-operative principles is testified to by the welfare and educational activities of the society. In the 1890s a pension fund for workers with an annual contribution from the society of £25 was established. This contribution was increased to £100 in 1913. In 1888 an educational fund was started with a grant of £10 and the next year an Education Committee was formed. A reading room was established at the factory with newspapers, books, periodicals and writing materials. Workers were offered facilities to attend continuation schools and technical courses of instruction.

For some years classes met in the factory and qualified instructors were engaged to teach English, drawing, mathematics, music, needlework, hygiene and history. A debating society met weekly. By 1890-91 there were fifty borrowers of books from the factory library which consisted of fiction, history, biography, travel, and science.

Games and sports were also provided. A bowling green was provided for older co-partners, and a recreation ground for the summer months added to the recreation room. In 1907 the society became a member of the Workers' Educational Association. As the society expanded three work places were set up and in 1908 a Social Club was in existence at the Willenhall workshop. The purchase of a piano led on to the formation of a dancing class. Temperance meetings were allowed, 'for those who stood for social and personal sobriety,' and the temperance movement played some part in shaping the policy of the co-operative. A George Stanton Memorial Scholarship Fund was founded. The society interested itself in the week-end school movement and the conferences organised by the Co-operative Co-partnership Propaganda Committee. Christmas cheer was provided for widows and families of workers 'who had gone to their long rest.' There was considerable interest in gardening and horticultural activity which the Education Committee encouraged with prizes and exhibitions. Football, cricket and tennis clubs were set up. Annual excursions for the workers were also provided. Between 1891 and 1923 the society contributed £1,300 to charity.

Halstead, who had been secretary of the Co-operative Production Federation, to which Walsall Locks and Cartgear belonged, was no independent witness, but it is difficult to disagree with him when he ends his history of the first 50 years of the society by saying that its jubilee marked an epoch in working class history, at least locally. 'The co-partnership had measured itself with the largest organisers in their own trade and held their place against the largest firms in Germany and America in the markets of the world.' But this was not its most important achievement. The Co-operative was a successful realisation of a reconstructed industrial system which had at its centre the needs and aspirations of its worker and members, not the private profit of a few individuals.

The successful Co-operatives no doubt encouraged other people. Dudley Bucket & Fender was particularly active in promoting local conferences on the advantages of industrial co-operation. The only emulators in the town were the Dudley Mat Makers Co-operative which was active in 1902 and appeared in Congress reports until 1905. Walsall Locks and Cartgear seem to have been operating in a more sympathetic environment. In 1892 three Co-operatives were set up in Walsall. The first was the Horse Collar and Leather Co-operative which had 39 members and £138 capital in 1895. In 1900 the value of its stock in trade was £414, but its membership was down to 36. It disappeared before 1905. Co-operation was also alive in the horse furniture trade with the setting up of the Walsall Bridle & Bit Co-operative and an Awl Blade Co-operative in Bloxwich . Both of these were short-lived, but the reports we have of them from *Sadlery & Harness* illustrate very clearly both the possibilities and the pitfalls of creating industrial co-operatives. Both were closely connected with Walsall Trades Council and the Padlock Co-operative.

The Awl Blade Co-operative arose from a two year dispute at which an employer refused to pay the higher prices paid by other employers and also declined to submit the case to conciliation or arbitration. As a result, their workers had decided to take the advice of the Trades Council and set up a Co-operative. A meeting of the operatives had been held at which both George Harrison, manager of the Padlock Co-operative, and Sam Welsh who was chairman of the Trades Council and also vice-chairman of the Conciliation and Arbitration Board, were present. At the December 1891 Trades Council meeting it was reported that estimates had been made of the sums required to purchase tools and materials, an appeal for capital made to the societies affiliated to the Trades Council, and it was expected that the men would be at work by the commencement of the new year. No other reports of this Co-operative, however, have been found.

The Bit Makers' Co-operative was also set up in 1892. The February Trades Council meeting was told that the Bit Makers' Society had decided to take up £100 of shares in the Co-operative and most of the members had taken up one £1 share. As however, the men could not pay the £1 all at once they were seeking loans at 5 per cent interest from Trades Council affiliated societies. The president of the Bit Makers' Society said that he and 13 others from different firms had been sacked and because of the hostility of the employers it was essential to start the Co-operative as soon as possible. However, the March Trades Council meeting was told that the commencement of the Co-operative had been greatly retarded by the action of Councillor Hykin. Hykin was treasurer of the Bit Makers' Society and would not pay out the £100 that that Society had decided to take out in shares of the Co-operative. Hykin, who presumably was opposed to the project, was successfully prosecuted and this was taken, 'As a warning that no doubt will have a salutary effect upon those who think that they can with impunity play ducks and drakes with working men's money.' The Co-operative Works were opened the next day. The premises in Hatherton Street were described as 'extensive and commodious and admirably adapted for the purpose.' A progress report in June 1892 stated that there were more orders than the Co-operative could execute because the society had not enough funds to buy materials and give the necessary credit. The trade was hostile and men in any way sympathetic to the Co-operative were being dismissed. This report was made to a meeting in Birmingham initiated by the Walsall Trades Council which proposed the formation of a Midland Counties Trades Council Federation. One of the motives behind this proposal was a widening of the basis for the procuring of funds for Co-operatives and the meeting went on to discuss the position of the Bit Co-operative and their particular need for capital to buy an engine to work their machines. It was also suggested that in view of this greatly increased area for raising capital and the hostility of employers that all bit makers should be called out and given work by the Co-operative. Again, however, this is the last report found of this Co-operative.

Finally, in this section on Productive Co-operatives mention can be made of the Wolverhampton Trade Union Boot & Shoe Co-operative known from the 1895 Co-operative Congress report, but about which no other information has been found.

To conclude, it is clear that industrial co-operation as an alternative to capitalism exercised the minds of very large numbers of people in the Black Country in the nineteenth century. Many hundreds participated in the setting up of such societies both long and short-lived. The Black Country also produced two of the most successful societies in Britain. This is a far from negligible record in an area too often dismissed as backward.

Consumer Co-operatives to 1884

The setting up of Co-operatives proceeded in waves during the nineteenth century. G.J. Holyoake in his *History of Co-operation* estimates that there were about 300 societies in England and Scotland in the 1830s. Among them, with the date of their establishment, was Stourbridge 1830, Dudley between 1830 and 1833, Wolverhampton 1832, Walsall 1832 and Bilston 1838. There was also a very short-lived Chartist Co-operative store in Bilston in 1842. Nothing more is known of these societies.

A second wave came in the 1860s. The Wolverhampton Industrial Society was formed in 1860 supported by a bevy of local clergy. In its first year it opened a new store in Stafford Street and was said to be growing strongly, but reports in the *Wolverhampton Chronicle* cease after 1861, although it was known to exists until at least 1864. It was joined by the Working Men's Co-operative Provision Store at 109, Merridale Road in 1865. This was started by 15 working men connected with the tin-plate department of the Merridale Works who agreed to contribute 6d. each per week until about £10 was contributed and then buy groceries. The Society began operations in the back kitchen of a member's house, but business increased so rapidly that a house in Merridale Street had been converted into a shop. Again, this is the only report found of this Society.

Also in this second wave of Co-operatives a Stourbridge Co-operative Society was formed in December 1861. A Lye Provident & Industrial Society followed which was a co-operative store in which profits were retained and converted into insurance premiums. In July 1863 it charged its store keeper with embezzling its funds, one of the hazards of the times when working class funds were inadequately protected.

This second wave merged into a third wave of Co-operatives in which successful consumer co-operatives were finally established in most Black Country towns. The Rochdale Pioneers in 1844 are usually credited with finding the key that opened the door to successful co-operation by payment of a dividend to the customer on purchases made. But changes in the law were necessary before working people could safely entrust their savings to their self-help organisations. The first was the 'frugal investment' clause of the Friendly Societies Act of 1846 which gave limited legal status to co-operatives. For other legislation the Christian Socialists were largely responsible. This included the Industrial & Provident Societies Act of 1852 which gave the same protection to Co-operatives as that enjoyed by Friendly Societies, particularly with regard to the investing and protection of funds. However, this did not extend to funds used for the provision of education which was a particular concern of co-operators. This was put right by an Act of 1862 which allowed application of profits to 'any purpose permitted by the law.'

In this twilight zone between the wave of unsuccessful co-operatives in the 1860s and the establishment of successful societies at the end of the 1870s, various other societies are mentioned of which nothing more is known. There is a list of 39 Black Country societies registered with the Registrar of Friendly Societies apparently in the decade 1863-73 among which are the following: Bilston Ironworks Provident Co-operative Society, and Bilston Miners' Provident Co-operative Society; Brierley Hill Industrial Co-operative & Provident Society and Brierley Hill Perseverance Co-operative Society; Cradley Heath Co-operative Provident & Industrial Society, Cradley Heath Chainworkers' Co-operative & Industrial Society and Cradley Heath & District Co-operative Society; Darlaston Industrial Provident Co-operative Society; Dudley Equitable Pioneers' Industrial Society, Dudley Port Industrial Co-operative & Provident Society, Kates Hill Working Men's Industrial Co-operative Society and Netherton Equitable Industrial Co-operative Society; Oldbury & District Industrial Progressive Co-operative Society; Oldswinford Co-operative Industrial Provident Society; Smethwick Provident Co-operative Society and (most remarkably) Smethwick and District Knights of Labour Co-operative Society: Walsall Co-operative Industrial Society and Walsall Provident Co-operative & Industrial Society; Wednesbury Co-operative Industrial Society, Wednesbury Co-operative Society and Wednesbury Working Men's Industrial Society; West Bromwich and District New Industrial Co-operative Society; West Smethwick & Spon Lane Industrial Co-operative Society; Willenhall Co-operative Industrial Society; Wolverhampton Industrial Co-operative Society and Wolverhampton Progressive Industrial Co-operative Society; Wordsley Brettell Lane Working Men's Co-operative Society.

Most of the above societies we shall return to as we consider their subsequent history, but others, it would seem, were registered, but did not thereafter function, or did so only briefly. In addition to those societies which did register themselves, there were others which did not. These can only be traced if they are mentioned in histories of subsequently successful societies; of these we have some examples. Having made the point that there was a considerable amount of mid-century Black Country consumer co-operation we can proceed to examine the societies which successfully emerged in the period up to 1914.

A society with a long lineage was the Soho Society. The first attempt at co-operation in Smethwick was in 1830 when the Handsworth Economical Union and Provision Company was started by workmen at Boulton and Watt's factory. This society lasted for more than twenty five years, but its demise is not recorded. In 1861, five or six years later, the Smethwick Co-operative Society was established. Its sixth report showed that it had 80 members and its annual trade was £560. A more ambitious enterprise was the West Smethwick Society established in 1866. This operated for nearly 21 years. At one time it had over 1,000 members and sales exceeded £7,000 a year. It also followed its predecessors into liquidation. But as it did, further attempts at co-operation were put in hand. Nine members of the old society met to establish a new one. They were Messrs Darlington, Griffin, Harrison, Jones, Levick, Malcolm, McKay, Poole, and Felix Smith. A name much favoured for the new venture was the Phoenix Society, indicating its arising from the ashes of the old. This however was rejected as likely to be an embarrassment to the new society and a name relevant to its unique situation in the area of the world famous Soho Foundry of Boulton & Watt was chosen instead.

In June 1887 a public meeting was held in St. Matthew's schoolroom and the name of Soho Co-operative Society adopted. About 50 people enrolled as members and subscribed over £17 as share capital. A provisional committee was elected already experienced in co-operative procedures. They

169

divided themselves into three sub-committees – finance, purchasing, and visiting. A shop in High Park Road was taken on an annual tenancy of £19-19-0d. A manager was appointed at £1-5-0d. a week with a house rent and gas free and a bonus of 3d. in the pound of all sales over £50 a week. The secretary was instructed to order two dozen copies of *Co-operative News*.

Arrangements were made with private traders to supply members with bread and coal and this was extended to clothing, drapery and boots. A difference of opinion with regard to coal raised an extremely important principle. It was moved that coal be paid for on the Saturday after delivery. But an amendment which was lost requested that payment be made on ordering. The society therefore was granting credit and this had been the cause of the downfall of so many societies. The arrangements with private traders suggest the correction of a feature which also was a potent cause of failure of societies, namely a limited range of goods on offer.

At the first general meeting held six months after inauguration the president and secretary, Messrs McKay and Griffin were re-elected and Felix Smith made treasurer. It was agreed to apply for membership of the CWS.

In March 1888 sales were £44 a week and it was decided to institute a 'checking system' whereby committee members took it in turns to do a monthly stint checking the business procedures at the shop. A sub-committee formed about the same time to enquire into the '..most expeditious way of conducting our business', recommended in June 1889 that business be conducted through a managing sub-committee, whose duties and remuneration were set out at length. These proposals were accepted. But difficulties continued. In the course of eighteen months there were five different secretaries of the society. In 1888 McKay resigned as president and was succeeded by Felix Smith. In October 1890 there was a serious fire which threatened the existence of the society. However, temporary premises were taken at 23 High Park Road and appeals made to members for continued support. It was 'hoped' that their insurance would cover the disaster. Whether it did or not the Society survived and sales were up to £80 a week by 1891.

The first annual tea and public meeting took place in March 1891 and was so successful that it became a regular function for many years. In the same year the CWS was persuaded to forward patterns and samples of drapery goods to be displayed to members on dividend night. This facility was so successful that the sale of drapery was instituted every Friday evening above the shop from 6-30 to 9-20pm.

By this time, the society was firmly established. Its history after 1884 will be followed with that of other local societies. This is possible because from that year statistics become standardised in the annual Co-operative Union Congress Report.

Dudley Co-operative Society was the first to establish itself permanently in the Black Country. This was in 1872. We hear no more of the previous Dudley societies nor the Kate's Hill or Netherton co-operatives but the new Dudley Society began operations in its first shop in Salop Street in October 1872. The first week's takings were £27. Little was known about the Society even in 1906 when Frank Bruff wrote his History of Co-operation in Birmingham and District. Bruff highlighted the fact that the society faced a serious crisis from June 1892 when a deficiency of £18,271 was found in the funds. By December 1905 not only had £15,781 of the debt been redeemed, but dividends and interest totalling £60,000 had been paid and since June 1897 a dividend of 2/-d. in the pound paid to members and non-members. The survival of the society through the Great Depression was a notable achievement. Its development after 1890 will, as with other local societies, be followed through Congress reports.

Walsall Co-operative Society developed in the unique circumstances of close contact between an active local Trades Council and the successful productive co-operative, Walsall Locks and Cartgear. A spin-off from this is that there is a detailed history of co-operation in Walsall by Fred Hall. An early Walsall Co-operative Society was set up in July 1829, he tells us, at a meeting attended by William Pare the noted Birmingham Owenite along with other members of the Birmingham Society. A pamphlet setting out the aims of co-operation survived in Hall's time. It noted that the poverty and ruin which had overwhelmed the poor was then spreading to the middle classes. (This was written when the second of what I have called the three Long Depressions after the Napoleonic Wars 1815-22; 1826-33; 1839-43 was creating mass unemployment and starvation – GB) The only salvation was

Co-operation. In contrast to Competition which created envy, hatred and malice and had brought society to its existing dire state, Co-operation produced the kindliest feelings based on the precept 'Love thy Neighbour as Oneself.' Co-operation recognised that labour is the source of all wealth. The way forward was for men to combine to save 6d. per week each and when the fund was large enough articles of constant consumption such as food, candles, soap, etc. should be bought and sold to members at retail prices. Profits should then be added to the common stock until a shop could be opened. Selling only for ready money, profits must rapidly accumulate and within a short time members out of work could be employed in their own trades and a ready market through co-operation be found for their products.

> Nor will they stop there, they have another and still higher object in view, for the attainment of which these are only the means, a sort of ladder, whereby they hope to attain an eminence from whence they may look down upon the petty jealousies, the rivalry and continual struggle for wealth, for vain and empty honours and useless distinctions, which are so strongly characteristic of the individual system... When that capital is sufficiently accumulated each society will rent or purchase a quantity of land in an eligible and healthy situation, on part of which buildings will be erected as dwellings for their members, and at a convenient distance workshops and manufactories. Connected with the dwellings will be public buildings, such as dining halls, reading and lecture rooms, libraries and schools in which the children of the members will be educated...

This was the full utopian Owenite Socialist programme. Pares and his colleagues would be particularly concerned to spread co-operative ideals into the Black Country for it was in Birmingham that other gigantic Owenite schemes such as the Grand National Consolidated Trades Union and the Labour Exchanges to which people brought the products of their labour and exchanged them for other goods through the medium of Labour Notes prospered temporarily. Walsall was not a large enough town to support such grandiose and unsustainable projects and the co-operative disappeared. Its legacy ten years later was attempts to establish in Walsall a branch of Owen's equally grandiose Association of all Classes of all Nations, which nationally supported the one Owenite colony established in England, Harmony Hall in Hampshire But in the Black Country members were more concerned to promote atheism, challenge the veracity of the bible and harry the 'religionists', particularly of the Church of England who were part of the established order repressing working people.

The next society known is one established in 1861 or 1862. In June 1862 the *Co-operator* stated that it had a membership of 166 and capital of £140. Four years later it was wound up. The secretary, H. Wood, explained:

> I have struggled hard for four or five years in the noble cause but at last I was obliged to give way, as nearly all the work lay on myself or my wife... the members would not support their own shop and preferred losing their own shares and those of other people than purchase... Yet it might have pulled through but that we gave credit and never had our capital available for trade purposes...

It seems clear that this society perished because there was an insufficient number of dedicated co-operators and also from the granting of credit.

The third co-operative established was the Walsall Provident Co-operative Industrial Society registered in September 1874. The proposal to start a co-operative led to correspondence in the *Walsall Observer*, when 'Live and let Live' deplored the suggestion, and pointed to the failure of previous societies. The nom-de-plume suggests that the writer was a private trader or shopkeeper. In February 1875 the society held its first tea meeting attended by 100 people. Mr Perry, the secretary gave a progress report on the society whose store was at 77 Dudley Road. A quarterly meeting in January 1876 chaired by the president S. Stringer heard that business was increasing, 5 per cent interest had been paid on share capital, a dividend of 1/3d. in the pound declared, and a 'handsome sum' carried to the reserve fund. But press reports later in the year indicated problems. There was a dispute between the manager of the society and its committee leading to a charge that the manager had withheld property belonging to the society. The society continued to exist until 1879, but thereafter does not appear in Congress Reports. It was, without doubt, yet another victim of the Great Depression, for both Samuel Welsh and George Harrison were among the 'few advanced men' who, Millerchip later wrote, were connected with the project and who so successfully managed co-operation in Walsall in the next decade.

The ultimately successful co-operative was, as we know, sponsored by the Walsall Lock Co-operative. The inaugural meeting was held in August 1885 with George Harrison, manager of the Lock Co-operative, D. Bailey manager of the Kidderminster Co-operative Society, E.L. Griffiths district secretary of the Midlands section of the Co-operative Union, and H. Blakemore of the Stafford Co-operative Society present. George Harrison moved the motion to establish a co-operative provision store in the town and raise the capital by means of £1 shares. Harrison's proposal that A. Cooper be elected secretary was also accepted. A committee was then elected consisting of G. Harrison, W.J. Dolphin, T. Millerchip, T. Anson, R. Webster, W. Anson Snr. J. Stanton, J. Newman, T. Rounds, R. Bonser. Sam Welsh was later proposed, who after protestations of having too little time, consented to join. Thus both the Lock Co-operative and the trade union movement were strongly represented on this first committee. The first known balance sheet, for the quarter ending March 1887, for what was by then known as the Walsall & District New Co-operative Society Ltd. showed sales at £130 and share capital £37. The store was at 226 Stafford Street.

The twelfth quarterly report showed that Sam Welsh was president, George Harrison treasurer, and H. Bland secretary. Sales were nearly £319 and share capital £111. The society grew slowly, but by 1890 was firmly established. Its sales were then nearly £2000 for the year with a net profit of £192. There were 150 members with a capital of £247. The average dividend for the year was 1/7½d.

Wednesbury Co-operative Society was important for its influence on neighbouring towns, The anonymous author of the centenary article on the West Midlands Co-operative Society in the *Wolverhampton Adnews* of 5 June 1986 states that a Wednesbury Old Society existed from 1887 to 1912 joined by the Wednesbury New Society 1895 until it merged with Walsall in 1925 and together with the Soho Society they serviced West Bromwich and Darlaston. Bruff in the 1906 Handbook deals only with the New Society stating that after the 'many failures that preceded its inauguration', it was founded in May 1895, 'By a few local enthusiasts, ably assisted by the Propaganda Committee of the Union and the CWS..' The faithful numbered but 87 and their capital of £70, although not sufficient to overwhelm one by its magnitude, was thought enough to make at any rate an unpretentious beginning. The first week's takings were £22, but by 1905 turnover was £15,000 and membership 700.

Bruff went on to say, 'Only those who know the poverty of the district the society serves can well appreciate the ungrudging labour which must have been given to realise the present results...'

Bruff has some significant things to say about the trading policy of the Wednesbury Society:

The Society does not believe in selling sweated goods, and to ensure that none shall creep in, purchases no less than 97 per cent of its goods from co-operative sources.

Wolverhampton Co-operative Society. The origins of this society are dealt with both by Bruff and an anonymous history recently unearthed by the indefatigable Ned Williams. Bruff tells us that the society commenced business in 1886 and the first year's sales were £1,313. By 1900 sales were nearly £20,000. In 1906 there were fine central premises in Stafford Street comprising a large hall with seating accommodation for 500, offices, restaurant, grocery, provisions, boots, hardware and drapery shops. At the rear were warehouses, a bootmaking and repairing shop and a bakery. These premises cost £4,000 and were owned by the society. They were lighted throughout by electricity. There were six other branches in the town, four of which owned freehold premises. The bakery produced 6,500 4lb loaves per week. Share capital was £11,631 and the reserve fund £366. Cash investment in other societies was £3,172. The society devoted 2½ per cent of its net profit to education.

The anonymous history of the Society to 1931 states that preliminary meetings to consider a society were held in 1885 in the caretaker's house adjoining St. George's Hall. The Society was registered in August 1885 as the Wolverhampton New Co-operative Society; this was changed in 1890 to the Wolverhampton & District Co-operative Society Ltd. The original premises were in Cleveland Road. The Society commenced business in June 1885 and the first balance sheet for the quarter July to September 1885 showed sales £34-10-1d, share capital £12-15-6d., profits £2-15-9d. and members 39. Beginnings could hardly have been smaller. Between September 1885 and March 1886 the society transferred its business to 15 Snow Hill. For the quarter to March 1886 sales had increased to £282 and the society was on firm ground. At the end of that year it had 159 members and a dividend of

1/2d. in the pound was paid. The first secretary of the Society was E. Bowyer and the first chairman F.H. Hill. In 1886 S.B. Ramsbottom was appointed salesman, presumably equivalent to manager. The first Board of Management was also elected in 1886 and consisted of E. Bowyer (secretary), H. Burrows (treasurer), Messrs Ashmore, Bailey, Drinkwater, Hossack, Hill (chairman), Kirtley, Martin, Scott, Solari, Thomas and Watson.

Continuing to make progress the Society moved again at the end of September 1887 to Bilston Street. Quarterly meetings at that time were held in St. George's Schools. Progress continued so that it was soon apparent that the Bilston Street premises were inadequate and the Society moved again to Cleveland Road where it traded between 1889 and 1891. These premises were not only sufficient for a shop, but also for a small warehouse, and also had a good cart entrance, necessary as the Society had acquired a horse and cart. Whilst at Cleveland Road sales doubled.

The most important development came in 1891 when a plot of land in Stafford Street (then part of the notorious area known as Caribbee Island) was purchased for £744 and the central premises opened on December 11th. the same year. The premises, when opened, consisted of grocery and boot departments, bakery, offices and hall which had expanded by 1906 to the premises described by Bruff.

From 1897 branches were opened elsewhere in the town. The first was a branch in Whitmore Reans in Hunter Street.

In January 1899 Tom Frost, the ubiquitous Labour activist who became the first Labour mayor of Wolverhampton, was elected president in place of E. Hope who had served the society for the preceding ten years.

About this time the Willenhall Co-operative Society was in financial difficulties and the question of the Wolverhampton Society opening a branch there was raised. But it was decided that it was not an opportune time.

In July 1900 a second branch was opened with a shop built on land acquired in Owen Road. The next year a site was acquired on Dudley Road. This adjoined the 'British Queen' and extended to the corner of Ranelagh Road. When purchased there was a disused Wesleyan chapel and outbuildings, also several cottages on the site. Part of the chapel was converted into No.3. branch and later became a branch confectionary shop. The upper part of the chapel was used as a flour room.

Another noteworthy acquisition was the taking over of the Whitmore Reans Coal Society in which many co-operators were interested. It was purchased at 19/6d. for each £1 share. This Coal Society is one which we should like to know more about as it was the only such society in the midlands.. Presumably it bought coal for its members at wholesale prices. Transport costs would probably have precluded it purchasing its coal from the Coal Mining Co-operatives operating at this time, and its coal would be bought in locally.

1902 was the year of the great Industrial Exhibition in West Park. Guarantors were sought for the event and the Society underwrote £100. Unfortunately, although as a spectacle and educationally it was a success, the abnormally wet weather led to financial losses and the Society had to find £95 of its guarantee. The local society had persuaded the CWS to take a stand at the exhibition and members of the local society had attended to publicise the Wolverhampton Co-operative, so the financial loss was in some measure compensated for. Also in 1902 the Bakery in Dudley Road was erected and equipped. The opening ceremony was performed on December 4th. by W. Colley, at that time chairman of the Bakery Committee, who served the society for 28 years.

In 1903 a system of delivering coal in 1cwt bags was adopted. This had not previously been done, apparently, but became general in the trade.

By 1906, when the Society reached its majority, sales had risen to £31,597 and the membership was 2,038. Besides the block of shops in Stafford Street, six branches had been opened 'with varying success.'

At the end of 1907 Tom Frost resigned after nine years as president. He had carried out his duties 'with marked ability and success', and was thanked by members and management for his 'splendid services.' His successor was elected the following year. He was A. Fullwood, who retained the post into the 1930s.

In 1910 it was decided to adopt the Collective Life Assurance Scheme promoted by the Co-operative Insurance Society. This remained in place until the adoption of the Society's own Death

Benefit Scheme in 1916. Also in that year the Society promoted a successful exhibition at the Drill Hall during which 150 new members were enrolled.

1912 saw the first of the Society's excursions – to Yarmouth. A train was booked and 300 members and friends enjoyed themselves. It was also the year of Lloyd George's National Insurance Act and the CWS formed an approved section with the local society acting as agents.

The next year was a quiet one, the most notable event being the formation of the Midland Convalescent Fund instituted with a large grant from the CWS in its jubilee year. Many Wolverhampton members availed themselves of this facility.

1914 opened successfully and gave promise of being one of the best years of the Society when catastrophe struck with the Great War.

Other societies before 1884

In the new upsurge of co-operation in the early 1870s we learn from the early co-operative journal *The Reasoner* in April 1871 of two Black Country co-operatives. The first was the West Smethwick Society. This, as we know, was set up in 1866, remained in existence for 21 years and was almost immediately replaced by the Soho society which established itself permanently. Smethwick might well contest with Dudley, therefore, first place in the Black Country for permanent co-operation. In 1870, we learn, the West Smethwick Society had 150 members; its grocery sales were £1593; butchery sales £253; shoes and clogs £71. Its share capital was £634 and it paid a dividend of 2/-d. in the pound. There was also a Willenhall Co-operative Society with 110 members, grocery sales even greater than Smethwick at £1777, a share capital of £576, paying a dividend of 1/6d. A notable feature of both of these societies is the relatively large share capital that they had accumulated. G.D.H. Cole wrote that some societies in prosperous periods had more capital than they knew what to do with. While this may not have been quite the case with these two Black Country co-operatives it is an indication both of the propensity to save of the more affluent working people who were the main customers of the co-operatives and also the availability of capital for expansion..

A *Labour Press* report of November 1876 gave details of the Bilston and Ettingshall Co-operative Society. At a tea party attended by 210 people at the Temperance Hall, Broad Street, followed by a meeting, the president, John Harper, gave a history of the society. In 1874 a few railwaymen met at a lodge meeting and four of them decided to start a society in Bilston. On the following Monday some gentlemen in Ettingshall asked why not a co-operative there? Fifteen working men then met to decide whether the co-operative should be in Bilston or Ettingshall. Apparently they decided that it should be a joint society. About 25 people contributed and £70 was spent on fitting out a shop. Smethwick friends helped with price lists etc. and a gentleman offered a £100 loan to buy stock. The society had grown until in 1876 it paid a 5 per cent dividend on a capital of £481. The times were not propitious, however and the society perished soon after, during the Great Depression.

A last report, from the *Labour Press* of June 1877, when the Depression was biting hard tells of more difficult times and makes no mention of Bilston. A midlands conference of co-operators was arranged in Wolverhampton by the Central Co-operative Board. Delegates attended from the counties of Staffs, Warwick, Derby, Leicester etc. Mainwaring of West Smethwick co-operative was in the chair. Thomas Jones, the secretary, gave a history of the Walsall Lockmakers which contained important details of the distribution of their income. Bailey of Smethwick, however read a paper on the Failure of Co-operatives in South Staffs. This he attributed to ignorance of co-operative principles and 'insufficient capacity.' This I take to be lack of a variety of goods, for he goes on to say that travellers of firms 'feared to call on Co-operatives' in case this offended other customers. The bright spot of the conference seems to have been the choice of Wolverhampton as the venue. 'The benefits of a Co-operative store in Wolverhampton are being talked about', the report ended. This gives us a first mention of a co-operative society in Wolverhampton in the 1870s.

Consumer Co-operation 1884-1914

From 1884 there is a continuous statistical record of all co-operatives in the report of each annual Co-operative Union Congress. By this time, the midlands had been divided into districts within which the

Birmingham and Stafford districts contained all the Co-operatives in the Black Country. We will begin with the situation existing in 1884 and then follow progress through five yearly periods.

Name of Society	Members	Share Capital (£s)	Goods Sold (£s)
West Smethwick	1024	3500	17782
Lye	473	3430	12084
Halesowen & Hasbury	405	2083	11800
Dudley	387	873	5966
Tipton	186	1869	3478
Cradley Heath	143	2372	2756
Bilston & Ettingshall	106	255	1800
Upper Gornal	55	86	3588

There are a number of surprises in this list. The first is the appearance of societies not previously traced – Lye, Halesowen & Hasbury, Tipton, and Upper Gornal. The second surprise is that all eight societies are in the 'villages' of the Black Country except the big town Dudley. The societies have been listed in order of members and, as might be expected, this correlates with sales except for Upper Gornal. With regard to capital, five of the societies seem to be reasonably well financed; share per member in these societies varied from over £7 per member in Lye up to £10 in Tipton and an incredible £16 in Cradley Heath. This last figure is for the most depressed area of the Black Country and adjacent Lye was hardly less so. The worst capitalised society was Upper Gornal, but its ratio of sales to capital was higher than any other society!

The Birmingham division report for 1884 stated that Dudley society was thriving and had opened a branch at Dudley Port. But Upper Gornal appeared to be declining. The Stafford district report stated that it was the third year of its existence and its members had visited other areas taking with them the *Co-operative News* and Central Board Tracts, but had difficulty in finding rooms in which to hold meetings to form further societies, because of the cost. It had however, met with Wolverhampton Trades Council and other friends to arrange a meeting which had led to the setting up of a committee in Wolverhampton.

In the period 1885 to 1890 co-operation proceeded steadily. Societies increased from eight to twelve, but the largest society in the Black Country, West Smethwick, disappeared in 1887 due largely to faulty accounting procedures it seems. It was replaced in the same year by Soho. However the Soho turnover of £4,385 in 1890 could not replace that of more than £16,000 of West Smethwick society in its last year of trading; another Society, Smethwick & District, was formed in 1890 but its first year's turnover was only £374. Despite their difficulties Upper Gornal and Bilston societies struggled on, although the turnover of both fell. Lye was another society which lost members and capital and suffered a reduced turnover; but its turnover of nearly £10,000 made it the second largest society in the area. Cradley Heath society disappeared in 1886, but this was offset by the growth of Dudley which opened branches at Woodside and Kates Hill and then extended to Cradley. Dudley's advance was phenomenal its sales rising from under £6000 in 1884 to over £82,000 in 1890. Halesowen & Hasbury was the third most successful society with a turn-over of nearly £14,000. It was joined in 1887 by the Halesowen & District Prudential Society whose turnover was only £3,395 in 1890. Tipton was another success almost doubling its turnover to £6,531. Of the other new societies, Wednesbury was a weakling with a turnover of only £262. Walsall New was a little better with just under £2000. Wolverhampton was girding its loins at over £6000.

The annual reports of the two divisions told of regular attempts to develop new societies and conferences to educate members in co-operative principles and practices. In 1886 the Birmingham divisional secretary, William Cope, sent a questionnaire to his fourteen societies on their educational facilities. Of those in the Black Country, only West Smethwick had an education committee and committed some part of the society's profits to education. Halesowen granted £2-2-0d. per annum for schools. Only Smethwick and Wolverhampton sold *Co-operative News*. Walsall pleaded that it was a young society and Wolverhampton might have said the same, but there was no excuse for Halesown and Tipton. It would seem that the loss of the West Smethwick society was not only a blow against co-operative trading, but also against co-operative educational principles.

At least one of the regular series of meetings and conferences held by each district seems to have borne fruit when a productive society of chain makers was set up in 1887 and a meeting at nearby Darlaston was held to discuss setting up a nut and bolt co-operative, although neither seem to have subsequently developed. But a Society was set up at Darlaston in 1889 according to the 1892 Congress report. But whether this was a productive or consumer co-op is not known.

A final noteworthy feature of the period is that the Knights of Labour started at least one co-operative society. There are two references to the Knights in the reports of the Birmingham district. The first was in 1889 when the secretary reported a society to which only those who were Knights of Labour could join. In 1890 a productive society at Cradley Heath was started by the Knights of Labour for the manufacture of buckets and sheet plate goods, but 'up to the present we cannot get any direct information as to how it is progressing,' the report states. Whether this was the same society or another one is not made clear. It is likely that this was the origin of the Lye Sheet Metal Iron Workers Co-operative (first noticed in 1892 and its name changed to Cradley in 1894) which existed until 1902.

The period 1891-95 was dominated by the difficulties of the largest co-operative, Dudley. Its phenomenal growth continued into 1891 when its turnover topped £100,000. Its sales were by then far greater than any society in the Birmingham and Stafford districts – twice as large as Kidderminster its nearest rival, and four times that of Birmingham. It was a bolt from the blue when the society failed to produce accounts for the 1892 annual statistical survey. The Birmingham District Report for the year said this:

> A great misfortune has overtaken the co-operative movement in the District, namely the Dudley Society to which the societies in the district were in the habit of looking to as a guiding star and worthy to be followed in all respects. Such a blow as that to our cause, so short a time after a similar case (presumably West Smethwick – GB), is a misfortune. But in the midst of our troubles we find that there are always amongst the ranks of co-operators men who will come forward and work for the grand principles of justice and unselfishness...

There was no mention of what these troubles were, but the *Co-operative News* of 30th July 1892 had the full story. A special members' meeting was told by the chairman, Isaiah Evans (who was none too kindly received) that the secretary, Mr Ball, had gone to Blackpool taking with him the keys to the safe and did not appear to be coming back. The safe was opened and the CWS contacted. They sent two auditors who examined the books and found various falsifications. The eventual deficiency was £18,271. The meeting was a stormy one and when the chairman was asked about the signing of blank cheques, he admitted that the committee 'had reposed unbounded confidence in Mr Ball.' As well they might, considering the results of the previous few years. Mr Mitchell, a representative of the CWS put the meeting in better temper by stating that if the present loss were put into a Suspense Account, the dividend halved and half future profits allocated to paying off the debt, the society could carry on, and in a few years would be as strong as ever.

The local Grocers' Protection Society thought this would be a good time to hold a meeting in Dudley and brought down a national speaker from Manchester to explain why co-operation could never succeed and why it produced more poverty than affluence. But of the 120 or so at the meeting about 100 were co-operators who met the speaker with derisory laughter and much interruption. When the speaker finished Isaiah Evans asked permission to go onto the platform and refute the statements made. As he walked down the hall, the meeting was hastily concluded and the Co-operators took the meeting over. Councillor W. Brooks (chairman of the Dudley Society) said amid applause, that the man who argued against co-operation was an enemy of the working classes. The meeting 'finally separated with almost unanimous expression of opinion in favour of co-operative principles.'

The accounts for 1893 show something of the scale of the disaster for the Dudley Society. Sales had been reduced by more than half down to £48,000 and the dividend slashed to 9¾d. Sales continued to fall, reaching a low of £40,000 in 1896. The members maintained faith with the society, however and the number of members fell only from 6,000 to 5,400, and share capital was maintained at about £15,400.

It might have been expected that neighbouring societies would have benefitted from Dudley's troubles, but this was not the case. The sickly Upper Gornal society with its £140 annual turnover disappeared in 1892; Lye, the third most successful society in 1885-90, disappeared before 1895. Of the two Halesowen societies, the Prudential was failing and disappeared in 1896 and the turnover of the more solid Halesowen & Hasbury Society fell from £14,000 in 1890 to under £9,000 in 1896.

Closures elsewhere were Bilston & Ettingshall in 1892 and Smethwick and District in 1896.

The other societies were, however, growing at various rates. Wednesbury picked up with sales rising from a ludicrous £6-8-0d annually for each of its 30 members in 1891 to £21-10-0d in 1894. Tipton sales rose from £6,531 in 1890 to £14,175 in 1896. Soho sales were virtually stagnant. Wolverhampton continued to grow from £6,000 in 1890 to £16,000 in 1894. Walsall sales jumped from £2,000 in 1890 to £3,000 in 1891 and £5,000 in 1895. Economically, the period was the tail end of the Great Depression, and general trade was bad for much of the time.

The last five years of the century was a period of better trade and employment, but fortunes varied. Two societies disappeared in 1896, one was the Halesowen and District Prudential and the other was the Smethwick and District Society. The poor situation with the Wednesbury society continued, although its sales more than doubled to a less than satisfactory £2,500 by 1900. Wednesbury co-operators, however, had had enough, and set up a new society in 1895. Sales of Wednesbury (New) were £2,000 in 1896 and tripled to £6,000 by 1900. Tipton sales declined to £12,000 and the Wolverhampton society stagnated, sales rising only £1,000.

There was vigorous growth elsewhere, however. Dudley's sales rose to £53,000, an increase of nearly one third, although this was still only half of the sales of its hey-day. Soho sales increased almost three fold to nearly £15,000 and Walsall sales rose 3½ times to £21,000.

Two attempts were made to set up new societies. In 1898 a Willenhall society was started in a town which had a previous co-operative tradition, but it was unsuccessful and the society had expired by 1900. A West Bromwich society was set up in 1900, but within four years it also failed.

Continuing with the outline of co-operative development up to 1914. The first five years of the twentieth century were years of good trade; 1900 a veritable *annus mirabilis*, the Boer War bringing prosperity to all trades. Walsall again led the way with sales increasing 3½ times to nearly £75,000. Wednesbury (New) sales more than doubled to nearly £15,000. Halesowen and Hasbury sales doubled to £20,000. Wednesbury (Old) almost doubled to £4,000 as did Soho to £37,500. In Wolverhampton however, there was only a small advance to £31,600, at Tipton a negligible rise and Dudley showed a decline in sales to almost £48,000.

The five years up to 1910 were years of depression, with dreadful unemployment from 1907 to 1909. Co-operative trade suffered accordingly. Dudley's sales declined to £46,000 in 1910 and Wednesbury (New) declined to £13,400. Tipton also declined to £10,000. Wednesbury (Old) showed a small advance to £4,500 but was losing members and capital. Halesowen & Hasbury showed a satisfactory rise to £26,000 as did Wolverhampton to £38,500. Walsall sales increased by 40 per cent and in this period cracked the £100,000 barrier to end in 1910 at nearly £116,000. Soho was the star performer in this period, however, sales nearly doubling to over £71,000.

The four years before World War One were years of economic advance and the Great Unrest. The local co-operatives benefitted from this and results in 1914 can best be expressed by the following table:

Society	Members	Capital	Sales	Dividend	Progress from 1910
Walsall	10,124	£67,015	£169,550	2/-d.	+ 47%
Soho	6,300	£32,610	£128,853	2/-d.	+ 80%
Wolverhampton	3,879	£33,313	£69,512	1/9¾d	Doubled
Dudley	6,816	£9,589	£59,259	2/-d.	+ 28%
Halesowen & Hasbury	1,472	£14,167	£35,126	-	+ 35%
Tipton	825	£5,849	£16,422	2/-d.	+ 58%
Wednesbury (New)	1,120	£7,076	£16,300	1/8½d	+ 22%

All societies (except Wednesbury (Old) which disappeared) grew at this time. Soho and Walsall benefitted particularly from expansion in the Wednesbury – West Bromwich area, and Walsall was also trading outside the Black Country. But with about 30,000 members and sales of less than £500,000 per annum, co-operation in the Black Country still lagged behind other parts of the country. In 1914 the national number of co-operators was over 3 million, so Black Country co-operators were 1 per cent of that total whereas Black Country people were about 2 per cent of the total UK population. On the other hand, the national average number of members per co-operative society in 1914 was 2,205 and four of our seven societies comfortably exceeded that number. Total national co-operative sales in 1914 were over £31 million and Black Country sales accounted for about 1½ per cent of that total.

Administration and Problems of Consumer Co-operatives to 1914

After 1900 the 'normal' co-operative dividend of the period came to be 2/-d. in the £ on purchases. In the 1880s it had tended to be lower and to fluctuate quite widely. For instance Lye society paid between 6d and 9d from 1884 until its demise in the early nineties. Soho's dividends began at 6d. in the later 1880s, by 1892 was 1/-d. and then rose steadily to 2/-d. Both Wednesbury (Old) and Tipton were extravagent societies in their early days. Wednesbury (Old) paid the highest dividend recorded in the Black Country of 2/9d. in 1887. Since the weekly purchases of its fifty members averaged only 1/6d. a week in that year it suggests that a small number of these members were controlling the committee and milking the society for their own benefit; but Wednesbury (Old) was a strange creature of which we should like to know more. Tipton seems to have paid more than 2/-d. through most of the 1880s and peaked at 2/8d. in 1892; it thereafter subsided to 2/-d. Dudley paid between 1/8d and 2/d. from 1884 until its disaster in 1892. Dropping to 9¾d. in 1893 it was 1/4d. in 1895 and back to 2/-d. in 1900 where it remained.

Soho, Walsall and Wolverhampton seem to have pursued responsible policies. Soho dividend ranged from 1/-d. to 1/8d. during the 1890s and by 1900 was 2-/d. at which it remained. The Walsall dividend ranged from 1/-d. to 1/8¾d in the 1880s and 1890s. It rose to 2/-d. in 1900 and remained at that rate. Wolverhampton was the one society that never reached a dividend of 2/-d. In 1886 it was 1/6d. It then fluctuated between 1/6d. and 1/3d. until 1894 when it rose to 1/9d. In 1902 dividend was 1/10d and in 1907 peaked at 1/10½d. In 1914 it was 1/9¾d.

The exception to the above figures was the years of heavy unemployment in 1905-07 when most dividends dropped below 2/-d.

Dividend policy is important in assessing the efficiency of societies. For private traders the key ratio is net profit to capital on which the dividend is paid. For co-operatives, however, the key ratio is net profit to sales, for it is on sales that the dividend is paid. The general co-operative profit/sales ratio was about 10 per cent (By examining five of the larger Black Country societies at ten yearly intervals I have established that profit/sales margins varied between 7.1 per cent and 13.2 per cent). With these margins a society paying 2/-d. in the £ dividend was thus distributing almost the whole of its annual yearly disposable income. This seems a rash policy; private traders would be ploughing back much of their profits into expansion. Because of the policy of paying out virtually all profit as dividend, reserve funds were always low. In 1890, just before the crash, the Dudley reserve fund was only £398. By 1914 when the reserves of both Walsall and Soho were over £3,000 these reserves would only have covered a fraction of the current dividend.

So we have now determined that neither profits nor reserves contributed very much to the expansion of Black Country co-operatives. What about capital? Here again was a vital distinction between private and co-operative capital. Private capital was permanent; co-operative capital was short-term and could be withdrawn at any time. Co-operative societies were thus in the position of building societies of today which borrow short and lend long.

Co-operatives, however, had much the same advantages as Building Societies today. Interest on Co-operative capital was invariably 5 per cent; the post office bank paid only 2½ per cent. The Co-operative society was therefore a natural home for working class savings, the dividend often being left to accumulate as capital. Only in the case of a panic would shareholders demand their capital. There is no record of this happening in the Black Country. As we have seen the disaster in Dudley led only to a small fall in share capital and with those societies that disappeared such as West Smethwick and

Lye there is no reason to believe that shareholders lost their money. Hence share capital could be used with reasonable safety as collateral for borrowings to expand. The co-operative movement was said to have 'more capital than it could use' at various times, and expansion usually came by loans from the Co-operative Bank, which had the security of the value of existing premises when they lent to established societies.

An indicator of the strength of a particular society was sometimes taken as the average amount of capital per member. For 1884 we have already seen the high holdings in the poorest parts of the Black Country such as Cradley Heath with nearly £17 per member and Lye £7. In 1890 Lye was the highest with more than £7 followed by Tipton which was down from £10 to £5. Other societies were between £1 and £2. By 1900 Halesowen & Hasbury was the highest with over £8 per member, followed by Tipton with £6 and Soho with £5. Halesowen & Hasbury retained the lead in 1910 with nearly £9 per member, but the larger societies were closing in with Wolverhampton at £8 and Walsall at £6. The lowest was Dudley with £2-10-0d. The overall Black Country average was just over £5 capital per member.

A quarterly report for December 1913 from the Walsall Society gives us a profile of the share holdings of 1,000 shareholders (presumably the share capital of other members were analysed in previous and subsequent reports):

Analysis of Shareholdings of Members 2001 to 3000

£	Number	Percentage
104-100	6	5.0%
99-50	8	5.0%
49-20	19	5.0%
19-10	17	5.0%
9-5	32	3.2%
4-2	133	13.3%
less than £2	785	78.5%

The maximum allowed by law for co-operative shareholdings was £200. No Walsall shareholding was more than £104 and the vast majority were either building up their share capital to £1 or holding an amount of less than £2. There is no reason to think that shareholdings in other Black Country societies would be much different. As we shall see, some societies took steps to limit the interest paid to shareholders who failed to purchase a minimum amount of goods each quarter.

A constant matter of concern was the amount of goods local societies purchased from the CWS. In theory, by cutting out the middle man, it would always be advantageous to purchase from the CWS. But the range of goods carried by the CWS was not infinite, local tastes and customs sometimes required local goods, and CWS goods were not always of the highest quality. Hence a society would lose trade if it did not cater for the tastes of its customers. For about seven years at the end of the century, the CWS statistical return requested figures for the amounts bought from Co-operative sources and goods from other sources. Societies had trouble with these figures and many did not give them. Figures for Black Country societies for 1900-01 show a wide variation, from Soho which bought 99 per cent of its goods from Co-operative sources to Dudley at 85 per cent, Walsall and Tipton at 76 per cent down to Halesowen & Hasbury at 38 per cent buying nearly two thirds of its goods from outside sources. From a Wolverhampton Society quarterly report of 1913 a full break down of goods showed that in drapery and outfitting 100 per cent of goods were bought from the CWS; for boots it was 92½ per cent and for hardware 89 per cent; for bakery and confectionary it was 71 per cent and for groceries only 67½ per cent. But groceries and bakery accounted for over 88 per cent of total turnover and the overall percentage of purchases from co-operative sources was about 70 per cent.

Education Committees

The first duty of a society was to have an Education Committee to spread the message of co-operation and also to contribute to charity, so the annual return always demanded a record of expenditure on these two items. Back in 1884 both West Smethwick (£13) and Bilston & Ettingshall (£3) contributed to education. Lye contributed only to charity, spending the large sum of £25 out of its £500 profits on this item. By 1890 the larger societies were developing, but of the nine, only Dudley (£21), Soho (£3) and Wolverhampton (£1) spent money on education and only Lye contributed to charity with the handsome sum of £49. By 1900 only Dudley and Tipton were not spending on education, although the former contributed £40 to charity. Walsall (£33) and Tipton (£30) were the biggest education spenders; most societies contributed to charity. By 1914 the position was much improved. The highest spender on education was Soho (£204) followed by Walsall (£190), Wolverhampton (£150)and Wednesbury (£58). Dudley was niggardly with £45. But neither Halesowen & Hasbury nor Tipton spent anything on education. Both Soho and Walsall were generous with charitable payments at over £80 each and only Halesowen & Hasbury contributed nothing. The charitable contributions were mainly to local hospitals. For instance, Walsall in 1913 donated £10 a year to the Walsall Cottage Hospital and 4 guineas each to three Birmingham hospitals and Lichfield Victoria Nursing Home. A donation to the Dublin Food Fund of 10 guineas in one quarter's accounts, however, suggests that some of the contributions recorded under this head might be political as well as charitable.

Education Committees worked closely with District Committees. The latter formulated policy for a number of co-operative societies and the local education committee implemented this policy at society level. Already by 1884 the two districts of No.5 Birmingham and No. 6 Stafford organised all Black Country co-operatives. We know more about the Districts because their reports appeared in the annual Congress report. The only Education Committee of which we have regular information is that of the Wolverhampton society, whose quarterly reports from 1909 include the activities of that Committee. But it must be assumed that educational activity sponsored by the Districts could only be successful if organised by local education committees.

Regular meetings and conferences were always a feature of the Districts' activities. For instance, in 1894 Stafford District had arranged a joint conference of Wolverhampton and Stafford societies at which there was a 'large attendance', as well as public meetings in Wolverhampton, Walsall and Willenhall. Conferences to publicise the virtues of productive co-operation were always a priority and sometimes, as in 1898 these were sponsored by Dudley Bucket or Walsall Cartgear. Another important theme was Co-operation and Trade Unionists, discussed in 1892. Other popular activities, we are told in the same year, were readings from novels, and courses of lectures on Health, Cookery and Dressmaking. In 1897 there was another conference on Co-operation and Trade Unions at Walsall, addressed by Millerchip, who was, of course, both. 'Goodly numbers' attended. 'Never was there a time when there was better feeling between them and us,' the report concludes. In 1898 J.F. Robson, the president of the Wednesbury society read a paper to a conference at Wednesbury on Loyalty to the Wholesale Society.

Details of the expansion of societies also appeared in the District reports. In 1898 Wednesbury, with a grant from the CWS, 'finished a block of buildings and have the finest provision shop in the town. Also a boot and drapery store and bakery house. There is a continual stream of customers all day long to the annoyance of their opponents.'

1900 brought comments on the 'unparalleled prosperity' of local industry and the emergence of a question which would become a key one – overlapping societies. In 1901 Birmingham District held a conference to discuss Mrs Llewelyn Davies' paper Co-operatives in Poor Neighbourhoods. This was a project of the Women's Guild and more will be heard of it. The Birmingham conference 'severely criticised' it. They objected to Co-operative Pawnshops and separate shops for the slums. A subsequent Stafford conference also mauled the women's proposals.

1902 brought a number of issues. The question of Co-operative Convalescent Homes was a 'chief topic'. Dudley Bucket sponsored a local conference on it. A resolution was passed of general approval but to wait for experience from Gilsland and Roden. Tea followed and a conducted tour of the works. Also in 1902 Halesowen and Hasbury society had decided to open a branch in Stourbridge after 'the District Committee had used its very best efforts to advocate the cause of Co-operation in that town.' The Birmingham District had also called a conference in West Bromwich 'where Brockhouse and others are earnestly attempting to encourage co-operation. As we know, this also was unsuccessful. In the same district, Birmingham Central co-operative failed. This was a medium sized society, but it could not be merged with the larger society because 'there was not sufficient to pay the creditors.' It was said to have been 'badly managed for years, and would not take advice.' The 1902 Education Acts also had ramifications within the co-operative movement. A conference was called in Wolverhampton on the Educational Programme of the Co-operative Union. It was necessary for the co-operatives to 'stir' owing to the 'present entangled state of the education laws.' Mrs Bridges Adams, secretary of the National Labour Education League spoke and 'an enthusiastic discussion followed.' Letters of apology were received from J. West B.A., B.Sc. of the Wolverhampton Higher Grade School and J.F. Robinson, clerk to the Wolverhampton School Board. This reflected the concern of the School Board, which was to be abolished and the fear that the Higher Grade School would be down graded. But in the absence of details of the Co-operative educational proposals or subsequent activities by the Wolverhampton society on this matter, we cannot judge the effectiveness of its intervention.

Renewed organised hostility to the Co-operative movement occurred at the turn of the century, but the 1903 report noted 'very satisfactory' reports from most societies and that they had not seen or heard of any Co-operative boycott. By 1904 the Free Trade v Tariffs controversy reached the local co-ops. A joint Birmingham-Stafford conference under the auspices of the Dudley Bucket and Fender Society after a paper by Councillor Tom Frost voted unanimously for free trade.

In 1905 it was reported that bankruptcy of the West Bromwich society had been avoided by its amalgamation with Wednesbury. By now districts were usually arranging four conferences a year. The first Birmingham conference had discussed 'Should there be Allowances for Retiring CWS Directors?' The general opinion was that it would be more to the point to have retiring allowances for CWS employees! The second was at Alcester on 'Small Holdings' because of 'great interest among local members in allotments or small holdings.' The third conference discussed 'Collective Life Assurance', and the fourth was the by then annual joint conference with Stafford district.

From 1906 Depression checked expansion and led to renewed conflict with private traders. Millerchip was sued for slandering the Clothing Manufacturers and heavy damages awarded against him. Societies were appealed to to help him pay these. Walsall and Cannock took the boundaries issue in hand the following year with a 'thorough discussion' on their spheres of influence. Walsall also opened a Training School for managers. A conference in Wolverhampton discussed another basic issue – Transfer of Members. A resolution was passed asking the CWS 'to take up' the question of transferring members and their share capital as 'many good members are lost for want of a recognised system of transfer.'

In 1907 Walsall moved into Lichfield when a small Lichfield society, started in 1904, was liquidated. The Birmingham report the next year noted with approval that the boundaries issue was being resolved by established societies opening branches in neighbouring areas instead of new societies being started; also the amalgamation of weak societies with stronger ones. Walsall progress, which also included the opening of the new central premises at a cost of £20,000, was celebrated and also the return of co-operation to Bilston. At the Temperance Hall, Wednesbury a conference had heard a paper by R. Micklewright of the local society on 'Why the Very Poor are not Co-operators and How to Help them.' Here again is the Women's Guild theme and the result was that 'No way was found of helping them.'

The 1910 report announced that Dudley was clear of debt, Councillor Millerchip had become Mayor of Walsall and the Walsall society had started a choir.

By 1911 the Great Unrest was beginning to be felt and a conference at Smethwick had discussed 'Is Co-operation Capable of Solving the Industrial Problem?' From this time, however, prosperity returned and subsequent reports deal mainly with progress of the societies. One other important issue was addressed, however. This was the question of credit. Again, this was a matter raised strongly by the Women's Guild and a local conference was held with the Women's Guild in 1911. In the same year the Walsall society took the bull by the horns and abolished credit dealing altogether. The next year it reported 'a good years's trade.' Because of the ending of credit it had been a test year and they had found that what had been lost by refusing credit had been made up with the cash when orders were placed, and also on deliveries.

Occasionally we get a glimpse of local Education Committees at work and from 1909 we have a complete record of the Wolverhampton committee from the quarterly reports of that society. The term education was interpreted widely. The committee took no responsibility for the training of employees in retail trade practice, nor committee members or ordinary members in co-operative principles. Rather were they propaganda or publicity committees attempting to convince the general public of the advantages of co-operation and also largely responsibility for the major publicity campaigns initiated by the society.

Such campaigns were always necessary when new premises or branches were opened. For instance, in December 1891, when new premises were opened in Wolverhampton, the mayor of Wolverhampton presided over the proceedings, apologies were received from the town's MPs and the Tory, Sir Alfred Hickman, proposed the toast of the Town and Trade of Wolverhampton. After six o'clock tea there were speeches followed by musical selections and then dancing from nine until 3 am. On the opening of the Willenhall branch in 1902 crowds of people witnessed a procession of waggonettes, brakes and vans through the principal streets of the town and the shop, decked with bunting and flags, was ceremoniously opened. The reality of the work behind such demonstrations is revealed from the opening of the Bilston branch in 1907 when we are told 'the whole district was worked up by Mr Griffiths (Co-operative Union), the employees, and all committees of the society, including the Women's Guild, who devoted several days to canvassing... every public hoarding and publication in the town contained some notification of the coming event.' On the opening day the usual procession and festivities took place. Even so, the branch was not successful and was closed by 1913.

The records of the Wolverhampton education committee after 1909 suggest something of a routine, punctuated by two important local annual events. The first was the Children's Sports Field Day. In 1909 this was held in a field in Park Lane and the Coseley Brass Band had been engaged. all Wolverhampton schools were to close at noon on 21st July to enable the children to take part and negotiations were proceeding with the county authorities for the same arrangements. Children were charged 2d. and adults 4d. of which 2d. was returned in refreshment. The children were organised by the local co-operative branches each given a different colour to distinguish them. On the day all were brought to the central co-operative premises and marched to the field. The 'track' events were mainly run as handicaps for boys over a range of ages. For instance, there was the 80 yards handicap for boys under 11, the 100 yard handicap for boys under 15 and a quarter mile handicap. There were also such events as egg-and-spoon races etc. Also included was a sack race for employees and committee members. 1,100 children and 400 adults attended this event in 1909 and the next year was pronounced 'even more successful.'

For some unrevealed reason the organisational feat of putting on such a large scale event was made even more stressful by holding it each year in a different field in various parts of the town. The 1912 sports were held 'in a field at the back of Oak Street.' In 1913 and 1914, however, they were held on the society's own premises on land at Goldthorn Road. The education committee decided in 1913 to inaugurate an essay competition offering separate prizes for boys and girls under 14 of 5/-d. and 2/6d. for the best essay on 'Impressions of our Children's Annual Field Day.' Unfortunately, there was only one entry and the competition had to be abandoned. The 1914 sports were recorded as 'a success in every respect' with numbers attending 'far in excess of any previous venture.' Perhaps the sports would have had a permanent home at Goldthorn Road if the war had not intervened.

The other yearly event organised by the education committee was the Annual Tea, Concert and Dance. It entailed considerable organisation for uncertain results. In 1910 it was pronounced 'not so successful,' but in 1913 it was 'the largest ever held,' and in 1914 when the event was limited to 300 it was 'a great success.'

The bread and butter of the education committee was the lectures they organised. Often these concerned CWS products that were in the news. For instance in 1909 Cocoa Lectures were arranged. At this time there was much public concern at the health hazard of adulterated cocoa beans and, of course, CWS products were noted for their purity. Similar lectures the same year were held on Soap and also Tobacco.

Lantern slides were the main 'visual aids' of the period, although moving pictures were developing. As early as 1906 a 'bioscope entertainment' was held at the Wolverhampton Co-operative Hall attended by nearly 500. Ned Williams records this as the first Co-operative cinematograph show in Wolverhampton. By 1910 regulations seem to have been tightened; for the Soap and Tobacco lectures there was cinematography at Willenhall, but this was not allowed in Wolverhampton which had 'illustrated songs' instead. The purpose of these lectures, it was said, was to educate the people in loyalty to CWS products.

From 1911 'tourist lectures' became popular with 'magic lantern' lectures on places such as Portsmouth and the Isle of Wight. These led on to talk of excursions which materialised in 1914 when a 300 seat train was organised to Scarborough.

The education committee moved outside the immediate area of the society. In 1912 lectures were organised at Codsall and Albrighton as well as Bilston, Bradmore and Central. 'Very satisfactory results in trade and members,' were reported. At the end of 1913 lectures were arranged at Whitmore Reans and Bushbury which were 'huge successes.' The committee believed that much of the progress of the society was due to these entertainments.

The committee also organised joint meetings such as one in 1910 when 40 people from the Education Committee, Women's Guild, Employees and Committee members met to discuss 'How to Improve Membership and Trade of the Society.'

Two other activities of the Education Committee deserve mention. The first is its role at Exhibitions. At the famous Wolverhampton Exhibition of 1902 which cost the Society most of its guarantee of £100 it participated in the 'notable movements' item when Freemasons, Oddfellows, Temperance and Trades took over a whole day to advertise their activities. Wolverhampton organised Co-operator's Day for the midlands and nearly 2,000 co-operators attended from Kidderminster, Birmingham and the Black Country. Each person who attended the events was presented with a souvenir of samples of CWS biscuits, cocoa and also an ash tray. In December 1910 it was the Wolverhampton Co-operative Exhibition organised by the CWS and the local society held n the Drill Hall. Exhibitions were promised for every day such as Spoon and Boot Polishing, Washing, Cake making and possibly a baby show. This in addition to the 'wonderful CWS working exhibits.' Lack of subsequent details from the education committee does not suggest that it was an overwhelming success.

The other initiative of the education committee resulted in a choir. This was first mentioned at the end of 1912 when it was said to be 'growing slowly.' In June 1913 the choir gave its first concert which was 'moderately attended.' In March 1914 it gave the final concert of its first season, but 'it was not well attended.' Presumably the choir became an early victim of the war.

The only other society for which records of an education committee have been found is that of Walsall for 1906 and also from 1913. By 1906 Walsall had the largest sales of any Black Country co-operative society at over £80,000 and it also had eleven branches throughout the Walsall area as well as its central premises in Stafford Street. The Educational Committee's report for the quarter ending March 1906 was its thirteenth, indicating that the committee had been formed in 1902; this was not until the society had been in existence for 15 years. Its activities were not extensive. The annual soiree at the town hall on New year's Day, 'did not receive the support it deserved, consequently showing an adverse balance.' A tea and concert in March 'proved to be a fairly successful meeting.' A bioscope entertainment and lecture also in March was free but 'it was not taken advantage of as much as it might have been... the bioscope being a treat in itself.' The balance sheet for the quarter showed that the committee had spent £76. The main items of expenditure were the ill-fated soiree £14, Wheatsheaf, the paper that was distributed free also £14, and Co-operative News £13. The expenditure was mainly funded by a generous grant of £50 from the society. The education committee of thirteen is notable for the inclusion of no less than five women reflecting, no doubt, the activity of the Women's Guild. The committee was also responsible for a choir.

By 1913 when regular quarterly reports have been found the society had grown. Its sales were more than £130,000. It had 16 branches and had spread to Sutton Coldfield and Lichfield. The main activity of the education committee was its children's classes on Co-operation. It had also held a series of propaganda meetings throughout Walsall which 'have been well attended and in every way were considered most successful.' It had also arranged a smoking concert for men only at which Mr J. Millington of Birmingham gave a 'forceful address' and a decision was taken to try to form a Men's Guild. The committee now included four women, of whom two, Mrs Haynes and Mrs Hutchins, had been on the 1906 committee. Expenditure on education, however, had only been £61, the main items of which had been the propaganda meetings (£20), publications (£14) and the expenses of the choir (£8). The grant from the profits of the society had only been £30.

Subsequent education committee reports for 1914 show that Men's Guilds were started in both Walsall and Sutton Coldfield. These reports also show the centrality of children's activities to the Walsall education committee. Despite the uncertainty caused by the war and the recognition that 'we may have to undertake work of a different character,' it was resolved to re-start the children's classes after the summer break and a children's gala was arranged in connection with a Pelsall shop.

The Co-operative Women's Guild

There was no more significant development within the Co-operative movement than the emergence of the Women's Guild. It was the first large scale organisation of working class women and as such stands high as a pioneer organisation of women's liberation. Moreover it was overwhelmingly a married women's movement and it often met, not in the afternoon when much genteel ladies' charity activity occurred, but in the evenings when negotiations with and support from husbands regarding child care and domestic duties was necessary and often very painful.

Overwhelmingly it was the women who spent the family income at the local store. It was the main task of the Guild, therefore, to spread the gospel of co-operation among these women. Yet in doing so the women discovered their own disabilities. Some societies, for instance, refused to admit women as members; many more accepted only one member from each family and this, invariably, would be the husband. So another main task of the Guild became the fight for women representation on all the committees of local societies up to the management committee which ran the societies and on to the regional and national committees of the movement. That it should also involve itself in the developing movement for women's suffrage came as a matter of course.

But beyond this, the Guild became deeply and obstinately involved in issues that were often far from welcome to the male rulers of the movement. Three of these became particularly important in these early years up to 1914. One was the campaign to abolish credit, the ruin of so many early societies. Second was the question of wages and conditions of co-operative workers which began with the concern for the female employees. Third was its concern to take co-operation from the areas where the aristocratic minority of reasonably and well paid workers lived, into the poorer areas of the slums.

The Guild began in 1883 as the Women's League for the Spread of Co-operation with a self-effacing platform designed not to outrage the chauvinistic susceptibilities of male co-operators and others. In 1889, however, having established itself within these modest limits, it embarked under a new president, Margaret Llewelyn Davies, on its programme of radical and liberating policies.

Our earliest knowledge of the Black Country Women's Guild come from reports of the annual conferences of the Guild. These took place at the same time as the main Co-operative Congress and were printed with the main Congress report. From these we know that that there were Guild branches in Dudley and Soho by 1893, but by the following year both had broken up. The report for 1893 also showed that a new branch had been formed at Walsall and there was also a branch at Wolverhampton, but it had seceded and would have nothing to do with the regional organisation of the Guild. By 1895 there appeared to have been no Guild branches in the Black Country, but the following year the Soho Guild was re-formed. At this time, when a Birmingham & Stafford district of the Guilds had been formed and one could have expected more detailed reports of what the local Guilds were actually doing, the Guild decided to move its national conference to a different time and place from that of the main Congress. With this move, the procedure of reporting the activities of local Guilds district by district disappears, to the great discomfort of the historian.

So we have to turn for Guild reports to the only societies which have adequate histories and these are the same societies for which quarterly reports survive; namely Wolverhampton and Walsall.

The history of the Wolverhampton Society states that the Guild came into existence as a result of the opening of the central premises in Stafford Street in 1891. A body of about 40 lady members undertook to raise the money to furnish the new premises by 'waiting on' every member of the society. They were so successful that they had money left over to buy a flag which 'waved proudly from the turret' on opening day. Wishing to follow up this success, 'The management committee was taken into consultation, and as a result of their joint deliberations, a decision was made to form a branch of the Women's Co-operative Guild.' This was in the year when the Guild nationally reported 98 branches of which 40 had been started in 1891. Whether Wolverhampton was the first Women's Guild formed in the Black Country, or whether the pioneers were Dudley, Smethwick, or even Walsall, it was the first to have a continuous existence from 1891. Unfortunately the History gives no details of the Guild's activities and so it is from the quarterly reports from 1909 that we find a record of its activities.

The run-of-the-mill activities of the Guild were social and they paralleled many of the functions of the Education Committee. For instance, an Annual Tea, Concert and Dance was organised which usually seems to have attracted about 100 people. Other socials were also organised throughout the year. The Guild also had an annual outing. In 1909 it was to Habberley Valley where they had 'glorious weather'. In 1910 it was an excursion to the CWS headquarters in Manchester when about 20 members visited Crumpsall's Biscuit Works and various CWS departments in Balloon Street. The next year 100 people visited the Wrekin. In 1912 a most strenuous outing to Yarmouth began at 3-45am and got back to Wolverhampton at 3-15am the following day. The next year the outing to Portsmouth attracted 50 people.

Special to the Women's Guild were the children's parties, usually organised around the new year. The one on 5 January 1910, for instance, attracted 80 children who were regaled with songs, recitations, a violin duet and a harp solo; scarcely rivetting fare for modern children, but presumably it was found acceptable. At the 1912 party it was reported that there were less children than usual but it was 'a great success.' In 1913 when co-operative activity was booming, the party attracted 150 children.

The normal activity was a fortnightly meeting at 7-30 pm in the Stafford Street hall which included Guild business and usually a speaker. Sometimes it was a fellow member such in 1910 when 'Our President (Mrs Perry) spoke on 'What is a Good Dividend?' or in June of the same year when 'Mrs Drysdale gave an excellent report of the Congress.' Or it might be a speaker from the local society such as the president, Mr A. Fullwood, speaking on the Collective Life Assurance Plan in 1910. Or outside speakers such as Miss Gough, vice-president of Dudley Trades Council who in 1914 addressed members on the ambiguously entitled subject of 'Reasons why Women Should and Should not be given the Vote'.

With regard to the national campaigns of the Guild, there were local Guild meetings in 1910 on Cash & Credit. It is reasonable to believe that this had some effect on the local society, although the most substantial success was in Walsall where, as we know, the local society banned credit from 1911. With regard to the other main campaign to bring co-operation to the slum areas, this was to be done by organising People's Stores which sold goods at less than the normal retail price in small quantities which the poorest people could afford, but on which there would be no dividend. Other proposals were a Loan Department with personal property as security, to tide poor people over inevitable misfortune; this was immediately derided as Co-operative Pawnshops. These proposals were never popular with the general co-operative movement and it was only in Sunderland that an unsuccessful attempt was made to set up such stores. There is no record of Wolverhampton Guildswomen taking up these proposals, but we do know that both the Staffordshire District (to which Wolverhampton Co-op belonged) and also the Birmingham District (to which other Black Country societies belonged), held Conferences on the proposals and decisively rejected them; Guildswomen would have been present at these.

One wonders also whether the proposals were as relevant for Wolverhampton as for some other areas since the Co-operative headquarters from 1891 was in Stafford Street. This had formed part of the notorious slum area called Caribbee Island until the slums were demolished under the 1875 Improvement Scheme. This remodelled the town centre, but only dispersed the slum dwellers to the periphery of the town centre. Hence the slums were never far from Stafford Street. But the Wolverhampton society does not seem to have taken steps to meet the demands of the poorest people which were for low prices, small amounts, and credit in times of need. Only the Penny Bank, which was an important feature of the society, might be said to have been an aid to savings in good times which might prevent recourse to the pawnshop in bad times.

There can be no doubt that the more prosperous years which underpinned the Great Unrest were years of quickening political and social consciousness and this was reflected in Guild activity. Particularly in 1914 the Guild joined the general campaign for improved social services for mothers and babies. In the summer it was calling for a baby clinic in Wolverhampton and proper maternity care. Also a demand for a woman doctor as the Assistant School Medical Officer of Health. In the autumn it was concern over high infant mortality in the town.

The prosperity of the years 1910-14 was also responsible for decisive improvements in hours and wages of co-operative employees, for which the agitation of Guildswomen can take much of the credit. In the spring of 1913 the Wolverhampton society accepted the minimum wage demanded by the Amalgamated Union of Co-operative Employees. This considerably increased the expenses of the society and led to the demand for better support from the trade union movement. The Women's Guild responded by holding meetings around such topics as 'Should Co-operators and Trade Unionists Unite?'

Also, from the autumn of 1913 hours of work were cut by $4\frac{1}{2}$. All co-op shops thereafter opened at 8-30am and closed at 7pm on weekdays and 8pm on Saturdays. This at a time when other shops regularly opened until 8pm and 10 pm on Fridays and Saturdays.

The prosperous years also brought a growth in membership of the Guild. We have no absolute figures, but a report of a meeting in 1912 to hear a report from the Birmingham Convention (a regular event for the Guilds) stated that 43 members were present. The report went on to say that the Wolverhampton guild compared favourably with 'any in the movement.' Early in 1913 the Guild reported a further increase in numbers.

With regard to the campaign of the Guild to get members onto all committees of the movement, we know that they had up to five women on the Education Committee at various times, but by 1914 there was still no woman on the key management committee of the Wolverhampton society.

Despite the success of the Guild in Wolverhampton, it should be noted that only one branch of the Guild was sustained. There is one mention, when the branch shop was opened in Willenhall, of a Guild there 'doing well,' but there was no subsequent mention of it. This contrasts with the situation in Walsall where, although we know far less about overall activity, the women there could sustain a separate Guild for a number of the branches of the society.

So, turning to the Walsall Guild, we note first the comments of Fred Hall in his book of the Walsall society, *From Acorn to Oak*. He traces the first Guild to October 1895 when the Management Committee granted the use of a room for the Women's Guild. The next reference Hall finds is July 1899 when a meeting resolved to form a Womens' Guild. The same year saw the opening of the Bloxwich branch at which the Women's Guild assisted with the initial propaganda and provided the tea on the day. The Bloxwich Guild seems to have been formed from this event. Mrs Haynes was the leading figure in the new Guild and Hall says:

> Mrs Haynes did a lot of self-sacrificing work when it was neither easy nor usual for women to appear on public platforms. On more than one occasion she stood on a soap-box at pitheads in the outlying districts and spoke in the open-air, in her endeavour to make new co-operators and to form new guilds.

In 1900 a management committee minute records that two Guildswomen were invited to serve on the Education Committee and these representatives were to be chosen by the Guild. Hall seems to have had access to the minutes of the Central Guild, but these now, unfortunately, are not available. Hall quotes only a couple of trivial incidents from these; and that is all.

We turn next then to the surviving quarterly reports of the society. These are available for one quarter of 1906 and then continuously from 1913. The report for the quarter ending March 1906 shows that there were three Women's Guilds. Central met at the Temperance Hall at 7-30 on alternate Monday evenings with contributions of 3d. per quarter. The secretary was Mrs Hutchins. Bloxwich Guild also met on alternate Mondays at the Bloxwich Co-operative Hall at 7pm. Contributions were

6d. per half year. The secretary was Mrs Wilcox. The third was the Walsall Wood Guild whose meetings were held in the Society's stores at High Street, Walsall Wood. Its secretary was Mrs Glover. But unfortunately there was no report of the activities of these Guilds. From the education committee report we learn that at a Tea and Concert at Leamore, the Bloxwich Women's Guild 'had charge of the tables' and also that there were five women on the education committee. These were Mrs E. Haynes, Mrs E. Alvey, Mrs M. Sarson, Mrs Hutchins, and Mrs S. Hall. An item of expenditure of £6 on the education committee balance sheet credited 'Guild' suggests that joint work with the education committee was important.

The next quarterly report, for December 1913, shows that there were seven Women's Guilds, the new ones being Pelsall, Bronwhills, Lichfield and Sutton Coldfield. All met on alternate weeks, but an earlier starting time seems to have been favoured with most starting between 6 and 7pm and the later 7-30 favoured only by Central and Sutton Coldfield. The secretaries were Central – Mrs Button, Bloxwich – Mrs Argyle, Walsall Wood – Mrs L. Adams, Pelsall – Mrs Smith, Brownhills – Mrs E. Critchlow, Lichfield – Mrs A. Barker and Sutton Coldfield with the only unmarried secretary, Miss Cresswell. Again, however, the notice of the Women's Guilds is only an advertisement and there is no record of what they did. From the education committee report we learn that there were four women members who were Mrs Haynes, Mrs Adams, Mrs Hutchins and Mrs Spanswick.

Nor do the subsequent quarterly reports through to the end of 1914 throw any more direct light on the activities of the Women's Guild. However, we know that an important part of the programme of the Walsall education committee was its work with children's classes, galas, and parties. It is inconceivable that these activities could have flourished without the participation of the active women within the society who would certainly be connected with the Guild. It seems, therefore, that there must have been a particularly close link between the Education Committee and the Women's Guild in Walsall.

Of the other Guilds which existed at Dudley, Soho, Tipton, Wednesbury, and Halesowen we know nothing.

Conclusions

For the Owenites of the 1820s, Co-operative trading was to be reinforced by education which would lead co-operators to understand that the retail store was only the beginning. It was to be followed by Co-operative production which in turn would lead to Co-operative communities and socialism. By 1844 the Rochdale pioneers, who were Owenites almost to a man, had scaled down their expectations somewhat, but their thoughts still lay in the direction of the old Owenite Institutions with their newspapers, reading rooms and lectures which they replicated with some success. It was at this time that the demand for 2½ per cent of net profits to be devoted to education appeared.

By the 1870s the situation was changed. The consolidation of capitalism had crossed socialist communities off the agenda as co-operators grappled with the problems of individual productive co-operatives. After the 1870 Education Act a largely literate generation developed. This meant that children's education would henceforward be confined to teaching co-operative principles. Other educational developments also strongly influenced the co-operative movement. The first was the University Extension of the 1870s. This aimed at bringing 'culture' to working people via University lecturers. From 1887 the Co-operative Union took in hand education of employees and committee members with courses in book-keeping and auditing followed in 1890 by correspondence courses and its own examinations in co-operating trading techniques. As a correction to this necessary but narrowing aspect of education Albert Mansbridge a CWS employee developed the Workers' Education Association which aimed to bring the political, trade union and co-operative movement together with the universities to develop small tutorial classes enabling greater student participation than the University Extension lectures. In 1899 Ruskin College was formed providing both correspondence courses on subjects germane to co-operation and the labour movement, together with the possibility for a small number of fortunate members to study full-time for one year at university level. These movements were all strongly supported by the Co-operative movement, but had the effect of channelling much co-op education outside the movement.

The first wave of Black Country co-operative societies in the 1830s accepted the full Owenite programme, as we have seen from the activities of the first Walsall society. The second wave in the 1860s struggled to survive and in the educational activities they undertook would have been influenced as much by the Christian Socialists as by Robert Owen.

When the third wave finally established co-operation in the Black Country from the 1870s, their educational aims were limited. As we have seen from the Wolverhampton and Walsall education committees from 1906, they confined their activities to the basic task of propagating co-operative principles among the general population to consolidate the co-operative presence. Only the Walsall Lock & Cartgear seem to have had an educational programme extending to libraries and social clubs, although these were confined to their own employees. Both the successful producer co-ops spent more on education than the consumer societies. Walsall Padlock kept closely to the recommended 2½ per cent ratio of net profits to education between 1900 and 1914. Dudley Bucket spent between 3 per cent and 2½ per cent in most years between 1900 and its take-over by the CWS in 1908. The consumer societies spent rather less. In 1900 Wednesbury (New) spent 1.7 per cent, Walsall (New) 1.4 per cent and Wolverhampton 1.2 per cent. Others spent less than 1 per cent or did not record their expenditure. In 1914 Wednesbury (New) spent nearly 4 per cent, but this was exceptional and its expenditure in the intervening years ranged from 1.9 per cent to 0.8 per cent. Wolverhampton was next best in 1914 at 1.5 per cent and Soho 1.4 per cent. Others were below 1 per cent including Walsall and Dudley. In defence of these smaller percentages it could be claimed that other expenditures by the societies had an educational element. Not least of these were the grants to the Women's Guilds which paid very large dividends not simply in the activities detailed above, but in the extraordinary affection and loyalty the Guilds inspired in their members which cannot be captured in print.

When all this is said, however, although the amounts spent on education were not negligible (Wolverhampton's 1.5 per cent in 1914 amounted to £150), the lack of training in co-operative practice and principles seems strange. The lack of staff training is notable, and parallels all too closely the general Black Country tradition of learning on the job, except for a narrow range of crafts. The paucity of education in co-operative principles for officials, committee members and rank and file co-operators must have had an important bearing on our final questions which concern the place of the societies in the local communities and why they did not grow faster.

The co-operative movement faced the in-built disadvantages in competing on price with private trade that they produced pure goods and that they tried to provide trade union wages and conditions. These disadvantages could be partly offset by utilising and/or developing a strong attachment to co-operative and socialist principles in a wide stratum of the population and also by the support of the local trade union and political movement.

The other set of difficulties were those of ideology and practice. Co-operators held that democratic workers' control was a superior system to that of private enterprise. The test of this contention lay practically in the range and quality of the goods that co-operatives provided and also the quality of the management that it produced.

With regard to developing a 'Co-operative consciousness,' we have seen the limitations of educational efforts. The co-operatives were, however, closely connected with the labour movement from the beginning. In Walsall William Millerchip, leading figure in both Locks & Cartgear and the local consumer co-operative, became one of the first Labour councillors in 1898; in Wolverhampton Tom Frost, who was president of the local society for many years, became a Labour councillor in 1902 and, after the Great War, the first Labour mayor. These are but two examples. The leadership of the local trade union movement could invariably be relied on, but the practical support of the trade union rank and file was more dubious. As we have seen, education committees and the Women's Guilds were constantly seeking to cement relations between Co-operators and the trade unions, but never with the success that the Co-operators thought they deserved.

This matter was brought out most sharply when trade union rates of pay and reduced hours were introduced in the years before the war. Although co-operative wages and conditions were generally better than in most private shops, retail societies and the CWS had to operate in an environment where 'sweated labour' produced much of the world's goods. One of the obstacles to higher wages was removed with the Trade Boards Act of 1909 when some of the worst of the sweated trades were regulated. In 1908 the Co-operative Union Congress accepted the principle of a minimum wage and in 1909 the AUCE scales of 6/-d. a week for boys of fourteen rising to 24/-d. a week at age 21, and 5/-d. for girls at 14 rising to 17/-d. at age 20 were accepted. In all this the Women's Guild was to the fore with a campaign for the fusion of the Co-operative movement with the trade unions; this foundered on the TUC connection with the Labour Party which would have violated the Co-operative movement's 'political neutrality' and alienated the majority of Lib-Lab and Liberal co-operators.

In 1910 the Women's Guild reported that 500 societies were paying the minimum wage; in 1911 it stated that locally only Birmingham and Soho paid these rates. Walsall reduced hours for all employees to 48 in July 1914. This would have meant opening shops at 8-30am and closing at 6pm with a half day closing. Previously shops had opened at 8-30am and closed between 6pm and 9pm on other days, the central premises remaining open until 10pm on Saturdays; such a reduction of hours would have involved considerable loss of trade, whether the society added to these losses by paying a minimum wage we are not told.

Wolverhampton, however, paid the minimum rate from the middle of 1913. Later in the same year it cut hours by 4½ closing at 7pm on week nights and 8pm on Saturdays. The Wolverhampton management committee report for September 1913 claimed that the wage increase had applied only to about a dozen people as other employees were already receiving the minimum rate. But the total cost of both measures was about £200 and Fullwood, the chairman addressed the following remarks to the trade unionists of the town:

> We need not point out the extra expenditure involved. That is apparent, but what we do wish to point out is the duty of all Trade Unionists in this town. It has been given to us as an excuse in the past that many Trade Unionists in this town were not Members of our Society and did not give us their patronage because we did not recognise the demands of the Union to the full extent; but now what is their excuse? In taking this step we have done for Trade Unionism what no other retail concern in this town can lay claim to and now we have to say that we have a just claim on Trade Unionists for their full and entire support for our movement. ... we hope our appeals may not from now be in vain and that the leaders also of the various Unions will give us their utmost support...

It is clear that trade union support was not what it might be, but could all the blame be placed on trade unionists' inability to recognise the ideological superiority of the movement, or their failure to see that there was a two shilling in the pound advantage by shopping at the Co-op? This leads on the the questions of the range of co-operative goods and also their quality.

The limited range of goods offered by the retail societies was always recognised as a weakness and various expediencies were tried to overcome this. In Wolverhampton in 1909, for instance, arrangements existed with various private tradesmen in the town to pay a co-operative dividend of 1/6d. on all purchases made. These included stationery and books from Rushton's, photography from W. White and the best known Wolverhampton photographer Bennett Clark, pianos and phonographs from Walton's, millinery from Mrs A.S. Garner, optical goods from Taylor of Penn Road, and clock repairs from W.H. Miller of Snow Hill. Wolverhampton was also willing to offer in 1910 a dividend of 1/-d. in the pound and £1 towards the rail fare to its members who went to Manchester to shop at the CWS where there was a 'vast range of goods not possible for local societies to stock.' Walsall adopted the same policy contracting with a private boot firm, butchers, a photographer, and an upholsterer to provide goods for a dividend of 1/-d. to 1/6. Fred Hall claims that this had the advantage of enabling the society to judge the demand for goods before providing them itself.

The vexed question of co-operative goods versus non co-operative led to great arguments at quarterly meetings. For instance, in 1906 Walsall had a resolution that only co-operative soap should be sold in future; the outcome is unknown. It could be argued that prospective customers tempted into a co-op shop would only return if they could buy their favourite goods there and might later be weaned into trying co-op goods. This argument was less important in the days of the infancy of packaged and branded goods, but it already applied to such things as soap, tea, tobacco and the CWS had its own Pelaw brand of polishes etc.

Beyond groceries, a basic necessity was bread the supply of which was in transition as home baking and small bakeries declined. Walsall opened a small bakery in 1895 but it soon became apparent that the installation of modern, expensive equipment was necessary after which regular reports told of expanded production, but also under utilisation of the plant. There were also other problems. In 1910 Wolverhampton reported that its bakery was 'a continued success despite outside attacks'. It also stressed that in a trade notorious for hours of 80 a week and more that Wolverhampton operated a 54 hour week and paid standard wages. The bakeries became one of the success stories of the co-operatives and by 1913 Wolverhampton was experimenting with a separate bread, confectionary and sweet shop on the Dudley Road.

Coal was another commodity in which co-ops increasingly dealt. But this could not be a co-operative product. By 1906 Walsall was advertising the delivery of best Cannock and Rugeley coal in bags or in loads. Wolverhampton, after absorbing the Whitmore Reans Coal Society in 1901 went on to buy its own wharf in 1910.

The other co-op staple, milk, is a mystery commodity in this period. Milk was in always in short supply during the nineteenth century, consumption was low and what was drunk was as likely to be condensed milk, courtesy of the developing canning industry, as fresh milk. In Wolverhampton in 1842 I estimated the supply of milk as sufficient to provide each inmate of the Workhouse with one pint a week and this was skimmed milk. This amount changed little through the rest of the century. As with other commodities, local co-op societies contracted with private traders to provide milk. In 1911 Wolverhampton society reported that for some time it had organised a commission trade with local dairymen, but, 'the last of them has now informed us that he cannot continue at present prices and therefore the supply of milk will be discontinued.' Fred Hall makes no mention of milk in his history of the Walsall society to 1914, but the minutes for the December 1914 quarter of the society record that a 'Dairy Depot is to be opened. This will supply members with yet another commodity (pure and unadulterated).'

Other co-operative departments consistently under-performed. For instance, of Walsall boot repair service it was said in 1914 that although it was the cheapest in Walsall it 'could cope with a much larger trade.' In Wolverhampton in 1910 it was reported of boots, hardware and drapery, 'We are sorry that they are not better supported.'

The justification for these complaints can be examined from the occasional report that shows the share of trade of the various departments. In Walsall in 1906 groceries accounted for 74 per cent of total sales, bread and confectionary 14 per cent, coal 7 per cent and drapery 5 per cent. By 1914 bread and confectionary had risen to 17 per cent but coal was down to 6 per cent The first available Wolverhampton return for the quarter ending September 1914 shows shares of trade as follows: Groceries 71 per cent, Bakery and confectionary 13½ per cent, Drapery and outfitting 9 per cent, Boots & shoes 5 per cent and Hardware 2 per cent. Coal sales are not shown. The ratio of profit to sales of these commodities varied somewhat. Profit on hardware was 21 per cent, on Outfitting and on Boots 17 per cent, Groceries was 16 per cent, Drapery was 14 per cent and Bread only 11 per cent. Since these Wolverhampton figures are for only one quarter they may be misleading, but there does not seem to be a much greater profit ratio to be obtained by branching out from groceries to other commodities. In fact outfitting, drapery, boots and the rest were important only for embryonic department stores developing at the central premises of the societies; and the economics of department stores are very different from that of grocery stores. It is clear that the way to growth was to duplicate grocery branches – a lesson not lost on the Liptons, Maypoles and Home & Colonial entrepreneurs then thrusting themselves into prominence. In looking for reasons why the societies did not grow faster, therefore, it is to the branch grocery store that attention should be focussed. Complaint was constantly made of the low average amount spent by co-operators. Soho seems to have been the most successful society in attracting the loyalty of its members. In 1890 members spent an average of £22 per annum. By 1900 it was up to £29. In 1914 it had fallen to £20. Walsall was the next most successful society, members spending in the same three years £13, £21 and £17. The Wolverhampton figures were £14, £13 and £18. Dudley members spent £16 each in 1890, but after their disaster it went down to £9 in 1900 where it remained in 1914. £9 is less than 3/-. a week when the grocery bill for a family of five would be about 9/6d. a week plus about 2/-d. for meat which would not normally be bought from the Co-op. Soho's £29 in 1900 represents 11/-d. a week which is very high, but from this time Soho expenditure falls. Dudley seems an exceptionally bad case. But with regard to the source of the goods bought, the Wolverhampton 1914 return shows that only about 66 per cent of groceries were purchased from CWS sources. This suggests that even active members were dissatisfied with some CWS products. If this were true for members it must have been a disincentive for non-members to shop at the Co-op and a partial reason for the slow growth of the movement.

The other main reason for slow growth would be if co-operative prices were higher than those of private traders. There is not enough data to compare prices directly. This leaves only a discussion the quality of the management of the co-operative societies which would be an important factor determining whether co-operatives were competitive or not.

Looking first at profitability, it is difficult to compare co-operatives with private traders. The only Black Country companies disclosing profits at this time are the large limited liability companies. Their results appear in the *Stock Exchange Gazette.* They are mainly the large iron and coal concerns whose fortunes were greatly dependent on the trade cycle. Other firms such as GKN, Chance, Kenrick etc. which have been the subject of books are also large, and over-affected by slump and boom. The co-operatives. as we have seen, did suffer during slumps, but as dealers in the necessities of life, were less affected. We have already noted that almost all co-operative profits were distributed as dividend and this might be considered a weakness compared with the prudent private practice of devoting at least half of profits to financing expansion. However, the co-operative habit of relying on the stability of its capital and borrowing from the CWS seems to have been just as effective in securing growth. For instance Walsall Co-operative's assets of land, buildings, machinery and fixtures were £9,000 in 1906 but by 1914 over £31,000. This reflected the co-operative habit of purchasing each new site, whereas the growth of the multiples like Lipton's was dependent on leasing each new property taken; the co-operative road would seem to be a superior managerial practice. Certainly co-operative expansion never seems to have been limited by a lack of capital. For much of our period there was a plethora of capital and the ability of the movement to safely offer 5 per cent interest on their savings to working class share holders represented a major economic achievement and a valuable welfare facility.

Regarding the entrepreneurial performance of the democratically elected management committees, although the record is mixed, there is little to suggest that it was inferior to the general run of private enterprise in the same field. That almost all productive co-operatives eventually failed is not surprising. They were either set up during a slump and thus doomed to failure or they perished during the Great Depression. The loss of the Smethwick retail society near the end of the Great Depression in 1887 from accounting deficiencies was a serious loss. The failure of the Soho Society, formed immediately after, to reach a comparable level of sales, suggests that it was more than accounting problems that afflicted the previous society. However, the disregarded plea of the Birmingham district for the Co-operative Union to examine the book-keeping problems of the Smethwick society, suggests that it might have been saved.

The failure of co-operation to take root in West Bromwich, Stourbridge and Bilston reminds one that co-operative enterprise depended on something over and above entrepreneurial flair; it required also a minimum base of ideological interest in the principles of co-operation.

The problems of the Dudley society deserve a business case study of their own. The expansion in the 1880s, (during the Great Depression, be it noted), was unprecedented in the west Midlands, and perhaps in the rest of the country. It suffered an £18,000 loss in 1892 from an embezzling executive. This loss, although substantial, should have been easily contained with the help of the CWS. That it should lead to the permanent loss of 50 per cent of the trade of the society and a downgrading of co-operative influence in the town both absolutely and in relation to other towns in an area where it had been the outstanding leader is inexplicable. The productive society, Dudley Bucket & Fender, was, of course a success from its beginning in 1888. Little is known of its managing personnel. President in the early 1890s was Mark Round. The manager and travelling 'rep' was John Round who was also delegate to the CWS Congress in the 1890s and from 1895 to at least 1906 he was a representative on the No.5. Birmingham District executive committee. There was also a Jabez Round on the Dudley

191

retail society committee at that time, but whether they were related is not known. The most regular Dudley Bucket delegate to the annual Co-operative Congress between 1895 and 1901 was Joseph Edwards, who was secretary of the society. Edwards, with Councillor Brooks, was a member of the 'alternative committee' that took over the Dudley retail society in its years of crisis from 1892. In 1907, the year before it was taken over by the CWS, Dudley Bucket employed 142 people and its profits were £2221 giving a 27 per cent return on its capital of £8,135. The records of both Dudley Bucket & Fender, and also the Dudley retail society until 1892, suggest that democratic self-government could also produce effective management.

For Wolverhampton and Walsall more information is available and more can be said of entrepreneurial performance. One stabilising factor was continuity of leadership, particularly in the key posts of president, secretary and general manager. In Wolverhampton after a shaky start which saw four secretaries come and go, Alfred Wood was appointed full-time secretary in 1901 and retained the post for more than thirty years. The presidency was held by E. Hope for ten years from 1889. He was succeeded by the highly efficient Labour councillor Tom Frost from 1899 to 1907. Frost was succeeded by A. Fullwood who was first elected to the management committee in 1894 and remained president until 1931 and beyond. H. Taylor remained vice-president from 1909 until after 1931. J. Hodgson, the general manager held the post from 1903 until his death in 1920. Given this firm administrative base, the growth of the Wolverhampton society was disappointing. Its sales grew 3½ times between 1900 and 1914 compared with the nearly nine-fold increase of Soho in the same period. On the other hand, Wolverhampton's profit to sales ratio was the highest of any Black Country society in the years after 1910, rising to 14½ per cent in 1914. This, however, might have been the effect of higher prices charged, and this would have had a retarding effect on the society's progress.

In terms of sales, Soho was the fastest growing society in the Black Country and by 1914 was second in sales only to Walsall. Unfortunately, neither of the two previous historians of the society has left us any information regarding the administrative personnel who were responsible for the massive growth of Soho in those years.

Walsall retail society grew nearly as fast as Soho, almost eight times between 1900 and 1914. The productive society, Lock & Cartgear, was also growing in this period into a vast concern. Already in 1900 it employed 201 workers; by 1914 this had risen to 250. Its profit levels fluctuated. In 1902 net profit was £708 on sales of £17,772 or a return of just under 4 per cent. In 1914 profits were £772 on sales of £21,115 or 3.7 per cent. For the period 1908 to 1913, however, profits averaged £1560 per annum giving a return of about 8 per cent.

Walsall co-operation produced a number of remarkable characters. One of the most remarkable of all was Sam Welsh. Sam was a Scottish radical immigrant to Walsall. He was secretary to the Walsall Cottage Hospital from its birth through the horrific and heroic period of the administration of Dorothy Pattison (Sister Dora) from 1865 to her death in 1878 and beyond. He was also president of the Walsall Trades Council in 1873 and leading spirit in both the inauguration and administration of the productive co-operative society, Lock & Cartgear, and also the Walsall retail society. Most remarkably of all, he was throughout this time the editor of the *Walsall Free Press*.

The other remarkable figure, with interests almost as wide as Welsh's was William Millerchip. Millerchip entered the lock trade as a half-timer at the age of ten in 1873. He quickly became a leading figure in lock trade unionism and after 1886 a leading figure with Juggins in the Midland Counties Trades Federation. Despite being refused membership of Locks and Cartgear in 1884 he became an employee of the society and by 1887 he was chairman of the directors of the society. He held this position until 1902 when he became secretary of the Lock & Keysmith's Union. In 1898 he became one of the first Labour councillors in Walsall and was mayor in 1908-9. From 1906 he was a magistrate. He resigned from the council in 1910 to become manager of the local Labour Exchange, a position he held until 1927 when he reached retiring age.

Locks and Cartgear were also well served by George Harrison who had suggested the Lock Co-op in the first place and became its first manager. This position he held until he retired in 1914 when his son, W.G. Harrison, succeeded him. With the influence of Sam Welsh and the partnership of

Millerchip and Harrison, together with the evidence earlier adduced, no further case needs to be made for the quality of the management of Locks and Cartgear.

The productive and retail societies in Walsall worked closely together. Sam Welsh became th president of Walsall (New) retail Society when it was set up in 1885 and remained so until at least 1889. George Harrison became the first and only treasurer until his death in 1917. The earlier years seem to have been difficult ones with three part-time secretaries and a series of managers. In 1905, however, H. Donaldson became the first full-time secretary and held the post until 1912. He was succeeded by T. Pearsall who remained until 1921. The business management situation was solved in 1897 when L. Pattison was appointed. Such was his zeal that he often went canvassing door-to-door for support and customers. He remained until 1910. In 1896 William Millerchip became president and held this position until he became manager of the Labour Exchange in 1910. Again we can note stability in the three key positions of president, secretary and manager from about the beginning of the century. By 1906, when we have the first quarterly report, we can identify other people on the management committee who gave long years of service to the society including William Abbotts (president 1910-20), Charles Deakin (brother of Joseph; management board member almost continuously 1904-36), H. Bland (a previous secretary), Joseph Thickett (railwayman and Labour councillor), and H. Hilliard.

The energy of William Millerchip was particularly prodigious. When he became secretary of the Lockmakers' Union in 1902 he had to sever his official connections with Lock & Cartgear because of the rule that only employees could be directors. He then flung himself into his duties as trade union and Co-operative society leader. As president of the retail society from 1896 he attended not only monthly meetings of the management board, but meetings of the departmental sub-committees of grocery, bakery, boot and shoe, and finance. He was a regular delegate to the Co-operative Congress from 1895 and from at least that year he was an executive committee member of the No.6. Stafford District of the Co-operative Union and chairman from at least 1902. In 1905 he was the Stafford District representative on the Sectional Choral Association Committee. In 1906 he was the District representative on the Exhibitions and Demonstrations Committee and the next year the District member of the Education Committee. In 1906 he was sued by the Clothing Manufacturers' Association for remarks he had made about sweated labour in a private firm and spent much time organising donations towards the heavy damages for which he was mulcted. In 1898 he became an early Lib-Lab member of the Walsall town council and in 1908-9 was mayor. In 1913 he became a member of the Co-operative Union Central Board and retained this position until 1938.

It is clear that there was an abundance of talent in Walsall committed to co-operative principles and the record suggests entrepreneurial ability, and flair. In the first five years of the society its sales rose four-fold from £500 per annum to £2,000. In the next decade sales rose seven-fold to £21,000. From 1901 to 1914 sales rose from £30,000 to £170.000 a rise of nearly six-fold. By 1914 Walsall was the largest retail society in the Black Country and there is little to suggest that a different form of management would have produced a better result.

The final answer to the question Why did not the Co-operatives Grow more Quickly therefore seems to be that up to 1914 Walsall, Soho, Wednesbury and Halesowen & Hasbury were growing as quickly as could be expected; only Wolverhampton and Dudley were lagging.

We have not been able to discuss the influence of price on the growth or retardation of societies, but it must be said that the co-operative movement catered largely for the working class aristocracy with highish and regular wages. Many of the poorest could afford neither co-operative prices nor co-operative principles. The middle class hated the co-operative movement and white collar workers shunned it from snobbery. This hostility to the movement was considerable up to 1914 and continued to exist after that. It must have been an important factor in retarding growth.

A final point must be made on co-operative success. It was only at a stage of the grocery trade when a profit of 10 per cent on sales could be made that co-operative shops could flourish. The trade during this time was being transformed by multiples like Liptons, Home & Colonial etc. specialising at first in a single (often imported) commodity. But in the Black Country at the time there was no such competition. In Wolverhampton, for instance, in 1914 only Blakemores had even two branches, other grocers operating with only one shop. The profit margin of 10 per cent continued into the 1930s and co-ops continued to flourish. But modern profit margins on co-operative sales are about 3 per cent, which does not provide an attractive dividend.

Regarding entrepreneurial flair we can take two examples. Thomas Lipton was a supremely successful private entrepreneur. He spent most of his life concerned with nothing but his grocery shops and making money. Then he spent the rest of his life buying his way into society and a title. Contrast this with the local co-operative entrepreneur William Millerchip who started work at age ten, worked unceasingly for co-operative and trade union principles all his life, presided over a local organisation which grew 350 fold and was on the board of management of a national movement with sales of £130m in 1913. Whose flair is more to be admired?

Bibliography: Co-operation to 1914

For this chapter I am indebted to Ned Williams (local historian of transport, work, etc.) who unearthed the *Wolverhampton Brief History of our Society* written in 1931 and who fed me regularly with material from *Co-operative News* in the library of the International Co-operative College at Loughborough.

Other histories used have been the first volume of *From Acorn to Oak* by Fred Hall for the Walsall Society, and for the Soho and earlier Smethwick societies, *The History of the Birmingham Co-operative Society 1881-1931* (Birmingham 1931) by an unnamed author, but written by T. Smith. Another source covering all Black Country co-operatives is Frank H. Bruff's *Co-operation in Birmingham and District* which he produced for the Handbook to the 1906 Co-operative Congress held in Birmingham. There is also *The History of the Walsall Locks & Cartgear Ltd. 1873-1923* by R. Halstead. The most thorough study of productive co-ops for the period is Benjamin Jones' *Co-operative Production* (1894 – Clarendon Press) which deals with Black Country productive societies. Mike Glasson, curator of the Walsall Leather Museum, sent me material on local productive co-operatives.

In the annual reports of the *Co-operative Union Congress* there are statistics for every co-operative society in Britain from 1884 to the present day. These give number of members, capital, turnover, profit, number of employees, wages paid, dividend and often much else. The series in Birmingham Reference Library runs from 1890. For the earlier figures I am indebted to the late Eddie Frow whose Working Class Movement Library, Salford, I always turn to first when I have a query on labour history.

Every Society issued a comprehensive report for each quarterly meeting which dealt with the democratic business of the society. For Wolverhampton these survive from 1909. For Walsall there is one report for 1906 and then a series from 1913. There must be reports from other societies yet to be uncovered.

From 1871 the main co-operative newspaper has been the *Co-operative News*. Later there was *Wheatsheaf*, distributed free and into which was inserted news of local societies. None of these inserts seems to have survived. Local newspapers carried regular reports of local co-operative activity. The main ones I have used have been the *Wolverhampton Chronicle*, *Walsall Observer* and *Dudley Herald*.

The *Co-operative Union Annual Congress Reports* from 1869 contain reports of the two Districts, Birmingham and Stafford, covering the Black Country from the 1880s, also reports of the relevant Education Committees and, for a short time reports of the Women's Co-operative Guild. Information on local Women's Guilds, however, has been disappointing.

All co-operatives were registered with the Registry of Friendly Societies and are recorded in each annual report of the Registrar. I was fortunate enough when researching friendly societies at the Public Records Office over twenty years ago to come across the document Industrial & Provident Societies registered 1850-1912 from which, I think, I have printed the definitive list of co-operatives registered in the Black Country during those years.

Eric Taylor in his unpublished Ph.D. thesis *The Working Class Movement in the Black Country 1863-1914* deals with co-operatives and he has biographies of co-operators, notably William Millerchip and William Abbots of Walsall in the *Dictionary of Labour Biography* Vol 1. Other sources used have been the labour newspapers *Reasoner*, *Labour Press* and *Flint Glassmakers' Magazine*, and Brian Stenner's *The Lockmakers*. Comparisons of Co-ops with private trade have been taken from Peter Mathias' *Retailing Revolution*.

Chapter 9

Women

Women, work and wages

The starting point in discussing the role and influence of women is the information contained in the ten-yearly Census data. From 1801 to 1901 the population of the Black Country increased from almost 100,000 people to almost 700,000. This was twice as fast as the national population growth of England & Wales. The greatest growth was between 1831 and 1841 when Black Country population grew by 38 per cent. But after this rates fell and by 1871 was below the national growth rate where it remained until 1901.

With the tempestuous growth of the Black Country one might expect to find a considerable preponderance of men over women. But this was never the case. In 1801 there were 98 females to every 100 males, in 1841 this ratio fell to its lowest at 94, but by 1901 there were about 350,000 men and the same number of women. This position may have been different among the Irish, the largest immigrant group of the century. But since, when Irish numbers were at their highest in 1861, they never accounted for 5 per cent of the population in Walsall and Wolverhampton and this dropped to little more than 1 per cent in Stourbridge and Dudley, if they did bring more men than women it would have had little impact on the general population trend.

Despite the rapid growth of the area, the Black Country was not an area of early marriage nor of exceptionally large families. The 1831 Census showed size of family varying from 5.5 persons in Wednesbury to 4.75 in Bilston and Wolverhampton. (The national figure was just under 5). With regard to marriage, in 1861 of people of marriageable age (15 to 75+) in the Black Country only 3 per cent of the 15 to 20 age group were married, at age 25 only 21 per cent were married, at age 35, 47 per cent, and by age 45 only 58 per cent of those of marriageable age were married. The marriage and re-marriage market remained active up to 75+ when 67 per cent were married. This leaves 33 per cent or one third of those of marriageable age who were obliged, or preferred, to remain single. The corresponding figure for 1901 shows an even larger number of persons of marriageable age remaining single at 38 per cent.(The national figures for England and Wales were 37 per cent single people of marriageable age in 1851 and 33 per cent in 1901).

The above figures must be taken into account when judging the extent and fairness of a 'natural' division of labour existing whereby a wife serviced her husband and family leaving her no time to participate in social or political affairs. For men engaged in unremitting, exhausting, physical labour for twelve hours a day at the beginning of the century and often eleven at the end, there was little enough time for 'leisure' activities. For women the round of child-bearing, washing, shopping, cleaning, mending and general family care left even less time for personal pursuits until at least her later years. By this time, however, she was usually prematurely aged and unable to use her leisure time productively.

Women were, of course, involved in the struggles of the bread winner to obtain and keep a job and avoid starvation, penury and exploitation. Other women were engaged directly in these struggles through their own employment.

The main trends of women's employment can be summarised as follows. In 1861 of all females of employable age about 30 per cent were gainfully employed in Wolverhampton and about 32 per cent in Dudley. Of these, the largest number were domestic servants. Of 2,149 women in domestic service in Wolverhampton 1,240 were girls under 20 and 909 were women over 20. The next most important occupation for women in Wolverhampton was that of making clothes which occupied 1,822 females. About 800 women worked around the mines and ironworks and in the factories. Of professional workers Wolverhampton had 139 teachers and 21 hospital nurses; Dudley had 67 teachers and 21 nurses.

What proportion of married women went out to work? In the registration district of Wolverhampton in 1861 more than 88 per cent of married women gave their occupation as 'wife' or 'widow' suggesting that about 12 per cent had paid employment.

By 1911, the last Census before the Great War, more information was available, but the general picture was little changed. In Wolverhampton County Borough nearly 31 per cent of all females over 10 years of age were gainfully employed. The largest category of employment was still domestic service, but this had fallen from 34 per cent in 1861 to 23 per cent of total female employment. The next largest category of employment was factory work at nearly 17 per cent. The only other large categories of female employment were dress at over 13 per cent and food and drink at 12 per cent. By now there were 571 teachers in Wolverhampton, 463 clerks (there had been only 9 in 1861) and 205 nurses.

Other towns varied somewhat in the percentage of women over 10 at work. In Dudley it was 27 per cent, in Walsall 33 per cent and in West Bromwich 27 per cent.

The 1911 Census gives the number of married women at work. In Wolverhampton of 11,866 women at work 9,136 were unmarried and 1,016 were widowed. This would mean that about 14 per cent of married women with husbands had paid employment, perhaps slightly higher than in 1861. Other Black Country towns give similar figures.

With regard to wages, it can be taken as a generalisation that women's wages were half that of men in most trades and sometimes less than half. By 1914 women's wages had risen, along with men's, to a historic high. This was due to a combination of factors such as the full employment of the years 1910-14, the Great Unrest and the Trade Boards Act of 1909 passed as a result of the scandal of sweated wages in the Black Country and elsewhere.

In 1914 the Trade Board rate for women chain makers as 2 3/4 d. per hour which should have provided for 54 hours work an income of over 12/-d. a week, but Tawney estimated the earnings of women chain makers at between 5/-d. and 8/-d. per week in 1913. This gives an average of only about 6/6d. The settlement of the Great Unrest gave women factory workers a 12/-d. minimum wage. Other national women's wage rates which might have applied in the Black Country were laundry workers 9/-d. to 12/-d, garment workers 3¼d per hour, clerks 15/-d. to 25/-d and Co-operative employees 17/-d.

In 1913 a Workers' Union enquiry into the wages of women workers at Kenrick's in West Bromwich showed that of 277 women, 120 earned between 6/-d. and 8/-d; no doubt many of these were young women. Another 50 earned between 8/-d. and 10/-d. A further 64 earned between 10/-d. and 12/-d. and 29 between 12/-d. and 14/-d. Only 14 women earned above 14/-d and up to the maximum of 21/-d. This is probably an average spread of women's wages in a large factory. The average is less than 9/6d. a week. This was before the 12/-d. minimum conceded by Kenricks as by other employers during the Great Strike. It was also, of course, a period of full employment.

What would such wages buy? If one takes a woman factory worker over 20 years of age earning 12/-d. in 1914 living in a household with a male income earner in work and paying one fifth share of a 5 family household now aspiring to spend the 28/3d. necessary to reach the minimum comfort level she would then pay into the family budget 5/7½d. a week or nearly 50 per cent of her wages. She would naturally want to spend more on clothes, entertainments, holidays, cosmetics, perhaps alcohol and and even tobacco. This ought to leave a margin for some savings. Her 12/-d. wage would also stretch to paying 1/-d. or 1/6d. for a rented room, if she decided to leave the family home, but in return for her independence she would then have to curtail some of her other expenditure.

Women earning more than 12/-d. a week would be correspondingly better off. How many women were likely to be earning more than the minimum wage? From the 1911 Census we can estimate that in Wolverhampton just over 10 per cent of women were employed in professional and clerical work likely to pay more than the minimum wage. If we then take the 16 per cent of the women employed at Kenricks as likely to be typical of the percentage of women paid more than the minimum wage in industrial work it could be that about one quarter of employed women were paid over the minimum in 1914.

This, it must be stressed is the optimum situation obtaining only from the settlement of the Great Unrest in July 1913. Even within this unprecedentedly favourable situation about 10 per cent of the female work force was widowed and an unknown, but large number, would be supporting children on a single female wage and so would be living in poverty. A further unknown number of women would be living in a household where the main male earner was incapacitated; again, such a household would be living in poverty unless there was another male adult earner supporting the family.

This optimum state of affairs underlines the significance of the settlement of the Great Unrest for the health and welfare of Black Country workers. But until the very last year of our period the general average wage for women in conditions of full employment was 8/-d. If we return to our budget above, it will be seen that a woman worker contributing to a family income would have only 2/-d. a week of spare income to spend on herself which was unlikely to leave room for any savings.

Much of the period from 1850 had, however, not been years of full employment but depressed years during which wages when in work could plunge to 4/-d. and disappear altogether if unemployed. Such were the years 1903 to 1908. Before that came the Great Depression of 1875-95 and earlier still the surprisingly large unemployment of the 1860s and several years of unemployment in the 1850s, the decades of Britain's industrial leadership.

The question therefore arises as to why women's wages were so low for so long. The general answer is that rising population provided a work force where supply usually exceeded demand. This was true for male labour and applied with even greater force to female labour in an area of heavy industry, where most jobs demanded heavy physical labour. In addition, because of the surplus of labour, male wages were fixed at an artificially low level for most of the century by the monthly meetings of the coal and ironmasters led by the Earls of Dudley. These meetings set not only the price of iron and coal, but also wages, which also determined the general wage level in the district.

The best survey of women's work in the West Midlands was a survey undertaken in Birmingham between 1904 and 1907 by Edward Cadbury, M. Cecille Matheson and George Shann published as *Women's Work and Wages*. The authors suggested that each grade of labour was paid slightly under its subsistence level. So for instance the cost of subsistence for teachers, including the cost of their prolonged education and need for access to cultural 'goods', was greater than the subsistence of an unskilled labourer. Thus in 1878 West Bromwich School Board paid its Certificated female teachers £55 to £65 per annum and Uncertificated teachers £35 to £45. Salaries in Board schools were higher than church school salaries, and the latter employed more uncertificated teachers. By 1892 female uncertificated teachers in the Black Country earned an average of only £42-10-0d. By 1914 a selection of salaries in Wolverhampton shows £55 paid to an uncertificated infant mistress and £60 for a certificated infant teacher serving at uncertificated salary until a vacancy occurred at the higher grade. Salaries in senior girls' schools ranged from £57-8-0d to £77-10-0d. Since most female teachers who married were sacked it is clear that a large proportion of unmarried female teachers had to maintain independent households and even with the higher salaries of 1914 it is questionable whether many pushed through the barrier of being paid at above their cost of subsistence.

Another factor keeping female wages low was lack of information and apathy. The report of Cadbury, Matheson and Shann stated that in Birmingham choice of jobs correlated heavily with the section of the working class that they came from. Most girls 'drifted' into their first jobs from ignorance of alternative work; the same was, no doubt, true for Black Country girls. This, together with the widespread feeling that their participation in the paid labour force was only a temporary phase of their lives, and the jibe that the married women were working for pin-money, meant that the scales were weighted on the side of employers paying low wages.

Thus many forces conspired to keep even skilled women's wages at subsistence level, and unskilled women's wages below that level.

Women in Trade Unions

To what extent were working women involved in the trade union movement? There were many complaints that women were difficult to organise and it is true that trade unionism in the Black Country made greatest strides when women organised women. The two most important Black Country women trade union organisers were Mary Macarthur and Julia Varley. Their achievements must be set against the national picture of women's trade union development. Female membership of all trade unions rose in two spectacular leaps. In 1886 it was 36,900. By 1896 it had nearly tripled to 117,888; this was the first period of the organisation of the unskilled. Membership then grew only slowly to 166,803 in 1906. Then there was another leap to 357,956 in 1914 as a result of the Great Unrest.

It is likely that the earliest female trade unionists in the Black Country were the domestic workers, notably in nails and chains. The tremendous strikes including the violence of 'dirgying' from 1850 to 1875 during the Great Expansion would have included women, but of their number and organisation nothing is known.

The first contact with the organised trade union movement was during the Great Depression when with female wages once again sinking to the starvation level of 4/-d. a week and no chance of winning wage advances, the local trade union movement attempted to protect wages by limiting women's work in various ways.

The first clash came in 1877 at the Trades Union Congress when W.J. Davis, the Birmingham Brassworkers secretary, spoke in favour of restrictions of work for women where heavy physical labour or degrading conditions of work pertained. Nails and chains and brickmaking were industries cited. This was opposed by the redoubtable Emma Paterson on the grounds that women should be allowed to earn their living without undue interference; chainmaking was 'not too hard for the females employed at it in the Black Country', she maintained. Davis riposted:

> We are not against women being employed at proper avocations, but it was inhuman to put the gentle, nay the lovable sex – those who had to nurse and nourish sons and daughters to conduct the world – to carry heavy weights, to use their feet as powerful levers, to do the work of the blacksmith, turn at the lathe or file at the vice. Laws and inspectors to prevent this degrading employment was humane statesmanship.

Emma Paterson was the female trade union pioneer who had formed the Women's Trade Union League in 1874 and had forced her way into the TUC from 1876. She remained until almost the end of her short life violently opposed to restrictions on the employment of women, arguing that men were pushing women out to protect male jobs and wages. The solution to low wages for women and degrading conditions was not legislation but trade union organisation.

The row continued. In 1882 Richard Juggins was supporting a Parliamentary Bill to prevent girls under fourteen working as blacksmiths after a Parliamentary Committee had stated that conditions as reported to them 'were a disgrace to the nation' and the statement of 'half nude women engaged in the work in company with men in the same state of undress' had been confirmed. The Women's Trade Union League demanded that males under fourteen should also be banned to prove that the Bill was not simply an excuse to restrict women. Parliament ended the argument by rejecting the Bill, not wanting 'to deprive thousands of young people of the means of earning a living.' At the 1887 TUC, Juggins 'finally threw off the mask' (the words of Barbara Drake) and moved on behalf of the Midland Counties Trades Federation 'to introduce such amendments to the Factory and Workshops Act as shall prevent the employment of females in the making of chains, nails, rivets, bolts etc., such work not being adapted to their constitution.' Only the two women at the TUC voted against this resolution.

The next year there was a compromise, however when Juggins, jointly with Clementina Black of the Women's Trade Union League proposed the historic motion unanimously passed that 'where women do the same work as men they shall receive equal pay.' Juggins explained 'that he had come to the conclusion that nothing but better pay would cure the evil, and they had therefore resolved to organise women as soon as possible.' Juggins 'then claimed the support of the Women's Trade Union League in forming a union at Cradley Heath.' Thus Barbara Drake.

We have no annual reports of the Midland Counties Trades Federation until 1889. The balance sheet for that year shows female branches of Chainmakers at Cradley Heath, Firebrick Makers at Lye, Nailmakers at Oldswinford, Spike Nail Makers at Halesowen and Spike Nail Makers at Sedgley. These same female trade unions appear in the annual reports for 1890 and 1891 and they are joined by the Female Brushmakers of Lower Gornal. But there is then a gap in the reports to 1896. From this time no female trade unions appear. Whether they disaffiliated from the MCTF or whether women were absorbed into the male trade unions is not known.

No mention of the strength of the women's unions appeared in the MCTF reports. One can try to estimate their relative strength as against men by comparing the amounts they paid in dues, bearing in mind that the women probably paid lower affiliation fees. For instance, in 1890 male Brushmakers paid £3-9-10d. and females £1-16-9. At Cradley Heath male chainmakers paid nearly £84 and women £8-11-0d, Fire Brick Makers at Lye £29 for men and £13 for women. From these, and other, affiliation fees it would seem that women paid up to almost one half of men down to one tenth. Whether this reflected relative memberships or whether women trade unionists accounted for more than these proportions is anyone's guess.

Nor are any of the names of these women trade union pioneers in the Black Country known. The Midland Counties Trades Federation annual reports do not even give the names of the secretaries of these women's societies affiliated to them. They are truly 'hidden from history.' But these were the years of the development of the 'new unionism' of the unskilled labourers; the years of the Dock Strike of 1889 which itself had been preceded by the historic strike of the Bryant & May match girls the previous year. It is clear that in these earliest days of female trade unionism Black Country women did not lag behind. In the 1890s small women's unions continued to develop, some men's unions were opening their membership to women and general unions were coming into existence based on a Socialist philosophy which made no distinction between men and women. The unions opening their ranks to women were largely those of which we have no local knowledge of female membership such as the Boot & Shoe Operatives and the Tailors. The new general unions after their great successes in the period 1886-90 had great difficulty preserving their existence. The most important of these unions for the Black Country were the Workers' Union and the two gasworkers unions – the Amalgamated Society of Gasworkers, and the Brickmakers & General Labourers (which was formed in Birmingham and became a national union) and the National Union of Gasworkers and General Labourers (which had started by organising London gasworkers and had become a national union active in Birmingham and the Black Country). On the whole, however, the later 1890s were a period of retreat for all trade unionists.

In 1903 Mary Macarthur became secretary of the Women's Trade Union League. She became involved in organising women in the Black Country as a result of the national sweating scandals (aggravated by the depression following the Boer War) which became centred on the chainmakers and other domestic workers in this area. In 1906 the National Federation of Women Workers was formed as a general union for women workers to counter the problems of the short life of many of the female trade union branches set up in previous years. In 1907 the NFWW absorbed the already existing women's branch of the Hammered Chain trade. The role of Mary Macarthur and the NFWW in the historic chain strike of 1910 to obtain the Trade Board rate has been fully dealt with in the section on the Great Unrest.

Following the chain strike came the other strikes of the years 1910-14. For these the women were organised mainly by the National Federation of Women Workers and the Workers' Union. Again, the details of these struggles are given in Chapter 7 of this work. The results were that by 1914 the National Federation of Women Workers had 10,000 members, of whom 1,000 were in the Black

Country branch. This is a large proportion of national membership and would have included many other workers besides chainmakers. The Lockmakers union stated, for instance, 'We leave the organisation of women in the trade to the NFWW.' But again, no names of ordinary branch members come down to us.

The situation of the Workers' Union is much the same. Set up in 1898, this union stagnated until the Great Unrest when it took the leadership of the strike movement and grew phenomenally from 4,500 members in 1910 to 150,000 in 1914. In the latter year the union had over 1,000 members in each of the six Black Country towns of Wolverhampton, Walsall, Dudley, Wednesbury, Smethwick and West Bromwich. Many of these would be women workers, but, again, we know nothing of their numbers, names or activities. Affiliated to Wolverhampton Trades Council in 1914 were two branches of the Workers' Union and also a Women's Section of that union, but this is all we know.

The greatest density of female trade union membership is likely to have been among teachers. We have charted the progress of the sectarian associations before the 1870 Education Act, the National Union of Elementary Teachers after 1870 and the National Union of Teachers after 1902. Membership figures are known only for 1896 and 1903. At the former date there were 201 teachers in the Wolverhampton branch and 270 in 1903. Women teachers outnumbered men by about three to one at the time of the 1911 Census, but again we know nothing of their numbers within the union. That some dissatisfaction was felt with the limited attention to women's interests is attested to by a branch in Wolverhampton in 1909 of a breakaway from the union – the National Union of Women Teachers.

The smaller teacher unions provide some further information. A Teachers' Guild of Great Britain and Ireland was formed in 1884 for headmasters and headmistresses. It appears to have had little influence in the Black Country until 1900 when Miss B. Foxley of Walsall Queen Mary's Grammar School was a member. More effective was the Association of Assistant Mistresses formed in 1885. Its only early members were three from the Dudley Proprietary School for Girls. By 1914, however it had 7 members each from Dudley and Wolverhampton High Schools, six from QMGS Walsall and one each from Halesowen Grammar and Oldbury, Stourbridge, and West Bromwich Secondary Schools.

Of other unions, we have traced twenty two female members of the National Union of Shop Assistants in the main Black Country towns in 1911. Other unions likely to have a small female membership are the National Association of Local Government Officers, the two other General unions (gas workers and general labourers), the Boot & Shoe Union, Printing & Bookbinding, Nurses and Co-operative Employees.

Once again, as with men, it is clear that Black Country women played a distinctive, as well as a not unimportant part in the development of trade unionism; especially bearing in mind that Black Country industry was small scale compared with areas such as Lancashire where trade union membership was denser. Particularly in the 1880s and again in 1911-14 Black Country women trade unionists stood at the forefront of progress.

Bibliography: Women

For further information regarding the economic position of women see my *Social Conditions in the Black Country 1800-1900* especially Chap 1 on Population and Chapter 7 on Wages, Hours, Cost of Living etc.

For the most comprehensive review of working conditions for women in Birmingham which also has relevance to the Black Country see Edward Cadbury, M. Cecille Matheson and George Shann – *Women's Work and Wages,* a Survey carried out between 1904 and 1907.

For women trade unionists nationally see Barbara Drake – *Women in Trade Unions* (1920). For the Black Country see Eric Taylor's thesis and chapters on Trade Unionism in this work.

My apologies to all women for the brevity of this chapter. It originally had two additional substantial sections. One was on Sister Dora (Dorothy Pattison) the Walsall nurse who became a legend among Walsall working people. The other was a history of women's suffrage in the Black Country. Both had to be sacrificed as this volume grew to unmanageable proportions. However, the latter has been published by me as *Votes for Women – the Struggle for the Vote in the Black Country 1900-1918*. Sister Dora, despite her life among working people is only marginally connected with the Labour movement and there is a most adequate biography of her by Jo Manton – *Sister Dora* as well as other biographies and much other material at Walsall Local History Centre.

'Pillar and Stall' working of the fabulous 10-yard coal seam in the Black Country thick coal, which, unfortunately, produced the highest death rates in Britain.

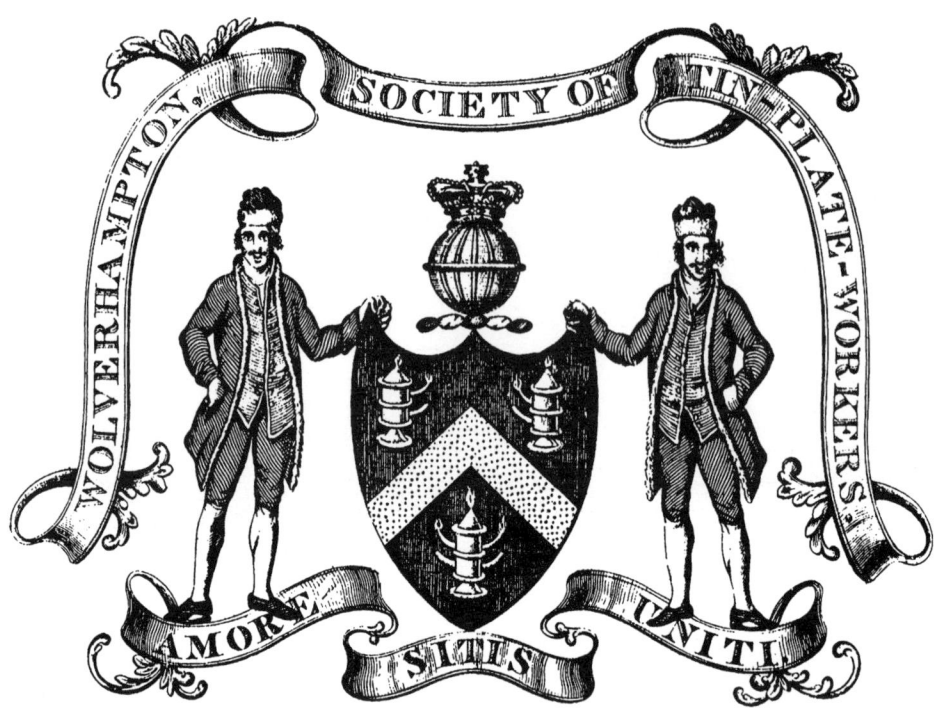

This is to certify that Mr
is a free Member of this Society
and is entitled to receive the Benefits
Stated in the Schedule

.... *Sec.y*

No .... Dated this .... Day of .... 18...
This Card is renewable in four
Months from the Date hereof.

Established in 1802 the Wolverhampton Society survived the repressions of the Combination Acts 1799-1824 (which made trade unions illegal), and produced two of the most spectacular strikes of the nineteenth century.

Wm. F. Hill　　　　　　J.V. Stevens　　　　　　A.W. Haddleton

C.C. Cooke　　　　　　Allan Granger

Five Liberal (later Lib-Lab) stalwarts of Birmingham Trades Council from the 1860s to 1900s.

Wm. F. Hill: Leader Affiliated Trades of Silversmiths, Electroplaters, and Brittania Metal Workers' Union. Trades Council member and official from 1882.

J.V. Stevens: Secretary Amalgamated Tin Plate Workers' Society and Birmingham City Councillor. Supporter of Tinplate Co-operative.

A.W. Haddleton: Flint Glassworkers' Union member and official from 1850. 1885-1895 secretary of the Trades Council.

C.C. Cooke: Started work at age 8. Founded public Lampman's Union 1870. President of Trades Council for three years. Member Aston Board of Guardians.

Allan Granger: Typographical Society member and official. Birmingham City Councillor 1881-1893. President Trades Council 1880-1887.

BIRMINGHAM LABOUR CHURCH.

THE TWELFTH ANNUAL MEETING

WILL BE HELD IN THE

TOWN HALL,

SUNDAY, OCTOBER 16, 1904.

B. SEEBOHM ROWNTREE

(Author of "Poverty: A Study of our Large Towns")

WILL DELIVER THE ADDRESS.

Chair will be taken at SEVEN o'clock by ... **T. GROOM** (Hon. Sec., Birmingham Cinderella).

Doors open at SIX p.m.

Organ Recital at 6-30 by Mr. **C. W. PERKINS**, (City Organist).

Labour Church Hymns.   Hymn Sheets provided.

Birmingham Co-operative Printers, 14, Pershore Street.

THE Labour Church is founded on the belief that the **Political and Industrial** life of a nation should be the outcome of its highest **Religious Ideal.**

Its members claim that sincere belief in the **Fatherhood of God** or the **Brotherhood of Man** must lead to a Political and Industrial Democracy.

By Political Democracy they understand **a government of the people, for the people,** based upon the principles of **Liberty, Equality and Fraternity,** and aiming at the **fullest physical, mental and moral development** of each member of the body politic.

By Industrial Democracy they understand an organisation of the industry of the people, by the people for the people, in which the **Land and Capital of the country** (the instruments of production) would be held and used **collectively for the Commonweal,** and men and women would **consciously co-operate** for the production of the life needs of their fellows.

Under such a system, with the enormous power of wealth production we now possess:—

(a) Every child could be secured the fullest possible opportunities of developing the powers within it.

(b) Every grown man and woman be able to claim, in addition to abundant leisure, the right to work which shall be worth the doing and worthily rewarded.

(c) And every old or infirm citizen be assured of peace and plenty so long as life shall last.

To this end the members of the Labour Church have devoted their energies, and hence must work for the overthrow of the present system of **competition, wage slavery, and monopoly** as not only opposed to, but destructive of their highest Religious Ideal. For in it men daily seek to gain by each other's loss; the few are made rich without working, while the many, in spite of incessant toil, are poor, oppressed and degraded; and an unending industrial war breeds hatred, misery and death throughout the length and breadth of our land.

To those who believe in a practical religion and despise a faith that does not lead to action, the members of the Labour Church fearlessly make their appeal, and believe that before all others they should receive help from those to whom the name of Christ is above all other names.

SOCIALISM IS RELIGION.

Early Twentieth Century Birmingham Trades Council Leaders

*W.J. Davis,
Founder of the Brassworkers' Society*

*W.J. Morgan,
President 1904-1909*

*J.E. Berry,
Secretary 1903-1910*

*J. Kesterton, President 1910-1912
and Secretary 1913-1918*

*Julia Varley,
first woman delegate to the Council*

*Dr Robert Dunstan,
Labour and Communist Parliamentary
candidate, Birmingham, 1918 to 1924.
(from a pencil sketch by M. Ivanoff, Moscow, 1924).*

*The first Hunger March, Birmingham to London 1922.
Unidentified, but known leaders were comrades Bridgen, Spencer, Waterer, Lewis and Burgess.*

Birmingham Trades Council Executive Committee 1928 (virtually the General Strike leadership)
Front row: *A. Lane, R. Edwards, C.G. Spragg, W. Lewis, E. Pardoe.* 2nd row: *C. Mann, Miss E.N. Cleaver (Treasurer), J.E. Corrin (President), W.T. Cardinal (Vice-President), F.W. Rudland (Secretary).* 3rd row: *H.G. Johnson, C. Watkins, H. Dawson, L. Bradley, W.L. Goodwin, S.L. Treleaven.* 4th row: *H. Shepperson, H. Parsons, G. Haynes, W. MacBeath.*

Birmingham District Communist Party leadership 1927
Back row: *Jack Thomas, Mrs Thomson, Adam Thomson, others unidentified but include Tom Roberts and Charlie Williams.* Middle row: *Bill Joss, E. Evans, Mrs Mitchell, Mrs Stokes, Daisy Vaughan, unidentified.* Front row: *Albert Darke (Wolverhampton), Billy Stokes, Jim Gardner, two unidentified probably from N. Staffs or Coventry.* Note the high proportion of five women.

Enthusiastic May Day procession in Birmingham in 1929 despite the pouring rain.

Birmingham – Labour's Victorious Six in the 1929 General Election.

Top (from the left):
John Strachey (Aston),
G.F. Sawyer (Duddeston),
A.G. Gossling (Yardley),
Wilfrid Whiteley (Ladywood).

Bottom:
C.J. Simmons (Erdington),
Fred Longden (Deritend).

Some early Black Country Labour MPs

T.F. Richards
First Black Country MP,
Wolverhampton MP, 1906-10

John Baker
Bilston MP, 1922-23 & 1924-31

J.J. McShane,
Walsall MP, 1929-1931

W.J. Brown
Wolverhampton MP, 1929-1931

Charles Sitch
Kingswinford MP, 1918-30

AN ADDRESS
TO THE
Working Classes of Walsall,
ON THE
OBJECTS AND ADVANTAGES OF SOCIETIES,
(Or Working Unions,)
ESTABLISHED ON THE PRINCIPLES OF
MUTUAL CO-OPERATION.

By a Member of the Walsall Co-operative Society.

To clothe the naked and to feed the hungry is good, but to teach men how to provide for themselves is much better.—KNOX.

Fellow Townsmen, and Brother Mechanics;

In offering to your notice a brief address, explanatory of the objects and principles of co-operation, I do not consider it necessary to say much by way of apology for the obtrusion. It is true, the subject might have fallen into better hands, some abler pen might have undertaken the task of pointing out the causes of the distress under which we are all suffering, and of stating and explaining the principles of that system of sociality, which, as opposed to merely selfish views, is calculated to promote the happiness, and to secure the independence of the working classes. But it is equally true, that as far as relates to our own town no one has yet attempted it, nor does there appear to be a probability that any of our fellow townsmen of the wealthier classes will undertake the performance of this great public duty. Be

—PRICE TWO-PENCE.—

Above: Sketch by G. Willott of the first shop in Hatherton Street used by the Walsall Society in 1886.

Left: First page of a Walsall pamphlet of 1829.

Left: The incredible Samuel Welsh founding editor of the Walsall Free Press 1859, initiator and secretary of the Walsall Cottage Hospital employing Sister Dora from 1863, founder president Walsall Trades Council from 1872, founder member 1873 Walsall Locks and Cartgear the productive co-operative that flourished for 113 years; founding chairman Walsall consumer Co-operative Society 1886.

Centre: The remarkable William Millerchip. Active in Locks and Cartgear from 1887; national secretary Lock Union from 1902; President Walsall Co-operative Society 1896-1910. Walsall Councillor and JP to 1910; Manager Walsall Labour Exchange 1910-1927 thereafter town councillor and alderman; a national leader of the Co-operative movement as member Co-operative Central Board 1913-1938.

Right: George Harrison. Manager Locks and Cartgear from its inception in 1873. Treasurer Walsall consumer Co-operative Society 1886-1917.

Part 2

The Birmingham and Black Country Labour Movement from 1914

Chapter 10

Birmingham Trade Unions and the War

The War and the City

The European War, as it was known at the time, was probably both the most tragic and the most heroic episode in the life of the city. Yet the records tell us all too little of this great saga.

Almost 12,000 servicemen perished in the conflict; this was about 5 per cent of the male population of Birmingham of military age between 18 and 45 years. The city council keeps the memory of their sacrifice green at the Hall of Memory; of the tears, anguish and anxiety of relatives and friends little was recorded. Nor were the sufferings recorded of the 150,000 men who enlisted in Birmingham, the large but unknown number of those who were wounded, and those who continued to suffer for the rest of their days.

On the civilian front, masses of men made munitions in factories turned over from peace production or in vast specially built factories paid for and controlled by the government, but run by private enterprise; at the end of the war munition workers were sacked, the government factories were often sold at knockdown prices and the miracles of production performed during the war years were very inadequately recorded. Vast profits were made during the war and the profiteer became the most reviled of creatures; but who these profiteers were in Birmingham and how much profit they made is almost unknown as only the largest of companies were public ones obliged to reveal their profits.

The war years were a liberating experience for many women. Mobilised to replace men they worked in factories, on the land, as conductors on the trams, on the railways, in voluntary social work, in large numbers as clerks and much else; but even before the war was over they were being sacked and returned to the home with only the vote (if they were over 30) to remind them of their emancipation.

Important democratic advances took place during the war. It could not be waged without the full co-operation of the trade unions which found themselves fully recognised by the government and the employers for the first time. Many war-time functions were organised locally. Committees for production and to organise recruiting; Tribunals to decide on the allocation of man and woman-power, and to rule on objections to Conscription; Committees to distribute food, fuel and other necessities Pensions committees and many others. Virtually all the records of these committees were destroyed and we have only limited press coverage of their activities.

Of other civilian problems the black-out and lack of entertainment caused irritation although air raids were not a serious threat. The city's vital industries were beyond the range of the aircraft of the day and Zeppelin raids occurred only three times, although they were widely spaced at yearly intervals from 1916. The last Zeppelin encountered on the British coast was brought down by a Birmingham man, Egbert Cadbury, son of the chocolate family.

Much more serious was the continual rise in the price of food and other necessities and the food shortages of 1817-18 as U-boats destroyed shipping faster than it could be built.

As the war progressed, the city became a centre for wounded soldiers and acute problems of the treatment of Discharged and Disabled servicemen arose. War weariness and the constant slaughter strengthened the peace movement, which had a presence in the city from the beginning. Celebrations at the ending of the war were muted by dissatisfaction with the system of demobilisation which discharged men not on the principle of first in first out but released first those who had jobs to go to.

Although the loss of so much of the record of the city at war has been deplored, Birmingham fared better than the Black Country and indeed most of the large cities of the country in that two historians R.H. Brazier and E. Sandford gathered such records as there were in 1924 and wrote *Birmingham and the Great War 1914-1919.* from which much of this preamble has been written. What follows is the reaction to the war of those organised in the Labour movement.

The Trades Council and the War

The war faced Labour movement activists with impossible dilemmas. Three views were possible. The majority view was that it was a war against Prussian militarism and expansion; when Germany invaded Belgium this view became almost unchallengeable since we had treaty obligations to defend that country. The second view was that war was an inevitable outcome of capitalist development; that this was a war between rival imperialist blocs for colonies. In Lenin's words the world had already been divided up into colonies and this was the new era of wars for the re-division of the world. Workers had no business killing fellow-workers for the benefit of their capitalist bosses. This remained largely an ideological view until March 1916 when Conscription was introduced and decisions had to be taken by those who were called up to fight. Conscription was also the catalyst for the even smaller group who were prepared to act on the self-evident truth that if all men refused to fight there could not be any war. They believed that the taking of life could never be justified under any circumstances. These men, together with many of the second view became Conscientious Objectors. Thus 1916 was a turning point and combined with increasing war weariness brought on by the ever-lengthening slaughter lists from the front led to a significant peace movement both in Britain and abroad which eventually brought the war to an end.

The overall development of this movement can best be traced through the minutes of the Birmingham Trades Council which, by a happy accident from the point of view of the historian, joined in July 1914 with the Labour Representative Committee (effectively the city's Labour Party) to become the Birmingham Trades & Labour Council. The same minute book thus records the activities of both the industrial and political wings of the Birmingham labour movement.

When war broke out the movement was committed to the resolution of the 1907 International Socialist Congress which stated:

> If war threatens to break out it is the duty of the working class in the countries concerned... to use every effort to prevent war which seems to them most appropriate... Should war none the less breakout, their duty is to intervene to bring it promptly to an end... to rouse the population from their slumbers and to hasten the fall of capitalist domination.

When it became apparent that war was near the following Manifesto to the British People was issued under the signatures of Keir Hardie and Arthur Henderson as representatives of the British Section of the International Socialist Bureau:

> The long threatened European war is now upon us... Whatever may be the rights or wrongs of the sudden, crushing attack made by the militaristic empire of Austria on Serbia, it is certain that the workers of all countries likely to be drawn into the conflict must strain every nerve to prevent their Governments committing them to war.
>
> Everywhere Socialists and the organised forces of Labour are taking this course. Everywhere vehement protests are being made against the greed and intrigues of militarists and armament-mongers.
>
> We call upon you to do the same here in Great Britain... Hold vast demonstrations against war in every industrial centre...
>
> There is no time to lose. Already by secret agreements and understandings... steps are being taken which may fling all of us into the fray...

Proclaim that for you the days of plunder and butchery have gone by; send messages of peace and fraternity to your fellows. Down with class rule. Down with the rule of brute force. Down with the War.

Demonstrations and meetings were organised. On the day after war began, 5 August 1914 a special meeting of the Birmingham Trades Council executive committee met at which the secretary, Councillor J. Kesterton, reported the steps he had taken to support the movement for the prevention of British intervention in the European war. He had conferred with the Independent Labour Party Federation and he had taken part in the Bull Ring demonstration the previous Sunday. He had also taken preliminary steps for a Stop the War agitation. However, the three national bodies of Labour – the Labour Party, Trade Union Congress and the General Federation of Trade Unions – called a Conference on Aug 4th. and Kesterton had attended that. This Conference had passed a resolution urging that parties throughout the country seek interviews with local authorities to discuss 'the inevitable dislocation of trade and the resultant unemployment and distress.' In other words, the national leaders of the Labour movement had forgotten all the fine words about resisting the war and were about to collaborate wholeheartedly with the government in the prosecution of the war.

The Birmingham labour movement followed suit. The Trades Council arranged a meeting with the Lord Mayor for Friday 7th. August. Its EC and the LRC met jointly the same evening and it was reported that the Town Clerk had met them, 'in a generous and sympathetic spirit' and had already put into operation some of the proposals of the deputation.

These proposals referred to measures against unemployment; for one of the first effects of the war was to throw many thousands of people out of work. Much of the work of the Trades Council in the first two months of the war was concerned with this unemployment. For instance, at the monthly Trades Council meeting on Saturday 16th. August it passed two resolutions. The first protested against attempts being made to induce University students and Boy Scouts to 'give their services free to farmers under the guise of patriotism' which was taking work away from farm labourers. The second resolution demanded that 'in the interests of the people the Government should take over the whole control of food supply in the country.' At its next meeting on 5 September the Trades Council protested at the Post Office allowing staff to be depleted (by recruitment) and overworking those who were left instead of taking on the unemployed. The National Union of Clerks seem to have had particular problems. They complained at that meeting about a food firm in the city sacking its clerks, and at the next monthly meeting an NUC resolution was passed protesting against victimisation of clerks at BSA where nine members of the union had been dismissed.

The question of unemployment was also the biggest problem of the Birmingham Central Citizens' Committee set up in the first days of the war. A Trades Council leaflet early in August noted that the Labour movement was well represented on the Citizens' Committee but went on to state, 'It is essential that every trade unionist exert himself in the scheme to prevent starvation in the city. Send in your names if you are willing to give your services to the great cause of caring for those who will otherwise suffer terrible privations from the war.'

This unemployment was serious, but short lived. The Intelligence Officer of the Birmingham Citizens' Committee (W.J. Ashley, the economic historian from the University) calculated that on 26 September, of a fairly representative sample of 18,500 workers, 3 per cent were unemployed and 22 per cent on short time, while 28 per cent were working overtime. Unemployment was worse among women that among men. Responsibility to relieve distress devolved on the Birmingham Citizens' Committee and their funds, apart from the amounts raised locally, came from the charity, the Prince of Wales Fund. Relief granted in the six months to February 1915 amounted to £42,000. Amounts then fell and by the quarter October-December 1915 payments were down to £7,650. By March 1916 total payments from the outbreak of war had been £171,000.

A report from the Birmingham Socialist Centre in September 1915 passed judgement on the work of the Citizens' Committee. It pointed out that besides relieving the distress of the unemployed it had also had to bear the burden of relieving the wives and families of servicemen who were left destitute as a result of the chaotic system of enlistment and consequent delay in paying dependents' allowances.

With regard to the unemployed, the report stated that the scale of relief was totally inadequate, payment to one adult being 5/6d. and two adults 8/-d. Rent could not be enforced, but the arrears accumulated. Even this pittance was paid not in money but in grocery tickets and officials ascertained the shops at which the tickets were exchanged and checked that they were spent on necessities. This method was a legacy from the odious Charity Organisation Society that had long been responsible for dispersing charitable aid in Birmingham and ensuring that it went only to the 'deserving poor'. Eventually, as unemployment fell, the Committee were left with 'the ineffectives, the unemployable and the chronic cases of poverty.'

The logic of their pro-war position ensured that the trade unions and Labour movement were quickly enmeshed in recruiting campaigns for the forces. But there was this dilemma. Although there was near unanimity in support of the war there was total opposition to Conscription. At this time it is difficult to comprehend this unanimous hatred of Conscription. But in 1914 it was the touchstone of British liberties that the lives of free men were not at the disposal of the state. It was the mark of the slave under the heel of Prussian militarism that our enemies were conscripted. The introduction of conscription into Britain would remove the very freedom we were fighting for. With such views it became incumbent on the Labour movement to help produce the recruits that the military machine required.

Brazier and Sandford give details of mobilisation. First came the recall of reservists to the colours. Of these, large numbers were serving with the police, the post office, the fire brigade and the tramway department. Then the various territorial battalions of the Warwickshire Regiment were mobilised. Then came the stream of enthusiastic recruits. By 10 October it was estimated that 3.35 per cent of the population of Birmingham had volunteered amounting to 28,521 recruits and this was among the highest percentages in Britain. After this there was a slump in recruiting.

Much has been made of the voluntary response to the war, but the amount of social pressure was considerable. It was not unknown for men who showed a reluctance to volunteer to be sacked and Birmingham city council, which made up the wages of those who volunteered refused the same concession to those who were conscripted.

In France the British Expeditionary force had encountered the Germans at the Battle of the Marne and retreated to regroup. By September 1914 the war had taken an entirely new turn with trench warfare replacing a war of movement. It was clear that the war would not be over by Christmas and that a never ending supply of cannon fodder would henceforward be required.

The first attempt to mobilise man and woman power was a National Register compiled from forms left at every house and filled in by all between the ages of 15 and 45. Over half a million forms were distributed during the first week of August and all were tabulated and sent to London in the first week in September. The next week 118,000 pink forms relating to men of military age were transmitted for the use of Recruiting Officers.

The national results, of the Register, which seemed to show 1,400,000 additional single men available for enlistment were interpreted in different ways. The army general staff was still thinking in terms of a short war and were scornful of 'shadow armies' for 'shadow campaigns' in the distant future. A seventy division force of 1,200,000 men could be sustained through voluntary enlistment, if recruitment were sustained. On the other hand demands were growing for the British commitment to be more equal to that of the French who maintained 108 divisions from a smaller population than ours. The National Register was accompanied by a strident Daily Mail campaign for Conscription; the TUC issued an equally determined blast against Conscription.

A last determined voluntary effort was therefore launched in November 1915 under the Derby Attestment Scheme. This scheme required 'pledges' from all men, both married and single, between the ages of 18 and 41 years that they would agree to be called up in 23 different age groups in such a way that all single men would be called up before any married men.

The attitude of Birmingham trade unionists to conscription at this time is summed up in a resolution moved at the Trades Council by Frank Spires (who was also the secretary of the LRC) in June 1915 stating:

> This Council declares its strongest opposition to the present agitation for Conscription believing conscription to be a violation of the principle of civic freedom hitherto prized as one of the chief heritages of British liberty and constitutes a grave menace to the freedom of the nation.

> It further believes that recourse to a compulsory system is uncalled for in view of the enormous voluntary enlistment since war began...
>
> The Council urges Parliament to offer instant resistance to any proposal to impose on the British people a yoke which is one of the chief causes of Prussian militarism against which hundreds of thousands of our fellow workers have volunteered for war.

This was countered by an amendment:

> While deprecating the present agitation for Conscription we believe the time has arrived for a National Register of all males in the U.K. and British colonies and provide military training for all physically fit men (not necessarily interfering with their occupations) and only in the event of the failure of the present voluntary system shall agitation for compulsory enlistment be encouraged by this Council.

The minute concludes, 'After lengthy discussion the amendment was defeated and the resolution passed with 4 dissentients.'

By November the Trades Council had rejected a motion by Erdington ASE that 'The Labour Party should find an alternative to Conscription and this should be a Citizens' Army on the Swiss Model.' and approved the appeal of the TUC, Labour Party and General Federation of Trade Unions to 'arrange great recruiting campaigns throughout the country as an alternative to conscription.'

The following account of this campaign in Birmingham is taken from Brazier and Sandford, but it must be added that there is little to confirm it from the minutes of either the local Trades Council or the Labour Representation Committee. It seems likely therefore that this campaign was sustained largely by those trade unions and Labour activists in the city with a particular enthusiasm for recruiting, notably the Brassworkers and W.J. Davis, rather than through the general machinery of the movement.

Recognising that this was the last chance to avoid conscription, a Birmingham and District Labour Recruiting Council was formed to organise a great campaign to secure the city's quota of recruits. This was set at 30,000 over the ensuing period. Beginning with a mass meeting at the Town Hall and messages from Kitchener and Austen Chamberlain, the campaign was carried on through press coverage and taken into the factories and workshops. The effect was almost immediate, recruiting, which had sometimes dropped as low as 100 a week in Birmingham, rose to 1,525 for the week ending 23 October and the following week was even higher at 1,661. Figures were boosted by a Group Enlistment System. This was part of the Derby Attestment procedure whereby single men volunteered to enlist when their age group was called up. An important feature of the scheme was that such attested men were able to appeal to a Tribunal and seek exemption if they were unfit, employed on work of national importance, or whose personal or family situation made it impossible for them to join the forces. The final date for enlistment under the group system was extended to Saturday 11 December. From Thursday of that week recruiting offices were besieged with would-be recruits and queues of men forming from 5-30am waiting to attest. Later, the group system was again extended to the day before conscription was to come into operation in March 1916 by which time it was hoped that all Birmingham single men would have attested. This would have justified the view that conscription was unnecessary.

The Birmingham target of 30,000 was over-fulfilled at the end of 1915, although not all single men had attested by then. But by this time the machinery of conscription was being put into place and the new era of compulsory enlistment began on 2 March 1916.

Meanwhile the main problem in the factories from the outbreak of war was the uncontrolled enlistment of skilled men into the forces and the efforts made by employers and the government to replace skilled labour with female and unskilled labour in their efforts to increase output. The political truce initiated by the Labour leaders nationally was endorsed in Birmingham and this disadvantaged unions at a time when both prices and profits were rising rapidly.

An early agreement affecting Birmingham was the Shells and Fuses agreement whereby the main engineering union, the ASE, agreed to permit the employment of women and semi-skilled men in factories engaged on war work. Also in March came the first general war-time agreement on industrial relations, the famous (or infamous) Treasury Agreement. By this the trade unions in the principal industries connected with the war agreed to give up the right to strike, to refer all disputes to government arbitration and abide by the findings. It further required the unions to give up all established trade union customs and practices concerning conditions of employment. This included agreement to the introduction of unlimited 'dilutee' labour on any class of work deemed necessary by the employer; the removal of all trade union restrictions regarding the employment of women, girls and youths; to assist and encourage speed-up in production; to give up all definitions of a normal day and all restrictions on overtime, night work or Sunday working; and to give up many of the safeguards regarding health and safety embodied in the Factory Acts. Thus the trade unions leaders were signing away all the rights of workers accumulated in 150 years of struggle. In fact the miners refused to sign the document and the ASE delayed until a further agreement was negotiated with Lloyd George stipulating that excess profits would be levied on engineering firms involved in war production and that relaxation of trade union practices would end when the war ended.

These agreements were made statutory in July 1915 with the first Munitions Act of the war. Strikes were made illegal 'in certain circumstances', and workers were forbidden to change their jobs without a 'leaving certificate' from the employers. This act also set up local Munitions Tribunals through which wage and other agreements were compulsorily arbitrated.

Such tight labour legislation fed the fears of those who believed that the liberties they were said to be fighting for were being voluntarily surrendered by their trade union leaders. Grievances at shop floor level therefore increasingly began to be settled by shop floor representatives rather than trade union officials and there came into existence the Shop Stewards movement. This was most powerful in Scotland where large scale stoppages occurred. These did not occur in Birmingham where shop steward organisation developed late and only in the big factories. Constant sources of friction were the unfair advantages the acts bestowed upon the employers, the differences between the treatment of war workers and the large number on non-war work and where that distinction began; also the ability of employers, especially in small firms and non-union firms, to avoid paying negotiated wage increases. So that while many stories of highly paid munitions workers were true, large numbers, particularly women, continued to be badly paid.

Birmingham engineers were in the best position to maintain their standard of living, but their experience suggests that other unions on less essential work would have even greater difficulty in maintaining living standards. The last advance for engineers had been in 1911 and negotiations were proceeding for an increase when war broke out. Prices rose immediately, but it was not until December 1914 that an increase of 2/-d. a week was agreed locally by the engineering employers. In July 1915 a further 3/-d. a week was obtained and in September 1916, local employers having refused a further advance the case was taken to the Committee on Production which awarded 3/-d. per week. Thus from the pre-war district rate of 38/-d. a week for skilled engineers the rate had risen to 46/-d. an increase of 21 per cent while the official Ministry of Labour index of retail prices had risen 46 per cent. The war also hastened the development of national wage negotiations and all subsequent wartime advances came from the Committee on Production and were national awards. Increases in 1917 were 5/-d. in April another 3/-d. in August, a Churchill bonus of 12½ per cent in October and another 5/-d. in December. In 1918 there was a 7½ per cent increase on the earnings of pieceworkers only and 3/6d. in August. Thus by the end of the war basic engineering rates had risen to 69/3d. plus the increase for pieceworkers. This represents a rise in basic rate over 1914 of 82 per cent when the cost of living had risen 103 per cent.

These basic rates would be augmented by a considerable amount of overtime and the standard of living of most civilian families rose, particularly with the removal of the bane of pre-war life, unemployment. Against this must be set long hours of work, the strain of war-time life, anxiety concerning relatives in the forces, and the grief of the bereaved.

Trades Council activity reflected both price and wage concerns. During 1915 the Council agreed to a request by he National Labour War Emergency Committee to hold a Conference in Birmingham in March on the Cost of Food and Fuel. In May the Council was resolving that the local Munitions Committee should have an equal number of trade unionists and employers. In June the complaint of the NUR of insufficient housing in Tyseley was taken up with the city council. Also in June there was a strongly worded resolution on prices to the city council from the Carpenters & Joiners:

> The interests of the community would be better served if instead of raising the prices of coal, gas and tram fares thus imposing further burdens on the people of the city, the Council should concentrate on protecting the public from the exploitation of Coal Owners, Millers and others and urges the City to call a Conference of City, Town and County Councils to take measures to end the unscrupulous and anti-patriotic exploitation of the people's needs in time of war.

An attempt was made to tone this resolution down, and it was also moved that the resolution lie on the table. But the original motion was passed with three dissentients. A particular scandal was the refusal of the government to raise the 5/-d. Old Age Pension and in June the Trades Council took up a national proposal that a 2/6d. increase should be found from the Prince of Wales Fund which by that time was no longer burdened with large unemployment claims. In July the Trades Council was protesting at a proposal to lower the school leaving age to thirteen for those who worked in agriculture. In fact. the city council had a good record in keeping children at school until they were fourteen during the war. At this time, the extreme pro-war faction felt a need to consolidate its position on the Trades Council and Councillor W.W. Saunders and W.E. Stevens moved:

> This Council pledges all support to the Committee on Munitions in its efforts to increase output of War Materials and bring about a speedy termination of the war in favour of the Allied Forces. It expresses its sincere thanks to the members of the various trade unions who by volunteering their services for military purposes have saved their country from the fate of Belgium and prepared us to meet a relentless and unscrupulous enemy.

This resolution was passed with seven votes against.

At the same meeting T.F. Fathers moved a protest at the 'unwarranted increases' in Birmingham rents and desired the Chief Assistant Overseer to make 'searching enquiries' with a view to revaluing properties where rents had been raised since 1 January 1915. This was part of a campaign that lasted throughout the war, despite the passing of a Rent Restriction Act at the end of 1915, and led to the formation of fifteen tenants' associations with 20,000 members.

In November Councillor Kneeshaw, a peace supporter, moved a comprehensive resolution at the LRC which represented the views of the Union of Democratic Control. It sought that at a future Peace Conference (a) no territory should be transferred without the consent of the inhabitants (b) no treaty should be entered into by Britain without the consent of Parliament (c) that future foreign policy should not be based on the balance of power but on the Concert of Europe with the setting up of an international Council. This resolution was carried by 20 votes to 14 indicating still considerable support for the view that the main task was to get on with the war rather than raise contentious questions about war aims.

The same month, the Trades Council executive considered a request from the No-Conscription Fellowship to appoint a delegate to a forthcoming N-CF conference. The EC resolved that no delegate be sent, but the full Council overturned this decision.

In December the Trades Council was protesting at the 'Junker like officials who manage the state controlled railways' for attempts to prevent lady clerks joining the Railway Clerks' Association, and the Carpenters & Joiners were regretting that the Labour Party did not obtain guarantees against further price increases before joining the government's recruiting scheme.

> 1916 opened with a determined last ditch stand to prevent conscription. John Kneeshaw moved:
>
> That this Council representing 70,000 working men reaffirms its unalterable opposition to Conscription. The agitation for conscription was never directed at securing national advantage, but for the purpose of undermining the Trade Union movement and undermining British democracy. We regard the proposed division of the nation's manhood into Married and Unmarried and impose conscription on the latter as a trick to divide the opposition to conscription. We repudiate such a trick and pledge ourselves to resist the introduction of this pernicious Prussian principle to the utmost extent of our powers.

John Beard of the Workers Union, one of the leaders of the war party, attempted to defeat this resolution with the following amendment:

> This Trades Council defers sending out a resolution as vital to this nation as Mr Asquith's pledge to married men until we have ascertained the views of the rank and file of our affiliated organisations.

This amendment was defeated and the resolution passed.

This continued opposition to conscription was strongly reinforced by the political wing, the LRC. On 10 January a resolution noted that a recent Labour Conference had 'decided unmistakedly' against conscription, congratulated the National Union of Railwaymen on its stand, and 'assured the Trade Union movement of its support for any further action taken to prevent conscription or make it unworkable if passed.' The LRC further resolved to hold a public demonstration against conscription, to apply to the Lord Mayor for the use of the Town Hall and set out its order of preference for speakers as J.H. Thomas MP, Philip Snowden MP, Robert Smillie, Robert Williams, Ramsay MacDonald MP and W.C. Anderson. But the national movement had no programme to 'make conscription unworkable if passed' and when after three weeks no reply had been received from any of the proposed speakers, the LRC dropped their protest demonstration.

But conscription continued as an issue. In July a motion reaffirming opposition in identical terms with Kneeshaw's motion of January was countered with the following amendment:

> This Council believes that it is the duty of every Trade Unionist and Socialist who believes in political action to support the State which claims him in this great crisis to work or fight to bring about the success of the Allies which our comrades are doing in France.

The amendment was defeated by 55 votes to 72 and the original policy confirmed by 70 to 55. This can be seen as a turning point in the alignment of the Trades Council to the view that the war should be stopped. The 'war party' led by the Workers' Union representatives of Councillor Beard and Julia Varley were from then on reduced to the claim that the Trades Council had been 'captured' by the Pacifists.

In July 1916 the Council, in conjunction with the local Workers' Educational Association, developed a comprehensive policy for Labour after the war. This included comprehensive training and employment plans for the war wounded; fulfilment of the pledge that servicemen should return to the jobs they left with Courts to decide contentious issues and where this involved the displacement of women men or boys, employment for them should be found or adequate means provided to avoid destitution including the extension of National Unemployment Insurance to all trades; immediate restoration after the War of all trade union rights; if any scheme of arbitration were adopted the Council favours the New Zealand model; further amalgamations of trade unions and local and national public utilities schemes to prevent unemployment. Finally, support for the growing shop stewards movement was expressed in the following way. 'For the maintenance of discipline and the prevention of friction in the workshop, small committees of Trade Unionists be appointed and recognised by the employers, such as already exist in several trades.'

In November the question of the conscription of wealth was brought up by T.F. Fathers. This demanded that the vast expense of the war be met by a levy on the accumulated wealth of the country. It supported the TUC suggestion for a Census of Wealth which would include the disclosure of bank balances, an estimate of productive and distributive wealth and property and real estate from which rents, interest and profits were paid.

The 1916 annual report of the Council highlighted the following work. Attempts to get the Old Age Pension increased from 5/-d. to 7/6d. which the government eventually conditionally conceded. Its work on prices, rents and housing. It also highlighted the 1916 Trades Union Congress which had been held in Birmingham. Arising from this Kesterton, the secretary wrote to Rudland, the president stating that he (Kesterton) had, as was usual, taken the minutes of the TUC and, which was also usual, had, at the end of the Congress been presented with the President's bell. He felt that this bell would be better in the hands of Rudland rather than himself. So, since he could not part with the original, he had had a replica bell made, by the same hands, which he now presented to the president 'for the perpetual use of yourself and your successors in the Presidential chair.' (This momento, the present secretary informs me, has long since been lost – GB).

Finally for the year 1916 it was recorded that the growth of the Trades Council had continued and by the end of the year 182 branches of 79 unions were affiliated representing nearly 100,000 workers.

1917

1917 brought many new problems. January saw indignation registered at the refusal of the government to raise servicemen's pensions and allowances. The secretary was directed to enquire from other trades councils regarding their experiences with the Discharged Soldiers' and Sailors' Association. The next month the Council heard that from the replies there seemed to be no advantage in setting up a DSSA and the best bodies to assist discharged servicemen were the trade unions. It was therefore agreed to ask all affiliated societies to set up sub-committees to deal with this matter.

In February the EC considered the proposed formation of a National Alliance of Employers and Employed. The Trades Council had sent a representative to a meeting of Workers' Representatives and had found that most of the big unions were represented nationally and a provisional committee had been set up to negotiate with the employers. The matter went to full council in April and was rejected out of hand. Its disadvantages outweighed its advantages it was said. The main concern was that employers would use the Alliance after the war to prevent the restoration of trade union rights.

The same meeting welcomed the Russian revolution, but resolution and amendment again clearly showed the positions of the war and peace parties. The resolution read:

> This Trades Council congratulates Russian trade unionists and people on the success of the Revolution. It trusts that the workers of Germany and other countries will take steps to depose their royal and militaristic dictators and oppressors, and urges on the British government the desirability of establishing a truly democratic government and restoring British liberties.

Opposed to this was an amendment moved by Councillor Beard:

> This Trades Council congratulates Russian trade unionists on the success of the Revolution and welcomes the declaration that they are prepared to defend their new, democratic, constitution from both within and without at the point of the bayonet. It hopes that the workers of Germany, Austria and Bulgaria will follow the example of the Russians and depose their royal and military dictators and also assist in ending the malignant rule in Turkey. It further welcomes the declaration of the new Russian government to rehabilitate Belgium, Serbia, Montenegro and Rumania, and expresses appreciation of the government of the USA in its decision to fight on the side of the Allies for Liberty, Humanity and endurable peace.

This powerful, patriotic amendment was lost and the original motion passed. In May an explicit anti-war motion was put to the Council by H. Potter of the Navvies' Union:

> This meeting is convinced that a lasting peace cannot be secured by a policy of conquest followed by a Commercial war, but only by a policy which lays the basis of a real Inter-national partnership. It condemns a long war of attrition which it considers would involve the victors as well as the vanquished in social ruin. It strongly urges that an attempt be made to ascertain whether we cannot now get by negotiation everything that the war was started to secure or defend, and demands that the people of this country shall not be committed without their knowledge or consent to the support of schemes of territorial aggrandisement which have not hitherto been regard as germane to the interests of the nation and which Parliament has neither debated or sanctioned.

It was then moved, 'That discussion on this resolution be postponed until the Enemy has withdrawn from all allied Territory.' This amendment was lost and the original motion passed by 43 votes to 29.

The Russian revolution had an immense impact on the country. A resuscitated United Socialist Council dominated by the Independent Labour Party and the British Socialist Party, both strongly anti-war by this time, decided to call a conference at Leeds to 'respond to the Russian government's call for peace' and work for a real international peace 'based upon working-class solidarity.' To obtain this the conference decided to set up Soviets in Britain, although little came of it eventually. Surprisingly, because it still appeared to have a pro-war majority, the Trades Council executive decided to send two delegates to the Conference. At the June full council an amendment regretting this decision was lost and the motion agreed by 77 votes to 55. A number of names were put forward, Rudland the president, Reynolds, Spires the vice-president, Cox, Keatley, Clynes, Beard, Hallas and David Jones. The last five withdrew their names, presumably because they were all pro-war, certainly Beard, Hallas and Jones were. Eventually Rudland and Reynolds both probably anti-war were elected. The LRC had earlier appointed two delegates, Fathers and Murray, to the Conference both of whom were anti-war.

In June, after the Conference, a letter was received from the United Socialist Council inviting the

Trades Council to organise a divisional conference on the same lines as Leeds. By this time, to the press, anything connected with Leeds was Bolshevism incarnate. This was reflected by the discussion on the executive. A motion that the matter lie on the table was defeated by 6 votes to 7, but a motion to read the letter to Council was lost by 7 votes to 6. Next business was then moved and carried by 6 to 5. At full council letters were read from the local ILP and BSP asking why the letter had not been discussed. The president replied that this had been defeated. The decision of the EC was then reversed and a resolution that the letter should be read was passed. The meeting then adjourned for a fortnight. When it reconvened, Rudland and Reynolds presented their report on the Leeds Conference. The secretary then read a circular from the Workers' and Soldiers' Council inviting the Trades Council to send a delegate to their district Conference on 18th. August. This was countered with a resolution that 'the question of Workers' and Soldiers' Councils is highly contentious and this Council is unable to vote without first ascertaining the views of its constituents.' This was lost and the resolution carried by 50 votes to 37. Rudland, Spires, Reynolds and Miss Stubbs were elected as delegates. The LRC also elected four delegates to this Conference, which was now being organised by a local secretary, Jim Simmons, on behalf of the national Workers' and Soldiers' Council.

Some local Conferences took place, but not the Birmingham one. It was banned by the police. But the preparations for the conference and the number of delegates elected throws considerable light on the anti-war movement in Birmingham at that time. This is dealt with fully in a subsequent section dealing with the activities of the political parties in the city.

The Trades Council annual report for 1917 focussed largely on the two issues of food and housing. The German U-boat campaign was now producing permanent serious food shortages and lengthy queues. The part that the Labour movement, including the Trades Council played in minimising these problems is fully discussed in a chapter on the Co-operative movement.

With regard to housing, the Trades Council fully supported the Tenants' Associations in resisting rent increases, both legal and illegal, and the evictions that followed inability to pay increased rents. The Rent Act of December 1915 had not only left loopholes which landlords could exploit, but some landlords took advantage of tenant ignorance to ignore the Act altogether. Kesterton, the secretary, said that he had written 5,000 letters and many cases had been taken to Court and won.

A new Rent Act of 1917 was a direct result of a case in Birmingham promoted by the Trades Council. This was Sharpe Bros & Knight v Chant where a tenant was advised to withhold rent in excess of the legal minimum and also deduct the excess amounts of rent that he had already paid. The landlord applied for an order to evict; this the County court refused. The landlord then went to the Court of Appeal which upheld the original decision. The new Act removed a widespread grievance in the city that even where rent reductions had been obtained under the 1915 Act it had been very difficult to recover the excess rent already paid.

However the 1917 Act did not entirely solve the problem and the Trades Council and the Tenants' Associations were applying for the Birmingham area to be declared a Munitions Area which would guarantee that no munitions worker could be evicted. Such an order was expected shortly, but Kesterton emphasised that although this would benefit munitions workers, the Trades Council was not for differential treatment for any section of workers and was campaigning for all evictions to be made illegal.

1918

1918 brought even greater stresses and problems for the Trades Council. January saw the LRC deciding on Parliamentary candidates for a post-war general election (Kneeshaw for Ladywood and Shann for Yardley), and the EC considering resolutions for a national system of rationing by need and not purchasing power, and another for a protest meeting on the cost of living.

In February the Trades Council left, or lost, their meeting place which had been throughout the war Queen's College in Paradise Street. They moved to Bristol Street Schools, although they received an invitation from the International Tailors to use their premises. An invitation to a Land Nationalisation Conference was accepted and Mrs Mitchell was appointed delegate to an Educational Conference under the auspices of the Birmingham Workers' Suffrage Federation. Three additional members to the Food Committee were also recommended.

In March the Trades Council passed a resolution requesting the TUC and Labour Party to prepare a Charter for Labour at the end of the war which should include repeal of the Defence of the Realm Act, Munition and Military Service Acts and the restoration of trade union rights. But a peace resolution expressing the view that the, 'Undue prolongation of the war... Brings within measurable distance the horrors of world famine...' and 'passionately appealing' to the House of Commons to 'accelerate those tendencies that betoken an earnest desire for the inevitable conference preliminary to a return to normal times.' was deferred.

April brought a clear indication that the war party was no longer prepared to coexist with the peace party. John Kesterton, the secretary, resigned. A meeting on the 6th passed unanimously a vote of confidence in Kesterton. Another meeting on the 13th. heard that Kesterton had accepted an offer from the Food Extra Rationing Committee to be their Labour Adviser. Disappointment was expressed at his resignation, but satisfaction with his new appointment for which he was 'exceptionally well fitted.' But at a third meeting Kesterton was criticised. He must have known of the offer of his new job, said one delegate. This was ordered to be expunged from the minutes. Willis of the Railway Clerks agreed with all the good things said about Kesterton, but thought that he tried to dominate the organisation. He then went to the heart of the issue. 'There had been a time when the Pacifists were in a minority on the Council. But they were not dismayed and strove manfully to convert that minority into a majority and they were not ashamed of their work...'

At a subsequent meeting Rudland, who had been the anti-war president, was appointed secretary and Frank Spires, also anti-war, became president. The views of the majority of the executive were thus brought into line with that of the anti-war majority of the delegates.

Issues brought about by the war continued to dominate Trades Council attention. In May the ASE No 1. Branch deferred resolution forecasting 'famine and revolution' if the war were not stopped was passed, and the same night a contrary resolution from an NUR branch demanding that the war be fought to a finish was defeated. Even the issue of Shop Stewards was at bottom a war issue. This was first brought to the attention of the EC by a letter from Mrs Mitchell of the National Federation of Women Workers). Full council decided that a national speaker should be invited to present the case for Shop Stewards and in July J.T. Murphy, the outstanding national shop stewards leader, 'Spoke for two hours showing the superiority of the Works System to the old trade union executives procedures.' The matter was renewed in September when a deputation from the Birmingham and District Shop Stewards told the Council that 45 factories, including all the large firms, were organised within the Shop Stewards movement. Suggestions for co-operation with the Trades Council ranged from a standing joint committee to regular quarterly meetings. But relations with the shop stewards were not finalised until after the war.

Meanwhile, at the June Council meeting standing orders were suspended to discuss the arrest of John McLean. McLean was the famous anti-war Communist educationalist, with enormous influence on the shop stewards movement in Scotland. The Council demanded his unconditional release and pledged themselves to 'resist this and other such Prussian acts having the object of suppressing our few remaining semi-liberties.'

In August the Council listened to John Mooney telling of the sentence of death passed on his brother Tom, an American leader framed by the police for his trade union activity. At the same meeting protests were made at the closing down of the press of the Socialist Labour Party, as the government campaign against anti-war activities intensified. A resolution protested that the government had arrogated to itself the right to suppress without warning any publication distasteful to it and was a serious menace to liberties and democratic rights.

Also in August the local campaign against the pro-peace Trades Council reached its climax with the formation of a breakaway trades council. An open letter from the executive of August 5th stated that an attempt was being made by a few extreme militarists of the British Workers' League to divide the workers of Birmingham. It linked this with a national threat by Havelock Wilson and others to set up a Trade Union Labour Party in opposition to the existing Labour Party due to be discussed at the TUC in the autumn. This new, and sinister move, the letter went on, had the hearty support of the *Birmingham Daily Mail* and the worst enemies of Labour.

It is interesting that no mention is made in this letter of the local leaders of the breakaway. These included W.J. Davis the Brassworkers Union leader who moved the unsuccessful motion for a new Labour Party at the TUC; John Beard and Julia Varley both Workers' Union officials; Eldred Hallas and Councillor Simpson controlling the influential local monthly journal of the Gas, Municipal & General Workers' Union; George Stanway, ex-president and Councillor Kesterton, ex-secretary of the main Trades Council.

The work of the Trades Council continued, however. New affiliations were announced in September and the next month the very significant addition to the Council of the Police & Prison Officers' Union occurred. By the end of the year the danger to the original Trades Council had passed. The annual report showed that thirteen branches had disaffiliated including the Brassworkers, but only three of 20 Workers' Union branches.

The final war protests came in October. There were complaints of inadequate forces' allowances. An appeal for Trades Council support for a Free Press, Free Speech and Release John McLean Demonstration from the Birmingham branch of the Workers' International Industrial Union was first passed to the LRC as being a political matter but also recommended to affiliated societies for their support. Also a strong protest was entered at the refusal of Havelock Wilson of the Seamen & Firemen's Union to allow ships to carry Arthur Henderson and other Labour leaders to France to consult with organised workers there.

At this point the war ended. There were no indications that it was drawing to a close and no celebrations when it did end. The Council went straight into post-war problems of housing, education, demobilisation etc.

One coincidence must be recorded. Just as the war started with the trade union and political sections being combined into a Trades & Labour Council, so the ending of the war coincided with the new Labour Party constitution which ended this partnership. By the end of the year the Council had reverted to its original title, which this author has used for convenience throughout the war, of the Birmingham Trades Council.

The activities of the Birmingham Trades Council have been followed at length because it claimed to be the authentic voice of labour in Birmingham. This claim is confirmed by the fact that official bodies, including the Ministry of Munitions, recognised that the Birmingham Trades Council was one of perhaps three other trade councils in the country which did genuinely reflect the opinions and power of the local trade union movement. At the outbreak of war the Trades Council claimed to represent 80,000 workers; by 1916 it claimed 100,000 workers. Each year the secretary reported that very few trade unions were outside the trades council. What percentage of the total labour force this represented we do not know, but the 1911 Census showed 400,000 men and women at work in Birmingham and this increased during the war. This suggests that rather less than 25 per cent of workers were in trade unions. This was about the average 'density' of trade union membership nationally in 1916, although for a large city like Birmingham it ought to have been higher.

It is interesting to compare Birmingham Trades Council progress with national trade union figures. By 1918 national trade union membership had increased, according to Mitchell & Deane, by 65 per cent compared with 1914. Birmingham Trades Council's claimed representation was 80,000 in 1914 and 100,000 by 1916 which thereafter changed little. This is an increase of only 25 per cent. But membership figures are not always the best guide. John Beard, the president of the Worker's Union, was always complaining that his secretaries had difficulty providing him with membership figures and he used finance as the key test of union progress. By this measure national trade union finances dipped in 1915 compared with 1914 and had only increased by 40 per cent by 1918. This was far less than the rate of inflation which had more than doubled prices. By this test of finance, Birmingham Trades Council emerges with a slightly better record. In 1914 its income was £416, and by 1918 this had increased to £771 or about 85 per cent.

If Birmingham Trades Council represented almost every trade union in the city, a considerable number of branches did not affiliate. This can be shown by noting the changing composition of the Trades Council between 1914 and 1918. At the outbreak of war affiliations to the Trades Council included 13 ASE branches and 20 Workers' Union branches. Other dominating unions were the building trades numbering about 30 branches from various unions and railwaymen with eight NUR branches and one Railway Clerks; also the important Brassworkers. This domination is expressed not in numbers, which are not available, but in financial clout. The largest contributor to the Trades Council income of over £400 was the numerous building unions with about £56. Next came the Railwaymen with £33 and the ASE with about £31. The Workers' Union branches contributed about £25, the two Gasworkers' unions £17 and the Brassworkers about £18.

By 1918 there were only 10 paid-up ASE branches and only 8 paid-up Workers' Union branches affiliated to the Trades Council. This was only to be expected with the Workers' Union branches whose leadership was spearheading the breakaway trades council, but is more surprising with the ASE whose branches in Birmingham had grown during the war from 14 to 24 and whose leaders were not embroiled in the breakaway. The important Brassworkers had also, of course, disaffiliated.

The financial heavy weight in 1918 was the three Rail unions contributing £150 of the £771 income. The next highest contributor was the building trades with nearly £45 followed by the Toolmakers with £41, and the ASE branches with £36. The rest of the income came in small amounts from a spread of trade unions which was much the same in 1914 as in 1918 of about 80 different Societies.

The Trade Unions and the War

For much of the war, the pro- and anti-war parties in the trade union movement continued to co-exist, kept together by the over-riding importance of the issues of wages, prices, rents, housing, call-up and conscription, food and coal shortages etc. Julia Varley, for instance, continued a member of the Trades Council executive throughout the war. Her Workers' Union duties, however, senior women's officer with twenty other women officers, took her all over the country and could have left little time for Trades Council duties.

Conscription in 1916 brought not only differences over attitudes to the war, but also friction between the skilled unions and those of the less skilled whose members bore the brunt of the call-up to military service and it is to the general unions that we now turn.

The Municipal Employees' Union had been founded in 1910 by Eldred Hallas and in 1914 he was the editor of the union's paper, *Municipal Employees' Monthly*. Hallas was stridently pro-war. In 1916 he became chairman of the Birmingham branch of the British Workers' National League, he collaborated closely with W.J. Davis in the setting up of the alternative trades council, and in the 1918 election was returned to Parliament for the Duddeston Ward on the ticket of the National Democratic Party. His paper up to the middle of 1915 mixed local issues with pro-war propaganda. For instance, in May 1915 Hallas gave the following figures for the feeding of school children. In the four weeks of May 1914 27,000 breakfasts had been provided. But in the five weeks to October 1914 the figure had risen to a peak of 366,000 and in January 1915 it was still 122,000. This had been due to the rise in unemployment at the beginning of the war and wives not receiving their allowances. On the war question he had attacked Ramsay MacDonald and Keir Hardie, criticised the Fellowship of Reconciliation, the ILP, the Union of Democratic Control and publicised Councillor George Shann's resignation from the Independent Labour Party because of its anti-war stance.

In June 1915 the MEA merged with the Amalgamated Society of Gas, Brick & General Labourers which had a membership of 13,500. This compared with a 1,600 membership of the MEA in 1913. The paper continued as the *Monthly Journal of the Amalgamated Society of Gas, Municipal & General Workers*. Joint secretaries of the new union were the secretaries of the old ones -John Simpson and Eldred Hallas, both pro-war. In December the paper was advertising the Mass Recruiting Meeting at the Town Hall chaired by Hallas organised by the Birmingham branch of the National Joint Labour Recruiting Council, which was trying to stave off Conscription.

In 1916 the union was advocating a minimum wage of 30/-d. for the unskilled and paying attention to female recruiting. By the end of the year it was deploring the secession of the skilled unions from the Allied Engineering Trades Federation and their forming a separate Birmingham Engineering Craft Unions Federation which excluded the general unions.

By March 1917 the union was embroiled in the question of Trade Cards being issued by the

215

skilled unions. 'They (the skilled unions) are indulging in the meanest kind of poaching. We will not forget.' The next month the paper reported a Conference of 50,000 General Workers requesting that the Government either withdraw the Trade Card scheme or allow all unions with members in munitions to issue Cards. The next month the paper reported the scheme withdrawn.

By July the paper was reporting that, 'Many Trades Councils have now become political debating societies captured by the pacifist ILP section.' It then announced the withdrawal of the Society from the Birmingham Trades Council. From the first Russian revolution in March 1917, the peace issue became a dominant issue with the paper. In July there was a whole page on 'German Psychology' designed to show the pacifists as dupes of the German war machine. In September another full page was devoted to 'too much politics in trade unions' presaging the moves in Birmingham to set up a rival trades council and a Trades Union Labour Party at national level.

In January 1918 the paper reported improvements in labourers' wages as follows:

| Engineering Trades 1913 | 27/-d. per week. | December 1917 44/-d. |
| B'ham Corporation 1913 | 28/-d. per week | 45/6d. |

This wage rise of 63 per cent compared with the Ministry of Labour index of all retail prices of a 90 per cent increase with more than a doubling of food prices.

But post-war and peace issues dominated 1918. In March the paper was advertising a series of meetings on post-war matters including Hallas speaking on 'Labour after the War.' But the same issue headlined, 'Proposals for a Trade Union Labour Party.' It went on to say 'The idea has a very emphatic support of the writer. (This must have been Hallas – GB) About 30 trade union officials have notified the secretary of the Amalgamated Musicians Union of their heartiest approval. If the idea were taken up widely it would be productive of enormous good.' By July Hallas was at total war with the Labour Party and its recent Conference. He criticised Arthur Henderson for saying that he would never serve in anything but a Labour cabinet and hit out at Ramsay MacDonald, 'If he had got in a pre-war Asquith cabinet he would have sung a very different tune.' Of the fraternal delegates Hallas said, 'Three or four continental socialists. Some anaemic if not actually pacifist.' By August, Hallas had been nominated to stand at Duddeston and in September the paper was raging, 'The ILP-cum-Conscientious Objectors-cum-Pacifists who constitute the Labour caucus of Birmingham have put forward an RAMC doctor to stand against Hallas. They use a doctor's uniform as camouflage to minimise the political effect of Hallas' stand for Country, Empire and our Allies.'

Hallas received Conservative support in the election and won with a substantial majority against a Liberal. He was one of fifteen National Democratic Party candidates elected.

It was the Workers' Union that bore the brunt of the almost inevitable conflict between the skilled unions regarding military call-up. Their main target was the Amalgamated Society of Engineers. The ASE organiser almost throughout the war was the Smethwick councillor George Ryder. His District No 9 was a vast one stretching across the Midlands and his monthly reports told little of the differences with the unskilled unions.

Once conscription started in March 1916, the question of who should be called-up assumed major significance. The skilled trade unions found that their members were being called up by military representatives on local Tribunals despite their being attested men under the Derby scheme who had volunteered for munitions work and were therefore exempt. This caused considerable unrest and in November 1916 with strikes in Sheffield and elsewhere the government instituted a scheme whereby every skilled man who had volunteered for munitions was to be issued with a Trade Card by his trade union which was a certificate of exemption from call-up.

This raised so many questions that in May 1917 Lloyd George negotiated with the unions the withdrawal of the card system and the institution of a Schedule of Reserved Occupations.

The reaction of the Workers' Union to these events is to be followed from their annual reports and also their paper the *Workers' Union Record.* Who was a skilled worker? the paper asked. Many in the Workers' Union had greater skills than some in the ASE, it was claimed. The dispute rapidly passed to the question of attitudes to the war. In April 1917 a leading article in the paper accused the skilled unions of poaching members, 'Who have only joined them because they offer a safe shelter to men who would do anything to save their skin.' The dispute continued after trade cards had been withdrawn. In February 1918 the paper was complaining that at a recent Man-power Conference the ASE wanted separate Conferences. 'Shop Stewards, Pacifists, Russians or any other old movement is being used to help them retain their privileges. They now discover that they want to stop the war. When they had Trade Cards they were great patriots.'

Criticising the Schedule of Reserved occupations the paper claimed that Arthur Henderson had said that all unions would be treated equally. But now they discovered that the ASE had its own 'secret' agreement with Henderson and they were now threatening to strike because the agreement was not being observed. The argument had now shifted from Cards to dilution of labour. 'The ASE says that all dilutees must go first. We ask, what is a dilutee? Is it a man who left school and entered engineering and who ever since has worked in engineering and can set his own tools? Should he go while a Class E ASE man stays?'

In March 1918 a party of fifteen Birmingham and Black Country members of the Workers' Union toured the battlefields of France. George Geobey reported he was glad to have had the opportunity to visit the scenes of destruction and fearful waste of wealth. 'One feels stronger than ever that there is little glory in war when one pictures its hideous suffering and brutality; but still all felt convinced that to avoid a repetition of all this slaughter the necessary thing is for the whole of the nation to continue using its full energies to make such repetition impossible.' Much of the energy of the union then seems to have gone into the amalgamation of the Workers' Union with the National Amalgamated Union of Labour and the Municipal Employees' Association. This was agreed in August 1918, but in fact it did not take place. The year ended with the not unimportant event of the opening of a union social club in Small Heath.

The other trade union leadership in Birmingham deeply committed to pro-war policies was that of the Brassworkers. The setting up of an independent Trades Council led by the Musicians' Union was paralleled by attempts to set up a rival national Labour Party dependent on the TUC. The main national protagonists were Havelock Wilson of the Sailors' and Firemen, J.B. Williams, national secretary of the Musicians' Union and W.J. Davis, by now the doyen of the TUC. It was Davis who moved the resolution at the 1918 TUC for a 'distinct political Labour Party for the Trade Union movement, based on the representation of and controlled by Congress...' By this time the new Labour Party constitution had been approved which set up local Labour Party branches open to all, through which middle class 'pacifists' would pour into the Labour Party as they had already done into the ILP, it was claimed. Davis began his speech to Congress with a history lesson showing how in 1906 the main miners' MPs were refused admission to the Labour Party because they refused to sign the constitution, whereas 'Philip Snowden and Ramsay MacDonald. who had never been in a factory or workshop in their lives were immediately accepted into membership.' He then turned to events in Birmingham:

> Let me give you an example of the working of the Labour Party constitution. The other day two great men went down to Birmingham. One of them had been in the Cabinet... They selected four Labour candidates. One was a railwayman and he, of course, was alright; but one was a lawyer and the other two were doctors. That is how the cuckoos come along. We had made some nice warm comfortable nests, and these men come along and take possession of them without contributing anything in labour or material to their construction.

Davis went on to attack Sidney Webb's view that this would bring 'brains' into the Party. 'We do not want "brains" imported into our movement (laughter and cheers) because we have commonsense and intelligence of our own.' Davis was fiercely attacked by, among others. a Birmingham delegate of the Bakers' Union. Davis returned to the rostrum:

> I would not have claimed the right (of reply) had it not been for the critic (from Birmingham) who charges me, with others, with dividing the Labour Party. The facts are that all the money contributed by the Trade Unions in the Birmingham district for organisational purposes was utilised to put pacifists in every possible position and nothing else (No!)... Our delegates could not get to the meetings, because they were working overtime upon munitions. The people who dominated the Trades Council did very little work (Oh! Oh!).

Davis concluded by saying that, as a consequence, the breakaway Birmingham trades council had been formed and he repeated the story that the new trades council represented 100,000 members and the old one only 20,000. Davis' resolution was seconded by E. Cathery of the Sailors' & Firemen's Union. It was clear that the resolution was going to be overwhelmingly defeated, so an amendment was put by the Operative Printers requiring that trade unions affiliated to the Labour Party form a federation to meet separately to formulate its own policy. This went part of the way to meet the objections of many who objected to the 'pacifist' influence of the ILP and distrust of intellectuals in general. But it was defeated by 3 million to 1 million votes. Davis' resolution mustered only about half a million votes and trade union allegiance to the existing, restructured Labour Party was overwhelmingly confirmed.

Bibliography: Birmingham Trade Unions and the War

The general history of Birmingham at war is: R.H. Brazier & E. Sandford – *Birmingham and the Great War 1914-1919*. The activities of the Birmingham Trades & Labour Council are well documented in their *Minutes* and *Annual Reports* for the period. Two works by Alan Clinton cover Trades Councils in general for this period, but also deals with Birmingham: *The Trade Union Rank & File, Trades Councils in Britain 1900-40;* and 'Trades Councils during World War 1' (in the *International Review of Social History* 1970).

Of the proceedings of the numerous Committees set up during the war such as the Citizen's Committees, and those dealing with Production, Manpower, Conscription, Pensions etc. hardly any record remains. But two reports from the early months of the war from W.J. Cashley, the Intelligence Officer of the Citizen's Committee, dealing with unemployment, have survived.

Information regarding the most important trade union, the Amalgamated Society of Engineers, is not to be found locally. It is in *The ASE Monthly Journal and Report*. Here are articles, and also the Monthly Report from each District. For my collection of Division No.9 Monthly Reports which cover Birmingham and the Midlands I am indebted to Edmund and Ruth Frow at the Working Class Movement Library, Salford, and the headquarters library of the AEEU at Peckham, London.

James B. Jeffreys' – *The Story of the Engineers* is also valuable in charting the complexities of war time legislation affecting the engineers.

For the *Workers' Union* which clashed with the ASE on both the treatment of its members and the alleged 'peace' policy of the ASE there is: Richard Hyman – *The Workers' Union;* and *The Workers' Union Record,* the monthly organ of the union.

Other important local trade union papers were the *Municipal Employees' Monthly* which became the *Monthly Journal of the Amalgamated Society of Gas, Municipal and General Workers.*

For the *Trades Union Congress* the annual reports for all the war years are important, but particularly for 1916 when the Congress was held in Birmingham and in 1918 when W.J. Davis of the Birmingham Brassworkers moved the unsuccessful resolution attempting to set up a rival Trade Union Labour Party. B.C. Roberts – *The Trades Union Congress 1868-1921* is also important for local participation.

Chapter 11

The Co-operative Movement in Birmingham in Wartime

Problems and duties

At the outbreak of war the Birmingham Co-operative movement consisted of two consumer co-ops. The larger, the Birmingham Industrial Co-operative Society Ltd. dated from 1881. The other, the Ten Acres & Stirchley Co-operative Society, although smaller, began in 1875. There was also a productive co-op, Birmingham Printers. A smaller productive society Midland Woodworkers was loosely associated with Birmingham, and the Planet Mutual Insurance Company which operated from Birmingham was sometimes considered part of the Co-operative movement. Birmingham was also the name of District No.5 which united about nineteen societies in Warwick and Worcester in divisional organisation.

A summary of the progress of these Birmingham Societies shows the following:

Birmingham Industrial Co-op	*1914*	*1915*	*1916*	*1917*	*1918*
No. of Members	29268	36426	42701	42381	41933
Capital £s	204222	279893	350860	400120	488752
Sales £s	560587	784194	1046670	1210673	1382557
Dividend (Av.for Year)	2/-d.	2/-d.	1/9¾d	1/5½d	1/5d.
Ten Acres & Stirchley Co-op					
No. of Members	8142	9559	10912	11693	11732
Capital £s	86294	112505	137044	167400	208598
Sales	194889	274713	342885	413590	448723
Dividend (Av for Year)	2/-d.	2/-d.	1/10d	1/8d.	1/7½d.
Birmingham Printers					
Capital £s	8348	8314	8931	11348	14532
Sales £s	9888	9713	11849	17608	30031
Net Profit £s	832	810	818	2067	4429

From the above figures it can be seen that the two consumer societies grew strongly in the first year of the war. But thereafter, war difficulties meant that sales just about kept pace with inflation. Birmingham Printers suffered severely from the unemployment at the beginning of the war and it was not until 1916 that growth began. Thereafter the society benefitted from the insatiable demand of the war bureaucracy for paper work, and the printers flourished.

The large increase in members at the beginning of the war was attributed by the consumer societies to the action taken by them in refusing to raise prices at the beginning of the war when some genuine shortages and panic stockpiling of food by consumers gave even honest retailers an excuse for raising prices considerably; unscrupulous ones charged what the traffic would bear and the term 'war profiteer' entered the vocabulary. Holding prices was the first war-time service rendered by the Co-operative movement to the citizens of Birmingham. But it involved both rationing their existing customers and refusing to serve non-members deemed guilty of stockpiling, and so it was something of a double edged weapon. As the war proceeded the Co-ops became the base from which the demand of the working class movement for food at reasonable prices and fair shares by rationing was based. This aspect is dealt with in detail below.

War problems hit the BICS immediately when 45 of their best horses were requisitioned for military purposes. This created bread distribution difficulties which were overcome by the purchase of two motor vehicles and establishing bread sales points from stationary carts.

Another immediate danger facing the Co-ops was the possibility of a run on their funds at the outbreak of war. This did not materialise, even though no new restrictions were placed on the withdrawal of capital. As the war proceeded competition for funds came from Government war and special loans. BICS paid 5 per cent on capital to those whose purchases were more than £3 per quarter and 4 per cent to non-purchasers on the outbreak of war. In November 1917 it slightly altered that to 5 per cent to purchasers of £3 of goods per quarter on savings up to £100 and 4 per cent on the remainder with 5 per cent to purchasers of £6 per quarter on savings up to £200 with interest of 4 per cent on the remainder. Non-purchasers also received 4 per cent on their capital. By this time, with prices doubling, the real yield was only half of its pre-war value. When the government began issuing stock at 5¾ per cent yield with a patriotic call to go with it, Co-op savings seemed to be in danger. This was met by stressing that Co-operative savings were for post-war development and that in the meantime this capital was invested in government stock. This, together with the fact that Co-operative savings were immediately available without penalty and the loyalty appeal of the movement seems to have kept savings attractive. The figures show that the capital of both BICS and TASCOS increased by about 140 per cent during the war, keeping growth ahead of inflation. The Co-ops also participated in government savings schemes by purchasing stock on behalf of employees who then repaid it by instalments. Thus during Birmingham Tank Week in 1917 BICS took up, at the request of 816 employees, £2784 of War Savings Certificates to be repaid in 31 weeks.

Both consumer societies opened new central premises during the war. TASCOS opened their new headquarters with an imposing block of buildings on the corner of Hazelwell Street and Umberslade Road in May 1915, the design being a 'free adaptation of Renaissance.' BICS opened its famous High Street premises which looked directly on to New Street and were central for the tram termini and all the principal railway stations. Seven storeys high with an 'Italian Renaissance facade' it remained the pride of the Co-operative movement until recent years. Both societies also opened other branches and outlets. Bread shops became particularly important in 1917 with grain shortages due to shipping being either sunk or transporting US troops to Britain. In that year TASCOS opened eight extra bread shops while BICS opened 31.

Political hostility to the Co-operative movement from the retail trade continued and was increased by the social stance adopted by the societies with regard to food supplies. There were continual Co-op complaints that the increasingly controlled food trade was dominated by representatives of the large, private suppliers at Whitehall. The main complaint was that Co-operative supplies were allocated with reference to numbers of members at a previous data point. This penalised the Co-operatives which were growing bodies and the resultant shortage of supplies curtailed this growth. Such discriminatory treatment was alleged most strongly with regard to the Excess Profits Duty of 1915 introduced as a result of widespread complaints of profiteering.

The retail trade had always objected to the fact that Co-operative surpluses were not subject to profits tax because they were mutual, democratically controlled bodies returning their surpluses to their members in the form of dividends. When the EPD was introduced the government inserted a special clause into the Finance Act to include Co-op 'profits.' Although this allowed the Societies to calculate the amount of surplus returnable to their members to include all new members joining in the period, it did not allow for the fact that an increasing proportion of the dividend represented not profit increases, but price increases. In the first year of its operation EPD cost the BICS £7,000. This made it necessary to reduce the dividend from 2/-d. in the £ to 1/10d.

From this time both dividend and prices (by lowering them) were manipulated to minimise EPD. Continual pressure by the movement led the government to introduce an alternative method of assessing EPD in 1917 on 'the dividend per £ sterling' and not, as previously, on 'the profit per member per annum.' This enabled the BICS committee to state that the Society's liabilities would be minimal. In fact, in 1918 the whole amount of excess profits duty paid of £8,714 was refunded. TASCOS also had their £1,564 EPD payments refunded.

Another grave problem was that of labour. The retail trades with their 'non-essential' workers contributed very largely to the armed forces. At the beginning of the war many Co-op employees voluntarily enlisted. Married men who enlisted from BICS were guaranteed their job back and granted half their wages during the war. Single men with dependents were given grants. Whether this continued after Conscription in 1916 is not known. By July 1915, 102 BICS employees had volunteered; by October it was 161. The Derby attestment and subsequent conscription continued to deplete the male labour force. BICS quarterly reports began to record deaths of enlisted former employees. In July 1916 four deaths were recorded. In subsequent reports deaths came in ones and twos. But these accelerated towards the end of the war. The quarter ending January 1918 recorded four deaths, the next quarter five, and the October 1918 report showed no less than 12 men killed in action, died of wounds or missing presumed killed. Deaths continued until the very end and the January 1919 report showed seven killed. In all, 35 former BICS employees are recorded as losing their lives while on service with the forces.

The drain of manpower was such that by October 1915 it was reported that male labour was 'almost unobtainable.' What had hitherto been very much a male preserve was now invaded by women. In 1914 BICS had employed 562 men and 69 women. By 1918 the figures were 500 men but 713 women. Wages in October 1915 were 32/-d. a week for men and 20/-d. a week for women. It is likely that this differential became narrower as percentage wage increases were granted during the war. The total effect on the standard of living during the war of either men or women is not known. From wage figures, however, it can be shown that the average wage which was about 23/6d a week at BICS in 1914 and slightly more at TASCOS, was about 36/6d. at BICS in 1918 and slightly less at TASCOS. The figures do not suggest that either men or women shop workers benefitted greatly from the allegedly 'high wage' economy of the war. Hours were reduced at both Birmingham societies during the war from 56 to 52½ by the expedient of closing the shops for an hour during lunch times.

Something of the strain of shop work in war time is captured by the historian of BICS:

Those were strenuous days! Long hours practically every day of the week. Then to stumble home, perhaps in almost pitch darkness, with an isolated street lamp showing a faint glimmer of light. Both the morning and evening papers contained nothing but war news. Apart from the columns of reports from the various fighting areas, large portions of space were devoted to explaining Food Orders, police court reports of infringement of these regulations together with a variety of other minor offences brought into operation by the Defence of the Realm Act. From the beginning of 1918 an important feature of every Birmingham newspaper issued on Saturdays was the Birmingham Weekly Food Bulletin which was a mine of information to the housewife as to what she had to do with her ration cards and the quantities of commodities she might hope to purchase therewith during the forthcoming week.

Every morning without fail the office mail included communications relating to Food Orders, notifications of further restrictions, calling up notices of employees and so on apparently endlessly. The indispensable men were now obliged to join some volunteer force for home defence purposes unless they were already serving as special constables...

It was no uncommon thing to find some buxom woman demanding as a right as a member to interview the secretary and, on gaining admission angrily flourishing a meat card in his face with a request to know how he expected a hard-working man engaged on munitions to live on, say 3oz. of steak for a meal.

If these were the strains of management, how much greater the problems of shop workers on their feet all day facing customers entitled only to inadequate rations and often without the supplies to provide even that. After work came other duties, statutory or voluntary and with it all the constant worry concerning loved ones in the forces.

Co-operative social organisation

Social and political activity is the life blood of the Co-operative movement. That political activity continued into war time is not surprising; what is surprising is that so much social activity continued. Brazier and Sandford tell us that the first casualty of the war in Birmingham was entertainment. But after the early months Birmingham became an important centre of wounded soldiers, a key rail centre of transit, and a city with thousands of servicemen on leave. All of these required entertainment and a network of welfare services. The Co-operative movement contributed to meeting these needs.

Co-operative social organisations comprised the Educational Committee, the well-known Women's Guild, and the lesser known Men's Guild. Early Education Committees were something of a misnomer; their main activity was to be a publicity committee for the Society, popularising co-operative principles in areas where these were unknown and organising the festivities connected with the opening of new branches. To some extent, the Women's Guild also performed these functions. There was also the Divisional Committee of the Co-op. This co-ordinated the activities of the societies in the district and was, in our case, the Birmingham No.5 District. One of the tasks of its executive was to arrange several conferences each year on co-operative principles and once it had decided on its annual programme it was the local education committees who carried it through.

These conferences proceeded throughout the war. The report for 1915 noted that in the larger urban areas 'new members have been enrolled by the thousand,' and it was the duty of the committee to educate them in co-operative ideals and make them co-operators, 'in the highest sense of the word.' Four conferences had been held, one at Dudley on 'What is our Aim?' The second at Birmingham on 'Joint Action with the Trade Unions and Labour Party,' the third at Kidderminster on 'The Future of Co-operation,' and a fourth at Warwick on 'What Co-operation Has, Is and Will do for the People.'

The 1916 District Report spoke of a survey of the whole district with the 'gratifying result that only one or two areas in the district lagged behind in co-operation.' Again, four conferences were organised during the year. 1917 was 'one of the most trying periods ever experienced by our movement' and transport difficulties meant that only two conferences were arranged. In the last year of the war four conferences were again arranged focussing either on post-war problems or topical issues such as 'Farming by Distributive Societies.'

The Education Committees were financed by the local societies. It cannot be said that BICS was particular generous to education during the war, its expenditure rising only from £771 in 1914 to £1062 in 1918. The record of TASCOS was better, its educational spending rising from £599 in 1914 until it was nearly equal to the much larger BICS at £1010 in 1918.

A separate report of the Educational Committee was included in the Societies' Quarterly Reports. The BICS reports on the outbreak of war showed both a Junior and Senior Choir. Both flourished throughout the war. A report for the first quarter of 1916 stated that the junior choir was preparing a concert in aid of wounded soldiers' funds. '...great enthusiasm prevails. Attendance and interest in rehearsals are splendidly maintained despite dark streets and other adverse conditions...the prospects of the choir were never more promising.' The senior choir had given two musical evenings, one was at the opening of a new branch at Stetchford.

Classes in Co-operative principles were also being held. In junior classes 86 girls and 85 boys sat for the examination. 91 certificates of merit were obtained and 142 pupils received certificates for attendance. Examinations under the Co-operative Union were also reported in Book-keeping, Economics, Industrial History and Co-operation (advanced). The July quarterly report showed that the committee was financing scholarships to four secondary schools in the city. It also organised scholarships for the Co-operative week Summer School valued at £4-4-0d. Candidates had to sit a paper on Co-operation. Four people were thus sponsored in 1916.

A traditional event organised by the Educational Committee and the Women's Guild was an Annual Children's Picnic in Sutton Park. This had to be abandoned in 1916 and it was recommended that the quarterly meeting should vote a sum of £50 to the Birmingham Children's Hospital in lieu.

The next year there was a falling away of the junior classes, only 58 sitting for the exam.

The choirs continued to arrange Musical Evenings which the cynical might regard as merely a cover for a talk. One such featured the chairman of the educational committee, J. Millington who spoke on 'The Ideals of the Co-operative Movement.' A Musical Programme was then given entitled 'Co-operation and Music.' The remark that, 'The hearty applause testified how much the whole programme was appreciated' reminds us that these were less sophisticated times. At another meeting Millerchip, the Walsall co-operator and member of the central board, spoke on 'Co-operation,' supported by the Junior Choir who were 'accorded a splendid reception.'

Another item appearing regularly on the Educational Committee's reports was Conferences organised in conjunction with the District Committees. These we have already discussed. Finally, each report mentioned briefly the activities of the Women's and Men's Guilds.

It is almost impossible to exaggerate the importance of the Guilds to the Co-operative movement. For detailed accounts of the BICS guilds we are fortunate enough to have the files of *Wheatsheaf*. We deal first with the Women's Guild, but reserve a fuller account of their activities for the chapter on Women.

At the outbreak of war six Women's Guild branches were reporting in *Wheatsheaf* – Aston & Perry Barr, Central, Erdington, Handsworth, Small Heath, and Sparkhill. In the next few months the total rose to nine with the addition of Harborne, Dudley Road, and Balsall Heath. This remained the total for the duration of the war. All the branches were active, although membership figures are sparse. In June 1916, Small Heath reported that they were 'doing good work despite difficulties.' Nineteen general meetings had been held with an average attendance of the very high figure of 80. Twenty five new members had been made in that year. At the 1918 AGM Small Heath reported 72 members with 25 meetings held and an average attendance down to 22. At Sparkhill in June 1918 the branch reported 112 members with average attendance at meetings of 58. In October 1918 Dudley Road membership was 42 with average attendances of 25.

Most branches had problems with evening meetings and the blackout, so in the winters at least Erdington and Central moved to the less preferred afternoon meeting.

After initial war difficulties had been overcome, the work of the Women's Guild branches became even more essential. The women popularised Co-operative principles, organised against food shortages, provided social activity not only for their members but also for wounded and other servicemen in the city, and as the war progressed, involved themselves in the political questions of peace and the post-war settlement.

Of the Women's Guild at TASCOS little can be said. Vickrage tells us that a Guild had been formed about 1901 which had a continuous existence from that time and four Guild branches had been formed before 1921, but he makes no specific mention of the Guild during the war.

That Women's Guild branches flourished during the war is perhaps not too surprising. What is a surprise is that Men's Guild branches flourished in wartime when the call-up and long hours of work made organising so difficult.

Credit for the development of the Men's Guild in Birmingham was given to Mr Macdonald in a *Wheatsheaf* report of Central Branch. This deeply regretted the departure of Mr Macdonald for work elsewhere. He had been largely instrumental in forming the first branch in Birmingham having 'brought the good news from Edmonton.' He was the first chairman of the branch.

Reports of the Men's Guild appear in *Wheatsheaf* from June 1915 when two branches were recorded – Central and Harborne. In January 1916 a new branch was reported at Sparkhill. By November 1916 a branch was formed at Small Heath and a Birmingham & District Council of Men's Guilds had been formed with a new branch reported from Pelsall and enquiries from Dudley. The secretary was E.W. Hampton. Harborne reported that it had been established in March 1915. Overtime prevented members attending. Thirteen had joined the army and present membership was 36.

In February 1917 Small Heath claimed to have a 'live' membership of 46. Complaints regarding sugar were being brought to the meetings. These were held fortnightly where they discussed such topics as Robert Owen, Income Tax, etc. In July 1917 Small Heath reported an Open-Air Social meeting and a visit to the Botanical Gardens in conjunction with the WEA.

The Men's Guild was particularly active during 1918. In March Central had 40 members and their secretary was A.D.K. McDonald. The Small Heath secretary was H. McGregor and Sparkhill's P. Lakins. Sparkhill reported that they had held 13 meetings and four whist drives; many members were working overtime, some had become special constables and others had joined the volunteers. Eight had recently joined up and total membership was 45.

In April 1918 the secretary of Harborne, C.E. Lowe, reported difficulties of members getting to meetings, but ten of them were 'keeping the flag flying'; some of them were on the Food Control Committee and some on the Pensions Committee; four were on the social committee with the Women's Guild and responsible for dances, lantern lectures, and 'whist drives that are the talk of the district.' It was time they thought of their own amusement, Lowe thought. Why not Co-operative Picture Houses?'

In August Central Men's Guild reported that it was in its sixth year of work and during that time 300 men had passed through its ranks. Vickrage mentions no Men's Guild activity at TASCOS, but suggests that two were formed in 1921.

It seems clear that Men's Guild branches, despite the additional difficulties of war time organisation of men, played an important role in developing co-operation during war time. One gets the impression, as with the Women's Guild, that the role of their members in the political struggles of the time are under-recorded in the reports of activity. It is likely that both men and women Guilds people played an important part in the development of the Co-operative Party in the final year of war.

The Co-operative Movement and the Food Question

And so we come to the most important contribution of the Co-operative movement to the history of the war years. The Co-ops as the only non-profit making, owner controlled, working class organisation, claimed the right both to act and speak on behalf of working people. In the former role it took the high moral ground, ignored as far as it could market economics, and distributed its supplies according to the principle of need not greed. Its claim to speak for working people was never admitted by the trade nor Whitehall, until the very end of the war when rationing became absolutely inevitable and a more favourable national food administration was in place under Lord Rhondda.

The first effect of the war was an immediate rise of prices, as we have noted. The two Birmingham Co-ops, with ample stocks, refused to raise their prices and quite rightly claimed that they had prevented even greater increases. In doing so, however, they had discriminated against both their own customers and potential customers in refusing to sell excessive amounts. The first two years of the war vindicated the Co-ops' claims to speak for the people with BICS membership increasing 46 per cent between 1914 and 1916 and TASCOS by 34 per cent. Early prices rises included not only food, particularly bread and sugar, but also coal which was in short supply.

By early 1915 BICS was complaining that many departments were not maintaining profits. One remedy resorted to in the summer was to sell mineral water to 'maintain staff and horses.' TASCOS, in the more rural south west of Birmingham, quickly resorted to agriculture, Gay Hill Farm in King's Norton being purchased in March 1915 for £1,500. Within a few months it was producing pigs, poultry and beef.

With the introduction of the hated Excess Profits Duty in 1916, both Co-ops resorted to price manipulation. TASCOS sold some of their groceries at almost cost price and dropped the price of bread to between 8d and 9d. the quartern loaf when the current market price was $9\frac{1}{2}$d. to $10\frac{1}{2}$d.

Conscription in 1916 which took off some fairly senior staff at BICS and supply allocation which did not take full account of the growth of members of the Co-ops led to a deterioration of service. By the end of 1916 the dividend at both BICS and TASCOS was down from 2/-d. to 1/9d.

Food problems became intractable in 1917 as a result of the German blockade and destruction of shipping. In November 1916 BICS had to announce that new members could be accepted only on the understanding that they would not be entitled to sugar, bread and coal. In July 1917 the BICS committee decided the only fair way to distribute sugar was to introduce sugar cards. All members of a family had to register on the principle of One Household – One Card. As shortages extended to other commodities the food card was extended to include sugar, butter or margarine, tea, bacon and ham with spaces for other commodities. These cards did not carry a right to a certain quantity of commodities, as this depended on the amounts allocated, but did ensure that members received only one allocation and not more by shopping at various Co-op branches. TASCOS claims that it instituted a similar scheme several months earlier.

By now, the food situation was getting desperate. Lord Davenport was at the Ministry of Food in the early months of 1917 advocating a voluntary system of food rationing comprising 4½lbs of bread, 2½lbs of meat and ¼lb of sugar and local food committees were asked to support this. But the labour movement nationally was demanding a proper system of rationing and in Birmingham the Trades Council, Co-operatives and Women's Groups were demanding a Municipal Food Service and in February 1917 formed a Food Vigilante Committee to back it. This was an important phase of the politicisation of the Co-operative movement in Birmingham. Food queues were now forming in Birmingham at 7am each morning (for that irreplaceable English institution the Sunday dinner at 3-30am). The government now began to fear food riots and revolution. They were vastly relieved when the great strikes of May 1917 led by the shop stewards movement failed to spread to Birmingham.

By mid 1917 the BICS quarterly report told of a 'grave alteration for the worse' in all food supplies. Butter supplies had averaged only 1oz per member per week and supplies of tea and bacon had been almost unobtainable. In that quarter, membership declined slightly for the first time due to both customer dissatisfaction and the refusal to guarantee new members food supplies. The BICS committee was 'more than ever convinced that the policy of restricted membership pursued during the past twelve months is the only possible policy under present circumstances.' The dividend was down to 1/5d.

The BICS half yearly report ending February 1918 summarised the food situation as follows. The general food question had become even graver. The national sugar scheme was in operation with the local Food Control Committee taking over control and distribution of tea, butter and margarine with a card scheme. The government had also taken over the distribution of other food commodities to wholesalers and retailers on the basis of past supplies, but without any attempt to regulate the supply to the public. The Society had attempted by means of food cards to ration the additional commodities of bacon and ham, lard, cheese, jam and syrup, condensed milk and meat. It admitted, however, that its card scheme could never be satisfactory while some members shared not only the limited but equitably distributed supplies available to the Co-op, but also went to other retailers to supplement their purchases. The Society ought therefore to press for the immediate rationing on a national basis of all the essential articles of food.

The food situation worsened in 1918. The Trades Council had passed a resolution at the end of 1917 demanding strike action if the food situation did not improve. There were food demonstrations at the big factories, notably Austin, and Metropolitan Carriage and Wagon. On 16 January 1918 Longbridge came out on strike. The immediate issue was the victimisation of the convenor of shop stewards, but the wages, housing, food and peace issues were by now inextricably entwined and a revolutionary situation was emerging. Meetings were held with Lord Rhondda seeking permission to work out a local scheme of rationing. As a result a ration of 1 oz of tea and 4 ozs of butter or margarine per person per week was devised controlled by the local Food Committee. This then led to a struggle for the control of the Food Committee seeking to replace worker control for the existing food retailer control. Early in February a national meat rationing scheme operated by the local Food Committee was introduced. Its complexity, with frequent changes in amounts, the inclusion of rabbits and poultry and the innovation of 'meatless days' (Wednesday and Friday in Birmingham) meant that it was not a success and food queues at butchers' shops grew.

On 24 February the labour movement organised a Day of Food Protest. A mass meeting at the Midland Institute demanded: a compulsory, national scheme of rationing; a cut in food prices; and fair and equitable distribution of food. Another resolution stated that workers organised nationally and internationally would stop the war if this was the only way of bringing the food shortages to an end. In the evening there was a meeting at the Town Hall when the war faction attempted to counter-attack. John Beard opposed the down-tools and anti-war resolution passed at the Midlands Institute. There was a storm of disapproval and another anti-war resolution was passed. Late in February the government began to provide more food for munitions workers via canteens in an unsuccessful attempt to divide munitions workers from the rest of the population.

Relief was at hand for the government, however. At the end of March 1918 the Germans launched their last desperate offensive and there was a patriotic reaction. Also, a government approved local system of rationing introduced in January 1918 was beginning to take effect. The BICS report for the quarter ending May 1918 noted that the rationing of sugar, tea, butter and margarine had led to a much improved situation compared with December even though the quantities allowed were meagre. This was reflected in improved membership figures. In the first half of 1917 no less than 1,580 members had withdrawn, although 1,501 had also been admitted. In the quarter to November 1917 810 withdrew and 548 joined. In the half year to February 1918 619 withdrew and 640 joined. But the quarter ending May 1918 again showed more withdrawals than admissions at 617 to 301.

The BICS report for the half year ending July 1918 stated that supplies to meet the normal ration were now adequate, but there were some shortages of other foods such as jam, marmalade, syrup, cheese and condensed milk. Rationing from the point of view of the commodities controlled by the Ministry of Food could be looked on 'as a distinct success.' To food problems was added that of coal. Coal supply which had been 1,500 tons in 1915 had sunk to 650 tons. A local rationing scheme had been prepared which the Society welcomed, but it doubted whether the ration proposed would be forthcoming in the winter. 1,079 members had withdrawn and membership had sunk below 42,000.

Much of the Birmingham experience of rationing, which had been watched with interest both at home and abroad, was incorporated into the national rationing scheme which began in July 1918. The foods rationed were sugar, butter, margarine, meat (including bacon and ham), lard, tea and jam. By this time the German offensive had been contained and the government could afford to release supplies from their food stocks to guarantee the rations.

The BICS report for the quarter ending November 1918 'rejoiced' at the Armistice ending the 'awful and unprecedented slaughter of men of all nationalities and the prospect of a return to civilisation and international sanity.' It welcomed the victory of allied arms believing it to mean the destruction of militarism everywhere and a new era of freedom and justice. It deplored the terrible price paid in killed and maimed and remembered in particular the 34 Co-op staff members who had made the supreme sacrifice.

With regard to the Co-operative movement the committee recorded the vicissitudes the movement had suffered during the war – large numbers of men taken from civilian employment, shortages of food and other commodities, unfair legislation, scant recognition from the government and representation on controlling bodies only towards the end of the war.

> Nevertheless the Society, with all its shortcomings, had proved itself to be a real people's institute standing by the people and trying to prevent their merciless exploitation and advocating equity and justice in the distribution of the necessities of life. The value of co-operation had never been so universally recognised. The Society looked forward to taking a share in the national life, once government controls were removed, commensurate with its importance and achievements.

The Co-operative Party

The grim experiences of war had convinced the Co-operative movement that it was time to move from its traditional non-political stance. The 'non-political' covered the fact that it was a Lib-Lab dominated organisation. The destruction of the Liberal Party by Lloyd George as he successively ousted Asquith, and moved on to head a 'national' coalition meant that many Liberals who had been pacifists, had operated in important institutions of state control during the war, and were involved in proposals for post-war reconstruction were beginning to look to the Labour Party as their new spiritual home. In addition the Co-operative movement had been radicalised by its experiences during the war and had taken its place as the consumer arm of the working class movement from the very beginning of the war when it became a constituent part of the War Emergency Workers' National Committee. All this eased the transition to open Labour politics.

A resolution agreeing to political action was passed at the Swansea Co-operative Congress in 1917 and resulted in the setting up of a Co-operative Representation Committee. This was supported by both TASCOS and BICS in Birmingham.

The BICS quarterly report at May 1917 put the position of the Co-operative Movement in the

National Life as follows, 'The Co-operative Movement is by far the largest distributor of foodstuffs in the country. It is the only organised body of consumers that exists; it has no selfish interests, the interests of the consumer and the interests of the citizen are identical, and yet to a large extent the movement has been ignored in the counsels of the nation... and this may also be said of local civic affairs.' The statement went on to say that it was therefore supporting certain moves at the forthcoming Co-operative Congress for direct representation of co-operators in Parliament and on local representative bodies. This was put as a resolution to the next quarterly meeting and was passed. TASCOS passed a similar resolution at its November 1917 quarterly meeting. This resulted in the formation of the Birmingham & District Representation Committee consisting of BICS, TASCOS, and the Soho, Smethwick Society together with the two productives, Birmingham Printers and Midland Woodworkers. It later became the Birmingham and District Co-operative Party.

The activities of the Co-operative Representation Committee can be followed from the minute book that survives from May 1918. In July a suggestion from the Trades Council political wing, the Labour Representation Committee, that there should be a standing committee of co-operators and trade unionists was accepted, as was an invitation from the Trades Council to send delegates to a conference on the Secret Treaties. In August a representative was sent to the Midlands Labour Conference. Various organisations sought support of the new organisation. In September there was extended discussion on the Whitley Councils and the Co-op, but no decisions were taken. Support for a proposed Birmingham branch of the League of Nations Society was deferred to a future meeting. Support was given to the Proportional Representation Society. Support for the Land Nationalisation Society was deferred until after a CWS Conference in Birmingham. Activities such as garden parties were being organised and resolutions supported such as one by Mrs Andrews that either food and milk prices be held down or that allowances for soldiers' wives should be reviewed every four months.

By October prospective Co-operative candidates for the post-war (which still seemed a long way away) parliamentary elections were being interviewed. The first two co-op hopefuls put forward were Frank Spires and Tom Hackett, chair and vice-chair respectively of the BCRC. The key question was the attitude of the candidates to the war. Hackett spoke first and said he was a Peace Man, but not a peace at any price man, but a peace by negotiations man. He suggested that the policy of the knock-out blow was unobtainable and said the earliest opportunity should be taken to put forward genuine peace proposals and end the 'present ghastly war.' Spires, who was one of the most prominent of Birmingham's peace men said that he was not a pacifist, but rather an anti-conscriptionist. He was no supporter of the 'knock-out blow' as that did not make for the end of all wars but rather tended to engender feelings of hatred and revenge. The policy of the Labour Party in endeavouring to bring about a more amicable feeling between the workers of all countries had his hearty support. After a full and free discussion the following resolution was carried, 'That this Council having heard the statements of the two candidates on the war, heartily supports their attitude and pledges itself to do all in its power to secure their triumphal return at the next election.' Subsequently, Tom Hackett (who was a leading TASCOS member) stood at King's Norton and Frank Spires at Sparkbrook, but neither, in the jingoistic atmosphere of the khaki election at the end of 1918, was returned.

Bibliography: The Co-operative Movement in Birmingham in Wartime

Each of the two Birmingham consumer Co-operatives has its own history: T. Smith – *History of Birmingham Co-operative Society* (1931); the same author's *Seventy Years of Service* (1951); Harry M. Vickrage – *75 Years of Co-operative Endeavour – A History of the Ten Acres and Stirchley Co-operative Society Ltd* (1950); and L & D Chew – *TASCOS Past & Present* (1991). The other general local history is Ned Williams' sumptuously produced and lavishly illustrated – *The Co-op in Birmingham and the Black Country* (1993). The main statistics of sales, capital, profits, dividend etc. come from the *Annual Reports of the Co-operative Union Congress*. These annual reports also contain the Reports of the No.5 Birmingham District. The quarterly and half-yearly Reports are the main source for the general progress and problems of the Societies. These are available at Birmingham Reference Library for 1914-18 for BICS. The most detailed accounts of the activities of local societies are to be found in *Wheatsheaf*, the monthly newspaper. This I have used for BICS. An important study of the food question in Birmingham and the part played by BICS is: Bryant Simon – *The Politics of Food in the First World War* (Unpublished M.A. thesis Warwick University 1987).

Chapter 12

Birmingham Women in Wartime

Women in Trade Unions

There is a widespread belief that women during the war earned very high wages. While this was true of a small minority, what follows will show that most women were abominably paid in 1914 and they remained badly paid in 1918. When the war ended, the reward for large numbers of these women was the sack.

As has been said, there is no record of the number of Birmingham women at work during the war, nor of the occupations they filled. The war fell almost exactly between the two Censuses of 1911 and 1921 and from these only a limited number of conclusions can be legitimately drawn. But such information as there is gives little credence to the idea that the war had a lasting influence on women's liberation. Even with regard to domestic service, where it is true that many women did escape its drudgery during the war, there were 20,000 indoor servants in 1911 and still 16,000 in 1921. In jewellery, a large employer of women which turned over almost its entire production to war needs, 13,000 women were employed in 1911, but only 7,000 in 1921. With regard to professional employment, there were 3,700 women teachers in 1914, but only 3,500 in 1921. Even in nursing, which must have expanded rapidly during the war, there were only 2,000 nurses in 1921 compared with 1,700 in 1911. Only in office employment was there a substantial and permanent improvement, female clerks increasing from 8,000 in 1911 to 20,000 in 1921. In the other 'liberating' area of women's work of public transport, 73 women worked on the railways in 1911, but only 38 in 1921. By this latter year there were only 5 female bus conductors in Birmingham and whereas 48 women had worked in road transport in 1911, the figure in 1921 was only 38.

For most women in Birmingham and the Black Country the main categories of employment at all times, including the war years, were in the factories, domestic service, and the preparation and sale of food, drink and dress. Most of these were low paid jobs.

With regard to women in wartime, there was a war within a war between employers who were determined not to concede equal pay for equal work under any circumstances, and some of the skilled trade unions determined to protect their male members interests by requiring that women who replaced men were not used as cheap labour.

The basic obstacle to women improving their economic situation in wartime was that had there been a 'free market' this might have been achieved; but the laws of supply and demand had been suspended by the government and women could neither strike to improve their wages nor leave their jobs for work elsewhere.

Another obstacle to improvement was the many categories of employment across which employers and government manoeuvred to keep wages down. There was employment in factories entirely given over to war production. These could be factories like the Austin with its 20,000 employees which was in the later stages of the war controlled by the government, or factories specially built and controlled either by the government or large em[oyers. It was in these factories where women had the best chance of approaching equal pay. It was also the sphere of employment for which government regulations favourable to women were enacted and the mistaken appearance given that such regulations applied to all women.

The next category of employment was in factories and occupations where part of the enterprise produced munitions, and the remaining output was for civilian use. Finally, there were the trades which continued to produce entirely for the civilian market. It was in these industries of food, drink, shop work, domestic work etc. comprising the majority of female jobs where government legislation never seemed to reach and where the small print of regulations would be found to exclude these workers.

This broad outline of labour legislation and voluntary agreement must be restated, for if there were problems of interpretation regarding men, there was even greater scope for procrastination and evasion with women.

The first broad wartime agreement came in the engineering industry in December 1914 when the Engineering Employers' Federation met with five main engineering unions who agreed that in return for suspending their rules regarding demarcation, overtime, dilution and the employment of women etc. 'standard rates of pay' would be observed in wartime and the status quo ante restored at the end of the war. With regard to women, an accompanying Shells & Fuses Agreement gave 'substituted' women the same 'rate' as the skilled man she replaced; but it said nothing about the wages of women who replaced semi- or unskilled men, nor which 'rate' was to apply to the 'substituted' women. It was also a voluntary agreement applicable only to employers who belonged to the Engineering Fed. Nevertheless, there were considerable numbers of women in Birmingham making shells and fuses who should have benefitted from this agreement.

The limitations of this arrangement led to the famous (or infamous) Treasury Agreement of March 1915. This officially outlawed strikes and the union surrender of all their rights and privileges was confirmed for the duration of the war. On the crucial question of the substitution of women for men, the Agreement laid down that the 'admission of semi-skilled and unskilled labour shall not adversely affect the rate customarily paid for the job.' Even the core of this agreement was flouted by paying women equal piece rates to the men they replaced, but not equal time rates, so that it can confidently be surmised that very few women achieved the same wage as men for the same work performed.

Another important ruling affecting women came in September 1915 and was known as Circular L2. This, together with L3 (which slightly amended L2) laid down that all 'substituted' women over the age of 18 'employed on work customarily done by fully skilled tradesmen' were to receive a standard wage of £1 for a normal working week and should also receive men's overtime, Sunday, holiday and night-work allowances. Again, the limitations regarding the number of women to whom these circulars applied and the scope for evasion, is obvious.

Besides wages, there were the questions of working hours, facilities and safety at work. Too many employers operated under the assumption that the Factory Acts had been suspended for the duration of the war. To these problems must be added the hardships of war – rationing and queues, anxiety and suffering regarding men folk in the forces, married women bringing up families as single parents, the blackout and fear of air raids etc. All this on top of the normal double shift of women of factory work and house work.

Within this minefield of problems, three main organisations struggled to improve the lot of women at work in Birmingham. These were the National Federation of Women Workers led by the hero of the Cradley Heath chainmakers and other women's struggles of 1910-14, Mary Macarthur; the Workers' Union with the redoubtable Julia Varley and her unprecedented team of twenty paid women organisers by the end of the war; and lastly the various unions that joined together during the war to form the Amalgamated Society of Gas, Municipal and General Workers.

At the beginning of the war the trade unions were preoccupied with general problems and little pertaining to women is known. Even Julia Varley's Workers' Union annual reports were confined to generalities. For instance her 1915 report stated that her work among women had been 'strenuous.' She had visited many towns including Glasgow and Edinburgh. She was also one of the referees on the Munitions Tribunal, the Citizens' Committee and most of its sub-committees in Birmingham; we know also that she was on the EC of the Trades Council. This appears to be the usual stretched programme of all engaged in women's work and it was not until 1916 that trade unionism among female workers in Birmingham increased from the reasonable, but not outstanding level of 1914. This advance is reflected in the reappearance in 1916 of the *Woman Worker,* the paper of the National Federation of Women Workers after a gap of several years, and the inauguration of the the Workers' Union monthly paper *Workers' Union Record.*

The main strength of the National Federation of Women Workers lay in the Black Country rather than Birmingham, centred on the Institute at Cradley Heath which had originated from the great Chainmakers' strike, although in Birmingham it had a sympathetic, long established presence at Bournville. Progress was resumed when the *Woman Worker* of June 1916 reported that a committee of women trade union workers had been appointed which 'gave Birmingham munitions workers a start in the Federation.' Their ranks had been strengthened by the addition of Mrs Lowen, Mrs Hunter and Miss Lloyd. 'Judging by the interest shown by the girls in the Federation it will soon be as strong in Birmingham as elsewhere.' The next month it was reported that the Birmingham branch 'had come to stay.' Two 'delightful' half days had been spent at Bournville where 20-30 women had listened to talks such as 'Women in Trade Unions', organised by the Women's Guild of the Ten Acres Co-operative Society. After tea there had been music and dancing. This set the pattern for the activity of the League which always tried to combine trade union with social activity. In September a report by Cecilia M. Mitchell stated that enquiries from munitions workers were still coming in who were expressing 'much dissatisfaction' with their conditions. They were hoping for good results from the TUC which was meeting in Birmingham that year.

The first results of wage improvements were reported in October starting, perhaps naturally, with Cadburys. Here the firm had conceded a war bonus. Girls over 18 earning under 26/-d a week would get another 3/-d. and those earning over 26/-d. would get 2/-d. There had also been applications from girls in other firms unloading brass rods and others on furnace work complaining about sulphurous, fumes all of whom were earning between 13/-d. and 15/-d. for a 54½ hour week. 'There is little doubt that these wages will soon be increased,' the report concluded.

The Workers' Union was also making progress in 1916. Julia Varley had now been joined by other women organisers and Miss Weaver, in May, reported the Tyseley branch membership was 'increasing rapidly.'

There was a certain amount of friction between the Workers' Union and the National Federation of Women Workers. The Amalgamated Society of Engineers had confirmed its opposition to the admission of female members and had effectively handed over the wartime organising of women in the engineering industry to the NFWW. The Workers' Union on the other hand, deeply involved in the organising of women in engineering, particularly during the significant strike period of 1910-14 which had seen such striking economic advances, had entered into a wartime agreement with the Midlands Engineering Employers. This they claimed was advantageous to the women, whereas the ASE maintained that the national agreements negotiated by them were undermined by the midland arrangements. The most ferocious attack on the role of the NFWW in the midlands came in the *Workers' Union Record* of September 1916 and was written by Julia Varley. There was also the overall complaint of the Workers' Union that ASE members which included semi- and unskilled men could be exempt from conscription while Worker's Union members, however skilled they became, were not exempt. These general differences inevitably affected the organisation of women.

Both bodies continued recruiting into 1917. In January Celia Mitchell of the NFWW reported new members at Drews Lane. They were a 'bright lot of girls.' and an office had been opened opposite the factory. General Electric women were doing well, but Kynoch girls must 'wake up'. Progress continued into February. Girls at Great King Street were 'a jolly lot' but they had no canteen, no place to eat and no place to warm food. At King's Norton Metal Works the girls were 'talking trade unionism all day long.' At GEC the management motto was 'everything on the cheap'. This report, by H.F. Harriet, ended 'Keep smiling. Everything comes to those who wait.'

In May there was 'a huge NFWW tea party' in Birmingham with 500 wounded soldiers as guests. 'Mrs Mitchell was in despair of feeding 4,000 people until three local Co-operatives came to the rescue.' The town hall was lent by the Lord Mayor. The Tramway Committee provided special cars to carry the soldiers from hospital and back. The Co-op Guilds, Women's Labour League and men's trade unions provided 'hosts of willing workers.' The soldiers arrived at 2-30 and Mrs Fawcett, national leader of the NUWSS, made a 'splendid speech' followed by the tea and entertainment. 'Everyone was sorry when the soldiers had to leave at 5-30 and it was noticeable that the special cars had to wait a long time while groups of wounded soldiers with pretty girls in pretty dresses arranged to meet at the big Trade Union meeting on Sunday afternoon.' From 7 to 10pm there was a social and dance and, 'Although there was a shortage of men everything went merrily and the only regret was that the Tommies had to go home before the fun was over.'

In July 1917 the *Woman Worker* head lines were 'Well done Birmingham.' Hundreds of girls had become recruiting sergeants for the great Trade Union army, it was claimed. At Kynoch's members of the Shop Committee were 'helping energetically,' and one young ASE member had recruited 100 women. An 'inspiring meeting' had been held at Lucas's.

A dispute at Warrington was highlighted in October where a conductress of 17 worked only nine hours a day, but on a split shift which meant that she had a long walk four times a day because there was no public transport. She wanted to leave but the Tribunal had failed to grant her a leaving certificate. The situation was almost as bad in Birmingham, it was stated.

An important decision had also been reached with regard to women's wages. At arbitration the Midland Employers' Federation had agreed that Ministers' Orders should be applied to women and girls employed by Federation members whether they were working on munitions or not. Up to this point Federation firms had paid the additional amounts to women on munitions exclusively, but not to women on private work as well as munitions. If this new minimum were applied it would mean that all women over 18 working for Federation firms would be paid a minimum of 5½d. an hour. But this agreement even if it were strictly observed, clearly had limitations and did not apply to most women.

Workers' Union sources reveal little about organisation of women in 1917, although the Union continued to grow rapidly. There is mention of a strike in October 1917 at Midland Rubber in Birmingham where the majority on strike were women who needed support from other trade unionists.

The third union largely involved in the recruitment of Women, the Amalgamated Society of Gas, Municipal and General Workers, dealt with women's pay in its *Monthly Journal* of January 1917. It claimed that equal pay for equal work with a time rate of £1 a week had been established in National Factories since the previous October. The reissuing of Circular L2 gave £1 for a 48 hour week for women 18 and over with an extra 6d. an hour for all additional work. 'This gives the majority of women and girls *on direct munitions* a decent living wage and the possibility on piecework of earnings undreamt of before the war.' Further information regarding women however, is as scarce in the ASGM&GW *Monthly Journal* as it is in the *Workers' Union Record*.

The National Federation of Women Workers continued to recruit during 1918. Mary Macarthur addressed a mass meeting at Birmingham Town Hall in January when Charles Sitch, the Chainmakers' secretary, who was also at this time the only man on the executive of the NFWW, reported continued low wages among women, citing pinafore adult workers earning between 9/10d. and 14/9d. for a 46 hour week. Steady growth of the Birmingham branch was reported early in the year (with a fancy dress dance in April) and also in December. But towards the end of the year reorganisation and election matters predominated in the paper, particularly Mary Macarthur's contest in Stourbridge.

References to women are also meagre in the *Workers' Union Record* in 1918. A large influx of members in the Birmingham area was recorded in January, but with no specific mention of women. In February organisation of men and women was recorded for the Screw, Nut and Rivet trade. This was one of the oldest, staple trades of Birmingham, but unlike the heavier Nut & Bolt trade, it had never before been organised. The most publicised work of Julia Varley was her visit to France in April 1918 to investigate charges of immorality against girls in the WAAC. Her conclusions were that conditions were as good as could be expected in wartime and the girls had been 'grossly libelled.' Much of the contents of the *Record* in 1918 were devoted to the union leadership's right-wing support for the war, the vendetta against the ASE and hostility to the Shop Stewards Movement.

The *Monthly Journal* of the ASGM&GW again carries little directly on women. Hallas, the editor, was as involved as the Workers' Union in right-wing policies of hostility to the Birmingham Trades Council, support for an alternative national Labour Party, and criticism of the existing Labour Party leaders.

Few conclusions can be drawn from this survey of the three main trade union bodies responsible for organising women in wartime in Birmingham.

It can be said that recruitment of women into trade unions was slow, but progress was greatest from 1916 to the end of the war. The national figures show that female membership of trade unions increased from 358,000 in 1914 to 1,100,000 in 1918. We also know that Workers' Union female membership was 5,000 in 1914, most of these in the midlands, and in 1918 it had grown to 80,000, more than any other general union; women constituted nearly one quarter of total membership at that time. One might hazard a guess from the evidence given above, that women trade unionists in Birmingham rose at least as fast as membership nationally, but otherwise we remain in the dark both with regard to the number in trade unions and the number who earned the legendary high wages of munitions workers.

Political women and the War: The National Situation

Before dealing with events in Birmingham, it is necessary to outline the national development of women and politics. Women participated in the general movement to prevent war. But they were more persistent than the men in attempting to stop the war once it had started and seeking or maintaining contacts with German, Austrian and other 'enemy' women.

It was natural that those involved in the strongest of women's organisations, the Suffrage movement, should take a leading part in shaping women's attitudes to the war. As we know, Mrs Pankhurst and daughter Christabel arbitrarily aligned the Women's Social & Political Union with those who supported the war, renamed the movement's paper *Brittania,* and in November 1917, again without consultation, renamed the the WS&PU the Women's Party. Sylvia Pankhurst, however, completely broke with her mother and was anti-war from the beginning. Although Mrs Pankhurst retained the support of some of the leading Suffragettes (Annie Kenney became the secretary of the new Women's Party and 'General' Flora Drummond its chief organiser) support for *Brittania* never approached that of its predecessor *The Suffragette* and Mrs Pankhurst herself moved increasingly into the highly exalted circle of generals and statesmen and lost much of her previous support.

The Women's Union of Suffrage Societies, largely middle class and with a basic Liberal ideology might have been expected to be pro-war, but in fact they inherited a Liberal tradition of preference of peace to war dating back to before the days of Cobden and Bright. The movement split down the middle in 1915. The following events led to this.

On the evening of 4 August 1914 a Women's Peace meeting was held. Among the organisations represented were the National Federation of Women Workers, the Women's Labour League, the Women's Co-operative Guild, and the National Union of Women's Suffrage Societies. The meeting was chaired by Millicent Fawcett. the almost legendary leader of the NUWSS. A resolution was passed at this meeting requesting mediation to stop the war by countries 'not yet involved' and support for the British war effort.

But the women were not content with resolutions. In co-operation with the International Suffrage Alliance, Emmeline Pethwick-Lawrence together with the Hungarian feminist Rosika Schwimmer toured the United States and interviewed President Wilson seeking his intervention to end the war. A Women's Peace Party was formed on the initiative of the American feminists at this time. In February 1915 women's leaders from Britain, Germany and Belgium met in Amsterdam to call a Congress of Women for April. From the British government's point of view, any peace activity was unwelcome, but a meeting involving contact with 'enemy' women was intolerable. 180 British women decided to attend the Congress at the Hague. The government withheld passports from all but 25 and even these were prevented from sailing across the Channel. Only three British women, Chrystal Macmillan (secretary of the International Suffrage Alliance) and Kathleen Courtney (a NUWSS organiser) who were already in Holland and Mrs Pethwick-Lawrence who travelled with the American delegation were able to attend the Congress. The German delegation was stopped at the Dutch border, but 28 women got through. In all 1,136 women from 12 countries participated. The main resolutions passed called for Continuous Mediation by a group of neutral nations, and a Women's Voice in the Peace Settlement. The resolutions of the Congress were to be delivered personally to the leaders of all belligerent and neutral nations of Europe and to the USA, and a formidable team of delegates was elected to carry out this task.

This was the Congress that divided the NUWSS and many of its leading figures became anti-war. Helena Swanwick who had been editor of *Common Cause* up to 1912 was a pacifist and became a leader of the Fellowship of Reconciliation. Maude Roydon who followed Swanwick as editor of *Common Cause* to 1914 also became anti-war. Kathleen Courtney and Catherine Marshall who were closest to the working class movement both repudiated the war and Catherine Marshall virtually ran the No-Conscription Fellowship as its male officers were called up and imprisoned. Only Millicent Fawcett of the NUWSS became pro-war and even inclined to some jingoism at times.

From the Hague Conference arose an International Committee of Women for Permanent Peace. In September 1915 the British branch named itself the Women's International League staffed largely by NUWSS women. This reported on peace women imprisoned in Germany, notably Rosa Luxembourg, and also those arrested in pre-revolutionary Russia. In June 1916 an important Women's Peace Crusade was created through the Glasgow branch of WIL with large numbers of women marching through towns – a hazardous thing to do with jingo soldiers inflamed by a jingo press likely to be encountered. The Russian revolution was a turning point and by January 1918 the Labour Party policy was to seek a negotiated peace.

The local effect of these events will be followed though the activities of the Birmingham women's organisations beginning with the Suffrage societies.

The Women's Social and Political Union and Women's Party

The Birmingham Women's Social & Political Union continued in existence during the war, but accounts of its activities are difficult to find in its paper *Brittania*. By 1916 the paper was reduced to a cyclostyled sheet still edited by Christabel Pankhurst with the uncompromising banner heading, For King, For Country, For Freedom. It soon reverted to printed form, but it suffered much from wartime paper shortages and the format and number of pages constantly changed. For 1916 the only local entry found is an announcement that Mrs Pankhurst would visit Birmingham in September. Nor can references be found in the paper in 1917 until the end of the year.

In November 1917, the name was changed from WS&PU to the Women's Party and from this time local fortunes seemed to have improved. By January 1918 a women's organiser had been appointed. She was Miss Isabel Green of 91 Kingsbury Road, Erdington. She promised a 'vigorous campaign' and delivered one. In February it was announced that the women of Birmingham and Coventry were 'Against Bolsheviks and for Country.' Motions had been passed by women in six factories in support of the government and protesting at the Amalgamated Society of Engineers motion of approval of the Russian Revolution. Mrs Pankhurst had been an early visitor to Russia after the revolution and returned with a decidedly adverse report. This she presented in January at a Birmingham meeting in the Temperance Hall. She also held two 'at homes' at the Midland Hotel.

Miss Green revived the tradition of open-air meetings at the Bull Ring. At her first meeting in February 1918 she was presented with flowers by the market women. She hoped to continue these meetings every Thursday (market day) at 1-15pm. Mrs Pankhurst returned to Birmingham in February for a week long campaign. She held a meeting at the Town Hall with 2,000 present and held successful 'at homes.'

The open-air meetings continued in February where the Engineers had held a meeting followed by 'Pacifist women demanding a negotiated peace.' Miss Green started a rival meeting and talked of 'Young fit men hiding in the factories and talking Pacifism. It was not British!' The next week the weather was not favourable and, 'the Pacifists were shivering in the cold afraid to start their own meeting due to what happened last week. They were waiting for Miss Green. The meeting on Peace by Negotiation was a failure.'

In March Mrs Pankhurst was back for Dreadnought Week and held a meeting at the Birmingham Hippodrome. The Women's Party continued to thrive. In April the weekly Bull Ring meetings continued, a concert and jumble sale was organised and indoor meetings were taking place at the Midland Hotel. In June Annie Kenney was in Birmingham for three days with a meeting at Solihull, a Town Hall meeting and a Patriotic Meeting at the Midland Hotel. Speakers classes were also being arranged.

In June the Women's Party was combating a strike of engineers at a Birmingham factory where a man named Cockbill had been imprisoned for 'impeding the production of munitions.' The strike was fomented by 'certain advanced and Socialistic members of the ASE,' it was claimed. 'Women munitions workers view this with alarm and we are informed that a counter-call for greater production has been issued.'

In the summer, the Women's Party took to organising factory gate meetings. In June there was a dinner hour meeting at BSA which attracted 'a large crowd of men and women.' At a meeting outside the Austin, Julia Varley spoke on her 'Enquiry into the slanders on the women of the WAAC.' There was also a meeting at Wolseley's where 'boys and girls were intensely interested.' In July there was a first meeting at the National Shell Factory and fortnightly meetings were reported at BSA. Miss Green also held a canteen meeting at 'one of our largest factories,' and a meeting at Kynoch's. These meetings were being chaired by two members from the Speakers Classes.

By this time the Women's Party was strong enough to take premises at 30 Paradise Street. The importance of the Birmingham branch can be judged from the fact that it was the first and longest weekly report appearing in *Brittania* at this time. Only eight or so other branches reported and these usually came from the large towns of Clydeside, Manchester, Sheffield, Liverpool and Bristol and smaller areas such as Hastings, Torquay and Bexhill.

Meetings continued throughout the summer. In July two large canteen meetings were held and at a meeting outside Vickers. Miss Green's 'denunciation of the shop stewards brought the wrath of some male, young advocates, but the women shouted them down.' At the end of July 'a large crowd in the Bull Ring was anxious to hear Miss Green speak on the strike. She appealed to loyal workers (not to strike).' In August 'General' Drummond came from London and meetings were held at Vickers and Kynochs where 'strong resolutions on how to beat the Hun' were passed. In August, factory gate meetings were continued at Vickers and National Shell Fuse. In the Bull Ring Miss Green 'explained the position of the Czech and Slovak armies in Siberia'. But 'at homes' were discontinued.

Activities continued into September. A Win the War Procession was arranged for 21st. but no report of it has been found. In the Bull Ring, Miss Horton 'explained the uncompromising attitude of the Women's Party to the alien question.' Miss Green 'spoke of the declaration of war by the National Federation of Women Workers against the Women's Party. She said this was a compliment coming from an organisation led by Pacifists and Bolsheviks. The crowd were indignant to hear that Mary Macarthur who aided and abetted strikes is chair of the Women's Advisory Committee which advises the Minister of Munitions on all matters concerning the employment of women in munitions factories.'

In October there was a Big Gun Week and Miss Green spoke at the main meeting in Victoria Square. Peace proposals were now being widely discussed. A large crowd at the usual Bull Ring meeting had come to hear 'what the Women's Party had to say about the German peace proposals. Miss Green dealt fully with the matter. There should be no peace until the Germans capitulate.' At another Bull Ring meeting Miss Green was complaining about the 'International Workers of the World who are making use of local Bolsheviks including members of the National Federation of Women Workers to spread their evil and destructive message in the tool shops and among workers in and around Birmingham.'

Early in November 1918 Miss Green spoke in the Bull Ring about the Allied Conference in Paris and 'the necessity to treat Austria as harshly as Bulgaria.' By the next week the war was over. *Britannia* interpreted this as 'a defeat for the attempts to spread Bolshevism and this had prevented any compromise peace.' Co-incidentally, the Town Hall had been engaged for a visit by Mrs Pankhurst. The hall was crowded and the occasion was turned into a Victory Celebration. The meeting was chaired by the Rev Arnold Pinchard (earlier an influential left-wing Church Socialist) who spoke on the Dangers of a Compromise Peace.

The next week the decks were being cleared for the forthcoming general election and the Birmingham Women's Party's attentions were diverted to Christabel Pankhurst's election in Smethwick.

The National Union of Women's Suffrage Societies

At the end of 1914 the NUWSS had a membership of 955, of whom 246 had joined during a recruiting campaign in June. The Society also had 4,640 non-subscribing members called Friends of Women's Suffrage.

On the outbreak of war, all members of the Society threw themselves into tackling the new problems raised by the conflict irrespective of their political attitudes to the war. In November funds were raised for a Workroom to relieve the initial unemployment among women arising from the war. It closed in March 1915 when its funds were exhausted and unemployment was no longer a problem. It had employed between twenty and thirty women for 27 hours per week at 3½d. per hour. Just before Christmas the Church League for Women's Suffrage had given the Workroom an order for little frocks to be given as gifts to those young German children living in Birmingham whose fathers had been interned. The Workroom was also used for social activity. Afternoon musical events were arranged, talks by Belgian women refugees telling of their escape from Antwerp etc. Another Workroom, Beaumont Hall, was opened in October organised by the Bournville Branch of the NUWSS, the Ten Acres & Stirchley Co-operative Women's Guild etc. It specialised in employing women between the ages of 30 and 50 plus. The hall, together with heating and lighting, was paid for by the Co-operative Society and deficits covered by grants from the Prince of Wales' Fund etc. A Dining Centre for expectant and nursing mothers was opened in the Jewellery quarter where unemployment was particularly bad. This also closed in March when unemployment lessened. The following comment highlights the general physical condition of the Birmingham poor at the outbreak of war: 'The ill-health of nearly all the women was very distressing – some were slightly consumptive, some anaemic but hardly one seemed healthy.'

The sensitive moral issues of the war were at first tackled by the NUWSS and the National Union of Women Workers (an umbrella organisation for all charitable and other societies dealing with women in Birmingham). They established Women Patrols in the neighbourhood of large military camps. The NUWW also established a League of Honour to guard 'young women and girls from the dangers arising from the excitement and dislocation of normal life due to the war, and especially to the aggregation of large numbers of soldiers...'

The political issues of the year were described as follows in the annual report:

...the crisis has not been without difficulty and peril to the unity of our Organisation. A considerable number of our members... were deeply desirous that the Union should attempt to give a moral lead to public opinion as regards its attitude – not on the war itself – but on the general principles which should form the basis of a future Peace in order to guard against any possible recurrence of the present catastrophe.

A large section, on the other hand, objected to the Union identifying itself with any views on any subject not directly concerned with the winning of the vote, and on which there must be wide differences of opinion. At the (General) Council meeting...resolutions were passed in favour of Goodwill v Militarism, Arbitration v Armaments, a United States of Europe v the Balance of Power, which might have been taken to express the wishes of the more Pacifist section.

However the decision of the Council not to take *action* on certain resolutions led to the deeply regretted resignation of the Hon. Sec., Miss Courtney, the Parliamentary Sec., Miss Marshall, the Press Sec., Miss Leaf and the editor of the *Common Cause,* Miss Royden and nine other members of the Executive, all of whom desired to be free to devote their time and energies to the great moral work of pacification.

The annual report for 1915-16 noted that while Suffrage work had not been entirely neglected most work had been connected with the war. The branch had been involved in medical aid to Serbia (where nurses and women doctors had taken part in the trek across the snow covered mountains into Montenegro), a Polish Refugee Maternity Hospital in England and a unit of nurses and women doctors which had been sent to Russia. A very large Motherhood Lecture Scheme had been inaugurated in co-operation with the Women's Co-operative Guild and most other women's organisations in the city dealing with health and welfare. Local action had been taken on the Report of the Royal Commission on Venereal Diseases.

With regard to the politics of the war, a large general meeting in Birmingham had decided to support a resolution in the name of Mrs Fawcett and the local leader, Mrs Osler, among others. This stated that in view of the differences of opinion in the Union as to the best means of promoting at that time the cause of International goodwill and future peace, the Council agreed that the propaganda of the NUWSS should be directed to Women's Suffrage only, and on political questions that divided the Union, individuals were free to work through any other organisation they thought fit.

In 1916-17 NUWSS activity continued to be directed to fund raising particularly for the Millicent Fawcett Hospital Units for Refugees in Russia and also the NUWSS Scottish Hospitals for Home & Foreign Service. The moral issue also absorbed much attention. An 'influential branch' of the National Council for Combatting Venereal Disease was set up to deal with both the treatment of the disease and dissemination among both sexes of knowledge and warning of the diseases. A powerful campaign involving the Women's Co-operative Guild and the Trades Council pressurising the Watch Committee to appoint women constables.

There was also activity as the Suffrage question came at last to fruition. This involved joint activity with the Conservative & Unionist Women's Franchise Association, the Friends' League for Women's Suffrage, and the Church League for Women's Suffrage. In February 1917, the national council of NUWSS accepted the recommendations of the Speakers' Conference to support the Electoral Reform Bill as the 'best terms at present available' and also accepted 'by our Labour friends.' The local Society also accepted this. Of these proposals the annual report said:

> It confers what is practically manhood suffrage on a six months residential qualification; and it gives an unequal but very substantial enfranchisement to women (a) on the basis of the municipal registers as householders, (b) as wives of male voters, (c) as University graduates. In order to meet the strong objection felt to the predominance of women electors, the qualifying age for women is fixed at 30.

It placed about 6 million women, compared with 11 million men on the Register. In view of subsequent discussion on reasons why the vote was eventually granted to women. it is interesting to read what the NUWSS thought at the time:

> The revolution in national opinion has been truly amazing... What has brought about this change? Largely, no doubt, the wider opportunity afforded to women by the War to prove conclusively that their active and patriotic service and devotion to their country... is in no way less valuable or less essential than that of men; but also the demonstration that the removal of the artificial restrictions on women's talents and activities will, as Suffragists have always maintained, materially augment the effective power and prosperity of the country.

On the political question, the Birmingham branch held their usual annual meeting to discuss resolutions for the national Council. After full discussion they supported full independence of salaried officials in their private time and independent action on the part of Societies on subjects other than women's suffrage. This continued a shift to the left of the Birmingham society and was rejected by the national Council. This shift is reflected in the columns of *Common Cause* in which there are no reports of Birmingham activity, but very regular announcements of forthcoming events. These indicate increasingly close contact with Labour organisations with Pacifist leanings. The most important were the two Women's Guilds of Birmingham Industrial, and the Ten Acres & Stirchley Co-operative Societies but also the Railway Women's Guild and the Socialist and Labour Churches.

The Birmingham NUWSS annual report for 1917-18 largely looked forward to the future. The bill enfranchising women at 30 and over was finally passed in January 1918 and much discussion ensued regarding the future of the organisation. A proposal to change the name was rejected on the grounds that the full achievement of equality with men on the vote had not been achieved. But the maintenance of a Society, working with other women's organisations to 'hold a watching brief' for the rights and welfare of women in the period of reconstruction after the war, was acknowledged.

In its local work, the continued move to the left was emphasised by the organisation of a Housing Conference in conjunction with the Women's Labour League which passed the following resolution:

> That this Conference of women, representing the Women's Co-operative Guild, the Women's Labour League, The Mothers' Union, the Women's Adult Schools, the Labour Churches, the Infant Welfare Centres, the National Federation of Women Workers, the Railway Women's Guild, the Women's Suffrage Society etc. etc. in the city of Birmingham urges the City Council to use all the powers they have and such as may be given to them to proceed immediately with the provision of houses to meet the acute need...

The leading local NUWSS activist at this time was the organiser, Carol Ring. When Catherine Osler, who had been president of the Birmingham NUWSS almost from its inception in 1868, had to retire from the NUWSS national executive, Carol Ring was elected in her place. It is likely that Carol Ring was already a Socialist at this time; *Common Cause* reports show that she not only spoke very frequently at Labour movement meetings, but in May 1918 chaired a George Lansbury meeting at the East Birmingham Labour Church.

By the time of the 1918-19 annual report the NUWSS was no more; in March 1919 it became the Birmingham Society for Equal Citizenship and Women Citizen's Association.

In July 1918 an important local conference had taken place on Women in the Metal Trades with representatives from four Trades Councils, 15 trade unions, 7 Works Committees, 8 Labour and ILP branches, 8 branches of the Women's Co-operative Guild and 10 different Suffrage Societies.

In the general election of December 1918 the NUWSS supported Mrs Corbett Ashby, a member of their executive, who stood as a Liberal candidate against Neville Chamberlain and Councillor Kneeshaw in Ladywood. Chamberlain won. The NUWSS regretted that they had stood a candidate against Kneeshaw 'who had always supported the enfranchisement of women', but the 'non-Party constitution of the Society, and the urgent need for obtaining representatives in Parliament of both sexes demanded all possible support for women candidates.'

With the end of the war the veterans retired and were honoured. Millicent Fawcett received an honorary degree from Birmingham University. Mrs Osler was similarly honoured, together with three vice-presidents of the NUWSS, Mrs George Cadbury, John Drinkwater, and Alfred Hayes. A Catherine Osler permanent scholarship at Birmingham University for women students wishing stay for another year to read for an MA was also inaugurated, and her portrait presented to the Art Gallery.

In summarising the work of the NUWSS during the war, the organisation involved itself deeply in welfare work for women and in doing so associated itself more clearly with the trade union and political organisations of the left. This cut across the Birmingham decision to propagandise as a Society only on Suffrage questions. The welfare work, however, expressed neither support for nor opposition to the war. The organisation never became stridently patriotic as did the Women's Social and Political Union. On the other hand, although associating more frequently with left-wing organisations it did not voice anti-war opinions either from 1916 when conscription strengthened such tendencies, nor later when feelings that the war was being unneccesarily prolonged and demands for a negotiated peace were wide spread.

Women's Co-operative Guild

It has been a difficult decision whether to include what is known of the Women's Co-op Guild in the chapter on Co-operation or this chapter on Women.

What is known of the Women's Guild comes from Wheatsheaf the monthly paper distributed in Co-operative shops with a local content; in this case a record of the activities of the Women's Guild of the Birmingham Industrial Co-operative Society only. There seems to be no record of the Ten Acres & Stirchley Women's Co-operative Guild.

At the beginning of 1915 there were nine Women's Guild branches – Aston & Perry Barr, Central, Erdington, Handsworth, Small Heath, Sparkhill, Harborne, Dudley Road, and Balsall Heath. It is possible that the last three were actually formed after the war started. This number remained constant throughout the war.

The branches held their usual weekly or fortnightly meetings, felt some responsibility for the two Co-op Choirs, and co-operated with the Men's Guild branches that developed during the war. Educational activities were also continued and developed with the Workers' Education Society, advertisements for whose activities were regularly reported in *Wheatsheaf*. We have noted elsewhere the Whist Drives and other activities to entertain wounded soldiers.

Reports of the progress of branches are infrequent, and therefore valuable. In June 1916 Small Heath reported 'good work despite difficulties.' Nineteen general meetings had been held in the year with an average attendance of 80. Twenty five new members had been made during the year. Black out problems led branches away from their traditional evening meetings and Erdington reported meetings changed to 3pm to 5pm on alternate Wednesdays and the hope of attracting 'those not able to get to evening meetings.' Central also changed to afternoon meetings before the end of the year.

In November 1916 Sparkhill reported meetings with speakers from the Union of Democratic Control and a talk on Women in Industry during and after the War. Harborne members were sewing for the Lady Mayoress's Needlework Fair at the Town Hall the next spring when proceeds would go to the Star and Garter Home for Disabled Soldiers.

In January 1917 Handsworth Guild reported its seventh birthday celebrations with 70 members and friends 'braving the darkened streets', to attend, and in February they heard an address on Russia by Mrs Chillingworth. Aston & Perry Barr branch celebrated its 11th birthday with a party in November 1916. In March 1917, Harborne reported that joint work with the Men's Guild was 'a great success.' In May, Erdington passed resolutions for a Maternity Centre and Creche in Birmingham and another for Adult Suffrage. Small Heath reported good meetings with the questions of Maternity Centres, a Municipal Milk supply and V.D. all taken up. A meeting with the NUWSS to consider industrial problems after the war had been held and there had been successful whist drives, the proceedings being divided between the Prisoner of War Fund, the Women's Hospital, the Women's Guild Hospital etc. Harborne Guild reported a marked improvement on the previous year and the great success of their wounded soldiers' party. In June Balsall Heath members were looking forward to their fortnightly rambles, but little other summer activity was recorded. In the autumn of 1917, Dudley Road reported a social afternoon with 30 wounded soldiers which had ended with the singing of Auld Lang Syne.

At he beginning of 1918 seven of the nine branches were regularly reporting activities in *Wheatsheaf* with social activities and wounded soldiers' parties. In June, Erdington reported a meeting with Miss Royden from the Union of Democratic Control. Sparkhill gave a full account of their activities. Their membership was 112 with an average attendance of 58. Five members were active on the local political council. One was on the Education Committee, one on the Agricultural Committee and one on the Emergency Committee. 'About a dozen' members had attended a BICS part-time week's school and four delegates were going to the national conference. Dispensary notes were purchased for members and sickroom appliances were available. In October a tenth branch was announced – at Witton.

As the war drew to a close attention turned more to electoral activity and the necessity to support the new Co-operative Party. Reaction to the Armistice comes from three branches. Aston & Perry Barr noted, 'On November 11th the Guild meeting had to be postponed until the following Tuesday owing to the armistice being signed.' Handsworth stated, 'November 12th being a holiday we had a social afternoon amongst the members who did turn up, which was merry and bright owing to the good news that had come at last.' Small Heath wrote ' December 4th being our social afternoon, was opened with a few well-chosen words by our newly appointed president (Mrs Rawes). It was felt we could not commence our meeting without referring to the deep feeling of gratitude that hostilities were at an end.'

What is surprising from these reports of the Women's Guild is that so little overt political activity is mentioned. Yet we know from the mainstream activity of the Birmingham society discussed in Chapter 11 how important were the women to Co-operative success, particularly on the question of food shortages.

The Women's Labour League

Cornish's Birmingham Year Book for 1914 records four WLL branches in Birmingham – Central, Handsworth, Saltley and Bordesley. The aim of the League was stated to be, 'To work for independent Labour representation in connection with the Labour Party and to obtain direct representation of Women in Parliament and on all local bodies.' The newspaper of the WLL was *Labour Woman*. The ninth annual conference of the League took place in January 1914. Here it was reported that district organisation was being set up for the Midlands. A list of women on local bodies showed that Mrs G. Williams of Saltley sat on the Birmingham Board of Guardians. Branches were especially involved in trade union work, it was stated, Saltley and Handsworth being particularly involved in collecting funds for the strikes of the Great Unrest which were still continuing at that period.

When war broke out *Labour Woman* also reported the activities of the Women's International Council of Socialist and Labour Organisations (British Section). It reported the International Socialist Women's Conference in Vienna in August 1914 and publicised the efforts of the German women, notably Rosa Luxembourg and Clara Zetkin, for peace.

The Women's Labour League affiliated to the Union of Democratic Control early in 1915 and district conferences were held on 'War and the Terms of Peace.' In May Mrs Hugh Gibbons and Miss Sophia Sturge reported in Birmingham on the Extraordinary Conference of Labour & Socialist Women held in Berne in March with representatives from Britain, France, Russia, Poland, Germany and the neutrals Italy, Switzerland and Holland. The main resolution had stated that 'War has its origins in the imperialist ideas of capitalist society'. War would be waged on this war and an immediate end was demanded without annexations. The Bolshevik proposals of a divided Russian delegation were defeated, however. These had called for a condemnation of all parties supporting the war and also that opposition to the war should be revolutionary in character.

Labour Woman introduced a column *Our Sisters Abroad,* which reported such items as the German anti-war journal *Gleichheit* still being published, and a Manifesto from German Socialist Women to the executive of the German Socialist Party declaring that the war was one of German expansion and demanding that the party return to the position of class war.

The tenth annual conference of the Women's Labour League took place early in 1916. A resolution proposed by Marion Phillips and seconded by Mrs Kneeshaw was passed reaffirming opposition to Conscription and, more to the point, pledged opposition to it if passed and agitation for its repeal. But another resolution stated that 'there were no grounds on which to adopt a policy of opposition to the War.'

It is difficult to assess the importance of the Women's Labour League in Birmingham during the war. District organisation existed throughout the war and midland district conferences were regularly called, but these were outside Birmingham until April 1917 when one was held at St. Saviour's Church rooms, Saltley. At this there were delegates from all League branches plus women from the Co-op Guild, Railway Women's Guild, the United Suffragists and the National Federation of Women Workers; 34 delegates in all. Two issues dominated the Conference. One was the ramifications of Conscription. Miss Margaret Haly, secretary to the Birmingham Women's International League and previously an organiser of the WS&PU, spoke on Industrial Conscription and proposed a one day strike to combat military Conscription. The other issue agitating women was the campaign against VD and a motion was passed:

> This Conference, representative of most women's organisations in Birmingham protests at the outrageous clauses in the Criminal Law Amendment Bill which makes it possible to detain in a home any girl under the age of 19 arrested by police for soliciting. It protests at this discrimination against women when men are equally guilty. This is a grievous and unjust interference with the rights of law abiding citizens.

After this there are no other references to the Birmingham Women's Labour League in *Labour*

Woman for either 1917 or the key year of 1918. Even in 1919 when a 'splendid first Conference under Labour Party auspices' of midland women took place it was in Smethwick and not Birmingham that it was held. Yet we know that a meeting of the Women's Peace Crusade took place in July 1917 in Birmingham with an estimated attendance of 12,000. The 1916 *Cornish' Birmingham Year Book* records three branches of the Women's Labour League of Birmingham Central, Handsworth and Saltley and in 1917 two branches, Central, whose officials were Mrs Kneeshaw and Mrs Mitchell and Saltley (Mrs Briden). But there are no entries for 1918.

Unless there is serious under-reporting of activities in Birmingham, a subsequent chapter will show that the Women's Labour League was more active in the Black Country than in Birmingham.

Workers' Suffrage Federation

This organisation arose during 1915 as an development from Sylvia Pankhurst's East London Federation of Suffragettes. Its organ was the *Woman's Dreadnought* which in 1918 changed its name to *Workers' Dreadnought.* Sylvia became convinced during the war that the suffrage would be conceded to women and the logical next step was for a women's organisation that would agitate for Adult Suffrage.

By April 1916 there was a Birmingham branch of the Workers' Suffrage Federation with fifty six members which met at the Stirchley Institute. A 'most successful' meeting had been held at the end of March and outdoor meetings were being held in the Bull Ring. Mrs Boyce wished to thank Miss Booth, Mrs Brooks, Mr and Mrs Durant, Councillor Hackett, Mrs Henderson, Mr Morcom and Mrs Ward for the success of the branch.

The same month we are told that the secretary was Miss Boden of 8 Richmond Road, Bearwood. She was arranging for the *Dreadnought* to be sold at local newsagents and would insist that they show posters. Branch meetings were held every Wednesday evening. Special donations of 1/-d. from Mrs Cann and 2/6d. from Mrs Ives were acknowledged. An 'excellent' meeting had been held in the Bull Ring on Wednesday 5th April and Mrs Boyce was leaving to go to Newcastle. Finally, it was reported that a branch of the League of Rights for the wives and relations of soldiers and sailors was to be formed.

Two delegates, Mrs Brookes and Mrs Pauden were elected to attend the No-Conscription Conference at the Priory Rooms on April 29th. *Dreadnoughts* were on sale at Mrs Ward, newsagent at 32 Bournville Lane, Stirchley. In May the full committee of the Birmingham branch was announced. It consisted of ten women – Mrs Harris, Mrs Sorrill, Mrs Manning, Mrs Chamberlain, Mrs Ward, Miss Bills, Mrs Brooks, Mrs Avery, Mrs Death and the hon.sec. Miss A.F. Boden now at 10 Sandhurst Road Moseley; there were also four men – Messrs Attwood, Durant, Morcom and Skett.

On Christmas Eve 1916 a great Peace meeting was held in the Bull Ring. From a prayer meeting in Priory Rooms a long procession of women marched through the principal streets of the city culminating in a meeting at the Bull Ring which ended with the singing of God Save the People. The speaker was Miss Haley. After the meeting they were surrounded by eager questioners including young soldiers.

Another Peace meeting was held on New Year's Eve. Miss Haley was again the speaker. 'A large crowd remained despite a heavy downpour,' the report stated.

In February it was announced that Miss Haley was doing four fortnightly lectures at the Stirchley Institute on Internationalism. In March Sylvia Pankhurst spoke with Miss Haley at the Priory Rooms. Before the meeting members were urged to volunteer to give out leaflets at factory gates etc.

In April the Workers' Suffrage Federation jointly with the Stirchley Labour Church organised a conference on Mothers' Pensions at the Stirchley Institute with Judge Neil as the main speaker.

For a time in 1917 the WSF secretary was Mrs Henson of 85 Watford Road, King's Norton, but by the end of the year Miss Boden again occupied this position.

In June Miss Boden was elected to the WSF Conference which was held in Birmingham in 1917 and by August the Birmingham branch was organising a People's Chamber for Peace, Socialism and Adult Suffrage.

The WSF held a national bazaar at Christmas called an Old Cockney Fair. Birmingham members were urged to send contributions to Mrs Durant of 176 Maryvale Road, Bournville.

From 1918 the name of the paper was changed to *Workers' Dreadnought*. But the only Birmingham activity recorded was packed meetings in March on the Montessori method of education.

Other Women's Organisations

Little can be said about other women's Labour organisations. The United Suffragists who continued the paper *Votes for Women* when the Pethwick-Lawrences broke with Emmeline and Christabel Pankhurst before the war, had a presence in Birmingham with an office at 13 Suffolk Street. Miss Julia Green was the hon.sec. In April 1917 *Votes for Women* tells us that members held meetings at this office, and the May issue states that at the Women's Labour League Conference in Saltley discussed above, there was a representative from the USA.

One organisation of some importance of which little is known is the Railway Women's Guild. This had branches in Birmingham and in 1918 the Saltley branch was affiliated to the Trades Council.

Two other women's organisations present in the city during the war were the Women's International League and also the Women's Freedom League, Of the latter Wiltsher tells us that it was associated with National Aid Camps which had a workshop in Birmingham distributing clothes.

A final word on the National Union of Women Workers This was the largest organisation of women in Birmingham. It was never a part of the Labour movement, despite the fact that before the war Julia Varley had affiliated her organisation, the Women Workers' Industrial Organisation, to it, and also the Suffragists and Suffragettes were affiliated to the NUWW.

During the war, the Labour women's organisations do not appear to have sought to affiliate to the NUWW and it remained a middle class charity organisation concerned with the welfare of women and children in the city. Its quarterly magazine, however, *Women Workers,* is the best source for the general activities of women in Birmingham during the war.

Bibliography: Birmingham Women in Wartime

Figures for women's employment are taken from the national Censuses for 1911 and 1921. For the Workers' Union see: Richard Hyman – *The Workers' Union;* and the monthly paper *Workers' Union Record* and the *Annual Reports.* For the National Federation of Women Workers see: *Woman Worker.* For the third group of Unions concerned with organising women see: *Municipal Employees' Monthly,* subsequently: *Monthly Journal* of the Amalgamated Society of Gas, Municipal & General Workers. For the general development of peace work among women during the war see: Anne Wiltsher – *Most Dangerous Women;* Jo Vellacott – 'Feminist Consciousness and the First World War' (in *History Workshop* No.23, 1987); and Jo Vellacott Newbury – 'Anti-War Suffragists' (in *History* vol 62, 1977). For the wartime activities of the Women's Social & Political Union (later the Women's Party) see their paper edited by Christabel Pankhurst: *Brittania.* For the wartime activities of the National Union of Women's Suffrage Societies see: Annual Report of the Birmingham & District NUWSS, and the newspaper *Common Cause.* For the Women's Co-operative Guild see *Wheatsheaf.* For the Women's Labour League see *Labour Woman.* For the National Union of Women Workers in Birmingham see their quarterly magazine *Women Workers.* For the Workers' Suffrage Federation see *Women's Dreadnought* (from 1918 *Workers' Dreadnought*).

Chapter 13

Birmingham Labour Movement Politics 1914-18

We have so far dealt with the activities of the Trade Unions, Co-operative movement and Women's movement during the war. We must now look at the general political movement during this time.

The Labour Party nationally supported the war from the outset. Its largest affiliate of individual members, the Independent Labour Party, was usually described as anti-war, but it contained members of varying views. Some, like Ramsay MacDonald, seemed to oppose the war at one time, but to support recruitment and the allied cause at others. Others were outright pacifists opposed to all wars. Many were Christian socialists or atheists opposed to the existing war as an imperialist one. For those who opposed the war there was the Union of Democratic Control set up in November 1914, advocating open diplomacy and a democratic peace. This organisation also catered for those who supported the war, but advocated an early peace by negotiation. The UDC was a joint creation of leading Liberals and leading ILPers such as MacDonald and Bertrand Russell. By the end of the war most of those Liberals were members of the Labour Party. Another organisation, also set up in 1914, the No-Conscription Fellowship, attracted the large number of people opposed to conscription whether supporters or opposers of the war. After 1916 the N-CF became the main support of conscientious objectors and closely connected with the main organisation supporting pacifists, the Society of Friends. Thus a wide range of organisations appeared which were respectable enough to cushion outright opponents of the war from many of the excesses of the war jingoes.

The position in Birmingham at the outbreak of war was even more complex than this. The Labour Party in the city was represented by the Labour Representation Committee which, as we have seen, joined with the trade union wing at the beginning of the war in the Birmingham Trades and Labour Council. Both the trade union and political wing supported the war initially, but within both wings there were, from the beginning opponents of the war. The ILP was the largest working class political party in Birmingham, but there was also the Marxist influence of the British Socialist Party (formed in 1911 by a merger of the Social Democratic Party with the more militant members of the ILP), and also the smaller Socialist Labour Party. There was, at the University, a Fabian Society branch. All of these co-existed quite happily within the Socialist Centre, an umbrella organisation co-ordinating Socialist activity within the city. There was also a number of Labour Churches; Central and Aston were called Socialist Churches and others continued with the older name of Labour Churches. The *Clarion* newspaper was influential in 1914 and its social organisations Clarion Cycling Club, Clarion Choir, and Clarion Social Club flourished. Finally there was a varied Anarchist presence in Birmingham. This arose from two sources; the earlier Anarchist influence of the 1880s when the Socialist League of William Morris was taken over by Anarchists and took root in Walsall (the Walsall Anarchist Bomb Plot occurred in 1892) from where it made occasional forays into Birmingham. The other source was the Syndicalism of the period of the Great Unrest (1910-14) which almost destroyed the British Socialist Party in Birmingham. Connected with this militant syndicalism was the Church Socialist League, two of whose national leaders, the Hon. Rev James Adderley, and the Rev Arnold Pinchard both with churches in Birmingham, led the local branch.

The Birmingham movement can best be dealt with by recording activities in the first two years of the war when majority opinion supported the war and then the period 1916 to 1918 when anti-war feeling accelerated.

British Socialist Party and the Socialist Labour Party 1914-1916

Both of these Marxist socialist parties were affected by Syndicalism. Roughly speaking, Syndicalists believed that socialism would come via the One Big Strike that would destroy capitalism, and not via the winning (or conquest) of power through Parliamentary institutions. Again roughly speaking, it could be said that Syndicalism usually arises in countries where the democratic or Parliamentary option does not exist and thus working class parties are illegal or have been retarded. Its surge in Britain from 1910 however, had been due to intense disillusionment with the performance of the Labour Party in Parliament and also the sudden appearance of the Great Unrest 1910-14, which with its massive strikes of the unskilled and semi-skilled, the Suffragette agitation and the mutiny of the generals and statesmen of Northern Ireland threatened to make Britain ungovernable. A further important factor was the arrival of Tom Mann from Australia preaching a typically British version of Syndicalism which stressed the importance of industrial action, but did not abjure political action and so thoroughly confused his supporters as to the relative weight to be attached to industrial and political action.

One of the most important people so confused was Leonard Hall. Hall had played an important role, from Birmingham, in forming the British Socialist Party in 1911. He had argued at the inaugural national Conference for equality of industrial and political aims. He had been unsuccessful, but had emerged with the second highest vote for the national executive of the new Party. From a maximum of nine Birmingham branches in 1912 with a midlands federation, the BSP was weakened from the right by those who regarded the industrial struggle as led by undesirable Syndicalists and Anarchists, and from the left by both Syndicalists and Anarchists who had a presence in the city both within and outside the local BSP. The Syndicalists found support both national and local in the *Daily Herald* and the Daily Herald Leagues that were formed in Birmingham and elsewhere. Leonard Hall gave up the struggle in disgust.

But the British Socialist Party was a not inconsiderable influence in the city in 1914. In the November 1913 local elections Norman Tiptaft in Soho polled 1,567 votes against the successful Tory's 1,802 votes. Eldred Hallas was a BSP city councillor.

When war broke out, the whole BSP executive supported the war and controlled the Party's paper, *Justice*. Both Tiptaft and Hallas became violently pro-war, but some local members were anti-war. This caused both confusion and weakness until 1916, when the anti-war party gained the ascendancy and published their own paper *The Call,* while Hyndman and the other pro-war leaders formed the National Socialist Party and continued to control *Justice*.

A man destined to play a considerable role in the Birmingham Labour movement surfaced in 1914 in the BSP. This was Fred Silvester whose particular interest was in Marxist education. He was active for the Central Labour College's classes for working class political education and opposed to the non-Marxist classes of Ruskin College. In October 1914 Silvester reported in *Justice* a lantern lecture by William Paul (a national Marxist lecturer who appeared frequently in Birmingham) on 'Mutual Aid' at the Bristol Street Schools. There was 'a large attendance representative of all the movement.' Silvester also reported that classes on Marxian Economics would begin the following week.

This interest in Marxist education led to contact with the Socialist Labour Party. This was a small sectarian organisation, most influential in Scotland in the factories. It differed from the Syndicalists in stressing the role of education in the development of Socialism, but was bitterly opposed to the 'fakirs' of the reformist Labour Party. It was also anti-war and thus a focus for 'pacifist' British Socialist Party members. In February 1915 Silvester reported a Birmingham Social Science Class organised by the Central Labour College and the Socialist Labour Party. It was followed by a social and dance at which 'all sections of the movement were there from the pinkest of social reformers to the reddest of social revolutionaries. The evening ended with Auld Lang Syne and the Red Flag.' This report was signed F.B. Silvester, hon. sec.

The Socialist Labour Party had maintained a precarious presence in Birmingham since the formation of the party in 1903. In January 1914 its secretary was G. Melbourne. The party met on the first Sunday of every month at the Coffee House, Spiceal Street (as celebrated a meeting place for the Birmingham labour movement as the Bristol Street Schools) and held open-air meetings in the Bull Ring every Sunday. By December 1915 Melbourne was still secretary, although the office seems to have been held by F. Knight earlier in the year.

The SLP's most celebrated member was William Holliday, a leader of the Birmingham Labour movement since 1898. Holliday held Bull Ring meetings opposing the war from the very beginning. In June 1915 he was jailed for three months for 'violating the Defence of the Realm Act.' A long letter from Silvester to the party's paper *Socialist* told how this sentence had been quashed on appeal. A committee had been formed in the city when Holliday had been sentenced which had been joined by all working class parties in Birmingham except the Socialist Party of Great Britain. An appeal for funds had been published in *Socialist, Justice, Labour Leader,* and *Forward*. The appeal had been heard in July and it was held that 'the speech was not prejudicial to recruiting.' But Holliday had not been granted costs. The list of those contributing to those costs however, occupied a whole page of *Socialist* and there remained a balance of £7 that was given to Holliday.

Holliday continued speaking in the Bull Ring. In November the SLP was 'countering the effects of the Town Hall recruiting meeting' when Holliday was heckled by Navvy Smith, 'A thorn in the side of the SLP and a notorious bible thumper trying to provoke Holliday to say something against DORA.' Holliday lost his temper and called Smith 'a bloody scoundrel.' Holliday was then arrested and charged with 'language likely to cause a breach of the peace.' This time the police made no mistake and Holliday went to jail where he died. The above report was signed 'SYLV' and in subsequent reports he gave either this shortened version of his name or signed 'F.B. Sylvester.'

By January 1916 Sylvester was secretary of the SLP branch. The *Socialist* only appeared once a month and the May issue made the most of the case in March when the Saltley branch of the Workers' Union had passed a resolution confirming 'its unabated opposition to Conscription.' and calling on the union executive to call a general strike if Conscription became law. Councillor Beard, the Workers' Union organiser, confident that this resolution had been passed by a 'mere handful' of malcontents, asked the branch to reconsider the resolution. About 200 members attended a reconvened meeting at which Beard spoke for about an hour, 'enough sentimental twaddle to drown not only the members present but anyone who came within a few miles of the meeting.' A good discussion ensued, 'and the true position of the workers was put by several members amongst whom were some who have had the advantage of being taught Marxian economics by Comrade Paul of the Socialist Labour Party...' Only five voted for the resolution put by Councillor Beard, we are told. Another plug for the SLP and its classes on economics and industrial history shows the report to have been written by SYLV.

In June 1916 the *Socialist* recorded the death of William Holliday. He died in prison at the age of forty six leaving a wife and eight children. Money had to be borrowed to pay for his funeral. He was buried in Witton Cemetery and it was proposed to erect a stone to his memory. His funeral service was conducted by James Stewart (president of the Bristol Sunday School but by then beginning to play an important part in the Birmingham labour movement). The *Socialist* said that Holliday was a fearless character who had many tough encounters with hostile crowds. 'Throughout the Boer War he had fought jingoes in the Market Place of Imperial Birmingham.'

Challinor in his *Origins of British Bolshevism* says rowdies tried unsuccessfully to break up a memorial meeting to Holliday in the Bull Ring on 28 May addressed by William Paul and James Stewart. Although there was a large number of policemen in the Bull Ring at the time ('some of them disguised as men'), the forces of law and order did not stop the violent disruption. 'What better tribute could they pay to the dead warrior of Labour...' said the *Socialist*.

Martin Durham in recent years found some personal recollections of a retired Birmingham blacksmith, Mr A., who remembered 'Bull Ring Billy':

> He was a labourer in a timber yard. That's all he was. 8 o'clock in the morning to 6 o'clock at night. Eighteen bob a week... A nice chap. Used to show yer the bumps what the police had done to him. Gee'im a good hiding when they got him down Moor Street Police Station. Went down like that (indicating with his sloping hands) from the first step and they gee 'im one on the back of the neck. Knock 'im out. Serve 'im out terrible. Fetch 'im in the morning, gee 'im three months and 'course the people what go to see him (in the Bull Ring) and he don't turn up, go round and get to know... A Socialist he was, a nice chap.

William J. Holliday, truly a martyr to the Cause of the working class.

In October 1916 the police raided the monthly SLP meeting. So ended 1916. The British Socialist Party had been weakened during the first two years of war. The formerly miniscule Socialist Labour Party had been strengthened by the defection of BSP members to it. Public opposition to the war had clearly been maintained, and the tradition of Marxist education in the Labour movement enhanced by fresh forces coming into the Socialist Labour Party in Birmingham.

The Independent Labour Party

At the outbreak of war, the ILP had been weakened both by defections to the British Socialist Party from 1911, and by continued dissatisfaction with the performance of the Labour Party in Parliament. There was more trouble in February 1913 when the Northfield branch withdrew from the local ILP Federation and formed a Socialist Society with members of the 'late BSP' and some Fabians. In May a special Finance Conference heard that in the past three years the number of ILP branches in the Birmingham federation had declined from 25 to 15.

The only branch contributing regular reports to the *Labour Leader* after the outbreak of war was the Erdington branch. In January 1915 the branch heard J. Simpson give 'a first class address' on Social Democracy and Imperialism and 'H.E. Smith presided over a good attendance.' Harry Brockhouse, from West Bromwich, was a regular visitor to the branch and it was Brockhouse who went as midland delegate to the 1915 ILP Conference where he moved a resolution that the ILP should take action, with neutral countries, to bring the war to an end and re-establish the International on a broad and lasting basis. If the war was right, it should be pursued; if it were wrong, it should be stopped, his resolution ended.

Bordesley Green branch reported a visit by Councillor Kneeshaw in March and Saltley was also operating, although with poor attendances due to overtime. In April, Central branch was re-established with Kneeshaw as secretary. Erdington was active in operating a sales drive by the *Labour Leader* and it was reported that Erdington was one of 46 branches nationally who ensured that every member received a copy of the paper each week. The next month Bordesley Green joined the scheme.

Erdington branch met weekly on Sundays and also sustained the local Labour Church where in May, J. Burley had spoken on 'Socialism and Christianity.' When the summer came Erdington organised rambles. By this time, Central branch felt strong enough to challenge Erdington in friendly competition.

By July 1915 the Birmingham ILP Federation was active, passing a resolution against Conscription; and under the heading of 'Birmingham's Great Day,' a conference of Trade Unionists arranged by the Union of Democratic Control was reported with Ramsay MacDonald as the main speaker.'We were proud of him. John Bull had campaigned all the week, but there were no disturbances even at the concert and social. The largest restaurant at the Colonnade Hotel was booked, but this was inadequate. Every spare chair in the hotel was utilised.' The report ended, 'The ILP in Birmingham is not dead.' Erdington even felt confident enough to indulge in some irony. 'We discussed the momentous question of whether to invest £1,000 of branch funds in War Loan, or donate 15/-d. to the (Labour Leader's) Special Effort Fund. The latter won the day.'

In August the Erdington Labour Church was evicted from its room. This brought the following comment. 'If the patriotic people of Erdington refuse to allow us the use of another room, why doesn't the Co-op provide one.?'

In September 1915, Keir Hardie died. A large commemorative meeting was held in October presided over by Harry Brockhouse, chairman of the Birmingham ILP Federation and with J. Simpson, Frank Spires and Bruce Glasier as the main speakers. Frank Spires recalled that at Keir Hardie's first meeting in the Bull Ring 20 years before there had been 200. His second meeting in the Bull Ring had drawn 15,000. Such was the measure of his influence over the Birmingham working class.'

By the autumn of 1915 the campaign against Conscription brought new life to the ILP in Birmingham. By November Central Branch was claiming that it was beating Erdington. They had made seven new members recently and quadrupled their membership in the past six months. Their members were determined in their opposition to Conscription. Erdington was advertising a Birmingham and Midlands Labour and Socialist No Conscription Council as being 'vigorous.' Handsworth announced its first public meeting since the outbreak of war; Kneeshaw spoke to 'a large audience' on 'Patriotic Plunderers' and an anti-Conscription motion was passed unanimously. In December the Birmingham No-Conscription Conference was reported with 'nearly every shade of Labour' represented. The Conference: opposed Conscription; sought increased pay for soldiers; employment for servicemen after the war at trade union rates of pay; a guarantee for forces' dependents against eviction and want; drastic measures against coal owners, shipping magnates, food speculators and others.

For the work of the Kings Heath ILP branch in 1914 and 1915 a Minute Book has survived. It shows some of the stresses and strains of a smaller branch. Already in May 1914 a meeting with 10 members present had discussed 'the position of the branch' and Kneeshaw had persuaded them that the branch 'was not too small.' When war broke out a branch meeting was called chaired by Comrade Sharp to discuss a report from a War Conference held by the Birmingham ILP Federation in the Priory Rooms addressed by Ramsay MacDonald and Bruce Glasier. Comrade Day said he could not agree with the line of Ramsay MacDonald (however he interpreted that – GB). Councillor Willard differed from Day saying that the war was due to the 'folly of our Secret Foreign Policy.' The decision reflected the divisions of the ten members present – the branch would not support the local recruiting meetings, but members were free to go if they wished.

In November 1914 there was another meeting attended by the Federation secretary to discuss whether the branch should continue to exist. Again the decision was that, 'by no means should the branch be allowed to drop.' The next problem was that the secretary said he had no time to attend to business and he was disheartened by the apathy of the members. It was then agreed that C. Holden should be secretary, but Holden said he was a civil servant and he questioned the advisability of his name appearing. He then agreed to become assistant secretary. At this meeting the Rev Morgan Whiteman was admitted a member of the branch. For the next meeting C. Pritchard was to be invited to discuss Non-Resistance and his attitude to the war.

Another meeting in November revealed that the branch was behind with its national affiliation fees, but this, of course, was not an unusual state of affairs. At the meeting Kneeshaw explained the attitude of the ILP national administrative council to the war, and again Sharp differed from the views of the NAC. At the December meeting eight members were present – Sharp, Ballard, Holden, Bennett, Clark, Francis, Thomas and Bengough. Ten copies of *Commonsense about the War* by George Bernard Shaw were ordered. This was a blast against the early jingoism of the war, but was basically a pro-war case for a 'democratic war.' Sharp then spoke on his differences with the NAC. There was no discussion but 'some members disagreed with a great many of the points he made.' Sharp was clearly taking a pro-war stance and others were opposed to him.

Nevertheless, in January 1915, Edward Sharp was nominated as a delegate to the 1915 ILP national conference the following Easter. The branch appeared to be veering towards a Pacifist opposition to the war. In January 1915 a Mr Wilson MA gave an address on 'Non-Resistance Policy', for which he was 'accorded a very hearty vote of thanks.' The next month a circular was read from the Society of Friends lecturing on 'Can War Ever be Right?' It was decided to take a speaker for the next meeting at Ruskin Hall.

In February 1915 the branch held its AGM. 'Reports showed that the position was not as good as we would like, but it was thought that things would get better...' Sharp was re-elected as chair. F.J. Bengough and A.S. Holden as secretaries, Ballard as Treasurer and Day as Trades Council representative.

In March 1915, Sharp took exception to the report of the Birmingham Federation and said he though he might have to resign from the Party. The wish of the meeting was 'that Sharp remain in the party, particularly as there is work he does on which all are agreed.' Nevertheless, the Minute Book records no more meetings. The next entry is for March 1918. The following month Bengough from the chair stated that the Kings Heath branch had not ceased to exist, but now was a suitable time to renew activity. The branch then consisted of seven men and one woman.

Returning to the activities of the other branches in the city, we find the anti-Conscription campaign being vigorously pursued in January 1916. The 'unalterable opposition' of the Trades Council was reported. Birmingham (City) ILP branch stated that it had only started less than a year ago, but it had already outgrown most branches in the district. Six new members had been made the previous week. Opposition to the war was expressed by Mr Toules moving a motion that the ILP disaffiliate from the Labour Party, but this was rejected. Erdington reported 'an extra good attendance' at the last meeting to hear W. Milner speak on 'War and Democracy'. 'His denunciation of Conscription was met with applause.' They also distributed 20,000 anti-Conscription leaflets. A Rotton Park branch began reporting. 'Weekly meetings were going splendidly.' A resolution demanding the Conscription of Wealth before the Conscription of People was carried unanimously. Five new members had been made.

Conscription began in February 1916 and a new stage of resistance began in co-operation with the No Conscription Fellowship. Erdington thanked the 'brave souls who came through the snow to make a success' of a meeting addressed by S. Palmer, secretary of the Birmingham No Conscription Fellowship. In March Erdington recorded as 'the best lecture of the season' one by Joseph Southall, the noted artist, who was to play a leading political role in Birmingham. He spoke on the 'Futility of War.' Erdington had found new premises for the Labour Church and at the end of March reported as 'very enjoyable' the last lecture of the season by H.E. Smith on 'High Minded Men and Women.' During the off-season, the Church had decided to invite NCF members to meet with them to 'maintain contact.'

In April the City branch reported that it 'bids fair to become the largest branch in the midlands.' Eight new members had been made at the last meeting, including Mr Wm.E. Wilson BD, author of Christ and War, and also Edwin Gilbert secretary of the Adult School Union. Erdington had passed a resolution demanding that the war should not be continued by economic means when military operations ceased. It had ordered a parcel of the Road to Peace leaflets and was sending delegates to the forthcoming No Conscription Conference. Several members of the NCF were present.

During the months after Conscription was introduced the *Labour Leader* was full of reports of the arrest of Conscientious Objectors including many in Birmingham and the Black Country. In May Erdington branch reported that it continued to 'forge ahead.' Three more had enrolled 'all of them enthusiastic for Peace and International Socialism.' The City branch was certain that 'the flowing tide is with us.' Most members were 'hard at it fighting militarism.' A. Barrett Brown and W.J. Chamberlain 'had the privilege of holding their end at the Mansion House.' These two well known Birmingham members were in the leadership of the NCF in London.

Erdington resumed social activity in the summer. A Sunday ramble to Blake Street in May 'would be long remembered.' Copies of *Tribunal* (the NCF newspaper) and Peace leaflets were distributed. 'We sang Socialist hymns by the Pool and collected a good crowd. Mrs Kneeshaw singing the Red Flag was enjoyed by all.' In June the weather prevented Erdington branch from taking their drive out to Hampton-on-Arden. But this enabled them to go to the NCF Conference and meeting where they enjoyed the speeches of national leaders and such local speakers as J.E. Southall, Frank Spires and Barrett Brown. Erdington reported that H.E. Smith, their star seller of the *Labour Leader,* was 'still breaking records'. At the same time a call went out for comrades to come forward to 'keep the branch machinery in order in view of possible eventualities in the next few weeks.' This referred to fears of the arrest of either comrades due to be called up, or branch officials as the government clamped down on peace activities.

At the end of June the Birmingham and District ILP Federation held its Conference. The main resolutions stated that Militarism and War were a subversive combination. Disputes should be settled not by force but by reason and arbitration. The principles of the recent International Labour and Socialist Congress at Copenhagen were endorsed. The principles of peace and fraternity should be taught in public schools. Working class organisations should engage in Peace propaganda. The Labour and Socialist Parties should influence their respective leaders to call an International Convention for Peace. The International Bureau should take opinions from its members as to the efficacy of strike action. Birmingham believed in the utility of strikes and instructed its members to report these to the International Socialist Bureau.

In July a Birmingham and Midlands ILP and NCF rally and garden party was held at the home of Henry Lloyd Wilson at Bournville. National speakers advertised were F.W. Jowett MP, Hon. Bertrand Russell and George Lansbury. The local speaker was the Rev J. Morgan Whiteman. There were children's sports followed by tea. For the rally, 800 had been arranged for, but 1,200 turned up. The two main issues discussed were Conscription and Peace Negotiations. The Ten Acres and Stirchley Co-operative choir provided 'a splendid contribution.'

In August Erdington affiliated to the National Council for Civil Liberties, which had been set up to protect the interests of Conscientious Objectors. In September a branch member was arrested. It was Ernest Tebbutt who was taken by night escort to Warwick. 'He is firm in his adherence to International Socialist principles,' the branch reported.

In October ILP branches, trades councils, trade union branches etc, were busy collecting for a Keir Hardie memorial and Erdington ILP heard a pacifist Congregational minister, Mr E. Bernstein.

In November the Birmingham military 'inquisition' suppressed the Rotton Park ILP monthly paper Birmingham *Forward*. Two police officers had called at the home of Hugh Lemon, secretary of the local UDC branch and also secretary of the *Forward* stating that they did not wish to arrest him, but warned him not to allow any copies of the current *Forward* to go out. Asked for their reasons, the officers replied that they were acting under orders, complaints having been received from local people. The previous night, under the orders of the military officer in charge of the Warwick and Midland District, detectives had visited four well-known Quaker JPs, 'active opponents of militarism and all forms of oppression' and demanded answers to ten questions such as: Have you been or are you connected with the NCF, the National Council against Conscription, the UDC or any other body publishing matter against conscription or recruitment; if so, in what capacity? Have you supplied any monies to such organisations; if so how much and when? Have you done anything to prevent the circulation of literature by religious bodies such as Quakers or Christadelphians? Have you been present at meetings etc. at which speeches have been made against conscription and recruiting? After convictions against such publications have you withdrawn your support from those societies?

Councillor Kneeshaw raised this matter the next week when the City Council reappointed the Watch Committee. He suggested that 'they should conduct police business in a British way and not leave Prussians living in this country to take control of their office.... There was an attempt at derisive closure of the matter, but Kneeshaw sturdily held his own and read through the ten questions, thus securing public attention to this latest instance of British Prussianism.'

Both Erdington and City branches continued reporting to the *Labour Leader* to the end of the year. In November City heard William Chamberlain talk on 'Tolstoy and his Message' and reported that the branch had seven members 'doing service in prison and plenty more well qualified.' Erdington reported a bitterly cold day in December when members turned out to hear Margaret Haley of the Women's International League. A resolution to the Government demanding peace negotiations was unanimously passed.

From the foregoing it is clear that there was considerable peace agitation in Birmingham during the years 1914-16. Additionally, some peace activity went unrecorded, as the single mention of the Rotton Park *Forward* reminds us.

Other Peace Organisations 1914-1916

Finally there are the peace organisations, some primarily Liberal orientated, others jointly sponsored by Liberals and ILPers which overlapped with the Labour movement.

At the outbreak of war, the Birmingham Lord Mayor elect was the Liberal Councillor, Harrison Barrow. He withdrew from this position, recognising that, 'The duties of the Lord Mayor must include those of a distinctly military character. As a member of the Society of Friends I could not conscientiously fulfil these.' Barrow became a member of the national council of the UDC. In 1918 he was imprisoned for six months and stripped of his offices on the city council. After the war, like many other Liberals, he joined the Labour Party.

Cornish' Birmingham Year Book of 1914 shows a Birmingham Auxilliary Peace Society. Its chairman was Joseph Southall and its hon.sec. Joseph Sturge. Other organisations in 1914 where anti-war feelings could be expected to exist were the Swedenborgian and Unitarian churches. The four Christadelphian institutions in the city were wholly pacifist, but also completely non-political. And in the 150 classes of the Midland Adult School Union anti-war members were to be found.

The International Peace Year Book for 1915 lists a Birmingham University War and Peace Society whose joint hon.secs. were Miss F.M. Pither and E.C. Wrigley. The Birmingham Peace Society continued to exist with Joseph Southall and Joseph Sturge among its officers. Its president was Dr Moore Ede, the Dean of Worcester and one of its secretaries was the Rev J.J. Ellis.

But the two most important peace societies were the Union of Democratic Control and the No-Conscription Fellowship. The UDC was formed on the outbreak of war and one of the first branches established was in Birmingham. In 1915 the International Peace Year book gave its local chairman as Harrison Barrow and Hubert Lemon its secretary. Its activities we have recorded through the *Labour Leader*.

The No-Conscription Fellowship was formed in December 1914. A local branch was immediately formed and it was on the initiative of the Birmingham branch that the important change of allowing both men beyond military age and women to be members was made in May 1915. Two Birmingham men made crucial contributions to the organisation, William Chamberlain and Arthur Barrett Brown. Again its activities have been followed through the *Labour Leader,* but after Conscription began in February 1916, it operated its own journal *Tribunal* to support the Conscientious Objectors.

Conscription and Conscientious Objectors

The Military Service Act, making men from 18 to 41 liable for compulsory military service, passed into law on 10 February 1916. For those of military age it turned an ideological battle into a physical battle. Protesters either joined the forces or they became Conscientious Objectors. The consequences of becoming a CO were not pleasant.

In March 1916 the No-Conscription Fellowship began to publish its monthly paper *Tribunal* edited by W.J. Chamberlain. Its aims were to acquaint NCF members and the public with the details of the Military Service Act and challenge its administration. The Act laid down that anyone registering a conscientious objection should appeal before a local Tribunal. These Tribunals comprised local people, including, in theory, representatives of the Labour movement. In practice these local Tribunals were usually identical with those set up to administer the Derby Scheme. Sitting with each Tribunal was a local military representative; usually a bellicose ex-officer doing his duty, as he saw it, of gaining as many recruits as possible for the army, and little equipped to deal with the subtle arguments of a middle class conscientious objector. From the beginning, both religious and political objections were recognised, although few Tribunals would accept either that political objection was part of the law, or grant equality of political with religious objection. Courts were empowered to make three judgements; absolute exemption, exemption from combat duties, and temporary exemption. Most of the cases heard were not of COs but those seeking exemption on grounds of hardship such as sole support of a family or essential to a family business etc. From March 1916 copious reports appear in local newspapers of tribunal proceedings from which much humour or indignation can be derived concerning their deliberations; but these local reports do not carry names and it is only when these local proceedings are picked up by the NCF and reported in the *Tribunal* that local individuals can be identified. Objectors who were dissatisfied could appeal to a County tribunal. There was also a national appeals tribunal, but only cases posing problems of principle tended to be referred to it.

Conscientious objectors faced numerous problems. The first was whether to recognise the local tribunal and appear before it. The next was what to do if they were granted non-combatant service; for to join the army in any capacity released another serving soldier for combat service. Usually, however, the CO was not granted any exemption; the dilemma then was to join as directed, or wait to be arrested.

Birmingham cases reported in the first two issues of *Tribunal* were those of an English born German who objected to fighting his blood relations whose case was dismissed; the second reported that a number of Birmingham NCF members had appeared before the tribunal, but none had been granted absolute exemption. Before March was out the *Tribunal* was suggesting that its initial target circulation of 100,000 might have to be revised upwards as Manchester was taking 1,500 copies and Birmingham, with possibly the largest circulation in the country, was taking 1,800 weekly.

In May *Tribunal* reported the Birmingham Trades Council resolution continuing to oppose conscription and supporting those who resisted any further extension of the Act, which was passed 55 votes to 30. By the end of May the first Birmingham CO was reported. He was W.R. Fleming. Procedure was that COs failing to report for military service were arrested either at home or at work by civilian police, charged (and often fined) and then handed over to the military at the county barracks. Here attempts with varying degrees of guile or physical force, were made to make the CO don an army uniform. If successful he was then deemed to be under military control. If he refused he was sentenced by a military court and then turned over to the civilian authorities to serve his term in a civil prison. Fleming was taken to Budbrook Barracks, Warwick where he was sentenced to twelve months detention, commuted to four months. It was in this early period that most of the excesses were perpetuated of leaving men who refused to put on uniform naked, or with only a blanket, in cold guard rooms for long periods, or submitting COs to the 'horse play' of hostile soldiers.

By the beginning of June *Tribunal* reported over 800 NCF members resisting military control. Nearly fifty had been transferred to France, some taken handcuffed with their military kit tied upon their backs. Once abroad and on active service COs could be charged with mutiny and sentenced to death. Many were, but all were said to have been commuted to imprisonment and no case has been authenticated of a CO being shot. If not given a death sentence COs could be, and some were, subjected to the barbarous penalty of field punishment tied to the wheel of a gun carriage.

Tribunal reported in June six men taken to Budbrook Barracks and there sentenced to four months hard labour to be served in Winson Green prison. None can be positively identified as Birmingham men, but some at least probably were.

Also in June the whole national committee of the No Conscription Fellowship had been arrested and fined £100 each. Most refused to pay and in July were sentenced to 61 days imprisonment. Both W.J. Chamberlain and A. Barrett Brown of Birmingham were among those imprisoned.

By August the Pelham Committee recommendations on Work of National Importance was in place. The committee had been set up when it was found that there was no agreement on what was work of national importance for those COs whose exemption was conditional on their accepting such work.

In September 1916, Chamberlain began a series of seven articles in the *Tribunal* on his experiences in prison under such headings as Reception, Chapel, Exercise, A Zeppelin Raid etc. This was later published in book form.

In October, both A. Barrett Brown and W.J. Chamberlain were called-up and appeared before the Birmingham Tribunal. Barratt Brown stated that he believed all war to be both un-Christian and immoral. He was then questioned with regard to his activities with the Quakers. The chairman said he regarded the appellant as a danger to the state, but thought he was the type of person who had caused the government to put a conscience clause into the Act. He therefore granted absolute exemption, although he disagreed entirely with the statements made.

Chamberlain's case was heard immediately after. He said he believed in the Brotherhood of Man and the doctrine of non-resistance as enunciated by the Christs of all ages. He was a Socialist, believing that Socialism and Christianity, rightly interpreted, were identical. He claimed that his work with the N-CF was work of vital national importance. He was asked whether he was a member of any religious body and replied that he was not aware of any such body he could conscientiously join since members of all alleged Christian bodies were at present slaughtering their fellows in the name of the Prince of Peace. The chairman said the decision was not to grant exemption. He did not look on the appellant as a conscientious objector nor his work of national importance.

Also in October *Tribunal* reported the prosecution of Councillor Kneeshaw under the Defence of the Realm Act for the possession of various leaflets and pamphlets seized at his house as being 'calculated to prejudice...' etc. Fines amounting to £54 were imposed.

In November a series of N-CF Divisional Conventions in place of a national conference ended with conventions in Scotland and Birmingham. In Birmingham, Barrett Brown presided over a fully representative conference on a Sunday afternoon, we are told. In the evening Bertrand Russell and Fenner Brockway spoke at a 'magnificent' public demonstration.

In December 1916 Chamberlain withdrew his appeal, stating that as nothing less than absolute exemption would suit his case, and in view of the fact that the Central Appeal Tribunal had recently recommended that absolute exemption be not granted to conscientious objectors, he felt it would be a waste of everyone's time for him to appear. By then Chamberlain was 'back at headquarters', although not as editor. He wrote, however, the main article in the December 21 *Tribunal* setting out the various international proposals for peace that had been made and calling on all Christian churches 'to lead the way out of the Hell into which the nations have been plunged.' His book, *A 'CO' in Prison,* was also being advertised at price 6d.

By the end of the year *Tribunal* recorded the national total number of men arrested and handed over to the military as 3,190.

Once Conscription began all peace organisations suffered crises of identity. Was their role to fight against Conscription and bring it to an end or was it to fight against the war? Was it protect the interests of the COs and expose the cruelties to which they were being subjected? Could these first two roles be pursued together? Were they pacifist organisations opposed to all wars at all times, or were they also Socialist organisations denouncing the war as an imperialist war?

The first change of NCF policy came in July 1916 after a new Military Service Act had 'clarified' the position regarding COs. This laid down that 'absolute exemption' was an option for Tribunals. But those not pleading before Tribunals or refused by the Central Tribunal were to be retained in military detention. Those in civil detention and willing to accept work of national importance under civil control were to be released. Those not deemed to be genuine COs and guilty of the double crime of cowardice and hypocrisy were to be subject to the full rigour of the law. The Joint Committee of Friends' Service Committee, NCF and Fellowship of Reconciliation pointed out that the Act did nothing for those already in detention (e.g. those sentenced to death whose sentences had been commuted to 10 years imprisonment), and it made proof of conscience a matter for Tribunals when it should be judged by the actions of the CO. By this time most of the NCF national committee were in Pentonville prison but they had decided that the time had come to throw the full weight of the NCF behind the peace movement and the aims of the movement should be: 1. Promotion of Peace and International Brotherhood by personal loyalty to conviction. 2. Resistance to the growth of Militarism and 3. Championship of Liberty of Conscience.

By October, the NCF emphasis was on Pacifism, Bertrand Russell writing that 'the NCF is a pacifist body.' Its aim was not to smash militarism, but to 'build, not to destroy, to win over, not to defeat; to bring the Kingdom of Heaven on earth – nothing less....' This could hardly be the last word and the argument continued.

Another source of conflict was the amount of attention being paid to individual cases of hardship compared with the general fight for principles. Catherine Marshall with her contacts in high places had established a relationship with General Childs. He had been specially deputed to deal with COs complaints. Both Barrett Brown and Chamberlain became indignant at this. Barratt Brown complained that the NCF had lost sight of its role and become bogged down in matters of detail. Chamberlain said that the Fellowship had degenerated into a society for the entertainment of Cabinet Ministers and War Office officials. He had never dreamed that the time would come when officers of the NCF would be in direct communication with the war office and be able to get the soldiers to do as they requested.

The other great organisation concerned with peace was the Society of Friends. Its problems were that the Society itself never pronounced on the war and many Friends served in the forces. Those who took the Pacifist position faced the problem that many pacifist Friends were also socialists and as the struggle against Conscription continued they were inevitably drawn into protecting the interests of all COs. The Friends, like the NCF also differed as to the amount of time to be devoted to the problems of individuals (whose sufferings were usually deemed minor compared with soldiers on active service) and the propagation of the principles of Pacifism.

Their weekly journal, *The Friend,* gives more information concerning COs in Birmingham than does the *Tribunal*. The main body of COs were dealt with by the early local tribunals. For instance at the Birmingham Tribunal of 24 March 1916 the following cases were heard and decisions made:

Name & Address	Verdict
Geo. L. BURTON, Bournville	Absolute Exemption.
John W. BURTON, Bournville	6 months exemption on account of youth.
C.H. COMPTON, Selly Oak	Exemption refused.
E.S. GALLIMORE, Selly Oak	Conditional on undertaking War Relief.
W.H. GAYNOR, Bull St. Birmingham	Cond. on joining Friends Ambulance Unit.
A. JESPER, Birmingham	Exempt from Combat Service only.
J.W.C. LAND, Bournville	Exempt on badge.
Walter T. LUNT, Moseley Rd	Exempt Combat Service.
Fred. C. MARLOW, Bull St.	Not given
G.A. PATCHING, Bull St.	Absolute Exemption.
Eric P. SOUTHALL, Bull St.	Exempt Combat Service.
K.W. SOUTHALL, George St.	Conditional on business grounds.
S. SMITH, Birmingham	Exempt Combat Service.
Arthur E. STREET, Birmingham	Conditional on health grounds.
Henry R. WALLIS, Bordesley Gn	Cond. on remaining a YMCA worker.
H. WOODHEAD, Bull St.	Exempt 1 month on business grounds.

Most of those who were only granted exemption from combat service gave notice that they would appeal. A week later the following cases were heard:

Gilbert BASSON, Birmingham	Exempt Combat Service.
Geo. L. BENTON, Bourneville	Absolute Exemption.
W.E. LITTLEBOY, Selly Oak	Deferred 1 month.
J.L. NICKALLS, Cotteridge	Conditional on remaining with War Victims.
W. ROWNTREE, Birmingham	Deferred for two weeks.
Henry WHITTAKER, Bournbrooke	Exempt Combat Service.

Detailed evidence for some of these cases was quoted in *The Friend*. For instance, Littleboy was asked why he wouldn't regard the needs of the country. He replied, 'The need of the country is a better understanding of Christ.' The Lord Mayor commented, 'It is the material need of the country, not the spiritual need that is in question at this Tribunal.' Littleboy then stated that he thought his work as an accountant plus the religious and social work he did was witness to the spirit of peace. The Lord Mayor replied that while Littleboy was raising spirituality the Germans were thundering at the gate. Littleboy was given a month to consider whether he would undertake alternative work.

In March there was a Warwickshire County Appeal Tribunal. Arthur C. Tonks of Severn Street Christian Society appeared before it. He said that he was not prepared to undertake any work connected with war. He had been dismissed from his employment for failing to enlist. His appeal was refused. No reason was given. Fredk. C. Marlow criticised the Birmingham Tribunal for its hostile attitude. He said he was prevented from bringing out any points he wished to have considered and was not allowed to have a friend with him. As soon as he said he was a CO a member asked him if he believed in Holy Communion and the laying on of hands. He said 'No' and a member then said, 'This is blasphemy.' The same member then said, 'Blasphemy – Go and get killed.' Marlow said he endeavoured to do only what his conscience bade.' Another member remarked, 'What a dreadful state of affairs if everybody was like that.'

At a Birmingham Appeal Tribunal Eric Southall was asked, 'Have you heard of the book The Yellow Peril.' Southall said he had, but had never read it. The member then said, 'It describes thousands of Chinese coming to Britain. Would it not be your duty to resist such barbarism?' Southall replied that he did not think it right to do wrong in a right cause. Another member then said, 'You have a comfortable home, haven't you. You look as though you have.' Southall protested that this was an unfair question. 'You would not wish me not to have a comfortable home?' he asked. Southall's employer A.J. Cudworth then spoke for him stating that although his business was not of national importance, he did not know what he would do without him. Finally Southall stated that he would not work anywhere else or with any of the Friends Units. His case was dismissed.

Another batch of Birmingham COs were heard in April. W.A. Blumson, E.J. Hickman and Maurice Oyston were given exemption conditional upon joining the Friends Ambulance Unit; Albert Griffiths, F.A. Honnick, H.G. Sears, G.H. Wooton and Edward P. Willcocks were Exempt Combat Service and R.V. Wadsworth had his case adjourned.

At a Warwickshire Appeals Tribunal in May it was stated that the Birmingham Corporation Refuse Disposal men were refusing to work with COs, as were men in some other departments. The Corporation was spending £100,000 annually to encourage men to enlist, it was alleged.

In June at the Birmingham Appeals Tribunal, Wilfred Littleboy's appeal against Exemption Combat Service was heard. He stated that in loyalty to God he could not become part of organised war. He was asked, 'If you worked under the Pelham Committee would not this bring about the peace and goodwill you desire?' He replied, 'No.' The next question was,'If all your countrymen took the same position would this keep the Germans out of this country?' Littleboy replied, 'This would liberate such a spiritual force as would advance the coming kingdom of God...' Then he was asked, 'Do you believe you are the sole judge of what work would help the country? Answer Yes or No.' He replied 'Yes'. 'I'm afraid your fellow countrymen do not accept this view,' he was told. 'I recognise that and they never will do so unless someone makes a stand now,' was Littleboy's last words. His appeal was dismissed. This case illustrates the unevenness with which genuine, Christian COs were treated. There was real reluctance to grant Absolute Exemption, even after June when the law had been clarified. Figures given to the Birmingham Tribunal in the first week of June showed that 397 applications had been received from COs. 150 appeals had been dismissed. 199 had been Exempt Combat Service and 37 had been exempted conditional upon undertaking work of national importance. Only five had been given Absolute Exemption.

In July there were details of Friends detained by the military. Percy Moore, William Rastall and Eric Southall had all been sentenced to 112 days hard labour.

By this time the main body of COs had been dealt with and subsequent Tribunals heard only occasional cases. Attention turned to the whereabouts of the COs.

Conscientious Objectors given Exempt Combat Service had a number of alternatives. They could be inducted into the army and be allocated to the Royal Army Medical Service or a special Non-Combatant Corps set up in March 1916. This was the first grade of objection; these men had made their point, would have nothing to do with killing, but were prepared to serve in the forces, even though this released another man to fight. The next grade was those who objected to all forms of military service, who had been sentenced to imprisonment and eventually opted for employment of national importance as decreed by the Pelham Committee under the Home Office Scheme. This was usually in camps of various sorts, employed in timber felling or other agricultural work, usually in exposed locations such as Dartmoor. Many of these men suffered severe privation. The last grade was the Absolutists who would accept none of these alternatives. Their fate was to be arrested, sentenced by the military to hard labour and handed over to a civil prison. When their sentence had been served they were released, immediately re-arrested and the process repeated. It was the hard labour and total isolation which broke the health or the spirit of so many COs and, of course, some prisons were worse than others. Some Absolutists took a poor view of the concessions made by the Alternativists.

By October *The Friend* was reporting the whereabouts of two types of COs, Friends and Attenders; the latter were usually No-Conscription Fellowship men. Arthur Tonks (Attender) was in Warwick Jail. Sidney Moore, and A.H. Pinfold (Att) were in Wormwood Scrubs and William Rastall was at Cheltenham Barracks. Privations at some of the Camps were so bad that they had to be abandoned. A camp at Dyce was broken up and the men given 8 days furlough. Among these were Alfred Hawkins, a Birmingham Attender and Howard Marten of Harrow, one of the men who had been sentenced to death in France. Two Birmingham Attenders, Wilfred Tonks and E.P. Willcocks were at Llanddeusant Waterworks and another Attender, A.C. Tonks had then been moved to Warwick Labour Colony.

In November there was a fresh crop of COs. Jesse Hodgetts, Ernest Horton and Cecil McDonald were deferred for one month. Robert Mason was exempt conditional on retaining his present employment and Arthur J. Sharp a NCF member was offered work with the Friends Ambulance Unit, which he declined.

In December 1916 there was another run down on the whereabouts of COs. Albert Griffiths, G. Douglas James, Sidney Moore, A.H. Pinfold, Edmund Pritchard, Wm. Rastall, and Eric Southall were all at Wormwood Scrubs. Tonks and Wellcock were still at the Waterworks. A.C. Tonks and Alfred Hawkins were at the Warwick Labour Colony. Wm.H.S. Hayden had volunteered for the RAMC provided he was not transferred to the fighting line. The Military Representative would give no guarantee of this, so Hayden accepted work under the Pelham scheme.

1917 – the year of the Russian Revolutions

Neither *The Call* nor the *Socialist* record very much Birmingham activity for the British Socialist Party and the Socialist Labour Party for 1917, although both continued to exist and some of their activity was reported by the *Labour Leader*.

Within the Independent Labour Party, Erdington continued to operate. In January at their annual tea and social they welcomed W.J. Chamberlain and his family. News was also given of one of the branch's COs. E. Tebbutt had served his first sentence at Wormwood Scrubs and had been removed to Weymouth where he received a second sentence of 8 months hard labour. He had been sent to serve this at Dorchester Prison. The Birmingham Social Science Class organised jointly by the Central Labour College and the SLP was holding a series of lectures on the Economic Basis of Imperialism. The lecturer was J.T. Walton Newbold (who was later to become the Communist Party's second MP).

In February, Erdington heard Miss A.T. Boden speak on 'Adult Suffrage' and it was announced that Mrs Howarth, in conjunction with the Women's International League was arranging a class for children 'to give them an interest in international affairs.' At a second meeting Tom Hackett spoke on Labour Problems after the War.

In March 1917 the Birmingham (City) branch held its AGM. 40 new members had been made. Seventeen of its members were COs. The branch had collected 300 signatures to a Peace Petition and conducted 'ceaseless peace and Socialist propaganda.' The East Birmingham branch announced a Tom Mann meeting at Saltley Picture Palace for 25th March.

The first Russian revolution took place on March 12th and its effects were evident by the following month. Erdington held a 'well attended' meeting and passed resolutions on educational reform, against industrial conscription, against violation of the right to asylum, against the introduction of agents-provocateurs and, 'last but not least,' approved the Manifesto of the Provisional Russian government. The City branch announced record attendances, as a result of which it had been decided that the branch should meet fortnightly. It was time for a 'Big Push' in branch recruitment and 'a committee had been appointed to draw up a plan of campaign.' The secretary at this time was J.W. Tonks.

In May Erdington went to a performance at the Repertory Theatre where John Drinkwater was the manager. 'We went wearing our red rosettes for Labour Day.' Rotton Park branch announced the beginning of their open-air season with meetings held every Sunday morning at the junction of Wellington Street and Winson Green Road, not far from the prison where many COs were serving their sentences.

At the end of the month the Labour and Socialist Convention to be held at Leeds on June 3rd. was announced. This celebrated Conference, and the local conference subsequently arranged but banned by the authorities, had considerable impact in Birmingham and it is proposed to break off the narrative here and bring the N-CF and Quaker reports up to this point before dealing with the Leeds Conference.

Two Pacifist bodies not so far dealt with are the Christadelphians and the Fellowship of Reconciliation. The Christadelphians were an important proportion of all COs. They had the good fortune to trace their pacifist credentials back to the U.S. civil war, and the good sense to petition parliament to grant them exemption in February 1915, a year before Conscription began. As a result, it is held that they automatically received Absolute Exemption when appearing before Tribunals. Many of them did, but by no means all of them. The vicissitudes of the Birmingham and Black Country Christadelphians are chronicled by Frank G. Jannaway in his book, *Within the Camp, being the Story of How and Why the Christadelphians were Exempt from Military Service*. As I have said, the Christadelphians isolated themselves from secular society, believing in an 'early personal advent of Christ to set up divine government over all the world.' They therefore played no part in the Labour movement.

The other Peace society so far unmentioned is the Fellowship of Reconciliation. This was set up 1915 and had an immediate Birmingham presence. By 1917 the International Peace Year Book gave FoR branches in Birmingham as Central, Bournville, Edgbaston, Erdington, Harborne, Kings Norton, Olton, Selly Oak, South Birmingham, Stirchley, Warley and University War and Peace Society. They held open-air services in Birmingham.

Returning to the two main Peace organisations, in January 1917, A. Barratt Brown was suggesting a new basis for N-CF membership of all men and women of any age likely to be called upon to change their jobs as a result of 'industrial conscription.' At the time of W.J. Chamberlain's visit to the Erdington ILP New Year party he was again in trouble with the authorities. On 5 January he was charged at Birmingham with being an absentee and the prosecuting officer asked for a heavy penalty as he had 'given the military a lot of trouble.' He went on that Chamberlain had written 'most seditious articles', whereupon Chamberlain said that this was irrelevant to the charge. In his defence Chamberlain said that twelve years ago, through the influence of Tolstoy, he had been converted to the Christian doctrine of non-resistance. In the same week Wilfred E. Littleboy, clerk to the North Warwick (Birmingham) Friends' Meeting was handed over to the military. He was accompanied by Hugh Gibbins, assistant clerk to the same meeting, who was himself arrested. The next week *Tribunal* was reporting peace negotiations around President Wilson's 'Note'. Chamberlain, who was in detention awaiting his district court martial, wrote thanking friends for the many letters he had received, but apologising for his inability to reply, 'as it is only light in this room for one hour a day.' He was later sentenced and sent to Wormwood Scrubs. Forcible feeding was reported in Wormwood Scrubs of a vegetarian who refused to eat meat. Barratt Brown (who had run into criticism from Catherine Marshall, among others) was producing a pamphlet to elaborate on his new scheme for membership of N-CF.

In February, Bertrand Russell was arguing in the *Tribunal* against the injustice to the Absolutists who were being rearrested after their first sentence had been served and given new sentences. Russell argued that these were the ones who had most convincingly demonstrated their conscientious objections and therefore should be granted Absolute Exemption, as provided for in the Act; this, however, was never granted. By this time 3,591 COs had been handed over to the military authorities. 2,221 had been court-martialled once, 437 had been court martialled twice, 31 three times and 2 four times. The Tribunal also drew comfort from the fact that at a Rossendale parliamentary by-election, the Peace by Negotiations candidate had polled 1,800 votes against his opponent's 6,000.

In March 1917, Barratt Brown, from the safety of Woodbrooke, was lamenting the N-CF policy of seeking amelioration of the condition of the Absolutists in prison as 'a lamentable lapse from its principles of No Compromise.' This brought a considerable correspondence from prisoners, both pro and con.

In April America's entry into the war led Bertrand Russell to write that although this might lead to a shortening of the war, it might both discourage a compromise peace by the now exhausted belligerents, and also lengthen the war by insistence on unconditional defeat of Germany.

In May, W.J. Chamberlain was court-martialled for the second time. He refused to plead or recognise the authority of the court. He said that if he could conscientiously do anything to further the war, he would be in the trenches. He could not therefore work on the land or in industry to make it easier for the authorities to secure men for military purposes. He regarded the acceptance of 'work of national importance' as fighting by proxy. A nation which attempted to destroy militarism by a greater militarism would find its second position worse than its first. He concluded by expressing his faith in the triumph of Love over Hate and of Brotherhood over the vile intrigues of financiers, diplomats and kings.

At a conference of divisional N-CF secretaries on 20 May. Mr Austin for the midland division said that branches were healthy, but waiting for a fresh stimulus, which he thought should take the form of an out-door campaign.

Early in June the *Tribunal* was commenting on the significance of the Leeds Conference.

The Friend in 1917 continued to give more details of COs than the *Tribunal*. In January more information was given of Littleboy and Hugh Gibbins (although their role as clerk and assistant clerk to the same meeting were reversed by *The Friend*). Both were fined 40/-d. and removed to Budbrooke Barracks, Warwick. Gibbins was arrested without prior call-up papers, a practice which *The Friend* reported as unusual, but not illegal. On 12 January, at lunch time, two military officers, and three detectives visited Woodbrooke Settlement in Bristol Road and after interviewing every man on the premises arrested seven of them as 'having failed to show any reason for not being in the army.' The seven were T. Corder, P. Catchpole, Charles Fish, William Corrin, Frank Dorrin, Stanley V. Keeling, Matthew Smith and Richard Porteous. They all came before the magistrates the next day, together with Robert B. Hurworth, who had been arrested at Woodbrooke on the 9th. They were all fined 40/-d. and ordered to wait an escort for having been absentees after 'having been deemed enlisted' at various places as far apart as Liverpool and Essex.

From this point, information regarding Birmingham COs in *The Friend* becomes scanty and we can turn to the Leeds Convention.

The Leeds Convention and its Aftermath in Birmingham

The Leeds Convention held on 3 June 1917 is widely held to be a failed revolutionary attempt to set up Soviets in Britain. The truth is more complex.

The Convention was called by the United Socialist Council. This was a body due to have been set up in 1914 consisting of the three main political bodies of the Labour movement, the Independent Labour Party, the British Socialist Party and the Fabian Society. It was not however activated until July 1916 when the first two parties joined, but not the Fabians. The Leeds Convention was its first major initiative. It was convened in spite of all the obstacles that the government and local authorities could put in its way and at least 1,500 delegates with a total audience of about 3,500 attended the proceedings. Unfortunately, any record of the delegates or their organisations does not appear to have survived, so we do not know what the representation from Birmingham was, although we know that some attended.

Four resolutions were discussed and passed. The first congratulated the Russians on their revolution; it was moved by Ramsay MacDonald. The second motion was moved by Philip Snowden. It hailed with the greatest satisfaction the declaration of foreign policy and war aims of the Russian Provisional Government, pledged the delegates to work for such a peace, and called upon our government to announce its agreement with the foreign policy and war aims of the Russian Provisional Government. These included no annexations, no indemnities, and the right of every government to dispose of its own destiny. The third resolution moved by Mrs Despard called on the government to place itself in accord with the democracy of Russia by immediately effecting a charter of liberties establishing complete political rights for men and women, unrestricted freedom of the press, freedom of speech, an amnesty for all political and religious prisoners, full rights of industrial and political association, and the release of labour from all forms of compulsion and restraint.

It was the fourth resolution, moved by and thought to be the brain child, of W.C. Anderson that was contentious. This called for the establishment in every town, urban and rural district of Councils of Workmen and Soldiers, for carrying out the foregoing resolutions and for the political and industrial emancipation of international labour. This resolution could mean all things to all men. To the war party it was red revolution, even though the Bolshevik revolution was not to occur until November 1917. For the ILP the Councils were simply co-ordinating bodies to the labour organisations already in existence. The idea of Soldiers' Councils was particularly worrying to the government at a time when ex-service organisations were already beginning to appear. The National Association of Discharged Sailors and Soldiers began in September 1916 and was linked to the trade union and labour movement; the National Federation of Discharged and Demobilised Sailors and Soldiers, linked to the Liberal Party, was formed in April 1917.

There could have been few participants in the Leeds Convention under the delusion that they were founding a revolutionary movement; what they did believe was that they were taking a significant step forward in uniting the forces for peace and shortening the duration of the war.

The real significance of the movement can only be judged by the support that it received locally, and in Birmingham evidence exists to show how wide that support was. The Leeds Convention elected half a provisional committee; the other half was to be elected at thirteen District Conferences. Several of these Conferences were held, others were broken up by rowdies, and some were banned, including the Birmingham one. But the Birmingham conference was organised, and the list of delegates remains.

The man entrusted with the organisation of the Birmingham Conference due to be held at the Priory Rooms on Saturday August 18th 1917 was Jim Simmons, who was to play a considerable part in subsequent Birmingham politics.

Private Jim Simmons had joined the army in 1911. The next year he became a Socialist. He was opposed to the war from the beginning, but served in Egypt, the Dardanelles and France. He was wounded three times and had his left foot amputated. In 1917 he was still in the army waiting for an artificial limb to be fitted and his subsequent discharge.

Simmons' letters show that he was in contact with Ramsay MacDonald as early as September 1915 and he continued to supply MacDonald with examples of anti-war feeling among the troops, and reported the soldiers' grievances which MacDonald attempted to redress through Parliament.

As a serving, disabled soldier Simmons was an ideal representative for the peace movement, but it was unlikely that he would be allowed to be a leading peace advocate without attracting the attentions of the police and military.

Private C. James Simmons was appointed secretary for the District Conference by the national provisional committee. Its agenda was to consider two resolutions and elect a district representative for the provisional committee. The first resolution was to endorse the first three motions of the Leeds Convention. The second resolution was to 'at once establish Workers' and Soldiers' Councils' locally'. Wherever possible it was suggested that the local Trades Council take the initiative, but elsewhere organisations should co-operate to set up Workers' and Soldiers' Councils.

As instructed Simmons sent out invitations to Labour organisations and recorded acceptances in a book. By the closing date 140 societies had elected about 220 delegates. The societies represented included ten Trades Councils, seven Labour Parties, 19 ILP branches, nine Fellowship of Conciliation, five Women's Co-operative Guild, five No-Conscription Fellowships, five National Federation of Women Workers, five Adult Schools, two Womens' International League, two Labour Churches, two Union of Democratic Control, and one Women's International League. Most of the delegates were from trade union branches. About twenty trade unions were represented including ten NUR branches, two ASLEF, seven ASE and seven Workers Union branches whose leadership was so opposed to peace activity.

All the important Trades Councils were represented – Birmingham, Coventry, Worcester, and six from the Black Country. The Labour Representation Committees of Birmingham and Coventry were among the Labour Parties.

Three days before the Convention was due to assemble Jim Simmons received a letter from the Birmingham Chief Constable, C.H. Nafter, enclosing a formal order under the powers conferred by the Defence of the Realm Regulations prohibiting the meeting of the Workers and Soldiers' Council 'in whatever place within the City, or whenever it may be proposed to hold same.' There were protests from the Labour movement and elsewhere at the banning and the *Birmingham Gazette* wrote an editorial protesting at the attack on freedom of speech. A series of letters followed in the local press in which the excuse for the banning of the meeting was widely held to be the scenes at the London Divisional Conference where a jingoistic mob had completely wrecked the interior of the Brotherhood Church, Hackney with the police looking on and doing nothing.

Nothing more was heard of Workers' and Soldiers' Councils in Birmingham, but it is clear that, as one would expect from what has already been recorded, there was wide support in Birmingham for the Leeds Convention and for local organisation to implement its decisions.

June to December 1917

ILP branches in Birmingham were active in June reporting back from the Convention and extending peace activities. The City branch held a meeting to hear a report from their delegate at Leeds. The following week the open-air season began and the branch reported a meeting on the War Aims of Russia at which there was 'not a suggestion of opposition from a large crowd.' Handsworth reported their 'longest branch meeting for twelve months' to hear J.W. Tonks talk on the Leeds Convention. A week later the City branch reported a talk at a Thursday meeting by Rev J. Morgan Whiteman on John Trevor, the founder of the Labour Churches; 'great times' were being had at a speakers' class on Fridays; and there had been a good open-air meeting on the Sunday with Councillor J.W. Tonks speaking on The 'Hun at Home.' Miss Whiteman took the chair. In the last week of June there had been a large crowd to hear 'our comrade' Private Simmons speak on 'No Patched up Peace.' There was 'no opposition, *Labour Leaders* were sold out, a collection totalled 8/8½d. Literature sales were 7/3d. and 8 new members have been made in June.'

Open-air activity continued throughout the summer. City branch had appointed Fred Longden their lecturer, but in July he was 'seized by the military.' The branch made nine new members that month. Erdington held three successful meetings in July. A Saturday meeting at New Street 'brought some anxiety, but it was the best of all.' In Handsworth they held the first public meeting since the war to a good crowd.

In August (usually a slack month) Henry Brockhouse spoke for City branch on 'A Democratic Peace' and for Bordesley Green on 'The Stockholm Conference – Why Labour should Attend.' City and Rotton Park branches had set up a joint committee to fight the new parliamentary constituency of Ladywood.

In September Bordesley Green held a meeting at the Mission Room, Humpage Road; Miss Chambers of the UDC spoke to a 'good crowd.' Rotton Park organised a solidarity march to Winson Green prison. Miss Gillian Chambers spoke to a 'good crowd' and Mrs Simmons took the chair. City announced 'splendid meetings' during the month including one at Small Heath Park Gates.

At the end of September Pte Jim Simmons was arrested – not in Birmingham but in Rochdale. A detailed report from that town stated that at the end of the season when their open-air activity had been very successful they had arranged for Private Simmons to address a series of meetings. Since other servicemen had addressed meetings in the town in uniform including the MP Brigadier-General Page Croft, they were, 'Expecting splendid meetings and an enthusiastic reception for Comrade Simmons'. He received both – and something else. At the end of the first meeting he was 'courteously invited' by the police into the Town Hall and his regimental number and other particulars asked for and given. The next night (Tuesday) both Simmons and the chairman were warned that if he spoke he would be arrested:

> This announcement called forth considerable resentment from the audience. The chairman opened the meeting and our good comrade delivered an uncompromising and fearless address on the need for a negotiated peace.
>
> The spectacle of a young soldier in uniform, who had given of his blood for his country, who had lost his foot in the fight for his country's liberty, standing with one leg supported by the seat of a chair, appealing to civilians for a common-sense attitude to the opening up of negotiations, appealing on behalf of his comrades of the three regiments he had served in, made a powerful impression on his large audience.

On Wednesday evening his chairman was just going to call on him when both military and civil police emerged. The MP asked him to step inside as they wanted to speak to him. The secretary of the Party requested to go with him. The police consented, but when he got inside he was separated from Simmons who was taken to the other end of the building – to the detention cells. It was not till late on Thursday morning that some comrades, having approached a Labour magistrate ... were able to see him for some minutes. Almost immediately after Simmons limped through the town on his crutches en route for Chester, and under military escort.

All the meetings that Simmons was to have addressed were held, it was claimed, and large audiences passed unanimous votes of protest at his arrest. The same issue of the *Labour Leader* found an old friend, identified only as P.D. who had known Simmons in the 'far away days before the war' when the Digbeth Parliament sat weekly in Birmingham. This was controlled by a Liberal government during its first two sessions. But, the Socialist Party gathered strength, defeated the Liberals in the third session and formed a government with C.J. Simmons in the Socialist Cabinet. 'I can see my dear old comrade as he stood up to introduce his first Bill. And now he lies in gaol. But he has helped to light a flame in England that cannot be put out.'

Back in Birmingham, October saw the reopening of the Central Labour Church. Good meetings were reported for Councillor Kneeshaw and Joseph Southall had spoken on 'Socialism and Art'. At the end of the month Erdington reported that their secretary had been arrested and was awaiting trial at Budbrooke Barracks, Warwick.

Branch activity continued to the end of the year. The noteworthy feature of November was that the East Birmingham Labour Church began its new session. In December, Jim Simmons spoke to a large audience on 'War Aims'. By this time however, he was ex-Private Simmons.

Tribunal continued to report on COs, but by the beginning of 1917 most had been dealt with and were in prison. The number of men nationally arrested and handed over to the military authorities, according to the records of the N-CF (which they claimed were more accurate than those held by the army authorities) was 3,249. By the end of July 1917 this had risen to 4,443. The circulation of *Tribunal* did not rise to 100,000 and more, as predicted, but settled down at about 20,000. Most of what *Tribunal* did print relevant to Birmingham concerned the two N-CF leaders A. Barratt Brown and W.J. Chamberlain.

Barratt Brown's resignation from the N-CF council necessitated a letter in July denying that he had resigned from the organisation and assuring people that he was still chair of the Midlands division and the Birmingham branch of the N-CF. Books for the Home Office Camps were always in great demand; in June 'a Birmingham friend' offered a selection that included Thorold Rogers – *Work and Wages;* Henry Clay – *Economics for the General Reader;* J.S. Mill – *Principles of Political Economy; Fabian Essays;* and Norman Angell – *The Great Illusion.*

N-CF support for the revolutionary movement epitomised by the Leeds Convention and in November by the Bolshevik revolution, led to much discussion, led by Bertrand Russell and Barrett Brown, as to what sort of revolution the N-CF supported. The July 19 *Tribunal* carried a supplement stating that the EC of the Friends Service Committee, N-CF and FoR had met and decided to publish individual statements which they hoped would 'stimulate thought on the subject.' One statement was by Barratt Brown headed, Revolution and Non-resistance, An Appeal for an Unarmed Revolution. This set out the full Pacifist case. 'We are of those who abjure the use of armed force in either civil or international war.' Violence was not only wrong, but futile for securing any worthy purpose. But violence that was necessary for war, was not necessary for revolution. Bertrand Russell took a similar view with a piece headed Pacifism and Revolution. Whether in fact these statements did stimulate thought is not known, but there was no contradiction or argument in subsequent issues of *Tribunal*.

The same issue gave 'news of our first editor' by permission of Mrs Chamberlain. He reported that his health was much better than when he was at 'the Scrubs' (where he served the first part of his second sentence). But he was still feeling the effects of confinement and 'I find that after my daily 45 minutes exercise, I feel as if I had walked at least 30 miles, and I am actually glad to get back to my cell!' He then gave his views on the controversy of whether the hard labour of their sentences was war work and to be resisted, with all the consequences that followed. Chamberlain was against this view. He considered that they were in prison because they refused to become in any way parties to the Conscription Acts. He had expressed his willingness to undergo any punishment the government thought fit to inflict and, 'Had the penalty been death, I would have accepted it.' Like Barrett Brown he pleaded for patience in adversity. He hoped the government would not keep them in prison long enough to prevent them fighting a tendency 'towards a belief in the power of force to effect reforms which I fear will be very strong among a nation of discontented workers trained in the use of arms.' The cry must never be 'to the barricades' but always 'to the ballot box'. In October Chamberlain was removed to Larkhill Camp, Salisbury Plain, where he expected to remain several weeks. Letters from all his friends were invited.

General matter in *Tribunal* illustrated what was fuelling the increased demand for peace in the middle of the year. One was the overwhelming support at the Labour Party conference for a Consultative Conference of the Socialists of Europe and USA. Also the decision of French, Italian, German and Austrian socialists to send delegates to such a meeting in Stockholm. The other was a Peace Note by the Pope, also in August, which had wide influence in Germany and Austria and had influenced a resolution in the Reichstag in favour of a peace without annexations or indemnities. Also in August was the third Battle of Ypres (Passchendaele) which quickly became bogged down in the mud and resulted in 300,000 British casualties.

The question of the extent to which the normal brutalities of prison life were aggravated by deliberate additional cruelties inflicted by governors and staff was always being raised. As we have seen, this issue split those Absolutists who thought that the main task was to propagandise for peace and that suffering was good for the soul. Both Barrett Brown and Chamberlain took this view and the extreme form of this position came in a statement issued on behalf of the Friends Service Committee at Christmas 1917 and signed by Barratt Brown, explaining why the Society of Friends had issued no appeal to the government for the release of the CO prisoners. One reason given was that to gain their release before the general public had been convinced of the correctness of the Pacifist position would 'injure the greater cause.' The statement ended by quoting George Fox, the Quaker founding father, 'there was never any persecution that came but we saw it was for good and we looked upon it to be good as from God.'

Not all N-CF members accepted that worse was better. Cases of forcible feeding were reported from other prisons as well as Winson Green – one case reported in October 1917 was of a prisoner forced fed continually from January. Cat and Mouse treatment was also reported from Winson Green, prisoners being released when their health had gravely deteriorated and rearrested when it had improved. When prisoners refused to obey orders they received solitary confinement. One case (not at Winson Green) was of a man confined in a cell 11' by 7' for fourteen weeks with one hour's exercise per *week* fed only on bread and water.

The normal regime of hard labour was designed to tax the strongest constitution whether it were mailbag sewing, stone-breaking or other work. Prisons were cold at most times, and in winter there were complaints of lack of blankets. In summer, during hot spells, where the small windows did not open, cells became furnaces, aggravated by the stench of the universal slop pail. If health wasn't broken, spirit could be by the regime of silence imposed and separation from other prisoners even at work. A debate in the House of Lords in November 1917 opened by Lord Parmoor exposed the cruelties inflicted on his nephew. Stephen Hobhouse, Replying to this debate, Lord Derby promised that there would be 'no more successive sentences.' But this promise had been made the previous year and was never kept.

Finally in December, there was a relaxation of prison rules. The period of exercise was extended from 40 minutes to 1 hour per day – 30 minutes in the morning and 30 in the afternoon. Prisoners were allowed to converse with a 'partner' during exercise, although they were not necessarily allowed to chose their partner. They could then walk in pairs instead of single file. Prisoners were allowed to receive and to write one letter a fortnight instead of once a month. One monthly prison visit of 30 minutes was reduced to 15 minutes. Prisoners at Wandsworth went en bloc to the Governor to protest at this strange 'privilege'. He wrote to the Home Office who decreed that visits should remain 30 minutes once a month. Prisoners were permitted to wear their own clothing, including an overcoat. They could also continue to wear prison underclothing. This was advantageous since they were only allowed one set of their own underwear, whereas prison underwear was washed in the prison laundry and a change provided. Lastly, prisoners who could afford it were allowed to pay other prisoners to clean their cells or utensils at a cost of 6d. per day. This 'privilege' was almost universally rejected by the COs.

Life in the camps and settlements also brought hardships, some perpetrated by hostile staff. The early camp at Dyce in the north of Scotland had to be closed down; at others prisoners opted to return to prison rather than stay in the camps.

In May 1917 there was an interesting report from the Dartmoor Settlement where a number of the Birmingham COs were:

> We have here a community of between 800 and 900 men representing all shades of thought and many with little in common except their determination to have no participation in war.
>
> While some form groups whose main ideas more or less coincide others have attained their position purely as individuals. Our settlement includes representatives of the Independent Labour Party, the British Socialist Party, the Fellowship of Reconciliation, the Society of Friends, Jews, Roman Catholics, Anglicans, Wesleyans, Unitarians, Congregationalists, Baptists, Plymouth Brethren, and International Bible Students, together with anarchists, atheists and agnostics.
>
> Practically all of these have been through the hands of the military authorities, sentenced to imprisonment, and after the genuineness of their conscientious objection has been recognised by the Central Tribunal, received a Royal Pardon conditional upon their accepting and performing with diligence and fidelity work under the Committee established by the Home Office for the employment of COs.

The report went on to categorise prisoners as men who were prepared to do work of national importance if it did not conflict with their consciences; and men who considered that they should have been given absolute exemption but came to the settlement as an alternative to prison or because of health or family reasons. The report did not criticise conditions at the settlement, but made two general criticisms. The first was that men skilled in trades and professions were given work for which they were entirely unsuited. Secondly the work was deliberately designed to involve the maximum of physical effort for the minimum return of value produced. It was recognised that this occurred because of a widely held theory of equal sacrifice i.e. that the sacrifices of COs should approximate to those of serving soldiers, but the artificial imposition of 'sacrifices' which were not imposed on other exempt categories such as business, health or age seemed illogical.

1918

Independent Labour Party activity quickened during 1918. Erdington and Rotton Park continued the most active branches. During the winter both branches reported their own meetings and also Labour Church activity. The Rotton Park Labour Church met at Dudley Road Schools. In January Frank Spires spoke on 'Open Diplomacy,' there was a speaker on 'Conscription of Wealth,' and Kneeshaw spoke on the 'Price of a People's Peace,' all with some form of musical interlude. This led to the formation of a William Morris Choir. By February the Stirchley Labour Church was active at the Stirchley Institute with Arthur Ponsonby MP speaking on 'The War for Liberty,' with Jim Simmons in the chair. Also in February City branch met and deprecated a proposal to stand a Labour candidate in Ladywood 'against the small band of Radicals who had been true to Internationalism.' Six new members were reported at this meeting.

In March, Kings Norton and Stirchley branches reported a highly successful Socialist Crusade week with Jim Simmons. He had spoken at six halls and outside the Bournville works. 'The final meeting saw a record crowd for Peace Now.' 30 new members had been made and there was as many to come. They were deeply indebted to the William Morris choir. Handsworth held a Social and Dance with proceeds to the Birmingham ILP Federation, which was again active. The Rotton Park Labour Church met each week. Kneeshaw seems to have been the main speaker for three weeks running. He was by then prospective Parliamentary candidate for Ladywood, thus allaying the fears of the Central branch, and at the third meeting he had a 'great audience.' The other meeting was a joint one with the UDC at which Roden Buxton spoke on peace and said that Lloyd George was 'now fighting a Commercial war.'

In April, East Birmingham Labour Church reported a meeting with George Lansbury and Rotton Park branch and he Labour Church continued with a full programme.

May brought the resumption of open-air meetings. Rotton Park opened with Kneeshaw, and Erdington started with a meeting at George Road at which 'Comrade Tonks and Harry Brockhouse gave excellent addresses.' Kings Norton and Stirchley opened with another Parliamentary candidate 'Comrade Councillor Tom Hackett.' He spoke on New Worlds for Old, 'made strong points on poverty and the back-to-back slums of Birmingham. The remedy was ILPism, he said. This met with the approval of a good crowd. Comrade Arthur Riley made an ideal chairman. The meeting ended with the Red Flag.' City branch commenced activity at Small Heath Park Gates where there was 'a big crowd and no opposition.' By this time the ILP was growing everywhere and at the end of the month the *Labour Leader* reported 34 new branches nationally during the previous quarter.

At the end of June came the Labour Party Conference and the final break-up of the war time coalition. All thoughts now were on the future and peace-time elections. In July, Kings Norton and Stirchley held a Garden Party at which Tom Hackett 'met several hundred voters.' Kneeshaw was busy at open-air meetings speaking on 'Labour and the Discharged Soldier.'

In August the Birmingham ILP Federation joined with the UDC to organise two meetings for Seymour Cocks 'of Secret Treaties fame.' Resolutions were passed to abrogate the secret treaties. The *Labour Leader* was now printing the weekly list of war casualties – 2,000 killed and 9,000 wounded and missing in the first week of August.

Kings Norton and Stirchley seem to have made much of the running in September. They held a Swimming Gala at which the Baths were packed. They finished their open-air campaign with a speaker from Newcastle-on-Tyne who addressed meetings at Cotteridge, Selly Oak, Austin Works village and Stirchley. 'The speaker was untiring and at the last meeting we had the biggest crowd of the season.' At the end of the month they opened their winter season with a Musical Evening and reported that membership of the branch had trebled since Christmas. Also at the end of the month the Birmingham ILP Federation organised a Conference on 'Peace and Democracy' at the Priory Rooms together with other Peace and Democratic bodies in the town. 140 delegates attended. The police were present, but did not stop the proceedings. J.N. Ballou JP presided. A resolution demanding Peace by Negotiations was moved by Dr Henry Hogkin and seconded by Tom Hackett. Joseph Southall, H.E. Smith and Harry Potter of the Navvies Union supported and Dr Dunstan the ILP candidate for Moseley stressed that it was a capitalist war. After the resolution was passed a Committee was set up to see that it was implemented. About this time South Birmingham ILP branch restarted, Bordesley Green and Small Heath joined forces and the local ILP Federation was said to be progressing 'surely, if slowly.'

During October Small Heath branch was holding successful meetings in support of Dr Dunstan. They claimed 80 members and sent out a call to 'make it 100.' At the beginning of November South Birmingham was also active. Kings Norton & Stirchley held two meetings with Tom Mann on 'The Russian Revolution' and 'Shortening Working Hours.' Both were received with 'great enthusiasm.'

On November 11th. the war ended. War casualties in the week ending 17 November were 6,500 killed and 18,000 wounded and missing. The *Labour Leader* made no mention of celebrations and the political work was intensified. For December 28 a great Birmingham Election Rally was arranged at the Central Hall with singing and music. Admission was free to all with TU cards or badges. All the Parliamentary candidates were to speak and 'Whatever the Result we will Fight on,' was the claim.

Turning now to the Pacifists in 1918, details of the activities of Conscientious Objectors is more enlightening in *Tribunal* than *The Friend*. The latter is most useful for the detailed lists of whereabouts of COs including a quarterly summary list. This material, with other sources, I have used to compile a list of Birmingham COs which is given as an Appendix. This list, however, is not complete.

In January A. Barratt Brown's absolute exemption was revoked. The case was brought by the military representative who wanted the exemption to be changed from Absolute to Work of National Importance under the Pelham scheme. This would, the military representative claimed, 'put him in line with every other CO.' It is likely that this unusual action originated at a higher level than the local tribunal for it hinged on the refusal to either use or recognise as legal, this category of absolute exemption. It emerged during the hearing that the Birmingham Local Tribunal had only ever granted three absolute exemptions. Barratt Brown did not appear before the Tribunal. He sent a letter stating that he had felt uneasy at having to apply under the Military Service Act for his certificate of absolute exemption as representing an acceptance of that Act and, while intending no discourtesy to the local Tribunal, he declined to accept its authority by appearing before it. The military representative while stating his case added that Barrett Brown 'was at Woodbrooke Settlement preaching sedition.' The chairman then said, 'Well we had better withdraw the exemption if he does not care to appear.'

In January the Labour Party Conference took place which accepted peace by negotiations and also demanded the release from prison of the COs. In the same month came the death in Shrewsbury Prison of Arthur Horton. He was on a starvation diet it was claimed, the prison was bitterly cold, he was not allowed to cover his bed with rugs at night, he had a dreadful cough that could be heard throughout the prison; the doctor said that he had a 'slight cough.' Similar conditions were reported at Winchester and Wandsworth.

By April 1918 some prisoners were being released on health grounds. Birmingham men were H. Goldy, N.C. Hill, and W.J. Chamberlain, all from Winchester Prison and W.P. Whitehouse from Exeter Prison. Chamberlain had suffered a breakdown which affected his eyes. 'He can only read and write with the greatest difficulty.' Barratt Brown was arrested and taken to Warwick Barracks where he was court martialled. He made his normal Pacifist defence, but for some unknown reason the court martial was quashed and another held. In April the *Tribunal* plant was raided and smashed up for printing a back page article-cum-leaflet: 'STOP THE WAR – It Need Not go on Unless the People Choose – Do not Remain Silent any Longer – COME OUT FOR PEACE'. The paper found new printers, but for another year its format was smaller as the whereabouts of the printing press was concealed from the police.

In April the new Manpower Act began calling up men aged 41 to 51. The *Tribunal* advised would-be COs. that they must apply to the local Tribunal for exemption forms as soon as they were called upon to report for medical examination. They were also warned that the only grounds of conscientious objection now was 'objection to the undertaking of combatant service'; the government and the military between them had finally and officially eliminated the category of Absolute Exemption.

In May Barrett Brown was again court-martialled, sentenced to 112 days hard labour and taken to Wormwood Scrubs. He was greeted by a number of Friends at Paddington. Harrison Barrow was also prosecuted, together with Edith Ellis and Arthur Watts of the Friends Service Committee, for printing without submission to the censor leaflets 'dealing with the war and questions of peace.' The men were sentenced to six months imprisonment and Edith Ellis to a £100 fine and £50 costs. There was an unsuccessful appeal in July and the two men were taken to Pentonville to serve their sentences.

By July W.J. Chamberlain seems to have been sufficiently recovered in health to begin a series of articles in the *Tribunal* entitled Fragments of History dealing with such topics as 'Freedom of the Press,' ' On Fighting to a Finish,' 'On Christianity and War' etc.

Also in July, the authorities hit on the idea of Exceptional Employment, in yet another vain attempt to solve the intractable problem of the Absolutists. This granted civilian employment in an almost endless list of trades (as opposed to the other alternatives for imprisoned COs of non-combatant service of various sorts in the forces, or penal employment under the Home Office Schemes). It was greeted with derision by the Absolutists, and none of the Birmingham Absolutists accepted it, although at least three others (A.J. Hawkins, Douglas J. James and G.H. Wootton) who had worked in the Camps opted for Exceptional Employment.

Yet another abortive attempt was made to placate the Absolutists in September 1918 when it was proposed to centralise all COs who had served two years in jail in Wakefield Prison, where locks would be removed from cells, and a work regime of semi-freedom instituted. Of the Birmingham Absolutists Southall, Look, Fletcher, Tebbutt, Westwood, Pinfield, and Percy Moore can be identified as being transferred to Wakefield. The scheme was viewed with suspicion from the beginning, reinforced by the issue of Home Office scheme type clothing and ration scales. Within a fortnight the Prisoners'

Committee issued a Manifesto declaring that instead of granting the COs the absolute exemption to which they were entitled they were being embroiled in a scheme to induce them to administer their own punishment by working a Scheme of Industrial Conscription. They would not undertake any compulsory work organised to facilitate the prosecution of the war. The government had again misunderstood their principles by taking for granted that they would accept any scheme which ameliorated the harsh conditions of prison hard labour. But for them the only two courses were absolute exemption which would allow them to serve the community without violating their consciences, or to serve their hard labour in prison. Among the signatories to this Manifesto was Eric P. Southall. The project was abandoned before the end of September and the COs dispersed again to other prisons.

In October Karl Liebknecht was released from a German jail and *Tribunal* heralded this as a good reason why our own political prisoners should be released. But Liebknecht's release was a result of a new German government seeking peace terms and Germany was already in the throes of revolution.

When war ended on 11 November 1918 attention then turned to the prisoners in jail and the future of peace organisations including the special case of the No-Conscription Fellowship. In January 1919 a new N-CF executive committee was elected. W.J. Chamberlain received the fourth highest vote and Hugh Gibbins became the midlands representative.

It was recognised government policy to release the COs. only when all servicemen had been demobilised. By December 1918 the only prisoners released had been on health grounds and 1,500 remained in prison. By March 1919 1,235 COs remained in jail and 3,410 on Home Office Schemes. But COs were still protesting at harsh conditions by hunger striking and then being released under the Cat & Mouse Act. In March hunger strikes were reported from Hull, Newcastle, Wandsworth, Winchester and Canterbury. At the latter prison, Wilson of Birmingham had been released under the Cat & Mouse Act.

By April 1919 the intent of the allies to prosecute a harsh peace, the British bombing of Egypt and further threats of war led *Tribunal* to proclaim The Failure of the Sword and the correctness of the Pacifist line. That month it was announced that all COs who had served two years or more would be released. In July *Tribunal* published a list of 55 COs still in prison. These included T. Gunton and H.P. Johnson, of Birmingham. On July 30th Winston Churchill stated that all COs had been released. This was not strictly true, but after this announcement the remainder were released and Cat & Mouse men told that they need not return to jail.

Discussion on the future of the N CF was well under way by this time. Members were divided between Bolshevik and anti-Bolshevik factions and there was a further rift as to whether an Anti-Conscription organisation was necessary or whether aims should be widened to embrace all Peace activities. W.J. Chamberlain put forward his own solution of dividing the Fellowship into two sections of anti-militarists and anti-capitalist militarists, but confessed his preference for '1,000 members who were against the use of armed force under any circumstances to 100,000 who were merely against the militarism of the capitalist.'

The national committee met on a number of occasions and eventually put forward proposals for the future. These entailed the dissolution of the existing organisation into three committees – one to initiate a new organisation to associate with all those resisting conscription, another to create a new group to form the British section of an international pacifist organisation and a third committee to deal with any attempt to introduce military training into the educational system. These proposals were put to regional conferences. At the midland conference in November Chamberlain moved the successful motion to accept the national committee proposals. In January 1920 a National Convention met for a final decision and the national committee's proposals prevailed. The No Conscription Fellowship then effectively ended, for the three committees produced little of substance and quietly died.

Conclusions

Although the number of Conscientious Objectors nationally was small (about 16,500 is the accepted figure) and those who resisted the Military Service Acts even smaller (6,312) their influence in opposing the war and gathering support for peace was considerably greater than their numbers. It is almost impossible to separate religious from political COs, because the former were invariably also Socialists or Liberals and the mass exodus of Liberals from their party to the Labour Party at the end of the war almost entirely blurs the distinction.

The impression from Birmingham is that the proportion of Conscientious Objectors in the city was greater than in almost any other area of Britain. A list of Friends and Attenders Detained by the Military or in Prison in May 1917 totalled 117, of whom 19 were from Birmingham compared with six from Manchester and 30 from Greater London. Other lists give similar findings. The final figures for the Birmingham Tribunal as given by Brazier and Sandford showed that it had dealt with 82 Conscientious Objectors and had granted 9 Absolute Exemptions at its 1,765 meetings between November 1915 and July 1919.

The Quaker influence was of long standing in Birmingham and the presence of the Cadbury family and the influence of the Colleges associated with them, particularly Woodbrooke, nurtured the Pacifist tradition. Several of the COs had worked at Cadbury's among them Bernard Edwards, Vernon Hill, Arthur Sharp and Charles Watkins. In addition 41 Cadbury employees served in the Friends Ambulance Unit.

The number of Absolutists from Birmingham cannot be accurately recorded. My list (see Appendix) shows at least 12 Absolutists who remained in prison from 1916 to 1919: Hill, Howdle, James, D.J. Littleboy, Percy Moore, Sydney Moore, Pinfield, Pritchard, Rastall, Sharp, Southall, and Watkins. To this should probably be added from the Friends Library List Griffin, and the two Looks.

These were the men who above all made sacrifices and showed considerable courage in upholding their principles. Others also went to jail for shorter periods, including national leaders W.J. Chamberlain, A. Barratt Brown and Harrison Barrow, all from Birmingham.

Finally with regard to COs. the No-Conscription Fellowship was an organisation unique in the world to which Birmingham men and women made a significant contribution.

Turning to the Birmingham labour movement in general during World War One, there was a small, vociferous minority who supported the war without reservations throughout. These included people who in the past had made a militant, Socialist contribution to the movement such as the leaders of the Workers' Union, particularly John Beard and Julia Varley. The leaders of the Brassworkers, notably W.J. Davis a national figure in the TUC, also vigorously supported the war. Other general workers' leaders Eldred Hallas and John Simpson led the war party and supported the British Workers' National League to combat the 'Pacifists.' Within the Trades Council a dominant support for the war faction in 1914 saw its support dwindle until John Kesterton and others left to attempt to form new organisations. But the list of those who could find any enthusiasm for the war was short. The vast majority of workers and their unions, notably the ASE, gave grudging support for the war, had their work cut out to support and protect working class interests and were gradually drawn into anti-war activities as the carnage continued and perceptions grew that the war was not about protecting 'poor little Belgium,' but for imperial expansion.

The stages of the growth of anti-war feeling are clear. At the outbreak only a few members of the Independent Labour Party and the even smaller number of socialists in the BSP and SLP. The exceptional importance attached to Conscription in 1916 and the theory that whatever else the state commanded it could not command our bodies, marks the first turning point in the development of resistance to the war. The Russian Revolution was the next turning point. ('We put people in jail for opposing the war, but in Russia the whole nation opposes the war', wrote the *Law Journal*). The publication of the Secret Treaties, which showed how the powers were proposing to stake out their spheres of influence, strengthened the claim that it was an imperialist war. By the time of the Leeds Conference in June 1917 majority support in the labour movement was for ending the war. The significance of Leeds is not that it failed to set up Soviets, but that it marks this turning point, certainly in Birmingham, of transition to a majority for peace. By January 1918 the Labour Party had approved a policy of peace by negotiations and, with a break in the spring when the German offensive took place, the peace movement continued to grow.

Of those in Birmingham who opposed war at an early stage we must, apart from the COs, mention Councillor John Kneeshaw's outstanding contribution from the ILP, F.W. Rudland on the

Trades Council and T.F. Fathers and Frank Spires of the Labour wing of the Trades and Labour Council.

The general conception remains that the 1st World War received public support throughout. This study of the Birmingham labour movement suggests that this is far from true.

Bibliography: Labour Movement Politics 1914-1918

For the British Socialist Party, *Justice* and *The Call*. For the Socialist Labour Party, *The Socialist*, R. Challinor – *The Origins of British Bolshevism*, and papers of Martin Durham. For the ILP see, *Labour Leader* and *Clarion*. Also Kings Heath ILP Minute Book Oct 1906 – May 1919. For the Peace Movement in World War 1 the standard works are: John W. Graham – *Conscription and Conscience* (1922); and John Rae – *Conscience and Politics* (1970). The former is a first hand account by a Quaker. The latter uses all the official sources and is seen as a 'corrective' to the more partisan work of Graham. But Graham comes nearer to the truth, in my view. Also: K. Robbins – *The Abolition of War;* M. Ceadel – *Pacifism.* For Quaker material there is the Library in London and also Woodbrooke College library. To their librarians I extend my warmest thanks. For the No-Conscription Fellowship: Thomas Kennedy – *The Hounds of Conscience;* W.J. Chamberlain – *Fighting for Peace* (1928). For the UDC: Swartz M – *The Union of Democratic Control in British Politics during the First World War;* article of the same name by H. Hanak in *Bulletin of the Institute of Historical Research,* Nov 1963. The main journals are: *The Friend; Tribunal* (N-CF); *UDC* (monthly). For the Leeds Convention see: Stephen White – 'Soviets in Britain' (in *International Review of Social History* vol xix 1974); and Jim Simmons' papers in Birmingham Central Library.

Appendix: Chapter 13: Birmingham Conscientious Objectors

Sources: *The Friend; Tribunal;* (Neither the two sources used nor I who abstracted them make any claim that these figures are complete – GB).

Abbreviations: FSB: Farm Street, Birmingham; Abs: Exemp Absolute Exemption: A: Attender; Bb: Bournbrooke; Bks: Barracks; Bv: Bournville; CM: Court Martial; CP: Civil Prison; ECS: Excused Combative Service: Except. Emp: Exceptionally Employed; FAU: Friends Ambulance Unit. HL: Hard Labour; HOS: Home Office Scheme; LT: Local Tribunal; Rlsd: Released; Res W: Reserve W.; sen: Sentence; SO: Selly Oak: Stirch: Stirchley: WS: Wormwood Scrubs.

ARTISS, J.T. – (A) Bb May 17 Catterick Camp. Aug 17 WS. April 18 Newcastle CP Jul 18 Newcastle CP. Oct 18 Newcastle.

BALLINGER, John – FSB. Jan 17 Budbrooke Bks. May 17 Left Wormwood Scrubs. Aug 17 Dartmoor Settlement HOS. Oct 17 Wakefield Work Centre. Jan 18 Knutsford Settlement. Apr 18 Knutsford. July 18 Water Orton, B'ham. Oct 18 Water Orton.

BROWN, A. – Barrett. Cott. April 18 Budbrooke Barracks. July 18 WS 1sen. Oct 18 Canterbury CP. June 19 Rlsd.

BUNNEY, John – (A) Bull St. June 16 4 months det. May 17 Portsmouth CP 2sen. Aug 17 Portsmouth CP. Canterbury CP 3sen. Oct 17 Canterbury CP. Jan 18 Canterbury CP.

BURTON, John W. – Bv, Mar 16 LT. May 17 WS. Aug 17 Portsmouth CP 2sen. Oct 17 Portsmouth CP. Jan 18 Portsmouth CP. April 18 Connaught Bks Dover 3CM. July 18 Canterbury CP 3sen (18mHL) Oct 18 Canterbury. Apr 19 Rlsd.

CANE, E.A. – (A) FSB. Oct 17 WS. Jan 18 Dartmoor. April 18 Dartmoor. July 18 Dartmoor. Oct 18 Dartmoor.

CHAMBERLAIN, William J. – Stirch. Jan 17 WS. Apr 18 Released from Prison & relegated to Army Reserve W.

CLAYFIELD, W.R. – (A) Stirch. Aug 17 WS. Oct 17 WS. Jan 18 Knutsford Settlement. Apr 18 Knutsford.

COMPTON, C.H. – (A) SO. Mar 16 LT. Jan 18 Newcastle CP 2sen (6 months) April 18 Newcastle CP. July 18 Newcastle. Oct 18 Newcastle.

COOPER, Wm. Arthur – W'ton. Mar 16 LT. Nov 16 Wakefield Work Centre. May 17 Belmont Workhouse, Sutton. Aug 17 Wakefield Work Centre. Oct 17 Wakefield WC. Jan 18 Wakefield WC. Apr 18 Wakefield. July 18 Exceptionally Employed. (Meeting House now given as York.) Oct 18 Excep. Emp.

DAVENPORT, A.E. – SO May 17 Dartmoor Settlement. Aug 17 Dartmoor Settlement. Oct 17 Dartmoor.

EDWARDS, Leonard – Stirch. July 18 Dorchester CP 3sen. Oct 18 Dorchester. Apr 19 Rlsd.

EVANS, G.A. – (A) Stirch. Aug 17 WS. July 18 Portsmouth CP.

EWAN, George A. – (A) Stirch. Oct 17 Dover Camp 2CM. Jan 18 Portsmouth CP. April 18 Portsmouth CP. Oct 18 Portsmouth. May 19 Rlsd.

FLEMING, W.R. – May 16 Budbrooke Barracks, 12m detention comm to 4 months.

FLETCHER, Ernest H. – B'ham. April 18 Dorchester CP 3sen (2yrs HL). July 18 Dorchester. Oct 18 Dorchester. Apr 19 Rlsd.

GIBBINS, Hugh – Bull St. Jan 17 Budbrooke Bks. May 17 Dorchester CP 2s. Aug 17 Dorchester CP. Oct 17 Dorchester CP. Jan 18 Dorchester CP. April 18 Dorchester CP. July 18 Dorchester. Oct 18 Dorchester. Apr 19 Rlsd.

GOLDEY, G. Henry – (A) Bull St. May 17 WS. Aug 17 Albany Bks 2CM. Oct 17 Portsmouth CP. Jan 18 Portsmouth CP. Apr 18 Released Res W.

GRIFFITHS, Albert – B'ham. Nov 16 WS (112dHL) May 17 Wandsworh CP 2sen. Jan 18 Crich Common, Matlock HOS. Apr 18 Crich Cm. July 18 Crich Cm.

HAYMAN, Eric – B'ham. B'ham Local Trib 19 Sep 18. Pelham approved his present work as of national importance.

HARRISON, J.G. – Cott. Jan 18. Armley Gaol 2sen. Feb 18 Released Res W.

HAWKINS, A.J.– (A) FSB. May 17 Dartmoor Settlement. Aug 17 Dartmoor Sett. Oct 17 Dartmoor. Jan 18 Dartmoor. April 18 Dartmoor. July 18 Exceptionally Employed. Oct 18 Excep. Emp.

HILL, Vernon C. – SO. Jan 17 Norton Bks. May 17 Chisledown Camp 2CM. Aug 17 Winchester CP 2sen. Oct 17 Dorrington Camp 3CM. Jan 18 Winchester CP 4sen. Rlsd Res W.

HORTON, Ernest E. – (A) Stirch. Dorchester CP 3sen. Apr 19 Rlsd.

HOWDLE, H.J..– (A) FSB. May 17 WS. Aug 17 Weymouth Camp 2sen. Oct 17 Dorchester CP. Jan 18 Dorchester CP. April 18 Dorchester CP. July 18 Dorchester. Oct 18 Dorchester 3sen. Apr 19 Rlsd.

JAMES, Horace W. – (A) Stirch. July 18 Newcastle CP 3sen (12mHL). Oct 18 Newcastle.

JAMES, Douglas G. – (A) West Bromwich. Nov 16 WS.

JAMES, Douglas J. – (A) Cott. Aug 17 Dartmoor Sett. Jan 18 Wandsworth CP 2sen. Jan 18 Dartmoor. Oct 18 Excep. Emp.

LEE, Arthur W. – (A) SO. May 17 Catterick. Aug 17 WS. Oct 17 WS. Jan 18 WS. Apr 18 Newcastle CP. July 18 Newcastle 2sen. Oct 18 Newcastle. Apr 19 Rlsd.

LEEK, A.B. – (A) B'ham. Oct 17 Dartmoor. Jan 18 Dartmoor. Apr 18 Dartmoor. July 18 Dartmoor. Oct 18 Dartmoor.

LOOK, C.E. – (A) B'ham. Jan 18 Dartmoor. Apr 18 Dartmoor.

LITTLEBOY, Wilfred E. – SO. Mar 16 LT. Jan 17 Budbrooke BKs. Aug 17 Dorchester CP 2sen. Oct 17 Dorchester CP 3sen (2 yrs HL). Jan 18 Dorchester CP. April 18 Dorchester CP. July 18 Dorchester CP. Oct 18 Dorchester. Apr 19 Rlsd.

MOORE, Percy H. – (A) Stirch. Nov 16 WS. May 17 Dorchester CP. Aug17 Dorchester C{P. Oct 17 Dorchester CP. Jan 18 Dorchester CP. April 18 Dorchester CP. July 18 Dorchester. Oct 18 Dorchester. Apr 19 Rlsd.

MOORE, Sydney C. – (A) B'ham Nov 16 WS. May 17 Exeter CP 3sen. Aug 17 Plymouth CP 4sen. Oct 17 Exeter CP. Jan 18 Exeter CP. April 18 Exeter CP.

PARRY, Frank R. – (A) FSB. Oct 18 Dorchester CP 3sen (18mHL). Apr 19 Rlsd.

PATES, E.G. – (A) Bull St. May 17 Portsmouth CP. Aug 17 Portsmouth CP 3sen. Oct 17 Portsmouth CP. Jan 18 Mountjoy CP, Dublin 4sen. April 18 Liverpool CP 4sen. July 18 Liverpool. Oct 18 Manchester CP. Apr 19 Rlsd.

PINFIELD, A.H. – B'ham. Nov 16 WS. May 17 Dorchester CP 3sen. Aug 17 Dorchester CP. Oct 17 Dorchester CP. Jan 18 Dorchester CP. April 18 Dorchester CP. 4sen. July 18 Dorchester. Oct 18 Manchester. Apr 19 Rlsd.

PRITCHARD, Edmund – B'ham. Nov 16 WS 112dHL. May 17 Dorchester CP 3sen. Aug 17 Dorchester CP. Oct 17 Dorchester CP. Jan 18 Dorchester CP. April 18 Dorchester CP 3sen. July 18 Dorchester. Oct 18 Dorchester. Apr 19 Rlsd.

RASTALL, William – (A) SO. June 16 112dHL. Nov 16 Cheltenham Barracks. May 17 Catterick. 3CM. Aug 17 Northallerton CP 3sen. Oct 17 Northallerton CP. Jan 18 Newcastle CP 4sen. April 18 Newcastle CP. Apr 18 Newcastle. Oct 18 Manchester CP. Apr 19 Rlsd.

SHARP, Arthur J. – Stirch. Jan 17 Budbrooke Bks. Aug 17 Dorchester CP 2sen. Oct 17 Dorchester CP 3sen (1 yr HL). Jan 18 Dorchester CP 3sen. July 18 Dorchester. Oct 18 Dorchester. Apr 19 Rlsd.

SMITH, Sydney – (A) FSB. Mar 16 LT. Aug 17 WS. Oct 17 WS. Jan 18 Wakefield Work Centre. Apr 18 Knutsford.

SNELL, A.B. – (A) B'ham. Oct 17 Oct 17 Dartmoor. Jan 18 Dartmoor. Apr 18 Water Orton, B'ham.

SOUTHALL, Eric P. – B'ham. Mar 16 LT. June 16 112days HL. Nov 16 WS. May 17 Dorchester CP 3sen. Aug 17 Dorchester CP. Oct 17 Dorchester CP. Jan 18 Dorchester CP. April 18 Dorchester CP 4sen. July 18 Dorchester. Oct 18 Liverpool CP. Apr 19 Rlsd.

TAYLOR, W. – FSB. Aug 17 WS.

TONKS, A.C. – (A) B'ham. Nov 16 Warwick Labour Colony. May 17 Dartmoor Settlement. Aug 17 Dartmoor Sett. Oct 17 Dartmoor. Jan 18 Dartmoor. Apr 18 Dartmoor.

TONKS, Wilfred – (A) B'ham. Nov 16 Llandeussant Water Works. Aug 17 Llandeussant WW. Oct 17 Llandeussant WW. Jan 18 Ll'sant WW. Apr 18 LlWW.

WADSWORTH R.V. Bv. Apr 16 LT. Oct 17 WS. Jan 18 Knutsford Settlement. Apr 18 Knutsford. July 18 Dartmoor. Oct 18 Dartmoor.

WATKINS, Charles L. – SO. May 17 WS. Aug 17 Portsmouth CP 2sen. Oct 17 Portsmouth CP. Jan 18 Portsmouth CP. April 18 Dorchester CP 3sen. Oct 18 Canterbury. Apr 19 Rlsd.
WHITE, Albert – (A) FSB. Apr 18 Knutsford Settlement. July 18 Knutsford. Oct 18 Excep. Emp.
WILCOCKS, E.P. – (A) B'ham, Nov 16 LLandeussant Water Works. Aug 17 Llandeussant WW. Oct 17 Dorchester CP 2sen (2yrs HL). Jan 18 Dorchester CP. April 18 Dorchester CP 3sen.
WOOTTON, G.H. – Bv. Aug 17 Wakefield Work Centre. Apr 16 LT. Oct 17 Wakefield WC. Jan 18 Wakefield WC. Apr 18 Wakefield. July 18 Exceptionally Employed.

Birmingham men still in the Hands of the Civil and Military Authorities at 9 May 1918, but of whom no further details are known. (Source: List at Friends Library London):

	Prison	Sentence
BANWELL, O.W.	Warwick	2nd
BENTON, J.W.	Portsmouth	2nd
BROADBEER, A.F.	Oxford	3rd
GRIFFIN, W.G.	Canterbury	4th
GUNTON, T.	Ipswich	3rd
JOHNSON, T.	Pentonville	–
JOHNSON, H.	Leicester	2nd
LOOK, H.W.	Winchester	4th
LOOK, W.	–	5th ?
REECE, E.W.	Newcastle	3rd ?
SMITH, H.	Wormwood Scrubs	1st
TURNER, W.E.	Winson Green	3rd

Appeared before Local Tribunals:
BASSON, Gilbert – Bham Mar 16 ECS.
BENTON, Geo. L. – Bv. Mar 16 Abs Exemp.
BLUMSON, W.A. – Stirch. Apr 16 – Cond. joining FAU.
BURTON, Geo. L. – Bv. Mar 16 Def.6 months (age).
DEARDON, J.W. – B'ham. Apr 16 Cond. join FAU.
GALLIMORE, E.S. – Moseley Rd. Mar 16. Cond. on undertaking War Relief.
GAYNOR, – Bull St. Mar 16. Cond on joining FAU.
GRAYLAND, Albert Edward – Bv. Nov 16 Cond. asked Cond granted. Ref. to Pelham Comm.
HICKMAN, E.J. – Apr 16 Cond join FAU.
HONICK, F.A. – B'ham Apr 16 ECS.
HODDGETTS, Jesse, – Bv. Nov 16 Cond asked Cond 1m. on joining FAU.
JESPER, A. – B'ham Mar 16 ECS.
JESPER, Wilfred – B'ham. Apr 16 Cond retain present Employment. (ILP)
LAND, J.W.C. – Bv. Mar 16 Exempt on badge.
LUNT, – Moseley Rd. Mar 16 ECS.
MACDONALD, Cecil – (A) SO. Nov 16 Abs. asked Con 1m given on engaging in work of nat.imp.
MARLOW, Fredk. C. – Bull St.
MASON, Robt. W. – SO. Nov 16 Abs asked Cond granted on continuing present empl.
NICKALLS, J.L. – Cott. Mar 16 Cond. remains with War Victims.
NURSE, Edmund. – Bv Apr 16 ECS.
OYSTON, Maurice – B'ham Apr 16 Cond.join FAU.
PATCHING, G.A. – Bull St. Mar 16 Abs. Exemp.
ROWNTREE, W. – B'ham. Mar 16 Deferred 2 weeks.
SEARS, H.G. – Bv. Apr 16 ECS.
STREET, Arthur E. – B'ham. Mar 16 Cond. on Health Grounds.
WALLIS, Henry R. – Bordesley Green Mar 16 Cond.on remaining in YMCA work.
WHITTAKER, Bb. – Mar 16 ECS.
WOODHEAD, H. – Bull St. Mar 16 Exempt 1 month on business grounds.

Court Martialled and Sentenced at Budbrooke or Lichfield Bks. but not identifiable as Birmingham men:
J. Arblaster, P. Coe, C. Deward, T.H. Pinfield (possibly A.H. Pinfield?), E. Woodward, S. Chiles, H. Dickason, A. Routley, Bird brothers, W.H. Jones, W. Ridley, R.C. Smith, G.A. Smith, L.J. Adams, G.O. Aston, G.R. Aston, L. Homes, A.E. Morley, R. Pond, Passant.

Friends Ambulance Unit 1914-19:
A list was drawn up in 1938 of all known people who served in the Friends Ambuland Unit. It is published in G.W. Young – *The Story of the FAU.* A copy is in Woodbrooke Library at F51.5. It lists 64 Birmingham men, only five of whom appear in the CO lists above. It is not known how many were registered conscientious objectors, but apart from over-age men, it must be assumed that most of them were COs.

National Statistics – Conscientious Objectors:
Total COs – 16,500 approx.
Number who resisted Military Service Acts – 6,312
Number of Men Court-Martialled – 5,790
655 men were court- martialled twice, 521 three times, 321 four times, 50 five times, 3 six times.
Number of Absolutists who served 2 years or more in prison – 843
Number of Men accepting work under Home Office schemes – 3,612

Chapter 14

Trade Unions in the Black Country 1914-1918

Outbreak of war

When the European War was unleashed in August 1914, the Labour Party was committed to the Socialist International resolution of 1907 which stated that if war broke out it was the duty of all Socialists in all countries 'to bring it promptly to an end.' The attitude of the Wolverhampton Trades Council had been determined by a resolution in 1913:

> That this Trades Council, believing that war is an enemy to human progress, emphatically declares itself against the growth of militarism nd heartily approves of the International Committee or Bureau, composed of representatives of various countries who, in the event of war being threatened, shall meet and come to an agreement whereby united action could be taken, so that in the event of war being declared between two or more countries the workers of the countries affected would be prepared to hinder it by a mutual and simultaneous stoppage of work.

However, when war broke out, all the European Socialist parties (except the Russian Bolsheviks) repudiated these vows and joined their own governments in support of the war. This included both the British Labour Party and the TUC.

The main resolution passed by Wolverhampton Trades Council on 31st. August 1914 did not express direct support for the war, but support for the recruiting campaign for the army that was to wage it:

> That having given full consideration to the decision of the national Labour Party to join in a campaign to strengthen the British army, this Trades Council hereby registers its approval of that decision and agrees to assist in carrying it into effect. It further agrees to place the Labour Assembly Rooms at the disposal of the organisers of the national campaign and urges all young men who are free from family responsibilities to give earnest consideration to the national appeal for their services.

Another resolution urged workers to 'stand by their organisations' to maintain trade union standards of wages and hours. Yet another resolution complained of the 'shameful attempts to debar Labour representation' from the local Citizens' Committee on which only 18 of the 144 members represented Labour and from an executive of 26 only one represented Labour. Thus both the trade union movement and the Labour Party in Wolverhampton became fully committed to the war.

It is to be assumed that all other Trades Councils in the Black Country also supported the war. Walsall is the only local Trades Council for which minutes have survived, but those for 1914 and 1915 are, unfortunately missing. However, a newspaper report of the annual general meeting in January 1916 shows both the extent of support for the war and also some of the tensions that were to weaken that support. The annual report of the secretary, G. Giles, stated:

> We owe a great debt to the sacrifices made by members attached to the Trades Council, one union enlisting 186 of its members. Some have laid down their lives, others have been maimed... Hats off to

the Staffords. We must assist the country to combat the devilish Prussian military machine... Walsall has been spoken of as a town reaping a golden harvest, but (this cannot apply) to workers not able to obtain sufficient to keep their families in decency. (It is) sheer impudence for ministers drawing £90 a week to ask labour leaders to discourage demands for higher wages when food prices have increased by 45 per cent.

The part played by this Council regarding recruiting stands out in bold opposition to the advocates of conscription.

The other Black Country Trades Councils existing at this time can be listed giving their dates of origin: Wednesbury (1875), West Bromwich (1891), Stourbridge (1901), Smethwick (1904), Bilston (1911), Willenhall (1911) and Tipton (1913). In addition, the war stimulated further trades councils and Oldbury (1915), Dudley (re-formed in 1916, date of origin 1897) and Halesowen (1918) all appeared during the war years.

At the beginning of the war mass unemployment was a main fear. Local committees were set up to alleviate distress with funds from the Prince of Wales' Fund. For some weeks unemployment was serious. An extreme example was that of Hobsons, in Wolverhampton. Here, the demand for carburetters for civilian aircraft disappeared overnight. Men were sacked and the works almost completely closed. Yet within a few weeks the firm was making carburetters for military aircraft the demand for which was unlimited.

The Workers' Union and Inter-Union Conflict

For the Workers' Union 1914 was a year of consolidation as the final 1/-d. from the Great Unrest became due bringing the minimum wage for labourers to 24/-d. a week; although the organiser, W.M. Adamson reported that, 'In a number of cases it has been necessary to put the Strike into operation to enforce the claim for better wages and conditions.'

As the war progressed, friction developed between the general unions and the skilled unions. This came to a head in 1917 when the short-lived prerogative of the skilled unions to issue Trade Cards of exemption from military service was in operation. A midlands conference in March of Worker's Union representatives from Birmingham and the Black Country, together with delegates from the Amalgamated Gasworkers, National Union of General Workers, and the more skilled unions of Carpenters & Joiners, Coachmakers, and Heating & Domestic Engineers, met to discuss the injustice of the engineering unions, notably the ASE, being able to issue exemption cards to all their members, some of whom were less skilled than men in the general unions. Such a privilege meant that the skilled unions were recruiting men who would normally join the general unions, and were indeed 'poaching' existing members.

The controversy was accompanied with some nasty accusations of men joining unions because 'they offer a safe shelter to men who would do anything to save their skin', and men who would be able to 'see his mother each night and go to the kinema and football matches; have his slippers warmed and a cosy bed to sleep in where, in his drowsy moments, he could think of Tommy Atkins...wearing a dish-like hat and standing in the trenches, and solemnly promise himself that his pals should have the biggest cheer he was capable of when they came back to the shop when it was all over.' Such accusations were not unconnected with the increasingly jingoistic position that Workers' Union leaders were adopting at this time against the growing 'pacifist' feelings after 1916.

From 1916 Workers' Union annual reports were abbreviated to save paper and news of recruitment and wage negotiation transferred to the monthly newspaper *Workers' Union Record*. But the complexities of negotiations between munitions workers working in munitions factories controlled by the government (the best paid), munitions workers in privately owned factories where other work might be civilian work, and factories wholly engaged in civilian work (usually the lowest paid) were such that no general picture of wage increases emerges. The one general statistic is that wages rose slightly less than the cost of living during the war.

Nor can the growth of Black Country trade unionism during the war be satisfactorily determined. Reports in the Workers' Union Record for March 1918 detailed branches in the West Bromwich district totalling nearly 1,700 members in twelve branches and the information that they were looking for a site for a Trade Union Working Men's Club. The next month a report from Wolverhampton showed that the Workers' Union membership had increased from 1,000 in June 1916 to 6,000. But complete figures are missing.

The Amalgamated Society of Engineers

Reports from the main skilled union, the Amalgamated Society of Engineers, are more enlightening, as there are monthly reports for almost every month of the war. The organiser for Division No.8 (from 1916 No.9) for most of the war was the Smethwick councillor George Ryder. But the division covered most of the midlands as far north as Crewe and south to Hereford and Worcester. However, most of the Black Country was within the Wolverhampton ASE district and some information is available. Ryder complained throughout the war of problems of negotiating with Black Country employers. In May 1915 he stated that there were three Employer Associations 'whose demands do not agree with each other and a large number of employers belong to none with their own ideas of wages and conditions.' Of the workers he wrote, 'I hope before my superannuation to convince some of the chaps in outside shops to put a proper evaluation on their abilities which is about 20-50 per cent more than they get at present.

By the end of 1915 Ryder was complaining that Black Country employers were prolonging negotiations beyond the end point of ASE procedure (which was a Central Conference at York) registering 'failure to agree' and referring the matter to the Committee of Munitions.

Wage rates in Birmingham continued to be higher than in the Black Country and in 1916 an ultimately unsuccessful effort was made to incorporate Blackheath, Old Hill, Halesowen and Cradley Heath in the Birmingham district to take advantage of these higher wages. The Ministry of Munitions, however, decreed that these areas should be in the Wolverhampton district.

During 1916 Ryder was faced with problems arising from specially built munitions factories such as the National Projectile Factory at Dudley and the National Fuse Factory at Tipton. Instead of these being controlled by the Ministry of Munitions they were administered by Harper, Son and Bean.

Excessive working hours were causing both absenteeism and unrest. By April 1916 Ryder was reporting 'an appreciable reduction in excessive overtime and week-end work,' arising from the report of Sir George Newman of the Health of Munitions Committee which argued that shorter hours might increase rather than decrease productivity.

Some social activity also went on. In March Ryder attended the Wolverhampton reunion which he reported as becoming larger each year. 1,500 attended and those without tickets had been unable to gain admittance. The next year 1,200 attended. In August the annual meeting of superannuated members was also reported as bigger than ever. 170 old members had been taken for a 25 mile drive to the Severn at Stourport. One was over 90 and his membership 'dated back before the Amalgamation' (i.e.1851). 'Another young fellow of 78 had been on the night shift at a large motor works and had done a 13 hour shift before joining us.'

On 1 May new regulations regarding war service badges and exemptions came into force and caused problems. In September it was holiday problems. The Midland Employers' Federation was 'flouting an agreement between the unions and the Engineering Employers' Federation which they usually observe.... Under normal conditions we would have struck. Attempts to take advantage of our reluctance (to strike) are particularly contemptible.'

In October Ryder reported 'a growing tendency for recruiting officers and industrial firms to think they can arrange matters without considering the wider machinery and the officers of the Minister of Munitions.'

By the end of 1916 the manpower situation was so chaotic that in November Ryder wrote:

I have been in constant trouble on matters arising from the vexed question of the position of skilled men in relation to the army. In reply to an anxious enquiry in the House of Commons the Rt. Hon. Mr Tennant could only venture that "God knows". Omniscience might suffice to answer the questions put by employers and members, but certainly would not make the answers tally. There is nothing in Holy Writ, the circulars issued by the Ministry of Munitions, and the conversation of recruiting authorities, or the decisions of tribunals, which enables one to give an opinion with authority. We have been officially instructed that certificated men are exempt from military service, but they are taken into the army. We are told there is a dearth of skilled men, and yet toolmakers are taken from the tool room of a national projectile factory, and the manager is informed that he can apply for their release. Men with years of training are removed from important munitions work, and others of military age and fitness waste time, money and material in trying to do the same job.

If it is the intention of the government to get the wrong man in the wrong place they are getting very able assistance.

In November 1916 Wolverhampton district was granted a 3/-d. increase on time rates plus 2½ per cent. Ryder wrote rather wearily, 'This necessitates again looking up the whole of Black Country employers who are notoriously evasive when asked for money.'

Some light on wage rates in the district does emerge at the end of the year when Ryder reported that the larger firms were paying 42/-d. on a 53 hour week instead of 32/-d. for a 56½ hour week. These two rates might therefore be taken as maximum and minimum for skilled men on time rates.

With Conscription having been introduced at the beginning of the year and the chaotic state of affairs described by Ryder at the end, the government faced considerable industrial unrest. It therefore appointed a Commission of Enquiry into Industrial Unrest. Its findings were published in July 1917. Wolverhampton Trades Council, the S. Staffs & Worcs Federation of Trades Councils and Cradley Chainmakers Association all gave evidence, and three of the Commission's 27 sittings were held in Wolverhampton.

The Commission identified the main areas of discontent as Conscription, the Trade Card System, the loss of trade union liberties, dilution of labour, leaving certificates, decreased differentials between skilled and unskilled men, rising food prices, liquor restrictions, industrial fatigue, and relations of employers and employed. It made a series of the most anodyne proposals for most of these ills. Only on the question of food prices was it militant, identifying it as the most urgent problem and demanding immediate reductions in food prices and a rigid check on profiteering. Neither of these proposals was attended to and the industrial problems of 1916 were summarised by George Ryder in his January 1917 ASE Report:

> 1916 has been full of trouble and hard work. Thank God it's over. The war, wages questions, dilution, substitution, debadging, the Military Service and Munitions Acts, the Tribunals and Arbitration Courts, the strange needs and duties of the time, with all the changes they have wrought in our outlook and work, accompany us into the New Year, and we have to do the best we can with the problems yet to face.

Unevenness of war work and leaving certificates were particular problems in 1917. In January about 40 ASE members in Cradley Heath had put in notices to leave 'in firms which refused to pay up' and had been granted leaving certificates. Usually when work was slack, workers were compelled to stay because the firm wanted to keep them and leaving certificates were refused. In March, temporary slackness was again emphasised with the 'annoyance it caused when men cannot get a discharge.'

Relations with employers in the Wolverhampton district remained fraught. In April Ryder reported that the Wolverhampton Engineering Federation 'always last ditchers' had contested the toolmakers rate and lost at the Munitions Tribunal. In June Ryder complained that a great deal of his time was occupied in trying to implement a national award as it affected youths of 18 to 20 in non-federated and uncontrolled establishments, the great bastions of low pay. Ryder exploded in August when he reported that the Midlands Employers' Federation to which 'all the ragtag and bobtail of the midlands trade' belongs and with which 'it was almost impossible to get any sort of decent uniformity of rates and conditions', had renamed itself the National Employers' Federation. 'Skilled men who meet these people in any part of the country will be well advised to resist their pretensions,' Ryder went on, and added that in Birmingham they were refusing to have any kind of agreement with firms in the National Employers' Federation which refused to observe the rates and conditions agreed with the Engineering Employers' Association.

In the autumn Ryder reported that 'the laggards were just getting round to implementing the last award as the new one is announced'. In October Ryder was sufficiently disillusioned to write,

'Stragglers must be dealt with by the men concerned. Employers will never pay up while men continue to work at the old rate.'

In November Ryder reported strikes in Birmingham and Coventry over recognition of shop stewards. There were no stoppages in Wolverhampton, but shop steward organisation was being developed.

One of Ryder's last acts as secretary of No.9 Division was to visit France at the invitation of the Admiralty. He paid glowing tributes to the cheerfulness and steadfastness of the British troops. But by this time Ryder was sufficiently affected by the growing feeling in the Labour movement that the war had gone on long enough, to be unable to bring himself to urge renewed support for the war, which was the intention behind the many invitations to trade union delegations to visit the front at the time, and to which Julia Varley had succumbed.

George Ryder relinquished office in November 1917 and his successor was not appointed until May 1918. During those vital months there were no reports from the Midlands division. The new organiser was C.R. Bates operating from Crewe. By June he was deeply immersed in Wolverhampton District affairs. Members at Harper Son & Bean together with its national factory outposts of Projectile at Dudley and Fuse at Tipton were demanding time and a half for Saturday work. This was being dealt with through the Ministry of Munitions and dates for Conferences were awaited. There were also problems at the Horseley Engineering Co. where a 1/-d. advance granted by the Committee on Production the previous December was not being implemented because the firm claimed that it paid over the district rate.

Shortage of labour, or determination to keep wage rates down had, unwisely, led the Horseley Engineering Co. to introduce Chinese labour. At first one was set on a planing machine. Bates asked for his removal. The firm then offered to pay the full rate to keep these men. Bates again refused. The outcome of this unusual case is not known, but the war was soon to end and there then was to be plenty of English labour available.

Meanwhile the dispute at the National factories had become enmeshed in other issues and a strike occurred at the National Fuse Factory in Tipton. This was over the arbitrary sacking of eighteen skilled men and their replacement by 5 discharged soldiers at 9d. per hour (39/9d. for a 53 hour week). A Conference between the firm and the Ministry of Munitions resulted in the rate of 81/-d. plus 7½ per cent being established for the ex-soldiers!

There was also a strike at Rubery Owen in Darlaston in October. This arose from a new costing system introduced by the firm. This went to a Conference, but the proposals were rejected by the men. Again the ultimate outcome is unknown as the war ended the next month.

But there was clearly a greater inclination to take industrial action towards the end of the war, either from frustration or increased militancy. Militancy is confirmed by a local Conference in August which requested the higher Birmingham rate and conditions for the Wolverhampton district. A local Conference with employers inevitably registered 'failure to agree' and the matter went to York. The source of this militancy might well be traced to the development of the shop stewards movement in the district with whom Bates recorded 'a splendid meeting' in October. Unfortunately there is no indication of the factories in the Wolverhampton district where shop steward organisation developed. But the *Wolverhampton Chronicle* report of the threatened strike of December 1917 for the recognition of the shop stewards movement specifically mentions, the 'important centres' of Coventry and Birmingham, Wolverhampton, Dudley and Walsall.

The next month Bates recorded the ending of the war. But with immediate unemployment there was neither time nor inclination for extended celebrations.

For Birmingham and the Black Country we can trace the growth of the Amalgamated Society of Engineers. Thus between December 1914 and December 1918 membership (branches in brackets where more than one) rose as follows:

Birmingham: (15) 3767 – (28) 11095
Wolverhampton: (4) 1332 – (6) 2463
Smethwick: (3) 721 – (4) 1328
Bilston 32 – 72

Oldbury 238 – 326
West Bromwich 126 – 348
1918 only (no branch in 1914)
Langley 187

Dudley 99 – 321	Old Hill 311
Walsall 46 – 129	Darlaston 180
Wednesbury 99 – 106	Great Bridge 315
	Willenhall 58.

These figures have been calculated from ASE returns and no guarantee of absolute arithmetical accuracy is given. They do, however, illustrate several interesting points. ASE membership in Birmingham increased threefold during the war. In the Black Country it increased $2^{1}/_{4}$ times. ASE membership in Birmingham was always higher than in the Black Country. Increases in membership in the two main Black Country engineering towns of Wolverhampton and Smethwick increased almost equally at about 85 per cent. The largest increase was $3^{1}/_{4}$ times in Dudley, but from a low base and the fact that two national munitions factories were in the area, the performance is not impressive. Walsall and West Bromwich increased about equally at more than $2^{1}/_{2}$ times, but again from a low base.

It cannot therefore be claimed that membership of the ASE, the main engineering union for skilled men, increased spectacularly in the Black Country during the war years, when the unions possessed unrivalled power.

Trades Councils – Walsall

Of the Trades Councils of the Black Country during the war, minutes exist only for Walsall and these only from 1916. Walsall was one of the more militant Trades Councils, but the range of matters dealt with was similar to that of the other Trades Councils of the area.

Much of the work was 'political' in defence of civil liberties. This inevitably involved the question of the Council's attitude to the war. Giles report at the 1916 AGM (already quoted) with its emphasis on 'crushing the devilish Prussian military machine' suggests unqualified support for the war, but the actual situation was more complex than that. For instance in March 1916, following the introduction of Conscription, the Trades Council protested at the treatment of the British Socialist Party, the Independent Labour Party, the Union of Democratic Control and the No-Conscription Fellowship at the hands of the Property Committee of the town council in refusing the use of the town hall for meetings of these anti-Conscription bodies. In May the Council protested at the imprisonment and removal to other parts of the country of the Clyde shop stewards and trade union leaders. The same month the Council endorsed, with only two against, a resolution passed at a National Council against Conscription meeting in Birmingham protesting against Conscription. This castigated Conscription as 'A conspiracy against the social, industrial and political advancement of the British people and more concerned with crushing British democracy than crushing Prussian militarism.'

However, in June the trades council received a visit from the local MP Sir Richard Cooper and, as a result manifestoes of the British Workers' National League were to be obtained. Both Cooper and the BWNL were patriotic and jingoistic. The same month a communication was received from a Peace Negotiating Committee. It was resolved that 'no action be taken at this time.'

In August, a speaker was accepted from the National Council for the Restoration of Civil Liberties. At the same meeting a resolution from the Russian Socialist Group in London was supported. This condemned the proposed compulsory mobilisation into the British army of Russian political and religious refugees. These refugees should continue to have rights of asylum and be permitted to go to destinations of their choice.

Civil liberties were also involved in a resolution that trade union officials should not be called up. This was to prevent the victimisation of 'awkward' shop stewards who were liable to be sacked, lose their protected status, and then be called-up. Before the end of the year one of the trades councils' own leading members was concerned when John Whiston was called up. His services were recognised by recording that he had co-ordinated the Great Strike in Walsall in 1913, had been the Workers' Union representative at the largest Walsall tube works for two years, then Workers' Union organiser for the Walsall-Dudley area, and had been the Walsall Trades Council secretary for two years. He had been called-up into the S. Staffs. regiment. The matter of his call-up was raised at Trades Council, but the chair ruled that the matter could not be discussed. In October Adult Suffrage was approved at the instigation of the local National Union of Women's Suffrage Societies.

The question of food prices occupied much time in 1916. In June there was a public open-air meeting at Town End Bank to protest at the cost of living. Here, support for a London Trades Council resolution that 'the government take control of the necessaries of life' was registered and 'the Conscription of Wealth' added. The president Joseph Thickett was elected delegate to a Conference in London on this subject. Sacrifices were evidently to be demanded of the inmates of the Workhouse, and in October the trades council objected to the proposal to deprive the inmates 'of their customary Christmas fare.' In November a call for a town's meeting on the food situation proposed by an NUR delegate was approved.

Representation on local committees in the town was sometimes important and sometimes not. In July delegates were elected to the Naval & Military Pensions Committee and also its executive as well as representatives on the Rents sub-Committee, the Midlands Industrial Council and the Prince of Wales Executive. The trades council secretary, G. Giles was a member of the local Pensions Committee and reported in November on the importance of the Labour Exchange finding work for discharges soldiers and sailors. But no representatives were elected to the War Savings Committee, 'The cost of living leaving no margin for workers to save', it was asserted. On the question of Pensions, the trades council supported the demand that pensions be paid to 'Little Mothers' i.e. daughters who assume financial and other responsibilities for a family where the mother dies and the father is serving in the forces.

During 1917 the food position worsened. In April an 'emphatic protest' was registered at 'the continued exploitation of workers in regard to the supply of essential commodities, beer included', and called for the resignation of the Food & Liquor Control Board. An amendment called on the Board of Trade to control all food prices 'to enable the poorer classes to obtain the necessaries of life, even if this means subsidising the trader for any loss'. It was also requested that the recently formed local Food Committee should set up Communal Kitchens 'to provide adequate supplies of food at reasonable cost.' In May a Food Vigilante Committee was set up by the local labour movement and regular reports of its activities given to the trades council. It dealt with such issues as widespread food adulteration, overseeing the local food distribution system (a national scheme of food rationing was only implemented in the very last months of the war). The beer question remained important. The restricted licensing hours imposed during the war seem to have been accepted as desirable and essential, but shortages of beer were resented. At a comprehensive discussion in August, the Food Controller was requested to review the town's delivery system and the licensing authority's attention was drawn to the fact that publicans were serving only their favoured customers and that Outdoor departments were being closed, forcing women into pubs who otherwise would not enter them. By December the long food queues were creating problems. The Vigilantes Committee called a special meeting from which letters were sent to the chief constable demanding that women and children in food queues be treated with equal respect, and the Tradesmen's Association was similarly requested to instruct members and assistants on equal treatment. This meeting also called for an immediate rationing system to be imposed.

Pensions was another much discussed matter in 1917. In January a replacement for Whiston was elected to the War Pensions Committee and correspondence discussed from the Old Age Pensions Committee. The next month this committee's complaint to the local authority that no case could be made out for paying Walsall pensioners less than the national scale, was supported. In November George Heafield, who had taken Whiston's place on the War Pensions committee was supported in his call for the resignation of the secretary of this committee over an unrevealed matter. Rents also continued to give concern. Cases were up taken, and sometimes won, under the Rent & Mortgages Act. Late in the year it was requested that Rent Controls be continued for two years after the war. Education, both existing and post-war was attended to. In September there was a protest at the use of Walsall teachers for a Sugar Registration Scheme. 'Teaching staffs in our schools are inadequate to fulfill their present duties', it was claimed. There were also protests at an Education Bill dealing with post-war education not being passed in the House of Commons. In September two delegates from the trades council attended a two day Conference at Ruskin College, which, at the time, was a leading advocate of a radical post-war education system.

Much of the rest of business at Walsall Trades Council in 1917 was connected with civil liberties and its attitude to the war. In March a London Trades Council resolution dealing with spying on the Labour movement was supported. It called for the withdrawal of regulations permitting competent naval, military or police authorities to attend private meetings or assemblies as an abuse of the Defence of the Realm Acts. Protests were also made when yet another secretary of Walsall Trades Council was called up. This time it was Evison. Victimisation was claimed on the grounds that the secretary of the Employers' organisation was exempt. But again the protests did not get very far.

Land Nationalisation was a natural demand at a time when the food supply was being expanded and some local authorities were buying land. Heafield attended a Land Nationalisation Conference in Birmingham in February. There was also a joint meeting between the trades council and the local Co-operative Society's education committee on the same subject in August.

A local branch of the National Association of Discharged Sailors and Soldiers was established early in the year and in March the Trades Council gave it their support. A deputation from the organisation attended the August Trades Council meeting; by this time it was called the National Union of Ex-Servicemen.

In June 1917 there was an early reference to support for the National Union of Police and Prison Officers. This organisation had been formed in 1912, and grew rapidly during the war years. Its activities culminated in the great Police Strike of 1919 when the union was crushed.

The attitude of Walsall Trades Council to the war was first considered in June when correspondence from the Sailors' and Firemen's Union requested support for its policies. The first of these was a demand that the British government give restitution to the relatives of all British and allied seamen 'murdered by submarines.' A second matter was support for its policy of refusing to carry any delegates to Russia unless they agreed that no settlement with Germany be made until it agreed to full restitution for the murders committed. The matter was nicely put to gain patriotic support. But the real question at issue was the recent refusal of Havelock Wilson's union to carry a Labour Party delegation, containing both Arthur Henderson and Ramsay MacDonald to an international conference. At first a motion was put to the trades council that the Seaman's Union action be supported. This was countered by a proposal that the matter lie on the table. This was defeated and a full-scale discussion ensued. The outcome was a motion that regretted the action of the Seaman's Union, and while not associating themselves with the actions of Ramsay MacDonald and his party, regarded the Union's action as 'not in the best interests of free speech.' This was passed by 45 votes to 3, indicating a large turnout of delegates.

Also in July, a motion must have been passed to send a delegate to the Birmingham district conference arising from the Leeds Conference in June where the setting up of Workers' and Soldiers' Councils in Britain had been approved, for at the August trades council meeting a motion to rescind this decision was defeated by 23 votes to 21. The Birmingham Conference did not take place. It was banned by the police. But Walsall joined the other Black Country trades councils that registered delegates to attend. These trades councils were Oldbury, Smethwick, Stourbridge, Wednesbury and West Bromwich. The non-registering trades councils were Wolverhampton, Dudley, Bilston, Brierley Hill, Rowley Regis, Tipton, and Willenhall.

After the banning of the Birmingham Conference a motion of protest was put to Walsall Trades Council, but a resolution to take no further action was passed by 20 votes to 6.

1918 was again dominated by the food question. Henry Skeets and Mrs C. Adams were both on the local Food Control Committee and the Trades Council's Food Vigilante Committee. Monthly reports of both Committees were given to the fortnightly Trades Council meetings. The two committees seemed to have worked amicably on most issues and in March the Food Control Committee wrote to the trades council congratulating it on the work of the Vigilantes Committee. The Vigilantes Committee was used to help get a fair share of supplies to the Co-op.

One of the main issues for both Committees was profiteering, although this matter first came to the Trades Council from the newspaper trade where a newly-formed Newsagents' Society successfully sought the help of the Trades Council against the 'monopolist newspaper wholesalers' of the town. As usual, when prosecutions did take place it was usually the small shop keeper rather than the real monopolist who suffered and the Trades Council was perfectly capable of defending the retailers when necessary; as in the case of a Mr G. Belo and his assistant who were fined in June for overcharging for bacon. The Trades Council demanded an enquiry into the case as 'entirely against the weight of evidence'. Profiteering was also behind the case of the great meat monopoly the Swift Beef Co. In May the trades council congratulated the local Food Committee for refusing to permit Swift's to distribute frozen meat to local butchers and insisting that it should be distributed through the local Butcher's Advisory Committee. It followed this with a resolution confirming its action against a trust which 'does not wholly look after the general interests of the community.' A final compromise decision from the national Director of Meat Supplies was that those butchers who wished to get their supplies through the local Meat Advisory Committee could do so, and those who preferred to get their meat from the Meat Importers' Committee could do that. This decision brought an effusive letter of thanks from the Walsall Butchers' Association which thought it owed the Trades Council 'a deep debt of gratitude', as its resolution 'had very great weight in bringing this important and critical matter to a satisfactory settlement.'

Another issue on which the two local committees seemed to have functioned together was the question of supplementary rations for workers performing heavy physical labour. The matter merged with that of Municipal Kitchens when Lloyd George allowed preferential canteen facilities in munitions factories in an unsuccessful attempt to split off munitions workers from others. An Arduous Work sub-committee was formed in Walsall and surfaced at the Trades Council in April when the sub-Committee pointed out that the Trades Council had appointed two miners, whereas they had been asked for a miner and an ironworker. The same Trades Council meeting passed a resolution deploring the fact that workers in controlled factories were allowed to have meat every day whereas other heavy manual workers were not. In May the women weighed in when a report of the Arduous Work Sub-Committee at Trades Council heard that representation had been made for women doing the work of men receiving supplementary rations.

Communal kitchens first came to the notice of the Trades Council in April when it was reported that Henry Skeet and others had gone to inspect a municipal kitchen in Nottingham and found it little better than a soup kitchen. After a discussion it was resolved to support a Communal Kitchen, but only 'one which was suitable for rich and poor alike.' By September the local Food Committee seems to gone off the idea of such kitchens, but the Trades Council passed a resolution stating that a National Kitchen was necessary in Walsall and asking the Food Ministry for assistance in establishing one.

Educational matters dealt with by the trades council in 1918 included a plea from the Uncertificated Teachers' Union for parity of treatment with certificated teachers which sounded plausible and was supported, but had to be withdrawn when the National Union of Teachers intervened to put the wider case of teachers in general. Henry Skeets was appointed to the town Education Committee in May.

Some progress was made on rents. In May the trades council resolved that the Rents Sub-Committee in the city be re-formed with a view to forming a Tenants' League for Walsall and a public meeting was called. At this time there already existed a Birmingham Tenants' Federation and a Sparkhill Tenants' Association, the trades council was told.

With regard to industrial matters, the trades council was drawn into the question of peaceful relations after the war. In May the Ministry of Labour sent the Trades Council a leaflet on the Whitley Report on Joint Standing Industrial Councils, and also an Enquiry by the Ministry into existing Works' Committees (Shop Stewards) shortly to be on sale at price 6d. The trades council ordered six of these reports. In October the council heard Mr Jackson, the Labour organiser from the National Alliance of Employers and Employed. He was accompanied by Harry Bagley of the Wolverhampton Trades Council who said that a a vote was being taken of Wolverhampton members regarding the advisability of joining the NAE&E. Jackson was thanked for his report but it was decided to defer consideration until delegates knew more about the matter. On November 18 a letter was read from the Chamber of Commerce asking for a round table talk on the subject of better relations between Capital and Labour. The council responded and there was an informal conference.

Further contacts were agreed, but by then the war was over and the rest is the story of post-war industrial relations.

The part played by the Trades Council in nominating a candidate for the general election at the end of the war is perplexing. Joseph Thickett who was a local councillor as well as president of the trades council during the war was eventually put up as a late candidate. But the question of a candidate had been raised at the Trades Council as early as March when Thickett was put forward, but for some unexplained reason rejected.

Finally matters associated directly with the war and international relations can be considered. In January an officer from the South Staffs Volunteers attended the Trades Council appealing for volunteers. In February the council decided to support Tank Week in the town. In May a protest at the introduction of conscription in Ireland about which there was strong feeling in the labour movement was allowed to lie on the table, although an appeal the same month for Home Rule for India was supported. In July the Trades Council refused to send a delegate to a Birmingham Conference on the Secret Treaties. When the war ended the following resolution was passed:

> That this meeting of the Walsall Trades & Labour Council learns with the utmost pleasure that an armistice has been signed, and hopes that ere long an honourable peace will be agreed which will be to the benefit of all nations. It also wishes to place on record its high appreciation of the splendid valour of the British and Colonial troops (especially the 46th Division which includes Walsall men) also the troops of the Allies and hopes that the government will see to it that the men who have acted so nobly, receive their just reward.

Other Trades Councils

Details of membership and composition of other Black Country trades councils is available from a compilation issued by the Ministry of Labour early in 1918 as a 'confidential Blue Book'. This originated as a request to the TUC by the Ministry of Labour for the supply of addresses of local secretaries of trades unions to enable the Ministry to nominate trade unionists for service on local war pensions committees. The work was handed over to the Fabian Research Department (which became the Labour Research Department towards the end of the war) in the summer of 1916 and completed by the end of 1917. Every trades council was asked to compile a list of all local trade union branches (whether affiliated to the trades council or not) together with the number of members and the name and address of the branch secretary. The lists were compiled with varying degrees of thoroughness, but each Black Country trades council participated.

The biggest trades council in the area, Wolverhampton, provided a comprehensive list of trade union branches, but very few membership figures. Where figures are given they show three branches of the Toolmakers' Union affiliated with 870 members, and four out of nine Workers' Union branches affiliated with 2,000 members. The Sheet Metal Workers with 1,200 members were not affiliated. Other affiliated unions with large but undisclosed memberships were the three railway unions, five branches of the ASE, and municipal, tram etc. workers. From other sources it was estimated in 1918 that trade union membership in Wolverhampton during the war had risen from 5,000 to 20,000.

Dudley Trades Council, believed to have been formed in 1897, was re-formed in 1916. Its return was meticulously compiled and membership given for most branches. Totals showed just over 4,000 trade unionists in the town with almost 3,000 of these affiliated to the Trades Council. The largest component was the Dudley branch of the National Federation of Women Workers with 800 unaffiliated members. Th largest affiliated unions were the Workers' Union with almost 450 members and the Brassworkers with 400. A 1917 annual report gives 3,330 affiliated members.

West Bromwich was one of the older trades councils in the area (1891), but was not large and its return gave no membership figures at all. From its affiliated unions it seems to have been dominated by five Workers' Union branches and four Gas & Municipal Workers' Union.

Smethwick, founded in 1904, also failed to give membership figures. But it was a strong trades council based on four Foundry Workers' branches and four branches of the ASE.

Stourbridge (1901) produced good membership figures. Thy showed almost 2,300 affiliated members with over 1,000 Municipal & General Workers, nearly 700 railwaymen, and 250 NFWW women workers dominating the Trades Council.

Rowley Regis Trades Council was formed only in 1915. It produced good returns showing nearly 2,500 affiliated members dominated by the Miners' Protection Society with 1,700 members.

Willenhall Trades Council (1911) showed about 2,000 affiliated members, but it was essentially a one trade council, the Lock & Key Makers providing 1,600 of its members.

Oldbury Trades Council was also formed in 1915. It also produced good returns showing an affiliated membership of just over 1,000 the largest components being nearly 600 Workers' Union and over 300 ASE members.

Brierley Hill Trades Council was formed even later, in 1916. Its return showed almost 1,200 affiliated members with the two general unions (Workers' and Gas, Municipal & General) providing almost half the membership. It is noteworthy that neither the Miners nor BISAKTA (the iron and steel workers' union) were affiliated in this predominantly iron and coal town. It was true generally in the Black Country that these two basic trades were generally absent from the local trades' councils.

The Bilston Trades Council return suggests that less than 250 members were affiliated of whom 200 came from a Workers' Union branch. This trades council was founded in 1911 and merged with Wolverhampton in 1926.

Tipton Trades Council existed only from 1913 to 1916. It lived long enough to render a return, but there were no figures attached to it. Conversely, Halesown Trades Council was formed only in 1918. Somebody provided the names of trade union branches in the town, but no membership figures were given.

It is clear from the above that trades council activity grew considerably during the war, and towards the end of the war a South Staffordshire and Worcester Federation of Trades Councils came into existence. But neither trades council activity nor trade union membership seems to have expanded as fast as either the opportunities or the necessities of wartime demanded.

Bibliography: Trade Unions in the Black Country 1914-1918

Very little remains on record of the heroic and tragic events of 1914-18 to which Black Country people and industries contributed. Records of the various civilian Committees and Tribunals such as Production, Conscription, Food, Pensions, etc. which gave a democratic gloss to the local war efforts have disappeared, in some cases deliberately destroyed. Rolls of honour of the military dead survive, some records of local regiments were compiled and some attempts made to record the deeds of those decorated for bravery.

In recent years, in response to a recent increased interest in local history in schools, both Walsall & Wolverhampton libraries have produced informative booklets on the first World War. For Black Country industrial history the most detailed is a history of Albright & Wilson who produced both chemicals and gases, R.E. Threlfall - *100 Years of Phosphorus Making*. Even the main industrial historian of the Black Country, G.C. Allen, could find little to write of World War 1.

For Trades Councils and dates of origins see Alan Clinton - *Trade Union Rank and File, Trades Councils in Britain 1900-40* (Manchester University Press) 1977 App 2. p.196.

For the Workers' Union see material at Modern Records Centre, Warwick University including annual reports; also *Workers' Union Record* from 1916, copy at Birmingham Reference Library and Richard Hyman - *The Workers' Union* (Clarendon Press) 1971.

For the Amalgamated Society of Engineers see material at AEEU headquarters, including monthly, quarterly and annual reports. Monthly Reports for the Midlands division were courtesy of the AEU Library at Peckham and Eddie Frow at the Working Class Movement Library at Salford.

Black Country details from the 1918 Board of Trade 'confidential Blue Book' giving details of trade union branches, their secretaries and membership were abstracted for me by Noreen Branson.

For other Trades Councils see: *A History of Wolverhampton Trades Union Council* - G.J. Barnsby (1994); 'The Re-formation of Dudley Trades Council' - G.J. Barnsby in *West Midlands Studies* vol 13, 1980; Walsall Trades Council Minutes, at Walsall Local History Centre.

Chapter 15

The Co-operative Movement in the Black Country 1914-1918

Progress and Problems

The general statistical position of all Co-operative Societies is recorded each year in the annual reports to the Co-operative Union Congress. The progress of the Black Country Societies during the war was as follows:

	1914	1915	1916	1917	1918
Dudley Co-operative Society					
Members	6816	6400	6741	7104	7115
Capital (£s)	9589	9678	10656	11273	13588
Sales (£s)	59259	69628	91513	124095	138588
Net Profit (£s)	6500	6814	9715	9873	8940
Average Divided (in £)	2/-d	1/10d	2/-d	1/6d	1/6d
Halesowen & Hasbury Co-op					
Members	1472	1472	1900	1906	1924
Capital	14167	14167	17422	16770	17141
Sales	35126	35126	42304	54096	59950
Net Profit (£s)	4099	4099	4341	1906	1693
Av. Divi. (in £)	–	–	1/9¼d	1/-d	6d
Soho (Smethwick) Co-op					
Members	6300	6806	8712	9320	9250
Capital (£s)	32610	41639	54028	62075	79649
Sales (£s)	128853	158491	213883	268698	285630
Net Profit (£s)	14961	17944	24176	23886	24332
Av. Divi. (in £)	2/-d	1/10½d	1/10½d	1/6½d	1/4d
Tipton Co-op					
Members	825	901	1051	1276	1314
Capital (£s)	5849	6387	6746	7790	8716
Sales (£s)	16422	22715	29656	43895	52773
Net Profit (£s)	1960	2819	3772	5124	6048
Av. Divi. (in £)	2/-d.	–	2/-d	2/-d	2/-d
Walsall Co-op					
Members	10124	11496	13462	14741	14043
Capital (£s)	67015	97259	114783	114475	12360
Sales	169550	230800	284394	332237	270036
Net Profit (£s)	21747	27917	33026	28255	25212
Av Divi (in £)	2/-d	2/-d	1/10d	1/3d	1/3d

Wednesbury (New) Co-op

Members	1120	1210	1440	1545	1608
Capital (£s)	7076	8738	9643	10802	18252
Sales (£s)	16300	19603	23064	34045	48902
Net Profit (£s)	1538	1842	2460	2794	4008
Av. Divi. (in £)	1/8½d	1/8¾d	1/8d	1/4½d	1/6d

Wolverhampton Co-op

Members	3879	5020	6251	6897	7015
Capital (£s)	33313	39794	49522	51758	68167
Sales (£s)	69512	109942	147300	155174	175762
Net Profit (£s)	10057	12185	13497	11213	12389
Av. Divi. (in £)	1/9¾d	1/10d	1/5½d	1/2¼d	1/4½d
Inflation	100	123	146	176	203

(Ministry of Labour Indices of Retail Prices – All Items.)

From the above figures it can be seen that Walsall was the largest Co-operative in the Black Country both with regard to membership and sales (although Soho sales exceeded Walsall in 1918 as a result of a very severe fall in sales in Walsall in that year). Soho was the second largest society followed by Wolverhampton. Dudley was the fourth largest society. Then came the Halesowen and Hasbury society followed by two small societies, Tipton and Wednesbury.

But with regard to increase in sales during the war the two smaller societies led the way with 321 per cent increase for Tipton and 300 per cent for Wednesbury. Wolverhampton's increase was 253 per cent, Dudley's 234 per cent and Soho's 222 per cent. Only Halesowen & Hasbury (171 per cent) and Walsall (159 per cent) failed to double their sales, the amount necessary to keep abreast of inflation. (The all items price index of the Ministry of Labour given above shows an increase from 100 in July 1914 to 203 in 1918).

All societies increased the number of their members during the war, the increases ranging from 180 per cent in Wolverhampton down to 104 per cent in Dudley. But membership was not necessarily an index of either efficiency or service. There were times during the war when societies discontinued recruitment of members in order to ensure fairness of distribution of supplies; at other times members left in large numbers when supplies were unfairly distributed to the societies. All societies operated policies of low prices and fair shares of available supplies. But such policies did not always bring new members or even satisfy old ones.

Share capital was the life blood of the Co-operative societies. Expansion was invariably financed from members' capital and loans from the Co-operative Wholesale Society. But the capital could be withdrawn at very short notice. The Co-operatives were therefore in much the same position as building societies which borrowed short, but lent long. Before the war this resulted in share capital receiving an interest rate of 5 per cent which was more favourable than any other savings source available to working people (and most other people as well). But the bane of all Management Committees was the shareholder who left his money in the Society for the interest, but refused to shop at the Co-op; these were not considered to be 'real' Co-operators.

With the war, new perils to Co-operative shareholdings appeared. Not only did the outbreak of war bring a surge in the buying of goods to hoard, but also the danger of withdrawal of capital on a large scale if public confidence in sources of savings was weakened. The Co-ops braced themselves for such an event, but it did not occur. No Society lost capital, although the increase in Dudley by the end of 1915 was only 1 per cent. The stationary Halesowen & Hasbury figure must be ignored as the same return for two years in the printed records must be a mistake. Other Societies had increases of 10 per cent to 20 per cent and Walsall led the way with a 45 per cent increase.

As the war proceeded another danger to capital arose. This was the increasingly high rates of interest offered on government stocks and loans. This does seem to have had an effect on Co-operative shareholdings. All Black Country societies increased their capital over the period 1914-18, but only Soho and Wednesbury substantially increased the real value of these savings, Wolverhampton broke even and the other Societies increased their capital by less than the rate of inflation.

There were considerable differences in the amounts of capital held by members. In 1914 the highest average share holding was at Halesowen & Hasbury with £9.62. This was followed by Wolverhampton at £8.59 and Tipton at £7.09. Three other Societies were between £5 and £6. But in Dudley the average share holding was only £1.40. By 1918 the highest average shareholding was at Wednesbury with £11.36. Wolverhampton was £9.72 and Walsall and Soho had increased holdings to £8 plus. Halesowen & Hasbury was £8.61, but this was a fall compared with 1914. Tipton also had fallen, to £6.63. Dudley had risen slightly but was still very much lower than other Societies at £1.90. None of the Societies, it will be noted, increased their average holdings by the rate of inflation.

With regard to dividends, the only Society managing to maintain dividends at 2/-d. in the pound throughout the war was Tipton. This was the smallest of the societies in the Black Country and this was achieved by distributing all profit as dividends. The other small society, Wednesbury, held its dividend fairly well from 1/8½d in 1914 to 1/6d in 1918, but like Tipton, its records are lost. Elsewhere, dividends were considerably reduced. This was caused both by falling profit margins as the price of foods was increasingly controlled by the government, and also by policies of deliberately cutting the dividend by holding prices down. We shall be able to follow these processes for the two large societies whose dividend was most affected, Walsall and Wolverhampton, from their quarterly reports.

Certain other information can be gleaned from these annual statistics printed in the Annual Co-operative Congress reports, although I have not given the details here. For instance the total wage bill and the number of employees is given from which one can calculate average wages. In 1914 these ranged from £73 per annum at Soho down to £42.50 at Tipton. By 1918 Soho was still paying the highest wages at £88.40 per annum. Tipton had risen to be the second highest payer at £80.60. Dudley and Halesowen & Hasbury each paid more than £71, but Wolverhampton paid only £68 with Walsall and Wednesbury at the bottom of the list with less than £61 per annum. It will be noted that none of these increases equalled the increase in the cost of living. However, we are not given the gender breakdown of these figures. In 1914, shopkeeping was a man's job. By 1918 most of these shop workers were women and girls. Co-operative workers would be paid trade union rates of pay and would be better off than many other shop workers. But if we take £71 as the average wage for a Co-operative work force predominantly female the resultant weekly wage of £1.37 is far removed from the alleged vast wages of women in wartime.

Midland District Co-operative Reports 1914-18

Co-operative Societies were grouped into Districts with a committee elected each year from member societies, which met to co-ordinate the activities of societies in the area. There were Black Country societies in both No.5 District Birmingham, and No.6 District Stafford. In the former were Dudley and Soho, with the remaining societies in Stafford district. Each Committee published an annual report which was also printed in the annual Co-operative Congress Report along with the statistics. It is to these reports that we next turn.

The 1914 Birmingham report stated:

> Never in the history of co-operation has the movement been subjected to so severe a test of the value of its principles as the year under review; and to say that in our own district it has stood the test nobly, really belittles the boon co-operation has proved to all classes of people in the great crisis which was, without warning thrust upon us. Not a town or village possessing a Co-operative store but has shown a tremendous lead in the steadying of prices of all commodities... Already the movement is reaping a rich reward from its straight dealing and some of our societies have had to record such great increases in membership as to make it really difficult to cope with the resultant increased trade.

As well as sharing in these membership increases, Soho was mentioned as having completed 'a magnificent new bakery and offices' which should ensure 'a tip top loaf'.

Another function of the Districts was to arrange a series of conference, usually every quarter, at one or other of the district societies. These discussed larger issues affecting all societies or matters raised at the national Congress. For these conferences national or regional figures of importance in the co-operative movement would usually open the discussion. Those attending would be activists in the societies, including the Women's Guild. In 1914 Birmingham District had arranged four such conferences, the last discussing Co-operation and the War Crisis.

The Stafford 1914 District Report made mention of the Walsall Society's 'phenomenal progress,' with 'remarkable progress' for most other societies. Wednesbury society was struggling with the problems of promoting co-operation in West Bromwich and 'better progress' was reported from its one branch in that town. Stafford District had also organised four Conferences. The first two mirrored peace-time concerns: 'Cash Trading & Emergency Funds', and 'Committees of Co-operative Societies and their Qualifications.' The other two concerned the war: 'Co-operative Policy during the War Crisis', and 'District Work – The Future Organisation & Development.'

These district committees functioned throughout the war with singularly little change of personnel. The two district secretaries were Frank Bruff of Birmingham and Henry Sanders of the Tamworth society. In the Birmingham district L. Evans represented Dudley in 1914 and 1915 to be replaced with A.H. Johnson for the rest of the war; Soho was represented by R. Hill in 1914 and A.W. Critchley in the last two years of the war. On the Stafford District committee, Sanders remained secretary and Wolverhampton, Walsall and Wednesbury were represented by the same individuals throughout the war, namely, A. Fulwood, H. Hilliard and W.J. Harris.

The 1915 Birmingham district report continued to report progress in membership. The old campaign against credit trading continued during the war and the hope expressed that 'No Credit' would soon be the general rule. By 1915 the question of closer relations with the trade unions and Labour Party was an important matter and one of the four Conferences in that year was devoted to this subject. The Stafford District reported 'pleasing progress' in 1915, 'notwithstanding many obstacles.' It singled out the progress of the 'cash trading societies.'

In 1916 Birmingham district reported a survey of its area to see where co-operation could be strengthened. It considered the worst served area was that where the boundaries of the two districts met, quoting the case of West Bromwich whose borders abutted Birmingham, but which had no society of its own. Little progress had been made, however, in this process of rationalisation. The Stafford district report elaborated on the 'many difficulties' reported the previous year and continuing – uncertainty and irregularity of the delivery of goods, depletion of staff and the substitution of less efficient labour in every department. Like Birmingham, it had continued to hold four conferences in the year. One of these had been held at West Bromwich to stimulate progress there. It reported that the Wednesbury society was making a special effort to re-establish co-operation in West Bromwich, and although it was an uphill fight, it now had four branches in the town. The fourth Conference had been on 'Agriculture and the Movement'; it resulted in a decision to consider the formation of a district agricultural society.

By 1917 Bruff was reporting the year as 'undoubtedly one of the most trying periods ever experience.' Quite the most important event, he considered, was the decision of the movement to enter directly the political field. 'Because of transport difficulties' only two conferences were arranged that year, one of them addressed by the Rev Arnold Pinchard was entitled the 'Opportunity & Responsibility of Democracy.'

Stafford district managed the usual four conferences in 1917. One was on 'Co-operation & Agriculture', the second on 'Some Weaknesses of Co-operation', the third on 'Shortages of Supplies, Cause and Remedies.' The fourth discussed 'Direct (Co-operative) Representation in Parliament and on other Public Bodies.' Walsall had joined with Cannock and neighbouring societies to secure a candidate at Lichfield 'in the Co-operative & Labour interest' at the post-war general election. A meeting had been held of Black Country societies in both districts to discuss the question of overlapping. After thorough discussion the unanimous decision was that 'amalgamation would not be acceptable or in the interests of our members at this juncture, but we shall, however, continue to work in harmony with each other and to co-ordinate our efforts and work towards a federation wherever practicable.'

The Birmingham district report for the last year of the war began:

> If any regrets are felt at the passing of the year 1918 they must certainly be quickly eclipsed by the hope that the present year will once more give to co-operation its proper opportunity and place in both

economic and ethical life. Half-stifled by an unsympathetic government, hedged in by almost innumerable restrictions, and altogether forced into a most deplorable ineptitude to serve its members in the way it would have liked, we at last, as co-operators may breathe the breath of renewed hope, and act with determination such as we have never before possessed.

Bruff continued that the lesson of the war was that societies must be more militant; no more apologetics, the war must be taken right into the enemy camp; Co-operation must be brought within the reach of all people, rich and poor; the position of Co-operation must be made unassailable in our land.

Stafford district reported that the year had been full of difficulties but it had been 'a grand year of advance.' Walsall society had begun to farm the 411 acres bought the previous year in conjunction with Cannock. Wolverhampton had purchased a property at Codsall and were about to start a branch there.

The spirit of the time had been struck by Bruff's Birmingham report. The movement had entered the war a predominantly Lib-Lab one. But the antagonism shown to the Co-operative movement during the war, the packing of the Food Committees with representatives of the private food trade (Lord Davenport, the first Food Controller, was a wholesale grocer), the refusal of the government to recognise the unique position of the movement, not only as the largest retailer of food, but also its ethical stance supporting fair shares for all by a government controlled system of rationing, all these things had politicised the movement. This had resulted in the emergence of the Co-operative Party in 1918 closely aligned with the Labour Party. Such a realignment was hastened by the break-up of the Liberal Party during the war into Asquith and Lloyd George factions resulting in large numbers of Liberals, both leaders and rank-and-file defecting to the Labour Party.

Walsall and Wolverhampton Societies

These are the only two Black Country societies for which records remain. For both there is a written history, the Walsall one comprehensive for the war period, the Wolverhampton one less detailed. The man source, however, is the quarterly reports of the societies, for both of which there is a complete series for the war years. The following narrative attempts to supplement the information given above, and illustrate differences between the war experiences of the two societies.

(i) Walsall

Despite rising prices, disruption of transport by the requisitioning of the society's horses, shortages of supplies, employees departing to the war etc. the society maintained its pre-war dividend of 2/-d. in the £ through to 1915. It was not until 1916 that the Management Committee's report began to seriously criticise the government. The occasion was the deduction of the first quarterly payment of the Excess Profits Duty of over £500 (on profits of £7000) and the fact that further monies would have to be found as the tax was retrospective to June 1914. The objection to EPD was that to tax Co-operative profits was to tax the 'savings' of working people when other forms of savings were not taxed, it was claimed. In addition the increased indirect taxes on food and other necessities imposed to pay for the war (which had the further effect of restricting consumption in war time) bore more hardly on the poor than the rich. The objection was not to increased taxation, because the war had to be paid for, but to the 'grossly unfair' distribution of taxation. 'This tax will probably continue until we organise ourselves (as the capitalist classes do) and obtain more adequate representation in Parliament,' the report concluded. This was prophetic not only with regard to a Co-operative Party, but the campaign by the whole co-operative movement against EPD. This not only led to the removal of the tax, but back payment of all that had been paid.

By December 1916 with short supplies recorded in the bakery, coal and milk departments, the society introduced its own rationing system. The specific cause was the shortage of sugar supplies. Members would be supplied with ½lb of sugar per person per household per week. This scheme covered nearly 40.000 people. The amount would be increased if supplies improved.

In June 1917 the dividend, which had averaged 1/10d in 1916, was lowered drastically to 1/3d. This was done to prevent the members being 'mulcted' of hundreds of pounds of EPD. Supplies were costing nearly twice as much as at the outbreak of war and if prices had been increased to the same extent 'profits' would have nearly doubled and 80 per cent of that would have been taken in EPD. To prevent this, prices had been lowered. 'Where there are no profits, there can be no excess profit.' The committee urged all members to protest at the tax which was 'wrong in principle and unjust in practice.'

Nor was this the only complaint. Sugar was the greatest cause of friction and discontent. The government had decreed that not more than half the quantity used in 1915 should be made available to suppliers. This penalised the co-ops, particularly Walsall whose members had increased from 10,000 in 1914 to nearly 13,500 at the end of 1917. But traders with less customers now had more sugar to spare and were enticing Co-op members away from the society. The committee appealed for loyalty from members. Membership did, indeed, continue to grow, but whereas it had increased by over 1,000 between June and December 1916, the increase to June 1917 was less than 500.

The next quarter over £2,250 was paid in EPD. Once again prices were reduced and profits minimised to protect members. Questions were being asked about the lack of Co-operative presence on Food Committees. Everything was being done to increase this, it was said, but some outlying authorities were refusing to appoint co-operative representatives.

From the middle of 1917 matters improved for the co-ops. Lord Rhondda replaced Lord Davenport as Food Controller, a Labour Party member, J.R. Clynes, became parliamentary secretary to the Ministry of Food and the Co-operative movement was freely admitted to the charmed circle of national food and rationing circles.

By the middle of 1918, the fear of starvation from German destruction of shipping was much reduced, and the government released stocks of foodstuffs. The June Walsall report stated that supplies of most foods had been more equitably distributed and the Co-op had fared 'as well as most people.' A national rationing scheme was being introduced (previously there had been the informal systems introduced by traders and a partial scheme controlled by local authorities). The Food Minister had given an undertaking that rationed articles would be supplied on the number of persons registered, and not on the datum period of 1914. Such a general rationing scheme had long been advocated by the movement. This national scheme was introduced just a few months before the end of the war and it was held that it had not been introduced before because of the opposition of the private food trade (notably the wholesalers) who had been making vast profits.

The strategy adopted over the Excess Profits Duty had also paid off. Under an 'averaging system' the whole of the £3,155 paid by the Walsall Co-op was returned to them. In view of 'the abnormal times through which we are passing', the whole amount was transferred to the Emergency Fund.

The June report concluded that it looked to 'a considerable increase in turnover by the return of those co-operators to their own shops who had been forced to trade elsewhere.' In fact the next report recorded a turn-over increase of nearly 6 per cent with a membership of 14,943; 218 members having joined during the quarter and 90 lapsed.

The society's quarterly reports are also the sole surviving record of the Educational Committee's activities and information on the Guilds.

Walsall had both Women's and a Men's Guild. The first available Walsall report for March 1915 reported that the Educational Committee had arranged a Social Evening which was an innovation. asking members of both Guilds to come and bring a friend. There had also been a tea for Belgian refugees where a crowded meeting listened to a lecture on Belgian Co-operatives, and collected nearly £2 for Belgian Relief.

Walsall Educational Committee also specialised in children's classes. The September report stated that a Children's Demonstration with 5,000 children participating was 'probably the largest ever seen.' Childrens' classes were being held in Walsall, Bloxwich, Walsall Wood, Sutton, Pelsall, Brownhills and Lichfield. There was also a proposal for an Adult Class. By March 1916 it was reported that this class had flourished, as had the Children's classes with 80 prizes and over 100 certificates awarded. Several meetings had been cancelled, however, as it had been found impracticable to hold meetings in the evenings. The June report stated that the Library had been overhauled and a new catalogue published in *Wheatsheaf.*

The Children's Demonstration in the summer was 'the largest we have had and one of the largest of any description held in the town.' But a joint winter programme of meetings had to be abandoned owing to 'the unsettled conditions.' In the autumn of 1916 a Children's Choir, which had been long rehearsing, gave their first concert. This had 'greatly pleased a good audience.' The choir was open to daughters of members.

In 1917, 300 children attended the winter classes and the annual demonstration 'passed off very successfully,' in spite of unfavourable weather. The children's choir was still flourishing and it was hoped to start another one at Bloxwich. In the autumn, the main adult success of the Educational Committee had been a visit by Professor Hall, the adviser of studies to the Co-operative Union, who lectured in the afternoon and held a public meeting in the evening, both well attended. The other main adult activity was the quarterly conferences arranged by the Stafford District, but organised by the local Educational Committees.

When children's classes resumed in the autumn they were 'a greater success than ever,' with an attempt to grade children according to their age and their 'knowledge of the text book.' Bloxwich had four classes starting with the under-10s and going on to a class for senior boys and girls 13 to 16. Two hundred children were enrolled in these Bloxwich classes. In most other places classes had been divided into junior and senior. The text books used were Our Story by Miss Isa Nicholson for juniors and for others a new intermediate text book, The Story Retold by Miss Julia P. Madams. Over 700 children in all were being taught the principles of co-operation.

By the winter of 1918 there were 911 children in the classes. A gardening class had also been started for the summer. The June report stated, 'The plots have had to contend with a long spell of hot, dry weather but the results are very satisfactory considering their original state.' There had been an outing to plots in other parts of the borough with differing soil conditions under the guidance of Mr Brayford.

During the summer of 1918 there were four children's demonstrations, gardening classes at Walsall and Bloxwich, children's choirs at Walsall, Bloxwich and Sutton. In the autumn the joint programme of meetings had been resumed and social evenings were being arranged once a month. The last quarter of the war reported 'a very busy quarter.'

The Educational Committee's Reports also publicised the Guilds. Unfortunately little is given except the bare details of their existence. In 1915 there were seven Women's Guild branches at Central, Bloxwich, Walsall Wood, Pelsall, Brownhills, Lichfield and Sutton Coldfield. There were also two branches of the Men's Guild at Central and Sutton Coldfield. By the beginning of 1919 there was an additional Women's Guild branch at Aldridge and another Men's Guild at Pelsall. Every quarterly report recorded the existence of these Guilds, the name of the secretary and the place and time of meeting. But no information regarding their activities, apart from that already given from the Educational Reports, was published. So we have no idea of the relative effectiveness of each branch, nor the numbers involved. This is a classic case of women's activities being 'hidden from history.'

In conclusion it seems remarkable how much social activity did flourish during war-time. In fact, the greater the problems of the Society as a whole, the more social activity it seems to have sustained. In three of the Women's Guild branches the secretary in 1915 was still in office in 1919. It is quite exceptional for a Society to support so many Women's Guild branches, most having only one. Considering the number of women in employment during the war, additional burdens of shopping, rationing, shortage of supplies and worry over members of the family in the services, it is remarkable that all these branches continued throughout the war. It is perhaps even more remarkable that Men's Guild branches survived with war-time work, overtime, civil defence duties, and call-up. Concern to pass on to children the principles of co-operation is also evident, despite the difficulties of the times. Again. Walsall was very successful in this regard.

(ii) Wolverhampton

Wolverhampton quarterly reports are available for the whole of the war period. The Wolverhampton society followed a cautious policy regarding dividends. The only time it reached 2/-d in the pound was in 1896 (the annual figures given in the quarterly reports differ slightly from those recorded in the Annual Congress reports). Thereafter it fluctuated between 1/11d and 1/6d. In 1913 it was 1/9d, in 1914 1/9½d, and it was raised again to 1/9¾d in 1915. The September 1914 report spoke of panic buying at the beginning of the war and a threatened run on savings. Supplies were rationed, membership restricted for a time, all demands on capital withdrawals met and the situation finally settled down. Record sales and influx of members continued into 1915. By September problems of supply were referred to as follows, 'The little troubles we have in supply and delivery of foods are matters which occupy a lot of our attention.' However, there were 'difficulties' with a bakery extension which persisted until the end of the war. The advertising of the numbers of loaves baked each quarter illustrates the difficulties of bread supply; in the September 1915 quarter it was 421,608 loaves.

Unbroken progress continued into 1916, but the increase in members was exceeding that of increase of capital. As a result, the restriction on interest on those savers who spent less than £3 per quarter with the society was lifted and all savings received 5 per cent interest. This had the desired effect of increasing capital. By October 1916 the problems of sugar and EPD were looming large. The society had been limited to 75 per cent of its 1913 sales for a membership that had doubled. The result had been a slight fall in quarterly sales, which was considered satisfactory in the circumstances. The introduction of the Excess Profit Duty led, as with other societies, to the holding or lowering of prices with a subsequent fall in the rate of growth of profits and a fall in the dividend to 1/8d. At this time income tax was being widened and large numbers of workers were paying for the first time. This led to an anti-Co-operative campaign demanding that dividends be taxed in the same way as private profits. The Wolverhampton society warned members that dividends should not appear on income tax returns.

In January 1917, the committee pointed out that EPD was the equivalent of 5d. off the dividend. The bread situation was very serious at this time. Delivery difficulties from a shortage of labour led the committee to urge members to collect their own bread wherever possible. Although members responded, it led to a fall in loaves sold from over 500,000 in March to just over 350,000 in September.

Sales continued to fall in the following quarter accounted for by great difficulties in getting supplies, particularly sugar. These problems, the committee admitted, were resulting in members taking their custom elsewhere, despite the operation of a sugar rationing scheme. The dividend again fell in 1917 down to 1/1½d. This general fall in the co-operative divi led the anti-Cooperative lobby to claim that co-op savings were not safe. The Wolverhampton society rebutted these allegations stating that prices had been deliberately been kept down, particularly coal, which was 2d. per cwt. and bread 1d a loaf cheaper than elsewhere.

By July 1917 sales were increasing once again despite increased problems with sugar. The small allotment made it necessary to refuse to supply new members with sugar and to limit the supply to old members. Amid all the difficulties, the campaign against credit continued with the bread and confectionery trade put entirely on a cash basis. To ease the bread situation an automatic plant was promised for operation within a few days, but there was no possibility of a projected travelling oven being completed.

At this time alterations in the capital structure of the society were proposed. The existing limit of £50 of shares per member was to be altered to £200 in the rules, but only to £100 at the present time. This, it was estimated, would give all the capital the society would need for post-war expansion and also assist the CWS which had invested about £11m in increased stocks and government War Loans. The existing 5 per cent interest was to be paid on all savings, but a 7 day's notice for every £50 invested was introduced. It was stressed that the financial position of the society continued sound even though there had recently been large withdrawals from many members 'to invest in other directions'. The dividend was increased by 3d. that quarter.

Sales were slightly down the next quarter and the divi with it. The committee pointed out this was because the prices of most commodities were now closely controlled by the government, some of them on such low margins that no dividend could be paid. Difficulties continued to the end of 1917. The fear was that members who had taken their sugar cards elsewhere would mean that any national rationing scheme would be based on existing registrations and the co-operative movement would be deprived of the registrations of those who went elsewhere only for sugar. Staffing difficulties were now being caused by lack of accommodation, and the society appealed for a house for a recently appointed boot manager.

Bread difficulties continued into 1918. At the beginning of the year about 400.000 loaves were produced, but this was down to 337,000 by June. The decrease puzzled the committee, especially as their loaf continued to be 1d. cheaper than elsewhere. By early 1918 food supplies 'remained much the same', but the distribution system was still changing. The society held that this had justified the rationing system they had adopted over the previous twelve months. Despite losing a considerable number of members because of the sugar misallocation, both sales and capital had increased over the previous year and 'quite 100 per cent more members had joined than had left the society.'

By June 1918 sales had increased 12½ per cent over the previous year and although much was due to higher prices it was achieved without many of the goods which were stocked in peace time. It was also pointed out that the small quantities in which goods were sold and the 'very many rationing schemes in operation', meant greatly increased shop and office costs. It was regretted that so many members had opted to register outside the society, but it was hoped that they would rectify this with the new ration book.

At the end of the war sales were still increasing, but there had been increasing problems with the coal supply. Short supplies in the previous period had led members to increase their orders. These were difficult to fulfil, firstly from a general shortage of labour and then because of the influenza epidemic which 'depleted our staff'.

So the war ended, without comment or celebration; too many problems loomed. In judging the success of the Wolverhampton society throughout the war, three criteria can be used. Total sales increased by 253 per cent between 1914 and 1918; adjusting this for inflation it represents a real increase over the period of 25 per cent. Membership in this period increased by 80 per cent and Savings more than doubled, keeping them slightly ahead of inflation in real terms.

As for Walsall, the Educational Committee and Guild reports are also included in the Wolverhampton society's quarterly reports..

Two of the Wolverhampton Educational Committee's stand-bys were the annual Tea, Concert and Dance and the annual summer Outing, both with the co-operation of the Women's Guild. In March 1915 the Committee recorded that the former had been held, the 300 tickets having been sold out, but the Excursion would have to be cancelled. Innovations, however, were a Mixed Reading Circle and Saturday afternoon visits to places of local interest. The other 'golden oldie' of the Educational Committee was the phenomenally successful Annual Field Day in which the majority of school children in the town participated. The usual elaborate preparations for the 1915 event were made with organising schools being allocated different colours to identify them. But at the last moment the event had to be cancelled because of 'inclement weather.' In the autumn the Committee was apologising for the 'abrupt termination' of the Saturday afternoon local outings, because of the 'impossibility of arranging permission' for such visits.

Even the annual Tea Concert & Dance for 1916 was questioned, but went ahead, although prices had to be raised to 1/-d for adults and 9d. for children. This still represented excellent value for two entertainments and a good tea, the Committee considered. Tickets were again limited to 300 for each of the two nights. It is from the Women's Guild report that we learn the event was 'numerically a great success.'

From the spring of 1916 the Committee was reporting that 'Educational work is very difficult under present circumstances. We hope the small amount of public work will be excused.' Work was proceeding through the Stafford District Association, however, and 'this ensures that we do not lose touch with the ideals of the movement.'

In the summer of 1916 the Management Committee cut off the quarterly grant to the Educational Committee for the duration of the war. It acknowledged the importance of the educational work, but considered that the use of the existing balances of the Educational Committee would ensure that its work was not curtailed. However, the next report of the Educational Committee stated that work was at a standstill and criticised the action of the management committee.

From 1917 the Educational work began to pick up. The Committee seems to have taken a leaf out of the Walsall book and arranged Children's Classes. These had been commenced at the end of 1916 and had been 'a decided success', the attendance averaging 120. For a new class starting in January an additional teacher had been engaged. Classes were held at the large Co-operative Hall, Stafford Street on Saturdays at 2-30pm. Members 'who wished to interest their children in the movement' were urged to enrol them.

The success of the 1916 'Annual' encouraged the Committee to continue with this event in a modified form. The tea had to be omitted, presumably because of rationing difficulties, but the entertainment was being strengthened. Two 'first class concert parties from Crewe and Manchester have been engaged at large expense', and for the subsequent Dance 'a good Quadrille band' had been engaged. Tickets were limited to 400 for each of the two nights. Admission to the two events was 7d. (including Entertainment Tax). The event was not entirely successful, however, as less than 300 attended on each night.

After this comparative failure the work of the Educational Committee seems to have tailed off again and for the 'Annual' in 1918 although only 250 tickets were printed, the event still 'did not come up to expectations.' It yielded a profit of £7, however, which was reserved for the entertaining of wounded soldiers.

After this the committee seems to have immersed itself in the question, through the District organisation, of the emerging Co-operative Party. and only the children's classes continued successfully. The report in December 1918 rejoiced that the war was over, announced an 'Annual' on the old lines complete with Tea, and successful Children's Classes. An Adult School, however 'was not exactly the success we anticipated'. More promising was the fact that four candidates had been supported at the General Election and two of them had been successful.

After a not too happy war experience, however, the Committee pinned its hope on the coming peace.

Turning to the Women's Guild, Wolverhampton differed considerably from Walsall in having only one, central branch. But, unlike Walsall, there is a separate Guild report within each of the society's quarterly reports.

At the beginning of the war the Guild reported that it had representatives on the Citizens' Committee and its ward committees, the National Relief Organisation. and the Women's Unemployment Sub-Committee.

By 1915 they were immersed in the question of the self-government of the Guild which bedevilled relations nationally between the Guild and the Co-operative Union throughout the war. The Union demanded that the Guild take up no question of which it disapproved; the Guild insisted on complete independence of action. As a result the annual national grant to the Guild from the Union was cut off. The Wolverhampton Guild was also supporting national Guild policy of No Member to Register for War Work until (a) all women seeking work were employed and (b) the Government guarantees trade union rates and conditions for women at work. By the end of the year the Guild reported 'steady progress'. It met on alternative Wednesdays at the Co-op Hall in Stafford Street at 7-30pm and during the quarter there had been a lecture by Mrs Cotterell (the Birmingham representative on the central committee) on 'Self-Government of the Guild', which Wolverhampton members fully supported; a lecture by Mrs Jenny L. Adamson (the local press secretary) on 'Women's Wages'; and a lantern lecture by Mr A. Wood (the secretary of the Wolverhampton society) on 'Cornwall.'

During 1916 the Guild lost its outstanding member, Jenny Adamson, who moved because her husband, a leading trade unionist, took a job elsewhere. Her loss was, 'Deeply deplored. We cannot afford to lose one so interested in our movement and the cause of Women's Rights.' Meetings continued throughout the year, the success of the annual party was reported, together with events such as a successful Whist Drive and Dance for the Wounded Soldiers' Fund.

In 1917 we get a first glimpse of the strength of the Guild when the July report records,'Considerable progress, membership being considerably over one hundred.' Activity in the first half of 1917 had included the usual New Year Social and Dance; the Children's New Year Party which was 'also well attended and greatly appreciated'. Also an entertainment for about 80 wounded soldiers to tea, followed by a musical evening, to which the soldiers contributed. 'The happy faces of the soldiers well repaid us for the time and trouble we had taken to ensure its success.' The Guild had also had a discussion on 'War Savings,' led by A.G. Walkden, the prospective Labour candidate for Wolverhampton West. 'After a good discussion it was decided to place our savings in the Society and for them to invest it in the War Loan through the Wholesale Society.' This decision reflected the general discussion and decisions in the movement throughout the war when there was 'patriotic' pressure on individual co-operators and Societies to invest directly in War Savings. The annual excursion took place in June when nearly one hundred members drove by brake to Clent in glorious weather and 'spent a most enjoyable day.'

Good progress was also reported in the second half of 1917. The Guild had heard a report from the sister in charge of St. Winifred's Home, Whitmore Reans catering for girls aged 10 to 16 at risk, and were so impressed that they decided to organise a Whist Drive and Dance for the Home. This, when held, raised over £50. Miss Herboldt of the newly formed Wolverhampton Educational League had addressed the Guild on the League's work which was intended to bring parents and teachers closer together and press for such things as open-air schools, children's libraries, play centres, after-care committees, maintenance grants where needed etc. After the meeting, several Guild members joined the League. But 1917 was also the year of maximum food problems and several members were serving on the Food Vigilance Committee and resolutions had been passed protesting at the price and scarcity of milk.

1917 proved a turning point and the Guild flourished further in 1918. Both the Children's Social at the end of the year and the New Year Social were a great success, seventeen new members joining at the latter. By March the secretary, Gertrude Page, was reporting that about 40 new members had joined since January and the branch had decided to set a target of doubling its membership. In asking for recruits the secretary said, 'In these trying times we cannot learn too much about the difficulties that the Co-operative Societies have to contend with, and at our Guild meetings a lot of the questions are fully discussed and it helps us to bear more patiently some of the trials we have to contend with. Several resolutions have been sent to the Local Food Control Committee, to Lord Rhondda and our local MPs, which have done some good.' The Guild seems to have been cultivating better relations with the Management Committee at that time. In February, several members of the Guild entertained the Committee and members; 'a most enjoyable evening was spent.' In March there was a deputation to the Management Committee 'to inquire the reason of the shortage of rationed goods'. Several criticisms and suggestions were made regarding the management of the shops. 'The management committee explained fully to us the difficulties under which they were working, and our only regret was that all members of the Society were not there to listen to the discussion.' Also in March James Whittaker, president of the local Trades Council, spoke on the vote and how it applied to women. Several Guild members joined the Labour Party at this meeting.

By September 1918 Gertrude Page was reporting a membership of 173. The money raised by the Guild, together with the Wolverhampton Women's Labour League, for St. Winifred's Home had been used to send the children to Wales for five weeks and also to renovate the Home. In May the Management Committee returned the compliment and entertained the Women's Guild when a sketch was given by several members of the Committee and other members sang and recited. Resolutions had been sent to the local MPs and others protesting against military training in the schools and also Regulation 40D of the Defence of the Realm Act. For the summer outing a party of seventy two people went by brake to Bridgnorth. It was unanimously agreed that the Guild should not close for its usual vacation in the summer and meetings would continue as usual.

At the end of the war the Guild had 217 members and claimed to be the biggest Guild in the Midland Section. We do not know, however, whether this was more than the aggregate total of the eight branches of the Women's Guild at Walsall. After years of agitating the Guild had finally had a member co-opted onto the Maternity and Child Welfare Committee of the Borough Council as well as the Heath Town Food Committee. The usual meetings and events were reported, and in addition, Women's Classes had been started. The end of the war was celebrated by the fortnightly evening meeting being superseded by a weekly meeting.

Conclusion

Some of the difficulties of assessing the profitability, efficiency and social success of Black Country consumer co-operation have already been touched on. It cannot be judged by its profitability or the dividend paid, as can private traders, for these were sometimes lowered to avoid Excess Profit Duty. Efficiency and service were undoubtedly affected by the difficulty of obtaining labour, but this would have applied to all retailers. With regard to the respective merits of the co-operative democratic system of management by elected committee compared with the managerial systems of private trade, there is no reason to believe that the Co-operative system was inferior before the war even by the sole criterion of profitability. During the war, for the two societies for which we have full knowledge, their general management committees showed remarkable continuity. In Walsall, of a fourteen strong committee in 1915, twelve were still serving on a thirteen strong committee in 1919; in Wolverhampton the nine strong management committee of April 1916 showed only one change in December 1918. Such continuity suggests that there would be no deterioration in managements skills. Some progress is indicated by the growth of premises. Walsall began the war with their central premises at Bridge Street, 16 branches, 3 coal depots plus warehouse, bakery and stables; it ended the war with the same central premises, 19 branches, the same three coal depots, two bread shops, a milk depot plus warehouse, bakery and stable. Wolverhampton began with central premises in Stafford Street, and five branches; it ended with the same central premises and five branches, but an additional confectionary branch and the beginning of the development of the Lichfield Street site for drapery and outfitting. In view of the difficulties of procuring and developing sites during the war, both societies made progress.

One index of efficiency might be the amount that customers spent with the society (although some allowance would have to be made for a possible increase in 'sleeping members' who left their money with the co-op, but did not buy from it). In 1914 sales per member per annum varied in the range £14.55 at Wednesbury to £23.86 at Halesowen and Hasbury, except for Dudley where it was only £8.70. For sales to have shown a real increase they would have had to increase by over 100 per cent per member because of inflation. Only Dudley, Tipton and Wednesbury achieved this. Elsewhere increases ranged from 51 per cent in Soho down to a distinctly modest 20 per cent in Walsall.

However, the increases in members and increases in sales are the two main indicators of the attractions of the co-operative movement. Considering membership first. It is true that in some quarters members left in alarmingly large numbers, but they could usually be replaced and there were few quarters when total membership actually fell. Overall, all societies increased their memberships during the war. Wolverhampton had the largest increase in membership between 1914 and 1918 at 80 per cent followed by Tipton at 59 per cent, Soho and Wednesbury at over 40 per cent each, Walsall and Halesowen in the 30 per cent range, with Dudley last at only a 4 per cent increase. With regard to sales, Tipton and Wednesbury both tripled sales; Wolverhampton (253 per cent), Dudley (234 per cent) and Soho (222 per cent) comfortably cleared the inflation barrier. But neither Halesowen & Hasbury (171 per cent) nor Walsall (159 per cent) increased their sales by the rate of inflation.

By these commercial criteria the Black Country co-operative movement had a successful war. But it was its political influence, the social and educational facilities it offered and the participatory democracy of its structure which were the great strengths of the Co-operative movement.

Walsall Locks & Cartgear Ltd

Finally, we deal with the one productive co-operative in the Black Country. Two sources of information are available for this Lock Co-operative. One is a History written for its fiftieth anniversary in 1923 by R. Halstead; the other source is the statistics in the Co-operative Congress annual report.

One might have expected that this productive unit would flourish in war time, but Halstead tells us that at the outbreak of war most of the trade was for export and these markets were abruptly cut off. The society was obliged to look for munitions work. In this they were successful, but Halstead does not tell us what this war work was. By this time, the lock co-operative had one of the largest factories in the industry with 250 workers; its machinery could easily be adapted to the making of small arms ammunition etc. even if it was not in the Chubb class which turned over to making armour plating for tanks and ships. Halstead also tells us that 55 of their workers joined the forces and 11 made the supreme sacrifice.

For further evidence of the development of the company we turn to the annual statistics. During the war its membership rose from 198 to 276. In theory all workers were co-partners, but there was some gap between theory and practice. This gap narrowed during the war, however, when of 290 employees, 276 were members.

Capital rose modestly from £7,515 in 1914 to £9,822 in 1918. Sales, however rose 3½ times from £21,115 to £74,730 and net profit rose even faster at 7½ times from £772 to £5925. Productivity (measured as the ratio between sales and the number of employees) increased from £84 to £258.

Average wages more than kept pace with inflation with a 165 per cent rise from just over £42 per annum in 1914 to £112 in 1918. Again, one must allow for the unknown gender change in these years in the workforce and also the fact that workers were usually members who received interest on their shares (7½ per cent in 1918) and also a dividend (amount not known), but even with these adjustments, the average weekly wage of £2-3-0d does not support the view of extravagantly paid war workers. It is higher, however, than that of shop staff which we estimated at £1-6-7½.

Halstead emphasises Walsall Locks & Cartgear's continued loyalty to co-operative principles. A long established Educational Committee seems to have remained in existence because educational expenditure rose sharply during the war from £19 in 1914 to a peak of £127 in 1917 and £108 in 1918. The society had a pension scheme and during the war provided for the families of men joining the forces. Its charitable expenditure also increased in war time from £20 in 1914 to £100 in 1917. Subscriptions included contributions to the Prince of Wales Fund, local hospitals and war-time charities. By the end of the war Walsall Locks & Cartgear had consolidated its position as a leading contender in the lock trade and accumulated the capital for expansion after the war.

Bibliography: The Co-operative Movement in Wartime 1914-1918

A main source is the statistics of every society contained in the annual reports of the Co-operative Union Congress. These reports also include District Reports of general progress of societies and educational work undertaken. For Walsall there is Fred Hall's *From Acorn to Oak,* a history of the society and for the productive co-operative. R. Halstead's *The History of Walsall Locks & Cartgear Ltd. 1873-1923.* For Wolverhampton there is *A Brief History of Wolverhampton Cc-operative Society* by H. Taylor who was vice-president of the Society at the time he wrote it in 1931. The other main source is the quarterly reports of the societies. For the Black Country for this period only the *Wolverhampton Quarterly Reports* (1914-1918) and the *Walsall Quarterly Reports* (1916-1918) have been traced. These also contain the reports of the *Educational Committees* and for Wolverhampton the *Women's Guild* reports too. For the national picture I have used G.D.H. Cole – *A Century of Co-operation* (1944).

Chapter 16

Black Country Labour Women at War 1914-1918

Women and the Trade Unions

The complexities of the war-time legal system which bound women at work and made it extremely unlikely that any but a few earned the reputed high wages of war-time have been explained in the chapter on Birmingham Women at War and will not be repeated here.

The immediate pre-war situation in the Black Country with regard to women and trade unions was that Mary Macarthur's National Union of Women Workers was strongly established at Cradley Heath and the south of the Black Country as a result of its leading the struggles of the chain workers culminating in the setting up of the Chain Trade Board in 1910. More strongly established in the Wolverhampton-Bilston-Walsall northern part of the Black Country was the Workers' Union as a result of the struggles of the Great Unrest of 1910-14. These had significantly increased the standard of living of unskilled and semi-skilled workers and the final instalment lifting the minimum wage of the unskilled man to 23/-d. a week was due in 1914. The same agreement raised female unskilled wages to 6/-d. a week at age 14 rising to 12/-d. a week at 21.

At the outbreak of war, the Amalgamated Society of Engineers, having refused to admit women to their own union, virtually agreed to hand over the recruitment of women in engineering to the National Union of Women Workers and there was friction almost from the start of the war between the NUWW and the Workers' Union as conflicting agreements were signed with different engineering employers' organisations. From the evidence available, it appears that large scale recruitment of women into trade unions did not begin until 1916. By this time, two further issues divided the two unions most directly concerned with the recruitment of women. The first was the issue of trade cards of exemption from military service. This did not directly affect women, but the other issue did. This was Conscription. This was opposed by the National Union of Women Workers and the union became identified with opposition to the war. The Workers' Union, on the other hand supported the war to the point of jingoism and Julia Varley was as vociferous as the men in this regard. Hence relations between the two unions were uneasy from the beginning and worsened as the war proceeded.

As has been said, recruitment of women into trade unions on a large scale does not seem to have started until 1916. Neither the 1914 nor the 1915 annual reports of the Workers' Union mentions women. Julia Varley was the only women's organiser at the outbreak of war and her 1915 report showed that she covered the whole of Great Britain, having visited Scotland and Ireland as well as many other towns. She reported that membership of the Women's Section continued to grow and she looked forward to 1916 when she hoped to be able to say that the Women's Section would hold 'a very important position' in the union. The extent to which this hope was fulfilled can be gauged by the fact that before the war ended there were twenty women organisers in the Workers' Union.

By March 1916 Julia Varley was reporting that she was negotiating, together with the men's representatives, for the adoption of the Birmingham scale in the engineering industry, and later in the same month negotiated, together with Miss Weaver, for the same objective with the Wolverhampton Engineering Employers' Union. In April Julia was addressing nut and bolt workers in Wolverhampton. 'It was like old times', she reported. 120 women's names were put forward for membership, 'with the promise of more.'

Emily Weaver was now taking over the work of organising women in the Black Country. She reported visiting Brierley Hill glassworks and starting a new branch for munitions workers at Dudley. In August she was reporting 'encouraging work' in Wolverhampton, Willenhall and Wednesbury. In September she reported one of the cases that were bringing the women into the trade unions; a Bilston tube firm was paying a 20 year old woman only 10/-d a week.

By September 1916 Julia Varley was making war on both the Amalgamated Society of Engineers and the National Federation of Women Workers. The occasion was an article in the ASE *Monthly Journal* criticising the Workers' Union for not bringing their agreements in line with those of the NFWW. Her reply was that the Workers' Union was negotiating better terms than those of the NFWW. She went back to 1913 and claimed that the NFWW had been willing to settle the great strike movement with a 10/-d. minimum wage for women at 21, whereas the final settlement by the Workers' Union was the 12/-d. minimum. Julia Varley now claimed that the NFWW had negotiated an agreement with the Midland Employers' Association for a minimum of 13/-d. from May 1915 while the Workers' Union had been negotiating for a 16/-d. minimum and, because of the action of the NFWW, had been obliged to settle for 15/-d. (Note that the 25 per cent rise claimed by the Workers' Union was less than the rate of inflation, which by the middle of 1915 was about 30 per cent – GB). The matter was vastly more complicated than this. Julia Varley claimed that she was against separate negotiation of women's wages as joint representation produced greater benefits for women. In addition joint negotiations made it less easy for employers to renege on equal pay agreements with regard to piecework rates for women taking over men's work. The multiplicity of employers' organisations in the Black Country and the infinite variety of occupations for women working in establishments completely producing munitions, partially producing munitions or not on war work emphasise the difficulties of those who had to negotiate the wages of women.

Towards the end of the year the Workers' Union reorganised and increased its branches in the Wolverhampton area. There had been a Women's Branch, but this had joined up with No.1. Branch because the female enamel workers who had formed the branch had been joined by men in that industry. The old Women's Branch had now been designated No.2. Branch. There was also a flourishing No.3. Branch and a newly formed No.4. Branch, all with mixed memberships.

With the reappearance of the *Woman Worker* in 1916 we can see the development of the work of the National Federation of Women Workers. In February Charles Sitch reported a 20 per cent increase for chainmakers, 3d on the minimum rate for hollow-ware workers and 1/-d. a week for Stourbridge laundry workers. In June a new branch was reported at Blackheath. 'We are at last coming to grips with the nut and bolt trade in Blackheath. A uniform price list has been compiled. Needless to say this represents a very considerable increase on the old one,' it was reported. In December members at Griffiths of Wolverhampton had obtained a 25 per cent increase in piece rates and 3/-d. a week on day rates. In Willenhall some members had increased their rates and an application was being made to the employers' association for a rise in all rates. In Dudley, as a result of the work of Mrs Hunter, meetings were being held. 'There are thousands of munitions workers in Dudley, and much is expected', the report said.

In 1917 reports are sparse from both the Workers' Union and the NFWW. The *Workers' Union Record* could report only a new branch at Greets Green in May where there had been a large influx of women members. There was not even an annual Workers' Union report for 1917.

The *Woman Worker* was hardly more enlightening. In August it reported, 'Sunshine in the Black Country.' Mrs Beaton had been organising in the Black Country for several months and although she had much to contend with, she could say that, 'the dawn of Trade Unionism was dawning in Dudley.' At Harper, Son and Bean there had been a dispute over wages which NFWW members had supported. For this they had been sacked. The Federation had been successful in getting the girls good jobs in other firms and a week's wages for all those suspended. The result was full recognition of the NFWW and friendly relations with the firm. A further dispute in Dudley in October was satisfactorily settled and in December a flying visit of Mary Macarthur to the midlands was announced where she was to address meetings at Cradley Heath, Lye and Dudley. But the Federation, as in 1916, was being more successful in Birmingham than in the Black Country.

Another union organising women in the Black Country was the Amalgamated Society of Gas, Municipal and General Workers. Its monthly paper reported a women's branch in Wolverhampton in 1916 with Mrs Wilkes as secretary. This paper also is short on women's activities, but does throw some light on women's wages. From October 1916 women of 18 and over in national factories were entitled to equal pay for equal work on piecework with a minimum time rate of £1 for a 48 hour week with an extra 6d. a hour for extra work. The report went on, 'This gives the majority of women and girls over 18 on direct munitions a decent living wage and piecework earnings undreamt of before the war'. But the beneficiaries were only the women on direct munitions in national factories and these comprised a very small minority of women workers.

In 1918 the *Workers' Union Record* was too full of its vendetta against the 'pacifists' of the ASE and NFWW to have much space for women workers. A strike was reported in March, however, at a factory in the West Bromwich district where a number of women joined the union and one of them was dismissed. The dispute was evidently about the piece rate for women. They went back to work when the firm undertook to pay according to Orders 492 and 781 and also to pay the day rate when women were were waiting for materials. The firm also agreed to compensate the dismissed woman with £2 a week for each week she was unemployed up to eight weeks or £1 a week if she got a job in less than eight weeks. Other than this, there is nothing else in the *Workers' Union Record* for 1918 on women workers. There seems to be no record of total female membership. We have only generalities such as that there were about 5,000 women members in 1914, mostly in the midlands, and 80,000 in 1918. This latter figure was about a quarter of union membership. We also know that as a result of the remarkable expansion of membership in Birmingham and the Black Country in the period 1910-14, the wartime growth of the union in this area was less than the national growth.

The *Woman Worker* provides evidence of greater activity on the part of the National Federation of Women Workers. In March it was 'pleased' that it had been able to negotiate a rate of 7d. an hour for women who were lifting gun shells weighing 60lbs. The next month it reported Charles Sitch organising pinafore workers who were paid only between 9/10d and 14/9d for a 46 hour week, or less than 4d per hour for an adult worker. Dudley Labour exchange was also criticised for withholding unemployment benefit from women workers. 'They seem to think no girl is unemployed who can join the WAAF.'

In May, Mary Macarthur was chosen as the prospective Parliamentary candidate for Stourbridge. In that month 'Stourbridge was up in arms' it was claimed because women had put in a demand for the Munitions Rate which was 23/-d. per week against the Trade Board rate of 4d. an hour at which they were paid. In August Mary Macarthur was addressing 'crowded meetings' at Cradley and Stourbridge.

In September 1918 the NFWW was recruiting at the National Fuse Factory at Tipton. The girls were 'waking up to trade unionism.' Nearly 200 women had joined, but the organisers 'would not be satisfied until all are in.' One grievance was that of the Viewers who wanted an increase on the present rates of 5/-d. on days and 10/-d. on nights. Another grievance was that they worked two five-hour spells per day without a break.

At the NFWW's bi-annual conference in October Mrs Garbutt of Cradley Heath was voted onto the executive with the largest number of votes. She moved a resolution demanding an extension of the Trade Boards system to all badly organised and low paid industries. She spoke as a chainmaker, she said. Women chainmakers could now earn 30/-d. a week or more, whereas before the Chain Board they could only earn 5/-d.

The next month, of course, the war ended. It is clear from the experience of these unions that although the trade unions negotiated the rates of pay which women received most unions found it hard work organising women, and the majority of working women, even those on munitions who had most to gain, remained unorganised.

Perhaps this conclusion could be reinforced by the testimony of one munitions worker from Walsall who worked at Kynoch's at Streetley and whose experiences are recounted in *Walsall at War*:

> I worked in the wadding shop. I pulled the cordite round and round and round (and) it went to the girl on the machine. She'd got the cartridge case and she put so many pieces of cordite into this cartridge case. My job was to put a tiny piece of wadding, cardboard only as big as my nail, on top of every one of these bullets. Then it had to go under this machine to be pressed down on top of the cordite.
>
> After the wadding I was transferred to the gauging shop and there was millions of cartridges and we had to 'steel gauge.' (It was) like the barrel of a gun and it was steel, about 4 inches long and fit into one hand. I can see myself doing it now, we used to sit in the cartridges, there was a 200 cwt cartridge box first then 100 cwt box – I got them on the side of me and we used to sit with the gauge in one hand and keep scooping the cartridges up. Every time you got a 'big head' on the cartridge you had to throw it out, because if not it back fired on our lads.
>
> QUESTION: How much were you paid for doing this, was it more than for the wadding?
>
> ANSWER: We weren't paid much, a whole week's wages was only £2-2-6d. I earned that one week for seven nights.... When it was getting towards the end of the war, I think they had enough cartridges as they thought and they sacked the boss...we all went on strike.
>
> Q: Was there a union at all?
>
> A: No, we automatically did it. There was unions, but they was only just starting, you see.

Finally, with regard to women in trade unions, there is a 'Gazeteer' of all known trade union branches, with the names of secretaries where possible, compiled by the TUC at the request of the government in 1916 and published in 1918. The TUC handed the job locally to the Trades Council. From the Black Country trades councils I have abstracted the following list of trade union branches with female secretaries. Not all these branches were necessarily affiliated to the local trades council. The list is regrettably short: Bilston Trades Council reported a National Union of Teachers branch whose secretary was Miss H.A. Altree. Stourbridge reported a NFWW laundry branch whose secretary was Miss D. Burrows. Stourport, where there was no trades council, reported another NFWW branch, secretary Mrs G.M. Walford. Rowley Regis Trades Council reported another NUT branch, secretary Miss Gertrude Jones, MA. Walsall Trades Council reported an affiliated branch of the Amalgamated Society of Tailors and Tailoresses whose secretary was Mrs Riley. and West Bromwich reported an affiliated branch of the National Union of Printing and Paper Workers' Union (Women's Branch), secretary Miss L. Teefer. Finally, Oldbury Trades Council reported a branch of the Soho Co-operative Women's Guild (Rood End branch) affiliated to it, secretary Mrs Forth. Other trades council, including the large ones of Wolverhampton and Smethwick had no women's branches to report.

Co-operative Women's Guild Activists

We have followed the activities of the Women's Co-operative Guild branches in our chapter on the Co-operative movement. In this section we will identify some of the members of these branches and the work they did both with the Guild and in the wider work of the Co-operative.

In Wolverhampton, the first woman to be a member of the management committee of the society was Mrs J.L. Adamson who was elected in April 1916. When her husband took the job of Workers' Union organiser in Ireland she left with him and was replaced on the management committee by another woman, Mrs M. Dale who was still on the board at the end of the war and far beyond. The secretary of the Women's Guild in January 1917 was Mrs Brindley. She was replaced by Mrs Gertrude Page in the July 1917 quarter and retained the post until the end of the war.

There was generally a number of women on the Educational Committee. In January 1918 these were Mrs Perry, Mrs Page, Mrs Dale, Mrs Brindley and Mrs Gardner on a committee of fifteen. They were joined in December 1918 by Mrs Diderage and Mrs Woolley.

In Walsall there were no women on the management committee until after the war. On the Educational Committee in September 1915 was Mrs Haynes, Mrs Hutchins, Mrs Adams and Mrs

Spanswick. They remained on the committee until March 1919 when they were joined by Mrs Dewsbury on a committee of eleven. The secretaries of the seven Women's Guild branches in September 1915 were Mrs Button – Central; Mrs Argyle – Bloxwich; Mrs L. Adams – Walsall Wood; Mrs Smith – Pelsall; Mrs J. Blakemore – Brownhills; Mrs E. Moore – Lichfield; and Mrs Alsopp – Sutton Coldfield. In March 1919, Walsall Wood, Pelsall and Sutton Coldfield still had the same secretaries. The other secretaries were Central Mrs Adams; Bloxwich Mrs Jordan; Brownhills Mrs Seedhouse, Lichfield Mrs Garrett; and the new branch, Aldridge, Mrs Goudie.

Of women's activities in other Black Country co-operatives societies we have no direct information. We do know, however, that the Soho Society had more than one Women's Guild branch, as the Rood End branch, secretary Mrs Forth, was affiliated to Oldbury trades Council.

Labour Women – the Political Activists

We have shown, in the chapter on Birmingham Labour Women, that the women's movement took more seriously than the men's their international obligations to end the war.

The main women's political organisation during the war was the Women's Labour League whose monthly organ was *Labour Women.* In January 1915 there was a special international issue with messages from women in Germany and other 'enemy' countries; British women were organised into a British Section of the Women's International Council of Socialist and Labour Organisations. This organisation reported regularly in *Labour Women* on such matters as protesting at the German hate campaign, and the Berne Conference of March 1915 with its delegates from Britain, 'enemy' and neutral countries which passed a resolution stating that the war had its origins in 'the imperialist ideas of capitalist society,' and urged War on War.

A branch of the Women's Labour League was formed in Wolverhampton in 1912, according to the *Wolverhampton Worker.* Its objects were to further Labour representation and appeal to the wives and daughters of trade unionists. Midlands District Conferences were held during the war and the July 1916 Conference was held in Wolverhampton at the ILP Rooms, Queen Square. Mrs Warden, the president of the district committee, was in the chair. The proceedings opened with the song, When will thou Save the People? and ended with a speech by Margaret Bondfield to a 'large and interested audience', on Trade Union organisation among Women. Unfortunately we are not told who the delegates were nor who the president of the Wolverhampton branch was who 'welcomed the delegates'.

The Wolverhampton branch was still thriving in March 1917 when the branch was publishing 'splendid little booklets,' which Mrs Dideridge said were making new members at every meeting. The branch had also recently consulted a large number of organisations in Wolverhampton for a conference on Education which had been arranged for the last week of April. In June the Wolverhampton branch was 'full of energy and initiative.' The local conference on education had been 'highly successful.' A much larger conference was being arranged around a programme devised by the Workers' Educational Association. By the end of the year the branch had organised a Women's Labour League Housing Campaign directed by Mrs Bigford.

Emma Sproson, Wolverhampton's most noted woman Suffragette and later to be its first woman town councillor, appears only sporadically in the war time record. She continued an ILP member and opponent of the war. She never appears as an activist in the Wolverhampton branch of the Women's Labour League. But she was well known beyond the borders of Wolverhampton. This is clear from the reference of the Erdington branch of the ILP in Birmingham which, having been prevented by the weather from going for their annual outing to Hampton-on-Arden, took the opportunity to attend the No-Conscription Fellowship where they 'derived much satisfaction from the speeches of Clifford, Allen, Fenner Brockway, Mrs Sproson...' It seems significant that Emma is named immediately after the two national speakers and first among the regional figures enumerated which included such Birmingham heavyweights as Joseph Southall (the painter), Frank Spires, Barrett Brown etc. Emma Sproson makes another appearance in a *Wolverhampton Chronicle* report of a local ILP Conference in February 1918 to discuss Rationing, when she said that rationing was an issue 'second only to the war itself.' But we still await a detailed account of the war-time activities of Emma (and her husband, Frank's) wartime activities.

No other Black Country branch of the Women's Labour League seems to have left any impression in print, so we turn finally to the 'non-political' activities of the National Union of Women Suffrage Societies and the violently political actions of the suffragette Women's Social and Political Union.

As has been explained fully in the chapter on Birmingham Women, the liberal, non-militant NUWSS split down the middle and many of its organisers became anti-war leaders in the No-Conscription fellowship and the Union of Democratic Control. The autocratic leaders of the WSPU, Emmeline Pankhurst and her daughter Christabel, immediately became pro-war and jingoistic, changed the name of their paper to *Britannia* and in November 1917 arbitrarily changed the name WSPU to that of the Women's Party.

At the outbreak of war there were the following branches of the National Union of Women's Suffrage Societies in the Black Country: Dudley (Mrs Powell, the Vicarage St. John's, secretary), Stourbridge (Miss E. Downing), Walsall (Miss Lowry), Wednesbury (Miss Westley) and Wolverhampton (Mrs Taylor).

As in Birmingham, the local NUWSS quickly engaged itself in general relief work, such as support for unemployed women and care for Belgian refugees without too much discussion as to attitudes to the war itself. But the NUWSS was clearly leaning towards co-operation with the labour movement's women's organisations notably the Women's Co-operative Guild. For instance, the Wednesbury branch NUWSS reported in November 1914 a Mending Party each week held at a room lent by the Wednesbury Co-operative Women's Guild, 'several of whom are members'. The Co-op women also offered a shop window to display 'our patched creations'. As the cold weather had not yet come the garments were undistributed, but it was suggested that they go to: those of children of school age to headteachers; some to the Central Red Cross centre in the town, of which the NUWSS secretary was a committee member; infant garments to the midwives, nurses and health visitors of the district.

I have not been able to consult *Common Cause* for the next two years and during this time there were no local printed NUWSS annual reports. By 1917 *Common Cause* is primarily useful for the list of organisations the NUWSS spokeswomen were visiting. In Birmingham, as has been shown, these increasingly included Labour organisations such as Women's Co-operative Guilds, Labour Churches, etc. the main speaker being the full-time organiser Carol Ring; also Mrs Osler the veteran secretary and visiting speakers. In the Black Country during 1917 Mrs Smallwood visited the West Bromwich Mothers' Union and Mrs Ring the Soho Hill Men's Movement. Nothing more is recorded.

In 1918, after celebrations on the granting of Women's Suffrage in March, the question of the post-war role of the NUWSS loomed large. In July at Walsall Temperance Hall, Lady Nott-Bower and Mrs Ring spoke on the subject of 'Child Welfare'; at West Bromwich Free Library Miss Rathbone and Mrs Ring spoke; and at Halesowen, Carol Ring spoke on 'Mothers and the Vote.' In December, the West Bromwich Society held its AGM. In March 1919 the NUWSS disappeared and became the Society for Equal Citizenship and Women Citizen's Association. The reaction of Black Country branches is unknown. From local directories we know that the Wolverhampton Women's Suffrage Society existed throughout the war. In 1918 its leading figures were Mrs Major (president), Mrs T. Graham and Mrs F. Carr (vice presidents) and Mrs F.D. Taylor of 107 Waterloo Road (secretary). This is still a very middle-class set-up and how it reacted with the local Liberal Party and the Labour movement is not known. Other NUWSS branches existed in the Black Country as the activity above indicates, but their existence is not recorded either in *Common Cause* or in local directories.

Turning to the Women's Social and Political Union, it would appear that the militancy and waywardness of Emmeline & Christabel had knocked the stuffing out of the Black Country movement before 1914. The Walsall Red Book records the presence of a branch of the WSPU from 1914 to 1917, but of its activity we have no record. No other town directory records a WSPU branch.

The Pankhursts' paper *Suffragette* disappeared on the outbreak of war and was replaced by *Britannia* with its masthead 'For King, For Country, For Freedom.' This did not catch working class interest and for a time in 1916 the paper was reduced to a cyclostyled edition. No Black Country activity is recorded up to the point when the WSPU was transformed into the Women's Party in November 1917. By this time the paper had added Bolsheviks to the villainous shop stewards and pacifists against whom they were waging war. This found support in the pro-war movement which was attempting to counter the growing anti-war movement in Birmingham and filtered through to the Black Country, no doubt, although there is little record of it either in *Britannia* or in the *Wolverhampton Chronicle* which would have been quick to record it whereever it occurred in the Black Country. The main impact of the Women's Party in the Black Country was Christabel's campaign for the Smethwick parliamentary seat in December 1918. Even for this it was the old WSPU big guns, such as Annie Kenney and Flora Drummond imported into the constituency who took the headlines and local female support is not recorded.

One final source of the activities of Labour women is the names of delegates who attended Independent Labour Party annual conferences during the war. These were, in 1917 from West Bromwich Miss Doreen Brockhouse who accompanied, I presume her father, Harry, who was a regular delegate. The next year the West Bromwich delegates were R. Micklewright and Miss I. Pugh. In Wolverhampton Mrs T. Jones was the sole Wolverhampton delegate in 1917 and Emma Sproson attended in 1918.

It is likely that Black Country Labour women's activities have been under-reported here and that further research might yield good results.

Bibliography: Black Country Labour Women in Wartime 1914-1918

For women in the Workers' Union see annual reports etc. at the Modern Records Centre, University of Warwick; copy of *Workers' Union Record* from 1916 at Birmingham Central Library; Julia Varley's biography in *Dictionary of Labour Biography* vol V. and Richard Hyman's *The Workers' Union* (1971). For the National Federation of Women Workers see *The Woman Worker New Series* from January 1916 (at Colindale) and annual reports of the Women's Trade Union League (at the London School of Economics). For the Amalgamated Society of of Gas, Municipal and General Workers see *The Municipal Employees' Monthly* for 1914-15 which became, after amalgamation, the *Monthly Journal* of the ASofGM&GW (at Birmingham Reference Library). The testimony of the Walsall munitions girl is taken from 'Walsall at War', *Walsall Chronicle* No.8. 1986 published by Walsall Local History Centre. The general Labour movement newspapers *Labour Leader, Clarion,* and *Justice* have been used, as well as the women's paper *Labour Woman*. The women's suffrage newspapers are: *Votes for Women* edited by the Pethwick-Lawrences of which British Library, Colindale holdings end in February 1918: the *Suffragette* ending in Oct 1915 when the Pankhursts' changed the title to *Brittania*. For the National Union of Women's Suffrage Societies see its organ *Common Cause.* Local material – Annual Directories, newspapers, principally the *Wolverhampton Chronicle* which covered most of the Black Country.

Chapter 17

Black Country Labour Politics 1914-1918

Attitude to the War

The Labour Party did not in August 1914 make a direct statement of support for the war; nor did the ILP make a statement opposing the war, but in reality, this quickly became the position. In the Black Country the trade unions and Trades Councils supported the war in the early years and it was not until the battles against Conscription took place at the end of 1915 and after its implementation in March 1916 that anti-war feeling began to gain the ascendancy in the labour movement.

Those who were anti-war from the beginning were few and far between and faced immense jingo and patriotic opposition. Such opposition as there was came mainly from the dissidents of the British Socialist Party who opposed their Party's leadership supporting the war, and also the ILP branches.

Little is known of the wartime activities of the British Socialist Party. Its paper *Justice* showed in July 1913 that in District IX (Birmingham & District) there were 13 branches including Black Country branches in Oldbury, Smethwick, Walsall, Wednesbury, West Bromwich and Wolverhampton. In January 1915 when divisional conferences were called it was found impossible to hold one in IX District. By October 1915 Div. IX. consisted of only three branches – Handsworth, Coventry and Walsall. A Walsall BSP branch existed in 1916. The Walsall Red Book shows a local BSP branch in 1917 and there might have been one in 1918 but no Red Book was published. In 1920 H. Ward of the Walsall BSP was the only Black Country delegate to the Convention that formed the Communist Party, so it is a reasonable supposition that the Walsall BSP functioned throughout the war.

There is no mention of Socialist Labour Party branches in the Black Country at any time during the war. Both nationally and in Birmingham the SLP strengthened itself at the expense of the BSP because of the SLP's anti-war policy. Its paper *The Socialist,* however, records no Black Country activity whatever, although there would be individual supporters.

With regard to the Independent Labour Party, many of the branches became impotent or ceased to exist when the war broke out. But such ILP branches that remained strong enough to be active were anti-war from the beginning. One of the most influential regional leaders was Harry Brockhouse of West Bromwich and both he and his ILP branch and Labour Church in West Bromwich actively opposed the war. Brockhouse was chair of the Birmingham and District ILP Federation and, as the ILP regained strength, the Midland ILP Federation. Both the nearness of Birmingham to West Bromwich and also because Erdington, City and later other ILP branches were active in Birmingham from the beginning of the war gave considerable scope for the activities of Brockhouse. The following activities are reported through the *Labour Leader.*

At the Annual Midland Conference of the ILP in January 1915 Brockhouse was elected president.

In February Brockhouse was at a West Bromwich ILP social where he presented an illuminated address to J. Micklewright for his services to Socialism, Trade Unionism and Co-operation.

The Birmingham ILP Federation arranged a series of conferences on the war and Brockhouse spoke at Erdington. At the Easter national conference of the ILP Brockhouse made his attitude clear when he moved a motion requesting that action be taken with neutral countries to bring the war to an end and re-establish the International on a broad and lasting basis. 'If the war is right it should be pursued; if wrong it should be stopped.'

In April 1915 a new branch was reported of Walsall and District with T.J. Allsop as secretary. The next month Stourbridge reported that throughout May it had held open-air meetings at Southwell's Coppice, Quarry Bank. There had been a 'fine send off on Labour Day' with John Kneeshaw speaking and the last week had a 'rousing speech from J. Bailey of West Bromwich. They reported that they had lost one or two members since the war, but had made 11 recruits in the last few months.

In June Brockhouse had a letter in the *Labour Leader* condemning the 'silly vanity' of those (Arthur Henderson and others) who had joined the Government. It should have been discussed by the Trade Unions and the ILP, he claimed. 'The ILP must not be tied to this Coalition, Capitalist government.'

In June 1915 Walsall branch reported that they had opened their out-door meeting programme with a visit from Bruce Glasier, who had received 'a splendid reception.' The branch scorned the *Labour Leader* campaign to see that each member received a copy each week, by saying that most of their members already did take it, and they were planning to hold meetings in the neighbouring villages and introduce the paper there. Wolverhampton also reported a 'very successful' meeting with R.C. Wallhead where there had been 'a large, attentive, intellectual audience.' There had been some opposition which the speaker had overcome. The meeting had been followed by an informal social in the branch rooms. In August Wallhead returned to Wolverhampton for a 'memorable' visit. The audience was 'highly appreciative of the high moral stand' of the ILP for Peace and Justice.

Less activity was reported for the rest of the year, but Brockhouse remained active, chairing a Birmingham memorial meeting for Keir Hardie. The West Bromwich Labour Church at the People's Hall, Lower High Street, continued to advertise its winter programme.

From the beginning of 1916 the battle against Conscription was being fought and lost and the ILP ceased to be the only force for peace. It is impossible to overstate the importance of the issue of Conscription to the people of the time. 'The greatest fight since Magna Carta' the *Labour Leader* called it. Conscription crossed the line that divided freedom from 'Prussian slavery.' The state had no right to control its citizens body and soul. Conscription negated everything that the war was about. Moreover, military conscription would inevitably lead to industrial conscription, it was held.

In the early part of 1916 West Bromwich ILP continued to monopolise Black Country reportage. In January R.C. Wallhead addressed a public meeting. 'Our only regret is that the audience was in the hundreds and not the thousands. The way he dealt with the Jingo Compulsionists was a treat.'

Conscription and Conscientious Objectors

During the period in 1915 of trying to prevent Conscription being passed the two organisations which would play an important part in opposing the war came into existence. One was the Union of Democratic Control. This organisation, largely Liberal at its inception, argued that a main cause of the war was the undemocratic nature of foreign policy. With the disclosure by the Russians after the February 1917 Revolution of the Secret Treaties drawn up by the great powers to define spheres of influence in the post-war world, this organisation gained considerable prestige. A branch was established in Wolverhampton in 1915 and in December held a Conference which was addressed by Langdon Davies.

The other, and more important organisation, was the No-Conscription Fellowship which led and organised Conscientious Objectors from March 1916 when Conscription became operative. Before this the *Wolverhampton Chronicle* was noting this organisation. In February it printed a letter from John T. Passant, the secretary of the Wolverhampton No-Conscription Fellowship stating that its members were opposed to all forms of compulsory military service on grounds of conscience and were prepared to suffer for their convictions. A report in the same issue noticed the Walsall branch of the N-CF whose secretary was John H. Taylor. The branch had passed a motion reaffirming its opposition to Conscription.

For the first few weeks, local Tribunals were inundated with applications for exemption for every possible objection including that of conscience. Tribunals were able grant three forms of exemption – Absolute Exemption, Exempt Combative Duties, and Conditional Exemption for various periods of time. Absolute Exemption was discouraged and eventually removed altogether. There were Tribunals in every town and a Wolverhampton and District Appeals Tribunal. The local Tribunals were of local people and were, in the main, ready made from the Tribunals set up to hear objections to Attestation under the Lord Derby Scheme which had been the last ditch attempt at voluntary recruitment before Conscription. Such Tribunals included a Military Representative, whose task was to see that as many men as possible were obtained for the army. In Wolverhampton the military representative was Major Capel Cure. The following extracts from the local press give the flavour of the proceedings of the Tribunals, but no names are given and for the details of conscientious objectors we have to turn to *The Tribunal,* the paper of the N-CF. In Wolverhampton the Vicar of St. Lukes asked exemption for a Church Army evangelist who had Attested as he could not be replaced. The chairman suggested that a woman be trained for the job. At Dudley a clothing manufacturer asked exemption for a clerk earning 20/-d. a week. The military representative said he could not be indispensable if he only earned that amount. Exemption was refused. In another case an art student said it was against his principles to mutilate the human form. He also was refused exemption. in Walsall a youth objected on the grounds of the Bible precept, 'Thou shalt not kill.' He gained Exempt Combatant Duties as did a strict Baptist who said he would rather die than take a life under any circumstances.

Wolverhampton Tribunal seems to have been lenient when it gave absolute exemption to a brewer's drayman who said he did not deliver to public houses. Capel Cure gave notice that he would contest the decision. A slaughterhouseman was given one month's exemption. Capel Cure remarked, 'It appears the slaughtering business is being overdone and the army underdone.' How conscientious objectors were dealt with is illustrated when a 24 year old pharmacist stated that human life was sacred in the sight of God and as a follower of Jesus Christ he must follow the precept of Love thy Enemies. The chairman (L.B. Moreton) asked why he didn't go to Germany and love them there. Major Capel Cure asked, 'If you were walking along a street and your mother was attacked, what would you do?' The pharmacist replied that it was a hypothetical question which he refused to answer. Another member (Ald. Craddock) said it was a pity he had not read the history of his Puritan forefathers who had shown a better spirit. The chairman then asked what he would do in the face of the atrocities in Belgium. 'I'd ask God for guidance and get it,' was his reply. Major Capel Cure then suggested that he be sent to the front. 'That will never happen,' he replied. He was eventually given Exempt Combatant Service. He said he would appeal. This man was on his way to becoming an Absolutist, who would not fight, would not accept non-combatant service, would not accept work which in any way assisted the war effort and who spent the rest of the war in prison.

Important political decisions were being taken at this time. In February the Labour Party conference confirmed its opposition to Conscription, but defeated a motion for its representatives to withdraw from the government. At Easter the ILP confirmed its opposition to the war and the British Socialist Party split in two with a majority in favour of immediate peace and the minority under H.M. Hyndman withdrawing to form a National Socialist Advisory Committee. The next month the Miners' national conference confirmed their opposition to Conscription and such was their power in wartime that they became a law unto themselves compared with the general trade union movement.

By April 1916 the *Labour Leader* and *The Tribunal* were reporting conscientious objectors (both religious and political) being arrested after failing to report for military service and being taken to military barracks. Here attempts (peaceful and not so peaceful) would be made to get them to wear military uniform, when they would be deemed enlisted. If they refused to do this they were then court-martialled and taken to civil prisons to serve their sentence.

The first Black Country conscientious objectors reported in *Labour Leader* were two brothers,

Luther and George Gee, A. Morley and J. Waplington all from Smethwick and G.R. Aston and G.O. Aston both from Wolverhampton. *Tribunal* gave further details. The brothers Gee, both schoolteachers and members of the N-CF, were arrested at their respective schools, taken before the Smethwick magistrates, fined £2 each, handed over to the military authorities and taken to Lichfield Barracks. Both had been before a military tribunal and been refused exemption.

At Lichfield Barracks on May 3rd. sentences were read out on 12 conscientious objectors who had been court-martialled the previous week. G.O. Aston, W.A. Cooper, R.E. Pond of Wolverhampton, L.J. Holmes, A.C. Morley and J.A.C. Waplington of Smethwick and J.C. Lovegrove of Walsall were all given 56 days hard labour, afterwards commuted to 56 days detention. G.R. Aston of Wolverhampton was given 56 days hard labour commuted to 46 days detention. B.C. Payne of Smethwick was given 56 days hard labour commuted to 49 days detention. R. Jones of Gornal was given 84 days hard labour commuted to 63 days detention. The brothers Gee were not informed of their sentence. Two weeks later courts-martial at Lichfield sentenced the Gee brothers to 56 days detention and Bell of Walsall was given 112 days detention commuted to 28 days. Later in May W.H. Turner and J.H. Westwood, both of Smethwick were court-martialled and both received 56 days detention.

John Kneeshaw, the Birmingham councillor, was present at the court-martial of the Gee brothers. who were the first to be arrested in the Birmingham district. The court consisted of six officers, the president of which was most scrupulous in taking evidence and seeing that the men received a fair trial. Their father gave evidence on their behalf and said he was responsible for their position as he had taught his sons to believe in the sanctity of human life and the common brotherhood of all men. Warfare was an iniquitous and futile method of settling international differences, he claimed. Luther Gee spoke of having made Jesus Christ his ideal and that war was in direct opposition to His life and teaching. Both were found guilty, but George Gee remarked that it was a pleasure to find a court possessed of such courtesy and consideration compared with their experiences at other Tribunals.

A considerable amount is known about William Arthur Cooper and a lesser amount about R.E. Pound. Both were masters at Tettenhall College and their claims for exemption were heard before the Tettenhall Tribunal on 18th March. Both were given exempt combative service. The military representative told Cooper that he was talking 'deep theology,' but agreed that his present work was a vocation. He was also puzzled why Cooper was prepared to help wounded soldiers in Tettenhall, but not in France.

Cooper was almost immediately called up, refused to enlist and was arrested in Tettenhall as a deserter by a 'very friendly policeman.' With others he was taken to Wolverhampton and tried. 'We were treated very well and the military representative evidently hated the job of having to appear against us.' The verdict, as they expected, was a 40/-d. fine and they were remanded to wait for an escort. 'We think we are going to Lichfield where we believe there is a sympathetic commanding officer who is doing nothing until he receives definite orders from headquarters. Everyone here has been very nice. We have the run of quite a lot of cells and we are allowed to write. Hardships have not yet begun,' Cooper wrote.

Cooper wrote a letter to *The Friend* on 20th April from Whittington Barracks, Lichfield, and was described as the Clerk of the Wolverhampton Preparatory Meeting. He said they were in a special guardroom which was infinitely better than the general one 'with its ordinary drunks and deserters.' They could get newspapers and send and receive letters. They had 'quite an amount of unofficial liberty' in their exercise (yard?) at the back. 'The army so far is any amount better than the Tribunals,' Cooper ended.

Soon after this 11 'privates of the South Staffs. regiment' were charged with 'disobeying the lawful commands of superior officers.' Herbert Darling spoke for all the accused by saying that they were not amenable to the Court because they were not soldiers. The president of the Court replied, 'We have nothing to do with that.' They were found guilty and sentenced on May 3rd. to 56 days hard labour commuted to detention. Two week later Cooper was reported at York where he was on his way to the Castle where he was to serve the remainder of his sentence. Visits by local Friends had been refused.

A further letter from Cooper stated that he was allowed to go into the city on 31st May and visited three Friends. The next day he was taken back to Lichfield, two weeks before his four weeks at York was served. At York Castle he had been placed in irons for over 20 hours. In the daytime his arms were fastened behind him. At night he was allowed fifteen minutes to undress and get to bed, after which his hands were placed before him and irons put on again. This report is ambiguous as to whether putting men in irons was standard practice at York Castle. His letter was written from 'the library' of Whittington Barracks where Cooper served the rest of his sentence. Life was pleasant, but 'a terrible waste of time,' he reported.

This is typical of the treatment of the earliest conscientious objectors. The military were not at all keen for their unwelcome guests to serve their detention in military barracks, and it was quickly arranged that COs would be transferred to serve their hard labour in civil prisons. The sufferings of COs in military hands varied considerably, as Cooper's example shows; when transferred to civil prisons the privations of hard labour and punishments for infringements of regulations were severe, but more uniform. COs also then had the option of accepting civilian work in camps, if their consciences would allow. Those who returned to prison time and time again were the Absolutists who would perform no work under compulsion. Other COs compromised and worked in the camps; Cooper was one of these.

By November 1916 Cooper was at the Wakefield Work Centre. Here the men were threatening to return to prison rather than serve in this Labour colony. Twelve men from the Centre were sent to work at a private quarry at 8d. per day. They then asked whether the men they displaced were called up. The Home Office refused to recognise the COs' right to question their conditions of work and stated that the ten men who had objected would be returned to prison and another ten men sent in their place. The COs then held a meeting and determined that they would all take the same stand. What that stand was and how the matter ended is not known. Of Cooper's colleague, R.E. Pond, nothing is known except his original court-martial sentence.

Returning to general political activity in the spring of 1916, the West Bromwich Labour Church reported a meeting with a new ILP midlands organiser, Harold Croft, in April. Stourbridge reported that it was holding its own in 'these trying times,' and their chief activity had been in co-operation with the local Committee against Conscription, the secretary of which was an ILP member. This is likely to have been Harold D. Wrigley, who was secretary of the Stourbridge N-CF in 1917.

In May, the West Bromwich Labour Church carried out a 'Peace Raid on 'Bromwich,' before breakfast on a Sunday. A 'Road to Peace' leaflet and 'No Conscription' literature was distributed. Lists of arrests of COs were published in the *Labour Leader* and those for May included H.W. Bell and A.E. Roberts of Walsall and W.H. Turner and J. Westwood of Smethwick. At the Smethwick ILP 11th AGM a further letter from Luther Gee at Lichfield Barracks was read and his 'splendid stand for Freedom' was recognised by his being unanimously elected as vice-chairman of the branch.

Stourbridge ILP opened its out-door programme, despite stormy weather, at Saltwell Coppice. 'The largest crowd we have ever had,' listened to Councillor Kneeshaw (Uncle Bill) speak on 'British Prussianism.' Later the same day Kneeshaw spoke at the Labour Hall to a large audience on 'The War so Far.' Suggestions for a Peace Conference to settle differences between nations was 'heartily applauded.' The Black Country branches were then distributing a series of Road to Peace leaflets. The first was entitled 'A Patched up Peace,' the second 'The Jingo View, the third 'Old Men and Young,' the fourth 'If the War Goes On,' and the fifth 'The ILP Attitude.' At Saltwell Coppice 'A crowd of 500 were disappointed when the advertised speaker could not appear, but Mr Keeble of Stourbridge and another from Oldbury held the crowd for over an hour while six dozen *Labour Leaders* and 10/-d. worth of literature was sold.' In the evening Harrison Barrow filled the gap at the Labour Church by speaking on 'The War – The Way Out.' At West Bromwich Dick Wallhead did an open-air meeting. 'We were astonished at the size of the crowd. The *Labour Leader* and *Forward* sold like hot cakes. Our literature was absolutely sold out,' it was reported. West Bromwich ILP was gathering signatures to a Peace Petition, 'with encouraging results.' The local clergy were being visited and asked for their support. At the Labour Church the *Labour Leader* was still being sold out.

In July the branches sent delegates to the Birmingham and District ILP Conference. This passed resolutions declaring that militarism and war was a subversive combination and disputes should be settled not by force but by reason and arbitration. The Conference also endorsed the principles of the International and Socialist Conference recently held at Copenhagen. There was also a Midlands Rally in the same month at which 800 people had been expected, but 1,200 turned up to discuss the two main issues of the 'Treatment of Conscientious Objectors' and 'Peace Negotiations.'

Activity continued through the summer and autumn. In August the West Bromwich branch had their first two conscientious objectors arrested and tried. 'The are both full of courage,' it was reported. The branch also had good meetings with F.C. Jowett and later a successful week-end with Fred Bramley whose theme was food and fuel prices. At night he spoke at the Labour Church. 'His oration has never been excelled in West Bromwich.' Success at West Bromwich continued into September with a visit from Mrs Muriel Wallhead where the branch's two conscientious objectors were introduced, 'and met a sympathetic reception from the audience.'

October saw a series of Keir Hardie memorial meetings including a large crowd at Smethwick Town Hall where Harry Brockhouse spoke on 'Twenty Years Personal Friendship with Keir Hardie.' A letter was also read from Councillor Simcox who was undergoing 18 months hard labour at Wormwood Scrubs. Several new members were made and literature sales were 'reminiscent of the old times before the war.' For the rest of the year activity continued in West Bromwich, but little is reported from elsewhere.

This very high level of peace activity in 1916, which had been triggered by the issue of Conscription alarmed the war party in the Labour movement. Already in July 1915 Victor Fisher of the pro-war section of the British Socialist Party had formed a National Socialist Defence Committee. Early in 1916 Fisher merged this Committee into the British Workers' Defence League. This was supported not only by most of the virulently pro-war Labour movement elements but also by wider Liberal and Conservative ministers and military men. The BWDL inevitably degenerated into a violently anti-Socialist organisation and stood candidates against Labour in the 1918 general election.

In May 1916 the British Workers' National League held a meeting in Wolverhampton with prominent national pro-war speakers. The chairman was John Beard who was the leading midlands official of the Workers' Union whose leaders were super-patriots, none more so than Beard. The local speaker was the Rev J.A. Shaw who had become a Socialist and supporter of the Labour Party in the pre-war years, but was pro-war and took upon himself the leadership of opposition to pacifists and conscientious objectors in Wolverhampton. The *Wolverhampton Chronicle* reported that there was constant heckling and interruptions at this meeting.

In November a British Workers' National League pro-war meeting was held in Bilston. J.H. Davies of Willenhall was in the chair and the Rev Shaw moved a resolution in favour of the continuation of the war which was passed. The *Wolverhampton Chronicle* reporter found it necessary to state that. 'the meeting passed off without disturbance.'

It seems clear that in 1916 not only was anti-war sentiment popular, but pro-war meetings were liable to be upset if the speakers claimed to be speaking on behalf of workers.

If 1916 had not been a good year for Labour patriots, 1917 was to be worse. In March there was the first Russian Revolution, in June the Leeds Convention with a resolution to set up Soviets in Britain, and subsequent Black Country support for a regional conference which the authorities found it necessary to ban.

By 1917 there was only a trickle of conscientious objectors through the Tribunals, as all of those in age groups up to 41 had been obliged to appeal when Conscription began. Wolverhampton Appeals Tribunal continued to provide such classic cases as a one eyed-man who had been certified as fit for military service and the Tribunal member who noted that his shooting eye was 'in a state of efficiency.' But information on Black Country COs is very sparse. There is nothing in the *Tribunal* where one would expect to find it as it would seem that many Black Country COs had political objections and would have been members of the No-Conscription Fellowship. *The Friend* also has few references although it attempted to cover all COs whether religious or political. Some information on the movements of W. Arthur Cooper are, however, available as he was an active and eloquent Quaker. By May 1917 he had opted for work under the Home Office scheme and was at the Wakefield Work Centre where he remained for most of the war.

ILP activity in the winter of 1917, as reported in the *Labour Leader,* again showed West Bromwich as the most active branch. In January it reported 'steadily increasing membership,' and meetings with Kneeshaw on 'Notes to President Wilson', and Maurice Reckitt on 'Guild Socialism.' In February Walton Newbold spoke on 'War and the Metal Trades,' with local examples. At the Labour Church Brockhouse spoke on 'What I Believe.' In March West Bromwich held a public meeting with W.E. Wilson on 'The Case for Disarmament.' Jingoes were present, but 'he knocked 'em,' the report stated.

The *Wolverhampton Chronicle* continued to report activity by the British Workers' National League. In January they held meetings in Wolverhampton and Willenhall. The former was at Shaw's church hall (All Souls). The main speaker was the national secretary, Victor Fisher, who urged his audience to 'get rid of all class hatred and bias.' A Birmingham speaker was Norman Tiptaft, once a militant Social Democratic Federation activist, but who subsequently managed to conceal all such youthful indescretions; he spoke on the need for greater output. They had 'a good reception.' At Willenhall the chairman was again J.H. Davies, secretary of the Gas, Municipal and General Workers Union, whose leadership was as jingoistic as that of the Workers' Union. The speaker was Charles Sitch leader of the Chainmakers Union at Cradley Heath.

In March 1917 pacifists hit back when the Wolverhampton branch of the Union of Democratic Control held a meeting in Wolverhampton. Harrison Barrow, the Birmingham Quaker, told the meeting that, in President Wilson's phrase, there could only be peace without victory, i.e. a negotiated peace. Father Darmody, the leading Irish Roman Catholic priest in Wolverhampton, presided at this meeting. His first point was to state that only the north east of Ulster was opposed to Home Rule. His second point was to refer to a recommendation of the Overseers of the Poor (Darmody was a long time Guardian of the Wolverhampton Poor Law). This was that discharged, disabled soldiers who could not obtain work should be exempt from paying the Poor Law rate on the grounds of poverty. This was taken to the County Court where the Bushbury parish clerk declared that this was the only exemption recommended on the grounds of poverty in fifteen years. The case was adjourned for further enquiries.

The British Workers' League, which was never short of finance, largely derived from aristocratic and military sources, seems to have made progress in the Black Country. By June 1917 a South Staffs Federation of the League was reported with 'large meetings' in Willenhall, Wolverhampton, Dudley etc. The Rev Shaw and Charles Sitch continued to be the main local speakers. At an outdoor meeting in Wednesbury in May Shaw said that there was an urgent need for patriotic labour to organise for victory over a dastardly foe. The intrigues of pacifists with the Russian socialist minority were deplorable, he claimed. A 'large crowd' was reported. A patriotic demonstration organised by the Brierley Hill Trades & Labour Council in the town hall was also reported at which Eldred Hallas from Birmingham was the speaker. In June another 'large meeting' was reported on Wolverhampton Market Square with Victor Fisher, the national secretary of the BWL, supported by local speakers Shaw and Tiptaft.

In July 1917 British Workers' League meetings were reported at Stourbridge, Oldbury, Halesowen, and Blackheath. At Oldbury, however, the League had 'found the pitch occupied by Pacifists.'

From this time, reports of BWL meetings become scarcer, although in November it was announced that Victor Fisher would be a Parliamentary candidate for the BWL in Stourbridge at the next general election.

The decisive turning point in peace activity in 1917 undoubtedly arose from the Leeds Convention of June 1917. This is often derided as the failed conference where unsuccessful attempts were made to set up Soviets in Britain. It is true that this was one of the main aims of the Convention. But the other aim was to rally support for a negotiated peace to end the war, and in this respect the Convention was crucial.

There does not appear to be a surviving list of delegates to the Leeds Convention. We therefore have no record of Black Country representation, although we know that delegates went from Birmingham. The aftermath of Leeds is also represented as equally disastrous with regional conferences called being broken up by jingoistic mobs or being banned. The latter was the fate of the

Birmingham regional conference called for August 1917. However, by great good fortune we have a full list of the delegates elected to this regional Conference preserved by Private Jim Simmons, the midlands organiser, who after World War Two became MP for Brierley Hill. This list shows the enormous support that existed in the Labour movement for activity to support the peace call from Leeds. In all 219 delegates representing 140 societies were elected. From the Black Country were the following: Walsall and Stourbridge Labour Parties; Stourbridge, Wolverhampton Netherton and West Bromwich ILP branches; West Bromwich and Stourbridge Labour Churches; Staffordshire District Council and Stourbridge branch of the National Union of Railwaymen; Stourbridge branch of the Associated Society of Locomotive Engineers and Firemen; Smethwick and Oldbury branches of the Workers' Union; two Smethwick branches of the Amalgamated Society of Engineers; West Bromwich branch of the National Union of Clerks; the No-Conscription Fellowship of West Bromwich; Oldbury Labour Representation Committee; Warley Institute Church; Stourbridge Union of Democratic Control; the National Amalgamated Lockmakers and Metal Workers' Trade Society; Smethwick branch of the Amalgamated Society of Woodworkers; finally, but most importantly, the following Trades Councils, Oldbury, Smethwick, Stourbridge, Walsall, Wednesbury and West Bromwich. The Birmingham regional conference was banned at the last minute by the chief constable of Birmingham, no doubt on the advice of the government. It is clear, however, from this list of delegates elected that there was widespread support across the whole of the Black Country labour movement for peace. This support was to grow in the final year of the war.

1918

In January 1918 the Labour Party adopted the policy of peace by negotiations. The next month there was an inter-allied Socialist and Labour Conference held in London to define war aims. The German military offensive in the spring of 1918 dampened peace activity for a few months. In March the Russians signed the Brest-Litovsk Treaty taking them out of the war. This created anti-Bolshevik hysteria, but also increasing demands for a negotiated peace. The food situation in Britain was also seriously deteriorating and, almost at the end of the war, a national system of rationing was devised. By August the allied offensive with tanks gave new heart to both peace by negotiation and also the one-more-push camp. Talk by then was of a coming general election, and when the war actually ended in November there appears to have been no time to celebrate it, as election and peace issues required immediate attention.

It is against this background that political activity went on in the Black Country. In January A.G. Walkden, a prospective Parliamentary candidate attended a joint meeting of Trades Council and Labour Representation Committee in Wolverhampton to discuss reconstruction, food questions, changes in the constitution of the Labour Party and the question of the League of Nations. Walkden had been a jingo, but was now being forced to acknowledge objective changes. Also in January the proposed Comrades of the Great War was said to have the support locally of Lord Dartmouth. This was a 'patriotic' organisation, eventually set up in August 1918, to offset the supposed revolutionary influence of the two other national organisations to which discharged servicemen looked for their welfare. These were the National Association of Discharged Sailors and Soldiers formed in 1916 associated with the Labour movement, and the National Federation of Discharged & Demobilised Sailors and Soldiers formed in 1917 and originally associated with the Liberal Party. Activity around this issue is reported from Stourbridge in January when an 'interesting and constructive' lecture was given by a discharged soldier, J.C. Scriven, on 'Money and Patriotism'. Scriven condemned those who rushed to the Tank Banks to put their money in War Savings at the highest possible rate of interest. Scriven suggested that it would be better for the government to pay for the war by reducing the capital of firms and taking sufficient securities from them. At West Bromwich ILP F. Bowers spoke on the 'Relations between Capital and Labour – Past, Present & Future.' A 'good audience' was reported with six new members made which brought the total membership of the branch to 107. The British Workers' League announced that they intended to stand candidates at the general election in every constituency where Pacifists were standing.

The food question dominated February with meetings at Wolverhampton, Walsall, Dudley,

Darlaston and Wednesbury to support a national rationing scheme and demanding increased Labour representation on local Food Committees. 900 delegates representing 200,000 workers assembled at a South Staffs and East Worcs. Federation of Trades Councils conference presided over by Charles Sitch which passed a resolution in favour of rationing all foods. In Wednesbury the *Express & Star* reported that a 'large number' of workers had left their employment to protest against food distribution in the borough.

In March 1918 election activity quickened. In Wednesbury candidates were nominated for the local seat and Alfred Short of Sheffield, a Boilermaker, was successful from a heavy weight short list of J. Baker of the Iron & Steel Union, H. Whitehouse of the miners, and J.T. Brownlie the president of the ASE. Also in March 1918 the *Labour Leader* reported a new ILP branch in Cradley. The report stated that with a number of new members enrolled and some transferred from Stourbridge 'this is a promising area.'

April brought no notice of activity, but May saw outdoor activity resumed. Stourbridge started on May Day at Saltwells Coppice with J. Bailey from West Bromwich as speaker. 30/-d. worth of literature was sold with orders for more. 'People want our message' (of peace) it was claimed.

In June the 'biggest ever' conference of conscientious objectors was held nationally and the Peace Society held its 102nd AGM. and we can return to the little information that we have on the Black Country COs. From 25th April, after the police raid when the printing press was smashed, *Tribunal* appeared in a smaller format, clandestinely printed and information on prisoners was more limited. W.A. Cooper continued at Wakefield where hooligans attacked the camp in May and nineteen COs were hospitalised.

In July, Luther Gee of Smethwick was released on health grounds from Winson Green prison; there is no news of his brother George. In October COs released from Winson Green included G.O. Aston of Wolverhampton and W. Millington of West Bromwich.

The end of the war brought no respite for the COs. Official policy was to continue their detention until all service men had been demobilised. This brought widespread hunger strikes and releases under the Cat & Mouse Act. One such release from Canterbury temporarily was Wilson of Birmingham in March 1919.

The most extraordinary case however was the arrest of the mother of John Waplington, the Smethwick CO, in November 1918. Mrs Waplington was charged under the Defence of the Realm Act 43b Regulation which made it a punishable offence for a mother to shelter a 'deserter' son. This law had created outrage among servicemen and had been repealed with regard to men on active service abroad, but it still applied in England. John was an absentee from Dartmoor Settlement and was found at home. Mrs Waplington defended herself against a prosecuting counsel, military police and two Home Office Officials. The Home Office officials demanded a severe sentence. Mr Waplington was fined £20 and his wife was sent to Winson Green for three months in the second division. Mrs Waplington said that for the previous six months her house was periodically searched by civil and military police. Sometimes at dead of night the family would be awakened and made to get up so that another search could be made for the son. Mrs Waplington was on the verge of a nervous breakdown when she was taken to prison. After three days she had to be removed to the prison hospital. She was released after 26 days 'very ill and broken in health,' but had no complaints against the prison authorities.

Turning to *The Friend*, there is news of Douglas G. James of West Bromwich in April 1918; he was then, however, described as a Cotteridge, Birmingham Attender and he was at the Dartmoor Settlement. A list in *The Friend* of May 1918 gives details of the following Black Country COs: A.H. Hinton of Smethwick was serving his second sentence in Newcastle Prison; H.A. Keeling of Walsall was serving his second sentence in Leicester Prison; J.H. Simcox of Smethwick was serving his fourth (?) sentence at an unknown prison; J.H. Taylor of Walsall was serving his second sentence in Wandsworth prison and with him was S. Turner of West Smethwick serving his first sentence. Finally, John Waplington was said to be serving his third sentence at Winson Green in May; but if the court case proceedings against his mother given above are correct it would seem that he must soon after have taken work under the Home Office scheme at Dartmoor and almost immediately absconded.

In July 1918 W. Arthur Cooper (now described as of York) was 'Exceptionally Employed'. This was civilian employment in an almost unlimited range of occupations, which had been one more ploy of the government to tempt the Absolutists out of prison and which had been spurned by them. It was, however, attractive to those COs who could square it with their consciences, as a release from the prisons or camps under penal control. Douglas James had also taken the Exceptionally Employed option by July 1918.

No other information has been found concerning the other Black Country COs. A list of fifty five men still in prison in July 1919 printed in the *Tribunal* contained no Black Country COs and in the same month the government announced that all prisoners were being released. A list of those known is given in an Appendix. We can return. therefore, to the political activity of the last six months of 1918.

The only mention of the ILP in the Black Country in the *Labour Leader* for the last six months of 1918 concerns the Wolverhampton branch. Here a national organiser, J. Austin Smith, visited the town for a week at the end of August. Meetings on Monday and Tuesday failed because of rain. On Wednesday he spoke at the Labour Rooms on 'Organisation.' Successful meetings were held on Snow Hill on Thursday and Friday, but a Saturday meeting was spoiled with the return of the rain. Smith's verdict was that the branch was making progress, but there was plenty of room for improvement. He urged the branch to 'put its back into it.'

The Khaki Election

Wolverhampton Chronicle coverage of the Labour movement was confined to electoral activity. In July W.B. Steer, president of the National Union of Teachers was adopted as Parliamentary candidate for Dudley. In November the Rev J.A. Shaw, standing as a British Workers' League and Coalition candidate in Wolverhampton East was asked why he left the ILP and Socialist movement. He said that he had never officially belonged to either. He could not become a member of the ILP 'without signing away my political liberty.' He advocated trade unionism 'in all seasons', but was against the rail strike of September which had been extended to Wolverhampton. Shaw warned against 'the types who supported Stockholm' and thought that the Germans could pay £10 billions in reparations. Shaw's chairman at this meeting was the Wolverhampton solicitor Randle J. Evans who, 'had been wounded in aerial fighting and had come from hospital to help him.'

On 11th December the *Wolverhampton Chronicle* gave a list of Black Country candidates. This showed the following Labour contestants:

W'ton East – No Labour candidate. Rev Shaw was defeated by the Liberal, G.R. Thorne.
W'ton West – Alexander George Walkden.
W'ton Bilston – Lt-Col (ret) John William Kynaston, physician and surgeon.
Dudley – William Bridgland Steer, schoolmaster.
Kingswinford – Charles Henry Sitch.
Stourbridge – Mary Reid Anderson (usually called Miss Mary MacArthur).
Walsall – J. Thickett, railway signalman.
Wednesbury – A. Short, boilermaker.
West Bromwich – Frederick Owen Roberts.

The Black Country constituency missing from this list is Smethwick, whose Labour candidate was J.E. Davison.

When the war ended Lloyd George hastened to call a 'khaki election' to ensure that he, as the 'man who won the war', should be returned. His own Liberal Party was irreparably split between supporters of the the previous prime minister, Asquith, and Lloyd George's Coalition supporters; the Tory party had participated in the wartime Coalition government; the Labour Party had withdrawn its members from the government and went into the campaign as a united body, although a small minority stayed with Lloyd George and called themselves Coalition Labour while the most right-wing pro-war Labour supporters appeared at the polls as National Democratic Party candidates. The key to winning a contest depended on having been a pro-war Coalition supporter of whatever shade and these candidates were said to have 'received the Coupon' which was a letter of support from Lloyd George.

The electorate, which now included women of thirty and above totalled 21 million but less than 11 million voted and of 4 million soldiers only 1 million were able to go to the polls. The elections were fought in a vengeful atmosphere of 'hang the Kaiser', and 'make Germany pay until the pips squeak'. In such an atmosphere and with little time for campaigning on the key issues of post-war reconstruction, Lloyd George and his Coalitionists swept the field. Out of 707 seats the Coalition won 473 (including 332 Coalition Conservatives and 127 Coalition Liberals). Non-Coalition Conservatives won 50 seats and Non-Coalition Liberals 36 seats. The Labour Party returned 61 supporters (up on the 42 MPs of the last general election in 1910) and obtained 21 per cent of the total vote. Not only was the anti-war group of Labour MPs led by MacDonald and Snowden defeated, but also Henderson and other Labour leaders who had supported the war.

The results in the Black Country, however, were startlingly different from the national picture. The Labour vote in the Black Country was 40 per cent, a percentage the national Labour Party was not to reach until the 1945 election. In nine contests in the Black Country, the Labour Party returned no less than four MPs. None of these constituencies had had Labour MPs in the past and it is difficult to say which of these successes was the most sensational. In West Bromwich, F.O. Roberts, a trade union leader defeated the sitting Coalition Conservative, Viscount Lewisham, by 11,572 votes to 9,863. In Wednesbury a new Conservative coalitionist received 10,464 votes against A. Short, the boilermakers' leader who polled 50 per cent of the vote in winning the seat with 11,341 votes; the Liberal candidate received a derisory 988 votes and lost his deposit. In Smethwick J.E. Davison, the Foundryworkers' official, stood against Christabel Pankhurst, the famous Suffragette leader and ultra-patriot during the war. Christabel stood as a Women's Party candidate and ruffled the feathers of the local Conservatives who were obliged to withdraw their candidate when Christabel received the Coupon from Lloyd George. Despite this, Davison the Labour man polled 9,389 votes to Christabel's 8,614 and won the seat. The fourth Labour success was at Kingswinford. This was a three cornered contest. The Liberal received 3,943, the coalition Conservative 7,509 but Charles Sitch, the chainmakers' leader won the seat with 10,397. This is perhaps the most understandable of the Labour Party gains as Sitch was a well known local Labour leader. But the other Labour successes were totally unexpected, and achieved by trade union leaders who were not local men. Nor were these successes a flash in the pan, as all these constituencies continued to return Labour members at each election up to the catastrophic year of 1931.

This early Parliamentary support for the Labour Party puts the Black Country high among areas of Labour support in Britain and contradicts a common impression of the Black Country as politically 'backward'.

In searching for reasons for these successes, it should be noted that some of these were areas where there had been a not inconsiderable peace presence during the whole period of the war, notably Smethwick and West Bromwich.

We can also see high levels of Labour support in some constituencies where Labour did not win.

In Dudley, the coalition Conservative candidate beat Steer, the Labour NUT candidate by 9,126 votes to 6,064 Labour gaining 40 per cent of the vote. Of all the Black Country contests it was in Stourbridge that Labour had the highest hopes of victory for here the candidate was the redoubtable Mary Macarthur, well known for her leadership of the Chainmakers during their epic struggles from the early years of the twentieth century. Here, however, a National Democratic Party stood a candidate against her because Mary had been an supporter of a negotiated peace. The NDP candidate was the one who received the Coupon from Lloyd George. Nor was he an ordinary NDP member, but Victor Fisher, the founder of the National Socialist Defence Committee in 1915 which evolved into the National Democratic Party as a breakaway from the British Socialist Party. A final handicap for Mary Macarthur was that she was not allowed to stand under the name by which she was widely known, but under her married name of Anderson. A Conservative and Liberal also stood in Stourbridge making it a four party contest which divided the votes fairly evenly. The Liberal won with 8,920 votes, Mary Macarthur came second with 7,587. The Conservative and NDP candidates each polled 6,690 votes.

In Walsall the sitting member was Sir Richard Cooper. Cooper, with some others had, during the war, invented a new political party, the National Party, demanding a more energetic prosecution of the war. During the election two of the main planks of its policy were a harsh peace for the Germans and opposition to Lloyd George's policy of spraying honours around to anyone who would pay for them and thus contribute to his personal election fund. Standing against him as the Labour candidate was Joseph Thickett, the local railway signalman. Cooper stood as a National Party candidate but he was also a Conservative. In the latter capacity he received the Coupon from Lloyd George. But whether he accepted the Coupon and indeed whether he stood as a Conservative are matters disputed locally. Thickett's nomination upset the local Liberals who were used to two-party politics. In the event, Cooper romped home with Conservative support and polled 14,491 votes. The Labour candidate Joseph Thickett followed with 8,336 votes and the Liberals trailed with 4,914 votes.

Wolverhampton East was the only Black Country constituency where a Labour candidate did not stand. Here the Coupon candidate was the Rev J.A. Shaw, the local pastor of All Souls Unitarian Church standing for the National Democratic Party under the older title of British Workers' League. Lloyd George himself came to a Wolverhampton meeting at the Grand Theatre to rally support for Shaw from Liberals and attempt to allay Conservative discontents at having to stand down to make way for Shaw. But Shaw was faced by a very strong local Liberal, George Thorne, and the Labour Party declined to stand. Thorne won the seat narrowly with 7,660 votes against Shaw's 7,138. The poll was the lowest in the Black Country at 48.6 of the electorate. This suggests not only that Conservatives were luke warm in their support of Shaw, but that Labour voters stayed at home in large numbers.

Wolverhampton West was the only Black Country constituency which had previously had a Labour MP. This was T.F. Richards who had won the seat in 1906 as a result of the national pact with the Liberals at that time. But Richards lost the seat at the next election in 1910. The Labour candidate in 1918 was Alexander George Walkden, general secretary of the Railway Clerks' Association, who had nursed the constituency from 1912 and who had been strongly pro-war. Walkden was faced by Alfred Bird, the Birmingham custard king, who had consolidated the Conservative hold on the constituency since 1910 and was the sitting member. Bird received the Coupon, although he had differences with Lloyd George during the war. One of Bird's handicaps was that he had been anti-women's suffrage and voted against it to the last. The progressive local Liberal, Price Lewis, had withdrawn his candidature in 1913 when Walkden was adopted as Labour candidate and the local Liberals were in no position to find an alternative candidate. So it was a straight fight between Conservative and Labour. Bird won comfortably with 13,329 votes to 10,158, but Walkden had won 43 per cent of the vote.

In Bilston the election was a martial affair. The sitting member was Brigadier-General T.E. Hickman DSO, who had won the seat at the January 1910 election as Colonel Hickman, Unionist. T.E. Hickman was the fourth son of Sir Alfred Hickman, the former MP for Wolverhampton West, who was the largest employer in Wolverhampton. Against Hickman the Labour Party fielded another military man, Colonel J. Kynaston surgeon and physician, who also was a local man who had a medical practice in the constituency at Hurst Hill.

Kynaston's election manifesto promised: A League of Nations and democratic control of foreign policy; Nationalisation of the land and vital services such as mines, railways and shipping; One million houses on Garden City lines and abolition of slums; just and generous treatment to returning servicemen; the 'fullest possible' Home Rule measure for Ireland; a national system of education from nursery to university; reinstatement of trade union customs and conditions; a shorter working day and compulsory minimum wage; and strenuous resistance to saddling consumers with the cost of the war. Hickman's policy was the usual 'patriotic', Union Jack and Empire one of Hang the Kaiser and make the Germans pay for the war. The Bilston campaign was a dirty one with Hickman accusing Kynaston of moral turpitude. After the election Kynaston sued Hickman for slander and libel, but the jury was unable to agree on a verdict.

Under these circumstances Hickman won the seat with 10,343 votes and Kynaston polled 6,744 votes. The war had ended with a decisive consolidation of the power of the Labour Party in the Black Country.

Bibliography: Black Country Labour Politics 1914-1918

Newspapers: *Tribunal, Labour Leader, UDC, Justice, Wolverhampton Chronicle, Express & Star*. For W.A. Cooper see *Friends at the Tribunals 1916-19* (Extracts from *The Friend*), copy at Woodbrooke College Library. Also information from Geoffrey Hancock, historian of Tettenhall, ex-teacher at Tettenhall College. For British Workers' League see Roy Douglas – 'National Democratic Party & British Workers' League' (in *Historical Journal*, vol. xv, 1972). For Midlands Regional Conference arising from Leeds Peace Convention see Jim Simmons papers at Birmingham Reference Library. For the origins of the ex-Service organisations see Graham Wooton – *The Official History of the British Legion*. For the 1918 election results: important material in my possession from Chris Roseblade with complete results for both municipal and general elections for Birmingham and the Black Country from 1918 to 1955; Michele Shoebridge – *Women's Suffrage in Birmingham & District* (Wolverhampton MA thesis, 1983); P.C.D. Page – *Candidacy & Campaigning in Wolverhampton Parliamentary Elections 1900-1918* (Wolverhampton MA thesis, 1987). For Joseph Thickett, Eric Taylor's entry in the *Dictionary of Labour Biography*, vol. 2. For the confused 1918 Walsall election Kenneth J. Dean – *Town and Westminster, A Political History of Walsall 1906-1945*. For the Bilston election details I am indebted to John Smallshire and his collection of material at Wolverhampton Central Library.

Appendix: Black Country Conscientious Objectors, World War 1

Sources: *The Friend, The Tribunal,* List at Friends Library, London, the *Labour Leader* (April 1916).
Abbreviations: Bks: Barracks; CM: Court Martial; CP: Civil Prison; ECS: Exempt Combative Service; Except Empl: Exceptionally Employed; FLL: Friends' Library List, nothing further known; HL: Hard Labour; HOS: Home Office Schemes; LT: Local Tribunal; Rlsd: Released; Res W: Released to Reserve W; sen: Sentence; WG: Winson Green; WC: Work Camp; WS: Wormwood Scrubs; 16: 1916 etc;

ASTON, G.O. – Wolverhampton Apr 16 CM, July 18 Rlsd WG.
ASTON, G.R. – Wolverhampton Apr 16 CM.
BELL, H.W. – Walsall Apr 16 CM.
COOPER, William Arthur – W'ton Mar 16 LT. Nov 16 Wakefield Work Centre. May 17 Belmont Workhouse, Sutton: Aug 17 Wakefield WC. Oct 17 Wakefield WC. Apr 18 Wakefield WC. July 18 Exceptionally Employed. (Meeting House now given as York). Oct 18 Excp. Empl.
GEE, George – Smethwick Apr 16 CM.
GEE, Luther – Smethwick Apr 16 CM, July 18 Rlsd WG.
JAMES, G. Douglas – W. Brom. Oct 16 WS. Apr 18 Dartmoor Settlement. July 18 Excp Emp.
JONES, R. – Gornal. Apr 16 CM.
HINTON, A.H. – Smethwick. May 18 Newcastle CP 2nd sen.
HOLMES, A.C. – Smethwick. Apr 16 CM.
KEELING, H.A. – Walsall. May 18 Leicester CP 2nd sen.
LOVEGROVE, J.C. – Smethwick. Apr 16 CM.
MILLINGTON, W. – West Bromwich. Oct 18 Rlsd WG.
MORLEY, A.C. – Smethwick. Apr 16 CM.
PAYNE, B.C. – Smethwick. Apr 16 CM.
POND, R.E. – Wolverhampton. March 16 Exempt Combative Service.
ROBERTS, A.E. – Walsall. Apr 16 LT.
SIMCOX, J.H. – Smethwick. May 18 Newcastle CP 4th sen?
TAYLOR, J.H. – Walsall. May 18 Wandsworth CP 2nd sen.
TURNER, S. – West Smethwick. May 18 Wandsworth CP 1st sen.
TURNER, W.H. – Smethwick. Apr 16 CM.
WAPLINGTON, J.A.C. – Smethwick. May 18 Winson Green CP 3rd sen. Nov 18. Absconded from Dartmoor Settlement. Arrested at home.
WESTWOOD, J.H. – Smethwick. Apr 16 CM.

Additional information concerning W.A. COOPER and R.E. POND. from Geoffrey Hancock, historian and late history master Tettenhall College. W.A. COOPER became headmaster of Ackworth Quaker School, Yorks after the war. Mrs Hancock attended this school. R.E. POND taught at Bishops Stortford after the war and eventually returned to Tettenhall College about 1950 until his retirement.

Chapter 18

The Birmingham Labour Movement 1919-1926

Ex-Service Politics

As we have seen, the end of the war brought neither time nor inclination for prolonged celebration; too many problems crowded in. Not least was that of the ex-service man.

While the war was in progress ex-servicemen had begun on their own behalf to address their own problems, and for the first time in recent British military history, organisations *of* ex-servicemen rather than charitable organisations *for* them emerged. The first was the National Association of Discharged Sailors and Soldiers (hereafter the Association) in 1916. The next year the National Federation of Discharged and Demobilised Sailors and Soldiers (henceforth the Federation) appeared. Both had agendas for change which could not but be political and alarm grew that both organisations would be captured by the left, especially the Federation which banned officers from membership unless they had come up through the ranks. Militancy was raised to a high pitch by a 1917 Act decreeing that ex-servicemen already discharged should be medically re-examined with a view to recall to the services on the principle that if a discharged man could hold down a job at home he could do a job in the army. The fear of militancy led to the creation of a conservative and patriotic organisation, towards the end of 1917, the Comrades of the Great War.

The demobilisation problems of 1919 together with the massive industrial unrest of that year, compounded by the effects of the Russian revolution and the threat of war against Soviet Russia brought into existence the avowedly political and left-wing National Union of Ex-Servicemen (henceforth NUX).

From the point of view of the establishment, it was necessary to bring the ex-service organisations under the control of Tory politicians and the generals. Unity proceedings were initiated in 1919. The carrot was to be the United Services Fund, established in the autumn of 1919, to distribute the surplus profits of the various service war-time canteens. These funds eventually reached over £10m of which nearly £2m was distributed by the British Legion. NUX, which was a party to the early unity negotiations, was not admitted to the administration of this fund. From this formidable financial base, negotiations were eventually concluded in July 1921 and the British Legion was brought into existence with Earl Haig, the architect of the slaughter of the war, as president, and the Prince of Wales as patron.

Ex-service organisations played some small part in electoral activity in Birmingham. None contested the general election at the end of 1918, but in the first post-war local elections in November 1919. A NFDDSS candidate, E.A. Peacy contested St. Paul's ward where he polled the respectable total of 974 votes to the Unionists 1403. Peacy next appears as a Conservative candidate in the same ward in 1920 when he beat the Labour candidate E.C. Taylor, who had been the leader of the Police

319

Strike in Birmingham in 1919, by 2562 votes to 1679. By 1920 the NFDDSS was in negotiations to form the British Legion. This body when it was formed proclaimed itself 'non-political' and so direct ex-service participation in elections ceased.

Further evidence of NFDDSS activity in Birmingham comes from a pamphlet in the central library dated 1920. It is a curious mixture of the early militancy of the organisation and its later approach to the unity negotiations. The pamphlet was written by Captain E.C. Whillier who describes himself as vice-chairman of the Birmingham District of the NFDDSS and chairman of the joint committee NFDDSS and Comrades of the Great War. The pamphlet is entitled *The Case for the Ex-Serviceman*. It has a most lurid cover of an ex-serviceman in chains while a smiling, bloated Will Dyson type capitalist in top hat and evening dress and his expensively attired female companion gloat over their enjoyment of his ill-gotten war profits. The pamphlet summarises its own conclusions under the headings of 'The Dangers, the Safeguards and the Demands of Ex-service Men.' While the demands are radical the general outlook is right-wing and chauvinistic. The dangers were said to be internal unrest and the possibility of Revolution; a German war of revenge perhaps in conjunction with the Russian war of propaganda; the struggle in the Pacific between the white and yellow races. The safeguards against these dangers were the maintenance of the fighting services and the existence of a contented mass of workers, especially the ex-service men. The demands of ex-servicemen to avoid these dangers were therefore: the right to work or adequate unemployment pay; the right of every family to a home and garden; the more equal division of the wealth of the community; equal rights and duties for all irrespective of wealth or position; statutory recognition of the ex-serviceman's right to preference in employment, government appointments, housing and adequate disability pensions; the right to administer all funds raised by or for ex-servicemen.

It was however the activities of the National Union of Ex-Servicemen that mainly featured in the *Town Crier*. In the first issue in October 1919 it was reported that discharged soldiers were joining the ILP and the black-leg proof NUX. There were seventeen branches in the district Jim Simmons stated. NUX members were instructed to act with local Trades Councils and not only were NUX branches affiliated to Birmingham Trades Council in 1919, but Harry Blanchard was on its executive council. Jim Simmons and Harry Blanchard were to be the main leaders of NUX during the following years. The next week details were given of a Saltley NUX branch whose secretary was J.A. Gould, and Central branch meeting at the Spiceal Street Coffee House whose secretary was Blanchard. There was also an Aston branch, secretary G. Rainbow. By the end of 1919 NUX branches were protesting at the proposed local war memorial, demanding that the money be spent on houses for ex-servicemen. This was supported by the Trades Council where NUX delegates raised the issue.

By 1920 there was an established column in the *Town Crier* by C.E. Leatherland, who was the third outstanding NUX leader in Birmingham. One of his early columns in February 1920 reported that the Labour Party nationally had appointed an Advisory Committee on Ex-Service Questions whose chief advisors were members of NUX. He also wrote of the constant pleas of distinguished Admirals and Generals for ex-servicemen to 'keep clear of politics' as a demand to keep clear of Labour politics and allow clubs to be built from the Canteen profits instead of using them for housing and other social purposes. Leatherland used his column to advise on all aspects of ex-servicemen and their families' welfare, particularly pensions.

An article by A.E. Mander, general-secretary of NUX, explained the origins of the organisation. The militarists had conceived a semi-military organisation with a chain of clubs throughout the country where soldiers and sailors could become 'patriotically and alcoholically intoxicated' to the tunes of Rule Britannia and God Save the King. For a mere one penny a month they were to have the 'pride and pleasure of remembering that they were heroes of the great war.' But for this they must organise as a 'class apart' from their fellow workers within a 'non-political' organisation. This was the old imperialist policy of divide and rule, continued Mander, and it was under these circumstances that NUX had come into existence. It was 'the ex-servicemen's branch of the general Labour movement'. Its tasks were to explain that wars were caused by the 'machinations of the Capitalistic, Militaristic master class' and to work to 'overthrow the system which had produced the war and the appalling conditions which followed the peace'. The success of NUX had been 'almost phenomenal' and they were currently engaged in welding an international organisation on the same principles, Mander concluded.

At Easter 1920 NUX held its first annual conference, in Birmingham. The presidential address was given by John Beckett, a founder of NUX in London, later a Labour MP and then a fascist with Mosley. He believed that in days when order had replaced anarchy, history would record a special place for NUX whose members had suffered the crimes and horrors of war and were resolved to make such hellish recurrences impossible.

Mander, the general secretary, reported on the origins of the organisation and believed that the class war began in earnest in October 1919 with the rail strike. All ex-service organisations then had to show their real colours. The Comrades declared their support for the government at all costs; the Federation declared itself neutral. NUX, on the other hand had supported the railwaymen and had received the commendation of the whole Labour movement, Mander asserted.

Ex-Private Jim Simmons moved a motion of condemnation of the peace treaties with his usual religious slant, stating that it was opportune that the Conference was being held at Easter because the day of the Resurrection of the working classes was at hand. The final resolution, carried unanimously, condemned the peace treaty and characterised the 'present imperialistic and capitalistic League of Nations as nothing but a League of Damnations calculated to serve no other purpose than that of engendering hatred and laying the foundation of another war greater than that which had taken its toll of Europe during the past four and a half years.' On behalf of Birmingham, Leatherland moved a resolution urging the use of ex-munitions factories to provide work for disabled ex-servicemen and the unemployed.

Turning to organisation, there was a 'heated discussion', between those who wanted the District Committees to have organising and executive powers and those who wanted the Districts to have only co-ordinating powers as in the Independent Labour Party. Birmingham was for the latter view, Leatherland being the chief speaker in its favour with Jim Simmons supporting him. The co-ordinating proposal, which was also supported by the EC, prevailed. It was also decided that the organisation should be open to women from the auxilliary services, wives of members and widows and dependents of ex-servicemen. In its final sessions conference approved affiliation to the Ex-servicemen's International. When officers were elected, Mander was re-elected as general secretary and Beckett as chairman after Leatherland and another candidate had withdrawn their nominations. On to the executive committee of twelve, Leatherdale and Jim Simmons were elected. The Conference closed with the 'singing of the Red Flag by one hundred and fifty lusty voices.'

By May 1920 the local NUX had embarked on a summer campaign of open-air meetings. C.E. Leatherland, by then the midland organiser, was the main speaker. A Small Heath branch, meeting at the Royal George Hotel, Garrison Lane weekly was by then well established. Central Branch were in new premises at the Rose & Crown Hotel where a weekly Wednesday meeting 'guaranteed a lively and interesting discussion' as well as dealing with all pension etc problems. Saltley branch met on Mondays at the Swan Hotel, Washwood Heath Road, and a new branch at Hockley & Lozells was expected to be formed.

As well as being active with the Trades Council, where Leatherdale and a Trades Council deputation went to the Tramways Committee in March requesting free travel on the trams for cripples, NUX members worked with other organisations. The same month Harry Blanchard successfully raised with the Saltley Citizens' Committee the question of war widows being entitled to be assessed on their husband's pre-war earnings where this was more favourable to them. In April Leatherland was pressing through the local Labour Party for an amnesty for service men imprisoned for military offences during the war.

For the Easter NUX Conference Birmingham NUX tabled a motion deploring the timid and compromising policy of certain sections of the Labour Party and called on workers to elect strong candidates who would not compromise.

Leatherland's column 'Notes for Ex-Servicemen' continued to appear in the *Town Crier* recording deputations, resolutions and social activity such as concerts and also the opening of a new branch at Selly Oak.

In May the local NUX organisation suffered a severe blow when Leatherland left to take up a journalistic appointment in the north. Harry Blanchard succeeded Leatherland (as midlands organiser presumably – GB) and G.F. Symons was accepted as NUX representative on the local Advisory Board responsible for the training of ex-servicemen. Surprisingly, Leatherland's column in the *Town Crier* continued and one of his first items was that the National Federation of Discharged and Disabled Sailors and Soldiers had narrowly voted against affiliation to the Labour Party by 140 votes to 131.

In July 1920 Leatherland was reporting a No Rent policy called for by the NUX executive requesting that members seek support by putting this to all Labour bodies. Blanchard was praised for taking up with the local Comrades of the Great War their proposition to adopt 'ex-enemy children.' Blanchard said he could never conceive of children being 'enemy'. NUX Also protested at new war medals and clasps for men who had served with the interventionist forces in Russia and Serbia. In August Leatherland deplored the Unity Conference where four large ex-service organisations (the Federation, the Association, the Comrades and the Officers' Association) were 'bowing the knee to the military and adopting a strong anti-Labour stance.' This at a time when 'every Guardians & Distress Committee meeting shows ex-servicemen driven to the Workhouse.'

By this time there was considerable militancy in Birmingham and the activities of NUX reflects this. In September Harry Blanchard, recovered from a recent illness, was leading 'vigorous outdoor activity' in the Bull Ring. Central branch had heard a report from the Birmingham Council of Action on its attempts to prevent interventionist war in Russia. Small Heath branch was campaigning for the October elections to the War Pensions Committees on which NUX demanded greater representation. Leatherland himself had appeared before the Watch Committee to demand why ex-servicemen were not allowed to put their barrows down for a few minutes in the Bull Ring while the affluent people of Edgbaston were allowed to block the streets by leaving their automobiles outside fashionable shops for hours. The question of ex-service street sellers was to remain an important one. Saltley branch was particularly active. In a special Sunday Field Day in October Jim Simmons had spoken for 1½ hours at Alum Rock Terminus on 'Traitors to Democracy' in the morning. In the afternoon at the Ward End Parliament Simmons and Blanchard had spoken on 'What we Fought For', and in the evening at Highland Road School Simmons had spoken on 'The Coming Struggle.'

The Unity proceedings of the other ex-service organisations and the general militancy of the time led to a national crisis in the organisation. This was revealed in a letter by Jim Simmons in the *Town Crier* of 8th October 1920. He said that as a member of the NUX executive he was amazed to learn that Mander, the general secretary, had virtually advised disbanding the organisation and that the Communists in Birmingham knew more about this than he did. This suggests that Mander's advice was for NUX to join the newly formed Communist Party. Simmons rejected this solution, maintaining that Red Jingoism was as bad as any other. NUX must remain, Simmons concluded 'to convert ex-servicemen from their dependence on employers to a sense of solidarity with Labour and to fight relentlessly militarism and war.' By this time, however, Harry Blanchard and the Central Birmingham NUX branch had joined the Birmingham Communist Party.

The same issue of the *Town Crier* carried a report by Leatherland on the first stages of a reorganisation of NUX on the lines suggested by the Ilford branch. These were that the national organisation be dissolved and that local branches form themselves into autonomous bodies which would affiliate to a central national bureau in London which in turn would affiliate to the Ex-Servicemen's International. It was further recommended that branches federate to one of eight divisions. These would elect divisional councils and officers which would be represented on a new National Council. Leatherland ended by stating that 'certain branches have transferred their members en bloc to Labour and Socialist bodies, but through the instrumentality of NUX 'tens of thousands of ex-servicemen have been saved from the clutching hand of the reactionaries and have been trained to take their proper stand inside the ranks of Labour.'

Leatherland continued to report the progress of the new NUX in the *Town Crier*. In November 1920 he claimed more than 120 branches in about half a dozen districts. G.F. Simons, the Saltley NUX secretary, had become the organiser for the midlands district. Leatherdale also quoted with approval a recent letter in the *Town Crier* from Jim Simmons pointing out that ex-servicemen 'are the men most fitted to preach the sacred cause of pacifism, the cause which alone can bring salvation to the whole of the nations of the world and the whole of the working-class populations of those lands.' It was this mixture of pacifism and class struggle that was to distinguish Jim Simmon's long contribution to the peace movement in Birmingham and the Black Country.

In December Leatherland was deploring the 'closing of the ranks of the reactionaries,' foreseeing the British Legion developing as an organisation of two or three million White Guards, 'all ready organised in branches and posts, each complete with its captain at the head (...the Comrades' scheme) and all...under government tolerance if not actual support and with the backing of the biggest jingoes in the country.' Leatherland ended by warning that the Labour movement had not taken the ex-service movement seriously enough. Proletarians were being led astray through weakness, apathy and ignorance into the ranks of the reactionaries. Here they were carefully tended, diverted from politics, taught to see everything through 'patriotic' and 'profiteeric' spectacles, condemning trade unionists as being responsible for unemployment, despising pacifism, and looking upon the Labour man as a fiend.

An 'enthusiastic' Midlands District conference of NUX was reported in February 1921. The Birmingham delegates were Jim Simmons, J. Hoare and G.F. Simon. The Saltley branch proposed the following set of principles: Anti-militarism, Anti-humbug, A New Social Order, Land and Backpay, No Secret Diplomacy, and Co-operation with Labour. Officers elected were Jim Simmons (president), J. Worrod of Coventry (vice-president) G.F. Simons (secretary) and H.B. Cresswell of Coventry (treasurer). At the Conference there was said to have been Communists, ILPers, Labour Party members and Trade Unionists. They had tacitly agreed that none of them would try to dominate the movement for their own ends. Unfortunately, no list of branches attending appeared in the *Town Crier* and it would seem that Birmingham and Coventry were the main strengths of the movement at that time.

In March Leatherland was pointing out the realities of the 'non-politics' of the other ex-servicemen's organisations. The Comrades were supporting a Coalition candidate at Moseley and a Lieutenant Smedley Crooke who was a well-known capitalist and the treasurer of the local Comrades, as candidates at the next municipal elections.

Leatherland's column continued to appear in the *Town Crier* until August 1921 when he was appealing for more ex service to stand as candidates in local elections. From this time NUX disappears from the records. To a great extent NUX had been caught between the millstones of the British Legion which came into existence officially on the first day of July 1920 with its ample resources to deal with ex-servicemen's problems, and the formation of the Communist Party on the last day of the same month 1920 which took some of the NUX branches and many of its militants.

But this was not quite the end of a Labour based ex-service movement in Birmingham. In August 1924 the *Town Crier* noted the existence of an Ex-Servicemen's Guild in Birmingham. It is fitting, perhaps, that the same issue of the paper gave news of the activities of C.E. Leatherland. He had been appointed to an important position at Labour Party headquarters in London as Parliamentary Correspondent to the Labour Press Service and *Labour Magazine* at a salary of £450 rising to £550. A short biography stated that Leatherland had joined the Royal Warwickshire Regiment in 1914 and served in France and Germany until 1919. He was demobilised with the rank of Company Sergeant-Major and had been awarded the MSM as well as being mentioned in dispatches. On leaving the army he became an official of Birmingham Corporation and had been one of the founders of the National Union of Ex-Servicemen. He left four years after to take up a post with the *Macclesfield Courier*. He had recently won two out of three gold medals awarded by the London Chamber of Commerce for their English Essay Competition. He had also secured third place in an Economics examination conducted by one of the monthly political reviews. His Macclesfield editor added very high praise.

The first Ex-Servicemen's Guild branch appears to have been at Mosley. A second was announced in October 1924 when its first social was 'a huge success.' The same month brought news of the once militant Capt. E.C. Whillier. By this time he was chairman of the Birmingham County Council British Legion. He wrote to the *Town Crier* noting that a letter had been published over the name of a Birmingham member of the Legion in the *Birmingham Mail* appealing for all Legion members in Birmingham and the West Midlands to vote Conservative. Whillier reminded all members that the British Legion must not be brought into the political arena, its members consisting of supporters of 'all the three great political parties in the State.'

References to the Ex-Servicemen's Guilds then become rare until the end of 1925. In November George A. Sutton, secretary of the Deritend Guild, wrote to the *Town Crier* complaining that the British Empire Service League was distributing gratis in the factories a glossy magazine 'Our Empire'. At Christmas 1925 the Ladywood Guild was still in existence under its secretary G.R. Stiles. And Jim Simmons was addressing meetings on 'Christmas in the Trenches.'

In the first half of 1926 the Guilds flourished. In January Jim Simmons wrote deploring the reactionary policies of the British Legion and the fact that NUX had been dissolved 'owing to traitors in the camp.' He now put his faith in the Guilds, of which there were several in Birmingham, he claimed. Simmons put forward a 9 point Charter which included adequate pensions, equal educational provision for other ranks' orphan children as that given to officers' children, homes fit for living in, access to the land rather than being shipped to the dominions as emigrants, democracy for serving soldiers and a national policy of peace. He thought there were sufficient Guilds to hold a Birmingham conference in the near future.

Jim Simmons' article produced a crop of letters on Ex-Servicemen's Grievances over the following weeks demanding, in the words of one writer, 'a strong, militant, independent organisation for Ex-servicemen.' Only one letter suggested that the remedy was to get inside the reactionary British Legion; when Simmons remonstrated with the writer he stated that he was, nevertheless, already a member of the Guild. Ex-chairman of the Rotton Park Guild wrote that he had enrolled thirty new members since September and the movement was therefore flourishing.

In March 1926 the conference urged by Simmons took place and a National Federation of Ex-Servicemen's Guilds was formed. The objects of the Guilds were approved much as Simmons had proposed them. There is, however, no mention of Guilds outside Birmingham being represented and it would seem that the two leading figures were Jim Simmons and Percy Shurmer, both of whom later became MPs and remained active in the ex-service peace movement.

Hands off Russia

The Russian Revolution was so central to the post-war history of the Labour movement, that something of its general development must be said.

The Russian revolution of February/March 1917 (the differing months are accounted for by the alteration of the calendar after the revolution) was welcomed by all classes in Russia outside the Tsarist bureaucracy as a release from an intolerable burden of dictatorship and repression, and monumental wartime incompetence which had led to the total breakdown of the war effort.

For similar reasons, the Revolution met with widespread support from all classes in Britain, above all the working class. 'Patriotic' support for the Russian revolution in Britain, however, depended on how quickly the new government could resume and wage more efficiently the war against Germany.

By the time the October/November revolution occurred it was clear that the army had collapsed totally, and that the mainly peasant soldiers had no intention of continuing the war. For the peasants and the small but influential working class the revolution had been for Peace, Bread and Land and victory went to the party which would satisfy these demands. The story between February and October is that of increasingly desperate attempts of the middle classes to coerce the Russian people into a renewal of the war and when these efforts resulted in military defeat, the inevitable rise of the Soviets and their domination by what had been in February only a small faction of the Russian Social Democratic Labour Party, namely the Bolsheviks under Lenin.

Britain refused to recognise the new Russian government, withdrew its ambassador and limited its contacts to an 'agent', Bruce Lockhart. Contacts in Britain were similarly limited to to a Soviet 'representative,' Litvinov. Lockhart recognised that the Soviet government was likely to remain in power and recommended recognition. But by this time defeated aristocratic, military and business interests in Russia were desperately demanding intervention to overthrow the Bolsheviks. In June 1918 British and allied troops landed in north Russia and seized Soviet territory. In August British, Japanese, French and USA troops were landed at Vladivostok. Foreign armed intervention had begun.

Three months later the Great War ended with the collapse of the central powers as the revolution which had begun in Russia spread and looked likely to become world wide. For the British people, therefore, the ending of the 1st. World War looked likely to hold the prospect of unlimited war against Russia and this they would not accept.

The Hands Off Russia movement therefore lasted from 1917 until 1924 when the Soviet government was finally recognised by the first Labour government in Britain. The Hands Off Russia Movement then became the Anglo-Russian Parliamentary Committee.

The movement to oppose armed intervention in Russia and for recognition of the Soviet government was widely supported in the Labour movement from the beginning. The first Hands Off Russia Committee was formed in January 1919, and a national Committee existed by the middle of the year. In Birmingham a Hands Off Russia conference was organised in November 1919 with 150 delegates. Rudland, secretary of the Trades Council and Labour Party took the chair and a resolution demanding normal relations with Russia was moved by T.D. Smith of the Socialist Labour Party. William Paul also of the SLP moved that a provisional local committee be formed and affiliate itself to the national Hands Off Russia committee. In the same month Lloyd George admitted that £100 million had been spent on supporting intervention forces in Russia and said that such expenditure could not continue. But Winston Churchill, who was paranoiacally opposed to the Bolsheviks, had controlled the War Office since January 1919 and intervention continued.

Agitation against intervention continued in Birmingham and district. In January the national Shop Stewards' leader, J.T. Murphy addressed a series of meetings at Aston, Small Heath and Tyseley. In March a Birmingham & District Labour Propaganda Committee for the Hands off Russia committee was formed. Its chairman was Councillor Taylor of the Police Union, and it consisted of representatives from various ILP branches, the Daily Herald League and three of the Labour Churches.

The Birmingham Hands off Russia Committee convened a delegate conference in May to consider what action could be taken. Rudland, who chaired the meeting, said that international intervention showed that the League of Nations was an organised hypocrisy with the object of crushing workers when they tried to free themselves from capitalist slavery. Direct action was fully justified under these circumstances. He was in favour of affiliation to the Third International because it was imperative that all workers get together. W.T. Cardinal moved a resolution expressing deep indignation at the government's hostile policy to Soviet Russia and apprehension at 'the attempts being made by the allied governments to prevent the German workers establishing a Soviet Republic'. Mark Starr of the S. Wales Miners was the main speaker. He was concerned that if intervention continued, the German workers would be crushed when they tried to emulate the Russians. The solution was to keep our capitalists occupied at home and he proposed a one day strike every week. Leatherland for NUX said that if there were no army there could be no intervention and cautioned that if unemployment grew men would return to the army. Starr, in his summing up, regretted that no one had taken up his suggestion of strike action.

This activity was stimulated by a Polish invasion of Russia. But it was the Polish capture of Kiev in May 1920, and the knowledge that Britain was providing arms to the Poles which galvanised the Labour movement. In that month action by dockers prevented the loading of the Jolly George with munitions to Poland. In August a National Council of Action was formed supported officially by the TUC and the Labour Party.

The Birmingham delegate to that Conference was F.W. Rudland. He reported back to 400 delegates at a meeting at Bristol Street schools the same month and an enthusiastic audience agreed to set up a Birmingham Labour Council of Action. Its aims were those of the national Council of Action – to end all military and naval intervention in Russia, to recognise the Soviet Russian government and establish unrestricted trading and commercial relations with Russia. The Council elected 12 representative trade unionists, six Labour Party and Co-operative members and six from other Socialist etc. organisations. An interesting mix of representatives included Kantor of NUX who had seconded the resolution, Davies of the Police and Prison Officers' Union, two women from the Women Workers, Mrs Longden from the Co-operative Women's Guild, three ILPers, including Chamberlain the editor of *Town Crier,* and a representative of the Shop Stewards. The one month old Communist Party had two official representatives, Miss Pendrie and Fred Silvester, although the total number of Communists on the Committee was five.

The ability of the government to intervene in Russia was limited by other factors besides that of the opposition of the entire Labour movement. Ten days after the capture of Kiev the Red Army began a counter-offensive which took it almost to Warsaw. There it was defeated and negotiations for peace began between Russia and Poland. In addition, by November the Red Army had entered the Crimea which meant that nothing but scattered bands remained of the White counter-revolutionary armies which the British and other governments had been so lavishly financing and arming.

In December 1920, Cardinal reported on the first year's work of the Birmingham Hands Off Russia Committee. Fifty public meetings had been held with leading figures of the Labour movement. Also numerous Trades Councils, trade union branches, Labour Churches and other Labour, Co-operative and Socialist organisations had been addressed. Three huge open-air demonstrations had been arranged in co-operation with the Trades Council, the ILP and the Communist Party. The first in June demanded that the TUC take industrial action against intervention in Russia. The other two demonstrations were in August as a result of the danger of war arising from the arming of the Poles. Cardinal's report concluded that the present times were very critical with peace with Russia still to be established.

The immediate danger of war ended in March 1921 when a trade agreement was signed with Russia which all knew was the first step to diplomatic recognition of the Soviet Union.

Hands Off Russia campaigns continued in subsequent years, but never at the same intensity as in 1920. In January 1921 a Town Hall meeting was organised under the joint auspices of the Hands Off Russia Committee and the Daily Herald League. Harrison Barrow was in the chair and the two main national speakers were Robert Williams and Ben Turner.

With the danger of war against Russia reduced, attention was turned to the famine in Russia. This was part of the general European famine that occurred in the wake of the war, but it was greatly aggravated by the wars of intervention. Lack of recognition of the Soviet government meant refusal of the British government to provide credits for food. An appeal by H.N. Brailsford in the *Town Crier* in April 1922 announced a May Day Appeal for Russia's starving millions and this was taken up by collections in the Labour movement in Birmingham.

In 1923 there was a renewed danger of war as right-wing elements stepped up their campaign against the trade agreement with Russia. An infamous note by Lord Curzon, the Foreign Secretary, in May demanded that the Soviet Union reply within ten days to various charges regarding fishing limits, compensation for British citizens executed before 1921. alleged violations of the trade agreement etc. Failing this the British government would consider the trade treaty at an end.

In June 1923 the Birmingham Hands Off Russia Committee organised a town hall meeting with Joseph Southall in the chair and main speakers Dr Dunstan, J.T. Murphy and J. Walton Newbold. Murphy said that the Curzon Note was merely an incident in a continuous policy from 1917 for the overthrow of the Soviet government. That Curzon was speaking not only for the British government but for all the international forces of reaction. A resolution was passed demanding the TUC and Labour movement put all possible pressure on the British government to grant full recognition to the Soviet government as the only way of avoiding a future rupture of relations.

Labour and Liberal pressure ensured that the ultimatum was withdrawn. This was not unconnected with the election results later in the year which returned 258 Conservatives, but 191 Labour and 159 Liberals and resulted in the minority Labour government which finally recognised Russia in 1924.

The Birmingham Police Strike 1919

The Birmingham Police Strike of August 1919 was a unique event in the history of the local labour movement. It was mercilessly crushed by the Home Office with the willing compliance of the Birmingham Watch Committee and the Unionist majority on the city Council, but the Labour members of the city Council and trade unionists continued the struggle for a number of years for the reinstatement of the sacked police officers.

The National Union of Police & Prison Officers (NUPPO) was created in London in 1913. But it was the poor wages and bad conditions in war-time that stimulated the growth of the Union. The first mention of a local NUPPO branch is in the minutes of the Trades Council for October 1918 where it is stated that an application for affiliation of a Police Union branch had been approved by the Trades Council executive and would be recommended to the full Council.

The 1918 annual report of the Trades Council stated that on hearing of the formation of NUPPO the secretary got in touch with the London Trades Council which was largely responsible for creating the Union. As a result the Birmingham Trades Council organised a meeting at the Corn Exchange for the formation of a Birmingham branch. This was attended by several hundred police officers. A branch of NUPPO was set up to which 90 per cent of the Birmingham force now belonged. From Birmingham the surrounding areas had also been organised and a Midland District Committee had been set up representing 85 per cent to 100 per cent of these forces.

These membership figures, especially of the surrounding areas which took no part in the subsequent strike, can be questioned, but the fact is that the Union at the beginning was almost a secret society. Evidence from the Walsall Trades Council minutes shows a much earlier connection with the Union. In September 1916 support for a rise in police pay was registered and a donation of 10/-d. was sent to the National Union of Police and Prison Officers. One delegate asked if this was a new organisation as no one in the district had heard of it. The President replied that if there was a member in the Walsall force he would not let anyone know. Walsall would not be the only area where the Union developed clandestinely.

The Birmingham Trades Council report continued; trouble had occurred because the Watch Committee had refused permission for representatives of the branch to attend a national conference at the Albert Hall and the Watch Committee refused to recognise the Union. They hoped wiser councils would prevail. They had not forgotten that it was the Watch Committee which authorised the use of police to visit workers' homes to find out why they were away from work. The report ended:

> We welcome the advent of the Police Union; as hitherto our police have been used principally in the interests of Capitalism and against the workers, irrespective of law or justice. We believe in just and impartial administration of the law; and this good understanding with our comrades, the Police, will do more than anything else to preserve the peace and ensure respect for the law.

An era of peace and solidarity between the police and organised workers was the last thing the government wanted and measures were already under way through carrot and stick to smash the union.

In fact, NUPPO had achieved one success in London and Lloyd George was not going to allow another. The grievances of the London police were the same as those of other forces – pay which had not been increased in war time although the cost of living had more than doubled, excessive overtime and work during the one rest day of the week without payment, and the excesses of discipline which varied with each force. The dismissal of a NUPPO official coincided with the approval of union objectives and on the 27th August 1918 an ultimatum was issued that unless the man was reinstated and their demands met, the London police would strike on 29th. August. These demands were ignored and to the utter astonishment of the police authorities, the government and the general public, the strike took place and by Friday 30 August almost the entire Metropolitan police force of 12,000 men and all the men of the City of London force were on strike. Government intervention was swift. Pay and pensions were considerably increased, the union official reinstated and an 'authorised organisation to represent the men was promised. The men returned to duty on the morning of the 31st.

An immediate effect of the strike was to raise membership of the union from 10,000 to 50,000 men, according to the *Police Review*. The sticking point for the government was recognition of the Union. Lloyd George had stated that he 'could not in war-time sanction the recognition of a police union.' This was interpreted by the naive as a statement that he would recognise such a union in peacetime, and in fact, by negotiating with the union he had already recognised it. The government set up a Representative Board and the union leaders at once set out to control it. But in July 1919 the government took decisive steps to outlaw the union. It set up a tame Police Federation with limited powers of complaint and divided into separate sections for constables, sergeants and inspectors. The bill went on: 'it shall not be lawful for a member of a police force to become, or after one month from the passing of this Act to be, a member of any trade union or association...having for its objects to control the pay, pensions or conditions of any police force.' It ended by stating that anyone contravening the Act would be dismissed, forfeit all pension rights and be permanently disqualified from joining any other police force. NUPPO was thus backed into a corner; it could either tamely disappear from the scene, or it could fight on the now limited issue of union recognition. It chose to fight and on 31st July 1919 issued a call for all NUPPO members to withdraw their services until 'full and frank recognition of our Union is conceded.'

Such were the events facing the NUPPO branch in Birmingham. At the end of May 1919 the reactionary Chief Constable, Charles Haughton Rafter, had jumped the national gun by issuing a Police Order stating that a threatened police strike by NUPPO had come to his notice and any Birmingham police officer joining such a strike would be dismissed and lose his pension. The Order went on to state, quite incorrectly, that an Organisation would be set up enabling men to make representation nationally on questions of Pay etc. Rafter ended by stating that the Order was issued with the authority of the Watch Committee. In fact the Watch Committee minutes for May disclose no discussion on this question and it was not until August that a copy of the Order was placed among the Minutes. The question of the police strike surfaced only obliquely in the Watch Committee minutes of 2 June when the pay rates of the police were set out. These showed that basic rates for a constable in Birmingham began at 43/-d a week and rose by 1/-d a week for nine years to a maximum of 51/-d. There was, in addition, a War Bonus of 12/-d. a week plus 2/6d. for each child together with traditional allowances of 1/-d. a week for boots and a 2/-d. rent allowance for those not living in police properties. These were not starvation wages, but they were earned through greatly increased unpaid hours of overtime, and police wages had seriously declined in relation to some wage earners.

On 23rd June there was a special Watch Committee meeting on Police Pay. Here it was revealed that the Home Office had approved pay scales starting at 70/-d. a week for the London police and was prepared to sanction the same rate for other police authorities. No question here even of the normal differentiation between London and provincial forces. Christmas was coming early it seems! Nor was this all. The pay increase was to be back dated to 1st April, and if this was not enough to head off a strike an immediate cash payment was sanctioned. It was not only the police who were to receive this largesse. Police pay scales were linked to those of firemen at a differential of 3/-d. a week in favour of the police. In August pay scales were raised for firemen to the same 70/-d. minimum as the police. No signs of economy here. By the middle of July the new police pay scales had been approved and an immediate cash payment of £10 authorised. The Birmingham police, like their colleagues in London and elsewhere had had their material grievances miraculously removed and the sole strike issue was now the principled one of recognition of the Union.

Despite all the difficulties, the Union call to strike was supported by the Birmingham branch and a limited number of police and prison officers joined the strike. It was led by Sergeant E. Taylor and D. D'Arcy, the secretary of the branch, who was a prison officer at Winson Green. The leadership made encouraging noises about the numbers on strike and the help to be expected from the Labour movement. But on 2nd. August a special meeting of the Watch Committee heard that the Chief Constable had been in touch with the Home Office and been informed that all striking police officers in London had been dismissed and similar action would be approved in Birmingham. Two sergeants and eighty seven men who had struck in Birmingham were then immediately dismissed.

The choices for NUPPO members at this time were stark. If sufficient men came out on strike the threat to dismiss all of them might be nullified; the police action was supported by the general Labour movement and if sympathetic strikes occurred they might still win. But among the police the strike was widely supported only on Merseyside and if the police were not supporting their own strike, it was virtually impossible for other union leaders to bring their men out in sympathy. Over the next few days more policemen did join the strike, but by then it was a lost cause.

Eventually three sergeants and 116 constables in Birmingham were dismissed for striking, which represented nearly 12 per cent of constables in the force. This was not as negligible a number as detractors both at the time and since have made out. The names of all those who sacrificed their jobs and pensions in support of a principle appear in an Appendix. In addition there were at least three prison officers dismissed from Winson Green.

The trade union and Labour movement gave as much support as was possible both during and after the strike, but in the nine months following the end of the war the economic situation had changed drastically. Unemployment was becoming widespread and this inevitably weakened the trade unions.

On 15th September 1919 NUPPO became an illegal organisation – the first trade union to be outlawed since the repeal of the Combination Acts in 1824, a matter that the TUC could not ignore. All that could be salvaged by then was a campaign to have the dismissed men reinstated. Who was ultimately responsible for these sackings; was it the Home Secretary or the local Watch Committees? Both prevaricated and maintained that it was the other, so campaigns were launched both nationally and locally.

When the *Town Crier* first appeared in October 1919 it joined the campaign for reinstatement. The second issue of 10 October carried a letter from David Davies, the treasurer of the Birmingham NUPPO branch stating that the men had been on strike for eight weeks and there was now no hope of reinstatement. He outlined NUPPO's growth locally claiming that it had 900 members (including 50 from the prison service) and 96 per cent had voted to strike in May 1919. In December the Labour group (22 strong) put a motion to the city council that the police should be reinstated. This was defeated by only 51 to 42, showing that sympathy with the police was wider than the Labour movement.

This was, it seems, the point when the campaign had most chance of success; for at the next Trades Council meeting it was complained that Labour members had left the meeting before the vote took place. An examination of the voting list, however, discloses that only one of the 22 Labour councillors failed to vote for reinstatement; that was G. Perry. Sgt. Taylor, who became a local councillor in January 1920, moved on behalf of NUPPO (which continued affiliated to the Trades Council) that their delegate to the TUC urge active steps to obtain reinstatement. He was disappointed with the attitude of the TUC and its Parliamentary Committee, Taylor complained. He might well be. The TUC was going through the motions of demanding reinstatement, but on the Parliamentary committee were such figures as W.J. Davis, the veteran leader of the Birmingham Brassworkers' Union and doyen of the TUC who was actively opposed to the strike.

In 1920 the campaign for reinstatement continued. In April the Birmingham branch of NUPPO was advertising in the *Town Crier* that several able speakers were prepared to address Labour organisations on the Aims & Objects of the Union. At this time NUPPO was running a national raffle in aid of the sacked men and this was advertised in Birmingham. There was also an appeal from the united Birmingham Trades Council and Labour Party for a ½d. levy on each member of all branches per week. This appeal was taken up by some branches of the Amalgamated Society of Engineers, but its total effect is unknown.

In March 1920 the Labour Group demanded from the Watch Committee a complete breakdown of all police who had struck giving their years of service, the amounts of their pay when dismissed, the pay they would have received if they had not been dismissed, details of the pensions they would have received and much more. When the Watch Committee eventually produced this document in May they complained of the amount of work it had involved. Years of service ranged from the 22 years of Sgt. Taylor who lost a pension of £140 per annum down to a constable with only one year's service. Most strikers were very experienced policemen, 41 having service between fifteen years and ten years. Every striker sacrificed a secure future for a very uncertain one.

In July support for the police continued with a march and mass demonstration through the city. Particular mention of support of the railway unions and also the postal workers was made. The postal workers represented 'fellow local State employees' whose union was also considered to be at risk if the police union was banned. The railwaymen, who were under a semi-military regime such as the police, also saw a risk to their unions and had been among the few workers nationally to strike on behalf of the police. The demonstration at Smithfield Market was large enough for there to be four platforms. Among the speakers was Councillor Tom Hackett, who was the only Labour member of the Watch Committee, but seems to have made no effective protest on that Committee. The resolution carried unanimously stated:

> This mass meeting of Birmingham citizens of all shades of religious, social and political thought earnestly request the Lord Mayor, aldermen and councillors of the city of Birmingham acting through the Watch Committee to immediately reinstate into the police service the police officers who were dismissed from the force for their action in August 1919. We are of the opinion that the steps these men took were the only steps they could take in defence of a principle which they had been led to believe by the Prime Minister they had the right to exercise...

The resolution, of course, had no effect. In October 1920 the Trades Council mounted another mass protest at the Town Hall. The meeting was chaired by the Rev Morgan Whiteman and the main speaker was Jack Hayes, the general secretary of NUPPO. Hayes was bitter and claimed that when the men had been bribed with a few pounds there were not enough men willing to strike for a principle. The matter of three Winson Green warders sacked and evicted from prison houses was also raised. In December Jack Hayes, was appealing for funds in the *Town Crier*.

The struggle continued into 1921. In February when the police budget faced cuts, it was claimed that the only real economy would be to reinstate the experienced, sacked policemen. The 1921 Labour group Report stated that efforts had been made to keep alive the question of reinstatement of the police and the group could be relied on to continue these efforts. But the issue was all but dead.

Only in 1925 was some measure of justice to the strikers proposed. In June, a Home Office circular canvassed the views of Watch Committees with regard to returning the pensions contributions paid by the dismissed strikers. The Birmingham Watch Committee opposed the proposal. But Alderman Bower, who was Labour lord mayor that year, objected strongly to this. The Watch Committee was therefore reconvened and their previous decision reversed. 'A step in the right direction,' the *Town Crier* commented.

The 1919 Police Strike was doomed to failure from the beginning. Once the pockets of the police had been stuffed with pound notes and their other material grievances met, there was no chance of a successful strike for the principle of a police union. The same tactic of legalised corruption has been resorted to successfully in recent years with the miners; if the miners could not win what chance did the police have? Particularly with the whole weight of legal, government and press opinion propagating that free trade unionism among the police was illegal. Only on Merseyside did a higher percentage of the police come out on strike, and it is therefore to the credit of the Birmingham police that so many men risked all for a principle.

With regard to the main players in the plot to destroy police trade unionism, the Home Office and upper ranks of the police had such characters as Sir Nevil Macready, Commissioner of the London police, who cut his teeth on Bengal and South African police affairs. Rafter, the Birmingham chief constable, was fanatically opposed to trade unionism. He at least never hid behind the Watch Committee or the Home Office in attaching blame to them for his actions; although he was quite capable of doing so as we shall see when we come to discuss his role on the use of spies against the labour movement. The Home Office did prevaricate, claiming that the ultimate responsibility for the police force lay with the local Watch Committee. The Watch Committee in turn blamed the Home Office. The actual position was that it was indeed the responsibility of the local Watch Committee whether the men were sacked or not; but if a sympathetic Watch Committee had not sacked the men it is unlikely that the Home Office would have provided the force with a certificate of efficiency the following year; its grant would then have been withheld and the force run by the Home Office.

But, of course, the Birmingham Watch Committee was not sympathetic to the strikers. The two key figures seem to have been Alderman Sanders, chair of the Watch Committee and Alderman James, chair of its Judicial Sub-Committee. Attendance at the main committee was usually about seven, of whom only one, Councillor Hackett, was a Labour member. How much of the contact between Sanders and James and Rafter the chief constable found its way on to the minutes of the

Watch Committee must be questioned, as the case of the May Police Order issued by Rafter and discussed above, shows.

The Watch Committee and Rafter were the driving force behind the determination to sack the police strikers in Birmingham. They were backed by a majority on the Council; but it was a small majority. Those of the 43 who voted with the 21 Labour councillors on the crucial vote to reinstate the sacked police strikers on the City Council in December 1919 included not only Liberals, but also Conservatives; and they seem to have included some of the leading Birmingham families. There were two Cadburys (Liberal and Independent/Progressive respectively), a Martineau (party affiliation not known), and a Kenrick (Conservative). Fifty one voted not to reinstate the strikers. It would have needed a turn round of only five councillors to have reinstated these men. There would then have been a position not dissimilar to the one in 1838 when the first elected Birmingham Town Council clashed with the Home Office over local democratic control of the police and lost.

Of the subsequent activities of the sacked policemen little is known. Edward Taylor was elected a city councillor in January 1920, but he survived only ten months. As a by-election victor he had to stand again the following November. He was beaten by Peacey the ex-NFDDSS candidate then standing as a Conservative. Taylor's career 'did not flourish' and Jack Hayes, the NUPPO general secretary, who subsequently became an MP, told the House of Commons on 12 July 1923 that Taylor had suffered 'untold privations.' Of the other strikers even less is known.

Unemployment

Unemployment was a problem in Birmingham from the end of the war. Indeed unemployment had begun to grow from 1917 when production of some types of armaments peaked and the munition factories began to sack workers, particularly women. Mass unemployment, however became intolerable in 1921 and 1922. It fell in 1923 and 1924 only to rise again in 1925 and 1926.

Up to 1923 we have no regular series of figures for unemployment in Birmingham and must use the national series of national unemployment of trade unions paying unemployment benefit. These show:

Year	1916	1918	1919	1921	1922
Percentage Unemployed	0.4	0.8	2.4	14.8	15.2

From 1923 we have actual figures of unemployment in Birmingham showing the numbers signing on at the Birmingham Labour Exchange and published each month in the Department of Employment *Labour Gazette*. I have averaged the January and June months to give an approximate annual figure. These show:

Year	1923	1924	1925	1926
Unemployment in B'ham	34543	33525	31878	33163
Percentage of Employed Pop (1921 Census)	7.8	7.5	7.2	7.5

Unemployment among women tended to be rather less; it was 6 per cent in January 1924 and 4½ per cent in January 1926. Juvenile unemployment was not negligible and seems to have fluctuated more than general unemployment. For instance there were 1513 young persons of both sexes unemployed in January 1924, but only 544 in 1926.

Something must be said about the cost of living and unemployment benefit after the war. The post-war 'boom' was also a period of rapidly rising prices. The Ministry of Labour Index of prices shows that prices had more than doubled during the war (1914 – 100; 1918 – 203). By 1920 prices were half as high again (249). The index then began to fall – down to 226 in 1921 and 172 by 1926. The effect of immediate post-war unemployment was cushioned by the 'donation' benefit of 29/-d. per week for all insured and non-insured men whether ex-service or civilian and 25/-d. for women, with 6/-d. for the first child and 3/-d. for subsequent children. This benefit ceased for civilian workers in November 1919; for ex-service men and women it ended in March 1921. Unemployed workers then reverted to the 1911 scale which was 7/-d per week (for insured workers only) aged 18 and above. In December 1919 the government raised these scales to 11/-d. for all men and women over 18 and 5/6d. for those aged 16 to 18. In 1920 a National Insurance Act brought most manual workers and also non-manual workers earning less than £250 a year into the national insurance

331

scheme and at the end of 1920 benefits were raised to 15/-d for adult males and 12/-d. for adult females. When the special ex-service scales ended in March 1921 benefit was set at 20/-d for men and 16/-d for women. Then in June 1921 as prices began to fall benefit was reduced to the previous scale of 15/-d. and 12/-d. To end this survey of benefits in this period up to 1926, the 1924 Labour government raised scales to 18/-d for men and women with 5/-d for a wife and 2/-d for each child.

Serious agitation of the unemployed began in Birmingham in 1920. In October there was a mass meeting at the Town Hall. Later in the month Alderman A.V. Stevens tried to move on the city Council a motion of censure on the police for their rough treatment of the unemployed demonstrators in the town. But 'the Liberals and the Tories stayed away,' and there was no quorum. In November there was a Church and Unemployment Conference in Birmingham attended by 80 people. Hugh Gibbins was the main speaker. The chairman, the Rev E. Leach, asked the church to face up to its responsibilities on unemployment.

The year ended with a stormy Town's Meeting on Unemployment. The *Town Crier* report of 24 December 1920 was written by 'Watchman', W.J. Chamberlain the editor, himself. 'The Lord Mayor among the Bolshies' he headlined a half page article. The meeting had been convened by the Lord Mayor (Ald. W. Cadbury) at the request of the Trades Council. 'The Chief Constable, with a large staff of uniformed and plain clothes police were also in attendance in close proximity to a small group of Communists, who were obviously there with a view to livening up the proceedings as opportunities occurred.' The proceedings were opened by the Lord Mayor who detailed steps taken by him and the various Council committees. In addition to two grants of £60,000 which would find work for only 1,000 unemployed men for about three months, application had also been made to the government for a grant of £500,000. The reply received from a minister was that the government hoped to make an announcement in a few days, but regretted that it could not say anything at the moment. Chamberlain reported, 'This characteristic government pronouncement produced the first symptoms of unrest among the audience, which indulged in various sarcastic remarks at the expense of the powers that be.'

The Town Clerk then read a letter he had received from Alderman P. Bower, chairman of the Labour Party, which, among other things, said, '...the present social system stands condemned by the fact that thousands of men, women and children were starving while the government were wasting the wealth of the country on wicked wars in various parts of the world (Applause).'

Councillor Shakespeare then moved the first resolution. It asked that the £120,000 already advanced by the Ministry of Transport for road building and repairs should be spent within two months instead of three, thus allowing more men to be employed. He was aware that this would only touch the fringe of the problem, but it would help the unemployed over the next two winter months. Frank Sharkey seconded the motion and widened the area of debate. He made a strong plea for those of the unemployed who were not capable of hard, manual labour. Only one class suffered the effects of unemployment. Others were unemployed all their lives and were having a jolly good time. The Duke of Northumberland was one of these unemployed, but there was no likelihood of distress in his household. Sharkey went on to suggest that landlords might consider not taking their rents while men were unemployed. He ended by saying that the government, by their senseless war against Russia, was depriving this country of much wanted trade. 'This vigorous speech brought much applause,' Chamberlain reported. The resolution was passed unanimously.

It was then the turn of the Bishop of Birmingham. He moved a resolution urging the government to put in hand large schemes of building and road making. He was 'not in first-class condition,' he observed, but he had considered it his duty 'as one who served the Lord' to be present at this meeting. God knows the government ought to economise,' he went on, but he would not be a party to economy at the expense of the workless. There must be no such thing as class, 'We are all one great family in the eyes of God,' he ended. Chamberlain commented, 'The audience gave His Lordship the benefit of the doubt and responded with a fair measure of applause.' This resolution was seconded by Yates of the NFDDSS who talked about the Empire being built by soldiers who are now unemployed and warned that unless the government hurried up there would not be an ex-servicemen's unemployment problem for they would all be dead.

At this stage J.W. Kneeshaw rose in the public gallery to move an amendment. This urged the government to open up trade with Russia and thus provide work. This was seconded by an ex-serviceman, but the Lord Mayor moved the amendment out of order.

The next speaker was 'Navvy' Smith a well-known populist lay-preacher and notorious 'patriotic' recruiting orator during the war. He was assailed with groans and hisses, but managed to move an amendment asking for government national factories for the employment of disabled ex-servicemen. Although it was a proposal meeting with general approval, the amendment was defeated, such was the detestation of the audience for the mover.

W. Brain then butted in for the Communists asking to be allowed to move a motion at the end of the meeting. This the chairman refused, stating that it would be passed on to the committee.

The next resolution was moved by the president of Birmingham Chamber of Commerce. In an uncharacteristic burst of generosity towards working men he proposed that unemployment benefit be raised to £1 for adults and £2 for a man and wife with adequate allowances for dependents. But he rather spoiled the effect by rattling the money in his trousers pockets and telling the audience that trade was bad and the country was overtaxed. Cries of 'Tax the Rich' was the reply to this. He also caused uproar when he urged that relief be given to 'the real unemployed and not to loafers.' There were indignant cries of 'Withdraw' and 'We were heroes during the war; now we are Loafers,' and 'The Duke of Northumberland is a Loafer.'

A resolution requesting that the Lord Mayor open a local relief fund administered by a broad committee and that a representative conference of midland Mayors and local councils be called to discuss measures against unemployment met with wide support, but also a great deal of cynicism.

Bill Brain then asked leave to move his motion. This again, the Lord Mayor disallowed and went on to discuss another resolution that he had received. But by this time there was so much uproar that he could not be heard, so he closed the meeting.

The moment the Lord Mayor left the chair, Bill Brain and Harry Shepperson mounted the platform. Brain took the Lord Mayor's place and drank a glass of water, proclaiming it 'the champagne of the unemployed.' He said the resolution he had wished to move was one passed by the Coventry unemployed. This called on the government to meet members of the Russian Trade delegation, ascertain from them what commodities Russia needed, and then open a factory in Britain to produce these goods. Instead of this resolution, however, he moved another one that 'the unemployment crisis, with its tragic results, is directly traceable to the private ownership of the means of wealth production.' This was seconded by Shepperson and unanimously passed. Chamberlain reported that although the audience by now had been reduced by about one third there was still 'quite a good crowd.' The meeting ended with the singing of the Red Flag. The Chief Constable stayed to the end and was heard to remark to a councillor, 'They have let off steam and there is no harm done.'

1921 opened with an unemployment and short time working figure of 58,488 in Birmingham. This meant 13 per cent of the working population affected by unemployment. With the large increase in unemployment focus changed to the non-insured unemployed – the sick, the aged, and others not entitled to unemployment benefit. The only resort of these unfortunates was admission to the Workhouse or receipt of the scanty amount of out-relief doled out by the local Poor Law Guardians. Such relief, unlike national unemployment benefit, came from the local rates which threatened to rise to intolerable levels as unemployment increased. A campaign then began to equalise unemployment and Poor Law relief scales with contributions from national taxation. In many parts of the country this involved occupation of Workhouses. Finally, in Poplar, the Guardians paying high relief scales refused to pay their precept for the London police and other purposes until rates were equalised between the poor London boroughs suffering from mass unemployment and the rich boroughs where rates were low. For this George Lansbury and other Poplar councillors went to jail, marched there with the Red Flag flying, were released after nation wide agitation, and by October a rate equalisation Act had been passed for London.

Birmingham contributed to these struggles. In September 1921 it was reported that there were Unemployed Committees in all parts of the city. They were firm for the relief scales agreed at the

National Administration Council of the Unemployed. This was the embryo of the emerging National Unemployed Workers' Committee Movement; at its April conference national relief scales had been agreed of 35/-d. per week for man and wife, 5/-d for each child, rent up to 15/-d a week and 1 cwt of coal per week.

Militancy in Birmingham, as elsewhere, was stimulated by changes in the unemployment insurance scheme in April 1922. An Act the previous year had raised the statutory benefit period from fifteen to twenty six weeks and introduced an 'uncovenanted' benefit for those whose statutory benefit was exhausted. But between statutory and 'uncovenanted' benefit there was a gap of five weeks; then they received five weeks 'uncovenanted' benefit, if still unemployed, then came another gap of five weeks followed by another five week's benefit and so on. The gap system affected about half the unemployed and drove them to the Poor Law guardians for benefit. The Poor Law authorities in turn were driven to protest to the government at the increasing burdens thrust on them and by July the gap was reduced to one week.

These burdens were additional to the not very frequent payments by the Birmingham Guardians of payments to those already receiving unemployment benefit who claimed that the miserly 15/-d was inadequate. At the beginning of May the guardians ruled that they would pay no more relief to anyone receiving benefit. On 10th May 1922 demonstrators assembling in the Bull Ring, Summerfield Park and elsewhere marched 20,000 strong to demand admission to the Workhouse. Outside the locked gates, the police attempted to disperse the demonstrators. After a short conflict they reformed to march back to the centre of the city. When they reached Great Charles Street the greatly reinforced police tried to prevent the demonstrators proceeding any further. Batons were drawn and the police clubbed down men and women. Still the crowd refused to disperse, reforming their ranks time and again until they reached the Bull Ring where a huge protest meeting was held and copies of the *Birmingham Mail,* which had made scurrilous statements about the unemployed, were burned. The meeting did not end until 10.30 pm.

A week later, on 17 May, another great demonstration of the unemployed took place in the Bull Ring. The leaders had previously been notified that unless they marched on a route determined by the police (off the main city streets) the march would be banned. When the unemployed attempted to form ranks to march, the police tried to disperse them and batons were again drawn and blood spilled. This time, however, there were missiles to hand for the unemployed to fight back with as the Bull Ring was under repair. Casualties were high on both sides, and this caused the police to desist. Eventually honours were fairly even. The demonstrators did not march, but the police were unable to disperse the meeting.

The Bull Ring baton charges were raised by the Labour group at the next City council meeting. Sharkey moved the suspension of standing orders to discuss the matter but he was ruled out of order. The Lord Mayor ruled that it could only be raised on the Watch Committee report or by a motion at the next meeting. The Labour councillors all walked out in disgust.

Militancy continued. At the end of May 5,000 unemployed marched from the Bull Ring to Summerfield Park 'headed by the inevitable Mr Skett carrying his Red Flag.' Again there was a provocative display by the police, 'Foot police every yard and mounted police.' Every road junction was heavily guarded by police. But the demonstrators were allowed to march to the Workhouse, where they were met by a large contingent from Smethwick. 'Several platforms' were set up to protest at unemployment.

In June, there was a One Week Unemployment Campaign. The same month there was a prosecution of James Sadler of Handsworth for refusing to undertake relief work at £2-0-2d per week. Sadler said he was a skilled navvy, the trade union rate was £3-5-10d and he was not going to work under the trade union rate. Sadler was bound over for six months.

It is not surprising that at this time, when unemployment was so serious, when unemployment and relief scales were at the same starvation levels as in Victorian times, when anger as the promised post-war land 'fit for heroes' failed to materialise, and when militancy was at its height (Britons had not yet learned to starve quietly), that the efforts of some organisations alleged to be concerned with the poor should be criticised.

The May Day issue of *Out-of-Work* (the organ of the National Administrative Council of the Unemployed) contained the following report from J. Spencer of Birmingham:

> Several of our Unemployed Committees fell away during the winter. Our next obstacle has been the Birmingham Unemployed Association. This is a charitable institution that doles out soup, buns, chunks of bread and also chunks of capitalism and expects the unemployed to swallow them all at once. The Council provided rooms to play games, but our boys found them and good results are coming from our agitation. We have now formed Committees under the NAC, but the Council won't find room for these. Several attempts have been made to get affiliation to the Trades Council. Seven of our representatives are on Boards of Guardians. Three of our delegates are on the Birmingham May Day Committee.

The attitude of the Trades Council to the unemployed movement can be illustrated from the proceedings of the February 1922 meeting where affiliation of the District Unemployed Committee, together with the waiving of the normal affiliation fee, was rejected by a 'big majority.' It was seen as a move by William Brain to increase the representation of the Communist Party on the Trades Council since Brain was both chairman of the Unemployed Committee and secretary of the Communist Party. It was also claimed that the majority of the Unemployed Committee were also Communists. In the following week's edition of the *Town Crier,* Brain replied with one of his vitriolic letters which so incensed Chamberlain the editor, and probably did his case no good with others:

> So, the affiliation of the Unemployed Committee is a subtle Communist move to swamp the Trades Council. Bah, you foolish, stupid people. In your nightmarish fear and hatred of Communism you are blindly destroying any attempt to stay further destruction of the workers' standard of life.

Communist controlled or not, the Birmingham unemployed organised a unique event in August – the first of the post-war Hunger Marches. On 9th. August thirty unemployed workers set out from Birmingham to march to London where they arrived on the 17th. They were welcomed by a big demonstration of the London unemployed. The reception they received from the authorities was cordial – in marked contrast to the reception of the early national marchers. They were received by the Minister of Labour and the Minister of Health who listened to them sympathetically and then told them the familiar tale of how difficult it was to do anything for them. After the interview the marchers were invited to take tea at the Ministry of Labour. Tea and sympathy indeed, but nothing else.

For the ten days that the marchers were in London they were accommodated and fed by the Poplar local authorities and given a civic reception at a mass meeting at Poplar town hall. In his speech the Mayor hoped that this was the first of many such marches to London. He did not have long to wait; by October the first national marchers from Glasgow were on the road.

By early 1923 relations between the trades council and the unemployed had improved. In January the Trades Council organised an Unemployed Sunday Rally at the Bull Ring. The speakers were the Trades Council president (H.G. Johnson), the Labour Party president (Ald. P. Bower, JP) and W. Brain the representative of the National Unemployed Workers' Committee Movement. The local movement was now affiliated to the Communist led organisation that was to organise the activity of the unemployed throughout the post-war years; it soon dropped the 'Committee' from its name and became the National Unemployed Workers Movement (NUWM). There were also moves to unite the three separate Unemployed Movements operating in Birmingham. Unemployed Sunday became the occasion in some towns for the unemployed to march to church and challenge the local clergy to assist their campaign, but that does not appear to have occurred in Birmingham.

If relations between the Trades Council and the unemployed were improving, the same could not be said of those between the editor of the Town Crier and Bill Brain. Chamberlain had made caustic comments on a letter of Brain's printed in the *Town Crier*. Brain retorted:

> I protest at the snivel (sic) that you tacked on to my letter. Not only was it snivel, but a weird mixture of whine and damned impudence... come down to the Bull Ring and tell the unemployed of their deficiencies. I know you have contempt for the NUWCM.

Chamberlain said that this was further proof of Brain's inability to conduct controversy according to generally accepted standards of decency and good manners.

In March, the national organiser of the NUWCM addressed 'the usual Saturday meeting' of the Birmingham unemployed. Wal Hannington was no stranger to Birmingham it was stated. 'Detectives were present at the meeting.' Rather surprisingly this report went on, 'We are not usually honoured by the police, but when Hannington speaks police appear.' In April 1923 there was further progress on unity when the Rotton Park Unemployed Committee and the Trades Council arranged a Conference to amalgamate all the local committees. This resulted in the formation of an Employed and Unemployed Workers' Committee. Chairman of this joint committee was William Brain and vice-chair was Councillor Shurmer. The treasurer was W.A. Exton the Smethwick Councillor, and the secretary was J.B. Guy the active secretary of the Rotton Park Unemployed Committee. The organiser was J. Spencer. The committee was completed by W.T. Cardinal and Miss Duffy.

By June, W.A. Dalley, the manager of the Labour Exchange, noted that 43,531 people registered for work the previous week and this was a reduction of 24,000 on the same week in 1922. This fall in unemployment was sufficient to dampen protest and little more is heard of the Unemployment Committees for the rest of the year.

But some of the Unemployment Committees remained in existence pressurising the City Council, Guardians and government to improve conditions. For instance, in April 1924 the Ladywood & West Birmingham Unemployed Committee was requesting that the winter coal allowance be continued throughout the year and that the three day waiting period for benefit be abolished.

In 1925 unemployment again fell slightly but National Unemployed Sunday was still being observed supported by the TUC and the NUWM. Speakers at the Birmingham meeting in June were J. Ganley, George Gull and Harry Shepperson. In Aston the Unemployed Committee organised a meeting in Aston Park.

At this low point of Birmingham unemployment it was still over 7 per cent of the employed population. Discontent was allayed by two factors. One was this comparatively low level of unemployment. The other was the semi- humane scales of benefit introduced by the Labour government, which the incoming Tory government was wise enough not to tamper with. 23/-d. per week for a man and wife plus 2/-d. for each child was an amount on which families would not face starvation, but only semi-starvation. Despite the mass unemployment of the 1930s and the economy cuts, the Tories never dared go back to quite the previous levels. And it is likely that this semi-starvation standard of living for the unemployed was a significant factor in heading off revolution in Britain.

Police Spies and the Campaign for Free Speech

Police spies smacks of the early nineteenth century Six Acts and Peterloo post-Napoleonic Wars period. It is strange to find exactly a century later the wide spread use of police spies and Birmingham perhaps the most important centre in Britain of this abuse. It is also strange to note that there seems to be no immediate precedent to this use of spies in the period 1914-18 when anti-war and pacifist movements active in Birmingham deemed by the authorities to be a threat to national security might more reasonably have justified the use of spies in the Labour movement. This post-war use of spies affected the developing Communist Party most, but it extended to all branches of the Labour movement.

An early protest came from an editorial in the *Town Crier* of 2nd July 1920 concerning the 'scandal' of police spies. Chamberlain recommended that these spies be pointed out at each meeting and a protest made. This makes it clear that the practice was already widespread. The use of spies led to the arrest of militants and their conviction from the evidence of these spies.

The issue unified the movement in Birmingham, but how to combat the problem led to arguments. Early in 1921 the Communist Party initiated a Free Speech Committee. At the meeting Jim Simmons moved a motion that the Committee be established by the Labour Party and represent the whole Labour movement. This amendment was defeated 34 to 22 and the original resolution passed unanimously. From the meeting Messrs. Whitehouse, Passey, Lyons and Davies were elected to the Committee. These were not the leading figures in the Labour movement, but at the meeting were such heavyweights as Joseph Southall, Fred Longden, Fathers, and W.J. Chamberlain as well as Bill Brain.

In February a leading national Communist, William Gallacher, was arrested and charged with 'attempting to cause sedition among the civil population.' Gallacher said that he had appealed to workers to organise industrially through Shop Stewards and Workers' Committees. But he was convicted on the evidence of a police spy and the stipendiary said that he was satisfied that what Gallacher said was a breach of Regulation 42. Gallacher was sentenced to three months in the second division.

The scandal became a national issue. In March when George Lansbury filled the Town Hall with a Daily Herald League meeting he said:
> You have got here a sort of judiciary which seems to have set about the... utterly hopeless task of crushing out opposition to the present order. It is a terrible thing that Birmingham should take the lead in attempting to suppress free expression of thought. Labour speeches are now being made in the presence of police reporters, and the words of Labour speakers are being twisted and garbled in order to fling men into prison.

The arrests continued. In May Jack Leckie, a leading Communist, was arrested while waiting for William Gallacher to come out of prison and was remanded for seven days without bail. When he was finally charged with the usual 'attempting to cause sedition among the civil population' it was for a speech he had made in Birmingham in January! Conducting his own defence Leckie challenged Birmingham's chief spy, 'Comrade' Freedman. Freedman alleged that at Bristol Street schools Leckie was in a wild and excited condition when making the speech which mainly consisted of abuse of Freedman and other police spies. Leckie called them 'dirty curs' and 'stinking spies'. Leckie was also accused of such remarks as 'Wake up, rebels! and the time will soon be near when the revolution will take place in England. Then we will be able to take our proper place with our Russian brothers and say, 'At last we have Britain for the workers.'

Leckie cross examined Freedman on the accuracy of his report and the type of shorthand that he used. Freedman was at a loss to reply until Leckie suggested that his shorthand was 'correspondence style' with which he agreed. Leckie then suggested that as he had sat next to Freedman until he mounted the platform and had made very rude remarks about Freedman and his profession, that he (Freedman) reported in a spirit of anger and retaliation. This he denied. The next witness was Detective-Inspector McArdle who had sat next to Freedman while he was writing his report. McArdle said that although he could not read shorthand, he had initialled Freedman's report as 'correct as far as it goes' after the meeting. Leckie unsuccessfully objected to this witness on the grounds that he had been present in court when Freedman gave his evidence. Leckie in his own defence claimed that it was a 'frame up' and it was because he was a Communist that he was being prosecuted. The stipendiary (Lord Ilkeston) said that whatever Leckie's intentions, it was clear that he had exceeded the limit allowed in making a speech of that kind. He sentenced Leckie to three months in the second division. Leckie said, 'Second division, thank you. I shall be a corpse before that time – or be free.' It must be stressed that this prosecution was not undertaken by the local police but by the Director of Prosecutions for whom W. Day led the case in Court. It is therefore clear that the use of police spies and these prosecutions were taking place with both the knowledge and approval of the government.

Four days later the three local Communists, Harry Shepperson, Jack Trotter and Bill Brain appeared in the same court headlined by the *Town Crier* as 'Another Field Day for Freedman'. The first two were charged with the usual 'attempting to cause sedition and disaffection among the civil population.' Brain was charged with the unusual crime of 'aiding and abetting sedition,' because he chaired the meeting in the Bull Ring on May 13 at which Shepperson and Trotter spoke. Brain's lodgings had also been searched where there had been found a 'huge amount' of literature, including the Theses of the Third International from which W. Day, who again prosecuted (although, on this occasion, it was not stated that he appeared for the Crown) quoted copiously. All three conducted their own defence. They didn't, of course, have any other choice; only in cases with wider implications could funds be raised through the Labour movement for defence counsel. Each defendant cross-examined Freedman. Brain suggested that Freedman did not take verbatim notes but inserted passages to agree with what he thought had been said. Shepperson asked whether he ever made a mistake to which Freedman replied 'No'. Trotter accused Freedman of deliberately lying. In summing up, the stipendiary said that the speeches of Shepperson and Trotter were not couched in such violent language as some with which he had dealt, but the object was the same. Brain had clearly committed an offence, he asserted. All three were sentenced to go to prison for six weeks in the second division. Brain asked that this be changed to first division, but this was refused.

'At the conclusion of the proceedings the women members of the Communist Party in court struck up the Internationale which was taken up by the prisoners and other Communists and kept going until the court emptied.'

Protests that followed stressed not only the gross injustice of jailing these men for nothing more than uttering revolutionary sentiments, but also the vindictiveness in sentencing them to the added privations of imprisonment in the second division which, among other things, limited their diet to little more than one of gruel, and increased the hours of heavy labour to which they were subjected. It must be stressed that these were ordinary working men hard put to earn a living at the best of times because of anti-Communist discrimination and made even more difficult by the years of unemployment. In addition all three were family men with children. The further sacrifices of rigorous imprisonment that these men were prepared to endure for their principles and the hardships it entailed for their families can hardly be over estimated.

In July 1921 the Trades Council mounted a meeting at the Town Hall to 'protest at the Emergency Powers Act and to defend the principles of Free Speech.' The *Town Crier* reported that because of a heat wave, the attendance was not large and consisted mainly of Communists. There was a platform of Trades Council speakers such as the president (A.P. Cassidy), Ald. J.V. Stevens, Sharkey, Rudland etc. but while Brain and Shepperson appeared on the platform they were not among the listed speakers. This led to chants from the audience of 'We want Brain.' Cassidy opened with a 'vigorous protest' at the initial refusal of the Public Works Committee to sanction the use of the Town Hall for a free speech meeting which had delayed the calling of the present meeting by one month. He then went on to a denunciation of the government's Secret Service department, and as 'disgraceful' in a free country the Emergency Powers Act which was nothing but 'class warfare'.

Rudland spoke on the EPA itself claiming that it was impossible to obtain justice when persons were charged with alleged offences under its suppressive clauses. When Stevens was then called on to speak there were renewed calls for Bill Brain to be allowed to speak. The chairman then stated that the meeting had been called under the auspices of the Trades Council and they had 'no intention of forming a platform for the Communists.' Stevens then moved, again with many interruptions, a motion which called for the repeal of the Emergency Powers Act and the immediate release of all those imprisoned under the Act. Frank Sharkey in seconding the motion said that he was not a Communist but it was everybody's duty to defend free speech including that of Communists. During the war there had been a mistaken slogan in the fight against Conscription of 'Single Men first.' Do not let the free speech campaign be 'Communists first,' before protests are made, he pleaded. When the next speaker was called the audience again demanded Brain. But Brain intervened to ask that Thirsk be given a quiet hearing after which 'I will give the chairman a chance to strike a real blow for free speech by calling upon me.' At the conclusion of Thirsk's speech, however, the chairman immediately took the vote for the resolution, which was passed unanimously, and closed the meeting. In the subsequent protests, Brain advised his supporters to disperse quietly. 'There is an army of police round the back,' he said, 'and I am not not anxious to go back to prison again. Let us wait until we can have a real free speech meeting.'

Chamberlain's contribution to this meeting was to append the following ironic paragraph to the *Town Crier* report headed 'Tribute to the Chief Constable':

> We should like to congratulate Chief Constable Rafter on the effectiveness of his anti-Labour Spy Department at Sunday's meeting. He left nothing to chance in his praiseworthy efforts to provide free board and lodging for any of the speakers who might quote Carson without acknowledgement. Standing by the chief note taker were three other police officers who, we suppose, were there for the purpose of swearing that the notes were a faithful record of the speeches. Our representative walked past the Council House yard prior to the meeting, and there he saw a little reserve force of police ready for any emergency. We understand that the police almost outnumbered the audience! Perhaps one of the Labour councillors will ask the chairman of the Watch Committee how many police were told off for Sunday's meeting, and at what cost to the ratepayers.

The next issue that arose was in December 1921 when the use of the Town Hall was refused to the Communists. This led to Labour protests at the City Council meeting led by Frank Sharkey and seconded by Jim Simmons. The latter felt constrained to include in his remarks the information that he was no Communist, in fact he spent most of his time opposing them, but he supported their right to free speech. At the end of the year there appeared in *Town Crier* a letter from Harry Blanchard, the secretary of the Birmingham Communist Party. He had complained to the Chief Constable of the large number of detectives (often twenty) who occupied seats at their Floodgate Street meetings while often over 100 men and women of the poorer classes had to remain standing. He was later rung up by the CID and told that their chief, Supt. Burnett, desired an interview. So, with another member of his executive, he attended. After making various excuses for the use of spies Burnett then threatened that if any disturbance of any kind occurred at a Communist meeting, he would arrest th whole of their executive. He went on to say that anyone as much as touching the sleeve of a police officer was committing an assault. Blanchard pointed out that the Communists had conducted a very vigorous campaign with great success under very trying circumstances in the past twelve months, both indoor and outdoor meetings, and not in any single instance had there been anything approaching a disturbance. Supt. Burnett agreed this was so. Blanchard pointed out that not only had they full control over their meetings, but the presence of detectives in such large numbers was irritating and resented by those who attended. Blanchard thought the trade union and Labour movement ought to be aware of this threat from the chief of the CID.

In 1922 the use of police spies shifted to the meetings and demonstrations of the unemployed, which have been described above, and protests continued. In February Chief Constable Rafter refused to meet a deputation from the Trades Council protesting at police spies. But the Emergency Powers Act, which had perpetuated the dictatorial powers possessed by the government in war time, do seem to have been interpreted less stringently in Birmingham from this time.

The abuse continued, however. In March 1923 the authorities seem to have been playing with the idea of a separate police force not under the control of the council, and suspicious Labour councillors demanded a report from the Watch Committee on the matter. In April Jim Simmons again raised on the city Council the question of the use of police spies at Labour meetings, but made no progress. So the matter was raised again more sharply on the Watch Committee of the 'Czarist methods of the anti-Labour chief constable.' Here the game of pass-the-parcel was played with the Watch Committee innocently protesting that it had no control over the chief constable. The matter was next taken to Parliament. Here the Home Secretary denied that police spies were employed under the instructions of the Public Prosecutor and the buck was passed back to Rafter who, it was said, was exercising his 'discretionary powers.' This led to the introduction into Parliament by the Labour members of a Freedom of Labour Bill. This Bill was rejected, the majority of Birmingham MPs not voting on the question.

In 1924 the Birmingham Free Speech Defence Committee was still in existence and widening its terms of reference. In May it protested at police note taking at Labour Party meetings (including the May Day demonstration) and also protested at the trial of Communists in India.

The issue of free speech then lay dormant until the autumn of 1925 when the Committee was reactivised by preparations for the General Strike. In mid-October 1925 twelve Communist leaders were arrested in an attempt to behead the militant national movement. In November they were charged with unlawfully conspiring to utter and publish seditious libels and incite divers persons to commit breaches of the Incitement to Mutiny Act 1797. The witnesses, of course, were note-taking police spies familiar to Birmingham. Five of the leaders were sentenced to twelve months and the remainder to six months in prison. The case was immediately taken up throughout the country.

The main protest of the Birmingham Free Speech Defence Committee was held in December at Digbeth Institute which was packed in spite of bad weather. Frank Sharkey was in the chair under a huge banner proclaiming 'Release the Twelve'. Oswald Mosley was the first speaker. He said the purpose of the meeting was to defend one of the oldest principles of the country which had been grossly violated by a class government in the interests of their class by proclaiming that violent expressions of opinion were sedition. These were the same people who had refused to prosecute

Carson, Birkenhead and Joynson-Hicks in 1913-14 when they not only proclaimed mutiny but went on to carry out acts of mutiny. Saklatvala, the Communist MP defended the taking of foreign gold as internationalist and indeed worthier than the capitalist gold that international bodies such as the Anglo-Persian Oil Company disbursed. Fred Londen moved the motion protesting against the sentences in view of the fact that the trial throughout was 'swayed by political bias' and demanding the immediate release of the men. J.E. Corrin of the Trades Council said that the seeds of the affair were sown when the solidarity of the workers frustrated the government's attack on the miners. Afraid to attack the trade union movement, the government had attacked the political section which they thought the weakest. The resolution was passed unanimously. And thus the stage was set for the General Strike.

The police spy issue continued into the period after the General Strike. But at this stage some attempt should be made to determine who was responsible for these undemocratic and indeed illegal practices during the post-war period, which were rife in Birmingham. Of Rafter, the chief constable, it can safely be said that he was an anti-Labour martinet who would have implemented any criminal code he was given to administer however harsh. He had considerable discretionary powers which he did not hesitate to use. But it is unlikely that he would have continued to use those powers had he not been convinced that his superiors were backing him in what he was doing. The most visible of these superiors was the chair of the Watch Committee. This was Alderman Sanders, who had occupied the same position during the Police Strike of 1919. The politics of aldermen are difficult to determine; councillors must present themselves every three years for re-election but not aldermen. By profession Sanders was a bullion dealer,but whether he was a Liberal or Conservative bullion dealer is of little moment against the fact that he was reactionary enough to continue to support Rafter in anti-revolutionary measures. But Sanders would need to be supported by higher authority and the Home Office not only supported but actively encouraged what was going on in Birmingham. The fact that prosecutions under the Emergency Powers Act and previous so-called 'sedition' Acts were initiated by the Public Prosecutor proves this. The same remarks apply to the man who followed Sanders as chair of the Watch Committee, Alderman James. He was chair from 1921 to 1923 and represented continuity of policy having been on the Watch Committee from about 1911. By 1921 he was sufficiently recognised as a Home Office man to be appointed to the National Police Council. James was followed as chair of the Watch Committee by Councillor Homer Muscott (1924-26). He was a Conservative with long experience as a member of the Watch Committee.

It would appear, therefore, that the reason why police persecution in Birmingham was greater than in other areas of the country was that here was a more pliant local organisation willing to collude with the Home Office and its dirty tricks department; and, at the end of the line, with sufficient reactionary Liberal and Conservative councillors to rubber stamp the illegal activities of the Chief Constable.

The Fight for Peace

As we have seen (Chapter 13) opposition to the First World War was particularly fierce in Birmingham. There was the traditional pacifism of the Quakers (recorded in the archives of Woodbrooke College), and the resistance of the No-Conscription Fellowship embracing all other strands of resistance from ILP ethical opposition to militant Marxist opponents of imperialism. Militants who sustained the war-time campaigns and survived to lead the post-war struggles included Joseph Southall, W.J. Chamberlain (editor of *Town Crier*), Councillor John Kneeshaw (who led not only the 'pacifists' on the City council but also opposition to war on the Trades Council), Rev J. Morgan Whiteman, and Harrison Barrow (the Quaker). To this list must be added the trade unionists who eventually made the Trades Council the focus of attempts (finally successful) to bring the war to an end – Frank Spires, T.F. Fathers, and F.W. Rudland (who became secretary of both the Trades Council and the Birmingham Labour Party).

From 1917 the local peace movement was strengthened by the appearance of Pte Jim Simmons who, having lost his lower leg in action, spoke for both the military and civil peace movements.

After 1918 the peace movement tended to be represented by the ex-service organisations, particularly the National Union of Ex-Servicemen (NUX). The left wing of NUX led by Leatherland merged into the local Communist Party in 1920 and the reformist wing led by Jim Simmons, the Christian socialist, continued for some time and then disappeared. Simmons reappeared in 1924 as the organiser of the Ex-Service Guild, and he was always central to the Peace Movement in Birmingham. In 1920 the Hands Off Russia Campaign united all peace activitists. It was in 1921 that the various strands of what might be called the traditional peace movement – pacifists, women, trade unions, and political parties came together to form what has always, since that time, been seen as the modern peace movement.

The feeling for peace, based on the sacrifices of the 1914-18 war remained very strong. In January Joseph Southall was commenting in the *Town Crier* that it was no surprise that Lloyd George was being offered the freedom of Birmingham as he had moved from being the architect of the slaughter during the war to the director of the Black and Tans; but the labour movement should not acquiesce in this outrage. Also in January there was a Midlands Conference and Demonstration on Ireland at the Central Hall with Arthur Henderson, John Bromley and Dr Marion Phillips. In March there was much discussion as to who was actually responsible for the 1914-18 war. Kneeshaw claimed that only three persons were ultimately responsible – Asquith the prime minister, Sir Edward Grey the foreign secretary, and Lord Haldane. No democratic decision to declare war could have been forced through the Liberal cabinet in 1914, he claimed.

In April a Birmingham Anti-Militarist Reunion took place. The male members of the audience were mostly conscientious objectors who had been imprisoned during the war. Messages were received from other countries and representatives of the Hague Conference which had set up the international No More War movement whose members were dedicated to resisting war service and campaigning for complete disarmament. Solidarity with Ireland continued with a meeting under the auspices of the Selly Oak branch of the Irish Self Determination League addressed by Frank Sharkey and W.J. Chamberlain.

In June 1921 the 15th. National Peace Conference was held in Birmingham. It was attended by 200 delegates from Labour, Co-operative and other organisations as well as the Peace Societies and the Friends. The Congress protested at the preparations being made for a new war. On the League of Nations it passed by a large majority an amendment in the name of the Birmingham ILP and moved by Joseph Southall. This refused to recognise the League and emphatically disapproved of the terms and conditions of the Treaty of Versailles. It called for general disarmament and the establishment of a 'real League of Peoples elected on a democratic basis.' In July it was announced, perhaps as a result of that Conference, that a branch of the Union of Democratic Control had been re-formed in Birmingham.

The concerns of the Peace Movement extended not only to Ireland but further afield to India. 'A fine demonstration' on behalf of Dominion status for India at the Town Hall led to a letter from Fred Silvester in the *Town Crier* confessing that he was rather disappointed with the speech of Annie Besant who 'seemed to be under the delusion' that dominion status would be freely conferred on India by the British government, whereas the truth was that this would have to be fought for both in India and in Britain. And dominion status would only be acceptable as a stepping stone to complete independence.

In April 1922 the Birmingham & District Anti-Militarists held a conference with Joseph Southall in the chair where Wilfred Wellock spoke on the 'Outlook for Pacifism.' By 1922 the No More War movement was calling for demonstrations all over Britain and throughout the world. A Birmingham Conference was called for May 27th. but I have found no report of it in either the *Town Crier* or *The Friend*. In June Major-General F. Maurice was 'preaching pacifism' at a League of Nations Union meeting at Bournville with Mrs George Cadbury in the chair. In August Birmingham answered the No More War call by mounting what was the greatest of mass peace demonstrations since the war. In a procession a mile long, led by a Salvation Army band, 20,000 people demonstrated for peace in Birmingham. Participating were wide sections of Birmingham opinion. There were Quakers, Boys' Brigades, Warley Institute Church, the Fellowship of Reconciliation, Birmingham Women's International League, League of Nations Unions, Free Churches Women's Temperance League,

Birmingham White Ribbon bands, Birmingham Unemployed Association and other unemployed organisations with separate contingents from Smethwick, King's Norton and Stirchley. In addition, of course were the Labour organisations – the Labour Party, the Trades Council, trade unions (including the National Union of Women Teachers and with the largest contingent, the National Union of Railwaymen), the Independent Labour Party, the Daily Herald Leagues, Co-operative Women's Guild, Sparkhill Men's Guild and its Comrades Section and the Birmingham Communist Party conspicuous with banners and bannerettes proclaiming 'No More War Except...' The procession proceeded to Calthorpe Park where there was a massive twelve platforms of speakers.

In September 1922 there was a danger of war in the Middle East and the Daily Herald League organised a crowded meeting at the Town Hall with the Rev Cosmo Gordon Lang and William Paul arguing against British involvement.

The 1923 *Cornish's Birmingham Year Book* records as peace societies, the Birmingham Auxilliary of the Peace Society whose chairman was Joseph Southall and the League of Nations Union with about 20 branches in Birmingham and District. The Women's International League (which had been brought about by protest at the 1914-18 war) was also active, holding its AGM in March. Peace activists participated in the record May Day parade in Birmingham, but the movement was at a lower level and when the national No More War demonstrations were called for on 28-29 July 1923, Birmingham seems to have managed nothing more than a meeting.

The No More War Movement continued active in 1924. This had been inaugurated by Wilfred Wellock in February 1921. Wellock, who had been a pacifist activist during the 1st World War, founded the No More War Movement in February 1921 through his paper *The Crusader* (later *The New Crusader*). In 1923 the name of the NMWM was changed to War Resisters' International. Wellock became an important figure in the post-war international Peace Movement with his attempts to find a synthesis of Socialism and Pacifism. He unsuccessfully contested the Stourbridge constituency for Labour in December 1923 and from that time was closely associated with the Black Country and Birmingham, where he came to live. The Birmingham No More War Movement held its AGM in April 1924 at the Guild House, Oozells Street and followed it with a public meeting. The president was a newcomer, the Rev John Lewis who. with Jim Simmons, became a pillar of the Christian Socialist movement in the city. Lewis was closely connected with the Marxist wing and after leaving Birmingham became one of the Communist Party's leading philosophy spokesmen. 1924 was one of the years when the consequences of the Versailles Treaty came home to roost. It was estimated that 40 per cent to 50 per cent of the German people were dependent upon aid with 3 million unemployed, the middle classes and pensioners rendered penniless from the inflation which had peaked in 1923 and wiped out all savings, and children deprived of schooling from lack of clothes to wear. The Christian Pacifists and Socialists spent considerable effort seeking contributions to a cause which was not high on many people's lists of deserving causes.

When the annual No More War demonstration was organised in September it was marred by heavy rain and obstruction from the authorities who refused to allow the procession to form in Victoria Square as advertised. Even without these disadvantages it is clear that the scope of the demonstration fell far short of that of 1922. 'Upwards of one thousand' were said to have marched to Summerfield Park. These included the No More War International Movement, Soho Hill Church, the Quakers, the Women's International League, the League of Nations' Unions, the Liberal Party, several Women's Sections of the Labour Party, the Guild Socialists, and the Communist Party. In the park there were two platforms from which a number of people, not particularly well-known either nationally or locally, spoke. The internationally agreed resolution was passed unanimously. It greeted the similar gatherings being held throughout the world, demanded the perfecting of organisation to remove the causes of war, the peaceful settlement of disputes, an all-inclusive League of Nations, and the development of an international sense of solidarity which would make war impossible.

In January 1925 the Birmingham Peace Council organised a Conference on Peace in Education. The speakers were the new Bishop of Birmingham, John Barnes (appointed by Ramsay MacDonald in September 1924), and the veteran peace activist Mrs H.M. Swanwick. The next month there was an FoR meeting addressed by Walter Ayles, a NMWM leader, on 'The Menace of the Next War'. Ayles reviewed the war and the subsequent 'peace' maintaining that this should have convinced everyone of the utter futility of war as a means of settling disputes. The main policy of the war-time allies seemed to be to isolate Russia. War could only be avoided 'by building up the true Christ spirit of love and fellowship', he concluded.

In July there was a large meeting at Carrs Lane organised by the Peace Council, Fellowship of Reconciliation and the No More War Movement to welcome the USA Fellowship of Youth for Peace delegation touring Britain. The chair was taken by J.D. Maynard and among the speakers were the Rev Leyton Richards, the Rev John Lewis and the secretary of the Young Socialist League, Miss D. Humpage.

As the youth movement grew in Birmingham it took up the peace question. In October 1925 there was a British Federation of Youth for Peace meeting at the Guild House, Oozells Street during Peace Week. Harold Bing, secretary of the Federation outlined the rise of the Peace Youth Movement from the movement in Holland resulting from the war. In the Christmas Day issue of the *Town Crier*, Jim Simmons wrote on 'Christmas in the Trenches.'

Peace activity continued strongly up to the General Strike. In April 1926 there was another 'Great Peace Conference' at the Digbeth Institute with Arthur Ponsonby. This was to further the cause of the Peace Letter to which there were already 50,000 signatures nationally. This arose from the belief that developments within the League of Nations now provided adequate machinery for Arbitration and the signatories would therefore 'oppose any government resorting to arms.' Jim Simmons chaired this meeting. A further meeting followed the next week addressed by Mr Styles of the National Federation of Ex-Servicemen's Guilds. Complaint was made of lack of support from the churches.

Adult Working Class Education

Adult working class education was a contentious issue throughout the inter-war period. The battle can be traced back to the 1870 Education which, eventually, sent all children to school and finally produced literate working men, many of them much concerned with further and higher education.

The first college for working people was Ruskin Hall (soon called Ruskin College) at Oxford, opened in February 1899. It was financed by a fairly wealthy, socialist American, Walter Vrooman who was doing on a small scale what Andrew Carnegie and others were doing on a larger scale – distributing largesse from their ill-gotten gains of industry. The College was run by a Council of Oxford academics and trade unionists and the students were mostly trade unionists. After two years Vrooman disappeared and the financing of this Labour College passed increasing to the trade unions and TUC. From 1906, the year of the birth of the Labour Party, the University, never friendly to the syllabus at Ruskin or to its principal Dennis Hird, attempted to control the College and work through the Workers' Educational Association (founded in 1903) as organs of working class education. The bone of contention was that Hird and his students were developing syllabuses based on the sociology of Darwin and the economics of Karl Marx. In October 1908 the students set up the Plebs League to negotiate with the College council, but failed even to convert the two right-wing trade union leaders on the Council of their desire to 'bring about a definite and more satisfactory connection between Ruskin College and the Labour Movement.' In 1909 the Council sacked Dennis Hird and the students came out on strike. The strike could not save Hird, but resulted in the setting up of an independent Labour College which existed, first at Oxford and then in London, until 1926. It ended when the TUC failed to support the Easton Lodge scheme, the offer of the Countess of Warwick, to give an estate for that purpose.

But before then, there had been friction between the Central Labour College and the Plebs League. In 1922 the National Council of Labour Colleges was set up with the priority of developing Labour Colleges in each area with administrative and teaching staff consisting largely of volunteers. The basic issue became therefore, Ruskin College and WEA offering 'objective' (bourgeois) education to workers or Labour Colleges offering 'working class' (Marxist) education.

The Birmingham activist most devoted to working class education was Fred Silvester. From 1915 to 1919 Silvester was secretary of the local Socialist Labour Party which specialised in the production of Marxist texts. In 1920 he was secretary of Birmingham No.2. branch of the Communist Party but he broke from the Communist Party soon after, partly on educational issues. During the war Silvester promoted the various classes organised by the SLP and reported in their paper *The Socialist*. In 1915 there were classes on Marxist economics and in 1916 classes on History and Economics. 1918 was the centenary of Marx' birth and despite war-time difficulties successful celebrations were held in June in Coventry and Birmingham organised by T.D. Smith for the Plebs League. The result in Birmingham was a continuation of the winter classes. These were held on Monday evenings at 110 John Bright St. They consisted of an economics class based on Marx' Wage Labour and Capital and an industrial history class based on Mark Starr's recent book *A Worker looks at History*. By this time there was a Plebs League branch in Birmingham whose contact man was Silvester of 8 Evelyn Road, Sparkhill.

After the war, in October 1919 Silvester announced in *The Socialist* a further extension of the Birmingham Social Science class now run jointly by the SLP branch and Plebs under the control of T.D. Smith. Smith was the other great local Plebs enthusiast. He lived at 12 Old Meeting Street, West Bromwich and was active in promoting workers' education in both the Black Country and Birmingham. Known as 'T.D.' he moved from the SLP into the Communist Party, but unlike Silvester, he remained a Communist to the last. Birmingham education benefitted in 1919 by the return to Birmingham of William Paul, an outstanding national lecturer, and another who moved from the SLP into the Communist Party. *Plebs Magazine* reported in November that W.W. Craik (one of the 1909 leaders of the Ruskin College strike) and W. Paul, 'Gave a fine send off to the Birmingham class,' and they were confident of record success. In December 1919 came one of the first clashes of the opposing ideologists when Mrs Elliot was congratulated at the Trades Council for challenging the affiliation of the No.1. Warehouse and General Workers' Union branch to the WEA and demanding that it change over to the Central Labour College, even though the challenge was unsuccessful.

Fred Silvester was a tireless controversialist in both the *Town Crier* and the *Plebs Magazine* – supporting Soviet Russia, defending Lenin and Trotsky against local critics, and preaching the class struggle and much else.

The Birmingham classes continued into 1920 now being organised by B.J. Rowland. Lectures included W. Hill on 'Ancient Slavery', T.D. Smith on 'Ancient Civilisations', W. Blain on 'Inorganic & Organic Evolution' and Silvester on 'Industrial History'. Slow progress continued into 1921. A *Plebs Magazine* notice in February showed the classes taking place at the ASE Club, 16a Spiceal St. To the class on Industrial History had been added one on Public Speaking. In April T.D. Smith was 'wondering' whether it would be possible to take a party of Plebians to France for the Paris Commune celebrations. Those interested were invited to write to Smith. No more was heard of this project. In December there was an optimistic report stating that Birmingham and Wolverhampton areas were active and it was hoped to form a District Committee.

1922 brought considerable advance. In January it was announced that the Birmingham Social Class was now called the Birmingham Labour College. The chairman was F.B. Silvester, the principal A.D.M. Taylor of the London Labour College, and the chief assistant tutor was T.D. Smith. The Birmingham College was linked to the newly formed Midlands division of the National Council of Labour Colleges. This comprised the colleges at Birmingham, Coventry, Smethwick, Walsall, West Bromwich and Wolverhampton; the divisional secretary was T.D. Smith.

In May 1922 Silvester, who was chairman of the Birmingham Labour College, opened a Karl Lieknecht-Rosa Luxembourg Club, (misinterpreted by some cultured bourgeois commentators as the Carl Rosa Club!). The Club, at 26 Digbeth, was a centre for discussion of Marxist literature and the promotion of working class education. Silvester was always ready to put what little money he had where his mouth was and hope that the future would solve its own problems, and this was a brave project. Silvester carried on a propaganda campaign, courtesy of the *Town Crier* editor, with such pieces as 'The Capital Levy Explained. This useful book by Hugh Dalton MA, DSc is now at the Agency price 1/-d.' and 'The Decay of Capitalist Civilisation. This is the book of the hour. If you want one you'd better hurry. I have a few copies left at 2/6 and 4/6d.' In May, the Birmingham College winter session ended with accounts of the two main classes of Economics, tutor Taylor, and

Industrial History, T.D. Smith. In addition Silvester was delivering a series of lectures for Water Orton Labour Party during the summer and T.D. Smith was lecturing for the Leamington NUR. These were important victories for the Labour College movement over the 'bourgeois elements' of the WEA and Ruskin.

1922 was the year when the builders' union AUBTW put considerable funds into the Labour College Movement thus joining the one other heavily committed trade union, the National Union of Railwaymen. In August the *Plebs Magazine* considered that the scheme adopted by the midlands No.6 Division of the Building Workers Trade Union was the biggest step forward since the founding of the Labour Colleges. The Labour Colleges suggested that the local secretaries of the NUR (who controlled the London Labour College) be contacted by the AUBTW secretaries to sponsor a conference with NCLC representatives to arrange comprehensive classes and scholarships under the auspices of the NCLC. Additionally, in the midlands joint conferences of the Labour Parties, Trades Councils and Co-ops should be held.

At the end of 1922 Fred Silvester seems to have changed the Club into a bookshop. He gave an account of the origins and naming of the shop in the *Town Crier* of 9 January 1923. The shop was at the same address as the Club, 26 Digbeth. When he opened this Labour Literature Agency he wanted to call it the Red Lamp. But other names were suggested to him, such as the Anti-Dope Shop until the more generally agreed title of The Bomb Shop was suggested. If Bristol could have its Bomb Shop, why not Birmingham? Especially as he couldn't afford to put up a red lamp. There had been predecessors Silvester said. A few years before there was the Labour Bookstall in John Bright Street. The bookshop was fathered by himself and mothered by the Labour Party and could not have come into existence at a worse time economically, Silvester went on. If people were serious about wanting more local council representation and MPs they wouldn't get it unless literature sales were better organised. He knew of four Labour Churches which sold no literature. As a member of the Labour Party he was prepared to devote his energies for little pay to the cause of emancipating the working class from capitalist exploitation. He hoped sufficient comrades would join him in making the Bomb Shop a success.

It is not many people who see their dreams come true, but Silvester seems to have realised most of the hopes he wrote about in *Plebs Magazine* of May 1917 when he said:

I want Sunday evening Marxist lectures, Marxian clubs, Marxian bookstores and libraries and a Marxian daily press.

Shortly after this Silvester fulfilled a further ambition. This was the self publication of his *Working Class Ballads, Songs and Poems*. Into this project he poured all his savings at a time when he was unemployed. The quality of the poetry of this working class militant who called himself Birmingham's First Bard is discussed more fully in the section of this chapter on Leisure and Pleasure. It is sufficient here to say that it is of a high quality and deserving to be better known.

The lack of local reports in both the *Town Crier* and *Plebs Magazine* suggest that, in spite of the optimism generated by the Building Trades participation which was putting 3d. per member into sending full time students on a two year course to the London Labour College and 9d. per member into the setting up of local educational facilities, 1923 was a year in which the Labour College Movement struggled to maintain its existence. This is understandable with unemployment in Birmingham said by the *Town Crier* to be standing at 100,000 in December 1922. This would have particularly affected the building trades union and its ability to find money for education.

Another educational agency was, however, in the field in 1923, This was the Labour Research Department with its Syllabus Series of booklets such as *The British Labour Movement* by G.D.H. Cole, and *The Development of Capitalism* by Maurice Dobb etc. These were available from sources of both the warring WEA and Plebs League.

The alliance of the Building Workers with the NCLC brought a major success early in 1924 when the Birmingham Trades Council was prised from the grip of the WEA and supported the Labour College movement. In September the Birmingham ILP Federation appointed two delegates to the local management committee of the Labour Colleges. The movement was also making progress with the editor of the *Town Crier*. Regular advertisements for the classes of the Plebs League began to appear for the first time in a journal which tended to lean towards the WEA with its heavy weight support at Birmingham University and also the Fabian Society in the city and at the University.

In November the Birmingham NCLC reported that it had had the assistance of William Paul and Dr Robert Dunstan during the year. This was the year of the rise and fall of the Labour government. Dr Dunstan had stood as the Labour candidate in both the elections and was unanimously readopted. The gap between the Labour Party and the Communists had not yet finally hardened. When it did, the Communist Party undertook its own educational programmes which was a further weakening element of the position of the Labour Colleges. The year ended with T.D. Smith appealing for more volunteer tutors – always a main problem of the Colleges whether they were flourishing or not – and welcoming the return of Fred Silvester to their number.

NCLC activities expanded in 1925. A 'very successful' Easter school was held at the Clarion Club House, Sheldon, with sixteen residents and a number of other students. This led to the organising of a summer school. But this was less successful; sessions were held on Metals in History, Economic Geography, and Law. A new divisional organiser was appointed in the autumn. This was Stuart Barr. He took over from T.D. Smith who for some unexplained reason went to assist Division 12 covering Northampton, Mansfield etc. Barr had his first major success at the end of the year when he persuaded the Labour Party to hand over their Speakers' Classes to the NCLC. Sparkbrook ILP Young Socialist League also joined NCLC classes.

But 1925 was a year when the superior resources of the WEA were revealed. The Birmingham City Council developed a scheme whereby free places and maintenance allowances were to be paid to students going to Ruskin College. Unkindest cut of all, Fred Silvester was organising WEA classes at Bristol Street Schools in the autumn on 'Communism'. William Cardinal opened on the 'Theory of Communism', followed by T.A. Jackson (taking the place of Dr Dunstan who was ill) on 'Capitalism v Communism'. The WEA year Book of the West Midlands showed that its classes had doubled during the year. The National Council of Labour Colleges countered with a directory in *Town Crier* which showed four divisional Labour Parties affiliated to it as well as one ILP branch.

1925 saw the beginning of a long series of articles in the *Town Crier* by J. Walton Newbold on the History of Birmingham and the Black Country. Newbold, who had been the Communist Party's second MP, but who was currently out of the party and very much at odds with it, has a connection with Birmingham the length and period of which are unclear. His articles were long, rambling ones with a great deal of non-local material, but his familiarity with the area should make it worth someone's while to collect together this contribution to the history of Birmingham.

Some hard information on the number of Birmingham NCLC classes comes in January 1926 when we are told that 12 classes were operating, although an advertisement in the *Town Crier* mentioned only six classes. In April there were more affiliations of ILP and Labour Parties to the Birmingham Labour College. It is clear, therefore, that up to the General Strike the Birmingham Labour College was experiencing one of its best years.

We can now turn to the activities of the local Workers' Education Association. Hostility between them and the Plebs began before the war. Silvester tells us that it was 1913 when he, together with William Paul, both members of the SLP, formed the Birmingham Social Science Class. Paul was the main tutor, until he was called up in 1917. Warfare with the WEA was thus declared in 1913. Silvester puts the core of the dispute in the *Plebs Magazine* of January 1918 thus:

> The bone of contention between the reactionaries who support the WEA and the revolutionaries who support the Central Labour College is – Can education in Social Science be non-partisan and impartial? Much space in the *Plebs* has been devoted to showing that this question can only be answered in the negative. The circumstances that led to the founding of the Plebs League and... establishment of the CLC were derived from the ideas in the heads of Oxford dons who, in the interests of their class – the Capitalist Class – desired to 'dope' the education given to working class students at Ruskin College. Their partisan efforts to impose bourgeois economics on the students met with a vigorous resistance. Since that time Ruskin College has been the central home of that emasculated teaching of sociology described as non-partisan and impartial of which the various branches of the WEA are the provincial depots.

The occasion of this philippic was an example of this 'impartiality' at Birmingham University. Here, according to Silvester, Dr Segal an expert on Russia, had been gagged by the University Senate, which included such liberals as Sir Oliver Lodge and Professor Muirhead, from concluding a series of lectures when his (Segal's) opinions were proving to be too revolutionary. This gagging, at the time of the Bolshevik revolution, was justified by the University on the grounds that 'present events in Russia are not clear.'

These lectures had not been arranged by the WEA, but L.W. Price, the secretary of the midland district of the WEA replied. He agreed with Silvester concerning the cancelling of Segal's lectures and considered the action of the Senate 'a regrettable and dangerous error of judgement'. But he thought that the 'deepening mystery of the Russian situation' at that time gave plausibility to the Senate decision and Segal himself had not claimed that he had been gagged. Price objected to Silvester's contention that the University decision was 'tarred with the WEA brush' and suggested that if Silvester would take a lesson from Segal and 'try to arrive at that state of mind which can meet opposite opinion without regarding them as deliberate perversions of fact', he also would be 'tarred with the WEA brush.'

The 1924/25 WEA annual report gave a history of the midland district. The first Birmingham branch had been formed in 1905, two years after the foundation of the WEA, and a midland district was formed the same year. A full time officer had been in place since 1907. The organisation had been particularly fortunate in their chairmen 'who had rendered invaluable services to the cause of education and to the development of our Association', the report went on. These chairmen were Dr Charles Gore (1906-12), Sir Oliver Lodge (1912-19) and Prof J.H. Muirhead (from 1919). All of these were closely connected with Birmingham University.

The 1922/23 report shows WEA classes in Birmingham centred on a King's Norton branch and taking place at Fircroft College. There was one Tutorial Class on Social Psychology, tutor A. Barrett Brown (soon to become principal of Ruskin College). There were also Preparatory Classes on the Growth of the Nation, Law, and Economic Geography. In addition there were Study Circles at Stirchley where Tom Hackett lectured on Modern Problems and Selly Oak where there was a class on Banking & International Finance.

Three years later Birmingham WEA activity was still centred on the King's Norton branch. Classes were now classified as either Tutorial or One Year. There were two Tutorial Classes – on Social History and Economics. There were five One Year Classes – three at Fircroft (Regional Geography, Literature, and Modern European History), Tom Hackett was still at Stirchley Institute but now lecturing on the Evolution of Society, and there was an Economics class at Northfield Institute.

It does not appear, therefore, that the WEA made great headway in this period. It was, and remains, an important source of working class education, relatively well funded with University and thus government money. But it can never escape the suspicion that such funds are available to divert the Labour movement from Marxist educational rivals and that those educated in WEA classes are drawn from middle class rather than working class students. As far as commitment and sacrifice for working class aims are concerned the Labour Colleges were valiant but disadvantaged competitors. None showed more commitment or made such sacrifices in Birmingham as Fred Silvester and T.D. Smith.

Women

The profile of women in the Labour movement after the 1st World War was, perhaps inevitably, lower than before. In the years before the war there was the suffrage movement. During the war, the women had been particularly tenacious in their international efforts to stop the war (see chapter 12) and as the men were called up took prominent parts in the No-Conscription Fellowship and general support for conscientious objectors. Women's participation in the war effort led to an improved economic condition (for some), increased participation in the trade union movement, greater equality both at work and with the granting of the franchise (to those over 30) accompanied, no doubt, by greater self-esteem.

Things began to go wrong as early as 1917 when peak production of certain types of armaments led to the sacking of women. Then came the period of demobilisation when women were pushed back into the home in favour of the men, and finally the economic crisis beginning in the middle of 1921.

Something of the old spirit, however, can be seen in a report in the *Town Crier* of October 1919 of the work of the Women's International League in Birmingham by 'M.H.' She outlined the origins of the movement from the international Peace conference at the Hague in the first six months of the war, and its development as an organisation for a constructive peace and for women's emancipation. In Birmingham there was a central study circle and district meetings at which it addressed the new, unknown problems of the future.

Early in 1920 there was news of social activity by the Women's Section of the Labour Party and of a children's party organised by the Women's International League. Women trade unionists in the Birmingham branch of the National Federation of Women Workers made a presentation to Councillor Mrs Mitchell the previous secretary of a branch formed in 1914. The new secretary was Mrs Pownall and the meeting was introduced to a new organiser from London, Miss Bromhall.

In May 1920 there was news of Mrs Carol Ring, the pre-war organiser of the National Union of Women's Suffrage Societies and wartime peace supporter. She had been to Austria on behalf of the Lord Mayor's European Famine Fund and reported on the plight of that country. The next month Mrs A. Howes was returned unopposed for Labour at a Washwood Heath ward by-election. Biographical details showed that she had been the first secretary of the Women's Labour League in 1910, also past president of the Co-op Women's Guild and a district and central committee member of the Railway Women's Guild. Towards the end of 1920 Chamberlain experimented with a weekly column in the *Town Crier* – From a Woman's Point of View by Labour Woman. This was said to be the first woman's column since Katharine Glasier's (presumably in the *Labour Leader* – GB). The column was not, unfortunately, productive of much news of the women's movement in Birmingham, dealing largely with domestic and home matters. In October Margaret Bondfield spoke to women at the town hall on the Special Unemployment Scheme, but it is not clear what organisation of women workers arranged the meeting.

Carol Ring continued her interest in foreign affairs and peace, making a militant speech in March at St. Stephen's Church under the auspices of a Social Services Committee, but little else of women's activities are recorded in the *Town Crier* for 1921.

In May 1922 there was a women's conference at the University on Higher Education for Women, chaired by Councillor Mrs Howes. This brought together many of the existing women's organisation in the city and there were representatives from the Women's Co-operative Guild, the Railway Women's Guild, the Women's International League and Labour Women's Councils as well as women from WEA branches, trade union branches and Adult Schools. Mrs Reynolds of the Birmingham Co-operative Society Education Committee gave the main address on the Purpose of Education stressing its necessity for every human being and belief that thoroughly educated persons would never remain individualists, but would strive to make the world a better place. Miss Adams of the Women's Section, the National Union of General Workers, currently studying at Ruskin, outlined existing facilities for working women including the Central Labour College, Ruskin, and colleges in Birmingham such as Woodbrooke. If local authorities were pressed they could do much, Miss Adams concluded. A session on Methods of Education by Miss F. Goddard of the Workers Union, a former student at Ruskin, brought oblique criticism of Marxist education and the Labour College movement by talk of education 'only in economics.' From the floor came trenchant criticism; the lack of money was a main cause of the lack of advance for women in higher education, as well as the widely held view that money spent on educating women was wasted. At least one delegate expressed the view that higher education for women would never be provided under the present system.

By 1923 Dr Margaret Dunstan was making an input into the movement in Birmingham; in March she spoke at St. Barnabas schoolroom on 'Birmingham under Private Enterprise'. This was in support of her husband whose memorable phrase 'this rotten and benighted city had penetrated the thick hides of landlords and capitalists of the city.' In April the Women's International League held its annual general meeting at the Priory Rooms. Both the president, Mrs H. Lloyd Wilson and the secretary Mrs Lennard resigned. Mrs Henson became the new secretary, Mrs Woodward treasurer, and the replacement of the president was left to the committee. A membership of 350 was recorded.

In May a Birmingham Labour Women's Advisory Committee was formed with Mrs Harrison Barrow as president. There was to be a delegate from each ward on the Committee. Officers elected were Councillor Mrs Howes chair, Mrs Cripwell treasurer, and Mrs Harrison Barrow secretary. Others on the committee were Mrs Bayes, Mrs Billington, Mrs Leonard, Mrs Manning, Mrs Stevens, Mrs H. Lloyd Wilson, and Mrs Webb. At this conference Mrs Fawcett and Mrs Howes gave a report of the national women's conference held at York.

In February 1924 the first annual conference of the Birmingham Labour Women's Advisory Council met at Digbeth. The guest was Mrs Margaret Bondfield, the first Labour woman minister. There were 457 delegates from Labour and Co-op organisations in Birmingham and district and a large number of visitors, 'Every seat in this large hall being filled long before the Conference commenced.' The main speakers were Mrs Bondfield, Parliamentary Secretary to the Minister of Labour, and Mrs H. Fawcett. Opening the conference, Councillor Mrs Howes said that this was the happiest moment in the lives of Birmingham Labour women; the wonderful attendance was a fine tribute to the work of Mrs H. Fawcett and the Labour Women's Sections in Birmingham and district. The secretary, Mrs Harrison Barrow gave an outline of the work of the Council since its inception and Mrs Raymond Beazley made 'an eloquent appeal' for delegates to realise the importance of reading and selling the literature of the Labour movement.

Margaret Bondfield, who was given a great reception on both entering the hall and rising to speak, spoke on Women in Industry. She started by contrasting this record gathering with the heartbreaking experiences of some former attempts to organise Birmingham women and 'make them pull their full strength in the regulation of industry.' Today the midland division had the third highest rate of unemployment among women, coming after London and Lancashire. A disturbing feature was the high number of married women who were compelled to seek employment for one reason and another. But the greatest tragedy of all was the number of boys and girls 'having their most formative years wasted by the evil of unemployment.

Dealing with the efforts made by the Labour government to alleviate unemployment among women. She was sure that the previous government had 'made a very grave psychological blunder' in insisting that all women trained in housecraft must undertake domestic service. Experience had shown that some women who had objected to the subject when undertaking the thirteen week course had subsequently changed their minds and voluntarily sought domestic work. But other retained their 'craft sense' that they would be needed in future in industry and resented being dragooned into the 'servile service.' The Labour government was removing this compulsion. She thought the new housing policy of the Labour government would bring work to many Birmingham building workers and she wanted Birmingham women to let the government know what they wanted in these new houses and she would guarantee that their voices should be heard. 'Brass taps, for instance. I wouldn't have a brass tap in the house. Women don't want to be polishing brass all day,' she asserted. Miss Bondfield next turned to the effect of foreign policy on employment. The recognition of Russia would open the vast markets of the East and better relations between France and Britain held out some degree of hope for German workers. She then dealt with Trade Boards and promised that those now moribund would be reactivated.

In closing she said that the Labour government was endeavouring to create a feeling of greater security for the whole population. Far too many old people had nothing to look forward to except the workhouse as a reward for years of toil. The keynote for the twentieth century must be social service, even to the point of sacrifice, for the common good. The motive of economic necessity must give place to the joy of service, so that all could work together.

After her speech, Miss Bondfield was closely questioned. Asked if she thought married women should be allowed to remain in industry she replied that on general principle she objected to any difference being made between married and unmarried women; the only test should be efficiency and suitability for the job. Regarding the Bill being brought before Parliament that month for women to be given the vote on the same terms as men, she reminded the questioner that the Labour Party was in a minority in Parliament and though they would do their best, she could make no promise of success. A question on domestic service was an oblique one, 'Does domestic service make good home makers?'

she was asked. Her 'diffident' reply was, 'There is a tradition that some men seek their wives among the ranks of domestic servants. I am not prepared to go further than that.' At the end of the conference Mrs Fawcett successfully moved a motion for the extension of the Trade Boards system to 'appropriate trades requiring such protection'.

In March 1924 the *Town Crier* was maintaining that the Co-operative Women's Guild was 'reviving its ancient glories.' Fifty people had attended a celebration of the 26th anniversary of the Central Guild. At the same meeting Councillor Mrs Sands was thanked for 'seven years hard' as president. In the same month the Bill for equal franchise ages for men and women had its first reading. Labour and Liberal MPs supported it. Only the Unionists had opposed it. Birmingham voting was as follows. For the Bill J. Smedley Crooke (Deritend) and Commander Locker-Hampson (Handsworth). Against the Bill P.J. Hannon (Moseley) and L.C. Amery (Sparkbrook) who had taken an active part in attempting to sabotage the Bill by voting for an amendment that it be passed to a Committee of the whole House. No less than 8 Birmingham MPs took the coward's way out of opposing the Bill by being absent. These were Sir Herbert Austin, J.B. Burman, Sir E. Cecil, both the Chamberlains (Austen and Neville), Jephcott (who in far distant days had been a pillar of the Labour movement), Sir F. Lowe and Sir A. Steel-Maitland.

Birth control was an issue in 1924. In July a letter from Rose Witcop in the *Town Crier* announced that as a result of the prosecution for publishing Margaret Sanger's pamphlet, the price was being reduced to 6d. and Birmingham organisations were invited to buy them and thus make the information available to those for whom it was intended – working women. In September the Warwickshire Labour Women's Conference passed a resolution that the Maternity and Child Welfare Act be amended so that birth control information be available at all welfare centres to all persons making application for it.

The Labour Women's Annual Conference in February 1925 was even larger than that of 1924 with 400 delegates and twice that number of visitors. The chief speakers were Miss Edith Picton-Turbervill and Miss Ishbel MacDonald. Councillor Mrs Howes, again chairing the conference, said that great progress had been made since the previous year and the Labour Party had broken through with one Labour MP in the city. But there was now a reactionary government in power. Their policies must be rejected, particularly the increase in armaments which was bound to lead to war. Children must be taught that war was not 'all brass bands and glory.'

Edith Picton-Turbervill spoke wittily on the need for women to have the franchise on equal terms with men. Never had women possessed so much power as they had today even with the restricted franchise. But only one in fifteen working women had the vote. In discussion a Wolverhampton delegate said that too many men were lukewarm on this issue, whereas another delegate reminded the Conference that men had been in the forefront supporting women's rights. In reply Mrs Picton-Turbervill said that the Labour Party was sounder on the franchise question than other parties and it was up to the women to ginger up the Labour Party. Ishbel MacDonald's theme was social services. She spoke of the Baby Clinic in London named after her mother started fourteen years before by members of the Women's Labour League. This had grown to 2,200 Baby Clinics throughout the country in 1924. Councillor Mrs Wilson (chair of the Maternity and Infant Welfare Committee) spoke on the work of the centre and the need for more than the two nursery schools existing in the city. Mrs Longden said she found that in the poorer quarters of the city mothers were so 'down and out' that it was difficult to interest them in Baby Clinics. Another delegate urged that Labour women press for pensions for widowed mothers. Mrs Fawcett moved an emergency resolution against the city Council's decision to build flats for working class families in slum areas. She wished she could take delegates to see the flats in Glasgow. Flats might be alright for middle-class people, but not for working class families. She also criticised the decision to build two bedroomed houses without bathrooms. She concluded by urging women to attend the city council meetings. "Nothing puts fear into the hearts of councillors more than a public gallery full of women.'

The issue of the flats escalated and the Sandwell Ward Women's Section of the Handsworth Labour Party protested, demanding that three-bedroomed houses with bathrooms were essential for working class families.

An example of women's work in a different field was a lecture by Mrs Lesley Lewis at the Broad Street Presbyterian Church in February continuing the series started by the socialist Dr John Lewis examining the foundations of Christian belief. Her lecture was on 'The Divinity of Christ.'

Reports of the annual meetings of the Labour Party Women's Sections appeared regularly in the *Town Crier* at this time giving the names of officers and committees, and also their social activity such as socials and children's parties.

In May the national Labour Women's Conference was held in Birmingham. Pre-conference publicity in the *Town Crier* concentrated on the remarkable growth of the national women's movement. and that this would be the largest ever gathering with 1,000 delegates expected. The delegates were welcomed to an informal At Home at the Town Hall on Monday. On Tuesday the delegates met in private and in the evening there was a charabanc tour of the City. The Conference proper began on Wednesday and in the evening was the great public meeting addressed by Ramsay MacDonald and the Labour woman MP, Ellen Wilkinson. The Conference continued on Thursday with a Town Hall reception and dance in the evening. On Friday there were visits to Bournville Garden Village and municipal departments.

The Conference Report showed 1,450 Women's Sections nationally with an estimated 200,000 women members of the Labour Party and 48 Women's Advisory Councils throughout the country. Details of work done during the previous year included, Maternity Care, the Nursing Profession, National Health Insurance, Penal Reform, Child Adoption, Women's Franchise, Factory Legislation, Housing, Education, Food Prices, and International Work. Resolutions before the Conference were on Equal Franchise, opposition to the proposal to establish Widows' Pensions on a contributory basis. and an ILP proposal to establish direct international contact between Socialist women. There was also a Peace resolution in the name of the Selly Oak Women's Section. This claimed that war was caused by the clash of capitalist interests, and the system of secret diplomacy; it pledged the Conference to support the Labour Party's endeavours to abolish both capitalism and secret diplomacy and to work for complete disarmament.

Separate ILP Women's Groups also existed, presumably affiliated to the Labour Party Women's Sections; in July 1925 there is a report of an ILP Women's Group outing to Evesham the coach being decorated with *Labour Leader* and *Daily Herald* posters and Socialist emblems.

We can end this review of 1925 by showing an example of how varied and painful were the disabilities which women suffered. A group of women who had been recently married had been dismissed from their jobs because the firms did not employ married women. When they signed on for unemployment pay this was refused. Instead they were sent to the Court of Referees. The following was the experience of one of these women who had been employed as a clerk for fifteen years and whose employment card was fully paid up for the whole of that period.

Q. What wages does your husband earn?
A. About £2 a week.
Q. How much does he give you?
A. 34/-d.
Q. Can you not manage on that?
A. No, I have to pay 15/-d. a week for rooms.
Q. Was it necessary for you to be married?
A. I don't understand you. (This was an accusation of what was then immorality – very serious in those days.)
Q. Were you forced to be married?
A. Certainly not.
Q. Well, why did you get married when you knew your husband could not keep you in comfort? (No reply.)
A. I suppose you thought you wouldn't get another chance if you didn't take this one. You are no spring chicken, you know. Your age is given here as 39.

This applicant's case was dismissed on the grounds that she had married knowing that the firm did not employ married women and she had therefore discharged herself. These cases were taken up by the Trades Council and referred to the TUC.

The women's movement continued to grow in the months up to the General Strike, as did the general movement in Birmingham.

This is an incomplete survey of the women's movement up to the General Strike. Still to come is the work of the Women's Co-operative Guild, the work of women in the trade unions, the work of women Labour councillors and work in other spheres. Each will be dealt with separately in this chapter. There is also the work that labour women did with the local National Union of Women's Suffrage Societies which turned itself in 1919 into the Birmingham Society for Equal Citizenship and Women Citizens' Association. Labour women also worked within the National Union of Women Workers, the umbrella organisation for all women's charitable work in the city; in 1919 this changed its name to the National Council of Women. These two important women's organisations were largely middle class in their origin and activities and were not part of the Labour movement.

It is clear, however, even from this survey, that starting from a low level immediately after the war, the women's movement grew very considerably in the years to 1926. The fact that women's work cannot be reviewed under a single heading suggests that not only did the movement deepen, but it also widened. Despite the sometimes justified feeling that the general labour movement in Birmingham was backward compared with some other parts of the country, it remains that by 1926 many more women were participating in both the women's and the general Labour movement in Birmingham than ever before.

Youth

The first Labour youth movement in Birmingham originated in 1924. The occasion of its origin was an increasing Labour input into sport and culture, the general strengthening of the movement at this time, and the particularly rapid growth of the Independent Labour Party. The first notice I have found comes from a letter in the *Town Crier* of 12 September by A. Norman Fowler. He states his interest in an article the previous week entitled 'Young Labour Advances', but suggests that before the Labour Parties in the city form a new youth organisations they should recognise that one already existed prepared to welcome any young socialist. This was the Birmingham Young Socialist League. Moreover, the three main lines of work suggested for the new organisation was exactly the lines on which the BYSL was formed. These were: Recreational, Educational and participation in Election Work. Any youth organisation formed in opposition to the BYSL would cause division in their ranks and Fowler suggested that the Labour Parties, instead of inaugurating opposing bodies, should persuade their juvenile members to join the BYSL. Fowler ended by stating that the League intended to set up branches throughout the city when strong enough, that it was affiliated to the ILP and that it was self-governed and controlled. By April 1925 there was a Sparkbrook branch of the BYSL and by May branches had been opened at East Birmingham and King's Norton. At the AGM of the Central branch, officers were elected as follows: President – Jack Wood, Vice Presidents – Leslie Skan and Bert Lane, Secretary Doris Humpage, Organiser – Arthur Smart.

Controversy dogged the movement from the beginning. In April 1925 Doris Humpage was complaining that the *Daily Herald* would not print a letter of hers which advocated a united youth movement around the Young Socialist League and complaining that 'differences as to tactics and quarrels concerning the abstruse theories advocated by the many doctrinaire sects that divide our Movement', should not be allowed to divert them from the struggle against the existing system. In May Doris Humpage enlarged on some of these differences when she wrote in the *Town Crier* that carrying banners only in demonstrations, 'Is far too little for so great a Cause.' That the movement needed 'education in all aspects of life.' It seems that the ILP was divided in itself, for there are reports of ILP members meeting with a Guild of Youth at the Clarion Club House. This was certainly not an anti-intellectual split. It is likely that the Guild of Youth grew out of the general Guild movement of the time, but might well be considered one of the 'doctrinaire sects' within the movement and might account for Doris Humpage's letter not being printed, as the Guild Socialists were supported by the *Daily Herald*.

BYSL activity continued throughout 1925. A varied summer programme included a ramble to Clent, and the reading of a G.B. Shaw play. In July came the reception to the delegates of the USA

Fellowship of Youth for Peace touring Britain. This was followed in September by a Peace Week of Youth with A. Norman Fowler as the secretary. In fact, Harold F. Bing, the organising secretary of the British Federation of Youth, spent three weeks in Birmingham at that time, claiming considerable success in mobilising young people in Birmingham. Peace was becoming a crusade, an adventure, calling for qualities of heroism and self-sacrifice, as war had in the past, Bing claimed, and a Youth Section of the No More War Movement in Birmingham was formed.

In September the *Town Crier* reported that the BYSL continued to flourish. Members were attending T.D. Smith's Economic Geography classes at the Clarion Clubhouse and they continued to hold weekly Tuesday meetings at the Guild House, Oozells Street. In October there was a meeting of the British Federation of Youth for Peace at the Guildhouse with Harold Bing. His theme was the rise and development of the Youth Movement. The Weeks for Peace were international, originating from Holland and the German Youth Peace Movement. Preparations were going ahead for a World Federation of Youth to be formed at a World Congress in 1928.

But by December, a letter to the *Town Crier* from L. Fisher of Aston Labour Party Youth Section said the youth movement in Birmingham was 'in a mess.' There was the BYSL, the Labour Party Youth Sections, the ILP Guild of Youth, and the Young Communist League. A programme was needed to suit all of them, Fisher said.

However divided it might be activities continued. At the end of the year there was a meeting of the No More War Youth Section which heard Professor John Stevens lecture on the German Youth Movement showing how it was trying to come to terms with its militaristic past. It was returning to expressions of the past such as medieval customs and folk dancing, but with a new emphasis on community, fellowship and internationalism.

Into 1926 the youth movement flourished, but it was the BYSL that made most of the running. it was also the BYSL that showed particular awareness of the issues of the coming General Strike. In the only report I have found of public activity in support of the miners before the General Strike, the Young Socialist League together with the Aston Labour Party held a public meeting at the Aston Theatre Royal with Duncan Graham a miners' MP, Arthur Ponsonby, and John Strachey prospective parliamentary Labour candidate for Aston. The meeting was chaired by D.D. Murden president of the local YSL. Not only were the miners supported, but government activity in setting up OMS (Office for Maintenance of Supplies) and agreeing to the proffered assistance of the Fascisti was condemned. The YSL also called on all socialists of both sexes from 15 to 30 to join with them in volunteering for Supply Services in the coming crisis to ensure such essential Labour services as the circulation of the Labour press and other activities.

At the second anniversary AGM of the BYSL in April 1926, it was announced that there were five branches – Central, E. Birmingham, Edgbaston, King's Norton and Duddeston. Officers elected were Jack Wood president, P.A.V. Bellows vice-president, Miss M. Ellsworth secretary, and D.D. Murden organiser.

Such was the state of the youth movement in Birmingham on the eve of the General Strike.

Labour Churches

The Labour Churches in Birmingham were unusual in that they developed from 1893 at a time when the general Labour Church movement was very much in decline. Labour Churches continued in Birmingham throughout the First World War, which was even more unusual. But to find a considerable number of such Churches continuing into the post-war years was unique.

The Labour Churches were invariably linked with the Independent Labour Party. During the early years of the war the Erdington ILP branch took the brunt of the hostility to its anti-war policy and it was the Erdington Labour Church that survived the longest. There are notices of its meetings in 1915 and 1916. Only in the darkest year of 1917 are there no notices of this Church and it is operative again in 1918. As war weariness grew, so did the ILP and by the end of the war there were four Labour Churches operating – Erdington, Rotton Park, Stirchley and East Birmingham (reopened in 1917).

The Labour 'Churches' met in secular premises and it is difficult to tell how their 'services' differed from ordinary ILP meetings. There are no records of these Churches. No leading figure appeared who could be identified exclusively with the movement. What we do have is an almost complete record of who spoke at each of these Churches for every week. This shows that virtually every national leader and most local cadres addressed the Labour Churches, and every activist in the City would have attended the Churches at some time or other.

Until the end of 1919 only the four established Churches seem to have operated. A typical report in October shows that the East Birmingham church met at Anthony Road Schools. Here the national secretary of the Coachmakers spoke to a 'large audience' on 'Labour and Education.' All existing educational institutions gave 'safe' education; working people should support the Central Labour College and the Plebs League, he said. No mention of 'prayers' or 'hymns'; and what permanent decoration of banners or pictures etc. suggestive of even a secular 'church' could be displayed in such premises? As far as this meeting was concerned it could have been an ordinary ILP meeting, except that it took place on a Sunday morning. By December a Tyseley Labour Church was in existence. Councillor E.W. Hampton, leading co-operator and later historian of the Birmingham society, spoke on 'Birmingham and the Co-operative Commonwealth.'

In February 1920 Hockley Labour Church was opened. A report by Councillor E. Taylor (leader of the 1919 police strike) in April stated that it met in Smith Street Schools every Sunday at 7 pm. On Good Friday a few willing workers had given a treat to about 280 children and on the previous Sunday Councillor Sharkey had dealt with the indifference of the workers towards their responsibilities. Those with known Christian beliefs regularly attended the Labour Churches. These included from Birmingham Jim Simmons, W.J. Chamberlain, and A. Barratt Brown, but although both Simmons and Chamberlain were speakers and chairmen at times, there is no indication that they participated in the work of organising the Churches, nor is there any indication of a committee that would be necessary to operate these not inconsiderable enterprises. It can only be assumed that it was done as part of the duties of the local ILP committee.

The Churches raised moral awareness. In January 1920 a report from Erdington stated that after a 'tip top address' on What is the Matter? with an appeal for a higher ideal of citizenship 'we heard the beautiful words of Walt Whitman which Comrade Tedstone read so effectively, we all felt strengthened to carry on the good fight'. But the next Sunday was politics with the Communist, W.T. Cardinal, speaking on Russia. The same Sunday ex-Pte Jim Simmons spoke at Rotton Park Labour Church on 'War,' claiming that diplomacy could have prevented the war and the terms on offer in 1916 could have ended it. Also the same week at Stirchley we have one of the few mentions of music, Miss Farnam singing two songs which were 'keenly appreciated.' The great attraction the following week was the Selly Oak Choral Union.

By 1921 more Labour Churches appear. It was customary for the Churches to close down during the summer and recommence in the autumn. The Churches, with the speaker, at their re-opening meetings in September 1921, were as follows: All Saints (Harrison Barrow), Aston (Clifford Williams – 'Love the Redeemer'), City Bristol Street (Wm Milner – 'Labour's Municipal Policy'), East Birmingham (George Hicks and Ex-Pte Jim Simmons), Ladywood (Harry Parsons), Rotton Park (Concert by the AEU male voice choir), Stirchley (J.W. Murby), and Sparkhill (F.R. Sharkey on 'Past, Present & Future'). A further notice in December 1921 shows two additional Churches operating. Aston (the AEU choir), and Erdington (W.A. Exton). There were thus ten Labour Churches in Birmingham at the end of 1921 and by February 1922 the total had risen to thirteen with Churches at Balsall Heath, St. Martins and Deritend, and West Birmingham.

Topics for discussion were infinite. In April 1922 at Erdington an address was give on 'The Religious Aspects of Free Trade,' in the course of which C.E. Fellows proclaimed that Protection was basicly anti-Christian. In the same week at West Birmingham W. Goodwin spoke on the Industrial Crisis and urged that all workers should be united in One Big Union.

King's Norton & Stirchley Labour Church captured big names. This church met at Stirchley Institute in semi-private circumstances. In March 1923 George Lansbury spoke, with Joseph Southall in the chair. Visitors were advised to 'come early.' In November Fenner Brockway, the national secretary of the ILP, was at the same church. On the same evening at the All Saints Labour Church

George Norwill gave the first of three addresses on 'The Psychology of the Study of the Mind,' and at Handsworth W.H. Milner was speaking on the 'History of the Birmingham Working Class Movement.' The Rev N. Micklem MA, of Selly Oak Colleges, was the speaker at Selly Oak Labour Church with soloist J. Smith, violin. The only other church to advertise music was Sparkbrook where G. Geoby, the trade union leader, spoke and W. Deakin was the soloist.

Two lists early in 1924 in the *Town Crier* show thirteen Labour Churches still functioning. Speakers from these two lists show the following. At All Saints J. Corrin of the Trades Council spoke to 'an interested and large audience' on 'Industrial Progress.' At Balsall Heath Harry Lennard read extracts from the letters of Rosa Luxemburg; and a fortnight previously W.A. Dalley had lectured on the poetry of Ernest Jones. East Birmingham had another celebrity Charles Roden Buxton, on Foreign Affairs. At Erdington W. Griffiths spoke on William Lovett and there was a reading from *News from Nowhere*. At Handsworth Councillor Jabez Hall addressed a packed church on 'The Church and the Workers'. At Harborne there was the first meeting of a new Church held at the Guildroom, The Circle, Harborne where a 'good audience heard an excellent lecture' by S. Dodd on Capital and the law of Reserves. At Stirchley Margaret Haley 'gave a thoughtful address' on the education of the workers. At Rotton Park Councillor A.E. Ager spoke on his experiences as a Labour councillor. At the other two Churches there were musical events. At Sparkbrook there was a musical programme by the Selly Oak Musical Society and at Small Heath the Bordesley Labour Church Male Voice Choir performed. Both played to large and appreciative audiences. Musical items were also more evident at the other Churches. All Saints had the Central Quartette, Balsall Heath had soloists as did Stirchley, and Harborne had three singers.

It is clear from these programmes that Labour activists in Birmingham had an enormous range of cultural, moral and political programmes offered to them every Sunday through the Labour Churches and that the modern Labour movement would not be able to sustain such a rich and varied diet.

At this time the *Town Crier* carried complete lists of the previous week's activities of all the Labour Churches with details of the next week's speaker. It would be tedious to repeat them, but some of the more interesting developments can be picked out. In 1925 Balsall Heath experimented with running two Churches, one at the Mary Street schools as well as the usual one at Clifton Street schools. At West Birmingham Jabez Hall spoke on 'Is Labour Anti-Christian?' This was a perfect type of subject for a Labour Church gathering, but this was at a W. Birmingham ILP meeting at a time, it would seem, when the local Labour Church was not operating. Why were not more of these topics taken at ILP meetings instead of in Labour Churches? Or was the demand for such discussion so considerable that both Labour Church and party meetings could be sustained by the local ILP branches? In fact, subsequent Sunday meetings of the W. Birmingham ILP were reported in the Labour Church column.

Selly Oak seems to have led the way with educational matters and when they had a speaker on 'The Evolution of Man' it was remarked that the subject was so vast that they had only time to deal with 'several stages' of man's progress. Mention of a lantern lecture comes in 1925 from Sparkbrook.

At the end of the 1925 session in April Erdington experimented with holding a meeting on the last Sunday of each of the summer months. Sometimes speakers failed to turn up. Often a satisfactory alternative speaker could be found in the audience, but at Erdington in October when a speaker failed to appear there was a gramophone recital. Also in October Jabez Hall took his talk on 'Is Labour Anti-Christian?' to the Handsworth Labour Church. Hall's final verdict was that Labour was not anti-Christian, but the report sheds little light on the relationship of the Labour Church to the Christian faith. When a Sparkhill speaker failed to appear Harold Bing, the organiser of the British Federation of Youth was on hand to speak on the 'Gospel of Youth.'

The Labour Churches had links with the cultural life of Birmingham and in October 1925 Stirchley had a visit from H. Humphrey's People's Theatre who gave a 'delightful performance' of G.B. Shaw's 'O'Flaherty VC.' This was subsequently repeated at a new Labour Church, City Road, meeting at the George Dixon schools.

The month before the local elections in November, the Labour Churches were given over to electoral activity with visits by candidates or councillors, appraisal of Labour policies or such items as

'The Responsibilities of Citizenship,' which was discussed on 1 Nov 1925 at yet another new Labour Church, Ward End, meeting at Sladefield Road schools.

So by 1926 the Birmingham Labour Church movement was stronger than ever with sixteen functioning Churches. It is most unfortunate that not one scrap of information seems to have survived regarding their personnel, their organisation, their philosophy, their procedures or their relations with other bodies. But it is clear that we are dealing with a movement of some significance in the life of Birmingham. No doubt there are continuities with the earlier practices of the Labour Churches in Birmingham from 1903 to 1914 whose activities are much better documented. But it is probably better to look for the emerging factors of the 1920s against the background of Radical Christianity in Birmingham. This includes the revolutionary Puritanism of the Joseph Priestley period of the 1780s, the Rational Religionists of Robert Owen of the 1830s who combined full blooded atheism with Owen's Natural Religion, the Chartist Church of Arthur O'Neil which shocked the tender consciences of the Anglican clergy in the 1840s, and the rationalism of the Secularists who spanned the whole period from the disappearance of the old Socialism in the 1840s to the rebirth of the new Socialism in the 1880s. Most of these elements would have co-existed happily in Labour Churches which were partly christian, but mostly secular.

Christian Socialism

The phase of Christian Socialism associated with the names of Charles Kingsley, F.D. Maurice and J.M. Ludlow who made important contributions to the development of the Co-operative and trade union movements in the 1850s appear to have had no direct impact on Birmingham.

Individual ministers can be found at all times associating with the Labour movement in Birmingham. But the first Christian organisation to avow that neither the church nor society could be considered Christian unless it was also Socialist and to have influence in Birmingham was the Church Socialist League founded by Conrad Noel in 1906. Among the co-founders were two important Birmingham figures – the Hon. Rev J.G. Adderley, vicar of Saltley and Rev Arnold Pinchard vicar at St. Judes. The Church Socialist League was an organisation exclusively for ministers of the Church of England; in doctrine it was very High Church. Its influence in Birmingham was to assist the formation of the British Socialist Party in 1911 and to associate itself, not, as one would expect, with the moderate elements in the Labour movement, but with the extremist left-wing Syndicalists.

When the war broke out both Adderley and Pinchard became supporters of the war; the Church Socialist League remained neutral on the issue. Both the war and theological differences broke the back of the League and it disappeared in 1924. Adderley was born at Hams Hall near Birmingham and after much service in London from the 1880s he took over St. Saviour's at Saltley, which was on his father's estate, in 1904. Here he remained until 1911 when he moved to St. Gabriel's, Deritend until 1918. After the war he left Birmingham and returned to London. He remained a Socialist for the remainder of his life and on at least one occasion returned to Birmingham to preach Socialism.

Arnold Pinchard remained in Birmingham after the war, but seems to have had no impact on the Labour movement. Both Pinchard and Adderley were acting enthusiasts, and Pinchard in particular had considerable influence on the development of the Birmingham Repertory Theatre.

The only minister to openly associate himself with the Independent Labour Party and to actively oppose the war was the Rev Morgan Whiteman and the only other known pacifist member of the ILP was E. Bernstein, a Congregational Minister.

The lone leader after the war who called himself a Christian Socialist was ex-Private Jim Simmons. We have seen the important role he played in the peace movement in Birmingham from 1917 as a disabled ex-serviceman; how he took one branch of the National Union of Ex-Servicemen into the social democratic camp when the other branch joined the Communist Party; his work as a Labour councillor and in almost every other sphere in these stormy years after the War. His insistence on his basic Christian belief underlying all these activities marks him as the most important Christian Socialist of these years.

In 1923 a national memorial was presented to Ramsay MacDonald congratulating the Labour Party on becoming the official Opposition party:

We, the undersigned, being priests of the Church of England... who have followed with deep sympathy the recent struggle of Labour to secure more effective representation in Parliament. respectfully offer our sincere congratulations to you and the 143 members of Parliament who, under your leadership, now Constitute the Official opposition, a development which carries with it momentous and far-reaching consequences to the nation...

Our particular calling, with its pastoral experience, gives us direct knowledge of the sufferings and deprivation, mental, moral and physical, to which millions of our fellow citizens are subjected in our present social and industrial order, and to find a remedy for which is the chief purpose and aim of the Labour movement. It is therefore a matter of great satisfaction to us that this increased opportunity is now open before you in the great assembly of the nation, and we shall support actively, in whatever ways are legitimately open to us, the efforts you will assuredly make for the spiritual and economic emancipation of the people.

This memorial was signed by the following twenty three Birmingham clergy: Rev W.J. Archer, St. Margaret's, Erdington; Rev J.W. Branker, Vicar of Selly Oak; Rev R. Bruce, St. Augustine's, Edgbaston; Rev E.L. Blood, St. Stephens; Rev C.A. Brown, St. Gregory the Great, Small Heath; Rev M.B. Charnock, St. Gabriel's; Rev G.B. Code, St. Bartholowmew's; Rev A.M. Coleman, Priest in Charge, Marston Green; Rev W.J. Cole, Vicar of Aston, Hon. Canon B'ham: Rev F.M. Downton, Assistant Priest of Temple, Balsall; Rev W.C. Ellison, St. Nicholas'; Rev Stanley Gibbons, Asst. Priest Northfield; Rev G.M. Harris, St. Paul's Balsall Heath; Rev H.A. Jones All Saints, Small Heath; Rev C.T. Kirtland, St. Margaret's; Rev Oliver S. Petit, Vicar of Yardley, Hon. Canon B'ham; Rev Herbert Raison, Principal Designate Queen's College; Rev Conrad Radford, St. Aidan's Small Heath; Rev E.A. Squire, Asst. Priest B'ham Cathedral; Rev S. Gladstone Stantion, St. Mary's Selly Oak; Rev W.G. Hargrave Thomas, Moseley; Rev F.A.C. Tidmarsh, St. Peter's Handsworth; Rev H. Wynne, St. Mary's Bearwood.

At least one of these signatories attempted to widen his church base when the Rev H.A. Jones invited members of the Sparkbrook Labour Party to his church in May 1924 to hear him speak on the text, 'I am come that they might have life, and that they might have it more abundantly.' He urged that the churches should be more active in social affairs. After the service, a large part of the congregation retired to the Church Rooms to discuss the sermon.

In 1925 Christian Socialism assumed organised form. Its two main pillars were the Rev John Lewis, soon to become a Communist, and the Rev Gordon Lang, described as the 'well-known Labour propagandist of South Wales.' This was to be a Gospel Mission centred on an organisation called the New Religious Fellowship. A decayed and empty Presbyterian Church in Broad Street had been restored and the Mission began in February 1925. Jim Simmons spoke there at a meeting of the Young Socialist League, but little more was heard of the Mission in the columns of the *Town Crier*. It persisted up to the General Strike, however, as John Lewis informed the author in an interview with him on the fiftieth anniversary of the General Strike.

One last important development in Birmingham was the appointment in 1924 of Bishop Barnes. This was the first ecclesiastical appointment of Ramsay MacDonald. Ernest Barnes, who had been born in Birmingham, became a pacifist after the outbreak of World War I and a keen advocate of the League of Nations. He supported the February revolution in Russia, but not the Bolshevik one. He was widely considered to be a dangerous socialist and heretic who opposed Genesis and supported evolution.

But the bishop was a disappointment to many Socialists in the town. In November 1925 Barnes made a presidential speech to the Union of Educational Institutions which was closely studied. The *Birmingham Mail* came to the conclusion that the bishop was a supporter of private enterprise. But Stuart Barr, the local organiser of the Labour Colleges claimed that to reach such conclusions the speech must have undergone 'drastic surgical treatment on the Editor's table.' However, Barr did find the bishop's speech ambiguous and asked, 'Where exactly do you stand, my lord, as in times like this clear thinking and frank expression of opinion are essential.'

As a footnote to this period, we can add that in January 1926 the Hon. Rev James Adderley returned to Birmingham to preach in the parish church on 'Religion and the Labour Movement.'

Leisure and Pleasure

Before the war Birmingham labour activists looked to Clarion for their relaxation and cultural pursuits. The paper was the centre for networks of Clarion Clubs, the most outstanding of which was the Cycling Clubs. But there were also drama, orchestral, choral, field clubs, Scouts etc. all of which touched Birmingham from 1900. One of the last Clarion initiatives before the war was the Fellowships many of which, including Birmingham, resulted in Clarion Clubhouses.

When war came and Robert Blatchford and all connected with Clarion took not merely a pro-war line, but an actively jingoist one, the influence of the paper and its circulation declined precipitously and the Clarion era came virtually to an end.

During the war there was little time for leisure or cultural pursuits and after the war new bases had to be found for such activists. Arising from the war were two cultural figures in Birmingham. One was the ILPer and painter Joseph E. Southall. The other was the worker-poet Fred Silvester. Southall came from a Quaker background (which included Joseph Sturge) of families which had lived in Birmingham since the seventeenth century. During the war Southall devoted his time to Pacifist activities and his talents to his two main anti-war books – illustrations for R.L. Outhwaite's Ghosts of the Slain and his own Fables and Illustrations. After the war he maintained his place as Birmingham's most illustrious painter as well as one of its leading Socialists.

Fred Silvester we have followed through his educational interests and support for Labour Colleges. Silvester self-published his Ballads, Songs and Poems in 1922 or 1923 dedicating them to the working class. Some of them are declamatory and imitative of William Morris, such as his Battle Song for Labour. But most of them are introspective written in various poetic and ballad styles likely to appeal to working class readers. An achievement worth preserving.

It was not until the youth movement began to develop that leisure facilities were again created. By the end of 1923 there were ten Labour football teams in existence. By March 1924 the Labour Sports Federation was making headway in Birmingham with five cricket teams registered as well as the football clubs and also the Ruskin Cycling Club to which Alderman Percy Bower had been elected president. By March there was a Saltley Labour Cycling and Athletic Club. Duddeston and Edgbaston Clubs appeared in 1925.

Regular reports of the matches of the Labour Football League appeared in the *Town Crier* and a league table in January 1924 showed West Birmingham and St. Martin's at the top of the table with eighteen points with ETU and Gem Rovers at the bottom with no points. But the top teams had played eighteen matches while Gem Rovers had played four and ETU only one. The League was clearly developing.

The development of a Socialist Football League led to arguments as to whether it should affiliate to the Birmingham Football Association. The secretary of the BFA argued in the columns of the *Town Crier* that it should. But a spirited reply by L.A.J. Byfield general secretary of the Birmingham & District Labour Football League likened the position in sport to the political situation in 1893 when the Independent Labour Party emerged and stood in 'glorious isolation'. So would it be in sport in 1924, argued Byfield – sooner or later capitalist sport would have to make way for Socialist sport under the control of the British Socialist Workers' Sports Federation. The 1924-25 season started in the autumn with at least ten teams.

1925 saw the emergence of the People's Theatre movement. An article by F.N. Moore in the *Town Crier* in February 1925 summarised the movement. Moore noted G.K. Chesterton's remarks that this was a national phenomenon; not only were people going to the cinema and the theatre but were also themselves acting. Chesterton put this down to the deadening routine of modern industry. This was also happening in Birmingham, Moore said. The Jewish Arts Society had recently produced two plays written by their own members, one 'remarkable for its poetry and characterisation.' At Bournville, a few weeks ago there had been an Authors' Evening when two plays, written by Cadbury employees were enacted. One of these, 'The Island Times' was outstanding. 'The comedy sparkled and the theme, that of the suffocating grip of the press on public opinion was originally treated.' The Community Players were also doing good work 'making the masses acquainted with the drama.'

But the centre of the movement, Moore claimed, was the People's Theatre Movement as envisaged by the Rev John Lewis, born a year ago and still flourishing at the Guildhouse. They were about to embark on a Shaw play, 'The Showing up of Blanco Posnet,' to be produced by the Shavian enthusiast, Hubert Humphries. Although centred on Ladywood, the People's Theatre Movement aimed to embrace the whole city in a scheme which would utilise the halls and schools of each district in little theatres where the best drama would be brought to the people. The Movement was a break from any existing dramatic society and constituted itself as a definite working class organisation; although it was prepared to co-operate with any other organisation bringing the best drama to the working class.

The versatile president of the People's Theatre Movement, Rev John Lewis, had already written a three act play entitled 'The Crucifixion of India' dealing with the crisis of nationalism in that country. The further development of proletarian plays and players, Moore concluded, depended on 'the awakened class consciousness of workers seeking a creative channel.'

An article in an adjoining column to that of Moore's explanation of the People's Theatre Movement contained a 'frank criticism' of the Birmingham Repertory Theatre by G.S.G. Although recognising the bravery of the Rep in putting on such Shaw plays as 'Back to Methuselah' and 'Heartbreak House' and the need for the Rep to keep itself solvent by mounting popular plays, G.S.C. found fault with both recent plays and also the middle class audiences and urged that the theatre could do worse than 'go into the highways and byways and bring the Great Unwashed into Station Street.'

When The Showing up of Blanco Posnet was staged, a review by R.G.Ll.T. in the *Town Crier* claimed that Hubert Humphries in the role of Blanco was 'outstanding' but could not compare with Miss M. Lacon as Feemy, who was a discovery of great ability.

Other leisure and cultural facilities appeared in 1925. By June there was a Birmingham Labour Motor Cycle Club. In January Edward Wright of the Handsworth ILP was suggesting a Labour Orchestra. By June it was a reality when the Birmingham Labour Musical Society held its first social and dance and gave an 'admirable' performance. More members were needed however and application was invited to E.P. Marley the secretary or H.G. Sear the president.

In May 1925 a letter in the *Town Crier* from Lionel Field suggested a central committee (on the lines of the London Labour Choral Union whose musical adviser was Rutland Boughton and whose secretary was Herbert Morrison) to create local Choral Unions and hold national and perhaps even international Labour Music Festivals. Birmingham's development was slightly different from this. A Birmingham Labour Musical and Dramatic Union appeared; although in March 1926 a report deplored the unwillingness of amateur musicians subscribing to the Labour Movement to give up a few hours a week to practice.

Within these musical and dramatic developments one senses the tensions of the 'cold war' of the time between the revolutionary and the Labourist points of view. The proposed tie up with the London Labour Choral Union controlled by Herbert Morrison would have been a victory for the reactionaries. Fred Silvester was always on hand to pour scorn on all who strayed from the revolutionary path. This he did in November 1925 in criticising the Rev John Lewis' conception of Hamlet as a progressive, by declaring him to be an 'irresolute petit-bourgoise and opportunist', in distinction to those who had taken the path of Lenin.

Cultural pursuits continued into 1926. Erdington Labour Dramatic Circle performed three plays at a gathering organised by the Water Orton Labour Party in January. These were 'The Dream Maker," The Old Rich' and 'The Noo System.' In February the Labour Orchestra was still practising but not yet ripe for the numerous performances it was asked to give. In May publications were advertised for the Workers' Theatre movement by the Labour Publishing Co. One was a volume of plays by Miles Malleson. Another was a good collection of plays from Harrap's, and books on producing, etc. In March the movement participated in the Bach Festival at the Midland Institute which brought a special visit of Rutland Boughton.

Finally, mention should be made of the Birmingham Repertory Theatre, which although not itself a Labour organisation, was progressive and involved numbers of people active in the Labour movement. Parties of Young Socialists regularly made bookings for plays. The theatre began life in 1907 under the title of the Pilgrim Players. The theatre in Station Road opened in 1913. Associated with Barry V. Jackson from the beginning was John Drinkwater. Drinkwater was a supporter of women's suffrage and was honoured after the war by Birmingham University as one of the vice-presidents of the National Union of Women's Suffrage Societies. Drinkwater was also anti-war. His first great success as a playwright was 'Abraham Lincoln' produced in October 1918 in Birmingham. It had a wildly enthusiastic reception and ran for a full month to crowded audiences. Within a few weeks it was revived. Staged within a few weeks of the end of the war and running on after its end, the play had a moving anti-war theme. The play was so good that it had to go to London and Drinkwater took the Birmingham Rep cast to the Lyric Theatre at Hammersmith where it opened in February 1919 and ran for four hundred and sixty six performances. Drinkwater then took the play to America where it had similar success and from that time Drinkwater's connection with Birmingham ended.

Other progressives connected with the theatre from the beginning were the brother Revs. Arnold and Lester Pinchard. Arnold Pinchard produced many of the early plays of the Pilgrim Players where his Mission Hall was the main venue of the Players. Both Arnold and Lester also acted in the plays. Arnold Pinchard's daughter Betty also acted with the company between 1913 and 1917 while Lester composed music and assisted musically.

After the war Jackson also embraced opera and he produced Rutland Boughton's Immortal Hour in 1921. Despite the brilliant productions and great glory that Barry Jackson was bringing to the British stage, the citizens of Birmingham did not respond. His iron resolve was finally broken by what was his most ambitious production – the first staging in England of Shaw's Back to Methuselah. Despite nationwide interest in the production, Birmingham people stayed away and in February 1924 Jackson closed the theatre and sought success elsewhere in England.

But the Civic Society took the matter up and schemes were devised to ensure that people took up tickets. Jackson then reopened the Rep in September 1924.

The Communist Party

It is difficult to convey the elation, enthusiasm and loyalty with which the Russian revolution was greeted throughout the world and particularly by working class militants. Tsardom had crushed every movement for freedom within its own vast domain and had been the Gendarme of Europe since 1815. Its overthrow in February 1917 was a matter of almost universal rejoicing. But its further development into a Socialist revolution from October was another matter. For the first time in history capitalism had been overthrown and Socialism was becoming a reality. Capitalists, landlords, money lenders and all other exploiters were being swept away and a Socialist state built and run by working people through Soviets of Workers, Peasants and Soldiers. Capitalism was not only the system that stole the worker's labour power and kept him in poverty, but also the system of boom and slump which brought mass unemployment and starvation. Above all, capitalism created wars of conquest and when all the world was divided between rival imperialists, capitalism had started the World War for the re-division of the world. All this would end with Socialism it was thought. The Revolution would spread across the world and all peoples would live as brothers and sisters in equality and peace. Such a vast project transformed working people into masters of their own fate and inspired them both to defend the infant Socialist state and also work to build the new Socialist society at home.

The founding of the Communist International in Moscow in March 1919 gave the impetus to the creation of Communist Parties throughout the world. Martin Durham in his 'Early Years of the Communist Party in Birmingham' (in *Essays in Birmingham Labour History*) describes how discussion on the formation of a Communist Party in Birmingham resulted in the setting up of a conference by the local ILP Federation in November 1919 which William Paul, the local SLPer opened. Subsequent discussions showed two points of view. One was led by Jim Simmons opposing Soviets and opting for a social democratic party, while W.T. Cardinal led the other faction supporting the creation of Soviets in Britain. In between was W.J. Chamberlain who held that it was too soon to decide between the two views. When put to a vote this was supported by 22 votes to 21. A considerable number of abstentions added to the impression that support for Soviets was considerable among activists.

At the last of these meetings in February 1920, the main speaker, Fred Longden put a motion favouring affiliation to the Third International. This was carried with only one vote against. It was then resolved to set up a committee comprising members of the ILP, SLP, Plebs League, Herald League and NUX. This Birmingham Joint Socialist Committee arranged meetings with each of the interested parties. In April William Paul addressed a joint meeting at which he explained the formation of a Communist Party was being held up by the main Socialist parties – ILP, BSP and SLP who were checkmating the efforts of the Communist supporters within their organisations. The only way out, Paul declared, was for local groups to set up their own Unity organisations. The following week a debate was scheduled between R.V. Harvey and Jim Simmons on 'Soviets or Parliament.' All sections of the movement were requested to attend these meetings, as they were all represented on the Joint Committee.

As a result of these and other meetings, in Birmingham, as elsewhere, an independent Communist Unity Organisation was formed. A statement from the Birmingham branch of the SLP stated at this time, 'we remain loyal (to the SLP – GB) for the present although earnestly wishing for Unity. We hope, however that the EC place no obstacle in the path of Unity...'

The Communist Party was formed at the Communist Unity Convention in London on 31 July and 1 August 1920. At that Convention Birmingham delegates were Fred Silvester and G. Smith from the Communist Unity Group, H. Stubbs from the Birmingham Shop Stewards' Movement and Bill Brain from the SLP. A further Convention at Leeds in January 1921 completed the unification of the Communist Party, but this brought no further strength to the Birmingham Communist Party, and perhaps its greatest local influence, as Durham remarks, was that the Birmingham delegates were Jack Trotter and Harry Shepperson who were to be active in the Party for decades; although another result was the election of William Paul, who was almost a Brummie, to the executive committee of the Party.

After the Unity Convention in 1920 *The Call* which had been the paper of the British Socialist Party became the organ of the new Party and changed its name to *The Communist.* In August it gave a Communist Party Directory. This claimed three branches – Birmingham No.1 secretary G. Wray, Birmingham 2 secretary F. Sylvester, Birmingham Camphill secretary R. Harris.

The Party was immediately plunged into united activity with the local Hands off Russia Committee and the Council of Action on which the CP secured six representatives. Huge meetings were taking place at this time. *The Communist* reported 'a remarkable demonstration' organised by the Trades Council for the Hands off Russia Committee on 8 August in the Bull Ring followed by another on 22 August in the same place where three platforms were set up and 'our comrades Shepperson, Rowland, Bram (Brain?), Palmer, Pritchard and Trotter spelt out the message of Communism.'

James Stewart became the first (unpaid) organiser of the Midland district in September 1920. He introduced himself at a Council of Action mass meeting at Calthorpe Park (the first meeting ever allowed in a Birmingham public park). There were three platforms, at one of which Arthur MacManus, the chairman of the CPGB, was the main speaker. MacManus, representing the National Council of Shop Stewards on this occasion, was scathing about Birmingham, claiming that it was a long way behind other cities and towns. Stewart followed the same line. He said he was about to take up the post of Communist Party organiser 'in this God forsaken hole,' and 'twitted' the police that their intelligence had not informed them of his appointment.

The CPGB received only a luke-warm welcome in the *Town Crier* and W.J. Chamberlain, its editor, was soon to find fault with the thrusting militancy of its members. William Brain, as we have seen, was constantly attacked. In January 1921 he was accused of 'infiltrating' Communists on to the Trades Council. (Strange how other people joined organisations, but Communists 'infiltrated' – GB). In the same month Harry Shepperson was attacked for criticising Councillors Shakespeare and Crump.

But the main problem facing the Party was police harassment. Much of this has been dealt with in the section on Police Spies and Freedom of Speech. Something must be added here, however. An unidentifiable (but before 1925) local report found in the Harry Shepperson papers recorded that Shepperson and Edgar Mobberley were charged with stealing articles from William Croxall. Croxall was a police spy who had been expelled from the Communist Party. He went to the Party HQ at Bradford Street where he was kept a prisoner for eight hours and brutally assaulted while the accused gained admission to his room at Bordesley and stole articles of food, documents and letters from his sweetheart. In evidence Maurice Ferguson, Midlands organiser of the CP, stated that Croxall was a police spy sent into the CP to obtain information. He had retained pamphlets related to the International Labour Defence and short-hand notes of various meetings which he had been repeatedly asked to return. Shepperson and Mobberley admitted going to Croxall's room, but insisted that they had taken only documents. Ferguson stated that after Croxall's expulsion a locked box was opened which contained letters showing Croxall's close connection with the police and letters in which his sweetheart urged Croxall not to give up his police work. When asked where the documents were, Ferguson refused to answer and when it was suggested that he was keeping stolen property he retorted, 'You didn't consider documents taken from German spies during the war to be stolen property.'

The Stipendiary said that both Shepperson and Mobberley had acted in a very high-handed manner. But he did not think they had any felonious intent. The summonses for theft were therefore dismissed.

It might appear that, on this occasion, Party members received the benefit of the law. But any idea that the police vendetta against the Party was being relaxed is dispelled by the tail piece. As Maurice Ferguson was leaving the court he was arrested by CID men and charged with regard to a speech he had made at the Bull Ring a few days previously.

Although Communist Party membership remained small compared with the ILP and the Labour Party, it had an immense influence on the shaping of the Birmingham labour movement. Nowhere is that influence more apparent than with the activities of the Communist who never lived in Birmingham – Dr Robert Dunstan.

Dunstan, who was born in 1877 was both a medical practitioner and a barrister. He served during the war in Mesopotamia as a Lieutenant in the RAMC. He was adopted as a Labour candidate for Moseley in October 1918 in circumstances as yet unknown. He had returned from the middle east in 1917, resigned from the Liberal Party and withdrawn his candidature from the Totnes division of Devon where he had contested the 1910 election as a Liberal Land Reform candidate and become 'the terror of the Landlords and Farmers by his outspoken denunciation of the housing scandal and starvation wages paid to workers in South Devon.' He was supported in Birmingham by the Trades & Labour Council and the Co-operative movement, in which he was active in London. His agent was Jim Simmons. Dunstan was then a left-wing member of the ILP. His election policy included A Peace which will keep the Peace, No Conscription Military or Industrial. A Tax on Land Values, and Abolition of all Taxes on Food. Like all the other Birmingham Labour candidates in this Khaki Election he was heavily defeated by the Conservative-Unionist candidate Sir Hallewell Rogers who polled 16,161 votes to Dunstan's 3,789. The Liberal trailed with 3,422 votes.

Dunstan had a charismatic personality and drew large crowds wherever he spoke. In 1919 he contested a by-election at Rusholme and more than doubled the Labour vote. In April 1921 the *Labour Leader* reported the death of Dunstan's wife in the influenza epidemic; he must have soon after married Margaret MacCallum who was also a medical practitioner, for both Mr & Mrs Dunstan became firm favourites in Birmingham.

For the 1922 election, called when the Conservatives refused to serve any longer under Lloyd George, Dunstan was nominated for Ladywood. This was a high profile constituency as he was directly challenging the Chamberlain interests and traditions represented by Neville Chamberlain. His election campaign was even more militant calling on citizens to end capitalist tyranny by using the political as well as the trade union weapon. He talked about smooth tongued statesmen weeping in public over the workers' sorrows but upholding the system of industrial capitalism that made workers wage slaves. Dunstan gave Neville Chamberlain a shock. He polled 10,589 votes to Chamberlain's 13,032.

At the beginning of 1922 Dunstan had set the city about the ears by calling Birmingham this 'Rotten and Benighted City.' This he substantiated with a series of scathing articles in the Town Crier exposing housing conditions, rack-renting landlords, an unjust rating system, the nearly 9 lbs difference in weight and more than 2 inches difference in height between boys of 12 at Bournville schools and boys at Floodgate Street schools, the inadequate education of working class children tipped into the labour market at 14 when middle class children were just beginning to acquire the higher knowledge necessary for a proper education, the scandal of the treatment of the unemployed, the grossly inadequate health facilities, the treatment of the elderly. And much else. In fact a survey of the lives of the poor from the cradle to the grave and all of it taken from the official statistics of the city.

Dunstan followed up his articles with meetings, and his week-end visits to Birmingham became mass demonstrations of support. In January 1923 Dunstan gave an illustrated lecture at the Town Hall on 'This Rotten and Benighted City,' and he continued a series of such lectures at the Dudley Road Schools the next month. In March Dunstan addressed the Trades Council on the Land Question and Dr Margaret Dunstan was talking of Birmingham under Private Enterprise at St. Barnabas schools where she said that her husband's phrase 'this rotten and benighted city' had penetrated the thick hides of the landlords and capitalists of the city.

Dunstan showed a considerable interest in the land question. He wrote a letter to the *Town Crier* in March 1923 setting out his objections to land taxation. The land should belong to the people, Dunstan claimed and its total value collected. The rating and taxation of land were Liberal tactics which prostituted the teachings of Henry George. He stood with the Commonwealth League – the land must belong to the people. This interest was very pertinent at a time when the Sydney Rating System was being put forward as an alternative to our own system. Dunstan subsequently wrote a series of articles for the *Town Crier* on the land question.

In June 1923 Dunstan was unanimously re-selected as candidate for Ladywood and at the election in November, which brought the first minority Labour government to office, he came even closer to toppling Neville Chamberlain when he polled 11,330 and lost by 1,554 votes.

Dunstan was still moving to the left. Early in 1924 he visited Russia and on his return he joined the Communist Party. He gave his reasons to a 'largely attended' meeting at Clark Street Schools. He also wrote a pamphlet for the Birmingham District Communist Party. Here he outlined his radical beliefs from his experiences as a medical student in London. The failure of the ILP was his main theme. They had disappointed him by refusing to affiliate to the Third International, subsequently manoeuvring into the Two and a Half International, and finally returning to the Second International. The history of the Labour government to date was also disillusioning with its imperialist actions in Egypt and India and the betrayal of the German working class through the Dawes Plan. The ILP now served not the interests of Socialism but the interests of its leaders. His visit to Russia had confirmed the reality of the Russian Revolution which in spite of the chaos left by the imperialist war, the blockade, intervention, civil war and famine, was successfully re-building society on a working class foundation. He had therefore decided to join the Communist Party, 'an organisation untouched with the glamour of political success, firmly representing the dispossessed in the class struggle, the Party which has opposed the reactionary policy of too many of the Labour leaders...'

From 1922 the Labour Party was rejecting at its annual Conferences affiliation of the Communist Party by large majorities artificially bolstered by the trade union block vote. The next step of the right-wing was to exclude individual Communists from membership of the Labour Party and prevent Communists in the trade unions, where they paid the political levy, from representing the Labour Party at any level. This proved more difficult than it seemed. But for Dunstan, once he had joined the Communist Party, the first effect was that his nomination for the Ladywood seat was not continued and Oswald Mosley was selected to fight the seat.

However, so great had been the impact of Dunstan on Birmingham and so considerable was the left-wing influence in the city that he was immediately nominated as a Labour candidate for West Birmingham.

The Labour government fell in October 1924 as a result of the Campbell case. J.R. Campbell the temporary editor of the Communist *Workers' Weekly* published an article during the Party's Anti-War Week. This called on the armed forces to make it known that they would never turn their guns on fellow workers either in military or class war. It also urged the organisation of Committees in barracks, aerodromes and ships.

Campbell was arrested, but when it was known that he was a disabled and decorated ex-serviceman the Director of Public Prosecutions was instructed to drop the case. Ramsay MacDonald made this a confidence issue in Parliament and lost the vote. The subsequent election might well have returned the Labour government with a larger majority. But a few days before the election the forged Zinoviev letter was published and the Tory opposition claimed that any Labour government would hand over the country to the Communists and Moscow.

The uncertainty as to the status of Communists standing as Labour candidates affected Dunstan. In his election address he called himself the Workers' Candidate. He stated that he was a member of the Labour Party and stood for the Labour policy of 1918, the New Social Order. He therefore advocated socialisation of the land without compensation, public control of the banks and credit facilities, giving control of mines and railways to the community and moving on to the common ownership of industry and the co-operative distribution of commodities. In fact, Dunstan was a Communist candidate with wide support in the Birmingham labour movement, particularly the ILP in West Birmingham. This support (and the very short notice of the election, no doubt) precluded any 'official' Labour candidate being nominated against him. Dunstan's opponent was the other Chamberlain – Austen and in a straight fight Dunstan polled the very creditable total of 7,158 against Chamberlain's 14,801. Dunstan was immediately re-selected for the West Birmingham constituency, and the struggle of the right-wing to oust Dunstan sharpened. But this belongs to the history of the period after the General Strike, so we return to the other activities of the Communist Party up to 1926.

The local Party participated in municipal elections only to a limited extent. In years when the Party was seeking affiliation to the Labour Party every effort was made to avoid standing against a Labour candidate and splitting the vote. Thus in 1920 Harry Shepperson competed against an Independent in Yardley where no Labour candidate stood. Not surprisingly he was comprehensively beaten in this Tory ward by 2,778 votes to 357. The next year however, in the same ward Shepperson did stand against a Labour candidate and polled more than him, the vote being Unionist 2298, Communist 759 and Labour 436. The vote probably reflects the standing of Shepperson in this ward, where he lived. Also in 1921 F.W. Robertson contested another no-hope ward, St. Mary's, as a Communist where no Labour candidate was standing. Here the result was: Independent 2557, Conservative 1274, Communist 666; again a very good Communist vote in a hopeless ward. In June 1922 the CP stood P. Palmer at a by-election in Yardley. He lost in a straight fight with a Ratepayer. Palmer subsequently left the CP and campaigned for the British Empire Union.

In 1923 at the November elections Robertson again stood in St. Mary's, this time as an Unemployed candidate with no Labour candidate. He polled 949 votes to the Conservative's 2270. Robertson was probably still a Communist at this time. The next year, 1924, he stood again in St. Mary's ward, but now he was a Labour candidate, however. But this time his vote was lower at 771.

This appears to be the entire extent of Communist participation in local elections up to 1926. No conclusions can be drawn as to support for the CP at this time; The Party was dogged, as it was always to be, by the dilemma that if it stood in a ward where there was any chance of being successful there would always be a Labour candidate standing and the Communist Party would be seen as splitting the vote. For this reason Communist policy was invariably orientated to seeking unity with Labour on both the political and the industrial field.

To this end they co-operated with, or created, the joint organisations through which they hoped to shift the Labour movement leftwards to the belief that capitalism could not be reformed, but must be abolished and be replaced by a Socialist society. This could only be done, Communists maintained, by supplementing Parliamentary action with direct action to remove a capitalist class that would never allow itself to be voted out of existence. We have followed the activities of the Party through Ex-Service politics, unemployed struggles, Hands of Russia etc. By 1926 the Minority Movement had been created for united action in the trade unions and the Left-Wing Movement to influence the Labour Party, but these are best dealt with in discussing the period beyond the General Strike.

With regard to the Communist Party it remains only to state what is known of its numerical strength in the period 1920-26. This is very little. There are no records of the membership in the Midlands in the national Party archives. The first indication of strength was the notice in *The Communist* stating that there were three branches in Birmingham at the inauguration of the Party in 1920. The fact that nothing more is heard of these three branches and subsequent activity shows only one branch in action suggests that this was optimistic. The only numerical estimate we have is a government one quoted by Durham of 100 in 1922, 80 men and 20 women. This would have come from a police spy who had to earn his corn, so this is likely to be exaggerated. Winnie Docherty says that the Local Party Committee which met at her house at that time contained ten or twelve members. This would give a ratio of about nine less active members to each activist, a ratio which seems rather unlikely at this time when the average age of members tended to be low under the influence of the Russian revolution. One would expect a higher proportion of activists, perhaps one in four or five, which would give a Party of forty or fifty. Figures for 1924 from Klugmann show two Local Party Committees in Birmingham in May 1924 and five local organisations. By May 1925 membership was growing and with still two LPCs there were now nine 'locals'. If we assume these locals to have the same average membership as the 162 locals nationally this would give a membership of 350 for the whole Birmingham district membership which included Coventry, the Potteries, the Black Country and several other towns. This is made plausible by the figure given by Carr that at the highest point of membership in September 1926 there were no more than 326 members in the whole Birmingham district. From this and other material Carr estimates membership of the Coventry CP at about 30 and my own estimate for Birmingham would be about 50. Another approach to membership is through sales of the *Workers' Weekly*. In March 1923 national sales rose to 50,000. and in April 1926 were 53,000. In early 1925, according to Arthur Swain's letter book, orders were between 27 and 29 quires per week and in June he placed an order for 28 quires until further notice. At 26 papers to the quire this amounts to 728 copies of which about 150 were sold in Smethwick. The remaining 578 copies were sold by 15 active comrades in Birmingham. The city thus sold about 1 per cent of *Workers' Weekly* circulation. If Birmingham sales were average for the total membership of the Party in Britain of 5,000, this would again bring us to a figure of about 50 members in Birmingham. The fifteen sellers representing the Party activists would suggest a slightly higher membership figure if my estimate of four to five less active comrades to each activist is valid.

Final mention must be made of the one charge of illegality which might possibly be levied against the Birmingham CP. This concerned Harry Emery who was a foundation member of the Party in Coventry. He moved to Birmingham in 1922 and became secretary of the branch. He was arrested in the same year for the part he played in a raid on the Birmingham Arms Factory to supply arms to the IRA. Emery was given bail, but he fled to Ireland from whence he made his way to Russia.

Bibliography: The Birmingham Labour Movement 1919-26

For the national development of the ex-services movement see Graham Wootton – *The Official History of the British Legion*. The only general history of NUX is an article in *History* vol 76, February 1991 by David Englander. Local accounts must be taken from the local press and mine has been taken from Birmingham newspapers, notably the *Town Crier*.

For national attitudes towards the revolution in Russia from the point of view of both the Government and the Labour movement I have taken contemporary eye witness accounts such as John Reed's *Ten Days that Shook the World*, M. Philips Price's *Reminiscences of the Russian Revolution*, W.P. and Z.K. Coates' *A History of Anglo-Soviet Relations*, *The Report of the Labour Party Delegation to Russia 1920*, R. Bruce Lockhart's *Memoirs of a Russian Agent*, and Lloyd George's *War Memoirs* vol 2.

The Birmingham Police Strike was comprehensively written up by Richard Shackleton in *Essays in Birmingham Labour History* (1983). His early death was a sad loss to the Labour movement in Birmingham. There is also a very fair but non-committal account of the strike by Chief Inspector John V. Reilly in *Policing Birmingham*. There are two general histories of the police strike: G.W. Reynolds and A. Judge *The Night the Police Went on Strike*, and A.V. Sellwood's *Police Strike 1919* published in 1919. Also 'The National Union of Police and Prison Officers' by V.L. Allen in *Economic History Review* vol ix No.1 August 1958. The half hearted way the TUC took up the case of the police is documented in the *Annual Report of the TUC 1919*. Several of the deputation who saw the Home Secretary were hostile to the strike including J.H. Thomas, J. Havelock Wilson, James Sexton and the Birmingham trade union leader W.J. Davis. Local details of the police strike come from the *Town Crier, Watch Committee Minutes* and *City Council Minutes.*

    Unemployment figures for Birmingham are taken from the Department of Employment *Labour Gazette.* Percentage unemployment is calculated from total numbers in employment given in 1921 Census. This would seem to give a more correct (although lower) percentage of unemployment than the Department of Employment figures taken from the number of insurance books issued. The cost of living figures are taken from the national *Ministry of Employment Index of Prices.*

    The standard eye witness account of unemployment between the wars is Wal Hannington's *Unemployed Struggles 1918-36* and unemployment and relief scales are taken from his book. The main Birmingham sources have been the *Town Crier* and the *Birmingham City Council Minutes.*

    For the Peace Movement in Birmingham the main source is the library of the Quaker Woodbrooke College. For the Birmingham Labour movement the main source has been the *Town Crier.* Vera Brittain's *The Rebel Passion* is useful for the international peace movement as is the biography of Wilfred Wellock by Andrew Rigby – *A Life in Peace.*

    The two main accounts of the Labour Colleges are W.W. Craik – *The Central Labour College,* and J.P.M. Millar – *The Labour College Movement.* For Plebs the main source is *Plebs Magazine.* For the Workers' Education Association see *WEA Annual Reports,* and its journal *Highway.* F.B. Silvester's *Working Class Ballads, Songs and Poems* has no date, but internal evidence suggests 1922 or 1923.

    The section on Women is taken entirely from the *Town Crier.*

    On the Youth Movement there is no general history of the period and the account is, again, taken from the *Town Crier.*

    For the earlier Labour Churches see my *Birmingham Working People.* For the Labour Churches after 1918 see the *Town Crier.* For a survey of radical Christianity to 1914 see my *Birmingham Working People.* For the Hon. Rev J.G. Adderley see I.P. Stevens' *Father Adderley.* For further information on Adderley, the Pinchards and the Church Socialist League I am indebted to the present Socialist incumbent of St. Saviour's Church, Saltley, the Rev Trevor Jones. For Jim Simmons see his autobiography *Soap Box Evangelist* (1972). For Bishop Barnes see the biography by his son, *John Barnes – Ahead of his Age.*

    For early Clarion activity see my *Birmingham Working People.* A good introduction to Joseph Southall is *Joseph Southall 1861-1944, Artist-Craftsmen* published in 1980 by Birmingham Art Gallery in connection with an exhibition of his work; at least it does fair justice to his Socialist activities, which is more than can be said of much written about Southall. Bache Matthews' *History of the Birmingham Repertory Theatre* covers the period 1907-1924.

    For the Communist Party see their paper *The Call,* the British Socialist Party paper from 1916 which became *The Communist* in 1920 on the formation of the Communist Party and became *The Workers' Weekly* in 1923. Also Martin Durham's 'The Early Years of the Communist Party in Birmingham 1920-24' in *Essays in Birmingham Labour History* edited by A. Wright and R. Shackleton. Also Frank Carr's *The Formation of the Communist Party in Coventry* (Warwick University unpub. MA thesis 1969). For branch membership figures see James Klugman *History of the CPGB* vol 1 and Henry Pelling *The British Communist Party.* Personal testimony of Winnie Docherty, daughter of Tom Lowe, foundation member of the Communist Party, eye witness to many of the events from 1920 when Winnie was fifteen years old and a participant in the movement since that time. Despite her age, Winnie's mind is razor sharp and it has been possible to verify so many of her statements that she must be considered a most reliable witness. But the most important source has again been the *Town Crier.* I have in my possession papers (and partial autobiographies) of Harry Shepperson and Arthur Swain; also some papers of Jim Crump.

Appendix: Birmingham Police Officers dismissed from the Force and forfeiting all pension rights for participating in the National Police Strike of 1919.

Name	Years of Service	Name	Years of Service	Name	Years of Service
CRESSWELL, Alf H.	7	HUSSELL, Horace	11	HAWKINS Arthur J.	13
HAYWARD, Fred J.	7	BAILEY, Joseph	11	LESLEY, Joseph	13
HUSSELBEE, F.W.	6	WOOD, Albert	10	LICKORISH, Chas Hy.	12
JARMAN, Frank	6	GREEN, Wm. A.	10	PRETTY, Chas. Fredk.	12
WALKER, Joseph	6	MORLAND, Saml.	10	BAYLEY, John	12
BAGGOTT, Thos. Wm.	6	SMITH, Fredk. W	10	OAKES, Albert	12
FULLER, Thos. Geo.	6	STONE, Arthur Hy.	9	WALTERS, Ernest	12
DEXTER, George	6	BULLOCK, Chas. W.	9	PARKER, John	11

Name	Years	Name	Years	Name	Years
DAVIES, Geo. E.	6	ALLEN, Jack	9	HIND, John	11
DOWELL, Horace	6	HUNT, Edw. Thos.	8	PUGH, Wm. Jos.	11
PADBURY, Wm. J.	6	GREEN, Arthur J.	8	SINCLAIR, Wm.	11
GRIFFIN, John T.	6	MILBURN, Geo. F.	8	BOOTON, Wm. F	11
HENDERSON, Harry	6	GOODE, Horace	8	JONES, Thomas F.	11
REDLEY, Fredk.	6	HOWES, Frank	7	HARRIS, Albert	11
HARDING, R.A.H.	5	DOVE, Gilbert	7	TAYLOR, Edward	22
PRIEST, Jos. Thos.	5	GODWIN, Herbert	7	DOUGHTY, Wm.	15
COMLEY, Alfred	5	EARLY, John	7	DAVIES, David	16
EVANS, Bernard H.	5	WALTERS, Wm. Chas.	7	THORPE, Chas. Wm.	21
EVANS, Austin	5	PRICE, Francis	7	SABIN, Fredk. V.	19
POTTER, Geo. Fredk.	5	PITTAM, Ernest	7	TEAHAN, John	19
BRAGG, Alf. Wm.	5	MOORE, Arthur, John	7	WARWOOD, Francis	18
CCLE, Herman	5	GILES, Algy. Leo.	5	HILL, Charles	18
D'NORTHWOOD, H.S.	15	PARKER, James	5	HOLMAN, Charles	18
WILSON, Edward	14	THORNE, Thos. M.	5	MARLOW, Philip	18
SHAW, Lewis	14	WILLIAMS, John	5	JACKSON, Henry	17
BINGLE, Geo. Wm.	14	FARMER, Wm. Ewart	5	MALONE, William	17
NEWMAN, George	14	JEFFCOTT, Thomas	5	WHAPPLES, John	13
CARTWRIGHT, Alfred	13	FRENCH, John	5	BEARDSALL, Thomas	5
WARRINER, J.J.L.	5	WALLACE, Edmund	5	CLANSEY, John	5
BARKER, Geo. Wm.	5	CROUCH, Fredk. B.	4	HARVEY, Geo. Edwin	4
MARSH, Joseph T.	13	WOODHOUSE, John T.	4	GARDNER, Wm. E.	4
MARSH, Joseph	4	HODGKISS, John	13	PRICE, John	13
WRIGHT, Geo. A.	4	BRUTON, Francis F.	4	FIELD, Hy. Allan	13
THOMPSON, Geo. M.	4	LEATH, Alf. E.	4	DAVIES, Arthur	17
BURKE, John	17	MOONEY, Thomas	17	THOMAS, Chas. Henry	17
BLACKHAM, George	16	MORLEDGE, John	16	MORGAN, Thos. J.	15
INGRAM, Arthur	15	MORRISON, Claude	15	BELCHER, Alfred	15
MATTOCK, John	15	OAKES, Albert	12	JONES, Robert	4

There are also 5 men (four with 4 years service and one with under 1 yr) whose names have been obliterated where the sheet has been stuck into a book. Total officers Victimised – 118. Source: Birmingham City, Watch Committee Minutes.

Chapter 19

The ILP and the Labour Party

The Independent Labour Party

Before the war the Labour Party consisted of affiliated organisations only; the 'home' of the individual Labour Party supporter was the ILP. When after 1918 the new Labour Party constitution allowed for individual membership and organisation by ward and constituency it was expected that the ILP would whither away – its left would go into the Communist Party and the centre and right into the Labour Party. This did not happen and, as will be seen, most of the national reasons for this were also present in Birmingham.

By the middle of 1918 the ILP had recovered sufficient strength to be able to organise a Federation for Birmingham. The ILP National Conference at Easter 1919 was 'the largest ever' with 369 delegates from 345 branches. These delegates included H. Leman, Joseph Southall and Jim Simmons from Birmingham. *Town Crier* reports showed continuing growth. In the Moseley constituency membership doubled, in Yardley it nearly trebled and four new branches were formed. Ex-Private Jim Simmons was appointed organiser. Labour Churches were full and Kings Norton ran a Socialist Sunday School. After the November elections the Birmingham Fed. ran a series of meetings on 'What is the ILP?' with a panel of speakers which included Councillors Hackett, Parnell, Milner and Jim Simmons led by the national figure, R.C. Wallhead. By this time the Fed. was deeply immersed in the Hands off Russia Campaign and it was organising the William Paul meetings on whether Socialism could come from Parliamentary action or Revolution; this was the crucial issue of support for the Russian Revolution and the Third International. At these meetings some members were outlining third alternatives. Fred Longden stated that Lenin saw nationalisation as steps to Communism and Parliament could then delegate industries to workers. Others were supporting Guild Socialism, which eventually became the policy of the ILP after rejection of the Moscow solution led to problems of the ILP differentiating its policy from that of the Labour party.

By 1920 unemployment was beginning to be an issue and, although the local elections in November 1919 had been satisfactory, the ILP tended to stagnate. At the Easter National Conference there were more delegates but they represented only 337 branches. Only one delegate attended from Birmingham; this was Miss E. Eastgate who would join the Communist Party before the year was out.

In March 1920 the Birmingham Federation elected its officers for the year. The chairman was Herbert Leman, vice-chairmen were Joseph Southall, William Cardinal and Fred Longden. The secretary was F. Moody and his assistant Jim Simmons. The treasurer was C. Baghurst and the literature secretary Miss D. Palmer. Members of the Council were Harry Shepperson, Miss Eastgate, Mrs Longden, Harrison Barrow and Duncan Whiteman. At this AGM it was also reported that the joint committee of the ILP, SLP, Plebs League, Herald League and NUX had been formed to continue discussions on whether to join the Third International. The same month the national ILP leadership withdrew from the Second (Socialist) International, rejected affiliation to the Third (Communist) International and called for the setting up of a Fourth International which would mediate between the two others. This caused dissatisfaction among the pro-Third International faction of the ILP and complaints were made that the discussion on this question was not published in the *Town Crier*. Did Chamberlain, the editor, deliberately withhold this material?

By May 1920 the question of intervention in Russia was coming to a head. A record meeting at the Town Hall was addressed by George Lansbury. He spoke of religion in Russia saying that most Russians were free thinkers and real religion could never be suppressed. On women, he said they were freer than anywhere else in the world, and of children that he had never seen so many looking well. The Revolution had been peaceful, he concluded, and the violence had been started by allied officials and support for the counter-revolution. Joseph Southall moved a motion deploring Poland's wanton attack on Russia and asking the TUC to force the British government to make peace. Southall also congratulated the dockers on the stoppage of the *Jolly George* (the ship carrying arms to Poland which was the turning point in the campaign to end intervention in Russia – GB).

ILP members Harrison Barrow and Joseph Southall were active in June in protest against lack of action against General Dyer who, at the Amritsar Massacre had ordered his troops to open fire killing between 400 and 1,800 Indians. A Bill of Rights guaranteeing the liberties of Indians was also demanded.

In July the ILP organised a great Freedom for Ireland demonstration marching through the city with Socialist and Sinn Fein banners flying and ending in the Bull Ring with 1,0000 people present. In September-October the local ILP was deeply involved in support for the Miners' Strike, bringing the South Wales Miners' Federation leader to Birmingham for whom local branches organised meetings.

The ILP continued throughout 1920 to be involved in the joint activity in this, one of the most militant years ever experienced, in Birmingham.

By 1921, with the Communist Party operating in the city, differences between the various factions in the ILP began to replicate the national situation. In March the Birmingham ILP Fed. rejected unanimously a proposal of the local Communist Party for joint discussions on the International, 'as a protest against the sabotaging of the Ramsay MacDonald candidature at Woolwich by these friends of capitalism disguised as Socialists.' At the 1921 Easter ILP National Conference there was a further fall of branches represented to 310. The Birmingham Federation was reported as consisting of twelve branches. Birmingham delegates were Miss Eastgate, then also in the Communist Party, and Jim Simmons.

The lack of reports of activity during the year suggests the ILP in the doldrums, although Labour Church activity seems to have been rising with about seven Churches active. Despite the smaller representation at annual Conference and the fall in the circulation of the *Labour Leader,* the ILP continued to comfort itself with reports of a rising number of branches from 753 in 1919 to 787 in 1921 and 792 in January 1922. However, at the Midlands Divisional Conference in January it was conceded that it had less branches 'mainly due to branches which were not functioning being erased from the record,' and in March the Midlands Division recognised that there was a financial crisis by dismissing Jim Simmons, its organiser.

At the 1922 National Conference only 215 branches were represented. Birmingham delegates were Joseph Southall, Fred Longden and Jim Simmons who were to make their presence felt. Southall supported a resolution in the name of the Aston and Preston branches that it requests the Labour Party to accept affiliation of the Communist Party. He was opposed by Manny Shinwell who quoted Tommy Jackson's apocryphal remark that the CP would 'shake the Labour Party by the hand in order to take it by the throat.' The resolution was passed after an amendment 'providing they accept the principles and constitution of the Labour Party' was incorporated. Southall went further and moved on behalf of the Birmingham branch:

> This annual Conference while being unable to agree with some of the methods of the Bolsheviks and adhering to the belief in persuasion rather than violence desires to express their intense sympathy with

the Bolsheviks in their anti-Imperialist struggles and gratefully acknowledges our continuing indebtness to them for publishing the Secret Treaties.

This was passed narrowly by 53 votes to 50. Fred Longden also moved a resolution, from Aston, requesting that the NAC 'continue consistently to promote an effective International.' In his speech Longden recognised the difficulties there had been at Vienna with extremes ranging from Ramsay MacDonald to Radek, the Bolshevik. He defended the action of the Bolsheviks in Georgia in suppressing the Mensheviks, which MacDonald had criticised. Previously, the Mensheviks had consistently suppressed the Bolsheviks, he claimed. Some of the most balanced minds in the Vienna Union were asking both MacDonald and Radek to put aside some of their doctrinaire attitudes, he concluded. Longden was supported by Southall who said that criticism of the Third International by leaders of the Second regarding the use of force by the Bolsheviks came ill from those who had turned jingo and supported the recent imperialist war (Cheers.) This Conference also officially accepted the industrial policy of Guild Socialism.

In May Fred Longden was adopted as prospective Labour candidate for the Deritend constituency. Longden was said to have been an active ILP member for eighteen years and the son of a Lancashire moulder who himself went to the foundry at the age of thirteen.

At the Easter Conference the ILP had officially admitted that it was in crisis financially, organisationally and politically. It was to be temporarily rescued by Clifford Allen who was elected Treasurer by a narrow majority. Allen set to work to restore the finances of the party by calling on his middle class allies from the Union of Democratic Control and No-Conscription Fellowship days for large donations. He appointed H.N. Brailsford editor of the party newspaper and in October it appeared as the New Leader. With regard to the problem of finding a role for the party and differentiating itself from the Communist Party on the one hand and the Labour Party on the other, its adoption of Guild Socialism was held to have achieved this and attempts were made to create closer relations with the trade unions. The formula worked. The financial crisis was overcome, the circulation of the paper increased and so did membership. But to what extent this was due to the organising abilities of Clifford Allen and how much to general increasing militancy arising from mass unemployment is difficult to judge.

While solving some problems, the Allen reforms exacerbated others. Members felt that the party was being swamped by middle class recruits without a clear Socialist perspective. This feeling existed in Birmingham where former Liberals, such as members of the Cadbury family, Harrison Barrow, and then Oswald Mosley were providing considerable sums of money and felt to be dominating policy with right-wing attitudes.

In Birmingham, the national campaign to reinvigorate the ILP under the slogan of 'Socialism Now,' coincided with the re-adoption of Dr Dunstan as Parliamentary candidate for Ladywood. In January 1923 there was an ILP rally with Dunstan, Jim Simmons and Fred Longden as the main speakers. Later in the month there was a Trade Union and Labour Conference at Digbeth organised by the Birmingham ILP Fed. with Ramsay MacDonald the main speaker and the president of the Trades Council in the chair. This was followed by a rally and concert at Moseley. MacDonald's weekend visit to the city was pronounced a great success with considerable sales of the *New Leader*. Also in January was Dunstan's illustrated lecture at the Town Hall on this Rotten and Benighted city when 'great crowds had to be turned away.' Recruits were also being made; Birmingham East reported twenty six new members, more on the books then ever before with lots of young people.

In February 1923 at Tyseley Picture House 'over seven hundred listened to Dr Dunstan give a moving address,' in which he dealt with land and rating and appealed for a better understanding of the Russian question. At this meeting the chairman, W.J. Chamberlain editor of *Town Crier,* appealed as a life-long ILPer for people to join the party.

At the Easter national conference an increased number of branches, 293, was represented. Harrison Barrow spoke on a resolution on public ownership of the drink trade. He supported Carlisle, the only town with a publicly controlled drink trade. There licences were down by half, as were convictions for drunkenness. The enormous power of the drink trade could only be combatted by ownership, not prohibition, Barrison maintained. After the conference Rotton Park branch claimed one hundred new members, a women's section and speakers' class formed, and an outdoor season started. Also several visits from Dr Dunstan and how it was 'truly marvellous how he in such a short time had won his way into people's hearts.'

By May 1923 the Birmingham ILP was beginning to make an important contribution to the city's politics, by inaugurating the ILP football league. E. Birmingham branch reported that it had set up a *New Leader* committee of twelve. The branch had taken part in the record May Day parade with a tableaux showing Life under Socialism. They hoped to have a branch of 300 by the end of the year.

During the summer Ladywood reported large open-air meetings with Dr Dunstan, and Deritend constituency was following suit. Here Jim Simmons 'made a speciality of the word *revolution,* nearly making hearers' hair stand on end as he propounded at length on the Party's desire for revolution. So many people have still to learn that a revolution is a *radical change* which can be brought about more effectively by ballot than by bomb. Jim Simmons is teaching them.'

From the autumn the ILP locally was concentrating on J.H. Hobson's Under-consumption theory which attributed unemployment to lack of money by workers to buy the goods they produced. This was the year when unemployment was the great issue.

The November 1923 general election brought celebrations for the first minority Labour government. In Birmingham Dunstan failed to unseat Neville Chamberlain by 1,554 votes, Longden failed in Deritend by 2,619 and there were advances elsewhere. But no break-through of a Labour MP. Reaction to the Labour government was at first enthusiastic and ILP recruitment continued. But it was later disillusionment with MacDonald and Snowden, the undisputed leaders of the ILP, which was to raise in its very sharpest form all the dilemmas of the ILP.

Meanwhile progress continued into 1924. In January the Young Socialists were set up. Rotton Park was reported as 'forging ahead' with its Labour Church crowded every Sunday. Dr Dunstan had been readopted for Ladywood and he promised to devote as much time as possible to the constituency. Erdington reported the formation of a cycling club in February. The same month a well attended Midlands Divisional Conference at Eaton chaired by Harrison Barrow showed good progress during the year. A unanimous vote of 'warmest congratulations' to Ramsay MacDonald was passed but trouble was presaged by Southall and Longden having passed with only three against a motion stating that since existing armed forces were a constant menace to peace, the ILP members of Parliament would oppose all votes of supply for these destructive agencies by whatever government it was proposed.

At the 1924 national Conference Southall and Longden with J.T. Durant represented 13 Birmingham ILP branches out of a national total of 772 branches. Again Southall and Longden were active in pressing pacifist view. Longden moved the reference back of parts of the NAC International Manifesto. This laid more stress on devastated areas than broken bodies and sought to place the blame for the war solely on the German government whereas all governments bore some of the blame. This obscured the real causes of war which had to be faced, Longden claimed. He was seconded by Southall. This led to a prolonged discussion in the conference during which Wallhead said that the matter had been put to all the European Socialist Parties by the International and the German party had accepted liability by endorsing reparations. Eventually Longden's reference back was defeated.

The national series of conferences on unemployment included one in Birmingham in June. This was attended by 270 delegates who discussed the ILP programme aimed at encouraging the Labour government to further action. It 'desired to bring to the notice of the government the immediate improvement that would accrue from the establishment of a 48-hour week,' and also asked for higher wages and further measures to deal with unemployment. Some delegates wanted more radical action, however. The Rev John Lewis on behalf of Ladywood ILP moved the nationalisation of the banking system. This was opposed by Harrison Barrow who said that this was not practicable at that time and he moved an amendment that necessary steps be taken 'to secure such control of the Bank of England as will enable the government to exercise a general control over the policy of inflation and deflation of credit.' This was defeated and Lewis's resolution passed. William Brain on behalf of the Communist Party said that he did not think MacDonald had any intention of challenging capitalism as the ILP seemed to think and moved an alternative motion which included scrapping the Versailles Treaty, a

44-hour week, a £1 a week increase for all workers, full maintenance for the unemployed, repudiation of the claims of Russian bondholders and large government credits for the development of Russo-British industry. He was replied to by Jim Simmons who said they were not discussing what might happen when a Lenin arrived in England, but what could be done now in the conditions under which a Labour government was operating. Brain's amendment was 'overwhelmingly defeated,' and the original ILP motion passed.

In July 1924 the Birmingham ILP Federation organised an aggregate meeting to consider a national campaign for the nationalisation of the banking system, opened by Rev John Lewis. In the same month a Birmingham for Socialism initiative was discussed. This was launched in October with a visit of John Wheatley the popular Minister of Health. The main local speaker was Oswald Mosley. 750 delegates from all over the midlands attended and it was, 'One of the most successful meetings ever held in Birmingham. Thousands were unable to gain admission to the Town Hall and an overflow meetings was addressed by Mosley... John Wheatley received a great ovation both inside the Town Hall and outside.'

By February 1925 when the annual Midlands Divisional Conference took place the Labour government had come and gone. But there was a 'healthy report of ILP progress, particularly in Birmingham.' Fred Longden, who was the midlands member on the National Administrative Council, chose, in his report to attack the International to which the ILP was affiliated (the Vienna Union, derisorily dubbed the 2½ International – GB) as spending most of its time railing at the Communists and not getting on with its proper business. A resolution on referring to the League of Nations the question of the assassination of Sir Lee Stack which had resulted in mass reprisals in Egypt was unsuccessfully opposed by Joseph Southall who said he had not the slightest faith in the League of Nations. Birmingham resolutions proposing the nationalisation of the armaments trade and demanding that the British government set an example and take the lead in reducing armaments, were passed. Other Birmingham supported resolutions on nationalising the Bank of England, a capital levy, proportional representation, raising the school leaving age to sixteen, prohibition of use of cars at elections except for the infirm and aged, were all passed. But one demanding that no candidate represent the ILP at elections until they had been at least six months in the party, was defeated.

Despite the disappointment of the fall of the Labour government the ILP continued to grow. The October 1924 election results had seen a break through in Birmingham with its first Labour MP, Bob Dennison, who won by 133 votes in King's Norton, beating Sir Herbert Austin. Of the three ILP candidates, Oswald Mosley almost toppled Neville Chamberlain in Ladywood losing by 77 votes after several recounts and claims of lost votes. Fred Longden lost by 782 in Deritend, and in Sparkbrook S. Potter almost doubled the Labour vote and came within 5,000 votes of beating L.S. Amery. Dr Dunstan polled over 7,000 as a Communist-Workers' candidate against 14,000 for Austen Chamberlain and, despite the Zinoviev letter, the Birmingham overall Labour vote improved.

At the Easter national conference a record 1,028 branches were reported against 772 in 1924 and the number of branches in the Birmingham ILP Fed. had risen from thirteen to eighteen.

The Birmingham ILP branches continued active in 1925 with a Women's Section organising meetings and charabanc outings and large Town Hall meetings such as one in September when Annie Besant and the Rev John Lewis were the main speakers; and, of course, the Labour Churches flourished. A feature of 1925 was the growth of the Left Wing Movement with which the left wing of the ILP was closely involved, especially Southall and Longden.

Progress continued into 1926. In February the Midlands ILP Annual Conference discussed the resolutions to be put to the national conference at Easter. Joseph Southall successfully proposed that sufficient time should be given to discuss fully foreign and Colonial policy and that a clear pronouncement against imperialism should be made by the ILP. Another resolution proposed by Southall was that once a Labour government with full powers was elected it should immediately call a conference of all the countries in the Empire to mutually determine how independence should be granted and to found a real Commonwealth based on equality. This was criticised as being impracticable, but was, nevertheless, passed. The anti-war theme was taken up by other Birmingham ILP branches. King's Norton wanted A. Ponsonby's Peace Letter endorsed, whose signatories vowed not to support or render war service to any government resorting to war. Perry Barr branch moved that disarmament should take place by international agreement in successive stages with immediate drastic general reduction of arms; this was carried. Joseph Solway, now secretary of the Birmingham Fed. moved that no ILP member of Parliament should ever vote for war credits. This, however, was defeated, largely on the grounds that MPs should be allowed to act according to their consciences. Solway also moved the immediate repudiation of the Dawes Plan. But after claims that MacDonald had only accepted it as a step to a final solution, the previous question was moved and carried. James Maxton presented a report on behalf of the National Administrative Council outlining ILP plans for its campaign 'Socialism in our Time.'

Maxton continued this theme at a crowded meeting at Birmingham Town Hall on the Sunday evening. Opening the meeting from the Chair Joseph Southall struck a militant note by supporting the growing Left Wing Movement. Speaking of the propensity of MacDonald and Snowden to pander to the customs of the upper classes, he said people were becoming tired of dress suits, top hats, and garden parties in the movement and wanted something of more benefit to the working class. Fred Longden took up the same theme. He said the ILP was not concerned with applying ointment to the wounds of the capitalist system but were concerned to change the system. He wanted to assure Communists that the ILP was not dead, and there were many in it who would struggle on the side of the workers as hard and as long as the Communists. When Maxton spoke he warned against the fatalism of both those who said that capitalism will always be with us and those who said it could only be replaced by force, although he personally thought that a violent revolution would probably be necessary.

The question of the function of the ILP even in this period when it was rapidly growing continued to perplex members. Sydney Potter in a letter to the *Town Crier* said that the ILP was the vanguard of the political working class movement. He favoured the school of thought which said that to fulfil this role it should lay less stress on numbers and recruiting and more on education of its present members.

The annual report to the 1926 national conference tried to clarify some of the issues facing the ILP. Reporting a record number of branches and members it stated that association with the Labour government had given the impression that it had modified its policies; it was now time to re-state its purpose and policy. The orientation of the Party would be towards a more militant Socialism. At home it would work with the trade unions and others for Socialism in our Time. Abroad, it was not satisfied with the policy of the Labour and Socialist International to which it was affiliated and it would press for talks with the Third International on the possibility of an all inclusive International. The report stressed the unique contributions it was making in educational and cultural matters with a national student as well as a national youth movement 9,000 strong; also the Arts Guild movement with a large number of art and craft groups, choirs, and dramatic societies under the direction of Miles Malleson.

When the Easter National Conference took place the Birmingham Fed. was reported as having twenty branches and there was the large number of nine delegates from Birmingham, including Solway, Southall, Oswald Mosley and Jim Simmons.

By the time of the General Strike, therefore, the general growth of militancy which had fuelled the development of the ILP showed no sign of abating and the ILP could justifiably look forward to further growth while renewing attempts to solve the contradictions of its relationship to the Labour and Communist parties, the development of a programme for 'Socialism in our Time', the question of its role in the movement, and solving the contradictions of the differing views of its members ranging from outright pacifists, advocates of co-operation with Communists at home and abroad, to supporters of the social democracy of Ramsay MacDonald.

The Labour Party

The new 1918 Labour Party constitution led swiftly to the setting up of Divisional and Ward Labour Parties in Birmingham. These undertook the electoral work previously performed by the ILP and, although individual members of the Labour Party were often also members of the ILP, this was the most important respect in which the influence of the ILP was undermined.

The khaki General election, taking place a month after the war ended, was a disaster for Labour, all twelve constituencies returning Unionists and Coalition candidates. Eldred Hallas, however, a trade unionist Lib-Lab with Lloyd George's Coupon was returned in Duddeston and A.R. Jephcott, another Lib-Lab was returned at Yardley calling himself Coalition-Unionist. Neither was recognised as a Labour MP. In other constituencies A.E. Ayton polled 5,211 to Steel-Maitland's 12,678 in Erdington; H.J. Odell polled 4,576 to the Unionist's 12,019 in Handsworth; Tom Hackett, the Co-operator stood as an Independent in King's Norton and won the respectable vote of 4,917 votes against Sir Herbert Austin's 8,809; in Ladywood, John Kneeshaw who had been the bedrock of Birmingham opposition to the war on the city council and on the Trades Council received only 2,572 votes to Neville Chamberlain's 9,405; Dr Dunstan polled 3,789 in Moseley to the Coalition Unionist's 16,161; and in Sparkbrook Frank Spires also stood as an Independent, beating a Liberal but losing to A.C. Amery by 3,014 to 15,225.

There were no Municipal elections in November 1918 and the next year's elections brought a considerable advance for Labour. The situation during the war had been that in December 1915 there were eight city councillors. By December 1918 this had risen to eleven including two Aldermen, Beard and Gregory. From the November 1919 elections the Labour Party emerged with twenty one councillors. With by-elections returning Frank Sharkey and the police strike leader Edward Taylor this quickly became twenty three. This was a sizeable opposition group on a Council of 120 members. Some of the old guard councillors had disappeared including John Kneeshaw and George Shann, and Councillor Percival Bower, who had joined the council during the war, was elected leader. Bower also became president of the Birmingham Central Labour Party. Bower became an Alderman in the summer and this caused an outcry because Bower had not been put forward by the Labour Party and was elected with opposition votes. Aldermen were viewed with suspicion as likely to become part of the establishment; once installed aldermen never stood for re-election and passed from the control of the local party. Simpson (one of the pre-war eight) had also been elected without Labour support, and both Beard and Gregory, the other two alderman, were also criticised. Bower and Simpson were requested to give up their aldermanic position; they both refused. The matter was taken no further. But a warning was issued of the need for co-operation between the Labour group and the party. The threat was also made that anyone else accepting aldermanic nomination without the agreement of the party would be expelled.

In October 1920 the *Town Crier* printed a brief summary of the activities of the Labour group in its first post-war year. At the first meeting they had argued that all war-time aldermen and councillors who had not faced election in 1919 should be obliged to go to the polls; also that meetings should be changed from afternoons to evenings to allow workers to attend. Both were defeated. In December they had moved a motion protesting at the dependency of local hospitals on charity and demanding the setting up of a National Health Authority. A proposal from the Watch Committee to introduce mounted police into Birmingham was successfully opposed with Liberal support. The reinstatement of the striking policemen was demanded repeatedly throughout the year. In January a proposal to spend £10,000 on work for the unemployed was opposed on the grounds that it was inadequate. In March the Labour councillors had raised the housing question. Councillor Taylor said that houses in his ward 'were not fit to bring up vermin in,' and a proposal to limit spending on housing to £1,500,000 was condemned. The question of police spies at Labour movement meetings was also raised. In May the 'failure' of the issue of Housing Bonds at 6 per cent (intended to finance the housing programme – GB) was raised and a capital levy to pay for housing was demanded. In June a proposal to pay council workers who joined the Territorial Army was opposed as subsidising militarism. Opposition to tram fare rises obtained wider support and was only defeated by the casting vote of the Lord Mayor. Underpaid teachers received less sympathy as Labour's demand for more pay for uncertificated teachers was defeated.

An important issue raised in 1920 was the Sydney Rating System. This rated land rather than properties and was much discussed at the time within the Labour movement. A particular advocate in Birmingham was Councillor Tiptaft, an erstwhile Labour militant long since become respectable as an Independent/Progressive, who moved the report back of a Finance Committee report which had considered, and rejected this System. Tiptaft claimed that the Sydney system had been adopted by 160 municipalities in Australasia and with rates at 17/-d. in the £ the Finance Committee should have gone more deeply into the matter. After further discussion the reference back was defeated. Then most of the Tory and Liberal councillors went home. leaving only about thirty councillors to discuss the rest of the business which included further grilling of the Watch Committee over the victimised Police strikers and police spies at Labour meetings.

Despite these efforts on their behalf, the working class seemed ungrateful and in the November 1920 elections the Labour Party received a severe set back. Aston was gained and a Tenants' candidate won Lozells, but six Labour seats were lost and Labour representation fell to 21.

In the light of the militancy of the time and the mass unemployed this defeat seems strange, especially as the Labour Party continued to win by-elections up to November. An example of this militancy was the May Day demonstration which was a record one with a mile long procession, splendid tableaux, and a 'fine muster of police spies.' F.W. Rudland in his annual report of the Borough Labour Party considered the electoral defeat as inevitable 'in view of the industrial crisis and its exploitation by the Government and the big employing combinations, backed by a reactionary press.' The *Town Crier* spoke of a 'strenuous and unscrupulous campaign of the reactionary forces', and warned that rates would rise.

At the November 1921 elections, however, there was a considerable victory. All Labour seats were held and six captured, bringing Labour representation back to 27. It was at this election that Harry Shepperson gained 759 votes as a Communist (after he had been rejected as a Labour candidate) and polled more than the Labour man at Yardley. When Rudland made his annual report Labour representation had risen to 29. He put the victory down to the work of the rank and file and the recognition of the 'absolute need for a proper canvass being taken.' He also pointed out that Labour's total poll in 1921 was only 1.134 votes less than the Unionist total, yet they held only 29 out of 120 seats. This was to lead to a strong lobby for Proportional Representation in the Birmingham Labour movement.

The 1922 May Day celebrations were just as successful as the previous year despite vile weather and the holding of it on May Day itself (Monday) instead of the nearest week-end. In jest, someone had suggested the police band to head the procession, but the chief constable, Rafter, took up the proposition and, as the *Town Crier* reported, there was the spectacle of the police band closely followed by the Communist Party with its banner. The lack of the usual tableaux made by people at work, was compensated for by large numbers of locked out engineers and the many Unemployed Committees in the city. The police band provided a final diversion by playing Rule Britannia and God Save the King. 'Ironic cheers and laughter from the locked-out engineers greeted the former and the Red Flag drowned the latter,' reported the *Town Crier*.

Friction continued to exist between the Labour group on the Council and the Labour Party rank and file. For instance at the 1922 Labour Party AGM protests were received from ILP and AEU branches that some Labour councillors had failed to vote for free speech when the question of allowing Communists to hire the Town Hall was discussed. A resolution was put asking them to explain their reasons for not supporting free speech. W.J. Chamberlain, the editor of *Town Crier*, in moving the resolution said that he did so on behalf of his branch, but he did not himself support it. He believed that another principle, the right of people to vote according to their conscience, was equally important as the principle of free speech. At the election of officers of the Labour Party for 1922 Alderman Bower continued as president and moderate members were voted to both the Trade Union and Socialist sections. Only the two vice-presidents, Sharkey and Longden, could be called militants.

Some councillors made individual expressions of militancy. In February 1922 Jim Simmons was apologising for an outburst at a Council meeting discussing unemployment where he had used 'unparliamentary language.'

F.W. Rudland's 1922 report of the Borough Labour Party told of Constituency parties still being organised in wards without local parties: also an increase in Women's Sections. Discussions organised reflected the increased emphasis on electoral work and had included speakers on Housing, Poor Law, the Drink Trade and Libraries. A serious complaint was that Labour councillors were blocked from membership of committees dealing with matters of most concern to working people and none occupied the chair of a committee and were therefore denied the most influential position.

At the November 1922 elections the Labour Party lost two seats. The municipal elections were closely followed by the general election. Although there was no break through with seats, Rudland was quick to point out that the Labour poll had nearly doubled since 1918 from 36,000 to 70,251; but for this they had no seats whereas the 106,892 Unionist vote had given them eight seats. 'No wonder our opponents are opposed to Proportional Representation,' Rudland concluded.

In 1923 there were problems with Councillor Jesse Williams. A month after being elected in November 1922 he gave notice that he would become an Independent. When called on to resign as a councillor he refused and he was expelled from the Labour Party. Once again, May Day in Birmingham was a 'record one.' During the summer at least one Labour Party branch, West Birmingham, was carrying out successful open-air activity. The annual Borough Labour Party report was signed by both Rudland and W.J. Chamberlain. It reported the formation of a thoroughly organised Labour Women's Advisory Council, responsible for organising the record Margaret Bondfield meeting in February. It also reported the failure to keep the Tenants' Associations non-political with the intervention of 'our political opponents.' The Labour Party therefore had no option but to urge these Associations to affiliate to the Labour Party. Several were already affiliated.

At the November elections two more seats were won. Alderman Bower's analysis of the results showed that 70,649 votes had elected 20 opposition Councillors, whereas 44.563 Labour votes had secured only two councillors. Bower also stressed that Liberals and Tories had been 'driven on to one platform' by the strength of the Labour Party and this new camp now contained 'brewers as well as abstainers, priests as well as ministers.' The annual election 'scare' this time was that the Labour party had been responsible for the shortage of bricklayers, which was allegedly holding up the building of houses.

The 1923 general election which had returned the first, minority Labour government had still not yet produced a Birmingham Labour MP. Part of the reason for this was revealed in the election expenses for that campaign. Sir A. Steel-Maitland, minister and local monopoly-capitalist had been the most extravagant, spending £1022 to Labour's £172. Neville Chamberlain spent £756 to Dr Dunstan's £251. Most constituencies showed similar divergences. But in King's Norton the Co-op candidate spent £522 to Sir Herbert Austin's £659 and Mrs G. Cadbury's £590 for the Liberals.

An interesting Council item in March 1924 was the Labour councillors' opposition to a proposal for the Council to guarantee £3,800 for Civic Week at the Wembley Exhibition. Jim Simmons referred to the exploitation going on in the letting of stands while Alderman J.V. Stevens thought the eventual expenditure would be nearer £10,000. In this case the Labour councillors had allies and less than a dozen councillors supported the motion.

Once again Birmingham's May Day was a record, although it reverted to the Sunday after the first of May. As reported by the *Town Crier,* 15,000 marched from Victoria Square to Summerfield Park. Headed by a National Union of Railwaymen band and a large contingent of NUR marchers, large numbers of other trade unionists followed led by the Birmingham Corporation Tramways band. 'The Trade Union section made a brave show with its banners and tableaux.' Then followed the political sections led by the Irish Pipers' Band and the 'fine' Birmingham Borough Labour Party banner. City Labour councillors and Poor Law Guardians led this section followed by contingents from constituency and ward parties in the city. It was a united May Day. The ILP sent 'a record muster' and the Communist Party was 'well represented'. Then came the Co-operative section, beating 'all previous records.' with Women's and Men's Guilds and Young Comrades' Circles. Finally, other organisations including the No More War Movement, National Guilds League, Labour Sports Clubs, Anti-Vivisection League, and Herald League, also marched. 'The various tableaux were so arranged as to give colour and interest to the whole length of the procession.' Those highlighted by the *Town Crier* were, 'The Beacon Light' of the NUR, 'Labour Sweeping On' and 'Sweeping Poverty Aside.' by the Transport & General Workers Union, St. Martin's & Deritend's 'grimly realistic tableau' entitled 'War of the Future' showing a whole family blotted out by poison gas, and the Communist Party's 'excellent tableau' by the Hay Mills & Yardley Group illustrating Internationalism, with Russia the central figure.

On arrival at Summerfield Park the massed bands and the AEU choir led the singing of the Internationale and speeches were then delivered from the four platforms. Notable events in 1924 were Oswald Mosley joining the Labour party in March and being nominated as parliamentary candidate for Ladywood in July on Dr Dunstan joining the Communist Party; also Frank Sharkey announcing in July that he could not afford to continue as a councillor because of the loss of earnings involved thus high lighting another way in which the Labour Party was disadvantaged compared with its Tory and Liberal opponents.

At the September Town Hall meeting where the Labour group reported on its work on the Council, discontents came to a head. Councillor Mrs Howes complained of the difficulty experienced in getting a Labour representative even on one committee. Alderman Bower said that large increases in rates had only been avoided by paring the estimates of spending committees and taking £100,000 from the trading concerns. Such cuts in the Health Services at a time when medicine and surgery were making giant strides were a false economy and could not be continued. Similarly with education, schools were deteriorating and there was a lag in secondary education. With regard to housing, they had 43,366 back-to-back houses and 58,028 houses without separate sanitation. Teddy Ager took up the housing theme. Only 5,500 houses had been built from the end of the war and since 5,000 houses a year were necessary to cater for the growth of the city they were actually 5,000 houses worse off. He believed the Wheatley Housing Act was the most effective social legislation ever passed; yet Unionists councillors were saying that they would refuse to administer it. Ager advocated the setting up of a municipal direct building department. Jim Simmons defended the creation of 'scenes' in the council chamber. These stirred up public opinion and forced the council to do things it would not otherwise do. Despite such dreadful social conditions and mass unemployment, the powerful Unionist and Liberal press was able to paint a picture of the Labour Party as the party of high expenditure and in November 1924 the Labour Party lost five seats to take representation on the council down to 20.

The Borough Party annual report, signed by Rudland and A.E. Ager as p;resident of the Party, highlighted the chaos at the count of the general election, particularly at Ladywood with its re-counts and claim of lost votes. The Labour Party demanded more counting agents and requested that in future counts take place in the constituency itself or that only a limited number of counts take place at the Council Chamber and Town Hall where all twelve of the counts have previously taken place. The Lord Mayor and the Town Clerk, to whom these complaints were made, agreed that more counting agents should be sworn in, but rejected the idea of all counts taking place in the constituencies.

There was the usual review of meetings organised and Town Hall demonstrations. The latter included a review of Labour's work on the council, one by the builders' leader R. Coppock on direct labour and one on foreign policy and unemployment. Among affiliations to the Labour Party during the year were more Tenants' Associations.

1924 had begun with the election of Birmingham's first member of parliament at the previous November general election, Bob Dennison. It ended, after the November local elections with a loss of five Labour seats, but the election of Birmingham's first Labour Lord Mayor, the controversial Alderman Percival Bower.

In February 1925 Jim Simmons won a by-election at Duddeston to take Labour representation up to 21.

The contradiction between the increasing strength of Labour organisations and poor local election results was again demonstrated with another 'record' May Day. Over 15,000 people were said to have marched from Victoria Square to Calthorpe Park. The *Town Crier* reported that from 2 pm almost every car arriving in the city centre carried its quota of Labour supporters wearing red rosettes. Again it was a united demonstration with a trade union section, a political section including all twelve of the Divisional Labour Parties, all the Women's Sections, Aston Youth Section, all the ILP branches, Guild of Youth, Young Socialists' League, Communist Party, Young Communist League and

Herald League. Then came a large Co-operative Section with its Women's and Men's Guilds and Young Comrades. Then the No More War Movement and National Guilds' League. There were eight bands and 31 tableaux many of them lovingly described in the *Town Crier*. Ishbel MacDonald was the main speaker. The May Day celebrations had begun on Friday evening with a crowded Town Hall meeting addressed by David Kirkwood.

The question of Proportional Representation continued to occupy the Labour Party. This time it arose from the national budget in April being passed by a government with the votes of only a minority of the people. The Home Secretary promised a Conference on Electoral Reform for 1926.

The 8th 1925 Labour Party report reflected on the fact that it was the child of the trade union movement whose Trades Council was celebrating its sixtieth anniversary. It went on to outline Labour representation in Birmingham since 1914. The report also recorded agreement between the Labour Party and Co-operative Party on joint candidates at elections. This was signed between the two parties both locally and nationally. John Strachey and Oswald Mosley had put forward their proposals re National Credit and the Banking System and its relationship with Poverty and Unemployment. It had been decided that the monthly executive meetings should be allocated as follows: three meetings for receiving Councillors' and Guardians' Reports, three devoted to organisation, an AGM, and the remaining five meetings to educational or special purposes.

With regard to the counting of votes, a final decision was accepted that three divisions should be counted at the Art Gallery, four in the Council House and five in the Town Hall. Where a majority was one hundred or less, special arrangements would be made for the candidates, or their agents, to check the form which contained the totals of each bundle of votes, but not to check the voting slips themselves.

A breakdown of Labour representation on council committees suggests that the situation was not quite as dire as indicated by Mrs Howes. On all committees there were one or two Labour councillors. On the Distress Committee, which had local sub-committees, there were five councillors and also five Labour co-options. On the local Pensions Committee labour councillors were represented on each of the ten sub Committees. On the Education committee there were three Labour councillors plus Miss Cleaver. But on other key committees of Finance and Watch and also Tramways there was only one Labour councillor.

A new departure was an Organising Committee Report for 1925. This reported the adoption of Model Rules for Constituency Parties, a card index of affiliated organisations and members containing 15,000 names, contact with members and collections of dues by means of a system organised on polling stations under a Captain with Street Stewards. Monthly propaganda sheets were also being distributed in some constituencies. An Information bureau and a speakers' club of 80 people paying contributions for weekly notes and other information were also operating. On the organisation of youth it reported an unsuccessful attempt to create one youth organisation for the city. In April a constitution for Youth Sections of the Labour Party had therefore been prepared, and there were currently eight Youth Sections. A Musical and Dramatic Union had also been formed with Central, Sparkbrook, and Selly Oak choirs with the AEU choir agreeing to affiliate.

It is clear that 1925 was a year of considerable advance both organisationally and culturally. Yet at the municipal elections in November the Labour Party lost another two seats bringing their representation down to 18, the lowest it had been since 1919.

At this point, six years after the end of the war, an assessment can be made. Any post-war optimism of a better world had been shortlived. The reality of wartime when, under government direction, several million men could be removed from the productive process and the bulk of industry turned to the non-productive task of churning out instruments of war and yet the social conditions of many millions, especially children, could be improved was not lost on working people. A peace time regime, similarly directed, would surely have little difficulty in building the houses and providing the work that would rapidly raise living standards. But the old, iron 'reality' was a return to free market forces perpetuating the gulf between the rich and the poor. Immediate post-war conditions favoured the raising of wages and living standards; unfortunately, it also increased the possibilities of raising prices even more. With the advent of mass unemployment in 1921 the main resources for working people to raise their living standards were struck from their hands. The two Birminghams continued. The one of the rich was fortified by the profits of increasingly monopolised industries in Birmingham and new industries; and buttressed by the possession of War Loans issued at high rates of interest and increasingly profitable as prices fell, particularly after the devaluation of the return to gold in 1925. Both the interests and the values of these classes were advanced morning and night by the anti-working class press, while both Austen and Neville Chamberlain in Parliament were living reminders of the continuation of the Chamberlain tradition.

These people, who saw the fine public buildings and large private houses in Edgbaston as the reality of life in Birmingham were genuinely shocked when Dr Robert Dunstan called Birmingham 'this Rotten and Benighted City,' and proved it with statistics of inadequate treatment of war pensioners, scandalous standards of poor relief and unemployment benefit, appalling housing conditions, vast differences in development between children in working class wards and others, equally unacceptable differences in death rates between rich and poor wards, hospitals dependent on charity, an inadequate education system and much else. Dunstan's description of Birmingham was the reality for tens of thousands of people, while the myth of a classless and prosperous Birmingham applied only to a minority. The only defence against Dunstan's flood of statistics was that conditions were not as bad as in some other large cities such as Liverpool or Glasgow; and with regard to inadequate war pensions, Neville Chamberlain justified this by claiming that these were higher than in other European countries, disregarding the fact that these countries had either lost the war, as with Germany and the central powers, or were poorer than Britain, such as France.

Birmingham Labour councillors can, no doubt, be justly accused of failing to protect and improve working class conditions in the city in these years after the war, but there was some genuine militancy regarding such measures as correcting the injustice done to the police strikers, the expertise of Harrison Barrow with regard to housing and Jim Simmons' work for war pensioners. But numbers were too small for the Labour councillors to affect the direction which the Unionist and Liberal councillors were determined to take the city in these years.

Bibliography: The ILP and the Labour Party

For the general development of the Independent Labour Party see R.E. Dowse – *Left in the Centre*. The *Labour Leader* which became the *New Leader* in October 1922 is a main source for the Birmingham ILP, the other being the *Town Crier*. National Conference Reports of the ILP are available on micro-film. Biographies of both Harrison Barrow and Joseph Southall are in vol 5 of the *Dictionary of Labour Biography* and Fred Rudland's in vol 7. Short biographies of local Labour candidates can sometimes be found around election time (November) in the *Town Crier* e.g. 30th October 1925. For Guild Socialism see Dowse. The best modern introduction is the series of readings edited by Ken Coates and Tony Topham entitled *Workers' Control*. For the Birmingham Labour Party see its *Annual Report* contained within the *Birmingham Trades & Labour Council annual reports*. *Birmingham City Council Minutes*. Chris Roseblade material recording and analysing Birmingham and Black Country election results both general and municipal from 1918 to 1945. This is in the possession of G. Barnsby (1996). For Norman Tiptaft's hidden socialist past consult the Index of my *Birmingham Working People*. For the total failure of Housing Policy up to 1925 under Neville Chamberlain's legislation see Carl Chinn – *Homes for People: One Hundred Years of Council Housing in Birmingham*. The *Town Crier* continues to be the main source.

Chapter 20

The Trade Union Movement in Birmingham 1919-1925

Trade Union Advance 1919-20

Lloyd George required all his wizardry to keep the Labour movement at bay in the post-war period. He hoped, as we have seen, to avoid post-war unemployment problems, and as an additional insurance, had granted fairly generous unemployment pay to both returning servicemen and munitions workers. Workers expected after the war higher pay and shorter hours as a reward for their efforts. For many workers, the latter did occur, but fell short of the 8-hour day the movement had been demanding since the 1890s. Roughly speaking hours fell from the 54 which many workers had gained during the Great Unrest of 1912-14 to 48 hours after the war; the former was a ten-hour day with four hours work on Saturdays; the latter a nine-hour day also with four hours work on Saturdays. In the large factories engineering workers worked the negotiated 47-hour week, which meant an early finish on Fridays. The 47-hour week remained until 1950. Building trade workers in Birmingham negotiated a 44-hour week in December 1920, but it was raised in 1926 to 46½ hours in summer and 44 in winter. These hours persisted until 1960. Even such well organised workers as Birmingham printers worked a 48-hour week, which was not reduced to 44 until 1938. Other organised workers such as railwaymen and transport workers also obtained reductions, but hours in these industries were notoriously long as were those of shop workers whose hours were reduced only in the larger shops. Against any reduction in hours must be set the increased strain of working with up dated technology and the effects of speed-up which became a main issue in Birmingham factories in the 1930s.

Controls over most of industry were almost immediately abolished after the war and the shadow factories sold. Only coal, agriculture and railways among major industries remained under government control.

The government wished to strengthen industrial relations after the war by extending Joint Industrial Councils, and the Federation of British Industries promoted, together with compliant trade union leaders, a National Alliance of Employers and Employed.

Fear of revolution drove much of government policy during the first three post-war years and this spectre almost materialised in August 1920 when the government announced its intention of sending troops to Poland. This resulted in the Hands off Russia Campaign, the formation by the TUC and the Labour Party of a Council of Action and the threat of a general strike. Lloyd George was saved by the Poles who at this time began to advance against the Russians and an armistice was signed in October.

The trade union movement in Birmingham grew during the war. The Trades Council increased its standing within the city and its main characteristic during the war was its gradual transition after 1916 from support for the war to outright opposition and champion of an early, democratic peace. Exactly how much progress the Trades Council made is difficult to judge. Its finances is the most important criterion. In 1914 its subscription income was £382 and in 1918 £771. If this is corrected for inflation, which doubled prices during the war, it represents a fall in real income. If one takes the number of branches paying subscriptions, however, these fell slightly from about 157 to about 151 in the same period. This says nothing about the size of branches and total members affiliated might have been smaller or larger. 1918 was the year when the pro-war elements, led by W.J. Davis and Kesterton attempted to set up a rival local Trades Council based on the TUC, and, nationally a new TUC divorced from the political movement. Both failed, but the effect on the Trades Council finances and affiliations was apparent in 1918. Whereas twenty Workers' Union branches were affiliated to the trades Council in 1914 there were only eight branches in 1918. There had been three branches of the two Gasworkers' Unions affiliated in 1914, but there were none in 1918. Davis's Brassworkers were affiliated in 1914 but not in 1918. These were the three unions with the most active pro-war leaderships and they had contributed between them 16 per cent of the Trades Council's income in 1914. There were other causes for falls in affiliation, however. Building during the war was greatly curtailed and so the bricklayers, carpenters, painters and labourers who were a mainstay of the Trades Council in 1914 had less branches affiliated and contributed almost exactly the same amount in 1918 as in 1914. What is surprising is that the Amalgamated Society of Engineers which grew considerably during the war had the same number of branches affiliated in 1918 as in 1914. The growth unions during the war, from the point of view of the Trades Council were the railway unions. Their affiliations rose from nine to fourteen branches and their contributions from £33 in 1914 to £144 in 1918 making them the largest contributors to the Trades Council's finances.

By the end of 1920 Trades Council income was down to £665. Building workers were back in force with 23 affiliations, so were the Gas Workers, but only seven Worker's Union branches paid dues and only seven ASE branches. Central branch of the National Union of Ex-Servicemen was affiliated and a feature of the Trades Council had been the political affiliations to it. In 1920, for instance, most of the ILP branches were affiliated (although only three had paid their dues) and other political affiliations were two Labour Clubs, the East Birmingham Tenants' Association, Birmingham University Fabian Society, Saltley Railway Women's Guild and Sparkhill Women's Co-operative Guild.

Allen Cassidy and Fred Rudland began their 1920 annual report as follows:

'It was a famous victory', and its hard won dead sea fruits – reduced wages, lowered standards of life, curtailment of personal liberty and unemployment... are now the special perquisites of the toilers. The master class have reaped a golden harvest from the shambles of Europe, and their ill-gotten gains in the shape of watered stock or over-capitalisation is one of the principal reasons why wages must now come down to pay interest on their investments. Then, of course, the infamous terms of the Peace Treaty strangles European trade and representative British manufacturers have exhibited greater business acumen than British statesmen by declaring that it would be better to give than to take a huge indemnity from our former allies to enable them to restart their industries and trade with us.

The report went on to state that the long discussed matter of a Trades Hall and Central Headquarters for the movement had again been postponed 'in these unsettled times' and the Trades Council had taken premises above one of the the Co-operative shops in Corporation Street. The invaluable services of the *Town Crier* were acknowledged. The Trades Council had organised six Conferences during the year on such topics as Public Ownership of the Liquor Trade, the Blind Persons' Act and Economic Freedom; they had been represented at three Council of Action conferences on Housing, Russia, and the Employment of Ex-Servicemen.

Some matters had been of constant concern throughout the year. For instance, on housing there had been meetings with the Housing Department and the Building Trades Operatives regarding a Direct Building Department for the Council. Also the Co-operative Builders Ltd. had been formed and approved by the Trades Council. Unemployment had caused much anxiety. As a short-term measure the Trades Council had agreed at the Town's Meeting with the raising of a Relief Fund which had reached £20,000 and there had been negotiations with the Salaries and Wages Committee concerning wages for unemployed men engaged on road making etc. Another matter had been Teachers' Pay. A new scale was offered which slightly improved pay but accentuated the difference between Certificated and Uncertificated Teachers while ignoring altogether Supplementary Teachers. With the help of the Labour councillors these matters were referred back and a slightly improved offer made which the teachers accepted under protest. Acknowledging the services of the Trades Council, the National Union of School Teachers made a £10 grant to Trades Council funds.

The amalgamation movement had been active during the year. The greatest was the formation of the Amalgamated Engineering Union from the ASE and other engineering unions. Other important amalgamations had been the National Union of General Workers combining Gasworkers, Municipal Workers, General Workers and the Federation of Women Workers, also the Amalgamated Carpenters from the two Carpenters' Unions, and the uniting of the Tramway Workers and the Vehicle Builders.

At the end of the report twenty three new affiliations were recorded, including the Brassworkers, who had been a party to the attempted Trades Council breakaway in 1918. But no record of disaffiliations is given. The annual report ended by stating that the Trades Council was stronger and more widely representative than at any time in its history. The executive committee contained three Communists, W. Brain (Foundryworkers), H. Shepperson (AEU) and H. Blanchard (Nat. Union Ex-Servicemen).

Both 1919 and 1920 were notable nationally for a great increase in the number of workers whose wages were determined by national negotiating machinery and also for the number of strikes. A major clash involving Birmingham in 1919 was that of the Ironfounders who were determined to negotiate separately from the engineers, to replace individual piece-work with group piecework and demand a 15/-d. wage increase. A strike began in September, but the employers were determined to resist and the strike caused much hardship. In December 1919 the foundry workers balloted on the employers' offer to pay a 5/-d increase, as agreed by other engineering workers and decided by a two to one majority to stay out. But union funds were exhausted and the leadership recommended a return to work, which took place at the end of January 1920.

Another strike in 1919 to affect Birmingham was that of the railwaymen who struck in September. The causes were complex but included demands for parity of conditions with footplate staff who had already negotiated through ASLEF a favourable settlement, including a 48-hour week. Terms negotiated by the NUR leadership were rejected once and the strike terminated in January with a 29-27 vote to accept only 'under protest.'

Another strike in 1920 was that of the miners. This affected Birmingham only indirectly. The first effect was that the miners were the pace setters for both a living wage and also nationalisation; if the miners failed it would have repercussions throughout the economy. The second indirect effect was that the miners' strike was the occasion for the re-enactment of the Emergency Powers Act, which the Birmingham police used with such devastating effect to hound and spy on the Labour movement.

The two years of 1919 and 1920 were the years most favourable for the Labour movement. They were the years of direct action, when the government was prepared to make almost any concessions to avoid revolution and when the labour market was most favourable to workers. It is therefore salutary to note the conclusions of Rudland's Trades Council annual report of 1920 speaking of reduced wages, lowered standards of life, curtailment of personal liberty and unemployment, as the 'dead-sea fruit', of the 'famous victory.'

Slump, Deflation and Wage Slashing 1921-24

In 1921 the economic situation deteriorated disastrously. By the middle of the year production was 20 per cent down on the previous year and unemployment had soared. It is difficult to discuss unemployment in Birmingham until 1923 from when regular monthly statistics appear in the *Labour Gazette*. For the previous years we only have the national figures based on trade unions paying unemployment benefit. These figures show unemployment at its lowest in 1916 at 0.4 per cent rising to 0.8 per cent in 1918 and to 2.4 per cent in 1919 and 1920. But in 1921 unemployment rose to 14.8 per cent and in 1922 to a maximum of 15.2 per cent.

Rudland prefaced his 1921 Trades Council Report with a quote from J.A. Hobson: 'Low wages, high taxes, long hours, insecurity of employment, and semi-military tyranny lingering in the workshops and poverty in the home – such are the fruits labour must expect from a long and successful war.' The report went on to say that the year had been dominated by unemployment and outlined the action the Trades Council had taken – demands for work or full maintenance, town's meetings to demand work provided by the local authorities and Guardians only to be told that these were national matters, fruitless appeals to national authorities, and demands that such public relief work as there was should be paid for at standard trade union rates. Other matters of outstanding importance dealt with had been the question of free speech and the EPA regulations, and the proposed Red International of Trade Unions. Rudland concluded that little could be expected of a House of Commons where 361 MPs were known to be members of the Federation of British Industries and that trade unionists must raise their sights to more than hours and wages. The past year had been one of great anxiety, but adversity could be turned to good account if workers would be wise and intelligent.

The *Town Crier* reported fully each Trades Council meeting and also other trade union business. An outstanding item in 1921 was a party at Birmingham Town Hall in September to celebrate the creation of the Transport & General Workers Union. In Birmingham this incorporated some of the gas and general workers, together with the United Vehicle Workers and some of the general workers to make it an important player in the field of public transport trade unionism as well as general unskilled and semi-skilled labour. There were no celebrations for the Workers' Union. The amalgamation that it had negotiated with the National Amalgamated Union of Labour arranged for 1919 had become unravelled and left the Workers' Union only the second largest general workers union. It tried to retrieve its fortunes by offering an over-generous unemployment pay scheme at the very moment that unemployment was going through the roof. 1921 was a disaster year for the Workers' Union and worse was to follow.

Another important item in 1921 was the Trades Council discussion on affiliation to the Red International of Labour Unions. Harry Pollitt put the case for joining, pointing out that the 'Yellow' or Amsterdam Trade Union International had been in existence for twenty years but had no machinery for international action and could not even stop international black-legging. It was also linked with the League of Nations which was in reality a League of Super Capitalists. The Red International was based on three principles, Pollitt went on, 1) That there could be no identity of interest between workers and capitalists 2) The Dictatorship of the Working Classes 3) Real representation of the rank and file on an international basis. After a lengthy discussion the following resolution was passed:

> This meeting of delegates from branches of industrial organisations in Birmingham calls upon the Trades Union Congress to sever its connection with the Amsterdam Federation of Trade Unions and to take immediate steps to be represented at the joint Congress of the International Council of Trade and Industrial Unions to be held in Moscow on July 1.

The resolution went on to urge trade union branches to support affiliation to the RILU and appoint delegates to a local committee of the British Bureau to attain affiliation. This motion was passed at a 'full attendance of delegates' with only two dissentients.

The next year, 1922, was also a year of mass unemployment. Rudland in his annual Trades Council report continued to speak of the 'bitter fruits' of the war and a growing realisation that the capitalist system had broken down. He saw 'a welcome spirit of revolt' among workers, even though he had to admit a fall in income as trade unions struggled with unemployment. The report ended with a most explicit commitment to socialism. 'From the present struggle we must learn our lesson and consciously and unitedly carry on the fight more effectively until Capitalism is abolished and the emancipation of our class achieved.'

Trades Council activity during 1922 was both militant and drastic. It was a year when wages in all industries were being attacked. The official cost of living figure had peaked in 1920 at 249 (1914 = 100). It fell to 226 in 1921 and to 183 in 1922. Falling prices reflected falling sales as Europe began to recover and markets were lost to us. In February builders were under attack and the Trades Council urged joint action among the building trade unions. In April it was the turn of the engineers 'in a period of unexampled depression and unemployment' to face demands for a worsening of wages and conditions. In this case, 'forces were divided' and wages reduced.

These and other attacks on wages and 'the seeming futility of trade unionism today' led the Trades Council to sponsor a conference for the unification of the trade union movement. The aim was to produce 'one thoroughly representative single body with full powers...to provide effective machinery for any emergency.' In following this eternal dream of the One Big Union a 'remarkably successful' national conference was held at the Midland Institute in October representing 67 Trades Councils with about another 60 expressing their support. This resulted in the formation of a National Federation of Trades Councils speaking on behalf of the rank and file and seeking direct representation at the Trades Union Congress. The latter seemed a reasonable demand seeing that the Trades Councils had set up the Trades Union Congress in 1868 and had been ousted in 1892 in favour of direct representation of unions because this would bring more money to the TUC, prevent double representation of members, and also keep at bay the greater militancy of the Trades Councils. However, TUC and national union leaders had no intention of allowing power to pass to to the more volatile, militant and penurious Trades Councils. The scheme was a mixture of syndicalist ideas and Communist Party policy. The proposals had been initiated in Birmingham by H. Parsons local organiser of the Birmingham Furniture Trades and the national conference had been chaired by Alec Gossip, the left-wing leader of the Furniture Trades Association. Nevertheless, despite its left-wing pedigree there was clearly very wide support for merging national unions into One Big Union under the control of a single authority while using the Trades Councils locally to carry through policy.

Unemployment and declining union membership assisted conservative trade union leaders in combatting this most radical proposal for trade union reform since the setting up of the TUC. The National Federation of Trades Councils managed only one annual meeting. This was in November 1923 in Birmingham and was organised by R. Palme Dutt of the Labour Research Department and chaired by Harry Pollitt of the RILU, both leading Communists. 103 delegates from 71 Trades Councils attended with support from others. Plans by then were less far reaching, however, and conformed to the ideas of the Minority Movement which had by then been set up by the British section of the RILU. Pollitt simply called for trade union unity around the natural central body of the TUC.

These ideas had too strong an impact for the TUC to ignore them entirely, however. Within a month of the Birmingham Conference, the TUC had called together the leaders of the largest Trades Councils, including Parsons of Birmingham, from which the idea of a Joint Consultative Council of equal numbers of NFTC and TUC delegates was thrashed out. With this the teeth of the National Federation of Trades Councils were drawn. Future meetings of the Joint Consultative Committee were to be strictly on TUC terms. The NFTC was dead.

Another matter to occupy much Trades Council time in 1922 was the Engineering Lock-Out. This arose from management determination to wrest back powers which the unions had acquired during the war and was waged around the question of the Management's Right to Manage. The villain of the affair was Sir Allan Smith, chair of the Engineering Employers' Federation and it was said that Birmingham Employers were less keen on a battle which started with the AEU but widened to a lock-out of all engineering workers. A previous survey by the EEF on restrictive practices had brought no expression of violent feeling that action should be taken on the issue, especially in areas such as Birmingham where restrictive practices were not widespread. The immediate issue became that of the employers' right to impose overtime and the AEU's insistence that the union be consulted. The lock-out began in March and continued until June. The April Trades Council meeting was devoted entirely to this dispute. Dempster, the AEU local organiser, said that 'management functions' was a camouflage for the real issue which was to drive the standard of living back to below the 1914 level and the employers had chosen a time when the union's funds were greatly depleted as a result of unemployment to attempt this. The standard of living of all workers was at stake. If the engineers went down the rest of the workers would soon follow.

The meeting then discussed a resolution in the name of the executive committee which had been passed by seven votes to five demanding that executive powers be vested in the TUC which should then call a general strike in defence of workers' living standards. H.G. Johnson, the president and member of the Railway Clerks Association said that he did not agree with the resolution and called on the vice-president, Bill Brain, to move it. Brain claimed that the employers had been preparing for this battle for eighteen months and a state of war existed between employers and workers. Councillor Frank Sharkey then seconded the motion. After this an amendment was tabled by A.P. Cassidy of the South Yardley branch of the AEU. This condemned the employers' 'brutal attack' on workers' conditions at a time of unexampled depression and unemployment; it criticised the government for not instituting an enquiry into the dispute under the Industrial Courts Act of 1919 and it called on all trade unionists to urge on their executives the need to empower the TUC 'to take the strongest possible action in order to bring the dispute to an end satisfactory to the workers.' Some in favour of the amendment argued that the resolution would be impossible to implement and others said they had no mandate from their members to vote for a general strike. But when the amendment was put it was defeated by 51 votes to 49. When the original motion was put the result was 51 for and 51 against. A recount ended 53 for and 53 against. The chairman gave his casting vote against the resolution.

Communist influence on the Trades Council was considerable at this time. There were three, Brain, Shepperson and Cardinal on the executive, but as there is, unfortunately, no record of attendance at Trades Council meetings we do not know how many delegates were Communists. In February Brain moved that Unemployed Committees be allowed to affiliate to the Trades Council free. This was seen by the anti-Communists as an attempt of the Communist Party to seek greater influence on the Trades Council. The executive therefore rejected the proposal (with three against) but the District Unemployment Committee was to be informed that the executive was always prepared to consider any representation they made on unemployed questions. At the full Trades Council Brain moved the reference back of this section. When Shepperson rose to support he was reminded by Cassidy that they were both members of the same AEU branch which had voted against affiliation of the Unemployed Committees. Shepperson retorted that this did not prevent him speaking in favour, although he would vote against. Johnson then made three points in favour of the executive decision. 1) that insofar as the unemployed were trade unionists they were already represented on the Trades Council, 2) that it was contrary to the constitution to allow non-unionists to be represented and 3) that if the motion were passed there was a grave danger of important unions seceding from the Council. Brain's proposal was negatived by 81 votes to 36.

That the last threat was no idle one is suggested by a protest from the Midlands District Council of the NUR in May complaining about 'disruptive tactics' on the Trades Council by delegates holding 'Communist views.' They also protested at recent attacks on the general-secretary of the NUR and other trade union leaders. If these tactics did not change they would advise all NUR branches to disaffiliate. The president of the Trades Council promised that 'serious attention would be given to the matter by the Executive'. The following year all three Communists failed to be elected to the executive and the sole Communist in 1923 was Jack Trotter.

Rudland's 1923 Trades Council report was much more low key than his previous ones. He began by referring to the general European situation five years after the war. He noted the sufferings of the Germans and called for the immediate withdrawal of British troops from Germany to set an example to France and Belgium, and asked for the support of German workers 'if only for the most selfish of reasons i.e. self preservation.' Rudland also welcomed the emergence of a strong, self-reliant Russia, 'in the face of internal and external war secretly promoted by the Allied Governments.'

Rudland's report went on to describe the many deputations to the city Council, Poor Law Guardians, Chamber of Commerce etc on wages, hours and conditions. Also meetings on Unemployment, the Rating System etc. and a conference addressed by William Gallacher on the Plight of the Germans. Financial assistance had been given to the Workers' International Relief Committee on behalf of Russian workers and £10 was raised by the sale of Russian peasant goods for the benefit of German workers. Councillor Frank Sharkey, for many years a Trades Council delegate was seriously ill and a subscription had raised £47 for him to get away and recover without anxiety.

Town Crier accounts supplement Rudland's report. In March the Trades Council had made some efforts to unify the various Unemployment Committees in the city. This was the time when the National Unemployed Workers' Committee Movement was well established. Rudland reported that the meeting had been a failure because other Committees would not accept the unification proposals put forward by the local Unemployed Workers' Committee because, they alleged, it was Communist dominated. Rudland's conclusion was that there was no hope of finding an agreed solution. Bill Brain denied that the UWM was the Communist Party in disguise and said that if Communists took a prominent part in the movement it was because they were more persistent in pressing the demands of the unemployed. Despite Rudland's pessimism, however, a couple of months later a Committee of the Employed and Unemployed was sponsored by the Trades Council.

Although Brain was no longer a member of the Trades Council executive, he continued an important member as a delegate of the Foundry Workers. His Communist views made it virtually impossible for him to obtain work. But in March 1923 he reported, in what was described as 'a humorous little speech,' his offer of a job on a scheme of the Board of Guardians which the Trades Council opposed because of the rates of pay. 'It is something of n international incident when I have work offered to me', Brain said, and this scheme was one whose sole purpose was to discover 'rogues, stiffs and vagabonds who were not genuinely seeking work.' The authorities knew he was a keen worker in the Unemployed Movement and they were 'trying to get him active in other spheres while they set about lowering the relief scales.' A.P. Cassidy urged that the Trades Council support Brain, or any other delegate who refused to accept the scheme.

The guest speaker at the March meeting was Dr Robert Dunstan describing his Land for the People scheme. Nationalisation of the land he rejected and said that this had been tried in Russia and failed; present policy there was along the lines that he was suggesting. This was that the whole of the land be taken into public control and rent paid for it by the occupiers. Land values should be collected annually and allocated to the local authorities according to need. This would abolish the existing grossly unfair rating system whereby slum dwellers in Birmingham paid £270 per acre in rates while the owners of unused land paid only 11/3d per acre. In answering questions Dunstan was careful to differentiate his scheme from that of the 'Single Taxers' or 'Taxation of Land Values.' These recognised the right of the present owners to the land and that Dunstan did not recognise. Nor did he suggest that the land was the only issue. Capital, industry and production would have to be controlled by the people. But the first step should be the control of the land. The effect of such a policy would be revolutionary in the sense that it would probably result in the reactionaries adopting violent methods to defeat the policy, but with the whole of the workers behind the policy such methods would be defeated by mass passive resistance in the form of a general strike. Dunstan was 'cordially received' and the policy he advocated was 'heartily supported' by the Trades Council.

1923 was the first year for which we have reliable unemployment figures for the city. 1922 had been the worst year at over 15 per cent unemployment nationally. In 1923 the Birmingham average figure of unemployment for the year was 54,543 equal to over 12 per cent of the working population.

In 1924 unemployment fell sharply to 33,525 which was still 7½ per cent of the employed population. Rudland's Trades Council report continued to stress the international situation. Wars to end Wars were snares and delusions as all history from the Spanish Armada to the Armageddon of 1914 showed. Whether victors or vanquished, all are involved in economic and industrial calamities. Each ruling class calls for lower wages and longer hours. 'The only way out of this was the establishment of one united Working Class International endowed with full powers to hold up all transport and supplies upon a declaration of war by any government, and the recognition of a uniform basis for wages and conditions in all countries,' Rudland declared.

Conciliation conferences regarding inter-union differences had occupied Trades Council time in 1924. A dispute between the Workers' Union and the Printing and Paperworkers had been solved amicably. Another between the Furnishing Trades and Vehicle Builders regarding recognition of FTA members employed in railway carriage shops had been referred to the national executives of the respective unions.

The first Labour budget, which had cut £30m taxes from the people's food, was welcomed. But minimum wage legislation was urged on the Labour government 'to stabilise wages at a reasonable level.'

An 'important meeting' on Housing had urged the City council to set up a direct building department.

'Valuable assistance' had been rendered to the Actors' Association in its efforts to organise a boycott against a visit of Sir John Martin Harvey's company to Birmingham in September, in view of the fact that Sir John was one of the founders of the Stage Guild formed by the employers to smash the Actors' Association and impose contracts of employment on artistes that would 'encourage the continuance of sweated conditions.' A 'pleasing sequal' to this had been a presentation to Arthur Bourchier on the occasion of his company's visit to the Theatre Royal of letters of appreciation for his valuable services to trade unionism and the Actors' Association presented by the Trade Council and the Labour Party.

When the Builders' dispute had begun in July the Guardians had ruled that all eligible for relief (e.g. dependents only) would be paid only by loan. This had been tried during the Engineering Lock-Out of 1922 and eventually reversed by pressure from the unions and the public. The same occurred this time. An emergency meeting of the Board of Guardians was called on the initiative of the Labour guardians which ultimately withdrew the 'obnoxious order.'

Some of the many other vital matters dealt with by the Trades Council were enumerated such as, Trade Boards, Factory Inspection, Teachers' Salaries, Rent Control, Working hours of Women and Young Persons, Strikers and the Right to Picket, Poor Law Disqualifications, the Unemployed and Task Work, ex-Police and Prison officers and much else.

The Trades Council annual report of 1924 devoted considerable space to developments arising from the Birmingham Conference two years previously which had set up the National Federation of Trades Councils. This concerned the conference between the TUC and the NFTC which the Birmingham Trades Council president, J.E. Corrin, had attended. This had set up a provisional committee of twelve representatives each from the TUC and the NFTC to constitute a link between the Trades Councils and the TUC. The secretaries of Trades Councils were to act as local Labour Correspondents to the TUC General Council and forward reports of local matters. Joint statements might also be issued and the Trades Councils would act as the circulating agency for special propaganda publications issued by the TUC. This 'tardy recognition' of the work of the Trades Councils was welcomed by Rudland, but he suggested that all national executives of unions should now see that all their branches were affiliated to the local Trades Council and arrangements made to see that fees were paid. In addition, if Trades Councils were to act as local agents of the TUC, there must be direct representation of the Trades Councils on the TUC general council. These direct representatives should be elected at regular area conferences, and thus the TUC would be in constant touch with all parts of the country.

Turning to accounts of trade union activity in 1924 as seen by the *Town Crier*, the big national dispute of the year was that of the Builders. It arose partly from an application for an increase in pay made possible by the fall in unemployment and partly by differences between building workers and employers in Liverpool. The position in Birmingham at the outset of the strike in July was outlined by the president of the Birmingham Building Trades' Operatives' Federation, Mr A. Lane, at a mass meeting in Southfield Market attended by 3,000 operatives. Lane said that the employers were claiming that large numbers of operatives were working under the old wages and conditions. This Lane denied. The great majority of men at work were working for the 172 employers who had signed a more favourable provisional agreement. Others were out solidly not only in Birmingham but throughout the county. If the employers therefore carried out their threat of a lock-out, they would find that there was no one in Birmingham to lock-out. The two sides were eventually brought together by the Minister of Labour and an agreement signed extending the date of the national stabilisation of wages. The dispute had lasted seven weeks.

A last item of interest in 1924 was that the Trades Council passed a tribute to Lenin on his death in January.

Unemployment fell slightly in Birmingham in 1925, the year's average being nearly 32,000 or 7 per cent of the employed population. It was particularly low in the first part of the year at 21,000 but rose sharply in the second half of the year to double at 42,000. This was the result, perhaps, of the return to the gold standard in May 1925 at the pre-war parity of $4.86 = £1; although 1926 was to see similar fluctuations of employment between the two halves of the year.

The 1925 annual report was its Sixtieth and Rudland devoted two pages to a history of the Birmingham Trades Council. Turning to the events of the year Rudland claimed that while the prospects of the people grew steadily worse during the year, the prospects of the class living on dividends grew considerably brighter with a tax remission of £36m. The principal matters of 'more than ordinary interest' were the following. The establishment of the Birmingham and District Council of Trade Unionists and Co-operators whose main work was to be to recognise the mutual interests of trade unionists and co-operators and to work out a joint programme of education and other matters. The looming General Strike was recognised. The 'exhilarating demonstration of solidarity' by the Miners and the TUC General Council was the subject of an 'inspiring debate' at the September meeting, together with the report of the Executive as to the arrangements made in the event of the mine-owners pressing to an issue their impossible demands for wage reductions. Trouble was avoided by the Government undertaking to subsidise the industry until the following May. The December Trades Council meeting had protested at the arrest of the Communist leaders as the Government prepared for the Strike and a fund for them had been started.

The TUC had called two Birmingham Area Conferences of Trades Councils. One had been a general meeting to discuss further measures of unity between the General Council and the Trades Councils; the other had been called to discuss the Blanesburgh Questionnaire on the Unemployment Insurance Act (the Blanesburgh Committee had put forward progressive proposals regarding the level of unemployment benefit – GB).

In July there had been 'an exceedingly useful and highly successful' Conference on Hours and Wages. This was 'an emphatic protest against any attempt by employers still further to depress the workers' standard of life, realising that the time was long overdue for a united stand for all-round improved conditions.' To give effect to this policy a Birmingham Trades' Union Council of Action had been set up whose first fruits had been an autumn Back to the Union Campaign. Some 20,000 leaflets had been distributed and meetings arranged, but 'uncongenial weather conditions' caused the campaign to be called off after three weeks and it was due to be reactivated the following summer.

The Trades Council year ran from March to the following February, but Fred Rudland's 1925 Report was dated April 1926. To it he added a Final Word as follows:

> At the time of going to press, the industrial outlook is threatening, and no one can say with any certainty what is likely to happen; but, so far as workers are concerned, a new spirit of determination to resist any further 'cuts' or increase of working hours is manifest, as also an exhibition of greater unity among all ranks than has previously been the case. Whether it be the miners, workers in the Engineering industry, or whatever section is attacked, it must be an 'all-in' struggle in order to stop the 'rot' and unitedly advance for all-round improved conditions. Your Executive is prepared to play its part on your behalf, acting under any instructions the TUC General Council may issue...'

The scene was set for the General Strike.

Trades Council Finance & Affiliations 1918-25

National trades union membership continued to rise after 1918, when it was 5 million, to 6.3 million in 1920. It then fell sharply to 4.9 million in 1920 and continued to decline more slowly to 4.1 million in 1925. With regard to Birmingham Trades Council its income was £771 in 1918 and this had fallen to £665 in 1920. The following year there was a large rise in income to £983, but it fell back to £679 in 1922 and remained within a few pounds of that figure until 1925. With regard to affiliated branches, the high income for 1921 was raised by 144 affiliated organisations and branches, which was slightly less than the 1918 figure. In the absence of any information regarding the size of trade union branches we can only judge the growth or decline of the Trades Council by this criterion of the number of affiliated societies paying their subscriptions. As given above, this suggests that the Trades Council did not share in the growth of trade unionism after the war, but from 1920 it did not suffer the heavy fall in membership that the national trade union movement suffered. We are here talking only of Trades Council membership, but it is likely that this also applied to general trade union membership in the city, in view of the fact that there were no basic industries in the city where falls in trade union membership were most precipitate.

With regard to the influence of individual trades and industries within the Trades Council, the 1925 figures show the railway unions contributing the largest amount to its £674 income at £126 of which the NUR gave £98. The second largest contributor was the building trades unions with £75. But both these contributions were smaller than they had been in 1920. Next came the Brass &Metal Mechanics with £60. Eight Post Office Workers' Union branches contributed £46 and the next largest contribution was by the engineering unions at £45. Printers and paper workers paid £39. None of the three major trade union amalgamations of the period dominated the Trades Council; the AEU contributed £29, the Transport and General Workers (mainly transport workers in Birmingham) paid £30, and the Municipal and General Workers (mainly gas workers) paid £20. The Workers' Union affiliated only seven branches and paid £18. This was no longer because of differences with the Trades Council, but because membership of the union was declining disastrously, although the Women's branch at Cadbury's survived. There are only two other mentions of women's branches – one was a Women's Section of the Municipal and General Workers' Union, and the other a Women's Section of the Gold Beaters.

Most of the Trades Council's income came from small unions, some of which can be mentioned here. The Council warmly supported the blind, whose numbers had been greatly increased by the war. The League of the Blind was always regarded as affiliated, although it did not pay subscriptions. There were three branches of the National Union of Clerks, but two were where one would expect them to be – at Cadbury's and in the Co-op and organisation of clerks remained difficult. The same can be said of shop workers. Of four affiliates of the National Union of Distributive Workers three were Co-op branches. Of the two affiliates of the Shop Assistants, Warehousemen and Clerks one was at Bournville, but a Central branch seems to have been quite large judging by its affiliation fee of £9. Three Life Assurance Unions contributed £13. Other unions were Bakers contributing £10, Brushmakers, ETU paying £5, Draughtsmen, Glass Bevellers, Gold & Silver Trade, Safe Makers, School Attendance Officers, Primary School Teachers, Tailors & Tailoresses, and Theatrical Employees.

Wages and the Standard of Living

Were the constant complaints of Birmingham workers affiliated to the Trades Council of the inadequacy of their wages justified? This is not the place to undertake a full survey of wages, but a start can be made by examining the minutes of the Salaries & Wages Committee of the Birmingham Corporation. These are particularly useful because most non-manual workers were paid according to scales determined by the City council, while the pay of the manual workers was largely determined either in direct negotiations with trade unions or by the acceptance of rates negotiated nationally or locally between unions and such employers' groups as engineers or builders. Hence what is true of manual Corporation wages applies in many cases to private industry.

After the war workers were looking for a considerable improvement over their pre-war conditions and their efforts can be followed through the Labour Committee minutes of Birmingham Corporation. Early in 1919 engineers and builders were granted the 47-hour week as negotiated by their unions. In May the question of an extra week's holiday was raised and in July manual workers in non-trading departments were granted 12 days per year, although holidays in other corporation departments were not standardised during the years up to 1925. In December the Corporation reviewed its de-casualisation policy in response to government pressure. Wage increases were granted through the year and the Gas Workers' Union was strong enough to raise the question of non-union labour; this matter was passed for discussion in other departments. Wage increases continued into 1920 and in October the West Midlands Joint Industrial Council negotiated a minimum wage of 61/6d. for Birmingham.

But everything changed in November 1920. The boom had broken, unemployment was mounting and prices falling. The Ministry of Labour Cost of Living Index which had been 203 in 1918 (1914 = 100) had risen in 1919 to 215 and soared to 240 in 1920. It then began to fall, and in 1921 was down to 226. In 1922 it plummeted to 183 and in 1923 it was 174 after which it showed a slight rise. In November 1920 a questionnaire went to all Corporation departments asking them to devise ways of reducing staff and from then on wage cuts were the order of the day. The first to bear the brunt seems to have been Lady Clerks and Typists whose wages were reduced as early as 1 July 1920 only those earning 25/-d. a week and less being spared. Those earning 28/-d. were cut to 26/11d, and those earning 35/-d. had a 12 per cent cut to 30/10d.

In April a questionnaire was sent to all departments requesting numbers of married women employees whose husbands were earning. Despite the fact that only nine such women could be found, all were sacked by the end of the month. Where workers were not on sliding scale agreements, these were forced on them in the stampede to reduce wages. Vehicle Builders set up a Joint Wages Board with employers and agreed an ½d. an hour decrease for every 10 point fall in the cost of living index with reviews every three months. By June 1921 male manual workers' wages had been reduced by 5/2d. per week and an enquiry was held as to whether it was right that women's wages should have fallen by that amount. The enquiry found that most female workers were cleaners and charladies earning 1/-½d per hour. So a sliding scale was devised for them which took their wages down by 8 per cent to 11½d. per hour. In October the engineers had their 12½ per cent bonus withdrawn in three monthly instalments. Between March and September 1922 non-manual council workers had salary deductions of over 19 per cent.

The effects of most of these cuts can be measured quite accurately. For non-manual Corporation workers salaries were cut between August 1921 and September 1922 by an average of 36 per cent for men and 47½ per cent for women. In the same period the cost of living fell by only 23 per cent.

With regard to engineering workers, wages paid by the Corporation averaged £2 in 1914; by November 1920 just before prices began to fall, the average wage was £4-10-0d. In other words throughout the most favourable period workers had known to press for wage increases – the war and the subsequent boom – wages had risen by 125 per cent, but the cost of living had risen by 149 per cent. By October 1922 in the depths of the slump engineers employed with the Corporation were receiving 56/-d. a week, an increase of 47 per cent over 1914, but the cost of living had risen by 83 per cent. By October 1922 Corporation engineering workers were getting 56/-d. an increase of 47 per cent compared with 1914 but the cost of living over that period had increased by 83 per cent. Tramwaymen's wage rates in 1914 were 43/6d. and in October 1922 64/6d, an increase of 48 per cent compared with the cost of living rise of 83 per cent And tramwaymen worked in an industry controlled by the government and subject to 'munitions' rates of pay. The unskilled benefitted most from the war, but these benefits must not be over-estimated. General labourers with the Corporation had a 109 per cent increase in their wage rates between 1914 when they were 26/6d, to 55/6d. in October 1922, compared with the 83 per cent rise in the cost of living over the same period. But the minimum wage in Birmingham fell from 71/-d. in October 1920 to 50/7d. in July 1924, a fall of 29 per cent compared with the fall in the cost of living over those years of 30 per cent So whatever advantages labourers had gained as a result of the war had been almost whittled away by 1924. Similar falls in wages greater than the decrease in the cost of living are recorded for building trade workers.

Prices continued to decline until 1923. In 1924 and 1925 prices rose, but these rises were miniscule and in 1926 prices fell again. Some cuts were restored during these years, but they also were miniscule and addressed mainly to rectifying anomalies that had occurred.

It is certain that workers in private industry in Birmingham fared even worse than Corporation workers, since with the Corporation we are dealing with a large and 'good' employer whereas the private sector contained many 'bad' employers. Trade union rates of pay were paid only by the largest private employers and the difference in wages in 1937 between employees in the motor industry working in factories employing over 10 workers and those factories employing under ten was more than 30 per cent – a reminder of how biased the official Ministry of Labour wage statistics are against workers. collected as they are predominantly from large factories.

Birmingham workers, therefore, had every justification for resisting wage cuts and believing that their standard of living was being deliberately lowered.

Bibliography: The Trade Union Movement in Birmingham 1919-1925

For an optimistic view of wages and hours see Eric Hopkins – 'Working Class Life in Birmingham Between the Wars', in *Midlands History* 1990. For hours and wages in the Birmingham engineering, building and printing trades see *British Labour Statistics, Historical Abstract 1886-1968* Tables 2, 3 and 4. For unemployment figures to 1923 national unemployment indices have been used as there is only occasional information from Birmingham Labour Exchanges. Since January 1923 local unemployment statistics have been published every month in the *Labour Gazette* and its successors. I have averaged two month's figures (one a winter month, January, the other a summer month, June) to give an annual figure of unemployment. To obtain percentages of unemployment I have taken from the 1921 Census the total occupied population figure. For the Birmingham Trades Council see their *Annual Reports* and reports of meetings in the *Town Crier*. For Birmingham Corporation wages and hours see *Salaries and Wages Committee* (often called the *Labour Committee*) *Minutes* and also *Council Minutes*. The standard trade union history for the period is Hugh Armstrong Clegg's – *A History of British Trade Unions Since 1889*, vol II, 1911-1933. The fullest study of a local trade union is Richard Hyman's *The Workers' Union*.

Chapter 21

The Labour Movement in the Black Country 1919-1925

Ex-Service Politics

We have seen (Chapter 17) how the Black Country was turned into a Labour stronghold after the 1918 general election with four Labour MPs and 40 per cent share of the vote, which was not equalled nationally until 1945. Labour MPs continued to be re-elected to these constituencies until the debacle year of 1931. In municipal politics, however, the Labour Party was at first less successful as Ex-Service organisations appeared and ex-service issues dominated the months after the war.

We have also seen (Chapter 18) the struggle for the minds of ex-service men and women between 'non-political' organisations tacitly accepting the existing capitalist system and led by generals, and a 'political' ex-service movement attached to either the Labour or the Communist Parties. The three organisations that first emerged – The National Association of Discharged Sailors and Soldiers, the National Federation of Discharged and Demobilised Sailors and Soldiers, and the Comrades of the Great War – were quickly brought into line with the assistance of the massive bribe of the Canteen Fund millions to form the 'non-political' British Legion in July 1921. The avowedly political National Union of Ex-Servicemen (NUX) either joined the newly established Communist Party in July 1920 (as did one of the Birmingham NUX branches) or co-operated with the local Labour Party. NUX disappeared in the next two or three years as the general question of unemployment overwhelmed questions of jobs and pensions for ex-servicemen.

Both the Federation and the Association established themselves throughout the Black Country. For instance, by April 1919 the NFDDSS was well established in Tipton and was starting a branch in Sedgley. In the summer of 1919 there were considerable riots in many towns, including Wolverhampton and Bilston. It is not easy to determine the real cause of these, but they involved ex-servicemen and their organisations and were undoubtedly connected with the grievances of ex-servicemen concerning jobs and their general treatment.

For instance, in June 1919 the *Wolverhampton Chronicle* reported an 'amazing riot' in Wolverhampton. It began at 10-50 pm on a Saturday night when P.C. Kyte saw four men on the footpath near the Grand Theatre arguing. He asked them to move on. But one of the men 'behaved offensively' and Kyte arrested him, whereupon the other three men 'set on' Kyte. The arrested man escaped but fell down in Lichfield Street and was recaptured. Meanwhile a hostile crowd of 3,000 to 4,000 gathered and demanded the release of the prisoner. The Chief Constable (Webster) then went to Queen's Square to ask the crowd to be reasonable. The man arrested was John Henry Mountford, aged 23. He was charged with being drunk and disorderly and assaulting the police. Mountford was a discharged soldier and it so happened that a Mr Shorthouse, who was the chairman of the Bilston branch of the NFDDSS, saw the incident and he stopped to investigate. While he was speaking from the Police Station steps, however, the cry went up that he was a detective and he was 'fired at' with a brick. Another member of the Federation with him lost his coat and hat and false teeth and fell and was trampled on. The trouble was assuming 'alarming proportions' and a fire hose was turned on the 'mob'. This served 'a useful, but not the desired effect and the air was full of flying bricks and stones.' Windows were smashed in the Town Hall. 'Finally the police collected in full force, charged with truncheons and the streets were cleared by 1-30 am. Sunday.' Mountford was not a member of the NFDDSS, but another man arrested during the riot was suffering from TB contracted during the war, and he was a member.

The same afternoon the Wolverhampton NFDDSS held a crowded meeting at the Labour Assembly Rooms and Mountford was made an 'honorary member'. W. Smith, the Wolverhampton president. said he regretted that the chairman of the Bilston branch had been knocked about. it was not Federation members who were to blame, but an 'unruly mob who got in town.' Mr Tope, another Federation official, said that the NFDDSS was always on the side of law and order. A resolution was carried to obtain legal assistance for Mountford.

When the case came to court Mountford said that he had had several glasses of beer at the Swan and another five at the George. He usually had five or six glasses a day and he could take 10 or 20 (laughter). He was not drunk at the time. He had not been in Lichfield Street for ten seconds when Kyte appeared. There was no shouting or loud talk. Two witnesses gave evidence of Mountford's sobriety. Francis James MM told of a previous incident in Dudley Street when Kyte ordered him to move on and he had reported this to an Inspector. James said that he and Mountford had a few drinks, but they were both sober. Kyte telling them to move on was the cause of the trouble, James claimed. Mountford moved away, but he, (James) paused and Kyte pushed him into an entry. Kyte struck at James and missed and James said that if that was his game... and struck and hit Kyte. Others gave evidence that Mountford was sober and that James struck Kyte. After 2½ hours the magistrates said there was no doubt in their minds that Mountford was drunk and disorderly. They regretted having to deal with a soldier and fined him 10/-d.

The next month a riot occurred in Bilston. On a Monday between 11pm and 2am a mob of 'some thousands' surrounded the Police Station and wrecked it. The trouble began, it was alleged, when two or three men the worse for drink assaulted two police constables near the Market Hall. Two soldiers home on leave then began to assault the police and a large crowd gathered. They demanded that the two constables (Turner and Pardoe) be turned out of the Police Station. William Baker (20), Samuel Dando (20) and Lilian Randall (18) were charged with assaulting the police, rioting and doing malicious damage mounting to £113. They were fined 30/-d. each and costs. Dando said that he was going to China the following week and they would have to run for their money. It seems clear that these light sentences reflected an uneasy civil situation, particularly with regard to demobilised servicemen, which the authorities were anxious not to inflame. The widespread military mutinies of January and February 1919 had not been forgotten and these ex-servicemen were probably among those who had been hurriedly demobilised as a result of these events.

In Dudley the DDSS Federation was active, claiming 2,500 members in August 1919. It held a Conference in December to discuss ex-servicemen's grievances. In Walsall not only was the Federation active, but also the militant National Union of Ex-Servicemen (NUX). Both the Federation and NUX clashed with regard to affiliation to Walsall Trades Council.

At the November 1919 municipal elections in Wolverhampton the DDSS Federation stood three candidates. James Whittaker, the Labour agent anxious about a split vote, reported to the Labour Party EC in September that the Federation intended to stand, but he could get no further information. The Labour Party seems to have negotiated with the Federation for the outcome was that two of their candidates did not face Labour opposition and they won seats in St. Mary's and St. James' wards. In Blakenhall, agreement could not be reached it seems and the NFDDSS candidate faced both a Labour and an Independent rival. He was roundly beaten by Dideridge the Labour man, and Mitchell claimed he had been beaten by the 'pacifists' at the Sunbeam factory.

The only other town in the Black Country where a NFDDSS candidate stood was in Lyndon ward, West Bromwich. Here there was no agreement with the local Labour Party, and the Federation and Labour men polled identical votes of 312; but the seat was won by an Independent with 502 votes. No organised ex-servicemen stood in the 1921 municipal elections in the larger Black Country towns nor in subsequent years.

But ex-service politics continued into 1921. In 1921 NUX suggested to the Labour Party support for a Conference demanding the immediate release of 'men serving terms of imprisonment for the violation of military law.' Many of these would be conscientious objectors who had opposed the war. The Labour Party agreed to share the expenses of the Conference.

In May 1920 at the national conference in London of the NFDDSS the delegates from Tipton, T.F. Lister and Councillor Douglas Pielou were prominent. It was this conference that took the decision to merge the three organisations into the British Legion. In September a new annexe to the Dudley Ex-Servicemen's Club at Wadhams Pool was handed over to the NFDDSS by the Patriotic Committee which, during the war, had provided 20,000 food parcels to prisoners of war and 200 gold watches to men who had been decorated. In the same month the Sedgley Federation branch had held its second annual parade. A 'good number' of Tipton and Dudley ex-servicemen had also attended the midlands divisional conference of the NFDDSS. Here the result of the political ballot was announced. An overwhelming majority demanded that the organisation be affiliated to no political party. They would not assist the police to recruit special constables, but mount their own pickets if ex-service interests were threatened. In November Dudley NFDDSS was protesting at postmen working overtime when some ex-servicemen were unemployed.

Politics were hard to avoid, however. In Walsall in September the NFDDSS joined with the Trades Council in requesting that the mayor call a town's meeting to discuss unemployment among ex-servicemen. In January it had been claimed that unemployment in Walsall was lower than anywhere else in the country.

NUX continued to exist in Wolverhampton. In December 1920 it wrote to the local Labour Party suggesting a special form of membership for its individual members. The matter was referred to the wards, but later NUX was told that the time was 'not ripe' for such a change.

The issues of ex-servicemen remained as urgent as ever, particularly with regard to jobs, pensions and homes. But by now the general issue of unemployment loomed so large that ex-service matters were shuffled off to the relatively well financed but politically neutered British Legion and direct ex-service political influence disappeared.

Hands off Russia

Intervention against the new Socialist government in Russia began early in 1918. In March, British troops were landed at Murmansk and the next month British and Japanese forces occupied Vladivostok. At first it could be held that these forces were to resist the Germans, but after May, when further large contingents of soldiers were landed at Murmansk, hostility to the new regime became open and aid to the White generals opposing the Bolsheviks increased.

It was the fear of servicemen at the end of the war that they would not be demobilised but sent to Russia that was behind the mutinies of February and March 1919 from which rapid demobilisation followed and thus made impossible full-scale war against Russia at that time.

But hostility to Socialism was inflamed by the capitalist press and no horror story of Bolshevik atrocity was too fanciful to circulate and be believed. This extended to the local press and the *Wolverhampton Chronicle* regularly printed such stories as Bolshevik slaughter of hundreds of boys, or the harrowing tale of Miss Lilian Picken of Codsall who had 'escaped' from the Bolsheviks. These were mixed with the confident predictions of superannuated generals that Bolshevik power could not be maintained.

With the defeats of the successive white counter-revolutionary generals attempting to overthrow the Bolsheviks, the prospects for British intervention seemed to be receding, although a number of Hands off Russia committees were formed at the end of 1919. But in April 1920, the well-armed Poles opened an offensive against Soviet Russia and occupied Kiev. Once again it seemed that Soviet regime could be overthrown by supporting the Poles.

Black Country resistance seems to have started in May 1919 when the Wolverhampton Labour

Party received a letter from Newcastle Labour Party asking their support for a special Labour Party conference to demand the withdrawal of British troops from Russia and the ending of the blockade. The reply was that although the Wolverhampton Labour Party had every sympathy with the proposal, such a conference would be too expensive in view of the coming annual conference. But a Wolverhampton Hands off Russia Committee was in existence before the end of the year, probably initiated by the Independent Labour Party, and the Labour Party agreed to elect six members to the Committee. In March the Wolverhampton Hands off Russia Committee held a public meeting with Colonel Malone (who had been elected to Parliament at the 1918 election as a Coalition Liberal, but had immediately gone to Russia and returned so enthusiastic that he joined the British Socialist Party and thus became a foundation member of the Communist Party and the Communist Party's first MP.). Protests at British intervention were made to the government and the Polish legation.

In May 1920 one of the significant episodes of the campaign occurred when London dockers refused to load the *Jolly George* with weapons for Poland. The Wolverhampton Trades Council sent its congratulations to the dockers.

At a Sedgley meeting, H.B. Lees-Smith, the prospective Labour candidate for Bilston demanded an end to attacks on Russia. If the Russians were left to themselves, the harsher aspects of the regime would disappear. The war in Russia was against the British working class, he maintained, and the Russian experiment must not be blotted out with blood and force.

By August 1920 the position was so serious that the Wolverhampton Labour Party and Trades Council joined together to form a Council of Action. This was in response to the national situation. On August 9th the Trades Union Congress and the Labour Party had met and unanimously passed a resolution stating that it felt certain a war was being engineered between the Allied Powers and Soviet Russia on the issue of Poland; that such a war would be an intolerable crime against humanity; that the government should be forewarned that if such a war occurred a conference would be convened to declare a general strike; and a Council of Action be immediately constituted to carry the decision into effect.

In Walsall the Trades Council passed a resolution in August 1920 stating that they would not be a party to a war on Russia. If such a war were declared they would carry on propaganda against such 'forced service' among the armed forces, delay the making of munitions, hold up all transport by land, sea and air, and advocate a 'down tools' among workers.

Such threats of direct action were sufficient to deter the government from intervention and the Poles, who by then had been chased from Kiev and were besieged outside Warsaw, were told that Soviet proposals for the settlement of borders were fair and should be accepted.

Another attempt to invade Russia had been thwarted, but the danger of intervention was by no means at an end. Hands off Russia Committees continued to exist. In October 1920 A.G. Walkden, the prospective Labour candidate for Wolverhampton West, told a meeting that the government had spent money on a 'wicked and foolish enterprise' and the money spent on war against Russia could have built 100,000 houses.

In January 1921 the Wolverhampton Hands off Russia Committee was asking the Labour Party for support for a lecture by Mrs Newbold. This was referred to the Women's Group. In 1921 the great famine occurred in Russia and Labour activists turned to organising relief. Emma Sproson arranged for a collection to be taken at the May Day demonstrations of 1922.

British government hostility to the Soviet government did not abate. When the wars of intervention finally ended and the Soviet government was firmly established, recognition was refused, trade boycotted and diplomatic means used to weaken the regime. In May 1923 C. Hindle moved a motion at Walsall Trades Council:

> That owing to the unwarranted interference in the internal affairs of the Workers' Council government of Russia in dispatching a Note containing an ultimatum couched in language calculated to elicit a strongly worded reply, with the possible breaking off of diplomatic relations leading to war, this Council organises an All-in Conference of workers with the object of forming a Council of Action in conjunction with other towns to be prepared to prevent a rupture between the two countries and realise the slogan – Not a Man; Not a Ship: Not a Gun.

After some discussion it was agreed to leave the matter with the secretary to draft a resolution embodying the sentiments of the resolution and, with the chairman, to call a meeting should it be deemed desirable.

It was not until the 1924 Labour government that Soviet Russia was recognised and trade encouraged. But with the return of a capitalist government the following year, the powerful Peace Movement that developed had always the possibility of intervention in Russia as a prime concern.

Unemployment

Problems of demobilisation and absorption of the workforce into peacetime industry can be illustrated by the Walsall experience. In January 1919 there were more than 2,000 unemployed. The bulk of these were said to be ex-munitions workers who lived in Walsall but had worked in factories now closed, outside the town . By September 1920 there were 1,218 workless of whom 500 were ex-servicemen. Despite this fall, the position was warranted serious enough to hold a town conference on unemployment.

In Wolverhampton unemployment was 1,543 in October 1919 and by mid-June 1920 it was up to 2,349. Despite this level of unemployment these were years when workers were determined never to return to pre-war standards of living. Conditions conspired to allow higher wages and shorter hours to be wrested from employers; but unfortunately, prices rose faster than wages and only limited gains in living standards occurred. At the end of 1920 an economic hurricane struck, mass unemployment returned, wages were reduced, and the dream of a land fit for heroes was blown away for ever.

By May 1921 unemployment in Wolverhampton had risen to 12,828 (8,835 men, 643 boys, 2925 women, 428 girls) and those on short-time numbered 17,629). This meant nearly 28 per cent of the labour force out of work and another 38 per cent with less than a full week's work. If one adds those on low wages this amounts to as horrific a degree of poverty as Wolverhampton ever experienced. Figures in other Black Country towns were almost as bad. In Walsall in mid-April 1921, 11,630 persons were unemployed (27 per cent of the work force).

Mid 1921 proved the worst period and in December 1921 Wolverhampton unemployment was 11,052 (25 per cent of the work force), as unemployment continued at a desperately high level. At the end of 1922 Dudley unemployment was 22 per cent, West Bromwich 13 per cent, and Smethwick 19 per cent. When regular series of unemployment figures become available in 1923 the January Wolverhampton unemployment percentage was 17 per cent and Walsall 14 per cent. In 1924 the percentage was much the same, although in some towns i.e. West Bromwich and Cradley Heath unemployment was down. In January 1925 Wolverhampton unemployment fell briefly to 10 per cent, but by June it was back to 15 per cent.

A summary of unemployment regulations and scales of benefit must preface any discussion on the reaction of workers to this unprecedented level of unemployment. The fairly generous post-war unemployment benefit scales were designed both to cushion ex-service unemployment and also to keep revolution at bay. These were 29/-d. for a man and 24/-d. for a woman with additional child allowances. These scales expired for civilians in November 1919 and for ex-service men and women in March 1921. In November 1920 civilian scales were 15/-d. for an adult man and 12/-d. for an adult woman with no additional benefits for a wife and children. Such scales could not provide even a subsistence standard of living for a married man with a family. Other sources of income were charity funds, work provided by the local Council, and out-relief granted by the Boards of Guardians in return for task work.

Immediately after the war local Councils were coerced by the unemployed either to set up Unemployment Committees or to re-activate the pre-war Distress Committees. At the Walsall Conference on Unemployment in October 1920 mentioned above, Councillor Talbot said unemployment could not be prevented but remedies must be devised. The Conference ended with a resolution to 'put into operation schemes already prepared,' whatever that meant.

But serious protest was contained until 1921. By that time, work schemes had been organised in Walsall and in January 1921 Hucker, the Labour councillor, moved that the unemployed be paid £2 per week with 6/-d. for each dependent. The Borough Surveyor said that ex-service men would get

44/-d. for a full week's work, and 34/-d. for three days work at 1/-d. per hour plus their unemployment pay of 10/-d.

In Wolverhampton the same week Councillor Dideridge moved an early meeting of the Distress Committee with a view to claiming money from the National Relief Fund (the long-standing Prince of Wales Relief Fund.)

By this time the unemployed had organised themselves. In April a large meeting on the Market Patch at Wolverhampton decided to send a delegation to the town council. An angry crowd was only reluctantly persuaded to disperse until after the deputation had been met. Emma Sproson, a member of the Unemployment Committee, said that if people were forced into the Work House it would cost £7 for a man, his wife and three children. The main demand of the unemployed was for a standard, subsistence rate of pay for work done, said Morey, one of the leaders. The deputy mayor (T.A. Henn) said it was wise for the unemployed to talk things over with the council and he accepted that the council and the Guardians should work together. At this council meeting the mayor moved that the area between the borough hospital and Rough Hills, which was owned by the council, should be levelled at a cost of £2,000. But schemes like this required money and permission from the government and Councillor Williams said that 50 per cent of these schemes were turned down.

At this time, the two Birmingham Communist leaders, James Stewart and Bill Brain, were active in organising the Wolverhampton unemployed. Stewart appeared before magistrates in April charged under the Emergency Powers Act of 1921 with 'using words likely to cause disaffection among the civilian population.' Stewart was prosecuted by the Town Clerk. Supt. Haynes, giving evidence stated that Stewart was introduced by Hill (the secretary of the Labour Party – GB). Stewart said he had been locked up before and expected to be locked up again. Pointing to a scar, he said he got that from a policeman. Appealing to ex-servicemen he asked where was the place fit for heroes to live? Men sticking it on £1 a week and almost starving. Then he made a 'venomous attack' on the police according to Haynes. They had no brains, only sawdust, but they must be watched. They carried something in their tail pocket and would use it. If they wanted promotion they should go to the Houses of Parliament where they would find 1,000 thieves to arrest. Referring to a man 'executed' in Ireland Stewart said he had promised James Connolly that he would carry on the fight 'until all kings are buried, all governments smashed, and the boss class trodden down.' The stipendiary said Stewart did not know the effects of his words on men more ignorant than himself. He was given one month's hard labour. The same week a special meeting of Wolverhampton council proposed relief schemes costing £81,000.

Walsall also was holding unemployed demonstrations. In January 1921 there was a large meeting at Town End Bank with a march to the town hall. J.J. Millington, a newly appointed member of Walsall War Pensions Committee raised the case of ex-servicemen who, if they obtained employment on demobilisation and then became unemployed received only £1 a week, whereas a demobilised soldier who did not get work received 29/-d. He, Millington, was in that position and he had £1 a week to maintain his family of six children. At the end of January unemployment figures in Walsall were 4,760. Of these 166 were disabled soldiers and 1309 women. There was a very large proportion of girls (548) to boys (197) out of work. It was estimated that an additional 1,500 were on short time.

Walsall had the additional problem of large numbers of miners who were on strike from the end of March 1921. By mid-April there were reports of the Walsall Guardians turning away starving miners and a motion being passed to give miners temporary relief. By then unemployment was up to 11,630. In the fifth week of the stoppage 4,000 miners were besieging Bentley Common, and Pelsall and Cannock miners were said to be resolute to stay out. The strike ended in June after 89 days. In September the workless were said to be faced with starvation and 2,000 unemployed marched on the Workhouse demanding monetary relief from the Guardians. Work schemes of £40,000 were approved by the town council. In October several hundred unemployed from Darlaston marched on the Walsall Workhouse demanding Wednesbury scales. These were higher than Walsall's, giving £1 cash and 9/-d.in groceries, whereas Walsall gave only 13/-d. and this in the form of a loan.

Unemployment dominated the May Day demonstrations in the Black Country. In Wolverhampton a unanimous resolution was passed demanding work or maintenance for all persons willing to work and declaring that unemployment was a national and not a local responsibility. In Willenhall there was an exchange of speakers with Wolverhampton at the Spring Bank football ground demonstration. In Dudley the Trades Council organised a service at the parish church and marched there from the Market Place demonstration. The vicar, A.H. Phelips declared that life was unlovely, insecure and in many respects intolerable. If these conditions were a product of the system of the last 300 years, the sooner it was modified the better. At Wednesbury Alfred Short, the local MP, and a Wesleyan minister spoke at a Labour meeting at the Town Hall. In Cradley Heath there was a special united service at St. Luke's church with non-conformist and church ministers addressed by the Dean of Worcester. The Dean said that Labour discontents included a sense of unfairness and injustice, with industry organised for profit rather than human welfare. Dr Ede said that wage earners must have a share in the organisation of industry. In Walsall at a large meeting at the Arboretum A. Hollender moved the resolution on unemployment and said they must smash the octopus that held the workers in its grip.

By August there was fresh cause for concern. The government decreed that those who had exhausted their period of unemployment benefit must wait until November before a second period could begin. This forced the unemployed back to the Guardians for relief. In September 1921 the Poplar Guardians, in London, refused to lower their scales of relief and went to prison flying the Red Flag. This was approved by Wolverhampton Trades Council and many others and stimulated action elsewhere.

A deputation from Wolverhampton went to the Minister of Health. Sir David Shackleton said that the government had greatly overspent on the national insurance fund and it was the duty of the local Guardians to relieve distress. Wolverhampton Trades Council then organised a deputation to the Guardians to discuss scales of relief, particularly for children, and relief for unmarried male applicants. Later in August a joint deputation of the Trades Council and the local Unemployed Committee met the Mayor to thoroughly discuss the existing distress. A.J. Weaver stressed the need for immediate assistance to children, especially with regard to boots and clothing. At present there were two hundred applications for boots to the fund administered by the Chief Constable. At this point the Chief Constable and the Director of Education (Warren) were called in. Warren said that there were about four hundred cases worthy of support for boots or clothing. The Chief Constable's report showed hundreds of families unable to provide boots and clothing. The British Legion had spent £100 on destitute ex-servicemen in the past three weeks and their funds were exhausted. The decisions of the meeting were that children should be concentrated on, Sunday concerts organised to raise funds, collections at Wolves matches be organised and an immediate appeal made to the National Kitchen Fund for boots and clothing.

Further light on the complexities of the national scheme was given to Wolverhampton in a letter from the Minister of Labour in August 1921. The previous November, he explained, a further 8 million workers had been brought into the national insurance scheme bringing the total to 12 million. The newly insured could obviously not meet the normal conditions for benefit so the act had provided for eight weeks benefit when four contributions had been made. Then in March 1921 it was enacted that persons in insurable employment for twenty weeks from the end of 1919 would be eligible for 16 weeks benefit from March to November 1921 and a further 16 weeks from November to July 1922. In July 1921 (under pressure from the unemployed, which the letter did not mention – GB) the periods of benefit in both these years were raised from 16 to 22 weeks. The Ministry of Health was now prepared to sanction loan expenditure for local Guardians and it was hoped that this would be sufficient to tide over these 'abnormal conditions.'

The Wolverhampton Trades Council and the Unemployed Committee at once sought a meeting with the local Guardians and suggested a scale of 36/-d. a week for a man and wife with 4/-d. for each child. The Guardians then sent a telegram to the Minister of Health saying that new relief scales were under consideration, a loan or overdraft was immediately required and guidance was requested. A reply the next morning stated that an overdraft would be considered if the amount were stated and the accounts submitted. Scales, it was stressed, should be sufficient to relieve distress, but not more than that of an independent worker maintaining himself. When the Wolverhampton Guardians reconvened Harrison said that the existing scales were 15/-d. for a man and wife with 3/-d. for each child. By the end of September they would owe about £10,000. S.R. Rhodes then moved that present scales be not departed from; their sympathies were with the poor, but the demands on tradesmen, struggling professional men and citizens would lead to bankruptcies if the scales were increased. Mrs Berrington remarked tartly on the amounts spent on picnics, charabancs and in public houses by working people. Morey and Mrs Dideridge, two Labour Guardians, demanded that the points raised by the Trades Council deputation should be considered. This was lost by 12 votes to 9. Councillor Williams dissociated himself from the hot heads, but moved application to the Ministry for a loan and scales of 30/-d. for a man and wife, 7/6d. for the first child, 6/-d. for the second and 4/6d. for any other. Rent and coal allowance to be made where necessary with a total limit of 65/-d. W.L. Pritchard opposed this saying that many people were in a worse position than those being legislated for. J.J. Darmody, the progressive Roman Catholic guardian, said he would not like his children brought up on the present scale, but he thought the new proposals too much. Rhodes then asked for his proposal to be amended to 1/-d. extra for children. This was passed when Williams' proposal was lost 16-5. Pritchard then moved that the additional 1/-d. be paid in kind and this was passed!

The Walsall Guardians were also meeting at this time to review their scales. The chairman, E.H. Barnett, said that while they were obliged to relieve those in distress, they were not called upon to provide money for the public houses, bookmakers, nor picture houses. These remarks brought protests from several Guardiands. At this point there was a telephone call from the Ministry of Health stating that they were not prepared to depart from the Relief Registration order of 1911. Relief on the scale proposed by Walsall would place the recipient in as good a position as an independent worker. The Minister considered that most relief should be on loan or in kind. The Guardians then had a lengthy discussion on relief work and everything was eventually referred to the finance committee. These decisions enraged a large crowd which had been waiting outside the Workhouse. Some said that while the Guardians were considering, men were starving. A considerable number in the crowd wanted a mass entry into the Workhouse. T. Bergin, the chair of the Unemployed Committee appealed to the men to wait until the next week when the whole position would be put to them.

The next week several thousand Walsall unemployed marched from Town's End Bank to the Council House. Tim Burgin and Harry Walker, local leaders of the Unemployed Workers' Committee, led a deputation to the town council. Burgin said, 'Charity we despise and it is work we require.' The mayor said that a special meeting was being called that week and the General Purposes Committee had been instructed to find what work schemes it could.

In Dudley at the end of September extra relief was suspended because of the refusal of the Minister to sanction a £6,000 loan to finance new scales.

In October work for the unemployed in Walsall was authorised for roads and application made to the Minister for work costing £37,000. In Wolverhampton the council's Unemployment Committee carried out work costing £34,800.

In December unemployed workers on relief works at Friar's Park Sewerage works, on the border of West Bromwich and Wednesbury, came out on strike because the authorities concerned would not pay the men 1/5d. an hour. A deputation went to Holborn House to interview the Guardians and requested the wage increase, also compassionate leave for Christmas, and extra coal, clothing and blanket allowances. The chairman said they would not alter the relief scales, nor give extra at Christmas, but they would make provision for blankets etc.

1921 was the worst year for unemployment until the 1930s, but very heavy unemployment continued thereafter until the comparatively good year of 1925, after which unemployment rose again.

For comparison purposes it can be said that in September 1921 the Minister sanctioned for Birmingham relief scales of 29/-d. for a man and wife, with 3/-d. for each child, to a maximum of 50/-d. 1921 was also the first year that the cost of living fell, but in the middle of the year it was still $2\frac{1}{4}$ times that of 1914. This meant that the 23/-d. a week minimum wage for unskilled workers negotiated during the Great Unrest in 1913 would in 1921 have to be 51/9d to provide the same standard of living. Lastly, Poor Rate expenditure in Wolverhampton rose from £53,394 to £90,973, a rate in the £ rise from 2/6¾ to 3/10d.

High unemployment and social tension continued into 1922. In Wolverhampton a Council debate took place in February around a resolution from the Mayor requesting that the government provide the funds for further schemes of work. Two Labour councillors, Dideridge and Davies went further by demanding from the Government either work or maintenance. The council was only providing work for 40 men out of 8,000 requesting it. Williams, a Labour Guardian, said the Guardians, while paying out £1,200 a week to the unemployed (which would rise to £2,500 if the Unemployment Donation ceased), were also providing £644 a week for relief of the destitute, aged and infirm, while the numbers on medical relief had risen from 368 in April 1920 to 1,026 in February 1922. The Mayor's motion was passed unanimously.

In April Poor Law estimates for the half year to September were reduced. At this time, Out-Relief was at £650 a week and relief to the unemployed at £50,000 for the half year. Also in April the Guardians cut 5/-d. a week from their relief claiming that this was a winter allowance for coal. A motion in May to rescind this decision and pay a 2/6d. coal allowance in the summer was defeated by 14 votes to 15.

The Wolverhampton Unemployment Committee continued to hold large meetings at the Market Place. In November as a general election loomed a crowd of 2,000 listened to the views of the contestants. Sir Robert Bird the Tory MP spoke for an hour despite interruptions. Walkden, the Labour candidate, said that the Tories were war-mongers and he would put this money to use for the unemployed and also support a Capital Levy. G.R. Thorne the Liberal MP 'was given a great reception from part of the crowd.' He said that Free Trade was essential for recovery and talk of Bolshevism in Britain was nonsense.

Unemployment in Wolverhampton which had been 10,000 in March 1922 was still over that figure at the end of the year.

In Walsall and district Unemployment Committees also operated. In February a meeting of Ex-Servicemen in Darlaston were addressed by the prospective Unionist candidate on Unemployment. William Brain 'of the Birmingham Communists' also addressed the meeting. Later in February the Darlaston Unemployed Committee held its own meeting at the Picturedrome. Joseph Butler, the assistant secretary, said they were not Bolsheviks; due to the objections of the Darlaston UDC permits for the unemployed to collect in the town on Saturdays and Sundays were being withheld by the Chief Constable of Staffordshire. Rose, the chair of Darlaston UDC, later claimed that he was not opposed to collections by the unemployed and said unemployment in Darlaston was probably worse than almost any other town. E. Dennison, the prospective Parliamentary candidate for Walsall at a meeting in March also felt it necessary to disclaim that he was a Bolshevik and he said that we were paying in unemployment for the bad Peace Treaty.

There was never any shortage of people to attack the amounts received by the unemployed. In August 1922 a Walsall unemployed man was summonsed for non payment of industrial school arrears. He claimed that he could not pay because he was unemployed. He had a wife and nine children and received £2 a week in benefit and relief. The presiding magistrate on hearing this said that very few men would ever work again if they thought they could receive that amount. The defendant replied that he would start work tomorrow, if he could get it. He agreed to pay 2/-d. a week off the arrears.

Wages of those in work were also closely scrutinised. Stokers at the Walsall Workhouse were receiving £3-7-5d for a seven day week on alternate day and night shifts. It was claimed that men would do the same work for £2! No doubt they would at existing rates of unemployment. McShane objected to any reduction, but eventually moved a reduction to £3-5-0d. This was defeated and the wage reduced to £3. The effects of unemployment were shown in June 1922 when for four posts at the Walsall Workhouse, 342 applications were received.

In June 1922 the Communist leadership of the Unemployed Workers led to them being banned from the Walsall Labour Club on the grounds that 'they had fallen into the hands of Communist extremists.' Not only the Club, but also the police were keeping an eye on the Unemployed Committee meetings, it was said. The matter was taken to the Trades Council. Here, A.J. Stanley, the secretary of the Labour Club said that it was clear that the Unemployed Committee 'had fallen into the hands of people hostile to the real aims of the Labour movement.' Alec Fox, the chair of the Labour Club said the club could lose its licence if rules were not complied with. Lawless, a delegate of the Unemployed Committee, said the unemployed were not jeopardising the club, the club committee were doing that and he emphasised that the Unemployed Committee was non-political. When C. Kitson, president of the Unemployed Workers tried to speak, Baldwyn, the Labour agent, said that the decision was irrevocable and there was no point in the Trades Council discussing it. The chair ruled that the discussion must cease amid protests from Kitson and others.

In September a meeting of the Walsall Chamber of Commerce met a deputation consisting of W. Millerchip, the superintendent of the local Labour Exchange and J. Whiston and H.D. Henshall of the Unemployment Committee to discuss the problem of unemployed youth. Millerchip said that 1,400 boys and girls between the ages of 14 and 18 were registered as unemployed and there was a problem in creating interest among these young people. Whiston said that he thought there were 2,000 in all roaming the streets. A draft scheme of education and tuition had been prepared and submitted to the Walsall Education Committee. A final resolution was passed expressing sympathy with the objective and undertaking to render assistance.

In contrast to Walsall, the Unemployed Committee in Smethwick always enjoyed close relations with the Trades Council. In April 1922 the chair of the Birmingham Board of Guardians was defeated by an Electrical Trades Union representative, who signed the Unemployed Workers' Committee manifesto on adequate scales of relief. The centre of activity for Smethwick Unemployed Workers was St. Stephen's church where Rev F.K. Roberts was the Socialist vicar, but by 1922 there were several Unemployed Workers' Committees where weekly meetings were held in such places as Holy Trinity Church, St. Chad's and the Central Schools. The activities of the Smethwick Unemployment Committees and all other Labour affairs were reported by W.A. Exton from 1919 until the end of our period and beyond in the Birmingham *Town Crier*.

1923 brought little respite from depression. In February a batch of rate defaulters was summonsed at Wolverhampton. 90 per cent of them pleaded unemployment as the cause. The magistrates F.H. Parkyn and F.J. Gibson were said to have taken 'a humane view and either adjourned the cases or made small orders against the offenders.' The local Labour agent, Davies, appeared for several of the defaulters. Typical cases were a man with a wife and three children with another on the way out of work for 17 months and two brothers unemployed for 2 years 4 months and 18 months respectively. By the end of February unemployment in Wolverhampton had dipped just below ten thousand to 9,404.

The cost of living fell to its lowest level and in July 1923 was 174, still 74 per cent above the pre-war level. Wolverhampton teachers' salaries were cut by 5 per cent In June the Council refused to close Unemployment Centres when the government temporarily ended a 75 per cent grant.

In July 1923 the Minister of Health approved a Wolverhampton scheme that, on the face of it, went much of the way to meet the Unemployed Workers' Committee Movement demand for work or maintenance. Wolverhampton borough and the UDCs of Bilston, Willenhall, Short Heath, Wednesfield and Heath Town (covering the Wolverhampton Poor Law area) agreed to provide work for all able bodied men who applied for relief. Such men would be given a card which they took to the local authority; if they accepted the work offered, they would receive the full scale of relief. The local authorities would incur no cost except supervision and the provision of tools. In August, the annual report of the Ministry of Health revealed that while between 1 in 23 to 28 persons were in receipt of relief as an average for the country, the numbers in West Bromwich and Walsall were between 1 in 7 to 10.

Unemployment Committees continued active in Smethwick in 1923. On May 1st a 'fine meeting' at Victoria Park with a very wide platform including the Rev J.S. Tute, Vicar of St. Chad's, passed a resolution sending fraternal greetings to organised workers of the world, declaring that there could be no quarrel between workers of different nations of the world, that war was produced by capitalism which also produced unemployment, slum crowding, poverty, starvation and premature death; it solemnly pledged itself to the fight against capitalism and to establish world-wide socialism. Most of the work of the branch was more humdrum however; a report in June showed regular meetings, the taking up of cases at the Labour Exchange and obtaining more money and back pay for unemployed, and an application for affiliation to the Smethwick Trades Council. In July 1923 a letter appeared in *Workers' Weekly,* the Communist paper, from the Smethwick Unemployed Committee stating that a comrade who sold the *Workers' Weekly* for about one hour on Thursday and Friday outside the Smethwick Labour Exchange had his benefit withdrawn and also his poor relief on the grounds that he was not unemployed. A deputation went to see the manager 'and he was kept all the afternoon, but he would not budge.' An appeal was made to the Guardians who also refused to change the decision even when it was pointed out to them that the claimant was not paid one penny for selling the paper.

The workless figures on 31 December 1923 for Black Country towns was Dudley, 4,746, Smethwick 4,882, Walsall 5,881 and Wolverhampton 7,805. Despite a slight fall in unemployment in 1924, the militancy of the unemployed rose to a peak in that year despite the existence of a Labour government which in August raised benefit scales considerably, but did little else to remedy the grievances of the unemployed. In Walsall, the Unemployed Committee put its demands to the Trades Council for their support in January:

> Pay for relief work to be raised from 11¼d per hour to 1/2½d
> Future relief to be paid in money and not tickets.
> The 'Gap' System to be abolished.

In Wolverhampton the unemployed were on strike from January. A mass meeting of 500 unemployed declared a strike from the 11th. On the 14th. a mass demonstration to sites where work was still being done was met with a barricade of police, but the men downed tools. After useless negotiations, the mass of 2,000 workers decided unanimously to continue the strike.

Payment of relief as a loan was another cause for complaint. The West Midland's Federation of Trades Councils in January heard of a conference of Labour Guardians to be called to discuss this question as the Dudley Guardians were now calling these loans in. This was not being done in Stourbridge, however, because the unemployed had crossed out the words 'on loan' and signed the form on the back instead of the front. In February, P.H. Lawless, secretary of the Walsall Unemployed Union, wrote a letter to the Walsall Guardians stating that men were being slowly starved to death by the system of refusing relief for two further weeks after men had been employed on relief works for one week. If the system was not changed the men would consider going on strike. This was too much for Alderman G. Warner, 'Strike! Well, that's the limit!' he said.

The Wolverhampton strike continued centred around four demands:
- Task work to be abolished or conform to trade union rates and conditions
- Relief to be increased by 25 per cent plus rent allowance.
- Boots for every day wear to be supplied to the unemployed.
- Relief to be granted as a gift not a loan.

The *Workers' Weekly* reported that at a huge Sunday demonstration of 6,000 on the Market Place it had been decided, with one dissentient, to continue the strike. The one dissentient was a local Labour Guardian, who, nevertheless, endorsed the demand for trade union rates of pay. Comrades H. Harrington and Bill Brain were holding large meetings every day and 'needless to say, are meeting with the usual amount of personal abuse from interested parties.' The unemployed were solid, none more so than the women folk who attend the meetings in large numbers. 'A word of appreciation is due to M. Hartshorn, a Labour Guardian who has thrown himself wholeheartedly into the struggle, and also to Councillor Mrs Sproson who is rendering splendid service. The unemployed are marching out from Wolverhampton to every village where task work is being enforced and have been successful in pulling the men out. They have forced the Guardians to give relief despite the strike,' the report ended.

At the end of January the strikers agreed to a truce while rallying other Labour forces in the town to their support. 'But Labour Councillor, G. Williams, who has led the attack on the unemployed movement, refuses even to meet them to talk things over,' the *Workers' Weekly* reported. On January 23rd a 'huge meeting' had passed a resolution congratulating John Wheatley on having been appointed Minister of Health and urging him to secure cancellation of all regulations permitting any form of task work or preventing any Board of Guardians from granting relief upon a full living basis when such is their desire.

By March 14 *Workers' Weekly* was reporting the unemployed in Wolverhampton 'absolutely fed up' with the state of affairs developing since they agreed to resume the task work on the old basis of four days per month pending the decision of the Board of Guardians in regard to the claim for increased relief and trade union rates of pay. 'Negotiations have been proceeding between the Board of Guardians and the Unemployed Committee with the Trades Council, but no headway has been made...' This report was by Bill Brain and goes on:

> The rank and file have become so impatient and exasperated with the Board even I, a Communist, have had to restrain them. However, we have resolved to be treated with contempt no longer and today, Monday, the task workers have come out to a man.... The spirit of the men is splendid and promises a fight to the finish.

On 28th March Bill Brain again reported in *Workers' Weekly*:

> The strikers have maintained the struggle except for about thirty faint hearts. Considering the baby-starving programme of the Wolverhampton Guardi-huns, the press campaign against us etc. the determination of the workers is one of the most astonishing demonstrations of solidarity I have ever witnessed. The Board operated their threat of cutting off out-relief and on Thursday a demonstration of 2,000 marched to the Workhouse to demand admittance. Many women and children were included and in spite of bitter cold, they besieged the workhouse until after 8pm. The children were crying for bread and all they were offered by the Wolverhampton Guardians of the Poor, led by a Christian Minister, was a spoil bank to be levelled at scab rates of pay. Women in the adjacent houses came to the rescue and brought tea and bread to the children.
>
> The strikers refused to conform to the clothes and bath regulations hence we decided to disperse and march there again next morning at 10am when the Board was sitting. Some of the marchers had covered six miles twice over on Thursday, the crowd were there again on Friday morning, the Guardians reaffirmed their decision thereupon we decided to expose the nature of the indoor relief they were offering. The strikers consequently went in, took the bath ceased to be the great unwashed and filled the place before half of them had entered. One hundred and three were admitted and another one hundred were lined up outside waiting their turn and a big crowd of supporters, men and women, were there. The hundred queued up again on Saturday, but were told "house full" come again Monday.
>
> Meanwhile the women were fighting for out-relief and in spite of official delays and obstruction many of them got it, the remainder are renewing their pressure. We are now, Sunday, informed that the Board are turning them out of the workhouse because, they assert, they have orders from the Ministry to do so on the grounds that the men are not properly destitute. Wheatley should give instant attention to this task work scandal because I believe the officials are doing things in his name which he would not stand for.
>
> I attended Trades Council meeting Thursday night and after much discussion the Council formally resolved that it was with us in the fight. At a special meeting the next morning a special joint committee with full powers, was elected to give daily attention to the position. This should help considerably.

The strike continued into April. On April 11 another report appeared in *Workers' Weekly* not signed, but presumably again by Bill Brain judging by the style as follows:

> The second strike of the unemployed against task work can now be regarded as over because, except for a handful of die-hards, the men have resumed work. They have resumed under the compulsion of sheer starvation, not only of themselves, but of their wives and children also. The local authorities let loose every form of terrorism calculated to undermine the men's spirits by visiting the men's homes for the purpose of frightening the wife with yarns of prosecution for neglecting the children. We challenged the Guardians or their agents in the NSPCC, to institute any prosecution knowing as we do that it would afford us publicity upon the facts of the fight that we have not been able to secure except from *Workers' Weekly*.
>
> The strike committee requested the mayor of Wolverhampton to call a town meeting to discuss the position, but he declined on the grounds that the matter simply concerns the Guardians and the unemployed.

Brain's report went on to say that the strike committee had asked W.M. Adamson, the Cannock Labour MP, to put a question in Parliament and Wheatley had declared that his information satisfied him that all cases of destitution had been relieved by the Guardians and no enquiry was necessary.

'Do these smug comments from comfortable Labour ministers mean they reject as untrue the information at the disposal of the Trades Council and unemployed committees and accept without question the reports coming from the bureaucracy of the Ministry of Health?' Brain asked. He ended by urging that the fight against task work be taken up all over the country and the joint council of the Trades Union Congress and the National Unemployed Workers' Committee Movement request the government to institute an enquiry into task work.

The local struggle against task work was indeed at an end. But the Wolverhampton struggle was taken up throughout the country. In May 1924 the National Federation of Trades Councils passed a resolution calling for the immediate abolition of task work (which included the degrading work of breaking stone – GB) and support for the Wolverhampton Trades' Council's demand for an immediate public enquiry into the alleged refusal of Wolverhampton Guardians to relieve cases of destitution. The TUC in the autumn of 1924 discussed the National Unemployed Workers Committee programme which included a scale of relief of 30/-d. a week plus allowances for a wife and children; also that no work be offered by local authorities under trade union rates of pay and conditions, was discussed but not agreed on. After this, the greater problem of the General Strike loomed. The raising of the benefit by the Labour government in August 1924 from 15/-d. to 18/-d. with additional allowances for a wife and children went some way to helping the short-term unemployed, but once this benefit was exhausted the problems of resort to the Guardians and the question of task work remained.

In 1925 unemployment fell in Wolverhampton by another thousand from an average of about 6,800 per week in 1924 to about 5,800 the next year. Unemployment also fell in Smethwick, but in both Walsall and West Bromwich it rose slightly. The protests of the previous year had alarmed the government, and in February 1925 the government (by this time a Tory one) made money available for the building of the much discussed Birmingham New Road. The same month Darlaston Unemployment Committee meeting at Darlaston Ex-Servicemen's Club was complaining to the Prime Minister that the benefit of ex-servicemen was being stopped under new regulations.

Amounts paid by Guardians continued to be under attack. In Walsall in March the case was cited of a young man unemployed for four years who received from the Guardians 10/6d. a week plus an unspecified amount for board and lodging; relief higher than this had to be approved by the Guardians. The next month in Wednesbury there was a case of four families evicted from condemned houses at Hitchin's Croft. The local Labour Party took this matter up and were told that the Council could not interfere with the decisions of a magistrate. Evictions were always a sensitive issue and mass meetings and a march of 400 to the Town Hall protested against these particular proceedings.

In June Wolverhampton Trades Council organised a general demonstration against unemployment around the time of Unemployment Sunday which was becoming an annual feature of the Unemployed Movement. John Baker MP told the gathering that unemployment was inherent within the present system. A. Short, the Wednesbury MP addressed a meeting, presumably at Wednesbury on Unemployment Sunday.

The same month a protest meeting was held on Wolverhampton Market Place protesting at the continuing refusal of the Guardians to meet the Wolverhampton Trades Council and the Unemployed. Allport, the chairman of the Trades Council, said that the action of the Guardians 'was very callous, very brutal and showed very little humanity.' Dan Davies, the Labour agent, however raised a different issue. 2,427 people had had their benefit refused by the Labour Exchange Committee because they had failed to convince the Committee that they had been seeking work *every day*. Walsall had not turned off a tenth of that number, Davies claimed. Davies said that it was easy for a man to read out a list of firms he had visited and the biggest liar got the biggest benefit. He urged the unemployed to impress upon the public that they were not prepared to lie down and starve while others lived in the lap of luxury. Councillor Hartshorne, a Labour Guardian, said the Board had given out only about a quarter of the amount paid twelve months ago and there had been reductions in relief since the protest of the unemployed the previous year.

In September a Wolverhampton man, Isaac Smith, committed suicide. He had been out of work for some time and had a letter to appear before the Labour Exchange Committee. He told his wife he was going out and would not be back until he had found a job.

The years 1921 to 1925 were years of maximum militancy regarding unemployment; years when the hardships of the Great War and the promised land fit for heroes contrasted most starkly with the reality of mass unemployment and slum housing. These were the years when, as Hobsbawm says somewhere, the poor had not yet learned to starve quietly for fear that worse would befall.

Adult Working Class Education

The contest between Marxism and Social Democracy in the general labour movement was replicated in the sphere of adult working class education.

The party which did most to popularise Marxist education before the war was the Socialist Labour Party, very sectarian, but the source of much of the Marxist material translated at that time. It was the SLP, (founded in 1903 as a breakaway from the Social Democratic Federation), whose students played a leading role in the break with Ruskin College (founded in 1899) over the issue of Marxist versus reformist education. They set up the Labour College movement with its monthly organ *The Plebs*. From this time there was a bitter struggle between the Labour College and its branches, and the Workers' Education Association which was associated with Ruskin College and reformist education.

The two pioneers of the Labour Colleges in this region were Fred Silvester of Birmingham and T.D. Smith. TD, as he was always known, lived most of his life in West Bromwich, but we find him associated at various times with Birmingham, Smethwick, Wolverhampton etc. as he taught classes and organised groups throughout the West Midlands and was for many years the full time organiser of the region.

Silvester was organising Social Science classes in Birmingham from 1917. In November 1918 there were classes in Smethwick and West Bromwich and although T.D. Smith is not mentioned it is almost certain that he organised them. It was in October 1919 that Silvester first mentioned T.D. Smith as the 'able and energetic comrade' organising classes with him in Birmingham. In December 1919 Silvester mentions a report from a Wolverhampton Conscientious Objector stating that there was a large Marxist class in Wolverhampton mainly composed of ILPers. TD went there to take a class on Industrial History and found 'an enthusiastic class of about 50.'

In December 1920 *The Communist* reported that the Communist Party branch in Walsall as well as fulfilling its normal duties had started a *Plebs* class. In January 1921 *Plebs* reported that this *Plebs* Class met every Sunday morning at the Labour Club and that a series of lectures was being given on Working Class Education by Birmingham comrades. The reporter was Charles Hindle of 3 Victoria Terrace, Ryecroft.

1921 was a turning point in the development of Labour Colleges with the formation of the National Council of Labour Colleges in October 1921 at a conference at the Clarion Club House, Yardley, in Birmingham. At this conference T.D. Smith was elected to the provisional committee. Two basic problems were that the WEA was making inroads into trade union schemes of education through a Workers' Educational Trade Union Committee; also that trade union finance was becoming vital at a time when mass unemployment was beginning to emerge and trade unions were finding themselves in straitened circumstances. Both challenges were met with the popularisation of IWCE (Independent Working Class Education). The most important early NCLC trade union success was the decision of the Amalgamated Union of Building Trade Workers (AUBTW) at its 1922 conference to devote 1/-d. per annum per member to working class education administered through the NCLC.

By January 1922 the Birmingham Social Science class had turned itself into a Labour College with Silvester as chairman, A.D.M. Taylor from London the Principal and T.D. Smith as Chief Assistant Tutor. This coincided with the formation of a No.6 Midlands Division with branches in the Black Country at Smethwick, Walsall, West Bromwich, Wolverhampton and Stourbridge. The secretary of this new division was T.D. Smith. At this time, the classes were feeling the effects of unemployment, and in March comrades were urged to 'rally round TDS and his gallant band of tutors and students all busily fighting for the unemployed with classes having a great struggle to keep going and secretaries hardly able to pay the train fare of lecturers.'

The AUBTW money brought grandiose plans for expansion. In August 1922 there were plans for the AUBTW secretaries (who were administering the scheme) within Div.6. to contact all NUR secretaries (the NUR had been one of the earliest financial pillars of the central Labour College) and the secretaries of the following Trades Councils to ask for joint meetings with Labour Parties and Co-operatives: Wolverhampton (including Tettenhall), Bilston, Walsall, West Bromwich, Wednesbury (including Darlaston), Brierley Hill, Dudley (including Gornal) and Smethwick. By November 1922 *Plebs* was reporting the Black Country undergoing 'a brightening process through educational conferences being conducted by Birmingham Labour College comrades. Although the revolution is not yet complete there are sufficient indications of NCLC success for this first campaign on behalf of IWCE to be distinctly heartening.'

But despite these encouraging noises hard evidence of NCLC classes in the Black Country during these years of high unemployment is difficult to find. An additional problem of the NCLC was that its insistence on Marxist education brought accusations that it was dominated by the Communist Party. A disclaimer by Eden and Cedar Paul (both Communists) in *Plebs* in June 1923 answering a query from Holland regarding the state of revolutionary education in Britain stated that the position had been discussed at the Education Committee of the 4th. Congress of the Communist International in Moscow the previous November where it had been explained that Marxist education in Britain was under the control of the NCLC and the Plebs League and that any attempt of the small Communist Party to control it would fail and be detrimental to the progress of both Communism and Marxist education. T.D. Smith continued as organiser of Division 6, and in December 1923 he was appealing in *Plebs* for more Labour Colleges without indicating which classes already existed.

Classes there must have been, however, in the Black Country. In February 1924 *Plebs* reported 11,000 classes nationally the previous year which was expected to rise to 17,000 in 1924. The Directory in the paper the same month gave Black Country secretaries in West Bromwich (D. Collins, 7 Clive St.), Dudley (A.V. Lewis 5 French Rd.), and Wolverhampton (J. Parkins 140 Chester St.). But a report from Division 6 in December showed that the only Black Country class had been at Wolverhampton.

In March 1925 a new class was 'being arranged' in Walsall, and the next month organiser T.D. Smith was 'taking advantage of the Tory threat to interfere with the political levy,' to circularise all working class organisations offering a course on the Law in relation to Trade Unions. The movement was obviously at a low ebb. Week-end schools and a summer school in Birmingham had attracted only limited attendance. But militancy was beginning to rise. In October 1925 Stuart Barr was appointed Division 6 organiser in place of T.D. Smith. TD was to 'assist' in Division 12. This was an area covering Northampton and Mansfield and how TD was to do this from West Bromwich is not explained. The new broom swept very vigorously. By December Barr was reporting affiliated classes in Stourbridge, Smethwick, West Bromwich, Walsall and Wolverhampton. The next month he reported additional classes in Dudley and Tipton. A week-end school and conference in Dudley in January had been a 'huge success bringing the whole local Labour movement into the work of IWCE.' Barr had also recruited the following new tutors to assist him: Joe Roche, W. Hindle, D. Rydderch, L.H. Burke, D. Collins and D. Murden. In February 1926 Stourbridge was reported as a Labour College. In March Dudley College was running three classes. The Labour movement was being stimulated to organise NCLC classes and after a talk by Barr, Tipton Labour Party had decided to start a class. At a Walsall Conference and week-end School Barr had lectured on Industrial Policy. The success of Dudley was largely due to the 'energetic nd painstaking' secretary Comrade Ward; a week end school on Imperialism was being arranged. Walsall was turning itself into a Rambling Club for the summer. The Walsall Labour College secretary was A.H. Fox and the West Bromwich secretary F. Able.

So by the time of the General Strike the thin years both in Birmingham and the Black Country seemed to be over and a vibrant movement of Marxist IWCE was developing. We can now turn to the WEA to see how it fared in the years 1919-26.

The Workers' Education Association

The WEA – the great rival of the NCLC in working class education – was enmeshed in contradictions of its own. Based firmly on the Universities, there were some parts of these establishments with no enthusiasm for educating working people. Others saw the development of higher education among working people as inevitable and requiring an organisation such as the WEA to 'guide' it into non-revolutionary channels. Others were enthusiastic about working class education and genuinely believed that objectivity in the social sciences was possible. Non-Marxists within the Labour movement were naturally drawn to the WEA rather than the NCLC. The advantages the WEA enjoyed were relatively generous funding and the provision of tutors with academic qualifications as against the do-it-yourself. worker-activist tutors of NCLC classes. But both depended on voluntary labour to initiate local groups and classes and to sustain them.

WEA annual reports for the West Midlands are available from 1921-22. The first shows classes in a number of Black Country towns during that year. The 1922-23 Report is more specific. There was a branch at Bilston whose secretary was J.E. Percival and there was one class, on English Literature. At Dudley there were two secretaries, R. Jones of Old Hill and H. Stansbie of Dudley. The branch ran classes at Brierley Hill (Economics), Cradley Heath (Psychology), Dudley (Literature), Netherton (Economics), Old Hill (Literature) and at Lye a class on Literature was 'being prepared.' At Halesowen there was also a 'preparatory class.' At Tipton, where the secretary was W.J. Cox a preparatory class on Social Psychology was advertised. In West Bromwich the secretary was F.L. Bullock. There were four classes at different venues in the town on Economic History, Literature, European History, and Biology. In Wolverhampton, whose secretary was W. Hulme, there was one tutorial class, on Economics, but a course of lectures had been arranged at the Co-operative Hall on 'The Nation and Drama', 'How to Appreciate Great Music', 'With Normans and Bretons for a Holiday', 'Art in Common Life' and 'The New Map of Europe Explained'.

The Report for 1924-25 contained a history of the Midland District. The movement had been founded in 1904, and spread to Birmingham in 1905, but there is no mention of classes in the Black Country until 1919-20 after the district had been divided into West and East Midlands in 1918. The 1925-26 Report shows a branch still at Bilston with a new secretary E.A. Moss. There was still one class, this time on Economics. Dudley had now only one secretary, Stansbie. Activity was at about the same level as the previous year with Cradley Heath doing Literature and hoping for a class on Economics. Dudley continuing its course on Literature. Netherton taking Social Philosophy, and Old Hill Economics. The Halesowen branch, its secretary still T. Scarlett had a class on European History. A new branch at Sedgley, secretary E.A. Moss, held two classes, Psychology and Literature. Another new branch, Smethwick, had not yet appointed a secretary and was attempting to organise a class. A third new branch, Stourbridge, secretary J.H. Woolridge, had taken over classes in Cradley and Lye, both on Literature. The Tipton branch carried on with one class in Psychology, but had also arranged a series of Gilchrist Lectures on 'How the Old Monks Lived', 'Flowers and their Insect Visitors', 'The Sense of Beauty', 'The Marvel of the Tiny', 'The Electron', and 'Caterpillars'. West Bromwich with a new secretary, H.E. Pountney, was reduced to two classes, Economics and Literature. A fourth new branch, Willenhalll, secretary T.E. Pace, had a class on Literature. Wolverhampton, secretary now Miss A.H. Everness BA, had expanded with four classes, Social Economics, Literature, Appreciation of Music, and Industrial History taken by the secretary.

It seems clear that WEA activity increased in 1925-26 as did NCLC activity, but one would not have thought for the same reasons. The NCLC advance was clearly associated with increased working class militancy as levels of unemployment fell, and the prospect of a General Strike loomed; the nature of their classes reflected this. The problem with WEA classes is to assess the number of manual workers who actually attended them. Usually the answer was, not very many, the classes being attended more by lower middle class professional people and white collar workers. On this question we have no information for the Black Country at this time. Increased WEA activity may, therefore, have simply reflected the increasing well-being of these sections of the community and unconnected with militancy of any sort.

Nor were the polemics and hostility between WEA and NCLC contained in the pages of *Plebs* and to a less extent, *Highway,* the respective organs of the two bodies, concerned with Black Country matters. It was Fred Silvester in Birmingham who maintained a campaign against the WEA ensconced at Birmingham University, but there are no echoes of this hostility in the Black Country.

Finally, although WEA classes in economics and history would have been taught with a distinct anti-Marxist bias, the wide range of WEA subjects were less susceptible to either Marxist or anti-Marxist interpretations; although it might perhaps be claimed by some that cultural and scientific subjects diverted workers from the class struggle. In the Black Country therefore the NCLC and the WEA co-existed without too much stress and the WEA was able to provide a wider range of classes for working people (whether they attended them or not) than the much more proletarian NCLC.

The Communist Party

The Communist Party of Great Britain was born on 31st July and 1st August 1920 at a Communist Unity Convention in London dominated by the British Socialist Party and Communist Unity Groups which had been formed mainly by Socialist Labour Party members when the official SLP leadership refused to continue unity negotiations. Other groups such as Daily Herald Leagues and Guild Socialists were also represented.

We have seen how the British Socialist Party had predominated in the Black Country before 1914, but the support of the BSP leadership for the war, followed by the split after the victory of the anti-war elements in 1916, led to a growth of the Socialist Labour Party during the war which had been anti-war from the beginning. At the Convention as delegates from Birmingham were Fred Silvester and Bill Brain who were SLP members and H. Stubbs representing Birmingham Shop Stewards. The sole Black Country delegate was H.H. Ward of Walsall representing the British Socialist Party.

The first branch Directory which appeared in the new organ of the Party *The Communist* in August 1920 recorded three branches in the Black Country – South Staffs whose secretary was George Bridgen with an address in West Bromwich; Walsall whose secretary was Joe Deakin, leading figure in the Walsall Bomb Plot of 1892, BSP member and later Labour Party stalwart; the third branch was West Bromwich secretary J. Ferguson. The first branch probably represented those SLP members and others who had formed the South Staffs Communist Unity Group and joined the Birmingham Unity Group prior to the Communist Convention.

Early Communist activity in the Black Country was however led by Birmingham Communists, notably James Stewart, the first organiser of the Birmingham District of the Party who had the dubious honour of being the first Communist to be arrested and imprisoned in Wolverhampton. Another who operated mainly in Birmingham was Bill Brain who led the Wolverhampton Unemployed Workers Committee. Brain is entitled to be claimed as a Black Country Communist, however, because he lived in Smethwick. T.D. Smith, the NCLC enthusiast of West Bromwich who was an SLP member became a foundation member of the Communist Party, but we know the names of few other activists. We hear nothing of activity in the S. Staffs branch but both Walsall and West Bromwich continued to function as branches (they made donations to the Russian Famine Fund in September 1921) and at some time a Wolverhampton branch was formed.

In 1923 the Communist Party entered a period of growth with the doubling of the circulation of its newspaper now called *Workers' Weekly*. In Wolverhampton a meeting was called in July to which 'all readers of WW and rebels generally' were invited to attend. It was held at the Labour Assembly Rooms addressed by Bill Brain and was to 'reconstitute' the Communist Party branch.

A Birmingham District Congress was held in February 1924 'with delegates from Wolverhampton, Walsall and Birmingham locals present' we are told. The main items discussed were the death of Lenin and the new Labour government. On the latter it was stated, 'If the Labour government is defeated in the House of Commons because it clearly and boldly fought the class fight this would be followed by an electoral victory undreamed of.' But, 'if it is cautious, denies its class basis and degenerates into a mere liberal hack it will be discredited.' On the general state of Party health Jack Trotter, who opened the Congress, started by saying that in spite of the immense difficulties of the past twelve months he was satisfied that the Party was now firmly established and would make progress in the coming months.

On the basis of rising militancy, the national leadership organised a recruiting drive in the autumn of 1924. Both Dr Robert Dunstan and a national organiser, William Joss, made tours of the Black Country. In September, Dunstan spoke at West Bromwich, Brain in Wolverhampton, and Joss at a mid-week meeting in Wolverhampton Market Place with 200-300 reported 'who stayed to listen in pouring rain.'

In January 1925 the executive committee of the Communist Party held an open session in Birmingham. In preparation for this, large meetings were organised throughout the district. These included one at West Bromwich Town Hall with leading Communists, Tom Bell, J.R. Campbell and Harry Pollitt speaking. Another was at the Co-op Hall in Wolverhampton, speakers J.T. Murphy and Bill Brain. Here, practically all theatre proprietors had refused to let their theatres to the Party and the Wolverhampton Bill Posters Association had refused to post 200 double crown posters the local party had printed for the meeting at the Co-op Hall.

At the end of January the Party organised a Lenin Week on the anniversary of his death. In Wednesbury a meeting had to be abandoned because the letting of the hall was cancelled at the last moment. The next week Bill Brain organised an open-air meeting in the Market Place. They found a large number of Tories there who began to sing God Save the King. This had the effect of attracting a crowd of about 900 and Brain reported a 'very successful meeting.'

In August 1925 the Party organised an Anti-War Week. Locally meetings were organised in Wolverhampton with Bill Brain and Wednesbury, J. Reynolds.

At this time the Communist Party was energetically trying to expand its factory base. From Wolverhampton a letter to the *Workers' Weekly* signed ALD (undoubtedly Albert Darke, the first known Wolverhampton Communist leader- GB) reported five factories in the Park Lane district of Wolverhampton making dry batteries on the low wages of female workers. Communists were chalking notices of a meeting by J.R. Campbell on Saturday August 22nd. The chalking extended into nearby Heath Town and the chairman of that Council ordered the chalkers to stop, but they took no notice as the chairman had no powers to stop them. Darke goes on to say that workers were becoming interested and were discussing the 'exploits' of Campbell (who had brought about the defeat of the first Labour government – GB).

At this time the Communists were the only part of the Labour movement preparing for the General Strike. The October 16 issue of *Workers' Weekly* carried the banner headline '26 weeks to go' and subsequent issues showed the decreasing number of weeks to show down. In October the government arrested twelve leading Communists and imprisoned them until the Strike was over.

In January 1926 Brain announced in the paper that a Communist Party group was to be formed at Dudley. During Lenin Week there were meetings in Wolverhampton Market Place and at the Co-op Hall addressed by Dr Dunstan, and there was a meeting in Tipton Market Place. In March it was announced that groups of the Left-Wing Movement were being formed in Birmingham and Wolverhampton and Dr Dunstan came to Wolverhampton to set this up.

It is clear that by 1926 the Communist Party was growing, but it is difficult to quantify the progress. We know that the Birmingham District acquired a bookshop in 1925 and this could only have been supported by progress in most parts of the district. We know that nationally the circulation of *Workers' Weekly* doubled between 1923 when it first appeared and 1925. We know from Winnie Docherty's papers that Smethwick sold 13 dozen papers weekly. This achievement must be seen against the background of a complete wholesalers' boycott.

Records show that total organisations within the Birmingham district rose from 5 'locals' in May 1924 to 9 in May 1925 and only three other Districts exceeded that number, but this tells us nothing of progress in the Black Country, unfortunately. The scanty evidence suggests an organised Party branch in Wolverhampton and perhaps Walsall or West Bromwich. In other towns would be groups of Communists working with their trade unions, Unemployed Committees etc. and exerting an influence beyond their numbers. But Communists were few on the ground.

The Independent Labour Party

After 1918 when the Labour Party constitution was amended to include individual membership it was expected that the ILP would whither away as its members joined either the Labour Party or the Communists. This did not occur either nationally or locally and from 1918 the ILP entered a period of growth, despite – or because of – its patchy record of resistance to the war. Progress is reported in the party paper *Labour Leader*.

The ILP, together with the Trades Councils were responsible for the post-war May Day rallies. In

1919 the Wolverhampton rally took place on the Market Place with Emma Sproson, Lawley, Shepherd, and Driver the main speakers. Four dozen *Labour Leaders* were sold and a 14/6d. collection taken for war widows.

In July the ILP was holding open-air meetings at Smow Hill with Williams and Micklewright. 'If local comrades would rally round we can attain our pre-war standard' it was reported. At this time the ILP was providing legal assistance for tenants with ejection orders against them. Wolverhampton continued to hold successful meetings at Snow Hill with speakers from West Bromwich. On July 9th J.H. George 'held a crowd spellbound for one hour, in spite of the local floral fete.' On 23rd. July was the 'best meeting of the season' with T.W. Wright. By the end of the open-air season on September 17th Comrade Arthur (again from West Bromwich) spoke for an hour, but literature sales and collections were 'only fair.'

In November the local Labour Representation Committees, dominated by the trade unions (providing the cash) and the ILPs, (providing the organisation), were responsible for the local elections in which considerable progress was made in Labour representation in 1919 in the Black Country.

1920 maintained much the same pattern, reports of May Day activity and elections in November but not much else, suggesting that the ILP was doing little more than holdings its own.

In Wolverhampton a 'splendid programme' was produced for May Day which included the annual demonstration and also a meeting at which the 'muster was fair but there was room for more.' Emma Sproson gave a short talk on the origin of the Red Flag and 'proceedings ended with a rendition of that well-known Labour song.' In Smethwick the Labour movement was allowed to use Victoria Park for the first time and there was 'a great May Day demonstration.' In November there were some Labour gains in the 1920 elections, but results were generally disappointing.

1921 began with a crippling blow to the West Bromwich ILP – the death of Harry Brockhouse at the early age of 52. Councillor Brockhouse was West Bromwich's leading Socialist. He was the eldest son of the head of the important West Bromwich firm of axle makers, J. Brockhouse & Co. In his early years he had been a teacher serving his apprenticeship as a pupil-teacher in a West Bromwich Board School. He gave up teaching to take a post at his father's firm and at the time of his death he had held an important position at Vickers of Sheffield for three years. An obituary written by A. Hobson, secretary of West Bromwich ILP, in the *Labour Leader* of 3 March 1921 stated that Comrade Brockhouse had started as a Liberal and Nonconformist. He had been converted to Socialism when he was 27 years of age by hearing an address by Carrie Martyn at Bilston. Prior to this he had founded a Democratic Club supporting Land Nationalisation a la Henry George. He was the chief founder of the West Bromwich Labour Church. At one time a member of the national administrative council of the ILP, he had inaugurated the system of District Councils and District Federations. For nineteen years he had been chairman of the ILP Midlands Divisional Council. Regarding Brockhouse's attitude to the war, Hobson's obituary says, 'In the *Clarion*'s best Fellowship days, Councillor Brockhouse was an ardent Clarionette, but was painfully compelled to sever his connection when the militarist bugle began to blow.' About four years ago the Co-operative Colony of Murcot had been founded near Broadway and Comrade Brockhouse had been actively associated with it until his death. In 1918 he had been elected Labour representative in Hill Top, the ward in which he lived. His main Council activities had been in connection with housing and unemployment. His 'rabid Socialist views', according to local Liberals would have ensured 'a big effort to oust him at the next local elections.'

In 1921 the Worcestershire Federation of the ILP was stimulating party activity in the Black Country. In April the 'usual open-air meetings' were being reported at Saltwells Coppice near Brierley Hill. In May Jim Simmons spoke there to an 'audience composed largely of locked-out miners.' A collection was taken for the Miners' Children's Fund. At the Worcestershire Federation meeting in May, Comrade Dearn of Langley was elected chairman, and Comrade Weston of the same branch was elected secretary. Comrade Downing of Netherton was also represented on the Divisional Council. The Netherton branch expanded into Dudley, and a Dudley & Netherton branch was formed. It held regular open-air meetings until the end of September. At the penultimate meeting Fred Longden delivered a 'powerful address listened to attentively and many expressed warm appreciation of the way the case against private enterprise was put.' At the last meeting Dearne of Warley 'dealt with the present economic crisis.'

In October there was a meeting to amalgamate the Worcestershire Federation with that of South Staffordshire. But there was a poor attendance 'because of the weather' and officials were not elected, Comrade Weston of the Worcestershire Federation carrying on as secretary. Local election results in November were good, only West Bromwich recording losses.

January 1922 brought news of a new ILP branch at Bearwood. Nationally the ILP was still claiming growth with 792 branches. But the Midlands Divisional Conference had to report losses as branches which had ceased to function were struck off.

There are few reports of Black Country meetings in 1922, but in March, Emma Sproson's status both as speaker and war resister was confirmed by news of a No More War Demonstration at the next anniversary of the end of the war where her name was associated with a galaxy of prospective national speakers such as Bishop Gore, Bevin, Clynes, Henderson, Lansbury, Russell and G.B. Shaw.

1922 was the year when the ILP leadership admitted crisis in the party, and from October the party organ was renamed *New Leader* and the party reorganised under the austere Clifford Allen. Matters improved almost immediately, but how much was due to Allen and how much to rising militancy in the Labour movement is a moot question.

In its anxiety to establish a distinctive role for itself as against the Labour Party, the ILP adopted Guild Socialism and in 1923 launched a campaign for unity with the trade unions around guild socialism in industry. One of the first of these Trade Union Conferences was at Dudley in March with R.C. Wallhead the main speaker. During the spring, ILP activity was renewed in Shropshire with the resuscitation of the Shrewsbury branch and a fierce, physical Parliamentary by-election in Ludlow. ('To cross the Shropshire border is to go back almost to feudalism').

By June the Stourbridge branch was taking 'a new lease of life with a steady influx of new members.' Two recruits at a Wilfred Wellock meeting said they must belong to the party of which J. Ramsay MacDonald was a leading figure. Wellock, the noted pacifist and prospective parliamentary candidate for Stourbridge, gave 'an inspiring address' dealing with the lot of the worker under capitalism and… a splendid crowd was roused to enthusiasm with the way he dealt with the Russian situation.' (At this time the *New Leader* was carrying advertisements for the First Workers' Loan to Soviet Russia. £200,000 of 5 per cent stock was being offered repayable in 1933 in 10/-d. £1 and £5 denominations – GB). By September a 'successful' conference of Black Country branches was held in Wolverhampton. A strong and representative committee was formed with Miss Widdowson of 177 Staveley Road Wolverhampton as secretary. In November Fenner Brockway was speaking in Walsall.

1924 was the year of the Labour government led by MacDonald and Snowden, both members of the ILP and with 32 other ILP members of Parliament. The ILP seemed at the peak of its power. In February a new branch was formed at Halesowen. In March a Midlands Conference sent 'warmest congratulations' to MacDonald, but Black Country participation was not specified. The same month Smethwick held a victory ball at the Baths Assembly Room and also a meeting at which Julia Varley, the Workers' Union veteran, spoke on the Labour Movement and Domestic Service. She urged girls who were refused unemployment benefit because they would not take up domestic service to protest not only about the wages but also the hours where some girls started at 6am and did not finish until 10pm. Another revitalised branch was Tipton which in April held 'an enthusiastic meeting.' at which, 'Our comrade Powis opened an interesting discussion dealing with the points raised at the opening of the branch by Mrs Sproson of Wolverhampton.' The points made were not specified but, no doubt, Emma Sproson was urging the Labour government to greater militancy.

In May, Wolverhampton comrades were said to be 'breaking new ground.' Mrs Sproson had addressed enthusiastic meetings at Tipton and Walsall and Comrades Frank Sproson (Emma's postman husband) and Ted Williams had addressed a meeting in Darlaston, the first ILP meeting ever held there, it was claimed. In June there were Unemployment Conferences throughout the country. One in Birmingham was very successful, but for the one scheduled for West Bromwich, I have found no report. In October Tipton reported a 'fine meeting' at Great Bridge Market Place at which Councillor J. Bailey and J.H. Dearne had spoken. A resolution supporting the Russian Treaty (the first recognition of the Soviet government – GB) 'was passed without a dissentient.'

Support for the ILP was at its peak at this time and it launched a Campaign for Socialism. The

Birmingham ILP organised a large and enthusiastic Conference in October which probably involved the Smethwick branch.

But the same month came the Campbell Case and the Labour government was destroyed. By this time the ILP was very divided concerning the performance of the Labour government. An editorial in the *New Leader* declared that a vote of Censure on the Labour government would have come anyway; the Liberals wanted to have it on the Russian Treaty, but the Conservatives organised it on the Campbell case. It was widely held that the Labour government would be returned at the forthcoming general election with an increased majority and a mandate for real socialist measures; and indeed it probably would have been, except for the forged Zinoviev letter which was published just before the election alleging that the Labour government was controlled by the Russians. The Labour Party increased its vote, but there was a landslide victory for the Tories at the expense of the Liberals who were almost obliterated.

The election campaign went well in the Black Country. In Stourbridge Wilfred Wellock, the ILP candidate, made 'fine progress'. At Hill and Cakemore, 'a previous black spot', meetings were crowded. There were 'big advances' in Cradley. In Oldbury there was a 'Liberal landslide in our direction.'

Ramsay MacDonald made a tour through the Black Country, recorded by Henry Nevinson. MacDonald's spell was such that he generated an almost religious fervour among many Black Country people.

In November, Emma Sroson, the only Wolverhampton ILP councillor, was returned at the municipal elections despite the united efforts of Tories and Liberals to unseat her. Once again she waved the Red Flag, which had so enraged them three years previously, from the Town Hall balcony. ILP branches and membership continued to grow. In 'wonderful Birmingham' 200 recruits were made at one election meeting where Oswald Mosley, Jim Simmons and other candidates spoke. Nor did it end after the election. In December an ILP Guild of Youth was formed in West Bromwich reminding us that the Guild had been formed in 1924 at the Easter ILP Conference and the ILP was spearheading cultural developments with the Arts Guild. A new ILP branch was also formed in Oldbury, secretary T. Standley, in December.

Progress continued into 1925. In May the South Staffordshire Federation of the ILP held its second annual general meeting in Dudley. Miss Widdowson, the secretary reported that six new branches had been started during the year in addition to the well-established branches at Wolverhampton, West Bromwich, Dudley, Walsall, Tipton, Halesowen and Willenhall. John Paton, the national organiser, urged branches to develop a Study Circle, a Women's Group and a Guild of Youth. 'After tea the delegates witnessed a very remarkable presentation of Shaw's Candida given by the West Bromwich ILP Dramatic Society.'

Smethwick ILP, which was in the Birmingham Federation, was equally active. In January it held a successful Educational Week. The same month at the coming of age of the Trades & Labour Council, the annual report reviewing its history saw 'the hand of the ILP in all its activities.' During the winter the ILP ran Saturday dances at the Baths Assembly Rooms on 'undoubtedly the best dance floor in Smethwick.' The ILP Rooms, besides carrying out its normal functions, performed 'rescue acts' when other premises were not available. So, it hosted a meeting of all Parliamentary candidates at the end of 1924, and saved the evening 1925 May Day programme when the open-air arrangements were rained off. The May Day 1925 procession saw not only an ILP contingent, but also sections from the well-established Socialist Sunday School and also, for the first time, the new Guild of Youth, both nurtured by the ILP. In December 1925 the ILP organised a large meeting in Smethwick to protest at the arrest of the Communist Twelve.

1926 began with a great meeting at Bilston Town Hall, 'Generally acclaimed as the finest meeting ever held in Bilston.' The speaker was Minnie Pallister supported by David Collins, the chair of the S. Staffs ILP Federation. 'Mrs Hattie Holland, our new Social Secretary made an able chairman.' Thirteen new members were recruited, making a branch totalling 85 members after only four months of existence. The S. Staffs Federation later reported that Minnie Pallister had also done 'excellent work' in her speaking tour at Wolverhampton, Willenhall, Walsall and West Bromwich.

Lastly, some indication of the development of the ILP in the Black Country can be gleaned from reports given at the annual Easter ILP national conferences. 1919 was a year of genuine growth. South Staffs. delegates present were E. Micklewright (West Bromwich) and W.G. Grant (Smethwick). There were Black Country branches in the three Federations of Birmingham, S. Staffs, and Worcestershire. Judging from the accounts, a thriving branch would contribute about £4 a year to national funds. In the Black Country, Smethwick paid £3-5-0, Walsall and Wednesbury nothing, West Bromwich £3 and Wolverhampton £8. In the Worcester Federation Cradley paid 15/-d. Langley 2/6d. and Netherton £1-15-0d.

At the 1920 Conference branches represented fell from 345 to 337. Harry Brockhouse was the only Black Country delegate. From the S. Staffs. Federation Walsall and Wednesbury branches were deleted, but in Worcestershire Blackheath branch was added, paying 2/-d.

In 1921 the national leadership was still claiming branch increases, but Conference representation fell to 310 branches. Councillor Egbert T. Lewis from Stourbridge was the only Black Country delegate. The country was reeling from mass unemployment and average national contributions fell. Under these circumstances West Bromwich contributed £3-10-0d, Wolverhampton only £1 and Smethwick but 6/8d. The Worcestershire Federation was more successful, Cradley paying 10/6d. Langley £1-15-0d. Stourbridge £4-10-0d. and Netherton (now expanding into Dudley) £6.

Branch representation at Conference again fell in 1922 to 215, another year of mass unemployment. There were three delegates from the Black Country, Grant (Smethwick) B. Covcoran (Stourbridge) and Harry Horton (Wolverhampton). The South Staffs Federation seems to have disappeared, and under the Worcestershire Federation was the two Staffs. branches of Wolverhampton and West Bromwich, as well as Langley, Netherton and Stourbridge.

1923 was an equally miserable year. Miss Florence Widdowson of Wolverhampton was the only Black Country delegate and the Worcestershire Federation showed the same five branches.

By 1924 there was an improvement. There were five delegates from the Black Country at the Conference: Mrs B. Corcoran (Stourbridge), and David Collins? (West Bromwich); Miss F.B. Widdowson now represented Wednesbury and Councillor Emma Sproson Wolverhampton, while Walsall made a first appearance with the influential J. McShane. The Black Country Federation was now known as Worcestershire & South Staffordshsire with three branches in Worcestershire (Halesowen, Langley Green and Stourbridge) and four in Staffordshire (Walsall, Wednesbury, West Bromwich and Wolverhampton). By 1925 the Worcester & S. Staffs Federation had grown to fourteen branches with new branches at Dudley & Netherton, Oldbury, Langley, Rounds Green, Tipton and Willenhall.

At the 1926 Easter ILP Conference on the eve of the General Strike five Black Country delegates attended from branches in all three of the restored Federations. The South Staffs Fed. now contained eleven branches.

Thus it seem clear that ILP activity in the Black Country showed the same pattern as that of other local Labour organisations – growth in the immediate post-war period followed by a sharp decline in the years of mass unemployment 1921-24, and then strong growth in the years leading up to the General Strike.

The Labour Party

The considerably increased influence of the Labour movement during the war years led to the emergence of a New Labour Party through a revised constitution of 1918. The new constitution had a number of aims. One was to change the position inherited from 1900 when the Labour Representation Committee was set up comprised of representatives of organisations only, mainly trade unions and Socialist societies such as the Fabian Society and the ILP. To this end, individual party membership was to be introduced and local Labour Party branches formed which would be subordinate to the party nationally. Particular attention was to be paid to the newly enfranchised women and branches of the Women's Labour League were to be converted into Women's Sections of the Labour Party.

To consolidate these changes there had to be changes in the national executive of the party. Until 1918 this consisted of 16 members, 11 of whom were from trade unions, one from trades councils, one from local Labour Parties and Women's organisations combined, and three from Socialist societies. This was to be changed to an executive of 23, consisting of 13 from trade unions and national affiliated groups combined. Another five were to be elected from local Labour parties, and four from Women's sections. Finally, the Treasurer was to be elected separately. The other key change was that although each section nominated its own candidates, they were voted on by the whole annual Labour Party conference. This obviously put the Socialist parties at a disadvantage and the grouping of them with the trade unions was meant to assuage the wrath of the militant pro-war trade unionists who had threatened to set up a separate Trade Union Labour Party as a result of the anti-war attitudes of the 'pacifist' Socialist societies, particularly the Independent Labour Party. In fact, matters turned out differently. The threat of a separate Trade Union Labour Party was snuffed out at the 1918 TUC, and the ILP far from disappearing in the period 1919 to 1925, increased both in size and influence.

The Black Country Labour movements adapted to these changes in different ways, but new Labour Parties emerged in each town whose main responsibilities were the election of a Labour MP, the adaptation of national policy to a local municipal programme, the election of local Labour councillors and the building of local organisation to achieve these ends.

We can begin to follow the vicissitudes of the Labour Parties through the general elections of the period 1918 to 1925 of which there were no less than four in seven years. The 1918 khaki general election returned 473 Lloyd George Coalition candidates and only 58 Labour MPs. However, as we have seen, four of these MPs were from the Black Country and the Labour vote in the Black Country was much higher than that for the UK as a whole.

These four MPs, F.O. Roberts (West Bromwich), J.E. Davison (Smethwick), A. Short (Wednesbury) and Charles Sitch (Kingswinford) were all trade union officials. They had been selected originally mainly because their trade unions would finance the candidate and the constituency. But they all turned out to be good constituency MPs and all of them were returned at all subsequent elections until 1931.

Before the 1922 election there was a sensational by-election victory in Dudley in 1921. This was due to the appointment of the local MP Sir Arthur Griffiths Boscawen as Minister of Agriculture. James Wilson, another trade unionist, was the Labour candidate and he overturned a majority of 3,000 to win by 276 votes. This was a puzzling change of allegiance, the Dudley seat having been either Liberal or Conservative since 1832. The press speculated that Boscawen was a protectionist 'dear food' man, and also that unemployment was a key factor; but when unemployment was worse in 1922, Wilson lost the seat to another Conservative.

The 1922 general election resulted from the Conservative determination to break from Lloyd George and form their own administration. The result was 344 Conservatives, 115 Liberals split almost exactly into two factions, and 142 Labour MPs.

In Walsall the maverick Sir Richard Cooper who couldn't make up his mind whether he was Coalitionist or National Party in 1918 resigned and was replaced in 1922 by his wife. The Labour candidate was R. Dennison. But the result was another sensation as Pat Collins, the showman, won the seat as a Liberal polling 14,675 to Lady Cooper's 14,349 and Dennison's 8,946.

In Wolverhampton West there had been a by-election in March 1922 due to the death of the custard king A. Bird. Walkden stood again, this time against the son, Sir R. Bird, but again the Conservative majority was about 3,000. At the general election of 1922 Walkden stood for a third time against Bird, but again failed to dent his majority. In East Wolverhampton, the Labour Party was still finding it difficult to obtain more than a toe-hold. In a four candidate contest G.R. Thorne, the local Liberal, retained the seat with 11,577 votes against the Tory C.H. Pinson's 9,410; W.T.A. Foot the Labour candidate polled 3,076 and the Rev J.A. Shaw, making a last appearance as a Lloyd George Liberal, polled 1,169. In the Bilston constituency (which included Sedgley, Coseley, Gornal and part of Tipton) John Baker, a nominee of the Iron & Steel Trades Confederation, stood in a straight fight with a Tory who had climbed Mount Everest, C.K. Howard Bury. Bury won the seat with 12,297 votes to the Labour man's 10,392.

In Stourbridge, no Labour candidate stood, and the Conservative was returned.

Another general election followed in November 1923. This returned the first Labour, minority, government with 191 seats compared with the Conservative's 258 and the Liberal's 158 seats. The circumstances of this entirely unexpected election were as follows. Stanley Baldwin, a new leader of the Tory party, claimed that he could not deal with unemployment without a policy of Protection. Since this violated pledges of his predecessor, Bonar Law, Baldwin felt a general election was necessary. The result was probably a verdict in favour of Free Trade, for the Tories lost nearly 100 seats. These seats divided almost equally between the traditionally free trade but hopelessly split Liberals and the Labour Party. But different issues probably decided the result, notably that of unemployment.

The four established Labour MPs in Kingswinford, Smethwick, West Bromwich and Wednesbury again retained their seat. In Dudley the electorate returned to traditional politics with a vengeance the Conservative winning with 10,227 votes, the Liberal 8,510 and Labour only 1,958 compared with 8,522 at the 1922 election.

In Walsall Pat Collins' personal popularity enabled him to increase his Liberal majority, but the poll of a new Labour candidate Lt. Col. A.C. Osburn fell by nearly 2,000 to 7,007.

At Stourbridge there was a Labour candidate in 1923. This was Wilfred Wellock, the well-known Pacifist. He had been a leading figure in the No-Conscription Fellowship during the war, and called himself a peaceful, revolutionary, Christian Communist. In 1921 he had founded the No More War Movement which in 1923 became the War Resisters' International and he edited the journal *The Crusader*. In 1923 he polled a respectable 9,050 in a three candidate contest won by the Conservatives with 14,764 votes against the Liberal's 13,269.

In Wolverhampton East the short period between the elections meant that the Labour Party could find no candidate to stand against the grand old man of Liberalism, G.R. Thorne, who was returned unopposed.

But in Wolverhampton West there appeared for the first time a man who was eventually to win the seat and have considerable influence on both national and Wolverhampton politics. This was W.J. Brown. He had beaten Emma Sproson to the candidature, doubtless because he was secretary of the Civil Service Clerical Association and could bring financial assistance to the constituency. His early history reads like a fairy story or something out of Superman. Born in 1894 in a Battersea slum, his father, a plumber, found, like other skilled men, the greatest difficulty in supporting a growing family and his ailing mother in times when full employment was rare. Brown senior moved his family to Margate, and W.J. became the support of the family as his mother's health deteriorated under the strain of an unsatisfactory relation with her husband. When he was eleven he won a scholarship to a Grammar School. Here the headmaster despised the scholarship boys and made W.J.'s life a misery until the day when he refused to take corporal punishment from the head and his father came to the school and 'taught the headmaster a lesson' after which there was no more trouble. Brown left Sandwich Grammar School when he was fourteen and a half and returned to Battersea on his own. Here he had a number of jobs whiling away time until he was old enough to take a civil service examination. At this time his real education began in the Battersea Public Library, Brown claims. At sixteen he sat for the Civil Service Boy Clerks' Examination and took 51st place out of 1,000 entrants.

The problem with Boy Clerks was that they were all sacked at the age of 18. But it so happened that there was a Royal Commission on the Civil Service in 1911 and W.J. contrived to organise the Boy Clerks and present evidence to the Commission regarding this injustice. Not only was he complimented on this presentation, but his suggestions to remedy this anomaly appeared in the proposals of the Royal Commission and were subsequently implemented. W.J. Brown was then elected secretary of his Boy Clerks' Association. During the war, which he opposed, he avoided call-up not by registering as a Conscientious Objector, but by spinning out the process of objection to service to the limit, at which point his papers were lost and the whole process began again. By then the war was over. This period Brown utilised to organise all clerical workers in the civil service and for the Civil Service Clerical Association to become the first white-collar organisation to affiliate to the TUC.

After the war, apart from supporting two sisters and a brother, he saved the life of his sister Grace by defying the verdict of a Harley Street specialist that she had dementia praecox and sending her to an old landlady of his who fed her up and restored her to perfect health. He also found time to found the Holiday Camp industry establishing the Civil Service Holiday Camp at Lowestoft in 1924 despite the refusal of his union executive to finance the project.

In these ways W.J. Brown graduated to politics and found himself contesting the Wolverhampton West seat in 1923 when he gave the sitting Conservative, a severe jolt by polling 15,740 votes to Bird's 15,990.

In the Bilston constituency John Baker again opposed the Tory member Colonel Howard Bury and would have won but for the intervention of a Liberal, the votes being Bury 10186, Baker 9085, Prentice 5205.

With their four MPs intact and near misses in West Wolverhampton and Bilston, the Black Country vote in 1923 could be said to reflect the increased support which led to the election of the first Labour government, despite disappointments at Dudley and Walsall.

By October 1924, however, there was yet another general election. Labour opinion had been divided as to whether a minority Labour Party should ever take office. Others held that it should form a minority government, enact measures favourable to working people which would at some point be defeated by a combined Tory/Liberal vote, go to the country on this issue and be returned with a working majority. Ramsay MacDonald, on the other hand, took the view that the Labour Party should take office and enact nothing that would offend Tories and Liberals and so convince the country that Labour was 'fit to govern.' The most important legislation passed by the first Labour government was in home affairs the Wheatley Housing Act which led to the building of the vast Council house estates of the inter-war period, and in foreign affairs the recognition of Soviet Russia, with all its implications for trade and employment.

It was indirectly in connection with the latter issue that the Labour government fell. In August 1924 J.R. Campbell, acting editor of the Communist Party paper *Workers' Weekly* published a 'Don't Shoot' appeal urging soldiers not to shoot at their their fellow workers if ordered to do so. There was no immediate danger of this occurring, but it was relevant to the coming general strike. For this appeal Campbell was to be prosecuted. Subsequent counsels decided to drop the prosecution, especially when it was learned that Campbell was a decorated and disabled ex-serviceman. The Tories seized on MacDonald's change of mind to oppose him and MacDonald made it a vote of confidence. The government was defeated and MacDonald called a general election.

This outcome was not necessarily fatal for the Labour government. As a minority government it would have been defeated at some time or another; it was also the more or less the preferred outcome of those who wanted radical legislation, an election, and an improved mandate for the Labour government; also the tide was flowing in favour of Labour. But the *Daily Mail* was to introduce a new factor at the last moment – the supposed Zinoviev letter. This was a forged communication allegedly from the president of the Third International urging various seditious activities on the British Communist Party. The conclusion drawn was that in view of the Russian treaty a vote for Labour was a vote to hand the country over to the Communists and Moscow. Even this might not have been fatal, for the Labour Party increased its vote. But a more profound consequence was the collapse of the Liberal vote which gave the Tories a large overall majority. The final result was Conservatives 412 seats, Liberals 40, Labour 151.

In the Black Country the four Labour MPs, Roberts (West Bromwich), Davison (Smethwick), C. Sitch (Kingswinford), and Short (Wednesbury), were again returned, all of them with increased majorities compared with 1923 and very large increases since they had first been elected in 1918.

The four Labour MPs were joined by a fifth – John Baker in Bilston who beat Col. Howard Bury by 14,583 votes to 12,840. This meant that Labour controlled half of the ten Black Country parliamentary constituencies. It is interesting to note that Bury played on the Zinoviev letter probably more than any other Black Country Tory candidate. He claimed that the country was faced with a very great menace which might upset their civilisation and Constitutional form of government. The Zinoviev letter was absolutely genuine, Bury claimed, and was a deliberate attempt to create civil war in this country. Baker, on the other hand, in his election address stressed unemployment and how the opening of trade with Russia and the curbing of expenditure on war would enable schemes of housing, afforestation, electrification etc. to provide work and revive prosperity. Baker also supported a capital levy, fair treatment of ex-servicemen and pensioners, adult suffrage, national ownership of the drink trade and support for the League of Nations. Clearly a radical pro-Russian policy was an advantage in Bilston, as it must have been in many other constituencies despite the Zinoviev letter.

In Walsall there was a four-cornered contest with an eccentric local doctor J.J. Lynch standing as an Independent. Both the Tory W. Preston, a local business man, and the Labour man Small (with the splendid non-Labour Christian names of Gladstone, Lothian, Rosebery) were also new candidates. Pat Collins suffered from the general Liberal decline and was defeated by Preston who played the patriotic and Zinoviev card. Preston received 15,168 votes, Collins 12,734, Lynch 622 and Small 11,474 thus increasing the Labour vote by 4,000.

In Dudley there was a straight fight between Cyril Lloyd and Stanley Baldwin's son, Oliver, standing for Labour. Lloyd won with 11,199 votes , but Baldwin had raised the Labour vote from under 2,000 to over 10,000.

G.R. Thorne bucked the Liberal trend and was returned once again in Wolverhampton East polling 11,066 votes to the Tory Sir T. Strangman's 10,013. This time a Labour man, D.R. Williams also stood and polled 5,188. In Wolverhampton West, W.J. Brown, still very much on the left-wing of the Labour Party, ran Sir Robert Bird almost as close as in 1923 with 17,046 votes to Bird's 17,886.

In Stourbridge in 1924 Wilfred Wellock again stood as the Labour candidate. This pacifist cum anarchist had originally rejected Parliament as a means of achieving Socialism and thought it would come through a general strike. His experiences of post-war Germany changed his mind, however, and he stood for a second time. He came second in a three candidate contest polling 14,113 against the Tory victor's 16,023 and the Liberal's 10,418 votes. Wellock had increased the Labour vote by nearly 7,000.

In all Black Country constituencies, therefore, Labour had improved its position substantially and also gained another MP. The brief reign of Labour brought greater prominence to two of the Black Country MPs. F.O. Roberts became Minister of Pensions and J.E. Davison became a Labour Whip, a post he held until his death in 1927.

Had there not been a Zinoviev letter, had the Liberal vote not collapsed, and had election results been as good elsewhere as they were in the Black Country the first Labour government might have continued until 1929, and the General Strike might not have occurred with all its adverse consequences for Labour. But history is not made from 'ifs' and the Labour movement had to face up to a further five years of Tory rule.

Local Elections to 1925

Having discussed the national political and economic situation and its effects on parliamentary elections in the Black Country, we can turn to the variations on these themes that occurred locally as reflected in municipal elections results, and also look a little closer at the problems of local Labour Party organisation.

It might be expected that areas with local Labour MPs would also have Labour local administrations. This was not to be, only three Black Country local authorities, Coseley, Sedgley, and Tipton were controlled by Labour in our period 1918-25, and some other councils were 'hung'. We know a considerable amount concerning both Coseley and Sedgley from the personal recollections of John Smallshire in his *Pioneering in Black Country Local Government 1850-1950*. These smaller areas were Urban District Councils or Rural District Councils where elections often took place only every three years when all councillors retired at the same time and a new council was elected; but in other UDCs and RDCs a single councillor was elected for each ward each year. Whichever system was adopted these elections were held in April each year whereas elections for the municipal Boroughs were in November.

In Coseley councillors were elected all together at three yearly intervals. In February 1918 a group met in Coseley which included two pre-war councillors, Matthew Wilkes and Arthur Wakelam, and set up the Coseley Labour Party with Sam Davies as chairman, and local headmaster Louis Williams as secretary. They chose thirteen Labour candidates to contest the 1919 local elections hoping to ensure control of the council at the first attempt. Of these, 11 were elected on to a council of 20 and control duly passed to Labour. In Hurst Hill they won one seat, in West Central ward and South East ward Labour won two of the five seats, in Highfields they won three, but most remarkable of all, in Spring Vale there was no contest and three Labour men were returned unopposed. Labour control continued until 1922 when, as Smallshire says, 'Louis Williams and his wife went to live in Sedgley and a few Labour councillors failed to cope with public office.' From 1923 to 1925 there were seven Labour councillors. With a small Council such as Coseley the lack of a majority might not mean loss of control if some of the eight Independents voted with Labour or if the Labour members were particularly dominant. One such dominant figure in Coseley was Sam Davies. Davies was a founder member of the Bilston Labour Party as well as chair of Coseley Labour Party. He had continuous membership of Coseley council from 1919 to his death in 1939. In 1924 Davies was chair of Coseley's Education, Health and Juvenile Employment Committees as well as the UDC representative on the Ministry of Labour Employment Committee. He also helped found Bilston Trades Council and was its president in the 1920s.

Another Labour controlled council in the Black Country was Sedgley. The miners of Lower Gornal were the driving force here. In 1919 eight Labour candidates stood and seven were elected, giving Labour, 'virtual control', as Smallshire says on a council of fifteen councillors. Among the splendidly proletarian victors were two bricklayers, a coal miner, a blacksmith, a fitter and a furnace builder, all six coming from Lower Gornal. In 1920 Labour gained two seats and thus had an absolute majority. In 1921 the common roll was abandoned and Sedgley divided into five wards with three councillors for each; Labour won ten of these seats with five shared between Conservatives and Independents. In 1923 there were 10 Labour members in a council of 20 and Smallshire maintains that Labour control continued until 1925.

Tipton UDC became another authority controlled by Labour. In this case also the council was totally renewed at triennial elections. In 1919 Labour had 8 successes on a council of 24. Also supporting Labour would be two Ex-Service councillors, D. Pielou, who was to make the transition from soldier-radical to Tory MP, and H.E. King. The 1922 results are difficult to interpret because no parties of candidates were given in the local press; one can only say that at least two Labour councillors were returned as was King on the Ex-Service ticket. But how many new Labour candidates won seats cannot be determined. When the council was next elected in 1925 again no parties were recorded but the *Tipton Herald* reported that Labour had won 'a decisive victory' with 16 or possibly 17 seats out of a council of 24. The paper went on to say that this caused little surprise as the local Labour Party had been campaigning assiduously for the previous twelve months. One outstanding result was the victory of W. Hill, (who was chairman of the Trades Council), over G.R. Peake who had been on the council for 47 years. Both men went to the same church, the United Methodist Church at Dudley Port, and Hill won because he had both the Labour and the Church vote, the *Tipton Herald* claimed.

Of all the local authorities in the Black Country in 1918 Smethwick seemed the best placed to achieve Labour control, and it came within a whisker of doing so. Already in 1915 it had six Labour councillors – George Ryder, Joseph Kesterton, Arthur Morris, Jesse Simcox, George Wilkinson, and Albert Willis. Also in 1915 Smethwick had the first Black Country Labour Mayor – George Ryder. In a six ward (18 councillors plus six aldermen) authority the strength of Labour in Smethwick was that most wards were winnable. But in both 1919 and 1920 results were disappointing, two contests being won and two lost. In 1921 Labour made progress by winning four seats and losing two contests to Unionists. In 1922 Conservatives or Independents won three of the contests and Labour the other three. Once again in 1923 the six wards divided evenly. In 1924 five wards were contested and Labour won only two. The following year five seats were again contested and this time Labour won four of them.

By 1925 none of the Labour vanguard of 1915 had survived but there were several Labour aldermen by then and there had been three Labour mayors. Smethwick also had two women Labour members, Mrs Flattery and Mrs Sands, both of whom were very active. Other leading members of the council from 1919 were Alderman C.F. Betts Labour mayor in 1924, W.E. Lawrence, W.J. Salmon, A. Morris, and W.A. Exton. Control of Smethwick council after the elections of November 1925 was on a knife edge Labour being the largest party with 12 seats, Unionists having 11 and Independent 1. Smethwick was therefore a hung council in 1925.

Wednesbury was another constituency with a Labour MP and thus might seem another area where the Labour Party might be successful locally. Its first two Labour councillors came in 1919 when all four wards were contested and F. Whitehead won Market Ward and F. Rotton Wood Green. In 1920, the election coincided with the coal strike and Labour gained another seat. In 1921, the first year of mass unemployment, Wednesbury Labour had a set-back retaining Town Hall ward, but losing King's Hill and failing to gain Wood Green. In 1922, another year of mass unemployment, Conservatives won in the three contested wards, but Labour was unopposed in Town Hall ward. By 1925 Labour in Wednesbury was still not progressing. In the four wards, which were all contested in that year, Labour won only one of them and the sensation of the year was the appearance of a Communist, T. Gee, who, in a straight fight with an Independent in Town Hall ward polled 536 votes to L.A. Dingley's 1,465. The *Express & Star* was clearly relieved that the Communist had been beaten, but they went on to report his speech after the count almost verbatim. Gee said 'Fellow members of the working class. When I entered this struggle I was not particularly keen to win because I think the working class struggle has to be carried out somewhere else beside the ballot box.' He was satisfied that there were over 500 rebels in Town Hall ward on which the Communist Party could build.

The other constituency with a Labour MP elected in 1918 was Kingswinford. The base of Charles Sitch, however, was among the chain makers covered by the Rowley Regis and Quarry Bank UDCs. In 1919 Labour won 8 seats in Rowley Regis (compared with two before the war) on a Council of 20 seats. Elections were triennial and in 1925 there were again 8 Labour councillors, but the Tividale ward had disappeared and the Council reduced to 17 seats. Cradley Heath was also a productive ward, returning C. Sitch and the Rev F. Pickles in 1919 and four out of 5 Labour councillors in 1925. Rowley ward returned all four Labour candidates in 1919 and two in 1925, one of these being the only councillor serving for the whole period, J.T. Kite.

Thus Labour in Rowley Regis had considerable influence on the Council from 1919 and by 1925 with eight seats all but controlled it with the opposition split among Conservatives 4, Liberals 1, and Independents 4.

A similar situation existed on Quarry Bank UDC. In 1919 Labour won 4 seats out of 12 seats with Lt. Cox of the Federation of Soldiers and Sailors, likely to support Labour on most issues holding 1 seat. In 1925 the Labour Party won 5 seats and, uniquely for the Black Country, there was still one Ex-Service representative, although by this time it was J.T. Whilley. With an opposition of 4 Conservatives and 3 Liberals in 1925 the Labour position was a strong one.

In adjacent areas Labour support was poor. It had only two seats out of 18 on the Brierley Hill UDC in 1925 and Stourbridge had no Labour councillors until 1922 when Samuel Wright won a seat in St. James' ward. The next year Charles Broughton won the St. Mary's Ward. Both were influential Labour members and by 1926 both were JPs. But these were the only two Labour councillors on a council of 6 aldermen and 18 councillors. On Kingswinford UDC there seem to have been no Labour councillors at all, unless there are any unidentified Labourites on lists which give names of those elected, but no parties. This is unlikely.

Turning to the larger Black Country towns, in West Bromwich in 1919 Labour won one seat and T.D. Smith who stood as a Socialist Labour Party candidate was defeated. In 1920 Labour won two more seats and Edmund Mynett (Spon Lane) and J. Shaw (Greet's Green) joined J.T.H Davies who won Greet's Green the previous year. In 1921 Joseph Bailey won Lyndon ward for Labour and in 1922 T.W. Wilson won Lyng. 1923 was a bad year for Labour, they won no seats and an Unemployed candidate standing in Lyng lost by 595 votes to 1113. In 1924 when things were improving Labour won two seats, J. Bailey (Lyndon) and A. Guest (Hill Top). In 1925 Wilson retained Lyng ward and in that year there were 5 Labour members on a council of 8 aldermen and 24 councillors.

Dudley was another large town where the Labour Party did not perform well. Of the 1919 elections the *Dudley Herald* commented that no women were nominated and the Labour threat to contest every ward did not materialise. In St. James' ward J. Price, the trade union leader, stood down when the Mayor (Councillor Adshead) was asked to continue for a second year. Labour stood two candidates and these were the only wards contested. Labour won both of them, Barney Norton, a Netherton iron worker taking Netherton ward and J.H. Molyneux winning a famous victory in St. John's. The next year there were two more Labour gains in Netherton when S. Payne and J.E. Willetts became councillors. By 1922 the tide seems to have reversed in Netherton when Barney Norton lost his seat to a Liberal. Even worse was to occur in 1923 when J. Bayliss and S. Payne lost a straight fight with Tories for two seats at Netherton. J.A. Taylor did, however, win a seat in St. Thomas' ward. In 1924 two Labour candidates in Netherton, J.B. Holden and D.H. Whitehouse, were beaten again for two seats by two Tories. In 1925 W. Timmins won a seat in St. Thomas' for Labour and Molyneux was returned for a third term with an increased majority. In Netherton the two seats went to one Liberal and one Conservative, but the standing of both opposition parties meant that the vote was split and the two Labour candidates came in the middle with Conservative and Liberal candidates both above and below them. However, in a two seat contest in St. Thomas' the only Labour candidate, W. Timmins, came top of the poll.

By 1925 therefore, it seems that Labour had only three Labour councillors, Molyneux, J.A. Taylor and Timmins, in a council of 28. The swing from Labour in Netherton, an area thick with iron works and coal mines, warrants further research, particularly in view of its proximity to Old Hill and Cradley Heath with their very different experiences of increased Labour representation.

The Labour movement in Walsall has its historian in Kenneth Dean. His book *Town and Westminster* deals with the political history of Walsall from 1906 to 1945. He notes that by 1914 the movement for political representation in Walsall included a branch of the Fabian Society, the Walsall Industrial Council, the Independent Labour Party, the British Socialist Party, the Socialist Club and the Walsall Labour Association. Lib-Labism had deep roots in Walsall and early labour representation on the local council included the Lib-Labs Alderman Dean of the miners, who died in 1910 and William Millerchip of the Walsall Lock Co-operative and national Co-operative leader, who resigned in 1910 when taking over as manager of Walsall's first Labour Exchange. The only two Labour councillors in 1914 were Joseph Thickett and H. Hucker, both railwaymen and both moderates. But this Lib-Lab tradition was also overlaid by a militant one. In 1888 Haydn Sanders of the Socialist League became one of the first Socialist councillors in Britain when he was elected on a revolutionary socialist programme. In 1892 the so-called Walsall Anarchist Bomb Plot resulted in the imprisonment of the Marxist leader Joseph Deakin. Deakin served five years in prison but came out to become a Trades Council leader and to be regarded as the real founder of the Walsall Labour movement. Also in 1919 the British Socialist Party still had a voice in Walsall and a Walsall member of that party, H.W. Ward, was the only Black Country delegate attending the founding Convention of the Communist Party in 1920.

At the first post-war local elections in 1919 Labour stood four candidates in Walsall, but only A.J. Stanley at Pleck won a seat. In Bridge ward a woman, Mrs C.W. Dewsbury, prominent Labour and Co-operative activist, was put up, but she was defeated. In 1920 Thickett retained his seat at Pleck with a majority of almost 1,000, W. Abbotts, the Co-op leader, won Leamore, and Daniel Cartwright, who was later to split the Miners' Federation, captured Bloxwich. In 1921 Timothy Burgin won Birchills and Hucker retained his Caldmore seat. 1922 was a disaster year; five wards were contested, none was won, and Stanley lost his seat in Pleck. This was largely due to rampaging Ratepayers who were screaming for economies and who captured three seats. Throughout this period Liberals and Conservatives collaborated to ensure that only a single candidate opposed Labour in each ward. An exception was 1923 when Labour fought itself in Bloxwich. D. Cartwright stood on the ILP ticket and won the seat, showing the strength of his personal following with miners. He polled 1,385 votes, beating the Ratepayer with 1,179 votes and reducing the Labour candidate, C. Kidson, to a derisory 59 votes. This was a bitter inter-Labour struggle and two years later in 1925 Cartwright formed his own Wednesfield and District Miners' Association.

1924 was a peculiar year. Five of the eight wards were uncontested and among these were two Labour wards – W. Smith at Bloxwich and Henry Hucker being re-elected unopposed at Caldmore because he was the Mayor elect in that year. In the contested wards Ratepayers (some of them now calling themselves Unionist Ratepayers) won two seats against Labour opposition. In Birchills, Burgin the sitting Labour councillor was defeated. There were again only three contests in 1925. In Leamore Mrs G. Cresswell became Walsall's first woman Labour councillor beating a Ratepayer by 26 votes. In Paddock ward Mrs Dewsbury fought a Ratepayer and lost by 669 votes to 1,312.

Thus the position of Walsall Labour on an eight ward Council of 24 councillors plus eight aldermen in 1919 was that Labour had only three councillors. By 1921 the number had doubled to six. In 1922 and 1923 it was down to five and in 1924 and 1925 it was back again to six. Scarcely an influential position on the council. Consolation achievements were that Henry Hucker became the first Labour mayor and Mrs Cresswell the first woman on the council.

It is noteworthy that in Walsall, once unemployment took hold in 1921, initiative on the Council passed to the Ratepayers, who joined with Liberals and Conservatives in the conspiracy to ensure that Labour was opposed by only one candidate. This is not surprising, of course, in view of the fact that the Ratepayers were Conservatives and Liberals in disguise and after 1925 the label of Ratepayer is dispensed with and members appear in their true colours of Conservative and Liberal.

Apart from this disadvantage, Dean discusses a number of weaknesses that the Walsall Labour Party suffered from, hampering its efforts to attain political control of the town. Two of these were difficulties in relations with the Trades and Labour Council and relations with the local Co-operative movement. Occasional differences did arise, but both bodies were affiliated to the Labour Party and the benefits to the Labour movement of co-operation between the three bodies was much greater than the disadvantages of the occasional problems that arose between them. The differences between those on the left of the Labour Party and those with right-wing views dominated Walsall labour politics as it did elsewhere. The former were represented by the ILP and the Communist Party. The ILP was constantly urging the Labour Party on to greater militancy and this would be the foremost consideration in their support of Daniel Cartwright. Cartwright was to remain on the council and be a thorn in the side of the Labour Party into the nineteen thirties. The Communist Party inherited the militant tradition in Walsall and was a force in both the organisation of the unemployed and also the trade union movement. But many of the leading figures in the Labour movement in Walsall were strongly anti-Communist and they were powerful enough to determine that labour politics in Walsall would be 'moderate' throughout the period.

Before finally discussing Wolverhampton we can briefly discuss the fortunes of the remaining smaller local authorities in the Black Country. In the two areas adjacent, Darlaston and Willenhall, Labour fared even worse than in Walsall. In Darlaston UDC each triennial election reported produced a list of names but without party labels with no identifiable Labour representation. In Willenhall, dominated by the lock trade, the Lockmakers' Union on a number of occasions discussed standing candidates, but nothing was done and again no known Labour councillors appear. In nearby Bilston elections were held each year and the Labour Party had a stronger presence. In the 1919 elections Labour won two seats (James Walton at High Town and H.A. Thomas at New Town) on a 15 seat council dominated by Economists. In 1920 W.T. Fellows was returned unopposed at Ettingshall and G.F. Vaughan in Bradley. This was the high point of Labour representation in Bilston. In 1922 Walton stood for re-election but by then had deserted the Labour Party and stood as an Independent. He was defeated by an Economist. There seems to have been little electoral activity in 1923 and 1924. But in 1925, following the victory of the Labour government, there was a flurry of activity which, unfortunately for the Labour Party, resulted in the reverse of their intentions – the defeat of their only councillor. This caused considerable, long-term damage to the party. Firstly, two Labour candidates standing in Bradley and Town Hall wards both lost. Secondly, in the only other ward contested, Ettingshall, John Fellows, the chairman of the party insisted in putting forward two Labour candidates instead of relying on the sitting councillor W.T. Fellows. Moreover, the Labour Party made the mistake of attacking Dr Bulgar the Liberal candidate as being an unreliable person to sit on the council. According to Smallshire, this enraged not only liberals in Bilston, but in Wolverhampton also and Liberals 'stormed the ward coming from all parts of the Black Country.' The result was that Dr Bulgar was top of the poll followed by an Independent and both Labour candidates lost.

At the other end of the Black Country, Halesown never had a strong Labour representation and in 1925 the council consisted of 10 Liberals, 4 Conservatives and 1 Labour. Oldbury fared rather better. In

1919 they stood in each of the six wards and captured two seats in Warley, the surprise of the election being the defeat of the leader of the council by E.A. Cooper the Labour schoolmaster in Warley South. By 1925 Oldbury had been much reorganised and had eight councillors in four wards. H. Mansell and W.H. Grice won the two seats in Central ward and W.B. Hay won one of the Broadwell seats. This gave the Labour Party three of the eight seats on the Council, a relatively strong position.

Finally we turn to Wolverhampton. Here, municipal politics have been exhaustively analysed in George Jones' splendid book *Borough Politics, a study of the Wolverhampton Borough Council 1888-1964*. There is also a complete set of Wolverhampton Labour Party minutes from 1907. Not the least of Jones' achievements has been to identify all councillors as Liberal, Conservative and true Independent, usually despite the labels they actually used of Progressive, Independent, Ratepayer etc. He can thus give the state of the Council for every year from 1887-88. Jones in his book, however, does not give the names of the councillors he has identified and it is to be hoped that he leaves his notes for posterity to mull over and agree or dissent from the conclusions he drew which must have cost him so much time. This lack of names is less important for the Labour Party as we have the researches of Chris Roseblade who has collated Black Country election results for the larger towns from 1919 to 1938. For our period 1919 to 1925 the position in Wolverhampton was as follows.

Pre-war there were three Labour councillors. To these in 1919 were added another three – H.J. Newman in Merridale, J.E. Dideridge in Blakenhall and A. Davies in Dunstall to bring the total to six on a council of 48. In addition two Ex-Service candidates out of three won seats and these could be expected to support Labour on most issues. Emma Sproson stood in Park ward but was defeated. In 1921 Labour won two seats, J.W. Kennedy, St. Mary's and G.T. Williams in Blakenhall, but lost a pre-war Councillor A. Bent. 1921 was a bumper year with three Labour victories, including Emma Sproson, the first woman councillor in Wolverhampton. This brought Labour representation on the council to 10. In 1922 it fell to 9, but rose to 10 in 1923 when two candidates (including Emma Sproson) stood as ILP candidates. As unemployment fell and militancy became possible Labour representation rose to 11 in 1924 and reached a high point in 1925. At this time the council consisted of 13 Labour, 21 Conservatives, 3 Independents and 11 Liberals. With 27 per cent of the seats on the council, Labour in Wolverhampton must be accounted the most successful of the large towns in the Black Country.

The existence of minute books for the Wolverhampton Labour Party enable us to follow the local problems which would also have been common to other Labour Parties.

The great advantage of the Labour Party everywhere was that it had a municipal programme. This centred around Council house building to improve the dreadful housing conditions, improved education for working people, hospital and health facilities not least for the young and the old, and trade union rates of pay and conditions for municipal employees. Opposition parties had no programme of any sort, and therefore could do no more than combine together to try to thwart Labour. Fortunately for the opposition, everything the Labour party wanted to do cost money and the charge of Labour 'extravagance' and the call to keep the rates down was a potent one, especially after 1921 when the depression struck.

To carry through the Labour programme required something else the opposition did not have – discipline. Tories and Liberals had the freedom to 'vote according to their consciences'. Labour Party councillors enjoyed no such luxury; if the Party programme was to be carried through, every member must vote for it and disciplinary means must be found to punish those who would not. Thus the Labour Party pioneered the Group System which the Tories and others would only follow in 1945.

A further problem for the Labour Party was that human nature being what it is, some Labour councillors would inevitably hanker for the independence of the Parliamentary Labour Party which had successfully asserted a complete independence from the Party Conference and in their superior wisdom would determine when, and even if, the Party programme should be implemented.

Efforts to cope with these problems had been made before the war by the setting up of a Consultative Committee comprising councillors, Labour Representation Committee members and others to discuss the monthly Council meeting agenda. After 1919 when the number of councillors doubled and then doubled again these problems became more pressing.

After the war, the LRC was transformed into the Labour Party and the Minute Books which commence in 1907 continue unbroken into the post-war period. In 1919 the Committee was concerned with getting local Council candidates nominated. The committee wanted all local councillors to retire since there had been no elections since 1913 and they obtained the agreement of G.R. Thorne for the Liberals, but presumably the Tories would not agree and only one councillor, as usual, retired in each ward. James Whittaker also negotiated with the Ex-Service organisations. Other election matters included negotiations with the ILP for the holding of out-door meetings at Snow Hill and in the constituencies, and the desirability of standing two women candidates (eventually only Emma Sproson stood). More general matters were protests to the Food Controller regarding the price of sugar, and sympathy with a resolution from Newcastle Labour Party asking for a special conference to demand the withdrawal of British troops from Russia and ending the blockade, but feeling that this would be too near the annual Labour Party conference.

In 1921 in response to a letter from the ILP regarding the Hands off Russia campaign in Wolverhampton, the executive agreed six Labour Party members to the Committee. Hands off Russia was the most explosive issue of 1920 and, among others, a meeting was held with Colonel C.J.L. Malone (who became the first Communist MP). Another issue was that of Ireland, and in December 1920 the local Labour Party agreed to send delegates to a conference in London on British Labour and the Irish Peace. Relations with NUX continued. Early in the year NUX proposed a conference around the issue of the release of all serving men who were still imprisoned for the violation of military law (this was largely a question of the release of the Conscientious Objectors); the Labour party agreed to sponsor the Conference and share expenses with NUX. At the end of the year NUX proposed that its individual members should be eligible for Labour Party membership, and this matter was referred to the wards. The final decision was that the 'time was not ripe for this change'. Considerable concern was shown for the 'destruction of child life in Central and East Europe', and a number of meetings were held.

On municipal matters interest was expressed in the Sydney Rating System and co-operation established with the Birmingham Labour Party to discuss its merits. In view of the extension of the franchise to women special attention from 1918 was paid to the development of Women's Sections within the Labour Party. Central to this question in Wolverhampton was the position of Emma Sproson, the town's leading Suffragette and War Resister. Emma was a handful for the Labour Party. As an ILP member she supported militant policies and was never averse to resigning from the Labour Party if she disapproved of what was being done. Her first resignation came in 1920 before she was a councillor. The reason for it is not made clear in the minutes of the EC, but a couple of leading members were deputed 'to wait on her', and she was persuaded to remain in the Party.

In early 1921 prices were still rising and the Labour Party executive took this matter up with the Bakers' Union. James Whittaker negotiated with Wolverhampton Co-operative Society to insert Labour Notes in their local edition of *Wheatsheaf*. Ominously enough, the first subject was to be Unemployment. Delegates were sent to a London conference in January and the next month the legal ramifications of door to door collections for the unemployed was being raised. The problem was compounded in May by the coal strike and by June collections were being made to the Miners' Children's Fund. In September, the national Labour Party declared Sunday October 9th. to be Unemployment Day and in Wolverhampton the local Party and the Trades Council organised a demonstration. November brought outstanding election results with three gains of Tom Frost (Blakenhall), Emmas Sproson (Dunstall) and A.A. Beach (St. John's). These victories brought the issue of wearing gowns at Council meetings to the fore. Previously there had been a decision to wear gowns, apparently, for this was rescinded by 20 votes to 4 at the Labour Party EC. Emma Sproson put forward a resolution that the councillors should themselves decide whether to wear gowns or not, but this was defeated 20-0.

Emma Sproson was prominent in 1923. She successfully moved that a collection be taken for Russian Famine Relief at the May Day demonstration. In July she was objecting to information getting out concerning EC meetings. In August she resigned her individual membership from the Labour Party, presumably in the belief that she would still be a member by virtue of the affiliation of the ILP to the local Labour Party. She complained that she and her husband were being boycotted by the Labour Party and she asked for it to be stopped. No such boycott existed, it was stated, and her resignation was accepted. However, the next month she withdrew the resignation.

1923 saw determined efforts to strengthen Labour Party organisation and also procedures for the conduct of the growing group of Councillors. The main officers of the EC in 1919-20 were Albert Bent (chair) and Charlie Hill (secretary) of the EC. After Bent's illness in 1921 Allan Davies became chair of the EC and Hill remained secretary in a partnership that was to last for many years. Other members of the executive in 1923 were Dark, Dean, Dideridge, Hollins, Hooper, Mead and a newcomer H.E. Lane, who was to be a councillor for 50 years. The ILP representative on the EC was not elected, but Emma Sroson was later chosen; she was soon complaining that she was not receiving notices of the EC. Mrs Jones and Mrs Palmer were appointed the Women's representatives pending 'reorganisation'.

An important task in the spring of 1923 was to select a new prospective Parliamentary candidate in place of A.G. Walkden, who retired after three unsuccessful attempts to win Wolverhampton West. The key question was who could provide the money to support a Parliamentary campaign. In April Allan Davies reported that whilst in London he had heard that W.J. Brown, general secretary of the Civil Service Clerical Association, 'was available', and his trade union was prepared to pay £250 per annum for electoral expenses. Brown was promptly invited to a Selection Conference where there were to be two other candidates, Emma Sproson and O.S. Willey. At the last minute Willey sent his apologies, saying that he could not attend because of a prior engagement! The two candidates were given fifteen minutes to speak and another fifteen minutes to answer questions. Brown was chosen by 34 votes to 17. Obviously, the local candidate stood no chance at all as she had no money to provide and Brown was an excellent candidate who might well have been chosen on his own merits, But it is interesting to speculate how Parliamentary as well as local history might have been changed had Emma Sproson become an MP.

In the summer Emma was again in trouble. She moved an ILP motion on the EC condemning Allan Davies for moving a motion on the Council that no Committee member be allowed to enter the fever hospital without the prior consent of the Medical Office of Health. This undermined the principle of democratic government, she asserted. This motion was lost by 11 to 3. Another motion was then moved protesting at the action of Councillor Davies, the statement he made with regard to Mrs Sproson being 'in conflict with the facts.' This was lost by a narrower margin of 7 to 5. This was followed by yet another motion moved by Mr Horton congratulating Mrs Sproson on her fight with the Health Committee and expressing confidence in her. At this point the meeting was adjourned. When it reassembled with Mrs Hartshorne in the chair, Councillor Williams moved a convoluted motion:

> That this meeting does not agree that Mrs Sproson acted in the best interests of the Labour Party in bringing this matter to the Town Council without first bringing it to the EC of the Party.

This resulted in a vote of 5 to 5, after which the original resolution was not put.

As a result of this and other experiences the constitution of the Consultative Committee was revised. The Committee was to consist of all Councillors plus seven from the two constituency Labour Parties. Meetings to discuss the Council agenda were to be held on the 1st Thursday of each month and special meetings could be called by any two councillors. Members of Committees were obliged to report on 'all matters of importance' coming before the Council. No Councillor should table any resolution for the Council that had not been discussed and agreed by the Consultative Committee. Nor could any question be asked at Council without first obtaining the opinions of the Labour members on the Committee. Finally, came the key clause, 'In all cases in which the policy or principles of the Party are affected a majority vote shall be binding upon all members.' Such a constitution strengthened collective control, but there were still problems of enforcing decisions, as the future was soon to show.

In 1924 the Consultative Committee principle was extended to Labour representatives on the Board of Guardians and the same constitution adopted. This was the year of the first Labour government. In the previous December at the General Election W.G. Brown in Wolverhampton West had failed to topple the Tory custard man, Bird, by only 241 votes and he was immediately re-adopted as candidate with the support of Mrs Sproson. The election of the first Labour Prime Minister was celebrated by having a special portrait of J. Ramsay MacDonald hung in the party Rooms.

Dissatisfaction with the performance of councillors began in February with a complaint against Councillor Williams by the Unemployed Committee. The Labour Party EC considered this matter but gave Williams a vote of confidence of 17 to 8. The next month there was trouble with the Consultative Committee. Councillors Allan Davies and Dideridge voted for an increase in the Town Clerk's salary despite a group decision to vote against this. A resolution of censure was then brought to the Labour Party. The councillors 'explained their position', but absolutely refused to give an undertaking to abide by Consultative Committee decisions. Censure was then carried by 25 votes to 2. Davies said he would withdraw his name as a delegate to the Labour Party, place the situation with his society (the ASLE&F) and abide by their decision. The matter was particularly serious as Davies was chair of the Labour Party EC at the time and Dideridge was on the EC. The affair dragged on. In May a resolution reaffirming that Davies and Dideridge must agree to abide by the Consultative Committee constitution before they could be considered representatives of the Party was confirmed by 13 votes to 3. In July a motion to rescind the decision regarding Davies and Dideridge was lost by 16 votes to 18. The margin was narrowing. In August D & D wrote to say that they would accept decisions 'if they were in conformity with the policy or principles of the Party.' This was not enough and a vote to rescind the decision was lost 4 to 6.

In August the matter was again discussed and a decision taken that the vote must take place not later than 9-30pm. (Some meetings went on until 11-30 pm by which time family men and moderates had gone home and only the young and militant remained – GB). It was moved by Talbot and seconded by Mrs Sproson that D & D 'cannot be considered to be representatives of the Labour Party.' An amendment was moved by Beach:

> For the sake of Party unity and in view of the approaching elections Municipal and Parliamentary and in recognition of past services and the need for Labour Party unity on the Town Council that the vote of censure be removed.

This persuasive resolution resulted in a tie 19-19. After several attempts to extend the discussion beyond 9-30 pm had failed a vote was taken and the censure was finally removed by 17 votes to 20. The next month Clause 5 was amended allowing the Consultative Committee to determine whether any local matter was of sufficient importance to be deemed a matter affecting the policy of the party; this was agreed by 16 votes to 1.

In October Emma Sproson again resigned 'as a public representative of the Party' This time the EC recommended this be accepted. But almost immediately she 'withdrew her resignation unreservedly.' At the Labour party meeting she was censured 29 votes to 2 for failing to observe the Consultative Committee resolution re. the election of aldermen and was requested to give some undertaking to observe CC decisions in future. Presumably she gave some such undertaking as she defended successfully her Dunstall council seat in November.

At this time there had been the Zinoviev Letter forgery which defeated the Labour government at a general election. W.J. Brown's position in Wolverhampton had been only marginally worsened; he lost again to Bird this time by 840 votes.

Other general matters dealt with by the Labour party during the year included protest at the Task Work imposed by the Board of Guardians, the purchase of a typewriter and duplicator, a resolution to the national Labour Party conference requesting that Health Authorities be allowed to provide birth control information, support for a No More War demonstration, and a protest at the wearing of Court dress by Labour Party parliamentary representatives. In some wards there were 'very few young men active workers,' and to attract more the organising of Debating Classes was suggested. With regard to the key question of work with women the Women's Advisory Committee was asked to help develop Women's Sections in wards where these were weak.

1925 was to be a year dominated by the Communist question. We have seen how militancy had been building up in both the national and local Labour movement as unemployment declined. The demise of the first Labour government only slightly affected this militancy which was to lead on to the enthusiasm of the General Strike. Cutting across this militancy was the question of relations with the Communist International and Communists in Britain. At the 1924 Labour Party Conference a three-pronged attack on Communists was mounted. Firstly, affiliation of the Communist Party to the Labour Party was decisively rejected. Secondly it was laid down that no Communist Party member could be eligible as a Labour Party candidate either nationally or locally. Thirdly, and passed by only a very small majority, no Communist Party member was eligible for membership of the Labour Party. These resolutions were easier to pass than to carry out; the predecessors of the Communist Party had been part of the structure of the Labour Party. Many Communists were also individual members of the Labour Party. The Communists were the leaders of the Unemployed struggles in the localities and worked with Labour Party members in the Minority Movement (which had been set up in June 1924) to further left-wing policies in the trade unions. To try to square these circles and pressurise the many local Labour Parties not at all keen to implement these resolutions, a sub-committee was set up 'to collect information throughout the year' from affiliated bodies.

These enquiries reached the Wolverhampton Labour Party in March 1925. The local party replied that it had no problems with Communists in the town and the local Communist party was not strong. They had not therefore considered it desirable to put the Conference resolutions into operation. The local Communist Party then wrote to the Wolverhampton Labour Party, presumably along the lines of a Communist Party Political Bureau statement at the end of March calling for resistance to the policy of expelling Communists from the Labour Party. It was agreed that this letter be left over until the Labour party conference agenda was considered. Continued support for Soviet Russia was emphasised in June when a letter from the Anglo-Russian Parliamentary Committee urging an increase in Anglo-Russian trade was supported. The same month a Communist Party resolution (whether this was the previous letter or something else is not made clear), was deferred until the report by the sub-committee of the national Party. Yet another complication was attitudes to the *Sunday Worker.* This was set up in March 1925, as a united front Communist-Labour newspaper and was particularly strongly supported by Labour Parties in Birmingham led by Joseph Southall, the artist. This excellent labour paper was inevitably labelled a Communist front, however. When the paper was brought to the notice of the Wolverhampton Labour Party in June it was agreed to recommend that the paper be taken up. In July the *Sunday Worker* prospectus was circulated and it was agreed to purchase 100 shares and recommend that the ward parties take it up. This was passed by 11 votes to 7. The Wolverhampton delegate to the national Labour Party conference was also instructed to support the motion on the *Sunday Worker.* Another matter which raised the Communist issue was the youth question which the local Labour Party had agreed to 'take up' in July 1925. There is no indication that there was a Young Communist League branch in Wolverhampton at the time, but young Communist militants might well have been in the ILP's Young Socialist League and strong opinions existed that one united youth movement was enough for Wolverhampton. But enquiries to the national agent brought the ruling that the YSL was not eligible for affiliation to the Labour Party. It was then agreed to defer the youth matter until a proposed national Labour youth organisation was formed. In October came the arrest of the twelve Communist leaders in preparation for the General Strike, and the Labour Party supported the nation wide protests that followed. Thus the burning question for right-wing ideologues of expelling Communists from the Labour Party had to be deferred until another year.

This chapter has traced the complexity of Labour organisation in the different towns of the Black Country. All shared the general determination in 1918 that a better world should be built. All were rendered virtually powerless when the slump and mass unemployment appeared at the end of 1920 and this dream disappeared. But by then the main party of working people – the Labour Party – had been established in every town and village and Parliamentary election results from 1918 to 1929 showed the Black Country to be a stronghold of labour. When the slump came considerable militancy was demonstrated headed by intelligent and determined leadership. This limited the ability of Conservative governments acting for the main business interests to try to solve the slump in the way they considered best by slashing wages. This militancy was both patchy and, in general, accorded with previous local traditions. This is demonstrated by the municipal election results. In 1919 only limited Labour gains were made reflecting a loyalty to those parties that had directed the war and won it, despite the mass slaughter it had entailed. Once unemployment engulfed the area it might have been expected that the Labour Party would come into its own. But instead the calls for economy blunted the Labour message of improved social services. As unemployment subsided somewhat from 1924 militancy again became possible. This brought, among other things, the first minority Labour government. Despite its shortcomings and the forged Zinoviev letter which prevented its re-election, this militancy grew to the point where it could sustain the most remarkable episode in the history of the British trade union movement – the General Strike.

Bibliography: The Labour Movement in the Black Country 1919-1925

For ex-Service politics and the development of the British Legion see Graham Wooton – *The Official History of the British Legion and The Politics of Influence.* National Union of Ex-Servicemen (NUX) activities can only be followed from the local and Labour press.

For Unemployment see the Ministry of Labour *Labour Gazette* (monthly) which gives occasional Unemployment figures until 1923 and thereafter a regular monthly series for the larger Black Country towns. Percentage figures for Unemployment are my own calculations from the table of total numbers of people employed from the 1921 Census. Cost of Living figures are also given in the *Labour Gazette.* Normally the annual average figure is sufficient, but between 1921 and 1923 the index fell so rapidly that it is necessary to have monthly figures to assess changes in the standard of living as the fiercest wage reductions ever known were implemented. See Wal Hannington – *Unemployed Struggles 1919-1936.*

Protests against these cuts have been followed from *Workers' Weekly, Labour Leader,* the *Minutes of Walsall Trades Council;* for Smethwick, the weekly column of W.A. Exton in the Birmingham Labour paper *Town Crier,* and from the local press – *Wolverhampton Chronicle, Express & Star, Dudley Herald, Tipton Herald, Walsall Observer, Worcestershire County Express.*

For Working Class Education see *Plebs* and *The Communist,* for the National Council of Labour Colleges. WEA West Midlands Annual Reports and *Highway* for the Workers' Educational Association.

For the Communist Party see: *Communist Unity Convention (1920) Official Report;* James Klugman – *History of the Communist Party of Great Britain* vol 1; The Party paper *The Communist,* from 1923 the *Workers' Weekly;* personal information from Winifred Docherty and also transcripts of interviews given by Winnie at various times.

For the Independent Labour Party see: R.E. Dowse – *Left in the Centre. The Independent Labour Party 1893-1940; Labour Leader,* after October 1921 *New Leader;* Henry Brockhouse – obituary in *Labour Leader,* March 1921 and the local press; ILP annual National Conference Reports.

For the the Labour Party see: G.D.H. Cole – *A History of the Labour Party from 1914* for national developments; The autobiography of W.J. Brown – *So Far...* (1943); John Smallshire – *Pioneering in Black Country Local Government 1850-1950* (in Wolverhampton Local History Centre); Material of Chris Roseblade in possession of G. Barnsby analysing local and general election results in the Black Country from 1885 to 1939; George Jones – *Borough Politics, A Study of the Wolverhampton Borough Council 1888-1964;* Kenneth A. Dean – *Town and Westminster, A Political History of Walsall from 1906 to 1945;* Councillor John Rowley – *Wolverhampton Labour Party 1907-1951,* an Introduction to the Records of the Wolverhampton Labour Party; Minutes from 1907; J. Ward – *Emergence of the Labour Party in the Black Country 1910-1922* (Unpublished Wolverhampton University MA thesis – 1993).

Chapter 22

Black Country Trade Unionism 1919-1925

The Trades Councils

By the end of the war the nine pre-war trades councils -Wolverhampton (formed in 1865), Wednesbury (1875), Walsall (1890), West Bromwich (1891), Stourbridge (1901), Smethwick (1904), Bilston (1911), Willenhall (1911), and Tipton (1913), had been joined by five others. These were Oldbury and Rowley Regis, both formed in 1915, Brierley Hill formed in 1916 and Dudley Trades Council, thought to have been formed in 1897, but which had to be re-formed in 1916.

As has been explained, much of our knowledge of trade unionism in the years from 1916 comes from a Gazeteer compiled by volunteers in 1916-17 from the Fabian Research Department (which became, towards the end of the war, the Labour Research Department). This was done at the request of the TUC which had been asked by the government to supply lists of local trade unionists throughout the country who could be nominated for service on local Pensions Committees. The results were handed over to the Ministry of Labour and published as a 'confidential Blue Book' in 1918. Where trades councils existed they were the obvious organisations to collect this local information. Where there were no trade unions, the task was more difficult. The Government wanted information regarding both affiliated and non-affiliated trade unions, the name and address of the secretary of each branch, and the number of members where possible.

The local returns from the Black Country were, as elsewhere, uneven. But valuable information information regarding the strengths and weaknesses of trade union organisation can be gleaned where numbers of members were given. Unfortunately large trades councils such as Smethwick, West Bromwich, Walsall and Wolverhampton gave no figures. But where figures were produced it seems that Bilston, for instance, had almost 600 trade unionists in the town 230 of whom were affiliated to the trades council which was dominated by the Workers' Union with 200 members. In Brierley Hill nearly 2,000 workers were affiliated to the trades council, but neither the miners nor the ironworkers who formed a significant part of the organised work force were affiliated. In Dudley a total of over 4,000 trade unionists was recorded, nearly 3,000 of them affiliated to the trades council; the largest affiliate was 800 members of the National Federation of Women Workers. In Rowley Regis about 2,500 were affiliated to the Trades Council which was dominated by 1,700 in the Miners' Protection Society. This was an exception to the rule that miners and ironworkers did not affiliate to local trades councils, and probably arose because the union was a rival to the Miners' Federation.

Where membership figures were not given one can judge of the spread of trade unionism, but not its depth. This spread shows the following.

The building trades were organised in all towns. The bricklayers belonged to the Operative Bricklayers Society. The painters were organised in the National Amalgamated Society of Operative

House and Ship Painters. Most carpenters belonged to The Amalgamated Society of Carpenters & Joiners, although there was a branch of the rival General Union of Carpenters and Joiners in Wolverhampton. Stone masons, plasterers, and plumbers were also organised as were builders' labourers in such organisations as the National Association of Builders' Labourers in Dudley and the Wolverhampton & District Builders' Labourers' Protective, Accident and Burial Society as well as, presumably, in the general labourers' unions.

Skilled engineers were universally organised in the Amalgamated Society of Engineers or the specialist trades unions of Steam Engine Makers, United Pattern Makers, United Society of Boilermakers, the Friendly Society of Iron Founders and the Electrical Trades Union. Important unions for less skilled local people were the National Society of Brass Workers and Metal Mechanics; the Lock, Latch and Key Union; Enginemen, Firemen and General Electrical Workers; the Galvanised Hollow Ware Association; and the Amalgamated Society of General Toolmakers.

Glass workers were organised in the two main centres of Brierley Hill and Dudley in the National Flint Glassmakers' Society.

Iron workers were organised in most Black Country towns in BISAKTA (the British Iron & Steel and Kindred Trades Association), but in Dudley and Bilston there were also branches of the Associated Iron & Steel Workers of GB. Puddlers and Forgemen were also organised and at Dudley there was a branch of the Midlands Blast Furnacemen, Cokemen and By-Product Workers' Association.

Postmen were organised in all towns in the Postmen's Federation and in Dudley and Wolverhampton there were branches of the Postal and Telegraph Clerks' Association.

Printers were organised in the Typographical Association in six of the main Black Country towns and there were branches of the Amalgamated Society of Lithographic Printers and also Printers' Assistants in Wolverhampton.

Railwaymen were organised in the National Union of Railwaymen in at least nine towns and ASLEF (Associated Society of Locomotive Engineers & Firemen), in four towns. There were branches of the Railway Clerks' Association in Walsall, Dudley and Wolverhampton.

The National Amalgamated Union of Shop Assistants, Warehousemen and Clerks had branches in at least seven Black Country towns and the Amalgamated Union of Co-operative Employees operated in five towns.

Teachers were well organised in most towns by the National Union of Teachers, although they were not often affiliated to their trades council.

For the unskilled and semi-skilled there was a wide variety of unions. The largest was the Workers' Union operating in all towns. Th next most important union was the Amalgamated Society of Gas, Municipal and General Labourers which competed with the Dock, Wharf and General Workers Union and the National Union of General Workers. The Amalgamated Association of Tramway and Vehicle Workers catered for transport workers. Council workers joined the National Union of Corporation Workers or the National Federation of Caretakers, but there seems to have been little organisation among white collar council employees.

This applies to white collar workers generally. There were branches of the National Union of Clerks in Walsall, Smethwick, Oldbury and Wolverhampton; insurance agents organised themselves in the National Union of Life Assurance Agents or the company societies of Royal Liver or Prudential; there were branches of the Musicians' Union in Wolverhampton and the National Union of Journalists in Dudley; hair dressers were organised in Wolverhampton and Stourbridge, but this was the total extent of white collar unionism.

The most specialised sector of Black Country trade union organisation was the leather trade of Walsall which had experienced a particular boom during the war. Nine trade unions such as the Amalgamated Society of Bridle Cutters and Fancy Leather Workers, separate saddle unions such as Gig, Saddle Tree and New Brown, and the Walsall United Patent Leather Dressers existed. But only two – the Amalgamated Society of Harness Makers, Bridle Cutters and General Leather Workers and the Fancy Leather Workers' Trade Society were affiliated to the trades council.

Finally, a word about women. The most important trade union was the National Federation of

Women Workers with large affiliates to Stourbridge and Dudley Trades Councils. The Soho Co-op Women's Guild was affiliated to Oldbury Trades Council, and there was a women's branch of the National Union of Printing & Paper Workers affiliated to West Bromwich Trades Council. Of the number of women in other trades unions discussed we know nothing.

Such was the spread of trade unionism in the Black Country at the end of the war as revealed by the 'Gazeteer.'

The activities of the trades councils after the war are difficult to trace. Records are rare, although proceedings of annual general meetings can usually be traced in the local papers for the immediate post-war period. But as the slump deepened after 1920 and trades councils became weaker, coverage of even the larger trades councils by the newspapers lessens.

A case in point is the Smethwick Trades & Labour Council, the only printed record of which is the Report & Financial Statement for 1919. This was the one year of advance after the war and concluded that 'it is well with Smethwick' with increased affiliates, including the National Union of Police and Prison Officers, 'which was an active affiliate during its brief career.' In industrial affairs it had supported the main strikes of the year – the Bakers, Railwaymen, Assurance Agents and Ironfounders. Other industrial matters attended to had arisen from the war – management of the Employment Exchanges, the Government training scheme for discharged and disabled men etc. In local affairs the trades council had intervened on public lighting, housing, municipal markets, the Profiteering Tribunal, feeding of necessitous children etc. It had organised a successful Women's Conference, and a conference of the S. Staffs & Worcs. Federation of Trades Councils. It gloried in its recently elected nine town councillors, four of whom were trades council officials, including the secretary C.C. Jones. The activities of Smethwick Trades Council can be taken as typical of the work of other trades council in 1919. Fortunately, although this was the one printed report of this trades council, its activities can be followed further through a weekly Smethwick column of W.A. Exton in the Birmingham Labour paper, the *Town Crier*.

Also in 1919 there was a short report of the Darlaston Trades & Labour Council from which the only useful information to be gleaned is that it met at the White Lion Hotel, the president was F.H. Hosser and the secretary George Oates. A fuller report of the Wednesbury Trades & Labour Council in the same newspaper (Tipton Herald) gave the officers for 1920 as G.W. Stokes (Workers' Union) president, S. Westwood (Amalgamated Toolmakers) Vice-President, J. Good (Workers' Union) treasurer, and B. Griffiths secretary. Resolutions were passed respecting the welfare of the Blind. the coal question and the demand for 14 days paid holiday per year.

Dudley Trades & Labour Council proceedings were more frequently reported in the *Dudley Herald* in the immediate post-war years. As has been stated, this trades council was re-formed in 1916 and the only existing document is a minute book which ends in May 1918. A report of the previous year's work in the *Dudley Herald* in February 1919 showed income at almost £31 compared with nearly £15 in 1918. 79 delegates had been elected representing 4,000 workers. An item on the Police Union noted that the trades council had been asked to provide a meeting place for them which had been very successful and that 'there was very good reason to think that the Union would receive a very warm welcome from the Trades Council.' The Council continued to grow in 1920 with 5,700 members affiliated, 90 delegates and income of £43. The two mainstays of the organisation were John Taylor JP (president in 1920) of the Anvil & Vice Makers and James Price (secretary since 1916). Both had been active in re-forming the Trades Council and both were leading lights of the Midland Counties Trades Federation. Strangely, reporting of this important organisation which gave a voice to the small trades of the Black Country and whose annual meetings were widely reported before the war, ceased to be reported after the war, although the MCTF remained in existence.

In January 1920 the *Tipton Herald* gave a very comprehensive report of another of the smaller organisations, the Tipton Trades Council AGM, and even listed the names and trade unions of all sixteen delegates present. Officials elected were the president W. Bourne (National Union of General Workers), vice-president Councillor Powis (Iron & Steel Trades Confederation), treasurer Councillor J. Brook (Boilermakers), and secretary F. Hyde. The executive was to consist of one representative from each affiliated organisation, namely, NUR, Miners, NUGW, ISTC, ASE, Workers' Union,

Boilermakers, Steam Engine Makers, Moulders, Brassworkers, Postmen, Teachers, Chainmakers, and Vehicle Builders. Income for the year came to about £23 and there was a balance of over £12 in the Co-op Bank. Bourne concluded 'There is no reason to be displeased at the past work' and he thought future work would be crowned with even greater success. His hopes were to be dashed. When the 1922 AGM took place all reports were of unemployed demonstrations, strong protests against the cuts of the Geddes Axe and regret that the Tipton Central School had been suspended. However delegates were again named in the AGM report and numbered nineteen, three more than in 1920. Attendance at monthly Trades Council meetings had also averaged nineteen.

Other reports in 1922 included those of Wednesbury, Brierley Hill and Stourbridge Trades Councils. At a monthly Wednesbury Trades & Labour Council meeting in February eighteen delegates were present including one from the National League of the Blind and no less than 5 from BISAKTA. The meeting heard reports from representatives on the Poor Law Guardians, delegates from the S. Staffs. Federation of Trades Councils, the Labour Party and the sub-committee of the Clothing Fund. A demand to the Guardians for adequate relief was passed at the meeting. The chairman of the meeting was Frank Aston (AEU No.1).

At the Brierley Hill Trades & Labour Council AGM the secretary, Councillor W.T. Trevis gave the sixth annual report. It had been the most difficult year the Council had faced, he said. The lock-out of the miners in March 1921 had added to the grim unemployment. Some work had been found on local schemes. Committees had been formed in all three Brierley Hill wards with the council to raise funds, investigate cases and distribute relief. The Trades Council had raised £34 for the miners. Over £1,000 had been raised in all and they wished to thank the UDC and local trades people. The next step was to organise the unemployed to put the position before the Guardians. They supported the Right to Work bill and protested at the Government paying only 75 per cent of the trade union rate for relief works. They were requesting that polling booth and election counting personnel should be drawn from the ranks of the unemployed. Officers re-elected included the president H.H. Chandler, vice presidents Lewis and Bullas, treasurer A. Bowen and secretary W.T. Travis.

For Stourbridge Trades & Labour Council we have only a report of a monthly meeting in February 1922 held at the Labour Club. It was attended by fourteen delegates. They protested at the high price of beer and supported the S. Staffs & Worcs. Federation of Trades Councils in its campaign against going back to pre-war conditions. The chairman, T. Broughton, said that it would need more than pious resolutions to prevent this. The only way was to elect working men to Parliament.

There was little let up in unemployment in 1923 and the trades councils were involved in the clashes between local Unemployment Committees, dominated in the larger towns by the Communist led National Unemployed Workers' Committee Movement and local council committees set up to deal with Unemployment, sometimes called by that name but usually known as Distress Committees. In the smaller towns, the situation was even more complex. For instance, at the Brierley Hill Trades Council in January 1923 the activities of the local Distress Committee were strongly condemned. This Committee, according to the secretary W.T. Travis, had been set up on the initiative of the trades council, but this had now disappeared and a new committee, not representative of the town had been set up. This new committee was controlled from the parish church and was boycotting the trades council, alleged Travis, particularly by holding its meeting in he afternoons when working men could not attend. Twynham, a delegate said that there had been too many Labour representatives on the old committee. Delegates on the old committee testified to its value; it had divided the town up into wards and had authority to dispense funds for relief. The Rector of Brierley Hill later denied that there was discrimination and said the new committee had been set up following an advert in the local press to announce its formation. The issue divided the Trades Council, the executive being strong for action against the new committee. Eventually a deputation was elected to meet the leaders of the new committee, but afterwards the deputation was divided as to its usefulness, and the matter was dropped.

At Willenhall Trades Council tribute was paid to the 'splendid work' of the local Unemployed Committee which had received £191 and had organised a Soup Kitchen, given treats to children, distributed stockings and still had a balance of £34. The chairman said the Committee was doing great work 'for our unemployed comrades.' The matter went to the local council where Councillor Pinson said he understood that the committee was unofficial and asked how it came to be collecting funds without authority. In reply the chairman said that this matter had been investigated and it had been found that everything was above board and the unemployed were on the committee. He would move a vote of thanks to the Unemployed Committee. Three other councillors, F.W. Evans, Aston, and T.H.P. Hyatt said they would associate themselves with such a motion, but the outcome is not recorded.

By 1923 reporting of trades councils' activities in the local press was becoming thinner. At the Dudley AGM, affiliations were down to 35 branches representing 3,000 members it was reported. At the Brierley Hill AGM 21 delegates attended, including four women. Income had been £17, but expenditure was £24. At the Tipton AGM 15 had been present.

1924 was the year of the first Labour government. The secretary, Hubbold, at the Dudley AGM foretold 'a glorious future' for the Trades Council under Labour. He had some grounds for optimism, for affiliations were up to 39 branches with 3,500 members. One of the reasons for their success was the policy of inviting prominent guest speakers who had discussed such subjects as 'The Versailles Treaty and its Effect on Trade,' 'Juvenile Unemployment,' and 'The Place of the Elementary School in relation to Democracy.'

Exton's report of Smethwick in the *Town Crier* begins:

> The annual meeting of the Trades & Labour Council was the biggest I have ever attended from all points of view. Never have I seen so many delegates at one meeting, and the number of public representatives included one MP, six Labour magistrates, two aldermen, nine councillors and two guardians. How's that for a small place like Smethwick?

The annual report by the secretary Councillor C.C. Jones stressed that despite the problems of the previous three years where unemployment had been higher than in any other town of its size only ten organisations had ceased to be members and three of those were due to amalgamations. The re-election for the third time of John E. Davison, and continued success in the local elections received a prominent place in the report and financial difficulties outlined. No figures of membership was given and we have only the remark, 'the Council has not failed to suffer from growing pains', to suggest that Smethwick, like Dudley Trades Council, was once again growing.

For 1925 I have discovered no AGM reports in the local newspapers of the Trades Councils discussed above. However, we have fuller knowledge of the two largest trades councils in the Black Country – Wolverhampton and Walsall.

For Wolverhampton there is my *History of the Wolverhampton, Bilston & District Trades Union Council* published for the Council's 150th year in 1990. This outlines the main work of the Council during the years 1919-25. In 1919 it was support for the miners, railwaymen and foundry workers on strike. In 1920 the May Day demonstration brought together the current demands of the Labour movement for reductions in the cost of living, a national housing scheme, continued rent restriction, immediate self-government for Ireland, work at trade unions rates of pay for all unemployed and justice for discharged servicemen; also the successful campaign to stop the wars of intervention against Russia. From 1921, unemployment was the dominant issue with great demonstrations and violence in the town. 1922 was the year when, in co-operation with Birmingham Trades Council, efforts were made to reorganise the trade union movement and achieve the age long dream of One Big Union. In 1923 W.J. Brown became the town's prospective Parliamentary candidate whose election in 1929 was to have outstanding national and local repercussions. 1924 was the year of support for the Labour government. In 1925 the annual Trades Council report showed that beside the main campaigns against unemployment and the No More War peace movement, action had been taken on support for Chinese and Indian workers against sweated conditions, protests at insufficient local housing, the demand for a direct labour building department, action on fair wages, protest at the refusal of the government to allow the Communist MP, Saklatvala to visit his native India, and protests at the arrest of twelve Communist leaders in the run-up to the General Strike.

With regard to the strength of the Wolverhampton Trades Council, in 1914 45 societies had been affiliated. This had grown to 58 in 1917. It continued to grow. By 1922 74 societies were affiliated and in 1924 it was 75 societies. We must assume that Wolverhampton Trades Council followed the national and local trend of losing membership in the years of greatest unemployment, but it would seem that Wolverhampton suffered less than many other trades councils. By 1924 growth had been resumed, again in the pattern we have observed for Dudley and Smethwick.

For Walsall Trades Council there are actual minutes for the years 1919 to 1924. These show war issues dominating activity in 1919. The poor quality, shortage and profiteering on beer brought protests. Profiteering was an issue throughout the year; another protest on beer in May stated that 'profiteering endangers the peace of the town'. In July there was a call for local JPs to implement the law allowing fines for profiteers to be twice the amount of the profit gained, and the next month demands that profiteers should be tried by local tribunals. Various issues directly concerning ex-service personnel were raised. In January there was a protest at the Health Committee offering work at only 35/-d. a week to ex-servicemen. In April there was support for a National Federation of Discharged & Disabled Soldiers and Sailors demand not to unveil a portrait of Carless, the Walsall deceased VC, until an adequate pension was granted to his parents. There was also indignation at the Government trying to push its responsibility for War Pensions on to charitable institutions with a unanimous vote not to support the King's Fund. On the urgent need for Housing, the Trades Council called in February for the immediate implementation of the local Housing Scheme. The next month a special meeting on housing objected to Council houses on the open spaces in the borough and demanded a Garden City either in the Birmingham Road or Sutton Road areas. Unemployment was a particular issue in Walsall from the end of the war. In March a resolution was passed demanding the immediate repatriation of enemy aliens in accordance with the Government's election pledges. In November the Trades Council was seeking a meeting with the Chamber of Commerce on this subject. In the early part of 1919 there was support for the Police and Prison Officers' Union. In February there were congratulations to the police on organising themselves and an invitation to join the Trades Council. In June support for the Union in its efforts to gain recognition was expressed. Anti-war sentiment was expressed with the Birmingham councillor J.W. Kneeshaw addressing Walsall Trades Council on behalf of the Union of Democratic Control and internationalism with support for Irish independence, the Hands Off Russia campaign and affiliation to the Indian Parliamentary Committee. Post-war collaboration between employers and employed had some support on the Trades Council and a visit of a Provisional Committee of Employers and Employed was agreed in April. But a request for support from the Industrial League was left lying on the table, and in August the Labour Organiser of the National Alliance of Employers and Employed was told that the Trades Council wanted nothing to do with that organisation.

The danger of war with Russia climaxed in 1920. In June alarm was expressed at Government policy on Poland and Ireland. In August a particularly militant resolution was carried unanimously stating that if the war persisted the Trades Council would 'carry on propaganda against the forced service of members of the armed forces, delay the making of munitions, hold up transport by air sea and land, and implement a down tools policy of all organised workers.' The local Food Committee continued to exist in 1920. In April protests were made at the ending of controls the next month, particularly price control. In May it was requested that Australian jam be released. Regular reports were made to the Trades Council by its representative on the Food Committee, M. Skeels. The issue of collaboration with employers was finally ended in September when the Alliance of Employers and Employed was told that the organisation served no useful purpose. In September the Trades Council was calling for a town conference with the NFDDSS, the Chamber of Commerce and all other interested bodies on Unemployment among Ex-Servicemen. Other items showing the range of Trades Council interests included the refusal to accept a lecturer from the USA to speak on Prohibition and a concern for the lighting of urinals in the borough (the trades councils, particularly Walsall's had been influential in the setting up of public conveniences). Co-operation with the Labour Party included the setting up of a *Daily Herald* Development Committee, the May Day demonstration and the nomination of Labour candidates for the November local elections. The two principal officers of the Trades Council at this time were Councillor John Thickett the president, and John Whiston, secretary.

Unemployment dominated Trades Council proceedings in 1921. In January they were calling for a return of a portion of the National Relief Fund to relieve unemployment in Walsall. In March there were complaints of the queues at Walsall Labour Exchange; the next month there was support for a Labour Party resolution demanding £2 a week per household in unemployment benefit, and 25/-d. for single men and women. In September a town meeting on Unemployment was demanded and the recall of Parliament to debate remedies. Later in the month there were complaints of the inacivity of the government 'in this grave matter'. Unemployment led on to the question of relief particularly during the miners' lockout of 191. Protests were made in April that the Guardians were granting relief to miners' dependents only in the form of loans. In September it was urged that where relief was given in kind it should be through Tickets which would 'equalise expenditure throughout the town'. Dissatisfaction was nationwide. The 'magnificent stand' of the Poplar Guardians in refusing to cut assistance to the unemployed was applauded and when these councillors were jailed financial assistance was organised for them. At this time the Trades Council backed a comprehensive national insurance scheme for sickness, accident, unemployment and old age paying 50 per cent of average national earnings with 10 per cent for a wife and 5 per cent for each child under sixteen. This to be financed 40 per cent by industry, 40 per cent by individuals and 20 per cent by the Government.

Unemployment again dominated Trades Council activity in 1922 and resulted in further moves to the left. Pressure on the town council regarding cuts in unemployment benefit brought a letter from the Town Clerk saying that the council was already requesting the Government to restore these cuts. In 1922 there were further threats to peace from the Turco-Greek war and Lloyd George's ultimatum in September to the Turks that they should advance no further. The excuse was plausible, but the main issue was British and French control of the Straits which had been used to supply arms and men in the wars of intervention against Russia and had denied both Turkey and Russia trade outlets through the Straits. Thus a resolution from the Trades Council demanding the recognition of the Soviet government claimed that 'there could be no advance in European civilisation until this occurred.' Continued affiliation to the Union of Democratic Control was another indication of he concern for peace. In domestic matters there was increasing concern at the weakness of national trade unionism and increasing interest in the Soviet and Communist dominated Red International of Labour Unions, a British Bureau of which had been set up in October 1921. Its campaigning issues in 1922 were a 'back to the unions' drive and the strengthening of the trades councils. Walsall was represented at a Birmingham Conference of the Red International of Labour Unions in October and the report of the delegates favourably received. One result was a letter from *All Power,* the monthly journal of the RILU seeking readers and the volunteering of a delegate, C. Hindle, to supply the magazine.

1923 saw a continuing concern with peace, the main issue being the Curzon Ultimatum. After the collapse of the wars of intervention against Russia, reactionaries had to face the fact that the Soviet Union (formed in 1922) had come to stay. In 1921, therefore, a limited Anglo-Russian Trade Agreement was negotiated. But this first step towards relations with the Soviet Union was never accepted by many on the right and by 1923 it was clear that there were enough differences to find an excuse to end the Agreement and return to the state of undeclared war. In September Lord Curzon, the Foreign Secretary, delivered a note to Moscow demanding that, unless certain demands were met within ten days, the British government would immediately consider itself freed from the obligations of the Anglo- Russian Trade Agreement. Whatever the rights and wrongs of the questions in dispute (and they included the release of British trawlers for violating a twelve mile agreement which the Russians enforced, but the English did not recognise, and also compensation for the family of a British citizen executed for treason), such matters could not be resolved in ten days and the Labour movement saw the Ultimatum as an attempt to renew the wars of intervention. In Walsall this led to a letter being sent to the trades Council from the Walsall branch of the Communist Party offering co-operation in the formation of a Council of Action in Walsall. The matter was discussed around the following motion by C. Hindle:

> That owing to the unwarranted interference of the British Government in the internal affairs of the Workers' Council government of Russia, in dispatching a note containing an ultimatum couched in

language calculated to elicit strongly worded Notes in return, and with the possible breaking of diplomatic relations leading to War this Council elect a committee to organise an all-in Conference of Workers with the object of forming a Council of Action in conjunction with other Towns to prevent a rupture between the two countries and realise the slogan: Not a man; Not a ship; Not a gun.

This motion was discussed and it was moved to defer the question. But it was eventually decided to leave the matter with the secretary to draft a resolution embodying the sentiments of the resolution and empowering the secretary and president to call a special meeting should it be deemed desirable. If a Council of Action was not formed in Walsall they were formed in many other parts of the country. The Soviet Union made some concessions immediately and suggested a Conference to discuss all outstanding issues, and with this and considerable pressure from the Labour movement the Ultimatum was abandoned. The call for Councils of Action was a national demand of the Communist Party and Hindle, who put the motion at Walsall and was a particularly active member of the Trades Council at that time, was likely to have been a party member.

Up to July 1924 when the Walsall Trades Council minute book ends, business was more local. The Trades Council joined with a local Labour Party and ILP committee for a joint summer propaganda campaign. The usual local matters, such as protests at the low pay of taxi drivers was addressed and two humane topics; the first was support for the Abolition of Capital Punishment; the second was support for an Animal Welfare Committee concerning humane killing, which resulted in a letter being sent to all the butchers in the town.

The Walsall Trades Council minutes, unfortunately, discuss neither the membership of the trades council nor its finances. The executive did make annual nominations of officers, which were invariably accepted at the annual general meeting, so we do know something of its officers. John Whiston remained secretary of the Council through from 1919 to beyond 1925. Thickett remained president until 1922 and in 1923 he became the mayor. A.H. Fox remained president from 1922 and J.W. Stanley was treasurer from 1921, replacing M. Skeels. Of its financial position we know nothing except that there was a special meeting to discuss financial difficulties in 1923.

It is likely that Walsall followed the local and national pattern of a seriously weakened position after 1920 followed by some recovery after 1924, but whether it did or not, the general conclusion can be drawn that of the nine Black Country trades council that emerged from the war, all of them survived the fearful slump of the early nineteen twenties.

In addition, they managed to sustain a Black Country federation of trades councils and reports of this body throw some further light on the personnel and influence of individual trades councils.

The first report found for the South Staffordshire & Worcestershire Federation of Trades Council was of a meeting held at Dudley in January 1922. The President, James Price from Dudley, was in the chair. Mrs Hunter JP of Rowley Regis was in attendance and other officers were Henry Bullus of Brierley Hill, the secretary and T. Lewis of Stourbridge the treasurer. Other trades council delegates present were H. Malugand, H. Bradley, Mark Fletcher and B. Norton of Dudley, R. Homer and S. Edwards from Rowley Regis, C.C. Jones and C.H. Ansell of Smethwick, D.H. Martin of Bilston, J. Newton, J. Gallimore, H.W. Chandler and W.H. Walkin from Brierley Hill, E. Potts and G. Orme of Wednesbury, W.J. Clarke of Oldbury, F.W. Dublin and W.T. Travis of Brierley Hill, N.A. Flowers and W. Hill from Tipton, W.H. Exton Smethwick, D. Collins West Bromwich, J. Freeth and P.S. Websdale of Walsall. From non-Black Country trades councils there were delegates from Bromsgrove, Kidderminster, Lichfield and Malvern. Henry Bullus gave the report for the previous year. Tipton was present for the first time and Willenhall had decided to affiliate, but no delegate was in attendance. Bullus went on to say that the year had been one of 'strenuous usefulness.' The last AGM at Stourbridge had been largely attended and a resolution of sympathy had been sent to Mary McArthur's relatives. An executive committee meeting at Malvern had been poorly attended because of the miners' strike; a resolution demanding more working class JPs was passed. The half yearly meeting at Cannock had been welcomed by the first Labour civic head. An E.C. at Lye had protested at the suggestion that Trade Boards were to be abolished. Electorally there had been the splendid bye-election victory at Dudley and this meant there were now 16 Labour MPs in the area; also two aldermen, 2 County councillors 112 councillors, twenty Guardians and eighteen JPs. After the report the main issues discussed were help to the unemployed by the Trades Councils, the lack of value of the Housing and Town Planning Association, the case of Bilston which had no Labour JPs, and the employer offensive to return to longer hours.

This AGM probably saw the organisation at its zenith. Almost all the Black Country trades councils were affiliated with the notable exception of Wolverhampton which continued throughout the period to stand aloof. Exceptional representation from Dudley, Brierley Hill and Stourbridge suggests that they saw the Federation of Trades' Councils as an alternative to the Midlands Counties Trades' Federation's important pre-war role of strengthening the smaller crafts through united action. As has been said, no accounts of the post-war activities of the MCTF have been found, although it continued to exist and by 1926 operated from offices in Walsall where the district secretary resided, although the general secretary remained the long-serving J. Taylor of Dudley (see Walsall Red Book for 1926).

When it came to the election of officers, the chairman said that he thought the honours should go round and C.C. Jones of Smethwick became the president. In historical vein it was noted that Price had been president for three years and Sitch for six years. This suggests that the organisation originated in 1913. Of Jones it was said that he had been born in Shropshire and connected with the Labour movement for 20 years. He had been secretary of Smethwick Trades Council for six years, and was secretary to the Smethwick and Oldbury branch of the National Union of Clerks. He was a Smethwick councillor and had been a delegate to the Federation since 1916. A new vice president, D.H. Martin of Bilston, was elected. Henry Bullus was re-elected secretary and E.T. Lewis treasurer. Mrs Hunter JP proposed thanks to the Ladies' Committee. Regret was then expressed that Mrs Hunter was about to leave for Canada. She was the district organiser of the National Union of General Workers (Women's Section), formerly the National Federation of Women Workers founded by Mary McArthur, and she had served in the area from Cradley Heath for nine years.

By the next AGM in January 1923 the organisation was in trouble and had been re-named the West Midlands Federation of Trades Councils. Five trades councils had withdrawn including two in the Black Country – Lye and Willenhall – and unsuccessful attempts had been made to persuade Wolverhampton to affiliate. Harry Bullus' report stated that they had tried to carry on despite the desperate slump. The July EC had passed a resolution on the causes of the Tipton Explosion. (This had occurred in 1922 in a shed where girls were dismantling small cartridges; the death toll was nineteen.) The October EC had discussed Work for the Unemployed and also the Legal 8-hour Day, but no other meetings were reported. The matter of gravest concern to the AGM was a deficit of £21. W.H. Watkins from Brierley Hill said that trade union branches could not afford to affiliate to their local Trades Council so how could they find the money to affiliate to a super-Trades Council? R. Homer asked what would be the position if all trades councils in the Fed paid their arrears. (Voice from the hall – 'We'd be in clover.') A committee was set up to consider the deficit. The previous year's officers were all re-elected. Twenty four Black Country delegates were present, the largest delegations being six from Smethwick, and three from Dudley with others from Bilston, Stourbridge, Tipton, Rowley Regis and Brierley Hill.

The venue for the 1924 AGM was the Workers' Institute at Cradley Heath. Black Country attendance again being about twenty four. Bullus reported a more successful year. It was the year of the Labour government and the area now boasted nine MPs three county councillors and one mayor. The heavy financial loss of the previous year had been turned into a surplus of £2-6-4½d. for which Bullus was given a hearty vote of thanks. Clem Jones of Smethwick was re-elected chairman, as were the other officers, Martin of Bilston (vice chairman) and Bullus of Brierley Hill (secretary). No mention is made of the treasurer. Bullus, in accepting re-election, warned that if his business continued to grow he would not have time to devote to the organisation and they would have to look round for a successor. Business included the passing of a motion from Councillor Travis JP urging that in view of changes in the Rent Acts, JPs should ensure that people have alternative accommodation before signing ejectment orders. A discussion on Unemployment suggested that every town should have a strong Unemployment Committee affiliated to the local trades council, as at Smethwick.

In 1925 the AGM of the West Midlands Federation of Trades' Councils was held at Walsall. There was again about 25 delegates from the Black Country trades' councils of Brierley Hill, Smethwick, Cradley Heath, Bilston, Rowley Regis, Stourbridge and Oldbury, but none from Walsall. Bullus' report told of continued efforts to organise the unemployed, and to abolish loan relief; also strong participation in the Back to the Unions campaign. Whilst regretting the demise of the Labour government, Bullus claimed that the movement continued to grow. Income for the year had been £47, but there was a slight deficit of £3. When it came to elections Martin of Bilston, who had been acting as president after Clem Jones had become a Labour Party agent in S.W. England, pleaded lack of time, and W. Salsa of Smethwick was elected in his place. Harry Bullus' business had continued to expand and he declined nomination; his place was taken by another Smethwick man, W.A. Exton. Frank Evans of Rowley Regis was elected vice president and John Wilson of Brierley Hill became treasurer. Bullus and Travis continued their association with the organisation by becoming auditors.

By 1926, therefore, the two main offices were occupied by Smethwick men from a small town, but an important Labour and trade union centre, while other offices were occupied by men from the smaller trades councils. The lack of representation from the larger trades council of Wolverhampton, Walsall and, after 1924 Dudley, weakened the Federation. The change of name from South Staffs. to West Midlands did not attract support either from from North Staffs or any other any other industrial area in the west midlands. The WMFTC remained an organisation of the small trades councils of the Black Country, the only other trades councils represented in 1925 being Lichfield and Tamworth. There was always criticism of the organisation, especially at the time of the financial crisis. Tipton paid its £1 affiliation fee for 1923 but threatened to withdraw if they were not satisfied; the deficit had been caused by the organisation trying to run before it could walk, it was claimed. But the Federation obviously served a need of the smaller trades councils and it experienced the general cycle of strength at the end of the war with full employment, crisis in the years of depression and some growth after 1924 leading into the General Strike.

Black Country Miners

We can next turn to the fortunes of some of the more important trades unions in the period 1919 to 1925 beginning with unionism in the two traditional Black Country industries of coal and iron.

For mining, it is difficult to ascertain the basic facts of the industry. G.C. Allen estimated that in 1872 28,000 miners produced about 9 million tons of coal whereas in 1913 10,000 miners produced about 3 million tons. Allen's figures are for 'south of the Bentley fault' which is the traditional boundary between the thick coal of the Black Country and the thinner and deeper seams of the Cannock coalfield. But there is a sort of No Man's Land north of the Bentley fault and south of the A5 of large pits many of whose miners lived in Walsall. The 1901 Census gives a complete breakdown of miners, and for nineteen towns in the Black Country there were 12,480 miners. The Censuses of 1911 and 1921 are defective in that the break down of miners is for the County Boroughs only. These show:

Miners in:	Walsall	West Bromwich	Wolverhampton	Dudley	Total
1901	2483	1179	88	1589	5347
1911	2563	1127	131	1619	5440
1921	2895	751	84	1426	5156

It will be noted that for 1901 miners in the county boroughs account for only 43 per cent of the total of miners and assuming this proportion remained constant the total number of miners would be raised to: 1911 – about 12,500 miners and 1921 – about 11,900 miners. This would suggest that the mining population which had halved between 1861 and 1901 remained fairly steady thereafter to 1921. In Walsall the number of miners in each decade actually increased slightly, reflecting increased output in what I have called No Man's land between the thick coal of the Black Country and the deep mines of the Cannock field north of the A5. My figure of Black Country miners for 1921 at nearly 12,000 seems on the high side; local press estimates of those on strike in 1921 were usually about

7,000, but there are too many coal towns in the Census not recorded in the Tables of Occupations for, nearly 12,000 not to be an unreasonable guesstimate.

It would also be best to attempt to establish the wages of Black Country miners and the cost of living before discussing their reaction to the most important events of 1919-25, namely the rapid fall in the cost of living during 1921 which coincided with the Miners' Strike of that year. Thick coal miners' wages from 1909 to 1913 had been 3/-11d per shift. The figure for 1914 is missing but the price of coal was rising and we might make the kindly assumption that wages rose to 4/-d. per shift. Flat rate increases during the war added a further 3/-d. per shift bringing the total to 7/-d. per day or a rise of of 75 per cent The cost of living had risen by 103 per cent in the same period. Thus wages had not risen as fast as prices during the war. With the post-war boom and shortage of coal a 2/-d. increase in 1919, another 2/-d. in 1920 and a final increase of 1/6d. January 1921 brought wages to a maximum of 12/6d. per day. But the cost of living rose rapidly during these years and at November 1920 was at its peak of 176 per cent above 1914. This compared with 175 per cent increase in wages by the end of 1920. Thus in the most advantageous period that the miners had ever known wages were still below the cost of living. The wage increase in 1921 lasted only one month. In February wages were reduced by 2/-d. and in March by another 1/6d. It must be emphasised however, that this was a period of rapidly falling prices and by March 1921 miners' wages were 137 per cent higher than in 1914 while the cost of living was 141 per cent higher. No doubt overtime, both during the war and in the post-war boom brought earnings above wage rates, but miners, like other workers, were seeking substantial improvements in the post-war standard of living. The only substantial permanent gain for the miners after the war was the reduction of hours from eight to seven per day.

Very pertinent to the question of wages at this time was also the price of coal and the mineowners' profits. From the end of 1917 the Government took charge of the pits and the price of coal was determined not by the market but by political considerations. National figures quoted by Page Arnot show coal owners' profit for 1909-1913 were 11¼d per ton and in September 1918, 3/6½. a rise of 378 per cent – far above the rise in the cost of living or miners' wages. In the following months profits were to rise even further and there is nothing to suggest from Black Country figures of output and productivity, despite the problems with mine drainage, that costs in these mines were markedly above the national average.

Apart from wages, two other main grievances during the war were 'wet working' in pits where clothes had to be wrung out on a number of occasions each day and the failure to honour the concessionary coal agreements, either on grounds of increased costs of transport, or as part of the never-ending struggle of owners to do away with free or cheap coal.

For all these reasons, the miners nationally formulated demands in January 1919 for a 30 per cent increase in *earnings,* a six-hour day and nationalisation of the mines. When these demands were not immediately met the miners balloted on strike action, which had majority support from Black Country miners. Events then followed with considerable speed. The famous Sankey Commission was set up in March 1919 and its findings considered by the Government in July. It granted immediately the 7-hour day and 6-hours at the end of 1920, 'if circumstances allowed'; also a 2/-d wage increase and 'continued control of the mines by the Government.' By August the Government had changed its mind and rejected nationalisation. The next month a MFGB conference re-affirmed support for nationalisation, but did not suggest strike action. Prolonged negotiations then proceeded with the Government and the owners. In October 1920 a short Datum Line strike occurred (against a proposal of the owners to tie wages to coal output). The Government then used the occasion to pass a draconian Emergency Powers Act. By the end of 1920 the slump had begun, the economic power of the miners had been stripped from them, and the initiative returned to the Machiavellian Lloyd George and the coal owners.

Added to this disastrous chain of events Black Country miners faced the fact that much of their coalfield was declining, only the actions of the Mines Drainage Commission kept some pits open, and they were faced with a unanimously hostile press which would brand them as destroyers of both their own livelihoods and the coalfield if they took any action to improve their economic position.

It is at this point that we can introduce the 1991 Wolverhampton MA thesis of Christopher J.

Horsnall entitled *Coal Mining Trade Unionism in the Black Country 1914-27*. He has my sympathy. Unlike historians of earlier mining trade unionism in the the area he has no trade union journal to assist him and virtually no records from either the Miners' Federation of Great Britain or from the local Miners' Associations. He is thus almost completely dependent on the hostile local press which was always ready to misrepresent both the actions and motives of the miners torn as they were between loyalty to the union, the need to protect their standard of living and the insidious, all-pervading and often false propaganda of owners and press that strike action would destroy the coalfield.

The onset of the slump enabled the Government to renege on its promises and announce an end to controls on the price of coal by March 31st and the end of pooling of profits by June 1921. This would mean that the mines would be virtually decontrolled, the owners once again assuming complete control, and any possibility of ameliorating the effects on wages between areas where profits were negative and areas of high productivity by any national scheme of profit pooling and national wage negotiation would be at an end. The mine owners announced the ending of all contracts of service (including those of enginemen and pumpmen) and negotiations by Districts which would cut some wages by 50 per cent The miners unanimously rejected District wage bargaining and after fruitless negotiations with the owners the great Lock-out of 1921 began in April.

The course of the Lock-out must perforce be followed through the baleful eye of the local press. In the first week of April the *Dudley Herald* explained away the average reduction of 4/-d. to 7/-d. per shift in the Black Country, compared with only 1/-d. in the Cannock coalfield, as 'due to the excessive amount of slack, up to 80 per cent in some cases', it claimed, from the Black Country pits. The *Wednesbury News* the next week carried two pieces of news. The first was that J.H. Thomas the NUR leader, announced that the Triple Alliance of railwaymen and transport workers would strike with the miners. (This promise was reneged on on Black Friday April 15 with Thomas playing a leading role.) The other news was that on the very first day of the Lock-out the King had declared a National State of Emergency (under Emergency Powers taken five months previously) and 'patriotic citizens' were urged to join a Defence Force.

The same week the local papers played the flooding card. The *County Herald* reported an 'ominous statement' at Dudley claiming that if one pumping station stopped working the mines of the whole of the Old Hill district would be drowned; much the same was true of the West Bromwich district, it claimed; Edward Howl, the general manager of the S. Staffs Mines Drainage Commission, stated that the Tipton district was already drowned out. These were alarmist reports. While not wishing to underestimate the effects of flooding, there were few proven cases of pits closing permanently as a result of the Lock-out and most pits opened after it. As the S. Staffs Mines Drainage Commission Report of 1920 showed, the effective drainage of the pits was hampered by the use of inefficient steam driven pumps instead of electric pumps and the fears of some local authorities whose towns floated on water that if their areas were de-watered there would be excessive claims on them for subsidence.

The *Tipton Herald* of 16th April explained why the Colliery Engine Winders were on strike together with the miners. They had been given fourteen days notice to leave their employment and then ordered to work on day to day contracts at existing rates of pay and to accept the results of the strike.

Horsnell deals with the main problems arising from the conflict: the inadequacy of strike funds; wrangles with the Poor Law authorities as the miners contended they were not on strike, but locked out; problems of legality and danger as miners worked outcrops and picked from from old workings for coal to sell; other workers put out of work, notably glass workers who needed the best coal. Also mass meetings of support for the strike and a mass meeting of enginemen, firemen, mechanics and underground deputies who warned the S. Staffs & E. Worcs Coal Owners Association that any victimisation after the strike would bring the men out again.

By the third week of the Lock-out a *Dudley Herald* leader was threatening:

> There is a mischievous element in trade unions today that must not only be scotched but killed.

At the end of April, the *Dudley Herald* and its satellite papers were taking a different tack and ignoring the strike altogether.

On May Day mass unemployment and support for the miners were the two main themes of the Labour demonstrations. But one must turn to the *Wolverhampton Chronicle* to find anything like adequate reporting of these events. In Dudley the Trades Council organised a march to the parish church headed by a Salvation Army band. The congregation was addressed by the vicar A.H. Phelips who said that the conduct of the miners during the dispute had been beyond reproach. Life was unlovely, insecure and in many respects intolerable. If these conditions were the product of the system of the last 300 years the sooner it was modified the better. Salvation lay along the lines of a return to the spirit of Christ, he concluded. In Cradley Heath, where the headquarters of the strike was at the local Workers' Institute, a special united service was held at St. Luke's Church with nonconformist and church ministers, addressed by the Dean of Worcester. He said the conditions of life that made Labour discontented were 1.A sense of unfairness and injustice, 2.A life of 'stinting', 3. The irksomeness of the present system of control, and 4. Industry was organised for profit rather than human welfare. Dr Ede followed asking how we could get the co-operative commonwealth. Not by class warfare. Wage-earners must have a share in the organisation of industry.

In May the local press was spreading the story that miners were earning £8 to £10 a week. Dan Cartwright challenged these reports and said that 80 per cent of miners were earning £4 to £5 a week. In the middle of May the *Dudley Herald* admitted that there was an impasse and made the following points: 1. That the coal industry would be bankrupted if the dispute went on. 2. That the pooling of profits was impossible. 3. The aims of the strike were political. 4. The government and mineowners' offer was fair and reasonable. 5. Nationalisation was at the back of the strike.

At the end of May the government made a new offer of talks with the miners and the coalowners. What was offered was little advance on the proposals that had caused the dispute. The two main miners' demands for national wage negotiations and a national profit pool to average out the enormous fall in wages which would occur in the least profitable pits were again rejected. A National Board was proposed, however, to give 'guidance' to the local Boards. The Government also offered a £10 million subsidy for a limited period. The miners put these new proposals to a national ballot and by 435,000 votes to 181,000 they were rejected. In the Black Country the S. Staffs & E. Worcs Miners' Association voted to return to work by a majority of 700, but the Old Hill miners gave a two to one majority of 383 to stay out. The enginemen and craftsmen agreed to abide by the miners' decision. The result of the ballot was announced on the 17th. of June. The next day Lloyd George withdrew the £10 million subsidy offer. But without hope of further assistance to the miners the dispute could not be maintained and the national executive was driven to negotiate a final settlement. The Lock-out ended on Friday 31st July.

The *Dudley Herald*'s verdict at the end of the strike was that the miners' stubbornness had cost the industry £500m. That the miners' grievances were no greater than those of other workers who had not been given a subsidy of £10m.

The terms on which the miners returned to work were that men over sixteen would receive 2/-d. a day less than the wage on 31 March with further cuts of 6d in August and a further 6d. in September. After this wages would be regulated by a local Wages Board. Taking the S. Staffs & E. Worcs Miners' Association's figures issued before the Lock-out occurred, the wage rate at March 1921 was 16/1d. This became 13/1d in September 1921. This was more than the 1914 wage plus 50 per cent (10/3d) offered before the lock-out began. But in September 1921 the cost of living was 120 per cent above that of 1914 and in real terms miners' were slightly worse off than pre-war as wages had risen by 118 per cent but prices by 120 per cent. So disappeared the dreams of a better post-war world for the miners.

Iron Workers

Iron making was the other traditional basic industry of the Black Country. Like coal mining, it was an industry in decline but, unlike coal, it was not temporarily reprieved by the war. Black Country iron production had peaked in 1856 at 777,000 tons. It nearly reached that figure again in the hectic boom of the early 1870s, but by 1900 was just below 400,000 tons. In 1913 production was 467,000 tons and it fell during the war to 413,000 tons in 1918. After the war production dived to 319,000 in 1919 and declined further thereafter. Iron workers were further disadvantaged by the enormous fall in the price of iron. This peaked at £33-4-11d. per ton in September/October 1920. By Jan/Feb 1921 it was just over £30 and by the end of the year the price had almost halved. Prices continued to decline throughout 1922 and the trough came in Nov/Dec at £10-15-11 a ton. Thus the price of iron had fallen three fold compared with the fall in the cost of living of only 40 per cent. Iron workers' wages were governed by the price of iron and the price falls catalogued above were those of the Midlands Iron & Steel Wages Board, whose figures were accepted by both workers and employers. From the records available it is not possible to follow the exact falls in wages exacted from the employers in this situation, especially as the sliding scale was usually represented by amounts per ton of iron produced. Taylor's *The Better Temper,* shows, however, that the Wages Board survived, despite the ironworkers' representatives threatening to leave at various times as some employers undercut the established Wages Board's rates of pay. In 1924 when the price of iron was up to £13 per ton a reorganisation of the Board more favourable to the workers' representatives was negotiated. The main post-war objectives of the Iron & Steel Trades Confederation of the 8-hour shift (instead of 12hrs), and direct labour thus ending the contract system of furnacemen and others paying their own underhands, had however been achieved. The course of wages has not been ascertained.

The Engineers

By 1914 engineering dominated the Black Country and of the many trades unions catering for the industry the Amalgamated Society of Engineers was paramount. Nationally this union almost doubled its membership during the war, but in the Black Country membership rose by more than this, from almost 2,700 in 1914 to over 6,100 in 1918. Engineers shared the mounting militancy towards the end of the war and when the 47-hour week was negotiated in 1919, only a small majority approved this, the minority being divided between those wanting 44-hours and 40-hours. Another result of this militancy was the desire for an amalgamation of all engineering unions which came to a conclusion in July 1920. This brought total membership of the new Amalgamated Engineering Union in the Black Country to nearly 6,700. The two most important engineering towns were Wolverhampton with nearly 3,000 members and Smethwick with nearly 1,200. Only Oldbury topped 600 members and West Bromwich 500. Walsall did not reach 400 nor Dudley 300. These figures suggest that the amalgamation was less successful in the Black Country than nationally; certainly the two main unions which refused to amalgamate, the Foundry Workers and the Boilermakers, continued a vigorous existence with co-operation with the AEU continuing in the old way via the Federation of Engineering & Shipbuilding Unions.

The course of wage reductions in the Black Country engineering industry can be followed approximately from the figures we have of the Birmingham District, bearing in mind that Black Country rates were slightly lower than Birmingham. Wages of Fitters and Turners peaked from 38/-d. in 1914 to 84/11¼d in April 1920, an increase of 124 per cent compared with the cost of living rise of 149 per cent By 1924 wages were down to 56/-d., 47 per cent above 1914 compared with the rise in the cost of living from 1914 of 75 per cent. Again, the real standard of living had fallen compared with 1914. Engineering workers also suffered disproportionately from unemployment. In October 1920 when the figure of unemployment taken from trade union returns showed 2.2 per cent, the engineering rate in the W. Midlands was 5.2 per cent. In January 1922 when the trade union figure was 16.5 per cent the West Midlands engineering unemployment rate was at 32.8 per cent the highest in the country. Such figures should be borne in mind when facile generalisations are made of the diversity of W. Midlands industry protecting it from the worst effects of unemployment. This was certainly not true of the first post-war slump.

The engineering employers took advantage of the weakness of the AEU to impose the Lock-out of 1922. The immediate issues for the employers were union consultation on the questions of over-time, the manning of machines, and union insistence on negotiating wages and conditions of apprentices. The real issue, however, was the complete assertion of employers' 'right to manage' in their own factories and, in some cases, the desire to crush the recently enlarged AEU. The issues in the Black Country can be followed from the divisional officers' monthly reports of the period printed in the

AEU *Monthly Journal.* In December 1921 R.F. Dempster the No 17 Divisional officer was reporting that Hickman's, the iron and steel firm, in Bilston had reduced wages of AEU members on the sliding scale applicable to the ironworkers. This had brought their wages below that of the AEU district rate. Hickman's had refused to alter this and the AEU members had been called out. In Wednesbury, Isaiah Platt had implemented the agreed 12½ per cent wage cut at one stroke instead of over a period. Again, negotiations had been fruitless and the men were called out. In January 1922 at Wolverhampton the Vulcan Manufacturing Co. was operating a 49 hour week and negotiations had failed to produce any result. The sanction imposed in this case was that 'union members were not free to start.' The same month Birmingham engineering employers had laid down a scale of reductions for boys of 3/-d. a week at fourteen rising to 9/-d. at twenty one, which also applied to Wolverhampton. In March this was disputed and taken to a conference with the Wolverhampton Engineering Employers where this was amended to link reductions in pay for boys to the male adult rate.

This raises the question of the attitudes of Birmingham and Wolverhampton employers to the 1922 Lock-out. Sir Allan Smith, the secretary of the national Engineering Employers' Federation, who was a solicitor and had never been an engineering employer, was widely regarded as the driving force behind the Lock-out. In March 1922 the Birmingham engineering employers were protesting at the autocratic attitude of their Federation and were proposing to hold local discussions with their Engineers. West Midland employers were not subject to the manning restrictions on machines prevalent in some areas of the country, nor was over-time a burning issue at a time of slump and mass unemployment. Local employers might therefore be regarded as not one hundred per cent behind the lock-out, although very firm to regain 'managerial control' in a situation so favourable to them. Unfortunately, the AEU monthly reports for Division 17 are not available for two crucial months of the Lock-out and there is very little in the local press. But engineers in the Black Country maintained discipline throughout the 13 week lock-out despite the impossibility of winning under such circumstances and suffering considerable hardship. The men went back on humiliating terms of conceding all the employers' demands including the 'right to manage' and control of overtime.

But demands imposed nationally were not always easy to impose locally. AEU Divisional reports after the Lock-out show disagreements in Wolverhampton over the operation of overtime on night shifts and a recommendation that members on night shifts ban overtime until pre Lock-out conditions are observed. There were also negotiations with firms which had refused to reinstate workers after the Lock-out; in most cases the excuse made was lack of work. In October the union was intervening in forbidden territory at Harper Sons and Bean at Tipton on behalf of an apprentice working short-time and only being paid for the hours worked. The union also complained that other Federated firms were not observing the Overtime and Nightshift agreements; this was denied by the employers. At the end of the year the Sunbeam shop stewards negotiated a new Payment by Results scheme unanimously endorsed by the workforce. 'The system is based on time not price, this being the desire of the men,' the AEU Divisional organiser reported. This represents something of a compromise between skilled men's traditional abhorrence of piece work and the needs of a modern industry.

However, despite damage limitation where unemployment was high and some successes with such firms as Sunbeam and Harper Sons & Bean in the motor industry where conditions were not too dire, the extent of the defeat from the Lock-out cannot be disguised and it showed in the fall in the figures of AEU membership. Nationally figures were down from 480,000 in 1920 to 234,000 in 1925. In the Black Country, membership fell from 6,600 in 1920 to 3,300 in 1925.

Locks

The Lock industry, important to Wolverhampton and Walsall but vital to Willenhall, illustrates a different tactic to the onset of the slump, of co-operation rather than conflict with employers. Indeed the industry is the only one I have found where both sides resurrected the tactics of the Great Depression of the 1870s and 1880s of attempting to hold prices by employers supporting the union and expecting the union in return to boycott firms which sold below the price list.

The fortunes of the National Amalgamated Lockmakers and General Metal Workers Union were at their lowest ebb in 1911 with 150 members and an income of £5. At this point it was reorganised with the help of G.R. Thorne, the local Liberal MP, and John Taylor of the Midland Counties Trades Federation. In 1912 a Wages Board was formed and by 1913, in the prosperous pre-war years the union had 1,000 members and had established the 54-hour week. 1914 brought patriotic support for the war, praise by both the the union and the MCTF for the decision of employers and employees to work together and a new strength – albeit practically forced on the union by the influx of women as the men enlisted – from the admission of women to the union. The above details come from the 1916 General Report which reviewed progress from 1911 to 1916.

The union's support for the war did not waver even after 1916 when the union tried to protect its skilled, married, men over 30 from conscription and failed, being told only that applications to the local Tribunal would be 'treated sympathetically.' The union later sought assistance with enlistment problems from the General Federation of Trade Unions and the Midland Counties Trades Federation. The 1917 Annual Report did, however, print in full the joint War Aims of the Labour Party and TUC which were critical of the prolongation of the war by that time.

From 1918 to 1921 we have no annual report. But we do have the EC minutes of the Willenhall branch, which was the largest branch, and included in its minute book is also the proceedings of the Wages Board. These sources show that in 1918 it was agreed that it was necessary to make Political Action an aim of the union and the Wages Board agreed to abolish the traditional charges for gas, coal, power etc. 1919 brought further advances: agreement with the Wages Board on the implementation of the 47-hour week from February worked by two shifts; and the total abolition of overtime, although where this was absolutely necessary the employees' representatives would have to agree it. Unanimous agreement was also reached on the Wages Board that Outworking should be abolished, except for Keymakers. A thorough review of the Price Lists was also undertaken. During this period of advance John Taylor, one of the two leading figures in the Midland Counties Trades Federation, was the secretary of the employees' side of the Wages Board, and there was something like consternation when he resigned at the end of 1919. However, his place was taken satisfactory by George Bellamy, the Willenhall branch secretary.

As men returned from the war and the number of women in employment fell, the old question of whether women should be members of the union surfaced. In March 1920 it was agreed that six month's notice be given for the withdrawal of the women to the MCTF but a month later that was changed to the affiliation of the women to the Women's Trade Union League. By October 1920 unemployment was beginning to bite and for the next few years this was to dominate union activities.

In the winter of 1921 union Unemployment Benefit to members had to be cut from 15/-d. to 10/-d. and a levy of 1/-. a week on all employed members (6d. for those on short-time) was made. In February came the first cut in wages of 5 per cent which the union endorsed as 'in the best interests of the Trade' to accept with another 5 per cent drop in March. In September the employers demanded a 25 per cent reduction, but this was negotiated down to 10 per cent. In October a Sliding Scale of wages was being negotiated which was eventually based on a 12 point change in the official cost of living. The Annual Report for 1921 said that it had been the worst year in the history of the trade for unemployment. £16,000 in state benefits had been disbursed and £6,000 of union funds. George Bellamy stressed that although reductions were never agreeable these had been negotiated amicably with the employers and regretted that other trades had not done the same. Bellamy also thought that the day was not far distant when trade unions would have to cater for their own unemployed and when this day arrived, 'It should not be a pittance, but sufficient for men to retain the vigour to do the work demanded,' when they eventually found a job. The union had also protested at its inclusion in the Pressed Metal Trades Board and argued that it was better served by the Joint Industrial Council into which the Wages Board had by this time been transformed. The union victory on this point was crucial to what followed.

It was also in 1921 that the union opened a meat shop, an activity that has puzzled many people. But it arose from the Unemployment Regulations of that year which limited the time that unemployed benefit was paid and the introduction of the infamous Gap before benefit was resumed at the commencement of the next financial year. To members thus excluded from benefit the union gave meat vouchers exchangeable at butchers' shops in Willenhall and Wolverhampton. This proved unsatisfactory, the holders of vouchers often receiving inferior meat. So the union opened its own shop in Willenhall. The directors of H & T Vaughan, the lock firm, provided the premises, transport and much else. Apart from providing unemployed voucher holders with good meat, the shop had the additional advantage of bringing other prices down, 'exorbitant prices elsewhere disappearing like magic'. But the success of the shop depended on union members and others purchasing their meat there, and this did not happen. In 1922 the shop was leased to Marsh and Baxter who then provided cheap or free meat for the appeals of the union for meat for the unemployed at various times during the winters. Such events as the Unemployed Workers' Christmas Dinner Fund, and parties for the children of unemployed workers etc., were also generously supported by the local Lock companies.

In 1922 unemployment fell from the levels nearing 25 per cent to chronic levels of about 15 per cent and the secretary paid tribute to the members who had refused to take work below the rate for the job. The union claimed that it had emerged from 1921 stronger numerically than ever before, although it did not give the figures. Few men remained outside the Society and a list of those who did was being compiled and would be published.

A serious problem during these years was the increase in the numbers of youths at work. In previous periods of unemployment, it was said, youths working with adults were the first to be laid off. Now the adult was sacked first and the youths did the work of the adults. This problem was eventually resolved by the JIC in 1925 agreeing that youths should be limited to one for every four craftsmen employed.

Co-operation between employers and the union had clearly paid off. It now became even closer. In 1924 an employer posted a notice that he was subject to competition from firms which sold below the Wage Board rate. He had therefore resolved to pay non-union workers in his factory 10 per cent less than union members. This example was clearly effective, for in 1925 the union announced that there were few non-unionists either male or female. 'In the major factories it is impossible for non-unionists to work.'

Was it possible, in the 1920s, for an industry to escape the worst consequences of an economic depression of almost unprecedented depth by class co-operation to maintain prices and allowing trade unions to punish recalcitrant employers? In most cases the answer must be 'No'. But in the case of the lock industry, where demand for the product remained firm during normal conditions of trade and where production was virtually confined to a small area and crucially to the small town of Willenhall, it might have been possible. The strains on both sides were enormous. Employers, absorbed by their own problems of survival, could scarcely ignore the heaven sent opportunity to smash the power of the trade unions which had grown through the war and the first two years of peace. Also the difficulty of establishing price lists for the many types of locks the industry produced and the certainty that such lists, if established, would be ignored by some employers in the industry, posed difficulties which had proved insuperable in the past. For the trade union, co-operation involved the repudiation of nationalisation as an ultimate aim and a conviction that the interests of employers and employed were complementary and not antagonistic. The Lock & Metal Workers Union was pulled both ways. It, rather reluctantly, admitted a political function for the union in 1918. But in the same year, when W.J. Davis (and some leading Black Country trade unionists associated both with Davis' pro-war attitudes and his connections with Birmingham small trades and attitudes to employers not dissimilar to the MCTF) attempted to form a 'new' non-political Labour Party based on the TUC, the Lock Union voted for the 'old', established, political, Labour Party. Class collaboration was never complete and when the outlawing of 'out work' proved impossible, one of the most potent sources of price-cutting re-appeared.

The success or otherwise of this policy of class-collaboration can only be viewed from the workers' side in this study. Regarding unemployment the emphasis on improved trade from 1922 was unusual among unions. High unemployment continued in the trade, but the finances of the union were maintained with relative ease with the help of the 1/-d. per month levy. At the end of 1921 union contributions from members amounted to £4,780 and Unemployment pay had been about £6,000; after other expenses had been met there was an excess of expenditure over income of £265.

The next year contributions from members dropped to £3614, but unemployment pay dropped below £2,000. Dispute pay rose considerably, however and the year ended with a slight loss of £11. In 1923 contributions were again lower at under £3,000 but unemployment pay fell to £803 and the favourable balance rose to nearly £1,000. By 1924 the union was growing again with contributions at £4,671; unemployment pay was rather higher at £1073 but there was a healthy balance of £2,194. In 1925 contributions were again higher at £4,952, unemployment benefit was down to £983 and the balance rose to £2,201. By that time, the assets of the union had risen from £12,140 in 1921 to £17,543 in 1925. On membership the union is more reticent. Stenner has found the peak figure of union membership at 4,563 in 1920. Membership figures reappear in the 1925 Annual Report; this shows membership at 2,046 in 1924 with a leap to 3,004 in 1925; this was largely due to an unexplained increase of women in the union from 354 in 1924 to 1,038 in 1925. Membership of the union was therefore halved between 1920 and 1924, but rose again the next year to make the total loss of membership only about one third, although this included some small union branches in other parts of the country by that time. If, as the records insist, there was a virtual closed shop in Willenhall at least by 1925, this is different from the experience of other unions and suggests that class collaboration paid off in this period, at least from the point of view of the work force.

The Workers' Union

The fortunes of those in the Workers' Union were different. This was the main, thrusting, Black Country and Birmingham based, Socialist orientated, high turnover trade union, catering for the unskilled and semi-skilled who were most prone to unemployment. This union had also defied the general belief that the wages of the unskilled were too low to support generous sickness and unemployment benefits and sustained just such a scheme. In the heady years of the Great Unrest in the Black Country, the national membership of the union had risen from 5,000 in 1910 to 150,000 in 1914. During the war membership more than doubled and by 1920 was at its peak of 496,000. But with the slump, membership more than halved in 1921 and nearly halved again in 1922 down to 140,000. Slight growth then occurred and by 1925 membership was 152,600.

In his 1921 annual report, the general secretary, Charles Duncan wrote:

> The year 1921 has not been a year at all, it has been a nightmare. It is remarkable that any union still exists able to pay its way, for no scale of contributions and benefits, and no set of trade union rules ever drafted, ever contemplated for a single moment a set of conditions as we have been passing through. To meet such a storm as this, contributions would require to have been trebled, if not quadrupled during the past five years. But nobody foresaw and consequently nobody made the necessary provision.

The financial consequences to the union were grim. Whereas the Out-of-Work benefit paid by the union in 1919 was less than £25,000, by 1921 it had risen nearly ten times to £231,700. This was one and a half times the total contributions to the Out-of-Work fund paid by members in the entire existence of the union. Another such year would have bankrupted the union. Much of this misfortune had been brought on the union by its own executive. When national insurance had been extended after the war and unions running their own unemployment schemes were permitted to become agents for the payment of the national scheme, the Workers' Union had engaged in a Dutch auction with other unskilled unions to raise their rates of benefits far higher than could actuarially be maintained. In 1922 Out-of-Work benefit paid out was down to £35,218, partly from improved trade but largely from reduction of benefits paid and levies on members. In the next two years benefits paid out again halved so that the financial position was partially retrieved. With its vast membership losses the Workers' Union suffered more than almost any other union.

Information regarding the fortunes of the Black Country branches of the Workers' Union is difficult to find despite the existence of the union's *Record* and a plethora of organisers. The only consistent record is of membership and finances. The largest centre of membership in the Black Country, was Wolverhampton. In 1921 it had five branches (membership not known) but paid nearly £20,000 to the union; by 1925 it still had five branches, but contributions were down to £2,374, indicating a very severe drop in membership. West Bromwich had six branches in 1921 including a Women's branch; in 1925 there were four branches and the Women's branch had disappeared.

Smethwick and Wednesbury were two other areas of considerable Workers' Union strength. Smethwick in 1921 had five branches, some of them very large; by 1924 there were four branches of unspecified strength. In Wednesbury there were five branches in 1921; in 1925 four, but one of these contributed £2,000 to the union. Some entries are difficult to credit. Walsall, for instance, had 166 members in 1921 but is said to have paid £7,000 to the union; in 1925 it was down to two branches but one of these paid £6,809. Halesowen branch had 859 members in 1921 and the same number in 1925; this suggests a branch not reporting each year and the same figure being used in the national records.

From these Black Country figures generalisation is all but impossible. The Wolverhampton financial figures suggest an almost ten-fold drop in membership. Another three main centres of union strength at Smethwick, Wednesbury and West Bromwich suggest a lesser fall, while the Walsall figures suggest little change. More research is needed.

Unemployment and Real Standards of Living

It is clear that the Depression of 1920-23 was of a severity comparable to both that of the worst years of the Great Depression (1876-1880 and 1884-86) and also to that of the other Great Depression of the early 1930s. One might say that the consequences were even more tragic, for there was a unanimous resolve among workers after the war never to return to the poverty and squalor of the pre-war years. Workers were also prepared to display a militancy equal to that displayed during the Great Unrest of 1911-13 to prevent such a return. Economic conditions, however, defeated them, although once conditions improved from 1924, workers were prepared to make the most militant action of all in the General Strike of 1926.

The effect of the Depression on Black Country living standards is not easy to trace. The following full sets of figures are for Birmingham and in using them it must be borne in mind that Black Country rates were usually slightly lower. This information can be indexed as follows:

	Wages	*Cost of Living*	*Real Wage*
Birmingham Engineers (Fitters & Turners)			
October 1914	100	100	100
April 1920	220	250	88
April 1924	147	175	84
Birmingham Building Workers (Bricklayers)			
Oct 1914	100	100	100
April 1920	267	250	175
April 1924	186	175	106
Birmingham Builders' Labourers			
October 1914	100	100	100
April 1920	333	250	133
April 1924	197	175	113
Birmingham Printers (Compositors)			
October 1914	100	100	100
April 1920	212	250	85
April 1924	195	175	111

SOURCES: Wages – *British Labour Statistics,* Historical Abstract 1886-1968, Tables 1,2,3 and 4; Cost of Living – *Labour Gazette* Ministry of Labour Indices of Retail Prices; also in *Abstract of British Historical Statistics,* B.R. Mitchell and Phyllis Deane p.478.

The striking feature of the above table is that the real standard of living for engineering workers dropped drastically. In view of the importance of engineering to the Black Country it is clear that the fate of large numbers of skilled workers in employment was a standard of living in April 1924, when the worst of the slump was over, lower than that of the prosperous immediate pre-war years.

On the other hand, Black Country council employed, unskilled workers fared rather better. Their wages were controlled by the West Midlands Joint Industrial Council for Local Authorities Non-Trading Services (Manual Workers.) This sliding scale comprised three elements – average pre-war wage, an amount to compensate for cost of living fluctuations, and a sum to secure to the workman an improved standard of living. This the scale achieved as the results below show:

Minimum Rates	July 1914	July 1920	March 1923
Wages	24/-d.	69/-.	49/-d.
Cost of Living	100	249	174
Real Wages	100	116	117

SOURCE: Wolverhampton Borough Council Minutes 12 Feb 1923 pp.266-7.

It must be borne in mind, however, that the increase in real wages of 17 per cent applied only to unskilled workers, other more skilled Council manual workers being governed by the outside rates for the trade; also, as we have seen, unskilled workers benefitted by the narrowing differential between the craftsman and his labourer.

The evidence is insufficient to determine whether a majority or minority of those in work had improved their standard of living between 1914 and 1925, but it would be a travesty of the truth to judge the matter only by these criteria, for we have now to consider the question of unemployment and the standard of living of those not in work.

Again, unambiguous evidence on unemployment is difficult to find. Until 1911 the only figures available were those of such trade unions as paid unemployment benefit. These are generally recognised as being too low. Between 1911 and 1921 there are monthly totals from the newly set up Labour Exchanges showing the numbers of *insured* workers unemployed. These can be set against the trade union figures and they roughly correspond; this is not surprising since both sources suffered from much the same defects. From 1921 virtually *all* workers became insurable and the Ministry of Labour then took to measuring unemployment by the number of insurance cards they held of those out of work and claiming unemployment pay; this, as we know from current experience, is an unsatisfactory way of measuring unemployment; nor is a realistic *percentage* of unemployment likely to emerge by dividing total employment cards issued by the number of unemployed. But even these official percentage figures cannot be used for calculating local unemployment as they are published only for wide areas such as the West Midlands.

The only satisfactory way to measure percentages of local unemployment is to relate them to the total number of persons in employment; such a figure is available, but only once in ten years, from the Population Census. Even this is suitable only for calculating male employment, since it can safely be assumed that almost every male of working age must sell his labour in order to live and he is therefore either employed or unemployed. Such a *rate of male adult unemployment* might be higher than the overall rate for men, women and youths, but it is the key rate because it is in most cases the wage of the breadwinner bringing up a family and, in most of these cases the only wage the family received. This rate could be worked out for all towns. I have worked out only the following:

Wolverhampton May 1921 – Adult Male Unemployment Rate:
No. Men 18 + 32,458: Total Males over 18 Unemployed 8,835
Percentage Males over 18 Unemployed 27 per cent

Is such an unemployment rate realistic given that the national unemployment percentage for the year stands at 16.6 per cent according to Beveridge (Full Employment in a Free Society, p.47)? Well, the same month according to the *Labour Gazette*, engineering unemployment was 20 per cent, but the highest rate was the West Midlands at 29.3 per cent Thus my figure of 27 per cent seems much more reasonable than the national figure. If we turn to June 1924 when the worst of the slump was at an end we have the following figures:

	Smethwick	Walsall	W. Bromwich	Wolverhampton
No. of Males 18 & over	22279	29997	22748	32458
Unemployed Males 18 & Over	4104	5701	3032	5818
% Unemployed Males 18 & Over	18	19	13	19

The Beveridge national unemployment figure for that year is 10.2 per cent. Again my male adult unemployed rate seems more realistic.

We can now return to the question of trying to measure the real standard of living in 1924 compared with 1914. The figures we have presented above show real wages varying between 16 per cent below 1914 to 13 per cent above the 1914 level, with no means of measuring how many Black Country people were above or below these levels. But if we make the generous assumption that more people in work increased their real wage, and that this average real increase was 10 per cent, we would still have to take account of the 17 per cent unemployed. These would be receiving the unemployment benefit introduced by the Labour government in 1924 which was 155 per cent above the levels of 1920. Under the 1924 regulations a man with wife and one child would receive 27/-d. per week in benefits. This would be about half the normal wage of a skilled man or two thirds that of a labourer. A notional 'average' real wage increase of 10 per cent between 1914 and 1924 might therefore well be cancelled out by the lesser income of the 17 per cent unemployed. In reality of course, real wages would vary from the worker in employment enjoying the real increase in income of 10 per cent down to the unemployed worker whose real income would be about two thirds that of a labourer in 1914. In addition a minority of workers would be receiving trade union unemployment pay and there would be the self-employed 'penny capitalists' analysed by John Benson.

Despite the weaknesses of the material used however, it would seem difficult to come to any other conclusion but that that the bulk of Black Country workers and their families had barely improved their real wage between 1914 and 1924; and in the years of unemployment and wage cuts of 1921-3 real wages slumped considerably. This explains the militancy of the unemployed between 1920 and 1924. The only real gain of the period was a fall in working hours.

Bibliography: Black Country Trade Unionism 1919-1925

For Walsall Trades Council there are *Minutes* to 1924, For Smethick there is Exton's column in the *Town Crier*, for Wolverhampton there is my *History of Wolverhampton, Bilston & District Trades Union Council*. Activities of other Trades Council must be picked out from the local press. Details of trade union branches in the Black Country at the end of the war come from the Ministry of Labour Blue Book of 1918 and made available to me from the Labour Research Department by Noreen Branson. For miners in the period see C.J. Horsnell *The Coal Mining Trade Unions in the Black Country 1914-1927* (Wolverhampton University Unpub. MA 1991) For the national picture R. Page Arnot *The Miners – Years of Struggle*. Cost of living figures come from the *Labour Gazette*. For iron workers see Eric Taylor *The Better Temper, a History of the Midland Iron & Steel Wages Board 1876-1976*. Many of the papers of the Midlands Wages Board are in the Modern Records Centre of the University of Warwick. For engineers, AEU membership figures are taken from monthly and quarterly Reports of the union. Engineering wages from *British Labour Statistics*, Historical Abstract 1886-1968. For the 1922 Lock-out nationally see James B. Jefferys, *The Story of the Engineers* chapter 9 and H.A. Clegg, *A History of British Trade Unions since 1889*, chapter 8. For the AEU locally see AEU *Monthly Journal*. For lock makers see Brian Stenner, *The Lock Makers, A Century of Trade Unionism*. Also records of the National Union of Lock and Metal Workers for access to which I am grateful to its general secretary Mr Ward. For the Workers' Union see Richard Hyman, *The Workers' Union* and *Annual Reports, Workers' Union Record* etc in the records of the union lodged at the Modern Records Centre, Warwick University. For the cost of living and unemployment figures see *Labour Gazette*. For the ways the unemployed might supplement their incomes see John Benson – *The Penny Capitalists*.

Chapter 23

The Co-operative Movement in Birmingham 1919-1939

We have seen (Chapter 11) the difficulties experienced by the Co-operative movement during the war and the contribution it made to keeping price rises to a minimum and developing a fair system of rationing.

At the end of the war it was hoped that rationing problems would disappear and the pent-up demand for goods would lead to a rapid expansion of the Co-operative movement as the 'land fit for heroes' was built. The reality proved different. 1919 brought continued difficulties with some foodstuffs and also coal. 1920 brought an advance, but from 1921 the worst slump since the Great Depression of 1875-95 occurred. This lasted until 1925. Then expansion was renewed until 1930 when the Great Depression hit Britain from the USA and the Co-operative movement was again engulfed in problems.

The Co-operative movement in Birmingham at this time consisted of the large consumer society Birmingham Co-operative Society and the smaller Ten Acres & Stirchley Society. There was, in addition, an industrial Society – Birmingham Printers. We will deal with the three societies in turn.

Ten Acres & Stirchley Co-operative Society Ltd

The varying fortunes of this intriguingly named society, invariably abbreviated to TASCOS, can be demonstrated through its vital statistics:

Year	1918	1920	1922	1924	1926	1928	1930	1932
No. of Members	11732	14992	14463	14800	18919	23685	29870	32247
Sales £s	446723	677101	358826	429410	644282	848970	929758	929316
Dividend in £	1/7½d	1/3d	4d	8½d	1/-d	1/-d	1/2d	1/2

From these figures we can see that after 1918 membership grew rapidly, but between 1920 and 1922 sales almost halved, the dividend almost disappeared and membership fell, although only slightly. By 1926 growth was very rapid until 1930 when the slump slowed sales and membership growth, but did not lead to the catastrophic falls of the early 1920s.

The day to day cares of running a society are reflected in the quarterly Directors' Reports. The coal shortage dominated 1919 with the society complaining that supplies allocated to it by the government were inadequate and raising the question of discrimination against the Co-op movement by boards dominated by rival grocery chains. But by the middle of the year a large increase in trade was reported enabling £1,250 to be put to reserves which had been frozen since 1914 at £6,000. The next year saw good progress, but 1921 brought the slump which nearly bankrupted the society. One problem was that at times of crisis the sales of non-food departments fell drastically. Thus early in 1921 the Directors reported that Drapery, Boots and Tailoring sales had fallen greatly due to unemployment whereas food sales continued satisfactory. This meant there was no alternative but to reduce staff where wage costs had risen from 1/2½d per £1 of sales to 1/10½. Falling sales meant a fall in profits and a fall in dividends. The July 1921 report stated that it had been the most depressing quarter ever due to the prolonged coal strike, the vast amount of unemployment and the constant fall in prices. Under these circumstances it was impossible to give dividends at the pre-war level. This was normally 2/-d. in the £ making Co-operative shopping most attractive to the more affluent working class family, although to what extent Co-operative prices were higher than in other shops is a matter not much discussed. The fall in the dividend, which was the only thing that mattered for those who had not imbibed 'Co-operative principles', led to a withdrawal of members. So that in this July 1921 quarter 499 members had withdrawn but only 324 had been admitted. The fall in dividend led to fears that shareholders' capital was at risk. Here again, the interest on Co-op shares of 5 per cent and upwards made it the most attractive investment available to working people. Elaborate explanations were therefore necessary to convince savers that the value of their shares had no connection with the dividend paid; this would only be the case if the dividend were paid out of capital, and this had never occurred. In addition, the writing down of assets, it was claimed, meant that existing assets of premises and transport were considerably undervalued.

But in the October 1921 quarter, for the first and last time, money was taken from the reserves to pay a dividend of 6d. The situation was worsening. The falls in prices were hitting the food department. Cheese was down from 135/-d. to 103/-d. per cwt. there were large reductions in the value of boots. Drapery, Tailoring, Millinery and Furnishing were all showing losses. Worst of all the Co-operative Wholesale Society had made large losses through the depreciation of stocks and this had fuelled rumours that share capital was at risk. Once again it was urged for 'luke-warm members' that there was not the slightest excuse for panic.

The slump continued relentlessly throughout 1922. In the January quarter profits were £2,824 on sales of £119,486 and the dividend was down to 5d. The directors felt that they had not had the loyal support of their members. 'The first consideration is reasonable wages and good conditions for our employees', they maintained. But this did not keep members. In that quarter 386 members joined but 553 left. In April, sales were below £100,000. In October sales reached rock bottom at £84,577; profits fell to only £789 with the dividend set at a derisory 2d. January 1923 saw the nadir of TASCOS fortunes with profits at only £768 and the dividend remaining at 2d. In that quarter 659 members left and only 232 joined. By this time there was demoralisation within the Society. The education grant which was usually over £300 was cut to £110. Affiliation fees to the Co-operative Party were suspended and the anti-political elements were successful with a resolution to contract the Society out of all political activity. By this time the deeds of TASCOS properties were lodged with the CWS.

Part of the problem was with two farms the society possessed. These were relics of the war years when feeding the nation and high food prices had ruled. But between 1920 and 1924 Allen's Cross Farm of 177 acres lost over £10,000 and even though its prospects for future profits were said to be good, the directors wanted to cut their losses and sell it. Problems with Birmingham Corporation regulations held this up, although portions were sold to speculative builders and TASCOS itself built some houses. Losses continued and the farm was not sold until 1928 when the Corporation bought it for £16,597 or 5d. per square yard. The Gay Hill Farm of 25 acres made a loss of £566 in 1923 and was sold in 1925 for £1,700. This entailed a loss of £750.

By the middle of 1923 the Great Slump was at an end and progress resumed. Between 1920 and 1923 TASCOS sales had almost halved. It could be said that this is not as bad as it sounds as the general price level during that time had also fallen by about the same amount. But the effect of this, the worst deflationary period ever recorded, on profit margins was sufficient to almost bankrupt TASCOS. The membership showed rather more loyalty than the protestations of the Directors suggest. About one third of the capital of the Society was withdrawn in these four years. This withdrawal did not mainly reflect a fear for the solvency of the Society; at a period of mass unemployment the most loyal of members had need to withdraw their savings, and unemployment was never higher than in the years 1921 to 1923. The final test of loyalty, that of membership, shows a fall from nearly 15,000 in 1920 to 13,633 in 1923 reflecting the depressing quarterly reports of more members out than in. But this is a fall of less than 10 per cent and shows not only the loyalty of Co-operators, but also continued satisfaction with rates of interest on savings even when the dividend had almost disappeared.

After the slump, prices continued to fall, but less precipitously. In 1924 the cost of living was 75 per cent above that of 1914 and by 1931 it was about 50 per cent higher. Sales topped the half million mark in 1925 and in 1930 reached almost £930,000. It was not to reach £1m, however, as the ensuing slump cut back sales, although not nearly as seriously as in the 1921-23 slump. The £1m was reached in 1934 and by 1938 sales had again increased by 50 per cent to over £1.5m.

The increased sales rapidly brought prosperity to TASCOS. In the January 1924 quarter the dividend was raised to 7d. By the end of the year every department had improved. There had been an 'extraordinary' increase in Coal sales of almost 100 per cent. Bread had increased by 11 per cent in April, and Milk was at its highest level ever, apart from December 1920. Butchery had increased 50 per cent due mainly to recently introduced travelling butchers shops. Boot repairs were once again in profit and Drapery and allied departments had shown the first increases for many quarters. The Building Department, which provided outlet for surplus capital, was lending on mortgages at 5 per cent with the proviso that £40 was spent with the Society every year. Profits which had been down to 2½d. per £1 of sales were then up to 11½d. Such growing affluence meant that previous promises could be honoured. A deposit of £100 was made to £250 promised to the Co-operative College, and the other £150 paid the next year. Large plans were laid to celebrate the TASCOS Jubilee in 1925.

New ventures were put into place. In 1924 the Midland Co-operative Convalescent Fund was joined giving members £3 benefit over a year for a contribution of only 1d per member per year. In 1926 an Employees' Pension Scheme was inaugurated offering half wages at age 65 (with a minimum payment period of five years) financed 40 per cent by TASCOS and 60 per cent by the employee. Hair dressing (for men and women) started in 1926. A nursery department began in 1927 when the Bournville Village nursery was leased from the Bournville Trust. These were innovative ventures as was the expansion into pharmaceuticals in 1928 with drug and optical departments, later expanding into photographic work.

A catalogue of expanding grocery premises and new shops during these prosperous years would be tedious, and has, in fact, been done by Vickrage. The basic fact is that sales almost tripled between 1923 and 1930. The effect of this can be measured by the dividend. From the 2d. at the end of the disaster year of 1923 it rose to 1-/d. in 1926 where it remained at that amount until 1929, rising to 1/2d in 1930.

The welfare of employees was always a main concern of Co-operative Societies. Employees were organised in NUDAW nd their pay was usually higher than elsewhere in the retail trade. The pension scheme was almost unique, it being unheard of in small shops, and in rival chains, such as Maypole and Home & Colonial applicable only to head office, managers, clerks etc. But wages were the second largest expense after the purchase of goods. In 1919 when TASCOS had 303 employees wages came to 6.3 per cent of total sales. In the disaster year of 1923 the number of employees had been cut back to 275, but their ability to resist wage cuts during the Great Deflation of 1921-24 was reflected in the fact that wage costs were then 11.5 per cent of sales. By 1929 it was still 11 per cent of sales on a greatly increased workforce of 796. The actual average wages for TASCOS shop workers were £2-8-0d. in 1919, and £3-11-9d at the height of the post-war inflation in 1921. Wages came down to £2-12-6 in 1924 where they more or less remained until 1929.

Hours of work were long. Shops opened five days a week at 9am. and 8.30 on Saturdays. They closed at 7pm on Monday, Tuesday and Thursday with a 12 noon early closing day on Wednesday. On Fridays and Saturdays the shops closed at 8pm. Allowing one hour for lunch this gives a 50 hour week. But again, it is an improvement on other shops where hours were longer and even with the big multiples, closing on Saturdays could be 10pm.

The ability of the Co-ops with their social responsibilities to compete in the retail trade against the bitter opposition of much of the private trade and important parts of the national press, is due to the devotion and sacrifice of many individual members and employees. but a catalogue of the names of long-serving employees and managers, committee members, long standing members etc. does not make exciting reading. TASCOS tried to honour their heroes during the Jubilee Celebrations in 1925 when they held a tea and social for the wives and husbands of members with twenty five years continuous service. Vickrage lists such people as E. Booth, secretary and chief executive of the Society from 1900 to 1944, and S.C. Adkins assistant secretary from 1919 to 1944 who then followed Booth as secretary. Also William Lygo a director for over 33 years between 1906 and 1948 and George Allen a director from 1910 to 1923 and then chair of the Education Committee until 1934. There were more such as these, but pride of place here must be given to two people. The first was Mrs M.E. Cotterell who was the first (and still one of the few) who served on the board of the Co-operative Wholesale Society. She was elected in 1922 and served for 14 years until she reached retirement age. She was a Birmingham city councillor from 1917 to 1922 and a leading member of the Women's Guild both locally and regionally. She remained active in the service of the Society until the 1950s when she was in her eighties. The other leading member was Tom Hackett. Hackett had first been elected briefly as a director in 1894 and in 1923 at the lowest ebb of the Society's existence he became president. This post he retained until 1946 with a break of only one year, when that other worthy veteran, William Lygo defeated him in 1930. Hackett had stood as a Co-operative and Labour candidate in the 1918 general election, but had shared the Labour defeat of that khaki election. Hackett was also chair of the TASCOS Education Committee from 1907 to 1923 and shared in all the social activities of the Society, to which we now turn.

TASCOS Social Activity 1919-1931

The research and publicity heart of a Society was its Education Committee; it was also the initiator or support of the social organisations of Guilds and children's activities on which the future of the Society depended. The Education Committee was elected every year and the 1919 Report of Arthur C. Senior outlines its activities in the difficult first post-war year. Junior Classes had been started at eight locations and it was hoped to start a self-governing Junior Guild. A week-end school had been held for teachers of junior classes.

A Social Club had been opened at Stirchley. Its large room had been used by the railwaymen during their strike and this room was likely to become a home for educational and trade union work. It had been intended to be jointly controlled by the Society and the ILP but, 'owing to peculiar circumstances,' the Education Committee had decided to take over the entire responsibility.

The Choral Society had taken first prize at the Birmingham district Co-operative Convention. It was to take many more prizes in subsequent years.

Arrangements had been made to fight both Parliamentary and Municipal Elections by a team headed by Mr S.T,Perry JP, national secretary of the Co-operative Party (and father of the famous tennis player). A week-end school had been held at Woodbrooke College promoted by the Midland Educational Society to discuss the problems of Parliamentary Representation and there had been 'splendid attendances and a healthy interest manifested in the subjects under consideration.' There had also been a Trade Union Conference addressed by F.O. Roberts, the West Bromwich Labour MP on 'Labour and Co-operation'.

Other activities noted during the year included satisfaction at the number of Co-op employees taking Co-operative Union Correspondence Courses, a Workers' Union event attended by 200 where a happy evening of games, dancing and music was interspersed with 'several interesting reports' from the secretaries of Men's and Women's Guilds etc, and the important announcement of Day Continuation Schools for the Society's young employees.

The work of the Education Committee was financed by the quarterly grant from the Society's profits. A typical distribution of profits from a prosperous quarter, the middle of 1920, showed net profits of £12,627. Of this £10,000 was allocated to the dividend at 1/4d. £314 went to the Education Committee and nearly £130 was devoted to politics – grants to the national Parliamentary Representation Fund and the Birmingham District Co-operative Representation Council (soon to become the Co-operative Party). The balance went to various reserve funds.

As hard times appeared the Society tried to keep up its educational expenditure. The January 1922 report showed profits down to £2,824 with a dividend of 5d, but the Education grant continued at £313, although political grants were down to £70. The Educational Committee's report stressed the unprecedented amount of unemployment and the apathy and indifference of many who felt it was hopeless to struggle against the economic circumstances. But the seven Women's Guild branches were still apparently flourishing as was the Junior Guild. There was stress on the papers of the Co-operative movement which it was the 'duty' of all Co-operative members and organisations to sell; these included *Co-operative News,* recently reduced to 1d., *Millgate Monthly* at 6d., *Women's Outlook* at 1½d., and *Children's Circle* at 1d.

In April 1922 profits were again down, but the Education and Political grants were maintained. Emphasis in the report was on economy. The usual summer Children's Parties would have to be cancelled 'owing to the abnormal depression in trade.' But the Children's Classes had continued well attended and 230 children had sat for the examinations, results of which would be published in the *Wheatsheaf.* By July 1922 future Children's Classes were in jeopardy 'unless voluntary teachers are forthcoming,' and the Women's Guild was to be financed by the Education Committee at 1/6d. per member per annum instead of by a fixed amount. When the dividend fell to 2d. in the October 1922 quarter, the Education Committee received £110 and no political payments were made. So serious was the position of the Society that a joint Propaganda Committee of representatives of the Directors and members of the Education Committee had been formed and carried out a series of meetings, notably in Shopping Fortnight in July during which a Trade Procession had been organised. In September there was a Garden Fete and Gala at the employees' sports field. It was also reported that the Children's Classes had been saved by volunteers coming forward and were being organised at six centres. Junior choir rehearsals recommenced in September with an average attendance of 50 and for its development they were greatly indebted to Mr Leech and Mrs Downes. There were also strictures at the 'very unsatisfactory state' of the sales of Co-operative publications.

By the January 1923 quarter the dividend was still 2d. and the Education grant was down to £90. But in April 1923 Tom Hackett could announce that the Society had 'turned the corner' and the Education grant rose to £106. It was not until October 1924, however, that the Education Committee could report that it did seem to be 'well on the road to better times.' Details of the five Children's Classes were given; they started at 6pm, were open to children between 10 and 14 and prizes were awarded for attendance and achievement. To previously reported activities had been added a Lending Library, a Literature Committee, two annual scholarships for a boy and a girl to attend a secondary school in the city, and a scholarship worth £100 a year to the Co-operative College.

There is, unfortunately, too little information on the progress of the Guilds – Men's, Women's and Mixed – for this period. No reports of their activities or finances appear in the quarterly reports of the Society. Presumably such news as there is appeared in the local pages of *Wheatsheaf,* which are now lost.

Birmingham Co-operative Society

The largest society in the city was the Birmingham Industrial Co-operative Society. In 1919 it was almost three times the size of TASCOS. judged by sales, and by 1930 it was getting on for five times larger. Its fortunes, however, closely followed that of TASCOS in the post-war period with recovery and development until 1920 followed by the problems of the dreadful slump until 1924.

The first post-war report of the General Committee showed that sales had risen by almost one and a half times since 1914, (although prices had doubled – GB). The sales force had been revolutionised. Of about 400 employees in 1914 only 11 per cent had been women; by 1919 there were more than 1,200 employees of which 60 per cent were women. On two of the main post-war problems, the Society was ambivalent. On demobilisation the additional labour was welcome, but as they were all men, there were some problems in integrating them into the labour force especially at a time when expansion was very difficult. By April 169 demobbed employees had been re-employed, but this was only 52 per cent of those who had enlisted or been conscripted. Another 48 men would never return, for they had made the supreme sacrifice. But it looks as if many who had experienced the war were not keen to return to the comparatively low wages and long hours of the retail trade. On the clamour, led by the food trade, to end price control and rationing the Society welcomed the removal of food controls in so far as they enabled consumers to change their retailer, but not until sufficient stocks had been accumulated to prevent large rises in prices. The main problem for the society was its coal supplies, and this continued to occupy much of its attention over the coming period.

There were a number of social benefits attached to Co-op membership. A Convalescent Scheme offered accommodation and fares, or fares only when an applicant had a 'ticket', together with expenses incurred at home by the absence of the patient. These were available for both members and their families and employees. But the benefits were not available to those with tubercular or mental disorders. There was also a long-established Emergency Fund for sickness or other distress. It was remarked that during the war, claims on this fund had almost ceased, but by October 1919 there had been four claimants who had been paid a total of £8-10-0d. In 1920 a Death Benefits scheme was adopted, based on amounts purchased from the Society, calculated to cost the Society ¾d per £1 of sales.

In this first year of peace employees benefitted from the 48 hour week being negotiated with the AUCE. There was also a generous wage award which, however, was rapidly eroded by inflation. The adult male minimum became 65/-d per week. Adult females 45/-d. Branch managers 80/-d. and Branch manageresses 55/-d. Motor drivers and delivery men received 70/-d. A long standing national Co-operative controversy was re-argued in 1919. This was whether Co-operative employees were entitled to a bonus, i.e. whether they were 'members' entitled to share in the dividend or simply employees. The Birmingham Society had adopted the progressive principle in 1889 that employees were entitled to a bonus, but only when profits allowed a dividend of 1/3d. With immediate pre-war dividends at 2/-d. in the £ the principle had lain dormant but now the dividend was coming close to the 1/3d. In October it was argued that the employees were entitled to their bonus even though the profits of the quarter were, as usual, estimated and not firm. But the issue receded after 1920 as dividends dropped disastrously and the bonus disappeared.

The second year of prosperity, 1920, was taken up not only with reports of expansion, but also fundamental problems. The coal shortage continued and after fruitless protests to the local authorities, BICS, together with TASCOS and the Soho Society organised a mass meeting of protest at the Town Hall, attended by 1,500 people. Here Co-operative complaints were vigorously aired. These were the continued use of a datum period of 1917 which penalised the rapidly growing Co-operative movement and the allocation of coal which was currently between 50 per cent and 75 per cent of Co-operative requirements. The Fuel Overseer was invited to the meeting and put his case, but this fell far short of the demands of the Co-operators. By July it was reported that supplies had improved somewhat, but that new coal customers were not being accepted.

Another alarming prospect was the re-opening of the campaign of opposition to the Co-operative movement by the national press and important sections of business. Their key demand was for the taxing of Co-operative 'profits' at the same rate as private profits. These attacks had been beaten off in the past, the last attempt being the excess profits tax during the war. But this time private enterprise attacks were buttressed by a recent Royal Commission on Income Tax which recommended taxing all Co-operative profits except for the amount returned to members in dividends. The Co-operative movement claimed that the net effect would be taxation on share interest (already taxed through the individual) and most other profit allocation, including reserve funds, dividend equalisation funds, insurance funds, charitable donations, political and similar grants etc. The results of mutual trading among members, it was claimed, were not profits but savings – a reduction of savings rather than an addition to income. Even if such surpluses were income, the majority of members of Co-operatives were not liable to income tax under existing exemption limits and the costs of collection of the amounts due and the large number of refunds made would make the taxation non-economic. This matter was one of supreme importance to the movement, it was concluded. It was designed by its competitors to impede the progress of Co-operation and undermine its financial stability. It should be fought by every legitimate means. A national campaign was organised. Locally meetings were held, MPs lobbied etc. and contributions made to the central campaign such as £200 by BICS in the July quarter.

A further difficulty for the Society was the miners' strike in the autumn which closed down the Coal Department and cost the Society £6,400. The Society, of course, supported the strike and many members were active in helping the miners and their families.

Of the rapid development of shops and departments in 1920, three must be mentioned. The first was the development of farming, soon to prove uneconomic. This arose as a result of resolutions passed when both wartime prices and patriotism were high. Blackgreaves Farm (230 acres) was purchased in 1919 at Lea Marston and the adjacent Lea Farm (488 acres) bought in 1920. THis was linked to the purchase of 262/4 Corporation Street for joint use by the Society and the Trades Council. Here the Society centralised the sale of agricultural supplies, offering everything necessary to allotment holders, gardeners, small holders, pig and poultry keepers, farmers etc.

A more successful project was the decision to enter milk retailing. Few societies sold milk at this time as it was considered turnover in relation to profit and dividend was too low. But the Birmingham venture was an instantaneous success and made profits for the society from its commencement in May 1920.

The third development was the purchase of five acres of playing fields at Barrows Lane, Yardley for £2.750. This proved a boon to employees and, when later extended, was used by the Society for some of its functions.

With inflation still raging, Co-operative employees received their second, and last, large wage increase in 1920. This amounted to an average of 8/4d. per week per employee, but the detail given is insufficient to calculate the amounts for male and female shop workers.

The democratic process with regard to employees was also extended in 1920 when another controversial Co-operative principle was addressed. This concerned the right of employees to be elected to the Management Committee with the subsequent danger that this Committee would be dominated by employees who might put their wages and conditions above that of the interests of the Society. To obviate this danger, disqualification was only partially removed, by allowing for only two employees to be eligible for election to the board, and requiring that they be elected by the whole membership.

All Societies were members of the Co-operative Union and through its Annual Congress policy for the whole movement was made. There were also local mutual support bodies interpreting Union policy and settling local problems. BICS belonged to the Birmingham District comprising in 1919 twelve retail Societies and three productive societies – Birmingham Printers, Midland Woodworkers and Alcester Needle Makers. Reports of the work of the District Committees were made at the Annual Congress and printed in its papers. The Birmingham District secretary was Frank Bruff of Birmingham Printers, and representatives of the Soho, Worcester, Dudley, Alcester, Kidderminster and Midland Woodworkers societies comprised the Committee. Three Conferences and a Convention had been organised during the year, Bruff reported. The Conferences took place in the area of a different Society each time and were addressed usually by the leading co-operators in the District. So in Soho a paper was read on 'The Future of the Co-operative Store' by a leading Soho member. In Dudley, the Dudley president spoke on the 'Duties and Aims of the Movement' and at Worcester Bruff opened a discussion on 'Sectional and District Boundaries.' The annual district Co-operative Convention, which had been postponed during the war 'was a huge success, despite the railway strike.' Business was combined with pleasure. In the morning a paper was read by the Birmingham assistant-secretary on 'The Problems of the Co-operative Movement in 1920' and in the afternoon'an 'inspiring address' was given by the Minister of Old Meeting church of Birmingham on 'The Humanising of Business.' Meanwhile a choir contest resulted in a win for the TASCOS choir with Oakengates second. In the evening 3,000 were present to hear the combined choirs give 'a magnificent rendering' of Elgar's 'Banner of St. George.' The verdict on the day's proceedings was, 'It is an undoubted fact that this Convention is an enormous help to the movement in the Central Midlands.' The income of the District Committee was about £45. Of this about £30 came from the Co-operative Union and the rest from subscriptions from its Societies. Its main expenditure was on payments to members to EC meetings and district conferences of about £35. The secretary received a 'salary' of 3 guineas per annum.

Subsequent District Reports followed much the same pattern – reports of Conferences on questions pertinent to the movement, the Annual Convention, and summaries of the progress of the societies within the District.

The state of education in each Society was also a matter of concern to the District, and for an account of this activity one returns to the Quarterly Reports of each Society. Social activity had stood up well to the disruptions of war and the first BICS Education Report after the war outlined the continuance of these activities. The main ones were the Musical Evenings, Junior Classes, the Men's and Women's Guilds, the Junior and Senior Choirs, Conferences and Week-end Schools. Subsequent reports showed these activities developing as fast as the Society itself. In 1920 the first Comrades' Circle for young people was formed at Harborne by the Women's Guild. At the end of 1920 there were 13 Women's Guilds and 7 Men's Guilds. By this time the Education Committee was complaining that it could no longer finance all its activities since its grant from the Society was dependent on profits and these were smaller than they had been pre-war when dividends were 2/-d. in the £. It therefore requested that the basis of the grant be changed to 10d. per member per annum. Subsequent Management Board reports do not record whether this proposition was put, but it does raise the question of how much the Education Committee did receive. BICS was fairly generous with its Education Grant, but the Rochdale Pioneers had considered that 2½ per cent of the profits of a society should be devoted to education. In 1920 we find that BICS profits were £158,843 and its education grant was £1,479 or 0.93 per cent of its profits.

To summarise the progress of the Society in the two 'prosperous' years of high inflation and difficulties of supply following the end of the war we find the following. The number of members had increased by 37 per cent Other indicators must be deflated for inflation which was 23 per cent between 1918 and 1920. Share capital rose by 57 per cent Sales increased by 50 per cent both being real gains against inflation, but net profit rose by only 24 per cent which was barely above the inflation rate of 23 per cent. As a result, the dividend fell in this period, from an average of 1/5d. in 1918 to 1/2d in 1920.

The Slump Years 1921-1924

The total devastation of the 1921 slump arose from the speed with which it developed. Inflation peaked in November 1921 at 176 per cent above pre-war prices. The price level then fell precipitously. In April 1921 it was down to 133 per cent and by December it was 99 per cent above pre-war levels. This generated an unstoppable demand for wages to be cut. In September 1920 national unemployment had been 1.6 per cent. By April 1921 it was 10 per cent and by July peaked at 23 per cent Nor can the cosy conclusion be drawn that unemployment in Birmingham was lower than the national average because of its diversity of employment. In April 1921 when the average national unemployment rate was 10 per cent the national rate in engineering was 15 per cent but engineering unemployment in the West Midlands was the highest in the country at 25 per cent and it rose to a peak of 33 per cent in June. By April 1921 the BICS quarterly report quoting official figures of 80,000 wholly unemployed and 40,000 partially unemployed, claimed that almost one third of wage earners in Birmingham were unemployed.

With the Co-operatives' high dependence on food sales they were protected from the worst results of the slump, but BICS first fall in sales was reported in the first quarter of 1921.

Sales continued to fall. In July 1921 prices were reported down by 20 per cent but wages had fallen by only 6½ per cent. By the middle of the year it was claimed that despite stringent economies expenses had been reduced by only 16 per cent whereas sales were down 30 per cent The dividend was then down to 5d. Withdrawals of share capital began to be heavy and measures had to be taken to try to restore confidence. Non-co-operative chartered accountants were called in to audit the accounts and their confirmation of the stability of the Society was advertised; special meetings between management and members and management and staff were called to restore morale and pleas for loyalty to the Society made.

The slump continued through 1922 and on to 1923. As previously planned developments came to fruition, no new expansion was undertaken and some premises were sold. Farm losses exacerbated the situation. The rate of decrease of sales, however, eventually fell to the level of that of the fall of prices, and special sales drives were undertaken such as a Shopping Fortnight and the very successful new form of weekly club which greatly helped the most affected departments of clothing and boots.

July 1923 was the first quarter in which revenue increase exceeded the fall in prices, but the dividend remained at 4d. Only in the last quarter of 1923 did sales rise by 10 per cent enabling the dividend to be raised to 5d. and only after two more quarters of sales increases of about 15 per cent was the dividend raised to 8d. and the expansion of the society could be resumed.

The support of the Education Department was crucial during these years of crisis. At the beginning of 1921 the Education Committee reported 13 Women's Guild branches and 7 Men's Guilds, '...which help materially to spread the gospel of Co-operation, making new members and discussing matters important to us all as both Co-operators and citizens.' The Senior Choir was making good progress and the Junior Choir rapid progress. There was an Adult Class on Co-operation where attendance was good, 'but one could wish for more.' Five Conferences had been held during the quarter and the annual general meeting was to be held, as usual, at the Town Hall.

The decision to purchase playing fields in the good days came to fruition in the bad years. A Playing Fields Committee was set up in the summer of 1921 offering facilities for Cricket, Tennis, Football and Harriers. For an annual fee of 4/6d. free admission to the playing fields was allowed. Subscriptions for football were 5/-d. for adults and 2/6d. for those under eighteen. Membership was limited and early application was advised. Social activities continued to develop during 1922. Guilds grew to 15 Women's and 8 Men's. An additional Senior Choir at Lozell's with sixty mixed voices was reported. The Comrades Circle at Sparkhill was 'very active,' and an additional Circle started at Erdington with the help of the Women and Men's Guilds. Additions to the library suggested a Marxist orientation with *The People's Marx,* Engel's *Conditions of the Working Class in England 1844,* and *Wages, Prices and Profits* (sic). 4 Junior Classes were maintained, a Children's Gala was organised and the Junior Choir was so successful that it was necessary 'to refuse any other applicants.'

But falling profits were affecting the Education Grant, which was down to £690 in July 1922 and the difficulties of the Society brought political reaction, for it seems to have been the Education Committee which the next quarter advised the Society to make no political grants for the time being.

In the first quarter of 1923, however, the Education grant was raised to £875. This seems to have had the effect of stabilising rather than increasing educational activity over the year. The Guilds remained static at 15 Women's branches and 8 Men's with total membership of 830 and 232 respectively. Two Adult Classes were maintained, mainly for Co-operative employees in Book-keeping and Salesmanship, but neither was wildly successful. An additional facility was a Recreational Hut at Lea Marston in the vicinity of the farms.

Growth Resumed 1924-1930

In 1921 profits had fallen from more than £150,000 the previous year to almost £50,000 and they remained at about that level for the next two years. But in 1924 profits bounced back to almost £100,000 and growth was resumed. The first decision taken at this time was that Co-operative goods should be priced competitively throughout the range of products sold. This silenced trade detractors and others who maintained that the Co-op dividend was bought at the expense of higher prices. This involved the Society in expensive additional publicity through the local press. Another important decision was to increase the number of Special Clubs from one to two per year. These each lasted 24 weeks and vouchers for 24/-d. were issued for each shilling that a member paid. The dividend was also paid on these purchases. Thus the clubs and credit schemes of private traders were improved upon and the money spent on clothing etc. where profit margins were highest in departments which had suffered most during the slump. To such innovations does T. Smith, the historian of the Society, credit its expansion to become the third largest Co-operative Society in Britain, after the two giant London societies.

Other publicity ventures during 1924 were the May Eve Parade of 100 Co-op vehicles, and the implementation of the Co-operative Congress decision that the first Saturday in July should be observed as Co-operators' Day throughout the world.

Development and improvement also went ahead in 1924 including a further $18\frac{1}{2}$ acres to the Playing Fields. But, despite the farms making a small profit, the poultry farm was closed down.

In 1925 space was rented at the prestigious annual National Trades and Industrial Exhibition at

Bingley Hall. This was so successful that extended space was taken in subsequent years. The dividend was gradually rising. It was 10d. in January and 11d. in July after an 'unparalleled' rise in sales of 35 per cent over the corresponding quarter of the previous year. It remained at 11d. until the end of the year with 5d. for non-members.

But the most important event of 1925 was the merger with the adjacent Soho Society of Smethwick. The economic depression hit the Soho Society more than most. Its sales fell from nearly £500,000 in 1920 to less than £100,000 in 1925. Consequently its profits fell from £34,000 in 1920 to £893 in 1922 and a loss of more than £2,000 the following year. Its share capital fell from £120,000 in 1920 to £30,000 in 1925 as poverty rose and confidence in the Society fell. It paid no dividend from 1923 to 1925. Only its membership remained steadfast, falling less than 10 per cent from 12,500 to 11,500 in this period. A merger was negotiated with Birmingham with the assistance of the CWS. Soho members received 10/-d. in the £ on their shares, which with subsequent pay-outs was raised to 15/-d. Much was owed to the CWS which had to be written off. All other creditors were paid in full. This is one of the few examples where Co-operative shareholders lost part of their capital. The causes must have been more complex than those given by Smith of poverty and unemployment in Smethwick being greater than in Birmingham.

The merger with Soho brought shops in Birmingham, Smethwick, Oldbury, Langley and West Bromwich into the enlarged Society. It also took the opportunity of shortening its name to the Birmingham Co-operative Society, abandoning the anachronistic word 'Industrial' from its title.

The early results of the merger are difficult to disentangle as the BSC had adopted a Standard Balance Sheet recommended at the Co-operative Congress and 'net profit' was assessed on the different basis of 'Net Surplus including Share Interest.' But whatever the accountancy vagaries they cannot alter the fact that 1926 was the most successful year in the history of the Society. Profits rose from £88,000 in 1925 to £227,000 in 1926, an extraordinary rise of over 150 per cent.

A 1926 list of premises operated by BSC shows another side of the merger. The offices and central emporium was in the High Street. Sixty six grocery establishments were operated, including fifteen inherited from Soho. There were thirteen Drapery departments (three from Soho), twelve Boot establishments (three from Soho), and four Tailoring establishments (two from Soho). There were twenty eight Bakers and Confectionary shops (three from Soho) serviced by three Bakeries (one from Soho); also two Furnishing Departments (one from Soho). Some activities had not been undertaken by the Soho Society. These included Twenty five Butchers shops, and six Fish, Fruit & Greengrocery shops. Six Coal Depots and Wharves, a Dairy Department and two Dairy Farms completed the list. There were also 272 Delivery Rounds.

1926 was the year of the General Strike. Its effect on the Society were summarised in the July quarter of the year. The increased sales would have been even larger but for the strike. The calling out of Co-op employees had disrupted the Society and there had been other effects such as the stopping of building. But £1,000 had been contributed by the Society to various Miners' Women and Children Relief funds.

Such a rapid improvement in the fortunes of the Society transformed the dividend. In 1923 it had averaged $4\frac{1}{4}$d, in 1924 $7\frac{3}{4}$d, in 1925 $11\frac{1}{2}$d. and in 1926 it hit the magic 1/-d. This then raised the question of whether it should remain at that point. Was 1/-d. enough to remain competitive, to cover depreciation and development, and to retain members and capital? If so, further increases in profits could be devoted to the education of members and the public in Co-operative principles. Birmingham Co-operators seem to have answered these questions in the affirmative, for the dividend remained at 1/-d. until 1930, despite continually rising profits.

1927 was another bumper year for the Society, its profits increasing by 27 per cent. An Employees' Superannuation Scheme became operative in January. About 100 boys from the Grocery Department had attended half-day release classes in 1926 and two additional classes had been created – one for boys in Butchery and Greengrocery and one for girls in Drapery and allied departments. A report from the AGM of the Superannuation Fund indicated that 940 males and 128 females had joined the Fund, this being 55 per cent of adult male employees and 26 per cent of adult females. Five employees had been elected to the administration of the Fund. Very extensive development of shops and premises were reported throughout the year. These included, opposite the main BCS premises in High Street, The Grand Louvre and also the Metropole Hotel.

In January 1928 it was recorded that the Society was then the third largest in Great Britain from the point of membership and fifth measured by sales. Further acquisitions in the City centre were made in 1928 when Midland Arcades was purchased for £85,000 on leases mostly 70 years unexpired. This property was bought as an investment on future development of the Society and in 1928 rents totalled almost £11,000 a year.

Expansion continued into 1929. £2,000 was contributed to the purchase of a national Co-operative newspaper, *Reynolds News*. Large capital investments of £200,000 were made in Birmingham Corporation five year loans, and improvements such as a model dairy capable of processing 100,000 gallons of milk per week and described as the best in Britain, and possibly Europe, were made.

From 1930 expansion came to an end. But the effects of the Great Depression of the 1930s on the Society were much less than those of the slump of the 1920s.

Education Developments 1924-1930

The Education Committee always devoted much effort to promoting the sales of Co-operative publications, usually without a great deal of success. In 1924 sales per quarter of *Co-operative News* were only 30 dozen. *Millgate Monthly* had sold 167 and presented 75 copies to the city Library. *Women's Outlook,* recently become a fortnightly, sold 57 dozen and *Our Circle* 12 dozen. To organise the first Co-operators' Day a joint Committee of four Management and four Education Committee members was formed. The Women's Guilds of Erdington, Hockley, Witton and Stechford organised Tableaux respectively on 'The Golden Crust' (this was the wrapped and sealed loaf of BCS), 'Following in Mother's Footsteps', 'Herald of Co-operation', and 'Co-op Milk'. A Speakers' Class had been reopened with Fred Longden continuing as tutor. It took the form of of a course of ten lectures on 'Ten Phases of Working Class Movements,' which students had to speak on the following week.

By 1925 the Education Committee was organising 22 Junior Classes with 1,000 children attending. Of the AGM at the Town Hall that year it was said that the Hall was not full to hear a lecture on Education, but all tickets had been sold. William Hampson (Casey) 'charmed with his playing, apt quotations and remarks.' Casey was a veteran violinist and comedian who had for many years entertained Labour movement audiences. The extension of the Sports Field which had now added bowls, a putting green and clock golf to its attractions, enabled, Co-operators' Day 1925 to be held on the Society's own Playing Fields. By the end of the year there were 20 Women's Guild branches and 8 Men's.

All sections of the Labour movement were expanding in the run up to the General Strike and the Co-op was no exception. The activities of the Education Committee were expanding as fast as the sales and membership of the Society were. Even sales of periodicals were up considerably; *Co-operative News* to 44½ dozen per week *Women's Outlook* to 17½ dozen per fortnight and *Our Circle* up to 14 dozen per month. The Junior Classes in 1926 attracted 1,700 children with an average attendance of 82 per cent. The three choirs continued to appear at Co-op functions and Musical Evenings. By the autumn there were 23 Women's Guilds, 10 Men's and 2 Members (mixed men and women's) Guilds 'all actively engaged in propaganda, educational and social work.' There were also 6 Comrades' Circles catering for the age group 14 to 25. The May Parade, on the eve of the General Strike featured a monster 230 Co-op vehicles, and a film of the event was made to show at the local cinemas.

The generally adverse effects of the defeat of the General Strike did not apply to the Co-op, and educational activity continued to expand in 1927. Musical evenings were popular with a speaker on a Co-operative topic being supported by a choir and solo items. The format was extended with two 'very successful' Social Meetings at West Bromwich Town Hall 'in recognition of the extension of trading and social activity in West Bromwich.' The series was then extended to five meetings, all well attended, with a maximum audience of 800.

The success of the Junior Classes was quite extraordinary. In 1927 there were more children than ever, and no less than 800 of them (300 more than the previous year) sat for a final Examination. 'The syllabus of study,' it was explained, 'is designed to suit the special needs of Birmingham children and deals largely with the affairs of Co-operation as they affect our Society.' A children's Painting Competition the same year brought more than 1,000 entries. Prizes to the children were presented at the annual Town Hall meeting and the two children with the highest marks were given Summer School Scholarships. As usual, the centre piece of the meeting was a speech by a CWS director. Was it this, or was it the 'lengthy programme of musical and other items contributed by our Joint Co-operative Choir and other artists of which the audience was keenly appreciative' which brought 'a good attendance' to such a meeting?

Co-operators' Day was also extended in 1927. A Gala and Demonstration was held at Sutton Park. 'Some 5,000 were present and the usual attractions of sports, Punch and Judy, band selections and other entertainments were thoroughly enjoyed.' There was also, of course, a speech by an MP on a Co-operative topic.

The less successful Adult Classes seem to have improved somewhat in 1927. A book keeping and apprentices' class catered for Society employees. An innovation, however, was a successful Psychology class held in conjunction with the WEA and an unsuccessful attempt to organise a class on the History of Birmingham. This, perhaps, marks a transition from the traditional role of the Education Committee as being solely the propaganda arm of the Society and disseminator of Co-operative principles, to a wider role of also providing more general educational opportunities to its members. Three classes organised by the Women's Guild in 1927, however, stuck to the old formula and were on the Principles of Co-operation.

Expansion of the work of the Education Committee continued in subsequent years. A Co-operative orchestra was formed in 1927 and two years later a Musical Council was formed, responsible for the co-ordination of the work of the two Senior choirs (the Junior choir having disappeared) and the orchestra. The Musical Council was also influential within the wider musical culture of Birmingham and it invited the Midlands Choral Association to hold its annual Summer Festival in Birmingham in 1929.

The Children's Classes continued to expand and in 1929-30 sixty five classes with an average attendance of 1,900 were organised. After the 1927 Gala Day at Sutton Park in 1927, the event became an annual Children's Day. When the children became too old for the classes they often moved into one of the ten Comrades' Circles. The Women's Guild had 31 branches by 1930 and constituted an entire district of the National Women's Guild. The Men's Guild extended to 12 branches by 1930 and the two Mixed Guilds continued to operate.

The grant to sustain these educational activities came from the expanding revenues of the Society. The grant in the disaster year of 1923 was down to £823. By 1926 it was over £2,000 and in 1930 £3,804. The 1923 grant amounted to 1.6 per cent of the Society's profits, but for all other years the education grant amounted to barely 1 per cent of profits. This was less than half the amount recommended by the Rochdale Pioneers, but on target for the 1 per cent which the Birmingham Society had set itself in 1884. The relative amount of the grant, therefore, did not increase in the years when, despite rising profits, the dividend was held at 1/-d.

The Birmingham Co-operative Party

Before 1918 every effort to involve the Birmingham Society in politics had been resisted. The Chamberlain tradition still pervaded the city, Co-operators were mainly from the skilled working class, and as likely to vote Liberal, or even Conservative, as Labour.

This changed during the war with the problems of supply, the domination of rival private food groups over food rationing administration, and continuing hostility of the grocery trade and press (national and local) to the Co-operative movement.

But the Co-ops occupied an ambiguous position with its leading cadres usually steeped in the Socialist principles of Robert Owen, but a mass membership concerned with little more than economical shopping and the divi. But the political situation changed during the war, the Liberals split and the Labour Party emerged as the second party.

The Co-operative Congress of 1917 passed a resolution requesting direct Co-op representation on national and local bodies and the Birmingham Societies – BICS, TASCOS, Soho and Birmingham Printers – almost immediately set up a Birmingham and District Co-operative Representation Council to achieve these aims. In the hastily called khaki general election of December 1918 Frank Spires of BICS stood in Sparkbrook, and Tom Hackett of TASCOS stood in Kings Norton. In the 'Hang the Kaiser' atmosphere of this election these candidates had no chance and were defeated along with the Labour candidates. In the local elections of 1919, however, three Co-operative candidates were successful – J. Hart (Selly Oak), E.W. Hampton (Balsall Heath), and W. Hood (Kings Norton). W.H. Harris also won in Smethwick.

Problems, however, arose inevitably between the Labour Party and trade unions over the allocation of seats to Co-operators. Despite painstaking efforts, agreements between the Labour Party and Co-operators on this matter continued to be difficult to achieve.

The position worsened during the post-war slump years when the anti-politics lobby within the movement campaigned to end the political grant using falling profits as an additional excuse. This was successful in TASCOS, but defeated in BICS. The situation was basically retrieved in TASCOS by an amendment to the constitution allowing the formation of voluntary parties within the area of the Society.

But it was not until after the 1924 General Election, at which Fred Longden of BICS stood, but was defeated, that long lasting agreement with the Labour Party materialised. This resulted in the election of Fred Longden in 1929 at Deritend as the first Co-operative MP in Birmingham. By 1930, in addition to its MP, the Co-operative Party had three Councillors on the city Council, seven magistrates and five co-opted members of the local pensions committee. The activity of propaganda for the Co-operative movement and election of representatives on public bodies was carried on by eight branches of the Co-operative Party serving seven parliamentary constituencies.

Industrial Co-operation

Midland Wood Workers

The ideal of the Co-operative Commonwealth envisaged the peaceful supersession of capitalist production by Co-operative production. This ideal, fostered by the earliest Co-operators under the influence of Robert Owen, was diverted by the spectacular growth of Consumer Co-operation following the success of the Rochdale Pioneers. This position was reflected in the Birmingham District where only three small Industrial Co-operatives operated in 1918 – Alcester Needle Makers, Midland Woodworkers, and Birmingham Printers. The first is outside our remit. Of Midland Woodworkers, little is known. They first appear in Co-operative Union records in 1912 with 46 members and a share capital of £231. Sales were then £670 and no profit was given. They had twelve employees who were paid a total of £300 or less than 10/-d. per week! In 1914 sales were up to £902, but employees were down to four. By the end of the war sales at £2,095 had just about kept up with inflation and seven employees earned £2-7-6d. a week. The Society reached its peak. In that year its turnover almost reached £10,000 and it employed 21 people. But the slump hit it hard. Its sales were halved in 1921 and its employees came down to six. By 1924 its sales had halved again down to less than £2,500 and in 1925 despite a rise in sales, its cash in hand and at the bank totalled only £9. No more is heard of the Midland Woodworkers. It may be that this Society performed a special function within the movement, or served the interests of a minority of its members, or perhaps produced particularly high quality products. But nothing of this can be gleaned from the records examined.

Birmingham Printers

More is known of the Birmingham Printers whose aim was to produce high class printing in the tradition of Baskerville in Birmingham and William Morris nationally. It was the brain child of Frank Bruff who was its first secretary and manager from its founding in 1902. Bruff also lectured on typography at the Birmingham Municipal Secondary School and his reputation for high quality printing brought orders from such customers as Birmingham University, Birmingham City Council, His Majesty' Stationery Office etc. Beginning with a capital of £110, this had risen to nearly £20,000 in 1919 when it had 279 members, employed 95 workers, had a turnover of almost £40,000 and made a net profit of £5,500. The slump hit its revenue and by 1923 it was at its lowest of £30,000 The Society had the reputation of never going on short time until 1932, paying above trade union rates of pay, providing good welfare facilities and working a 48-hour week between the wars. The Society was a workers' co-operative providing its members with secure and renumerative employment while selling high quality goods in a very competitive market. The success of a workers' co-operative is not therefore to be judged by the capitalist yardstick of profit, but by the satisfaction it gives to its members. The main achievements of Birmingham Printers seems to have been that it retained it members and share capital during the 1920s on a slow growth of revenue from £30,000 in 1923 to £35,000 in 1930. This was accompanied by a large increase in employment provided from 114 employees in 1923 to 144 in 1926. This could not be sustained, however, and employment fell to 133 in 1928 and 122 in 1930. A similar pattern was repeated in the 1930s. After the worst ravages of the 1930s slump revenue was still only £32,000 in 1935, but 146 people were employed. By 1938 revenue was £38,000 but employees only 115. Profits play a minor role in worker-co-operative balance sheets. Those of Birmingham Printers rose from a low of £1,185 in 1922 to £1,904 in 1930. But although net profit is of less importance to an Industrial Co-operative it needs to be sufficient to cover expenditure considered desirable. For instance in 1919 the Birmingham Printers' net profits were £5489. From this it was possible to pay a dividend of 1/-d. to 279 members holding a share capital of nearly £20,000 as well the normal interest on the shares costing £875. Then £1,829 was paid as a bonus on wages. £150 was spent on Education, which was 3 per cent of net profit, compared with the 1 per cent allocated by BICS and most other consumer societies. £113 were spent on 'charitable uses' and 3 guineas was the Society's subscription to the Co-operative Union. However, the fall of profits to below £2,000 at which they remained until 1930 made these 'extras' impossible to maintain. 1921 was the last year that a bonus on wages was paid and not until 1929 was a dividend (of 3d) paid. No educational expenditure was possible until 1929 when it was allocated £41. Virtually all the surplus was absorbed by the payment of interest on the share capital. This was the price paid for high wages, secure employment and good working conditions.

Birmingham Co-operative Personalities

Private industry and retailing depends on attracting intelligent and resourceful management by the payment of high wages. The Co-operative movement, however, relies almost entirely on Management Committees whose members are prepared to work for an ideal without pay. This idealism extends to many employees and all those who organise and participate in the the political and social organisations of the Society. Typical of those who devoted their lives to the Co-operative movement was William Roberts. He was among the band of railwaymen at Saltley who set up the Society in 1881. On inauguration he became Shareholder No.1. and also President. Except for the period 1888-98 when he was an auditor to the Society, he held the Presidency unbroken and unopposed until 1922. He thus saw the Society through its early struggles and the difficult war period of 1914-18. When he retired he was thanked for his 'incomparable services' and given the Freedom of the Society. When he died in 1927 a Management Committee obituary stated, 'It could be accorded to few persons to serve their fellow men and women for so long in a position of great trust and responsibility.' It stressed his absolute integrity and devotion to the Co-operative movement.

William Roberts was followed as president by Joseph Millington. Millington's services to the Society began in 1890 when, as a Midland railwayman he had been transferred from Derby to Birmingham. He was then a prominent NUR member and had served on its executive. Millington remained an active trade unionist. He was associated with the Birmingham Trades Council for many years, was its president from 1899 to 1902 and on its executive committee for sixteen years. At the turn of the century he was an original member of the local Labour Representation Committee which after 1906 became the Labour Party.

About 1905 Millington left the railway to become a Relieving Officer with the Aston Board of Guardians, on which he had served as an elected member for seven years. From about 1895 He was a member of BICS management committee and from 1912 he was vice-president of the Society. Whilst holding this position he was also a member of the Education Committee, and its chairman from at least 1916 until July 1920. When the Co-operative movement entered politics it was inevitable that Millington should be involved and he was on the executive committee of the Birmingham & District Co-operative Representation Committee in 1918 which became the Co-operative Party the next year. Millington also served the Co-operative movement nationally on the Midland Sectional Board of the Co-operative Union for many years and from 1912 was elected representative on the central Board of the Co-operative Union. In 1922 he was the natural successor to Roberts as president of BICS.

General Secretary of BICS during this period was James McDowall. He had joined the society as a clerk in 1903, became Secretary in 1907 and served in that capacity until 1948.

George Diddams was another veteran with fifty years service to the Society in 1930. Frederick Cornforth was another. He joined the Society in 1883, was first elected to the management committee in 1893 and served on this committee for 35 years.

Arthur Green BSc was a teacher first elected to the management committee in 1913. With a break for war service he continued to serve throughout the nineteen twenties and was vice-president of the Society from 1922.

John W. Whatmough joined the Society as a clerk in 1905 and became the teacher of the classes in Management etc. run by the Education Committee for its employees. He became assistant-secretary of the Society in 1911, retaining that position into the 1930s.

William Luckcuck was first elected to the management committee in 1914. His particular interest was the Co-operative Party on whose national executive he served for several years.

Arthur B. Round was the first employees' representative elected to the management committee when the rules were changed after the war to allow employee representation. He had previously been a member of the Education Committee. He became the Society's representative as a director of Birmingham Printers. His artistic and musical abilities had been utilised as early as 1906 when he became the director of the first of the Society's choirs.

W.T. Cardinal was elected to the management committee in 1924. In the General Strike of 1926 he was the only prominent Co-operator who participated in the leadership of the strike by virtue of his being vice-president of the Trades & Labour Council at that time. He was also the only Communist in the leadership of the strike. He remained militantly left-wing after he left the Communist Party, leading the minority faction on the Trades Council who opposed collaboration with the employers after the strike. This meant that he was usually defeated for president, but retained the vice-presidency of the Trades Council. Presumably he also advocated radical views on the management committee of BICS on which he served for many years. He eventually left Birmingham to become a director of the Co-operative Wholesale Society.

Edward Curtis, who succeeded Millington as chair of the Education Committee in 1921, first joined the Committee in 1914. Prior to that he was secretary to the Senior Choir. He was a member of the Midland Co-operative Choral Association and wrote six songs for a new Co-operative song book. Another of his interests was Guild work. He was the first secretary of Small Heath Men's Guild. From 1919 he served on the National Council of the Men's Guild and in 1929-30 he was its President. Curtis was active in urging the publication of the BCS annual Handbook and for eight years was the editor of the local pages of *Wheatsheaf*.

For the Co-operative Party, the best known figure was Fred Longden who became the first Birmingham Co-operative Party MP in 1929. During the war he had been one of the many Birmingham War Resisters who were imprisoned.

For Birmingham Printers, the inspirational figure was Frank Bruff secretary and manager from its inception in 1902. For the annual Co-operative Congress held in Birmingham in 1906 a Handbook was produced to which Bruff contributed the first local history of eighteen pages entitled *Co-operation in Birmingham and District*. With Bruff should be associated Thomas Smith. Smith was a pre-war Guildsman. He began working for the Society in 1917 and joined the 'secretariat' of MacDowall and Whatmough who, together with two typists, were the office 'brains' who administered the society for many years. For the Jubilee year Smith wrote the *History of the Birmingham Co-operative Society 1881-1931*. Subsequent historians have been greatly indebted to him.

Women and the Guilds

It is necessary now to try to pay adequate tribute to the women who contributed to the Society in this period. Most Co-operative customers are women, but apart from their work in the Guilds, women played a less active part in the administration of the organisation. The Co-op was a man's world, and even the advantages won by women during the war were gradually eroded. So, for instance, whereas the majority of employees were women in 1919, by 1927 men again predominated when only 715 out of 3,201 employees were women. Of the nineteen departments into which the Society was divided by 1931, only one was headed by a woman. This was Mrs K. Kendrick, a graduate of Birmingham University with lengthy London and provincial experience in the catering trade who controlled the Restaurant, started in 1916.

The two main elected bodies of the Society were the Management Committee and the Education Committee. On the former women were few. For instance, the 1920 Management Committee of 14 contained three women, Mrs A. Andrews Mrs M.J. Rawes, and Mrs M. Williams. Annie Andrews was first elected in 1917 and served through to the 1930s. Mary Rawes was first elected in 1916. They both had a background of work in the Women's Guild. On the 1931 Management Committee there were only two women, Mary Rawes and Mrs Andrews. But Mary Williams had the distinction of being the first woman to be elected to the management committee. She served two spells; one from 1909 to 1920 and the other from 1922 to 1927. Apart from her Women's Guild work she was for many years on the Boards of first the Aston Guardians and then Birmingham's. She was also a JP.

A better proportion of women was elected to the Education Committee and after 1925 they were in a majority . Mrs F. Stein was an outstanding example of those who served the Society. She was secretary of the Education Committee from 1911 and immersed in Guild and Junior Classes. She resigned in 1923 from ill-health and was at that time said to be taking no less than five of the Junior Classes herself. She, however, was given the 'freedom' of the Education Committee and still serving in 1931 as an Honorary Member.

The Swinglers were a Co-operative family. Edith Swingler became the first secretary of the first Women's Guild branch in Birmingham in 1900, Mrs C. Swingler was the first chair of the branch. She was said to be the only woman who dared appear at Quarterly Management Committee meetings, such was the domination of men at that time. Edith was still a member of the Education Committee in 1931. Her husband had been a member of the original committee of 1881.

Mrs F.S. Lakins joined the Education Committee in 1915 and was still there in 1931 having served five years as vice-chair. Miss E. Lewis joined the Education Committee in 1920 and took considerable responsibility for the Junior Classes; she took on the enormous task of being responsible for the examinations each year. Mrs J. Turner (1918-25) was another who joined the Committee during the war. After 1925 there seems to have been an infusion of new blood and new names such as Mrs L. Burrell, Mrs M. Pegg and Mrs E. Shuker appear.

Of the dedication and work of the women in the rapidly growing Women's Guild branches much could be said. From lists of secretaries of Women's Guilds in the 1920s we can pick out familiar names. Mrs Pegg was secretary of the long established Erdington Guild in 1926 and Mrs Corrin (wife of the chairman of the General Strike Emergency Committee?) secretary of the Cannon Hill Guild. Women also served as secretaries of Mixed Guilds; Miss E. Lewis was secretary of Acocks Green Members Guild in 1927, but this seems to have been a temporary expedient. Women also serviced the Comrades' Circles and in 1927 four of the six Circles had young, unmarried secretaries – the Misses C. Hazlewood (Aston), M. Smith (Erdington), W. Newcombe (Small Heath) and M. Miles (Nechells).

By 1931 there were no less than 31 Women's Guild branches operating within the Birmingham Co-operative Society area. The history of every one of these branches could be written from the reports from each branch printed in the monthly *Wheatsheaf*. Here one can only summarise the activities of these extraordinary bodies, the most important women's organisation in the Labour movement. The Women's Guild branch was a school of democratic action and empowerment for working class women starting typically with a young, timid, inexperienced housewife and taking her through confidence building stages until many were capable of speaking before mass national audiences and taking national and even international positions within the Co-operative and Labour movement. And always while she was facing the tasks of bringing up a family, coping with a sometimes hostile husband, and dealing with sickness and often unemployment.

The democracy of the Guild was exemplified by the fact that it elected and re-elected its officers not just once a year, but twice. Delegates and often officers were elected to area and divisional Guild organisations and conferences, culminating in the National Women's Guild annual conference. Also delegates and representatives were elected to the Education Committee of the Society, and the quarterly effort made to persuade people to attend the Management Committee meetings and influence the proceedings. Then there was representation on sports and social committees and ad hoc committees for anything from the opening of new shops, special problems of the society, to organising the local Co-operative Day with its floats and processions on the first Saturday of July.

All these and many more activities were submitted to the democracy of the Guild by being reported back on at the weekly branch meeting.

Social, business and political matters were usually skillfully contrived by branch officers. Christmas was the occasion for branch parties and also children's parties. Each anniversary of the branch was another occasion for a party to which members of all other Guild branches would be invited.

The main business of the weekly meeting was a talk. Usually this was on a topic of local interest to women – hospital administration, after-care committees for fourteen year old school leavers, health welfare centres for mothers, penal reform, local councillors dealing with their work, slum clearance, parenthood etc. Sometimes the talk was on Co-operation from a member of the Management or Education Committees – the work of the departments, the need to inculcate co-operative principles, or the history of co-operation. Sometimes it was on a cultural subject – literature, poetry, plays, gardening etc. A favourite lecture was 'Flowers in the Guild Garden' as every Women's Guild branch in the country was allocated a particular flower.

Other talks broached or embraced the political. Peace and the League of Nations was a frequent topic; international affairs were popular – starvation in Europe after the war, the state of India, China, Africa and our colonies later; also the growth of international co-operation, usually stressing its phenomenal growth in Russia.

There was, however a reluctance in some branches to become directly embroiled in political matters. This could be circumvented by talks about Co-operative politics and the Co-operative Party and the necessity for the movement to have Parliamentary representation to protect consumer interests. But there was also the annual participation of the more active women in supporting Co-operative or Labour candidates in the local elections and also in general elections which were frequent up to 1931. The Co-op was inevitably political.

After the talk and the ubiquitous tea, other business would be discussed. Visits to such institutions as the Society's bakery or milk depot, or private institutions such as laundries (the Guild urged the Society to provide a laundry, but it was never able to), or Cadbury's, or Fircroft or Woodbrooke for week end schools, or the annual outing.

There were always good causes to support. It might arise from a talk from the head of the Blind Institute and funds would afterwards be raised. Or money and clothing collected for miners' families as in 1921 and 1926 when they were on strike, or from 1929 when unemployment began to devastate mining communities in South Wales and the Midlands. A permanent commitment was the upkeep of a cot at Woodlands in memory of Miss Llewelyn Davies, the national leader of the Women's Guild from 1889 until 1921.

Such is an imperfect impression of the scope of the activities of the Women's Guild branches. Usually meetings were well-attended. Recorded attendances suggest an average of 40-60 for meetings with 80 not infrequently being reached. On only two occasions have I found reference to meetings being cancelled because of sickness. Both were from influenza – the first from the epidemic of 1919 and the second from an outbreak in 1929. Occasionally a speaker failed to turn up, but the branches had resources to deal with this. Sometimes the reports made by members at each meeting were discussed in greater detail than normal. Sometimes one of the Guildswomen present would volunteer to speak. Or the meeting was turned into a social or a whist drive. Or if all these failed members would amuse themselves. This was in later years elevated to an institution called Sing, Say, Do or Pay where members either performed or paid a forfeit. At first members were shy and elected to pay, but were soon 'brought out of themselves', reports record.

Continuity of office appears to have been less than might have been expected. Between 1919 and 1925 all the secretaries of Guild branches had changed and between 1925 and 1930 only two secretaries retained office – Annie Corrin at Cannon Hill and Mrs Gledhill at Handsworth.

As mothers of many of the children attending Co-operative Junior Classes, Guildswomen felt a responsibility to the next stage of the movement, the Comrades' Circles of young people. These catered for members of Co-operative households between the ages of 14 and 21. The first Circle was formed in Birmingham in 1920 and by 1925 there were five Circles and in 1930 seven. Children of leading Guildswomen can be recognised in J. Gledhill president of Handsworth Circle in 1930 and Constance Shuker, secretary of Aston & Lozells Circle. Girls played a leading role in the Comrades' Circles. Three had female secretaries in 1930, Daisy Aspery at Handsworth, Winifred Newcombe at Small Heath, while Constance Shuker was not only secretary at Aston & Lozells but was also secretary of the federation of the seven Circles and making a regional and national contribution to the movement.

Organisation of youth was as difficult in Birmingham as it was elsewhere and the types of activities suitable to the Circles was often discussed. An example of this was in 1929 when Comrade Tranter of the Small Heath Circle wrote to the paper *Our Circle* calling the Circles a waste of time. Small Heath immediately called a meeting inviting not only other Circles, but also the Labour Party Young Socialists' League, and the ILP Guild of Youth, demanding that Tranter justify his remarks. Tranter's case was that dreadful housing and social conditions were causing youth to seek degrading kinds of pleasures such as picture houses and dancing, neglecting their real job of using the resources available from the movement to change these conditions. Others present denied that picture houses or dancing were degrading and a hot discussion was continued. At Aston & Lozells Circle it led to a debate with the ILP that 'The Guild of Youth plays a more important part for the Realisation of a Co-operative system than does the Comrades' Circles.' This motion was strenuously contested by Comrades Shuker and Paul. Tranter was invited to the Witton Circle and seems to have so charmed his audience with his case for politics in the Circles that Witton agreed that they should have at least two political speakers each half year. Continuing Women's Guild interest in the youth question is evidenced by, for instance, the visit of Constance Shuker to the Bearwood guild to talk about the importance of the Circles and a consequent decision for the Guild to hold a meeting and invite young people with a view to forming a Comrades' Circle in Bearwood; also a visit of the Circles to Aston & Perry Barr Women's Guild to debate the motion 'Is the Modern World Degenerating Morally?'. Social activities continued to predominate in the Circles, however. A particular feature of 1929 was a winter Games League participated in by all Circles consisting of whist, crib, table tennis, draughts etc. which caused considerable excitement and was eventually won by Wards End.

The Women's Guilds also had contact with the 11 Men's Guilds that existed by 1930 and the two Members' (Mixed) Guilds. This included co-operation in the main social events events of the year such as Christmas children's parties and Co-operators' Day, and also in the political campaigns to protect the business interests of the Society, the activities of the Co-operative Party, and local and Parliamentary elections.

From the above it is clear that the loss of the activities of the Guilds whether Women's, Men's, Mixed or Comrades' Circles is not the least of the losses arising from the modern decline of the Co-operative Movement.

Conclusions

Judged from the two main indices of success, the two main consumer Co-operative Societies in Birmingham enjoyed spectacular success in the period 1919-30.

Beginning with membership figures, TASCOS rose from 13,208 in 1919 to 29,870 in 1930 or by 126 per cent. Birmingham Co-operative Society figures increased in the same period from 47,868 to

152,668 an increase of 219 per cent, although it had absorbed the Soho Society which had over 11,000 members at the time of merger. Sales had increased at TASCOS in these years from £548,895 to £929,758 or 69 per cent and at BCS from £1,621,113 to £4,110,854 an increase of 154 per cent. With the sales figures account must be taken of inflation. In 1919 prices were at 215 (1914 = 100) but down to 158 in 1930, so sales in 1930 were worth almost 25 per cent more in real terms. This was reflected in the greatly increased number of shops and other facilities opened by both Societies. However this represents a serious tightening of profit margins, reflected in the fact that whereas dividends before the war had usually been 2/-d. after the war 1/-d. was not exceeded until 1930.

This expansion in the ten years after the war can be compared with rates of growth in other periods. For instance growth was greater than for the period 1930-38 when membership grew by about 50 per cent and sales by 60 per cent with TASCOS performing slightly better than BCS; dividends, however, had risen to 1/5d. at BCS in 1930 and 1/4d. at TASCOS. The growth of 1919-30 was, however, dwarfed by the expansion of the period 1900-1914 when membership increased in both Societies by about 600 per cent and sales by more than 850 per cent.

The membership figures for 1930 raise the question of the influence of Co-operation in the City at that time. Combined membership of TASCOS and BSC totalled 182,535. The population of Birmingham at the 1931 Census was just over 1 million people and the national average family size was 2.1 children plus two adults. Assuming that only one person per family held a share nearly three quarters of Birmingham families would hold a share in the Co-op.

Impressive as these figures are, the aim of ardent Co-operators was to build the Co-operative Commonwealth in which people bought all the goods they needed at the local Co-op store made in Co-operative factories and financed by Co-operative savings. Other indices showed how far they were from realising these dreams.

The normal rate of interest on capital with the Co-op was 5 per cent and this represented as good and safe a return as was available for small, working class savings. Thus the average shareholding of members was an indicator of the extent of working class savings and also a reflection of the economic situation as members were able to leave their dividend with the Society or were, reluctantly, forced to eat into their savings. Savings per member were usually higher at TASCOS than in BCS reflecting, perhaps, the more affluent area of operation of the smaller society. The figures in 1919 were £13 at BCS and £19 at TASCOS. This reflected war time conditions with full employment, but few durable goods to to spend savings on. In 1925 the figures were down to £9-10-0d and £15-17-6d reflecting the withdrawal of savings during the slump of 1921-24. By 1930, however, at the end of the more prosperous period savings were only marginally higher at £10 for BSC and nearly £16 for TASCOS. Nor were the figures for 1938 significantly higher. But when allowance has been made for deflation we find the cost of living about 22 per cent lower in 1930 than in 1918 and so the figures for savings are little changed in real terms.

Another indicator of loyalty to the Society and the satisfaction it gave to its members is the average purchases made. In this respect also, 1918 seemed to be the best year, when annual average purchases amounted to nearly £34 per annum at BCS and nearly £42 per annum at TASCOS. This had fallen to £15 and £32 in 1925 and by 1930 had only risen to about £27 and £31. But again, when deflation is taken into account there is little real change. Taking 1930, therefore, weekly expenditure by members was about 10/-d. per week. This was less than half of the food bill necessary to keep a family of four, so it is clear that the percentage of expenditure on all items by the average Co-operative member was small.

From the point of view of the seeker for the Co-operative Commonwealth the situation was even worse when one considers the goods purchased by Co-operative members which were made in Co-operative factories. This was an index closely watched and after the standardised balance sheet was introduced an item 'Value of own Production and Services (Wholesale Prices)' was introduced. In addition, at least once a year the percentage of Co-operative produced goods for each department was published. If we take these two indices for BCS we find the 'Own Produce' was 30 per cent of total sales in both 1925 and 1930. The second index gives percentages of goods purchased from Co-operative sources by departments. For Jan 1925 these were: Grocery 68 per cent: Bakery 56 per cent:

Confectionary 17 per cent; Boots 53 per cent; Drapery 52 per cent; Tailoring 69 per cent; Furnishing 54 per cent; Butchery 5 per cent; Fish, Fruit & Greengrocery 0.1 per cent; Restaurant 44 per cent; Dairy 1 per cent; Coal 44 per cent; Farm 30 per cent. These figures of goods bought from Co-operative sources must be correlated with the percentage of the Society's revenue the department was responsible for. The figures for October 1925 showed the following: Grocery and Provisions was far and away the most important source of revenue at 49 per cent of the total of £544,000. Then came the Bakery with £74,000, the Dairy with £40,000, the Butchery £38,000, Drapery £36,000, Confectionary £29,000, Coal £18,000, Boots £13,000, Furnishing £10,000, Tailoring £9,000, Fish, Fruit & Greengrocery £9,000 and the Restaurant £5,000. From these two factors – percentage of Co-operative input and contribution to the Society's revenue – the Society's strategy can be worked out. It is clear, for example, why Fish, Fruit & Greengrocery was not a favourite option for the Society – it produced only 2 per cent of the Society's revenue and practically none of it was purchased from Co-operative sources. Departments with high Co-operative inputs such as Tailoring and Furnishing provided only 4 per cent of the Society's sales, however.

Despite this plethora of statistics from the annual Co-operative Union report and from the Societies' quarterly reports, we are still without the information necessary to finally judge of the efficiency of the Societies. For this we would need to know at what prices each Department bought it goods and at what mark-up rate they sold them. Also we need more information on whether Co-operative prices were really competitive with other local retailers.

One's impression is that only in limited areas was Co-operative selling on a large enough scale to compete effectively with the large retailers. Grocery and Provisions was one of these Departments but this only at the expense of about one third of their goods being non-Co-operative produced goods. Other departments such as Bread and Milk also seem to have been competitive. Other Departments had wider profit margins but made a smaller contribution to total sales. Drapery (women's wear) always fared better than Tailoring (men's wear), but both made a negligible impact on the local clothing trade. Furnishing was even more disappointing, representing only about 2 per cent of BCS sales.

It can be concluded that the majority of Co-op members did only part of their weekly shopping at the Co-op; they might have had bread and milk delivered and perhaps coal, but for the rest of their shopping they went elsewhere. It was a minority of members who took the Co-operative message that the Society could provide all their needs. It was from this minority that the democratic management of the Society was drawn, and who participated in its social and political work.

The Co-operative Commonwealth was impossible of realisation. But within the parameters to which it was confined, the Co-operative movement touched the lives of most of the people of Birmingham during its considerable expansion in the period 1919-31. For many thousands it represented a commitment to a Socialist ideal for which they could work and sacrifice.

1930-1939

These general comments are not invalidated by a short survey of the period to the second World War. Co-operative fortunes in Birmingham during the slump of the 1930s were very different from that of the 1920s. In 1930 BCS experienced a fall in sales from £4.2m to £4.1m but TASCOS sales rose from £857,000 to £930,000. 1931 was the worst year. BCS sales dipped below £4m to £3.8m. TASCOS fell to £923,000. But against this must be set the fall in prices. This was not as great as the 1921 fall, but it was substantial enough to offset the fall in revenue. Thus in 1930 prices fell by 8 per cent compared with 1929. In 1931 they fell another 4 per cent and in 1932 a further 3 per cent. There they stabilised until 1935 when prices began to rise again. Thus we find Directors of Societies unbelievingly explaining to themselves and their members that despite national unemployment peaking at 2¾ millions and Co-operative revenues falling, their overall, real position was actually improving. Between 1932 and 1938 (the last full year of peace) BCS sales increased 75 per cent to £6.5m. while TASCOS sales increased 66 per cent to £1.5m. Both Societies made relatively equal progress. BSC membership grew to 228,577 in 1938 an increase of 41 per cent while TASCOS membership rose by 45 per cent to 46,698 in 1938. Increases in capital in those years were 30 per cent at BCS and 35 per cent at TASCOS. Both Societies paid moderate dividends much in line with each other; in 1932 these were BCS and TASCOS both 1/2d. and 1938 BCS 1/5d. and TASCOS 1/4d.

Features of BCS growth over this period were: the opening of a laundry in 1931 when the society celebrated its 50th. birthday in style at Bingley Hall; the claim to have been the first bakery to introduce first wrapped and then sliced bread; a return to the funeral business; entry into pharmacy; considerable development of travel and holiday facilities; and the proliferation of shops on the new Council estates, over eighty new branches having been opened between 1931 and 1939. This enormous growth consolidated the BCS position as the third largest society in Britain and raised questions of c-ordination, efficiency and democratic control by the members that go to the heart of the purpose of Co-operative trading.

TASCOS made similar progress on a more limited scale under Tom Hackett, the Society's president, who was a works foreman at Cadbury's. This cemented close contact between Cadbury employees and TASCOS, and a nursery was started in 1927 on property leased from the Bournville Trust; a very novel development. The Society was also one of the first to enter pharmacy and optical services and also ran a funeral parlour.

By 1939 the Co-operative movement in Birmingham was at the height of its power and influence. Its subsequent history is rather different.

Bibliography: The Co-operative Movement in Birmingham 1919-1939

The main sources for the Co-operative movement in Birmingham for this period are: *The Co-operative Union Annual Congress Report,* and the *Quarterly Reports* of the Societies. For the latter, quarterly reports for the Birmingham Co-operative Society are complete for the period, but not those for the Ten Acres and Stirchley Society. *Wheatsheaf,* the monthly magazine of the national movement had local pages and these are the source for monthly reports of the activities of the Women's and other Guilds. These local pages exist for BCS but not TASCOS. All the above material is at the Birmingham Central Reference Library. Both the Birmingham consumer societies have their historians – T. Smith's jubilee *History of the Birmingham Co-operative Society 1881-1951,* and *75 Years of Co-operative Endeavour – A History of the Ten Acres & Stirchley Co-operative Society* (1950). A later history is Ned Williams' – *The Co-op in Birmingham and the Black Country.* There is much historical material at the headquarters of the Central Midlands Co-operative Society at Central House, Hermes Road, Lichfield, WS13 6RH and I wish to thank the Officers for allowing me to use this source.

Chapter 24

The Co-operative Movement in the Black Country 1919-1939

The Co-operative movement in the Black Country ended the war as it had begun it, with seven consumer societies – Dudley, Halesowen & Hasbury, Soho, Tipton, Walsall, Wednesbury and Wolverhampton – and one productive society, Walsall Lock & Cart Gear. By 1930 two of these consumer societies had disappeared. Soho into Birmingham Co-operative Society and Wednesbury into the Walsall Society. We propose to deal in turn with the differing fortunes of each of these societies.

Dudley Co-operative Society

The Dudley Society lived in the shadow of its past. In the 1880s it was one of the fastest growing Societies in Britain, sweeping through the Black Country villages of Cradley Heath, Netherton, Quarry Bank, Brierley Hill etc. with an almost messianic Co-operative fervour which increased sales from under £6,000 per annum in 1884 to over £82,000 in 1890. Then came the crash in 1892 when the secretary of the society, James Ball, absconded leaving a deficiency of more than £18,000. This amount was soon repaid and handsome dividends restored, but the Society never regained its previous momentum.

In the first year of peace the Society suffered a large decrease in membership, it falling from 7,115 in 1918 to 4,839 the next year. Sales, however, continued buoyant and the dividend remained at 1/6d. In 1920 membership rose to 5,900 and sales rose to a maximum of £230,306. But this was barely keeping pace with inflation and the dividend fell to 1/5d.

During the subsequent three years of economic depression, Dudley also suffered, but not nearly to the same extent as, for instance Soho which the depression drove to bankruptcy or other societies which barely escaped that fate. In 1921 sales fell to £188,841 and in 1922 to a low point of £139,584, but the dividend paid in both years was 1/4d. very much the largest in Birmingham and the Black Country. By 1921 there was a slight rise of sales to over £140,00 and the dividend remained at 1/4d. These results are remarkable for the slump and deflationary years during which, for instance, the Wolverhampton dividend fell to 2¾d.

Progress continued until 1927 when there was a slight blip, the dividend falling to 1/3½d. despite both sales and profits being higher than previous years. The dividend fell further to 1/1½d in 1928 despite a considerable rise in sales with profits up from under £40,000 in 1927 to £48,000; but despite the fall, the Dudley dividend was exceeded only by Tipton in the Black Country.

From 1929 the 2/-d. dividend was restored, despite, paradoxically, a fall in both sales and profits. 1930 was a bumper year when sales rose by more than 50 per cent and profits even more. In 1931 sales declined slightly, heralding the depression of the 1930s but the dividend remained at 2/-d.

The record of the Dudley society for these years is thus one of bucking the trends. It survived the slump of 1921-23 with minimum damage, it grew strongly through the more prosperous years of 1924-30. Its subsequent history was the fall in revenue in 1931, marking time for the next three years and moderate growth after 1934. But the 2/-d. dividend remained until 1939. Thus the Society also avoided the worst effects of the 1930s slump.

During the period of strong growth in the mid 1920s the 1918 membership figure was not exceeded until 1926, but after that it almost doubled to 13,883 in 1931.

Of its educational and social activities little can be said as no quarterly reports for this period survive. We do know, however, that educational provision never reached 1 per cent of profits. It was highest in 1919 at 0.76 per cent, in 1925 it was a miserly 0.37 per cent and only slightly improved in 1930 at 0.41 per cent.

Such information as we have regarding its personnel come from Ned Williams' research. Its leading public figure was James Molyneux, in 1929 treasurer of the Society, and also the first Labour councillor in Dudley after the war. Others were Charlie Williams and Ted Bennett Snr.

Halesowen & Hasbury Industrial Co-operative Society

The recent discovery by Ned Williams of a periodical 1892-96 of William Cope's called the *Birmingham & District Co-operative Record* enables the origins of the Halesowen & Hasbury Society to be dated at 1871. Ned Williams recounts the legend of the double name arising from rival factions of Primitive Methodists from Hasbury, and Birmingham Street Methodists from Halesowen only agreeing to work together with the double name.

In 1883 another Society had been formed in Halesowen. This was called, according to the Co-operative Union annual returns, the Halesowen & District Prudential Co-operative Society. The two societies co-existed until 1896 when the Prudential disappeared.

By 1914 Halesowen & Hasbury had 1,472 members and it ended the war with 1,924 members. The Society had not had a good war. No dividend is recorded for 1914 and 1915. Its increase in membership came in 1916 when it rose to 1,900 and it paid a dividend of 1/9¼d. But in 1917 its dividend was down to 1/-d. and the next year to 6d. This was less than any other Black Country society. Its net profit fell from £4,341 in 1916 to £1,906 in 1917 and fell further the next year to £1,693. Misfortune continued after the war. Membership slumped to under 1,700 in 1919 and the dividend fell to 4¾d. In the only other prosperous post-war year of 1920 membership rose only slightly to 1,751 and the dividend languished at 7¼d. H & H appeared doomed come the slump. But this did not occur. In the first year of the slump, 1921, the dividend fell to 6d. but by that time others were lower – Wednesbury 3d. and Wolverhampton 4d. and only Dudley at 1/6d. was riding high. In 1922 the dividend was maintained, but Soho was down to 2¼d. and Wolverhampton to 2¾d. In 1923 the tide turned and the dividend was raised to 7¾d. and in 1924 to 10¼d. From 1925 it was 1/-d. and there it remained until 1929 when it was raised to 1/2½d. At this point it was the highest dividend paid in Birmingham and the Black Country except for the 2/-d. of Dudley and Tipton. In 1931 they raised it even higher to 1/4½d. How had this remarkable turn round been achieved?

Ned Williams makes it clear that three men were central to the transformation. One was George Albert Roper who became president of the society in 1925 and continued to 1952. The second was H.G. Adams, the secretary after the war. Thirdly A.J. Hayward the General Manager. A.J's regular Monday visit to every shop set the style and his attention to detail and efficiency was legendary, particularly after he swopped his Regulation motor-cycle for a Clyno car in 1925.

The transition was sufficient to attract the attention of *Co-operative News*. This outlined the position in 1918 with a bank overdraft of £9,063, an overdue trade account of £5,445, members debts of £900 and a suspense account of £1,692. By 1921 the bank over draft was less than £1,500, the suspense account had been cleared and capital increased. 1922 was the worst year, however, with net profit down to its lowest level at £1,973. Economies were made and wages cut, but in true Co-operative fashion sackings were limited. In 1920 there had been 40 employees and this was cut to 34 in both 1921 and 1922 rising thereafter to 126 in 1930.

Revival began in 1923, but the Society had boundary problems, it being hedged in by the larger societies of Dudley and Birmingham. These problems were amicably overcome through the Co-operative Divisional machinery.

From 1925 to 1930 the Society was in a position to grow strongly. Membership increased from 2,124 to 5,926, and capital from £23,139 to £56,350. Sales rose by 160 per cent, but the real indicator of its efficiency was the 268 per cent increase of net profit which had taken the Society from the verge of bankruptcy to being one of the strongest (although the second smallest) in Birmingham and the Black Country.

Soho Co-operative Society

Unlike Halesowen & Hasbury, the Soho Society had had a good war. By 1918 it was the second largest society in the Black Country. It was situated in an area where the Labour movement was strong returning one of the four Black Country Labour MPs at the 1919 general election and almost enough Labour councillors to form a majority on the Smethwick council. After the war the Soho society continued to surge ahead. But by 1925 the Society was bankrupt and had to seek rescue from the Birmingham Co-operative Society. What had gone wrong?

In one sense it was a victim of its own success. Immediately after the war the Society opened shops at Langley and Oldbury; the district of West Bromwich was ceded to Soho from the Wednesbury society and work started on a large store at Handsworth. The problems can be seen by the economics of the Handsworth branch. When started in 1919 it was estimated to cost £22,848; when it was opened early in 1921 inflation had taken the cost to almost £36,000. Thus Soho was hit more than most by excess capacity when the slump came. It was also said that unemployment in Smethwick was worse than other towns in Birmingham and the Black Country, and although this cannot be demonstrated it is certain that unemployment in Smethwick was as bad as elsewhere. There was the further problem, also faced by other societies, of large accumulated stocks having to be written down during the slump as sales dropped. Other societies could offset this problem to some extent by upvaluing their fixtures and fittings. But much of Soho's properties were so recent that their falling value only added to the problem. Lastly there was the withdrawal of capital which threatened to undermine confidence in the Society.

The strenuous efforts made to avoid catastrophe are outlined in Tom Smith's *Birmingham Co-operative Society* but the problems were so serious that when the upturn came for most societies in 1924, Soho's problems only worsened. Sales, which had been over £470,000 in 1920 fell to £182,000 in 1923, but fell even further in 1924. Capital, which had been at a maximum of £120,000 in 1920 had halved by 1922 and halved again to £30,000 by 1925 when the Society was taken over. Even worse, net profit fell from a maximum of £34,000 in 1920 to a loss of £2,293 in 1923. As a consequence the dividend fell from 1/2¼d in 1920 to 2¼d in 1922 and in the two following years no dividend at all was paid.

These disastrous results had repercussions for both the CWS and adjacent Societies. As sales fell, Soho's indebtedness to the CWS rose. If the Soho society failed, doubts would be cast on the solvency of adjoining societies. The two Birmingham Societies were therefore informed of the crisis and negotiations proceeded with the CWS. In November 1922 it was reluctantly agreed that the Soho Committee should suspend the withdrawal of capital. In April 1923 the Society came under the supervision of the CWS. In December 1924 negotiations were opened for the Society to be taken over by the Birmingham Co-operative Society. Soho shares were valued at 10/-d. in the £. which subsequent pay outs raised to 15/-d. and the merger became effective from July 1925.

There seems to be little evidence that the failure of the Soho Society arose from bad management. The General Manager, B.G. Lloyd, had been in charge since 1897 and had thus contributed to the great successes of the Society. The Secretary, F.E. Scurrah, had been appointed in 1919. We do not know who the other key figure, the President was, but quite exceptional efforts had been made by the Management Committee to involve the membership, Guilds etc. in improving the position of the Society, but all these efforts failed.

Tipton Co-operative & Industrial Provident Society

Tipton was another small society, but it had an extraordinary record of high dividends which continued into the post-war years. It was founded in 1871. In 1884 (one of the worst years of the Great Depression) it had 186 members who held an average of £10 each of shares, it sold £3,478 worth of goods and paid a dividend of 1/1½d. It was paying a 2/-d. dividend from at least 1902 which rose to 2/6d. in 1905, fell the next year back to 2/-d. subsequently fluctuated to as low as 1/6½d. in the next few years, to rise again to 2/-d. in 1912 to 1914. It continued at 2/-d. throughout the war – a remarkable achievement and the best record in the Black Country.

But this seems to have been achieved by devoting more of the profit to dividends than seemed prudent to other societies. During the war in 1914, for instance, it paid 10 per cent (2/-d. in the £1) of its total sales in dividends when the ratio of profits to sales was 12 per cent. Wolverhampton's sales /profits ratio was 14.5 per cent but it only felt able to pay a dividend of 1/9¾d (about 9 per cent). But Tipton had quite a good war and it was still paying its 10 per cent dividend when its sales/profit ratio was down to 11.5 per cent at the end of the war. In the two 'prosperous' years after the war the sales/profit margins fell to 9.8 per cent in 1919 and the dividend was reduced to 1/10d (about 9 per cent) and in 1920 the profit/sales ratio fell to 6.7 per cent and the dividend was reduced again to 1/4d. (about 6.7 per cent) which meant that all of the profit was spent on the dividend.

Then came the bad years. In 1921 (the worst year) profits/sales ratio dropped to 2.5 per cent and the dividend was dropped to 10d. (4.2 per cent); but that cost £625 more than the profits that year. To pay it, the already inadequate reserves were raided and they fell from £1,800 to £625. In 1922 the position improved marginally. The profits/sales margin rose to 5.8 per cent and an improved dividend of 10½d. absorbed 4.2 per cent. 1923 saw another increase in the profit/sales margin, but the dividend was again raised – to 1/-d. Thus almost all of the profit was again absorbed by the dividend. It should be noted that Walsall paid 6d. dividend in 1923 and Wolverhampton 4d.

In 1924 when most societies were turning the corner Tipton's profits/sales margin fell to the abysmal level of 3.6 per cent yet it persisted in paying a 5 per cent dividend which meant it paid more in dividend than it received in profit and the reserves again had to be used reducing them to nil. The Society continued to live dangerously without reserves and again paid more in dividends than profits in 1925. In 1926 the Society raised the dividend to 1/8½d., although this only just enabled the dividend to be covered by the profit and put £50 to reserves. From 1927 the situation improved with profit margins widening and another £150 put to reserves. In 1928 the 2/-d. dividend was resumed and the reserves doubled to £400. But only by 1930 would more cautious Management Committees consider their societies were completely safe when the 10 per cent dividend was well covered with a 13 per cent profits/sales margin with a (still inadequate) reserve fund of £1,200.

It seems, therefore, that Tipton just 'got away with it'. But there must have been a degree of good management behind the risk taking policy of returning virtually all profits to shareholders. This is confirmed by the survival of the Society and its position at the end of the 1920s which enabled it to continue to pay high dividends combined with a more cautious accountancy approach.

Wednesbury (new) Co-operative Society

Co-operation was of fairly ancient lineage in Wednesbury. We have noted three Societies registered in the 1860s (see Chapter 8) and Wednesbury was also a centre of Owenite Socialism in the early 1840s. Wednesbury 'Old' Society had been founded in 1887, but those impatient at its slow progress founded the 'New' Society in 1895 and the two societies co-existed until 1912. In that year the 'Old' Society had 229 members and the 'New' 985. But the 'Old' paid a dividend of 2/-d. and the 'New' only 1/4½d. The extraordinary feature of the 'Old' was its lack of capital, often this being less than the total of members. In the year of its demise the 'Old' had 229 members with £111 of share capital and the 'New' a more normal 985 members with £5,706 capital. In 1913 the 'Old' had disappeared and the 'New' had 1,012 members and a capital of £5,887 so it had not profited greatly from the fall of the rival Society. One cannot but speculate that the 'Old' had been run by a clique of members for their own benefit, perhaps based on a single factory, or was idiosyncratic in other ways.

The 'New' Society seems to have been prudently managed. In the first three years of the war it paid a dividend of just over 1/8d. It then fell to 1/6d in 1918. But these were the difficult years of 1917-18 when everyone's dividend fell (except Tipton's!). Both share capital and sales more than doubled during the war thus beating inflation. By 1918 its net profit was £4,008, a profit/sales ratio of 8.2 per cent when its dividend was 7.5 per cent. Wednesbury looked forward to the coming of peace with confidence and in the first two years it seemed to flourish. The Stafford District report for 1919 stated that Wednesbury was doing 'extraordinary trade', especially in fish and had bought a new hall for propaganda. In 1920 it was reported that its four West Bromwich shops had been transferred to the Soho Society, but that it was doing more trade than ever, despite the transfer. This was true, but inflation was rising so rapidly that in real terms sales were falling. Thus in 1920 the profits/sales ratio fell to 6.7 per cent and although the dividend was dropped from 1/6d. to 1/3¾d this represented almost all of the profit.

But much worse was to follow. In the crisis year of 1921 the Society made a loss of £388 and the dividend was lowered to 3d. Sales had fallen by almost half, although prices were falling so rapidly at that time that the real fall was much less. But in 1922 sales fell by more than half to £22,000 and the trading loss was a record £8,286, despite the desperate ploy of doubling the dividend to 6d. at a time when the reserve fund had been exhausted in 1921. The situation eased a little in 1923, but losses were still substantial at £3,265 and no dividend was paid. 1924 was the year when most Societies saw an improvement, and sales at Wednesbury did rise marginally from £18,500 to £19,750, but the trading loss also rose marginally to £3,451. The end of the road had been reached. Like Soho it had to be absorbed, and in 1925 Wednesbury (New) passed to the neighbouring Walsall Society.

Under the amalgamation terms Walsall paid 7/6d. for every 'New' share and a further 7/6d was paid to those who continued their membership into Walsall and traded to the extent of £5 per year. Thus most members, who had been loyal to the Wednesbury Society (membership fell only from 1,695 in 1921 to 1,610 in 1924), received 75 per cent of their share capital from the Walsall society.

Walsall & District Co-operative Society

A characteristic of the Walsall Society was the militancy of its management. In the second quarter of 1919 the Management Committee report stressing the role played by the Co-operative movement during the war and pointing to the dangers ahead argued:

> Locally, nationally and internationally representatives of the Co-operative movement have had to combat the false ideas of legislators that the consumer existed for the benefit of the private trader. Nearly all industry and trade is based on this assumption and it is quite impossible to over-rate the dangers from which this country has escaped through the persistent efforts of the Co-operative movement and its influence on prices.
>
> The struggle of the future is not with the small shopkeeper or tradesman... but with the large trusts and combines who seek to control the supply, the prices and all the amenities of life...
>
> The Society holds out the hand of fellowship to all those who do not ask privilege for themselves and who seek their own in other's good.

In the first quarter of 1920 the anti-capitalist spirit was even stronger:

> Within the last few years we have seen the most colossal profiteering the world has ever known, and today organised capital is more deeply entrenched than ever. If there is any faith in the workers' cry for control in industry and the means whereby they live then we submit they must co-operate to bring about that change.
>
> We must choose between patronising and bolstering up the capitalistic system of trade and industry, and that of a co-operative system which is working for the good of each and all.

This militancy was tempered with a realism in running the affairs of the Society which enabled it to strengthen its position as the largest Co-operative in the Black Country, a position it had held since at least 1910.

The swift growth in 1919 and 1920 of sales and profits intoxicated Societies. In Walsall the growth in sales was 76 per cent in 1919 and 24 per cent in 1920. This was real growth in excess of inflation which was 6 per cent in 1919 and a further 16 per cent in 1920. Despite this, the Society held the dividend at 1/3d. in 1919 where it had been since 1917 and only raised it to 1/4½d. in 1920, arguing that the building of reserves and the development of the Society came before dividends. Reserves, which had been about £3,000 during the war rose to nearly £8,000 in 1920.

When the economic blizzard struck in 1921 sales fell only slightly, but the dividend was dropped to 9¾d. In 1922 there was an enormous fall of 40 per cent in sales from £557,000 to £334,000, although this was softened by a fall in prices of 19 per cent. Management response was not typical. The dividend was raised to 11d. to pay for which 50 per cent of the reserves were raided. In 1923 sales fell slightly, but caution returned to the Committee and the dividend was lowered to 6d. This was nearer to the ratio that the Society usually observed of distributing only half of the net profit. In 1924 sales almost levelled off, but with a rush of blood to the head the dividend was doubled to 1/-d and almost the whole of the profits were spent in dividend. 1925 saw a more serious drop in sales from £333,000 to £306,000, but sanity returned and the dividend was lowered to 7d. thus observing the prudent ratio of distributing only half the profits.

1926 was the year of the General Strike, which affected the Walsall Society more than others because of the large number of miners in the area covered by the Society. Indeed for the second quarter of 1926 no dividend was paid. Nevertheless sales rose strongly during the year to £376,000, partly from the absorption of the Wednesbury Society, and the average dividend for the year was raised to 8d. Prosperity returned in 1927 when sales reached £421,000 and the dividend was raised to 10½d.

1928 was the year of the absorption of the Cannock Society. Cannock's problems began when they made a net loss in 1921 of £2,833. The dividend was lowered from 1/1¾d to 7½d. but to pay this the reserves were reduced from £5,371 to £785. Unfortunately there was a massive loss the next year of £7,918 and the dividend was lowered to 3d. Improvement came only in 1925 but the Society then imprudently raised the dividend to 1/6d. or 7.5 per cent of sales when the net profit on sales was only 4.3 per cent and all reserves had disappeared. By this time bankruptcy or amalgamation with another Society were the only alternatives. Adjacent Walsall, with whom close relations had always existed came to Cannock's rescue and the two Societies merged. Although Cannock brought with it a debt of £6,000, the Society was considered sufficiently sound for 20/-d. in the £ to be paid on the Cannock capital.

The effect of the merger on the Walsall Society was immediately apparent. In 1929 membership of Walsall had risen by 10,000 to 32,000 and sales reached £500,000 for the first time. In 1930 sales almost reached £750,000. Sales fell in 1929, the first year of the 1930s Slump, but rose thereafter to £1.370,000 in 1938 with the dividend rising from 1/-d. in 1928 to about 1/6d. in the later 1930s. During the years 1919-30 Walsall consolidated its position as the leading Society in the Black Country, increasing its lead over the next largest Society, Wolverhampton, from being about twice as large to being about three times as large, although some of this trade was being done outside the Black Country.

Much of the success of the Walsall Society must be put down to good, if rather unorthodox, management. The key figure was William Abbotts, who must come close to William Millerchip as the leading Black Country Co-operator. Abbotts was born in 1873, left school at the age of ten and spent 31 years with the London & North Western Railway as an active trade unionist. He joined Walsall Co-op and in 1902 was elected to the Education Committee and soon became its chairman. In 1910 he followed Millerchip as president of the Society. In 1919 he left the railway service to become full-time Adviser to the Walsall Co-op at a time when he was still president. From 1920 he served on the Midland Sectional Board and subsequently served on most Co-operative Union committees including the United Board. He was a JP from 1915 and a Labour member of Walsall Council through much of the 1920s. He died suddenly in 1930 still heavily involved in the affairs of the Society. From his appointment in 1919 as Adviser, Publicity Agent and Propagandist to the Society, Abbotts was virtually the general secretary. His vision, energy and ability helped steer the Society through the difficult years of 1921-24. Other leading members who were on the Management Committee in 1920 and still there in 1930 were T. Gwinnett, A.E. Hinks and H. Skeels who shared the positions of chairman and vice-chairman during the 1920s and gave the requisite stability and competence to the Society' management.

The Walsall Society's Quarterly Reports are available for the period 1919 to 1925 and they contain the reports of the Education Committee. 1919 Reports told of the resumption of the Junior classes on 'Co-operation'. Their low attendance in February was due to 'a further outbreak of influenza'. But in March good examination results were reported. There were Junior choirs at Walsall, Bloxwich and Sutton. Week-end Schools were very important. The August report stated:

> It is quite impossible to convey to our members the value of these Schools. Generally speaking, it is the active, responsible persons in the Co-operative and Trade Union movements who are most regular attendants at these schools. No form of tuition could be more useful or valuable to them in their work.

The New Year Whist Drive was a popular regular feature. The financial report at the end of the year showed income at £206 of which £150 came from the Society.

In 1920 the Education Committee was trying to form a bridge from the Junior Classes to full membership of the Society by means of a Junior Guild catering for ages 14 to 21. This was operating by 1921 and achieving 'considerable success.' From 1921, with the onset of the slump, Education Committee grants were so reduced that the Children's Classes could not be financed, but they were resumed the following year.

From 1921 the Education Committee was elected as recommended by a national Co-operative committee. Four members were elected from he general membership of the Society, three from the Management Committee, two from the Women's Guild, one from the Men's Guild, one from the heads of departments and one from the employees.

The Children' Classes continued and prospered. In 1919 there had been 600 children in the classes; by 1935 there were 1,000 children aged 10 to 14 attending 33 free classes, sitting examinations and gaining prizes. The Classes were supplemented by an annual Childrens' Demonstration with floats and fancy dress which in 1925 numbered 6,000. This was absorbed into the the Co-operators' Day celebrations of July of each year from 1924. These Childrens' Demonstrations became so large that they were taken over by the Management Committee who eventually turned them into a day trip to the seaside; in 1936 nearly 8,000 children were taken to Rhyl.

After 1925 Quarterly Reports fail us and we turn to Fred Hall's book *From Acorn to Oak*. The Junior Guild, designed to keep adolescents in touch with Co-operative principles, did not flourish in the 1920s. Only in the 1930s did a Comrades' Circle and a branch of the Woodcraft Folk come into existence. It was the same with music and drama. With regard to music it was not possible to follow up the initiative to form an orchestra until 1932. In 1936 there was a Junior Choir in Walsall, a Male Voice Choir in Brownhills and an orchestra class. There was also a drama class by 1936.

The Education Committee took over other regular duties. It became responsible for more systematic programmes of Employee education classes after 1924. It had an overall responsibility to support and provide a grant to the Guilds. It sponsored an annual Members' Excursion which began in 1924 with a visit to the National Exhibition of that year which was such a success that it continued thereafter. It also took responsibility for a booklet outlining the Winter Activities of the Society and its social organisations with titles such as 'Why You should Join the Walsall Cop-operative Society,' which served the dual purpose of informing members and use as a recruiting aid. Finally it had been responsible since 1901 for the local pages, ranging from four to twelve, in the monthly national Co-operative journal *Wheatsheaf*. For a short period in 1910 there was also a local journal the *Walsall & District Monthly Record*.

This vast load of Educational work was carried out on a voluntary basis and it was not until 1931 that it was professionalised by providing the Committee with an office and a full-time secretary.

The final question with regard to the Educational Committee is the extent to which the Society supported its work financially. The £300 educational grant of 1919 represented 0.8 per cent of net profit. The grant fell to £200 in the slump year of 1923 but it represented a higher percentage of net profit at 1.2 per cent. In the good year of 1928 the grant rose to £475 but this was a lower percentage of net profit back to 0.8 per cent. The grant in 1931 was £1,005 and this was 1.2 per cent of net profit. Throughout the 1920s, therefore, grants were below the Rochdale Pioneers recommendation of 2½ per cent of net profits to be devoted to education. But this was still very good in relation to what other Societies in Birmingham and the Black Country and elsewhere in the country were paying. From 1932 to 1938, however, Walsall educational expenditure exceeded 2 per cent of profits and in 1933 almost hit the Rochdale target at 2.4 per cent. This must be counted exceptional support for education.

Next we turn to the activities of the Guilds in Walsall. We have already commented on the extraordinary number of Women's Guild branches that Walsall maintained, while regretting that very little is available with regard to the activities they undertook. This position prevails into the 1920s. We know that in 1919 there were eight Women's Guild branches in Walsall – Central, Bloxwich, Walsall Wood, Pelsall, Brownhills, Lichfield, Aldridge, and Sutton Coldfield. There were also three Men's Guild branches – Central, Sutton Coldfield, and Pelsall. By 1936 there were 24 Women's Guild branches with a total of 1,000 members and there were also 11 Men's Guild branches. Lack of knowledge of the work of these Guilds arises from the fact that only their existence is advertised in the Quarterly Reports of the Society and more detailed reports were published in the local pages of *Wheatsheaf* now lost to us.

The chapter in Hall's book *From Acorn to Oak* on the Guilds does little to fill the gap. The Women's branches were always larger than the Men's and they both co-operated in the arranging of some social and educational functions. Hall concentrates on the Central Women's Guild branch which had been formed in 1899 and was always particularly active in the field of child welfare and housing. Guildswomen had also been active on the Board of Guardians and the Public Assistance Committee. Some, like Mrs Hutchins had become JPs. Such a summary pays scant respect to the importance of the Women's Guild.

Finally, mention must be made of the development of the Co-operative Party. Walsall co-operators suffered the frustrations and unfairness of the war period and were among those who attended the conference in 1917 which decided on the formation of a separate Co-operative Party. A Political Council was formed in Walsall and William Abbotts became its chairman and most influential figure. By 1919 the Political Council was in a position to run a municipal candidate, and in 1921 Abbotts, standing in Leamore, became the first successful candidate of the Co-operative Party in Walsall.

During the slump years of the early 1920s those opposed to the Society participating in politics were successful in getting a motion through the Quarterly meeting that the Society should disaffiliate from the Co-operative Party. This position continued until 1931 when a Co-operative Political Council was again formed. This was based on individual members paying a subscription of 1/-d. a year with the support of the Walsall Society and all its auxilliary bodies. Despite the problems of collaboration with the Labour Party, Co-operative candidates continued to win seats on Walsall, Brownhills etc. councils, and Staffordshire County Council.

Wolverhampton Co-operative Society

Wolverhampton is the last of the Black Country consumer societies to be dealt with. Its sources are considerable with Quarterly meeting proceedings available for the whole period 1919-31 as well as a history of the Society up to 1931 written by H. Taylor, the vice-president of the Society at that time. The quarterly reports are particularly useful, because they contain both the Educational Committee reports and the only full account we have of the activities of Black Country societies' Guilds.

The Wolverhampton Society was the second largest in the Black Country after Walsall. During the war it had the usual problems of Co-operatives; in 1914 its dividend was a normal one of about 1/10d. but from 1916 it fell and by 1918 it was down to 1/4½d. At the end of the war it was as enthusiastic as other societies on the prospects for growth.

The first quarterly report after the war outlined the prospects and problems. Sales were increasing at an unprecedented rate, and the amount of capital members could invest was raised to £200.

> ...we have been keeping on building new records of trade, and to such an extent that we feel convinced that much more trade is awaiting us did we provide the facilities for coping with it, because there is no getting away from the fact that much congestion does exist in all our places of business, which is not pleasant to our members, or yet conducive to encourage new members to come in.

The Committee then opted not only for expansion, but on a scale 'in keeping with the dignity of the present dimensions of our business and provide adequate accommodation for any future development.'

This particular report gives a unique view of the effect of the 1919 influenza epidemic on the

Society. Thirty grants had been made averaging £5-7-6d. per grant and showed the death rate of the Society membership being as high as 17 per 1,000. (The overall death rate in England & Wales was 14 per 1,000 in 1919 – GB).

One cannot think that the trading figures, good as they were, gave grounds for such extreme optimism regarding trade. Indeed, the dividend was dropped to 1/-d. in 1919, this being 5 per cent with the profit/sales ratio being only 5.6 per cent. The next year, 1920, sales actually fell by £17,000 to just over £200,000, and the dividend was again lowered to 9½d; but this was at least a more prudent ratio of about 4 per cent when the profit/sales ratio was 7½ per cent.

But much worse was in store for the Society. The slump descended and in 1921 for the first time in the Society's history there was a loss – of almost £6,500. The dividend dropped to 4d. Losses could be covered in only two ways, either by using the Society's reserves or else (if the CWS would allow it), to increase loans from the CWS Bank. Wolverhampton chose the latter path, its overdraft at the bank rising from £2,000 to nearly £25,000. In 1922 there was a further but smaller loss of £1,819. The dividend to be paid out of non-existent profits was reduced to 2¾d. This was raised by increasing the bank overdraft to £30,000 and also raiding the reserve fund which fell from £1,403 in 1921 to £225 in 1922.

1923 saw a return to profitability even though sales fell to their lowest point at £126,000; the dividend was raised to 4d. This was amply covered by a profit/sales ratio of 4.6 per cent. Sales rose continuously from 1924 to 1930, although strangely, membership reached its lowest point of 6,254 in 1924. The dividend continued to rise reaching 1/-d. in 1927 and 1/2d. in 1929. By 1938 the dividend was 1/6d. The period from 1925-1931 was one of very considerable prosperity, membership doubling from 6,254 in 1924 to 12,752 in 1931 and share capital nearly tripling from £82,750 at its lowest point in 1922 to £234,546 in 1931. Capital per member rose from a low of £13-8-0d. in 1923 to £18-8-0d in 1931 and £30-4-0d in 1938.

The turn-round of the Society's fortunes was attributed, in large part, by Taylor, to the appointment of a General Manager, Mr E. Ashton, in May 1922; by implication this means that the failure to appoint a general manager after the death of the previous one, Mr Hodgson, in 1920, was a major cause of the Society's problems in 1921 and 1922.

During these desperate days of crisis the Management Committee continually called for loyalty from the members, particularly for the Bakery, 'our greatest productive asset', as it was described. Here the manager was Mr Bailey 'who had won many gold and silver medals' in open bakery contests and yet sales still lagged.

It was not until 1926 that the Management Committee had 'the greatest pleasure' in submitting a Quarterly Report. This was also the year of the General Strike. The only reference to it in the Quarterly Report was under the delicate heading of the 'Coal Crisis' during which despite high prices and moderate quality the Society had been able to meet the needs of all its members for coal.

By October 1927 trading conditions were so good that the Management Committee was reporting a surfeit of capital. 'It must be remembered that when the Capital gets to a larger sum than is required for ordinary trading purposes, the 5 per cent interest becomes a serious consideration', the Directors reported. But there was no intention of reducing interest or limiting amounts and they were considering how best to use this capital. The eventual solution was to invest it in Co-operative enterprises such as the CWS, the Co-operative Building Society and the Printing Society. By 1930 the Society had over £36,000 invested with the CWS as well as £22,000 in loans. This was virtually the whole of the Wolverhampton Society's investment and loans, the only others over £100 being £110 to the National Publishing Society and £100 to the Leicester Self-Help Boot & Shoe Society.

By 1928 a situation had arisen that was a Co-operative accountant's dream. Overall sales were 16½ per cent up. But sales in Boots, Hardware, Outfitting and Drapery had increased by 35 per cent Even the Bakery was flourishing at last, despite prices having fallen by 12½ per cent in the preceding year. This had been assisted by a new Catering Department and 'there are very few large parties in the district during the summer months that we are not asked to cater for, and receive numerous testimonials afterwards.' 1928 was also the year that the single shop of the Bridgnorth Society was taken over, 20/-d. in the pound being paid on its capital. By 1929 it was confirmed that 'all departments are prosperous.'

During these prosperous years the Society doubled the number of its shops from seven to fourteen. But it proceeded with considerable caution, perhaps a legacy of the difficult days; butchery was not attempted until 1929, and milk delivery not until 1932. Only in 1931 was the Emporium ib Lichfield Street opened. Progress had been good, but other Societies, such as Walsall had expanded faster.

A fuller account of the Educational and Guild activities of the Wolverhampton Society can be given than for other Black Country Societies.

In 1919 the Educational Committee was occupied with trying to restore conditions to 'normal' pre-war activities. By the autumn of 1920 it could report much success in that regard. Two Childrens' Field Days had been carried through in Wolverhampton and Codsall, and Childrens' Classes had been formed. These met at the Co-op Hall every Saturday at 2-30pm under three separate teachers. In addition, a Junior Guild had been formed, secretary George Hands, of which much was expected. Later in 1920 the Educational Committee reported the formation of a Men's Guild. A successful Employees' Concert and Dance had also been organised. The football team of the Junior Guild had organised a football match for funds for the unemployed. A monthly rota had been arranged for the Sports Ground at Goldthorne Hill to supervise the organised games there every Saturday.

The budget of the Committee for 1919 showed that it was operating with a surplus of about £100, a grant from the Society of £150 and sales of various goods and tickets amounting to about another £150 bringing total income to roughly £400. Most of this had been spent and the balance at the end of the year was down to £26. In 1920, the Society increased its grant to the Educational Committee to £350 enabling the Committee to extend its work.

But by the autumn of 1921 the Committee was reporting that its work had 'not been so strenuous' quoting the summer holidays and the suspension of Classes over the period. But the real reason was the depression and unemployment, 'which seems to be curtailing all progressive activity,' the Committee complained. This affected the attendance at and limited opportunities to hold successful concerts and socials. Quarterly budgets began to shrink. In the third quarter of 1921 spending was under £40 and the next quarter nothing was spent. The main reason was that the Society was making a loss and grants to the Educational Committee ceased in 1921.

The situation continued to deteriorate and even the Children's Annual Field Days at Wolverhampton and Codsall came under review by the Management Committee which finally decided that the Codsall one should go ahead.

Educational Committee reports became briefer and budgets disappeared from then. Events organised failed to make a profit and even attendance at the Childrens' Classes fell off and were a cause for concern.

But the autumn 1923 Report contained the following item. 'The popular Saturday night Whist Drives in the Large Hall are now in full swing and much appreciated by large attendances. The prizes are good and useful and the sociability of these large gatherings is one of their attractions.' These Whist Drives were to prove the salvation of the Educational Committee.

In 1924, as industrial conditions improved the Educational Committee was reporting a 'very strenuous quarter'. The Weekly Whist Drive had now been linked with a Dance and, 'become an institution, our Members to the number of over 300 weekly, enjoying to the full what is provided for them.' The annual Tea, Concert and Dance had been renewed and it was hoped to organise a day excursion to Aberystwyth on Whit Monday. The Children's Classes had been consolidated and at a New Year's Social the children had given a 'very nice' concert. Above all, Propaganda Meetings had been resumed in various parts of the town. Other successes followed in 1924, notably the Children's Annual Field Day at Hordern Recreation ground which proved 'an exceptional success,' 1,600 children and 500 adults taking part.

From 1923 when the Wolverhampton Society returned to profitability it would have been expected that the Educational grant would have been restored. But this was not the case. No Educational grant was made between 1921 and 1929. Only in 1930 was a grant of £100 made which was repeated the following year. The result was that the Educational Committee was forced to raise its own expenditure. Without the Whist Drive proceeds activity would have remained at a very low level. Unfortunately, however, the Whist Drives, successful as they were, were very expensive to organise. A half yearly budget for July 1928 will show this. All but £4 of the £348 income, came from the Whist Drives. Total expenditure was £350, but of this, Whist Drive expenses were £295, leaving only £55 of genuine expenditure. The main items of expenditure were nearly £12 in subscriptions to worthy causes, £12 for Children's Classes expenses, and £15 to the Employees' Annual Social.

Despite this slender financial base, the Committee added to its activities in the latter part of the 1920s. A choral society was formed in 1928. Also education for employees was belatedly organised. Junior employees attended a class studying Arithmetic, Commercial Correspondence and Business Methods. Older employees taking correspondence courses or attending the local Technical School had their expenses reimbursed.

The budget for the second half of 1929 showed the Whist Drives again contributing almost the whole of the budget at £402, but expenses were only £128 so that worthwhile expenditures could be made. These included nearly £300 to the Children's Field Day, £40 to the Musical Society and £7 towards Employees' Classes. Propaganda expenses came only to £4-6-5d. By this time the Committee had added to its usual commitments an Annual Carnival.

The annual report for 1930 signed by J. Jones, who had been the Educational Committee chairman since 1920, spoke of pride at the record profits of the Society. He reported Children's Classes larger than ever, successful Conferences organised by the Stafford District, the Co-op Hall packed for lectures and concerts, successful Propaganda meetings, and widespread social activity. The half-yearly budget showed the Whist Drives contributing £416 and the Musical Society £22 to income, but, at last, there was a £100 grant from the Society. The largest item of expenditure was again the Children's Field Day which had cost nearly £340.

The overall impression of the period is of an enormous amount of work undertaken by the Educational Committee. But one wonders what more might have been achieved if the Society had funded the Committee from 1923 and contrasts the Wolverhampton situation with that at Walsall where by 1931 there was a full-time Educational organiser.

Finally we turn to the Guilds in Wolverhampton. We have already noted the difference between Wolverhampton and Walsall where the latter supported a large number of Women's Guild branches whereas Wolverhampton had just one. This situation continued with only some modification into the 1920s.

The first Women's Guild report for 1919 stated that meetings were held alternate Wednesdays at the Co-operative Hall, Stafford Street at 7-30pm. The secretary was Mrs G. Page of 3, Crowther Street, Park Village. She reported the previous quarter as 'the most progressive the Guild has ever experienced.' New members were joining every week and the total stood then at 257. Meetings had heard speakers on such topics as 'Credit trading,' 'Housing,' and 'Co-operative Capital'. In February there had been a 'Surprise Night,' with Mrs Walton in the chair. Mesdames Jones, Lewis, Nunn, Ballard and Griffiths had given a sketch 'Dear Girls,' which had been 'highly appreciated.' Other members sang and recited and 'a most enjoyable evening was spent.' Also in February there was a Fancy Dress Dance 'voted one of the best events the Guild had ever held.' In March the Guild Annual Tea and Dance had been held 'when close on 300 members and friends sat down to a splendid tea followed by a dance. Also 'Mesdames Dale and Page had attended the first national conference of Co-operators and Trade Unionists in London.'

The next report showed meetings taking place every Wednesday. Mrs Page and the president (Mrs Dale) had been re-elected and a committee of Mesdames Drysdale, Hoppi and Minshall elected. Guild numbers were then 299. 'Several gentlemen have joined us as honorary members and we should be pleased to welcome any others who are interested in the work of the Women's Guild.' In April there had been an address by a Co-operative Insurance agent which resulted in several women transferring their policies to the Co-op. In May Mrs Whalley of the National Union of Women Workers had talked on the 'Education Bill,' discussing medical treatment, nursery schools, maintenance grants etc. This had resulted in a resolution to the local education committee demanding more secondary schools for workers' children. 'May 28th was a red-letter day in the history of the Guild.' In the afternoon a conference of the Stafford District Women's Guild was held attended by 80 delegates. In the evening

Fred Bramley of the TUC had spoken on 'Trade Unionism and Co-operation,' and this was reckoned 'one of the finest meetings ever held in the Co-op Hall.' In June about 130 Guild members went to Stourport for the Guild outing. It was also announced that a Codsall branch of the Women's Guild had been set up. Finally, Mrs Page reported that the Guild would not be closing down for the summer and invited other Co-operative women to join what 'I think we can claim is the largest Guild in England, although 299 is a small number out of 7,000 (nationally).'

Reporting on the work in the spring of 1920 Gertrude Page wrote on the significance of the Guild:

> The couple of hours spent in the Guildroom every Wednesday is not a waste of time. It enables women to learn and understand many of the Co-operative and Labour problems that face us at the present time and helps one to take a more intelligent view of matters; and now that women have the vote, it is necessary that they do all they can to educate themselves, so as to be able to judge for themselves the right person to vote for.

The list of subjects discussed reinforced her point. 'The Irish Question,' 'The Education Act,' 'Save the Children,' 'Sources of Unemployment,' 'The Miners' Lock-out,' and 'Women Magistrates and Jurors.' Other usual events were held. The Annual Tea and Dance was a success, the Annual Outing, to Malvern, had been arranged, although how they were to get there they did not know in view of the railway dispute. A Whist Drive had been held for the *Daily Herald* Fund, and a Sick Visiting Committee had been revived to visit Guild members.

By the summer of 1920 membership had soared to 450. As well as the weekly meetings at which 'questions of national and local importance' had been discussed, some members had also attended two-day schools, official classes and conferences. The new Codsall Guild had also been visited.

Optimistic reports continued into 1921. Highlights had been an afternoon on the sports field at Goldthorn Hill in August including a football match between the Women's Guild and the Junior Guild. All the usual events had been held. A Glee Club had given a excellent Concert. Various local Councillors had addressed meetings and appealed for assistance in the November elections. At the Guild elections Mrs Dale and Mrs Page had been re-elected, Mrs Nunn became vice-president and the committee was Mrs Hands, Mrs Bassett, Miss Woods and Mrs Huckin.

But by 1923 Guild reports were becoming attenuated with subjects for discussion reflecting the slump, such as strong protests at the cutting of milk to nursing mothers. These years took their toll of membership and by the beginning of 1924, despite making 25 new members, total membership was down to 175.

Activity revived in 1924, however. In June a successful 'At Home' had been held where special invitations had been sent out to all Labour Party Women's Sections and a 'most enjoyable' social evening was held resulting in many of the women joining the Society. A new project was a Fruit and Flower Show scheduled for the autumn.

By the summer of 1925 the Guild had a new secretary, Elizabeth Bowyer, who had been elected to the town council the previous November. She reported 'e very successful year.' Whist Drives had been held to assist Guild members who had been widowed during the year and others who were sick, and the usual activities had been carried out.

1926 and 1927 were years of progress for the Society, but Guild reports are still too short to assess progress and no membership figures are given.

By 1928 Mrs R. Beddows was secretary. She reported on the subjects discussed in the spring quarter – 'Life and Work of Charles Dickens,' 'Clothes,' 'Health,' and the 'Wages Question;' she summarised social activity in the autumn to be the Annual Harvest Festival in September, the Annual Tea in October and a Monthly Social. The absence of mention of summer activity suggests that the Guild closed down. Mrs Beddows' next report covered the winter session with the stress on No More War as a key topic for discussion. Social activities had been the Monthly Social, a Whist Drive in November, A 'Sing, Say or Pay' in December and the Children's New Year Party and Members' New Year Party in January.

In 1929 an attempt was made to continue through the summer, but attracting speakers proved difficult.

A slightly longer report in 1930 from Mrs Beddow stated that 1929 'had not been a very bright one for the Guild.' This was partly because several Guild members had lost their husbands and whist drives organised to raise funds to assist them had been unsuccessful and had left the Guild in debt. But the Annual tea, Concert and Dance in October had been successful and the money had been given to the widows. On January 1st. the Children's New Year Party had been followed by the Carnival Dance for members. This was the first time the two events had been held on the same day and was 'a huge success.' Talks in November and December had included 'Co-operation and Trustification,' 'Peace Pageant', 'Through Trade to the Co-operative Commonwealth,' 'Hints on First Aid,' and 'Factory Legislation.'

In a last report in 1931, Mrs Beddows was still hoping for 'better things,' although she reported the membership figure to be 250. The big event of the year was to be the Guild 40th Anniversary Party.

Through all the Women's Guild Reports there is no mention of finance. In other societies the Guild was financed by the Educational Committee, but there is only one reference to financial aid to the Women's Guild in the Wolverhampton Educational Committee reports. Since the Educational Committee had to finance its own activities, it must be assumed that the Guild also had to do the same. Subscription to the Guild was 2/-d. per member in 1921; with membership then at about 400 total income would be £40. In 1924, after the Great Deflation, subscriptions were set at 1d. per week; assuming membership then down to 250, income would be about £50. By 1931 subscriptions were again set at 2/-d. per annum which, with membership still at 250, income would only be £25. The Guild did not seem too successful in raising additional money, witness the failure of their whist drives compared with the hugely successful ones of the Educational Committee. The best financial period seems to have been the middle twenties which might have allowed for some risk taking with events, but the 1931 income of £25 seems quite inadequate to support a thriving and expanding Guild.

But three other Women's Guild branches in the area of the Wolverhampton Society in the 1920s must be mentioned. A Codsall branch of the Women's Guild was formed in the optimistic years of 1919-1920, for the Wolverhampton Guild reports that in July 1920 a visit was paid to the Codsall Guild where Mrs Dewsbury of Walsall addressed them on 'The Part the Guild has played in National Life.' In the autumn Mrs Dale, Mrs Perry and Mrs Page visited 'the new Guild Branch at Codsall,' and reported that good progress was being made. The fact that a Children's Annual Field Day and Outing was held in Codsall in August 1922 suggests that the Guild was still in existence at that time. But we have no further information on this Guild branch and it must be assumed that it perished during the slump years.

Once better times returned, a Guild was set up in Bilston and opened by the Guild president for the District, Mrs Adams, on September 22nd. 1924. The secretary was Mrs Hill of 6 Priestfield Street and the Guild met every Thursday at 7-30pm at the Scouts' Hut, Proud(s) Lane, Bilston. The first report told of a successful first Social in October and hopes to hold socials once a month. Women co-operators from Bilston and Bradley were cordially invited to join. A report in 1928 stated that twelve recruits had been made since their formation and the total then was 35 members. This suggests that the original Guild branch had not survived and had been re-formed in that year. A further notice in 1929 announcing the success of their first Annual Tea and Dance confirms this.

In January 1930 another new branch was formed. This was at Merry Hill meeting at the new Mission Hall, Merry Hill. The secretary was Mrs Hoppitt of 'Highfield', Coalway Road. Officers and a Committee were elected, after which the Guild was officially opened by Mrs Adams of Walsall, the secretary of the District. Recruiting from among the 100 who had attended resulted in a membership of 40 at the end of the Social evening. During the summer there were outings to Broadway and Evesham and into the Lickey Hills. These alternated with meetings addressed by the Labour mayor (Allan Davies) and the Co-op stalwart Alderman Tom Frost. Membership fee was 2/-d. per annum. A further report in 1931 by Mrs A.J. Smith, the secretary, stressed that the greatest achievement of the Guild had been the number of women in Merry Hill and area who had become members of the Guild for the first time. Two outstanding events had been the Children's Party on 30th December 1930 and the 'huge success' of the Fancy Dress Ball in January 1931.

In 1930 the Bridgnorth Women's Co-operative Guild branch came into existence. The secretary was Mrs D. Hill and it seems to have been the only Wolverhampton Guild branch that met in the afternoons. Its venue was the room over the Bridgnorth shop, every Wednesday. After a series of successful meetings its first outing was to visit the CWS Convalescent Home at Roden, 'which all thought a very beautiful place.' This was followed by Tea at the Co-operative Cafe, Shrewsbury. 'It had been a very enjoyable day.'

This brings us to the end of our period and reports from 1931 Quarterly meetings bring no more accounts of the Bilston and Bridgnorth branches, suggesting that as the new slump descended only Wolverhampton central and Merry Hill Guild continued to meet.

Two further Guilds must also be reported. These were the Men's Guild and the Junior Guild. It is not clear when the Men's Guild was formed and for information concerning it we must turn to the reports of the Educational Committee. In 1921 it was said to meet on alternate Tuesday nights and its continued success was thought to depend on interesting Co-operative employees in its activities. A further report in 1922 stated that its affairs had 'taken a turn for the better.' The secretary was Joseph Jones, who was also secretary of the Educational Committee. But after 1922 there is no mention of the Men's Guild and it must be assumed that it, also, was a victim of the Great Slump.

The basis on which the Junior Guild was formed suggested a more solid foundation of support. It was an Educational Committee decision in 1920 to form a Young People's Guild and Social Club which should be entirely democratic and self governing, and, if possible, self supporting. George Hands, the secretary, in his first and only independent report stated that:

> Our meetings commence at 6-30 each Tuesday night. Table games, skipping and boxing are in progress until 7-15; business is discussed until 8 o'clock (one of the young people generally being in the chair and it is very encouraging to see the enthusiastic way they enter into discussion). Refreshments are then partaken of, which are provided by the Committee and sold at cost prices, making just a slight profit. The rest of the evening is spent in singing and dancing, Miss Tatton being engaged to teach the former from 7-45 to 8-45.

Two very successful social evenings had been held to which each member had been able to bring a friend. At a conference in Birmingham on 'The Young People's Guilds,' the Chairman of the Co-operative Union had congratulated Wolverhampton on being the one Society in the midlands carrying out the methods advocated by the Co-operative Union. there were about 170 members on the register, 140 of whom had paid their annual subscription of 1/-d.

Subsequent reports came from the Educational Committee. In November 1921 it was stated that the Guild had met most Tuesdays during the quarter. That the Tennis and Cricket Sections had been wound up for the season and its equipment stored. Football was then in full swing and the Guild could boast of a good Junior Football Team. But ominously it was noted that, 'The industrial situation has affected the attendances and also lessened our opportunities to hold successful socials.'

The February 1922 report told of two socials not being the success anticipated because so many of the members were unemployed and the fact that Mr Hands was moving from the area and having to give up the secretaryship. But the football team was continuing successful. In August 1922 it was stated the the officers had not been able to work together and there had been resignations, but members had taken advantage of the long evenings 'and have put in full time at the sports grounds where various outdoor pastimes have been indulged in.'

The Guild lasted until the end of 1923 when it was reported, 'Unfortunately the Guild has had to be suspended for various reasons for the present, but we are hoping to reopen it again very shortly, with a well-organised series of Lectures and Social Events.' This was not to be, however, and the slump thus brought an end to leisure facilities for more young people in the town.

Walsall Locks and Cartgear

The last Co-operative to be noted is the one Productive Co-operative in the Black Country area. We have seen in previous chapters how Walsall Locks and Cartgear was set up in 1873 as a result of a trade dispute in the years of the Great Expansion. Remarkably, it survived the Great Depression and by the 1890s had taken part in the general transition of the trade from domestic to factory production, had beaten the competition from the largest firms in Germany and America at their own game and become one of the largest producers of locks in Britain. In addition, from the beginning it adhered to Co-operative social principles, was an exceptional spender on education and welfare provisions, as well as being a self-governing enterprise owned by its members.

During the Great War it successfully diversified into munitions work and by 1918 had a capital of nearly £10,000, sales of almost £75,000 and profits of £6,000 to share between its 276 members.

The profits reflected war profiteering (1914 profits had been less than £1,000) and these high profits did not continue. By 1922 profits were down to £3,400, but the Lock Co-operative did not suffer the severe problems of the Consumer Co-operatives in the Depression of 1921-23. Profits fell to a low of £2,200 in 1923 when deflation had brought prices to their lowest point, but thereafter profits continued to grow until by 1928 they were at their maximum of £4,870. Unlike the Consumer Co-ops, however, the Lock Co-operative was badly affected by the 1930s slump. Profits fell from 1929 and in 1932 a loss of £610 was made. But the position was retrieved in the more prosperous years of the later 1930s. By 1936 profits were nearly £4,000 and in 1938 were over £6,500. The stability of Walsall Locks is demonstrated by the stability of its share capital. Whereas the Consumer Co-operatives faced ruinous runs on their capital in the 1920s slump, Walsall Locks suffered a loss of capital only in 1922 when it fell to £15,809; thereafter it rose continuously until by 1931 it was almost £18,500 and by 1938 over £21,300.

The stability of Walsall Locks is also exemplified by its capital reserves. Again, in contrast to the Consumer Societies, it put money to its reserves every year from 1921 to 1931, these growing from £12,600 in 1921 to over £17,000 in 1931; thereafter they remained at virtually the same figure into 1938. Conversely with its Loans and Overdrafts; these fell during these years from about £6,00 in 1921 to about £5,000 in 1931.

The number of members varied only slightly from 350 in 1921 to a low of 312 in 1923 up to 340 in 1931. This can be compared with the number of 'employees' each year. These were 353 in 1921, a low of 283 in 1922, building up to 359 in 1930. In 1938 there were 428 employees. The near coincidence of the figures of members and employees suggests that almost every employee was a member of the Co-operative and almost all members worked at the Co-operative. This was not necessarily the case, because some retired and previous employees might have wanted to retain their capital in the Co-operative when they had left its employ; we do not know whether it was the policy of the Co-operative to allow or encourage this to take place. But every employee a member and no one outside the Co-operative being a member is likely to have been largely the case.

The question of the remuneration of the members is important but complex as the Society never declared an annual dividend. We are thus left to assume that members depended almost entirely on their wages. These we can calculate. Taking a 'bad' year as 1923, the average wage was £109 per annum and in the 'good' year 1928 it was £114, but since we know neither the gender nor the age structure of the work force it is impossible to calculate the wage of adult male or female workers. Until 1923 the Co-operative paid an annual bonus to its employees. But in 1923 this amounted to only £4 per employee per annum. This was a normal amount and could thus never be a serious increment to wages.

Although, in the absence of an annual dividend, it is difficult to see how the net profit was distributed each year it can be noted that he average shareholding in Walsall Locks was considerably higher than in the Consumer Co-operatives. Taking Wolverhampton as one of the more affluent Societies, in 1925 the average shareholding of members was £15-10-0d. But the average shareholding in Walsall Locks the same year was over £51. Thus each employee/member had a fairly substantial holding in the Co-operative which both paid him a weekly wage and the profits and assets of which the members were the ultimate owners.

As was the tradition with Walsall Locks, a generous part of the profits continued to be devoted to education, welfare and charitable causes such as the local hospitals. In 1918 Educational expenditure was 1.8 per cent of profits, and in 1922 2.1 per cent. For the succeeding four years it broke through the Rochdale Pioneers' recommended 2.5 per cent barrier to average an extraordinary 4.2 per cent. In the years 1927 to 1930 it was 2.5 per cent for each year. With the slump of the 1930s educational expenditure ceased altogether until 1935. Charitable expenditure was also particularly high at Walsall Locks. In 1921 it was £100 as against £120 for Education. In two years, 1922 and 1927, charitable expenditure exceeded that on education. In other years charitable expenditure in the 1920s ranged from £75 in 1926 to £125 in 1929. In the three bad years of 1931-34 neither educational nor charitable contributions were made, but in the later 1930s charitable expenditure was usually £50. This continued to equate roughly with educational expenditure and it was not until 1937 that educational expenditure was more than double that of charitable contributions.

With nothing but the bare Co-operative Union annual statistics to guide us it is impossible to say how the Co-operative coped with the technical, business or human problems. All that can be said is that by 1938 it was still a profitable undertaking, demonstrating that a Co-operative self-governing enterprise paying competitive wages within the trade and returning its profits to its worker-members could compete with the most advanced capitalist companies. Walsall Locks continued to exist and thrive until the Thatcher plague descended and destroyed the Black Country metal industries.

Summary and Conclusions

The first post 1st World War decade was characterised by booming business in 1919 and 1920 accompanied by very high inflation which, in real terms, offset most of the increases made. There followed a most devastating slump accompanied with an unprecedented fall in prices in 1921 to 1923, accompanied by mass unemployment, which shattered all dreams of a country fit for war-time heroes to live in. Economic conditions improved from 1924 and a more prosperous period followed until 1929 when the effects of the great 1930s slump began to appear.

In the inflationary period 1919-20 Societies were encouraged to lay large plans for expansion which only exacerbated their later problems. During the slump most Societies were brought to the brink of bankruptcy and two of them – the previously thriving Soho Society and the smaller Wednesbury Society – had to be amalgamated with larger Societies.

As they struggled out of the slump each of the Societies made their individual contributions to the members and communities that they served and it is with these contributions that this conclusion is concerned. In comparing Societies we have taken the years 1924-1930 as the only period of both price stability and reasonably prosperous economic conditions.

In this period, judging from total annual sales, we find that in 1924 Walsall was the largest Society followed by Dudley and then Wolverhampton. Then came the two smaller Societies, Halesowen & Hasbury and Tipton. This situation remained the same in 1930, but by then the gap between them had lessened because Halesowen & Hasbury had more than tripled its sales, both Dudley and Tipton had increased their sales about 2¾ times, Walsall had increased by 2¼ times and Wolverhampton had only just doubled its sales.

Comparing the Societies by the number of members, we find the same order in 1924 as for sales, except that Wolverhampton had more members than Dudley, but by 1930 this position had been reversed and by both sales and number of members the original position had been restored. However, between these dates the rates of growth of members had again varied widely. Halesown & Hasbury had again led the way by increasing membership 233 per cent from 1,780 to 5,926. Dudley followed with a 143 per cent increase from 5,312 to 12,891. Other rises were lower. Walsall's was 89 per cent from 19,430 to 36,758 despite having absorbed the Cannock Society. Wolverhampton's increase was 84 per cent from 6,254 to 11,511 and Tipton, surprisingly, had only a 62 per cent growth from 1,169 to 1,897 members.

Other important indices of development are the increase of capital and the amount of shares held by each member. With regard to capital over the period 1924-1930 the growth rates were as follows. Again, Halesowen & Hasbury led the way with a 188 per cent increase. Walsall followed with 140 per cent Tipton and Dudley were about level with 131 per cent and 130 per cent increases respectively. Wolverhampton was bottom of the list with an increase of only 124 per cent. With regard to capital per member, however, Wolverhampton headed the list with £15 in 1924 and £18 in 1930. Halesowen & Hasbury followed in 1924 with £11 per head, but by 1930 this had fallen to £9-10-0d. Walsall was third in 1924 with £10-10-0d. per member and by 1930 had raised itself to second place at £13-8-0d.

Fourth came Tipton with £7-15-0d. share capital per member in 1924 rising to an affluent £11 in 1930. Dudley lagged a bad last its share capital per member being £6-13-0d. in 1924 which fell to £6-6-0d. in 1930. To what extent share per member measured member loyalty to the Society coupled with active efforts to increase share capital, and to what extent it reflected the prosperity or otherwise of different towns, is not at all clear. The much greater share density of the producer co-op Walsall Locks and Cartgear at £50 plus, reflects, of course a very different situation.

The most important index of 'consumer satisfaction' would seem to be the dividend paid. In this respect Tipton was a clear leader with an average dividend between 1924 and 1930 of about 1/9d. Dudley came second at about 1/7¼d, Halesowen & Hasbury third at about 1/1d, Wolverhampton fourth at about 11½d. and Walsall fifth at about 11d. Two caveats must be entered however. Tipton was lucky to avoid bankruptcy during the slump period of 1921-23 partly from the payment of over-generous dividends and Walsall, bottom of the dividend league, might be regarded as the Society offering greatest security for its members' capital.

The other index of Co-operative efficiency is the extent to which its Educational expenditure furthered the ideal of the Co-operative Commonwealth. In this regard, Walsall held the palm, with a thriving consumer society in the town together with the only productive co-operative in the Black Country. By 1931 with a full-time Educational officer and over 3 per cent of its net profits devoted to Education, it stood alone. Second came Halesowen & Hasbury with 2.2 per cent of its profits spent on education in 1930. Dudley came next with regular educational expenditure, but this averaged less than 0.5 per cent of its profits. Wolverhampton, as we have seen made no educational expenditure from its profits between 1924 and 1929 and Tipton never contributed one penny to educational expenditure. This does not necessarily mean that education was not undertaken. Wolverhampton Educational Committee managed to self-finance considerable activity. Of Tipton less is known. Back in the 1890s it had a Family Club, whether this continued into the 1920s or whether it ever had a Women's Guild are not at present known.

The Educational achievement of Walsall must be stressed. It came nearest to the Rochdale Pioneers' aim of spending 2½ per cent of profits on education; its educational activities spread beyond that of being the propaganda arm of the Society: it provided education for its employees, and also classes and courses for its members; by the 1930s it was supporting numerous Women's Guild branches totalling about 1,000 members (compared with about 250 in Wolverhampton) and the unprecedented number of 11 Men's Guild branches. This is a record that few Societies in the country could equal.

Co-operation 1930-1939

Black Country Co-operatives were as little affected by the slump of the early 1930s as Birmingham. All societies' sales fell between 1930 and 1931 but only Tipton with an 11 per cent fall and the industrial co-operative Walsall Locks and Cartgear at 19 per cent suffered severe falls. Sales of both these societies continued to fall in 1932, but by then sales of Dudley, Halesowen & Hasbury, Walsall and Wolverhampton societies were in excess of their peak 1929 levels. All societies recovered strongly in the following years and the position in 1938 (the last full year of peace) was:

Sales (£000s)	Dudley	H & Has	Tipton	Walsall	W'ton	Locks & C
1932	426	184	51	748	274	61
1938	693	375	63	1,370	525	107

In order of merit for increases in sales it can be seen that Halesowen & Hasbury led the by way more than doubling their sales. Both Wolverhampton and Walsall nearly doubled their sales. Tipton had their problems in this period sales increasing by only 25 per cent. Lock and Cartgear rallied strongly with a 75 per cent increase in sales.

If we take the 'consumer satisfaction' index of dividend paid Dudley takes the palm. Throughout the nineteen thirties in slump and boom it paid 2/-d. in the £. Tipton matched it until 1932 when its profligacy caught up with it and subsequently Tipton paid about 1/7d, although this continued the highest dividend in the Black Country apart from Dudley. In 1938 the dividend of all the other three consumer societies was 1/6d. The question again arises of whether a 1/-d. dividend is enough to keep existing members happy leaving reserves for expansion. So we can next look at membership.

Dudley did not reap a rich reward for its generous dividend policy its membership increasing only by 24 per cent. Halesowen & Hasbury had the highest membership increase between 1932 and 1938 of 73 per cent. Walsall came next with 56 per cent then Wolverhampton with 48 per cent. Tipton's membership increased by only 6 per cent.

What about increases in capital? This combines confidence and loyalty to the society together with, presumably, the degree of affluence or poverty of the society's catchment area. The figures show only Halesowen & Hasbury doubling its capital between 1932 and 1938. Dudley followed with 68 per cent, then Walsall 66 per cent, Wolverhampton a disappointing 58 per cent and poor Tipton only 12 per cent.

Topping most of the above indices it would seem that Halesowen & Hasbury could be adjudged the most successful society in the years 1930-38 as it had been in the period 1924-29. Walsall continued to be the largest Black Country co-operative society followed by Dudley, then Wolverhampton. Tipton was a special case. It was the smallest of the Black Country societies by far and logic suggests that its best interests would have been served by merging with Dudley. However, despite its problems of lack of growth, it maintained the second highest dividend in the Black Country. Unfortunately the society seems to have left absolutely no evidence of its activities and so nothing can be said of the nature of its problems.

With regard to promoting the co-operative commonwealth and meeting the Rochdale criterion of devoting 2½ per cent of net profits to education, we can look at the Black Country figures for 1938 as typical for the period. These show Halesowen & Hasbury leading with 2.3 per cent followed closely by the productive co-op Walsall Locks & Cartgear at 2.28 per cent. Walsall consumer society had slipped to 2 per cent but this was much in excess of Wolverhampton spending 0.8 per cent but whose Education Committee was expected to be self funding. Dudley spent 0.7 per cent, and Tipton continued, as ever, to spend absolutely nothing on education.

Bibliography: The Co-operative Movement in the Black Country 1919-1930

The *Annual Co-operative Union Congress* Statistics are again the main source. Fred Hall's *From Acorn to Oak* is a main source for the Walsall Co-operative Society. For Wolverhampton there is the *Brief History of Wolverhampton Co-operative Society* written by its vice-president H. Taylor in 1931. For both Walsall and Wolverhampton there are the *Quarterly Reports* of these Societies for the period 1919-1931. A new and valuable source is Ned William's sumptuously produced book *The Co-op in Birmingham and the Black Country (1993)*.

Chapter 25

The General Strike in the Black Country 1926

The Miners

One difference between the General Strike in the Black Country and in Birmingham was that a considerable body of miners existed in the Black Country, so we shall deal with them before discussing the wider aspects of the General Strike and then return to the misfortunes of the miners after the General Strike had been betrayed.

As with the 1921 Miners' Strike it is difficult to trace the numbers of miners or their conditions. My estimate from the 1921 Census of 12,000 miners in the Black Country, including the No Man's Land between the Bentley Fault and Watling Street, north of which the Cannock coalfield proper begins, had probably been slightly depleted by the 1921 Strike and subsequent flooding, but the larger pits continued to develop. The No Man's Land in Walsall Wood, Brownhills and Aldridge contained such pits as those of the Walsall Wood Colliery Company employing over 1,000 miners, the Aldridge Colliery Company with over 1,800 men in two pits and Harrison's at Brownhills and Wyrley employing nearly 2,000. Within or marginally outside the Black Country, the Earl of Dudley operated the Baggeridge pit employing nearly 1,000; at Hamstead Pit, West Bromwich 800 were employed and at Hilton Main north of Wolverhampton over 1,300 miners worked. These large collieries employed over 9,000 miners. Then there were medium sized, traditional Black Country pits employing 200-300 men such as Old Park, Dudley with 260 employees, and Shrubbery, West Bromwich with 280. Other pits employed 100-200 men and this trailed down to Poxon and Read of Wednesbury who employed four men and Richard Perrins of Bilston who employed only two men – one underground and one above ground.

Wages can be followed only by taking South Staffs & Salop wage rates, which includes the Cannock coalfield where wages were higher than in the Black Country. Wage rates given are an average for all employees:

	1914	1918	1919	1920	1921	1922	1923	1924	1925
Wages (per shift)	5/-d	11/2d	12/6	16/10	12/8	7/7d	7/7¾	8/3½	8/8¼
" (index no.)	100	223	250	337	253	152	153	166	170
Cost of Living	100	203	215	249	226	183	174	175	176
Real Wages	100	113	116	135	112	83	88	95	97

It will be seen that real wages rose to a maximum of 35 per cent over pre-war levels in 1920 but fell when prices fell in 1921. As a result of the miners' strike in 1921 wages fell to 83 per cent of the pre-war level in 1922 and had still not reached the pre-war level in 1925. It must again be stated that these figures apply to S. Staffs & Salop miners which included the larger and more prosperous Cannock coalfield. Black Country wages and standard of living would undoubtedly be lower.

To estimate average earnings from these figures we need to know the number of shifts worked. The maximum that could be worked was six per week for 52 weeks making a total of 312. Few would want to work this maximum even if the pits were open, but in 1924 we know that in S. Staffs & Salop pits worked an average of 282 shifts or almost 5½ per week. This would give average earnings in 1924 of almost 45/-d. per week for those in continuous work. But because the pits were open this did not mean that all miners were working. National figures for unemployment show 3 per cent of miners unemployed in 1923, nearly 6 per cent the following year, and 11½ per cent in 1925. The bulk of this unemployment would be borne by miners in the export trades, but it is likely that the figure of 45/-d. for earnings in 1924 would have to be deflated by about 3 per cent for unemployment to accurately reflect earnings.

Figures for the S. Staffs and E. Worcs. coalfield alone are rare but there is one of 1924. This shows that 1,732,112 tons of saleable coal was raised and sold at an average price of 14/2.84d per ton. Comparable figures for the Cannock coalfield were just over 6m tons raised at a selling price of 18/7d. The national output that year was 267m tons sold at an average price of 18/10d. The differential between the price of Black Country and Cannock coal suggests that there might be a similar difference in wages.

The miners' trade unions involved in the 1929 strike were the West Midlands Miners' Association which was the Old Hill Miners' Association, renamed after the 1921 strike. The second was the S. Staffs. & E. Worcs. Miners' Association organising the central part of the coalfield. Relations between the Old Hill miners and the S. Staffs and E. Worcs. had before the war been cool, the Old Hill men working an area that was still prosperous. These differences had healed as the Old Hill area also declined. But both associations had some large pits in the areas they organised. The third unions was the Pelsall Miners' Association which organised not only Black Country miners but those in the large pits in the No Man's Land north of the Bentley Fault. The Pelsall miners always associated themselves with the more prosperous Cannock field and eventually they became part of the Cannock Miners' Association. Thus all three associations had some large pits to bolster trade union organisation.

Much is made of poor trade union density in the Black Country and this applied also to Black Country mining. Horsnall quotes the example of only 587 trade unionists out of 2,000 Old Hill miners on the eve of the General Strike. But the Black Country was predominantly an area of small units difficult to organise and this applied also to its pits. The Black Country miners, as with other local trades, found their own solutions to such disadvantages. In this case, the problem appears worse from the fact that only underground workers were organised in the unions. Nor does it seem that pit ballots were held authorising the strike. But when the strike was called both non-union miners and surface workers answered the call of the Miners Federation of Great Britain and despite overwhelming pressures most remained faithful to the end.

After the 1921 strike national coal production increased until 1925, the year of the return to the gold standard, when production fell sharply to 243 million tons (still above the level of the immediate post-war years), but receipts decreased to just under £200m (from a peak in 1920 of £397). The main fall was in the coal exporting areas. Once again the mine owners saw this as an opportunity to abolish the two main post-war gains of the Miners' Federation of Great Britain – national, as opposed to local pay settlements and the seven hour working day. For their part the miners were prepared for total resistance, coining the slogan not a penny off the pay, not a minute on the day and sought the assistance of the TUC. With the assurance that there would be a general strike if the miners' conditions were worsened, negotiations between the miners, mine owners and government proceeded.

The uneasy peace established in the coal industry after the 1921 strike came to a head in June 1925 when a joint committee of owners and miners broke up after failing to agree on measures to modernise the industry. The owners then terminated the existing agreement on 31 July 1925, after which there would be pay cuts, estimated by the MFGB to be between 6 per cent and 23 per cent and local wage negotiations only. It was also made clear that the 7-hour day must go. In the Black Country this wage cut was estimated at 18 per cent. The miners refused to discuss such a proposal.

Negotiations then proceeded via the TUC to resurrect the Triple Alliance of Miners, Railwaymen and Transport Workers and it was extended to the Engineers and Boilermakers. All these unions faced certain wage cuts if the miners were defeated. The strike was averted at the last minute by Baldwin announcing a Commission of Enquiry supported by a subsidy to the industry for the period covered by the enquiry. To the jubilant workers this was Red Friday overcoming the shame of Black Friday in 1921 when the Triple Alliance had collapsed leaving the miners to fight alone.

Official figures for S. Staffs and Salop showed that in 1924 profits had been 10d per ton (compared with national profits of 1/2d). In the period of the subsidy (August 1925 to April 1926) profits were 1/3¾d but if the subsidy of 2/10¼d. per ton were discounted the district produced coal at a loss. The Samuel Commission satisfied neither owners nor miners. The owners wanted immediate wage cuts; the miners wanted no cuts until the industry had been reorganised – after which, they believed, wage cuts would not be necessary. Unlike 1921, there were no sharp falls in the cost of living to justify wage reductions. Deteriorating economic conditions were blamed on the return to gold and also the Dawes Plan which helped to greatly increase German coal production. Notices went out that wages would be reduced at the end of April. The proposed cuts in the Black Country were again about 18 per cent. The miners had no intention of being starved to bear the whole brunt of the industry's ills. They demanded a continuation of the subsidy. The Government refused. The General Strike was on.

The General Strike

There are no surviving trade union sources for the General Strike in the Black Country, and so Emile Burns' collected reports in his *The General Strike May 1926: Trades Councils in Action* provides much of our information for this area.

From Burns' report for Wolverhampton we learn that no preparations had been made beforehand, and a Special Executive meeting of the Trades & Labour Council met only on the first day of the strike and an Emergency Committee of three men was appointed to sit continuously with full powers to co-ordinate the activities of the unions involved. The first wave of workers called out consisted of 1,500 transport workers, and an unspecified number of members of the Typographical Association, NATSOPA, ETU, some AEU and Allied Trades and Building Workers.

The Emergency Committee consisted of representatives of each affected union. It first met the next day, Tuesday 4th May, and was faced with the problem of interpreting the general circular sent by the TUC while waiting for instructions from the individual unions to cease work. The Committee was divided as to its functions, some thinking that it had powers to call the men out. The majority view, however, was that its job was to carry out the instructions of the TUC and obtain concerted action locally on that basis. But this presented problems, since different unions were sending different instructions to their branches, this being most evident in the building trades.

The central Emergency Committee met every afternoon in the Labour Rooms. A separate strike committee was formed of the railway groups (there were important railway engineering shops in Wolverhampton) which met daily at North Road Club. The central Emergency Committee eventually consisted of four Trades Council members, a representative from each of the building trades and the North Road joint committee.

To overcome the lack of reliable information, lines of communication were set up south to Birmingham, north to Manchester and beyond, and west through Shrewsbury to North Wales. Volunteer dispatch riders were appointed to act for the TUC in every town between Dudley and Oswestry, receiving reports each day from each strike committee, sending out official information from the TUC, supplying them with speakers where necessary and forwarding information to London for the General Council of the TUC.

A local bulletin of 500 of each issue was published for six days from 5 May. Open meetings were arranged every day at the Market Place with a good supply of local speakers assisted by the miners from Cannock. There were national speakers at the week-end. A meeting on Sunday May 9 packed the Theatre Royal with 2,500 people, with an overflow meeting of 1,100 at the Co-op Hall, Stafford Street. Even so, thousands were unable to obtain admission.

As in the rest of the West Midlands there were differences of opinion as to whether car workers were included under transport and therefore among those to be called out. In Wolverhampton the matter was settled when the Vehicle Builders received definite instructions to withdraw their labour. The other unions involved then acted on the principle laid down by the TUC that where one section of the labour force was called out in a given factory then all should strike. Thus the important car industry was closed down.

All building workers, except those engaged on housing, hospitals and sanitation were ordered to strike. This caused dissatisfaction in Wolverhampton where 'the whole of the industry was determined to stand by the miners.' The Strike Committee therefore had the greatest difficulty in keeping within the TUC instructions, and on Saturday 8 May, a meeting of building workers instructed local officials to send a telegram demanding the withdrawal of all building workers.

The town's power supply from the Commercial Road power station received a great deal of attention. The TUC requested that local arrangements be made to supply homes, hospitals, bakeries etc. but the management refused to negotiate with a deputation and instructions were eventually received to withdraw all men from the power stations.

From figures provided by the manager of the Labour Exchange on Monday 10 May, it is estimated that 35,000 workers took part in the General Strike in Wolverhampton.

The only other Black Country town report published by Emile Burns was a short one on Wednesbury. Here the strike was organised by the Trades Council acting with its affiliated trade union branches. It issued a Bulletin each Sunday, the first selling 750 copies and the second 1,000. The position on May 12 was given as 'No weakening. The position was magnificent. The trouble has been since the termination.'

Emile Burns' information can be supplemented from other sources. The *Birmingham Worker*, bulletin of the Communist Party reported on 7 May that the Council of Action that had been formed was in continuous touch with Tipton, Darlaston, Walsall and surrounding areas. 'Even non-unionists are affected by the spirit of working class unity and are on the streets with the organised workers. Mass demonstrations are being held and enthusiasm runs high. The formation of a Workers' Defence Corps is contemplated. The unemployed, who are rendering valuable assistance, are seeking representation on the Council of Action.'

The *British Worker* (the TUC paper) carried two reports on the strike in the Black Country. The first issue on Wednesday evening 5 May reported the stoppage in Birmingham and district as complete. Not a man on the railways or other transport was working. The biggest trouble was to keep at work those who were not involved. The 7 May issue reported that the West Bromwich position, according to the local Trades Council, was regarded as eminently satisfactory. Councillor Guest, the agent, reported that the response to the call to cease work had been complete. The main difficulty had been to keep men and women in who wanted to strike in sympathy with the miners. The opening of the new Labour Rooms had been of great advantage to the local strike committee.

In the TUC library there are reports from Wolverhampton and Walsall, and also a report from Ellen Wilkinson and J.F. Horrabin of their tour through the Midlands. The latter report gives valuable testimony of the position in Wolverhampton towards the end of the strike. It states that there was a ready and unanimous response to the call in every occupation. Public opinion was strongly in favour of the strikers. Not a tram or bus was running. Some attempts had been made by the town Council and Chief Constable to intimidate tramway and busmen without success. Three Midland Red buses had tried to run, but were withdrawn by inducements. The Typographical men had been persuaded to go back by the editor of the local paper the *Express & Star*. Police and strikers were on good terms. Food was supplied by road and there were no shortages. In Wolverhampton, Wilkinson and Horrabin had addressed two open-air meetings on the Market Place of 6,000 each. The figures they give for the indoor Sunday meeting was 4,900 at the Royal Theatre and 2,000 at the Co-op Hall. At New Invention they had addressed 2,000 at an open air meeting. In Bilston 1,500 had listened in Oatmeal Square. Their general observation was that they had been immensely struck by the complete stoppage and the peacefulness of the workers in every town through which they passed. The response was magnificent everywhere.

A report to the TUC from Walsall of May 6 was on special notepaper headed Walsall Trades Council National Industrial Crisis Committee. The secretary was John Whiston and the chairman A.H. Fox. They reported the position in Walsall as 'splendid.' A wonderful demonstration had been held with a huge meeting. All were out who had been called out. In addition, several thousand engineers had decided that they were on transport work and had come out. The local strike committee was very efficient and was publishing a local newspaper. Public opinion was on the side of the strikers.

The recently released Cabinet Papers on the strike are disappointing. Police intelligence in 1926 was no better than in the nineteenth century. The Midlands reports are sparse and refer mainly to Birmingham. On May 5 it was reported that 'iron and steel works were stopped generally in the Midlands.' This affected particularly Brierley Hill and Bilston in the Black Country. 'Newspapers were practically all suspended except for a few scrappy publications.'

The Home Office report for May 6 stated that journalists were on strike in sympathy with the printers. The *Express & Star* was publishing a foolscap sheet with the aid of volunteers. About 2,500 men had come out at the Sunbeam Works. McManus was expected to hold a Communist meeting in the town on Saturday, but the police would not allow him to speak. There had been some interference with working railwaymen who were being given police protection.

On May 7 a Home Office report stated that in Wolverhampton more engineers were out and that 400 specials had been enrolled with more coming forward. The electrical workers might come out, but in that case the power station would be run by volunteers. The Home Office summary for May 10 reported that a patrol had found a detonator on the GWR line near Cradley Heath.

Turning to the local press, the *Express & Star* ran a badly produced, duplicated 1d sheet on 4, 5 and 6 May. The first reported hopefully that arrangements were being made to run charabancs and buses in certain areas under police protection and it was hoped to run a skeleton GWR train service from Wolverhampton to Birmingham. A Communist meeting of about 800 had assembled at the Market Place and had been immediately dispersed by the police. Pickets at the garage of C.F. James in Sweetman street were reported and one of his charabancs in Stafford Street had been stopped, police arriving in time to prevent a disturbance. Such contrasting snippets of national news were reported as the arrest of the Communist MP, Saklatvala in Hyde Park for a 'seditious' speech and the arrival of the Prince of Wales in Paris from Biarritz. Local news on Thursday May 6 was that engineers and body builders at Black Country motor works were out and that all was quiet in Dudley, Darlaston, Walsall and Willenhall.

By Friday 7 May the *Express & Star* was producing a two page printed sheet with more local news. Wolverhampton tramways were still firmly out. The Star Engineering Works at Bushbury and Frederick Street were closed although only 50 per cent of the men were trade unionists. The Sunbeam Moorfield Motor Works were at a standstill. Guy Motors had 500 to 600 men out and 200 men in. At A.J. Stevens (AJS) 50 to 60 AEU men were out, but the firm was carrying on. In Brierley Hill 2,000 men were out in iron and bricks. In Walsall between 1,000 and 3,000 hands were idle, but all large works were able to continue. In Bilston the Springvale steelworks was closed and hollow ware workers would have to go on short time next week. In the Rowley Regis area 6,000 workers were idle, but at Halesowen all workers were continuing. In Dudley all was quiet with 300 men out. At Brierley Hill 1,500 men were out at the Earl of Dudley's works, 300 at Harts Hill Ironworks and 90 at the Brettell Lane Ironworks.

On Saturday May 5 the *Express & Star* managed to print four pages. An advertisement from Beattie's (the large department store in the town) showed that they at least had prepared for the General Strike. It stated that the strike had threatened for months and the store had ample stocks to meet demand for three months. In Wolverhampton the paper reported the continued total absence of trams and buses, but otherwise the town was normal. Bushbury parish church had given over its Institute to the strikers (mainly railwaymen) and these men had decided to march to church as a body on Sunday. AEU men had stopped work at Clyno, but this firm was carrying on. A short service for industrial peace was being held every day at St. Peter's Church in the town centre at 12.30pm. The grand Theatre would be closed the following week because the company, which was to have produced

'The Jazz Marriage', had transport difficulties. In Willenhall most factories were on a three day week because of shortage of fuel. At Dudley on Friday night there had been an attempt to stop a charabanc taking workers home, but despite a large crowd the vehicle had got through.

On Monday May 10 another four page paper appeared. There had been no peace moves over the week-end and the position remained the same. Many Black Country works were managing to keep open. At Harper Sons and Bean three works with 2,500 men had to be closed in Dudley, Tipton and Smethwick because finished cars could not be dispatched. 3,700 men had signed on at Dudley Labour Exchange since the strike began. Joseph Ball, a miner of Cross Street, Dudley was given one month's hard labour for allegedly assaulting two police officers and committing an offence against the Emergency Powers Act. He incited the crowd by shouting, 'Come on lads. Let's have a go! We're not frightened of you!' The crowd rushed the police who drew their staves. Several women said, 'Cheer up, lad.' when sentence was passed. Sunbeam and the Star were at a standstill. At AJS it was said, 'There is a sort of ebb and flow at our works but we are able to carry on; about 800 are on duty and about 600 on strike. At Wednesbury two local MPs, A. Short and C. Sitch had addressed 3,000 workers at Cradley Heath on Saturday evening. Two hundred men were on strike at Henry Meadows of Wolverhampton, leaving 38 at work. In Tipton the road men were on strike and at W.G. Allen's in the same town an unsuccessful attempt had been made to prevent a steam wagon loaded with iron plates from entering the works. This issue of the *Express & Star* found space for a remarkable Red Scare story: A Paris paper had published a letter from its German correspondent stating that the General Strike in Britain had been planned in secret many months before in Moscow!

On the last day of the strike the *Express & Star* reported the Wolverhampton situation little changed. Strikers were still coming out. For instance, 129 at ECC, and other works were closing because of lack of transport. At Bilston, lorries leaving goods stations still had to have police guards. At Walsall the Board of Guardians had published their scales of relief for the families of strikers. These were for wives 10/-d., for wives with one child 14/6d., with 3/6d. for every additional child. Rent relief of 50 per cent could be allowed. Half the relief was to be paid in cash and half in kind.

The *Express & Star* voiced the opinion of the employers and much of its reportage was mendacious or misleading. An example is the paper's report of May 10 that at Guy Motors a secret ballot in the presence of two trade union officials had given a 75 per cent vote in favour of a return to work. This issue also reported that men at Bayliss, Jones and Bayliss were returning to work. The next day the paper reported that 87 men had reported to work at Guy's while between 500 and 600 men were 'affected' by the strike and 250 had been 'outside' (i.e.picketing) when the firm opened. Guy, the managing director, admitted that the meeting at which the ballot had been taken 'was not largely attended' due to the pickets telling the workers that the meeting was not being held. Guy was a particularly active employer in attempting to break the strike. Even this amended version of the Guy story is likely to be only an approximation to the truth, and the facts of the so-called return to work at Bayliss, Jones and Bayliss are now never likely to be known. Another clear example of misleading reporting was an item on May 12 headed 'How men were going back to work before the good news came.' Here the whole country was scoured for news of men returning to work before the end of the strike, but all that could be found was such items as 'Birmingham – a 12 minute train service to Dudley,' or, 'Stoke-on-Trent – a number of tramway and omnibus employees have returned, but the response is extremely limited.'

But the press is cowardly as well as venal; while the capitalist system is under serious threat the endless strictures on workers are suspended. But when profits and property are once again secure, editors again thunder against the wickedness and criminality of striking workers. This was so in 1842 when Chartists controlled the Black Country in the general strike of August in that year, and so it was with the *Express & Star* in 1926. The May 12 editorial spoke only of 'unbounded relief' at the ending of the strike; but the following day it was, 'The Law Victorious,' and 'Did the TUC ever consider the legality of their action?... It can hardly be imagined in any way a victory for the unions... The forces of law and order have triumphed in Britain as they always will'. Much more of this sort was to follow in the days and weeks ahead.

The General Strike of 1926 is the most important episode in the history of the trade union movement in Britain. Employers and the Government had provoked the strike to curb the power of the trade unions and bring all wages down. The right-wing Labour leaders feared the strike, had tried to avoid it, and wanted it ended at the earliest possible moment before it got 'out of hand'. It showed with the starkest clarity that society only existed through the labour of working people. During the strike Trades Councils exercised powers of decision and control normally carried out by employers and police. Thus the strike taught lessons of democracy and workers' control. It was also a magnificent example of workers' solidarity and comradeship, contrasting sharply with the selfishness of capitalism. Above all, in a society of mass poverty, deprivation, and high unemployment a successful conclusion to the strike held the promise of fundamental changes in society. Most strikers realised therefore, however dimly, that the project they were engaged on was of great significance. Hence the Nine Days had an atmosphere of gaiety, solidarity, determination, and mass participation which is rarely captured by strike reporting. Some observers, however, did begin to catch this atmosphere. Here is John Strachey writing in the *New Leader* after the strike and referring to the Labour parliamentary candidates who left London for their Birmingham constituencies on the Saturday before the strike began:

> When they reached the headquarters of their divisional Labour Parties they found unexpected crowds gathering around the banners of local parties and trade unions. As they marched with their comrades through the streets of the city, unprecedented masses of people lined the route and followed them to the park where the May Day demonstration was held. They did not realise that, almost literally, these great crowds were not to disperse until fourteen days later when they were dismissed at another demonstration. The whole city swayed with the quiet vibrations of these impressive masses.

Ellen Wilkinson also wrote graphically in *Lansbury's Labour Weekly* of May 22 of her experiences in the midlands:

> We got to Coventry that night to find the town in the hands of the local Soviet. We spoke to one of the largest open-air crowds I have ever seen. The engineers were very disgruntled at not being called out.. Wolverhampton, not on our list, demanded a meeting and within one hour we got a large crowd to listen despite pouring rain. They and Walsall were in the same position as Coventry...

Much of this mass participation went unrecorded, but it is quite certain that almost every urban area saw meetings and demonstrations perhaps larger than they had ever seen before. Throughout the strike the hunger for news and desire for mass communication were such that enormous meetings could be called during the day. Often these were Communist meetings which the police promptly broke up. The solidarity of the strike made mass picketing possible and overwhelming public sympathy was manifest at crucial moments.

In view of the particular efforts made to break the strike at what was thought to be its weakest link, namely in transport, this atmosphere of solidarity might be illustrated by detailing the determined efforts made in Wolverhampton to get the buses back on the road. On Monday May 10 it was decided to attempt to run ten buses manned by volunteers. At 6-30pm when the attempt was to be made, a crowd, estimated by the *Express & Star* at 1,000, assembled at the Cleveland Street bus depot. Police, including mounted specials, cleared a way for the volunteers and it seems that some of the buses got away. At 9pm the crowds 'still numbered several hundreds.' At 7-30am the next day the first bus, manned by three men in plain clothes and one uniformed policeman, set out. It was later claimed that ten buses were running. All that day, strikers in Queen Square 'thronged the pavements as densely as if waiting for a royal procession.' On Wednesday, the *Express & Star* returned to the events of the previous day. 'The first day of the volunteer bus service will be long remembered', it stated. The report went on to tell of huge crowds in Prince's Square during Tuesday night, and photographs confirmed the enormous numbers who protested against this attempt to break the strike. The transport workers of Wolverhampton remained firmly on strike to the end.

In Bilston too, masses of workers demonstrated, although we only have the *Express & Star* reports to go on. 'Bilston tramway and railway workers gathered in fairly large numbers on Monday 10th. when attempts were made to remove supplies from the railway depot to various factories. A number of volunteer lorry drivers, including several undergraduates in plus fours evidently enjoyed the experience. There was no attempt at molestation.'

In the great pre-strike May Day demonstration the festive mood was shared by Wolverhampton's Communists, but this did not prevent arrests taking place. Albert Darke and John Foster were charged with 'wearing service uniform in such a way as to bring it into contempt.' Darke wore RAF uniform with a red band; on the shoulders he wore red badges. Foster was in the uniform of a line regiment and was similarly decorated. The case was heard after the strike had ended. Inspector Churchward gave evidence that on May 1 the Labour Party was holding a demonstration from St. James's Square. As the procession moved off Darke joined it with a placard reading 'Don't Shoot.' At 7-45 the same evening at a Communist Party meeting Darke was similarly attired and Foster carried a red flag. The two Communists were defended by Randle Evans, a noted Labour Party progressive solicitor, who submitted that his clients were wearing uniform in the course of a bona fide military representation forming part of a tableau. They were not there to bring contempt upon the uniform. The chairman of the bench of magistrates (consisting of W.H. Pritchard, Sir Charles Marston and Alderman Tom Frost the Labour JP) said that the court could not tolerate that HM uniforms should be used in a contemptuous manner. Albert Darke was fined £6 and given time to pay, and Foster was fined £1. If the strike had still been on the sentences would have been much more severe.

Further information regarding the role of the Communist Party in Wolverhampton came from a personal interview of the author with Ralph Prescott who joined the party in 1924. He states that Wolverhampton Communist Party had considerable influence on Wolverhampton Trades Council; Albert Darke, the local Communist Party secretary, was a delegate. The most important way of exerting the Party's influence during the General Strike was through meetings on the Market Patch. These were invariably broken up by the police. He particularly remembers one meeting at which he was chairman. He spoke from the steps of the old market Hall which formed an excellent elevated platform. He had not been speaking long when he was hauled down by the police. Albert Darke jumped up and took his place. As Prescott was taken away to the Town Hall, mounted police dispersed the crowds with batons in the fiercest struggle he had ever seen. Prescott and Bill Smith, another Communist arrested with him, persisted in asking what they were charged with, but the police would make no charge and they were both released after the crowd had been dispersed. When the strike ended the Party directed its efforts to raising money for the miners. Cannock was at the heart of this struggle and miners' choirs came to the Market Patch to sing and raise funds. The Communist Party came out of the strike with increased prestige, says Prescott, and it exercised influence far greater than its number, a fact of which the police were well aware. In 1926, however, there were only about nine members of the Communist Party in Wolverhampton, and it was obviously not strong enough to be a decisive influence on the strike.

As in other parts of the country, the first reaction of many to the end of the strike was a feeling of elation, for they supposed that they must have won. But disillusion was swift and was followed by the struggle to return to work. In Wolverhampton the Emergency Committee met as usual on the afternoon of May 12 and had posters displayed in front of the Labour Rooms advising men not to return to work until instructions to that effect came from their unions. This caution was well justified. The railways, Guy's Motores, the ECC and Midland Red buses were 'requiring men to sign documents giving away rights which their fathers and grandfathers had fought so dearly for, and it is quite evident that the employers of this country are prepared to use this crisis as a method of breaking down trade union bargaining.' Other employers were taking men back 'only as work became available.' Apart from the railways, however, it is not possible to assess the extent of victimisation in the Black Country.

In evaluating the strike, Postgate, Wilkinson and Horrabin classified areas into four classes. Class I was towns where response was near to 100 per cent. Class II was where the strike was wholly effective but with weaknesses in some sections. Class III was towns with serious weaknesses, and Class IV towns where the strike broke down. Midland towns in Class I were Birmingham, Kidderminster, Lichfield, Stafford, Stoke, Worcester and Wolverhampton. In Class II were Coventry, Shrewsbury, Smethwick, Stourbridge, Walsall, and Wednesbury. No midlands towns were in the other two classes.

The Wolverhampton Emergency Committee summed up the strike as follows:

...the Trade Union movement are indeed to be congratulated upon the splendid stand made on behalf of their more unfortunate brothers the miners, and with very little exception, the whole of the workers stood solid and were prepared to fight to the bitter end, so that when the news came through on Wednesday May 12th that the strike was over, it came as a shock, as the situation then looked as if it would last indefinitely.

On Sunday May 19 Wolverhampton Trades Council held a meeting at the Market Place. The *Wolverhampton Chronicle* informs us that there was a crowd of 300, but this increased after the first half hour. R.H. Allport, the chairman of the Trades Council said they met 'to offer thanks for the solidarity of the working class.' Dan Davies, the local agent for the Labour Party said, 'If the strike had lasted another week, we would have entered into another era of struggle.' This latter statement is highly significant. The day before the strike was betrayed by its leaders, the TUC had called out the second wave of workers – all the engineering and shipbuilding workers not already affected. This call was just beginning to take effect. The solidarity of the strike from start to finish, not least in the Black Country, suggests that this unique chapter in working class history would have ended very differently had the strike continued.

The Miners fight on alone

The General Strike had been called off with none of the main demands of the miners addressed. These were: no wage cuts until the mines had been reorganised after which cuts should not be necessary; no return to eight hours which would make the British miner's working day the longest in Europe except for Upper Silesia (as the Samuel Commission pointed out); national negotiations which would allow wages in the worst hit, export coal fields to be equalised from the profits of the still prosperous areas. These demands not being met the miners felt, therefore, that they had no alternative but to continue the Lock-out.

The first problem was the sustenance of the miners and their families. The miners' unions had never supported large strike funds and, as we have seen, many miners and all surface workers were not members of the union. Horsnell quotes from local newspapers stating that the funds of the West Midlands Association were exhausted by the second week of May and the funds of the S. Staffs & E. Worcs. Association ran out by the end of May.

When union strike pay ran out, the miners' second resource was to the Poor Law. As in the 1921 strike, some Boards of Guardians attempted to deny any responsibility for men on strike and thus hasten the starvation of the miners. But such die-hards were over-ruled and Boards of Guardians were compelled by public opinion, if not their own humanity, to support wives and children, and where men were receiving nothing from strike funds, a minimum amount which could support a family was estimated. The Walsall scales were 14/6d. for a wife and child with 3/6d. for each additional child. A rent allowance of 50 per cent might or might not be allowed. When strike pay ended Walsall Guardians considered 30/-d. a week sufficient to maintain the largest family. The Stourbridge Guardians allowed 17/-d. a week for a miner, his wife and three children and the maximum, however large the family, was 26/-d. In June the Vicar of Cradley complained that the miners in that town were receiving no relief from the Guardians. Thus relief was arbitrary, varied from one town to another, and was insufficient.

The third source of sustenance for miners and their families was from fund raising. There was a central MFGB fund whose monies were distributed, mainly for trade unionists, according to the number of miners in each district. There were also local funds meant for all miners on strike organised by each of the Miners Association with the local Trades Councils responsible for factory and street collections. Some local friction was bound to arise (as those of us who collected for the miners in 1984-5 found). Kingswinford broke away and formed its own collection in an area where there were few miners and a relatively prosperous area from which to collect. Apart from such problems the funds were a major source of assistance.

Both the West Midlands Association and the S. Staffs. & E. Worcs set up central funds from which the MFGB dispersals were distributed. Substantial amounts of this came from the Miners' International. By October 1926 £1,275,077 had been contributed from Europe, Canada, America,

Australia and almost every coalfield in the world. Soviet Russia had contributed one third of this. It was fitting that a donation for the Black Country miners from Russia was addressed to Cradley Heath where the struggles of the chain makers in the the early part of the century would be well remembered and whose Institute was the headquarters of the miners of the district.

In the S. Staffs & E. Worcs area fund raising was in the east of the district the responsibility of the West Bromwich Trades Council and in the West by Brierley Hill Trades Council. When the West Bromwich & District fund closed in February 1927 over £3,500 had been collected, £2,300 of this came from places of work. This was a considerable contribution.

Wolverhampton Trades Council presumably supported both Black Country and Cannock miners and was also an area which others could 'raid' as when miners from Walsall came to Wolverhampton and collected £28.

Walsall Trades Council collected for the Pelsall Miners' Association as well as miners in the thick coal.

Labour women were a particular source of strength. It was they who initiated the scheme of Miners' Lamps Days and it would not only be Brierley Hill Trades Council that organised Lamp Days when thousands of miniature miners' lamps were sold to raise funds.

A traditional additional source of help was the Soup Kitchen. These were first opened when unemployment rose in the aftermath of the General Strike. Reports from the *Walsall Observer* of 22nd May showed that unemployment in Darlaston had doubled since the end of the strike. Councillor Hucker, the local NUR secretary stated that only 45 per cent of workers at the Bescot goods depot had been allowed to resume work. At Ryecroft, largely passenger traffic, about 50 per cent were back, but only 5 per cent of cleaners. Most station workers were back dealing with parcels accumulated during the strike. Railway services were still restricted to conserve coal, and trades dependent on fuel such as iron and steel, tubes etc. were almost at a standstill.

A Distress Fund was initiated by the Walsall Trades Council with John Whiston as secretary. Whiston was not only secretary of Walsall Trades Council but also secretary of the Workers' Union who had 90 per cent of their 1,000 men and women membership in Walsall out of work because of the strike. Soup kitchens were immediately opened at Hednesford and other parts of the Cannock coalfield. It was decided to resurrect the organisation that had been so successful during the 1921 miners' strike starting with feeding children until the Council could be persuaded to provide school meals.

By the end of May it was claimed that all children in Pelsall and Cannock Chase were being fed, either by volunteers or by the County authority under the Provision of Meals Act. In the past fortnight the miners had received 10/-d per week from strike funds, but these funds were now exhausted. Walsall Wood estimated that it had 800 children to feed and a local committee had been formed. In the New Invention, Essington, Short Heath district there were 1,000 children to feed; again, a local committee was at work.

In early June Soup Kitchens were opened in Bloxwich and Leamore by the Walsall Miners' Distress Committee to feed the families of about 2,000 members. Meals were served largely in public houses. Appeals were made for money as that week's meals had been prepared on borrowed money.

Such activities continued in Walsall and the rest of the Black Country until the end of the lock-out.

The Return to Work

Once the General Strike was ended the government lost no time in putting forward proposals even more onerous than those suggested by Samuels. The 7-hour day was to be repealed, wage cuts of 10 per cent were to be immediately enforced, followed by further cuts within three weeks, subject to a minimum wage of 45/-d. District negotiations were to begin. These proposals were rejected by the MFGB, but local offers were made. Cannock Chase Coal Owners offered the Pelsall and Cannock miners work at 8-hours (with half an hour for dinner) and at wages at 46.64 per cent above the 1911 level (or about 7/4d. a day). This was rejected by both the Cannock and Pelsall miners.

The next attempt at a settlement came in June. It was stimulated by legislation to suspend the seven hour day for five years passed through Parliament in June and gaining the Royal Assent on July 8th. It was an offer of talks by the chairman of the Mining Association to the chairman of the MFGB, but these talks did not materialise when it was clear that the owners were not prepared to make any concessions.

The Lock-out was never complete in the Black Country either on the side of the miners or the owners. Some owners were prepared to offer work at the old terms. One such was S. Evers & Co. of the Homer Hill Colliery, Cradley Heath. But Evers manufactured fire brick and were desperate for coal to continue production. Many small coal proprietors would have been in similar straits. Some larger owners also would be anxious to maintain their coal output for iron production etc. Such was the Earl of Dudley; he offered Baggeridge workers an 8-hour day plus 46.67 per cent on 1911 rates, almost the same percentage that the Pelsall miners had rejected. Hingley & Co. made the same offer and it was unanimously rejected at a meeting at the headquarters of the West Midlands Miners' Association.

July saw another intervention by Church leaders suggesting that negotiations be re-started on the basis of the April wage and Government support during the negotiations. This was rejected by both owners and the Government. It also went to a ballot of the miners who also rejected, albeit by the small margin of 333,000 to 367,000, negotiations. But most 'No' votes came overwhelmingly from South Wales, Yorkshire and Lancashire. Other districts voted for the proposals including the Midlands and within that district both Black Country Associations and Pelsall.

A MFGB Special Conference in August 1926 voted rather less narrowly (428 to 360) for the re-opening of negotiations with the owners. But the owners were adamant in refusing concessions and subsequent overtures to the Government made it clear that the time for subsidies had long since passed.

At the beginning of September the MFGB Conference revealed how serious the position was. The last payment of strike pay by the union had been 3/-d. per man and there was currently in hand only 1/8d. for the following week. The suffering of miners and their families was intense and some miners were returning to work. District totals showed 36,785 had returned. This was less than 5 per cent of the total membership of the Federation, but it masked serious differences between districts. The Midlands was the worst district accounting for more than half of that total at work. In Nottingham the local association was controlled by George Spencer MP who had already negotiated with local owners. He was expelled from the MFGB and set up his own breakaway union in that area. Sam Edwards reported that 840 men had gone back to work in the West Midlands Association, but few of them were union members. Henceforth, the hopes of the owners and Government rested on starvation and breakaways from the MFGB.

The mine owners pressed home their advantage and in mid-September the Mining Association closed off any hopes of national negotiations by the districts refusing to the Association powers to negotiate with the miners, thus precluding anything but local negotiations. A special MFGB conference at the end of September reconsidered the position. The number of miners back at work had increased to over 81,000 and the Midlands share of that total was 34,000. But a militant South Wales motion intensifying the strike by calling out the safety men in all pits was carried. This went to a district vote and was confirmed by 460,000 votes to 284,000. The 60,000 Midlands vote, however, was cast with the minority.

The government met this renewed militancy with increased repression under the Emergency Powers Act, arresting pickets, and banning meetings in the coalfields such as A.J. Cook's meetings in Staffordshire. By mid-October the new militancy was getting results, the Ministry of Mines admitting 26,000 less men at work with a large decline in those working in the Midlands.

This brought a new initiative from the Government early in November with the significant concession that the owners would pay 'temporarily' the April 30th rate of pay. A Special Miners' Conference eventually decided by 432 to 352 that these terms be accepted; but when put to the Districts it was rejected by 461,000 votes to 313,000. In view of the smallness of the majority, the fact that miners at work totalled a quarter of the MFGB membership, and the dangers of further breakaways, the Conference decided by 502 to 286 to recommend all districts to open negotiations locally. By November 30 all miners were back at work.

Most mining trade unionists in the Black Country remained loyal to the MFGB to the end, however. In mid-October the *County Express* gave voting on an alleged offer of 'a return to work on the 1921 agreement pending a settlement on a national basis.' Four hundred West Midlands Association miners at a meeting rejected this, as did 300 Pensnett miners and a majority of other members of the S. Staffs. & E. Worcs. Association who attended meetings. The Lock-out in the Black Country ended on November 30 with a joint statement by H.S. Whitehouse and Sam Edwards, the leaders of the two Black Country unions and the opening of negotiations with the mine owners for a local settlement. The Lock-out had lasted 31 weeks.

The Settlement in the Black Country

In December 1926 a joint negotiating committee of the two Black Country trade unions met with the Salop, S. Staffs. & E. Worcs. Coal Owners Association. The first offer from the owners was an 8-hour shift with 32 per cent on basis rates. This gave an average wage of 6/7d. per shift. This represented a fall from the August 1925/April 1926 S. Staffs & Salop rate of 8/6¾d or 23 per cent together with the extra hour's work. The unions would not accept this and at a second round of conferences in February the owners improved their offer to 57 per cent on basis to the end of March down to 47 per cent to the end of June with a minimum wage of 40 per cent plus of basis rates and a subsistence wage of 6/2d. This offer was accepted and in March a District Wages Board was formed. Sam Edwards claimed that basis plus 40 per cent was as good as any settlement in the country but this was estimating average pay at 7/-d. per shift.

The District Wages Board was formed much as previous ones before national wage settlements began. It consisted of six each of miners and owners, with the chairmen and secretaries of the miners' and the owners' organisations as ex-officio members. There was also an independent chairman. Wages for July 1927 and subsequently were to be based on the average price of coal over the previous three months. The two miners' associations remained separated but acted together as a Miners' Combined Association on the Wages Board. The agreement was to continue until June 1931 and thereafter could be terminated by three months notice of either side.

The determination of wages thus returned basically to movements in the price of coal. This had the twin disadvantage the miners had always fought against of ignoring the movement of the cost of living, and a built in determinant that the standard of living of the miners would never rise unless the cost of living fell. This, together with the extra hour on the day, and the loss of protection from national negotiations illustrates the enormity of the defeat.

The importance of the real wage can be illustrated as follows. If Sam Edwards basis plus 40 per cent (i.e. 5/-d in 1911 plus 2/-d = 7/-d.) is taken as the settlement of the Lockout and compared with the cost of living of 100 in 1914 against 168 in 1927, the real wage is 83 per cent of the 1914 standard of living. This is what it had dropped to in 1922 after the strike of the previous year; the real wage had then crept up to the 1914 level in the months before the General Strike only to be plunged back to the 1922 level as a result of the 1926 Lock-out.

Something must also be said about the absolute standard of life this average of 7/-d. per day would give. For a full week's work of six shifts it would equal 42/-d. In 1914 when miners earned an average of 5/-d. a shift or 30/-d. a week, the Rowntree Poverty Line for a family of man, wife and three children was 35/3d. Adjusted for 1928 prices this Poverty Line was 59/7d. The 1927 settlement gave Pikemen 9/2¼d per shift or 55/1½d per week, although he might do slightly more than one 'stint' per shift; thus even the most skilled miner's wage was not above the poverty line if he had a wife and three children. When one takes into consideration unemployment, short-time working, and loss of work from sickness and accident, it is clear that apart from the more prosperous war years and the two boom years of 1919 and 1920, Black Country miners' standard of living was below the 1914 level through most of the 1920s. And from 1927 they did not have the advantage that other workers had of reduced hours of work.

Bibliography: The General Strike in the Black Country 1926

For miners in the Black Country virtually the only source is the local newspapers, notably the *Walsall Observer* and the *Staffordshire County Express* with its local satellite editions for Stourbridge, West Bromwich, Dudley etc. These sources have been used by Christopher J. Horsnell for his Wolverhampton University MA thesis 1991 – *The Coal Mining Trade Unions in the Black Country 1914-1927*.

The other main source is the *Annual Reports of the Minister for Mines*. Unfortunately, the Black Country coalfield had so shrunk by 1921 that few separate figures for this area are given, and for wages the nearest category is for South Staffs. & Salop, which included the higher paid Cannock miners. Sometimes there are details of output, costs, prices and profits for the Black Country alone which I have used. Much of this material appeared in the *Colliery Year Book & Coal Trades Directory*. This began in 1922, but it was not until 1926 that it began to publish full material. This Year Book also published complete lists of coal mines, their owners and often their output and number of miners employed. From this Black Country mines can be picked out.

The miners were organised in three main associations – the Old Hill Miners' Association (to become the West Midlands Miners' Association after 1921), the South Staffordshire & East Worcestershire Miners' Association and the Pelsall Miners' Association. The latter organised some miners in the 10-Yard Black Country seam around Walsall, but mainly organised miners in what I have called the No Man's Land between the Bentley Fault roughly marking the end of the 10-Yard Black Country seam, and Watling Street which marks the beginning of the Cannock Coalfield. There is now a very useful book discussing this No Man's Land – *Coal Mining in Walsall Wood, Brownhills and Aldridge* (Walsall Local History Centre 1994). All three Associations were affiliated to the Miners' Federation of Great Britain.

For the General Strike in the Black Country the main sources are – Emile Burn's collected reports in his *The General Strike May 1926: Trades Councils in Action*, R. Page Arnot's *The General Strike*, and Ellen Wilkinson, J.H.F. Horrabin and R.W. Postgate *Workers' History of the Great Strike*. Also General Strike documents at the TUC Library and the Cabinet papers for the period at the Public Records Office (mainly PRO CAB 27/331). Much of the material here appeared in G. Barnsby – *The General Strike in the Black Country,* published on the 50th. anniversary of the strike. The interview with Ralph Prescott, a Communist Party member at the time of the General Strike was with the author.

For the Miners' Lock-out after the General Strike see R. Page Arnot's *The Miners: Years of Struggle* for a sympathetic general picture. But the total absence of miners' trade union records either locally or nationally means that we are totally dependent on what the hostile local press printed.

Chapter 26

The General Strike in Birmingham,
Monday 3rd May to Wednesday 12th May, 1926

Causes of the General Strike

The General Strike of 1926 was unique to Britain, and indeed, to the world. It was not a strike for higher wages or better conditions for those on strike. It was exclusively a strike in support of miners whose standard of living was threatened, and the perception that if the miners were defeated then the standard of living of all workers would be lowered. In other words, workers laid their jobs on the line for the altruistic purpose of supporting fellow workers for the sake of the common good. Behind such action is the concept of class consciousness. Tories can never understand class consciousness. Their creed is self-consciousness; only such actions that benefit themselves have validity. Moreover they see class consciousness among working people as the direst threat to their system of values, a threat to be stamped out. Such were the thoughts of politicians, industrialists, newspaper proprietors, the middle class in general and many working people also when, to their utter astonishment, the TUC called the General Strike on the 3rd of May 1926 and the response of workers in Birmingham, as elsewhere, was virtually 100 per cent.

    The General Strike ultimately failed. But when the forces arraigned against the strikers were joined by forces at the heart of the strike – leaders of the Trades Union Congress responsible for calling the strike and Labour's political leaders, many of whom had no thought except to prevent the strike taking place and when it did take place, devoted all their energies to ending it – one can see that the miracle is not that it succeeded, but that it happened at all. As H.A. Clegg in his *History of Trade Unions Since 1889* says, the General Strike is the most important episode in British trade union history and the only comparable example of the willingness of working men to sacrifice for a cause was the First World War.

    The problems of the miners went back to the 1921 Lock-out, when, outmanoeuvred by Lloyd George setting up the Sankey Commission which promised nationalisation of the mines, the miners struck only after the short post-war prosperity had ended and the depression with its fall in coal production, prices and wages was well under way. This ensured that the miners had no chance of winning especially after Black Friday, April 15th, when railwaymen and transport workers' leaders refused to activate the Triple Alliance to help the miners. The Lock-out dragged on from April to July, but the miners were inevitably defeated leaving them with the statutory 7-hour day as their only gain from the war.

    The return to the Gold Standard in 1925 presaged a general attack on living standards with the Prime Minister, Stanley Baldwin, saying that 'all workers of this country have to take reductions in wages to help put industry on its feet.' In June the coalowners gave notice of termination of the 1924 national agreement with the miners, and demanded a return to local negotiations, reductions in wages and the end of the minimum wage. These proposals were rejected by the miners who then put their case to the TUC General Council. The General Council pledged that the miners would not be left to fight alone and the transport unions undertook to place an embargo on all movement of coal if the Lockout took place. At this point the Government moved in and offered a 9-month subsidy to the industry and a full enquiry into the Coal Industry by a Royal Commission. This was celebrated by the trade unions as Red Friday (31st July 1925).

The Royal Commission was set up, but whereas the Sankey Commission of 1919 had contained equal numbers of miners and coalowners and had recommended nationalisation of the mines. the Samuel Commission was a very different animal. It consisted of the lawyer Sir Herbert Samuel, a general turned banker, a cotton employer, and the economist William Beveridge. Its eventual limited proposals satisfied neither side. To miners it offered no safeguards for either wages or hours of work and proposed only the nationalisation of mine royalties.

Meanwhile militancy was growing in the unions. Negotiations to extend the Triple Alliance through an Industrial Alliance were started by the TUC and at the TUC Scarborough Congress in September 1925 a resolution empowering the TUC to call a General Strike was remitted to its General Council, elections to which that year had brought a swing to the right.

The Samuel Commission reported in March 1926. There followed two months of fruitless negotiations between the Government, coalowners and miners. In April the coalowners posted lockout notices to expire on 30th. April. On Saturday May 1st a special conference of Trade Union Executives approved the TUC General Council's proposal for a General Strike in defence of miners' wages and hours to begin at midnight on Monday 3rd. of May. The Government replied by declaring a State of Emergency.

Negotiations with the Government continued with increasing desperation on the part of some General Council leaders who desired at almost any cost to avoid a General Strike and wanted only a continuation of the government subsidy while reorganisation of the coal industry, as suggested by Samuel, began.

Eventually, at 1.05am on Monday May 3rd, the government broke off negotiations under the pretext that printers at the *Daily Mail* had refused to set up an editorial condemning the General Strike. Despite further grovelling of the General Council in condemning the action of the *Daily Mail* printers, the Prime Minister had gone to bed and the lights were out at Downing Street. The General Strike began as day shifts ended on Monday May 3rd and night shifts failed to turn up for work.

Preparations for the Strike

Despite the jubilation of Red Friday (31st July 1925) the Government was intent on making preparations for the coming struggle, and the trade unions knew that when the coal subsidy ended the prospect of a general strike would return.

The Government made the most of this respite. In September 1925 the Organisation for the Maintenance of Supplies was formed. This organisation, it was claimed, had no official connections. A Birmingham Area Branch was set up in February 1926 with a brief to enrol volunteers to serve in a possible 'national emergency.' It was, of course, a strike breaking organisation to which the emerging Birmingham fascisti, British Empire loyalists and other right-wing groups flocked. The Government also drew up detailed plans for the continuance of essential services in the event of a strike. The country was divided into ten districts each headed by a Civil Commissioner. One of these districts was the West Midlands with Lieut-Colonel G.E. Stanley MP as Commissioner. These districts were then sub-divided, Birmingham being one of these sub-divisions. Since most local authorities, including Birmingham, were Conservative, the Government made the local authorities their agents for such an emergency. In November 1925 Circular 636 was issued by the Ministry of Health (Minister Neville Chamberlain the anti-strike Birmingham MP) requiring local authorities to set up organisation to secure the maintenance of public services 'during an industrial emergency.' In January

1926 the Birmingham City Council appointed an Emergency Sub-Committee consisting of Aldermen Sir David Brookes, Gregory, Sayer and Martineau and Councillors Lee, Muscot and Shakespeare with the Lord Mayor and Alderman Williams ex-officio. Of these members three were Labour. When the emergency materialised, Councillor Shakespeare, a railway guard, resigned. But Alderman Joseph Gregory a former organiser of the National Union of General Workers, turned blackleg and continued on the Committee. Alderman Percival Bower also remained a member of the Committee. His position was anomalous. Not only was he Lord Mayor, but he was the first Labour Lord Mayor of Birmingham. He had often been at odds with the local Labour Party and some believed the presence of the City's first citizen on the Committee would provide a conduit through which could be mitigated or negotiated differences between the Committee and the trade unions. This proved to be a myth, power was in the hands of the government approved Alderman Sir David Brookes (the leader of the Unionist group on the City Council), and the Chief Constable (Charles Rafter), who was controlled by the Home Office. The Birmingham Emergency Committee delegated various responsibilities to sub-Committees and Corporation departments with full powers to use Corporation staffs. With the solid support of the Employers' Associations in the City and the Birmingham Chamber of Commerce, and the virulent detestation of the working class movement by the two newspaper groups in Birmingham, it seemed that long before the strike took place, an iron ring of opposition had been put in place which would make it impossible or madness to contemplate a General Strike.

This view would be reinforced if one turned to the problems of the trade unions with regard to strike preparations. Birmingham, with its myriad of small firms was notoriously difficult to organise. Any preparations the trade unions made would be interpreted as provocation and proof that the unions were determined to organise a general strike which would then be misrepresented as opening the way to Bolshevism and the overthrow of the Constitution. Around these issues the trade unions, despite the universal desire to support the miners, were split into a moderate majority, and a vigorous left-wing led by an emerging Minority Movement supported by the Communist Party. However, the increasing militancy of the trade union movement in Birmingham, as recorded in Chapter 20, was offset by a loss of electoral support and the determination of the national Labour Party to remove the Communists and all their influence from its ranks.

Such proposals for preparations as were made in Birmingham were usually initiated by local Communists. The most controversial was a proposal for Workers' Defence Corps under the control of Trades Councils, which the national Communist Party saw as essential for protection against the local fascisti, the OMS, and the perceived determination of the state to destroy the trade unions and Labour movement in the coming struggle. The matter was brought up at the Trades Council by Bill Brain in November 1925 and his proposal was passed by 39 votes to 34. The idea of Workers' Defence Corps were ridiculed by the *Town Crier* and the right-wing and advantage was taken of the Trades Council AGM in January 1926 to rescind the resolution. G. Ackland on behalf of AEU No.9 Branch argued that the proposal for Workers' Defence Corps was incorporated into a composite motion which had outlined a number of proposals for Trades Council action; that the proposal was impracticable and not in the best interests of the trade union movement. A.P. Cassidy, the seconder, said Brain had taken advantage of the Council to 'get in a bit of Communist propaganda.' Corrin, the president, speaking on behalf of the Executive, said they had considered the proposition and concluded that it was an impossible one; there was no need for such Defence Corps. Such bodies would create more bother than they prevented. If the Communists wanted Workers' Defence Corps let them form them themselves. Corrin concluded. Brain and Cardinal (another Communist) defended the proposal, but the resolution was 'passed with an overwhelming majority.' How large 'overwhelming' was we are not told, but total attendance seems to have been about 140 at the AGM. In the elections for officers that evening Brain stood in a straight fight against Corrin for the presidency. Corrin received 104 votes and Brain 34. W.T. Cardinal stood for the Vice-Presidency. In this case six nominees were voted on and Cardinal was elected with 38 votes against his nearest rival's 37 votes. No Communists were elected to the Executive Committee. Shortly after Bill Brain, who had been a member of the national executive of the Communist Party in 1924, was asked to move to the North East where he played a prominent part in the General Strike in Northumberland and Durham. Cardinal thus became the only Communist on the Trade Union Emergency Committee in Birmingham, so it could hardly be held that the General Strike was a 'Communist Plot' in Birmingham.

Considerable support remained in Birmingham for the left-wing demand led by the Communists for adequate preparation for the strike. Government preparations included the arrest of twelve leading Communists in October 1925 and sentences which kept some of them in prison for the duration of the strike. These arrests brought strong protests from most of the Labour movement in Birmingham, including the Trades Council which also supported the appeals of the International Class War Prisoners' Aid petitions for their release and for financial support for their families. The decision of the Labour Party at its 1925 Conference aimed at preventing trade unions from sending Communist delegates to Labour Party conferences etc. was also vigorously opposed including a debate at the March 1926 Trades Council meeting protesting at the Birmingham Labour Party's attempts to enforce this ban on Communists. This was only defeated by a compromise amendment by S.L. Treleaven that the matter be referred back to union branches who, preferably by referendum, should consult their members and resolve the matter once and for all.

The only other attempt at preparations for the strike seems to have been when the Young Socialist League together with the Aston Divisional Labour Party called a 'Rally to the Miners' on 18th April at Aston Theatre Royal. This meeting called for organisation for the by now inevitable General Strike, and the Young Socialists offered themselves as volunteers. Speakers at the rally included miners' MPs and John Strachey, who was prospective Labour candidate for Aston. Official preparations for the General Strike began only on Saturday May 1st when the General Council of the TUC made the Trades Councils their local agents and a meeting of the Birmingham Trades Council proposed the creation of a small committee representing the Birmingham Trade Union and Labour movement.

The next day, Sunday 2nd, a special meeting of the Trades Council executive committee met to sketch the outline of an Emergency Committee that would 'sit daily and, as far as possible, control and co-ordinate the industrial position on behalf of the workers.' W.J. Chamberlain attended to offer his services as a publicity agent and the paper he edited, the *Town Crier*, became the official organ of the Emergency Committee. A Publicity sub-Committee was set up consisting of Chamberlain and the President and Secretary of the Trades Council. No statement to the public was to be made without the approval of this sub-Committee. The secretary F.W. Rudland, outlined instructions from the TUC General Council. The Emergency Committee was to act on the instructions of the General Council; 'all our people' should avoid the possibility of conflict with the authorities; 'all our friends' who attempt to speak should keep strictly within moderate limits; 'The great mass of our people' should endeavour to make the best use of their enforced idleness to get into the country or parks for recreation and relaxation and no demonstrations or meetings should be held unless authorised by the Emergency Committee. It was proposed and accepted that the Trades Council representation on the Emergency Committee should be its officials and five others. Those elected were the president, vice-president and secretary J.E. Corrin (full-time organiser of the T&GWU), W.T. Cardinal (Workers' Union), Rudland (Typographical Assn) and J. Stuart Barr (minutes secretary and organiser of the National Council of Labour Colleges). E.C. members elected were H. Dawson (Brassworkers), S.L. Trelevean (Life Assurance Workers), C.J. Mann (Distributive Workers), George Haynes (Bakers) and Walter Lewis (ETU).

On Monday May 3rd the delegates elected by the Trades Council called a meeting with the officials of the trade unions involved in the General Strike to complete the formation of the Emergency Committee. Nine were eventually elected, equal to the number of Trades Council representatives. These were Councillor A.E. Ager (District Secretary of the AEU), H. Ayres (NUR), Charles Brett JP (Sheet Iron Workers), Councillor James Crump (area secretary T&GWU), George Geoboy (Workers' Union), Jabez Hall JP (Iron & Steel Confed.), Eldred Hallas (General & Municipal Workers), T.C. Pearson (Printing & Paper Workers), and C. Spragg (Building Trades Operatives). Deputies were allowed and several were used when members were otherwise engaged, including T. Hurley for Eldred Hallas who became ill early in the strike and died a month later. Two co-opted members were Chamberlain the *Town Crier* editor, and Allan Young the Birmingham Labour Party organiser.

This was the very moderate Emergency Committee which saw Birmingham through the General Strike. Only three had left-wing credentials, Cardinal the Communist, Stuart Barr of the NCLC, and

Rudland the Trades Council secretary. Most were decidedly right-wing, such as Councillor James Crump as his son, Jim Crump jnr, (a leading Birmingham Communist from the 1930s) never tired of explaining. Hallas was a renegade having been elected a Birmingham MP in 1918 on the Lloyd George National Democratic Labour coupon. But it must be said that despite its right-wing character, every one of the Emergency Committee worked devotedly throughout the Strike, all thought it was a victory when the strike was called off, and all denounced the ultimate sell-out.

This moderation was emphasised during the further proceedings of this meeting which finalised the Emergency Committee. W. Lewis of the printers, opposed the idea of using the *Daily Herald* as the organ of the TUC while the *Daily Mail* was closed down; Labour publicity must be secured on a voluntary basis, he maintained. No such scruples bothered Winston Churchill who used the facilities of the *Morning Post* to print the anti-strike *British Gazette* and many considered the refusal to use the *Daily Herald* as the organ of the Strike was one of the cardinal strategic errors of the campaign.

The meeting adjourned and reconvened later as the first meeting of the Birmingham Emergency Committee. This meeting raised the next essential matter after that of publicity. This was the issue of permits for food and other essentials to be moved. Hallas moved that this was such an important matter that it should be dealt with by the full Committee and not a sub-Committee. This was accepted and referred to the next meeting which was arranged for 2-30 pm the next day Tuesday 4th May.

The Nine Days of the General Strike

Day 1: Tuesday 4th May

The main primary sources for the conduct of the General Strike in Birmingham are the original minutes of the Emergency Committee (reprinted on the 50th anniversary of the Strike), the correspondence of the Birmingham Emergency Committee with the General Council of the TUC, the Cabinet Papers relating to the strike, and the various news bulletins and papers both pro- and anti-strike produced at the time. These will be dealt with for each day as far as possible.

The first staggering surprise to both trade unionists and the government on the first day of the strike was the total and absolute response of all the workers called out. The TUC strategy was to call out a 'first-line' of transport workers, printers, such productive trades that were large users of coal such as iron and steel and heavy chemicals, and building workers except those engaged on housing or hospitals. Electricity and gas unions were asked to withdraw men providing power (but not light). Sanitary and health services, hospitals, Poor Law institutions etc. were not to be affected and food supplies were not to be interfered with. If this were not sufficient to win the strike, a 'second line' would be called out later. On the first day not a bus, tram or train moved in Birmingham.

When the Emergency Committee met at 2-30pm on the first day they were overwhelmed with applications for permits to move food and this was the first item taken. A motion by Hallas that permits be issued only to trade union labour to transport and load and unload food was accepted. The resolution that the whole Emergency Committee should be responsible for issuing permits was immediately found impracticable, George Haynes was appointed Permit Officer, and left the meeting immediately to attend to his duties.

W.J. Chamberlain then reported that the stoppage in the printing trades was so complete that it was almost impossible to issue a Strike Bulletin as intended. (Chamberlain had been hoping to use the Leicester Co-operative press which printed the *Town Crier*). However, he had been assured that a short bulletin would be considered for broadcasting and he was given permission to draft one. Chamberlain was to draft several such bulletins for the BBC but John Reith took upon himself the role of government agent and nothing from the strikers' side was broadcast.

Some of the agenda dealt with tricky points of Permits e.g. moving of drainpipes on a Birmingham city project by union labour, but no guarantee that union Labour would move them from the station to the municipal depot; perishable goods being moved from the station; a request by the Corporation Electric Supply Building Department for permission to use 'a few Painters and Joiners'; a successful application to carry out some repair work at a factory which was 'out' in order to avoid a lengthy lay-off at the end of the strike, etc.

The rest of the Agenda dealt with other pressing problems. A delegate from the Wolverhampton Emergency Committee sought information and advice. This given, a Despatch Service was set up to liaise with the West Midlands. A delegate from the Woodworkers raised the question of a small number of workers being 'out' in a factory when most were working. This very common problem was avoided on this occasion by informing the delegate that his information was out of date and all were out. A deputation from the Foundry Workers stated that having come 'out', they had now received instructions from their union to return to work, and they had come to the Emergency Committee to explain the position and avoid any misunderstanding. The Committee agreed that there would be no recriminations. This cancellation had been ordered by the General Council and put the Foundry Workers' Union in the unwanted position of black legging on both the railway and steel workers because of confusion as to whether they were in the first line of workers called out.

The Cabinet papers gave a report of the Chief Constable of Birmingham to the Home Office at noon 3rd May stating that with regard to food supplies the Trades & Labour Council were taking control of the position and had set up a committee to consider applications for the handling of food; A sympathetic strike had started at the railway carriage works and local newspapers had been issued in Birmingham that day. This last item referred to the morning papers. There were to be no other normal papers until the end of the strike.

Day 2: Wednesday 5th May

On the second day of the strike the Emergency Committee met both in the morning and afternoon. By this time it was the inevitably confused situation in manufacturing industry and the role of the Emergency Committee which dominated the agenda. H. Dawson reported that with regard to the GEC the question was one of great seriousness. Confusion existed with regard to the interpretation of instructions. Some branch secretaries had given orders which violated instructions of the General Council. Dawson considered that the Emergency Committee was the responsible body and could not tolerate any local trade union official interfering. Councillor Ager said that there had not been interference, it was a legitimate mistake due to general instructions being acted upon and then subsequent instructions being received. Rudland questioned the policy of the General Council saying that the more general the strike the sooner it would be over. Treleaven defended the General Council stating that they were conserving financial resources. Councillor Crump thought the position would rectify itself as workers not on strike but affected by it became unemployed and reported to the Labour Exchange. To deal with this particular problem Hurley suggested that the unions concerned should get together to settle it. Thus was born the first of several industrial sub-Committees which co-operated with the Emergency Committee. But the Emergency Committee in this case used the specific General Council instruction that where some men were out all would be called out. This could conflict with specific instructions to unions, as we have seen with the Foundry Workers, and was a source of weakness throughout the strike.

A special problem was Cadbury's. They were (and are) a so-called 'good employer' and in their role as Liberals were active in urging a negotiated settlement throughout the strike. But their paternalism was strictly limited and they were ruthless in trying to break the strike on their own premises. As manufacturers of food they were early applicants for Permits, but a delegation of trade unionists from the works told the Emergency Committee that the Permit to move cocoa and chocolate should be revoked as they were delivering to well-known firms that were blacklegging. In addition they pointed out that the Administrative Staff were blacklegging in the Electrical Department. The chairman (Corrin) explained that the Permit had been granted with strict conditions which had now been violated. The Permit was withdrawn.

In a difficult position were the Builders. They first sent a deputation to the Emergency Committee pointing out that the Committee's definition of Housing was different from that used by the Building Trade Unions. They asked the Emergency Committee to alter its definition and allow repairs only to houses in receipt of the Wheatley or Chamberlain subsidies, mainly Council housing. The proposition was accepted.

The last question taken in the morning was that of factories where only one or two workers were on strike. Here it was decided that the union or unions concerned should consult with each other and use their own discretion. Obviously, the danger of victimisation was considerable where only a few workers were on strike.

The afternoon session was equally hectic. A letter from the Transport Group Joint Strike Committee (the second of the Emergency Committee's sub-Committees) requested a representative from the Transport & General Workers Union to act in conjunction with Haynes as a Food Permit Officer. More controversial Permits were discussed. Councillor Ager wanted to know what the position of his AEU members was now that a decision had been taken by the Vehicle Builders to call all their men out. G. Bowen was interviewed as to why this decision had been taken and said that Vehicle Building was allied to Transport and there was scarcely any alternative. It was agreed that these matters be discussed at the joint meeting of the Engineering Trades scheduled for that evening. The local Plumbers sent a deputation stating that the branch had agreed that their men should come out and seeking its endorsement by the Emergency Committee. This was agreed, except for plumbers at hospitals. Unions actively engaged in the strike were seeking representation on the Emergency Committee and such requests from both Woodworkers and Vehicle Builders were deferred. The question of unions in Utility Services was raised and, as with other 'trades', it was recommended that all unions involved should consult on matters of policy. Administrative matters dealt with at this afternoon session included arranging despatch riders, responsibility for distributing the national strike bulletin *British Worker,* and a sub-committee to arrange meetings.

Dunlop's was another of the 'paternal' employers causing concern. There had been no trade union organisation in the company until 1925 when strikes occurred over methods introduced to speed up production. Within a short time rubber workers and others joined the Transport & General Workers' Union and Ernest Bevin (the union's general secretary) took a personal interest in affairs at Port Dunlop. The firm had maintained that trade unionism was unnecessary as it operated a Factory Council; it even maintained that the strikes had been settled not by the intervention of the trade unions, but the Factory Council, even though the union had obtained eight delegates out of thirteen at elections to the Factory Council. Bevin said the union had no objection to the Factory Council, but he did not believe that any person, however clever, could secure justice by weight of argument alone, and negotiators must be economically independent and meet employers as equals. As might be expected under these circumstances, Hart of the Heating & Domestic Engineers reported to the Emergency Committee that the situation was developing 'chaotically' at Dunlops. Many of his own men had ceased work although they had instructions not to strike. The Carpenters & Joiners had been called out and the power-men were going to finish at the end of the shift. The Emergency Committee decided that the power workers be instructed to remain at work, and that communication be made with the firm to explain how the 'unfortunate position' had arisen.

Another key item arose from the fact that the Chief Constable, like the City council, despite their total opposition to the strike were obliged to negotiate with the strikers. Rafter sent Chief-Superintendent Burnett to the Emergency Committee to discuss co-operation to keep the peace and actions likely to create trouble. W.T. Cardinal pointed out that because of the size of the dispute there would be many more pickets than had ever been seen before. The Superintendent 'noted' the point. He also told of two men arrested in John Bright Street charged with intimidation. Later, the chairman and secretary of the Emergency Committee were deputed to look after all trade unionists in conflict with the police during the strike.

The first report from Birmingham to the TUC General Council was drafted at this meeting. It stated:

> Everything in Birmingham in regard to the stoppage is proceeding satisfactorily. The extent of the stoppage is much greater than anyone ever anticipated and all road, passenger and carrying traffic, both trams and buses has been stopped.
>
> Commercial road transport has, in practically all cases, responded loyally to the call. On the railways the stoppage is complete. Traffic locally and clerical staffs have unanimously answered the call.
>
> In the factories, the difficulty now is to keep people at work; all want to be out and in the fight.
>
> Newspapers have failed to appear and the well-known provincial organ in Birmingham this morning is

represented by a Roneo foolscap sheet. We are issuing daily bulletins; a complete chain of despatch riders is in operation, and the whole of the districts are kept acquainted with every development.

The Committees ordered by the Council have been set up and are doing their work in Birmingham. Birmingham has full confidence in the General Council; we accept their directions and await victory.

(signed) J.E. Corrin, Chairman.

Reports reaching the Cabinet dated 5th May included one from the Home Office stating that there were no serious disturbances in Birmingham, although some strikers had interfered with transport goods and passengers; that police protection had been given at Port Dunlop and a military guard had been asked for by Kynochs and BSA; the Communists were arranging to produce a newspaper. A report from the Engineering Employers' Federation the same day noted that Patternmakers had ceased work in Birmingham and it was anticipated that more AEU men would come out on the 6th.

The *Birmingham Mail* also published a broad sheet on Wednesday 5th May, and a pathetic effort it was – one single side of a Roneo sheet. One third of it was devoted to the national strike position. The second third dealt with the local situation and then there were a very few race results and two cricket scores. The sheet was attributed as being printed and published by Sir Charles Hyde, Bart. at 6 Cannon Street Birmingham. Hyde was the owner of the *Post* and *Mail* and virulently opposed to the strike. The local intelligence claimed that the situation in Birmingham had improved with emergency train services running. Midland Red had instituted services on the Londonderry-Hagley Rd. route but as a consequence of opposition they were withdrawn. Arrangements for the delivery of food were working satisfactorily; about 120 tons of fish had reached Birmingham by lorry, prices being about 20 per cent up. Response to the call for volunteers had been good, some firms offering batches of 20-50 employees. The Torchlight Tattoo was carrying on as usual and large numbers of charabancs were running to and from from Victoria Square to Station St. Motor drivers were urged to give lifts to foot passengers.

Day 3: Thursday 6th May

The Emergency Committee continued to meet twice a day. Each session dealt with controversial Permit applications and the morning session finalised the Emergency Committee's Permit Officers as George Haynes of the Bakers together with a Railwayman and a Transport Worker. The report of the Engineering Trades Advisory Committee held the previous evening was considered. It had recommended that union labour at the Austin, Lanchester, Wolseley, BSA and Daimler factories be called out to 'regularise the position.' This was accepted by the Emergency Committee. The next item raised the question of the relation of the Co-op movement with the strikers. The Co-operative Union, incensed by the remarks of the miners' leader Arthur Cook that the Co-ops were the third arm of the labour movement, had specifically distanced themselves from the General Strike. However, relations with the Birmingham Co-operative Society and the strikers were good, and permits to move food and even soap were readily granted. On this occasion a permit to move 1,000 tons of coal was granted. But a permit for a few men to carry out repairs to the Co-op dairy and bakery was refused. This did not prevent the Emergency Committee accepting the offer of the Co-op to take messengers as Co-op vehicles moved round the area. A final important matter at this session was a report from the Circulation Committee of the *British Worker*, the TUC paper printed on the *Daily Herald* press, that it would be sold through the normal newsagents.

Administrative matters dealt with at the afternoon session of the Emergency Committee included receiving instructions from the General Council; the preparation of a report by Stuart Barr and arrangements for it to be conveyed to London; preparation of another futile bulletin for the BBC, and the receipt of messages from towns such as Shrewsbury with information exchanged on the Birmingham position. With regard to the conduct of the Strike two further industrial sub-committees were set up, a Furniture Trades Advisory Committee and also a Public Utility Advisory. The existence of area Strike Committees was also revealed when the Aston Strike Committee brought up the question of indentured apprentices and the position at Lucas and the GEC. These matters were referred to the Engineering Advisory Committee. Further arrests were also dealt with. Five men arrested at Springhill claimed that thy were simply marching down the street in a group when police jumped out of a car and arrested them. Corrin, Rudland and Haynes were deputed to interview the chief constable on this matter.

The Cabinet Papers for the day show a report from the Chief Constable of Birmingham. He noted a considerable improvement in both main and local rail services. Good services of local charabancs were being maintained despite many attempts at obstructions. More men of the Electrical Trades Union were out, but normal conditions prevailed at the Corporation Power and Light Stations. The number of engineers and general workers coming out was increasing, but no factories were stopped. A second issue of the *Birmingham Worker* had been published by the Communists and 2,000 copies had been sold. No serious disturbances had occurred beyond attempts by men to interfere with vehicles and six men were in custody. There was no shortage of food and fuel; a train load of petrol was expected the next day and guards had been doubled. Liaison officers stated that the strikers were believed to be getting tired of the strike.

Day 4: Friday 7th May

The proceedings of the morning session of the Emergency Committee began with the reading of a 'wire' from the TUC. This authorised local committees to open negotiations with employers offering to 'supply light and power for such services as housing, street and shop lighting, social services to be maintained for food, bakeries, laundries, and domestic purposes.' The results were to be reported back to the TUC. To carry out these instructions the Emergency Committee referred the matter to its Electricity Supply Council consisting of delegates from the AEU, Workers' Union, General & Municipal Workers, ETU, T&G and Blacksmiths, but it is no wonder that the TUC was phoned as to the interpretation of its instructions. This item overlapped with another. This was an interview of W. Lewis with the City Electrical Engineer who would give no guarantee that only essential services would be provided with light and power. This information was to be sent to the TUC by Courier.

The report from the deputation to the police was heard and deemed unsatisfactory. It was therefore decided to appoint a delegation of Cardinal, Crump and Rudland to interview the Chief Magistrate of the City, the Labour Lord Mayor, Bowen.

A deputation from the Clerks at Cadbury's was heard and it was decided that they come in line with other workers there and strike.

Banking was discussed when a delegation from the Co-operative Society and the NUR discussed indemnities from the Emergency Committee for local payments made to strikers in the eventuality of cheques not arriving in time from the unions. This was a sore point with the Co-op Bank as in some districts there were still payments owing for money advanced for the 1921 Miners' Strike. It was agreed that the chairman and secretary should pledge on behalf of the Emergency Committee that, together with the NUR, they would 'in so far as it lay in their power', agree to such an indemnity and guarantee the payments.

Other business that morning revealed the existence of a Selly Oak Strike Committee; the granting of a Permit for a theatrical company to move to Manchester; and agreement that a member of the editorial staff should sit on the Emergency Committee to facilitate the approval and production of Strike Bulletins.

At the afternoon session that representative, Oswald Mosley, was already present. The first item on the agenda was taxi and passenger transport. Parkes, the organiser of the Transport Workers urged drastic action such as stopping the supply of petrol. This was not thought possible, but would be raised at the meeting with the Lord Mayor.

Confusion with regard to instructions in the Building Trades was raised and a Building Trades Advisory Committee set up. In the meantime, the decision that Plumbers remain on strike was endorsed. There were also problems with ETU members at Aston. In the case of Verity's it was decided that this was a purely union matter and referred to the ETU but at Moss Gears the men should remain out. A call from the Stirchley Joint Strike Committee asking the Emergency Committee to call out all foremen members at factories on strike brought the reply that this would have to be dealt with by each separate union.

Publicity was discussed. T.C. Pearson complained that he had only been able to obtain 70 quires of the TUC paper the *British Worker* the previous day and the demand was much greater than the supply. Walsall was also having supply problems and when Whiston came to Birmingham to seek the help of the Emergency Committee he was referred to T.C. Pearson and his sub-Committee. Statements for the BBC were still being prepared and one from Strachey was amended and approved. Speakers were coming from London for the week-end demonstrations and the TUC asked Birmingham to supply transport from Rugby.

A deputation from the Clergy, led by the rector Rev Leyton Richards, was received by the Emergency Committee. It reported that clergymen and ministers from all denominations in the area had met and declared their conviction that nothing but harm could come from prolonged industrial strife. It called on the government to resume negotiations for a settlement on the basis of the strike being called off if Lock-out notices of the coal owners were withdrawn and the subsidy resumed 'for a shorter or longer period.' They would do all they could for peace, they asserted. No reply is recorded by the Emergency Committee, but it would have approved, as these were the very points on which the Government had broken off negotiations.

Finally, during this afternoon session, Rudland and Cardinal had left for their meeting with the Lord Mayor. It could not have been a very long one, for they were back in time to present the results to the Emergency Committee. He was powerless, the Lord Mayor said. The position was outside his jurisdiction. Under the Emergency Powers Act nine-tenths of their power had been taken away, and with regard to the Police, the Home Office was in control.

The Birmingham report to the TUC on the 7th May read as follows:

> We are pleased to be able to report in the Birmingham district solidarity is being well maintained. No trams or buses are running. All railwaymen, including traffic and goods staff, locomotive men and firemen, and the particularly pleasing feature of the Railway Clerks' Association, are all out. Newspaper have failed to appear in Birmingham: do not accept statements which have appeared to the contrary. Birmingham's well-known organs are simply represented by typewritten Sheets. Slight disturbances have taken place; mainly due to the unjustified and autocratic attitude of the police. These matters are being seriously taken up with the authorities and the Trade Union Committee is determined that matters shall not get out of hand. Industrial paralysis is spreading, and on every hand, the workers are welcoming the fact that the time is coming for them to come into line. Difficulty is being experienced at the moment to keep the development of the dispute in line with the instructions of the General Council, because of the over-anxiety of the workers to be in the fight. Meetings are being held in all localities. A magnificent spirit is being displayed, and arrangements are being made for a monster demonstration on Sunday in Calthorpe Park at 3.0pm.

In London, the Cabinet received a Home Office report dated 7th May which gave a Birmingham City Police Report. This stated that there had been an improvement in main line and local services and a good number of men were returning to work. No trains or buses were running but a good charabanc service was being maintained. The number of engineers and general workers striking was increasing, mostly from the AEU. There had been no disorders. Eight men had been arrested yesterday for intimidation and destruction of vehicular traffic and fined £5 each. Two railway pickets had been fined £3 each. There was no shortage of food or petrol and no attempt had been made to interfere with the transport of food by road. Recruiting of specials was good.

Day 5: Saturday 8th May

The week-end brought no respite for the Emergency Committee and it met twice on both Saturday and Sunday. The Saturday morning session was attended by the two main speakers for the Sunday demonstration, Morgan Jones MP and Mrs Adamson. Jones explained that they were sent officially from the TUC, but the idea had originated from a meeting of the Parliamentary Labour Party which had decided that members of parliament would be better employed by going out to the regions than continuing their Parliamentary duties. Forty or fifty MPs had then been placed at the disposal of the TUC. Cardinal, who was in the chair in the absence of Corrin, welcomed the guests, handed them over to the Propaganda Organiser and a Co-op car was placed at their disposal.

Police provocation was the next item dealt with. The headquarters of the Communist Party at Hockley Hill had been raided and five Communist trade unionists (Tom Lowe, Jim Gardner, Miss

Clarke, T. Gee and Eskell) had been arrested. It was agreed that the case be referred to a solicitor, Mr Bickley, and the Emergency Committee accept responsibility for the bail and defence. The next provocation had been the starting of a small bus service by the Fascists with the co-operation of the police. This was referred to the TUC with a recommendation that action be taken by the TUC to withdraw power.

Rumblings of the problems at Cadbury's surfaced when a deputation from the East Staff Branch at Bournville of the Shop Assistants, Warehousemen and Clerks together with the Stirchley Strike Committee wanted to know if the decision to bring out the clerks at Cadbury's had been endorsed by the TUC. Mr Chapel of the Stirchley Strike Committee stated that the Clerks' official had received instructions from Head Office that his members should not be brought out. It was agreed that attempts be made to contact the TUC, that in the meantime the strike decision should stand, and that there should be a meeting at Cadbury's that afternoon to explain the situation.

Problems with regard to carrying of food by the Co-op had arisen and it was agreed that Cardinal and a representative of the Co-op should interview the TUC with regard to the matter.

The statement regarding the renewal of negotiations submitted the previous day by the delegation of Clergymen and Ministers had also been made nationally headed by the Archbishop of Canterbury and it was agreed that the Lord Mayor be approached to place the matter before the Birmingham City Council.

The afternoon session of the Emergency Committee began with a deputation from the Central Ironmoulders on the position of their men who were on strike but who had now been ordered back to work by their union. They wanted their union's decision to be ignored and the strike action endorsed by the Emergency Committee. This was agreed, the action of the men in coming out being in accordance with TUC instructions. A letter was also read from the Gas Fitters and Allied Workers calling on the TUC to extend the strike by calling out all men engaged in the production of all power used for industrial purposes.

It was also reported that the Co-op problems had been solved by their representatives in direct talks with the TUC; but it was still resolved that Cardinal, with Mann, should seek an interview with the TUC to raise several questions needing attention.

More police provocation was reported by Treleaven at New Street – the police using sticks and kicking men without provocation.

Finally, it was decided to instruct all Area Strike Committees to continue to arrange entertainments, sports etc. for men and women on strike.

The Home Office report for the 8th May stated that a Corporation bus service started that morning run by volunteers from Hagley to the centre of the city was working smoothly with protection. The *Birmingham Post* had been issued that morning with 14 columns of print. Over 233,000 copies had been sold as far afield as Shrewsbury and Leamington. Communists Headquarters had been raided and persons were found printing the fourth number of the *Birmingham Worker*. The printing equipment and printed copies had been seized. There was a great demand for and shortage of the *British Gazette*. 50 drivers of Allied Transport Ltd and 600 workers at Cadbury's had returned to work. Main and local railway services were improving.

Day 6: Sunday 9th May

The Sunday morning session of the Emergency Committee heard a report from its Building Trades Advisory Committee stating that the TUC had handed over the conduct of the dispute to the Building Trades Federation. A resolution was passed agreeing that the status quo (i.e the men remain out) be maintained until Monday afternoon when the Advisory Committee would meet. The arrangements for picketing by various societies were approved and a Co-op charabanc had been arranged to pick up pickets for the Austin; other unions were welcome to use it.

Police provocation was becoming serious. It was agreed that all provocative actions by the police should be recorded so that the Home Office could be pressed for an enquiry after the strike. For the present it was agreed that complaints against the police should be handed to the Emergency Committee with copies for the Lord Mayor and the TUC. In addition the Chief Constable was to be asked to remove one particularly obnoxious constable deliberately provoking trouble. The Lord Mayor was also to be asked to convene a meeting of magistrates. It was suggested that a government notice posted all over the City ought to be counteracted by a poster from the Emergency Committee, but no action was taken. (This was probably the Chief Constable's notice of 7 May stating that under the Emergency Powers Act it was an offence punishable with three months imprisonment with hard labour and £100 fine, or both, to prevent the working of any public building, railway, passenger vehicle, factory, electric generating station etc. – GB).

Corrin reported on a meeting at Cadbury's the previous afternoon. Strikers were suffering from fears of intimidation, he asserted. At a Transport Workers meeting 18 had voted to go back to work and 7 to meet him on Monday morning. Sheet Metal Workers were fairly solid and the ETU solid; all other workers at Cadbury's were wavering.

In the afternoon all were at the Demonstration and the Emergency Committee reconvened at 7pm. A report of the demonstration was given by Corrin who spoke of the magnificent crowds and wonderful contingents. 20,000 people attended the rally which was completely peaceful, although the police took exception to remarks by Councillor Percy Shurmer and he was arrested.

A report was given by Cardinal and Mann of their meeting with the TUC. They had received some instructions on the electricity question. With regard to engineering this was to be the second line of attack and definite instructions could be anticipated immediately. With regard to unlicensed vehicles the TUC suggested that the men keep cool, as this could not very materially affect the strike. The police had also been discussed and the TUC agreed that under the Emergency Powers Acts the powers of local authorities had been curtailed. Cardinal and Mann had raised the question of another meeting with the TUC regarding the appointing of a deputy Emergency Committee in view of the probability of some members of the present Committee being arrested.

Cardinal and Mann had also taken advantage of their visit to London to interview the national Permits Committee at Unity House. Definite instructions would be conveyed to the Birmingham Permits Committee; the opinion of the national Permits Committee was that the government should be responsible for the bulk movement of food and local permits would not be necessary. With regard to daily deliveries of bread and milk these men were to be treated in the same way as shop assistants. These were most serious abdications of the powers of the TUC to pursue the General Strike. But this was not the only item of bad news, for the last item discussed at the Sunday evening session was a weakening of the local situation.

This was a report that the strike at Cadbury's had collapsed. In the Manufacturing and Distributive divisions of the firm, the workers, represented by the Workers' Union and the Shop Assistants, Warehousemen and Clerks were to return to work on Monday. The reasons for this were various. Rumours of another department starting work had broken the spirit of the strikers, but the active support of the Departmental Chiefs on behalf of the firm had been a determining factor. The delegation of six from the factory requested the advice of the Emergency Committee on this matter. During the discussion a letter was received from Mr Elvin, general secretary of the NUC, advising Mr Summers at Bournville that all NUC members should be withdrawn. The Emergency Committee stated that it was with regret that they heard of the capitulation at Cadbury's but they could not recognise the return to work; when the dispute was over the matter would have to have very full and careful attention.

The Sunday report to the Cabinet dealt with the following items. Despite the police raid on the Headquarters of the Communist Party on Friday a further number of the *Birmingham Worker* had appeared that day. The *Sunday Mercury* had published an eight-page paper. The attendance at Calthorpe Park was put at 10,000. The four minute bus service from Harborne under police protection was still running. Corporation tram and bus inspectors had agreed to report for work on Monday. The Corporation now had sufficient skilled volunteers to maintain all services including gas and electricity, if necessary. Councillor Sawyer, a railway guard and member of the Watch Committee, had been arrested for saying at a public meeting that the Special Constabulary was 'nothing more than a body of traitors.'

Day 7: Monday 10th May

The morning session of the Emergency Committee dealt with the usual routine matters – complicated Permit issues, reports received from outside districts (in this case Bristol, Worcester and Cardiff, all reporting the situation satisfactory), and various letters from union branches being passed to the appropriate sub-Committee.

Problems persisted with publicity. Six cars were requested to attend at 110 John Bright Street at 7am to collect the *British Worker*.

Two offers of recreational premises were accepted. The first from the Rev Leyton Richards offered Digbeth; publicity for this was to be published in a Bulletin. The other was the offer of the Clarion Club which was accepted and notified to the Yardley Strike Committee.

There were two calls to extend the strike. One, from the Saltley Strike Committee demanded action from the TUC to cut off 'pressure supplies' to the BBC. The Workers' Union also requested the withdrawal of power in Birmingham because some trams were running. This was referred to the Engineering Advisory Committee.

Picketing was discussed and at last the Labour Lord Mayor was proving useful. A letter from him stated that pickets would be allowed to carry out their legal duties and those cleared from Tenant Street would be allowed to return. He asked that details of any future infringements of pickets' rights should be reported to him.

Finally the Transport Group Joint Strike Committee reported that workers who refused to take jobs on the railways during the Strike were having their unemployment pay stopped. This was referred to Mr Dalley, the manager of the Unemployment Exchange.

The morning session of the Emergency Committee had seen a number of members unavoidably absent. The afternoon session was better attended and more decisive. Questions of black leg labour were again raised. Mr Taylor of the UPW wanted protests to be made to the Postmaster General on labour being used to blackleg on the railwaymen by carrying mail long distances. This was referred to both the local and the national Transport Committees and a protest sent to the Postmaster General.

Harry Shepperson reported on the case of the five Communist trade unionists whose case had come up that morning and was adjourned until Friday. Also on police provocation Councillor Shurmer was asked to procure particulars of the cases that had occurred in Calthorpe Park.

The manager of the Labour Exchange came to the Committee to say that there was no truth in the report that Unemployment Pay was being refused to workers who refused to blackleg on the strike. All people being offered jobs would be informed that a dispute was in progress and they were entitled to refuse to accept the job. Dalley had been a leading member of the Labour movement but that was no guarantee that his subordinates were not violating the law on this matter.

Pointers to the intensification of the Strike were offers of clerical assistance from the Railway Clerks' Association and the offer of the use of an Oliver typewriter which was accepted with thanks. The Birmingham ILP also raised the question of stewards at all meetings. Cardinal proposed that all future meetings be guarded by stewards to keep clear of trouble. This was accepted and also an Organisation sub-Committee was set up consisting of Cardinal, Hall, Haynes and Treleavan.

But this was the day when the second line was being called out by the TUC and this was the item that dominated the agenda. The session began with a telegram from Ernest Bevin stating that all men engaged in transport were now to be called out except Co-operative bread and milk men. Then it was agreed that the local Engineering Advisory Committee hold a special and urgent meeting later that afternoon to consider the implications of the TUC call out of the engineers. Ager stated that an earlier EAC meeting had requested that the Emergency Committee agree to immediate instructions being issued in the following terms:

> Industrial Crisis; Engineering Section.
>
> Definite instructions have been issued by Trades Union Congress General Council that all men engaged in Engineering and Ship Building shall, unless otherwise ordered. refrain from starting work on Wednesday 12th May. This applies to all Unions.

This statement was to be signed by the officials of all unions concerned and issued to the members of these unions. The resolution covered the motor and cycle industries, but Corporation workers were to remain at work.

The resolution was moved by Cardinal and accepted by the Emergency Committee. All the signs were that a successful extension of the strike would take place; a despatch from the TUC was read stating that 'in the vital services the Movement is being strengthened daily'; reports from other districts read that afternoon showed Leamington and Cheltenham 'satisfactory' and Rugby 'splendid'; from Gloucester it was stated that at Gloucester Aircraft they were 'out to a man.'

By the late afternoon, the *Birmingham Strike Bulletin* for May 11th was on the streets. It included the following item:

Government defeated in Parliament.

Tom Johnson MP for Dundee, in the House of Commons moved the deletion of the regulations providing for the arrest without warrant for certain acts.

The motion was carried by 316 to 75. Keep strong now and we will win through.

The implausibility of such a defeat in Parliament and the use the Government might make of it led the Emergency Committee to pass the following motion. 'It was agreed to get in touch with Unity House as to the authenticity of the statement re Government Defeat.'

The Home Office report to the Cabinet for Monday May 19th stated that the Midland Division was generally quiet with a few arrests for stone throwing in Birmingham. At Birmingham two houses had been raided under Regulation 33 and were being searched. They were occupied by persons who had been publishing false news such as 'Government defeated in Parliament.' There were also six remands of persons arrested for seditious publication. Tramwaymen were steadily returning and trams had begun on several routes that day. Buses were being run by volunteers, but a number of bus drivers had offered to return. Engineers at the General Electric Company went back that morning, but the men were being called out that night from the Corporation power works. Dunlop's had reopened that night and more strikers had returned at Cadbury's.

Day 8: Tuesday 11th May

When the morning session of the Emergency Committee began the first item was to discuss the fact that all its members had been arrested the previous afternoon. Corrin stated that he had been called out of the room and told that the police were in charge at 180 Corporation Street (the HQ of the Birmingham Labour Party) where the *Birmingham Strike Bulletin* was published. Stuart Barr, Rudland and he then went to 180 and found that the machinery had been dismantled and all copies of the *Bulletin* confiscated. Later the police raided 262 Corporation Street (the HQ of the Trades Council where the Emergency Committee met). Inspector Burnett said that the statement regarding the Government defeat was untrue and he had instructions to arrest the Emergency Committee who were to report to his office at 11am on Tuesday. This the Committee did and were charged. Corrin stated that although a sub-committee produced the Bulletin, the Emergency Committee took full responsibility for it.

Allan Young in explaining how the offending item had come to appear stated that confirmation of it had come from Charles Sitch at Stourbridge. Oswald Mosley thought that Tom Johnstone had probably brought forward a motion in Parliament, but the figures had been transposed; he would ascertain whether this was the case. It was agreed that no blame be attached to the Bulletin staff.

In regard to defence, Rudland said that the Emergency Committee was due to meet Mr Ladd, solicitor, at 7pm with Mosley and Strachey in attendance. Cardinal moved that the Bulletin be issued that day in the name of the Emergency Committee; this was agreed. Auger of the Railwaymen's Joint Strike Committee then revealed that they had received the news of the Government defeat from Coventry, who had received it from the *Cricklewood Workers' Gazette*. Corrin then suggested an announcement in the next *Bulletin* regarding the Government defeat, but that it first be shown to a solicitor. This was agreed.

The afternoon session of the Emergency Committee began as usual at 2-30pm. Complaints regarding delays in telegrams and phone calls were discussed with the Postal Workers and taken up with the TUC.

The key question of electrical workers at the three big power stations was discussed. The management had requested 24 hours notice of strike action whereas the TUC notice was for immediate action. It was agreed that the strongest possible picket line be mounted at Summer Lane, Nechells and Dale End that evening and the next day.

Parry for the tramwaymen reported that these men had been threatened with the loss of their jobs if they did not report for work the following day and it was quite likely that they would all return. Parry asked whether the power supply was likely to be cut off in support of the tramwaymen. He was given a copy of the instructions issued to workers in electrical undertakings. Ager raised the question of some brass workers still working and this was referred to the Brassworkers' Union.

A report on the position in Birmingham was given to a courier who had been sent by the TUC and it was agreed that a further report the next day be sent through Dr Tucker of the TUC who had come from London to Newcastle and reported the situation 'satisfactory' in all the towns he passed through.

Mrs Fawcett met the Committee to discuss ways in which women could aid the strike. She suggested that women be represented on the Emergency Committee, that a Central Committee of Women be formed to co-ordinate work of the various districts, that women be used for propaganda purposes, assistance at social evenings etc. It was agreed to consider these proposals alongside the report of the Organisation Committee.

Cardinal next presented the Organisation Committee's report. The appointment of an Interview Committee, a Vigilance Committee and a Propaganda Sub-Committee was suggested and agreed. A deputy Emergency Committee was then appointed, 'in the event of the present Committee being put out of action.'

On May 11th there were three representatives of the TUC (W.A. Robson, J. Wedgwood and Martin Kingsley) independently reporting on the situation in Birmingham. They sent two reports to the TUC. The first mainly concerned Cadbury's. They had met George Cadbury junior and other members of the Cadbury family. It was explained that many of the strikers had returned to work and most of the girls had never come out. The engineers were still on strike but Cadbury thought the strike would peter out. It was agreed that there should be no victimisation. On the wider aspects of the position, the Cadbury family was most anxious to assist in rallying moderate opinion on the lines of the Archbishop's appeal or the Newcastle Resolution (where the local Council, the bulk of whom were businessmen, had declared in favour of negotiations). The delegation then saw the Town Clerk and the Lord Mayor. Both of these were moderates and anxious for peace, but there was no possibility of getting a resolution on the Newcastle lines through the Birmingham council of businessmen; the employers were determined to resist the strike and fight to the end led by the Chamber of Commerce and the Engineering Employers' Association, the Lord Mayor stated. The *British Worker* was on sale in the streets, the delegation reported, together with the *Post* and *Mail* and *Gazette*, the latter very moderate in tone compared with the others; also the *British Gazette* was available.

The TUC delegation's second report dealt with the arrest of the Emergency Committee suggesting that 'the local police appear to have been somewhat embarrassed at having to make the arrests.' With regard to the numbers on strike they could give no estimate, partly because the Emergency Committee was occupied at the Law Courts and secondly because the second line were not due to strike until the next day. Oswald Mosley said, however, that Birmingham was 'astonishingly solid', and from others at HQ 'naturally anxious to stress the hopeful side', they gathered that this was the general view. But it was admitted that the case of the tramwaymen was difficult and they had problems with getting the electricians out, partly 'because they were under contract to give seven days notice', although Mosley was addressing a meeting that evening where he hoped to 'swing them over.'

The Cabinet received a Ministry of Labour report on the 11th. May which read as follows:

No sign at present of any break. The temperature, however, is much lower and the confidence shown earlier by the strikers is less marked. This is due to several causes. The men see trams, buses and trains running... and they are very dissatisfied as to the position of the AEU and the T&GWU some of whom are out and others still working. They think the TUC have some more cards to play and want to see the strike extended to gas and power. Unless there is something more done men will start to dribble back towards the end of the week, especially in the transport trades.

The strikers realise now that they must lose, but the local officials tell them that they have really won, as the mass support given when the general strike was called shows that the whole trade union movement is solidly on the side of the miners. They feel now that if the men now working are asked to come out there would not be the same response.

The Prime Minister's week-end speech is having a marked effect in the Midlands. People are remarking on his statement that if the general strike is called off there is no reason why negotiations on the coal question should not be brought to a satisfactory conclusion.

Day 9: Wednesday 12th May

At the morning session no one knew that this was to be the last day of the strike, and the routine business of the Emergency Committee went ahead. It was agreed that someone from 180 Corporation Street should attend the Vigilance Committee. A proposal that the TUC be asked to equalise Strike Pay for all those in trade unions which were unable to pay according to rules, was agreed. Cardinal reported that Co-op transport men had unanimously decided to remain at work; a meeting with McDowell of the Co-op was taking place at 12-30pm and he would report back the result. Cardinal also suggested that the matter then be left with the TUC who would be informed through a special courier that night. Mann then suggested that all permits be withdrawn except for bread and milk; this was agreed.

With regard to electrical workers Hurley reported that Swan, the chairman of the joint industrial council, had circularised all electricity workers requiring 7 days notice before striking and Dale End workers had agreed not to come out. Hurley reported, however, that all ETU men in Coventry were out.

A letter and resolutions were received from Aston Strike Committee. The letter reported intimidation of Workers' Union members at GEC; no action was taken. We are not told what was in the resolutions, but no action was taken on them either.

Finally a communication was received from Mr Summers, midlands organiser of the National Union of Clerks re. Cadbury's. It was agreed that a report be sent to the TUC regretting that Elvin, the national secretary, had changed his instructions and again ordered the Cadbury clerical workers back to work.

When the afternoon session of the Emergency Committee began, Rudland reported the calling off of the General Strike. This had come from reliable sources – Trade Union head offices etc. But it was agreed that communication be made with the TUC direct, and a sub-committee of Corrin, Rudland and Cardinal was set up to receive the official TUC communication.

It was then agreed that the Emergency Committee remain in being to deal with possible victimisation of men and unions.

The Chairman (Corrin) next moved that a Victory Celebration be arranged for the following Sunday in Summerfield Park and that the Printers' Union be approached to prepare a Victory Bulletin. Corrin thanked the members of the Emergency Committee for their co-operation and hoped the Committee would continue to exist after the strike. These thanks were extended to the political side of the movement. 'The comradeship displayed had been remarkable.' Special appreciation was then made of the work of Corrin, Rudland, Cardinal and Stuart Barr (Minutes Secretary). The meeting closed with agreement to re-convene the next morning.

The Birmingham Emergency Committee report dated 12th May to the TUC was written before the Strike was called off and summarises the position that morning:

> ...Owing to the wire sent by you re. the position of electrical workers not arriving at all, the position here was made exceedingly difficult and though everything has been done since the weekend we have been unable to secure anything like a complete withdrawal of labour. In the meantime the tram and busmen have shown signs of wavering and owing to an ultimatum issued by the authorities asking for a return of uniforms etc. many of the men have reported back for duty, and indeed this morning the tramway service has been restarted on a fairly extensive scale. The key industries however are still standing firm and the Emergency Committee is confident that despite the possible effect on the 'morale' of the men the position is very satisfactory...

Facts in relation to the arrest of the Strike Committee will be found in Strike Bulletin No.7 herewith enclosed. The full Committee comes up for trial on Friday next and are at present out on bail on securities of £20 each...

The Home Office report to the Cabinet for 12th May was written after the strike had been called off and is therefore, understandably, brief:

Little information is available as yet to the effect of calling off the strike. In Birmingham strikers generally assume that they will return at once, but are waiting definite instructions from their unions.

Engineers. In Birmingham about 1,700 struck this morning, but 120 already on strike returned. The electrical engineers in the Corporation power works decided last night to strike but stayed at work after all.

The Long End to the Strike

The General Strike was called off by the General Council of the TUC about midday on May 12th. For political leaders such as Ramsay MacDonald, and trade union leaders such as J.H. Thomas, the strike was a disaster which should never have occurred and their main aim was to end it as soon as possible. Once the government broke off negotiations and the strike was on, a compromise could only be arranged through a third party. Such a person appeared on the fourth day of the strike when Sir Herbert Samuel, chairman of the recent Royal Commission on the Coal Industry, returned from Italy and offered himself to Baldwin as a mediator. He was told that anything he negotiated would be unofficial and could not bind the government. Nevertheless Samuel contacted J.H. Thomas and secret negotiations were conducted at the house of Thomas's friend Sir Abe Bailey, the South African mining magnate; the miners were not told. On 10 May an agreed draft of Samuel's recommendations, which included wage cuts, was put to the miners who refused to accept them. It was a slightly modified version of this document that the Negotiating Committee put to the General Council. They were all too ready to believe that proposals which the government had no intention of implementing and which were unacceptable to the miners were sufficient guarantees to call off the strike. It was not even peace with honour, it was unconditional surrender. Nor did these surrender terms include any guarantees against victimisation of strikers or the withdrawal of lock-out notices for the miners. The result was that strikers were obliged to rely on the local organisations they had built up during the strike. Nationally, there were more men on strike on the first day of peace than there had been on the last day of the strike.

In Birmingham, the Emergency Committee met in morning session as usual on Thursday 13th May. The first business was arrangements for Sunday's demonstration, which it was agreed would be called in the name of the Trades & Labour Council and not in the name of the Emergency Committee. Then came reports of victimisation of strikers: Avery's had written a letter to all employees terminating their employment and stating that individual applications must be made for renewal of employment. A similar letter had been issued by Tangye's and it was decided to send a deputation to the Engineering Employers' Federation on this matter. Corporation Departments were making similar demands and a deputation was arranged to see the Lord Mayor. Some unions were dealing with victimisation at a national level, including Printers and Railwaymen. The third item on the morning agenda was arrangements for the defence of the Emergency Committee at the following day's prosecution. Lastly a telegraphic report to the TUC was agreed giving the position in Birmingham and seeking advice.

The afternoon session was occupied almost entirely with victimisation reports. The delegation which had interviewed the Lord Mayor reported that the Tramway Department was 'taking a very serious view of the action of members of the T&GWU' and would discuss the matter at a meeting of the Tramway Committee the following Tuesday. Cardinal had replied by stating that the deputation were not there as supplicants and unless the Department was prepared to act honourably there was the possibility of guerrilla warfare. By now some workers were back on strike; Vehicle Builders at Kyott's Lake Road working for the Tramways Department had gone into work at 12 noon and came out after working only one hour. The men had been told that they must make individual application to return to work and this they absolutely refused to do. There was a report from the Engineering

Employers' Federations stating that there would be no victimisation, but it would take some time to absorb everybody. No vindictiveness would be shown to any individual. This report was accepted as was a proposal that all engineering cases be handled by the Engineering Advisory Committee. Finally a telegram was received from the TUC stating that strikers must be reinstated on the basis of complete maintenance of wages and conditions operating before the strike; otherwise strikers should not resume work.

The last Home Office report to the Cabinet of 13th May dealt mainly with the problems of the return to work:

> Railwaymen at Birmingham and elsewhere have decided not to go back to work except on the basis of the status quo. They object to signing GWR notices that they are not relieved of consequences of having broken their contracts, and at Birmingham a resolution was passed that they should not return to duty till the notices are withdrawn.

> Dunlop Rubber Company's men at Birmingham reported for work but were told that the Company was not yet ready for them. 400 BSA engineers applied to return and were referred to the Labour Bureau; they declined to go there and demanded reinstatement at old rates of pay.

On the morning of Friday May 14th the Emergency Committee was in court. The Committee met in the afternoon when it was reported that ten leading members had been fined £10 each – Corrin, Cardinal, Rudland, Dawson, Crump, Barr, Ayres, Young, Strachey, and Plummer. Eight were bound over for six months – Ager, Brett, Geobey, Hall, Haynes, Treleaven, Spragg and Mann. Pearson and Lewis were discharged. This was a very different result from what could have been expected if the strike had still been on. The question of whether there should be an appeal against these sentences was raised and the matter left with Oswald Mosley to take soundings with KCs in London. The meeting also heard the result of the Birmingham Communists' trial. Gardner had been fined £10 and the others fined £5; again very light sentences, especially for Communists.

The Emergency Committee met on Saturday morning and twice on Monday. These sessions were mainly taken up with receiving information from Mosley and discussion of a possible appeal.

The last meeting of the Emergency Committee took place on Tuesday May 18th. Its main business was to take a decision with regard to an appeal. A letter was read from Mosley stating that Counsel had 'distinctly advised' against an appeal and intimated that they would be 'let down by any barrister in the circumstances'. After discussion it was agreed on a motion put by Cardinal and seconded by Mann that no appeal be made. On the question of raising the money to pay the fines, it was decided to apply to individual unions, but the matter was referred to the Trades Council meeting taking place that evening. In this way the Emergency Committee disappeared back into the organisation that created it.

Victimisation had been the main issue facing workers after the strike and both the WEA booklet *The Nine Days in Birmingham* and Paul Hastings deal with other cases not discussed above. There were some notable individual cases. Councillor G.F. Sawyer, Watch Committee member and Poor Law Guardian arrested for calling all special constables 'traitors' had his case dropped but was not allowed back on the railway until a week after others had been taken back. Another railwayman, H. Ayres a foreman goods supervisor with 30 years unblemished service with the LMS was sacked and was eventually reinstated only by the personal intervention of J.H. Thomas the NUR secretary. F.W. Rudland, secretary of the Trades Council and the Emergency Committee, was deprived of his magisterial appointment. Two people suffered permanent victimisation. Councillor Percy Shurmer, a Post Office engineer was dismissed after a £10 fine for 'inflammatory speeches.' It took him six months to find alternative work – with the Co-op. Margaret Clarke, a part-time teacher at Bourneville Day Continuation School was dismissed for her part in the production of the Communist *Birmingham Worker*. Despite a petition from her students denying knowledge of her politics. She was sacked by the Education Department because 'she had made no expression of regret for her acts or views,' when she came before the Education Committee.

There were a number of verdicts on the the strike. Speakers at the post-strike Victory Rally in Summerfield Park where 5,000 listened to speakers from three platforms naturally stressed the achievements of the strike. Oswald Mosley said that they celebrated the workers' victory. With one hand tied behind their backs they had whipped the Government. They were celebrating one of the greatest events in the history of the world. They had used only their industrial power, and not all of that. What could they not do if they used both industrial and political power? J.E. Corrin's view was that the workers had no cause to regret the steps they had taken. They had compelled the Government to reopen negotiations.

By May 21st W.J. Chamberlain had had time to reflect on events and reviewed the course of the strike in the *Town Crier*. He thought that it would take some time to draw conclusions that could be profitably used in the future, but he had received many letters giving various views as to how a future General Strike should be conducted and his own view was that:

> ...we have seen the first and last General Strike in this country for at least a generation. Not that I believe the strike was a failure. On the contrary, I believe the amazing success of the strike will make it unnecessary in the future. The powers that be have been taught a lesson which they will not soon forget. There may be occasions in the future when it may be necessary to threaten a General Strike – to stop a war for instance. But if such an occasion should arise, the threat will be enough to curb the maddest die hard or war-monger.

This was the verdict of a moderate socialist, anti-Communist, pacifist, and conscientious objector of World War 1.

The other main verdict came from the 1927 annual report of the Trades Council:

The year under review will be long remembered for the heroic struggle of the Miners against the Mine-owners and Government in their combined attempt still further to depress the standard of life of all those in the mining industry. Still more memorable was the remarkable response by the rank and file of other great industries when the call came to demonstrate in a practical fashion their sympathy with the miners. Coming as it did at a trying and exhausting period for most of the Trade Unions, with weakened membership and depleted funds, the most optimistic must have had grave doubts as to what extent the call would be obeyed. With practically everything at stake, and asking nothing for themselves, the magnitude of the response was akin to the miraculous...

The spirit of malignity and materialism, the natural product of the late war, had for a time possessed many, and one despaired of ever again witnessing any manifestation of loyalty to great principles or recognition of the holy bonds of universal brother-hood. Whatever the outcome of the immediate object in view, the response was superb. It...revealed to us our tremendous power once united, and constituted a grave warning to any Government or set of employers who try the patience of the people too far.

What could have been

The General Strike is the most important episode of the British trade union movement. It is unique also in world trade union history. It will therefore always be studied. Two basic questions to be addressed are firstly, was the Samuel Memorandum a sufficient reason to end the strike, and secondly, whether the forces at the end of the strike were sufficient to have carried the strike forward. The motives of those who called off the strike were various. There were those, led by J.H. Thomas and Ramsay MacDonald, who never wanted the strike and sought any excuse to call it off. Others, who were frightened that the strike was 'getting into the wrong hands', joined them. This view was well expressed by Charles Dukes, secretary of the General & Municipal Workers speaking in January 1927 at a Conference of Trade Union Executives:

> ...every day that the strike proceeded control and authority was passing out of the hands of responsible executives into the hands of men who had no authority, no responsibility...

Others convinced themselves that the settlement guaranteed negotiations re-starting more or less at the point they had reached before the strike began. Others knew that if the strike proceeded it would inevitably be 'politicised'. Others, no doubt, believed that the strike had reached its limit. Such diversity of views came together to call the strike off with the same unanimity that had agreed to start it. Clearly, in retrospect, the Samuel Memorandum was totally inadequate as a basis for the settlement of the strike, as the miners, who rejected it, realised. The settlement was clearly a betrayal of the miners.

Whether the settlement was also a betrayal of the General Strike depends on the answer to the second question of what was the balance of forces when the strike was called off on May 12th. We can begin by comparing the contrasting objectives of the Government and the miners.

The Government was determined to represent the strike as a threat to Parliamentary government, a Bolshevik plot to subvert the Constitution led by the Communist Party and the Minority Movement. The Government activated the Emergency Powers Act on the Saturday before the strike began. Regulation 21 made it an offence for any person to attempt to cause mutiny, sedition or disaffection among His Majesty's forces, police or civilians, or to impede the supply and distribution of food, water, fuel, light or other necessity. To implement these regulations the Government had control of the armed forces, took control of the police and supervised a whole, long prepared, system of local government control built around the OMS. The issue of the *British Gazette* for 5th May set the tone by alleging that if the strikers won, the rights and destinies of the nation would not be in the hands of Parliament but a small minority of trade union leaders. By Day 3 the Government, in the person of Sir John Simon was declaring the strike illegal. Justice Astbury followed this up on 11th May by reaffirming Simon's view and declaring that strike pay was therefore illegal. On the first Sunday of the strike Cardinal Bourne put the official Catholic view of the strike that 'it was a sin against God.' On the last day of the strike a decree was issued under the EPA allowing the Government to confiscate any monies sent from abroad to the strikers. Thus, for the Government, the strike was political from the very beginning, justifying the use of the armed forces to crush it.

In direct contrast, for the miners it was an industrial struggle and nothing else. Some of the miners, including its leader A.J. Cook, were Syndicalists, some were Communists, but there is no evidence whatever that any such miners were in a position, even if they had wanted to, 'subvert the Constitution' or pursue any other political aim.

But the official obsession with the Communist Party makes it necessary to examine its role in the General Strike both nationally and in Birmingham.

Twelve Communist leaders were arrested in October 1925 and faced the extraordinary charge of belonging to an illegal organisation because its aim was to overthrow the Government by force and therefore it was seditious. These arrests were protested against in Birmingham, as we have seen, and in most other parts of the country. Nevertheless five were sentenced to 12 months, which effectively kept them out of the General Strike, and the other seven to six months in prison. This was the first attempt to remove those Communist Party, Minority Movement and Unemployed Workers' Committee leaders whose policies were allegedly to overthrow the Government. But what was the policy of the Communist Party and what strength had they to impose their policies on the Labour movement? At the beginning of the strike there were about 5,000 Communists which grew to nearly 10,000 during and immediately after the strike. They were a drop in the ocean of trade unionists.

But it was the Communists who recognised most clearly that Red Friday was a temporary retreat by the Government and that the coming struggle would be a political one. Each week their paper the *Workers' Weekly* gave a countdown viz. in August 1925:

34 WEEKS TO GO

Thirty four weeks to what? To the termination of the mining agreement and the opening of the greatest struggle in the history of the British Working Class.

WE MUST PREPARE FOR THE STRUGGLE

In January 1926 the Communist Party formulated its own eight point policy of preparations. Two of these were achieved before the strike began. The others were, a working agreement between the General Council and the Co-operative Wholesale Society; the formation of Factory Committees; a campaign for 100 per cent trade unionism; a common policy for all trade unions of £4 a week of 44 hours; and better relations between the General Council and the NUWCM to counter attempts to use the unemployed as black legs. The most controversial, point was, organisation of Workers' Defence Corps composed of trade unionists and controlled by Trades Councils to protect working class meetings from fascists and reactionaries and an effort by the General Council to put the workers' case to the workers in the Army, Navy and Air Force. This was scarcely a programme to 'subvert the constitution.'

Once the strike had begun, it was the Communist paper *Workers' Bulletin* that the Government was most determined to suppress. But the makeshift leadership moved its meeting place around and managed to produce their Bulletin for 10 consecutive days. What was the content of these Bulletins? The first was on the first day of the strike. It commented on the success of the call-out, the justice of the strike and called for 'this criminal' Government to resign. It ended with the slogans 'Every Man Behind the Miners', 'Not a Penny off the Day', 'An Injury to one is an Injury to all', and 'No Government has the Right to Order Men and Women to Starve'.

On the second day of the strike the Communist Party executive issued a statement. Its main message was that the Government had dropped the pretence of serving all classes and must resign and be replaced by a Labour Government. It also called for the nationalisation of the mines without compensation, under workers' control.

The main item in the Bulletin on the third day of the strike was a reported revelation by Baldwin that on the eve of the strike the TUC was prepared to discuss with Birkenhead a settlement which contained a proposal for a reduction in miners' pay.

At the weekend two Bulletins were issued. The first quoted the Government seizure of stocks of newsprint as evidence of the extremes to which it had now been reduced and claiming that the Constitution under EPA was 'anything the Government chose to make it'. The second Bulletin welcomed the General Council statement that any negotiations with the Government must be 'free from any conditions', and the strike would not therefore be called off on a basis that 'may involve a reduction of wages', for the miners.

The Bulletin the next day 10th May deplored the refusal of the General Council to accept Russian workers financial aid as 'a blow to the wives and children of British workers and a wanton insult to Russian workers.'

When the strike was called off on 12th May the Communist Party sent telegrams to all parts of the country stating that in spite of previous promises and the unanimous demand of workers, the General Council had called off the strike without any guarantees from the Government. The Communist Party advised: Refuse to return to work. Reject the Samuel Memorandum. When the leaders fail, the workers must take things into their own hands.

Such were the activities of the Communist Party nationally during the strike. There were no illusions that there was a revolutionary situation nor that the Communists could lead it. What was expected was that nine days of struggle would convince workers that the Government was not a neutral agency protecting the interests of all classes, but an agent of the employers prepared to use the full force of the state to end an industrial dispute. It was at this stage that the betrayers of the strike acted and called it off.

We can now turn to the role of the Communist Party in Birmingham. We know that it was small, not likely to have been more than 30 or 40 strong, but with a number of very active cadres. The most important activist was Bill Brain, but he was posted to the North East at the beginning of the strike where he played a leading role there. Only one Communist was on the Birmingham Emergency Committee and thus directly involved in the running of the strike. This was W.T. Cardinal, who was vice-president of the Trades Council. Despite his being a Communist he was entirely integrated into the Emergency Committee, played a leading role throughout the strike, and was arrested with all other members of the Committee. The other known pre-strike Communist activists were Jack Trotter, Harry Shepperson and Tom Lowe all of whom were victimised during the strike. Their main activities during the strike were participation through their union branches, speaking at Communist Party and other meetings, particularly in the Bull Ring, the distribution of the *British Worker,* and the Communist Party's *Bulletins* and the production of the party's local paper the *Birmingham Worker.* It is from events arising from the last publication that we learn of other activists. On Friday night 7th. May the police raided the headquarters of the Communist Party at Hockley Hill. They ransacked the building and arrested five Communists – James Gardner, Thomas Lowe. Margaret Clarke, Thomas Gee, and Harold Hesketh. They were charged with publishing false accounts of disaffection in the armed forces in the *Birmingham Worker.* Like the Emergency Committee they also were lucky in that they were tried after the strike had been called off. Gardner was fined £10 and the others £5. The sort of treatment they might have expected was exemplified by the case of Jack Trotter who was tried during the strike for a speech in the Bull Ring in which he had said the Government knew that the army was not reliable and that special constables were 'a bunch of hooligans.' Trotter refused to plead saying that the prosecution was an attempt to crush the working class movement. He was sentenced to three months in gaol, and despite the support of the Emergency Committee and Birmingham's lone Labour MP, Robert Dennison, he had to serve out the whole of his sentence. Margaret Clarke later expanded on the raid of Hockley Hill:

> While Jim Gardner was District Organiser we had produced a number of factory papers for various towns in the area including the *Cadbury Worker*. These became the District paper when the strike began and those for Wolverhampton, Walsall, Stafford etc. were merged into the *Birmingham Worker*.
>
> We were raided at the District Office where we produced the paper on the Friday night.... They arrived with a terrific amount of noise, charged the door and broke it down and stormed up the stairs – their excuse being that we might have had weapons. They questioned everyone in the building, took what papers they wanted, and took us off to the Central Police Station. Their object was to create as much noise as possible – and fear. Since we had all the lights burning it was obvious we were not trying to hide. We were kept all that night in the cells...
>
> Next day we were brought before the Stipendiary and remanded on bail. I was bailed first by Mosley's wife, but I told the Stipendiary that I should refuse bail unless it was found for all of us. Jim was released about 5pm and went to see about the publication of the next issue of the *Birmingham Worker*.
>
> When we went before the Stipendiary on the Monday morning the police opposed bail on the grounds that a further *Birmingham Worker* had appeared after we had been arrested. But on the Stipendiary asking whether any seditious material had appeared in this issue and on being told that there was none, bail was granted. The case was adjourned until the Friday.
>
> On the Friday our case was brought up after that of the Trades Council...

Mosley paid all the fines.

The only surviving *Birmingham Worker* is a copy of issue No.3 dated Friday May 7th. It is a four page duplicated sheet and to judge of the magnitude of this achievement it should be compared with the barely one sided duplicated sheet of the *Birmingham Mail* on the 5th of May and the best the *Birmingham Post* could achieve of two printed pages on the day after the strike ended. The front page of the *Birmingham Worker* reiterated its proposal of the previous day that the best response of the General Council to the appearance of the official *British Gazette* would be to allow production of the *Daily Herald*. Next came an explanation that its newsgathering and production had been so improved that it could produce a four-page paper which it hoped, but could not guarantee, to continue throughout the strike. It then printed the TUC message that this was a legal and peaceful industrial dispute. Other items on the front page were the arrest of Saklatvala the Communist MP, the 'pathetic' Government attempt to procure scab labour by stating that they 'would not be unprotected by the state from subsequent reprisals' and a report that the police had dispersed a crowd in the Bull Ring. The second page contained nine reports of local, regional and national news about the strike. Th third page was given over entirely to the national CP Bulletin on The Political Meaning of the General Strike, which we have already quoted; this carried on to the fourth page which ended with other national reports and the news that the American Federation of Labour was supporting the strike. None of its matter could be construed as seditious or advocating violence.

This review of the activities of the Communist Party nationally and locally suggests that although the party made a significant contribution to the General Strike, it was too small to play a decisive role, and had neither the power nor the intention of overthrowing the state by illegal means. But this was the belief not only of the Government, but those trade union leaders who saw the control of the strike 'slipping into the hands of those who had neither responsibility nor authority'. In the case of Birmingham there is no evidence of either sedition or control of the strike passing to hands other than those of the Emergency Committee. Thus we come back to the question of whether local forces were sufficiently strong to have survived a further phase of the strike, with its possibility of victory.

Had the Negotiating Committee of the General Council of the TUC possessed the temper of the Birmingham Emergency Committee there would have been no sell-out of the General Strike on May 12th. The Birmingham Committee was resolutely united from beginning to end of the strike. No distinction can be found between left, right and centre, all were committed to the strike. All workers who participated in the strike were entitled to the protection of the Emergency Committee; this included the five Communists arrested in the raid on the party, speakers in the Bull Ring as well as picketing strikers. Police victimisation was always high on the Committee's agenda. During the strike the Committee was quick to learn the political nature of the struggle they were waging. The derided Workers' Defence Corps of the Communists, rejected in January, were soon found necessary to protect meetings etc. through a Vigilance Committee. Also a Propaganda Sub-Committee to combat government political propaganda was formed, and an alternative Emergency Committee elected in view of the probability of the arrest of the existing Committee. An important additional potential source of strength was the mobilisation of women and no doubt, if the strike had continued, youth organisations and trade union branches would similarly have volunteered their services.

The general organisation of the Emergency Committee compared well with other such Committees throughout the country. The full committee met twice a day. It had a wide range of of organisational sub-committees and Advisory Committees for such trades as Transport, Engineering, Building, Furniture Trades, Public Utilities etc. There were also area strike committees of which we would like to know more – Aston, Selly Oak, Small Heath, Stirchley, Yardley and perhaps others; these were likely to have been of greater importance as the strike continued and spread.

A second vital source of strength to the Emergency Committee was its total unity with the political wing of the Labour Party. The Emergency Committee was created by the Birmingham Trades & Labour Council. The secretary of both organisations was Fred Rudland and joined with him on the Emergency Committee was the other key Labour party figure, Allan Young the Labour Party organiser, and two Councillors Ager and Crump. They were joined by W.J. Chamberlain who was a moderate socialist and one of the team which edited the *Birmingham Strike Bulletin* from the actual premises of the City Labour Party; associated with Chamberlain was the two very influential Labour Party members Oswald Mosley and John Strachey. It was therefore unlikely that a wedge could have been driven between the trade union and political wing of the Emergency Committee.

A third source of strength was the relationship of the Emergency Committee with the Birmingham Co-operative Society. The Co-operative movement experienced problems during the General Strike due to its twin features of being both a trading organisation and a political body with close relations with the trade unions and the Labour Party. As a result the relations of some Strike Committees with their local Co-ops were less than fraternal. This was not the case in Birmingham, however. One official activity was the meeting of financial obligations of the strikers by the Co-op Bank against indemnities by local unions. In Birmingham, the Co-op Bank cashed £28,000 for 36 union branches and recouped all of it. The grant of credit to Co-op members on strike was another traditional source of strength which would have been more important as the strike proceeded. Other contacts seem to have been more informal. The historian of the Birmingham Co-operative Society is non-committal regarding these relations, stating only that the Management Committee of the BCS met daily during the strike and had open access to the Emergency Committee at all times. The support of the Co-op through the provision of messengers, transport of individuals, coaches to convey pickets etc. was therefore, presumably, unofficial. Had the strike continued, however, the organisations of the Co-op such as Women's and Mens' Guilds, the Co-operative Party, Comrades' Circles etc. responsible for this activity would have been drawn more directly into the strike. And the crucial question of the supply of food to more than just the customers of the Co-op would have arisen.

Another source of strength was international solidarity. The strike as a unique event created enormous interest abroad. Would donations from the Russians have continued to be refused by the General Council of the TUC if the strike had continued? Evidence of substantial payments in the pipeline from European, American and Australian sources led the Government to activate the Emergency Powers Act by prohibiting the cashing of such donations, but ways could have been found to counteract this. One thing the Government could not have prevented was the refusal of foreign dockers to load ships to Britain or to unload ships from Britain, or other manifestations of the solidarity of foreign workers with British workers.

A vastly important factor was that of the public attitude towards the strike. Sympathy with the miners was widespread among both the working class and middle class; the inconveniences of the strike were borne with good humour to the end. In addition the Government was not popular. It was a minority Government that had defeated the 1924 Labour government on the issue of the Campbell case, in which Campbell, acting editor of the *Workers' Weekly,* had first been charged with sedition for printing a 'Don't Shoot' article addressed to the armed forces but subsequently not prosecuted. A more important indication of the unpopularity of the Government was that the post-strike elections were markedly in favour of Labour. Ager, Auger. Corrin, Lewis and Mann, all Emergency Committee members, were returned to the City Council with a total Labour gain of eight seats. Neville Chamberlain, one of the hard men of the strike, was chased from his Ladywood constituency to an ultra safe haven at Edgbaston. Before the end of 1926 Oswald Mosley was in Parliament increasing a Smethwick Labour majority from 1,253 to 6,582. At the General Election of 1929 Birmingham captured six of the twelve seats breaching the Chamberlain hegemony over the City, and recording the biggest swing to Labour in the country. If these were the results of the defeat of the General Strike what would have been the fruits of its success? Despite the attempts of the Government to claim that the general public did not support the strike the reverse appears to have been the case in Birmingham.

However, not only opponents of the strike, but some supporters, hold the view that the General Strike in Birmingham peaked on 8th May and was then disintegrating, so the position on the ground on May 12th must be examined. Weaknesses there were, notably the position at Cadbury's and the capitulation of the tramwaymen. Large claims were also made of the number of trains running, but the number of railwaymen returning to work in Birmingham was negligible. Truncated local newspapers were appearing, produced by managerial staff, but nothing more could have been done because the printers remained solidly on strike. When the second wave of strikers were called out at midnight on 11/12th May there were reports of workers not coming out at factories such as GEC and Dunlop, but what significance can these reports have, even if true, when the strike was called off the same day? There is no reason to believe that the main body of engineers would not have obeyed the strike call, as all other workers had in Birmingham. Nor was the situation at Cadbury's and that of the tramwaymen necessarily irreversible. Relevant to the latter is the Battle of Bearwood on the last day of the strike when Midland Red determined to run 30 or 40 buses. They did run, but only with the assistance of masses of Staffordshire police, a convoy of 60 cars driven by special constables as despatch bearers, 10 motor loads of special constables some wearing steel helmets, a motor ambulance section, and 20 Birmingham police with 2 superintendents and 2 inspectors. More such pyrrhic victories could hardly have been afforded if the strike had continued. This solidarity of the busman could hardly have failed to influence the tramwaymen in the same union. In addition, not all the tramwaymen were back at work, Washwood Heath and Coventry Road depots forming a hard core of resistance. If this were not sufficient the cutting off of electric power could have immobilised the trams.

Power was a key to the success of the strike. It is said that power workers at the three main Birmingham generating stations were loath to strike and even if they had, the authorities claimed they had sufficient trained men to keep the power stations running. The latter may have been wishful thinking, but the issue of the electricians coming out was only raised seriously when the second line was called out on the last day of the strike; and even before this some electricians at the power stations had agreed to strike.

The other two key issues in winning the strike were food and petrol. The local Emergency Committee had already been deserted by the national Strike Committee which had abandoned food distribution nationally to the government without a struggle. Demands for greater control of food supplies would have been raised if the strike had continued. The issue was linked with petrol. Transport was flowing freely throughout the country and this irked many strikers. This could only be remedied by cutting off supplies of petrol and such demands were raised in Birmingham.

But all this raises again what the strike was about. It was not to paralyse the country and overthrow the Government. It was not an attempt to coerce the Government by starving the general public and depriving either the public or hospitals etc. of light and power. The strike could have been won with both food and power supplies in the hands of the government; although it would have been won more quickly if they had been controlled by the strikers. For this was a limited industrial dispute that only the Government could solve. The miners' demands were strictly limited. It was to return to the status quo ante where wages were not reduced or hours lengthened until the reorganisation of the coal industry had been at least begun. For this to be done, the continuation of a Government subsidy was necessary. These were modest enough demands. The Government set its face against these demands. It was prepared to use all the forces of the state not to have to concede such demands. But it would not have been the end of the world if they had been forced to concede these demands. They had done it once on Red Friday and it could and should have been done again. It would still have left the Government with plenty of scope to bamboozle the miners and deny them their full demands; but the miners were not to be fooled at that stage of the proceedings.

The further question arises as to the power of the Government to take effective measures at the next stage of the strike if the General Council had not capitulated. The Government had in fact shot its bolt in treating the strike as a revolution instead of an industrial dispute. What further measures could the Government have taken? They had already taken dictatorial control of the whole country. And how could they have used these measures? They could have arrested the TUC Negotiating Committee, as it threatened to do, and jail them. But an alternative committee would have emerged as it did in Birmingham. It could have stepped up police violence on pickets, let loose the specials, and ultimately used the army and killed people. This had all been done in the past and there were elements such as Churchill, fascists and some employers itching to do this. But what would public reaction to all this have been from a Government vowing that it was protecting democracy?

It can only be concluded that Government policy was an elaborate bluff. It would have had the greatest difficulty in coping with a further stage of the strike and would have been forced to address the miners' demands.

But it is not the intention here to argue that the General Strike could have been won. The more limited aim has been to show that in Birmingham the forces to take the strike through to the next stage were present. Whether this was so in other areas remains to be demonstrated. But, as a generalisation it might be claimed that if Birmingham could have coped many other areas with greater reputations for militancy ought to have been able to have continued the strike.

Unfortunately the Government's bluff terrified the national leaders of the strike and it was called off. In using World War 1 imagery in describing the self-sacrifice of men who struck not for their own advantage but for their comrades, the miners, we might use the same Great War expression regarding the General Strike – Lions led by Donkeys.

Bibliography: The General Strike in Birmingham Monday 3rd May to Wednesday 12th May 1926

My serious interest in the General Strike in the West Midlands was first stimulated in 1975 when the History Group of the Communist Party initiated a research programme for the celebration of the 50th anniversary of the strike. Out of these activities came the book 1926 – *The General Strike* edited by Jeffrey Skelley which included two regional studies of Paul Hastings on *Birmingham* and mine on the *Black Country*. The Communist Party programme also included regional meetings and a very detailed questionnaire for surviving participants in the strike. Unfortunately these were few, but I possess four completed questionnaires from Wolverhampton, N. Staffs, Coventry and Jim Crump's, the son of Councillor James Crump who was on the Birmingham Emergency Committee. Other research inspired by the 50th. Anniversary came from the WEA and resulted in *The Nine Days in Birmingham*, a booklet published by Birmingham Public Libraries in association with the WEA. Other earlier accounts of the strike had been on the 60th Anniversary of the Trades Council *An Historical Sketch of the Birmingham Trades Council 1866-1926* by W.A. Dalley, who was the manager of the Birmingham Labour Exchange at the time of the General Strike; the next account was in John Corbett's *The Birmingham Trades Council 1866-1966*.

First among the primary documents for the strike is the unique (as far as I know) full and complete *Minutes of the Birmingham Trade Union Emergency Committee*, a Souvenir Copy of which was published for the 50th. Anniversary. Also copies of the Emergency Committee's *Birmingham Central Strike Bulletin* and the Communist Party's *Birmingham Worker*. Surviving copies and other miscellaneous posters and literature relating to the General Strike are recorded in the Birmingham Central Reference Library under BRL 331861 fol.1926.

Something of the Emergency Committee's relations with the Co-ops is to be found in the *History of the Birmingham Co-operative Society Ltd 1881-1931* by the Co-op activist T. Smith, and H.M. Vickrage – *75 Years of Co-operative Endeavour – A History of the Ten Acres and Stirchley Co-operative Society* (1950).

Three invaluable contemporary accounts of the strike containing important references to Birmingham are *The General Strike* by R. Page Arnot, *The General Strike May 1926: Trades Councils in Action* by Emile Burns which were both published by the Labour Research Department before the end of 1926, and *A Workers' History of the Great Strike* by R.W. Postgate, Ellen Wilkinson MP, & J.F. Horrabin, published by the Plebs League in 1927 which classifies the response in each area putting Birmingham in Class I where the response was 'near to 100 per cent.'

Correspondence of the Birmingham Emergency Committee with the General Council is in the TUC Library. Professor John Foster researched the Cabinet Papers and kindly abstracted references to Birmingham and the Black Country for me. Anti-strike activities are best researched from the proceedings of the Birmingham City Council and the archives of the Birmingham Chamber of Commerce.

General histories of the strike are numerous and the main works are discussed in Margaret Morris's *The British General Strike 1926* a pamphlet published by the Historical Association in 1973 and her more comprehensive Penguin of 1976 *The General Strike*. The accounts I have found most useful are R. Page Arnot's *The Miners: Years of Struggle*, which covers not only the General Strike but the months when the miners had to fight alone; also James Klugmann in the volume edited by Jeffrey Skelley, noted above. One of the most recent accounts of the strike, the indispensable *History of British Trades Unions Since 1889* by H.A. Clegg I found disappointingly thin on the General Strike.

Chapter 27

The Black Country Labour Movement 1927-1939

Parliamentary Representation

In the 1923 general election (which returned the first, minority Labour government) the 'usual' four Labour MPs at Kingswinford, Smethwick, Wednesbury and West Bromwich were returned. These four were also returned at the 1924 election (which can fairly claim to have been lost by Labour as a result of the forged Zinoviev letter) and were joined by John Baker at Bilston. In 1927 at a by-election Wilfred Wellock, Labour pacifist and creator of the No More War Movement, was returned at Stourbridge.

In the 1929 General Election, when the second Labour government was returned, the same six were joined by Oliver Baldwin the Tory prime minister's son at Dudley, the local man J.J. McShane at Walsall, and W.J. Brown a very stormy petrel at Wolverhampton West. This meant that nine out of the ten Black Country seats were held by Labour. The one exception, Wolverhampton East was held by the Liberal, Geoffrey Mander, who was to play an honourable and leading part in the fight against Appeasement.

At the 1931 General Election dominated by the betrayal of the Labour leaders MacDonald, Snowden and Thomas, every one of these seats were lost. Wednesbury was regained at a by-election in 1932 and was retained at the general election of 1935 when there were also Labour victories at Kingswinford (Wilfred Wellock again) and West Bromwich. So from 1935 to the outbreak of war there were only three Labour MPs in the Black Country and it was not until 1945 that the Black Country was to sweep the board with ten Labour MPs out of ten.

Municipal Representation

Local representation varied widely over the Black Country, but the Parliamentary experience of reduced Labour representation between 1931 and 1938 was repeated as the following will show.

Smethwick

Smethwick suffered more severely than most after 1931, perhaps because Sir Oswald Mosley had been their MP and the support the local party had given him until he finally formed the British Union of Fascists. Even in 1933 there were still 15 Labour councillors compared with 15 Tories and 2 Independents and the Labour Party all but controlled the Council. But thereafter the Labour party steadily lost seats until by November 1938 when the last municipal elections before the war took place, Labour had only 9 seats, the Conservatives 19 and Independents 4.

West Bromwich

West Bromwich was a town where the Labour Party had no chance of controlling the local Council during the 1920s or the 1930s. In 1933 the state of the Council was 10 Labour, 10 Conservatives, 11 Liberals and 2 Independents. By 1938 it was 11 Labour and 23 others.

Stourbridge

This was another town where Labour exercised little influence. In 1928 when Labour influence was high elsewhere, Stourbridge had only two Labour councillors. By 1938 the situation had considerably improved but the state of the Council was 8 Labour and 16 Independents.

Halesowen

Halesowen was another hopeless town from Labour's point of view and in 1938 had only 1 Labour councillor to 19 Independents.

Rowley Regis

This was a town where Labour influence increased in the later years of the 1930s. There had been 6 Labour councillors in 1933 and this had risen to 13 in 1938 compared with 19 Independents.

Dudley

This was a town where the Labour Party tended to have about one third of the representation on the Council. At the peak of its influence in 1929 Labour held 13 seats compared with 17 Conservatives, 7 Liberals and 3 Independents. Labour representation fell to 10 in 1931. But by 1934 there had been something of a transformation and Labour at 18 had overtaken the Tories on 16. Unfortunately 1935 and 1936 were two disaster years when the Tories won six seats and the situation in 1937 was 11 Labour, 24 Conservative, 3 Liberals and 2 Independents.

Walsall

With Walsall we can follow some of the problems of creating an effective Labour Group. In 1933 Labour was in a minority of 15 to 25, but it was noted that the minority was getting its way with regard to slum clearance, wages on Council house building etc. The old story of the bundle of sticks (the Labour Party 15) being unbreakable whereas the single sticks (the opposition) could be broken one by one. But the Labour group did not always act in concert. In 1933 nine Labour councillors resigned from the Public Assistance Committee (the important committee which not only determined out-door relief rates under the Means Test, but administered the whole previous Poor Law system of the the Workhouse, hospital, and childrens' homes.) without consulting other members of the Labour group. Without such machinery some Labour members such as Mrs Cresswell and A.J. Stanley became laws unto themselves and even by 1939 there was no agreed procedure by which Labour members acted together and were disciplined if they voted against group decisions.

The Labour Party also faced an Anti-Socialist Alliance throughout the thirties formed to ensure that only one opposition candidate stood against Labour.

Labour also faced problems with the powerful Walsall Co-operative Society. It came to regard the Leamore seat as its own and in 1932 when Councillor Hamson, chair of the Public Assistance Committee having resigned refused to stand again for election and a non-Co-operative candidate was nominated there was considerable friction.

Danny Cartwright was also a thorn in Labour's flesh. Cartwright was the rebel leader of the Bloxwich miners' breakaway union from the Miners' Federation. He was elected at Bloxwich in 1920 and made the seat his own. In 1923 he stood as Labour/ILP and humiliated the official Labour candidate who polled only 53 votes. He was then returned unopposed every three years until 1938, neither Labour nor Tory being willing to brush with him.

In 1934 Labour were opposed by George Cotterell an ILP candidate and in 1936 his wife, Mary, stood. They polled votes of 364 and 257. But it is noteworthy that after the ILP committed suicide nationally by disaffiliating from the Labour party in 1932 the ILP in Walsall retained a greater presence than in other Black Country towns. George Cotterell stood again at a by-election in 1939 polling the more respectable vote of 565 to the Labour vote of 846 and the anti-Socialist's 920. Cotterell also stood in 1945 polling 1,404 against Labour's winning votes of about 2,000 in an election for two seats.

By 1935 Labour held 16 seats and Independents 24. In 1936 the Labour Party besides being opposed by a Rent & Ratepayers' Association also faced two unemployed workers. But these polled derisorily Laffan in Pleck gaining 24 votes and Wakelam in Palfrey 13. By this time both the Labour Party and the Co-operative Party were experiencing financial difficulties and the opposition also seemed to be having problems in finding candidates, and decreasing stomach for a fight. The result was that an increasing number of both Labour and opposition councillors were being returned unopposed. In 1935 there were five No Contests, in 1936 six, in 1937 seven and in 1938 eight. The state of the parties at Nov 1938 was Labour 13, Others 27. In 1939 a series of by-election worsened the Labour position still further.

Wolverhampton

We can consider the fortunes of Wolverhampton from the time of the enlargement of the borough from 48 seats to 52 seats in 1927. In the larger borough the Labour Party gained no further seats and had twelve councillors and one alderman. In 1928 Labour lost one seat in St. Mary's where the best known local Communist, Albert Darke contested. Darke was not responsible for this loss, however, as his vote of 110 and the Labour vote of 527 combined did not equal the Independent's vote of 724.

In 1929, the year of the election of the Labour government when Labour could be expected to be doing well, the Labour Party regained one seat. In 1930 Labour lost one and gained one. In this year the energetic and leftist, Ted Lane, who eventually served fifty years on the Council, was elected. In 1931, the year of the betrayal of Ramsay MacDonald, most sitting Councillors were returned unopposed. In 1933 the Council was again enlarged to sixty seats and at the elections of that year Labour held 14 seats.

Wolverhampton Labour Party suffered the same difficulty as Walsall. An Anti-Socialist Alliance existed in the town and between 1919 and 1950 no Conservative ever opposed a Liberal in a contest against Labour.

The failure of this anti-Socialist alliance in the Parliamentary field led to another series of Labour difficulties in the thirties. In 1929 W.J. Brown had been elected on a minority vote of 21,103 against Bird the sitting member who polled 17,237 and a Liberal's 4,580. The failure of the Labour government to stem the tide of unemployment or to act in a remotely Socialist way on any matter led W.J. Brown to join with other left-wing critics, notably Sir Oswald Mosley and John Strachey in Birmingham, Oliver Baldwin at Dudley and J.J. McShane of Walsall to demand proto-Keynesian measures to end the crisis. The refusal of the Cabinet to approve the Mosley Manifesto led to Mosley's resignation from the Cabinet and his proposal to form a New Party. W.J. Brown resigned from the Parliamentary Labour Party in March 1931 and whether he actually joined the New Party is not entirely clear. But as the New Party quickly turned into the British Union of Fascists, Brown's connection, if any, was fleeting. His resignation from the Parliamentary Labour Party was regarded as resignation from the national Labour Party. This Brown and his supporters denied. The resultant controversy split the local Party. When the issue was decided against Brown he formed his own Independent Labour Association in Wolverhampton financed by the support Brown was receiving from his union the Civil Service Clerical Union.

The serious weakening of the local Labour Party can be seen in subsequent municipal election results. In 1932 Elizabeth Bowyer stood as an Independent Labour Association candidate in Blakenhall/St. Johns ward and came second with 798 votes forcing the official Labour candidate into third place with 418 votes to the winning Conservative's vote of 872. William Lawley, the leading supporter of Brown in Wolverhampton, won St. Matthews for the ILA. M. Ansell of the ILA stood in Graiseley ward but was beaten into third place by the successful Labour candidate. George Crane, a leading Communist engineer also stood in the 1931 election at St,Georges, but polled only 175 in a straight fight with the successful Labour Candidate, Beach, with 1,363 votes. This was at the tail end of the Communists' Class against Class policy and no other Communist was to stand in the years up to the war when the CP was seeking good relations with Labour.

In 1933 J. Hill stood for the ILA at Blakenhall and came a bad third at 491 votes to a successful Trade Union candidate, J.A. Sandbrook, with 1,525 votes. An ILA candidate stood in St. Matthews ward, but came second in a contest where there was no Labour candidate. In 1934 J. Hill won another seat at St. Matthews. By this time it was recognised by both Labour and the ILA that ILA influence extended only to the St. Matthews ward (where they eventually held all three seats) and St. James where Edward Bradley (later to defect to the Fascists) won a seat to make the ILA maximum total of four councillors. In 1935 William Lawley retained St. Matthews, but his wife failed to take St. James.

1935 was the last year of the Independent Labour Association and the period 1931-35 is difficult to assess with regard to the number of seats held by Labour. It seems perverse to regard ILA seats as opposition seats as on most issues the ILA voted with Labour and was indeed to the left of many official Labour councillors. By 1936 when the ILA was no more and its remaining councillors had Labour/Co-operative labels the Labour Party had thirteen councillors and two aldermen on a Council of sixty. By 1939 the Labour group had 19 members. This was one more than the Conservatives but left Labour a minority on the council which also contained 15 Independents and 8 Liberals. In 1931 the Labour Group had adopted model rules of procedure approved by the national conference of 1930, and although these could not cope with the major breakaway of the ILA, they sufficed for lesser matters and gave a framework for the maximisation of the Labour Group's influence as a minority party on the Council in a way that was not possible in Walsall. The latter years before the war also saw a replication on a smaller scale of another Walsall problem – that of uncontested elections. In 1934 there were only four contests in Wolverhampton out of twelve. In 1935 there were eight contests, in 1936 only four, in 1937 five again, and in 1938 only three contests.

In conclusion it can be said that the Labour Party wielded considerable influence on the town Council in the inter-war years. But the Conservative-Liberal-Independent anti-Socialist alliance held firm to the very end, and this meant that there were no progressive Liberals with whom Labour could co-operate and Labour therefore remained some way from having control of the Council.

Wednesbury

Wednesbury was a town where Labour eventually gained control after 1925 and then lost it. In 1928 there were 6 Labour councillors to 10 other. In 1929 there was a Labour majority. This majority continued in 1931 and 1932 when Labour representation was falling elsewhere. The Labour majority reached its peak in 1935 when the council position was 13 Labour and 3 Others. 1936 was a disaster year when Labour lost three seats and with it their majority. The next year there was no change and in 1938 Labour lost another seat. The position then was Labour 6 and Others 10.

Coseley, Sedgley and Bilston

Not even the ingenuity and personal knowledge of John Smallshire can give a clear picture of the position in Coseley and Sedgley in 1939, because of the apparent lack of some election results and the problems of interpreting election results where no party affiliations are given. In both UDCs the Labour post-war majorities were whittled away, but this did not necessarily mean that Labour lost control of these councils. In Coseley numerical Labour control ceased in 1922 and in Sedgley (according to Smallshire) in 1925. But after that Councillor Pratt was chairman of the UDC in 1930 and was succeeded by Councillor Dews, 'both Labour men of some standing'. Smallshire further writes of Sedgley:

> At this time Labour could only rely on seven and then five councillors, but the opposition was of mixed character. were not Tories as such but Economists, sometimes called Ratepayers and all types of Independents, some of them former Labour members. The small band of experienced Labour councillors still maintained a strong hold on the administration, but were sorely tested on policy.

Whatever the actual position was in 1938 in Coseley and Sedgley, Labour councillors continued to be elected and it might even be claimed that a 'Labourist' culture prevailed on these councils.

Lastly I want to deal with Bilston which, although it never had a Labour majority on the Council showed considerable militancy in the 1930s and also illustrates the problems of poverty, unemployment and an appalling environment which applied to all areas of the Black Country but which have not been adequately covered in this section dealing with local government electoral representation.

After the imposition of the Means Test in 1931, Fenner Brockway, a national ILP leader, was working on a book entitled *Hungry England* when Ben Bilboe – a new name in Bilston radical history – and others persuaded him to come to Bilston. The following are some of his conclusions:

> In Bilston I get the impression of a district devastated by war. There are large waste stretches pocked with holes and ridges just as though they had suffered a heavy bombardment... There are houses in ruins...there are houses with cracked walls and roofs only prevented from falling down by wooden beams propped against them. So looked the towns of Flanders before they were repaired.

On housing Brockway writes:

> I find it difficult to describe the first house I visit. It would be more suitable to chickens that human beings, The walls and roof are cracked. There are a small scullery and living room on the ground floor, dark, damp, stuffy places. There are steep narrow stairs...a dirty brown stain streaks the wall where the rain has come through. The two bedrooms are in the same desolate condition with rotten, falling wallpaper... In the living room is a plain table, an old horsehair armchair and two kitchen chairs. In the rooms above, two iron bedsteads with a few clothes on them and two chairs. There are no carpets or linoleum on the floors.

> 'That's all I've got out of the war,' says the man with a bitter laugh. I was gassed and shell shocked – for this. I have been refused a pension, though I lost my job because I couldn't stand it through the effects of gassing...'

The rent of this house was 6/9d. The man had previously been employed for eighteen weeks after a long period of unemployment and his six day 'waiting period' for benefit had been extended. 'We should have starved if the British Legion had not given us 10/-d. for two weeks.' Their means test income was 29/-d. After paying the rent and 3/-d. for coal there was little more than 19/-d. for food, clothing and everything else. If the whole of this 19/3. had been spent on food alone it would scarcely have provided an adequate diet. But this ex-soldier's income was princely compared with others as Brockway found ploughing on to houses without gas or electricity, (some using candles rather than oil lamps because candles were cheaper) with fetid, filthy communal toilets. All this in the centre of British engineering skills! Brockway commented. A miner of 64 out of work for twenty months and his wife received only 15/3d. A labourer in a steelworks, usually earning £2 a week but injured and receiving £1 a week compensation plus 7/6d. from the PAC to keep six children only one old enough to work; the housing conditions of this usually employed man were dreadful, showing the impossibility of keeping a large family even on £2 a week.

There was also the problem of long-term unemployment for both skilled and unskilled men in the iron trade where five out of six works at Bradley were closed. A representative of the men serving on the Conciliation Board which adjusted wages every two months on a sliding scale according to the price of iron gave the following percentages of unemployment in the iron trade:

Jan 1930	Jan 1931	Jan 1932	June 1932
19%	41%	64%	43%

This, of course, is not the whole picture. But it would be a foolhardy person who would try to minimise the poverty and the hardships suffered by the majority of working people in the nineteen thirties.

It was in these circumstances that Ben Bilboe appeared on the scene in Bilston. Born in 1902 in a caravan at Ironbridge, his father was an itinerant stallholder who travelled the fairs such as Pat Collins. During the war he enlisted under-age in the Welch Fusiliers and was sent to India. Here he learned that his wife was pregnant and requested compassionate leave. This was refused and he deserted making his way back to England as a stoker via Hong Kong, USA and Australia. He then gave himself up to the military authorities and was eventually granted an honourable discharge and given his medals.

With a wealth of worldly experience Ben Bilboe, like so many others, found it difficult to get permanent employment. He worked successively as debt collector, rent collector and friendly society agent. By the time of the General Strike he shared a large, rambling house opposite Bilston Football Club with his twin brother Harold and his family. Ben's elder brother, Bill, joined the Communist Party as did Harold, but according to John Smallshire who knew Ben well, although he sympathised Ben never became a member. But by 1930 the house in Queen Street was the Bilston headquarters of the National Unemployed Workers' Committee Movement and this was tantamount to being a Communist, particularly in the eyes of the *Bilston and Willenhall Times*.

The role of the Unemployed Workers' Movement was the double one of helping the unemployed to obtain their rights (crucial after the Means Test of 1931) and also to agitate for local schemes of work to employ at least some of the unemployed. The Bilston branch of the UWM grew steadily. The Bilboes were joined by other Communists, Labour Party members, ILPers and non-party people. One of the few schemes of work which did get off the ground was land donated by the Bradley ironmaster, Luther Greenway. for a childrens' playing field and park. Ten men were employed to move 10,000 tons of slag heaps eleven feet deep and seven feet high and told by Walter Hughes to put their hearts into it and get it done quickly because it was costing the council a great deal. A further vast area of 1st World War landscape at Loxdale Street became known as 'Poverty Bonk.' When efforts to gain money from the government to level this area failed, the UWM decided to put up its own candidates for the local elections. In 1932 they contested all five wards in Bilston. All were dubbed Communists by the Bilston and Willenhall Times. None of the UWM candidates was elected. Ben Bilboe polled best in New Town with 287 votes against the Labour candidate's 463 and the triumphant Unionist's 769. In three wards the Labour Party did not oppose the UWM candidates, but their maximum vote was 150. Horace Winmill, a card holding Communist opposed W.T. Fellows, the Labour leader of the Council; he polled 109 to Fellows' 902. The *Bilston and Willenhall Times* was jubilant at the rout of the 'Communists.'

1933 was Charter Year when Bilston became a Non-County Borough. This involved a change of election date from April to November. The parties took a general decision not to contest the April elections, as all Councillors would have to be re-elected in November. The UWM, however, decided to stand Ben Bilboe against just one Labour councillor, Harriet Holland, who epitomised for the militant UWM the right-wing views of most Labour councillors. Bilboe lost, however, by 336 votes to 581. The local newspaper this time reported that Bilboe stood as an UWM candidate and not a Communist. In the November 1933 election, Harold Forrest stood as an official Communist candidate.

When work schemes were initiated they were plagued with complaints that wages were below trade union rates and also claims of favouritism in choosing workers involved and excluding militants such as UWM members. When a Loxdale scheme was finally started it was called by the UWM the 'Loxdale Slave Labour Scheme' and a campaign was initiated to turn it into a 'Work for Real Wages Scheme' and demands that there be a rota of men to ensure work sharing.

In September 1933 general discontent with such schemes was so widespread that Bilston Unemployed Workers Movement combined with UWM branches in adjacent towns to stage a demonstration at the Loxdale site. Leaders involved included Henry Millichip who had been organising the unemployed in Willenhall since 1931, Councillor William Bradshaw of Darlaston secretary of the Labour Club there and campaigner against the Means Test, and Councillor George Stokes of Wednesbury, a veteran leader of victimised workers and the unemployed. Bernard Moore, the Birmingham organiser of the NUWCM was to be the main speaker. Contingents from the above mentioned towns, together with the Bilston unemployed marched to the site and a crowd, estimated by the hostile *Bilston and Willenhall Times* at 'about a thousand', gathered at the protest. A large body of police was mobilised and it was rumoured that the men working on the site were to be called out. There was considerable tension at the meeting, therefore. This rose to a climax when, after previous speakers it was announced with 'a great deal of chanting, whirring of rattles and ringing of bells' that Ben Bilboe would speak for Bilston, in the enforced absence of Bernard Moore.

Bilboe began by asking everyone to take off their caps and sing the Red Flag. This they did. What he subsequently said could not always be heard but was alleged to include, 'These men must come off the site.... I know what you want.... You are waiting for me to give the word Go.... There will be a time to go and then I shall be with you.' By this time the police alleged that the crowd was getting out of control and moving towards the gates of the site. Bilboe was hustled off the platform. The crowd continued for some hours, but was eventually dispersed by the police.

Bilboe was issued with a summons to appear at Bilston Magistrates' Court on 20th October to answer a charge of 'Uttering at a mass demonstration on Monday 25 September certain words which constituted a breach of the peace.' On the day of the hearing he marched to the court accompanied by men and women with banners and preceded by a jazz band. He was pronounced 'a man likely to persist in inciting others to a breach of the peace,' and was ordered to enter into recognisances of £50 to keep the peace for twelve months and to find two sureties of £10 each, with the alternative of three months imprisonment. He refused to be bound over and stated that he would appeal.

Immediately before the hearing Bilboe had been nominated a UWM candidate for the November local elections. On the Saturday before the Monday poll Bilboe was arrested and taken to Winson Green prison. The Bilston Communist Party and the NUWCM led the protests at his arrest and conducted Bilboe's election campaign.

To the surprise of many Bilboe was returned for one of the three seats of New Town Ward with 887 votes. He was sandwiched between two Conservatives who polled 1,052 and 880 respectively. Unsuccessful were a Conservative and Harold Forrest the Communist who nevertheless polled 580 votes more accurately reflecting the true support for Communists if people had a choice of voting both Labour and Communist. Mrs Bailey the Labour candidate with 550 votes and Mrs Holland an Independent with 390 votes also lost. In High Town, Harold Bilboe stood as a Communist but polled only 175 votes. After the election Ben Bilboe was required to sign a declaration of acceptance of office, but he was still in gaol and his fellow New Town ward councillors, both Tories, had to take the form to him at Winson Green. A tremendous campaign continued to have Bilboe released with street chalkings changed each day to indicate the days he had spent in gaol.

When Bilboe was released he was joined by Labour councillors W.T. Fellows and J. Roberts in opposing the Loxdale scheme unless men were paid at trade union rates of pay. This was defeated by 15 votes to 3. In December the Council heard a UWM delegation of Harold Benboe, Aubrey Pugh and G. Harris who put the full demands of the NUWCM of: work at Loxdale at trade union rates of pay also further schemes at such rates for house building and slum clearance; abolition of the Means Test; extra winter relief for the unemployed; maximum operation of meals for children; reduction of rents by 25 per cent and cancelled arrears for the unemployed; end of police hostility; free use of a Town Hall room for UWM meetings and free use of the municipal baths for the unemployed.

Bilboe's success could only be limited because most of these demands could only be met by national legislation. Nevertheless he continued to lead a militant protest movement. In June 1934 he put the following motion to the Bilston Borough Council:

> 1. Scale of Transitional Payments. This Council calls on the County Council to recognise an agreed scale of payment to unemployed persons not less than the amount paid to those on ordinary benefit and not taking into account family incomes...

> 2. That in view of working class resentment against the Loxdale Instructional Centre this council tenders to the Ministry of Labour the necessary notice for the liquidation of the present scheme of labour recruitment and in view of the essential nature of the work being done other arrangements to be made for the continuance of the work on the basis of full time employment at recognised trade union rates of pay.

> 3. In view of the increasing interference of the national government in the expenditure of local government on social services, particularly Unemployment, Housing, Child Welfare and Education and at the same time the national budget showing definite increases in providing for war services... this Council views with alarm the danger of war and deplores the refusal of His Majesty's government and other Imperialist States to accept the proposals of the Union of Soviet Republics at Geneva for total disarmament, or partial disarmament. We appreciate the efforts of the Soviet government against war, and in view of the other governments not agreeing with the disarmament proposals put forward, welcomes the new proposals...for the transformation of the present conference into a permanent Conference on Peace... This Council accordingly calls on HM Government to accept these proposals and abandon its support for the German and Japanese aggression against the Soviet Union (while) at the same time (curtailing) financial assistance for the elevation of the social services at home.

With this and similar motions linking economies at home with war preparations abroad, Bilboe plagued the local council, but with only a small Labour minority on the council and improved, although still dire, unemployment figures the peak of militancy in Bilston had passed.

Ben Bilboe came up for re-election in 1935. By then he had become an official Labour candidate and fighting New Town ward again Bilboe topped the poll with 1,002 to the Conservative's 717 and Hattie Holland the Independent's vote of only 204.

With a secure base in Bilston, Bilboe turned to the County Council. In 1937 he chose the No.2 Bradley seat occupied by the president of the local Conservative Party, Toole, who had held it unopposed since 1925. Bilboe won the seat by 926 to Toole's 780. At Stafford Bilboe co-operated with his old Means Test allies H.G. Millichip of Willenhall and C. Pratt of Sedgley.

In the November 1937 Bilston borough elections, Toole also lost his Bradley seat to George Jones. At that time Labour held five seats, W.T. Fellows having been elected an alderman. But Fellows died in the summer of 1937. This left Ben Bilboe, the two brothers Jones, both active Methodists, and John Roberts. At a by-election in 1937 they were joined by the Rev Luke H. Jenkins in Town Hall ward.

Bilboe brought his normal militancy to the county council. At a council meeting in May 1938 he opposed air raid precautions as meaningless and a waste of public money unless accompanied with policies to oppose fascism and appeasement. On this occasion he was trying to move that councils be allocated an overall sum and spend some on air raid precautions if they wanted to. Bilboe was ruled out of order by the county council chairman and he refused to accept the ruling. Amid uproar Bilboe was told that if he continued to defy the ruling he would be asked to leave the chamber. Bilboe still refused, the police were sent for to eject him and the meeting adjourned. When, later, Bilboe agreed to apologise to the chairman he prefaced it with reasons why he acted as he had, but was told that only an unconditional apology would do, and this he subsequently gave. Bilboe found an extended field for his radicalism at Stafford in defending rural workers. He was again 'named' at meetings and threatened with police eviction when he denounced such practices as paying county council roadmen by cheque monthly when they could scarcely live week by week, and leaving workmen employed in remote rural areas to make their own way home for many miles either spending their hard earned money on rare buses, or walking until they almost dropped.

In 1938 Bilboe had to defend his Bilston seat. There were no other contests that year, but at all costs, a candidate to oppose the radical socialist Ben Bilboe had to be found. Eventually a Conservative stood, but Bilboe swept home by 1.197 votes to 485.

When war broke out there were 13 Conservatives, 2 Independents and 5 Labour on Bilston Council. Smallshire describes the five Labour as 'three dedicated Christian Socialists, a fried fish merchant with strong local community backing and Marxist-Atheistic Ben Bilboe with his shabby clothes and worn boots.'

Against Fascism, Appeasement and War

From 1933 when Hitler came to power in Germany local Labour movements found themselves much more deeply involved in foreign affairs. Hitler destroyed first the German Communist Party (for which he was thanked publicly or privately by most Conservatives), but then went on to destroy the Socialists and the trade unions, which raised the concern of the whole Labour movement. Hitler's continuing persecution of the Jews gave concern to all liberal people, although a natural disinclination to believe that such horrors were occurring in the middle of Europe and a latent anti-Semitism in Britain damped down protest and resistance.

Millions more did not want to think about politics, certainly not about another war, or support any action which might provoke the aggressive powers of Germany, Italy and Japan. It was in this atmosphere that appeasement flourished.

Within Parliament there was not only the question of to arm or not to arm but, after 1936, when the issue had been decided in favour of arming, the Labour Party faced the problems not only its own pacifist minority who opposed rearmament, but also whether to vote arms expenditure to a Tory government which (a) gave luke-warm support at best to the League of Nations and (b) would spend the money to arm unilaterally and use the arms on imperialist ventures to put down justified colonial protest and revolt. In this context the Black Country MP who performed best was not Labour but the Liberal MP, Geoffrey Mander of Wolverhampton. Mander was a firm supporter of the League of Nations Union and he contrasts the activities of Sir Austen Chamberlain who had long experience as Foreign Minister and who was a leading member of the League of Nations Union until he died in 1936, with that of his half-brother, Neville, who was the architect of Appeasement.

The Peace Ballot 1935

The Peace Ballot of 1935 was the most remarkable amateur public opinion poll ever organised in Britain. It originated with the League of Nations Union inviting other national bodies to serve on a National Declaration Committee to sponsor a ballot on collective security and international disarmament. Thirty eight bodies agreed including the Liberal Party, Peace Associations, Churches, Women's organisations the TUC the Labour Party and the Co-operative Party. Local broadly based Declaration Committees were then formed and volunteers called for to distribute ballot forms to every household of every polling district in the district and then collect the completed form. It seemed a crazy project particularly in view of the powerful opposition to it. The Conservative Party was split, some supporting the ballot and others vehemently opposed it. The Conservative national newspapers did their best to ignore the ballot the *Daily Express* advising its readers to tear up their ballot papers. Even some pacifists were luke-warm about the project because it was not a Peace ballot; and the sheer volume of work involved in visiting houses, often many times, and explanations of what the ballot was about were mind boggling.

Yet the ballot exceeded all expectations. Nationally 11½ million people voted in the ballot. This was more than 50 per cent of all those who voted in the general election of 1935.

The questions asked were as follows:
1. Should Britain remain a member of the League of Nations?
2. Are you in favour of an all-round reduction of armaments by international agreement?
3. Are you in favour of an all-round abolition of national military and naval aircraft by international agreement.
4. Should the manufacture and sale of armaments for private profit be abolished?
5. Do you consider that if a nation insists on attacking another, other nations should compel it to stop by:
   (a) economic and non-military measures?
   (b) if necessary military measures?

The key questions were 1 and 5. To the question Should Britain Remain in the League of Nations no less that 97 per cent answered Yes. Nothing could be more emphatic. The most controversial question was the fifth. On question 5(a) of whether the League should impose non-military sanctions 9½ million voted Yes. Even more significant was question 5(b) asking whether military action against an aggressor would be approved; here the Yes vote fell to 6½million and the No vote rose to over 2 million, But even this was overwhelming support for military action against Japan, Italy and Germany if their aggressions continued.

Local results mirror almost exactly the national results. The problem is, however, to discover what the local results were. The local press followed the national papers in ignoring the ballot as far as possible and publishing results in such small print that they are very difficult to find. For instance, neither the Walsall result from the *Walsall Observer* nor the Wolverhampton result from the *Express & Star* has been found. But we know that Walsall had a broad local committee which included the Vicar of Walsall, the Chamber of Commerce. James Leckie the local Liberal MP, Walsall Grammar School, the Civic Guild of Help as well as Walsall Labour Party, Trades Council and Co-operative movement, including the formidable Womens' Co-op Guild branches.

It is clear, however that almost every village and town in the Black Country participated in the ballot many of them showing higher than national results. For instance, at Cradley Heath, home of the chainmakers, 70 per cent of the registered electorate voted. At Hasbury, Rutley and Illey no less than 84 per cent voted. In Stourbridge participation was lower but still reached almost 50 per cent. These three results have been dredged from the murky depths of the microfilmed Wolverhampton

Express & Star, but its pages fail to reveal either reports of the Wolverhampton campaign, the organisations involved or the result. We only know from this newspaper, that the Wolverhampton League of Nations Union AGM in April expressed 'disappointment' at the result of the ballot. The amount of work to be done had been seriously under-estimated; some houses had had to be visited four times; widespread ignorance of the ballot was encountered, some people believing that it was the League of Nations itself running the ballot. Yet there is no reason to believe that the Wolverhampton poll was below the national average of 37 per cent of the electorate participating in the poll particularly as we do have a report from neighbouring Bilston. Here we have the most detailed results of the campaign and know that of the town's 45,226 electors, 63.2 per cent voted in the ballot. The ballot in Bilston seems to have been largely organised by the town council and local churches; the result was declared at the Town Hall by the Mayor, with other councillors present, including Ben Bilboe. Over 500 comments were made on the ballot papers. Six people thought the League of nations was 'hopeless, helpless and useless'. Others thought that Britain should rely on its own strength and ignore the League. Of 70 comments on war itself 69 condemned it, and six would not fight at any price. Others commented that if war broke out the politicians and armament makers should be the first to go 'over the top.' The one who supported war stated that he would 'rather die in battle than of slow starvation.'

The Smethwick result we know from the Birmingham labour paper the *Town Crier*. Here 14,468 people voted out of an electorate of 44,797 or almost 33 per cent; as in Wolverhampton, regret was expressed by labour activists that it had not been possible to organise for more people to vote. We also know of ballots at Darlaston (where 36 per cent of the electorate voted), West Bromwich, Willenhall, Wednesbury, Lye and Wollescote. Hostile editorial comment regarding the Darlaston result suggested that although support for the League of Nations was overwhelming among those who voted, if the other 64 per cent had voted they might have overturned that result; but this ignores the fact that however high the participation nationally, support for the League remained in the high 90 per cent wherever a ballot was taken.

Dudley distinguished itself by declaring its results as early as December 1935, being only the second town with populations of more than 60,000 to do so. Here 13,873 ballot papers were distributed and 7,075 collected. The cost of the ballot in Dudley was £24 and the number of volunteers 346. It had a vigorous local committee headed by the Venerable Dr A.P. Shepherd, Archdeacon of Dudley and he was supported by other Churches, Girl Guides, Toc H, the Teachers' Training College, the Girls' High and the Grammar Schools etc. as well as the Labour movement.

With regard to the national result of the ballot the extraordinary thing was the unanimity with which people voted across all areas of Britain. Nationally, 97 per cent of participants voted Yes to the first question; in the known results in the Black Country it was 98 per cent. On the controversial question 5b regarding the use of force to deter an aggressor the national Yes total was 74 per cent; in the known Black Country results it was 75 per cent, although there were large numbers nationally and in the Black Country who abstained from answering this question.

There is no known copy of the national results of this unique Peace Ballot in the existing archives of the League of Nations Union. What can be said is that the ballot showed mass support for the League of Nations and its machinery of sanctions both economic and military. Had Neville Chamberlain had the same faith in the League and determination to help make its machinery work, the Second World War could have been avoided.

Appeasement, Spain and World War

Already, while the Peace Ballot was being organised, Appeasement was well under way. Hitler's occupation of the Saar, and Italy's preparations to invade Abyssinia occurred early in 1935. The first stage of German rearmament was met with reassuring noises from the national press, echoed by the *Express & Star* that Britain had nothing to fear from this. The core of appeasement was implacable hatred of Communism and the belief that Hitler would attack and destroy the Soviet Union, an event which would strengthen Britain's imperial position. Only a small section of the Conservative Party, led by Winston Churchill, understood the menace of fascism to Britain from the beginning.

By the end of 1935 the infamous Hoare-Laval Pact was offering Italy the whole of Abyssinia and although public uproar in Britain forced the repudiation of the Pact, proposed oil sanctions were not implemented by the British government and the fascist powers were again given the green light for continued aggression.

The event which mobilised the vast support of the Peace Ballot was the so-called Spanish Civil War. This began in July 1936 when a rebellion by army officers against the legally elected government of Spain invaded the country from Morocco and tried to overturn the government. The limited support for the rebellion led first to air support and then military support for Franco on a vast scale from German and Italian armed forces. To this the British and French governments dreamed up a fantasy of Non-Intervention. This was an alleged neutrality favouring neither one side nor the other. Its effect, however, was to prevent the elected government of Spain from buying the arms it required while turning a blind eye to the decisive aid the rebels were receiving from Germany and Italy.

The almost total domination of the right-wing leadership of the Labour Party and trade unions nationally met increasing dissatisfaction in the localities after 1935. The main right-wing principles were total resistance to any demand for United or Popular Fronts together with opposition to the Soviet Union and Communist Parties everywhere. The divisions and strains that this brought can be illustrated from the minutes of the Wolverhampton South West Constituency Party Minutes. In June 1936 Wolverhampton AEU No.5 branch passed a resolution supporting the affiliation of the Communist Party to the Labour party 'in view of the menace of Fascism and War.' This was acknowledged by the SW Labour Party EC, but no action was taken. The branch followed this up requesting that the local Labour Party support the application of the Communist Party to affiliate to the Labour Party. When put to the vote the result was six for and six against; the chairman, Councillor Beck then gave his casting vote in favour, and so, the local Party was committed to support affiliation at the national conference in October.

A month after the 'civil war' in Spain began in July the Labour Party considered its response to the Spanish Workers' Appeal for assistance and decided to hold a public meeting in St. George's ward. In September the Wolverhampton Peace Council asked the Labour Party to support a meeting it was calling. The reply was that no delegate would be sent and later when the Peace Council asked the Labour Party to receive Mr Chubb to speak to the EC the matter was left to lie on the table. The Peace Council persisted and the result of another letter to the EC was a statement that the Labour Party would not affiliate to the Peace Council, it would not support a United Front and it would not purchase the Peace Council's pamphlets.

This hostile attitude to united action continued into 1937. In January the whip was removed from the local League of Youth who were actively supporting united action. At the end of the year the EC rejected an invitation to support a local conference of the International Brigade and a Spain Campaign appeal was also rejected.

Hostility continued into early 1938. In January the local Left Book Club organised a China Week and the Labour Party would not co-operate with this. In the same month the Spain Medical Aid Appeal was rejected. But attitudes were clearly changing. In February in response to an appeal for a Crusade for Peace and Security at the end of the year, the EC replied that it had insufficient funds to support the Week, but it would take and distribute leaflets. It was also agreed to support the Boycott Japanese Trade movement. In April, in appealing for volunteers to support a campaign in St. George's ward those invited included Left Book Club members. In April the Labour Party executive called a special meeting on the Popular Front and after May Day it was agreed that the May Day Committee of the East and West Wolverhampton Labour Parties and the Bushbury Labour Party be continued as a May Day and Spain Aid Committee. But this was almost death bed conversion stuff; by then Spain had been cut into two and Munich was only a few months away. By September the position had so improved that it was agreed to read a letter from the Wolverhampton Communist Party; co-operation with a committee composed of two Communist delegates, two Labour Party, two Co-operative Party and one Liberal Party member were agreed.

Some activity by the Labour Party in 1936-7 did take place. The National Council of Labour called for the setting up of joint Labour committees to raise money for Spain and such a committee of the local Labour Party and the Trades Council was formed. But it remained an internal affair and had little impact on the town. The Trades Council opposed Franco from the beginning and collections were regularly made, but with the inability of the Trades Council to initiate or take part in Popular Front activities the impact was limited. It was the same in May 1937 when 4,000 Basque children were evacuated to Britain. A separate committee composed mainly of Labour Party members was set up and united activity discouraged.

Early Aid Spain activity originated around two centres. Geoffrey Mander the Liberal West Wolverhampton Liberal MP was not only active in criticising Non-Intervention in Parliament, but was also active in his constituency. His speeches and persistent questioning in Parliament were reported in the national press, and because of his national status, in the local press as well. Mander was not afraid to associate with Communists nor any other organisation criticising government policy on Spain in particular and Appeasement in general. It was no credit to the Trades Council that they vetoed the proposal for Mander having a mandate to speak on behalf of all democratic organisations in Wolverhampton at a National Conference on Spain in April 1938.

The other centre for the initiation of activity on Spain was the Wolverhampton Communist Party. It was a small, but growing party, and by 1938 its secretary was the highly efficient George Crane, later to become a leading national AEU figure. Within a month of the outbreak of the Spanish rebellion, the Communist Party had held two meetings on Spain. The outstanding national contribution of the Communist Party was the organisation of the British section of the International Brigade. Two members of the Party in Wolverhampton fought in Spain. One was William Scott who worked at Goodyear's, was a member of the Transport & General Workers Union, a former member of the Labour Party and a local personality. The other was Jerry Ward. It was also the Communist Party which initiated the local Aid Spain Committee with other left-wing people almost as soon as the rebellion broke out. This was the centre of collections for Spain. The Committee made Sunday morning collections of food and money, held regular meetings on the Market Patch and arranged public meetings. It participated in all the main campaigns – for the Youth Foodship, support of the Basque children, the Midlands Ambulance for Spain and the final Midlands Foodship in 1939. Unfortunately the amounts collected cannot be estimated.

The most important ally of the Wolverhampton Communists on the Spanish issue was the local branch of the Left Book Club. The LBC was founded in May 1936 by Victor Gollanz and it caught the spirit of the times. Each month for 2/6d. a specially written, topical book could be purchased. Some of these books had a permanent influence. One can quote Edgar Snow's *Red Star over China,* the Dean of Canterbury's *Socialist Sixth of the World,* and A.L. Morton's *People's History of England.* Others were extremely influential at the time, Haldane on air raid precautions, books on the U.S.slump, on unemployment and poverty in England by Wal Hannington and Ellen Wilkinson's classic of Jarrow the *Town that was Murdered.* C.R. Attlee contributed *The Labour Party in Perspective* and there were books on fascism and resistance in Italy, Germany and Japan. Groups were formed to discuss the books in 50,000 towns and villages. Large rallies were held. The Left Book Club politically educated a whole generation. The LBC would have been important if it had educated only the middle classes who were turning to left political thought and action, but it coincided with a great political awakening of working class people, especially the young and energetic. Above all the LBC became a spearhead of the movement to aid Spain and to build a Popular Front against Appeasement and war.

The Wolverhampton Left Book Club reflected all these trends. One of its leaders was Basil Chubb, a Communist teacher at Wolverhampton Grammar School who was sacked at the beginning of the war for attending demonstrations. Another leading light was a teacher at the Girls' High School. Meetings were held at one of the flats of an idiosyncratic, property owning Communist, Geoff Brotherton, who, it can be readily believed, did not attend the meetings himself, and urged the participants to keep quiet because of other tenants of the building. Later, according to W. Hood whose essay is the only written source of information on the Wolverhampton Club, it acquired permanent premises in a converted barn in Hartley Street. But Hood's witnesses are the proletarian members John Smallshire and the Laws brothers Chris and William, who all testify to the large working class element in the Club and its influence in promoting the Popular Front activities in the town from 1936.

In other Black Country towns Aid Spain and resistance to Appeasement was confined to declarations and personal contributions. In Smethwick the local Labour Party remained on the left after the Mosley debacle but generated little activity and drifted to the right. The Trades Council was eventually split into an industrial and a political section, but this brought no improvement in activity and influence. Wednesbury, on the contrary, had a strong Labour Party with a Labour MP after 1935, but it was right-wing and generated little Spanish Aid activity.

West Bromwich was one of the Black Country towns generating considerable Spain Aid activity. This was largely due to the activities of William Laithwaite who came to West Bromwich in 1936 and invigorated left policies. Active in the Labour Party and the Trades Council, he also became chair of the Unemployed Committee and active in the local Left Book Club. Laithwaite created a left-wing opposition to an essentially complacent, right-wing Labour Party on the issue of Spain. Laithwaite, who is described by Peter Drake as a 'sleeping Communist' co-operated with the West Bromwich Communist Party and the Left Book Club to generate considerable Spain Aid and Popular Front activity in West Bromwich.

'Sleeping Communists' were not a rarity – people who agreed with Party policy but thought they could be more influential outside the Party, or lived in areas where there was no Communist presence. Sometimes they were in the Labour Party but gradually became disillusioned and took themselves and others into the Communist Party. Such a one was Bill Shakespeare who was in the Old Hill Labour League of Youth but took himself and many fellow LLoY members into the Communist Party. Jim Westwood had been a Labour councillor on Rowley Regis UDC since 1931 but disillusionment over Spain and appeasement led him to join the Communist Party and influence many others. Arthur Williams of Blackheath served in the International Brigade and was wounded. At Oldbury Elsie and John Evans were militant Communists deeply involved with Quakers in the adoption and care of Spanish and German refugees, and who on the jubilee of George V in 1935 flew the Red Flag with the hammer and sickle from their council house and refused permission for their children to attend street parties. These are just a few examples that can still be collected in 1997. They indicate that Aid Spain penetrated every corner of the Black Country and touched hearts in the same way that Vietnam was to affect a future generation. But we will end with the example of the Bennett brothers in Walsall, their wives Noreen and Lou who, with Bill Brain and others developed an influential Communist Party able to sustain a bookshop and whose Labour movement created the most powerful Aid Spain movement in the Black Country. Both C.A.(Dusty) Bennett and his brother Don fought in Spain with the International Brigade. Dusty was killed at the Ebro in July 1938; his brother Don returned and took part in the campaign against Appeasement and remained active in the Communist Party in Walsall in the post-war years.

The other major contribution of Walsall was its care for the Basque children. They arrived in England 23 May 1937 and by June a Walsall Committee for the Relief of Spanish Children was in existence meeting in the Council House. Meetings were chaired by the Mayor and held in the Council House. The first Mayor concerned was the Labour Mayor Councillor A.J. Stanley who was enthusiastic for the cause, and he was supported by the very influential Alderman Pat Collins the Liberal fair owner, who became the next mayor, as well as other members of the Walsall Town Council. This official committee remained in existence until November 1939 and was a broad based, humanitarian committee such as existed elsewhere in the country. Almost simultaneously a Midland Joint Committee for the Care of Spanish children was set up. Representatives at an early meeting in July 1937 included the mayor of Walsall, the deputy Mayor of Wolverhampton, councillors from Aldridge, Willenhall, Coseley and Darlaston, with apologies from the mayors of Oldbury and Wednesbury. But Walsall's overall contribution to the care of Basque children was the greatest. This was largely because Walsall became the site of one of the three Homes set up in the district, the other two coming under the control of the Birmingham equivalent of the Walsall Committee.

The Walsall Home was at Aldridge Lodge, Bosty Lane, Barr Common, Walsall. John Whiston, the secretary of Walsall Trades Council and a Walsall town councillor was seconded to become Superintendent of Aldridge Lodge and a main objective of both the Walsall and the Midland Committee became the upkeep of Aldridge Lodge. The Walsall Labour Party, trade unions and Co-operative movement, especially the Women's Guild responded strongly to the challenge and it was perhaps inevitable that Walsall's contribution should be the greatest as the Home was situated there.

Aldridge Lodge was one of a series of Homes set up by the National Joint Committee for Spanish Relief which was chaired by the Conservative MP, the Duchess of Atholl. How the Walsall Home came into existence we do not know, but, as we have seen, minutes of the Walsall and Midland Committees exist from July 1937 and we can follow the fortunes and problems of Aldridge Lodge from this time, particularly through the reports of the superintendent which are with the minutes.

The Lodge was capable of accommodating about thirty children. The children were educated by a Spanish teacher. They studied Spanish language and literature, arithmetic and geometry, the geography of Spain and the world, physiology and hygiene, civics, singing and 'gimnasia'. They were soon to be taught English by one of John Whiston's sons. There were problems with religious education because although Roman Catholicism was the religion of the Basque people, churches here were likely to be pro-Franco and Spanish speaking teachers in England convent trained.

The children were well-behaved, but the long winter evenings brought problems of occupying their time. The Walsall Co-operative Women's Guild had set up a sewing party, provided the children with night clothing and given each boy two pairs of stockings and the girls the wool to knit their own! A Garden Party in September was visited by about 1,000 people and made valuable contacts for the children as well as producing about £20 profit.

At Christmas the children had a real Xmas dinner and attended parties at Walsall and Bilston Girls' High Schools, Etheridge Infants' School Bilston. Walsall Picture House, Alexandra Theatre and Cadbury's in Birmingham etc. The ever-generous Alderman Pat Collins sent fruit, nuts and crackers for the Xmas dinner.

There was a small turnover of children who returned to Spain or left for other homes, also pressure on space as Aldridge Lodge was asked to take children from Homes closing down. Each child was allocated 10/-d. a week which was paid either by the National Committee or from local funds. This was considered 'quite adequate' for Aldridge Lodge and was, of course, much more than the children's allowance for the unemployed.

Great emphasis was laid on the health of the children which at Aldridge remained mostly good. Health was an important issue when children were transferred between Homes and Aldridge reported problems in May 1938 as a result of taking six children from a Salvation Army Home in Brixton that was closing down. On examination, the heads of all the girls were found to be verminous and scabies and impetigo was also diagnosed. Strong complaints were sent to the National Committee that children should be transferred in that state.

By August 1938, some children were being educated at local schools and the older ones were attending evening classes. At this time the superintendent reported the Home, 'contented, although there is only Mrs Whiston and myself here now.' But it was more than Mrs Whiston could do to supervise the cooking and attend to the children's clothes, in addition, Whiston said, 'although I have had to attend the girls it is not a proper thing for me to have to do.' Help was urgently needed.

Aldridge Lodge was a well run Home. Eleanor Rathbone MP, one of the vice-chairs of the National Committee, visited it in September 1938. She was 'more than satisfied' and 'did not know how we managed to carry on by ourselves.' She promised to do what she could to get assistance. The Home also passed muster with an Inspector of Education who also commented favourably on the cleanliness of the home and took away paintings and woodwork done by the older boys for an exhibition of work by Spanish children for an exhibition in Paris. The Lord Mayor of Birmingham on a visit was so struck by the difference between Aldridge Lodge and Elford Hall (one of the two Birmingham run Homes) that he was going to take it up with his committee.

By this time fascist aggression in Spain had been successful and in March 1939 the Republic was defeated. Some children went back to Spain and others to their families in exile in France; many had been adopted by English families. But it was estimated in September 1939 that about 1,000 of the original 4,000 Basque children remained. The financial situation at Aldridge Lodge became serious and the National Committee was informed that unless funds were forthcoming the Home would have to close in August. The Whiston's volunteered to take a cut of £1 a week in their wages, but this was refused. The National Committee was concerned that a good home like Aldridge Lodge should have to close and promised to do what it could, but their funds were almost exhausted.

For some time the Homes had considered raising funds by the children performing Spanish songs and dances. A boy was sent to Aldridge Lodge to see if the boys there could be taught Basque dances and they proved adept at it. A Spanish teacher of music was also sent to Aldridge Lodge and a choir was formed. Concert parties were formed to tour summer resorts and some Aldridge Lodge children joined a concert party serving the North Wales and Lancashire seaside resorts.

Temporary relief came from Birmingham when a considerable quantity of food and some money was transferred when Elford Hall closed. Also Corbyn Cadbury, treasurer of the Midlands Refugee Committee guaranteed any money needed by Aldridge Lodge until September. In September, when war was declared, five homes on the east coast had to be closed and the National Committee sent four children to Aldridge and five more were expected. By October, the financial position was getting worse by the week and Whiston wrote, 'Only this week I received a letter from our most generous and loyal subscriber the Walsall Co-operative Spanish Children's Committee saying that they could only continue their present commitments for another four weeks.'

The Home was still open in January 1940 when Whiston's last report stated that 17 children had been returned to Spain and a spate of adoptions of children locally, brought their numbers down to nine and the Home was to close. By that time the Walsall Committee for the Care of Spanish Children had contributed £1,575 to the upkeep of Aldridge Lodge.

In September 1939 Hitler invaded Belgium and Chamberlain declared war on Germany; the struggle of anti-fascists to prevent war by collective action through the League of Nations had failed.

Bibliography: The Black Country Labour Movement 1927-1939

For Parliamentary and Municipal elections there are George Jones' *Borough Politics* for Wolverhampton and Kenneth Dean's *Town and Westminster* for Walsall. Also for Wolverhampton is John Rowley's history of the Wolverhampton Labour Party in his introduction to the Labour Party papers held in the Wolverhampton Archives. I hold a collection of elections results for Birmingham and most of the Black Country from 1918 to 1939 and beyond compiled by Chris Roseblade, who, tiring of the delights of Wolverhampton has migrated to the Far East. For Coseley, Sedgley, Willenhall and surrounding areas there is John Smallshire's admirable *Pioneering in Black Country Government* in MS binding at Wolverhampton Archives department, and, of course the local newspapers. W.J. Brown's *So Far* is the Wolverhampton MP's personal testimony with regard to Oswald Mosley and his New Party and also on the national scene is Robert Skidelsky's biography of Mosley.

For continuing poverty in the Black Country see A. Fenner Brockway's *Hungry England* and a piece I have not used, J.B. Priestley's 'English Journey' reprinted in the *Blackcountryman* Vol 3 Summer 1970. On Unemployment there is another piece I have not used a University thesis of which I have no further details by David Round on *Local Responses to Unemployment in Wolverhampton and Salford 1929-34*.

On the Peace Ballot there is *The Peace Ballot Official History* by Dame Adelaide Livingstone and the reluctant local newspapers.

For an overall view of Spain and Appeasement there is the Wolverhampton Liberal MP Geoffrey Mander's *We were not all Wrong*.

For local Spain Aid the indispensable source has been Peter Drake's 1977 Birmingham University M.Litt thesis, *Labour and Spain*. For the Left Book Club in Wolverhampton there is a useful essay by W. Hood with personal testimony from John Smallshire, Chris Laws and Ms D.M. Overton. My own personal witnesses on the struggle against Appeasement have been Don Brayford, Charlie Johnson and Ms J. Fisher.

The episode of the Basque children and Aldridge Lodge has been taken from the John Whiston papers at the Walsall Local History Centre. These include the minutes of the Walsall and the Midland Committees for the Care of Spanish Children and also the minutes of the Walsall Trades Council. the Midland Federation of Trades Council minutes 1927 to 1969 and much else.

Chapter 28

Birmingham from General Strike to World War 2

The Trade Unions 1927-1939

The first task of the Labour movement after the defeat of the General Strike was to limit the damage of the Tory Trade Disputes and Trade Unions Act of 1927. This created a new category of 'illegal strikes' which went far beyond the banning of general strikes. The Act also severely restricted picketing. It also prevented Civil Servants from belonging to trade unions with political connections with either the TUC or the Labour Party. Finally, in an attempt to cripple the finances of the Labour Party it decreed 'opting in' instead of 'opting out' of unions' political funds.

The TUC did not make this resistance any easier. An inquest on the conduct of the Strike, which should have been held at the September Congress, was delayed until a special conference in January 1927. Here those who had called the strike off shielded themselves from the charge of treachery by blaming the Communist and Minority Movement who had 'made it impossible for the General Council to resist the call for a general strike' as C.T. Cramp, NUR leader put it. There followed a general witchhunt of the Left by both the TUC and the Labour Party. And by this time, even people like Rudland, who had loyally led the Strike in Birmingham and expressed the same disgust as all Birmingham leaders and rank and file when it ended, had come round to the view that the General Council had had no alternative but to call off the strike.

Birmingham Trades Council organised a vigorous opposition to this Blacklegs' Charter, as it was called. A Conference of about 700 trade union delegates set up a Trades Union Defence Committee in April 1927. At a town hall rally addressed by Mosley and Will Thorne a Trade Unionists' Covenant was proclaimed and in an impressive ceremony all in the hall rose and repeated it sentence by sentence vowing to defend trade union and political rights. The next month a Midlands demonstration of 10,000 marched to Summerfield Park in pouring rain and burned copies of the Bill. There were demands by the Communists and Left-wing Movement for the TUC to set up a Council of Action and call another General Strike until the Bill was defeated, and a more moderate call by the ILP for a 24-hour strike.

Despite all this opposition, in January 1928 ten branches of the Post Office Workers and Post Office Engineers had to leave the Trades Council. Trade Unionism was in the doldrums where it remained through the Slump of the early 1930s.

Right v Left 1927-1929

The Russian revolution continued its considerable influence over the British Labour movement. Its ability to sustain itself despite vast foreign military intervention was followed by the beginnings of Socialist construction and the ability to create full employment. By 1927, Soviet support for national liberation movements at a time when both India and China were in revolt against imperialism was important. All this created problems for the right wing which controlled the national Labour Party and, from 1927 the TUC. Leading the left forces were the small Communist Party, much of the still influential Independent Labour Party, and the left in the trade unions. Many of these trade unionists were organised in the Minority Movement and the political forces in the Left-Wing Movement. For the right wing these were always considered to be Communist inspired and controlled bodies. In addition, the Third International analysis of the world situation that capitalism was in its final stages and its revolutionary overthrow imminent, led to the British Communist Party adopting sectarian tactics which were often far from helpful.

An important early battle in Birmingham was that to replace the popular Dr Dunstan who had already stood three times as a Birmingham Labour parliamentary candidate, forcing Neville Chamberlain to move from Ladywood to the Edgbaston constituency. When Dunstan joined the Communist Party in 1924 Oswald Mosley became the candidate in Ladywood but left wing forces in West Birmingham Labour Party nominated Dunstan. He stood in the 1924 election as a Workers' candidate without Labour Party opposition because by that time Communists had been excluded from standing as Labour Party candidates. This was far from the liking of the many members who criticised the actions of the late Labour government and Dunstan was promptly re-nominated as prospective Parliamentary candidate by the left-wing in West Birmingham. A leading figure in support of Dunstan was Joseph Southall, artist and pacifist, member of the ILP and Labour Party. He was also a local and national leader of the Left Wing Movement and the newspaper that supported it, the *Sunday Worker*.

Shortly after the 1924 election, the West Birmingham Labour Party had selected another candidate which the left refused to recognise and Dunstan continued to campaign in Birmingham. In 1926 this candidate, Capt. Brennan, withdrew his candidature and Dunstan's supporters saw an opportunity to heal the breach and have Dunstan reinstated as the only candidate. This failed, however, and Labour parties throughout the country were being disaffiliated for supporting Communist/Labour prospective MPs. Southall protested vigorously in the *Sunday Worker* against charges that Communists were 'disruptive' and stating that the real disrupters were those who would weaken the Labour Party by removing 'some of its most gallant and faithful champions.' At a Left-wing Movement Conference in September Dunstan received powerful support including a message from George Lansbury, then in Moscow, stating that the selection of a new candidate for Birmingham West (O.G. Willey) was disgraceful. The ILP Midland Guild of Youth also refused to endorse Willey. A campaign to restore Dunstan's candidature involved members of Labour Parties in Edgbaston, Moseley (Fred Silvester) Handsworth (Miss Eastgate) and Sparkbrook as well as Cardinal of the Trades Council.

Support continued for Dunstan into 1927 and it was not until the end of that year that expulsions could be considered. Leading members such as Southall, Miss Eastgate, Silvester, Symes, Mrs Luckett, Jim Crump Jnr and several others were recommended to be expelled by their local parties. But such was their support that this misfired. The Edgbaston party not only refused to expel Southall and Crump, but re-elected them as Chair and Secretary of the divisional party.

In Moseley, the divisional party refused to expel Fred Silvester. In Yardley Mrs Luckett was supported by the divisional executive. In March 1928 the Borough Party recommended to the national executive that Edgbaston and Moseley divisional parties be disaffiliated and new parties set up. The matter thus went to the national Party Conference in October 1928, which happened to be held in Birmingham. Elaborate attempts to assure delegates that the 'Birmingham problem' was a limited one of a few rebels were made and new parties for the dissident areas were authorised.

Purging was even more difficult in the trade unions. Bill Cardinal, vice-president of the Trades Council, was not a direct member of the Labour Party. But he was considered by the NUR sub-council representing 18 branches in Birmingham to be 'a person unsuitable to be a delegate of the Trades Council.' He was only saved by the fact that he had recently been elected to the national executive of the Workers' Union. It was not until 1929 that right-wing domination of the Trades Council was consolidated. H.G. Johnson of the Railway Clerks replaced Corrin as president beating Cardinal only by 66 votes to 58 and Councillor C.G. Spragg became vice president after Cardinal had inexplicably withdrawn his name for that office.

Completing right-wing domination of the Labour movement in Birmingham, W.J. Chamberlain became very anti-Communist and this was reflected in the *Town Crier,* the paper becoming the voice of the establishment. Even the traditional outlet of opposition, readers' letters, became truncated, and weeks would pass without any letters appearing.

The substance of the disputes affecting right and left in Birmingham must now be set out.

The Independent Labour Party remained a powerful force in the City. It maintained a Federation of branches which covered the whole of the City. Its policy was always to the left of official labour and included at this time the demand for a Living Wage. It also contained a powerful pacifist element. For instance, at a Midland ILP Conference in March 1927 Southall proposed a resolution to the national conference that all Labour MPs should vote against war credits. The ILP was part of the strong anti-war movement in Birmingham which, among other things hosted annual World Peace Conferences at the Quaker College, Woodbrooke.

The ILP also performed the extraordinary feat of sustaining Labour Churches. The number fluctuated but seems to have been at its maximum of 11 at the end of 1927 and in to 1928.

The youth movement of the ILP was the Guild of Youth. Naturally more radical than its adult organisation it jostled for influence within the city with the Labour Party's Young Socialist League, and the Co-op's Comrades' Circle. It was the constant concern of the right-wing in the adult movements that no United Front should be formed with the small, but well-financed Young Communist League. Such Labour sports organisation as existed was sustained by young people; a Labour Football League was formed, but could not be maintained and its teams moved into other youth leagues.

The activities of the ILP in Birmingham were therefore very wide ranging at a time when, after the failure of the first Labour government and the General Strike, ILP policy moved to the left. The Living Wage was adopted in 1925 as an answer to unemployment and incorporated into a policy of Socialism in our Time in 1926. The question of co-operation with the Communist Party therefore continued to be a matter of vital concern.

As we have seen, the Birmingham ILP was heavily involved in the National Left-Wing Movement set up by the Communist Party in 1926 as a natural home for victims of the right-wing purges of members of disaffiliated Labour Party branches and trade union members. Both the Birmingham ILP Federation and its Guild of Youth were affiliated to the organisation. According to its secretary, Fred Silvester, the Birmingham Left Wing Labour Group had been formed to oppose within the Labour movement Imperialism, Militarism, and Liberalism; to insist on equal rights for all sections as members of the Labour Party and to work for control of Parliamentary leaders by the rank and file. The remainder of Silvester's letter in the *Sunday Worker* was a spirited defence of Dr Dunstan.

In July 1926 a Birmingham Left Wing Conference was held at which there were 95 delegates from 10 trade union branches, 10 Labour Party organisations, 7 Socialist organisations, the Sunday Worker Committee, the Teachers' Labour League, the Daily Herald League and Birmingham Labour College. The meeting was chaired by A.E. Smith, the president of Sparkhill Labour Party. Greetings were read from A.J. Cook, the miners' leader, Joseph Southall and Bill Cardinal (vice-president of the Birmingham Trades Council and E.C. member of the Birmingham Co-op). Resolutions were passed unanimously on a Socialist policy for Industry, Unemployment, National Health, Housing and Education, also foreign policy and the British Empire. A resolution urging the reversal of the 1925 Labour Party Conference decision to exclude Communist Party members from membership of the Labour Party was passed by 36 votes to 7. A resolution on the General Strike moved by Dr Dunstan urging TUC changes in organisation and leadership to 'prevent a recurrence so tragic as surrender', was carried with three dissentients. The rest of the Conference was concerned with the Miners' Lock-out, then still continuing, and the meeting ended with the singing of the Internationale.

Left Wing activity was also carried on through the Sunday Worker Committee which organised a mass meeting at the Grand Theatre in October 1926.

1927 was the tenth anniversary of the Russian Revolution and the Left Wing Movement took the initiative in September in calling a broad conference to elect delegates to take part in the Moscow celebrations. Southall at this time likened Britain to a beleaguered city with war mongers closing in but the imperialists dividing the citizens into two hostile camps called Socialists and Communists. A subsequent meeting in October elected Miss D. Jones (UDAW, Co-op and Labour Party), W.D. Buxton (Workers' Union), Jim Crump (AEU) and W. Rogers (NUC) as delegates to Moscow.

In September 1927 the annual Left Wing Movement national Conference took place and J. Stuart Barr of the Birmingham Labour College was elected midlands representative on its committee. Expulsions continued from the Labour party and in August the Teachers' Labour League had been disaffiliated. Criticism of the Labour Party by Left Wingers now came to match the vitriol of the right wing. Southall (still vice-president of the Birmingham borough Labour Party) suggested that the Birmingham Labour Party was being taken over by employers of labour who had originally been Liberals. This letter caused a national sensation, but Silvester followed it up talking of 'A' and 'B' taking secret control of the Birmingham Labour movement. Both were social pacifists and their wealth had enabled them to swing the movement to social reform instead of Socialism. One of those referred to was undoubtedly Harrison Barrow who was a large scale grocer. Alderman Bower, the very right-wing leader of the Labour Party in the Council chamber, was also amassing wealth and was soon to be expelled for his capitalist activities and increasingly Tory views.

The Herald League was a long established organisation in the City associated with Left Wing activity. In September it organised a Town Hall meeting and the *Town Crier* refused to insert an advertisement for the meeting. The national circumstances were as follows. George Lansbury had resumed daily publication of the paper in 1919, but it was always in financial trouble and in 1922 financial responsibility was taken over by the Labour Party and the TUC. From then on the paper instead of remaining a radical one became the mouthpiece for official right-wing policy. The League continued in existence. Chamberlain's excuse for refusing the advertisement was that the League no longer existed nationally as it had been banned by the *Daily Heald*. This was indeed the case and thus another part of the left-wing had been suppressed.

Organised Left Wing Movement activity continued into 1928. S.M.B. Potter, a Labour parliamentary candidate for Sparkbrook, had spoken at a Saklatvala meeting in the previous autumn and had only just escaped being expelled for this. In March 1928 Potter began to address meetings purporting to show that certain officials of the Birmingham Labour Party and a newspaper 'claiming to be its official organ', were in receipt of subventions which did not pass through the audited accounts of the Party and the donors sit on Committees 'to which they have not been elected and have no right to attend.' Whether Potter proved his point or not it fuelled the view that the rich controlled the Party.

In September 1928 a successful Third National Conference of the Left-wing Movement was held with Birmingham representation. But problems lay ahead. By this time the Labour Party was banning not only Communists, but also organisations 'ancillary or subsidiary' to the Communist Party. A 'black list' of seven organisations included the Left Wing Movement, the Minority Movement, the National Unemployed Workers' Committee Movement, the League against Imperialism, International Class War Prisoners' Aid and Friends of Soviet Russia, all of which had active branches in Birmingham.

But the Labour Party was spared the task of banning the Left Wing Movement in the city. On the eve of he Wall Street crash the Third International was elaborating a theory that capitalism was again in its final crisis and the policy called Class against Class was accepted by the world movement including the British Communist Party. The new policy characterised the British Labour Party not as a Socialist Party but as the third party of capitalism and reversed the policy of seeking Communist affiliation to the Labour Party to one of direct hostility. One of the first victims of this change was the Left Wing Movement. It was the Communist national secretary of the movement, Ralph Bond, who suggested that Communists should be withdrawn from the Left Wing movement because it had been formed to work with Labour Party members. Such a course dismayed members of the Movement and split even the Communists. The resistance was led from Birmingham. Southall protested at the virtual liquidation of the Movement without consulting its members. Silvester wrote to the *Sunday Worker* the same month (April 1929) stating that even the Communist Party executive committee considered that the Left Wing Movement had useful work to perform and he (Silvester) urged all secretaries of Left Wing Movements to contact him and re-establish the organisation. The editor of the *Sunday Worker* (William Paul, a Communist) thought that the re-establishment of the organisation was impracticable at that time, although he agreed, rather contradictorily, that united action between Communists and Left Wingers in all localities was essential.

Silvester continued to elaborate his views. The action of the Communist Party seemed to have cleared the way for a new Left party for those not willing to join the Communist Party, he claimed. This could be a new Left Wing Committee Movement enabling co-operation with the Communist Party to continue in the form of a Left Wing United Front.

The Left Wing Movement continued to exist. In June 1929 an article in the *Sunday Worker* by Silvester explained that George Bridgen had contested the general election as a Left Wing candidate in the disaffiliated constituency of Moseley polling 675 votes against the 'scab' official Labour candidate's nearly 16,000 and almost 34,000 for the Unionist. Was it wise in these circumstances, Silvester asked, to have withdrawn Dr Dunstan from West Birmingham where the 'carpet bagger' O.G. Willey had been defeated by 43 votes? (Dunstan had stood at Bethnal Green in London where he polled 1,300 votes – GB). Silvester reiterated his belief that a Left Wing Movement could be sustained to work with the Communists and revive those 'depressed as a result of workers' support for official Labour.' (Labour in Birmingham had achieved a stunning success with six seats won – GB).

Discussion continued in the *Sunday Worker* on the future of the Left Wing Movement, but by the end of the year the matter was settled when the Committee announced that the paper would close and its support transferred to the *Daily Worker* which began publication in January 1930.

The history of the Left Wing Movement demonstrates the falsity of right-wing claims that its members were tools of the Communist Party. Leaders like Southall and Silvester were among the most experienced and popular of Birmingham political leaders. Both had their distinctive political views. Silvester had been a member of the Communist Party but found it unsuitable as a vehicle for his views. Southall, the pacifist, had put his views strongly in his 1927 article comparing the situation to a beleaguered city. He went on,'The rottenness of the Second International has now been revealed. Either we unite with our Russian comrades or we are lost. Anti-Communism must go.' If leaders held such distinctive views there is no reason to believe that the rank and file were less sophisticated with regard to their relations with Communists. There was, and continued to be, a large number of political activists holding views between those of the Communists and those of the ILP. Within a few years these were to be organised in their own party – the Socialist League.

The National Minority Movement

The Minority Movement was a similar such body meeting a real need for trade unionists. MM was formed in 1924 to organise left trade unions and individuals within existing unions. It was affiliated to the Red International of Labour Unions and stood for the overthrow of the capitalist system. The hand of MM can be seen in a March 1925 resolution at the Birmingham Trades Council for support for a proposed Anglo-Russian Trade Union Committee to set up a new Trade Union international. MM influence continued not only in the Trades Council, but in the MM groups set up for each industry such as engineering, rails, building etc. The MM held its annual Conference in Birmingham in January 1927, but its condemnation of the TUC general council as 'betraying the General Strike' raised the ire of the right. By the end of the year Chamberlain was roundly condemning the Minority Movement in the *Town Crier* and right-wing unions were complaining to the Trades Council of the 'disruption' caused by left wing motions brought to Trades Council. At the 1928 TUC MM was outlawed.

Elections to 1929

Refusal of the right-wing to co-operate with Communists and the left had particularly dire consequences when unemployment began to rise again in 1928 and it was necessary to campaign for programmes of work creation and higher benefits. Hostility extended into every sphere of activity –

the Peace movement, opposition to Imperialism, the youth movement, sport and culture. Yet these were good years electorally for the Labour Party and much more would have been achieved if the movement had not been so decisively split.

In 1927 four seats were gained by Labour on the Birmingham City Council. In 1928 it was four gains and one loss giving Labour 36 seats on a council of 72 Tories, 9 'Independents' and 4 Liberals. The 1929 elections brought neither gain nor loss. But before that, in June, at the General Election Labour won an astounding victory which seemed to end once and for all, the Joseph Chamberlain influence which had held Birmingham workers in thrall for fifty years, first to Liberal influence and in later years to Tory-Unionist support. Six Parliamentary seats were won out of twelve. Bob Dennison, Birmingham's previously lone Labour MP was defeated by 491 votes, and Willey failed to win West Birmingham by only 43 votes. The successful candidates were John Strachey in Aston, Fred Longden in Deritend, G.F. Sawyer in Duddeston, Jim Simmons in Erdington, Wilfred Whiteley at Ladywood and A.G. Gossling at Yardley. Important also for Birmingham was the fact that Oswald Mosley was re-elected at Smethwick with an increased majority. The second Labour government was formed and a new era begun.

The Rise of the Labour Government

The second minority Labour government was in a stronger electoral position than the first had been. In December 1923 there had been 191 Labour MPs to 258 Tories and 158 Liberals; in 1929 Labour had 287 seats compared with 260 for the Tories and only 59 for Liberals. The basic issue of the election had been unemployment; unfortunately Labour took office just as the world slump was developing. National unemployment in 1929 was 1.2 million, by 1931 it was 2.6 million. Birmingham unemployment rose from 31,500 to 60,500 in January of the same two years.

The strains within the various sections of the Labour Party increased. The ILP insisted that the government implement part of its Socialism in our Time programme immediately. The Prime Minister, Ramsay MacDonald and his Chancellor Snowden, in both of whom there was probably no spark of Socialism left at this time, were determined to pursue orthodox economic policies which ordained that spending must be cut as revenue fell, and this meant cuts in wages and unemployment benefit.

The first crisis came with the so-called Mosley Memorandum of February 1930. Sir Oswald Mosley, Labour's high flying recruit, who had sat in Parliament as a Tory and then an Independent from 1918 and become a Labour MP in 1926, had been appointed Chancellor of the Duchy of Lancaster with special responsibility for unemployment in a Cabinet Committee on that subject. Mosley presented his famous Memorandum to the Cabinet. It included Keynesian measures of deficit budget spending to create jobs. Also control of imports and Empire preference. These proposals were rejected out of hand by the Cabinet as impractible violations of the laws of orthodox financing. The Memorandum also contained measures for a small cabinet to be responsible for government during the crisis, and it was these proposals that first alerted the wary to the authoritarian implications lying behind Mosley's thinking. Mosley popularised his proposals at meetings in Smethwick and won support for his ideas in his constituency and in Birmingham.

Pari passu with this argument went increasing ILP dissatisfaction with the Labour government. At the ILP Conference held in Birmingham in April 1930 the 'rebel' view was overwhelmingly endorsed that ILP MPs. would not be bound by Parliamentary Labour Party rules but would vote according to decisions made by the ILP Conference. The confusion this created can be seen from the position of Jim Simmons, one of the more influential Birmingham MPs who came under Mosley's influence. He was in favour of Mosley's economic policy, but opposed the ILP decision not to be bound by Labour Party decisions in Parliament. As a pacifist he also reserved the right to vote according to his conscience on matters of war and peace and was not therefore a member of the ILP group.

In June Mosley resigned from the government for which action he received an enthusiastic welcome in his own constituency and considerable support in Birmingham. At the Labour Party conference in October, Mosley's proposals were discussed and when voted on lost by only 1,046,000 votes to 1,251,000. Mosley was also voted on to the party executive in place of J.H. Thomas. By December the Memorandum had been refined into a Manifesto and discussion raged in the Birmingham Labour movement. Jim Simmons signed the Manifesto despite 'rumours that a new party was about to be formed' but stressed his continued support for the Government in and out of Parliament. John Strachey was part author of the Memorandum and he supported Mosley. W.J. Chamberlain, who was now back in his Watchtower and determining the policy of the *Town Crier*, was opposed to Mosley. His criticism followed the lines of the 'rebels' in the ILP, whom he usually violently opposed. If state money was to be used to develop new industries and modernise old ones then tax payers should receive the full benefit of such 'rationalisation'. That meant public ownership and control i.e. Socialism, Watchman avowed.

As the controversy continued the Mosley group demanded a National Labour Party Conference to discuss their policy. Meanwhile demands were continuing within the ILP for a complete break with the Labour Party and the Midlands ILP Conference in January 1931 faced resolutions from Birmingham City branch supported by the Birmingham ILP Federation for disaffiliation from the Labour Party. At the ILP Conference at the end of January 1931 32 branches were represented out of a nominal number of 55 branches. The resolution was put by Joseph Southall and much of his support came from the Left Wing Movement within the ILP. The motion to disaffiliate was, however, lost by 37 votes to 11. Watchman was naturally pleased as a member of the ILP favouring continued affiliation, but he acknowledged that logic was on the side of Southall and his supporters; the ILP was riding with one foot on a horse going to the left and the other foot on a horse going to the right. Southall was honest enough to maintain that the performance could not be continued. The further argument that if it disaffiliated from the Labour Party the ILP would 'commit political suicide' was a dishonest one, Southall maintained. However, these 'illogical and dishonest' arguments prevailed at the national ILP conference at Easter 1931.

In February 1931 Jim Simmons was still supporting the Mosley Manifesto despite misgivings on some points. He strongly supported the idea of a five man emergency Cabinet with other Ministers responsible for departments and all other MPs serving on Committees. This was greatly superior to the existing procedures whereby 300 MPs had recently been kept in an 18-hour continuous debate on an Agricultural Land Utilisation Bill about which most of them knew very little, Simmons maintained.

But at this point the situation changed drastically. Mosley further refined his policy into a large pamphlet called *A National Policy*. After more defeats for his policy within the Parliamentary Labour Party, Mosley announced that he was forming a New Party under that name based on his National Policy pamphlet. Mosley's belief that he would take a large part of the Labour movement with him into his New Party was gravely mistaken. He took with him only five MPs – himself, his wife, Oliver Baldwin (son of the Tory leader), Robert Forgan and John Strachey (who resigned within a few weeks). Mosley quickly shed his left-wing views and became the leader of British fascism.

Strachey was repudiated by Aston Labour Party. At a New Party meeting at the Astoria Theatre, Aston, early in March, a large crowd of Labour supporters heckled Strachey and demanded that he resign. Cynthia Mosley and Sir William Morris, the car magnate, were also given a bad time by the crowd. The secretary of the New Party, Allan Young, made attempts to recruit Labour Party agents in Birmingham, but apart from the defection of Dan Davies he was unsuccessful.

Labour support seemed unaffected by the Mosley defection. Birmingham' May Day was again considered a record with a mile long procession, huge crowds lining the route and 20,000 people at Aston Park.

The Fall of the Labour Government

Unemployment peaked in the first half of 1931 at almost 3 million. Snowden, determined to present a balanced budget, convinced that taxes on business would only worsen matters, and harassed by Tories and Liberals to reduce expenditure, needed a weapon to convince recalcitrant Labour and ILP members that there really was no solution except to cut wages and benefits. He chose to set up a Committee to advise on reductions in Government expenditure. Its chairman was the retiring chairman of the Prudential Insurance Co. and it became the notorious May Committee. This provided the Chancellor with the worst possible scenario for the future and proposed cutting national expenditure by £96 million of which £66.5m was to be found by cutting 20 per cent from unemployment benefit. The ploy misfired. What had been a manageable crisis became an unmanageable one as the financial world was led to believe that Britain was on the brink of bankruptcy. £50m of borrowings swiftly drained away as foreign owned sterling was withdrawn. The New York Federal Reserve Bank would only lend a further £80m if the main proposals of the May Report were implemented. MacDonald knew there was no chance of persuading Labour MPs to accept such measures, especially as many were discussing the alternative of going off the Gold Standard. In August, with Parliament in recess, MacDonald resigned, leaving his colleagues to assume that this would result in a Tory or Tory/Liberal Coalition government. Instead he formed a 'National' Government of Tories and Liberals with himself as Prime Minister and Snowden still Chancellor of the Exchequer.

Birmingham reaction was summed up by Watchman in the *Town Crier* in a series of headlines. 'MacDonald and Snowden Choose the Wrong Road', 'Mistaken Sense of Duty Ingloriously ends Great Careers', 'United Labour Movement will Rally Behind Henderson', and 'The Power of High Finance Must be Broken'.

Watchman's predictions were confirmed. MacDonald called an election for 27 October 1931 and a united party had high hopes of victory. Tom May was chosen to contest the Aston seat formerly held by John Strachey. Jim Simmons was re-selected at Erdington. Simmons was particularly affected by MacDonald's defection. He had 'venerated' him, he wrote, recalling the days in 1917 when Simmons, a wounded serviceman and opponent of the war, was assisted by MacDonald.

But Labour had misread the mood of the electorate. Every Labour seat in Birmingham was lost. It was the most devastating defeat the party had ever suffered. The local elections the next month only confirmed the misery. Nine seats were lost, bringing representation on the Birmingham City Council to 89 Tories, 21 Labour, 3 Liberals, and 6 'Independents'.

Between 1931 and 1934 the Labour movement in Birmingham was at its lowest ebb. Socialists continued to wage bitter war on Communists as agents of the Soviet Union. Communists pursued sectarian policies in the belief that the further left a person's view the greater the danger to the working class because they were 'agents of imperialism.' The Independent Labour Party caught between these trends disaffiliated from the Labour Party in 1932.

It was not until the danger of Fascism was recognised and fuller employment made trade union organisation in the factories possible from 1935 that advances could be made. In the meantime, in these bleak years, the problems of working people were neglected.

Unemployment

One of these areas of neglect was the unemployed. Unemployment in Birmingham in the 1930s was considerably lower than it had been in the crisis years of 1921-23. In 1931, according to the Census of that year, 62,000 Birmingham people were unemployed or 12.4 per cent of those employed; the national figure in 1931 was 21.5 per cent. By 1933 Birmingham unemployment fell to 8.5 per cent while national unemployment was 21.3 per cent. Unemployment in Birmingham continued to fall until 1936 when it was just under 25,000 or 4 per cent (national figure 14.3 per cent). Despite this comparative advantage, unemployment in Birmingham was serious, particularly when cuts in benefit were implemented in 1931 and the Means Test introduced.

The militancy of the Birmingham unemployed in the period 1921-23 and the organisation of the first Hunger March from Birmingham to London, under the auspices of the National Unemployed Workers' Committee Movement has been recorded in Chapter 20. By 1925, when unemployment had fallen to about 32,000, NUWCM branches were beginning to disband and Deritend which turned itself into a Sunday Worker's League branch. might not have been alone.

In August 1926 Harry Horner, national organiser of the NUWCM suggested that the organisation concentrate on Birmingham targeting the Birmingham MPs Austen Chamberlain, Neville Chamberlain and Steel-Maitland, as Ministers responsible for Unemployment. But a campaign could not be sustained in the aftermath of the General Strike and with unemployment falling. Such a campaign was sustained, however in 1928 when unemployment again began to rise. In July a Birmingham Unemployed Campaign reported such activity as a mass meeting in West Birmingham and seven other meetings in the City.

Early in 1929 th NUWCM organised the second National Hunger March around the 'Not Genuinely Seeking Work' clause the invocation of which allowed local Public 'Assistance' Committees to deprive people of their benefit. The Lancashire contingent reached Birmingham on Feb 11th. Hannington tells what followed. There was a large reception Committee two miles from the city centre and the marchers proceeded to Digbeth where they were served a splendid meal provided by the local Co-ops. When they marched to the Workhouse, where they were to stay, unusually large numbers of police accompanied them. Once inside the Workhouse they were locked in casual cells, the police still making trouble by denying the marchers the service of their first aid men to attend to the feet of the marchers. They then left the Workhouse in protest, preferring to remain on the streets for the night. The police then rushed at the marchers, drawing their batons, and several men were seriously injured. After a fierce struggle the men were finally locked in the Workhouse. In the morning a huge protest against the police was staged in the Bull Ring and the marchers moved on to the more peaceful town of Stratford-on-Avon. Support for this march was wide, although it was officially boycotted by the Birmingham Trades Council and Labour Party.

But by November 1929 bitterness had returned and A.E. Smith, secretary of an NUWCM branch in Birmingham was complaining in the *Sunday Worker* that, 'NUWCM work has again been sabotaged by police activities and the local Labour Party which has had our local committee ejected from their Committee room.'

Agitation was renewed in 1931. A motion from Harry Shepperson was carried that the Trades Council receive a deputation from the NUWCM. Bernard Moore, the local NUWCM leader, explained that the campaign was around the slogan of 'Not a Penny off Unemployment Pay: Not a Worker off benefit: Down with the National Government.' Jim Crump stated that this was an opportunity for the Trades Council to lead the unemployment movement. The Trades Council agreed to be represented on a deputation to the General Purposes Committee and to nominate a speaker at a meeting of the Unemployed at the Town Hall, although it was stressed that the NUWCM was a proscribed organisation. The Town Hall meeting on 7 October was so crowded that many could not get in. But it was an unhappy meeting leading to charges of Communist 'wrecking tactics', which Communists on the Trades Council strenuously denied. The delegation to the G.P. Committee of the City Council on October 11th included John Strachey, Shepperson, Moore and the two Trades Council nominees. They were accompanied by thousands of unemployed who had marched from the Bull Ring. The delegation demanded that the Council refuse to operate the Means Test, restore outdoor relief scales and extend Public Works schemes, many of which had been postponed. The next day, when the demonstrating crowds had disappeared the G.P. Committee rejected all the delegates' demands.

On October 14th further large meetings and demonstrations throughout the City lasted all day and deputations went to the Lord Mayor and the Labour Exchange. Police brutality increased. A large force of police kept marchers on the move and refused to allow them to congregate before the Council House. On 20 October the Mayor refused to meet Moore, Strachey and Lily Webb, but they were detained in the Council House while police dispersed the demonstrators outside. Later in the day the two Communists Moore and Tom Roberts were bound over as 'disturbers of the peace' after a meeting at Gosta Green, but released in time to lead another march to the PAC offices the next day. Jack Trotter was bound over on 26 October for accusing the police of wilful perjury over the arrest of Moore. Lily Webb suffered a similar fate for a speech in the Bull Ring urging the unemployed to crowd the streets and besiege the PAC office.

In November Edward Newman, secretary of Selly Oak NUWCM, F. Johnson and B. Bywaters were bound over for inciting a crowd outside Selly Oak Labour Exchange. In December Newman, Tom Roberts, J. Gough and Lily Webb were fined for obstruction. Moore and Shepperson were charged with assault while leading a delegation to the Council House on December 11th. Moore was sentenced to ten months hard labour and Shepperson to nine months.

The agitation continued into 1932. In March a Petition organised by the Handsworth Council of Action contained nearly 41,000 signatures. To it was attached the death certificate of a man who had committed suicide because of unemployment. The Petition presented by Councillor Shurmer to the Council called on it to refuse to operate the Means Test and demanded a town's meeting. In July Harry Shepperson was given 6 months imprisonment for 'inciting certain persons to assault the police,' during a Bull Ring meeting. And in November Jack Trotter was sentenced to a horrifying fifteen months hard labour for 'incitement.'

This was the end of large scale militancy over unemployment in Birmingham. Whether it was ended by the fall in unemployment or by the 'police terror' in the City is a moot point. But it cannot be too strongly stressed that this savagery against the leaders of the unemployed, usually Communists, was perpetrated on ordinary working men (and their families) who at the best of times had difficulty obtaining work because of their beliefs. Heroism is not too strong a word for those who made sacrifices most of their lives and were prepared to suffer the additional horrors of imprisonment for the cause they believed in. Conversely the tradition of police brutality in Birmingham continued from the nineteenth century into the twentieth. It was ably led by the Chief Constable Sir Charles Rafter, successive Stipendiary magistrates, and the City Watch Committee. This violence must be recognised as excessive even by the standards of the day, and roundly condemned.

Trade Union Activity 1927-1939

The trade union unity generated by the General Strike was shattered almost immediately. The Trades Council and unions split into right and left as one group sought peace with employers as the way forward, whereas the left wing saw militancy as the only means to protect living standards.

Nationally the TUC inaugurated the Mond-Turner talks and conferences. This was followed up locally by Fred Rudland calling a meeting suggested by Alexander Ramsay of the Engineering Employers, of trade union officials and local employers to discuss the industrial situation. The idea of Industrial Peace was widely supported by Birmingham employers under the chairmanship of Sir Eric Geddes. Dunlop's opened a hall for their new works council called the Temple of Peace.

Meanwhile Rationalisation was the order of the day. The economies to be achieved by rationalisation in the new industries can be demonstrated by productivity at the Austin where the number of employees per car per week fell from 55 in 1922 to 10 in 1927 and 7 in 1933. Much rationalisation took place in the name of the Bedaux System, a crude time and motion system.

Despite the weakening of trade unionism after the Labour laws of 1927 opposition to Bedaux took the form of unofficial strikes in the years before the Slump. In 1927 200 workers at Lucas, Formans Road struck against reduced piece work earnings as a result of Bedaux. In May 1928 there was a similar strike at Moulded Products of Castle Bromwich. In March 1929 there was the first large scale strike in the country against Bedaux at the Austin, Longbridge. 5,000 men staged a stay-in claiming that their earnings would be reduced from £7 to £3. The stay-in was organised by a Committee led by W. Tegryn Bowen a former Welsh miner who had only been at Austin's for three months; the vice-chair was another ILP militant, S. Beardsmore.

After the General Strike, the Birmingham Trades Council took up the TUC vendetta against the Communist Party. In April 1927 a letter from the Minority Movement asked the Council to appoint delegates to their Fourth Annual Conference. A letter was then read from the TUC stating that any Trades Council affiliated to or associating with the MM would not be recognised by the TUC. Symes then moved and Trotter seconded a motion of protest to the TUC. Cardinal supported this stating that the TUC had no right interfering in matters over which they had no control and proposed that two delegates be sent. The resolution was opposed by NUR delegates and Corrin, the president, who felt there were sufficient other opportunities to discuss trade union affairs.

As we have seen at the Trades Council AGM in January 1928 Cardinal was pursued by the Birmingham Sub-Council of the NUR representing 16 branches for attending a Left-Wing Conference and supporting Dr Dunstan but next business was moved. Also in January Tom Lowe moved a resolution protesting against the Peace in Industry policy of the TUC and this was passed.

The right-wing of the Trades Council won a decisive victory at the 1929 AGM when H.G.

Johnson beat Cardinal for the Presidency by six votes after Corrin had resigned. This was also the year of the Communist turn to the Class against Class policy.

The Labour government, the slump and unemployment led to a temporary cessation of strikes, but these resumed in 1932. In May 10,000 Lucas workers staged a lightning strike against a points system based on Bedaux. When in August 1932 Lancashire cotton workers struck against the Six-Loom System (instead of two) they received the whole-hearted support of Birmingham Trades Council who in October organised a Conference on the Bedaux System and condemned all such systems of speed-up.

Just as important was the successful 11 week strike from March 1933 at Hope's Windows of Smethwick against the Bedeax System. Here the strike was led by Tom Roberts, a Communist, and organised under the principles of the Minority Movement and the Red International of Labour Unions. These principles were 1.A Central Rank and File Committee with all power to conduct the strike backed by Committees in every shop. 2. Mass pickets, dinner-hour meetings, and bulletins to encourage the strikers and gain outside support. 3.Absolute insistence on recruitment to the appropriate trade union. 4. Insistence that a National Unemployed Workers Committee Movement representative be co-opted to the Central Strike Committee to prevent scabbing. All power to the local strike committee, meant that full-time trade union officers could not intervene and order the men back to work while negotiations proceeded with the management. This, it was alleged, was what happened in the Austin strike of 1929 with the result of an unsatisfactory settlement. During the Hope strike, trade union officials were encouraged to assist and benefit from the increased trade union membership, but they were not allowed to interfere. Substantial economic gains were made and when the trade unions stated that under their constitutions they could not recognise shop committees, all members of these committees were turned into shop stewards. These tactics were to pay handsome dividends in the future.

Despite these signs of increasing militancy the right-wing redoubled their efforts to drive Communists out of the trades councils, as they had been driven out of the TUC. By 1934 the victory of Hitler in Germany the previous year was leading the Communists to change their policies again and they were demanding a United Front. The Trades Council rejected overtures dismissing them as Communist 'manoeuvres' or 'plots'. In this they were abetted by the *Town Crier* whose reporting at the time was totally right-wing with opposing views given little scope in the paper.

Matters came to a head in 1935. The Trades Council in pursuance of the TUC ruling that 'disruptive elements' should not be allowed to be delegates to Trades Councils put the matter to a ballot of its affiliated unions and the purge was endorsed by them. In May, the Trades Council then passed the following resolution by 75 votes to 54:

> No person shall be eligible to act as a delegate to the Birmingham Trades Council if he or she is a member of the Communist or Fascist Parties or any subsidiary organisation of these parties, or a member of an organisation proscribed by the General Council of the TUC.

It was ironic that this motion should be moved by Bill Cardinal who until 1927 had been a Communist but then moved steadily to the right and became president of the Trades Council in 1934 and 1935. Of other possible Communists only Tom Lowe and his daughter Winnie remained on the Trades Council executive after 1936. Tom might have been persuaded by his duties as organiser of the local Foundry Workers to resign from the Communist Party and he also became a member of the executive of the Birmingham Labour Party. Winnie perhaps followed her father and became treasurer and minute taker of the Trades Council. But both at heart were Communists and rejoined the Communist Party later. The ban lasted until 1942 when the Russians entered the war. But contact with Communists could not be avoided. Appeasement and the war in Spain became too important for bans and proscriptions to hold. In addition, as trade unionism grew the issue of free speech outside factories became a dominating issue, and those attempting to distribute leaflets or hold meetings were usually the 'disruptive elements' who had to be defended.

In the 1930s the police operated a ban on meetings at factory gates. One of the firms 'protected' from 1931 was Lucas's at Great King Street. After the strike of 1934 the ban was temporarily lifted but then reimposed. In October 1935 the Birmingham Council for Peace and Liberty was formed to fight the ban. In April 1936 two Communists, Bert Williams and a Cambridge undergraduate John Cornford were fined by the Stipendiary for obstruction when distributing leaflets, despite evidence of Peace & Liberty members that there was no obstruction. On appeal, the Recorder vindicated the rights of individuals to distribute leaflets and gave costs against the police. Despite this, the police continued, albeit more carefully, this practice.

Trade union growth continued, and the key factory remained the Austin. In November 1936 another strike against speed up both revealed the position left by the 1929 strike and how the lessons of Hope's were being learned. The 5,000 men who came out were mostly non-union and there was no leadership in the factory. The leadership had to come from outside said the *Town Crier* and it was a Communist leaflet which urged the setting up of a strike committee, picketing, and the necessity to join the union. There were also other weakness, the paper pointed out, such as inter-union rivalry, and a condescending attitude to the strikers. Clearly much still remained to be done to make Austins a union firm.

Two years later in September 1938 Austin Aero workers at the 'shadow factory' were on strike. Here were 6000 workers mostly highly skilled many earning only 36/-d. per week. This was the fourth time in two years that there had been strikes at the Aero, the *Town Crier* said. Trade union membership seems to have been low, although there was organisation within the factory which had called the strike. The strike was therefore 'unofficial' and the policy of Lord Austin was to prevaricate until the men drifted back to work, it was claimed. This did not happen and a week later the strikers supported the strike committee's call to return to work. This was the second strategy of management once it was clear that the strike could not be ignored – to get the men back to work while endless negotiations proceeded. The point at issue was the basic rate of pay. This was unimportant some argued, it was the total sum in the wage packet that mattered. But from the basic rate was calculated piece rates, overtime rates, holiday entitlement etc. and thus it was the key to what was in the wage packet. The settlement of the strike was clearly partial and it could even be represented as a defeat.

Such struggles on a smaller scale were taking place in other factories during this period when trade unionism was being strengthened in Birmingham.

From 1937 politics figures much more prominently in trade union affairs. The 1937 Trades Council report regretted that the British and French governments had not taken a 'courageous stand' at Geneva and called the bluff of Hitler and Mussolini when they could have been stopped. 1938 was the year of Munich. 'The humiliating spectacle of a British Premier, against the wishes of his advisers, waiting on Hitler at Berchtesgarten and returning with an ultimatum! has only made war more certain", lamented Spragg and Rudland in the 1938 Annual Report, By the following year war was a fact.

In attempting to assess the progress of trade unionism in Birmingham in the period 1918 to 1939, it seems reasonable to assume that Trades Council fortunes fluctuated in much the same way as most individual trade unions. Trades Council income continued to be spread over a number of trade union groups with no one industry predominating. In 1938 the rail unions again seem to have contributed the largest share of the £621 income from affiliation fees at about £85 followed by the many building trade unions with almost £70. The AEU contributed nearly £60. Of the two general unions the Municipal and General contributed £58 and the Transport & General Workers £46. Brass & Metal Mechanics at £42 were the only other sizeable contributor.

Trades Council income for selected years was as follows:

1922	1923	1926	1927	1933	1936	1937	1938	1939
£983	£679	£675	£370	£355	£425	£555	£621	£640

The 1922 figure shows income at its highest when the cost of living was at its highest. 1923 was a slump year but the cost of living had fallen by about 5 per cent. Income continued stable until 1926. The effect of the General Strike is seen by the drastic fall in income of no less than 45 per cent. There followed the slump of the 1930s when income continued to fall. From 1936 income rose considerably under the influence of fuller employment, but in the last full year of peace income had not reached the 1923 level, although allowing for a fall in the cost of living of about 10 per cent between 1923 and 1938 in real terms income was about the same. This is scarcely an impressive performance for the inter-war years. It was to take another war to restore Birmingham Trades Council to its former stature and influence.

The Struggle to Prevent War 1932-1939

The inter-war years were dominated by the struggle to preserve peace and in one sense the surprise is not that World War 2 broke out when it did, but that it did not break out earlier. From 1919 the struggle was to stop the war against Russia. In 1924 the Labour government signed a trade treaty with the Soviet Union, but this was not ratified in Parliament and in 1926 the Arcos Raid on the Soviet Trade Mission on the familiar grounds that it was an espionage centre led to a further fear that militarists and those who had had their property confiscated would lead a further war against the Soviet Union. In addition there were colonial demands for independence which imperialists felt it necessary to subdue notably in India, China and Egypt. Under the second Labour government there was a temporary respite when establishing diplomatic relations with the Soviet Union was approved in Parliament against the votes of all but three Tories. But by 1930 the slump and world-wide unemployment brought the menace of fascism which was to lead to war.

The Peace forces in Birmingham were considerable. There were the Pacifist Quakers in their Cadbury strongholds who held annual peace conferences which always had an international element. There was the powerful pacifist element in the Independent Labour Party with its experience of 1914-18 war resistance; its three main spokesmen tended to be Jim Simmons, the disabled war veteran, W.J. Chamberlain, Quaker and ILPer who occupied the powerful position of editor of the *Town Crier,* and Joseph Southall, Birmingham's famous painter, who became the conscience of the ILP. They were joined by Wilfred Wellock, war resister and pioneer of the No More War Movement, who became a Stourbridge Labour MP. Then there were the militant anti-war and anti-imperialist elements, usually led by the Communist Party, but always overlapping with many other sections around which the campaigns for the United Front and later the People's Front were waged.

The Peace movement in Birmingham, as elsewhere, tended to be divided. In 1931 Watchman in the *Town Crier* was accusing the No More War Movement of collaborating with the Communists. This was vehemently denied by Will Rowe (secretary of the Birmingham Council of the NMWM) and also Wilfred Willock who quoted in evidence that the local NMWM was not affiliated to the National Anti-War Council. In June 1932 Will Rowe explained that a renewed danger of war arose from the fact that the Japanese had been allowed to invade Manchuria because they were seen as an ally against Communism, and the success of the Russians in avoiding unemployment during the slump was attracting working people to their doctrines and capitalists in Britain were even more anxious to destroy the Soviet Union. At a large War Danger Conference at Digbeth with 240 delegates representing 78 organisations a Birmingham Council of Action was set up. It condemned the League of Nations as 'an instrument of war' and decided to send delegates to the Anti-War Conference at Geneva. By the end of the year Watchman was quarrelling with the decisions of the No More War Movement annual Conference at Sheffield which, in his opinion would split the movement by bringing in questions of what the movement would do once war broke out, instead of concentrating solely on how to prevent war.

Peace had a particular attraction for young people at this time. In August 1933 a Birmingham Youth Peace Conference was organised jointly by the Labour League of Youth, the Co-operative Comrades Circles, the ILP Guild of Youth, the Young Communist League and the No More War Movement. it was held at the large house and gardens of Mr and Mrs Sargeant Florence, prominent citizens both of who were active in the Peace movement. The main speaker was an Indian who saw British imperialism as the main war danger. The Conference passed a resolution demanding immediate complete disarmament. 1933 was also the year of the famous Oxford Union debate when the gilded youth of the nation voted 275 to 153 that they would not fight for King and Country, and when Tory big guns and the military were brought to Oxford to overturn the decision they were beaten by 750 votes to 188.

The highlight of 1934 was the 24th. National Peace Conference which was held in Birmingham in June. It opened with an address by G.P. Gooch, the historian, on 'The International Outlook'. This led Joseph Southall to ask whether they were at a Peace Congress or a League of Nations Congress. The Congress satisfied nobody. The Pacifists were accused of disrupting the Congress because their views were not accepted. When collective security was discussed the various views that the League of Nations was either a League of Imperialists or completely ineffectual were voiced. One result in Birmingham was that certain religious views were clarified. The Bishop of Birmingham, Dr Barnes, was in favour of Britain disarming, unilaterally if necessary. The Rector of Birmingham, Guy Rogers, also supported disarmament refusing to believe that that the resources of reasonableness and Christianity had been exhausted. Discussion in Birmingham was stimulated both before and after the Congress. Canon Tredennick was challenged to debate by the League of Nations Birmingham Youth Groups for his 'notorious' statement to a British Legion parade at Sparkbrook that war was inevitable unless Britain was fully armed. There were plenty of other clergyman 'followers of the Prince of Peace' sharing this view.

But 1935 saw the most remarkable peace manifestation in Birmingham. This was the National Peace Ballot. It arose from the League of Nations Union deciding to organise a national poll on the League and Collective Security. it invited other national bodies to serve on a National Declaration Committee which would sponsor and organise such a Ballot. Thirty eight organisations responded including Churches, Peace Societies, women's organisations, the Liberal Party, the Labour Party, the TUC and the Co-operative Movement. The Conservative Party did not support it nationally, but left local organisations free to do so if they wished. The Ballot required organisation at Constituency and ward levels throughout the country and a vast army of volunteers. There was almost no money to fund it. Would it be successful? What percentage of people would participate? In Birmingham by January 1935 there was organisation in nine of the city's twelve Divisions and most of the Wards. All political parties in the city were participating and at Ballot HQ, 168a Corporation Street, they were 'quietly confident.' The Ballot was staggered throughout the country. When it was Birmingham's turn in February 1935 6,000 volunteers had been enrolled but a further 550 were required. Everyone over eighteen years was entitled to vote and the Ballot went on for a fortnight. The results were announced in March. The questions and the numbers replying were as follows:

	For	*Against*
1. Should Great Britain remain a member of the League of Nations.	275,523	6,479
2. Are you in favour of an all-round reduction of armaments by international agreement?	259,007	21,681
3. Are you in favour of the all-round abolition of national military and naval aircraft by international agreement?	226,486	51,449
4. Should the manufacture and sale of armaments for private profit be prohibited by international agreement?	249,353	27,197
5. Do you consider that if a nation insists on attacking another the other nations should combine to compel it to stop by		
(a) economic and non-military measures	246,077	16,960
(b) if necessary, military measures	184,914	56,375

The Poll was a huge success. 284,004 people had voted representing 43.3 per cent of Birmingham people aged 18 and over. In the days before scientific opinion polls were possible, this was the largest poll undertaken in Britain and was a massive exercise in democracy and democratic participation by the population on the most important matter of all, war or peace.

Opinion in Birmingham mirrored opinion elsewhere. Overwhelming support for the League of Nations. Massive support for reduction of arms by international agreement and only slightly less support for complete disarmament. Very large majorities for ending the private sale of arms, this at a time when the USA Senate was hearing evidence of incitement of wars by arms salesmen and manufacturers and a similar enquiry was to be held in Britain. Lastly the vexed question of what to do with an aggressor; another vast majority for sanctions and smaller but considerable support for the taking of military measures if all else failed.

Although it was never tested on this scale again this probably remained the public view and bitter experience proved that they had been correct. However the British government took the opposite road of attempting to appease the fascist powers in pursuit of its wider campaign to destroy the Soviet Union.

Spain, Fascism and War

The Peace Ballot of 1935 came at a turning point in the international situation. 1935 was an election year. The Labour Party could not afford to be called the peace party if the Tories were re-arming; nor could it afford to be called the war party if the Tories were disarming. The same dilemma faced the Tory Party. but Baldwin neatly solved it by standing on a peace policy and then immediately reversing it and starting a large re-armament programme after he had won. In Birmingham the Labour Party was punished for its indecisive policy and split ranks by again failing to win a single seat. G.F. Sawyer came nearest in Duddeston, but even here the Tory majority was 3.262. The Labour Party had to console itself with the thought that it had polled one third of the votes, but had not won a seat. The local elections had set the dismal pattern, when the Labour Party had lost four seats.

In July 1936 General Franco began his armed revolt against the democratically elected Spanish Republican Government, and from this time began a political crusade to save Spain which captured the minds and hearts of progressive people in a way that has only been matched since with the war in Viet-Nam.

At this time the organised Labour forces in Birmingham were aligned roughly as follows. The Labour Party and trade unions were sympathetic to the Republican cause but not willing to take any steps likely to involve them in co-operation with the Communist Party. The Co-operative movement took the same line but was a little more flexible. The Independent Labour Party had finally taken the plunge in 1932 and disaffiliated itself from the Labour Party. It had also broken with the theory of gradualism and called itself a Revolutionary Socialist Party. Instead of attracting the vast following that it had hoped, this destroyed the ILP, as most well- and ill-wishers had prophesied. ILP branches disappeared and with it went almost all the Labour Churches and the main driving force for Socialism within the Labour party which it had been since 1893. Its renunciation of gradualism and embracing of revolution led it to associate in Spain not with the main Republican cause but with the minority POUM anarchists in Catalonia.

The Communist Party officially renounced its Class against Class policy, with its total opposition to the Labour Party as the third party of capitalism, from the Seventh Congress of the Communist International in 1935. From this time the British Party reverted to its normal policy of seeking affiliation to the Labour Party and the industrial policy of building up the existing trade unions. In 1934 the Soviet Union joined the League of Nations and from that time the Communist Party stood unswervingly for the prevention of war by Collective Security through the League of Nations. Thus the Communists had a consistent and largely correct policy for avoiding war which, together with the energy and initiative of its increasing membership, attracted both working and professional people and continued to give the party an influence far beyond its numbers.

The war in Spain played a part in the setting up of the Birmingham Council for Peace and Liberty in October 1935. The main issue at the time was free speech in the city, but the Council played a leading part in the subsequent struggle against appeasement under the leadership of Mrs Newth.

The initial rebellion of army officers led by Franco was a failure and within weeks he found it necessary to seek arms from Germany and troops from Italy. The reaction of the British government to this was the policy of Non-Intervention. Such a policy treated both the democratically elected government and the rebels on 'equal terms' and denied the republican government the right to buy arms. Under these circumstances the only government willing to supply arms was that of the Soviet Union. Then to prevent these arms and supplies reaching Spain a sea blockade was set up! Under these circumstances the influence of the Soviet Union increased considerably thus feeding the paranoia of those, including the Labour Party and trade union leaders who were obsessed with the 'Communist menace.'

Almost from the beginning of the rebellion a wide Aid Spain movement spread throughout the country. In Birmingham it was spearheaded by the Council for Peace and Liberty. Associated with its committee were the two Communist organisers in the city, Jim Crump and Bert Williams, also Joseph Southall of the ILP, and Julius Silverman, Harrison Barrow, and Duncan Jones who were all Labour Party members. Mrs Newth the secretary, a history teacher at Edgbaston High school and her husband, a lecturer at the University, were also Labour Party members. The chairman was Councillor W.E. Wheeldon of the Birmingham Co-operative Society. Other active supporters were John Kennedy, John Cornford, Margot Heinemann and George Thompson, all Communist academics, Lucy Hutchinson a curator at the Art Gallery and Dr Leys and his wife. Youth and enthusiasm to chalk on walls, distribute leaflets and organise was provided by the Young Communist League, the Labour League of Youth and university students.

The Council for Peace and Liberty made it clear from the start that its aim was not only to raise medical supplies and food for Spain, but also to pressurise the British government to recognise the Spanish government. In August the Council organised its first city centre demonstration in the Bull Ring. Here it was announced that both the Labour Party and the Trades Council in the city were backing an appeal by the National Joint Council of Labour to raise funds for Spain. The medical profession was raising the question of ambulances for Spain at this time and this was taken up in Birmingham by Dr Leys. Another united Bull Ring demonstration at the end of August passed resolutions in support of Spanish democracy and marched to the Spanish Consulate. In October there was a great Town Hall meeting addressed by Ellen Wilkinson and John Langdon-Davies. Jim Crump took a collection of £120 stated to be the largest yet collected outside London. Taking up the Spanish slogan of They Shall Not Pass, the meeting ended with a torchlight procession through the city centre led by Ellen Wilkinson.

In December the Council produced its own pamphlet Rebellion in Spain written by Helen Grant, a lecturer in Spanish at Birmingham University, It had a postscript by the Council demanding a change in British government policy.

Important events which influenced the anti-fascist struggle must now be outlined before we leave 1936. Strengthening the case for unity was the victory of the left in France. About the same time came the first fruits of appeasement. In March Hitler marched into the Rhineland. Excuses could be found for this act of aggression; it was, after all, German territory it could be argued. In May the Italians defeated Abyssinia and Haile Salassie was taken into exile by a British warship. This was a blatant act of aggression where Britain and France had failed to activate the League of Nations to implement sanctions, not even on oil, where Mussolini was thought to be vulnerable. Excuses were made that Britain was not willing to risk a war against Italy.

Attitudes to the Soviet Union were moved two ways during 1936. Sidney and Beatrice Webb's book *Soviet Communism – A New Civilisation?* argued not only the superiority of a planned economy, but that Soviet democracy was superior to western democracy. This appeared to be confirmed when the new 1936 Soviet Constitution was ratified offering not only western freedoms of speech and action, but Socialist freedoms of full employment and welfare from th cradle to the grave. On the other hand, the first of the great trials took place in Moscow, that of Zinoviev and accomplices. Most people found it almost impossible to believe that leaders of the revolution had been plotting and spying for the west for many years. Yet the Fifth Column of those within waiting to betray the cause became familiar from the Spanish rebellion and later in France and Norway. Also the Soviet Union lived with the constant fear of attack by the western powers. Sir Walter Citrine (TUC secretary, leading opponent of the united front, and one of the first to take an 'honour' from the capitalist state) slated the Webb's book and his review was reprinted in the *Town Crier,* while Watchman became an implacable opponent of the United Front in Birmingham.

In 1936 the Communist Party campaigned throughout the year for affiliation to the Labour Party. The party in Birmingham was growing fast and now had its own premises and bookshop at 42 Holloway Head. Both Harry Pollitt and William Gallacher (with his new status of the only Communist MP) came to Birmingham to argue the case. At the Labour Party Conference in October affiliation was defeated by 1,728,000 to 592,000 votes. The majority was bloated by the block vote of the trade unions, notably the two main anti-communist unions, Ernest Bevin's Transport & General Workers and the Municipal and General Workers' Union. This result was of little use to the many active Labour Party members and trade unionists who were already involved in joint united front work with the Communists. An earlier result of this dilemma was the suspension of the National Advisory Council of the Labour League of Youth on constitutional grounds, but these were connected with the amount of independence enjoyed by the League and its current tendency to united front activity. It was vigorously opposed by the Birmingham LoY branches.

1937 was also a year dominated by events in Spain. The increasing use of German and Italian troops with their aircraft and tanks while the Republic was denied arms was having its inevitable effect. In April Guernica was razed to the ground by German bombers prompting widespread horror throughout a world not yet inured to mass bombing; it also brought the immortal picture by Picasso. By October all of northern Spain was in fascist hands.

In Birmingham 1937 began with a Spain Week organised by the Birmingham Council for Peace and Liberty. It included a Spain Exhibition at 166 Corporations Street, the showing of the film 'The Defence of Madrid' and a Conference at Digbeth, speaker Professor Harold Laski on 'Spain, the Next Step.' Birmingham people were asked to give money and food for Spain, learn the facts, read and sell pamphlets about Spain and organise meetings at local Co-op Guilds, trade union branches, political meetings and League of Nations Union branches.

1937 was the year when most of the volunteers to the International Brigade went to Spain. Of the two Birmingham organisers of the Communist Party Bert Williams was allowed to go to Spain where he served as a political commissar for some months. Jim Crump was requested to stay behind and organise the volunteers. A decision to accept international volunteers had been made by the Spanish government in October 1936. One of the first Birmingham men to volunteer was Dr C.C. Bradsworth who became medical officer in Madrid to the International Column and played a pioneering role in the development of treatment of the wounded. Another anti-fascist doctor, Duncan Leys, was refused permission to go to Spain by the Birmingham City Council. All prospective volunteers for Spain were screened by Jim Crump. This became an illegal operation from January 1937 when, in the name of 'non-intervention', the British government banned the volunteers. Crump screened men for both their political reliability and also their suitability for combat action. Volunteers reported to the Communist Party headquarters in Birmingham and, if accepted made their way to London and then by various stratagems to France where they were passed on by anti-fascists to Spain, sometimes having to cross the mountains between France and Spain on foot. Crump rejected more men than he approved, but in all 22 volunteers went to Spain from Birmingham and another eight from surrounding districts. Of these, five were killed.

Returning to events in Birmingham, the success of Spain Week was followed up by other united action. The Spain Exhibition went round the city, starting with Kings Norton Divisional Labour Party taking it. The Women's Committee Wool for Spain at 42 Holloway Head appealed for warm clothing after disclosing that the winter was particularly severe and that one third of Madrid had been bombed by the fascists with thousands homeless and epidemics threatening.

In February the Trades Council demanded that the arms embargo on Spain be lifted. The same month John Cornford was killed is Spain. Although not a native of Birmingham his few months work as a Communist had made an important impact on the City. As a memorial to him it was proposed by the Council for Peace and Liberty (CPL) that the lorry it was raising money for to give to the Spanish government, together with the medical supplies and equipment with which it would be filled would be raised in the name of John Cornford.

In March a deputation representing almost every divisional Labour Party in the city and headed by the chair of the City party, Harrison Barrow, met Attlee in the House of Commons to demand a more active policy on Spain by the Parliamentary Labour Party. Attlee managed to convince them that the position was 'very difficult.' Attlee himself was the only Labour MP who visited Spain and a company of the British battalion was named after him. The Cornford Lorry was paid for in March with a topped up collection of £125 taken by Isabel Brown at a united town hall meeting organised by the CPL in conjunction with the Spanish Defence Committee. Reports in the *Town Crier* testified that every division and ward Labour Party branch was collecting, organising dances and bazaars and in many other ways supporting Spanish Aid.

In May the Trades Council was protesting at the 'German invasion of the Basque territory.' Later in the month another Bull Ring demonstration organised by the CPL was chaired by Jim Simmons with such leading Labour figures as J.W. Crump (Jim's father.) under the slogans 'Remember

Guernica Save Madrid!' An Ambulance for Spain Fund was launched in June at the Priory Rooms by the CPL with a platform of Harrison Barrow, the Dean of Canterbury, the Rector of Birmingham Canon Guy, Willie Gallacher Communist MP, Joseph Southall and Miss Lloyd Williams of the 'Save the Children' Spanish Fund. The Dean of Canterbury brought a harrowing eye witness report of German bombing in Spain and told how at Guernica attacking planes had followed the bombers shooting down the fleeing population for a distance of five miles.

In July a Labour Party Spain Conference was addressed by David Grenfell, a member of the National Council of Labour. Speakers demanded the right of the Spanish government to buy arms and an end to non-intervention. Grenfell defended the Labour leaders against charges of betrayal and said that outright challenge to government policy would have to face charges of Labour being prepared to make war on Germany and Italy. The most militant response the conference could think of was a deputation to Transport House to urge a national demonstration to help Spain.

Following these unsatisfactory exchanges, in August the Labour Party and the Trades Council set up a Birmingham Spanish Aid Committee with the function of assisting and co-ordinating all the efforts being made in the city to help Spain. One of its first public actions was a great Town Hall rally protesting at the British government appointing Agents in those parts of Spain occupied by the Franco forces and calling for aid for Spain. The main speaker was Hugh Dalton and from his speech it was clear that the focus was passing from aid as a humane and democratic gesture to the Spanish people to a necessary measure of self defence against fascism.

The events of these years brought a rapid politicisation of the general public, particularly young people. Two attempts to cater for this were the Penguin 6d. books with their Specials such as *Searchlight on Spain* by the Duchess of Atholl which sold 100,000 copies in a few weeks in 1938 and also *Picture Post* with its graphic pictures of the war in Spain. Another development from 1936 was the immensely successful Left Book Club (LBC) set up by Victor Gollancz. This was attractive to the middle class and intellectual recruits to political activity. The first mention of the Club in Birmingham in the *Town Crier* was in February 1937 when it announced that 'nearly one hundred Birmingham men and women mostly under forty' went to the national rally of the Club at the Albert Hall. Here Gollancz stated that 140,000 members had been made in eight months. Other speakers were John Strachey, Richard Acland Liberal MP, Professor Laski, D.N. Pritt KC and Labour MP, and Harry Pollitt. Greetings were received from General Miaja in charge of the defence of Madrid, from LBC members fighting in Spain, the Indian National Congress, and 114 Radical MPs of the French Parliament. The platform represented the national leadership of the Unity Campaign soon to be launched. By June 1937 there were twelve Left Book Club groups in Birmingham. Their function was to encourage the purchase of one book per month for 2/6d. and to create discussion groups to talk about current politics. Left Book Club members were from the beginning devout supporters of the Spanish Republican government, opponents of appeasement and believers in the People's Front. They very much widened the circle of people involved in anti-fascist politics. But their insistence on unity fell foul of the national and local trade union and Labour Party leaders who would have no truck with the Soviet Union and the Communist Party.

The question of unity was the overriding consideration if war was to be prevented and it is to this that we finally turn in discussing the events of 1937.

The early part of the year was dominated by efforts of the Socialist League to create a united front with the rump of the Independent Labour Party and the Communist Party. When the ILP made its disastrous decision to disaffiliate from the Labour Party in 1932, those members opposed to this decision formed the Socialist League as a purely educational body affiliated to the Labour Party. As such it had a presence in Birmingham. But as it elaborated radical policies that the executive of the Labour Party increasingly rejected, it could not resist the temptation to constitute itself a party especially after Sir Stafford Cripps became its leader in 1933.

By January 1937 a formal agreement between these three parties was reached and a series of mass meetings throughout the country began. The Birmingham meeting was held in early February. The chairman, Frank Horrabin, spoke for the Socialist League claiming that the joint Manifesto was a call for unity of all working class forces under the banner of the Labour Party and the trade unions.

Wal Hannington for the Communists said that in the past five years the British government had done everything in its power to assist international fascism; from Japan to Manchuria to Germany and Abyssinia it was one long record of betrayal. 'Don't wait until you are forced to talk about unity in a Fascist concentration camp,' he concluded. Fenner Brockway speaking for the ILP said the inaction of the Labour movement over Spain was 'a blot on working class history' and indicating that the ILP would willingly return to the Labour Party if there was any chance of its structure being democratised. The meeting ended with an appeal for all organisations of the working class to demand unity.

These powerful appeals were widely discussed in the *Town Crier*. Jim Simmons and Watchman were for unity within the Labour Party, but critics declared that it would take too long to change policy, especially in view of the block vote. Others argued that capitalists would not allow Socialism to be implemented in Britain and they would do what the German capitalists had done and crush the Labour movement.

The answer of the Labour Party executive was to caution all Labour party members that the Communist Party was a proscribed organisation and appeal for its own brand of unity – within the Labour Party. We have seen that the response of the Birmingham Labour Party was to criticise national inaction with regard to aid to Spain and its tacit support of non-intervention.

At the end of January 1937, the Labour Party executive expelled the Socialist League from the Labour Party. In March the Socialist League dissolved itself to avoid further hassle for its Labour Party members. But this did not end the Unity Campaign, nor did it solve the question of Sir Stafford Cripps who, for the time being, remained a member who was difficult to expel because of his brilliance as a Labour Party MP and also his personal popularity. In May J.S. Middleton, the national secretary of the Labour Party wrote to all divisional Labour Parties reminding them that the League had been expelled, but continued to function and pursue what he called 'the so-called Unity Campaign.' However, the same week the Birmingham Council for Peace and Liberty was holding a united demonstration in Birmingham with Jim Simmons in the chair and the *Town Crier* was full of reports of joint activity on Spain.

As a general war loomed the dilemmas of the Pacifists deepened. As we have said, the leading pacifists in Birmingham tended to be those who had gone through the First World War. In June a Peace Convention met in Birmingham called by the Parliamentary Pacifist Group, the Peace Pledge Union and other organisations. It was presided over by Wilfred Wellock who set out three principles: The nature of modern warfare rendered civilisation and warfare incompatible terms; War was War whether it was for defence, aggression or for collective security; the road to peace lay in constructive action through Justice, Generosity and Goodwill. The first resolution stated that war was a Crime against God and Man and all had the right to renounce participation in war preparations and war. This was passed unanimously. The second resolution called on the British government to call a World Conference at which the economic and territorial grievances of all countries should be discussed and settled by mutual adjustments. This also was passed. But a third resolution calling for a strengthening of the League of Nations by founding its authority 'on the moral authority of world public opinion rather than upon the armed coercion of collective security or an armed police force,' ran into trouble from the ILP delegates led by Joseph Southall. The ILP wanted to get rid of the 'sham' League of Nations and replace it with a real one, It was a thieves' kitchen of treaty breakers directly responsible for the triumph of Nazism in Germany, Southall declared. Another resolution demanded total disarmament and the ending of all treaties and commitments with other powers, but this was virtually rejected by urging that the education of public opinion must be the driving force behind any attempt to reduce arms. A separate political Peace Party was rejected. A motion rejecting Conscription was seconded by a delegate from War Resisters' International on the grounds against it used in the First World War, namely that it was incompatible with democracy. It was a form of British fascism. it was claimed.

Wellock continued to argue the pacifist case in August when the Parliamentary Labour Party had abstained from voting for the Army, Navy and Air Force estimates. Wellock thought the Labour Party was no longer the Peace Party; the Labour Party thought it would be inconsistent to urge the Government to more active measures against fascism and deny the means necessary to carry them out. Watchman supported Wellock.

In August the Bourneville Works Council held the 15th Boeke International Conference on Problems of War and Peace. This was a Trust established by Miss Beatrice Cadbury who renounced her share of profits made by Cadbury's through war. She had married Mr Boeke who ran an international children's school in Holland. Sixty delegates attended from many countries. H.N. Brailsford, the lecturer for the week, concentrated on the development of the League of Nations to prevent war.

Pacifist ranks were split, however, when Watchman wrote in defence of the Labour Party policy and was criticised by Wellock.

The No More War Movement continued active at this time with meetings throughout the city. New local figures were John Ballinger and Councillor Mrs Lennard of the Women's International League. In November there was a Birmingham League of Nations Week with meetings every day.

The next development in unity came when the Birmingham and District Co-operative Party used the occasion of its annual Town Hall demonstration to invite Sir Stafford Cripps to talk about the recent Labour Party Conference. This had partly met widespread criticism of the block vote and right-wing trade union leaders controlling the party by allowing a larger number of constituency representatives on the NEC. This had partly been achieved by the Socialist League and the Unity campaign and also the criticisms of the Birmingham Labour Party, Cripps maintained, and he considered the Bournemouth Conference to have been a turning point in the development of the Labour Party.

Arising from the increasing middle class interest in the Soviet Union a Society for Cultural Relations with the Soviet Union was formed. It held a remarkable three day Midlands Congress for Peace and Friendship in November, It opened with a session for businessmen at the Chamber of Commerce. Messages of support were received from George Bernard Shaw and Sir Norman Angel. Canon Guy Rogers chaired sessions of the Congress and defended the position of a Christian supporting a so-called atheist country. Edith Summerskill spoke on the enormous develops in health. Dudley Collard defended the Soviet penal system as a fair one, remedial rather than penal. The Earl of Listowel emphasised that the only way of avoiding war was the co-operation of Britain and France with the USSR.

1938 – Czechoslovakia, the Final Betrayal

In Spain the Republican government continued to resist against impossible odds. By April the fascists had cut Spain in two. In July the Republic launched its last offensive on the Ebro, but this was eventually defeated. In September the International Brigades were withdrawn and in March 1939 the Republic was finally defeated. Aid to Spain from Birmingham continued to flow. A Spanish Refugee Children's Fund supported both the Quaker colonies in Spain and also three children's homes in the Birmingham area which were partly furnished by the Birmingham Co-operative Society. A Birmingham Labour Party initiative to form a Council of Action to support Spain would have put all the Labour movement's resources and full-time officers behind the campaign, but it was frustrated by national trade union opposition. Nevertheless a united committee sponsored the Birmingham Food Ship at the end of 1938 and both the local Trades Council and the Labour Party continued to collect aid for Spain and also supported its right to buy arms and an end to 'non-intervention'.

But the struggle against the whole policy of appeasement probably detracted from the campaign on Spain. In February 1938 the split in the Conservative Party over appeasement became open when Anthony Eden resigned as Foreign Secretary and the possibility of Forming a Popular Front including Winston Churchill emerged, despite the loathing with which Churchill was regarded for his actions during the General Strike and earlier.

In March 1938 Hitler's troops marched into Vienna. At the same time Hitler was raising the question of 'uniting' the 3 million Germans in the Sudetenland of Czechoslovakia. In May the *Town Crier* printed a statement by the Labour Party E.C. rejecting any consideration of a Popular Front. It quoted the difficulties of co-operating with Conservatives on the right and the Communist Party and ILP on the left; in this they might have had a point, but they failed to deal with the main point which was their continued support of non-intervention in Spain and their refusal to consider an alliance with the USSR. But in May the Birmingham Labour Party by a large majority rejected the policy of their EC and supported a Popular Front. In June the League of Nations Union brought Winston

Churchill to a Town Hall meeting; the chair was taken by the Lord Mayor and other speakers included Canon Guy Rogers. Churchill said that three things were necessary, the immediate re-arming of Britain, support for the Covenant of the League of Nations, and co-operation with all those who supported peace and freedom.

Also in June the United Peace Alliance held a meeting in Birmingham attended by Co-operators, Labour Party members, Communists and others. The United Peace Alliance was the brain child of the editor of the Co-operative Sunday paper *Reynold's News*. Its policy was one of strengthening the League of Nations, guaranteeing the independence of Czechoslovakia, by arms if necessary, to combat fascism in Spain and Air Raid Precautions in Britain. The Alliance had the advantage of not proposing alterations to political structures as did the Popular or United Fronts, and this was made more important as the time for Parliamentary elections was drawing near. Alfred Barnes, chair of the Co-operative Party Conference, spoke for action to defeat fascism, but ruled out a Popular Front, which was a product in Europe of proportional representation, he claimed.

In September 1938 the Communist Party held its 15th Congress in Birmingham 'occupying the Town Hall' as the *Town Crier* reported with its call for a Popular Front embracing not only the working class, but middle class and professional people, farmers and workers in the countryside, and the Churches, particularly the Roman Catholic church whose hierarchy was still supporting Franco. On the Friday night there was a moving memorial meeting to those who had died in Spain. The next night there was community singing, Unity Male Choir singing British, Spanish, Soviet, and what was then little known, Chinese and Chinese Red Army songs. The *Town Crier* was greatly impressed with the discipline, elan, determination and pageantry of a Party which had grown to nearly 16,000 members, of whom probably near to 150 were Birmingham members.

The shameful events of the autumn of 1938 made world war inevitable. The Czechs refused the demands of Hitler to annex the Sudetenland. They had treaties with both France and Russia to come to their aid if attacked. Despite this Chamberlain flew to Berchtesgaden and negotiated with Hitler to meet his demands on Czechoslovakia. When he returned, together with France and ignoring Russia, he put irresistible pressure on Czechoslovakia to cede large parts of their country to Hitler. On 30 September the Munich Agreement was signed giving large parts of Czechoslovakia to Hitler in return for which Chamberlain brought his famous 'peace in our time' document that Germany had no further territorial claims on Europe. In March 1939 Hitler occupied the rest of Czechoslovakia.

In Birmingham in January 1939 the Labour movement was involved in the great council house tenants' Rent Strike with a 42,000 signature Petition to the Birmingham City Council refusing to pay rent increases. A national all party deputation went to the Prime Minister on the eve of his talks with Mussolini seeking assurances of an end to Italian intervention in Spain, no recognition of belligerent rights or any other measure of starving the Spanish government into submission, and the protection of British ships plying their legitimate trade with Spain. Five Birmingham people were on the deputation, Councillor Silverman, Dr Killick, Messrs Sweetland and Tyler and Mrs Griffiths. Chamberlain and Halifax refused to meet the delegation. The last great battles in Spain were being waged. Birmingham Council for Peace and Liberty was still holding Town Hall meetings on Arms for Spain, but the great national campaign led by the Labour Party was Foodships for Spain. Birmingham was allocated a Food Ship. Ten days before the campaign was due to end the £1,000 appeal had raised £375 and Birmingham eventually joined with the Midland Food Ship. At this time there was a youth initiative with the formation of a united National Youth Campaign of Service for Peace and Democracy with a policy of changing the government's policy to one based on collective security around the League of Nations. An appeal to support the youth was signed by a broad spectrum of people including A.E. Ager, Christopher Cadbury and Bert Williams.

Early in 1939 the Popular Front agitation was renewed by Sir Stafford Cripps with his Memorandum and Petition. The former demanded greater efforts to remove the Chamberlain government. His Manifesto was rejected by the Labour Party national executive who had now developed a defence that (a) a United Front was impossible because of the proximity of the next general election and (b) those who advocated a Popular Front were hob-nobbing with right wing parties and thus betraying Socialism of which they (the executive) had suddenly become the unsullied guardians. Cripps immediately launched a nation-wide campaign for his ideas. On January 25 he was expelled from the Labour Party. But Cripps was supported by the Birmingham party which addressed the EC as follows:

> The Birmingham Borough Labour Party wholeheartedly supports the memorandum submitted to Divisional Parties by Sir Stafford Cripps.
>
> It believes that only unity of all opposition forces can defeat the Chamberlain government. To achieve this defeat is the most important task facing the Labour Movement in the present international situation made more threatening by the fall of Barcelona.
>
> In these circumstances this Party protests against the high-handed and undemocratic action of the national EC in expelling Sir Stafford Cripps.

Cripps held a Birmingham Town Hall meeting in February and the *Town Crier* confessed to a doubt as to how this Popular Front would be able to agree on a government to oust Chamberlain. Opponents of Cripps mobilised a recently formed liaison committee of the Labour Party and Trades Council originally formed to discuss deteriorating local election results in the City and how to combat them. It was pointed out that the majority supporting Cripps on the Labour Party executive was small (44 to 26) but if all the 181 delegates, more than half of whom were trade union delegates, attended the decision could be reversed. However, the trade unionists continued to stay away and the decision stood.

Meanwhile the Birmingham Trades Council at its February meeting was rejecting Conscription. The argument that Conscription destroyed democracy was linked to other recent government measures such as the appointment of twelve area 'dictators' to control the city in wartime and police control of local Air Raid Precautions. The adoption of totalitarian practices was no answer to totalitarianism, said the mover of the motion, Hoddinott of the Shop Workers Union. Despite a debate recognising the seriousness of the international situation and a desire to resist fascism the motion was passed with only two dissentients.

In February the Birmingham branch of the National Union of Journalists convened an all-Party Conference on Press Freedom attended by over 500 delegates from 180 organisations including 23 Labour Parties, three trades councils, Co-operators, Communists, the Church, the Birmingham Unionists (Tories), the RSPCA, to name only a few. Norman Birkett KC chaired the conference and speakers included MPs from all parties. Discussion ranged over the Official Secrets Act and the 'subtle influences' which could reduce us to the state of the fascist press. Welcoming the recent changes made to the 1911 Act a resolution was passed that 'further amendments were necessary to preserve and protect the liberty of the subject.' This was moved by the Civil Service Clerical Union and seconded by Jack Trotter the Communist. The Conference ended in 'perfect harmony', said the chairman.

In March the *Town Crier* carried advertisements for a new Labour Book Service. This was meant to counteract the still growing influence of the Left Book Club. Its selling point was that it offered two books per month for 2/6d. But it came too near the war to make an impact.

On March 17 Chamberlain was in Birmingham speaking to the Conservative Association justifying Munich and receiving the plaudits of his supporters. But by March 31st after rumours of German troop movements Chamberlain made his remarkable guarantee to Poland that it would be supported by Britain if Poland were attacked by the Germans. This was a pledge that Britain had no means of fulfilling, unless it were in agreement with the Russians. So Chamberlain was reluctantly led to the leisurely and long-drawn out negotiations with the Soviet Union which having come to nothing by the middle of August, was followed by the bombshell of the Soviet-German Non-Aggression Pact; under no circumstances could the Soviet Union allow itself to be faced with the hostile western powers of France and Britain as well as fascist Germany.

In April in Birmingham the Labour Party demanded a Labour councillor on the Emergency Committee destined to rule Birmingham in war time, but this was refused by the mainly Tory council. The tenants' agitation was coming to a head. 14,438 tenants voted in favour of a strike and only 1,093 against. The Aston League of Youth sent a protest to the national executive of the Labour Party who, alarmed at the success of the National Youth Campaign and its support for the Popular Front, had disbanded the National Advisory Committee of the League of Youth and cancelled its Easter Conference.

Support for an end to appeasement and agreement with Russia widened. A Town Hall meeting of the broadly based International Peace Campaign brought local Labour Party leaders (Harrison Barrow and Joe Johnson its president) together with the Birmingham Liberal Association and the AEU, the engineering union leading the struggle to end appeasement, to initiate a national campaign under the slogans, 'Peace-Willing Nations must Unite' and 'Russia must be Included.' At this point the national Labour leaders put the Left Book Club on its proscribed list.

Resistance to Conscription continued with a wide range of objections aired in the *Town Crier*: Those most affected had no vote to express an opinion; it was the thin edge of the wedge to totalitarian conscription of all labour; conscription of labour should not be accepted until wealth was also conscripted. One of the largest Trades Council meetings ever held voted unanimously that voluntary methods were better than conscription for defending the country. 24,000 engineers in the Birmingham and Coventry districts of the AEU vowed to fight conscription. A Town Hall Protest against Conscription meeting was held in June, the main speakers being Jennie Lee, Fenner Brockway and Joe Johnson. Pacifism had a moderate revival. A No Conscription League echoing the the Fellowship of the first World War was set up, secretary John Ballinger, supported by Quakers and Socialists, offering advice to those who wished to become Conscientious Objectors.

In June the Youth Pilgrimage reached Birmingham. It was welcomed by contingents from Birmingham and all over the midlands to a Pageant at he Embassy Rink. The policy of the National Youth Campaign was: National Security required opposition to any further aggression: Youth will give its services Voluntarily, but only for a policy of collective security: and the formation of a bloc of Peace Loving Powers including the Soviet Union. Speakers included Gabriel Carritt and John Gollan, both Communists and also Ted Willis, chairman of the Labour Party League of Youth National Advisory Committee, soon to be a spectacular recruit to the Young Communist League and later a renowned television writer.

The political gloom of the summer was relieved only by the magnificent victory of the Council house tenants against the differential rent scheme and its accompanying means test. The ten week rent strike was met with allegations that it was a 'red plot', but on July 3rd the Council capitulated and the scheme was withdrawn. To some extent it was a red plot. Jessie Eden was an inspiring vice-president of the Tenants' Federation and the secretary was Ted Smallbone, a returned International Brigader. Mrs N. Williams who edited the Federation's journal *The Tenant* which reached a circulation of 40,000 was the wife of Bert Williams the Communist District Organiser. Other Communist leaders were John Corbett, Sid Atkin and George Bridgen. It was an impressive example of the organising skills of Communists. But the campaign was run on United Front lines. It was supported by the local Labour Party, the Trades Council and Co-operative movement. Above all it was the tenants both political and non-political who made the struggle possible.

By August war was inevitable and it was appropriate perhaps that the last Peace initiative in the city had been that of the youth. In the week before the war the *Town Crier* front page declared 'Peace or War – we Stand by our Faith'. It believed that the existing world chaos was the result of Capitalism and only the establishment of a world Socialist Commonwealth could end the sacrifice of the common people on the altar of greed and ambition.

The next week the war which never should have been and which could have been prevented if the principles of Collective Security endorsed by the people of Birmingham in the Peace Ballot of 1935 had been followed, was a reality.

A Joint Manifesto of the Labour Party, the Trades Council and Co-operative Party in Birmingham declared:

> Responsibility for the war rested largely with the British government which had failed to tackle Nazi and Fascist aggression.
>
> Now that the war was a reality it was confident that all members of the Labour movement would render the fullest possible service to the Nation and Democracy.
>
> Our fight is against Nazi aggression and not the German people.

Strenuously as we fight fascism abroad we must be equally vigilant in our efforts to resist dictatorship at home particularly by preserving the right of free speech and the right to criticise.

When peace comes we must guard against the evils of Versailles and the peace treaty must embody the principles of: the rights of all peoples to participate in the unlimited wealth which modern science provides; the establishment of a world Court of Justice in which every nation will have equality of status; agreement that all nations undertake rapid and progressive disarmament.

Bibliography: Birmingham from General Strike to World War 2

The main source for Labour politics in Birmingham is the remarkable weekly newspaper the *Town Crier*. For the story of its development see Peter Drake's 'The Town Crier: Birmingham's Labour Weekly 1919-1951' in *Essays in Birmingham Labour History* edited by Anthony Wright and Richard Shackleton (1983). The other essays in this volume applicable to the period are David Rolf's 'Birmingham Labour and the Background to the 1945 General Election', and Marion Large's 'Sources of Labour History: Primary Material in the Social Sciences Department of Birmingham Reference Library'.

The Labour movement newspapers used apart from the *Town Crier* are the *Sunday Worker* united left-wing journal 1925-29, the ILP paper called *New Leader* after 1926 and the Communist newspapers *Worker's Weekly* to 1927, *Workers' Life* to 1930 and thereafter the *Daily Worker*.

The 1930s are covered by two excellent Birmingham University theses – Paul Hasting's *The Labour Movement in Birmingham 1927-45* (1959) and Peter Drake's *Labour and Spain: British Labour's response to the Spanish Civil War, with particular reference to the Labour Movement in Birmingham* (1977).

Two books mentioned in bibliographies to previous chapters are John Corbett's *The Birmingham Trades Council 1866-1966* (1966) and Jim Simmons' *Soap-Box Evangelist* (1972).

For the Birmingham Trades Council and the Birmingham Labour Party there are full sets of *Minutes* and also the *Annual Reports*.

Biographies of Birmingham leaders in the multi-volumed *Dictionary of Labour Biography* for the period 1927-39 include Alfred Barrett-Brown (vol VIII), Harrison Barrow (vol V), James Crump Snr (vol V), John Fallows (vol II), Fred Longden (vol II), Cynthia Mosley (vol V), Fred Rudland (vol VIII), Percy Shurmer (vol II), Joseph Southall (vol V), and Wilfred Wellock (vol V). Potted biographies of local election candidates can often be found in the *Town Crier* in October of each year.

The books most important to me for general background have been A.J.P. Taylor's *English History 1914-45*, Ben Pimlott's *Labour and the Left in the 1930s*, G.D.H. Coles's *A History of the Labour Party from 1914*, Noreen Branson's *Britain in the Nineteen Twenties,* and Branson and Margot Heinemann's *Britain in the Nineteen Thirties*. All except Pimlott were eye witnesses and participants in the events they describe. I was a concerned and committed onlooker from the time I left school in 1934.

Chapter 29

Conclusions

Socialism is an elastic concept. It ranges from the bureaucratic state owning, controlling and planning all aspects of economic activity, as practised in the late Soviet Union to ideas of a just and fair society currently advocated by New Labour.

What is certain is that socialism and capitalism are two sides of the same coin. Where there is capitalism it generates opposition to the flaws that have always accompanied it – the creation of unacceptable inequalities of riches and poverty, and its development through boom and slump, creating mass unemployment and poverty for every generation of working people. For these reasons Socialism is as old as capitalism itself.

This book begins in 1850 when, despite the unprecedented wealth it had created, the poverty and suffering capitalism had produced raised legitimate fears that it would destroy itself and working people with it. In fact the reverse was to be the case. Capitalism stood on the threshold of its greatest expansion making Britain the Workshop of the World. But during the years up to 1850 various theories of Socialism had developed characterised by Marx as Utopian, the most important of which in Britain was the Socialism of Robert Owen.

Once it was clear that capitalism was in a new stage of growth, however, socialism lost any mass appeal it might have had and such class conscious workers as there were developed a hybrid ideology of Secularism and others devoted their efforts to building new craft trade unions and the other institutions of self-help in Britain.

But by 1875 capitalist development had run out of steam in Britain, as in other parts of the capitalist world, and the Great Depression began. This created mass unemployment everywhere and destroyed the basic industries of coal and iron in the Black Country. It took ten years for new Socialist parties to develop. When they came they represented the two tendencies of Marxism and Social Democracy. The Great Depression followed the usual pattern of capitalist crises of being both destructive and also creative. New export led growth in the Colonies created Imperialism epitomised by the desertion of Joseph Chamberlain in Birmingham from free trade Liberalism to protectionist, imperialist Toryism.

This stage of capitalist expansion continued through to the Boer War with its profits and jingoism until another massive slump occurred from 1905-08, after which there was prosperity until 1914. Through these years the new forms of socialism survived and developed and by 1900 it was clear that masses of people were rejecting capitalism for socialism.

Politically and electorally the period 1900-14 brought massive changes. Locally Labourists and Socialists won seats on local councils, Poor Law Guardians and School Boards. Nationally the Liberal Party was attempting to retain the vote of working people by offering a welfare state of Old Age Pensions and limited health and unemployment insurance. But by now Socialism had a secure presence and Gladstone junior negotiated the famous pact allowing some Labour candidates a run without Liberal intervention which resulted in 29 Labour members being returned to Parliament in 1906, including Fred Richards in Wolverhampton, which secured the permanence of the Labour Party.

This was also the period of the 'cheerful Socialism' of Clarion with its cycling and social clubs, Cinderellas and Fellowships and the (relatively) peaceful co-existence of Marxists and Social Democrats in such co-ordinating centres as the Birmingham Socialist Centre.

Meanwhile the organisation of the semi- and unskilled in trade unions from the late 1880s and renewed prosperity from about 1908 led to the Great Unrest which substantially raised the standard of living of those who had invariably lived at poverty or below subsistence levels.

The Great War of 1914-18 produced contradictory changes. In the first place it meant full-employment, wages which almost kept pace with inflation and overtime working that ensured rising real incomes for civilians in work and improved health of children. But it further undermined Britain's economic position in the world. In the first two years of peace the lack of competition from Germany and the central European powers allowed trade unions to raise wages, but, unfortunately prices increased almost as fast and rises in real incomes were therefore limited.

From 1921 unemployment rose accompanied by the most vicious fall of prices and cuts in wages ever known. Thus did the hopes of a land fit for heroes disappear.

But the sufferings endured during the war and the promises made of improvements after the war were such that outraged workers were prepared to take militant action to try to preserve standards of living. This militancy survived the disappointments and fall of the first Labour government in 1924 and continued in the optimism and idealism of the General Strike. Even the betrayal and defeat of the General Strike could not entirely douse this militancy and a second minority Labour government was elected in 1929. It was the slump of the 1930s and Ramsay MacDonald's decision in 1931 to form a 'national' government rather than resign honourably when massive cuts in wages were decreed by the bankers as necessary to control the slump, which finally extinguished militancy.

The Labour Party had been all but destroyed, the Independent Labour Party committed hari-kari in 1932 when it disaffiliated from the Labour Party; with it went the Labour Churches in Birmingham and the Black Country and much of the cultural activities.

From such a defeat there could be no quick revival. A successful struggle against fascism and appeasement in the 1930s was made impossible by the implacable hostility of the Tories to the Soviet Union and the blind hatred of right-wing Labour and trade union leaders of Bolshevism abroad and the Communist Party at home.

It would take the horrors of World War 2 and the alliance with the Soviet Union to rehabilitate the Labour Party and restore the credibility of Socialism in Britain.

The contest with capitalism continues. It has been the purpose of this book to record the struggles and aspirations of past Socialists in Birmingham and the Black Country who devoted their lives to the service of working people, in the hope that it will inspire and assist the present and future generations in furthering the same struggle.

Index

Adams, Mrs 19
Adams, W. 19
Adult Working Class Education 343-347, 402-409
Amalgamated Engineering Union 383-385
Amalgamated Society of Engineers 26, 270-276
Amalgamated Society of Carpenters and Joiners 383-385
Anarchism 53, 59, 243
Appeasement 540-541, 559
Aucott, Wm 76
Auxilliary Peace Society 250

Bailey, J. 11
Baker, G. 18
Baker, J. 313, 417, 418
Barrow, Harrison 561, 564
Basque children 543-545
Battison, T. 11, 12, 16
Beard, John 209, 211, 214
Bellows cutting 37, 38, 40
Bennett, C.A. (Dusty) 543
Bennett, Don 543
Birmingham
    and the Great War 204, 215
    Council for Peace and Liberty 556, 561, 562
    Secular Club 7
    Repertory Theatre 359-360
Blatchford, Robert 56, see also Clarion
Bradlaugh, Charles 5, 11, 12, 17, 19, see also Secularism
Brain, William 387, 403-404, 409-410, see also Communist Party
Brass Workers 98-99, 217
British Legion 319
British Secular Union 18
British Socialist Party 243, 244-246, 305
British Workers' League 213, 311

Brockhouse, Henry 63, 411, see also ILP
Brown, W.J. 416-417, 425
Bruff, Frank 465
Builders and Building Trade Unions 31-33, 83-84

Capper, James 76
Cardinal, William 369, 465, 548
Cartwright, Daniel 422
Cattell, Christopher, Charles 5, 7, 8, 115
Chain Trade 38, 39, 40, 94-96
Chamberlain, W.J. 554, 559
Chartist Land Company 4
Christadelphians 250
Christian Socialism 125, 356-357
Clarion 56-60, 114-120, 243
Communist Party 360-365, 386, 409-410, 426-427, 561, 567
Conscientious Objectors 250-255, 306-309, 313-314, 317
Conscription 206, 207, 215, 306-309
Cook, Samuel 4, 5, 20
Co-operation 161-194, 219-227, 283-303, 451-471, 473-490
    Birmingham 219-221
        Birmingham Co-operative Society 455-462
        Ten Acres and Stirchley 451-453
        Industrial 463-464
    Black Country 161-194, 283-303, 473-490
        Bilston and Ettingshall 195
        Cradley Heath 175
        Dudley 170, 473-474
        Halesowen and Hasbury 474-475
        Lye 175
        Smethwick 174, 175
        Soho 174, 177, 475
        Tipton 175, 177, 476
        Upper Gornal 175

Walsall 170-172, 177, 287-289, 477-480
Wednesbury 172, 476-477
Wolverhampton 172, 289-294, 480-486
Education Committees 179-184
Food Question (1914-1918) 224-226
Guilds – Women's 222-223, 466-468
– Men's 223-224
Industrial Co-operation 162-168, 486-488
Party, Co-operative 221-227, 294-295, 462-463
Cost of Living 139-146, 384-385, 447-448
Crump, Jim Snr 563, see also Transport & General Workers' Union
Crump, Jim Jnr 561, 563

Davis, W.J. 214, 217, see also Brassworkers' Union
Davison, J.E. 314, 415
Deakin, Joseph 52, 53, 54-55, 113, 409
Depression – see Economic Conditions
Dunstan, Robert, Dr 378, 409, 548-549, see also Communist Party

Eastgate, E., Miss 369
Economic Conditions 3-4, 17, 20, 70, 73-75, 97, 109, 137-139, 271, 390-391, 554-556, 558
Ex-Service Politics 319-323, 393-395
Ex-Servicemen's Guild 323
Exton, W.E. 419

Fabian Society 55-56, 125, 243
Factory Acts 37
Fellows, Alf 52
Fellowship of Reconciliation 215, 256
Forcible Feeding 261
Free Speech 336-340, 557
Freethought Temperance Hall 12
Frost, Tom 178, see also Wolverhampton Labour Party

General Elections 314-316, 372, 373, 375, 378, 415-418, 552
General Strike 493-499, 505-529
General Workers' Trades Union 99-100
Glassworkers 40, 41, 42, 96-98
Grand National Consolidated Trades Union 32
Great Unrest 147-159
Guild Socialism 412

Hallas, Eldred 211, 215
Hands off Russia 324-326, 395-396, 434-436
Hansom, Joseph 32
Harrison, George 165, 193
Hardie, Keir 215
Harvey, William 27
Hingley, Noah 38
Holland, A. 18, 19
Homer, Thomas 39
Humphries, Joseph 34
Hyndman, H.M. 50, 61

Independent Labour Party 50, 63-68, 125-132, 246-249, 259, 262, 305-306, 309, 314, 369-374, 410-414, 549, 561

Ironworkers 25-26, 75-78, 383, 441-442

Jones, John 6, 11, 12
Juggins, Richard 42, 46, 90, 93, 96

Kesterton, John 213
Kimberley, Thomas 25
Kneeshaw, J.W. 209, 210, 249, 434
Knights of Labour 88-90

Labour Churches 121-124, 243, 260, 353-356
Labour Party (and LRC) 314-316, 374-380, 416-425, 552-554
Lane, Jonathan 7
Leeds Convention 257-259, 311-312
Left Book Club 341-343
Left Wing Movement 549-551
Leisure 358-360
Lewis, John, Rev 372
Lock Co-operative 34-35
Lockmakers 34, 35, 91-92, 443-446
Longden, Fred 369, 371, 465
Lowe, Tom 556
Luckcuck, William 465

Macarthur, Mary 148-152
MacDonald, Ramsay, J. 215, 465
Mander, Geoffrey, MP 539
Mann, Tom 50, 60
Martyn, Caroline 31
Mayer, H.V. 8, 11, 12, 15, 17, 19
Master and Servant Acts 26, 38
Midland Counties Trades Federation 84-87
Midlands Secular Union 7, 11
Millerchip, William 188, 192-194
Millington, Joseph 464
Miners 23-25, 69-74, 154-156, 438-441, 491-493, 499-502
Minority Movement 551
Midland Social Democratic Association 18
Mooney, Tom 213
Mosley, Oswald, Sir 373
Murray, John 6
Municipal Elections 375, 376, 378, 418-420, 531-538, 542
Municipal Employees' Association 217
Murphy, J.T. 213
Musicians' Union 216, 217

Nailmakers 36, 37, 92-94
National Amalgamated Association of Ironworkers 26
National Association for the Protection of Labour 31
National Association of Discharged Sailors and Soldiers 319
National Association of Miners 24
National Association of Puddlers, Rollers & Millmen 26
National Council of Labour Colleges 343
National Council for Civil Liberties 249

National Federation of Discharged & Disabled Sailors & Soldiers 319, 394
National Unemployed Workers' Committee Movement 555
National Union of Ex-Servicemen (NUX) 319-324, 393-395
National Union of General Workers 398
Newbold, J. Walton 346
Newth, Mrs 561
No-Conscription Fellowship 243, 249, 251, 252, 265, 309, 312
No More War Movement 342
North, John 18
Nuts and Bolts 43, 90-91

Oldbury Freethought Temperance Hall 11
Operative Carpenters and Joiners 32
Owen, Robert 3

Parliamentary Representation 132-136, 314-316, 531, 551
Pacifism 565-556
Peace Activity 340-343, 558-560
Peace Ballot 539-540, 560
Peoples' Theatre Movement 358-360
Perry, Edward 29, 30, 31, 33
Piggot, Thomas 76
Police Spies 336-340
Police Strike 326-331, 366-367
Pollitt, Harry 384
Popular Front 566, 568
Practical Miners' Association 25
Price, E. 7
Prices 143, 208, 384
Print Workers 43
Proportional Representation 379

Quakers 250

Railwaymen 99, 383
Reddalls, Mr 15, 17, 18
Red International of Labour Unions 384-385
Rents 209, 212
Republican Club 11, 12, 13, 14
Republican Conference 15
Roberts, F.O., MP 415, see also General Elections
Roberts, Tom 555
Roberts, Wm. 464
Rudland, Fred 382, see also Birmingham Trades Council
Russell, John 18

Sander, Haydn 52, 53
Scholey, E. 5, 11, 12, 16, 18, 19, 30
Secular Chronicle 17
Secular Union, S. Staffs & E. Worcs 11, 12, 14, 16
Secularism 4-9, 11-17
Sharrocks, Wm. 57
Shaw, J.A., Rev. 153, 415

Shepperson, Harry 555, 556
Shop Stewards 213, 361
Shopworkers 44, 101
Silk, John 5, 11, 19
Silvester, Fred 345, 346, 548, 560
Simmons, Jim 258, 259, 340, 354, 356, 369, 378, 565
Sitch, Charles 415
Sitch, Thomas 95
Slump – see Economic Conditions
Smith, Thomas 465
Social Democratic Federation 49, 50, 51, 110-114, 243
Socialist Churches 243
Socialist Labour Party 124, 244-246
Socialist League (1880s) 50, 52-55
Socialist League (1930s) 564-565
Socialist Party of GB 125
Southall, Joseph 369, 370, 549, 561
South Staffs Mill and Forge Wages Board 26
Spanish Republic, Aggression against 541-544, 561-564
Sproson, Emma 301, 403, 412, 413, 424, 425
Standard of Living 139-147, 390-391, 447-449
Syndicalism 244

Taylor, Eric 23, 36, 76
Teachers 43, 279, 390
Tinplate Workers 27-31, 81, 82
Tommy (Truck) 36
Trades Councils
    Birmingham 204-215, 389-390, 547, 556-558
    Bilston 281
    Brierley Hill 281, 432
    Darlaston 431
    Dudley 104, 280, 431, 433
    Halesowen 281
    Oldbury 281
    Rowley Regis 281
    Smethwick 280, 429, 431, 433
    South Staffs & E. Worcs 104, 431, 436-437
    South Staffs & Worcs Federation of 431, 436-437
    Stourbridge 280, 432
    Tipton 281, 431, 432
    Walsall 103, 276-280, 429, 434-446
    Wednesbury 104, 431, 432
    West Bromwich 281
    West Midlands Federation of 437-438
    Wolverhampton 103, 280, 429, 433-434
    for 1926 see General Strike
Trade Unions and the War 271
Trades Union Congress 105-107
Transport & General Workers' Union 384
Trumper, Oliver 11, 12, 20

Unemployed Workers' Committee Movement 334, 335, 401, 402, 405
Unemployment 139-147, 205, 331-336, 383-384, 387, 388, 397-405, 447-449, 554-556
Union of Democratic Control 215, 243
United Front 564

Upton, W. 11
Varley, Julia 210, 214, 215, see also Workers' Union
Vaughan, Mr 35

Wages 208, 216, 383-385, 447-448
Walkden, A.G. 314, 415
Wallwork, Daniel 5, 20
Walsall Anarchist 'Bomb Plot' 54-55
Walsall Free Discussion Group 16, 17, 19
Watkins, Anthony 18
Watts, Charles 6
Wellock, Wilfred 412, 416, 418
Welsh, Sam 46, 192
Whiston, John 543-545, see also Walsall Trades Council
White Collar Trade Unions 100-103
Whittall, Mr 5
Whittaker, James 59, see also Wolverhampton Borough Council and Trades Council
Whittaker, Joseph 121
Williams, Bert 567

Wilson, James 415
Women 147-152, 347-352
    Birmingham Women in Wartime 229-242
    Black Country Labour Women at War 297-303
    Labour League 240-241, 301
    Other Women's organisations 242
    Political activity 233-234
    Suffrage Organisations
        National Union of Women's Suffrage Societies 236-238, 302
        Women's Social and Political Union 234-236, 302-303
        Workers' Suffrage Federation 241
    Trades Unions 229-233, 297-300
    Work and Wages 195-198
Workers' Education Association 345-348
Workers' Union 216, 217, 272, 273, 387, 446-447

Youth Movement 353-353, 358, 372, 378, 549, 559, 568, 569
Youth Peace Movement 343

Sponsors of this book

Prof. John Saville, Hull
Prof. Chris Wrigley, Nottingham
Sandra for John Rowan, Birmingham
Kath Barker, Brighton
Dorothy Thompson, Worcester
Stan Newens MEP, London
Max Bennett, Codsall
John Smallshire, Wednesfield
Joe & Kay Ball, London
Sheila Gillett, Rickmansworth
Sidney Barnsby, Watford
Arthur Hale, Rickmansworth
Walsall Local History Centre
Carlo Piccirelli, Halesowen
Doug Matthews, Halesowen
Simon Murphy MEP, Wolverhampton
Ross Cranston MP, Dudley
Roy & Vida Henning, Havant
Robin Corbett MP, Birmingham
Prof. John Stewart, Birmingham
Councillor Theresa Stewart, Birmingham
Jenny Jones MP, Wolverhampton
Sir Richard Knowles, Birmingham
Terry Davis MP, Birmingham
Ken Purchase MP, Wolverhampton
Andy Goodall, Wolverhampton
Francis King, Wymondham
Sylvia Heal MP, Birmingham
Eric Hobsbawm, London
Bill Moore, Sheffield
Graham Taylor, Wembley
John & Elizabeth Hazlehurst, Bristol
Bob & Jean Hazlehurst, Wolverhampton
Nick Matthews, South Africa
Chris Game, Birmingham
Stan Henderson, Dartmouth
John Charlton, Newcastle-on-Tyne

H.K. Greenhalgh, Solihull
Graham Stevenson, Birmingham
Ken Evans, Wolverhampton
Eddie Dare, London
Stewart Maclennan, Glasgow
Colin & Alison Hale, High Wycombe
Bert Hogenkamp, Amsterdam
Lynne Jones MP, Birmingham
Jon Bloomfield, Birmingham
Tony Atienza, Bury-St-Edmunds
Ruskin College, Oxford
Nick Kelleher, Wolverhampton
Wolverhampton Trades Union Council
Liz Anderton, Wolverhampton
Councillor S.J. Waltho, Dudley
Fircroft College, Birmingham
Doreen & Phil Sheppard, Wolverhampton
Councillor Paul Hickman, Stourbridge
John Upton, Birmingham
John Tomlinson MEP, Walsall
Wolverhampton Grammar School
Councillor J. Hampson, Upper Gornal
Maureen Green, Wolverhampton
Prof. John Benson, Wolverhampton
Co-operative History Group, Birmingham
Bilston Community College
Mel & Frank Reeves, Wolverhampton
Sir David Perris, Birmingham
West Midlands Co-operative Society
Don Watson, Dumphries
Mike Beazley, Birstall
Ewart A. Edmonds, Birmingham
Harold Smith, London
Bill Kirkpatrick, Warlingham
Derek Robinson, Birmingham
Stanley G. Taylor, Willenhall
Selwyn Evans, London

Unison branch, Selly Oak Hospital
GMB 94 Dudley branch
Maureen Whitehouse, West Bromwich
Unison, Sandwell Health branch
Co-operative Union, Manchester
Dave Holmes, Bilston
John Goodman, Coventry
Councillor S. Austin, Birmingham
Councillor Tim Oliver, Walsall
3GMBATU Shop Stewards, Albright & Wilson, Oldbury
Ian Pearson MP, Dudley
Thos C. Charlton, Sutton Coldfield
Dennis Turner MP, Bilston
Philip Davis, Telford
Gisela Stuart MP, Birmingham
Larry Moody, Wolverhampton
Walsall MBC, Leisure and Community Services
TGWU Midlands Region, West Bromwich
Ned Williams, Wolverhampton
Kenji Tomizawa, Tokyo, Japan
Graphical, Paper & Media Union, Birmingham & West Midlands branch
Unison, West Midlands Gas branch
Mrs P. Palmer, Birmingham
Mrs D.L. Broughton, Birmingham
Mrs L.D. Shakespeare, Birmingham
GMB Birmingham & West Midlands Region
Northern Herald Books, Rastrick
Iron & Steel Trades Confederation, Sutton Coldfield
TGWU/ACCTS, Wolverhampton
Alan & Irene Rickman, Birmingham
TGWU Birmingham Power & Eng. District Committee
TGWU Aston Cross Branch, Birmingham

Malcolm Chase, Leeds University
TGWU 5/908 Birmingham
Paul Tennant, Birmingham
Dudley Borough Council Libraries
MSF Wolverhampton Central Branch
Barbara Lloyd Taylor, Billericay
S.J. Haycock, Kingswinford
Birmingham Trades Union Council
Rudi Achtelstetter, Holzhausen, Germany
Councillor Albert Bore, Birmingham
Councillor Ian McArdle, Birmingham
Christine Crawley MEP, Birmingham
TGWU 5/905 Birmingham
Colin F. Fitzer, Birmingham
Donald Bateman, Bristol
John Fox, Birmingham
Paul Tyler, London
Cyril Pearce, Huddersfield
M. Hayman, Birmingham
R. Stevens, Nottingham
M.J. Payne, Birmingham
TGWU 5/905 Birmingham
Colin F. Fitzer, Birmingham
Donald Bateman, Bristol
John Fox, Birmingham
Paul Tyler, London
Cyril Pearce, Huddersfield
M. Hayman, Birmingham
R. Stevens, Nottingham
M.J. Payne, Birmingham
UNISON Wolverhampton General Branch
NU Lock & Metal Workers, Willenhall
Dave Lyddon, Keele University
Marian Hall, Birmingham
Ray & Marion George, Wednesfield
Chas. Collett, Whittington